[redacted]

PUBLIC HEALTH

Administration and practice

PUBLIC HEALTH

Administration and practice

George Pickett, M.D., M.P.H.

Professor and Chair, Department of
Public Health Policy and Administration,
School of Public Health, University of Michigan;
formerly Director of Health, West Virginia;
Director of Health and Welfare, San Mateo County, California;
Director of Health, Detroit and Wayne County, Michigan

John J. Hanlon, M.S., M.D., M.P.H.†

Professor, School of Public Health, San Diego State University;
formerly Assistant Surgeon General, U.S. Public Health Service;
Director, Community Health Services, Philadelphia;
Commissioner of Health, Detroit and Wayne County

NINTH EDITION

with 19 illustrations

TIMES MIRROR/MOSBY
COLLEGE PUBLISHING

ST. LOUIS • TORONTO • BOSTON • LOS ALTOS 1990

Editor: Pat Coryell
Editorial Assistant: Loren Stevenson
Editing and Production: Editing, Design & Production, Inc.
Book Design: Candace Conner
Cover Design: Elise A. Stimac

NINTH EDITION

A division of The C.V. Mosby Company
11830 Westline Industrial Drive
St. Louis, Missouri 63146

Printed in the United States of America

Library of Congress Cataloging in Publication Data

Pickett, George E. (George Eastman, 1935–
Public health: administration and practice / George Pickett, John J. Hanlon. – 9th ed.
p. cm.
Hanlon's name appears first on earlier ed.
Includes bibliographies and index.
ISBN 0-8016-2501-7
1. Public health. 2. Public health administration. I. Hanlon, John J. (John Joseph), 1912–1988. II. Title.
[DNLM: 1. Public Health Administration—United States. WA 540 AA1 P52p]
RA425.H29 1990
362.1'068—dc20
DNLM/DLC
for Library of Congress 89–12721
CIP

GW/RRD/RRD 9 8 7 6 5 4 3

To John and Frances Hanlon

Preface

When the first edition of this book appeared, more than four decades ago, public health and indeed the world were very different. Having endured the global trauma of World War II, there was widespread enthusiasm and hope for a peaceful, prosperous, and stable future in a world without disease, rich with energy, devoid of pollution, endowed with justice for all, and without poverty of psyche or soma.

World War II had, as had its predecessor, brought with it amazing advances in the biological and physical sciences: antibiotics, new surgical techniques, advances in virology, a better understanding of mental illness, and, moreover, nuclear energy to be used for peaceful purposes. It also ushered in a new era in which the industrial and economic power of the United States was expected to fuel the world's economy. Millions of returning veterans had experienced the benefits of an organized system of health care. This stratified system employed trained paramedics at the front line, who were backed up by field stations equipped to do emergency surgery and a tertiary care system which could bring the most up-to-date medical technology to all members of the armed forces without regard to their rank, income, or ethnic group. These returning veterans and their children moved into the ranks of industry, business, labor, politics, education, and public health in the ensuing 40 years. They had experienced a different environment than that of their parents and they had different expectations of their government. The epidemics of lung cancer due to smoking and of AIDS were as yet unknown.

Public health departments at that time fit a classic American model: a physician, a nurse, and a sanitarian provided a limited array of services intended to protect the public against communicable diseases. More than 80% of the nation's population lived in areas served by a public health department. There was a clear line of communication from the Surgeon General of the U.S. Public Health Service to the state health officer to the director of the local health department. Faced with a threatened outbreak of typhoid or polio in a community, an epidemiologist from the Centers for Disease Control in Atlanta could be on a train within 24 hours. Medical care was widely available for those with a modest income, as well as for veterans. In many communities there were public hospitals which provided medical care for the poor. In others, the local welfare budget paid for needed care, provided that need could be proved to the local policy makers. Mental health care (but few treatment services) was provided in large state hospitals. The state and local health departments were responsible for the sanitation of the environment: milk and food inspection, sewage systems, and the water supply.

By 1989, all of that had changed. Health care for the poor (both employed and unemployed) was a major issue in every state legislative body, with nearly 37 million people in peril because they had no insurance with which to buy their way into a zealously entrepreneurial and private medical care system, even though state and federal expenditures for health care for the aged (Medicare) and the poor (Medicaid) were nearly three times greater than the entire federal budget in 1950. And matters appeared to be getting worse: the price of medical care continued to rise faster than virtually all other segments of the economy, as benefits for workers and the poor became more and more constricted. The mental health system had been drastically changed, with state hospitals playing a minor role and community mental health centers attempting to care for larger and larger populations of chronically mentally ill people, living in but hardly with the community, and growing numbers of homeless individuals, AIDS patients, and the victims of substances such as alcohol and "crack."

Environmental health services had been splintered into numerous agencies both at the federal and state level. Separate agencies were created for occupational health programs. In only a handful of states is the state health department the lead environmental agency. In some states there are departments of natural resources, environmental protection agencies, agriculture departments, occupational health programs, toxic waste authorities, environmental review boards, and radiation control agencies involved in providing environmental health services, along with the state and local health departments, the police, and the fire department. In spite of the efforts, there is serious concern about the rising tide of environmental pollution and a growing perception that it may not be possible to live in a risk-free world.

Public health agencies themselves have been reorganized dozens of times since this book was first written. Umbrella human service agencies have been formed and then dissolved, and umbrella environmental agencies have been established which effectively split the traditional concerns of public health, assigning some to social welfare organizations and the others to environmental protection agencies, which many think are not the same as environmental *health* agencies. At the end of 1988, the Institute of Medicine published its long-awaited study *The Future of Public Health** and described the scene as one of "disarray." It is true—there is confusion about the purposes of public health in the United States. While public health continues to provide an enormous range and variety of services, directly touching the lives of 60 to 70 million people each year, and indirectly providing services which protect all of us, the public and its elected leaders are not clear about what is intended and who should do it. While there is no dispute about the desire to prevent dangerous communicable diseases, there is less consensus about the role of government in preventing or otherwise controlling such diseases as heart disease, cancer, substance use and abuse, and injuries. While there is widespread conviction that medical care costs too much and that those without adequate access have a right to obtain it, there is disagreement about the responsibility of government for needed reforms and programs and who should pay how much. Public health has not been intimately involved in these discussions in most states. While there is grave concern for the number of mentally ill people who are living in abominable circumstances in every community of the land, there is confusion about the role of institutions in providing protective and treatment services. While there is a consensus that pollution must be controlled, there is disagreement about how to do it and who should pay.

The disarray of public health foreshadows the disarray that will emerge in other sectors of society in the few short years before this century gives way to the next. It is apparent that the most important problems of society cannot be solved by traditional, single agencies and it is becoming apparent that continually reorganizing the agencies of government will not make solutions easier. New and more efficient approaches to transorganizational policy formation and implementation are needed if the public's health is to be protected within the boundaries of the resources and the social policies of the nation. It is to this task that public health must turn its attention in the 1990s. It is for the purpose of helping to prepare the leaders of that effort that this book has been written.

The book is intended for graduate students in public health, community health, and health administration programs, as well as students in nursing, medicine, dentistry, and other health professions who need some knowledge of the public health effort in the United States. While its title includes the word "administration," this is not a "how-to" book. It is really a more descriptive and analytical source. The skills of management are better acquired in course work, as an apprentice and through books specifically intended to cover such topics as organizational behavior, public sector financial management, and human resource management.

Part One consists of four chapters which describe the historical, philosophical, and scientific roots of public health. The five chapters of Part Two discuss the basic tools of public health (epidemiology, prevention, and the law) and its organization in the United States. Part Three provides an overview of the management of public health in the United States as well as a chapter which briefly describes how public health is managed in other countries. (This is a much neglected subject in the United States and the reader is encouraged to examine public health systems in other countries to gain better insight into the U.S. system.)

In Part Four, although the separation of infectious diseases from noninfectious diseases is at first seemingly arbitrary, it does have some conceptual basis. Health efforts directed at chronic diseases involve a different social purpose—that of not only protecting the individual against disease but the public's purse as well, which is somewhat different

* Institute of Medicine: The future of public health, Washington, DC, 1988, National Academy Press.

from the social mandate to protect everyone from other people's infectious diseases. A new chapter dealing with AIDS is included. The disease had scarcely been recognized at the time the last edition was written.

Part Five includes chapters dealing with occupational health and safety, injury control, and public health nutrition. (The latter subject can be treated as an environmental issue or as a welfare issue, but was chosen to be included here.) Part Six includes four chapters which are devoted to different segments of the developmental life span: pregnancy and perinatal health and child health—traditional concerns of public health for more than a century—and adolescence and aging—emerging areas of concern and interest. It is significant that there is not a chapter dealing with the group between adolescence and the elderly, namely the working age, adult population of the country. While many of the activities of public health protect the health of adults, they have not been singled out as an area of special concern in this country, unlike the socialist nations which prize their workforce or other nations with national health insurance.

Part Seven describes the public role in the behavioral arena, including mental health, substance use and abuse, and violence. Part Eight describes the personal health services programs of the public sector, with distinct chapters dealing with public health nursing and organized efforts to assure access to medical care.

When this book was first written by John Hanlon, he was able to write authoritatively about the entire range of public health, and he contributed to the initial development of many of the topics covered. Now, of course, there are numerous monographs written by specialists in each of the areas covered by this book, and there is an array of journals covering virtually every topic described here. It is a little audacious for a single person to attempt to cover so much. With the exception of the two chapters on environmental health contributed by Dr. Barry Rabe, however, that apparently is what this book represents. However, it is much more than that. It includes the ideas and reflections of hundreds of current public health professionals who have shaped the thoughts of the author during the past 25 years.

Most importantly, the book includes a large amount of the wisdom of John Hanlon, who was an extraordinary person, both professionally and personally. It includes ideas which have been listened to and assimilated from the many people whose friendship has been experienced because of John's enthusiasm and thoughtfulness. The author has enjoyed the rich experience of learning from the best of the present as well as the past, and it is their wisdom which shapes this book.

GEORGE E. PICKETT

Contents

PART ONE

Roots of public health

Before embarking on a study of public health in the United States, it is necessary to consider the roots of public health: its origins, its historical evolution, and its meaning at the dawn of the twenty-first century. These introductory chapters will describe the philosophy and purpose of public health, review the impact of culture and society on health status and vice versa, provide a historical perspective on the evolution of public health, and offer a brief overview of the global or international nature of public health problems and programs. The purpose of these chapters is to broaden understanding of the unique nature of public health and thereby make more comprehensible the more detailed discussions in subsequent chapters of the organization of public health, the problems assigned by society to its public health agencies, and the policies that are explicit or implicit in the organization and application of public health resources.

CHAPTER 1

Philosophy and purpose of public health

PUBLIC HEALTH AS A PROFESSION

Throughout the world there are now large numbers of people from many professions engaged in the field of public health. They are unusual in that their common bond is the conviction that the public's health can be improved by altering conditions—behavior, the environment, biological interactions, and the organization of services—that might otherwise, at a future time, have an adverse impact on health. Unlike most professions, which have a common body of knowledge and a shared educational experience to bind their members together, the public health profession has an intended outcome as its common ground, as the cohering force that binds its members together in a global effort. Their training and educational backgrounds are widely diversified: medicine, nursing, law, engineering, sociology, statistics, management, psychology, microbiology, dentistry, economics, accounting, political science—virtually every type of professional education from administration to zoology, from meteorology to social work, can be applied in the field of public health.

Public health workers are often described as idealistic and dedicated, but they can be found in many settings, including industry, government agencies, academic institutions, and private practice. They are increasingly well paid in a competitive environment that values education and skills. There is a persistent argument about who is a public health professional. Deans of schools of public health maintain that their graduates are public health professionals regardless of the setting in which they work. The American Public Health Association tends to define a public health worker as someone who works in a public health organization, regardless of training. Some argue that the chief executive officer of a hospital or a nursing home administrator is involved in public health work, while others assert that these are personal care agencies, which are more often than not involved in a profit-making enterprise. Is a pediatrician immunizing a child a public health practitioner for the moment?

This book is not about the education of public health professionals or the practice of preventive medicine; it is about public health as an organized, social effort, centered in official agencies but intimately involved with voluntary and not-for-profit organizations, intended to protect, promote, and restore the people's health.

What can be accomplished by public health workers in the face of an environment made increasingly hazardous by our own actions, human behavior that often leads us to risky actions or inactions, biological threats such as cancer, heart disease, diabetes, and AIDS, and an often ambivalent political process for allocating scarce resources among competing social needs such as education, health, highways, welfare, and national defense? One is reminded of a statement by the Irish parliamentarian Edmund Burke (1729-1797) in the face of repeated criticism: "Those who carry on great public schemes must be proof against the most fatiguing delays, the most mortifying disappointments, the most shocking insults, and what is worst of all, the presumptuous judgments of the ignorant." Sir Henry Cole once showed this statement to his close friend public health pioneer Edwin Chadwick and commented that Chadwick should have it pinned to his sleeve as an epigraph.

An essential point to be made is that despite all handicaps, spectacular successes of far-reaching consequences have been achieved during an amazingly brief historical period. At the time of Cole's comment to Chadwick in the midnineteenth century, the average age at death in large English cities was only 36 years for the gentry, 22 years for tradespeople, and 16 years for the laborers. More than half the children of the working class and a fifth of the children of the gentry died before their fifth birthday. Since then, the average life expectancy at birth has increased in the United States and several other countries to well over 70 years, and the death rate before the fifth birthday has decreased about 95%.

The late Milton J. Rosenau justified patience on the basis that the recorded history of civilization encompasses relatively few generations. Only 3,500 years have passed since the time of Moses; and if the average length of a generation has been about 35 years, there have been only about 100 generations from Moses to the present. When one considers that the modern era of the biological sciences is scarcely 140 years old, most of the progress in public health has taken place in just the past 3 to 4 of those 100 generations—a blink of the eye in the course of human history.

Public health necessarily has been closely identified with medicine. The practice of medicine is commonly regarded as one of the oldest professions. Yet modern medicine is hardly more than a century old. Indeed, it has been said that not until 1910 did the average patient in the United States have a fifty-fifty chance of being diagnosed correctly.[1] Effective treatment was something else again. Now medical knowledge and techniques become outdated with accelerating rapidity. The modern public health movement, although presaged by occasional and sporadic earlier glimmerings, is fairly recent too.

It also is important to realize that these developments have not occurred by themselves. They have been intimately related in conception and development to a broad and multifaceted philosophic and social revolution that has had as its driving force a growing adherence to the concept of justice. These developments have been a critical part of a broad spectrum of social reforms that includes public education, public welfare, racial and sexual equity, the rights of labor, the humane care of the mentally ill, and penal management, to mention only a few.

These relationships have prompted Beauchamp[2] to conclude that "while many forces influenced the development of public health, the historic dream of public health that preventable death and disability ought to be minimized is a dream of social justice." Public health must really be regarded as an ethical enterprise, an agent of social change, not just for the sake of change but to make possible the achievement of other social goals. For much of its history, public health has striven for this goal through professional application of scientific and technical knowledge. Dubos[3] has pointed out that changes in the human environment require new adaptive responses that if inadequate result in ill health and other consequences. Changes, hence the need for adaptation, are constantly occurring, since both we and our environment are dynamic, not static. New factors are introduced into the human environment not only by technical innovations and geologic or climatic changes but also by ever evolving human wants, habits, and aspirations. Perhaps the greatest challenge results from the fact that although science may provide solutions to problems inherited from the past, it seldom if ever can do the same for problems of the future—because it does not know what they will be. Public health workers must always be ready to contend with the unknown problems of the future. They must think and be ready to act prospectively, in contrast with those in therapeutic professions who think and act on a retrospective basis. This often places public health workers in a difficult position, since so many other professions and most public officials are unaccustomed to this point of view. As stated by Draper and associates[4]:

> Public health not only involves, it actually *demands* confrontation with received wisdom and the established powers. All this is not to say, however, that being controversial is a *sufficient* qualification for being effective today in public health, but it certainly seems to be a *necessary* qualification. But if persuasion and sometimes open conflict are not occurring, we should realize that we have lost a "public health movement."

DEFINITIONS OF PUBLIC HEALTH

To define *public health,* it is first necessary to attempt to define *health.* The traditional, dictionary definition of health is "freedom from disease or pain." The constitution of the World Health Organization defines health as "a state of complete physical, mental, and social well-being and not merely the absence of disease or infirmity." Neither definition is particularly helpful for purposes of this discussion.

Until recently, many people pursued health as an ultimate goal in itself. Increasingly, however, it is realized that health has value only to the extent that it promotes efficiency and makes possible a satisfactory total living experience. It is the quality of life that is meaningful, not merely the quantity. Health in and of itself is of little if any use. Its true value lies in the worthwhile activities made possible by virtue of it. Furthermore, it is erroneous to think of complete and lasting health as attainable or even desirable. Dubos[5] used this as the theme of his provocative book *Mirage of Health*. He emphasized that health and happiness, so long regarded as absolute and permanent values supposedly achieved by some in the golden ages of the past and still sought after in our time, appear to be illusions. As he indicated, complete freedom from disease, stress, frustration, and struggle is incompatible with the process of living and evolution. In this vein, he mused:

> Life is an adventure in a world where nothing is static, where unpredictable and ill-understood events constitute dangers that must be overcome, often blindly and at great cost; where man himself, like the sorcerer's apprentice, has set in motion forces that are potentially destructive and may someday escape his control. Every manifestation of existence is a response to stimuli and challenges, each of which constitutes a threat if not adequately dealt with. The very process of living is a continual interplay between the individual and his environment, often taking the form of a struggle resulting in injury or disease.

He concluded wryly that "complete and lasting freedom from disease is but a dream remembered from imaginings of a Garden of Eden designed for the welfare of man."

Health is better understood as a continuum. A *disease* or *injury* is any phenomenon that may lead to an *impairment*. *Impairments* are abnormalities of body structure at the organ or system level, such as decreased lung capacity due to cigarette smoking or a broken bone. Impairments may lead to *disabilities*, which are disturbances at the level of the whole body. For example, impaired lung capacity may lead to a disability if the normal demands of the individual exceed the residual capacity of the lung to provide adequate ventilation. In turn, a *disability* may lead to a state of *dependency* at the level of the individual's environmental or social interactions. A *dependency* is a condition that requires external resources, such as a cane or an attendant or medicine, to carry out activities of daily living.

Health in this continuum may be defined as "the absence of a disability."

What is *public health?* There have been many attempts to define it. Chronologically, these definitions present a word picture of the evolution of the field. Early definitions were limited essentially to sanitary measures invoked against nuisances and health hazards with which the individual was powerless to cope. Thus initially insanitation and later communicability were the criteria followed in deciding whether a problem fell within the purview of public health. With the great bacteriologic and immunologic discoveries of the late nineteenth and early twentieth centuries and the subsequent development of techniques for their application, the concept of prevention of disease in the individual was added. Public health then came to be regarded as integration of sanitary science and medical science. As will be discussed later, it has more recently come to be regarded as a social science.

In 1920 Winslow,[6] a strong advocate of this broader viewpoint, enunciated what became the best known and most widely accepted definition of public health and its relationship to other fields. For analytic purposes it is presented here in outline form:

> Public Health is the Science and Art of (1) preventing disease, (2) prolonging life, and (3) promoting health and efficiency through organized community effort for
> (a) the sanitation of the environment,
> (b) the control of communicable infections,
> (c) the education of the individual in personal hygiene,
> (d) the organization of medical and nursing services for the early diagnosis and preventive treatment of disease, and
> (e) the development of the social machinery to insure everyone a standard of living adequate for the maintenance of health,
>
> so organizing these benefits as to enable every citizen to realize his birthright of health and longevity.

Winslow's definition was timely and comprehensive. It allowed inclusion of almost everything in the fields of social service as they related to health and well-being. In addition, it provided a concise summary, not only of public health and its administration, but also of its historic development.

The definition had some shortcomings, however, which have become more apparent as social expectations have changed. The emphasis on prolonging life has begun to alter as longevity has approached the outer limits of what may be possible and quality of life has taken on added importance. Winslow did not include medical care per se and made no mention of the broad field of mental health. (He perhaps can be excused for the now unacceptable use of the pronoun *he.*) Winslow included social change to assure everyone an adequate standard of living, an appropriate goal of public health, but it is also a goal of education and welfare agencies and thus lacks a distinguishing capacity.

Working with the definition of health presented above, *public health* may be defined as *the organization and application of public resources to prevent dependency, which would otherwise result from disease or injury.* This definition refers to *dependency,* not impairment or disability. It may appear to be unnecessarily conservative as a statement of purpose, but it defines a purpose that can be agreed to by a broad spectrum socially and politically. The prevention of some diseases and injuries and their resulting impairments may be considered practically impossible in many circumstances, and since an impairment may not create a functional disability, it may have little social or public consequence. Even a disability, so long as it does not interfere with social interaction or require the consumption of additional resources, may not be of social concern. But dependencies, by definition, are a matter for social or public concern. It should be noted that the best and often the only way to prevent dependency may be to prevent the disease in the first place, as is true of measles, lung cancer, and AIDS.

It is evident from these definitions that there has occurred a gradual extension of the horizons of public health. In conformance with the advances of medical and scientific knowledge and keeping pace with social and political progress, public health work has expanded from its original concern with gross environmental insanitation to, in sequence of addition, sanitary engineering, preventive physical medical science, preventive mental medical science, the positive or promotive as well as social and behavioral aspects of personal and community medicine, and more recently, the promotion and assurance of comprehensive health services for all.

The inevitable and continuous extension of the boundaries of public health was clearly recognized a third of a century ago by Mountin,[7] who stated:

> The progressive nature of public health makes any restricted definition of the functions and responsibilities of health departments difficult. More than that—there is a real danger in attempting to narrow down a moving or growing thing. To tie public health to the concepts that answered our needs 50 years ago, or even a decade ago, can only hamstring our contribution to society in the future.

This perceptive statement still remains valid.

THERAPEUTIC MEDICINE, PREVENTIVE MEDICINE, AND PUBLIC HEALTH

A short discussion of the distinctions between therapeutic medicine, preventive medicine, and public health is appropriate. To a major extent, the practice of medicine has been concerned with diagnosis and treatment of damage already done—the realignment of a broken limb, the healing or removal of a diseased organ, or the readjustment of an unsettled mind. It is important to note that treatment accepts the existence of an impairment and includes some degree of dependency. The nature of the problems necessitates an individualized approach that is important in its own right. Preventive medicine is concerned with the prevention of disease in the individual. Thus it consists of four areas of action:

1. The prevention by biologic means of certain diseases, such as specific communicable and deficiency diseases
2. The prevention of some of the consequences of preventable or treatable diseases, such as syphilis, tuberculosis, cancer, diabetes, and hypertension
3. The minimization of some of the consequences of nonpreventable and noncurable diseases, such as many genetic conditions
4. The motivation of improved health in individuals by changed lifestyles that minimize the potential impact of behavioral and other health hazards

Because of the increasing number of possibilities for the application of preventive concepts to the early diagnosis and treatment of incipient or established diseases, preventive medicine should be regarded as a component of good clinical medical practice. As a result of the increased teaching of community and family medicine, the development of comprehensive care systems, and emphasis on continuity of care, there is a growing tendency by private physicians to incorporate preventive medicine into their practices.

It is possible to go further, however, and encourage the development of constructive and promotive health in which the center of interest is still the individual but now as a social or community integer, a member of a family and of a social group. It is notable that the emphasis in public health has changed from the physical environment, or sanitation, to preventive medicine and, more recently, back to the individual and the environment but now in terms of the individual's relationship with the complex social and physical environment.

It would be preferable, of course, if medical practitioners served in a total sense—as personal or family health counselor, therapist, and provider of all preventive and health education and promotive services. To be able to do so, however, would require some philosophic reorientation, some reorganization, more time, and a more extensive use of allied health personnel as well as automated and electronic technology. A method increasingly used is personal health hazard appraisal or risk assessment. This useful tool of prospective medicine is discussed in Chapter 17 in relation to health maintenance. Its wide acceptance and use will probably depend on effective cooperative efforts of public health organizations, schools of medicine, practitioners of medicine, educational institutions, and insurance and similar companies. Already it serves as an important concept in the national health program of Canada.[8]

From what has been said earlier, it is evident that public health goes a step further than therapeutic or even preventive medicine. Its patient is the entire community or indeed the world, and its armamentarium is more extensive than those of the other fields. Therapeutic care systems use only the tools of medicine and surgery, with the occasional adjunctive input of psychology. Health problems, such as alcoholism or low birth weight, are seen as medical problems requiring medical solutions. Public health has a much broader purview. It is a multidisciplinary endeavor, and solutions are crafted from a wide variety of skills and professions: the law, medicine, engineering, psychology, political science, education—whatever works and is acceptable and affordable.

There are several other important distinctions between public health and medical care. The priorities of public health are socially determined; the priorities of medical care are unrelated to social goals except by coincidence. This is not to say that one set of goals is necessarily of greater value or a more accurate reflection of personal or social needs: they are simply different.

Medical care in the United States seeks to maximize the chance that the best possible outcome will occur. To that end, it is often unlimited by any resource constraints, and marginal benefits may be sought at enormous cost. Public health, on the other hand, seeks to minimize the chance that the worst possible outcome will occur. Public health accepts risk as an essential component of life and tries to manage it in a calculus that combines, implicitly if not explicitly, an estimation of both benefits and costs. The eradication of smallpox was the result of such a calculus. Similar calculations resulted in a different approach to measles, since eradication appeared to carry too high a price for the marginal benefits that might be obtained. These calculations may produce a different answer at some time in the future if technology or other factors change. The therapeutic system, however, should and does insist on absolute protection of each individual patient, although its success will be variable. This contrast in approaches can lead to real conflicts between professionals in the therapeutic system and their counterparts in public health who may be concerned with the optimal allocation of scarce resources.

The distinctions between therapeutic care and public health are profound and important, and they are not widely understood. Clinicians often do not understand why a public health agency may decide not to apply a particular screening device in an effort to find people who may have a particular disease, such as glaucoma or cancer of the colon. Public health workers may not always appreciate a therapist's willingness to use every tool available to correct an impairment. These different perceptions, which are often manifest in the confusion of the general public about public health goals and objectives, are at the heart of many current health policy dilemmas. They will become more apparent in the chapters that follow.

SCOPE OF PUBLIC HEALTH

During recent years, the perimeters of public health concern have been expanding rapidly. Whereas not long ago many would have limited the scope of public health matters to general sanitation and the control of infectious disease, today all aspects of Winslow's famous definition are not only included but even surpassed. With reference to our environment, public health workers now think in the broadest possible terms—the total ecologic relationship between people and their environment. As for personal health services, public health agencies are already deeply involved, not only in problems of distribution and quality of health personnel and facilities, but also in the assurance of adequate comprehensive health care for all. This has been evidenced by a spectacular increase in significant legislative actions and programs during recent years.

In general, public health is concerned with four broad areas: (1) lifestyle and behavior, (2) the environment, (3) human biology, and (4) the organization of health programs and systems. Most of the activities of public health also fall into one of the following nine categories (adapted from a report of the Sun Valley Forum on National Health[9]):

1. Preventive health services for all age groups, including screening, early detection, immunization programs, health education and other activities
2. Coordination of public health services to bring the resources of other public sector and community services to bear on complex problems
3. Assuring access to care, especially for low-income, minority, and geographically isolated populations
4. Prevention or control of physical, chemical, and other hazards to health
5. Health status assessment, including surveillance of diseases, measurement of health status and assessment of service utilization trends
6. Quality assurance of individual professionals, institutions, and organizations, including public sector service systems
7. Catalyzing the development of needed services, such as long-term care programs for AIDS victims
8. Such other functions as community health planning and advocacy
9. Management of public sector programs and service systems

These categories include a wide variety of services, many of which are discussed in subsequent chapters. Obviously many public health agencies do not find it possible or necessary to engage in all of these activities. In many communities an agency other than the official public health department may be responsible for services that are considered to be in the broad field of public health, such as mental health, substance abuse, or personal health care services. Variation across communities may reflect either differences in real needs or differences in social determination of what matters.

Because public health is a term applied to a concept as well as to an agency, and because local and state public health agencies are so variable, it is necessary to find an abstract way to define what public health is in practice. This has given rise to the very useful concept of a *governmental presence in health.*[10] This concept, paraphrased, states that government, whether at the state or local level, is responsible for assuring that an agreed-upon set of standards and services is available and met in *every* community. There may be numerous agencies involved, such as the local health department, a community mental health center with its own board, a federally funded primary care center, a local hospital emergency room, and the district office of a state department of natural resources. But all of the people in each community are served by a unit of government, usually a local health department or a part of the state health department, which is responsible for the public's health and whose job it is to ensure that all the agreed-upon services are available and that whatever standards exist are met. Inherent in this concept is the need for an agency that can function across organizational boundaries, forming necessary coalitions in order to meet the needs of the community.

HEALTH AND GOVERNMENT

Some object to the concept that the protection and promotion of the public's health is an appropriate concern of government. Social and political philosophy did not always encourage this concept. The Roman Empire was notable for its concern for the protection and enhancement of the health and well-being of its own people. During most of history, however, the prevailing attitude has been to regard any such action as unnecessary and dangerous pampering of the masses. Indeed, this was one of the basic points made by Malthus[11]—that not only should the genetically and otherwise inferior be allowed to die according to nature's plan, but the conditions of the poor should not be improved lest they lose a sense of responsibility and moral restraint. Subsequently, lack of positive action was also justified on the basis of unwarranted and improper interference on the part of government in the private rights of the individual. Beck-Storrs[12] describes the dilemma in her discussion of the beginning of public health legislation in England in the late nineteenth century against a background of liberalism and individualism. She points to the conflict between the concept of public health and the prevailing idea of freedom of the individual:

> It suddenly dawned upon Englishmen that the modern apostles of health challenged the tradition of local government. They thought that they were called upon to make a decision between two evils, namely, either to let disorder and disease continue as before, or to suffer the monster of a civilized state.

She points out that public health threatened the Englishman's "right to be dirty" if he were so inclined. The affluent and the legislators, in the face of widespread communicable disease, were willing to agree to certain changes to protect themselves, but they did not want to go too far. The recommendations of The Royal Sanitary Commission, which was established in 1869, required the services of inspectors—but how could their authority be limited? To control the spread of infectious diseases, a system of compulsory notification would be necessary. Rules would have to be enforced for slum clearance. Minimum specifications for low-cost housing for workers were likely to force landlords and landowners to spend more money than they had intended. According to Beck-Storrs:

> Here for the first time in the modern period, arose the problem of state supported welfare measures which threatened to interfere with the economic activities of private citizens. And this happened at a time when economic liberalism was believed to be the principal reason for the prosperity of the 19th century.

To the extent possible, the government of England attempted to present the desired changes in a positive context—rights rather than restrictions, protections rather than prohibitions. Thus the state was empowered to ensure that people were no more likely to have their wells poisoned through the neglect of their neighbors than they were to be robbed with impunity. Health inspectors were given the responsibility of surveillance over drainage and sewerage systems, water supplies, bathhouses, and washhouses, as well as health conditions in workshops, mines, and bakeshops. Under the existing circumstances, the inspectors were natural targets of a public highly sensitive to its freedoms. Success depended on their training and tact and also on whether the instinctive resentment against such invasions of a person's private affairs could be overcome. The Royal Sanitary Commission, anticipating this reaction, therefore recommended "employment of only well-trained men, capable of administering on a national level the measures instituted by the proposed central authority." It may be worth observing parenthetically that this recommendation is as valid now as it was at the time it was made (except for its restriction to men).

In the developing United States, attitudes were if anything even more individualistic. As Roemer[13] has pointed out, the Western world's negative attitude toward government has deep roots, especially in America, where the colonists revolted against a domineering British monarchy. One result was the explicit limitation placed on the central government in the Constitution and the absence of Constitutional reference to health as either a personal right or a governmental responsibility. Roemer also emphasizes that the medical profession, having much earlier achieved independence from feudal landlords and religious authority in Europe, was doubly suspicious of governmental interference. As a result, as Shryock[14] has reasoned, medicine had little tangible impact on

American society before 1875. Indeed, this held true into the early twentieth century.[15] More recently, however, medicine and related fields, by either their presence or their absence, have had an increasingly significant influence on the problems, nature, and even survival of society. This, no government can afford to ignore.

Few now question health as a human right and its protection as a governmental responsibility. Thus the Director General of the World Health Organization stated that "social justice demands that all citizens of the world should reach an acceptable level of health that permits them to lead socially and economically productive lives."[16]

This clear, simple statement presents governments with a number of problems, however. It is realistically impossible to assure all people of health. Chance plays a role, as does individual human behavior. People do like to ski down slopes, and there is no society in which the use of potentially damaging substances, such as alcohol and other drugs, is unknown. There are three ways in which government can attempt to assure some equity (fairness based on need) and equality (equal benefits without regard to need) in access to at least a reasonable chance of being healthy: (1) through providing public health programs, (2) through providing access to good medical care, and (3) by altering the social and environmental factors that influence health status. These are complementary approaches, not mutually exclusive ones.

The first approach is usually taken, although resource constraints and different opinions about the value and appropriateness of some interventions limit its scope. The second is accomplished in part, both through the organization of public delivery systems and through payment for services needed by those whose access may be blocked by socioeconomic factors. But most governments, and the United States in particular, have not been able to develop acceptable controls on the amount or nature of the medical services to be made available. The third approach, altering the social and environmental factors that influence health status, is extremely difficult in a pluralistic society, since it involves the forced transfer of resources between individuals and groups. The public education system is the most highly developed and ubiquitous approach to altering social factors, but it suffers from various inequities, as do the welfare system, various taxation systems, and other social systems designed to promote an often vaguely defined concept of social justice. In recent years, the Reagan administration introduced the concept of a "safety net"—a set of government activities that were not intended to function as an equalizing force in society but only to provide a floor below which no one could fall. Unfortunately, there is little agreement about where that floor should be or how to maintain it. It has proven to be a porous net, indeed.

The existence of such programs is evidence that society does not believe that a reasonable assurance of health can be maintained without the intervention of government. Many actions, functions, and services would not be carried out if there were not a collective determination to do so. For example, while market forces might theoretically cause industry to protect its workers from exposure to hazards, history shows that in fact they often do not. Private practice may be an effective delivery system for personal health services, but many people cannot purchase needed services without government support. Thus while many parents might immunize their children to protect them against dangerous communicable diseases, many would not, and the public's health would thereby be jeopardized.

Many public health activities require the legal power of government: the police power that allows, in fact requires, government to curtail the rights of individuals to protect society in certain circumstances. These are not functions that can or should be carried out by nongovernment agencies. The exercise of such power requires adherence to concepts of fairness and due process that cannot be assured privately. In addition, many of the welfare functions of government cannot be carried out reliably without public sector responsibility for doing so. Private and voluntary agencies have a commendable record of providing such services in the United States, but they are inherently vulnerable to discriminatory decision making, which can erode their social purpose.

The essential organizing force is that of government. It is not a sufficient force to assure social justice, but it is an essential one.

HEALTH AND ECONOMICS

Even cursory thought or observation leads to an understanding of the relationship between economics and health. The social and economic status of individuals and entire groups has a profound impact on health status and vice versa. In addition, increasing attention is being paid to the economics of intervention: does the cost of a public health program produce benefits that are equal to, less than, or more than the costs of the program? Such questions provoke intense discussions about the appropriate criteria to be used in judging the value of a public health program. Brenner[17] has carried out and published a series of provocative studies that show the relationship between periods of economic recession and increases in spontaneous abortions, fetal deaths, depression, alcohol consumption, suicide, admissions to mental institutions, and cardiovascular and cerebrovascular disease.

Public health programs have an opportunity cost; that is, the money used for such purposes cannot be used for other purposes, such as personal and discretionary consumption, public education, or highway maintenance. A decision to consume resources for one purpose denies people the opportunity to spend those same resources on some other need. It is appropriate to ask what the benefits are of such decisions.

Most people appreciate the reduction in human suffering that has resulted from the public health movement. It must be realized, however, that the further removed one is in time and space from the threat of personal suffering, the less consideration is likely to be given to it. Success in public health work tends to mask its value.

It is difficult for people to attach value to something prevented. What would be the cost of providing services to thousands of poliomyelitis victims if an effective vaccine were not available and used? When there appear to be no or very few cases of such diseases, people soon forget what they were like. Many physicians are no longer familiar with measles, a disease easily recognized by their grandparents. The occasional consequences of such a disease (encephalitis, deafness, prolonged and severe illness) are little understood by those who have not seen them. It becomes difficult for younger elected officials to vote for appropriations to continue to prevent things that do not occur and that they have not seen or experienced.

The costs of all services have persistently increased. Proportionately speaking, the expenditure for public health services represents an area of considerable expansion. This has caused some to point to public health programs as an added economic burden to the taxpayer. It is important to demonstrate that money spent wisely for public health services may represent not an increase but an eventual decrease in the net bill for personal and community welfare and protection. The construction and maintenance costs of public water purification and sewage disposal plants are admittedly great. The costs, however, do not necessarily represent a net addition to the taxpayers' economic burden. Their absence would cost a greater sum for individual facilities, for increased medical care, and for lost earnings resulting from the illnesses that would not be prevented. Single or repeated outbreaks of hepatitis, for example, would cost a community much more in the long run than would the measures designed for their prevention. A sound financial policy for public health services therefore must take into consideration not only the humanitarian and social gains but also the economic advantages that may be attained.

Beyond the inevitability of these expenditures there is the added factor of the economic value of the lives made possible or continued by public health endeavors. To many, the thought of placing a monetary value on human life may seem distasteful. Essentially, reactions to life and death are based on emotion and sentiment, and ordinarily people avoid any thought of an economic value for a human being. Yet to be realistic, life does have a monetary value. The death of a parent brings to society as a whole, as well as to the particular family involved, an economic loss that is real and irreparable. This may manifest itself in a lowered standard of living for the family, the necessity of public financial aid, or the loss of a trained worker. Furthermore, government recognition is given to the value of a life, and one seldom hears objections to the concept of income tax exemptions for dependents.

In addressing himself to this question, Fuchs[18] makes several telling observations:

> What, then, is the justification for such an inquiry? The principal one is the fact that the question of the contribution of health services is being asked and answered every day. It is being asked and answered implicitly every time consumers, hospitals, universities, business firms, foundations, government agencies and legislative bodies make decisions concerning the volume and composition of health services, present and future. If economists can

help to rationalize and make more explicit the decision making process, can provide useful definitions, concepts and analytic tools, and can develop appropriate bodies of data and summary measures, they will be making their own contribution to health and to the economy.

In the same vein it must be recognized that, whereas members of appropriating bodies may be humane and sympathetic, collectively they must be analytic and practical. As a result, it is becoming increasingly difficult to gain legislative support for public health programs. This was illustrated in June 1980 when the Secretary of Health and Human Services announced that the Medicare program would no longer pay for heart transplant operations, which cost about $100,000. The Secretary commented, "I don't like the idea of assessing the value of a human life. At the same time we have to find out what the costs are. We have to ask, 'Will we buy this or will we buy something else?'"[19] Similar comments have been made with reference to kidney dialysis, the treatment of acute leukemia, the use of interferon, long-term care, and an ever growing number of other types of medical care. It is obvious, therefore, that the public health worker increasingly must be in a position to validate proposals and actions in economic terms.

It is unfortunate that many results of public health programs, although of great social value, are largely of an intangible nature; for example, diseases and deaths prevented, problems avoided, and the like. This makes it all the more imperative that health program planning and evaluative procedures incorporate from the beginning a consideration not only of economic costs but also of the anticipated benefits. Such cost-benefit considerations can be of inestimable value both in obtaining public understanding and support and in making budgetary presentations.

In attempting to do so, however, one is immediately confronted with two fundamental problems: (1) problems of definition—What is health? What is incapicitation? etc.—and (2) problems of measurement—How does one measure something that is not there? What base line can one use? The seriousness of these problems varies with time, place, and circumstance.

As far as countries in general are concerned, the World Health Organization has found the following among the obstacles to adequate quantification: (1) the widespread inadequacy of health and demographic statistics, (2) common exclusive reliance on input rather than output indicators, (3) the lack of an adequate measure of development of national welfare, and (4) the tendency of scientific disciplines to proceed in isolation from political science, economics, and sociology in studies that require a comprehensive approach.[20]

ECONOMIC VALUE OF LIFE

Many have tried to evaluate human life and to price its economic worth. One of the earliest attempts was that of Sir William Petty (1623-1687), who originated many ideas later used by the political economist Adam Smith in *Wealth of Nations* and other works. Petty[21] derived his estimate as follows:

> Suppose the People of England be Six Millions in number, that their Expense at £7 per head be 42 Millions: Suppose also that the Rent of the Lands be 8 Millions, and the yearly profit of all the Personal Estate be 8 Millions more; it must needs follow that the Labour of the People must have supplied the remaining 26 Millions that which multiplied by 20 (the Mass of Mankind being worth 20 years purchase as well as land) makes 520 Millions as the value of the whole people; which number divided by 6 Millions makes about £80 the value of each Head of Man, Woman and Child and of adult Persons Twice as much; from whence we may learn to compute the loss we have sustained by the Plague, by the Slaughter of Men in War and by sending them abroad into the Service of Foreign Princes.

In 1876 Sir William Farr[22] made more scientific computations using the life-table technique, which by that time had been developed. Subsequently this approach was applied more extensively and effectively by Dublin and his associates.[23] More recently this "human capital" approach has been improved and refined by a series of analysts* prominent among whom are Fein,[24] Mushkin and Collings,[25] Klarman,[26] Rice and Cooper,[27] Hartunian and associates,[28] and Landefeld and Seskin.[29] Landefeld and Seskin, in addition to broadening the methodology by adding the concept of "willingness-to-pay" (or in some situations one might add "willingness-to-act"), have presented a brief review of the nature of the contributions of the

* Each of these has published a number of articles and in some cases books on the subject. The specific references made here are to especially significant contributions.

others to whom reference has been made. Reference should also be made to a special issue of *Public Health Reports,* "The Cost of Disease and Illness in the United States in the Year 2000,"[30] and to a report of the National Academy of Sciences, Institute of Medicine, *Costs of Environment-related Health Effects.*[31]

As a crude analogy, the human body could be considered similar to a machine. Its proper function depends on various physical and biochemical components. It might be compared to an internal combustion engine with limbs in place of pistons and the endocrine system acting as the carburetor. Superimposed is the supervisory function of the human mind. In like manner, the human body may be regarded as an economic unit brought into existence for measurable, potential, productive purposes.

A machine must pass through several phases before it is ready to be of productive value. First, it must be built, which presupposes the existence of a factory in which it will be installed. Its construction therefore involves from the start a considerable capital outlay for factory site, labor, and tools. On completion, the machine must be prepared for use or function. This involves a series of installation expenditures for inspection and checking, for transfer to the site where it is to function, and so on. After this, it is ready to become productive, and the extent and efficiency of its usefulness will depend on its original quality or lack of structural defects, the correctness of its installation, and the manner in which it is routinely cared for while in use. It must be carefully and repeatedly lubricated, fed the proper fuel, inspected, overhauled, and replaced. Its ultimate economic value can be determined only after the costs of construction, installation, and preparatory expenditure and effort are deducted from the gross value of its productivity.

It is the hope of the manufacturer that the machine will continue to function with relative efficiency at least long enough to produce sufficient items for sale to offset all of the capital investment and the installation and maintenance costs. In other words, from the moment the machine is purchased, the curve of the cumulative investment in it continues to rise, and the curve of cumulative productive value lags for a considerable period. It is not until these two curves cross that the manufacturer can breathe easily and begin to reap a net benefit from the use of the machine. If any untoward circumstances develop before the two curves cross, the manufacturer will suffer a loss.

Many things may go wrong after purchase. The machine may have been defective, it may have been damaged during transportation and installation, or it may have worn out prematurely as a result of improper use or care. These are only a few of the undesirable potentialities the manufacturer must constantly guard against. Even after the two curves cross, all is not necessarily clear sailing, because the longer the machine is used the greater is the tendency for parts to wear out and for maintenance and repair costs to increase. Sooner or later a time is reached when these costs become greater than the value of the items produced, and the two curves cross again. Continued use is no longer economically profitable. The machine has now passed into the phase of obsolescence.

If one sets aside for the moment the very real but unmeasurable social and spiritual values of human life, there are some similarities with the foregoing example. With humans and their societies, however, there are many complex variables to be considered in approximating the average value of future earnings and the ultimate economic value of life. Time, place, and economic conditions are critically important. Related to these are varying labor force participation rates, variations in salaries for different age groups and the sexes, whether the value of housekeeping is included, continued but varied extensions of life expectancies, social programs that provide substitutes for earned income, and many other factors. Illness or other difficulties that may affect not only the individual but also those close to him or her can also alter productivity. Table 1-1 presents some of the chief items that contribute to the debit and credit columns of a human life.

If one considers some but by no means all of these factors, the cost of raising a child to the age of 18 years in the United States and then financing him or her through a public college is in excess of $150,000. This figure considers only direct costs. If the "lost" earnings of a parent who chooses to remain at home to raise children instead of gainfully working are added, the total cost may be as much as $500,000. Costs are greater for urban than for nonurban families and are lowest in the north central states and highest in the western states.

These variations indicate again the complexity of the problems encountered in attempts to quantify life from an economic viewpoint. Both the philosophic difficulty and the need for some practical approach have been stated succinctly by Muller[32]:

> Observation of society shows that there is no one mode of valuing life or of comparing the social worth of a year in the lives of two different individuals. A pecuniary standard is adopted whenever reference to comparative productivity loss is used as a guide to health policy, and this is in tune with the workings of institutions in which money talks—i.e., markets. Yet this standard is biased by social discrimination factors influencing productivity and earnings of different race, age, and sex categories.

TABLE 1-1 Factors in the socioeconomic value of human life—summary

Capital cost*

1. Economic incapacitation of mother
2. Risk of death to mother
3. Risk of injury to mother with immediate or subsequent effect on her economic value
4. Immediate costs of childbearing
5. Risk of infant death
6. Risk of infant illness or injury
7. Interest on capital investment

Installation cost†

1. Shelter, clothing, and food
2. Value of time mother devotes to child care
3. Education—family and community contribution
4. Medical and dental care and health protection
5. Recreation and transportation
6. Insurance
7. Sundries and incidentals
8. Risk of death during first 18 years
9. Risk of disability during first 18 years
10. Interest on installation costs

Period of productivity‡

Credit

1. Earning potential
2. Interest on earnings
3. Noneconomic potential

Debit

1. Risk of disability during productive period
2. Medical costs
3. Risk of premature death
4. Risk of becoming substandard or antisocial
5. Interest on debit items

*The investment that society has in each infant by the time it is born.
†The investment that society has in each individual at 18 years of age.
‡The return that society can expect from its investment, with the risks involved during this period.

ECONOMIC VALUE OF HEALTH PROGRAMS

The increasing use of cost-benefit analysis has by now provided many examples of the economic justification of public health programs. About a half century ago, an appropriation for an intensive diphtheria immunization program in New York City was shown to result in savings of more than $500,000. About the same time and in the same city, a $500,000 appropriation for an antipneumonia program saved at least $5 million annually. Also at that time in Detroit a special appropriation of $1 million for an early case-finding program against tuberculosis resulted in savings of over $5 million each year. A more recent example is found in an analysis of the risks and costs of immunizing children against measles, mumps, and rubella (German measles).[33] There were 2,872 cases of measles in 1983 compared to an estimated 3,325,000 that would have occurred without immunization. For rubella the count was 3,816 versus 1,500,000, and for mumps, 32,850 compared to 2,100,000. The authors estimated that the cost of caring for these patients would have been $1.4 billion if the diseases had not been prevented, compared to only $14.5 million for the care of the cases that did occur plus $96 million for the immunization program itself: a 13:1 ratio of benefits to cost. A cost-benefit study of screening blood donors for human immunodeficiency virus antibodies showed a benefit to cost ratio of 1.2:1.[34]

It is important to spend a moment examining some definitions.[35] The two terms commonly used are *cost-benefit analysis* and *cost-effectiveness analysis.* The latter involves a comparison of two or more approaches to achieving the same end result: for example, the use of seat belts and shoulder restraints compared to the use of air bags to save a life. Cost-benefit analysis is more complex but allows the comparison of quite different programs, such as screening for breast cancer versus restaurant inspection programs. In a cost-benefit analysis, the benefits must be reduced to a common unit, usually dollars, in order to develop a ratio of benefits to costs.

There has been an enormous increase in interest in such studies in recent years. A search of the Medline database at the National Library of Medicine revealed 155 articles involving cost-benefit analysis and prevention in 1986 and 1987 compared to none in 1974 and 1975. A similar search of a database covering health administration and planning literature revealed 136 published articles in 1986 and 1987 compared to just 14 in 1974 and 1975. These included an analysis of a domiciliary care experiment in Pennsylvania,[36] a study of the costs of a suburban paramedic program in reducing deaths due to cardiac arrest,[37] a report on the cost-effectiveness of cervical cancer screening,[38] and a study of community programs to prevent dental caries in Spain.[39]

Mushkin and her colleagues[40] estimated the economic cost of illness in the United States in the year 2000. Their results are shown in Table 1-2. They assumed improvements in certain death rates, an increase in the available work force, and a reduction in disability and in loss of work time caused by illness. They point out that the "gain in economic resources through the prevention or cure of diseases and postponement of death to an old age takes the form of added numbers of workers and added work time."

The value of all the costs was estimated at more than $2 trillion. Can that burden be reduced? In the years since the beginning of this century, reductions in mortality have been extraordinary. Table 1-3 shows the gains that have been made in controlling communicable diseases. Can the same gains be accomplished in reducing the incidence of noncommunicable diseases in which human behavior and social and environmental factors play leading roles? Table 1-4 shows the estimated years of life lost before age 65 to 13 leading health problems in 1980. These calculations were part of the deliberations at a Carter Center Conference in 1984.[41] Note that this table uses the concept of "years of potential life lost by age 65." A simple count of the number of deaths due to a cause obscures the fact that a death occurring early in life destroys more years of life than does a death occurring late in life. Thus a 20-year-old who dies in a motor vehicle collision costs society 45 years of working life—the economic return on social invest-

TABLE 1-2 Total costs of illness in year 2000, in billions of 1975 dollars and year 2000 dollars*

	Indirect costs				
Mortality indicators	**Mortality**	**Morbidity**	**Total**	**Direct**	**Total costs**
			Year 2000 dollars		
Mortality: single year loss	21.5	336.1	387.6	1,013.6	1,401.2
Mortality: present value of future earnings loss discounted at 10%	356.4	366.1	722.5	1,013.6	1,736.1
Mortality: present value of future earnings loss discounted at 2.5%	715.2	366.1	1,081.3	1,013.6	2,094.9
			1975 dollars		
Mortality: single year loss	5.2	89.5	94.7	416.4	511.1
Mortality: present value of future earnings loss discounted at 10%	87.2	89.5	176.7	416.4	593.1
Mortality: present value of future earnings loss discounted at 2.5%	174.9	89.5	264.4	416.4	680.8

From Mushkin, SJ and others: Public Health Rep 93:493, Sept-Oct 1978.
*Assuming constant labor force participation rates and including household values. Direct costs deflated by the medical care price index and indirect costs deflated by an index of average earnings. Productivity increase of 2% assumed.

ments in that person; 1,000 such deaths result in a loss of 45,000 years. Similarly, 1,000 deaths at age 50 due to lung cancer result in a loss of 15,000 years of life before age 65.

The concept is repugnant to some analysts, because it seems to imply that there is no social value to a life past 65 years of age. That is not the point. Death rates begin to increase sharply after age 65, and since all life ends in death, it is difficult to determine just what would be considered a "premature" death. Fixing the end-point at 65 simply makes the concept of unnecessary loss easier to measure. (Given increases in longevity, it would be just as sensible to increase the age to 70.) The total, for all of the listed causes, is 12,247,000 years of potential life lost, plus an unknown amount attributed to mental illness.

The conference considered the potential for reducing the loss due to many of these causes of death. For each category, the participants considered known risk factors and techniques for modifying risks. Many of the categories comprise several different phenomena, and the results vary widely among these component parts, but it is reasonable to assume that more than 50% of these years of life could be saved if present-day techniques could be fully applied. No one knows what the cost would be. What is a year of life worth? Does the answer to that question depend in part on whose life it is? Would 5 million years of life be worth $1,500 each? That would be $7.5 billion—about the amount currently being spent by all of the state and local health departments in the United States. Answers to such complex questions are urgently needed. But it must be emphasized that such numbers will not provide a simple answer to the complex questions society must face as it determines how it should intervene and why. Other values must be considered in making such decisions, as indicated by Hilbert[42] in his closing presidential address to the American Public Health Association in 1976:

> The mother in an environment harboring a dying infant, a wayward son, a prematurely aging husband, and a house falling into shambles thinks not in terms of epidemiological justifications or bacteriological samples proudly presented in tabular form. She thinks of happiness never quite attained, satisfaction never fully gained, frustrations never totally banished, poverty never surmounted, needs never fulfilled, and of health never fully realized. When preventive public health with all its ramifications extends its imagination to the creation of a new dimension that reaches into the hearts and lives of all mankind, then may come the hope that this preventive health cathedral may attain completion.

PUBLIC HEALTH AND NATURAL SELECTION

One other aspect of public health merits attention at this point. Public health programs save lives. Many of the lives saved are continued with

TABLE 1-3 Decline in deaths due to selected communicable diseases, 1900-1985, United States

Cause	Death rate per 100,000 1900-1904	Predicted deaths 1985	Actual deaths 1985	"Savings"
Typhoid	2.7	6,446	0	6,446
Measles	3.1	7,401	4	7,397
Scarlet fever	2.1	5,014	4	5,010
Whooping cough	3.7	8,833	4	8,829
Diphtheria	3.1	7,401	0	7,401
Poliomyelitis	.8	1,910	3	1,907
Tetanus	.8	1,910	23	1,887
Tuberculosis	55.0	131,308	1,752	129,556
Syphilis	9.1	21,725	80	21,645
Malaria	3.5	8,356	13	8,343
TOTALS		200,304	1,883	198,421

From (1) Mortality statistics, 1935, Washington, DC, 1937, US Government Printing Office; (2) Vital Statistics of the United States, 1985, Volume II—Mortality, Part A, Washington, DC, 1988, National Center for Health Statistics.

impairments severe enough to cause disabilities and dependencies, which may result in substantial social costs. Public health and medical care activities also save the lives of those born with severe impairments. People with diabetes and blood disorders and other problems can, with good support, live relatively normal lives. They can have careers and families. Their children are often likely to have the same impairments that they have. In an earlier era, those with such impairments did not survive to adulthood, or if they did, they were not likely to have children. Some have criticized public health for interfering with the process of natural selection, which is thought to select for life those with advantages and to pass over those who have such impairments. Huxley[43] referred to public health as "unnatural," calling it the very essence of the myth of progress. Bowes[44] concluded that a few "good old-fashioned epidemics" such as the Black Death might be desirable, because they tend to reduce the number of those with mental or physical impairments. There have been many other such statements. Most of the forceful writing on the subject comes from an earlier era, but the concern is often expressed in different terms today: in concern for the quality of life as well as its quantity, for living wills, for the right to die. Any society must learn to discuss such issues in an enlightened manner. But the idea that public health is counterproductive in its preservationist tendencies is particularly troublesome.

Who are the "fit"? Would a "good old-fashioned epidemic" select just those with severe impairments, or would everyone be at risk? As will be shown repeatedly in this book, the poor and minority groups tend to be most prone to disease, injury, and premature death. But does that reflect their environment or their genes? Kings and queens, merchants and artists, lawyers and physicians, geniuses and athletes, all have their share of impairments. In most instances uncontrolled disease strikes blindly, producing a variety of illness in all components of a society. Disease and death have often entered palaces and mansions through the front door. Edgar Allen Poe described the situation vividly in *The Masque of the Red Death.* The egalitarian nature of uncontrolled disease is also well illustrated at Stratford-on-Avon, where the birth of William Shakespeare is recorded in a church register. Several lines above is the entry "juli 11, 1564, Oliverus Gume—*hic incipit pestis* [here

TABLE 1-4 Health impact of 14 leading health problems, single listed causes, United States, 1980

Cause	Deaths	Preventable deaths	Years of life lost by age 65	Direct costs (by billion dollars)
Alcoholic illness	10,000	9,000	191,000	10.1
Arthritis and musculoskeletal diseases	7,000	2,100	49,000	12.6
Cancer	418,000	280,060	1,809,000	11.6
Circulatory diseases	934,000	625,780	1,607,000	25.6
Dental diseases	0	0	0	15.6
Diabetes mellitus	35,000	3,205	145,000	3.7
Digestive diseases	48,000	26,456	301,000	9.3
Drug abuse	1,000	900	21,000	.8
Homicide and suicide	51,000	45,900	1,317,000	.6
Infant mortality	47,000	14,400	3,043,000	4.7
Infectious diseases	66,000	33,000	763,000	5.7
Respiratory diseases	60,000	45,729	232,000	12.2
Unintentional injuries	104,000	93,600	2,769,000	15.5
Mental illness	?	?	?	?
TOTALS	1,781,000	1,180,130	12,247,000	$128.0

From Working Papers, Health Policy Consultation, Carter Center, Emory University, Atlanta, November 26-28, 1984.

began the plague]." During the year 1564, the village suffered 242 deaths from plague. This probably represented one third to one half the population of Stratford-on-Avon. During the plague's early phases, a vulnerable, helpless infant was born who by chance alone was spared, subsequently to write some of the greatest plays in the English language. So far as history can tell us, William Shakespeare was no more "fit" than Oliverus Gume.

So who are the fit and the unfit? Observation indicates that the definition varies with time and place. Steinmetz was a congenital cripple; Toulouse-Lautrec was afflicted with hereditary osteochondritis fragilitas; Mozart, Chopin, and many other great figures in the arts and sciences died at early ages from tuberculosis. Still others died of syphilis. Many great artists and scientists have died of AIDS. Are these creative and industrious people "unfit"? Citizens of the United States can least afford such labeling, since most are descendants of persons who by one standard or another would once have been considered undesirable or unfit. The reasons have varied: religious, political, ethnic, economic, social, and cultural—whatever reason was most expedient at the moment.

Although some people and even groups suffer from physical or other handicaps, it is false reasoning to suppose that they are necessarily "unfit." The Bantu people, from whom so many American blacks have descended, carried the gene for sickle cell anemia. While an unfortunate trait in many climates, that gene provided resistance to malaria in the Bantu's original climate, enabling them to survive while others did not.

No health worker would deny that the profession makes it possible for many to live who otherwise would die. Each Olympic tournament sees new records established. The descendants of immigrants are taller and of greater physical stamina than their forebears or their counterparts in their countries of origin. This is not meant to deny the need to apply the increasing knowledge of genetics in personal and marital counseling. However, one cannot help but ponder the potential magnitude of the benefits that would accrue to the human race from a truly vigorous application of present knowledge. Rosenau had this in mind when he wrote concerning preventive medicine and public health:

> It dreams of a time when there shall be enough for all, and every man shall bear his share of labor in accordance with his ability, and every man shall possess sufficient for the needs of his body and the demands of health. These things he shall have as a matter of justice and not of charity. It dreams of a time when there shall be no unnecessary suffering and no premature deaths; when the welfare of the people shall be our highest concern; when humanity and mercy shall replace greed and selfishness; and it dreams that all these things will be accomplished through the wisdom of man. It dreams of these things, not with the hope that we, individually, may participate in them, but with the joy that we may aid in their coming to those who shall live after us. When young men have vision the dreams of old men come true.

Some people may dismiss this as impractical idealism. But the achievement of the greatest success and satisfaction in a social field such as public health demands a full share of idealism. As a final word of caution, however, it must be realized that idealism and pragmatism are not necessarily immiscible, as are oil and water. In fact, their admixture is sorely needed now more than ever before in this incredibly rapidly evolving age. The prefacing statement by Lowell[45] in his book *Conflicts of Principle* is as timely and pertinent now and to the present public health purpose as when he wrote it half a century ago:

> People often call some men idealists and others practical folks as if mankind were by natural inclination so divided into these two groups that an idealist cannot be practical or a man of affairs have a lofty purpose, whereas in fact no man approaches perfection who does not combine both qualities in a high degree. Without either he is defective in spirit and unscientific in method; the idealist because he does not strive to make his theory accurate, that is consonant with the facts; the so-called practical man if he acts upon the impulse of the occasion without the guidance of an enduring principle of conduct. Hence both lack true wisdom, the idealist more culpably for he should be diligent in thought and seek all the light he can obtain. It is useful to repeat that many men have *light* enough to be visionary, but only he who *clearly sees* can *behold* a vision.

REFERENCES

1. Blumgart HL: Caring for the patient, N Engl J Med 270:449, Feb 27, 1964.

2. Beauchamp PE: Public health as social justice, Inquiry 13:3, March 1976.
3. Dubos R: The dreams of reason, New York, 1961, Columbia University Press.
4. Draper P, Best G, and Dennis J: Health and wealth, R Soc Health J 97:121, June 1977.
5. Dubos RJ: Mirage of health, Garden City, NY, 1960, Doubleday & Co, Inc.
6. Winslow C-EA: The untilled field of public health, Mod Med 2:183, March 1920.
7. Mountin JW: The health department's dilemma, Public Health Rep 67:223, March 1952.
8. A new perspective on the health of Canadians, Ottawa, 1974, Ministry of National Health and Welfare.
9. Manning B and Vladeck BC: Update: the role of state and local government in health, Health Affairs 2(4):134, 1983.
10. Model standards: a guide for community preventive health services, ed 2, Washington, DC, 1985, American Public Health Association.
11. Malthus TR: An essay on the principle of population as it affects the future improvement of society, London, 1798. Reprint, London, 1926, Royal Economic Society.
12. Beck-Storrs A: Public health and government control, Soc Stud 45:211, Oct 1954.
13. Roemer MI: The influence of government on American medicine, Oslo, 1962, Gyldendal Norsk Forlag.
14. Shryock RH: The interplay of social and internal factors in the history of modern medicine, Sci Month 76:221, April 1953.
15. Shryock RH: Medicine and society in America: 1660-1860, Ithaca, NY, 1960, Cornell University Press.
16. Mahler H: Health for all, WHO Chron 31:491, Dec 1977.
17. Brenner MH: Estimating the social costs of national economic policy: implications for mental and physical health, and criminal aggression, Report to the Congressional Research Service of the Library of Congress and the Joint Economic Committee of Congress, Washington, DC, 1976, US Government Printing Office.
18. Fuchs VR: The contribution of health services to the American economy, Milbank Mem Fund Q, 44:65, Oct 1966.
19. Schwartz H: How much is a life worth? Wall St J, Sept 15, 1980.
20. Interrelationships between health programmes and socio-economic development, Public Health Papers No 49, Geneva, 1973, World Health Organization.
21. Petty Sir W: Political arithmetic or a discourse concerning the extent and value of lands, people, buildings, etc, ed 3, London, 1699, Robert Clavel.
22. Farr W: Contribution of the 39th annual report of the registrar general of births, marriages, and deaths for England and Wales, 1876.
23. Dublin LI, Lotka AJ, and Spiegelman M: The money value of a man, ed 2, New York, 1946, The Ronald Press Co.
24. Fein R: Economics of mental illness, New York, 1958, Basic Books.
25. Mushkin SJ and Collings FA: Economic costs of disease and injury, Public Health Rep 74:795, Sept 1959.
26. Klarman H: Syphilis control programs. In Dorfman R, editor: Measuring benefits of government investments, Washington, DC, 1965, The Brookings Institute.
27. Rice DP and Cooper BS: The economic value of human life, Am J Public Health 57:1954, Nov 1967.
28. Hartunian NS, Smart CN, and Thompson MS: The incidence and economic costs of cancer, motor vehicle injuries, coronary heart disease and stroke: a comparative analysis, Am J Public Health 70:1249, Dec 1980.
29. Landefeld JS and Seskin EP: The economic value of life: linking theory to practice, Am J Public Health 72:555, June 1982.
30. Mushkin SJ and others: The cost of disease and illness in the United States in the year 2000, Public Health Rep 93:493, Sept-Oct 1978.
31. National Academy of Sciences, Institute of Medicine: Costs of environment-related health effects, Washington, DC, 1980, National Academy Press.
32. Muller CF: Economic costs of illness and health policy, Am J Public Health 70:1245, Dec 1980.
33. White CC, Koplan JP, and Orenstein WA: Benefits, risks and costs of immunization for measles, mumps and rubella, Am J Public Health 75:739, July 1985.
34. Eisenstaedt RS and Getzen TE: Screening blood donors for human immunodeficiency virus antibody: cost-benefit analysis, Am J Public Health 78:450, April 1988.
35. Warner KE and Luce BR: Cost-benefit and cost-effectiveness analysis in health care: principles, practice and potential, Ann Arbor, 1982, Health Administration Press.
36. Ruchlin HS, Hirsch S, and Morris JN: Pennsylvania's domiciliary care experiment: II. cost-benefit implications, Am J Public Health 73:654, June 1983.
37. Urban N, Bergner L, and Eisenberg MS: The costs of a suburban paramedic program in reducing deaths due to cardiac arrest, Medical Care XIX:379, April 1981.
38. Mandelblatt JS and Fahs MC: The cost-effectiveness of cervical cancer screening for low income elderly women, J Am Med Assoc 259:2409, April 22-29, 1988.

39. Manau C and others: Economic evaluation of community programs for the prevention of dental caries in Catalonia, Spain, Community Dent Oral Epid 15:297, Dec 1987.
40. Mushkin SJ and others: The cost of disease and illness in the United States in the year 2000, Public Health Rep 93:493, Sept-Oct 1978.
41. Amler RW and Dull HB: Closing the gap: the burden of unnecessary illness, New York, 1987, Oxford University Press.
42. Hilbert MS: Prevention, Am J Public Health 67:353, April 1977.
43. Huxley A: Brave new world, Life p. 63, Sept 20, 1948.
44. Bowes GK: Epidemic disease: past, present, and future, J R San Inst 66:174, July 1946.
45. Lowell AL: Conflicts of principle, Cambridge, MA, 1932, Harvard University Press.

CHAPTER 2

Historical perspectives

A LOOK AT THE PAST

Although the primary purpose of this book is to consider the current practice of public health, it is also important to consider its history.* This is not merely to pay tribute to those who went before, although Osler[5] once claimed it to be a sign of a dry age when the great men of the past were held in light esteem. Beyond this, historical review provides insight into the significance of current events. Many circumstances and events of the past help to explain some present-day problems and trends that otherwise might be puzzling.

In the United States, government involvement in health affairs is peculiarly Balkanized, with medical care, public health, and mental health each evolving along different tracks with their own policies and constituencies. In recent years, environmental health has been separated somewhat from public health.

The principal events that helped to shape the federal government's involvement in health affairs will be described in this chapter. A more detailed discussion of the development and present organizational relationships of state and local public health agencies will be found in Chapters 6, 7, 18, and 23.

PRIMITIVE SOCIETIES

Little is known about the prehistoric origins of either personal or community hygiene. Some hints may be gleaned, however, from a study of tribal customs and rules of contemporary primitive groups. With few exceptions they have a certain amount of group and community hygienic sense, usually derived from experience with survival. Rules against the fouling of family or tribal environments are almost universal. Many have taboos against the use of the upstream side of the campsite for excretory purposes. Burial of excreta is not uncommon. However, this practice is sometimes based on superstition rather than sanitary concepts. Many groups have elaborate provisions for disposal of the dead. Almost all primitive people recognize the existence of disease and engage in forms of voodoo or tribal dancing (psychosomatic medicine), temporary banishment (isolation and quarantine), or smoke and noise (fumigation) to drive away the evil spirits of disease. Such practices are not just a matter of historic curiosity. Many people in the United States still wear amulets, copper bracelets, and other objects thought to prevent certain diseases or suppress their symptoms. Folk medicine is widely practiced throughout the world.

* For two extensive and scholarly presentations of this subject, see *A History of Public Health* by Rosen[1] and *The History of American Epidemiology* by Top.[2] Also see *Health in America: 1776-1976.*[3] For other references, see Hanlon and others.[4]

CLASSICAL CULTURES

Archeologic evidence and other records show that Minoans, 3000-1430 BCE*, and Myceneans, 1430-1150 BCE, built drainage systems, toilets, and water-flushing systems. Herodotus wrote that Egyptians of about 1000 BCE were the healthiest of all civilized people. They had a considerable sense of personal cleanliness, possessed numerous pharmaceutic preparations, and constructed earth privies for sewage and public drainage pipes. The Hebrews extended Egyptian hygienic thought and formulated in Leviticus, about 1500 BCE, what is probably the world's first written hygienic code. It deals with a wide variety of personal and community responsibilities, including cleanliness of the body, protection against the spread of contagious diseases, isolation of lepers, disinfection of dwellings after illness, sanitation of campsites, disposal of excreta and refuse, protection of water and food supplies, and the hygiene of maternity.

* BCE and CE, meaning Before the Common Era and during the Common Era, are ecumenical terms used by both Jewish and Christian writers.

The Athenian civilization circa 1000-400 BCE is of interest for two reasons. It was there that personal hygiene was developed to a degree never previously approached. Much concern was given to personal cleanliness, exercise, and dietetics in addition to environmental sanitation. In contrast with present-day public health thought, however, the weak, ill, and crippled were ignored and sometimes destroyed. It is important to realize that this was essentially a culture of a minority of nobles, and the benefits of the culture were not available to the majority, who were poor farmers or slaves.

The Roman component of the classical civilization that succeeded Athens is well known for its administrative and engineering achievements. At its zenith it had laws for the registration of citizens and slaves; for a periodic census; for the prevention of nuisances; for inspection and removal of dilapidated buildings; for the elimination of dangerous animals and foul smells; for the destruction of unsound goods; for the supervision of weights and measures; for the supervision of public bars, taverns, and houses of prostitution; and for the regulation of building construction. A supply of good and cheap grain was assured to the population. Numerous public sanitary services were provided. Many streets were paved, and some even had gutters and were drained by a network of underground conduits. Provision was made for the cleaning and repair of streets and for the removal of garbage and rubbish. Public baths were constructed and extensively used. An adequate and relatively safe public water supply was made available by the construction of magnificent aqueducts and tunnels. It is of interest to note that several of the aqueducts and subsurface drains *(cloacae)* constructed by the Romans are still in use, having been incorporated into the present-day water and sewerage systems of Rome and other cities.

The Roman civilization, like that of Athens, rested on a majority of poor farmers and especially on enormous numbers of slaves obtained by military conquest. When the limits of conquest were reached and the supply of new lands and slaves diminished, the civilization weakened, and the vaunted legions were disastrously defeated by Gothic hordes in CE 378 at Adrianople. This led to the beginning of Western civilization based on quite different concepts of society, religion, government, economics, agriculture, and technology. These changes were so drastic, however, that a transitional period was inevitable.

THE MIDDLE AGES

The transitional period, which lasted from about CE 500 to 1500, is especially interesting from a hygienic and epidemiologic viewpoint. Classical ideology was dualistic and held that full spirituality could be achieved only by freeing the spirit from the body and from the material world. It regarded the world and the flesh as evil. The Western philosophy that eventually developed is pluralistic. As Quigley[6] described it, "Western ideology believes that the material is good and the spiritual is better but they are not opposed to each other since the material world is necessary for the achievement of the spiritual world." In other words, after all, God made the body as well as the spirit. It took time for such philosophies to spread and become accepted. Therefore there was a period from the final collapse of the Roman Empire, about CE 500, to the early part of the tenth century that has been somewhat unfairly called the Dark Ages. One of its characteristics was a reaction against anything reminiscent of the Roman Empire. Many people, especially early monks and anchorites, believed that the Athenians and Romans, despite their dualism, pampered the body to the detriment of the soul. Therefore they preached the belittlement of worldly things. This became known as "mortification of the flesh."

So intense was the reaction that it even included a significant change in attitude toward sanitation and personal hygiene. It was considered immoral to view even one's own body; therefore people seldom bathed and wore notoriously dirty garments. This is said by some to have been partly responsible for the eventual widespread use of perfume in this period. Diets in general were apparently poor and consisted of badly prepared or preserved foods. This gave rise to the widespread use of spices and the search for trade routes to obtain them. Sanitation was ignored. Refuse and body wastes were allowed to accumulate in and around dwellings. Slops were thrown onto the roads or streets, hence the famous cry *Gardez, l'eau.* These and other dangerous customs carried over even into relatively recent times, as depicted so well by Hogarth's prints of life in eighteenth-century England.

However, as time passed, some significant medical and hygienic developments occurred. Generally they were reactions to the disastrous effects of uncontrolled nature or ill-conceived habits and customs. Terrifying pandemics of disease occurred that were among the most intense experiences in the history of humanity. During the seventh century a new religion, Islam, appeared. It attracted many followers in Africa, the Near East, Asia, and to some extent the Balkans and the Iberian peninsula. Like Judaism, it placed great emphasis on cleanliness.

However, after the death of Mohammed, it became a religious custom to make a pilgrimage, or hajj, to Mecca, in present-day Saudi Arabia, the place of the prophet's birth about CE 570. During each great hajj, among the many thousands who converged on the small city were some from far-off Asia, including India, which was and still is the endemic center of cholera. Cholera naturally spread rapidly among the thousands of pilgrims, who disseminated it along their homeward routes of travel and throughout their respective homelands. Thus each hajj was almost invariably followed by a pandemic of cholera.

Complicating this, beginning in CE 1095, were the hordes of Christian crusaders who converged on the Middle East from all parts of Europe and whose wanderings inevitably resulted in periodic seeding of the European continent with the vibrio of cholera, as well as other agents of disease. The vibrio prospered in a gradually urbanizing Europe, whence centuries later it was transferred to America by the invading settlers. During the period from 1830 to about 1880, cholera repeatedly reentered America, spreading along the water routes and accompanying the prospectors to the gold fields of California. At one time or another, most settlements were affected by cholera, often resulting in the death of one third to one half of the population.

During the early Dark or Middle Ages, leprosy spread, probably from Egypt to Asia Minor and eventually throughout Europe, aided by the Crusades and other great migrations. It apparently was a far more acute and disfiguring disease than is presently observed in most of the Western world, and because of the terror to which it gave rise, laws were passed to regulate the conduct and movement of those afflicted. In many places lepers were declared civilly dead and were banished from human communities. They were compelled to wear identifying clothes and to warn of their presence by means of a horn, bell, or clapper and by crying the word *unclean.* This had a twofold result: it was an effective isolation measure, and it usually brought about a relatively rapid death from hunger and exposure, as well as from lack of treatment and care. These measures, inhuman as they were, almost eradicated leprosy in Europe (but by no means in the world) by the sixteenth century and may be regarded as an early, although unplanned, application of epidemiology.

The Black Death

No sooner had leprosy passed its zenith and begun to decline than an even deadlier menace appeared in the form of bubonic plague. Its spread is illustrative of a momentous ecologic phenomenon. The origin of the source was the vast plain of central Asia. The four biologic factors were (1) the bacterium *Yersinia pestis,* which infected (2) fleas, which lived on and infected (3) marmosets and (4) humans. The people who were infected were Mongols whose traditional life was nomadic. Their leader, Ghingis Khan, lived at a tent capital, Karakorum. In 1219 he gathered an army that was mobile by means of fast ponies and began a vast sweep of conquest that eventually included western Asia, the Middle East, Egypt, the Balkans, and eastern and central Europe.[7] With them they brought *Yersinia pestis,* which had been transferred to them from the marmoset. Conditions of living compounded by the chaos of conquest then resulted in the transfer from infected humans to rodents, predominantly rats, in the areas conquered.

From then on the spread of plague was rapid and repetitive, compounded by other military activities, crusades, dislocated populations, and trade. Probably nothing ever came so close to exterminating the human species, according to Hecker.[8] During the 1340s more than 13 million people died from the disease in China. India was almost depopulated. Tartary, Mesopotamia, Syria, and Armenia were said to be covered by dead bodies. At the plague's peak, Aleppo lost about 500 people and Cairo from 10,000 to 15,000 people daily. In Gaza 22,000 people and most of the animals were carried off within 6 weeks. Cyprus was depopulated, and ships without crews were often seen in the Mediterranean and in the North Sea, drifting aimlessly and spreading plague when they drifted ashore. It was reported to Pope Clement VI that half the population of the known world had died. The figure given was about 43 million. The total mortality from the Black Death is thought to have been over 60 million. Europe, particularly during 1348, was devastated. Florence lost 60,000 people, Venice 100,000, Marseilles 16,000 in 1 month, Siena 70,000, Paris 50,000, St. Denys 14,000 and Strasbourg 9,000. In many places in France only 2 out of 20 people survived.

In Avignon, where 60,000 people died, the Pope consecrated the Rhone River so bodies might be thrown into it without delay, since the churchyard was full. In Vienna, burial in churchyards or churches was prohibited; the dead were arranged in layers by thousands in six large pits outside the city. (In a main square in Vienna can be seen an elaborate monument commemorating the end of the great epidemic.) Crossing the channel, the Black Death destroyed half the population of medieval England and at least 100,000 in London alone. Hecker[8] states that as many as 200,000 small towns and villages in Europe may have lost all of their inhabitants. "Morals deteriorated everywhere, and the service of God was, in a great measure, laid aside. . . ."

It is estimated that Europe's tribute to plague in the midfourteenth century was about 25 million, and this one horrifying visitation was just a beginning. Plague continued to ebb and flow like a tide, periodically sweeping over the European continent. For example, in London in 1603 over one sixth of the population died, in 1625 another sixth, and in 1665 about one fifth. During 1790 Marseilles and Toulon lost 91,000 people; in 1743 Messina lost 70,000; and in 1759 about 70,000 died on the island of Cyprus. It must also be realized that great as these figures are, they are proportionately enormous in relation to the populations of those times.

Out of these terrifying experiences, and despite the view of divine or cosmic causation of disease, certain groping attempts were made to forestall the apparent inevitability of epidemic disaster. In 1348 the great trading port of Venice banned entry of infected or suspected ships and travelers. In 1377 at Ragusa (present-day Dubrovnik) it was ruled that travelers from plague areas must stop at designated places outside the port and remain free of disease for 2 months before being allowed to enter. Historically this represents the first quarantine measure, although it involved a 2-month interval rather than the 40 days that the term implies. This procedure is of particular interest in that it indicated a vague realization of the existence of an incubation period for a communicable disease. Six years later, in 1383, Marseilles passed the first quarantine law and erected the first quarantine station. These are historic landmarks in public health administration and epidemiology, but unfortunately their effectiveness was impaired by the fact that, although great attention was paid to humans, the role of the rat and the flea had not yet been discerned.

Other diseases

Some mention, even if necessarily inadequate, should be made of the rapid dissemination of syphilis throughout Europe and the Near East after the discovery of America, where it is commonly thought to have originated. Some measure of its incidence and seriousness is indicated by its vernacular name, the *great pox,* which was used to distinguish it from smallpox, a more formidable but more familiar disease. It is curious that little historic reference is made to the other diseases that are known to have existed with incidences far exceeding any now occurring, such as diphtheria, the streptococcal infections, the dysenteries, typhoid, typhus, and others. The most probable reasons are that, in the first place, people undoubtedly became accustomed to their inevitable endemicity and accepted them as part of the routine risk of life, and in the second place, they were so dramatically overshadowed by the tremendous impact of the great periodic pandemic killers as to merit relatively little mention in the historic writings of the times.

The people of Europe emerged from the Middle Ages and in fact came all the way to recent times with little substantial comprehension of any principles of public health other than those of crude, inhumane, and inefficient isolation and quarantine.

RENAISSANCE AND REASON

In a period marked by expanding trade and population movement and concentration, the risks presented by disease were necessarily magnified. The great pandemics of the Middle Ages therefore must have caused considerable social and political frustrations that could lead only to attitudes of fatalism and general disregard for the welfare of individuals. In this regard Hecker[8] commented:

> The mind of nations is deeply affected by the destructive conflict of the powers of nature, and . . . great disasters lead to striking changes in general civilization. For all that exists in man, whether good or evil, is rendered conspicuous by the presence of great danger. His inmost feelings are aroused—the thought of self-preservation masters his spirit—self denial is put to severe proof, and wherever darkness and barbarism prevail, there the affrighted mortal flies to the idols of his superstition, and all laws, human and divine, are criminally molested.

The way of life of a people likewise has a significant effect on their state of health or illness. In this respect Erasmus wrote to Cardinal Wolsey's physician describing the average English household of the sixteenth century:

> As to floors, they are usually made with clay, covered with rushes that grow in the fens and which are so seldom removed that the lower part remains sometimes for twenty years and has in it a collection of spittle, vomit, urine of dogs and humans, beer, scraps of fish and other filthiness not to be named.

Winslow,[9] in his precis of the modern public health movement, points out how long it has taken the human race to improve such conditions, presenting examples as disgusting as the preceding from England in 1842 and New York City in 1865. Indeed, even now in many parts of the world, circumstances such as these may be seen.

Gradually some began to doubt that disease was a punishment for sin. (It might be noted, however, that this stigma has only recently been removed from cancer, leprosy, and tuberculosis, and, even so, not everywhere. The AIDS epidemic has rubbed raw such ancient feelings.) By the end of the Middle Ages, several diseases had been differentiated. Among them were leprosy, influenza, ophthalmia, trachoma, scabies, impetigo, erysipelas (St. Anthony's fire), anthrax, plague, consumption, syphilis (the great pox), smallpox, diphtheria and scarlet fever (considered as one), and typhus and typhoid fever (also considered together).

The people of Europe emerged from this stunted period of history slowly and cautiously. The Enlightenment was characterized by a refreshing curiosity and, at first, a timorous willingness to inquire into the causation of disease. An increasing number of outstanding thinkers appeared, among whom were Montaigne, Paracelsus, Galileo, Spinoza, Bacon, and Descartes, to mention a few. Each in his own way hammered at the bars that imprisoned the minds and bodies of men. Their combined efforts resulted in remarkable subsequent accomplishments, especially in the late eighteenth century and throughout the nineteenth century. The concepts of the innate dignity and the rights of humankind began to be emphasized more and more. The search for scientific truth was at last advocated for its own sake.

THE EIGHTEENTH AND NINETEENTH CENTURIES

The plight of children

Meanwhile, other changes were occurring. Among them were the development of nationalism, imperialism, and industrialization, with both their benefits and their tragic and degrading concomitants. As artisans and farmworkers began to concentrate in larger cities, and the first tenets of capitalism began to find their expression in small factories, the crowding of the industrial revolution changed the face of Western Europe, making it vulnerable to fresh attacks of epidemic disease. Humans were seen as an expendable resource, and lives were sacrificed on a scale probably unprecedented since the building of the pyramids.

In England a legally condoned practice of apprentice slavery developed whereby pauper children were indentured to owners of mines and factories. The socially accepted pattern was for parishes to assume responsibility for orphans and pauper children. This responsibility was met at first by paying private "nurses" for taking the infants and younger children into their homes for a few years and putting them out to work as apprentices when they grew older. Partly because of the increasing numbers and partly as a remedy for frequent abuse of young children, parish workhouses began to be established in the late seventeenth and early eighteenth centuries as a substitute for parish nurses.

Theoretically the workhouses were intended to provide some training for the children, but this was kept at a minimum and was largely concerned with inculcating the ideals of obedience, labor, industry, virtue, and religion. As George[10] surmises, it was hoped that the workhouses would "cure a very bad practice in parish officers, who to save expence, are apt to ruin children by putting them out as early as they can to any sorry master that will take them, without any concern for their education and welfare."

In her authoritative review of life in England in the eighteenth century, George presents a picture of these methods and ideals in practice by describing the London Workhouse in Bishopsgate Street in 1708:

> . . . thirty or forty children were put under the charge of one nurse in a ward, they lay two together in bunks arranged around the walls in two tiers, "boarded and set one above the other . . . a flock bed, a pair of sheets, two blankets and a rugg to each." Prayers and breakfast were from 6:30 to 7. At 7 the children were set to work, twenty under a mistress, "to spin wool and flax, knit stockings, to make new their linnen, cloathes, shooes, mark, etc." This work went on till 6 PM with an interval from 12 to 1 for "dinner and play." Twenty children were called away at a time for an hour a day to be taught reading, some also writing. Some children, we are told, "earn a halfpenny, some a penny, and some fourpence a day." At twelve, thirteen or fourteen, they were apprenticed, being given, at the master's choice, either a "good ordinary suit of cloaths or 20s, in money."

When children reached the age of apprenticeship, their lot became infinitely worse. A writer on the Poor Laws in 1738 said the following:

> A most unhappy practice prevails in most places to apprentice poor children, no matter to what master. Provided he lives out of the parish, if the child serves the first forty days we are rid of him for ever. The master may be a tiger in cruelty, he may beat, abuse, strip naked, starve or do what he will to the poor innocent lad, few people take much notice, and the officers who put him out the least of anybody. . . . The greatest part of those who now take poor apprentices are the most indigent and dishonest, in a word, the very dregs of the poor of England, by whom it is the fate of many a poor child, not only to be half-starved and sometimes bred up in no trade, but to be forced to thieve and steal for his master, and so is brought up for the gallows into the bargain. . . .

Children apprenticed to chimney sweepers fared among the worst. In 1767 Hanway, a leading reformer of the period, described the miseries of their neglect and ill-treatment, of their being forced up chimneys at the risk of being burnt or suffocated, and of their being forced to beg and steal by their masters. As he wrote:

> Chimney-sweepers ought to breed their own children to the business, then perhaps they will wash, clothe and feed them. As it is they do neither, and these poor black urchins have no protectors and are treated worse than a humane person would treat a dog.

In apprenticing children in large groups, it was usual to require that for every 30 normal children, one idiot must be accepted. The unfortunate children, forced to work from 15 to 18 hours a day (sometimes literally chained to their machines), fed a minimum of food scarcely fit for consumption, and housed under the most crowded and filthy conditions, usually were released from their sufferings and abuse by early death.

As mentioned in Chapter 1, in 1842 Edwin Chadwick pointed out that more than one half of the children of the working classes died before their fifth birthday and that in cities such as Liverpool the average ages at death of the various social classes were 36 years for the gentry, 22 years for the tradesmen, and 16 years for laborers.[11]

Sanitary conditions

During this period the condition of the streets of most European cities became deplorable, caused in part by nightmen and scavengers emptying their carts in the streets instead of the places assigned for the purpose. The accumulated filth of the eighteenth-century house was in many cases simply thrown from the doors or windows.

> Although eighteenth-century London was incredibly dirtier, more dilapidated and more closely-built than it afterwards became, was there no compensation in its greater compactness, the absence of straggling suburbs, the ease with which people could take country walks? This is at least doubtful. The roads round London were neither very attractive nor very safe. The land adjoining them was watered with drains and thickly sprinkled by laystalls and refuse heaps. Hogs were kept in large numbers on the outskirts and fed on the garbage of the town. A chain of smoking brick-kilns surrounded a great part of London and in the brick-fields vagrants lived and slept, cooking their food at the kilns. It is true that there was an improvement as the century went on. In 1706 it was said of the highways, tho they are mended every summer, yet everybody knows that for a mile or two about this City, the same and the ditches hard by are commonly so full of nastiness and stinking dirt, that oftentimes many persons who have occasion to go in or come out of town, are forced to stop their noses to avoid the ill-smell occasioned by it.[10]

These conditions under which so many people lived and worked had dire results. Smallpox, cholera, typhoid, tuberculosis, and many other diseases reached exceedingly high endemic levels, and the contamination of streams became so bad as to prompt the statement in Parliament in 1859: "India is in revolt and the Thames stinks." Southwood Smith pointed out at the time that the annual slaughter in England and Wales from typhus and typhoid fevers was double the number of lives lost by the allied armies in the battle of Waterloo. With reference to smallpox, it has been estimated that in eighteenth-century Europe, as many as 1 person in 10 died from smallpox, half of them children. Annual death rates varied from 1% or 2% to as high as 33%. An unpocked face was rare, since about 95% of the Europeans who survived had had smallpox.

These conditions were not confined to England, and they concerned the inheritors of the Age of Reason in many lands. Increasingly liberal views of the nature and role of man were expressed, especially by philosophers and writers such as Smith, Hume, Bentham, and Mill in England; Montesquieu, Voltaire, Diderot, and Rousseau in France; and Jefferson, Franklin, Dickinson, and Samuel Adams in the American colonies. In a very real sense, the broader concerns of these men and others like them constructed the political and social platform on which it was possible to promote and develop sanitary reforms and other measures for the protection of the public health.

ENGLISH SANITARY REFORMS

Concern with the economic consequences of existing social and sanitary conditions began to appear, providing leaders in sanitary reform with forceful arguments. Thus Chadwick[11] reported the following:

> This depressing effect of adverse sanitary circumstances on the labouring strengths of the population, and on its duration, is to be viewed with the greatest concern, as it is a depressing effect on that which most distinguishes the British people, and which it were truism to say constitutes the chief strength of the nation—the bodily strength of the individuals of the labouring class. The greater portion of the wealth of the nation is derived from the labour obtained by the application of this strength, and it is only those who have had practically the means of comparing it with that of the population of other countries who are aware how far the labouring population of this country is naturally distinguished above others. . . . The more closely the subject of the evils affecting the sanitary condition of the labouring population is investigated, the more widely do their effects appear to be ramified. The pecuniary cost of noxious agencies is measured by data within the province of the actuary, by the charges attendant on the reduced duration of life, and the reduction of the periods of working ability or production by sickness. The cost would include also much of the public charge of attendant vice and crime, which come within the province of the police, as well as the destitution which comes within the province of the administrators of relief. Of the pecuniary effects, including the cost of maintenance during the preventible sickness, any estimate approximating to exactness could only be obtained by very great labour, which does not appear to be necessary.

Public health went unrecognized in a legal sense in England until 1837, when the first sanitation legislation was enacted. It established a National Vaccination Board and appropriated 2,000 pounds for its support. As a result, a few vaccination stations were set up in the city of London. This modest beginning was followed in 1842 by Edwin Chadwick's momentous *Report on an Inquiry into the Sanitary Conditions of the Labouring Population of Great Britain*, one result of which was the establishment in 1848 of a General Board of Health for England. Significantly, the same year saw the appointment, as first medical officer of health for London, of John Simon, who 7 years later was to assume that office for the nation as a whole.

The middle of the nineteenth century witnessed an extraordinary unfolding of knowledge about biology. So far as is known, bacteria had not yet been seen, and their existence was unknown. In 1850, working with epidemiologic data, John Snow studied a complex epidemic of cholera in London and, based on the empirical evidence he had laboriously collected, deduced that the disease was caused by a microscopic living organism that was propagated in the intestine and spread through the community sewerage system.[12] It was an extraordinary accomplishment. There were many others, continuing into the twentieth century with incredible velocity. In 1867 Lister described antisepsis. In the 1870s Louis Pasteur discovered how microorganisms reproduced; he also developed the first scientific approach to immunization. In that same decade, Rudolf Virchow, a German physician and eminent social scientist, developed the science of pathology, which led to an understanding of disease processes. Robert Koch clearly enunciated a set of postulates that were to shape the study of the causes of disease for decades to come. So extraordinary was this time that Osler wrote[13]:

For countless generations the prophets and kings of humanity have desired to see the things which men have seen . . . in the course of this wonderful 19th century. To the call of the watchers on the towers of progress there has been the one sad answer—the people sit in darkness and in the shadow of death. Politically, socially and morally the race has improved; but for the unit, the individual, there was little hope. Cold philosophy shed a glimmer of light on his path, religion in its various guises illumined his sad heart, but neither availed to lift the curse of suffering from the sin-begotten son of Adam. In the fullness of time, long expected, long delayed, at last science emptied upon him from the horn of Amalthea blessings which cannot be enumerated, blessings which have made the century forever memorable, and which have followed each other with a rapidity so bewildering that we know not what next to expect.

Osler alluded to political, social, and moral improvements. They were necessary if the biological discoveries were to lead to real improvements in public health. The Enlightenment was replete with new social thinking as well as scientific inquiry. The ravages of the industrial revolution were inescapable as scholars looked about them in the growing metropolises of Europe. What they saw struck some as inhumane and others as wasteful. The state, which had previously intervened only for war, was questioning its role. Was it now to intervene to achieve an equitable distribution of resources among some or all of its people? Or to assure an equal distribution (a different concept)? Was it to intervene out of utilitarian motives or for mercantile purposes? Or could the state intervene in the affairs of its citizens for the sake of beneficence? The answer has varied from time to time and in different places, but any answer was different from that which had preceded.

Changes in social policy, a subject of political science, made it possible to translate the new biological knowledge into effective public health programs. Now, for the first time in modern history, the state both chose to intervene and had the ability to do so. As superstition and intuition founded on an inadequate understanding of science gave way to knowledge, the state, in its various communities and nations, could choose to alter the course of epidemic disease. Legislation was passed concerning factory management; child welfare; care of the aged, the mentally ill, and the infirm; education; and many other aspects of human life. It was not long before the horrors of previous conditions were forgotten and the standards of order, decency, and sanitation began to be taken for granted.

Pride was based on real achievements, which had an undoubted effect on the health of the town, and in which London was a pioneer among large cities. The foot-pavements, the lamps, the water-supply, the fire-plugs, the new sewers, defective enough by later standards, were admired by all. . . . Beneath the pavements are vast subterraneous sewers arched over to convey away the waste water which in other cities is so noisome above ground, and at a less depth are buried wooden pipes that supply every house plentifully with water, conducted by leaden pipes into kitchens or cellars, three times a week for the trifling expense of three shillings per quarter. . . . The intelligent foreigner cannot fail to take notice of these useful particulars which are almost peculiar to London.[11]

The seeds of sanitary and social reform spread rapidly to other large urban centers of England. However, benefits to the smaller towns and rural areas were slower to arrive. As early as 1830, Chadwick had recommended the employment of local sanitary officers, including medical personnel, for adequate coverage of the nation. His proposals originally met with considerable opposition, some of which continued even when he demonstrated the economic soundness of the costs incurred.

ENGLISH INFLUENCE ON AMERICA

Conditions and developments in Great Britain may seem to have been unduly stressed. However, any discussion of backgrounds must necessarily emphasize those extraterritorial developments that have exerted the greatest influence on North America. It is true that many advances had been made elsewhere, notably in the Low Countries, in Germany, and on the Scandinavian peninsula. By midnineteenth century, France had long since embarked on significant studies and activities relating to public health and sanitation, and many scientific papers were being published. The establishment of the *Annales d'Hygiene Publique* gives testimony to this. The work of the Belgian Quételet was already widely known, and Pettenkofer in Munich and Virchow in Berlin had far-reaching influences.

Nevertheless, the early intimate ties—social, economic, and otherwise—between the North American continent and Great Britain made events in the latter of particular significance to the former. The relationship was aptly described in 1876 by Bowditch,[14] first president of the Massachusetts State Board of Health:

> But by far the greatest influence has been exerted upon us in America by England, who, by her unbounded pecuniary sacrifices and steady improvement in her legislation, and her able writers, has far outstripped any country in the world in the direction of State Preventive Medicine.... The consummate skill in the discovery, removal, and prevention of whatever may be prejudicial to the public health, shown under the admirable direction of Mr. Simon, late Medical Officer of England's Privy Council, and by his corps of trained inspectors is wholly unequalled at the present day, and unprecedented, I suspect, in all past time in any country on the globe.

Although scientific research may have progressed further in some other countries, the application of the new knowledge, especially in terms of administrative organization and procedure, occurred more rapidly and more successfully in England than elsewhere. Since administrative organization depends to a considerable degree on legal procedure, it is noteworthy that America from the beginning followed the pattern set by English law. Thus when the time came for American communities to pass sanitary ordinances, they did so in the tradition of the English common law.

COLONIAL AMERICA

Certain public health problems were recognized early by the colonists in North America. They had good reason for being conscious of the threat of disease—many of the early settlements had been completely obliterated by epidemic diseases, particularly smallpox. Among these were the colonies at Jamestown and probably the colony at Roanoke Island. On the other hand, ironically, it was probably because of disease that colonial powers were able to establish footholds on the American continents. The settlers of the Massachusetts Bay Colony, for example, came to a territory in which the natives were by no means peaceful. Yet by the time the Pilgrims landed at Plymouth, the Native Americans of the surrounding countryside had been all but eliminated, apparently by smallpox introduced by the Cabot and Gosnold expeditions. Smallpox also played a role in the weakening and eventual conquest of the Aztec Empire in South America. In this instance it is known to have been introduced by a servant of Narvaez, who joined Cortez in 1520.[15] It has been estimated that during the early periods of colonization of Central and North America, the Native American population was decimated by diseases introduced by the invaders, whether peaceful or otherwise.[16] In the Caribbean and the southern colonies in North America, smallpox as well as yaws, yellow fever, and malaria were spread by the slave trade with ill-fated consequences.[17]

The registration of vital events is essential to efficient public health awareness and practice. It is of interest that its recording was an early concern of the New England colonists. As early as 1639, an act was passed by the Massachusetts colony ordering that each birth and death be recorded. Subsequent acts outlined the necessary administrative responsibilities and procedures. Not only was the information made available locally, but copies had to be made by the town clerks and transmitted to the clerks of the county courts. The law also specified fees and penalties. Similar laws were enacted at about the same time by the Plymouth colony.[18]

Most of the early activities of a public health nature in America were concerned with gross insanitation and attempts to prevent the entrance of exotic diseases. For example, as early as 1647 the Massachusetts Bay Colony passed a regulation to prevent pollution of Boston Harbor. Between 1692 and 1708 Boston, Salem, and Charleston passed acts dealing with nuisances and trades offensive or dangerous to the public health. In 1701 Massachusetts passed laws for the isolation of smallpox patients and for ship quarantine, to be used whenever necessary. The difficulty with such measures was that no continuing organization or even committee existed to assure ready recognition of undesirable situations or noncompliance with the requirements of the enacted legislation.

In the century during which the American colonies drew together and eventually formed a federation of states, little progress of a public health nature was made. Recognition must be given, however, to at least one notable person of the period. The multifaceted Dr. Benjamin Rush wrote that political institutions, economic organization, and disease were so interrelated that any general social change produced accompanying changes in health.[19] Regretfully there are still many today who seem unable to grasp this simple concept. After the American Revolution the threat of various diseases, particularly yellow fever, which caused the abandonment of the national capital in Philadelphia, led to widespread interest in developing legislation to establish permanent boards of health. Permissive legislation of this type was passed in 1797 by the states of New York and Massachusetts, followed in

1805 by Connecticut. There is some controversy over who established the first permanent local *board* of health. A *board* of health is not an operating agency with paid staff. Boards were made up of prominent citizens who were to advise the elected officials of the community about public health matters. They had no executive authority and no budget for programs. Boston is commonly said to have organized the first in 1799, with Paul Revere as its chairman. However, this has been contested by the cities of Petersburg, Va. (1780), Philadelphia (1794), New York (1796), and Baltimore (1793). As an example of function, by the end of the eighteenth century New York City, with a population of 75,000, had formed a public health committee concerned with the "quality of the water supplies, construction of common sewers, drainage of marshes, interment of the dead, planting of trees and healthy vegetables, habitation of damp cellars, and the construction of a masonry wall along the water front."

THE NINETEENTH CENTURY IN AMERICA

Between 1800 and 1850, while the United States expanded greatly in size and population, public health activities remained essentially stationary. Threats to public health and welfare and the resulting incidence of disease, however, did not. Many epidemics, especially of smallpox, yellow fever, cholera, typhoid, and typhus, repeatedly entered and swept over the land. Tuberculosis and malaria reached high levels of endemicity. In Massachusetts in 1850, for example, the tuberculosis death rate was over 300 per 100,000 population; infant mortality was about 200 per 1,000 live births; and smallpox, scarlet fever, and typhoid were leading causes of death. As a result, by 1850 the average life expectancy in Boston and most of the other older cities in the United States was less than that in London, which was then the object of criticism. Indeed, life expectancy declined during this period. Shattuck[20] reported that the average age at death in Boston decreased from 27.85 years in 1820-1825 to 21.43 in 1840-1845. In New York, the average age at death decreased from 26.15 to 19.69 during the same period. The American social scene was the subject of scathing comments by visitors from abroad who were impressed with the crudity and "barbarism" of life in the United States and the generally unkempt appearance of its communities. As so often has happened, improvements in sanitation and public health were delayed by lack of progress in other fields. Thus the British hygienist Newsholme[21] described this period of American social history as follows:

> The rapid growth of cities tended to out run the forces of law and order and to smother under the weight of numbers any attempts at civic reform. Before public health measures could be adopted or enforced, other more pressing problems had to be solved. An effective police force, the first requisite of community life, did not make its appearance in the Atlantic seaboard cities until 1853, and satisfactory fire prevention came even later. Protection against the dirt and filth of human aggregation, which threatened the life of every man, woman, and child, had to wait upon the adequate enforcement of law and order.

The inadequacies of the times were reflected in the low quality of medical care. Professional teaching facilities were few and inadequate. Many "physicians" were self-designated and itinerant. The prestige of the medical profession was at its lowest ebb, and its ranks were disorganized and split by the development of numerous healing philosophies and cults.[22] Healing agents used included not only empirical remedies left over from medieval Europe but many newly discovered ones, often borrowed from the Native Americans. This state of therapeutic affairs led Holmes[23] to remark that "if the whole materia medica as now used, could be sunk to the bottom of the sea, it would be all the better for mankind—and all the worse for the fishes."

Medical care was not an issue of great importance at this period in American history. Medical education was largely a proprietary business or based on apprenticeship; physicians were poorly prepared and had little of the burgeoning European base of biological sciences behind them; public expectations were appropriately low; and the services, such as they were, were cheap. Since medicine was of such poor quality, there was little need to consider securing its services for the poor, and if that did become necessary, it was inexpensive to arrange. Early approaches to formulating public health policy were thus devoid of any social concern about organizing or paying for personal medical care. This remained the case until the 1920s, when it first became apparent that medical care was now worth obtaining and often too expensive for many people. By that time, however,

American medical practitioners were well organized as a "Sovereign Profession"[22] and quite able to prevent public health practitioners from providing medical care, even to those who were unable to pay for private services. Public concerns about medical care, when they were subsequently expressed, found their voice through the traditions of social welfare, not public health. (See Chapter 31.)

The Shattuck report

American public health in the midnineteenth century is most notable for the extraordinary *Report of the Sanitary Commission of Massachusetts.*[20] Its author, Lemuel Shattuck (1793-1859), a most unusual man, led the diversified life of teacher, historian, book dealer, sociologist, statistician, and finally, legislator in the state assembly. Although a layman, he had a keen interest in sanitary reform as a result of gathering and tabulating the vital statistics of Boston. Because of his persistent complaints regarding the lack of sanitary progress, he was appointed chairman of a legislative committee for the study of health and sanitary problems in the commonwealth. From this committee, and essentially from Shattuck's pen, came the report. With remarkable insight and foresight, it included a detailed consideration of the present and future public health needs not only of Massachusetts but also of the nation as a whole. This most remarkable of all American public health documents, if published today, in many respects would still be ahead of its time.

The content of the Sanitary Commission report may be appreciated when it is realized that there were no national or state public health programs when it was written, and such local health agencies as existed were still embryonic.

Among the many recommendations made by Shattuck were those for the establishment of state and local boards of health; a system of sanitary police or inspectors; the collection and analysis of vital statistics; a routine system for exchanging data and information; sanitation programs for towns and buildings; studies of the health of school children; studies of tuberculosis; the control of alcoholism; the supervision of mental disease; the sanitary supervision and study of problems of immigrants; the erection of model tenements, public bathhouses, and washhouses; the control of smoke nuisances; the control of food adulteration; the exposure of nostrums; the preaching of health from pulpits; the establishment of nurses' training schools; the teaching of sanitary science in medical schools; and the inclusion of preventive medicine in clinical practice, with routine physical examinations and family records of illness.

Unfortunately, although the report presented the principal concepts and modes of action that would ultimately form the basis of much of today's public health practice, its importance was not appreciated for nearly a quarter of a century. One of the earliest appraisals of it was given in 1876 by Bowditch,[14] first president of the State Board of Health of Massachusetts, in an address before the International Medical Congress of Philadelphia:

> The report fell flat from the printer's hand. It remained almost unnoticed by the community or by the profession for many years, and its recommendations were ignored. Finally, in 1869, a State Board of Health of laymen and physicians, exactly as Mr. Shattuck recommended, was established by Massachusetts. Dr. Derby, its first secretary, looked to this admirable document as his inspiration and support. In giving this high honor to Mr. Shattuck, I do not wish to forget or to undervalue the many and persistent efforts made by a few physicians, among whom stands pre-eminent Dr. Edward Jarvis, and occasionally by the Massachusetts Medical Society, in urging the State authorities to inaugurate and to sustain the ideas avowed by Mr. Shattuck. But there is no doubt that he, as a layman, quietly working, did more towards bringing Massachusetts to correct views on this subject than all other agencies whatsoever. Of Mr. Edwin Chadwick, I need say nothing. You all know him. Fortunately for himself, he has lived to see rich fruits from his labors. That was not granted to Mr. Shattuck.

The comparison of Shattuck, the American, and Chadwick, the Englishman, is of more than passing interest. Shattuck's report consisted essentially of straightforward, unembellished, unillustrated statements of fact, followed by specific and detailed recommendations. This contrasted with Chadwick's report, which included many vivid descriptions of the appalling conditions that existed. The latter caused an immediate emotional response on the part of all who read or heard of the report. One wonders if Shattuck's report might have had a more immediate effect had it provided readers with mental images of existing conditions for contrast with further mental images of desirable conditions attainable. On the other hand, although Chadwick's report brought about a prompt reaction that resulted in the establishment of a General Board of Health in 1848, the response was not long-lasting. Chadwick's overenthusiasm and impatience demanded immediate action, for which the British people were not yet ready.[24] Much antagonism and resistance developed, which resulted in the demise of the General Board of Health after only 4 years of existence. This reversal caused an unfortunate delay in the ultimate development of a sound national health program in Great Britain. The reports of Chadwick and Shattuck therefore, remarkable as they were, provide examples of administrative failure, one because of underpromotion and the other because of overpromotion.

DEVELOPMENT OF OFFICIAL HEALTH AGENCIES IN THE UNITED STATES

Official public health action occurs on three levels: local, state, and national. It is not surprising, however, that in the United States it began on the local, and specifically on the urban, level, since it is there that people and their problems are concentrated. Except for international affairs, most activities of the new nation's government were carried out at the local level: first in the cities, then at the state level, and finally in counties and rural areas. The roles of state and local health departments continued to unfold and change with an increasingly variegated pattern emerging.

Local health departments

The first half of the nineteenth century saw a gradual trend toward the more or less full-time employment of persons to serve as the functional agents of local boards of health, which now were increasing in number. This represented the first step in the formation of full-time local health *departments,* as distinct from *boards* of health. Some of the earliest were established in Baltimore (1798), Charleston, S.C. (1815), Philadelphia (1818), Providence (1832), Cambridge (1846), New York City (1866), Chicago (1867), Louisville (1870), Indianapolis (1872), and Boston (1873). The last illustrates the lag, in this instance three quarters of a century, that often occurred between the formation of a local board of health and the establishment of a functional agency. As might be expected, the initial activities of these early health departments were determined by current epidemiologic theories, which placed particular emphasis on the elimination of what were thought to be environmental hazards. For example, at the midpoint of the nineteenth century the population of New York City had reached 300,000, but its board of health was concerned only with crowded living conditions, dirty streets, and the regulation of public baths, slaughterhouses, and pigsties.

Public health organization on the rural level developed under somewhat different circumstances and much later than in urban areas. (See Chapter 6.) In 1910-1911 one of a series of severe typhoid fever epidemics occurred in Yakima County, Wash. Because it was uncontrolled by local authorities, L.L. Lumsden of the U.S. Public Health Service was requested to bring it under control. Lumsden not only solved the particular epidemiologic problem but also suggested ways of preventing its recurrence. One strong recommendation he made was the establishment of a full-time staff to deal with all public health matters.

Meanwhile, the Rockefeller Sanitary Commission,[25] which had been active in hookworm control in the southeastern United States and in Central and South America, concluded that no single disease or sanitary or public health problem could be successfully attacked without concurrent efforts aimed at all phases of public health. As a result, it recommended the establishment of local full-time public health staffs. Thus there occurred the coincidence of the same idea at almost the same moment at two different places for two different but related reasons, resulting in the establishment of the first full-time county health departments in Guilford County, N.C., in June 1911 and in Yakima County, Wash., in July 1911.* The basic soundness of the principle is indicated by the subsequent growth of local health units, which now serve most of the population of the nation.

State health departments

Repeated outbreaks of yellow fever and other epidemic diseases caused Louisiana in 1855 to establish a commission to deal with quarantine matters in the port of New Orleans.[26] Some therefore claim priority for Louisiana in the establishment of a state *board* of health. However,

* Some difference of opinion exists with regard to priority: many contend that Jefferson County, Ky., was the first, in 1908.

in terms of the more usual concept of the general functions of a state board of health, Massachusetts,[27] despite its delayed response to Shattuck's recommendations, is considered to have established the first true state board of health under the Act of 1869.*

> The board shall take cognizance of the interests of health and life among the citizens of this Commonwealth. They shall make sanitary investigations and inquiries in respect to the people, the causes of disease, and especially of epidemics, and the sources of mortality and the effects of localities, employments, conditions and circumstances on the public health; and they shall gather such information in respect to these matters as they may deem proper, for diffusion among the people.

In determining policy at early meetings, the board, under the leadership of Bowditch, concerned itself with public and professional education in hygiene, various aspects of housing, investigations of various diseases and measures for their prevention, methods of slaughtering, the sale of poisons, and conditions of the poor. It decided also to send a circular letter to local boards of health to inquire about their powers and duties and to collect for publication the number and prevailing causes of deaths in the most populous cities and towns in the state. The board requested each community to designate a physician to act as correspondent. In 1878 the Massachusetts Department of Health merged with the Department of Lunacy and Charity because of political pressure and a desire for "economy." As a result, matters dealing with public health were effectively submerged by the weight of the other two interests. Eventually, however, this situation was reversed, and a sound program was made possible by reestablishment of the health agency as an entity.

Most states did not attempt to combine mental health and other programs with public health activities. Public health involved exercise of the police power functions of the state, not its welfare or "caring" role. (See Chapter 9.) Massachusetts had determined that, unlike public health, which was largely the responsibility of local communities, mental health was a "caring" activity that was a state responsibility. Since there was no scientific basis for the treatment of the mentally ill and no private practice until much later, the state emerged as the dominant provider of services. By the time private mental health services became available, the role of the state as the principal caregiver was well established. The private sector in mental health has never established the sovereignty once realized by physicians generally, and the public sector has followed a separate track from that followed by public health. (See Chapter 27.)

* Act of 1869, General Court of Massachusetts.

It is interesting to note that the second state health department was established a year after the one in Massachusetts on the opposite side of the continent, in California. By the end of the nineteenth century, 38 other states had followed suit, to be joined during the early decades of the twentieth century by the remainder.

National health agencies*

The Marine Hospital Service. To consider the history and development of the Public Health Service, the most important federal health agency, it is necessary to return to the year 1798. The United States of America had just come into existence. Although still largely undeveloped, it was already vigorous and enterprising, one manifestation of which was its expanding maritime trade. Sailing ships for world commerce were coming down the ways at an ever-increasing rate, and the merchant marine was becoming one of the nation's most important resources.

The farmer of Virginia and the tradesman of Boston had firm roots in their respective communities, which they supported through taxes. The merchant seaman, on the other hand, led a precarious existence somewhat resembling that of the itinerant or vagabond. Often he had neither a permanent home nor a permanent route. His ship was the closest substitute for a home, and it might be in New York harbor one week, in Charleston the next, and in Liverpool within a month. Despite this, he too was an American citizen and deserved whatever security and assistance his nation could provide its citizens. For a period, however, things did not work out that way. Like anyone, the sailor was subject to injury or illness. In fact, because of the unusual hazards of his occupation, he was

* For a detailed account of the history of the agencies discussed in this section, see *The United States Public Health Service, 1798-1950* [28] and *A Profile of the United States Public Health Service, 1798-1948.*[29] An up-to-date history is currently being prepared in the Office of the Surgeon General.

subject to greater than average risk. Furthermore he was underpaid, and whatever he received at the end of the journey was more often than not quickly spent in the taverns and brothels that thrived in the vicinity of the wharves. As a result, he usually found it difficult or impossible to obtain or pay for whatever medical or hospital care he needed. Because he paid no local or state taxes and generally was not a member in good standing of whatever port city he happened to be in when ill, responsibility for him was usually avoided by the local authorities.

The young American Congress quickly became aware of this problem, and the first bill introduced at the first session of the first Congress addressed it. Because of several circumstances, however, a Marine Hospital Service Act was not passed until June 1798. Titled "An Act for the relief of sick and disabled seamen," the new law required "the master or owner of every ship or vessel of the United States arriving from a foreign port into any port of the United States [to] render to the [tax] collector a true account of the number of seamen that shall have been employed on board such vessel . . . and shall pay to the said collector, at the rate of twenty cents per month, for every seaman so employed; which sum he is hereby authorized to retain out of the wages of such seamen." The money was to be used by the President "to provide for the temporary relief and maintenance, of sick or disabled seamen in the hospitals or other proper institutions now established in the several ports of the United States, or, in ports where no such institutions exist, then in such other manner as he shall direct." The President was authorized "to nominate and appoint, in such port of the United States as he may think proper, one or more persons, to be called directors of the marine hospital of the United States, whose duty it shall be . . . to provide for the accommodation of sick and disabled seamen. . . ."

Since the money was placed in the custody of the Treasury Department, the anomalous situation came about, that, until 1935, most federal public health services were carried out under the aegis of the Treasury Department. The small sum of 20 cents a month is of particular interest in that it represented the first prepaid medical and hospital insurance plan in the world, under the administrative supervision of what eventually became a public health agency. In 1884 the monthly deduction was discontinued and replaced by a tonnage tax, which is still collected but now goes into the general Treasury, from which the few remaining Public Health Service hospitals and outpatient clinics are supported through appropriations.

At first, physicians who served the plan were also engaged in the private practice of medicine, but before long the need became so great that physicians were employed full time. Originally, sailors who needed hospital care were placed in whatever public or private hospitals existed at the ports. However, as in the case of physicians, the demand for hospital services soon became so great that within 2 years (by 1800) the first Marine Hospital was constructed at Norfolk, Va. This was followed by similar hospitals throughout the country, at first at certain seaports and later at a number of places along inland waterways. Most of these hospitals were closed in the 1970s as part of a general attempt to control the costs of medical care.

It is interesting that a medical director or supervising surgeon for the Public Health Service was not appointed until 1870. Compensation was a salary of $2,000 plus travel expenses. This developed eventually into the position of Surgeon General.

The Port Quarantine Act. The growing concern of the federal and state governments with epidemic diseases led to the passage in 1878 of the first port quarantine act. At that time, entrance into the country was limited to its ports, which represented the nation's first line of defense against epidemic diseases. Since the incidence of these diseases was invariably greatest at ports, the physicians of the Marine Hospital Service had the greatest opportunity to become knowledgeable about them. In addition, since epidemics usually began at and frequently spread from ports, states developed the custom of asking and authorizing federally employed Marine Hospital Service physicians to aid in the control of local outbreaks. It was logical therefore to assign responsibility for port quarantine activities to the Marine Hospital Service. Much later, this responsibility was extended to international airports.

The law of 1878 embodies another important feature in authorizing investigation of the origin and causes of epidemic diseases, especially yellow fever and cholera, and the best methods of preventing their introduction and spread. With little delay, control measures were initiated at ports of origin. Marine Hospital Service physicians were attached to the U.S. consular service in major foreign ports, and a system of reporting communicable disease through the consular service was put into effect. In 1890 domestic quarantine was added to provide for interstate control of communicable disease. This was an immediate outgrowth of another particularly devastating epidemic of yellow fever that entered at New Orleans and spread throughout the Mississippi Valley. Between the time of the Louisiana Purchase in 1803 and the beginning of the twentieth century, New Orleans experienced no fewer than 37 severe epidemics of yellow fever in addition to constantly recurring outbreaks of cholera, plague, and smallpox.

In 1890 Congress gave the Marine Hospital Service authority to inspect all immigrants. This was intended first to bar "lunatics and others unable to care for themselves," but the following year "persons suffering from loathsome and contagious diseases" were added. In that year Congress provided quasimilitary status for the personnel of the Marine Hospital Service, who were given commissions and uniforms.

The National Quarantine Conventions. At this point one should turn back a few years to the midnineteenth century. Those concerned with public health in America felt a need for closer, more effective working relationships to solve problems of mutual concern. Because of the efforts especially of Wilson Jewell, a health officer of Philadelphia who had attended the Conference Sanitaire in Paris in 1851-1852, a series of National Quarantine Conventions was held.[30] The first, a 3-day meeting, was held in Philadelphia in 1857. The 54 members in attendance discussed many subjects of common interest, including prevention of epidemic diseases such as typhus, cholera, and yellow fever; port quarantine; the role of stagnant and putrid bilge water, putrescible matters, filthy bedding, baggage and clothing of immigrant passengers, and air that has been confined. It was recommended that immigrants not previously protected against smallpox be vaccinated. The second convention, held in Baltimore in 1858, was noteworthy for proposals for a uniform system of quarantine laws and the organization of a Committee on Internal Hygiene or the Sanitary Arrangement of Cities. Two more conventions were held, in New York in 1859 and in Boston in 1860. The outbreak of the American Civil War precluded further meetings for several years.

The American Public Health Association.[31] The seed planted by the quarantine conventions did not die. On April 18, 1872, after the end of the war, 10 men, including Elisha Harris and Stephen Smith, met informally in New York City to reactivate interest in national meetings for the consideration of public health matters. Meeting again at Long Branch, N.J., in September with several additional representatives, they chose a name, adopted a constitution, and elected Dr. Stephen Smith first president of the American Public Health Association.

Since the National Quarantine Conventions were concerned primarily with quarantine matters, the formation of the American Public Health Association represented a considerable advance in that the scope of interest was greatly broadened. This was reflected in its earliest meetings, at which papers were presented on many aspects of sanitation, the transmission and prevention of diseases, quarantine, longevity, hospital hygiene, and other diverse subjects.

The American Public Health Association remains an active and vital force in public health after nearly 120 years, with 50,000 members and 23 sections representing interests ranging from health administration and medical care to environmental health and social work. *The American Journal of Public Health,* an official publication of the Association, is one of the best sources of information about public health. The Association's numerous other important publications include *The Control of Communicable Diseases in Man,* one of the best known handbooks of its type in the world.

The National Board of Health: its birth and death. An early concern of both the quarantine conventions and the American Public Health Association was the need for a national board of health. Smillie[32] described the circumstances that led to the ultimate formation of such a national board, its controversial 4 years' existence, and its painful, premature death from politically inspired financial starvation. Meetings were held in Washington in 1875 and attended by representatives of many state and city health departments for the purpose of considering plans for the formation of a federal health organization. The meetings degenerated into a jurisdictional dispute involving the army, the navy, and the Marine Hospital Service, the three existing federal agencies that already provided certain services in this field. In 1878 a devastating epidemic of yellow fever swept over much of the country. Since the disease was known to have entered through the port of New Orleans, the Louisiana authorities were charged with laxity. As a result, not only the army and the Marine Hospital Service but also the American Public Health Association sponsored legislation for a national health department. The bill proposed by the American Public Health Association was finally passed by Congress in 1879. It transferred from the Marine Hospital Service all health duties and powers, including maritime quarantine, but not its staff and executive powers. The act created a board of presidential appointees consisting of seven physicians and representatives from the army, the navy, the Marine Hospital Service, and the Department of Justice. About 2½ months later another act was passed that gave the board extensive quarantine powers and authorized an appropriation of $500,000 for its work. This second act included an unfortunate clause that limited the powers to 4 years, requiring reenactment of the bill for the work to continue. (Note that this is a common practice in legislation that establishes new programs and agencies, and it has caught public health workers by surprise more than once. While those who struggled to obtain passage of the bill work to implement it, the opposition may devote its attention, quietly, to the fact that the authorizing legislation will expire in a few years. Such programs must be reauthorized and, if sufficient doubt and disaffection develop during that time, it may prove difficult to do.)

The membership of the first board was notable; included were J.L. Cabell, J.S. Billings, J.T. Turner, P.H. Bailhoche, S.M. Bemiss, H.I. Bowditch, R.W. Mitchell, Stephen Smith, S.F. Phillips, and T.S. Verdi. The 4 years of life of the National Board of Health were marked by an ambitious and efficient program of studies and services, marred by the persistent and vociferous opposition of Joseph Jones, secretary of the Louisiana Board of Health, who objected to the presence of "Federal agents and spies." Jones seized every opportunity to belittle and misrepresent the activities of the National Board of Health. Intent as he was on destroying the new organization, he was saved the trouble by John Hamilton, the Surgeon General of the Marine Hospital Service and an *ex officio* member of the Board. Hamilton, although professionally inept, possessed considerable political astuteness. He realized that the National Board of Health would pass out of existence unless the law of 1879 was reenacted in 1883 and that in such an event its powers and functions would revert to the Marine Hospital Service. Accordingly, he worked quietly and effectively to prevent reenactment, charging misuse of funds, extravagance, and incompetence.

From the beginning, one of the members of the board, Stephen Smith, had favored conferring all national public health duties and powers on the National Board of Health but incorporating into it also the officers, staff, and activities of the Marine Hospital Service and any other agencies concerned with public health matters. Smillie[32] analyzed the situation in the following terms:

> He foresaw that Congress would lose interest in the National Board of Health, but would continue to support a service agency that had full-time career officers and was incorporated as an integral part of national government machinery.
>
> In retrospect we realize that Stephen Smith was right. The unwieldy board of experts, each living in a different community and attempting to carry out administrative duties, with no cohesion, no real unity of opinion and no central authority, was an impossible administrative machine. A centrally guided service, such as actually developed, had unity and purpose, but unfortunately lacked intelligent leadership. The public health policies for a great nation for many years were determined solely by the opinions—sometimes the whims and personal prejudices—of a single individual. It would have been a much better plan if Dr. Stephen Smith's half-formulated plan of 1883 could have been carried out, thus salvaging the really important features of the National Board of Health and incorporating in it a service agency with a full-time personnel, an esprit de corps, and a strong central administrative machine. The members of the Board of Health selected by the President of the United States because they were public health experts, should have been continued as a Board of Health and should have served as a permanent policy-forming body, advising and aiding their administrative officer. The Marine Hospital Service was the most logical existing national agency with which to vest this national public health function. The Surgeon General should have been made the executive officer of the board, and all actual administrative responsibility should have been centered in him. It was a great opportunity to have organized a close-knit, effective National Health Service, but there was no single man who had the vision or the power to solve this simple problem.

The National Board of Health died, and the United States has never had a cabinet level health department or an official comparable to the minister of health in most other countries.

The Public Health Service. In 1902, recognizing that the responsibilities of the Marine Hospital Service had been greatly broadened, Congress renamed it the Public Health and Marine Hospital Service and gave it a definite form of organization under the direction of the Surgeon General. The reorganization act was of further significance in that for the first time the Surgeon General was authorized and directed to call an annual conference of all state and territorial health officers. In 1912 the service was renamed the U.S. Public Health Service.

From this point on, the Public Health Service grew rapidly under the impetus of an increasingly complex society, several wars and national emergencies, and economic depressions. In 1917 the National Leprosarium at Carville, La., was established. In the same year the service became responsible for the physical and mental examination of all arriving aliens. The year 1917 was also noteworthy for a congressional appropriation of $25,000 to the Public Health Service for studies and demonstrations in rural health work in cooperation with the states. This modest appropriation represented the beginning of a new administrative approach to federal-state public health relationships. In 1918, because of problems brought to public awareness by involvement in World War I, a Division of Venereal Diseases was created, with power to cooperate with state departments of health for the control and prevention of these diseases. In 1929 a Narcotics Division, later expanded to become the Division of Mental Hygiene, was created, with hospital facilities at Lexington, Ky., and Fort Worth, Tex., for the confinement and treatment of narcotic addicts.

The Social Security Act. The 1930s were years of great social ferment. In 1935 the Social Security Act was passed. It set in motion many developments of far-reaching consequence. Title VI of the act, which related to the Public Health Service, was written "for the purpose of assisting states, counties, health districts, and other political subdivisions of the states in establishing and maintaining adequate public health service, including the training of personnel for state and local health work. . . ." Associated with the act was an appropriation that made possible grants-in-aid to the states and territories according to budgets submitted to and approved by the Surgeon General. This created the difficult administrative problem of determining an equitable basis on which to distribute grant-in-aid funds. Although subject to frequent adaptation, an attempt was, and is, made in general to allocate these funds on the basis of four factors: (1) population, (2) public health problems, (3) economic need, and (4) training of public health personnel. This allocation of funds has been of educational value for state legislators, since many grants-in-aid must be matched by state and local appropriations if the funds are to be used. Results were rapidly forthcoming. Within a year after funds were first made available, not only was there a great increase in the number of new local health departments, but in addition many states began to strengthen and expand their health programs significantly. In 1938 a second Federal Venereal Disease Control Act was passed, designed to promote the investigation and control of venereal diseases and to provide funds for assistance to state and local health agencies in establishing and maintaining adequate programs. One significant result was the breaking of a long-standing "silence barrier" concerning these diseases by Surgeon General Parran.

In 1939, as part of President Roosevelt's program for the reorganization and consolidation of federal services, a Federal Security Agency (now the Department of Health and Human Services) was created for the purpose of bringing together many of the health, welfare, and educational services of the federal government that were concerned with personal and social security. After 141 years, only 9 years less than the life of the nation itself, the Public Health Service left the anachronistic administrative jurisdiction of the Treasury Department. At that time the service had 8 divisions, each under an assistant surgeon general:

- Division of Scientific Research (including the National Institute of Health and the National Cancer Institute)
- Division of Domestic Quarantine (including State Relations)
- Division of Foreign and Insular Quarantine
- Division of Sanitary Reports and Statistics
- Divison of Marine Hospitals and Relief
- Division of Mental Hygiene
- Division of Venereal Disease Control
- Division of Personnel and Accounts

Meanwhile many other developments of consequence occurred. In 1946, at the end of World War II, Congress passed the Hospital Services and

Construction (Hill-Burton) Act, which gave the Public Health Service administrative responsibility for a nationwide program of hospital and health center construction. This marked the first major attempt to develop hospitals as a part of national policy. For many years thereafter, Congress appropriated substantial amounts of monies for this purpose. State or local funds had to match federal contributions by 1:⅔. In 1954 Congress extended the program to permit federal assistance in the construction of other types of health facilities in addition to hospitals and health centers. Included were general hospitals, mental hospitals, tuberculosis hospitals, chronic disease hospitals, public health centers, diagnostic and treatment centers, rehabilitation facilities, nursing homes, state health laboratories, and nurse training facilities. By 1965, however, such programs were felt to contribute to the rapid increase in the cost of medical care. By 1974 the programs had been eliminated, and federal legislation addressed instead the need to prevent new hospital beds from being built and to reduce the number already available.

Research: the National Institutes of Health. The research activities of the Public Health Service date back to 1887, when a one-room Laboratory of Hygiene was established in the Marine Hospital on Staten Island.[33] Initially this laboratory was devoted to bacteriologic studies of returning seamen. It grew slowly to become the National Hygienic Laboratory, later renamed the National Institute of Health, in Bethesda, Md., about 10 miles from Washington. From these humble beginnings developed the largest medical research center in the world. Fortunately, from the start it was developed with great skill, imagination, and foresight. Originally organized into three divisions of chemistry, zoology, and pharmacology, the National Institute of Health's functions were expanded in 1912 by an act that authorized it to

> study and investigate the diseases of man and conditions influencing the origin and spread thereof including sanitation and sewage, and the pollution directly or indirectly of navigable streams and lakes of the United States and may from time to time issue information in the form of publications for the use of the public.

Under consistently able direction, it attracted and developed a steady stream of outstanding investigators, including Carter, Sternberg, Rosenau, Goldberger, Frost, Leake, Armstrong, Stiles, Lumsden, Francis, Spencer, Maxcy, Dyer, Benacerraf, Nirenberg, Axelrod, Anfinsen, and Gajdusek, to name only a few. The contributions of these scientists and their coworkers caused William H. Welch to state publicly that there was no research institute in the world that was making such distinguished contributions to basic research in biology, medicine, and public health. Testimony to this is provided by the fact that, through 1976, the research of 66 Nobel laureates throughout the world has been financed by the National Institutes of Health. Included were several members of its staff. Prior to World War II, the work of the institute was heavily oriented toward public health. In recent years, however, it has become much more heavily involved in basic and clinical research related to therapeutic medicine. The relatively modest federal investment in public health research is supervised by the Centers for Disease Control (see below).

In 1937 Congress indicated its concern over a health problem of increasing importance by passing the National Cancer Act, which provided for the establishment of a National Cancer Institute for research into the causes, diagnosis, and treatment of cancer; for assistance of public and private agencies involved with the problem; and for the promotion of the most effective methods of prevention and treatment of the disease. In subsequent years public and congressional concern led to the establishment of a series of additional institutes, which by now include:

- The National Cancer Institute
- The National Eye Institute
- The National Heart, Lung and Blood Institute
- The National Institute of Allergy and Infectious Diseases
- The National Institute of Arthritis and Musculoskeletal and Skin Diseases
- The National Institute of Child Health and Human Development
- The National Institute of Dental Research
- The National Institute of Diabetes and Digestive and Kidney Diseases
- The National Institute of Environmental Health Sciences
- The National Institute of General Medical Sciences
- The National Institute of Neurological and Communicative Disorders and Stroke
- The National Institute of Aging

Partway through this development it was recognized that the specialized institutes should be interrelated, so in 1948 the overall name was pluralized to become the National Institutes of Health. It now constitutes the greatest biomedical research complex in the world, supporting research not only within its many walls but also in many universities and other pertinent organizations in the United States and other nations.

To accelerate research and its confirmation and final application, the Public Health Service in 1953 completed and opened the National Clinical Center on the grounds of the National Institutes of Health in Bethesda, Md. This is a research hospital of almost 600 beds, with twice as much space for laboratories as for patient care. When a problem is selected for study, the methods of approach are determined by a research team, which may include scientists from more than one institute and from other research organizations. Special provisions are made so that outstanding laboratory scientists and research physicians from other institutions in the United States or abroad may work in the center for periods ranging from a few months to a few years or more on problems of their own choosing.

To return for a moment to 1956, another significant event was the transfer of the U.S. Army Medical Library to the Public Health Service and its later development into a greatly expanded National Library of Medicine on the grounds of the National Institutes of Health. In 1968 the library became a constituent of the institutes complex. An innovative activity of the library has been the development of the computer-based system MEDLARS (Medical Literature Analysis and Retrieval System). This is a computerized bibliographic service designed to assist users in the library itself, in medical centers in the nation, and abroad by means of satellites, in obtaining bibliographies and abstracts of material pertinent to their area of interest. The service is increasingly important because of the inability of conventional methods to keep current with the tremendous growth of medical literature.

To further meet these needs, a National Center for Biomedical Communications (named after the late Senator Lister Hill) and a National Medical Audiovisual Center were developed. In 1968, recognizing the importance of international collaboration, Congress established the Fogarty International Center for Advanced Study in the Health Sciences as part of the National Institutes of Health. Here, leading scholars in the health field from any part of the world may study and carry out investigations in residence.

Mention should be made of several other important post-World War II additions to the Public Health Service. One was the National Office of Vital Statistics, later renamed the National Center for Health Statistics. It provides a vast amount of detailed data concerning health, illness, injuries, death, and the utilization of health services.

Of great significance was the establishment during World War II of the Communicable Disease Center in Atlanta, Ga. This renowned institution, now known as the National Centers for Disease Control, has grown to become not only one of the world's great epidemiologic centers but also an outstanding training center for various types of health personnel and a leading center for health communications and educational methods. In 1954 the Taft Sanitary Engineering Center was established in Cincinnati, Ohio, as a focus for research and training in environmental health. In 1966 this institution and the responsibility for water pollution control were transferred to a new Federal Water Pollution Administration in the Department of the Interior and subsequently in 1971, in company with most of the other environmental programs of the Public Health Service, to a new Environmental Protection Agency. In 1971 a National Center for Toxicological Research was established in Pine Bluff, Ark., under the direction of the Food and Drug Administration, which by this time had become part of the Public Health Service.

Legislation. Congressional interest in health has not been limited to research. During recent years, Congress has shown increasing concern about the prompt application of acquired knowledge for the well-being of the people. The 89th Congress was especially notable in this regard. It had the distinction of being known as the most "health-minded" Congress in the history of the nation.[34] An astounding number of legislative acts were passed by it and subsequent Congresses, which radically altered the evolution of public health in the United States. Many of the changes will be discussed in subsequent chapters.

Forgotson[35] has observed:

> The deep and long-term significance of the 1965 federal health legislation . . . lies in the changing role of government in the direction of widening the responsibility of the public sector (as exemplified by the Medicare amendments) and in developing new patterns of medical service and continuing education (as exemplified by the Regional

Medical Programs). The introduction of systems engineering and operations analysis into the total health endeavor will permit the development of sound priorities, effective controls, and improved administration. Comprehensive legislation covering every facet of resources and services makes 1965 the turning point in health legislation.

Not every change has resulted in growth or expansion of the Public Health Service or its parent agency, now the Department of Health and Human Services. Because of its growing concern about environmental matters, Congress formed the Consumer Protection and Environmental Health Service in the 1960s in an effort to consolidate and revivify its environmental health programs. This agency included the Food and Drug Administration and had a broad mandate but little power. The new agency did not include water pollution, which was moved to the Department of the Interior at the insistence of Congressman Dingell. Senator Muskie held hearings concerning the environment at which the complaint was voiced that the Public Health Service concentrated too much on research and not enough on the control of pollution, which was largely left to the states. As a result, a new agency was created, the Environmental Protection Administration, to which most of the Public Health Service programs in environmental pollution were transferred. Substantial new authority was lodged in the new agency, and its budget grew rapidly.

The cumulative effect of the foregoing developments has been a remarkable growth in the size and usefulness of the health component of the Department of Health and Human Service. This growth may be illustrated in terms of expenditures. In 1900 the budget of the Marine Hospital Service was about $1.4 million. In 1950 the budget of the Public Health Service was almost $120 million; by 1960 it was about $300 million; and by 1988 it had reached more than $12 billion.

The federal role in health affairs has changed from a simple concern about the vulnerability of port cities to an extensive involvement in virtually every aspect of public health and medical care. As will become apparent in subsequent chapters, the changing nature of the federal role has often resulted in confusion at the state and local level where services are actually provided. Federal initiatives have been launched to provide an important focus on emerging problems or to provide for effective management of a particular responsibility lodged in an existing or new agency or program. But most of the action takes place in the states and their communities, where the federal structure may make little sense in an operational setting. For example, federal involvement in mental health grew from concern about drug addiction to research programs carried out at the National Institutes of Health and has since been placed in a separate Alcohol, Drug Abuse and Mental Health Administration, which has both research and service responsibilities, the latter carried out through the mechanism of grants-in-aid to the states and local mental health programs. The activities have been persistently separated from other public health activities, a phenomenon replicated at the state and local level. Federal involvement in medical care grew largely from the welfare, not the public health focus of the Department of Health, Education and Welfare in the 1960s, and this separation has continued as well. The more recent shift of environmental responsibilities to the Environmental Protection Administration makes sense from a federal point of view but is often confusing at the point where community concerns are usually expressed.

Figure 2-1 shows the current organization of the Department of Health and Human Services. The

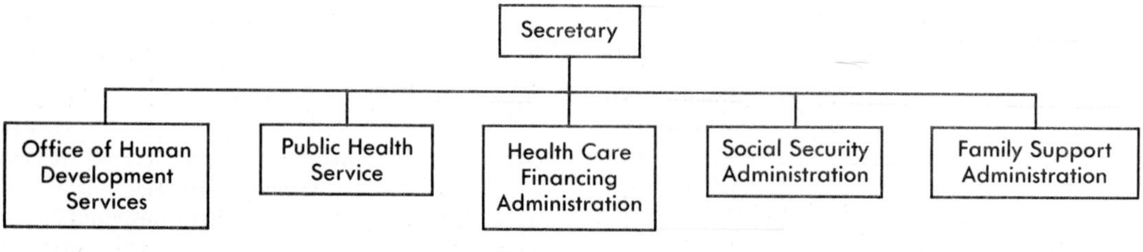

FIG. 2-1 The United States Department of Health and Human Services.

figure includes the Social Security Administration; the Health Care Financing Administration, the other major health-related component of the department, which is responsible for the administration of the Medicaid and Medicare programs as described in Chapter 31; the Office of Human Development Services, which includes major programs on Aging, Children and Families, Native Americans, and Developmental Disabilities; and the Family Support Administration, which includes federal welfare programs for children and families as well as other related activities. The Public Health Service is one of five major components of that agency. Figure 2-2 shows the six major subdivisions of the Public Health Service itself, as of 1988. It is likely that these structures will be changed again in the 1990s as Congress and the President continue to wrestle with the complex problems of a federal role in public health.

The Children's Bureau. The conception, establishment, development, and fate of this specialized agency provide a valuable case study for students of public administration. Although on the surface it is concerned with matters of a noncontroversial nature, the bureau from its inception has been a principal in many disputes and the target of several administrative and ideologic struggles.

The idea of a separate Children's Bureau was first suggested to President Theodore Roosevelt. As pointed out by Julia Lathrop,[36] who served as the first chief of the bureau from 1912 to 1921, it was no coincidence that

> this bureau was first urged by women who have lived long in settlements and who by that experience have learned to know as well as any person in the country certain aspects of dumb misery which they desired through some governmental agency to make articulate and intelligible.

Support came promptly from the National Consumers League, the National Child Labor Committee, and many national women's organizations and church groups. Arguing for a center of research and information concerning the welfare of mothers and children, they maintained an active lobby and pressure group in Washington until their goal was ultimately obtained. An effective argument was that the federal government had already set a precedent by establishing centers of research and information in other fields relating to national resources and that it might well become similarly concerned with its most important resource, the mothers and children of the nation. Between 1906 and 1912 many bills concerned with the establishment of a Children's Bureau were introduced, and extensive hearings were held. Both Presidents Theodore Roosevelt and Taft supported the movement, which incurred little opposition. Eventually Congress was spurred to final action and passed a measure* sponsored by Senator Borah on April 9, 1912.

One reason for delay was controversy over the placement of the bureau in the federal government's structure. The three possibilities suggested were the Bureau of Labor or the Bureau of the Census, both in the then Department of Commerce

*37 Stat 79, 737, 1912.

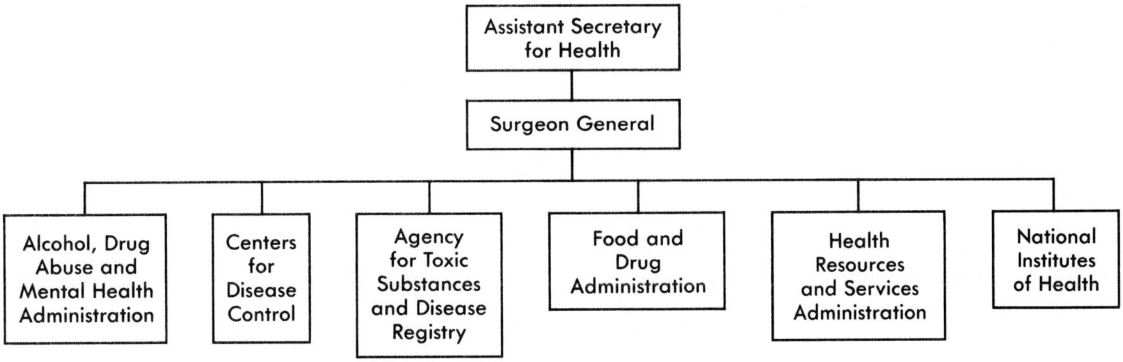

FIG. 2-2 The United States Public Health Service.

and Labor, and the Bureau of Education, in the Department of the Interior. It is significant that the U.S. Public Health Service, then in the Treasury Department, was not considered, apparently because of the submergence of the health aspects by the broader social welfare aspects of the proposed bureau. The failure on the part of the Public Health Service to concern itself with the problem at the time was to lay the groundwork for subsequent controversies over administrative jurisdiction and organization.

The act that established the Children's Bureau placed it in the Department of Commerce and Labor. When this department was divided the next year, the bureau was retained by the Department of Labor. The act directed that the

> said Bureau shall investigate and report . . . upon all matters pertaining to the welfare of children and child life, among all classes of people, and shall especially investigate the questions of infant mortality, the birth rate, orphanages, juvenile courts, desertions, dangerous occupations, accidents, and diseases of children, employment, legislation affecting children in the several states and territories.

Although originally given authority merely to *investigate* and *report,* the Children's Bureau trained a highly technical staff of experts who rapidly gained in experience. The bureau thus became the natural agency to be entrusted with new programs dealing with problems of maternal and child welfare. During the early years of its existence, the Bureau, in accord with congressional direction, followed a path of extensive and fruitful scientific research and dissemination of information. Many studies were made of the effect of income, housing, employment, and other factors on infant and maternal mortality rates. These studies led to the White House Conferences on child health, the first of which was held in 1919. Meanwhile, evidence gathered in some of the investigations was used by the National Child Labor Committee in obtaining passage of the Federal Child-Labor Law in 1915. This law, with the Children's Bureau designated as the administering agency, was effective from 1917 to 1918, when it was declared unconstitutional by the Supreme Court.

Study of maternal and infant care problems of rural areas led to the introduction of proposed national legislation to encourage the establishment of maternal and child welfare programs by means of grants-in-aid to the states. The Children's Bureau, designated in the bills as the administering and supervising agency, quickly found itself the subject of attacks from several quarters. It was argued that the adoption of the Sheppard-Towner Bill would provide an entering wedge for socialized medicine, would centralize power in the hands of federal bureaucrats, and that personal, family, and states' rights would be violated. The American Medical Association, the Anti-Suffragists, the Sentinels of the Republic, and several other organizations arrayed themselves in opposition to the bill.

During the hearings, a controversy that had begun to smolder between the Public Health Service and the Children's Bureau broke through. Some of the opponents of the bill were willing to compromise by favoring administration by the Public Health Service. The decision depended on whether the chief concern of the bill was with health or with general child welfare. Congress, deciding on the broader viewpoint, retained the Children's Bureau as the administering agency when final approval was given in 1921. One authority[37] has pointed out that unquestionably the bureau was able to maintain its position "by right of discovery and occupation and that the Public Health Service had been derelict in not promoting this type of work with sufficient vigor to maintain its belated claim to jurisdiction." This conclusion merits careful reading by present-day public health administrators. When a new health program is proposed, one of the first concerns is where to place it, and the proposing or initiating agency usually is favored.

The Sheppard-Towner Act established a pattern for maternal and child health programs throughout the country. It provided federal grants-in-aid assistance to states to attack problems of maternal and infant welfare and mortality. The states were given authority to initiate and administer their own plans subject to approval by a Federal Board of Maternity and Infant Hygiene, consisting of the Chief of the Children's Bureau, the Surgeon General of the Public Health Service, and the Commissioner of Education. Before the passage of the act, 32 states had established divisions or bureaus of child hygiene. During the following 2 years, an additional 15 states developed programs of this nature.

Although it is difficult to prove, the Children's Bureau is generally given major credit for the increased interest and action.

The original act provided for a 5-year program. In 1926 a bill was introduced for an extension of the act to 7 years. This provided opponents with another opportunity for attack. The 2-year extension that was granted signaled the end of the program. The importance of the federal aid was well illustrated by the fact that after expiration of the program, 35 states decreased appropriations, 9 states eliminated appropriations, and only 5 states reported increases for maternal and child health programs.

With the adoption of the Social Security Act in 1935, the Children's Bureau not only regained its lost functions but added to them. Under Title V, Part 4, of the Social Security Act, the Children's Bureau was given responsibility for the administration of programs dealing with maternal and child health, crippled children, and child welfare services. To implement these programs, the bureau was allotted an annual budget of $8.17 million for grants-in-aid exclusive of administrative costs. In 1939 this sum was increased to $11 million and in 1946 to $22 million. Within 10 months after the grants-in-aid became available, all of the 48 states, the District of Columbia, and the then territories of Alaska and Hawaii submitted requests and plans for approval. In this way, state maternal and child health programs received a much needed financial transfusion.

With the entrance of the United States into World War II and the subsequent draft of a large proportion of the male population, many wives, expectant mothers, and infants found themselves in somewhat precarious economic positions. This was reflected in their inability to pay for private obstetric and medical care. The Children's Bureau made Congress aware of the problem; and as a result, an Act for the Emergency Maternity and Infant Care for the Wives and Children of Servicemen was passed. The Children's Bureau was designated as the administering agency. The bureau had attempted, to the best of its ability and using some of its grants-in-aid funds, to do what it could to alleviate the situation. Congress decided to take action by means of supplementing the grants-in-aid funds of the bureau. As a result, a series of appropriation acts were passed, involving a total of more than $130 million. The use of these sums made possible the provision of much needed obstetric care for about 1.2 million expectant mothers and pediatric care for about 200,000 infants. It is of interest that the Children's Bureau quickly made the services as comprehensive as possible within the limits of the legislation. Another significant result was that the staffs of the Children's Bureau and of many state health departments obtained valuable experience in health care administration.

The Children's Bureau continued to expand its leadership in many fields, including audiology, perinatal mortality, prematurity, rheumatic fever, epilepsy, cerebral palsy, mental retardation, juvenile delinquency, nutrition, the problems of children of migratory workers, and children's dentistry.[38] It shared significantly in the momentous legislative advances of the mid-1960s. Because of increased awareness and concern about the relatively high rate of perinatal mortality, as well as premature births, handicapping conditions, and mental retardation, Congress passed the Maternal and Child Health and Mental Retardation Planning Amendments of 1963. This law authorized project grants to meet up to 75% of the cost of projects to provide comprehensive maternity care for high-risk mothers in low-income families and to provide care for their children. Two years later, in 1965, when Section 532 of Title V, Part 4, of the Social Security Act was amended, provision was made for the development of high-quality comprehensive health services for children and youth.

The combined objective of these two pieces of legislation was to reduce maternal, infant, and child morbidity by assisting communities to organize and use their services and resources to maximum efficiency. For improved maternal and infant care, funds were used for the establishment of prenatal and postpartum clinics, hospitalization, medical salaries or fees, salaries of public health nurses, health education, and various other services. The Social Security Amendments of 1965 made possible some major departures from traditional public health services. Comprehensiveness and continuity of care were stressed. There was no separation of preventive and promotive health services from treatment and rehabilitation, nor were services limited to particular illness categories. All health problems of the children involved were covered by the program, either by direct services or by referral to appropriate resources. Medical, dental, and emotional health problems were all included, and since particular emphasis was placed on children of families often unaccustomed to seeking care, outreach casefinding was provided. These two programs were especially needed in areas where there were many people of low incomes and where there were likely to be few practitioners of medicine and dentistry, a situation common to city slums. These efforts attempted to bring convenient, well-organized, comprehensive health services to those who needed them the most and obtained them the least. In the process, health agencies in many cities developed new, interesting, and effective working relationships with medical schools and other organizations in their jurisdictions. Furthermore, wherever programs were subsequently developed under the aegis of the Economic Opportunity Act to assist the socioeconomically disadvantaged, attempts were made to coordinate them with the maternal and child health programs.

Despite these valiant efforts, those in the position to watch noted that the bureau's identity was being whittled away. Early in 1963, soon after its fiftieth anniversary, the Children's Bureau became part of a new Welfare Administration in the Department of Health, Education and Welfare. Subsequently, in August 1967 it became part of another new major unit in the department, the Social and Rehabilitation Service, which also included the functions of the former Welfare Administration, the Vocational Rehabilitation Administration, the Administration on Aging, and the Mental Retardation Division of the Public Health Service. This new agency was designed to join under single leadership both the income-support programs for those in need and the social service and rehabilitation programs required by many individuals and families. The health functions of the Children's Bureau are now located in the Bureau of Maternal and Child Health and Resources Development of the Health Resources and Services Administration of the Public Health Service.

The Food and Drug Administration. The first efforts of the federal government to bring about control and supervision of the quality of foods were in 1879, when a bill was introduced in Congress to prohibit the adulteration of food and drink. This and several subsequent efforts came to naught, and 27 years passed before successful action was achieved. The present Food and Drug Administration grew out of a unique combination of efforts.[39] The major roles were played by a dedicated and determined public servant, Dr. Harvey Wiley of the Bureau of Chemistry of the Department of Agriculture; several concerned professional societies, notably the American Medical Association and the American Pharmaceutical Association; two widely read popular magazines, the *Ladies Home Journal* and *Colliers;* and a well-known crusading writer, Upton Sinclair. The greatest share of the credit for the ultimate success of the movement goes to Wiley for his tireless campaigning and to Sinclair for his famous book *The Jungle.* The book became an overnight best seller, was translated into 47 languages, and made its socialist author a wealthy man.[40] Despite great opposition from lobbies representing the canning industry, drug and whiskey interests, and those who manufactured and sold a vast array of proprietary medicines, bills were introduced and finally passed by Congress; and on June 30, 1906, the Pure Food and Drugs Act was signed into law by President Theodore Roosevelt.

The legislation resulted in establishment of a program to supervise and control the circumstances of manufacture, labeling, and sale of food. The responsibility was given to the Bureau of Chemistry of the Department of Agriculture, with Dr. Wiley in charge. Subsequent acts greatly broadened the program to include not only food, meat, and dairy products but also pharmaceuticals, cosmetics, toys, and numerous household products and appliances. In 1927 the Secretary of Agriculture recommended the establishment of a Food and Drug Administration to administer all of the accumulating responsibilities. As time passed, it became increasingly obvious that the legislation needed updating. As a result, on June 25, 1938, President Franklin Roosevelt signed the present Federal Food, Drug, and Cosmetic Act. Two years later the agency was transferred from the Department of Agriculture to the Federal Security Agency (now the Department of Health and Human Services) as an integral unit. Subsequently, in 1968, it was made one of the basic components of the Public Health Service.

SUMMARY

There appear to have been three critical turning points in the history and development of public health in the United States. It is interesting that they have been about 50 years, or two generations, apart: the 1860s, when the Shattuck Report began to exert an influence; the 1910s, when the groundwork was laid for so much of the public health development since; and the 1960s, when public health really began to broaden its horizons and abandon the barrier between it and medical care and when Congress decided to make undreamed-of accomplishments possible. It would appear that public health has now come of age.

This brief, historical perspective on the development of public health in the United States sheds some light on the current situation: the continued separation of medical care from public health, the similar separation (but for entirely different reasons) of mental health and public health, the recent reorganization of responsibility for the environment, and the at-times confusing interplay of the organizations established by Congress and those that are actually responsible for the administration of public health programs in the states and their communities.

There have been four major eras: the colonial phase, characterized by boards of health in port cities; the Shattuck era, with the development of organized health departments and the impact of the new biological sciences; the early twentieth century, with the development of state and local health departments serving most of the population of the United States; and the late twentieth century, with the expansion of public health concerns into medical care, community mental health, chronic diseases, and health behavior and a new concern for the impact of the environment on health. The next decade promises to be filled with at least as much change as the country wrestles with a growing awareness of its limited resources and its nearly insatiable demands for improved health.

REFERENCES

1. Rosen G: A history of public health, New York, 1958, MD Publications, Inc.
2. Top FH: The history of American epidemiology, St Louis, 1952, The CV Mosby Co.
3. Health Resources Administration: Health in America: 1776-1976, Washington, DC, 1976, United States Public Health Service.
4. Hanlon J, Rogers F, and Rosen G: A bookshelf on the history and philosophy of public health, Am J Public Health 50:445, April 1960.
5. Osler W: The functions of a state faculty, Maryland Med J 37:73, May 1897.
6. Quigley C: The evolution of civilizations, Indianapolis, 1979, Liberty Fund, Inc.
7. Chambers J: The devil's horsemen: the Mongol invasion of Europe, New York, 1979, Athenum Publishers.
8. Hecker JFC: The epidemics of the middle ages, London, 1839, Trübner & Co.
9. Winslow C-EA: The evolution and significance of the modern public health campaign, New Haven, 1984, Yale University Press (originally published in 1923).
10. George MD: London life in the XVIIIth century, New York, 1925, Alfred A Knopf.
11. Richardson BW: The health of nations, a review of the works of Edwin Chadwick, vol 2, London, 1887, Longmans, Green & Co.
12. Snow J: On the mode of communication of cholera. In Snow on cholera, New York, 1936, The Commonwealth Fund.
13. Osler W: Quoted in Ravenal MP, editor, Forward to a half century of public health, New York, 1921, American Public Health Association.
14. Bowditch HI: Address on hygiene and preventive medicine. Transactions of the International Medical Congress, Philadelphia, 1876.
15. Prescott WH: History of the conquest of Mexico, New York, 1936, Random House, Inc.
16. Woodward SB: The story of smallpox in Massachusetts, N Engl J Med 206:1181, June 9, 1932.
17. Marr J: Merchants of death: the role of the slave trade in the transmission of disease from Africa to the Americas, Pharos, Winter 1982, p 31.
18. Chadwick HD: The diseases of the inhabitants of the commonwealth, N Engl J Med 216:8, June 10, 1937.
19. Rosen G: Benjamin Rush on health and the American revolution, Am J Public Health 66:397, April 1976.
20. Shattuck L and others: Report of the Sanitary Commission of Massachusetts, 1850, Cambridge, MA, Harvard University Press (originally published by Dutton & Wentworth in 1850).
21. Newsholme A Sir: The ministry of health, London, 1925, GP Putnam's Sons, Ltd.
22. Starr P: The social transformation of American medicine, New York, 1982, Basic Books.
23. Holmes OW: Writings, vol 9, Medical essays, Boston, 1891, Houghton Mifflin Co.
24. Beck-Storrs A: Public health and government control, Soc Stud 45:211, Oct 1954.
25. Boccaccio M: Ground itch and dew poison: the Rockefeller Sanitary Commission, 1909-1914, J Hist Med 27:30, Jan 1972.
26. Gillson GE: Louisiana State Board of Health: the formative years, Baton Rouge, 1966, Louisiana State Board of Health; Gillson GE: Louisiana State Board of Health: the progressive years, Baton Rouge, 1976, Moran Industries, Inc.

27. Rosenkrantz BG: Public health and the state: changing views in Massachusetts, 1842-1936, Cambridge, MA, 1972, Harvard University Press.
28. Williams RC: The United States Public Health Service 1798-1950, Washington, DC, 1951, Commissioned Officers Association of the United States Public Health Service.
29. Furman B: A profile of the United States Public Health Service, 1798-1948, Washington, DC, 1973, National Library of Medicine.
30. Cavins HM: The National Quarantine and Sanitary Conventions of 1857 to 1860 and the beginnings of the American Public Health Association, Bull Hist Med 13:404, April 1943.
31. Bernstein NR: APHA, the first one hundred years, Washington, DC, 1972, American Public Health Association.
32. Smillie WG: The National Board of Health, 1879-1883, Am J Public Health 33:925, Aug 1943.
33. Harden VA: Inventing the NIH: federal biomedical research policy, 1887-1937, Baltimore, 1986, The Johns Hopkins University Press.
34. Rusk H: Congress and medicine, The New York Times, Nov 20, 1965.
35. Forgotson E: 1965: the turning point in public health law—1966 reflections, Am J Public Health 57:934, June 1967.
36. Lathrop JC: Children's Bureau, Am J Sociol 18:318, Nov 1912.
37. Key VO: The administration of federal grants to states, Chicago, 1937, Public Administration Service.
38. Eliot MM: The Children's Bureau, fifty years of public responsibility for action in behalf of children, Am J Public Health 52:576, April 1962.
39. Janssen WF: Food and Drug Administration: 75 years later, Public Health Rep 96:487, Nov-Dec 1981.
40. Kantor AF: Upton Sinclair and the Pure Food and Drugs Act of 1906, Am J Public Health 66:1202, Dec 1976.

CHAPTER 3

The determinants of health

When the Titanic sank in 1912,

> 4 first class female passengers . . . of a total of 143 were lost. Among the second class passengers, 15 of 93 females drowned; and among the third class, 81 of 179 female passengers went down with the ship. The third class passengers were ordered to remain below, some kept there at the point of a gun.[1]

Social class is a powerful determinant of health.

In most of the chapters of this book, the variables of life that affect health are discussed in order to explore specific problems, policies, and programs. There are, however, certain "cross-cutting" variables that will appear in almost every such instance. The purpose of this chapter is to review those cross-cutting, or common, variables and to explore their impact on health status generally.

The title of the chapter is misleading—"The Determinants of Health." Most of the discussion, like most of the research, addresses the determinants of ill health, or disease and injury, rather than health. There are books and articles exploring the epidemiology of cancer, heart disease, diabetes, AIDS, violence, child abuse, alcoholism, rabies, teen-age pregnancy, and injuries. But there are virtually no such discussions of the epidemiology of health or vitality. An explication of the epidemiology of disease or injury will not necessarily lead to an understanding of health. Disease and injury are the result of complex interactions between people, agents (bacteria, guns, or cigarettes), and their environment. People who are caught up in what appear to be similar circumstances may be affected differently. Perhaps the most important and interesting manifestations of the peculiarities of vitality are the differences seen in aging. Some people are frail and dependent at the age of 70, while others lead vigorous, independent lives into their 80s. Far too little is known about what determines these differences, and understanding them is taking on increasing importance as more and more people live into their ninth decade. (See Chapter 26.)

Of necessity, this chapter will present information about the determinants of ill health; this provides only hints about the determinants of health, however. Workers who are exposed to a persistently dusty environment are likely to develop diseases that produce disabilities and, in turn, dependencies. (See Chapter 1.) Controlling the dust will prevent the disease–disability–dependency sequence but may not result in a healthy worker. It is known that overweight people are more prone to develop diabetes, but thin people are not immune to the problem.

There is an enormous amount of variability within groups. In general, people in the age range 75 to 79 have more restricted activity days due to disability than do people in the age range 70 to 74, but there is more variability within both of those groups than there is between the two groups. If that seems confusing, consider two groups of children, one of fourth graders and one of third graders. The average weight of the fourth graders will be somewhat greater than the average weight of the third graders by 2 to 3 pounds. But the difference between the largest and smallest children within each group will be considerably greater than that small intergroup difference.

Within a single group, or classification, of people, it can be stated that those who do not smoke, drink little or no alcohol, exercise regularly, and restrict their consumption of fatty foods have a higher probability of being healthy and living longer. But those phenomena, known as risk factors, that increase the probability of disease or ill health do not, by their absence, produce health.

Health is a more complex state of being than is sickness or disability. The latter can be caused by a single event. For example, exposure to a high dose of ionizing radiation will invariably result in death. Health, however, is the result of a much more complex formulation, and a surprising amount of it is not understood. The principal factors can be grouped into four categories: environmental factors, life-style variables, sociopolitical organization, and biologic variables, or as some would say, luck.[2] (The luck, good or bad, of having a particular set of parents affects not only the biologic field through genetic expression, but the life-style and environmental fields as well.) Like all classification schemes, this one should be viewed as a utilitarian device—to be employed only so long as it is useful. It has no inherent validity. The purpose of such schemes is to facilitate discussion, although they also provide some hints as to what sorts of policies may be needed to alter the circumstances of health and disease in society.

Which comes first? People's genes can certainly affect their health. People with the gene that causes red blood cells to form sickle shapes (the hemoglobin chain folds up inside the cell) are vulnerable to severe health problems, especially when the oxygen content of the air they breath is reduced. (They have an advantage in malaria-infested areas, however, since the parasites cannot live as well in sickle cells as they can in normal cells.) Similarly, some people are genetically predisposed to develop diabetes, cancer of the colon, heart disease, or Alzheimer's disease.

Genes, part of the biologic field, are perhaps unique in this classification scheme, since there is little question of whether they cause the problem or the problem causes them. This is less true of many of the life-style variables, such as tobacco use or alcohol consumption. Lung cancer does not cause someone to smoke: it is a result of the behavior. But it is not clear just what causes such behaviors. Are they, in fact, personally determined characteristics, or do environmental and social factors play an important role? Poor people are more likely to die of lung cancer than are the affluent, and poor people are more likely to be smokers than are affluent people but does smoking cause the difference, or does the difference in income cause the smoking, or partially cause it? Are the poor less healthy because they are poor, or are they poor because they are less healthy? The question is important. If genes are the primary determinant of some forms of arthritis, genetic research is important for prevention of the disability and dependency associated with arthritis. But if life-style is the more important variable, then other forms of research and policy formation will prove to be more useful. If socioeconomic status is the most important determinant of low birth weight or smoking, improved medical care can only accomplish so much: policies concerning income distribution, employment, and education will be necessary if the problem is to be resolved.

The question of which comes first has been a riddle for many years. Recently, evidence has accumulated that suggests poverty itself may initiate the cycle of ill health, disease, and injury. (See below.) Most health problems have an array of ingredients that can be categorized into all of the four fields: biology, life-style, environment, and the organization and distribution of services in society. It is not always possible, nor is it always necessary, for an attack on the problem to focus on the central ingredient. An oblique or even peripheral attack may work. For example, some people have a genetic defect that does not allow them to metabolize phenylalanine effectively. By-products accumulate in the blood that, in the newborn, can cause severe mental retardation. The genetic defect cannot yet be corrected, but the pregnant woman and the newborn child can be placed on a diet low in phenylalanine, an environmental and life-style intervention, thus avoiding the problem. It is also possible to survive a noxious, insanitary environment if life-style patterns are developed to protect against the diseases present. Even the impact of poverty on health can be ameliorated through the social organization of programs and services designed to protect the victims from disease and injury.

Social attitudes or technology may necessitate oblique rather than direct attacks on some health problems, but policies can be better formed and debated if the complete sequence of the determinants of ill health is understood.

THE ENVIRONMENT

The role and significance of the environment as a determinant of health have changed considerably over the past hundred years. The nature of that change is not always appreciated fully.[3]

Prior to the industrial revolution, sanitary measures had a limited impact on the incidence of disease in society. Nutrition and warfare were more important determinants. Individuals and families were susceptible to diseases that were carried by food, water, or sewage, but the limited size of towns and cities meant that such problems rarely caused epidemics in large groups of people.

With the crowding that occurred as an industrial society developed, however, the environment took on a new and ominous significance. Lindheim and Syme[4] write:

> Conditions in the new industrial towns of the nineteenth century were truly deplorable. The most elementary traditions of municipal service and housing amenity were missing. Thousands of worker's dwellings were built back to back with two rooms out of four on each floor having no direct daylight or ventilation. Privies, foul beyond description, were usually in the cellar. It probably is no exaggeration to say that never before had such vast masses of people lived in such savagely deteriorated, ugly, and debased environments. In these circumstances of undernourishment, debilitation, unventilated living and working accommodations, and squalor, diseases such as typhus, cholera, yellow fever, and tuberculosis all took heavy tolls.

In the new industrial towns of England and Western Europe, life was "mean, brutish and short." Villerme[5] reported that life expectancy in Mulhouse, France, in the period 1823 to 1834 was 28.2 years for "manufacturers, merchants and directors," 17.6 years for factory workers, and 9.4 years for day laborers. Similar reports in England indicated a range of 16 years to 45 years. (Life expectancy at birth is a tricky concept. It seems difficult to imagine that day laborers could have lived only 9.4 years, but people were classified according to the occupation of the father in most cases, and if infant and childhood mortality rates were very high, the average age at death for all people in that class would fall into the childhood range.)

Prior to the eighteenth century, class differences in mortality were narrower. All people lived close to danger, from plague, pestilence, famine, and war. Class distinctions may have affected the distribution of wealth and power, but they had little to do with sickness and health. The organization of cities and the use of human capital to generate wealth through manufacturing changed all that. Differences in life expectancy between social classes began to widen, a phenomenon that has varied over time.

Worldwide environmental differences have a major impact on health. The prevalence of diarrhea and respiratory infections in infants and young children in developing countries results in some significant disparities in mortality rates and, some opine, in birthrates as well. Environmental circumstances also affect adults. In many developing countries, air pollution hangs heavily over major metropolitan areas, since people attempt to heat themselves, cook their meals, and engage in manufacturing with uncontrolled, open fires. Water supplies are inconstant and generally unsafe. Sewage disposal is primitive. Basic sanitation combined with pollution control programs could lead to significant improvements in health status in such environments.

In developed countries, a different set of circumstances prevails. While there is justifiable apprehension about the modern environment, much has been accomplished. Between 1970 and 1985, significant amounts of the so-called categorical pollutants have been removed from the air, even though the population has increased (Table 3-1).

Housing concerns have changed considerably too. The conditions described in Chapter 2 are rarely seen in the United States in the late twentieth century. New issues have arisen, however:

> The sanitary housing model which was drawn up to deal with 19th century conditions still hangs on in outdated Public Health and Housing Legislation, but there has been little recent attempt by governments to revise this to take account of 20th century problems and knowledge.[7]

TABLE 3-1 Air pollution, according to source and type of pollutant: United States, 1970 and 1985

Type of pollutant	Emissions in millions of metric tons per year: 1970	1985
Particulate matter	18.1	7.3
Sulfur oxides	28.2	20.7
Nitrogen oxides	18.1	20.0
Volatile organic compounds	27.2	21.3
Carbon monoxide	98.7	67.5
Lead	203.8	21.0

From Table 54, National Center for Health Statistics: Health United States 1987, Hyattsville, MD, 1988, US Department of Health and Human Services.

A little bit of good housing goes a long way: a safe water supply, sanitary sewage disposal systems, and a reasonable system for ventilation and heating will suffice. Spending still more money on the house itself will not further enhance the health status of its inhabitants.

Lindheim and Syme[4] assert that crowding, per se, in the developed nations of the world, does not contribute to ill health. Caution is necessary in evaluating such an assertion, however. It is clear that those who live in unusually crowded circumstances, even in well-developed countries, have higher rates of morbidity, mortality, and dependency due to illness and injury. But is it the crowding that causes the ill health, or are both caused by some other factor or factors? The environmental field, as it affects health, is a result of the interaction between the natural environment and the human-made environment. Its impact on health status is mediated through the social environment—poverty, public services, the educational system, and employment.

As stated above, new environmental problems have arisen: radon in the soil and building materials, indoor air pollution as a result of more tightly insulated houses and the use of synthetic building materials, the contamination of drinking water due to sanitary (or *in*sanitary) landfills and buried chemical tanks, falls in high-rise housing developments, and lack of open space for children.

Environmental factors that affect health include the following:

Life support

Food
Water
Air

Physical factors

Mechanical
Acoustical
Electrical
Thermal
Ionizing radiation

Biologic factors

Microorganisms
Toxins
Biologic wastes
Biologic antagonists
  Animal
  Plant
Allergens

Psychosocial factors

Crowding
Demands
Physical time

Chemical factors

Inorganic
Organic
Product complexes
  Combustion products
  Macromolecular products
  Industrial wastes
  Agricultural wastes (including fertilizers, pesticides, and herbicides)

Some of these factors, in proper form and amount, are helpful and even necessary, but in the wrong form or amount or at the wrong time or place, they are dangerous. Others are always hazardous.

It is possible to examine the discrete impact on health of individual environmental factors. This is frequently done in occupational settings in which comparable groups of workers with different exposures to one or more potentially hazardous factors can be compared. Studies have also been carried out comparing the incidence of respiratory disease or hearing loss in people living close to major highways and similar groups of people living in more rural or protected settings. In recent years, several studies have been conducted of the health status of people living adjacent to sanitary (or not so sanitary) landfills, toxic waste disposal sites, or nuclear energy plants. Such studies have been perplexing. In spite of the known toxicity of many chemicals in the laboratory setting, it has been difficult to show convincingly that people who live in close proximity to such hazards are harmed by them. The environment in which a person lives reflects several other variables that also affect health status, such as socioeconomic status and life-style, and it is very difficult to separate the phenomena.

The environmental field is full of hazards. Their complexity is increasing as technology provides us with new products and processes. Their proximity and pervasiveness become more threatening as there are more of us living in the same space. The cost of protecting people from environmental hazards increases accordingly. There is no safe environment: even in the most idyllic setting (in which very few people could live), wastes are generated, storms and fires occur, and accidents happen. Public policy formation will have to balance the conflicting requirements of economic growth and development on the one hand, and an optimally safe environment on the other.

LIFE-STYLE

Individual behavior has received an increasing amount of attention in recent years as a major determinant of ill health. Prominent factors are smoking,[8] the use of licit and illicit drugs (including alcohol, the most commonly used legal drug, next to aspirin and vitamins),[9] exercise, diet,[10] and more recently, sexual practices.[11] Questions of behavior, or life-style, were highlighted in the Surgeon General's report *Healthy People* in 1979.[12]

The impact of life-style on health status is enormous. Table 3-2 shows the impact of selected life-style phenomena on premature death and years of life lost before the age of 65. Most of the deaths are thought to be preventable.

The National Center for Health Statistics collected data on a variety of behavioral factors from a national probability sample of adults in 1985.[14] Some of the findings were:

Over half (55.4%) of all people over the age of 18 ate breakfast "almost every day." This was less true (42.6%) for those aged 18-29 than for older adults.

Almost a quarter (24%) of all adults in the United States were 20% or more above their desirable body weight. Most of these (55.8%) were trying to lose weight.

Most women (87%) over the age of 18 knew something about breast self-examination, but only 37.3% of them said that they performed the examination at least 12 times a year.

Only 40% of all adults reported that they exercised regularly. For those aged 18 to 29, the figure was 58.2%, but for those age 45 and over, only about 30% reported regular exercise.

About a third (30%) of all adults smoked cigarettes. The percentage was highest (38%) for males aged 30 to 44. Females were nearly as likely as males to be current smokers. In the age group 18 to 29, 31.7% of females smoked compared to 32.3% of males.

Nearly one quarter of all adults had consumed five or more drinks in one day on at least five occasions in the past year: 35.2% of males reported such behavior versus just 12.3% for females. Of those who said they were current drinkers, 16.9% reported that they had driven a car at least once in the past year when they thought they might have had too much to drink.

Slightly more than one third of all adults reported regular use of seat belts. Females reported slightly more use (37.5%) than did males (33.8%).

Studies of sexual behavior show similar patterns: large numbers of people either engage in practices that they know to be hazardous or avoid practices that they know to be beneficial.[15]

Other life-style factors have a profound effect on health status. People who live alone have higher mortality rates than do those who live in a stable relationship with other people.[16,17] People who are employed live longer than those who are idle. Thin people live longer than fat ones. People who sleep well each night live longer than those who do not.[18]

Life-style, or behavior, has been credited with or blamed for a substantial proportion of the illness and injury that causes dependency in modern times. As is the case with the environmental field, this was not such a common notion prior to the eighteenth century, when all people were more endangered by infectious diseases, nutritional problems, and warfare. But as these phenomena have become less important in the daily lives of

TABLE 3-2 Major precursors of premature death, United States, 1980

Precursor	Potential years lost before age 65	Deaths
Tobacco	1,497,161	338,022
Overnutrition	292,960	289,502
Alcohol	1,795,458	99,247
Handguns	350,683	13,365
Unintended pregnancy	520,000	8,000

From Amler RW and Eddins DL: Cross-sectional analysis: precursors of premature death in the United States. In Amler RW and Dull HB, editors, Closing the gap: the burden of unnecessary illness, New York, 1987, Oxford University Press.

people in the industrialized nations, life-style has become more important. The question of which comes first, discussed at the beginning of this chapter, is particularly important in considering the impact of life-style on health status (see below). Another important question concerns the phenomenon of "blaming the victim."[19] By blaming illness on selected life-styles, policymakers and apologists relieve the government and the medical profession of responsibility for many of the health problems of modern society and turn attention away from the social and political phenomena that cause or encourage unhealthy life-styles.

BIOLOGY

Biologic phenomena were the dominant determinants of health and disease in earlier centuries. (See Chapter 2.) The plague, leprosy, smallpox, and syphilis are only a few of the infectious diseases that have had a powerful effect on human history. That the determinants of health do not operate independently of one another is evident when considering the way in which environment, life-style, and sociopolitical organizations influenced the spread of these epidemic diseases.

When an infectious disease is very common, biology can be considered the dominant determining factor. For example, when many people had tuberculosis, it was not necessary to understand a great deal about individual variation. But as living conditions improved and the great plagues of history faded into the past, environmental conditions and life-style issues became more important. Why did some people get tuberculosis and others not?

Biology, as a determinant of health and disease, is not just a matter of pathogenic microorganisms. The interaction of these microorganisms with the human environment created by changing lifestyles has been a dominant phenomenon of the latter part of the twentieth century. Infectious diseases have by no means disappeared as important determinants of disease: consider AIDS, herpes infections, Legionnaire's disease, Lyme disease, and toxic shock syndrome.

These newer biologic phenomena offer opportunities for intervention that are equally exciting and worrisome. The biology of the human being, the host, has considerable influence on the situation. Genes not only cause diseases directly, but they provide a complex environment of protective devices against both infectious diseases and the so-called chronic diseases. They also control the way humans age, which can range from such abnormal conditions as progeria to the increasingly common phenomenon of the centenarian.

Genetic researchers have unraveled many genes and identified specific loci that appear to protect against specific diseases or increase the probability of their development. Many arthritic conditions can be traced to certain molecular configurations at the major histocompatibility locus of a chromosome. While many metabolic disorders are a result of genetic abnormalities, other genes provide protection against such diseases as cancer and Alzheimer's disease: when these genes are "turned off," disease often occurs.

At the present time, it is not possible to alter genetic structure in humans, but that surely will be possible in the near future. That power, of course, will raise a number of serious ethical and public policy questions. Even now, genetic research is leading to both exciting possibilities and difficult problems. It is now possible to examine the chromosomal structure of cells taken from the amniotic fluid surrounding a living fetus to determine the existence of several serious, even lethal, diseases. Should the presence of such a marker result in abortion? Certain genetic markers heighten the susceptibility of some people to certain chemicals. Should they be denied employment in an area where such chemicals are used, or should additional efforts be made to control the emission of the chemicals into the work environment? Sickness insurance is based on the notion that disease and injury cannot be predicted accurately. Since people cannot plan for such phenomena, as they can for housing, food, and clothing, insurance is necessary: it protects against the unanticipated event. But if genetic analysis can determine an increasing number of such eventualities, what is the meaning of an insurance program? If you know that a given individual has a 67% probability of developing systemic lupus erythematosus, is that an unexpected event? Should such individuals pay a higher premium? If everyone's chances can be determined, will each person have an individually determined premium rate? Will poor people have much higher premium rates than others? If so, who will pay them? Moreover, if risk can be predicted, insurance will no longer make sense: why insure someone whose fate you already know? If equity were the guiding principle, then government would have to intervene with a universal insurance program.

Gender should also be considered a biologic factor that has a substantial impact on disease and health status. There are many sex-specific differences in the incidence of disease. Some, such as hemophilia (a genetic disease carried by females but affecting only males), are the direct result of biologic characteristics. Others have a more indirect relationship. For example, females have about a hundredfold greater chance of developing breast cancer than do males. That corresponds to the greater size of the female breast and, presumably, the number of breast cells at risk. There may be additional biologic factors, such as hormonal variations, or life-style differences, such as breast-feeding, that have an effect on the incidence of breast cancer, but most of the difference can be attributed to the larger number of cells at risk in women. Other conditions are more difficult to understand at present: prior to 1950, cancer of the colon was more commonly diagnosed in women than in men; since then, the sex distribution has reversed. Is this due to more colon cells at risk in men, different dietary habits, the use of laxatives, or childbearing, or is it based on genetic characteristics? Other gender differences in health status seem more readily explainable. Deaths due to motor vehicle accidents and homicide are much more common in men than in women, usually attributed to different life-style and environmental variables.

Women live longer than men. At all ages after infancy, females have lower mortality rates than males do. The differences are large. In 1985, white females had a life expectancy at birth of 78.7 years, compared to 71.9 years for white males. Furthermore, 86% of white women born in 1985 could expect to survive to the age of 65, compared to 75% of white males.[6] (Note that such estimates are based on the incorrect notion that the mortality rates of 1985 will remain the same over the next seven decades, something that surely will not happen.) Many years ago, the gender difference was reversed. Even today, in underdeveloped countries, women have higher mortality rates than men. Stein and Maine[20] have postulated that this is because women in many nations are the victims of historic discrimination; with industrialization, they are recruited into low-paying and hazardous occupations; and the combination of factors results in high mortality rates compared to men. In developed countries, on the other hand, women have a significant advantage. Some have questioned whether this will change. Nearly as many women as men now smoke cigarettes; they are entering the work force in increased numbers; and they face an increasingly hazardous life. If some of the excess mortality suffered by men is the result of the stress of the male role, what will happen to women as they combine the role of parent, spouse, and employee? Verbrugge[21] has found that women in such situations appear to enjoy a relative advantage. Employed women with children, whether married or unmarried, have fewer restricted activity days a year than unmarried women who are unemployed, with or without children.

It remains difficult to separate biologic factors from environmental, life-style, and organizational factors. Until proven otherwise, women appear to be biologically more durable than men.[22]

THE ORGANIZATIONAL FIELD

The organizational field, which was considered in the Canadian report,[2] was not considered in the U.S. report *Healthy People*.[12] It is interesting to speculate on why that difference occurred. As noted in Chapter 2, public health in the United States has rarely been involved in the delivery of personal health services. (See also Chapter 31.) The U.S. government has long maintained that the system of medical care in the United States is superb. To consider organizational issues that might adversely affect health would have challenged that dearly held notion and raised questions about the responsibility of government to intervene in such matters—long considered a private affair. Yet the peculiar nature of the U.S. medical care system has clearly contributed to the poor health status of U.S. citizens, and this was well understood 50 years before the Surgeon General's report ignored the issue.[23] Organized as a purely private market, with no social insurance programs, needed medical care has been (and still is) beyond the reach of many poor families. The official government organization for health, the public health department, has been precluded from providing the needed services in most communities. (See Chapter 7 and Chapter 31.)

Other organizational problems adversely affect health status. School systems, for example, usually have a separate tax base. In many states, it is unclear whether the public schools or the public health department is responsible for school health services, and they are frequently unsatisfactory. (See Chapter 24.)

Hospital emergency rooms in the United States were managed as part of the not-for-profit hospital enterprise until relatively recently. By custom, and sometimes by law, the hospitals could not employ physicians. Thus medical staffing in most emergency rooms was erratic and often provided by untrained and reluctant volunteers. Ambulances were operated by funeral parlors, using their hearses when they were not otherwise occupied and drivers who had not had even basic first aid training. The results were deplorable. The situation began to improve in the 1970s, with major federal grants to the states to develop organized emergency medical care systems, but the programs have since declined. Rising costs coupled with the growing number of people who have no sickness insurance and concerns about medical liability have caused many hospitals to close their emergency rooms.

Physicians succeeded in outlawing nurse midwives in most states, claiming they were poorly trained. Subsequently, a growing number of physicians have withdrawn from the practice of obstetrics, leaving an increasing number of women with nonexistent or poor prenatal care.

Public health evolved separately from mental health in the United States. In most states and communities, the public health agency and the mental health agency are separate entities with little or no effort made to coordinate services. Both are separate from the state Medicaid programs, which are the largest payors for medical care services for the poor. Mental and physical health care are kept separated by such historical antecedents, to the detriment of good medical care and public health. (See Chapter 27.)

Organizational problems in medical care and public health are plentiful. They not only impede the effective delivery of needed services, both preventive and therapeutic, but they preclude effective policy analysis and problem solving at the state and community levels.

POVERTY

The reader will have noticed a constant theme throughout this chapter: whether discussing the effects of life-style, environment, biology, or the organization of services, low-income people are consistently at a disadvantage. They have more of virtually every health problem, with higher rates of morbidity, mortality, and dependency.[24,25] Poverty and a lack of education affect the biologic dimension through malnutrition and a residue of diseases and injuries that accumulates over a lifetime. Poverty has a powerful impact on the environmental dimension, degrading the quality of housing, increasing the risk of injuries, exposing people to excessive environmental hazards such as pollutants and animate vectors of disease, and subjecting them to excessive crowding and noise pollution. Poverty alters the behavioral dimension: the poor smoke more than the nonpoor and are less likely to value prevention highly, since day-to-day survival is more of a problem than prevention of some future catastrophe. Organizationally, although the poor have a number of official support systems intended to constitute a "safety net," they generally have poorer transportation systems, poorer schools, and less effective access to necessary health and social services.

At birth

Blacks in the United States have an infant mortality rate nearly twice that of whites, and this has been so since the beginning of the century. While both white and black rates have declined, the gap remains (Table 3-3).

Note that the table refers to nonwhite rather than black infant mortality rates. For many years all nonwhite births were grouped without further distinction. The actual white and black infant mortality rates in 1985 were 9.3 and 18.2 respectively.[6]

Many people have pondered the meaning of these differences. Joel Kleinman[26,27] has been a leading analyst for many years. He has considered a wide array of variables that are associated with low birth weight and high infant mortality rates, including age of mother, parity, education, and spacing between children. The most striking difference is prenatal care and that is related to the socioeconomic status of the mother and her education.

Childhood

If they survive birth and the first year of life, low-income and minority children face an increasingly hazardous existence. Death rates for white and black children are not the same (Table 3-4). The previously discussed sex difference is also apparent in the table.

The disparity remains for virtually all causes of death: violence, infections, congenital anomalies, and metabolic disorders. Lower income children suffer more bed days of disability due to acute conditions than do higher income children. They are more likely to need to see a physician, and they are more likely to use a hospital emergency room than a private office.[28]

Low-income children are also more likely to be exposed to environmental hazards, including lead paint, atmospheric lead, fires, motor vehicle injuries (often as pedestrians), and falls.

Adulthood

The problem is not diminished in adulthood. Working-age people with low incomes are more likely to lose work days due to illness and injury than are people with high income (Table 3-5).

Access to needed health care services is impeded by poverty, racism, and low socioeconomic status.[29-32] The situation has improved considerably since 1965, with the advent of the Medicaid program for the poor and the Medicare program for those over 65, but given the fact that the poor have more than their share of illness, they should be using more health care services than the nonpoor. Such is not the case.

The income of the poor simply does not permit the access needed to overcome the disadvantages of being poor. Families have a certain amount of disposable income — the money left over after taxes, social security payments, and other mandatory expenses. Poor people, by definition, have less disposable income than the affluent do. In most categories of expenditure, people have a range of choices to make: they can vary their housing costs, their transportation costs, their food costs, and their entertainment costs. But they cannot alter the amount they must allocate for medical care. While it may be true that high-income people can consume more expensive medical care than can low-income people, this does not appear to be the case in the aggregate. For years, the federal government has measured how families spend their disposable income. Three model families have been constructed: a low-income family, a middle-income family, and a high-income family. Table 3-6 shows how their money was spent in 1981. (Such data have not been published since 1981. It is not known whether the distribution of expenditures has changed since then, but the pattern shown in the table had persisted for many years prior to 1981, and there is no reason to suppose it has changed.)

There have been other approaches to studying the same problem. They all indicate the same pattern: (1) the proportion of the family budget consumed by medical care expenses has been increasing; (2) the amount required for medical care is fairly constant across income groups; (3) the poorest people, who have the greatest need for medical care, have the most difficult time affording medical care. The poor are faced with the choice of either reducing expenditures in other categories and thus dropping below subsistence levels, or foregoing the purchase of medical care.

Blacks have higher mortality rates from cancer and cardiovascular disease than whites do, and they smoke more: 41% of black men versus 32% of white men and 32% of black women versus 28% of white women.[33] An analysis of premature mortality by census track showed higher levels in low socioeconomic areas than in high ones.[34] Minority groups have more tuberculosis than do non-

TABLE 3-3 White and nonwhite infant mortality rates, United States, selected years, 1915-1984

Year	White	Nonwhite	Relative risk
1915	98.6	181.2	1.8
1925	68.3	110.8	1.6
1935	51.9	83.2	1.6
1945	35.6	57.0	1.6
1955	23.6	42.8	1.8
1965	21.5	40.3	1.9
1975	14.2	24.2	1.7
1984	9.4	16.1	1.7

From Relative risk calculated by dividing non-white rate by white. National Center for Health Statistics: Vital Statistics of the United States, annual publications.

minorities.[35] And, needless to add, low-income and minority people have greater exposure to hazardous conditions, both in their housing and at work.

So which comes first? Are people impoverished by illness, which prevents them from working, or are they unable to work because of illness and injury? Do poor people have more risk factors (smoking, drinking, poor diet and environment) because they are poor, or are they poor because of their behavior? Should the poor merely be encouraged to "shape up," or does society share responsibility for their illness and dependency? Should the poor be offered programs to help them stop smoking, or should they be offered jobs to help them escape poverty?

These amount to two separate questions: What are the determinants of illness and disease? If we can know that, what can be done about them?

Insofar as the first question is concerned, there can be little doubt that poverty is the greatest single determinant of illness and injury and the dependency related to them in modern industrialized communities. Careful long-term studies of large groups of people have shown that mobility between classes does not account for the differences in health status.[36] Haan[37] concluded that "socioeconomic position is one of the most persistent and ubiquitous risk factors known." He found that socioeconomic status carried a relative risk factor for poor health of 1.7 to 1 even after adjustments for many variables. The new "Black" report[38] (named for the chair of the committee responsible for the earlier report) has confirmed and extended its earlier findings.[39] According to Lock and Smith[40]:

> New evidence since the Black report has tended to confirm its conclusions that it is socioeconomic deprivation itself that harms the health of the poor. . . . Poorer people have higher death and sickness rates just because they are poor—and because they are less likely to have a job and more likely to live in poor housing and to have had a poorer education. They do also smoke and drink more, eat poorer diets and exercise less, but these differences in lifestyle do not account for all the difference in mortality. Furthermore, as new evidence shows, their material deprivation limits their ability to choose healthier lifestyles—healthier diets, for instance, are more expensive. Policies to combat inequalities in health by concentrating on the individual are thus, the report says, "misguided."

Marmot and his colleagues[41] write: "One has to get the causal chain in perspective. People's mate-

TABLE 3-4 Death rates for all causes of death, United States, 1985, for black and white children

Age (yrs.)	White males	Black males	White females	Black females
1-4	52.4	89.0	39.7	70.3
5-14	29.9	41.3	19.4	28.1

From National Center for Health Statistics: Health United States 1987, Hyattsville, MD, 1988, US Department of Health and Human Services.

TABLE 3-5 Number of days per person per year of activity restriction due to acute and chronic conditions, by family income

	Age		
Income	18-24	25-44	45-64
Less than $10,000	11.0	24.4	49.1
$10,000-$19,999	12.6	13.2	28.2
$20,000-$34,999	10.7	17.8	24.8
$35,000 and more	8.3	9.3	11.4

From National Center for Health Statistics: Health United States 1987, Hyattsville, MD, 1988, US Department of Health and Human Services.

rial conditions of life and their place in the social structure have a powerful influence on their behavior, which in turn affects their health."

The literature on social class and behavior is extensive and complex. People who expect to be able to shape their lives, to control the events that affect them, are more likely to try to shape those events than are people who feel that they have little control over such phenomena. Nursing speaks of the "locus of control"—the place where control over your life is exercised.[42] Those who manifest an expectation that their locus of control is internal are more likely to adopt a healthy life-style, provided they are reasonably healthy to begin with.[43]

The poor have more health problems than the nonpoor because they are poor. They have a less healthy life-style and environment because they are poor. They do not have access to needed health services because they are poor. The circle is of iron and it is unrelenting.

The second question, what can be done about the determinants of disease, is simpler to answer but more difficult to translate into policy. Treating and preventing poverty would do wonders for community health status. (One very effective way to reduce the prevalence of poverty would be to eliminate racial discrimination.) Public health, both as an organized social practice and as an individual profession, can attack poverty and discrimination as can the other principal agencies of the state: welfare, education, mental health, law enforcement, and economic development. Progress is slow, however, and, as has been witnessed in the United States during the 1980s, regression is possible. Employment policies, as well as the elaboration of priorities for public health programs, can have both direct and indirect effects on poverty and the illness it causes.

Beyond that, however, public health can deal obliquely with the consequences of poverty. It is unlikely that the impoverishment of women in the United States and other countries will be rectified quickly. But public health programs designed to meet the needs of young women can decrease perinatal mortality and morbidity and increase the probability that a child will survive childhood. (See Chapter 22.)

It is unlikely that low-income people can achieve full and satisfactory employment in a safe working environment in the near future. But organized public health actions and the authority of the state can reduce the hazards of work and better organize services for those who are harmed.

One of the problems with traditional typologies of the determinants of health and disease is that they exclude the role of the state—social action. In recent years, the focus has been on life-style, as if people choose their life-styles freely, knowing all the facts and having a full range of choices available to them. Such is, unfortunately, not the case. The community, acting through its organized agencies, including first and foremost its public health agencies, can act to decrease the probability that the hazards of life will affect people adversely. When that cannot be done, the community can act to reduce the damage inflicted by hazards. And when that cannot be done, the

TABLE 3-6 Family budgets for consumables, 1981

	Income		
Item	**Lower ($)**	**Middle ($)**	**Higher ($)**
Food	4,545	5,843	7,366
Housing	2,817	5,546	8,423
Transportation	1,311	2,372	3,075
Personal items	1,316	1,841	2,666
Medical care	1,436	1,443	1,505
Other	644	1,196	1,972
TOTALS	12,069	18,241	25,007

From US Bureau of Labor Statistics: autumn urban family budgets and comparative indices for selected urban areas, annual (Supplements to the Bulletin, 1570-5), 1981, Washington, DC.

community can act to organize the resources needed to treat and aid those who are harmed by the hazards of life.

The community can do these things, if it will.

REFERENCES

1. Lord W: A night to remember, New York, 1955, Henry Holt & Co.
2. Lalonde M: A new perspective on the health of Canadians: a working document, Ottawa, 1974, Ministry of National Health & Welfare.
3. Burby RJ and Okun DA: Land use planning and health, Ann Rev Public Health 4:47, 1983.
4. Lindheim R and Syme SL: Environments, people, and health, Ann Rev Public Health 4:335, 1983.
5. Antonovsky A: Social class, life expectancy and overall mortality, Milbank Memorial Fund Quarterly 45:31, April 1967.
6. National Center for Health Statistics: Health United States 1987, Hyattsville, MD, 1988, US Department of Health and Human Services.
7. Ranson R: Relating housing standards to health hazards, J Royal Society of Health 107:231, Dec 1987.
8. Centers for Disease Control: The health consequences of smoking: a report of the Surgeon General, Washington, DC, 1989, US Department of Health and Human Services.
9. National Institute on Alcohol Abuse and Alcoholism: Sixth special report to the US Congress on alcohol and health, Washington, DC, 1987, US Department of Health and Human Services.
10. Public Health Service: The Surgeon General's report on nutrition and health, Pub No 88-5021, Washington, DC, 1988, US Department of Health and Human Services.
11. Institute of Medicine: Confronting AIDS: update 1988, Washington, DC, 1988, National Academy Press.
12. Office of the Assistant Secretary for Health: Healthy people: the Surgeon General's report on health promotion and disease prevention, Washington, DC, 1979, US Department of Health and Human Services.
13. Amler RW and Eddins DL: Cross-sectional analysis: precursors of premature death in the United States. In Amler RW and Dull HB, editors: Closing the gap: the burden of unnecessary illness, New York, 1987, Oxford University Press.
14. National Center for Health Statistics: Health promotion and disease prevention, United States, 1985: data from the National Health Survey, Series 10, No 163, Hyattsville, MD, 1988, US Department of Health and Human Services.
15. Darrow WW and Pauli ML: Health behavior and sexually transmitted diseases. In Holmes KK and others, editors, Sexually transmitted diseases, New York, 1984, McGraw-Hill.
16. Berkman LF and Syme SL: Social networks, host resistance and mortality: a nine-year follow-up of Alameda County residents, Am J Epid 109:186, Feb 1979.
17. House JF, Robbins C, and Metzner HL: The association of social relationships and activities with mortality: prospective evidence from the Tecumseh community health study, Am J Epid 116:123, July 1982.
18. Belloc NB and Breslow L: Relationship of physical health status and health practices, Prev Med 1:409, Aug 1972.
19. Beauchamp DE: Community: the neglected tradition of public health, Hastings Center Report 15:28, Dec 1985.
20. Stein Z and Maine D: The health of women, International J Epid 15:303, Sept 1986.
21. Verbrugge LM and Madans JH: Social roles and health trends of American women, Milbank Memorial Fund Quarterly 63:691, Fall 1985.
22. Wingard DL: The sex differential in morbidity, mortality, and lifestyle, Ann Rev Public Health 5:433, 1984.
23. Falk IS, Rorem CR, and Ring MD: The costs of medical care, Chicago, 1933, The University of Chicago Press.
24. Rudov MH and Santangelo N: Health status of minorities and low-income groups, Pub No (HRA)79-627, Washington, DC, 1979, US Department of Health and Human Services.
25. Heckler M: Report of the secretary's task force on black and minority health, vol 1, Executive summary, Washington, DC, 1985, US Department of Health and Human Services.
26. Kleinman J: Trends and variation in birthweight. Paper presented at the annual meeting of the American Public Health Association, Los Angeles, Nov 1981.
27. Kleinman JC and Kessel SS: Racial differences in low birth weight: trends and risk factors, New Engl J Med 317:749, Sept 17, 1987.
28. National Center for Health Statistics: Current estimates from the national health interview survey, United States, 1986, Series 10, No 164, Oct 1987.
29. Aday LA and Andersen RM: The national profile of access to medical care: where do we stand? Am J Public Health 74:1331, Dec 1984.
30. Wilensky GR and Walden DC· Minorities, poverty and the uninsured. Paper presented at the annual meeting of the American Public Health Association, Los Angeles, Nov 1981.
31. Yelin EH, Kramer JS, and Epstein WV: Is health care use equivalent across social groups? A diagnosis based study, Am J Public Health 73:563, May 1983.

32. Shulman NB and others: Financial cost as an obstacle to hypertension therapy, Am J Public Health 76:1105, Sept 1986.
33. Morbid Mortal Week Report 36(suppl 25):404, 1987.
34. Morbid Mortal Week Report 37(suppl 10):155, 1988.
35. Morbid Mortal Week Report 36(suppl 6):77, 1987.
36. Fox AJ, Goldblatt PO, and Jones DR: Social class mortality differentials: artifact, selection or life circumstances, J Epid and Community Health 39:1, March 1985.
37. Haan M, Kaplan GA, and Camacho T: Poverty and health: prospective evidence from the Alameda County study, Am J Epid 125:989, June 1987.
38. Whitehead M: The health divide: inequalities in health in the 1980's, London, 1987, Health Education Council.
39. Department of Health and Social Services: Inequalities in health, London, 1980, Department of Health and Human Services.
40. Lock S and Smith R: Inequalities and the new Health Education Authority, Br Med J 294:857, April 4, 1987.
41. Marmot MG, Kogevinas M, and Elston MA: Social/economic status and disease, Ann Rev Public Health 8:111, 1987.
42. Wallston K and Wallston B: Who is responsible for your health: the construct of health locus of control. In Saunders G and Suls J, editors, Social psychology of health and illness, Hillsdale, NJ, 1982, Lawrence Erlbaum.
43. Rakowski D: Personal health practices, health status and expected control over future health, J Community Health 1:189, Fall 1986.

CHAPTER 4

World health: problems and programs

The twentieth century will be remembered chiefly, not as an age of political conflicts and astonishing technical inventions, but as an age in which human society dared to think of the health of the whole human race as a practical objective.

Arnold Toynbee

HEALTH: A GLOBAL ISSUE

The ultimate measure of a nation is its people. All else—including agricultural, mineral, industrial, and economic potential—is of value only to the extent and manner in which it may be related to people. The quantitative measure of a people is the population, especially the number of people who are able to function independently. An important qualitative measure of a populaton is the degree of illness or health and the rates of survival or death. Four factors cause the growth or decline of population: the number of births, deaths, immigrants, and emigrants. The first two are of major social, economic, political, public health, and medical importance to every nation. And as populations increase in size, and the technology of transportation and communication expand, the interrelatedness of changes in one country or region to those in the rest of the countries of the world becomes more apparent. It is fundamental to any consideration of international health problems that there be an adequate base of accurate statistical data relating to the number of people in each nation, as well as the rates and manner in which they are born, live, and die. (See Chapter 8.) Unfortunately, this is not commonly available. The student of international health problems is confronted at the outset by gross inadequacies in this respect and is forced to think, plan, and function to a considerable degree on the basis of impressions, estimates and generalizations.

It is not the purpose here to evaluate the completeness, accuracy, or comprehensiveness of various national or international vital statistics. However, it should be recognized that understandably the most highly developed countries have the most exact and adequate vital data, whereas the least developed and youngest nations, many of which have the most outstanding health problems, tend to have the least satisfactory information about their people. In addition, vital statistics are sometimes treated in a political manner, resulting in underreporting of information thought to reflect badly on a nation's mores or capacity for effective governance and making comprehension of world health problems even more difficult.

One might generalize that population enumeration and birth and death registration are relatively accurate and complete in the countries of northern and western Europe, parts of central and southern Europe, the British Isles, North America, Australia, New Zealand, and Japan. Conversely, they are less accurate (to varying degrees, of course) in most countries of Central and South America, most of Africa and the Middle East, and parts of Asia.

GENERAL OBSERVATIONS

Despite these limitations, there is sufficient information to indicate considerable variation among countries with regard to the fertility, health status, and longevity of their populations. For detailed information the reader is referred to the various statistical and epidemiologic reports of the World Health Organization.[1] In evaluating these variations, one must realize that many biologic, environmental, and social factors are involved. Thus climate, the nature of the soil, food consumption and habits, genetics, folk customs, and habits of work or exercise may affect the fertility, health status, and mortality experiences of populations. Beyond these there are, of course, the influences of public health personnel, facilities, medical and nursing services, housing standards and occupational conditions. In the broadest sense, economics, agronomy, education, and national political policy are probably the most important factors.

The key factor in determining the size of a population is the extent to which it can reproduce and maintain or increase itself. Various methods have been devised to measure this, the most common of which is the birthrate. In general, there is an inverse relationship between birthrate and either economic development or the degree and effectiveness of centralized planning by government (or a combination of the two) (Table 4-1). There is also a relationship between the birthrate of a country and the extent of general education and social status of women in that society.[2] It may be difficult to determine which comes first. But it seems generally true, at least in developing nations, that birthrates will remain relatively high so long as there is not an effective and universal education system and the social status of women is inferior to that of men. If that situation is altered favorably, birthrates decline. Lacking such changes, technologically based programs of birth control, unless they can be enforced by a strongly centralized government, have little durable effect on fertility. Birthrates have declined rather consistently in Western Europe and the British Isles, North America, and Japan. By contrast, birthrates have tended to fall more slowly or to increase in the countries of Asia, Africa, and Central and South America.

The birthrate in itself is neither a true measure of human fertility nor indicative of the extent to which the number of births is sufficient to maintain or increase the population of a nation. Because of this, additional indices, such as the rate of natural increase and fertility rates, have been devised. The rate of natural increase is simply the annual excess of births over deaths per 1,000 population. In general this rate is highest in the countries of Africa, the Middle East, Asia (except for Japan), and parts of Central and South America and is lowest in northern and western Europe and North America.

Even the numerical excess of births over deaths, however, is not a conclusive indication of the ability of a country's population to reproduce itself. A particular country at a given time may have an extremely large excess of births over deaths, yet its birthrate, especially when determined in relation to the number of persons of childbearing age, may not be high enough to maintain the present population eventually. This can occur when a country has a temporarily high proportion of young adults as a result of immigration or as a result of a mass delayed reproductive action, such as occurs during a period of warfare followed by the return home of

TABLE 4-1 Relationship of economic development and selected health status indicators, 1985

Economic development	Annual % population change	Birth rate per 1,000	Death rate per 1,000	Infant mortality rate*	Child death rate per 1,000†	Population per physician	Daily calorie supply
Low-income economies	1.9	29	10	72	9	5,770	2,339
Lower middle–income economies	2.5	36	11	82	11	8,230	2,514
Middle-income economies	2.3	32	10	68	8	5,080	2,731
Upper middle–income economies	2.0	28	8	52	4	1,340	2,987
Industrial market economies	0.6	13	9	23	<1	530	3,417

From World Bank: World development report, 1987, Washington, DC, 1987, Oxford University Press.
*Deaths of infants under 1 year of age per 1,000 live births.
†Children aged 1-4.

large numbers of young men. As a result of such circumstances, the birthrate may temporarily be much higher than the death rate, but the gross number of births may not be large enough to maintain such an age distribution permanently. There results eventually a population with a relatively high proportion of older persons and a concomitant fall of the birthrate, even below the level of the death rate.

As a result of these influences, it is fair to expect not only continued variations in population numbers, rates of increase, and density, but also significant accentuation of the differences in these factors among the nations and regions of the world. North America, the United Kingdom, Japan, the USSR, and Western Europe will probably experience stabilized or even decreasing populations unless net reproductive rates increase, death rates decrease even more than they have, or major immigrations occur. Most of Africa, the Middle East, Central and South America, South Central Asia, and Southeast Asia, on the other hand, appear destined to experience great and unsupportable increases in population if present fertility rates continue. In addition, barring the influence of other factors, these increases will be greatly magnified if death rates decline. There are many factors that might change or even reverse these trends. Important among them are improved education and standards of living combined with improved social status for women and improved health status generally. Historically, birthrates decline after improvements in public health and other social support systems that lead to a decline in infant and child mortality rates.

The crude death rate is one of the most common and convenient indices of the state of health of a community or nation. On the world scene, despite inadequate information, it is readily observed that in general the highest death rates occur in the countries of Africa, the Middle East, Asia, and parts of Central and South America. Significantly lower death rates are found in Western Europe, the USSR, the British Isles, Australia, New Zealand, North America, Japan, and a few countries in South America. It is immediately apparent that the national or regional variations in death rate essentially parallel the variations in birthrate and are related to economic development and the central role of government.

Progress in combating preventable disease and reducing mortality has been closely related to economic and sociopolitical development. It is generally claimed, in the literature from Western democracies, that health status indicators are best in the developed capitalist nations; that improved health status is related to wealth. In general this is true, but there are a sufficient number of exceptions in socialist countries to force some reexamination of such simple dogmas. Both Cuba and Costa Rica, for example, have relatively good mortality indices. Both are small countries, both have a low gross national product per person, but one is capitalistic and the other socialistic in terms of the central role of government in economic planning. Generally, death rates are lower in developed countries and higher in less developed and developing nations; they are also lower in more urbanized nations than in nations that are predominantly rural, with agricultural economies. That is not to suggest that heavy industrialization and urbanization necessarily produce improvements in health status or that rural living is unhealthy. It is, rather, a comment on the influence of community wealth on community health.

Although this relationship appears to apply to many specific death rates, it is by no means universally true. Certainly the relationship applies to the infant death rate and maternal mortality, as it also applies to the specific rates of death from almost all of the communicable diseases that can be controlled by public health, sanitation, and immunization methods. Until fairly recently, it was thought that the reverse was true for the so-called chronic, noninfectious, and degenerative diseases, such as cancer, heart disease, diabetes, and chronic pulmonary disease. However, as rural populations crowd into the urban areas of underdeveloped and developing nations, these problems of affluence are found to be related more to social structures, environmental conditions, employment, life-style, and the distribution of wealth. As living conditions improve marginally and more people survive the disease and injury threats of infancy and childhood, patterns of chronic disease very similar to those of the more industrialized and developed nations are becoming apparent.

The developed nations of the world have had the opportunity to face epochs serially: infectious diseases, then chronic diseases, and finally, diseases related to life-style and the environment. In developing countries, all three epochs appear to be crowding in on the population simultaneously. While most of the efforts of the international community are focused on infectious diseases in the developing world, population growth and urbanization are combining to push the epochs of disease into a continuum of calamity. In recent years, for example, a marked increase in lung cancer mortality rates has been observed throughout the world. This seems largely due to the decision of cigarette makers to concentrate their marketing efforts on underdeveloped nations as their markets in the industrialized and market economies dry up, accompanied by the general levels of poverty in those countries—a condition that is related to the prevalence of cigarette smoking.

In addition to birthrates and death rates, but as a function of the latter, average expectation of life should be considered briefly. The average life expectancy varies considerably among the nations of the world, from a low of about 34 years in Gambia and Sierra Leone to a high of about 76 years in Japan, the Netherlands, and Norway. As would be expected from the preceding consideration of death rates, the average life expectancy is much greater in Western Europe, the USSR, the British Isles, North America, New Zealand, and Japan than it is in most of the rest of the world. There are, however, several exceptions to this general picture.[3]

The differences among countries and regions are significant at all age levels but appear to diminish consistently as older ages are approached. The obvious conclusion, substantiated by age-specific death rates, is that the greatest risk to life in the lesser developed and less advantaged areas is experienced by infants and young children. In the poorer, less developed nations, up to one half of infants die, and deaths of children between 1 and 5 years of age are 12 to 15 times greater than in the developed nations. Survivors, however, have a reasonable chance of attaining a relatively advanced age.

One other important aspect of the variation in death rates and life expectancies relates to differences observed among the races. It is probable that differences are related more to social and economic factors than to racial characteristics. In general, they appear to be more circumstantial than inherent. This is exemplified by the fact that blacks in Europe and North America, although subject to a somewhat lower life expectancy and higher death rate than whites, nevertheless are in a decidedly more advantageous situation than blacks who live in Africa. Furthermore, the discrepancy between the rates for whites and blacks in the Western Hemisphere has narrowed somewhat although it has stabilized in recent years. That the problem is not simple is indicated by the situation in Hawaii, where the life expectancy of native Hawaiians is significantly less than that for other races living on the same islands.[4]

EXTENT OF WORLD HEALTH PROBLEMS

Any attempt to understand world health problems must conclude that the sciences of biology and climatology are essential. The cultural development, physical development, eating habits, clothing, housing, and, at least to some degree, methods of political organization of humans are partly determined by biologic and climatic factors. This applies especially to our reaction to the environment. By like token, most of the preventable illnesses to which we are subject involve other biologic beings: bacteria, viruses, protozoa, helminths, insects, and the like.

Some examples may serve to illustrate these points. Human beings share with the mosquito the unfortunate characteristic of being a suitable host for *Plasmodium falciparum,* the microorganism that causes malaria. The mosquito is an essential host in the life cycle of the plasmodium. Barring any interference, therefore, most of the people infected with malaria are to be found in areas of the globe where the climate supports mosquitos, and that means warm, moist, tropical and subtropical regions. If humans with the plasmodium in their blood move to an area where suitable mosquitos can be found, the disease may make a sudden and unexpected appearance. Moreover, if humans alter the ecology of their community by impounding water and using it for irrigation, they may inadvertently support the introduction of mosquitos, and thus malaria, into regions where it was previously unknown.

In contrast to malaria, pulmonary infections such as influenza and the common cold occur more often in less temperate climates with wider variations in temperature and seasons. These problems often lead to more serious lung diseases and chronic impairments. Once again, climate and biology combine to produce characteristic patterns of illness and morbidity. Typhus fever requires conditions that are not too cold to prevent propagation of the louse vector but cold enough to cause people to wear heavy clothing. When these climatic conditions are combined in an environment where sanitation is poor and clothing is rarely cleaned, as in times of war or other significant population upheavals, the louse thrives, typhus occurs, and humans die or are disabled.

The most common serious infectious diseases occur most frequently in warm climates. If the factors of biology and climatology are correlated with degree of economic development and applied scientific knowledge (and indeed, the latter would appear to be a function of the former), one observes a broad zone on the world globe, with necessarily indefinite borders and certain exceptions, that in general overlaps the equator about 20 to 25 degrees both north and south. This zone includes the areas in which the bulk of preventable infectious diseases and premature deaths now occur.

To most of those who reside permanently outside the zone, the extent of preventable disease seems incomprehensible. Nevertheless, as Russell[5] said many years ago, "Nothing on earth is more international than disease." A few examples may serve to illustrate.

Intestinal infections

The most widespread diseases result from infection by human feces. Included are infectious diarrheas, intestinal parasites, typhoid and paratyphoid, bacillary and amebic dysentery, infectious hepatitis, and cholera. Infectious diarrheas kill several million infants and young children (one third of deaths in this age group) each year in Africa, Asia, and Latin America.[6] The number of people affected by intestinal parasites is enormous. The World Health Organization estimated that worldwide in 1971 there were 650 million people with the roundworm *Ascaris,* 450 million with the hookworm *Ancylostoma,* 350 million with amebiasis, and 350 million with trichuriasis.[7]

These are old estimates. The topic is not as popular as it once was, and such estimates are less commonly attempted. They do little to advance knowledge of the problem or its solutions, but they do convey a sense of the magnitude of the problem. Some idea of the damage inflicted by such parasites may be gained from an old extrapolation by Stoll[8]: the 650 million people with roundworms probably contained 18 billion adult ascarids, which would equal the combined weight of almost a million adult men; would consume enough food from the intestinal tracts of their hosts to feed the entire population of Ecuador or Cambodia; and would produce 30,000 to 40,000 tons of eggs each year, which could and to a large extent do infect other people. This is the sort of journalistic feat rarely attempted in these more scientific times, but a valuable effort nonetheless. As Stoll observed, "Helminthiases do not have the journalistic value of great pandemics like flu or plague . . . but to make up for their lack of drama, they are unremittingly corrosive."

The tremendous amount of malnutrition and anemia, with concomitant increased susceptibility to various communicable diseases, that results from the burden of helminthic infestations constitutes an ongoing disaster. A somewhat bizarre parasitic infestation, dracontiasis, is worthy of mention for its unusual nature and its handicapping effect. The organism is a nematode, *Dracunculus medinensis,* or the guinea worm, acquired by drinking water containing the minute crustacean *Cyclops,* which has ingested the larvae that the adult worm has discharged into the water. Eventually the adult worm, which is sometimes as long as a meter and develops in the tissues from the swallowed larva, surfaces, usually on the human foot, and completes the cycle by discharging more larvae into the water. In the process, general symptoms as well as severe crippling may result. An estimated 50 million people are affected by it.

It is impossible even to estimate the numbers of cases and deaths from salmonellosis, shigellosis, the complex of so-called food poisonings, and infectious hepatitis. It is certain, however, that their incidence is tremendous. Cholera was reported in 34 countries in Asia, Africa, and Europe in 1987, with a total of 48,507 cases.[9] The disease waxes and wanes but can move with great rapidity. The Director General of the World Health Organization once said that one fifth of all deaths in the world were attributable to faulty environmental conditions. The number of people without a safe water supply or facilities for the disposal of human wastes is astonishing at the dawn of the twenty-first century. In Africa, the nations report that in rural areas only 20% of the population has a safe water supply. In North and South America, only about 30% of the people living in rural areas have potable water. Sanitary facilities are available in rural areas of Africa for considerably less than 50% of the population and, in many countries, for less than 10%. In the Americas, 16 of 23 countries reporting indicated that less than 50% of the people living in rural areas had adequate sanitary facilities.[10]

Vector-borne diseases

The large group of vector-borne diseases commands attention. Malaria occupies the predominant position. It is still probably the leading cause of death in the world despite strenuous national and international efforts to control if not eradicate it. The successes of the 1950s and 1960s have been thwarted by a combination of mosquito resistance to insecticides, escalating costs, population movements, and in some areas national and international strife. In 1984, 5.3 million new cases were reported, not including Africa south of the Sahara.[11] (Cases from that area are not published because reporting is inadequate, but from the data, it appears that more than 5 million additional new cases must have occurred in that region.) Half the world's population (2.227 billion people) live in areas where antimalarial activities are carried out, but the disease persists; 389 million people (8% of the world's population) live in areas with no specific measures against malaria, although the disease is endemic; 28% of the world's population live in areas where the disease never existed or has disappeared; 16% live in areas where it has been eliminated.[12] The situation has not improved during the past 15 years according to the World Health Organization reports. Technical problems in recent years have been related to the resistance of mosquitos to insecticides and the resistance of *Plasmodium falciparum* to drug treatment.

Trypanosomiasis, or sleeping sickness, spread by the bite of the tsetse fly, is of particular importance in a broad band across sub-Saharan Africa. If not treated early it is usually fatal. During the colonial era of the early twentieth century it became widespread. Epidemics, especially in Uganda and Zaire, were estimated to have caused the deaths of half the population. In company with malaria, it bars effective use of tremendous areas that many consider to contain some of the world's best agricultural and grazing land. The total area involved is about 4.5 million square miles, half again as large as the continental United States. Chagas' disease is a form of trypanosomiasis that exists in rural Mexico, Central America, and parts of South America. About 15 to 18 million people are estimated to be affected in South America.[13] It is spread by the bloodsucking Reduviidae, or kissing bugs. Although Chagas' disease is not nearly as serious as its African counterpart, cardiac complications are common.

Bilharziasis, or schistosomiasis, spread by snails, affects the populations of large irrigated parts of northern Africa, northeastern South America, Japan, and southeastern China. It has been estimated that in the Middle East about 30 million people, or 90% of the rural population, suffer from this debilitating disease, which generally reduces productivity by at least one third. In Egypt about three fourths of the population is affected. Lower Egypt is affected more than upper Egypt as a result of large new areas irrigated in relation to the high Aswan dam. Worldwide it is estimated that 200 million people are infected.[13]

Filarial infestations are another cause of physical incapacitation and economic loss. *Wuchereria bancrofti,* spread by several species of mosquitos, is found in most tropical countries, especially in Indonesia, northern Australia, parts of South Asia, Japan, Africa, the West Indies, the northern coast of South America, and the eastern coast of Brazil. In addition *W. malayi* occurs in the Malay peninsula, Sumatra, Borneo, New Guinea, India, Indochina, Sri Lanka, and southern China. Onchocerciasis, a type of filarial infestation spread by the black fly *Simulium,* is endemic to parts of Mexico, Guatemala and Venezuela, parts of Central Africa, and especially West Africa where "river blindness" from the disease has led to depopulation of fertile river valleys. The total number of people affected by onchocerciasis has been estimated at 20 million.[14] With reference to blindness in general, there are estimated to be about 30 million blind people in the world, over 24 million of them in the less developed countries.[15] Among the major causes, in addition to onchocerciasis, are trachoma, xerophthalmia from vitamin A deficiency, gonorrhea and syphilis, measles, cataracts, and glaucoma. Prevalence rates in some areas are very high; for example, upper

Ghana, 6.5%; Egypt, 2.6%; Chad, 3% to 5%; rural northern Sudan, 4.5%; India, 1.5%; Pakistan, 4.3%; Yemen, 4%; and Uganda, 1.8%.[16]

The plagues

Four other diseases, plague, leprosy, tuberculosis, and acquired immunodeficiency syndrome (AIDS), merit comment. Historically so important (see Chapter 2), human plague has not been eradicated. Its incidence varies from year to year, with sporadic cases reported from many nations. In 1985, 483 cases were reported from nine countries, with 51 deaths.[17] Some countries report cases nearly every year: Bolivia, Brazil, Burma, Ecuador, Madagascar, Peru, the United States, Vietnam, and Zaire.

Leprosy, another historic disease, currently claims about 15 million victims worldwide. Only about one fourth receive any treatment. Southern India has the largest concentration; about 3% of its population is thought to be infected. Other areas severely affected are China, many parts of Africa and southeast Asia, and several nations in Latin America. The recent development of drugs such as rifampicin and clofazimine combined with dapsone, as well as efforts to develop an effective vaccine, may spell some hope for effective treatment and prevention.

Tuberculosis, which may rightly be regarded as a disease of poverty, still claims at least 3.5 million new patients each year, more than half of whom die from it. Its incidence and prevalence closely parallel the degrees of economic disadvantage among the nations. The World Health Organization and other international agencies have been gradually breaking the chain of infection by means of early casefinding followed by chemotherapy and by extensive vaccination programs. Use of the Bacille Calmette-Guerin vaccine (BCG), not usually recommended in areas with a low incidence of the disease, is part of the World Health Organization's Expanded Program on Immunization (EPI). The ultimate weapon, of course, is economic improvement.

Acquired immunodeficiency syndrome (AIDS) was unknown to the world as recently as 1980. (See Chapter 16.) First found in Africa and thought to be related to a mutation of a peculiar retrovirus that originally affected monkeys, the disease was reported from every region of the world in 1988 (Table 4-2). By June of that year, 96,433 cases had been reported to the World Health Organization. The disease is probably more prevalent than indicated by present reports, since some nations are reluctant to acknowledge its existence, and it is clearly increasing rapidly. Worldwide totals are expected to be in the millions by the turn of the century.

POPULATION GROWTH

No discussion of world health can be viewed in perspective without consideration of the other major phenomenon of our history—the growth of the world's population. It has been estimated that the total population of the world was about 5 million people in 6000 BCE (Before the Common Era, as noted earlier, a more ecumenical term than BC). By the beginning of the Common Era, sixty centuries later, it had increased to 250 million people, a rate of increase of about 6.7% per century. During the next sixteen centuries the population increased at a rate of 4.4% per century to about 500 million people. Then an acceleration began: the population doubled during the next 2½ centuries and then doubled again in less than a century. It took all of our long history to reach the current figure of 5.2 billion, but it will require only 40 more years to double that figure at the present rate of growth, and if that rate continued, the population would reach the staggering and insupportable total of 26.6 billion by 2095. But that will not happen. Such extrapolations never continue over the long run. They cannot.

Overall, the annual rate of growth in the world's population is about 1.75%,[19] which added about 91

TABLE 4-2 Cumulative reported cases of acquired immunodeficiency syndrome by world region, 1988

Region	Cases
Africa	11,530
Americas	71,343
Asia	254
Europe	12,414
Oceania	892
TOTAL	96,433

From Weekly Epidemiologic Report 63, June 3, 1988.

million people in 1989. The growth rate was about 2% per year in the 1960s. During the 1970s the growth rate declined slightly in developed nations but increased in the developing world, which constitutes about 75% of the total world population. Then population growth decreased slightly in developing nations, but given the large population base that exists, larger numbers of people are added each year (Table 4-3).

The dynamics of population growth

When population growth data are studied, it becomes apparent that many forces in addition to public health are involved including area limitations; climate; present size, spatial distribution, and age structure of the population; present and potential resources for food; availability and use of efficient agricultural implements, machinery, and techniques; availability and quality of housing; policies and practices with regard to public health and education; existence, availability, and use of natural resources and sources of energy; methods of verbal and physical communication, with special emphasis on farm-to-market roads; trends toward urbanization and industrialization; tax and financial structure, especially the availability of short-term and long-term loans at reasonable rates of interest; policies relating to the composition, full employment, and adequate compensation of the labor force; and a multitude of cultural factors. This is not the place to attempt a review of these and the many other factors involved in population and world demographic trends, or the policies involved in international population planning. A substantial literature has developed during the past 30 years dealing with international aspects of population policy, family planning programs, and basic consideration of population growth as a major problem for the world in general and developing nations in particular.* A few additional comments are relevant here, however.

Population growth and public health

Without doubt, public health measures have contributed to the increase in population during the past century. They have done so in four ways: (1) by improving the probability of conception once sexual intercourse has occurred, through improved health status, (2) by increasing the chances of survival among infants and children, (3) by preventing the premature deaths of many young adults who constitute the most fertile component of a population and the group with the longest period of future fecundity, and (4) by greatly reducing the number of marriages dissolved by the death of one partner.

Understandably, there is concern over the ability of public health programs to reduce mortality rates in the face of continued high birthrates. Yet it has

* Among the better serial publications are *Studies in Family Planning, International Family Planning Perspectives,* and *Population and Development Review.* See also Appleman P, editor: *An Essay on the Principle of Population,* New York, 1976, WW Norton; Reining P and Tucker I, editors: *Population: Dynamics, Ethics, and Policy,* Washington, DC, 1975, American Association for the Advancement of Science; and Bulatao R and Lee R, editors: *Determinants of Fertility in Developing Countries* New York, 1983, Academic Press.

TABLE 4-3 Population estimates for the year 2000, regions of the world

Region	Population	Percent of total	Annual growth rate	Percent increase (1950-1983)
World	6,246	100	1.9	86
Africa	846	14	2.6	132
Asia	3,705	59	2.1	98
Latin America	560	9	2.6	135
North America	296	45	1.3	56
Europe	511	8	0.9	33
Soviet Union	289	5		
Oceania	9	<1	1.9	90

From Bureau of the Census: World population, 1983: recent demographic estimates for the countries and regions of the world, Washington, DC, 1983, US Department of Commerce.

been demonstrated repeatedly that improved health status will result in an increased rate of natural increase in a population followed several years later by a gradual and voluntary decline in fertility. The reasons for this phenomenon are extremely complex, and there is little agreement as to its dynamics, but empirically it seems to be axiomatic that a population increase will precede a declining birthrate. This makes the argument for a comprehensive rather than a single-factor approach to improved community health all the more compelling. It also indicates that, rather than restraining the application of public health practice, broader and more intensive support is warranted.

The task of improving world health is indeed awesome. John Evans and his colleagues[20] have described the obstacles to progress: the uneven distribution of health services, lack of appropriate technology, pharmaceutical policies that result in an inadequate supply and poor distribution of the most needed supplies, bad management, poverty, and inadequate or inappropriate government programs to finance needed services. One of the most serious problems in world health is the imbalance of health personnel of all types. There are different types of imbalances: numerical, qualitative, and distributional.[21] Some countries clearly have an insufficient supply of virtually all health workers. Others have an oversupply, which can lead to expenditure problems and a drive toward increasing use of invasive techniques to ameliorate insignificant or even nonexistent problems. This is not just a problem of the industrialized market economies; some developing nations have invested heavily in health personnel training and have an oversupply problem.

Qualitative imbalance is difficult to identify objectively, but surely exists in regions where the accessible health workers are not trained to handle the problems of the community. In addition, in virtually all countries, there is a consistent pressure for physicians, as well as other health workers, to specialize in increasingly narrow fields. Specialization appears to be a universal response to status needs, as well as a desire to master a body of knowledge. As the knowledge base in the biological sciences increases in size, students and practitioners must narrow their focus in order to remain proficient.

Distributional imbalances occur in almost all nations, as physicians and other health workers try to establish practices in urban areas, leaving rural areas without adequate access. Government policies have not always been successful in correcting such imbalances. Unfortunately, in many underdeveloped and developing nations, the same propensity for investment in tertiary care that is seen in the United States and other developed nations occurs. Countries with inadequate primary care, poor sanitation, and continuing high infant and child mortality rates have devoted significant proportions of their investment to high-technology medical care and the training of specialists. Such practices have been supported by American medical schools, which are better at exporting such technology than they are at developing a basic infrastructure of primary care.

Worldwide, there has been a significant increase in the number of health care professionals over the last three decades. The annual growth in the supply of physicians during this time has been 3.9% in developed nations and 7.1% in developing nations.[21] Still, numerical, distributional, and qualitative imbalances exist (Table 4-4).

Variations within regions are even more striking. The ratio in Ethiopia was 88,120 people per physician in 1981. In the middle-income countries, the range was from 760 in Egypt to 3,120 in Honduras, with 2,700 in Jamaica. In the upper middle–income countries, the range was from 300 in Hungary and Poland to 1,200 in Mexico. In the industrial-market countries, the figure for Spain was 360 and for the United States, 500.[3]

Variations such as these do not reveal the true picture of imbalances. Countries with a very low population-to-physician ratio may use physicians for many tasks that are performed by nurses in

TABLE 4-4 Population-to-physician ratios by regional income, 1981

	GNP per capita	Population per physician
Low-income countries	200	17,350
Middle-income countries	1,290	5,080
Upper middle–income countries	1,850	1,340
Industrial-market countries	11,810	530

From World Bank: World development report, 1987, Washington, DC, 1987, Oxford University Press.

other countries, whereas a much higher ratio of population to physicians does not necessarily mean that either a qualitative or numerical imbalance exists, since other types of health personnel may be well utilized, particularly as primary care workers. In addition, in many parts of the world, traditional healers are extensively used as primary care providers, although they are not enumerated in official counts of the size of the health work force.

Public health training, as it is known in the United States, is not a major feature of the health work force training policies of underdeveloped and developing nations. The evolution of public health practice and education in the United States is unique in its separation from medical care. (See Chapter 2.) In most other countries, public health training is provided in the medical school environment. As of 1985, there were 216 graduate institutions providing training in public health in 54 countries.[22] Most such programs, while influenced by the American model with its emphasis on epidemiology, environmental health, health education, and health administration, tend to focus on primary care. In the United States, primary care customarily connotes the use of "entry-level" physicians: general and family practitioners, pediatricians, internists who have not subspecialized, and obstetricians. In other parts of the world, primary health care "is essential health care based on practical, scientifically sound and socially acceptable methods and technology made universally accessible to individuals and families in the community"[23] and it includes at least

> education concerning prevailing health problems and the methods of preventing and controlling them; promotion of food supply and proper nutrition; an adequate supply of safe water and basic sanitation; maternal and child health care, including family planning; immunization against the major infectious diseases; prevention and control of locally endemic diseases; appropriate treatment of common diseases and injuries; and provision of essential drugs. . . .[23]

This blend of primary medical care and basic public health practice has been the policy of the United Nations since the Alma-Ata conference of 1978. It has continued to provoke discussion about national and international health policies as they affect developing and underdeveloped nations.

Walsh and Warren,[24] concerned because the aspirations of the Alma-Ata conference seemed unattainable using the methods advocated, described various approaches to the improvement of health status in developing countries. Using the Alma-Ata definition of *comprehensive primary care,* they stated that its provision to everyone in the near future remained unlikely because of the lack of resources. They defined *basic primary health care* in more limited terms: the use of health care professionals in clinics to treat illness. This they found inappropriate, ineffective, and unaffordable. A *multiple disease control strategy* would focus on nationally selected priority issues with a series of unrelated programs designed to control specific diseases. Such programs might concentrate on selected vector-borne diseases, basic water and sanitation programs, and nutrition supplementation. The programs might come together in the Ministry of Health at the national level but would have little or no interaction at the local level. That is, they would not be decentralized and would not involve treatment of basic illnesses. Walsh and Warren's favored strategy was *selective primary health care,* a strategy that involved the careful definition of problems based on mortality and morbidity. They recommended measles and diphtheria-pertussis-tetanus immunization for children over 6 months of age, tetanus toxoid for all women of childbearing age, encouragement of long-term breast feeding, the provision of chloroquine (an antimalarial) for episodes of fever in children under 3 years of age in areas where malaria was prevalent, and an oral rehydration packet for the treatment of diarrheal diseases. It should be noted that Walsh and Warren worked for the Rockefeller Foundation at the time, and a number of authors attacked their recommendations as being short-sighted and reflecting a traditionalistic policy. Others have attempted to show that comprehensive primary care is both feasible and practical.[25] Nonetheless, no one has yet found a way to solve the significant resource problems involved in implementing the World Health Organization's approach to primary care, and there is some evidence that the resource problem has become worse in recent years.

Decisions regarding program choices should be based on two fundamental considerations:

1. The costs and benefits of different approaches, and
2. The political feasibility of the program.

In recent years, there have been some encouraging trends even while resource problems have continued or worsened. Many countries have established planning units within their ministries of health. These have been strengthened by the assignment of personnel from other parts of the government, such as finance, and also by the provision of advanced training in planning and administration, both within ministries and through temporary assignments to other countries. (See Chapter 13.) Equally important has been the concurrent establishment of broad-based planning or development units, with health representation included, reporting directly to the head of government. These are fundamental steps, not only for the avoidance of duplication or conflicts of interest but also for the assurance that critically important views and actions are not overlooked.

Efforts continue to address work force imbalances. With the urging of the World Health Organization and the Pan American Health Organization, attention has shifted from expansion of facilities and personnel for hospital-based therapeutic care, largely in urban centers, to improvement and extension of relatively rudimentary health care services by primary health workers. Preferably such personnel are locally recruited and often supported by their communities. Included are many types with many names: medical or health assistants, sanitarians, nursing auxiliaries, midwives or birth attendants, feldshers, barefoot doctors, and many others. Another change that has occurred is the legitimization in many places of so-called traditional healers and some of their procedures. In many instances traditional healers have received training in certain aspects of scientific medicine and public health, and in return certain traditional medications and methods have been adopted by practitioners of scientific medicine and public health.[26] The goal, of course, is better distribution of more and better health care.

ECONOMIC, SOCIAL, AND POLITICAL RELATIONSHIPS OF WORLD HEALTH PROBLEMS

From what has been presented, it is clear that most of the preventable disease in the world is concentrated in what is commonly referred to as developing or underdeveloped areas or countries. It is not possible to speak, think, or act on the health problems of these countries or areas within an isolated substantive framework. Large proportions of the human beings who live in these areas, and they constitute most of the population of the earth, eke out a miserable existence under circumstances that are undesirable from many different standpoints, of which ill health is only one. Their housing is inadequate, their economy unbalanced, their food supply precarious, their methods of performing daily tasks primitive, their educational horizons limited, and their daily work relatively inefficient and unproductive.

What is cause and what is effect? McKeown,[27] in his study of population growth in seventeenth century England, concluded that food shortages led to high mortality (both through their impact on health and because of wars fought for land) and low fertility. As changes in agriculture increased the calories available per person, sanitary measures began to have an impact, leading to a decrease in deaths due to infectious diseases. Whether a similar analysis is directly applicable to the developing nations of the late twentieth century is unclear.

Widespread preventable disease unquestionably serves as a barrier to progress in any direction, be it economic, social, or political. A population that is chronically ill and malnourished understandably has decreased productivity. Billions of days of work are lost annually because of intestinal and arthropod-borne diseases. The loss in countries where malaria is widespread has been reported to be from 5% to 10% of the total labor force, with the greatest incidence of the disease occurring at the peak period of agricultural production. It was estimated by Russell[5] in 1948 that any nation importing products of a highly malarious country paid the equivalent of a 5% malaria tax.

Widespread disease also serves as an effective barrier to the development of agricultural lands and natural resources. The effective settlement of such areas as Sumatra, Borneo, central Africa, large parts of South America, and until recently, the Terai of India, Pakistan, Nepal, and large parts of Sardinia, to mention only a few examples, has been prevented by disease, primarily malaria and other insect-borne diseases. The accomplishments in the last two locations give some indication of the potential elsewhere. The control of malaria in

Sardinia during the 1950s paved the way for the resettlement of about 1 million Italians from the mainland. Similar measures in the Terai have made it possible to open this great fertile area to agricultural development. For the world as a whole, the malaria eradication program begun by the World Health Organization in 1955 has accomplished much, although, as has been mentioned, there have been recent setbacks in some areas. Even greater success has been achieved in the fight against smallpox, which has been eradicated from the face of the earth.[28]

For the individual, educational and intellectual development is difficult if at all possible when the body is chronically drained of its energy by illness and parasites. This was illustrated in the Philippines some years ago when it was found that malaria control reduced school absenteeism from about 50% daily to 3%. At the same time industrial absenteeism was reduced from 35% to under 4%. Uncontrolled disease and the environmental and social conditions that allow it effectively discourage investment from within or without, as well as industrial development. Such circumstances are not conducive to democratic forms of government and often lead to political instability.

These phenomena form a vicious circle with difficult access for corrective measures. Widespread endemic disease shackles a population with indigenous poverty, and poverty supports widespread endemic disease. Whether to focus first on the poverty and later on the disease or vice versa is unclear both theoretically and politically. It is perhaps easier politically to focus on the disease problems first, using one of the strategies discussed by Walsh and Warren, but it is not clear whether that effort alone can overcome the phenomenon of poverty. The situation is characterized by multiple factors, as was described clearly over 10 years ago[29]:

Economic stagnation
Cultural patterns unfavorable to development
Agricultural underemployment and lack of alternative employment opportunities
Poor quality of life due to scarcity of essential goods, facilities, and money
Isolation caused by distance and poor communications
An unfavorable environment predisposing to communicable diseases and malnutrition
Inadequate health facilities and lack of sanitation
Poor educational opportunities
Social injustice including inequitable land tenure systems and a rigid hierarchy and class structure
Inadequate representation and influence in national decision making

To these should be added:

Suppression of women
Inequities based on race, ethnic background, or religious affiliation

Some of these relationships are illustrated by the data presented in Table 4-1. Many more people live in the less developed countries than in those that are more developed. The relationship between income and health status is clear. Many more variables could be added to the table and the cycle would still be apparent: literacy, percent of calories coming from protein, the population per hospital bed, etc. The relationship of gross national product, or the economic status of a nation, to these factors oversimplifies a complex situation, as has been discussed above. To some extent, the degree to which the national government, or state governments in a federalized system, control economic and social planning has an important impact on health status. Per capita wealth data mask the way income is distributed in the country: whether there is a significant gap between the lowest and highest income groups, and the size of the middle-income group. Roemer[30] shows how the use of the Gini coefficient (named for the Italian scholar who developed the concept) can increase the precision with which the way wealth affects health can be estimated. The Gini coefficient would be 0 in a society where income was equally distributed and 1 where the highest income decile had all of the income and the other nine-tenths none. When the simple calculations that relate life expectancy and infant mortality rates to GNP per capita are adjusted by the Gini coefficients, the correlations are much stronger (Table 4-5).

The solution to the problem is not easy. Certainly it cannot be accomplished by an attack on health problems alone. In fact, such an approach would carry with it certain real dangers, if it were to succeed at all. Advancement must be made in many fields simultaneously. The statement of Myrdal[31] at the Fifth World Health Assembly in 1951 is still worthy of note in summarizing the complexity of the situation and outlining a guide for effective, lasting action:

> The task of social engineering is to proportion and direct the induced changes in the whole social field so as to maximize the beneficial effects of a given initial financial sacrifice. One important corollary to the theory of cumulative causation is that a rational policy should never work by inducing change in only one factor; least of all should such a change of only one factor be attempted suddenly and with great force. This would in most cases prove to be a wasteful expenditure of efforts which could reach much further by being spread strategically over the various factors in the social system and over a period of time. What we are facing is a whole set of interrelated adverse living conditions for a population. An effort to reach permanent improvement of health standards aimed to have a maximum beneficial effect on the well-being of the people will, in other words, have to be integrated in a broad economic and social reform policy. Such a policy will have to be founded upon studies of how in the concrete situation of a particular country the different factors in the plane of living are interrelated and how we can move them all upwards in such a fashion that the changes will support each other to the highest possible degree.

This concept and similar increasingly frequent views have resulted in the World Health Organization position on primary care.[23]

INTERNATIONAL HEALTH ORGANIZATIONS

Health is a community affair. The action occurs at the local level where the people, their problems, their communities, and their governmental structures are found. Therefore international health work cannot be thought of as a field unto itself. It has meaning only in its relation to the many national and local components of the total world health picture. It is with this reservation that certain aspects of the development and present status of international health activities are presented.

World Health Organization

Movement toward international cooperation in health goes back several generations, based initially on concerns about epidemic disease.[32] The first

TABLE 4-5 GNP per capita (adjusted), life expectancy, and infant mortality rates for 20 countries, about 1973

Country	GNP per capita (U.S. dollars)	Gini coefficient	Gini adjusted GNP per capita	Life expectancy	Infant mortality
India	110	.461	239	49	139
Sri Lanka	100	.358	279	68	50
Turkey	340	.544	625	56	153
Ivory Coast	330	.516	640	44	138
Colombia	370	.546	678	61	68
Zambia	380	.488	779	45	150
Malaysia	400	.497	805	59	39
Brazil	460	.553	832	61	110
Peru	480	.571	841	56	54
Iran	480	.473	951	51	160
Mexico	700	.558	1,254	63	61
Jamaica	720	.558	1,290	70	27
Taiwan	430	.317	1,356	62	18
Costa Rica	590	.429	1,375	68	68
Chile	760	.487	1,561	64	71
Venezuela	1,060	.591	1,794	65	52
Albania	480	.252	1,984	69	87
Cuba	510	.242	2,107	72	29
Yugoslavia	730	.333	2,192	68	44
Bulgaria	820	.206	3,981	72	26

From Roemer MI: National strategies for health care organization: a world overview, Ann Arbor, Michigan, 1985, Health Administration Press.

crystallization was the First International Sanitary Conference in Paris in 1851. It is significant that each of the 12 participating countries was represented by a physician and a diplomat. In 1903 plans began to be formulated to establish a permanent international health agency.[33] This became a reality in 1907, when 12 nations signed an agreement to create the Office Internationale d'Hygiène Publique. Meanwhile, for the same reason (concerns about epidemic disease), representatives of 21 American republics met at their first International Sanitary Conference in Mexico City early in 1902. On December 2, 1902, the International Sanitary Bureau was established. This organization has functioned continuously with several name changes and, as the present Pan American Health Organization (PAHO), is the oldest functioning international health organization. It also serves as the western hemispheric regional office of the subsequently established World Health Organization.[34]

In 1944, while World War II was still in progress, a conference was held in Montreal to discuss the future of international health efforts. A constitution for a World Health Organization was signed by 61 nations on April 7, 1948, and the organization came into official existence. By 1987 the World Health Organization had a membership of 166 nations, which made it the largest of the specialized agencies of the United Nations. In addition, about 120 nongovernment organizations maintain official relations with it.

The constitution of the World Health Organization, particularly in view of its definition of health as "a state of complete physical, mental, and social well-being and not merely the absence of disease or infirmity," has been aptly referred to as the Magna Charta of health because of its affirmation that health is "one of the fundamental rights of every human being, without distinction of race, religion, political belief, economic or social condition" and its recognition that "the health of all peoples is fundamental to the attainment of peace and security."[35]

With regard to its structure and management,[36] the headquarters of the World Health Organization is in Geneva, Switzerland. Regional offices are located at Brazzaville, for Africa; Washington, D.C., for the Americas (Pan American Health Organization); New Delhi, for Southeast Asia; Copenhagen, for Europe; Alexandria, for the eastern Mediterranean; and Manila, for the western Pacific. It is financed by prorated and special contributions from active member nations and from the United Nations Technical Assistance Board. Its budget for 1988-1989 was $634 million. An annual World Health Assembly, usually held in Geneva in May, serves as the agency's legislative body. Each member nation is allowed three delegates but only one vote at the Assemblies.

The erosion in the value of the dollar during the mid-1980s caused a sharp reduction in the purchasing value of the World Health Organization's budget. In addition, the United States adopted a policy toward the United Nations and its related agencies that resulted in a payment of only 5% of the World Health Organization's budget during 1985-1986 by the United States, rather than the expected 25%, leaving a budget hole of nearly $100 million. At the end of the biennium, the United States raised its contribution to 18% of the organization's budget, still leaving a shortfall of $38 million during a time when developing nations were experiencing severe budgetary difficulties and the new epidemic of AIDS was spreading throughout the world.

An executive board has the responsibility of implementing the decisions and policies of the Assembly and deals with emergency situations in the name of the Assembly. Normally this technical nonpolitical group of 30 health experts, who are elected at the Assembly, meets twice a year. A secretariat, headed by a Director-General, includes a technical and an administrative staff located at the Geneva headquarters and in the regional offices. It is responsible for the day-to-day work of the organization. There are five assistant Director-Generals and six Regional Directors. The staff (not including PAHO) was 4,384 in 1987. The World Health Organization provides for regional committees composed of representatives from member states in each region. These regional committees formulate regional policies and supervise the activities of the regional offices. In addition, panels and committees on various pertinent subjects involve more than 12,000 experts in various fields to advise the World Health Organization and keep it up to date on current scientific research.

The mission or purpose of the World Health Organization has been summarized as follows[37]:

1. It is the one directing and coordinating authority on international health work. It is not a

supranational ministry of health; rather, it is a worldwide cooperative through which the nations help each other to help themselves in raising health standards.

2. It provides to member countries various central technical services; that is, epidemiology, statistics, standardization of drugs and procedures, a wide range of technical publications, etc.

3. Its most important function is to help countries to strengthen and improve their own health service. On request it provides advisory and consulting services through public health experts, demonstration teams for disease control, visiting specialists, etc.

The current priorities of the World Health Organization, through its "Health for All by 2000" campaign, are the application of primary care, environmental health, control of infectious and diarrheal diseases, maternal and child health care, nutrition, injury prevention, and occupational health.

The functions and activities of the World Health Organization are extremely broad. For the first time in international affairs emphasis has been placed not on quarantine, checking epidemics, and other defensive measures, but on positive, aggressive action toward health in its broadest sense. The World Health Organization, although related to the United Nations, is a separate, independent agency with its own constitution, membership, and sources of funds. As yet, it is too early to determine with assurance what the future holds for this organization.

Pan American Health Organization

The beginning of the twentieth century saw the establishment at the Second American International Conference in Mexico City of the International Sanitary Bureau (1902), subsequently renamed the Pan American Health Organization. Its headquarters is in Washington, D.C. As has been mentioned, this was the first permanent international health agency and the longest lived up to the present. It was organized to be governed by an elected council and a Director-General. It is supported by annual financial quotas contributed by each of the American Republics, augmented from other sources. In 1986-1987 its budget was $111 million, of which about two thirds came from assessments of member nations and the remainder from the World Health Organization, other United Nations sources, and miscellaneous inter-American, national, and private contributions.[38] Under the provisions of the Pan-American Sanitary Code, which was ratified by all 21 of the American Republics in 1924, the Pan American Health Organization became the center for coordinating international action and information in the field of public health in the Western Hemisphere. It holds an annual conference of high quality, which is attended by delegates from all member nations. Through those member nations it has been given the responsibility and authority to receive and disseminate epidemiologic information, to furnish technical assistance on request to member countries, to finance fellowships, and to promote cooperation in medical research. It has done much to promote professional education in Latin America. It also serves as the regional office and agent in the Americas of the World Health Organization.

United Nations Children's Fund

The United Nations Children's Fund (UNICEF) is an agency whose history and activities have been intimately related to those of the World Health Organization. At the demise of the United Nations Relief and Rehabilitation Administration in 1946, certain of its funds were transferred to a newly formed agency organized to assist especially the children of war-torn countries. The program gradually expanded to include other activities and other areas, particularly underdeveloped countries.

This agency has spent large sums of money, especially on food and supplies, for the promotion of child and maternal health and welfare activities throughout the world. Beyond this, however, and usually through partnership with the World Health Organization, it has been carrying out large and significant programs of BCG vaccination, yaws control, and malaria control demonstrations. The promotion of family planning in developing countries has been one of its major activities in recent years. Organized originally as a temporary emergency agency, it has filled such a need and attracted such support that in 1953 it was given permanent status and named the United Nations Children's Fund. One of its most interesting and valuable enterprises has been the International Children's Center, established in the late 1940s.[39] The center brings together and coordinates the efforts of many disciplines: pediatricians, social workers, psychologists, educators, and health and social administrators. It is concerned with all three aspects of child development: physical, mental, and social. Its international activities are fourfold: teaching of child welfare problems and methods, medical-social research work, documentation and publications, and cooperation in matters of child welfare.

Bilateral health assistance

So far, consideration has been given to the development of what have been commonly referred to as the multilateral organizations in public health; that is, organizations whose financing, staffing, policymaking, and operations are entered into and shared by more than two, and usually many, nations. In addition, another type of international health cooperation exists that is carried out by what are referred to as bilateral agreements and organizations. This comes about when two nations, for reasons of mutual interest, agree to work together on certain matters dealing with public health.

The U.S. government became significantly involved in bilateral international public health activities as a result of World War II. In 1942 the Foreign Ministers of the American Republics recommended that steps be taken to solve the environmental sanitation and health problems of the Americas and that to this end, according to capacity, each country contribute raw material, services, and funds. The United States was asked to accept the responsibility of leadership.

Cooperative health programs were promptly established with 18 nations of Central and South America. The activities of each were financed by contributions from both the United States and the other governments concerned, and the programs were determined jointly by an official of the host government, usually the Minister or Director-General of Health, and the chief of the group of professionals assigned by the United States to the host country.

From the beginning the program had four areas of emphasis: (1) the development of local health services through health centers; (2) the sanitation of the environment, with particular emphasis on water supply, sewage disposal, and insect control; (3) the training and full-time employment of professional public health workers; and (4) the education of the public in health matters. It stressed complete community health development under full-time trained directors with active community participation.

At the end of World War II the United States organized a succession of agencies. These underwent a series of reorganizations and eventually in 1961 constituted the Agency for International Development (AID) within the U.S. Department of State.

AID coordinates its health planning and programs with the Office of International Health of the U.S. Public Health Service and with the World Health Organization and assists other nations by providing, among other things, technical and material assistance in a wide range of public health programs. At present, public health personnel financed by AID are engaged in numerous types of health programs in various countries throughout the world, in cooperation with the various assistance programs of the World Health Organization and other United Nations–related agencies, other nations, and private foundations. Many public health and related workers from the United States, representing a wide spectrum of professional disciplines, are involved in its programs. One of the most significant contributions of AID and of its predecessors has been the field of training. Fellowships for advanced training in the United States and elsewhere have been granted to several thousand professional health workers of other countries, and many thousands more have been given in-service training in connection with ongoing cooperative health programs. Because of the location of AID within the Department of State, many public health professionals and citizens of other countries have been suspicious of its programs, sometimes seeing them as elements of U.S. political strategy and occasionally finding evidence that people on AID assignments have been debriefed by State Department personnel and Central Intelligence Agency staff. Because of these problems, some organizations have been reluctant to become intimately involved in the work of AID, and some public health professionals will not accept AID assignments.

In addition to the United States, several other nations provide technical and material assistance in health and other fields on a bilateral basis. Among these are Sweden, the United Kingdom, the Federal

Republic of Germany, France, the USSR, and the People's Republic of China.

Nongovernmental agencies

No summary of international health cooperation would be complete without mention of the contribution that has been made by nongovernmental agencies. As far as "shirt-sleeve" technical assistance is concerned, undoubtedly the earliest endeavors were those of the various church missions and medical missionaries. In addition, there have been philanthropic foundations with interest in international health based on the highest altruistic motives. Among the many that might be mentioned are the Unitarian Service Committee; the American Friends Service Committee; the various Catholic Mission groups; the American Bureau for Medical Aid to China; the Foreign Mission Agencies of the Baptist, Methodist, and Seventh Day Adventist churches; and the Near East Relief agency. As is true of the Agency for International Development, these organizations are not without their critics. Although they vary considerably in their motivation and methodology, many are seen as elements of a colonialist mentality with proselytizing motives having little to do with the well-being of the host countries. In addition, there has been some darker suspicion that a few such organizations were part of a campaign of economic exploitation, which thrived on the dependency of population groups. But these criticisms are part of historical revisionism, which is apt to recast institutions of an earlier time according to present-day perceptions. The organizations provided an enormous amount of material and intellectual aid even if some of it was misdirected given present-day theories and practices.

Among the foundations, the Rockefeller Foundation is the best known in the field of international assistance in health. It has operated in almost all countries of the world in the seven decades of its existence. Its significant contributions are many and include such activities as the control of malaria and yellow fever, the development of recognized centers of learning in medicine and public health, the provision of postgraduate fellowships to many individuals, and the demonstration of sound methods of organization and operation of health programs. The Rockefeller Foundation has been joined by several other foundations, notably the Kellogg Foundation, which has been especially interested in improving professional education in the Latin American countries.

Conclusion

To some, it may appear that the programs of international health are too many, too varied, too dispersed and too confusing. Although this may be true to some degree, it has been by no means unexpected or undesirable. The field of international cooperation for social and economic development is still rather new. Indeed, there are still many individuals in the world who do not comprehend the mutual cause-effect and supportive relationships that exist between the efforts to improve health and the achievement of socioeconomic development. This in itself represents one of the greatest challenges to health workers on both the domestic and the international levels. It has been necessary and logical to approach international health with a combination of caution and courage and often on the basis of trial and error, rather than attempt to establish prematurely a fixed pattern that might have misled future growth and thought. In recent years a process of pulling the pieces together has begun in both the multilateral and the bilateral areas. It is to be expected that the future will see an ever more logical organizational approach to the tremendous problems that still exist in public health throughout the world.

Finally, it must be realized that there will always be an important place for all three types of international health work: multilateral, bilateral, and nongovernmental. Each in its way augments the efforts of the others. Sound, effective, and cooperative correlation of all of their activities may result in the ultimate achievement of the universally desired goal of world health.

REFERENCES

1. Weekly Epidemiologic Record and World Health Statistics Annual, Geneva, World Health Organization.
2. Caldwell J: A theory of fertility: from high plateau to destabilization, Pop Development Review 4:553, Dec 1978.
3. World development report. Washington, DC, 1987, World Bank.
4. Gardner RW: Life tables by ethnic group for Hawaii, 1980, Research and Statistics Report 47, Honolulu, March 1984, Hawaii State Department of Health.

5. Russell P: A lively corpse, Trop Med News 5:25, June 1948.
6. World Health Statistics Annual, 1986, Geneva, 1986, World Health Organization.
7. Health, Sector Policy Paper, Washington, DC, 1980, World Bank.
8. Stoll NR: This wormy world, J Parasitology 33:1, Feb 1947.
9. Weekly Epidemiologic Report 63, May 13, 1988.
10. World Health Statistics Annual, 1986, Geneva, 1986, World Health Organization.
11. Weekly Epidemiologic Report 61, May 2, 1986.
12. Weekly Epidemiologic Report 60, Nov 1, 1985.
13. Vector control in primary health care: report of a WHO scientific group, Technical Report Series 757, Geneva, 1987, World Health Organization.
14. Onchocerciasis, WHO Chronicle 30:18, Jan 1976.
15. Zahra A: WHO's communicable disease programme, World Health, Nov 1980, p. 3.
16. Data on blindness throughout the world, WHO Chronicle 33:275, May-June 1979.
17. Weekly Epidemiologic Report 60, Sep 5, 1986.
18. Weekly Epidemiologic Report 63, June 3, 1988.
19. Bureau of the Census: World population, 1983: recent demographic estimates for the countries and regions of the world, Washington, DC, 1983, US Department of Commerce
20. Evans JR, Hall KL, and Warford J: Shattuck lecture—health care in the developing world: problems of scarcity and choice, New Engl J Med 305:1117, Nov 5, 1981.
21. Mejia A: Health manpower out of balance, World Health Statistics Quarterly 40(4):335, 1987.
22. World directory of schools of public health and postgraduate training in public health, ed 3, Geneva, 1985, World Health Organization.
23. World Health Organization and United Nations Children's Fund: Primary health care. Report of the International Conference on Primary Health Care, Alma-Ata, USSR, September 6-12, 1978, Geneva, 1978, World Health Organization.
24. Walsh JA and Warren KS: Selective primary health care: an interim strategy for disease control in developing countries, New Engl J Med 301:967, Nov 1, 1979.
25. Boland RGA and Young MEM: The strategy, cost and progress of primary health care, Bull Pan Am Health Organ 16:233, 1982.
26. Morinis EA: Two pathways in understanding disease: traditional and scientific, WHO Chronicle 32:57, Feb 1978.
27. McKeown T: The modern rise of population, New York, 1976, Academic Press.
28. Henderson DA: Smallpox eradication: a WHO success story, World Health Forum 8(3):283, 1987.
29. Djukanovic V and Mach EP: Alternative approaches to meeting basic health needs in developing countries, Geneva, 1975, World Health Organization.
30. Roemer MI: National strategies for health care organization: a world overview, Ann Arbor, Michigan, 1985, Health Administration Press.
31. Myrdal G: Economic aspects of health, WHO Chron 6:207, Aug 1952.
32. Goodman NM: International health organizations and their work, New York, 1952, Blakiston Division, McGraw-Hill Book Co.
33. Howard-Jones N: The scientific background of the international sanitary conferences, 1851-1938, Geneva, 1975, World Health Organization.
34. Acuna HR: The Pan American Health Organization—75 years of international cooperation in public health, Public Health 92:537, Nov-Dec 1977.
35. World Health Organization: Basic documents, ed 22, Geneva, 1971, The Organization.
36. Director General: The work of WHO, 1986-1987: Biennial report of the Director-General, Geneva, 1988, World Health Organization.
37. Division of Information: The World Health Organization, Geneva, 1967, World Health Organization.
38. Annual report of the Director, 1986, Washington, DC, 1987, Pan American Health Organization.
39. Berthet E: Activities of the International Children's Center, Am J Public Health 48:458, April 1958.

PART TWO

The basis for public health

Public health work, by definition, is carried on mainly under governmental auspices. This is not meant to suggest that only governmental agencies can influence the public's health. Quite the contrary: the countless decisions that occur in the market places of goods and ideas have an enormous influence on community health—sometimes good, sometimes bad. Nor is the protection of the public's health solely a governmental concern: voluntary agencies have been an important part of public health in the United States.

Collective decisions to prevent the dependency which can result from disease and injury, however, require a formal means for deliberation and policy formation. Once the policies are agreed to, the protection of individual and collective rights becomes the responsibility of government. The distinction between a right and a privilege lies here: privileges are a personal matter, rights must be protected by government.

Public health policies are determined in the social arena. In this respect they are different from private health affairs which can be resolved without regard to social values. Consulting a psychoanalyst to improve sexual satisfaction or a surgeon to change the tilt of a nose is a private decision. Protecting the public against a dangerous communicable disease or the inhalation of tobacco smoke in a restaurant is a public issue. The methods used to determine such policies—public health policies—are those of politics. A word all too often laden with pejorative overtones, politics is the process society uses to make decisions when values may be in conflict. When you decide what to eat for dinner, it may be an objective, scientifically based decision. When two people decide what to eat, the decision is political. And when a million people consider what to do about air pollution vis-a-vis industrial development, or mandatory testing for illicit drug use versus personal freedom, science can only sharpen the issues and reveal some of the consequences of the choices. The decision, however, involves conflicting values and can only be arrived at through the political process.

The chapters of Part Two discuss the science of public health as it is applied in a political environment. Decisions about preventive interventions clearly involve trade-offs: choices involving costs and benefits and choices involving personal freedom and communitarian values. The concept of prevention lies at the heart of public health and is discussed in Chapter 5. The form or organization of public health is described in Chapter 6, and the function of public health is the subject of Chapter 7. Separating form and function, or the anatomy and physiology of public health, disintegrates the discussion of public health, but makes the subject more manageable. The form or anatomy of public health in the United States is reflective of the federal nature of our government in which the states have a relationship with the national government which is quite different from the relationship of local governments to either their states or the federal government in Washington. The term *presence* is used to discuss the function of public health—the governmental presence in health. It is a subtle and complex notion which may be unique to the public health role in the United States. Presence has two different meanings: 1) the fact of being present, in a place; and 2) the quality of that presence. A person or a piano can be present without having much presence. Bogart had presence whenever he was on screen; Vladimir Horowitz, together with his Steinway, has presence. In every community of the United States there is, officially, a public health agency present which is responsible for certain tasks. It may be a local health department, a regional or district department, or the state health department. It performs certain required functions, for example, inspection of restaurants, provision of immunizations for children, issuance of certain permits, testing people for communicable diseases. Beyond that, however, there should be a governmental presence in health—an organization with a leader whose job it is to protect the community's health, to measure its problems and its health resources, to draw attention to its needs, to sound an alarm when necessary, to urge, exhort and encourage, and to provide leadership in health for the community.

Public health policies are based on the measurement of health status and certain legal principles. The measurement of health status and the legal principles which lie at the base of the public health effort are discussed in Chapters 8 and 9.

CHAPTER 5

Prevention

How much is an ounce of prevention worth? Folk wisdom says it is worth a pound of cure, but how much is a pound of cure worth? Everyone knows what prevention means: it means to keep something from happening. But what? Death? Disability? Pain? Inconvenience? Spending money? Would you pay different amounts for each of them? Would it be worth $100,000 to prevent a death but only $25,000 to prevent the loss of an eye or a finger? How much to prevent the inconvenience of an illness? If it cost $5 plus some time to save $35 in medical bills, would you still spend the money? If it cost $30 to save $35 and you could prevent some inconvenience due to flu during the winter, would it be worth it?

Consider the policymaker's role: if you could save $1 million in lost work time or sickness benefits by getting people to lose weight or stop smoking, what would you do? Inform them? Persuade them? Provide an economic incentive to change behavior? Or would you consider prohibiting certain forms of behavior or perhaps banning the sale of tobacco products or cholesterol-containing foods?

If a new procedure (breast cancer screening, for example) could save some lives, should that procedure be included in insurance programs? In the Medicare program? How many lives for how much money?

If you could prevent a debilitating lung disease by finding people who were susceptible to it and preventing them from being employed in an environment where they would be exposed to a chemical that would trigger the disease, would you do it?

These are just a few of the questions that make the simple concept of prevention a difficult area for scientists and policymakers alike.

THE PURPOSE OF PREVENTION

Prevention is indeed a complex notion. Its definition is relatively simple: anticipatory action taken to reduce the possibility of an event or condition occurring or developing, or to minimize the damage that may result from the event or condition if it does occur.[1] Yet what the event or condition to be prevented may be varies considerably from one discussion of the notion to another, often without the discussants realizing that they are talking about different things. When Congress talks about paying for preventive health services in the Medicare program, it usually bases its decision on whether or not the procedure will save program money. That was the rationale behind including immunizations against a common form of pneumonia in the reimbursement program. When the American Heart Association or the American Cancer Society campaigns for dietary changes, they are interested in reducing the incidence of disease. When people see their dentist for a prophylactic checkup, they are usually interested in avoiding subsequent pain and inconvenience.

Depending on the purpose of the policymaker, the priorities for prevention may be different. To save work days, the targets may be the common cold, influenza, and unintentional injuries. To prevent deaths, the target may be heart disease. To save years of life in working age people, the targets may be injuries and violence. To save money, the targets might be certain genetic disorders such as thyroid disease or hyperphenylalaninemia. (That's as hard to spell as it is to pronounce. It's sometimes known as phenylketonuria or PKU.) To prevent utilization of the medical care system, the targets might be the common cold and preventive checkups themselves, since they are among the most common reasons for visiting physicians. Once you visit a physician, there is the risk that you will use more services, some of them expensive.

Prevention is the purpose of public health. Let's begin with some definitions. To repeat some of the discussion in Chapter 1, in both Hippocratic terms and in ancient Chinese writings, good health involved a state of balance between internal phenomena and the external environment. Perturbations in the balance resulted in ill health or disease. Much later, the Cartesian, or mechanistic, concept of health led theorists to believe that the human system was guided by universal laws that could be understood through scientific analysis and that governed all systems.[2] For more than 200 years, medical science pursued this simple, systematic notion of health and disease with considerable success. Robert Koch promulgated a set of postulates that led inexorably to a proof of causation: this germ caused that disease. Even then, however, it was clear to some that things were not so simple. Many people were exposed to smallpox: some got the disease, others did not; some died and others survived. Why? In more recent times, it has become evident that many people have been exposed to tuberculosis, but some are harmed far more than others. Habits (life-style), environment (housing and crowding), and biology (stress, other diseases) all play a powerful role in the development of tuberculosis. How do you explain osteoarthritis, or the frailty of some elderly people and the exuberant vitality of others?

There is growing acceptance of the notion that human beings and their environment constitute a very complex system. Some theorists have suggested that it cannot be understood; that the system is characterized by chaos rather than order; that there are so many variables entering into the system that minute perturbations of a seemingly inconsequential variable may result in cataclysmic changes in the system's balance, whereas at other times, major perturbations may have little consequence for the health of the system.

As discussed in Chapter 1, good health is a condition found along a spectrum (see illustration on this page). A disease or an injury results in an impairment. An impairment is an abnormality at the organ level: a tear in a muscle, destruction of some liver cells, thickening of the arterial wall, or a rash on the skin. Such an impairment may not be noticed at all. Smokers have usually damaged their lungs. If the damage is light enough and demands on their lungs are not too great (no marathons), the impairment may not be noticed. If the impairment is visible or severe, or demands on the organ are high, a disability may result. A disability is a disturbance at the system level and becomes apparent because there is evident functional limitation. Most people over the age of 20 have several impairments and at least a few disabilities: a crooked finger from an injury, limited motion in a joint, acne, a visual defect, or sinusitis.

Disabilities may not cause someone to become dependent. Dependency is a condition in which resources that have an opportunity cost have to be consumed in order to cope with activities of daily living. An "opportunity cost" means that, because a resource has to be consumed in one way, there is no opportunity to spend it for some other purpose. If an individual has to wear a hearing aid to function adequately, the money spent on it is unavailable for other purposes, such as a vacation or tuition. Paraplegia as a result of an automobile accident is a severe state of dependency with a significant opportunity cost. A cut finger may represent a temporary state of dependency for a violinist, less of one for a typist, and practically none at all for a baseball umpire. The resource used may be money to pay for treatment or buy a wheelchair, or time (an adult shopping for a partially dependent parent). Dependencies have social consequences due to their opportunity costs.

Health is the absence of disability (but is not quite the same as the presence of ability). Public health is the organization and application of public resources to prevent dependency that would otherwise result from disease or injury. To prevent is to take anticipatory action. Prevention is the basic purpose of public health. Yet it is by no means the exclusive province of public health, any more than education is the exclusive province of the school system. Prevention is unique among important human endeavors. Law is practiced by lawyers, music is played by musicians, medicine is practiced by physicians, crops are grown by farmers, but prevention is the result of many workers:

Disease or injury ⟶ Impairment ⟶ Disability ⟶ Dependency

Adapted from Wood, PHN: Appreciating the consequences of disease: the international classification of impairments, disabilities and handicaps, WHO Chron 34:376, 1980. The definitions and purpose of this schematic are quite different from those of the original authors.

physicians, lawyers, engineers, dentists, nurses, psychologists, statisticians, epidemiologists, microbiologists, anthropologists, meteorologists, physicists, teachers, political scientists, and many others.

The social purpose of education is served by many people and agencies, but the lead role, the recognized profession, is teaching. Such is not the case with prevention. Even if the lead role in the prevention of dependency due to disease or injury is given to public health departments, the mix of professions and disciplines involved is extensive. Dental disease has been prevented through engineering and chemical changes in the water supply; sexually transmitted diseases have been prevented through contact tracing and education; food-borne diseases have been prevented by means of legislation. Most of the preventive interventions of public health do not involve the practice of medicine by physicians.

Because of its interdisciplinary nature, the work of public health is poorly understood by many people. Most organizations are identified either by the profession or discipline of their principal workers or by their products: the highway department, the police department, libraries, or the welfare department. The outcome of their work is fairly clear. Public health, however, has as its outcome something that did not happen, and it is achieved by a mix of skills that robs the agency of easy identification. Most organizations are characterized by their methods or their inputs. Public health is organized around intended outcomes, and those outcomes are as heterogeneous as the disciplines that make up the public health work force.

TYPES OF PREVENTION

Prevention may take place at any point along the spectrum from the prevention of disease or injury to the prevention of impairment, disability, or dependency (see the illustration on this page). *Primary* prevention involves prevention of the disease or injury itself. Improved highway design, school education programs concerning smoking and substance abuse, and immunization against poliomyelitis or measles are examples of primary prevention.

Secondary prevention blocks the progression of an injury or disease from an impairment to a disability. Use of the Papanicolaou smear to look for early cellular changes that are thought to be precursors of cancer is a good example of secondary prevention. An impairment has already occurred, but disability may be prevented through early intervention. Treatment of certain streptococcal infections with penicillin can prevent the occasional development of rheumatic fever and serious heart disease. Early detection of high blood pressure can reduce the probability of a heart attack or a stroke.

Tertiary prevention blocks or retards the progression of a disability to a state of dependency. The early detection and effective management of diabetes can prevent some of the dependencies associated with the disease, or at least slow their rate of progression. Prompt medical care followed by rehabilitation can limit the damage caused by a cerebrovascular accident (stroke) and the same is true for heart attacks. Good vehicular design can reduce the dependency which might otherwise occur as a result of a crash.

While the purpose of public health is to prevent dependency, choosing an intervention point (at the primary, secondary, or tertiary level) is a function of knowledge, resources, acceptability, effectiveness, and efficiency. As noted in Chapter 1, aiming public health at the prevention of dependency appears to be inappropriately conservative to some people. It seems to accept an unnecessary amount of pain and disability. Yet preventing some impairments or disabilities would be terribly expensive given present knowledge and the benefits that might be realized. Although the frequency and severity of injuries can be reduced, preventing all injuries would mean avoidance of all risk, a situation

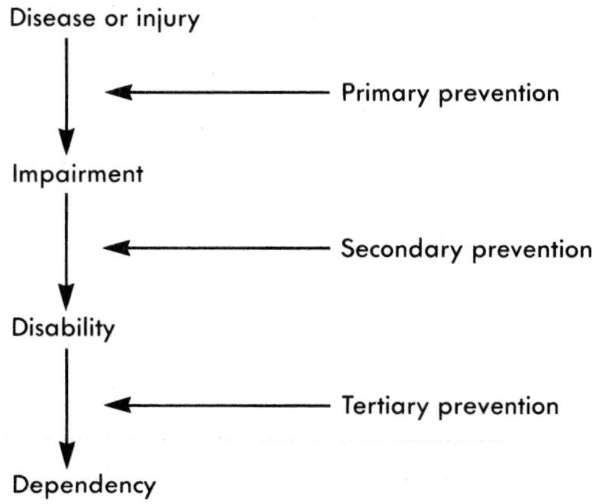

tantamount to death, not life. The primary prevention of high blood pressure (hypertension) is not always possible given present knowledge, but the secondary prevention of disabilities and the tertiary prevention of dependency are both possible and practical. If research makes primary prevention possible, the costs and benefits of such interventions, together with their practicality and acceptability, have to be considered.

The prevention of dependency may best be accomplished by intervening at the beginning of the process. German measles (rubella) is a fairly inconsequential disease with little morbidity and disability. In itself, it would not warrant the major effort made to prevent it, primarily through immunization. However, the consequences of rubella infection in pregnant women are severe, leading to fetal death or severe developmental disabilities that often require a lifetime of institutional care for the child. The goal of the immunization program is the prevention of dependency, and the most effective and acceptable point of intervention is at the primary level. Secondary preventive interventions are not available, and tertiary prevention would involve either abortion or long-term institutional care in many instances.

PREVENTION AND SOCIAL WELFARE

In recent years, public health concepts of prevention have been applied to an increasing array of social problems that may not, in a narrow sense, be thought of as health problems, even though they may lead to dependency due to disease and organ impairment: violence and the use of illicit drugs, for example. There is substantial interest in such phenomena, since their impact on society has become increasingly apparent. Violence (murder, suicide, and motor vehicle crashes) is the leading cause of death in adolescence and young adulthood. The use of illicit drugs and alcohol is among the major health problems of the twentieth century.[1,3] These problem areas will be discussed in subsequent chapters.

THE SUCCESS OF PREVENTION

Just how much has prevention been worth? The health status of entire population groups has improved dramatically during the past century or two. The Prevention Index is a measure of the extent to which people have adopted 21 selected health-promoting behaviors. In a series of national surveys, the national score has increased from 61.5 in 1984 to 65.2 in 1987.[4] In a later chapter, the improvements in infant and maternal mortality will be discussed in detail. The improvements have been extraordinary, even though serious disparities between groups still exist. Reductions in common communicable diseases have been equally remarkable (Table 5-1). Some of the leading causes of death in children in the 1980s were not even on the list of the top 10 causes of death a few decades ago because of the much greater frequency of some of the infectious diseases at that time (Table 5-2).

More recently, dramatic changes in adult mortality rates have been observed (Table 5-3). Life expectancy at birth increased from 48 years for white males in 1900 to 72 years in 1985; 19 years were gained during the first 6 decades, and another 5 years in the 2½ decades since then.

Until recently it was commonly said that the gains in life expectancy had been the result of reductions in infant mortality and childhood deaths. Average years of life remaining for 40-year-olds increased just 3 years, from 28 to 31, in the 6 decades from 1900 to 1960. However, beginning in the 1960s, death rates for adults began to decline sharply, principally because of a reduction in deaths due to cardiovascular disease. During the past 25 years, 40-year-olds have gained another 4 years. In other words, of the 5

TABLE 5-1 Decline in deaths from selected communicable disease, United States, 1900 and 1985

Cause of death	Deaths per 100,000 population per year: 1900	1985
Typhoid	2.7	0
Measles	3.1	0
Diphtheria	27.4	0
Pertussis	11.3	4
Diarrhea and enteritis	113.1	27
Syphilis	3.9	0
Tuberculosis	195	0.5

From Mortality statistics, 1900-1904, Washington, DC, 1906, US Bureau of the Census; Vital statistics of the United States, 1985, vol 2—Mortality, Part A, Washington, DC, 1988, National Center for Health Statistics.

years of life expectancy at birth that have been gained by white males since 1960, 4 years, or 80% of the total, have been gained through declines in adult mortality. During the prior 60 years, only 3 of the 19 years gained, or 16%, were attributable to declines in adult mortality. These recent changes are unparalleled in the course of human history. The increase in longevity for 40-year-olds is equivalent to that which would have been realized if all forms of cancer had been eliminated in 1960.[5]

Are these changes the result of public health and deliberate preventive interventions? To some extent they are, but health is a function of balance, involving numerous external and internal variables. Most of the major changes in health status either preceded the ability of government to intervene in a deliberate manner or occurred for a mixture of reasons, usually lying outside the realm of public health as it is known. McKeown, Record, and Turner reviewed declines in mortality in England and Wales during the twentieth century. They concluded that "the decline in mortality owed a good deal to specific medical measures but was also influenced considerably by general improvements in standards of living, particularly in respect to infant feeding and care."[6] Similar reviews of events have led to the same conclusions in the United States. Declines in deaths due to most infectious diseases began before specific medical treatment was available and before immunizing agents were used. The beginning of the decline in deaths due to cancer of the cervix preceded the use of the Papanicolaou smear. And declines in deaths per miles driven began to occur before seat belts and other safety features were required.

As the determinants of health (see Chapter 3) are often to be found outside the realm of human biology, so are the changes that lead to improved health status. When the modern age of public health began about 100 years ago, the equation seemed simpler. John Bigelow, in 1860, at the time of the Fourth National Quarantine and Sanitary Convention in Boston, said:

> The day is rapidly approaching when clinical doctors will scarcely be needed and when sanitarians will take their place, and when we shall not so much attend to the health of the human body as to the condition of the body politic.[7]

More than 100 years later, Jeremy Morris, a British epidemiologist, wrote that secondary prevention is second best; to begin at the beginning we must begin with social deprivation.[8] The notion of health as a state of balance among both internal and external forces means that the access points for intervention are complex and multitudinous. As in chaotic systems, unexpected changes can lead to results scarcely anticipated by analysis. In the long sweep of history, it appears that changes in standards of living, advances in education and literacy, and changes in the politics of human relations have had more to do with longevity than have specific preventive interventions. American dietary habits have changed considerably over the past 50 years, and average blood cholesterol levels have decreased. This appears to be the result of millions of individual decisions made by people for a wide variety of reasons. While public health

TABLE 5-2 Mortality in the 1- to 4-year age group, United States, 1925 and 1984

Cause of death, 1925	Rate per 100,000	Cause of death, 1984	Rate per 100,000
Diarrhea and enteritis	109.8	Accidents	12.9
Accidents	57.7	Motor vehicle accidents	6.9
Pneumonia	44.7	Congenital anomalies	6.7
Diphtheria	43.0	Malignant neoplasms	4.0
Tuberculosis	28.9	Homicide	2.4
Pertussis	28.6	Heart disease	2.4
Measles	14.4	Influenza and pneumonia	1.5
Scarlet fever	11.7	Diarrhea and enteritis	0.1
Motor vehicle accidents	11.7	Nephritis	0.2
Heart disease	8.9	Tuberculosis	0.0

From U.S. Vital Statistics Publications.

agencies and voluntary health associations now recommend such dietary changes, the decline began before such efforts. Throughout this book, the reader will find evidence suggesting that the distribution of income, employment, education, and societal relationships, including discrimination, are at the heart of the most complex and persistent health problems. Interventions in such arenas can have profound effects, but they are glacial in their rapidity. They lie largely outside the purview of organized public health. Nevertheless, there is much that can be done.

SOME EPIDEMIOLOGIC CONCEPTS

Epidemiology is often referred to as the "queen science of public health." It is the study of the distribution of disease and injury in population groups. (For a complete lexicon of epidemiologic terms, see Last.[9] There are many good textbooks of epidemiology.[10-12] Interestingly, epidemiology is not usually defined to include the study of health or wellness in population groups. The causes of health cannot be inferred simply from the study of disease and injury. Why, for example, do some people age well while others develop severe dependency patterns? The causation of vitality is an important and neglected area of study. See Chapter 26.) While a thorough discussion of epidemiology is beyond the scope of this book, some basic concepts are essential to the further understanding of prevention.

The *incidence* of a disease is the number of new cases occurring during a defined time: 22 cases of measles per week, for example. From this figure, an incidence rate can be calculated. If there were 5,000 people in the community, the measles incidence rate would be 4.4 per 1,000 people at risk. (See Chapter 8 for a more complete discussion of rates.) If the average *duration* of a case of measles were 14 days, then, provided the incidence stayed constant at about 22 new cases each week, the *prevalence* of measles during any one day would be 44. Prevalence is the number of cases in the community (village, city, state, nation, or world) at a particular time. It can be estimated by multiplying the incidence by the duration of the disease (22 cases per week equals 3.14 cases per day, or $3.14 \times 14 = 44$). The prevalence *rate* would be 8.8 per 1,000 people in the example just given.

Incidence, prevalence, and duration are important concepts in many areas of public health. They apply to chronic as well as to acute diseases. If the monthly incidence rate of new cases of AIDS is 50 per 100,000 people and the duration of the disease before death is 24 months, the prevalence rate for AIDS will be 1,200 per 100,000 people during any month. Several phenomena can change these figures. Earlier diagnosis has the effect of lengthening duration of the disease. So does improved treatment. If either occurs, prevalence will increase even though incidence may remain constant. If the incidence of new cases declines by one half as a result of public health efforts and the duration increases twofold because of earlier diagnosis and improved treatment, the prevalence of the disease may appear to remain constant.

The rising number of elderly people in society is partly a function of decreased infant and childhood mortality rates, which leave more adults alive on their 65th birthday. If at the same time longevity is increasing, duration (the length of time people live after age 65) will expand. When you multiply the higher "incidence" of aging by its longer duration, the prevalence of aging, or the number of people over the age of 65, increases dramatically.

Preventive interventions may reduce the incidence rate of a disease or an injury or, by means of early detection procedures and rapid treatment, its duration. Either would result in a decreased prevalence rate.

Screening is the use of a test to separate a population group into two fractions: one with a higher than average chance of having or developing the disease in question and the other with a lower than average chance. Those with a higher chance are said to be in a high-risk group. Screening does not establish a diagnosis. Those who are determined to be in the high-risk group should

TABLE 5-3 Average years of life remaining by age and year, United States, white males

	Year		
Age	1900	1940	1980
0	48	67	72
40	28	31	35
65	12	13	15

From Vital Statistics of the United States, U.S. Department of Health and Human Services, selected years.

undergo more specific testing to determine the presence or absence of disease.

The difference between the high- and low-risk groups may be great or small. For example, gay males and intravenous drug users have a much greater risk of developing AIDS than do heterosexual and non-drug-using males. The difference is sufficient to warrant special programs of education and screening in the gay male community. The differences between gay and heterosexual women, however, do not warrant such programs for gay women.

Screening for disease has been a popular form of prevention. Until recently, most people applying for a marriage license have had to have a test for syphilis. Most states require the testing of a blood specimen from all newborns to see if they are at high risk for one or more metabolic disorders that might lead to severe mental retardation if left untreated. Annual chest X-ray examinations were once common as a means of screening for tuberculosis, and some people advocate yearly tests for occult blood in the stool to detect those who may have colon cancer. Generally speaking, screening tests have not proven to be a useful form of prevention, however. Problems inherent in the concept limit its usefulness.[13]

All tests have at least two problems: (1) they cannot detect all of the people who may have the disease, and (2) they identify some people as being at high risk who do not have the disease. The former problem is related to the *sensitivity* of the test and the latter to its *specificity.* When sensitivity is very high, specificity is decreased; that is, an increased number of people are identified who do not have the disease—false positives. If sensitivity is decreased in order to avoid that problem, more people who do have the disease are missed—false negatives.

The problems of false positives and negatives can be serious. A false negative test for AIDS at a blood bank could lead to a disaster. A false positive test for AIDS could be psychologically devastating. There may be serious economic consequences as well. Testing for occult blood in the stool results in a substantial number of people without disease undergoing expensive X-ray examinations and other procedures, which have some physical risks as well as economic costs attached to them. The problem can be seen in Table 5-4.

Consider a condition that has a prevalence of 0.5% (5 cases per 1,000 people at risk). In a population of 10,000 people, a screening test with 90% sensitivity and 80% specificity (a fairly good test) will identify 45 of the 50 people with the condition but incorrectly label 98% of those who test positive (1,990/2,035). Similar tables can be constructed using a wide range of figures. Depending on how serious the consequences of either a false negative or a false positive may be, the net benefits of such procedures may be small or even negative.

THE STRUCTURE OF PREVENTIVE INTERVENTIONS

Preventive interventions can be aimed at the host, the agent, or the environment. Humans are the hosts of concern to public health. The agent of disease or injury may be a virus, a carcinogen, or a motor vehicle. The environment of interest may be a mosquito-infested swamp, a chemical plant, a campus party, or poverty. This traditional model includes most of the ingredients in the equation leading to impairment, and even very complex disease and injury phenomena can be analyzed in such a system. The primary prevention of dependency due to a motor vehicle crash may be accomplished by modifying the driver's behavior (the host), by improved highway design (the environment), or by building safer cars (the agent). The same process can be applied to AIDS. Education has been shown to modify behavioral patterns in at least some gay males. The agent, the human immunodeficiency virus (HIV), cannot be prevented primarily at the present time, but tertiary intervention can slow the progress of the disease. Some environmental changes may prove effective in preventing the spread of the disease, such as the use of sterile

TABLE 5-4 Sensitivity and specificity

	True status		
Test result	**Positive**	**Negative**	**Total**
Positive	45	1,990	2,035
Negative	5	7,960	7,965
TOTAL	50	9,950	10,000

needles by drug users or restrictions imposed on the operation of gay bath houses.

An alternative model for considering preventive interventions was developed in 1974 by the Canadian Ministry of Health.[14] The *field theory* concentrates on four fields: biology, life-style or behavior, the environment, and organization. The important additions were the focus on human behavior and the inclusion of the organizational field, or the ways in which society decides to organize its resources to prevent or treat a disease. The added focus on behavior became popular in the 1960s as increased attention was paid to cigarette smoking, exercise, the use of alcohol and other drugs, nutrition, and other life-style factors, including sexual practices. The United States followed the Canadian report in 1979 with *Healthy People*.[15] The U.S. approach differed from the Canadian primarily in its avoidance of the organizational field. Using the resources of the government to organize and finance preventive or treatment interventions was an unpopular notion at that time.

Both the Canadian and the U.S. proposals for improving health emphasized the role of personal behavior in determining health status. During the 1970s the same assertions were made by organized medicine in the United States, and life-style interests became an important part of the public health litany. Others countered that emphasizing personal life-styles obfuscates the role that organized interest groups play in perpetuating disease patterns: the tobacco and alcohol industries, for example, or the failure of the Medicaid program to adequately support prenatal and child care.[16] Concentrating on life-style has been referred to as "victim-blaming" and leaves untouched those socioenvironmental conditions that encourage and support unhealthy life-styles.

The utility of such models is evident when policymakers consider a particular health problem. They result in a methodical approach to prevention and avoid the possibility that the only methods considered will be those reflecting the resources of the agency or the disciplines of the planners. For example, a county medical society may consider the provision of good prenatal care the best way to improve the outcome of pregnancy. Consideration of the environmental setting, however, raises questions about housing, nutrition, and pollution. Life-style considerations help focus on the use of tobacco and licit and illicit drugs.

A useful approach to prevention can be developed by combining the field theory and the primary-secondary-tertiary typology. Lung cancer, for example, might result in the analysis shown in Table 5-5, while a consideration of the potential for intervening in AIDS might produce an analysis such as the one shown in Table 5-6.

The model may direct attention to some aspect of social structure that lies far outside the domain of the agency making the analysis, thus producing a better outcome than might be obtained if the planning process considered only those types of interventions that used the resources and disciplines of the agency. An analysis of the opportunities for intervention in highway fatalities, for example, might focus attention not just on the emergency medical care system, but on highway design, vehicular safety, and the problems of drug use, some of which are normally within the immediate purview of a public health agency.

Clinical practice and social policy

Prevention has become a popular notion in recent years. As noted in Chapter 2, nations have gone through several eras of disease: first the era of infectious diseases and sanitation, followed by the era of chronic diseases such as cancer and heart disease as more people lived past the age of 40, and finally the era in which a more complex environment interacts with life-style factors to produce a third stage of disease. It is this last transition in the United States, coupled with the growing realization that medical care can do little to reverse the dependency associated with such diseases, that has provoked increased attention to the potential for prevention. It has become a maxim, plausible but

TABLE 5-5 Preventive interventions in lung cancer

Field	Prevention* Primary	Secondary	Tertiary
Biologic	0	0	+
Environmental	+ +	+	0
Life-style	+ + + +	+ +	0
Organizational	+ + +	+	0

* +, least opportunity; + + + +, most opportunity.

unproven, that the prevention of disease will cost less than its treatment.

For many years physicians have been urged to practice preventive medicine. Recently there has been considerable interest in including preventive health services in medical insurance plans with the expectation that they will save money by avoiding the costs of treatment. Those who do not espouse prevention in this climate are the present-day heretics. Yet preventive interventions are not without their costs, both direct and indirect. Physicians are encouraged to provide preventive health services in order to comply with what are thought to be the present standards of practice and to avoid the liability that might be present if a disease developed that might have been detected at an earlier time. Clinical standards are not the same as public health policy, however. It is known that the use of X-ray mammography in women over the age of 50 can result in a decreased probability of death due to breast cancer. The American Cancer Society, surgeons, and radiologists urge that women over 50 have an annual mammogram. Screening of women eligible for Medicare would cost approximately $1.5 billion. The Congressional Office of Technology Assessment found that routine mammography reduced the chance of dying by 20%, down from 3 per 1,000 in women aged 65 and older. Savings of $2,000 per case were possible when the breast cancer was found early, but only if those savings were 100 times greater than the cost of the screening test would they be sufficient to offset the added costs to Medicare. That is not the situation at this time.[17]

A few years ago, a drug known as cholestyramine was widely heralded as a marvelous way to reduce blood cholesterol levels. If used according to the research protocol, it was said to reduce heart attacks by 20%. From the clinician's point of view, this might be a significant gain. However, looked at from a public policy perspective, the use of cholestyramine on a national scale might result in 4,877,000 healthy males rather than 4,850,000, an improvement of just 0.56%. To prevent some form of heart attack in 27,000 men (many of whom would recover) would cost $44.7 billion, or an average of $1,655,555 per person. Would prevention be "better" than treatment?

TABLE 5-6 Preventive interventions in AIDS

Field	Prevention* Primary	Secondary	Tertiary
Biologic	0	0	+ +
Environmental	+ +	0	+
Life-style	+ + + +	+ +	+ +
Organizational	+ + +	0	+

*+, least opportunity; + + + +, most opportunity.

Clinicians may screen for certain diseases in order to optimize the probability of achieving the best possible outcome. They assume that they and the people with whom they are working are perfectly effective and that false positives and false negatives will not occur or that, when they do occur, they will be wisely managed. From the public policy point of view, however, the goal may be to minimize the probability that the worst possible outcome will occur, and a different decision will be made. Clinicians are often puzzled at the reluctance of public health officials to embrace preventive interventions that make sense to them from a clinical point of view. The difference is partly the result of different objectives and partly the result of a different understanding of the effectiveness of screening.

The importance of prevalence

Prevalence, as noted above, is a function of the incidence and duration of a problem. Prevalence has a profound effect on prevention. It changes the assessment of what works, and it alters the benefits to be obtained.

In Table 5-4 the results of a screening program to detect people at high risk for a disease with a prevalence of 0.5%, or 5 of every 1,000 people, were shown. Using the assumptions of that model, 90% of the true cases in the community were found, but 98% of those who were identified as being at high risk did not have the disease. If control measures reduced the incidence of the disease, leading to a prevalence of just 0.1% (1 case per 1,000 people), the results would change dramatically (Table 5-7). In this case, 99.6% of all those identified as being at high risk would not have the disease.

When tuberculosis was very common, mass chest X-ray screening programs were effective. Many people had the disease, and the problems of sensitivity and specificity did not produce an unacceptable burden of false positives and false negatives. As the incidence and duration of tuberculosis both declined as a result of improved public health methods of contact investigation and prophylaxis and improved medical treatment, prevalence declined. Mass X-ray screening programs became inefficient and ineffective: the cost per new case identified became very high, and the number of false positives and false negatives increased. A skin test became a more common and effective screening tool, because it had greater sensitivity and specificity as well as a lower cost. Incidence and duration continued to decline, so that population-wide skin testing programs were no longer practical or effective, and selective screening programs were carried out in high-risk groups. In a sense, identifying a high-risk group based on some demographic or other variables (the homeless, for instance, or patients with AIDS) has the effect of increasing the prevalence of the disease within the group to be screened, making the procedure more accurate.

Prevalence also has an important effect on the economic evaluation of a screening program (see below). When prevalence is high, the benefits of preventing a disease or an injury versus treating it when it occurs are relatively high. As prevalence declines, this relative advantage for prevention declines, unless some other factors change as well. This can be offset by developing less costly interventions or by increasing the prevalence of the condition through the identification of high-risk groups.

Prevention versus postponement

Acute diseases—infections and injuries, for instance—can be prevented. Other conditions, especially those that seem to be associated with aging, may not be preventable. Some concomitants of aging are inescapable: a loss of elasticity in the skin, thinning of the hair, a gradual loss of elasticity in lung tissue. In addition, the number of functioning kidney cells or liver cells may decrease with age, possibly because of repeated insignificant viral infections or perhaps simply because of the aging process itself.

These changes lead to a gradual diminution in functional reserve capacity. For most vital functions, there is more than enough organ reserve to accomplish the tasks of the day: metabolic conversion of toxic chemicals or elimination of certain metabolites. If the reserve capacity is diminished over time, however, demand may exceed the remaining capacity of the organ under certain conditions, and a disability, perhaps even death, may result.

The lens of the eye thickens and joints wear out over time. In some people these changes begin earlier or progress faster than in others. Some people become dependent early in life, some only toward the end of life. If these changes (impairments leading to disabilities not necessarily due to disease or injury) lead to dependency, preventive interventions may be considered, partly to improve the quality of life, partly to decrease expenditures for medical care. It seems unlikely that these concomitants of aging can be prevented altogether. If their onset can be postponed, they will begin later in life and the impairment may never result in an apparent disability. If the onset can be postponed until after death, of course, the dependency can be effectively prevented. As matters stand now, the most common forms of arthritis associated with aging cannot be prevented, but their progression can be retarded and the onset or duration of dependency postponed. If either the incidence or the duration is reduced, prevalence decreases, and the societal burden of dependency is reduced, not to mention the individual's agony and pain.

The progression of chronic impairments can often be retarded with the functional effect, both to the person and to society, of prevention. Chronic lung disease, which can lead to severe patterns of dependency, is a function, at least in large numbers of people, of the number of cigarettes smoked during a lifetime: pack-years of exposure. Quitting smoking, even in middle or old age, prevents additional damage and slows progression. If dependency is postponed until after death, it has been effectively prevented. Postponement is another, and important, form of prevention.[18,19]

TABLE 5-7 Sensitivity and specificity

Test result	True status: Positive	True status: Negative	Total
Positive	9	1,998	2,007
Negative	1	7,992	7,993
TOTAL	10	9,990	10,000

Prevention as a discipline

Physicians often consider prevention as a form of medical care. The American College of Preventive Medicine and the Association of Teachers of Preventive Medicine consider preventive medicine to be one of the recognized clinical specialties. From the preceding discussion, however, it is apparent that prevention is the result of many different disciplines and professions. In fact, most of the diseases that have been prevented over the last few hundred years have been prevented as a result of initiatives taken or changes occurring in society that have had little to do with medical care or preventive medicine.

Those who specialize in preventive medicine have a difficult time deciding whether other physicians should or should not be encouraged to practice preventive medicine. Orthopedic surgeons do not encourage other specialists to practice orthopedics; in fact, they discourage them from doing so. But should a preventive medicine specialist discourage pediatricians and internists from incorporating preventive services into their practices? From the standpoint of the public's welfare, of course not; from the standpoint of the specialist, however, such discouragement would seem to be a prudent form of self-protection.

More broadly, the question can be phrased in the following terms: is prevention a discrete endeavor that should be organized in the most effective and efficient manner, or should it be incorporated into all aspects of life—the grade-school class on biology, the high-school class on sexuality, the nutrition program, the exercise program, the sermon, the political campaign?

A former Assistant Secretary of Health in the U.S. Department of Health and Human Services (at that time, the Department of Health, Education and Welfare) said that his office had

> resisted the easy organizational approach to this commitment [to prevention]; we shall not create a new agency for prevention or request new legislation on prevention. Rather we shall see to it that the concepts of prevention permeate every one of our programs be they educational or service or research.[20]

This seemingly sensible concept does not always yield the results one might hope for. For many and very complex reasons, treatment of existing diseases attracts considerably more attention and money than their prevention. People tend to be willing to spend more of their resources to deal with something that hurts or that makes them fearful than they are to prevent something that does not now bother them. Moreover, prevention of disease and injury often involves sociopolitical changes or individual life-style changes that are difficult to accomplish and are often opposed by others: either those who may benefit from the situation (producers, distributors, builders) or those who feel that personal liberties are at stake. The result is that much more is spent to treat heart disease, or even to create new hearts or transplant second-hand ones, than to prevent heart disease.

Several groups in the United States have argued persuasively for a new reimbursement scheme that would provide an incentive for physicians to incorporate more preventive health services into their practices.* However, there is ample evidence to support the notion that creating a payment source for a new medical service results in the overprovision of that service. Medical care is very sensitive to price: services for which itemized reimbursement is available tend to be provided in a repetitive manner, often with little or no apparent understanding of the epidemiologic concepts underlying such services. Moreover, many preventive health services are neither labor- nor capital-intensive and are provided by primary care practitioners routinely. Offering to pay for them as a separate item would result in increased payments for services that are, to an unknown extent, being provided without extra charge now.

It can be argued that prevention involves much more than just medical care, and that other providers may be better qualified to provide preventive health services: counseling regarding nutrition, exercise supervision, and programs dealing with smoking cessation and drinking patterns, for example. A separate preventive health services system may be a useful consideration: one that is guided by epidemiologic principles and managed by people trained in prevention rather than in therapeutic medicine. Such a system might be provided on a capitation basis or with vouchers, with the specific services to be provided based on

* The American College of Preventive Medicine is considering different approaches to paying for preventive health services, and a Preventive Services Task Force is pursuing the same question.

an epidemiologic and economic evaluation of their utility and benefit. Research is needed to determine whether more efficient and effective preventive health services could be delivered in this manner.

The question remains of whether people will actually pay for preventive health services, however they are offered. A number of researchers have studied the "marketing" of preventive health services, but these studies have been confined to discrete services requiring manipulative or invasive procedures.[21] The question should be extended further to a consideration of behavioral changes. It is clear that many people are willing to pay a substantial amount of money for activities that they consider to be in their own best interest: exercise clubs, weight loss groups, smoking cessation programs, screening services such as blood pressure and blood cholesterol determination. Generally speaking, however, the people most likely to take advantage of such services when they are offered are the people least likely to be at high risk for the diseases under consideration.

Some studies have shown that copayments in an insurance program deter the use of routine preventive health services. The higher the copayment, the greater the deterrence.

There are two approaches that might be taken to better understand the marketability of preventive health services. Certain services are popular and involve the discrete performance of a technical task by a trained provider. Glaucoma testing, blood tests for certain diseases and risk factors, Papanicolaou smears, and several other procedures have a ready market, willing providers, and little proven utility. They can and should be left to the marketplace, with the expectation that improved general education about health will better equip consumers to understand the value of their decisions. Other procedures have little marketability generally yet have considerable social value: screening newborns for certain metabolic disorders, immunizing children against several infectious diseases, immunizing certain high-risk groups against hepatitis, the use of restraint systems in automobiles, screening blood donors for HIV infection, and well-managed hearing and vision screening programs in elementary school. These programs merit careful consideration as public sector investments in prevention.

A federal panel has been formed to review the therapeutic procedures that are included in the Medicare program. Similar panels, including appropriate experts, should be formed to consider for which preventive health services reimbursement should be provided through public and private health insurance plans. This is a different task, however, from considering those services listed above, which are community health services and do not involve a one-to-one clinical interaction. Such programs warrant similar careful evaluation. It is interesting to note that such community health services are often debated intensely: community water fluoridation, passive restraint systems, and no-smoking areas, for example. This sort of scrutiny and debate have rarely if ever been accorded the application of a new medical or surgical procedure that is sold in a private practice setting.

THE ECONOMICS OF PREVENTION

At the beginning of this chapter the question was asked, "How much is an ounce of prevention worth?" It is a complex and puzzling question. Earlier editions of this book asserted that prevention programs had clearly demonstrated their value as both life and cost savers. But the evidence is far from overwhelming.

In England, Murray[22] found that dental health had improved significantly between 1970 and 1980; the number of "sound" teeth in school children markedly increased, but there were more fillings. Manpower resources, which had increased during the same 10 years, remuneration for services, and attitudes toward dental health and dental practice had all contributed to the increased provision of dental health services. Others have noted the same trends, in the United States and elsewhere.[23]

Louise Russell[24] presented a similar, bleak picture for the prevention community in 1986. She agreed that many chronic degenerative diseases may be prevented, or their progress delayed, but asserted that they might very well result in the expenditure of more, not less, money. There are several complex notions that must be considered in evaluating the costs and benefits of either preventive or therapeutic interventions. Some economists maintain that the future costs of routine medical care that may be obtained by a "saved" individual must be considered a negative benefit—a cost. The discounting of future benefits to their net present value is also a troublesome concept for preventionists. Simply put, anticipated future benefits must be discounted to their present value and compared to the current costs of achieving those benefits. Given the choice between receiving $1,000 now and that same $1,000 in 10 years, now is better: the $1,000 will be worth considerably less in 10 years. Therefore, spending $1 million a year to reduce the future incidence of a disease should be compared to the monetary value of the benefits thought to be possible 20 or 30 years in the future, and those future benefits must be discounted downward by some percentage amount for each of those years. For example, if it is thought that an effort would result in a $5 million savings in 20 years, and that the real growth in the value of money would be 6% during those 20 years, the future benefit is only worth $1,652,565 in present-day terms, producing a benefit-to-cost ratio of approximately 1.7:1. If you add the costs of medical care for the "saved" people during the 20 years (say, $1,500 a year for each person, or a total of $30,000 each), the net gain from the preventive intervention can erode quickly.

Russell's argument is valuable but incomplete, as she acknowledges. Disability, dependency, and the pain and grief accompanying them have their own value, and human lives cannot be so simply reduced to a price. Moreover, Russell asked, "Is prevention better than cure?" but therapeutic medicine rarely provides a cure and always assumes a period of dependency, sometimes severe and sometimes lengthy. While the future cost to society of dependency is not usually counted as a charge against the health care program, it is a cost nonetheless. The dependency costs associated with treatment may, in fact, be more substantial than the costs of medical care.

There is much to be learned about the evaluation of preventive interventions. The techniques of cost-effectiveness and cost-benefit analysis are valuable tools in public health and preventive medicine, but the assumptions that must be built into the calculations have not been well developed yet, nor has there been general agreement about some of the assumptions involved in such work. While that work progresses, it is appropriate to be cautious in asserting that preventive interventions will save money: lives yes, disability and dependency, yes—but money? That is another question and perhaps not the dominant one.

THE RATIONALE FOR INTERVENTION

When is it appropriate to intervene, to restrict human freedom in order to produce an individual or communal benefit?

Governments have had a long and tortuous history of intervention, and the U.S. government is no exception. A group of scientists in the federal government, in 1986, concluded:

> It should be a primary responsibility of government at all levels to ensure the thorough and objective assessment of conditions offering potential harm to the public. Depending on the nature of the determination, it may then also be the responsibility of government to facilitate educational, service or regulatory actions to help manage the risks.[25]

The fact that the report was published privately suggests that this may not be considered official policy.

There are several reasons for government to intervene. Government may intervene for paternalistic reasons or for utilitarian reasons, for example. Paternalism is the restriction of the liberty of a class of individuals to confer a benefit on that same class, whether they want it or not.[26] Utilitarianism justifies intervention on the grounds that it serves the utility of the state, usually through maintaining a more productive work force or a more fit army. In the present day, interventions usually are based on concepts of beneficence, equality, equity, or utilitarianism. Beneficence justifies intervention on the grounds that it is good to benefit another. Equality justifies intervention in order to attempt to distribute benefits and burdens equally. This is the basic rationale for public education in the United States. Equity justifies intervention in order to distribute the benefits of society in proportion to need. This is, or should be, the goal of a national health policy, but it is extremely difficult to accomplish. Utilitarianism would be used to justify mandatory helmets for motorcycle riders: their injuries cost us money; therefore we can require that they take steps to prevent such injuries.

Beauchamp[26] argues that intervention is justified for communitarian reasons—that the entire community benefits when disease and injury are prevented.

The rationale for intervention varies from epoch to epoch, from era to era, from place to place, and from person to person. A somewhat mundane analysis of a proposal to intervene in order to prevent disease or injury would suggest that the following questions be asked:

1. Is the problem well defined, and is its natural history understood?
2. Are the causes of the problem understood?

Who is likely to be affected and who not?
Is the proposed intervention likely to produce the intended effect? What is the evidence that that is so?
Have the consequences of intervening been determined?
Are the consequences of not intervening understood?
Are the resources available?
Is the proposed intervention acceptable to the public that is to be affected by it, and have the ethical aspects of the proposed intervention been considered?
On balance, are the anticipated benefits worth the cost of the intervention?

It is instructive to contemplate just how much uncertainty there may be in answering any of these questions and how sensitive the overall equation is to that uncertainty.

Most societies are more willing to support an intervention that affects someone else than one that affects them, especially when they may benefit from the former. Considerations of social justice would argue that there should be equity in the distribution of both the benefits and the burdens of intervention.

THE ORGANIZATION OF PREVENTION

Prevention, as noted above, is not the exclusive domain of any one profession or organization. Unlike highway construction and maintenance, the management of libraries, and the work of police agencies, prevention does not have a clearly defined locus in government. The organization most closely allied with that function is the public health agency—the governmental presence in health—which exists in every community. But that organization usually does not include the functions of mental health, often has nothing to do with health services for the medically indigent, and frequently has little to do with substance abuse or highway safety. The state agency responsible for purchasing medical care for the poor, Medicaid, has only recently begun to look at the effectiveness of its programs in terms of the health status of the population with which it is concerned; it has been principally a financing agency.

TABLE 5-8 Objectives for the nation, 1990, and draft priority areas for heath objectives for the nation, 2000

Objectives for 1990	Objectives for 2000
High blood pressure control	Prevent, detect, and control high blood cholesterol and high blood pressure
Family planning	Improve maternal and infant health
Pregnancy and infant health	Reduce adolescent pregnancy and improve reproductive health
Immunization	Immunize against and control infectious diseases
Surveillance and control of infectious diseases	Prevent and control sexually transmitted diseases
Control of sexually transmitted diseases	Prevent and control HIV infection and AIDS
Toxic agent control	Reduce environmental health hazards
Occupational safety and health	Improve occupational safety and health
Accident prevention and injury control	Prevent and control unintentional injuries
Fluoridation and dental health	Improve oral health
Smoking and health	Reduce tobacco use
Misuse of alcohol and drugs	Reduce alcohol and other drug use
Nutrition	Improve nutrition
Physical fitness and exercise	Improve physical fitness
Control of stress and violent behavior	Reduce violent and abusive behavior
	Improve mental health and prevent mental illness
	Prevent, detect, and control cancer
	Prevent, detect, and control other chronic diseases and disorders
	Maintain the health and quality of life of older people
	Improve health education and access to preventive health services
	Improve surveillance and data systems

Some states have attempted to pull together these various functions and agencies to facilitate planning for more effective preventive interventions. Virginia, for example, has passed a statute that attempts to coordinate several state agencies in developing a statewide plan for disease prevention and health promotion.[27] The Surgeon General's report *Healthy People* in 1979[15] was followed by *Promoting Health/Preventing Disease: Objectives for the Nation* in 1980.[28] The latter important document, the result of the work of hundreds of public health professionals, developed 227 recommendations in the 15 areas discussed in *Healthy People.* Table 5-8 presents both the objectives for the year 1990 and a draft list of priority areas for the year 2000.

During this same time, a different but related effort was under way involving the official state and local health agencies, the Centers for Disease Control of the U.S. Department of Health and Human Services, and the American Public Health Association. The collaborative project produced model standards for preventive health services throughout the nation in response to a congressional mandate that the states demonstrate what they were able to accomplish with federal grants for preventive health services.[29] The model standards had a profound effect on both state and local public health agencies and resulted in a series of major planning initiatives. The second edition of the model standards, in 1979, attempted to cross-reference the standards to the *Objectives for the Nation* document. In community after community, local health departments began to analyze their work in terms of the standards described in the new reports.[30,31] In California, the standards were adapted to state circumstances and used to negotiate revised program standards with several county health departments.[32] As the Office of Disease Prevention and Health Promotion of the U.S. Department of Health and Human Services began to consider new standards for the year 2000, even greater interest was expressed in the effort, and an extensive series of nationwide hearings was held to gather fresh insights into the process.

In spite of all this effort, however, little seems to have been directed toward improving public understanding of the complex notion of prevention. Little attention and even less progress have been made in developing new ways to discuss, plan, and form policies for prevention, which must clearly cut across the boundaries of numerous public and private agencies if they are to be successful. While interest is higher and commitment greater than it has ever been, the organization of public resources to prevent the dependency associated with disease and injury has not met the challenges of the end of the twentieth and the beginning of the twenty-first centuries.

REFERENCES

1. Torjman SR: Prevention in the drug field. 1. Essential concepts and strategies, Toronto, 1986, Addiction Research Foundation.
2. Noack H: Concepts of health and health promotion. In Abelin T, Brzezinsky ZJ, and Carstairs VDL, editors, Measurement in health promotion and protection, European Series No 22, 1987, WHO Regional Office for Europe.
3. McIntire MS, editor: Injury control for children and youth, Elk Grove Village, IL, 1987, American Academy of Pediatrics.
4. Prevention index '87: a report card on the nation's health, Emmaus, PA, 1987, Rodale Press, Inc.
5. Cole P: Personal communication, 1986.
6. McKeown T, Record RG, and Turner RD: An interpretation of the decline of mortality in England and Wales during the twentieth century, Pop Studies 29:391, Nov 1975.
7. Rosenkrantz BG: Public health and the state: changing views in Massachusetts, 1842-1936, Cambridge, MA, 1972, Harvard University Press.
8. Morris JN: Epidemiology and prevention, Milbank Q 60:1, Winter 1982.
9. Last JM: A dictionary of epidemiology, Oxford, 1983, Oxford University Press.
10. Hennekens CH and Buring JE: Epidemiology in medicine, Boston, 1987, Little, Brown & Co.
11. Mausner JS and Kramer S: Epidemiology: an introductory text, Philadelphia, 1984, WB Saunders Co.
12. Morris JN: Uses of epidemiology, ed 3, New York, 1975, Churchill Livingstone.
13. Whitby LG: Screening for disease: definitions and criteria, Lancet 1974(II):819, October 5, 1974.
14. Lalonde M: A new perspective on the health of Canadians: a working document, Ottawa, 1974, Ministry of National Health and Welfare.
15. Public Health Service: Healthy people: the Surgeon General's report on health promotion and disease prevention, Washington, DC, 1979, U.S. Department of Health, Education and Welfare.
16. Beauchamp DE: Community: the neglected tradition of public health, Hastings Cent Rep 15:28, December 1985.

17. Kolata G: $1.5 billion is seen as the cost of screening for breast cancer, New York Times, November 25, 1987.
18. Olshansky SJ: Pursuing longevity: delay versus elimination of degenerative diseases, Am J Public Health 75:754, July 1985.
19. Rowe JW and Kahn RL: Human aging: usual and successful, Science 237:143, July 10, 1987.
20. Cooper T: Keynote address to the National Conference on Preventive Medicine. In Preventive medicine, USA, New York, 1976, Prodist.
21. Quelch JA: Marketing principles and the future of preventive health care, Milbank Q 58:310, Spring 1980.
22. Murray JJ: Conclusion: the changing pattern of dental disease and treatment. In Murray JJ, editor, The prevention of dental disease, Oxford, 1983, Oxford University Press.
23. Glass RL and others: The first international conference on the declining prevalence of dental caries, J Dent Res 61:1303, special issue 1982.
24. Russell LB: Is prevention better than cure? Washington, DC, 1986, The Brookings Institution.
25. Task Force on Health Risk Assessment: Determining risk to health: federal policy and practice, Dover, MA, 1986, Auburn House Publishing Co.
26. Beauchamp DE: Public health and individual liberty, Ann Rev Public Health 1:121, 1980.
27. Governor's Task Force: Coordinating preventive health, education and social programs, House document No 5, Richmond, VA, 1987, Commonwealth of Virginia.
28. Public Health Service: Promoting health/preventing disease: objectives for the nation, Washington, DC, 1980, US Department of Health and Human Services.
29. American Public Health Association, Association of State and Territorial Health Officials, National Association of County Health Officials, US Conference of Local Health Officers, and Centers for Disease Control of the US Department of Health and Human Services: Model standards: a guide for community preventive health services, ed 2, Washington, DC, 1985, American Public Health Association.
30. Axnick NW and others: Survey of city/county public health agencies to determine the development, use and effect of program performance standards, Am J Public Health 76:692, June 1986.
31. Schaeffer M and Abrantes A: Standards for local public health services: where stand the states? Am J Public Health 75:649, June 1985.
32. Spain C, Eastman E, and Kizer KW: Model standards impact on local health department performance in California, Am J Public Health 79:969, August 1989.

CHAPTER 6

The organization of public health in the United States

THE POLITICAL SYSTEM

Until recent years, many regarded political science as a static description of formal organizational structures such as legislatures or political parties, along with normative political theory. Political scientists now describe politics as a dynamic system. The political process is the system used by people to negotiate policy when differences exist, especially differences in values regarding such things as welfare, the criminal justice system, education, and health. The institutions of government, especially the elected legislative bodies, serve as the forums in which the search for policy occurs. The administrative agencies of government often provide an opportunity for more in-depth, often narrower debate about the fine details of the policies as they have been developed by elected officials. The nature of these institutions and their relationships must be understood to gain an understanding of the political process and thus the role of government in health.

The basic outline of this system is contained in the Constitution. It is a federal system that is defined as "one where the governmental powers are divided by terms of a written constitution between a general government and the governments of territorial subdivisions, each government supreme within a sphere marked out in the Constitution."[1]

In this country the territorial subdivisions are states. Traditionally they tend to be apprehensive of the powers of the national government. It is often overlooked that not until the American Revolution was almost won did the original 13 colonies think seriously about union. Many influential people insisted that each colony should be a distinct and separate nation. The Continental Congress ultimately solved the problem by devising a union of states. The decision was made by a narrow margin of votes.

The politically dominant state

In forming a union, the colonies did not surrender their individual rights and prerogatives. Instead they took the attitude that most governmental problems would continue to be met and solved best on a separate and independent basis. Relatively few matters of common interest and concern were to be referred to the federal government established by their union.

They recognized that they had common interests in matters of defense, international diplomacy, and finance. Federal departments were formed to deal with these issues: War, State, and Treasury. Subsequently, as additional common problems developed or were recognized, other federal agencies were established.

The powers of the federal government are limited and specific. They were originally defined in Article I, section 8 of the federal Constitution. The first ten amendments to the Constitution, known as the Bill of Rights, were concerned with limiting the power of the federal government and protecting individual liberty: freedom of religion, the right to bear arms (the Second Amendment, which appears to support organized militias in the states, not individual gun-bearing), freedom from unwarranted search, protection against double jeopardy and self-incrimination, the right to a fair trial by a jury, protection against excessive bail, and the protection of additional rights not mentioned in the Constitution. The Tenth Amendment stated, "The powers not delegated to the United States by the Constitution, nor prohibited by it to the States, are reserved to the States respectively, or to the people." This amendment has enormous significance for the understanding of public health. Health is not mentioned in the Constitution as a function of the national government. The authority of the national government is contained in three places [italics added]: (1) the Preamble to the Constitution, which states, "We the people of the United States, in order to form a more perfect union, establish justice, insure domestic tranquility, provide for the common defense, promote the general *welfare*, and secure the blessings of liberty to ourselves and our posterity, do ordain and establish this Constitution of the United States of America"; (2) section 8 of Article I where it states, "The Congress shall have the power to lay and collect taxes, duties, imposts and excises, to pay the debts and provide for the common defence and general *welfare* of the United States"; and (3) section 8 of Article I, which states that Congress has the power "to regulate commerce with foreign nations, among the several States, and with the Indian tribes." These provisions, dealing with the common welfare and the regulation of interstate commerce, paved the way for the expansion of the national government in the health field since the 1930s, but its increased role has been implemented almost exclusively through the states, not directly by federal action. The Tenth Amendment made that clear. In contrast, most state constitutions explicitly recognize the police power of the state and the responsibility for the welfare of its citizens. The police power role authorized the control and abatement of nuisances, which can span the gamut from a weed-infested vacant lot to a badly run nursing home. The welfare role of the states is far more explicit than that of the federal government. By direct inclusion in their constitution of language from England's Elizabethan Poor Law of 1601, the local communities of each state were specifically assigned responsibility for the "aid and support of those not otherwise provided for." That role continued in one form or another until very recently. Even today, many states assign responsibility for medical care of the poor and general assistance to county government.

The authority of the states has been eroded in the last 50 years by the expansion of the national government's taxing and spending programs, but as previously noted, the federal interest has had to be carried out through the states and the local units of government: air pollution policy is developed at the national level, but it is implemented through state agencies; the federal Medicaid program has been implemented through the states, as have programs to control lead poisoning, to cope with toxic wastes, and to treat venereal disease. Even the vital statistics reporting system, developed at the national level, depends on voluntary compliance by the states. It is the fiscal carrot, which often becomes a stick, that makes it possible for congressional or presidential interests to be implemented through the state governments, as will be discussed later.

Intergovernmental relations

For many years public health programs in the United States were organized and operated along relatively simple lines. Relationships among the official health agencies of the three levels of government were usually quite clear. They might be summarized as follows:

1. In accord with the federal Constitution, each sovereign state determined the form and function of its official health agency.
2. The local health agencies, as they were developed with the approval of and some support from the state, served in effect as agents of the state health department.
3. The national government dealt essentially with interstate and international matters and on request assisted the states in various types of emergencies.

A number of forces led to significant and lasting changes in these relatively comfortable arrangements. Prominent among these forces were (1) changes in the national economy; (2) changes in the revenue potentials of the different levels of government; (3) societal needs and demands; (4) population changes in numbers, concentration, and mobility; and (5) scientific and technologic developments. The economic depression of the 1930s and the responses of the Roosevelt administration signaled the transition between the established roles of the past and the rapidly emerging roles of the future. Certainly of the five forces mentioned, the first—economic fluctuations—accelerated, if it did not indeed trigger, the other four. It is interesting to observe how essentially the same process appears to be recurring at the present time, although the direction of change seems to be somewhat reversed.

Public health organization on all three levels of government paralleled the socioeconomic development of the nation. For a long time the concept of government involvement in any type of health activity was either not considered a possibility at all or, if implemented, was viewed as an unwarranted intrusion into personal and private affairs. This was especially so on the local level. Government operation of a postal system was understandable and welcomed; roads were accepted with the reservation that they be constructed and maintained locally; but health matters were one's own business. As the nation grew in size and complexity, it became increasingly evident that such restrictive views could no longer serve the best interests of the people. Not only were areas of government action expanded, but the respective roles and relationships of the federal-state-local partnership were more definitively determined. Those roles have continued to change, with the locus of responsibility for health policy formation shifting from the local to the state to the federal level and back to the states again. In its major study of public health in the United States, the Institute of Medicine[2] described what it thought those roles should be in the 1990s. The institute concluded that the states were and should be the central force in public health; that they bore "primary responsibility for public health." The roles assigned to each level of government by the institute were as follows.

The states:

- Assessment of health needs in the state based on statewide data collection
- Assurance of an adequate statutory base for health activities in the state
- Establishment of statewide health objectives, delegating power to localities as appropriate and holding them accountable
- Assurance of appropriate organized statewide effort to develop and maintain essential personal, educational, and environmental health services; provision of access to necessary services; and solution of problems inimical to health
- Guarantee of a minimum set of essential health services
- Support of local service capacity, especially when disparities in local ability to raise revenue, administer programs, or both require subsidies, technical assistance, or direct action by the state to achieve adequate service levels

The federal government:

- Support of knowledge development and dissemination through data gathering, research, and information exchange
- Establishment of nationwide health objectives and priorities, and stimulation of debate on interstate and national public health issues
- Provision of technical assistance to help states and localities determine their own objectives and carry out action on national and regional objectives
- Provision of funds to states to strengthen state capacity for services, especially to achieve an adequate minimum capacity, and to achieve national objectives
- Assurance of actions and services that are in the public interest of the entire nation such as control of AIDS and similar communicable diseases, interstate environmental actions, and food and drug inspection

Localities:

- Assessment, monitoring and surveillance of local health problems and needs and of resources for dealing with them
- Policy development and leadership that foster local needs and that advocate equitable distribution of public resources and complementary private activities commensurate with community needs
- Assurance that high-quality services, including personal health services, needed for the protection of public health in the community are available and accessible to all persons; that the community receives proper consideration in the allocation of federal and state, as well as local, resources for public health, and that the community is informed about how to obtain public health, including personal health services, and how to comply with public health requirements

It remains to be seen whether these recommendations will be incorporated into the statutory base of public health in the United States. Their implications and utility will be examined in the remainder of this chapter and in Chapter 7.

Changing roles

The interpretation of the respective responsibilities of the state and national governments under the Constitution has changed considerably throughout United States history. Many people today regard the federal government as the ultimate source of power and money. Although this view was held with increasing justification until 1981, this was not always the case. The original concept of state supremacy has been briefly discussed. The principle is not dead.

For a considerable period of U.S. history, the federal government seemed somewhat distant to the average citizen. This early relationship has been described by Brogan[3]:

> It should be remembered that it was quite easy for the settler in the Middle West to have no dealings at all with the government of the United States. He paid no direct taxes; he very often wrote no letters and received none, for the good reason that he and his friends could not write. Yet the only ubiquitous federal officials and federal service were the Postmasters and the Post Office. . . . True, the new union had built the National Road, down which creaked the Conestoga wagons with their cargo of immigrants' chattels. It fought the Indians from time to time and it had at its disposal vast areas of public lands to be sold on easy terms and finally given away to settlers. But no government that had any claim to be a government at all has had less direct power over the people it ruled.

With increasing urbanization, education, mechanization, travel, industrialization, and interstate and international problems, the national government came more and more into focus in the citizens' eyes. At the same time there began to develop a blurring of the image of local and state government. Much of this had to do with increased needs and demands in relation to sources of revenue. There was a period when local governments were essentially self-sufficient, but as the demands made on them increased, they looked more frequently to the state governments for assistance.

By the 1970s, many states began to be featured in the national news media as providing the leadership needed to solve complex problems. State governors were younger, better trained, and nontraditional in their political roots than they had been in the nineteenth and early twentieth centuries. A new breed of administrators was functioning at the state level too—a younger, more independent (independent of traditional political ties, that is), and better trained work force with business and public administration training.[4] For a period of time, mayors of major cities seemed to hold the lead roles in public policy formation, particularly during the Johnson years (in the 1960s), as federal grants-in-aid were channeled directly from national agencies to the mayors rather than through the states. This began to change again with the Nixon administration and more strikingly with the Reagan administration, placing more emphasis on state-level officials.

As the locus of health policy formation has shifted back and forth, the federal and state governments have acquired much of the authority that once lay at the local level.

There are many methods short of total assumption of power and function that may be used to achieve a practical measure of centralizaton. Perhaps the simplest is the offering of advice and information by a federal agency to the states or by the states to the local governments. This is so common in the field of public health as to have become one of the prime activities of state and federal health agencies. It is only a short step from the transmission of printed advice and information to visits of state and federal consultants, followed by the lending of personnel, especially in the face of local shortages. Federal personnel may be assigned to direct state or local health programs. Field staff assigned by state health departments to assist local units may assume the authority to supervise local health programs. A variation is a program of inspection and advice, often without authority, to bring about compliance with state or federal recommendations. The inspecting and advising officials may merely report their findings to the central authorities, who may then promote additional legislation that often gives them increased supervisory powers. This has occurred, for example, in matters of hospital construction and inspection of sanitary and environmental installations.

Requirements for periodic fiscal and service reports are justifiable to obtain information concerning problems and programs. Theoretically a state or local health department has the right to organize its records and reports any way it sees fit. However, after the right to require certain reports is obtained, the next step is to standardize them. In more than one instance this has resulted in a change in the local program itself, the local personnel following the path of least resistance, especially if financial grants are involved. This has occurred in varying degrees as a result of requirements for reports of communicable diseases and for standardized fiscal reports of state and local health departments to federal health agencies. Another technique is to appoint a local official as the representative of a state or federal agency. Thus many local health officers have appointments as collaborating epidemiologists of the Public Health Service or inspectors for the Food and Drug Administration and follow the national agency's procedures.

State health agencies often have a direct role in the selection and appointment of local personnel. While the local health officer may be appointed officially by the local board of health or elected officials, approval by the state health officer is often required. In some states local health officers are appointed and removed directly by the state board of health or the state health director. The local health officer serves as the state health officer's representative in carrying out state laws.

By virtue of the local health officer's probable designation as registrar, births and deaths will be reported to the state health department on forms developed by the National Center for Health Statistics. If appointed a collaborating epidemiologist, the health officer will send weekly reports to the Centers for Disease Control of the Public Health Service, as well as to the state health department. The maternal and child health program may necessitate operation, inspection, and approval of clinics and hospital facilities, based on standards developed and required by the federal Maternal and Child Health Program or, since 1981, by the state program director. Protocols for testing and counseling people with AIDS, and arrangements made to provide necessary treatment, are often supervised by the state agency. Arrangement for the use of X-ray equipment and for hospitalization of persons with tuberculosis will in most instances be made with the state agency. Finally, it will probably be convenient, if not necessary, to obtain educational materials, biologics, and even office forms and supplies through the state health department.

All this may appear to virtually destroy any independence of action and thought by the local health officer, but the relationships also represent needed resources. Considering the limited resources available in the majority of local health departments, the involvement of the state is necessary to adequately carry out state laws. This is not true in the larger, more fully developed local health agencies, and they have customarily resisted strong state guidance and control, often turning directly to federal sources of money and technical assistance.

The federal government cannot dictate to the states the manner in which they should organize their governmental structure, establish their policies, or conduct their programs. However, actual dictation of these matters is not necessary for federal agencies to play a part in the direction of public health services throughout the nation. The significance of holding the purse strings is well understood by all. Among many examples of federal influence on state government's organizational structure are the rapid formation of state maternal and child health divisions after the passage of the Sheppard-Towner Act and, more recently, the establishment of separate environmental protection agencies by many states soon after such an agency was formed on the federal level.

Grants of federal money by the federal government to state and local organizations have gone a long way towards standardizing public health policy in the United States. Their influence will be discussed more fully in Chapter 7.

ORGANIZATIONAL STRUCTURE

The organizational structures of the state and national governments are basically similar. Each has three branches: the executive, or administrative, the legislative, or policy-making, and the judicial.

All local governmental units are creations of the state. As a result, the character of the various local units varies from one section of the country to another. The state-local government relationship is defined as a unitary system; that is, powers are conferred on subdivisional governments by the legislature of the state government.

There were 83,166 units of local government in the United States in 1987: 3,042 counties, 19,205 municipalities, 16,691 towns and townships, 14,741 school districts, and 29,487 special districts. The number of local government units has declined steadily during the last several decades, mostly due to the consolidation of school districts. In the last few years, there has been some increase due to the formation of special districts, a number of which have public health purposes, such as hospital districts, health districts, and sanitation districts.[5]

Cities and counties

Most local health departments in the United States are part of county or municipal units of government. While the forms of government vary somewhat from state to state, cities generally have broader discretionary powers than counties do. Cities have a charter, a sort of municipal constitution, which empowers them to do almost anything that state law does not prohibit them from doing. Counties are often more limited: they can do only those things specifically permitted to them by the state. Many of their functions are required by state law, and the elected or appointed officials responsible for such functions are agents of the state.

Cities, unless prohibited by state laws, can raise taxes, borrow money, issue bonds, make and enforce local laws, and operate a health department or municipal hospital if they choose to. They can also decide *not* to operate such programs and rely on either the state or the county for such services. There are several forms of city government. The "weak mayor-council" form of municipal government has an elected council, one of whose members (often the one who received the most votes in the general election) serves as the mayor. In a "strong mayor-council" form of government, the mayor is elected as the chief executive officer, and the mayor and council have separate executive and legislative functions. A city manager form of government is common in small and intermediate-sized cities. The elected council employs a professional manager to supervise the administrative functions of the city.

Cities have a variety of revenue sources available to them but are having an increasingly difficult time obtaining sufficient funds to maintain services. They often have the authority to use an income tax, but that may drive residents and commuters away. They use property taxes, but an increasing amount of municipal property is either exempt from taxation (church property or federal, state, and local government buildings, including schools and universities) or has too little value to yield much money. Sales taxes can often be imposed, but there are limits to the amount that can be levied, and sales taxes are a heavy burden for inner city residents, who must spend virtually all of their income on taxable items.

Counties are the universal unit of American government except in Connecticut and Rhode Island, which do not have counties. They are the administrative subdivisions of states. County boundaries were drawn to encompass all the territory and therefore all the people of the state. The county seat, usually a principal town or city in the middle of the area, serves as the "capital." Originally, the boundaries were drawn to make it possible for any citizen with a horse to get to the county seat and back in a single day. As the western states formed, this was no longer possible. Counties now vary in size from Kalawao, Hawaii, with 14 square miles, to the 20,117 square miles of San Bernardino County in California, which is larger than the states of New Hampshire, Vermont, Massachusetts, Rhode Island, and Connecticut combined. Loving County in Texas had fewer than 100 people in the 1980 census, compared to Los Angeles County with over 7 million citizens.

In spite of their role as administrative arms of the state, counties have at times seemed almost irrelevant. The five counties of New York City have yielded virtually all authority to the city. As noted, some counties are very small. They usually lack a chief administrative or executive officer, and they have limited authority, but they serve a unique and increasingly important function. As the role of state government has increased, and municipalities have found it increasingly difficult to obtain the revenue needed for city services, the counties' role as administrative subdivisions of the state has become more important. They usually have a single elected body, variously called county supervisors or commissioners or, in some places, the county court. While the county's elected body may appoint a county manager and several county department heads, many important county officials are independently elected: the sheriff, the assessor, the county clerk, a county attorney, and often a drain commissioner, for example. Coordinated governance can be difficult with responsibility diffused. The structure of county government is usually prescribed by the state, as are the procedures to be used, the nature of the tax base, and the role of the principal elected and appointed officials. Formed to serve a rural society and economy, counties have found it difficult to manage their affairs effectively and efficiently as they have become more urbanized.

The principal source of revenue for county government is the property tax, arguably the most unpopular of all taxes. It is an expensive and difficult tax system to administer fairly. High property taxes deter commercial development and outrage citizens, who like the fact that their homes are appreciating in value but object to the notion that they should pay more taxes.

Counties customarily have had a closer relationship with state government than have cities. Big city mayors are often political rivals of governors and are able to negotiate directly with state legislative committees. The mayors are important to federal officials as well and have exercised considerable power with executive branch officials. The health officers of major cities are responsible for large agencies, usually with large and well-trained staffs and substantial budgets. They are the action points for most of the major public health problems in the country: medical care of the indigent, waste disposal, AIDS, the homeless, and high infant mortality rates. Their programs and problems are often as large as those of the state health officer, but they are also often different problems. While the state agency may be involved in the licensure of health facilities, hospital cost containment, and rural sanitation, municipalities are more likely to be concerned about the homeless, medical care for the indigent, solid waste disposal, and hospital closures.

County health officers have been more dependent on the state for personnel, technical assistance, and policy guidance, both because their departments are often small and because they are responsible for the execution of many state health laws. Usually it is the county that runs elections, counts the votes, collects the property tax, and supervises law enforcement. These functions necessarily tie county government to the state legislators and the governor.

Special districts

Special districts are the most varied of all local units of government. They are usually established to deal with a particular problem, such as water, sewage, air pollution, and the like. To finance the specific undertaking, special districts have their own property tax base and often charge fees for their services. The most ubiquitous and important of the special districts are the school districts. They are of considerable importance in public health. (See Chapter 24.) Usually the superintendent of schools is separately elected or is appointed by the elected school board of the district. The school district has its own tax program, usually relying on the property tax. School districts often receive a substantial amount of state aid also.

There are various approaches to consolidating government units. In some areas of the United States the number of such units is appalling. In San Mateo County, Calif., there are 19 cities in a row between San Francisco and Palo Alto. Each has a mayor and a city council, most have an engineer, a police chief, a city clerk, and a city hall, and many developed their own municipal bus systems in the 1970s. There are also a number of special districts in the county. Other areas have even more separate jurisdictions. In many areas of the country, a large city comprises most of the county or sometimes more than one county: Miami and Dade County, Detroit and Wayne County, Los Angeles and Los Angeles County, Memphis and Shelby County, for example. In some such areas, the public health functions have been consolidated. In others, they remain separate: the citizens pay property taxes to support both a county and a city health department but receive services only from the city. In some areas, the county, the official agent of the state, is only a small fringe of territory around a major city. In its recent report *The Future of Public Health*, the Institute of Medicine,[2] in order to promote a clear line of accountability, made the explicit recommendation that "public health responsibility should be delegated to only one unit of government in a locality."

Various forms of metropolitan government have been developed. Some have involved the dissolution of one or more government units and the formation of a single larger unit. More often, the governments in a geographic area develop a series of contractual agreements for sharing certain services. Occasionally some services are split off from the units and a new government is formed to execute certain functions such as solid waste disposal, for all the units. In recent years, not-for-profit corporations have been formed to carry out some government functions.

Consolidation of government units is an extremely difficult political task. Attempts to consolidate school districts arouse intense feelings, and most small incorporated towns resist their elimination or absorption into larger cities. Yet the problems of multiple jurisdictions are real: lack of coordination, excessive tax burdens, wasteful duplication of scarce resources, and inconsistency in the administration of laws. Despite the shortcomings of county government, it is increasingly apparent that, given expanded powers and efficient organization, they could be used to streamline the work of government at the local level. Whether the voters will support such streamlining, however, is problematic. While most citizens complain about government inefficiency and high taxes, they are reluctant to vote for consolidation.

LOCAL PUBLIC HEALTH ORGANIZATIONS

In the 3,042 counties of the United States, there are 3,233 local health departments. More than half (1,789) are single-county units. There are 871 health departments in cities and towns, 226 health departments serving combined city-county jurisdictions, 125 multicounty health departments, and 222 listed as "other."[6] The towns with health departments are located in Connecticut, Massachusetts, and Pennsylvania. There is no single form for those listed as "other." They appear to be similar to the other classified units, but, due to local idiosyncrasies, use different names. Delaware, Hawaii, Rhode Island, and Vermont have no official local health departments. Several states have very few: Maine (3), Nevada (2), New Mexico (3), and Vermont (1). Some states have an enormous number of local health departments: Connecticut (119), Georgia (159), Massachusetts (357), Ohio (141), and Pennsylvania (244).

Given the federal structure of U.S. government and the role of the states in creating health policy and programs, the variation is not surprising. There have been several attempts to classify the approaches taken by the states in the organization of a public health delivery system.[6,7] Mullan and Smith[6] classify state-local health agency patterns as centralized, decentralized, shared, or mixed. In centralized systems, local health departments are operated by the state agency. In decentralized systems, local health departments are formed and managed by local government. In systems with shared organizational control patterns, the state exercises some authority over the local health department (as by appointing the local health officer or requiring submission of annual budgets and program plans), and the local government manages the budget, provides buildings

TABLE 6-1 Classification of states with local health departments by type of state-local interaction

Centralized	Decentralized	Shared	Mixed
Arkansas	Arizona	Alabama	Alaska
Florida	Colorado	Georgia	California
Louisiana	Connecticut	Kentucky	Illinois
Mississippi	Idaho	Maryland	Kansas
New Mexico	Indiana	Minnesota	Massachusetts
South Carolina	Iowa	North Carolina	Michigan
Virginia	Maine	Ohio	New Hampshire
	Missouri	West Virginia	New York
	Montana		Oklahoma
	Nebraska		Pennsylvania
	Nevada		South Dakota
	New Jersey		Tennessee
	North Dakota		Texas
	Oregon		Wyoming
	Utah		
	Washington		
	Wisconsin		

From Mullan F and Smith J: Characteristics of state and local health agencies, mimeographed paper, Baltimore, MD, 1988, Johns Hopkins University School of Hygiene and Public Health.

and other resources, and sets policy within state guidelines. In states with a mixed pattern, both centralized and locally governed agencies may be found. The mixed form usually exists in a state where local health departments are the preferred delivery system for public health services, but some counties cannot or will not assume the responsibility, usually because of their small size and lack of resources. In these cases, the state health department often provides a public health presence through a district office. Table 6-1 lists the states in the four categories.

Organizational structure

To carry out its mandate, the official public health agency in rural or small urban situations requires only a relatively simple type of organizational structure. Legal responsibility for the public's health is commonly given to a local board of health, the members of which are usually appointed by the locally elected officials—in cities by mayors and in counties by boards of supervisors or their equivalent. The board of health usually appoints and employs a county health officer, frequently subject to approval by the state health department. Increasingly state health departments have established standards and qualifications that must be met by those appointed to local public health positions. This type of state supervision has met with relatively little local resistance, since in many instances local units of government have found it necessary to turn to the state health department for assistance in finding capable candidates.

The employment of all other personnel is customarily the responsibility of the local health officer but is subject to merit system and equal opportunity regulations if they exist. Depending on the size and nature of the jurisdiction, the health officer's staff usually consists of one or more workers in environmental health, public health nursing, health education, and office management. Nutritionists, public health dentists, and representatives of other professions may be employed, even in small local agencies, again depending on local needs, wishes, and resources. The workers in environmental health may consist of combinations of engineers, professionally trained sanitarians, or sanitary inspectors trained on the job.

Usually, approximately one half of the funds and one half of the positions of the local health department are devoted to public health nursing. Even the smallest local health unit will or should have several nurses on its staff. One of the nurses, selected on the basis of training, experience, and ability, should be appointed as supervising nurse. Where several clinical workers are employed, one should be designated to serve as office manager and to supervise the work of the others. All members of the staff are ultimately responsible to the health officer, who in turn is responsible to the board of health or the elected government body.

When funds and candidates are not available to employ the necessary personnel, or when employment of full-time employees is not practical, as is often the case in staffing clinics, the gap may be filled by the part-time employment of private practitioners or by the use of services of district or state agencies. Wherever possible, however, the employment of full-time personnel is recommended. At least the health officer and the supervisory staff should have specialized training in public health.

In larger local units of government, more extensive personnel and organization are obviously required. In general, the distribution of types of personnel per unit of population is similar to that followed in the smaller areas; various numbers of different types of specialists are added to meet the needs of the particular situation. The larger and more complex programs necessitate a more formalized organizational structure with the bringing together of similar and related functions into divisions and bureaus. Although there is no standard organizational structure, certain functional units are almost universally encountered. Thus there usually exist units responsible for health statistics and records; environmental health; maternal and child health; public health nursing, either as an entity or integrated with the activities of several of the other divisions; laboratory service; epidemiologic service, or disease control; and health education. Increasingly, one also finds units for adult health, chronic disease, and substance abuse. Mental health is usually the responsibility of a separate agency, although some communities have combined the two successfully. Each category large enough to make up a unit should have its own director and possibly subdirectors. The direct professional service activities of those in the top administrative positions become greatly reduced, giving way to functions of a managerial and supervisory nature.

With the increased trend toward core city–suburbia complexes, as well as metropolitanization, a growing movement is under way toward merger of even large city and county health departments. About 11% of all local health departments involve two or more government units.[6] The establishment of public health organizations on the basis of larger units of local government or combinations of units has been necessitated by a consideration of the number of people and the size of area required to raise enough public tax funds to support at least a minimum staff of qualified public health workers. The trend toward combination, although politically difficult, can result in greater efficiency and improved public service.

Expenditures

Given the many forms of local health departments and their variable accountability to their state health agencies, it is impossible to describe accurately or completely the expenditures of local health departments or their sources of revenue. No single data collection system can provide the necessary information. The Public Health Foundation (an organization established by the Association of State and Territorial Health Officials in 1981 to conduct research and provide services for public health agencies) collects and publishes data about expenditures of state public health agencies. In recent years, the foundation has attempted to gather more accurate information about the expenditures and programs of local public health agencies, but it must depend on each of the reporting states to obtain that information from the local health departments—a task that cannot be accomplished uniformly at the present time, given the zealously guarded autonomy of many local health departments. In 1985, according to information provided to the foundation by the participating state health agencies, local health departments spent $3 billion. More than half ($1.7 billion) was spent on personal health services, most of which was for maternal and child health programs. About $293 million was spent on environmental health programs, $58 million on laboratory services, $248 million for resource development (including health planning, regulatory activities related to health services, and evaluation or quality control), and $154 million for general administration. The remaining expenditures ($538 million) could not be allocated to specific program areas based on the information collected.

Nearly half of the $3 billion dollars identified came from state health agencies. It included $825 million in state funds and $502 million in federal grant and contract funds received by the states and transferred to local agencies. Local health departments used $1.2 billion of local tax money, plus other revenue from fees and grant and contract activity.[8]

While by no means typical, the 1988 budget of the Palm Beach County (Fla.) Public Health Unit will serve to illustrate the diversity of local public health funding. (Local health departments in Florida are part of a centralized system. Relatively little of the total budget comes from local sources, but the variety of sources of revenue is typical of large, well-developed health departments.) The total budget for fiscal year 1988 (October 1, 1987, through September 30, 1988) was $26,652,351. It came from the following sources:

General revenue of the state	
General	$6,330,294
AIDS patient care	379,000
School health	205,198
Improved pregnancy outcome	667,513
Federal funds	
Family planning	240,136
Child health	33,610
AIDS	129,199
Hypertension	37,041
Nutrition program administration	250,000
EPA grants	128,300
Child health improvement program	50,000
Sterilizatio.	11,337
AIDS testing and counseling	31,891
Fees	
For enforcement	361,784
Personal fees	87,280
For primary medical care	623,475
Other sources	
Interest on trust fund	100,000
Primary care	3,000,000
Sexually transmitted diseases	198,675

State lab revenue	561,459
Tuberculosis control	95,851
Immunizations	48,947
Supplemental food supplies	1,763,703
Pharmacy	452,929
County support	
General appropriation	5,611,055
Fees	1,618,556
Building rental	1,595,148
Maintenance of buildings	481,134
School board	55,000
County air pollution	398,308
County toxic substance control	83,102
Epilepsy foundation	18,000
Primary care grant	716,898
Headstart dental program	1,700
Sabal Palm (private grant)	27,398
Robert Wood Johnson (grant)	87,879
Communications	170,551
Total	$26,652,351

The budget is made up of 12 different state contributions or allocations (each representing separate state laws), 9 federal grant programs, numerous fees (each with separate requirements), and 13 different local actions (10 of which are county agency contributions and 3 from private foundations). From that revenue, $21,283,954 was budgeted for a wide variety of services as follows:

Public health—control and regulatory programs	
Immunizations	$ 536,163
Sexually transmitted diseases	353,082
AIDS	111,156
Tuberculosis control	405,393
Communicable diseases control	287,697
Private water systems	32,693
Public water systems	379,237
Bottled water	26,154
Swimming pools	307,313
Individual sewage disposal	496,931
Public sewage systems	235,388
Solid waste disposal	170,003
Water pollution control	268,081
Food hygiene	1,013,478
Group care facilities	379,237
Migrant labor camps	104,617
Housing safety and sanitation	130,771
Mobile home parks	32,693
Occupational health	26,154
Consumer product safety	26,154
Sanitary nuisances	241,927
Air pollution control	536,163
Radiologic health	19,616
Toxic substances	111,156
Rabies control	13,077
Arbovirus surveillance	13,077
Emergency medical services	13,077
Vital records	268,081
Personal health services	
Chronic disease services	286,327
Nutrition services	805,293
Family planning	702,313
Improved pregnancy outcome	3,684,791
School health	2,113,801
Dental health services	1,355,180
Comprehensive child health	2,765,493
Comprehensive adult health	3,032,187
Total	$21,283,954

Many of the 36 separate program areas listed represent several programs, each with their own federal, state, or local statutory authority, regulations, procedures, and staff. The activities could be grouped differently or separated into smaller programmatic units, but the general picture that emerges portrays the complex and broad nature of the activities of a modern local public health department and provides some hint of the administrative complexity involved. Each of the program areas has its own budget, with sublines for personnel, overtime, part-time work, employee benefits (health insurance, retirement, Social Security, workers' compensation, and unemployment benefits), supplies (paper, typewriters, computer supplies, medicines, telephone usage, electricity, water, reprographics, postage), and equipment. And each line in each program must be carefully monitored. The end result is an agency with an incredibly complex accounting system and one that touches the lives of virtually every citizen in its community, often in many different ways.

STATE HEALTH AGENCIES

A recent discussion by Clarke[9] of the role of states in health services delivery describes a situation somewhat similar to that encountered when trying to describe the role of local government in health:

> The role of states in the delivery of health services is a difficult one to assess. The states are involved in such a wide variety of health activities, have such different

administrative structures as well as varying competence and sophistication, that it is almost impossible to characterize "the states" in anything but abstract terms.

In addition, states by their very nature are subject to certain conflicts and limitations. It is true that they are sovereign and subject to the federal Constitution only up to a point. As sovereign governments they have comprehensive authority that includes the protection of the health, safety, and general welfare of their citizens. Yet they lack the considerably greater federal fiscal power and the public intimacy that local governments may have. Nevertheless, they are sufficiently large and accessible to attract the attentions of a wide variety of special interest groups. These and related factors have led to criticism, especially by academics and federal officials, of state governments as inept, corrupt, inefficient, and lacking in social leadership.

These attitudes, common in the United States, are not supported by the facts. State health departments developed on their own initiative, many of them when federal activities were limited. They played a major role in the development of public health laboratories, sanitary engineering, and the formation of networks of county health organizations. Despite accusations of program limitations, the scope of their health activities is, in the words of Clarke, "truly awesome, and capable of reaching into almost every facet of health care delivery." Most public health programs espoused and supported by federal agencies had their origins in one or more of the states. Occupational health, maternal and child health, the use of public hospitals for the medically indigent, compulsory immunization of school children, screening for vision and hearing defects, early detection programs for heart disease, cancer, and diabetes, civil service systems, program budgeting, and affirmative action all had their origin in the states and were later incorporated into national policy. Moreover, at the present time, the formation of public health policy has clearly shifted back to the states from its 30-year sojourn in Washington, and state legislatures are deeply involved in the most critical public health problems of the present and future.

Organizational structure

In fulfilling their many responsibilities, each of the 50 states has developed its own unique pattern. Some have strongly centralized organizations, whereas others have decentralized to varying degrees. The subdivisions or functional units within the structure of state health departments vary greatly, both in number and in manner of emphasis and arrangement. No two state patterns are identical, but some similarities are to be noted. Thus the Association of Management in Public Health found that in two thirds of the states the director of public health had a span of control encompassing seven divisions or bureaus. This conforms essentially with the findings of The Public Health Foundation,[10] which are presented in Fig. 6-1. Shown is the structure of a hypothetical state health agency with the programs most frequently found within each of the organization's components. Figure 6-1 shows a so-called "umbrella agency" with the public health component highlighted. Umbrella agencies have been formed in recent years in an attempt to gain greater coordination of health programs. An ever increasing number of official state agencies have become involved in one or another aspect of public health: departments, boards, or commissions concerned with medical care, mental illness, medical care cost containment, the control of toxic substances, and emergency medical services; crippled children's agencies; social service organizations; substance abuse agencies; education departments; new environmental protection agencies; departments of agriculture and natural resources; industrial development agencies; the state police; special cancer control commissions; and many others. As many as 30 different state agencies can be identified that have some responsibilities related to public health. Many agencies share responsibility for specific health activities such as injury prevention, health education, or health planning.

Unfortunately, most attempts to improve coordination by combining several human or social services functions under an umbrella agency have resulted in administrative consolidation with no real functional improvement in activities. The head of such an agency, often referred to as a secretary, is an appointee of the governor in most instances and rarely has specific training in public health. There is little evidence that community mental health programs have become better integrated with the work of public health or primary care organizations or that environmental protection functions have become more effective as a result of the formation of umbrella agencies. In some re-

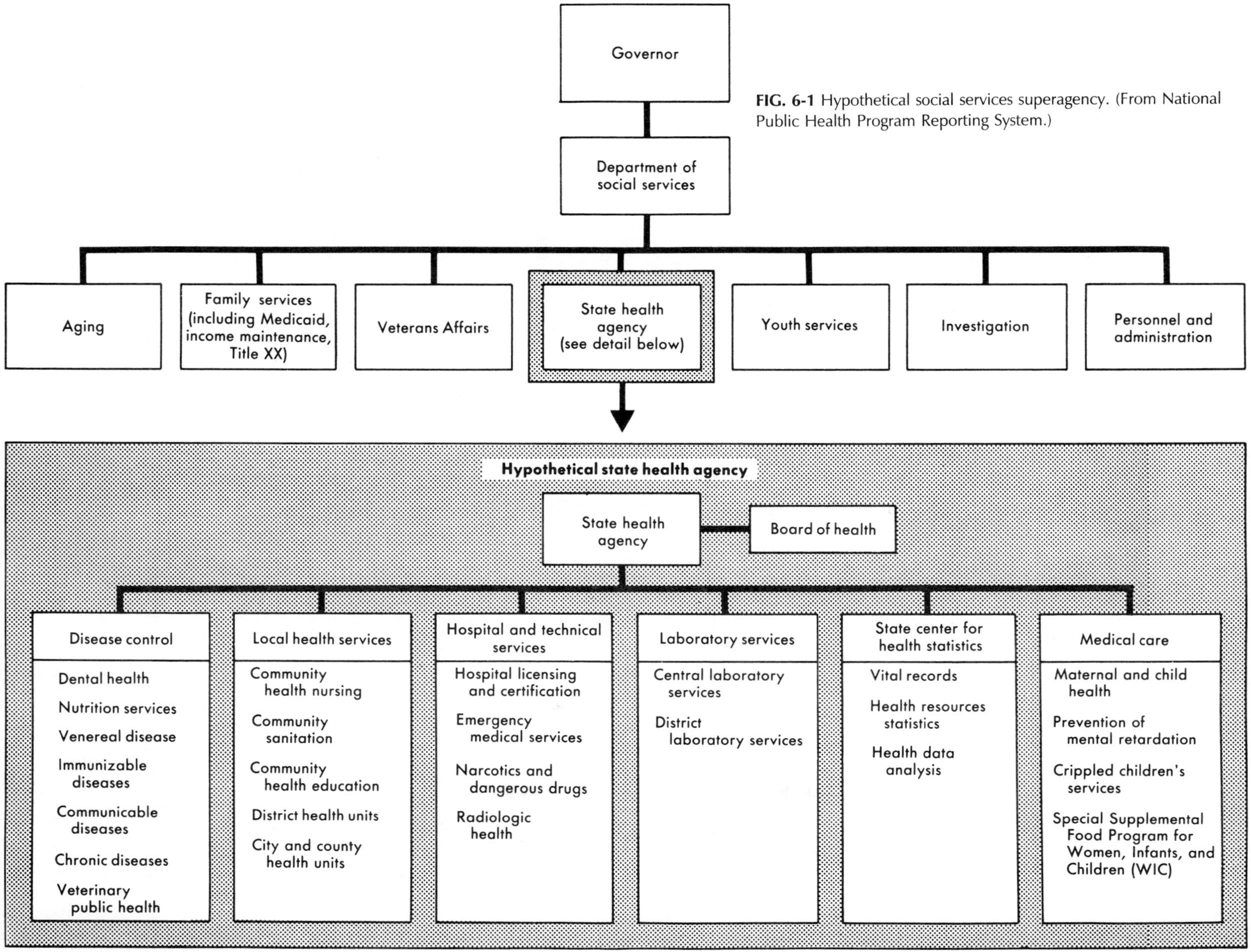

FIG. 6-1 Hypothetical social services superagency. (From National Public Health Program Reporting System.)

spects, such agencies have resulted in an organization that is more responsible politically to a governor and less controlled by a traditional board of health. Thus they are more subject to sudden changes in policy emphasis and direction, if a succession of governors focuses on different problems. The result is a large, often disparate agency, with ephemeral policies and changing leadership, at a time when the most important public health problems require consistent direction and the highest professionalism available. This negative appraisal of umbrella agencies to date does not mean that the concept is wrong. In practice, however, the agencies have not had the intended results. Given a general reluctance to experiment with new forms of public administration, this is not surprising. In 1986, there were 21 umbrella or "superagencies" and 34 free-standing state health agencies.[10]

State boards of health play a very small role in public health policy formation. As recently as the early 1970s, 40 states had policy-making boards of health. They were created by statute, and their membership was prescribed in law, usually consisting of physicians with a few other health professionals and an occasional representative of the general public. The board members were appointed by the governor but usually served for a fixed term and could not be removed unless they were guilty of improper behavior. In three states (South Carolina, Alabama, and Mississippi) the state medical associations were the state boards of health. Only Alabama persists with that indefensible structure, which assigns public policy-making to a private, membership organization with a fiduciary interest in the work of the agency.

By 1980, only 27 states had a policy-making board of health.[11] Since 1900, all state health agencies have been reorganized by statute at least once. Between 1961 and 1970, 10 were the subject of new statutes, and between 1971 and 1980, 23 were reorganized (including some that had been reorganized during the prior wave). In those last 23 reorganizations, 13 resulted in the disestablishment of a policy-making board of health. Of the policy-making boards that remained, 80% of the members were men and 90% were white. Consumers held 29% of the positions and physicians and dentists 40%. The loss of boards of health has made state health agencies more accountable to elected officials but has exacerbated their ephemeral nature.

In a 1987 survey, the National Conference of State Legislatures[12] asked, "What are the major health issues in your state?" The answers were as follows:

- Care of the medically indigent
- Malpractice
- Certificates of need for new health facilities and programs
- Long-term care and Alzheimer's disease
- Medicaid and other medical assistance programs
- Professional licensure
- Organ transplants and donations
- AIDS
- Health insurance
- State employee health plans
- Hospitals

There are few issues on the list that would have appeared there 30 years ago. Virtually none of the problems listed can be solved by a public health agency alone. Long-term care requires the collaboration of public health, mental health, Medicaid, and social services. AIDS requires the close and effective collaboration of education, mental health, Medicaid, and social services, as well as public health. Medical care for the poor requires the same agencies. Environmental health concerns and hazardous waste management did not appear on the list, but such problems are pressing in on the states, and they too cannot be solved by a single agency of state government. While most of the nonpublic health agencies that need to be involved appear to have a clearly demarcated scope of primary responsibility and the ability to carry out their functions as independent agencies, public health problems are different: they require the involvement of many different disciplines and organizations. Umbrella agencies were intended, in part, as a response to that requirement, but they have not succeeded in facilitating either problem analysis, policy analysis and formation, or program implementation. New experiments in the organization and administration of public health programs at the state level are needed if these problems are to be resolved in the future.

Expenditures

As shown in Table 6-2, expenditures of state health agencies in 1987 totaled $10.3 billion: $6.6 billion in programs or activities directly managed by the state agencies and $1.5 billion transferred to local health departments to support locally managed activities. In 1987, 29% of the total reported expenditures of state health agencies and local health departments came from federal grants and contracts; 46% came from state funds; 14% came from local funds; and 11% came from fees and reimbursements. Total expenditures increased by 62% during the 6-year period, an average of 8% per year: federal grants and contracts increased 60%, state funds 71%, local funds 27%, and fees and reimbursements 110%.

The largest single source of federal funds was the U.S. Department of Agriculture, for a supplemental nutrition program for women, infants, and children (WIC). Virtually none of this money ($1.7 billion in 1987) is used to provide personal services: it is used to buy food and is similar to other forms of restricted income transfer. When these funds are subtracted from the total, federal funds for public health services increased by 33% during the 5-year period, or about 5% per year.

The most common source of federal funds for public health services is the U.S. Department of Health and Human Services, but other federal agencies are also involved, as shown in Table 6-3. Many of the entries have many different grant-in-aid programs, each with its own statutory authority, policies, and procedures.

FEDERAL PUBLIC HEALTH ORGANIZATION

The many federal agencies that have responsibility for one or more aspects of public health fall into four categories. The first is concerned with broad health interests. The only example is the Public Health Service. The second is concerned with special groups in the population. Examples are the Administration on Aging, the Agricultural Extension Service, the medical divisions of the army and the navy, and the Veterans Administration. The third category includes agencies concerned with special problems or programs, such as the Office of Education, the Federal Trade Commission, the Bureau of Labor Standards, the Bureau of Labor Statistics, many bureaus within the Department of Agriculture, the Bureau of Mines, the Maritime Commission, the Social Security Administration, and the Bureau of Employees' Compensation. The fourth category is concerned with the international health interests of the United States. In addition to the office of International Health of the Public Health Service, there are the Agency for International Development of the Department of State and the international health activities of several other departments such as Defense and Agriculture. Their functions range from direct personal or technical service to regulation, research, education, and grants-in-aid.

The Public Health Service

The Public Health Service is recognized as the focal point for health concerns at the national level.

TABLE 6-2 Expenditures of state health agencies and local health departments, fiscal years 1987 and 1981

	1987* ($ million)	1981† ($ million)
Personal health services	6,882	4,312
Environmental health services	733	526
Health resources	758	484
Laboratory services	299	219
General administration	602	332
Not allocated by program area	993	455
TOTAL	10,267	6,328

*From Public Health Foundation: Public health agencies, 1989: an inventory of programs and block grant expenditures, Washington, DC, 1989, The Foundation.
†From Public Health Foundation: Public health agencies, 1981: a report on their expenditures and activities, Washington, DC, 1983, The Foundation.

TABLE 6-3 Federal funds for state and local health department activities, 1987

Funding source	Amount
Department of Health and Human Services	1,014
Alcohol, Drug Abuse and Mental Health	95
Centers for Disease Control	180
Health Resources and Services	504
National Institutes of Health	25
Health Care Financing	161
Other	50
Department of Agriculture	1,652
Environmental Protection Agency	71
Other federal	80
TOTAL	2,816

From Public Health Foundation: Public health agencies, 1989: an inventory of programs and block grant expenditures, Washington, DC, 1989, The Foundation.

The Public Health Service is directed by the Assistant Secretary for Health. It is organized into six functional units (Fig. 6-2): (1) the Centers for Disease Control, (2) the Food and Drug Administration, (3) the Health Resources and Services Administration, (4) the National Institutes of Health, (5) the Alcohol, Drug Abuse, and Mental Health Administration, and (6) the Agency for Toxic Substances and Disease Registry. In addition, the Office of the Assistant Secretary has several staff offices directly related to it. These are concerned with management; with health policy, research, and statistics; planning and evaluation; intergovernmental affairs; and health promotion. There are also offices for legislation, international health, population affairs, and other special concerns. For decentralization of services and more effective assistance to states, 10 regional offices are maintained: in Boston, New York, Philadelphia, Atlanta, Chicago, Kansas City, Dallas, Denver, San Francisco, and Seattle. In addition to a National Advisory Health Council, a number of special advisory councils and committees composed of nongovernmental experts are available to many of the institutes and programs. Each year the Assistant Secretary for Health or a representative meets at an annual conference with the state and territorial health officers and with certain other special groups.

Historically, the Public Health Service has been directed by the Surgeon General of the Public Health Service, the ranking officer in the Commissioned Corps. The position originated in the days of the Marine Hospital Service (see Chapter 2). During the administration of President Lyndon Johnson, the professional appointment of the Surgeon General, as a career officer, was seen as an impediment to the influence of the President's office on health policy, and the position of Assistant Secretary for Health was created and placed in charge of the health affairs of the Department of Health, Education and Welfare. At times the two positions, Assistant Secretary and Surgeon General, have been held by the same appointee; at other times the Surgeon General has been a symbolic leader, with political direction supplied by the Assistant Secretary.

The six components of the Public Health Service function in a variety of ways. To a considerable extent, the responsibilities of the Health Resources and Services Administration and the Alcohol, Drug Abuse and Mental Health Administration are met by means of grants and contracts with other governmental agencies, private institutions, and individuals. One exception is the Indian Health Service in the Health Resources and Services Administration, which provides hospital, clinical, and other health services for Native Americans on reservations and for Eskimos. The National Institutes of Health and the Centers for Disease Control carry out extensive intramural and extramural

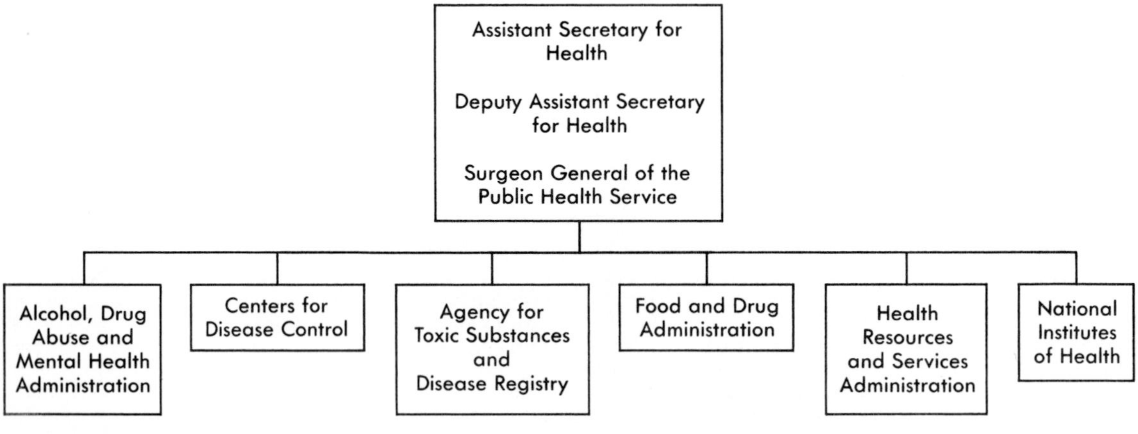

FIG. 6-2 The U.S. Public Health Service.

research, both on their own and by means of grants and contracts in the United States and other parts of the world. In addition, the Centers for Disease Control serve directly as the epidemiologic surveillance and emergency unit for the nation, and the National Institutes of Health have the added responsibility of the National Library of Medicine, the Fogarty International Center for Advanced Studies in Health Sciences, the National Center for Biomedical Communications, and the National Clinical Center. The Food and Drug Administration, by means of its field and laboratory staff, maintains surveillance over the safety and efficacy of foods, food additives, pharmaceuticals and other drugs, cosmetics, and a wide variety of consumer goods including toys and flammable fabrics. It is also responsible for the control of quackery.

The Department of Health and Human Services

In the years that followed establishment of the Federal Security Agency in 1939, various federal health programs, in addition to the Public Health Service, were transferred to it. Most significant among these were the Children's Bureau and the Social and Rehabilitation Service from the Department of Labor, the Food and Drug Administration from the Department of Agriculture, the National Office of Vital Statistics from the Department of Commerce, the health and medical functions of the Bureau of Indian Affairs from the Department of the Interior, and the Administration on Aging. Eventually, on April 11, 1953, Congress established a Department of Health, Education, and Welfare as part of President Eisenhower's reorganization of the Executive Branch of the government. The purpose was to bring into closer functional relationship and to improve the administration of the important health, education, welfare, and social security functions then being carried on by the federal government. The department was not truly an administrative or functional unity, however. It consisted of units of different organization, expertise, and interests. Most units had strong traditions and histories that antedated the department considerably. Many had separate strong and effective congressional ties and public or professional constituencies and did not hesitate to use them unilaterally. Yet, there was a clear need for a more effective operational relationship among those working in the components of human services. Awareness of this, and the consequent chronic administrative frustration, is evidenced by the many reorganizations that have occurred during the past two decades. In 1979, Education was removed and established as a separate Cabinet-level department. The remainder was retitled the Department of Health and Human Services (Fig. 6-3).

Other federal agencies

The Department of Education is engaged in several activities related to health. It promotes programs of health education and school health and safety, engages in investigations relating to medical examination of school children and their teachers, promotes school lunch programs, and administers a grant-in-aid program for vocational education in health.

Several units of the Department of Agriculture engage in programs concerned with health. The Animal and Plant Health Inspection Service is concerned with the cause, prevention, and treatment of diseases of domestic animals, which naturally have an influence on many phases of human health. Federal meat inspection services are administered by the Food Safety and Inspection Service. The Plant Protection and Quarantine Service, although primarily concerned with the protection of crops from parasitic insects, necessarily contributes much knowledge and service to the control of insects affecting humans. The largest public health programs of the Department of Agriculture are in the Food and Nutrition Service division. The division is responsible for the food stamp program for welfare recipients, the supplemental nutrition program for high-risk women, infants, and children, and for much of the school-based nutrition program.

With the establishment of the Environmental Protection Agency at the end of 1970, most of the environmental health activities and responsibilities of the Public Health Service were transferred to it. (See Chapter 18.)

Federal agencies in international health affairs

Originally the interests of the U.S. government in international health affairs were limited to measures designed to prevent the introduction of certain diseases. Developments in world history, economics, and methods of transportation, however, have made it necessary to adopt a broader

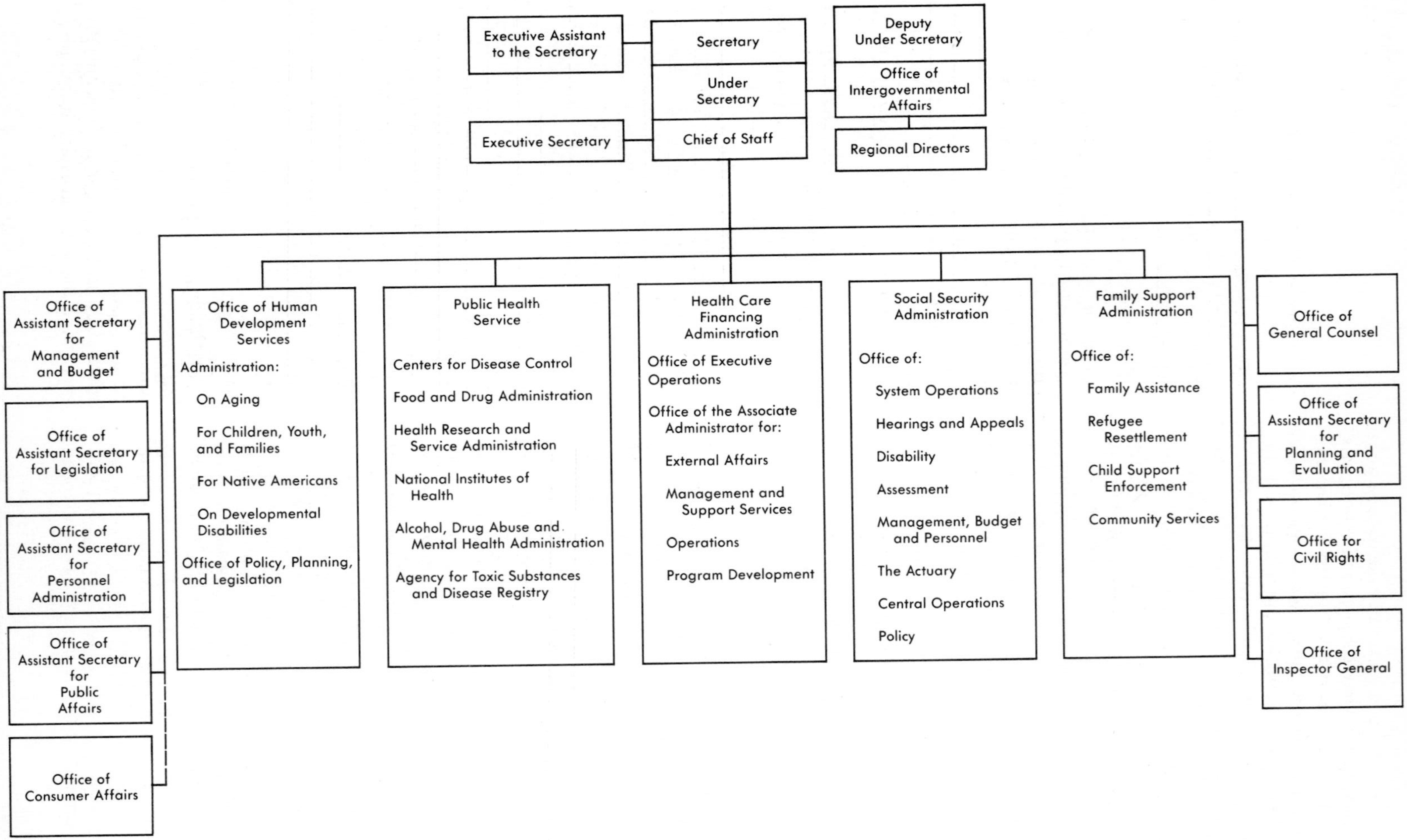

FIG. 6-3 The U.S. Department of Health and Human Services.

viewpoint and to assume responsibilities of great significance to international public health. These newer responsibilities are of two types: first, participation in development of public health programs in other nations and, second, participation as one of a number of partners in the promotion of worldwide health. The most important federal agencies involved in these activities are the Office of International Health of the Public Health Service and the Agency for International Development of the Department of State.

The Office of International Health of the Public Health Service was established to coordinate and give general direction to all service activities in the international health field; to maintain liaison with agencies in this field; to represent the service at international health conferences; to direct a program of international exchange of health personnel and educational material; to draft sanitary conventions and regulations and reports required by international agreements; to collect and distribute data relating to foreign medical and health institutions; to supervise special health missions to foreign countries; to advise the Department of State regarding development of plans, programs, and policies for consideration by the World Health Organization and the Pan American Health Organization; and to advise the offices of the Secretary of Health and Human Services and Surgeon General on international health matters. In relation to the foregoing, the U.S. government has representation in the World Health Organization, the Pan American Health Organization, and the Anglo-American Caribbean Commission.

The bilateral international health activities of the U.S. government are centered in the Agency for International Development of the Department of State. In the planning, staffing, and conduct of its health programs, it relates not only to the Office of International Health of the Public Health Service but also to other significant parts of the U.S. government, to bilateral health assistance programs of other nations, and to any other official or nonofficial organizations concerned with health assistance to developing nations. Much of its work is carried out by means of contracts and other cooperative arrangements with state health departments, universities, schools of public health, schools of medicine, and professional associations or organizations.

THE FEDERAL FINANCIAL ROLE

As noted at the beginning of this chapter, constitutional support for a federal role in public health is slender: two references to support for the public's welfare and a preemption of state authority in regulating interstate commerce. The Tenth Amendment allocates all other power and authority, anything not assigned to the federal government by the Constitution, to the states or to individuals. How then has the federal government established a mandatory health insurance program for the elderly, welfare programs for the poor, supplemental food programs for high-risk infants and their mothers, uniform reporting of vital statistics, an occupational safety and health program, control over food and drugs, standards for air quality, a school lunch program, a standard definition for human immunodeficiency virus (HIV) infection, and uniform procedures for testing our milk supplies? Through the use of grants-in-aid. Using the power to raise taxes and the requirement to be concerned about the public's welfare, Congress can raise money that it can then give to the states for specific purposes, provided the states want to carry out those purposes. The President, as the Chief Executive Officer, appoints a Secretary of the Department of Health and Human Services and a Surgeon General of the Public Health Service who organize the divisions and bureaus to administer those laws. Rules are adopted by the agency that further spell out the manner in which the congressional purpose can be achieved. A state or local unit of government or, in some instances, a private organization can apply for funds and, if they agree to adhere to the rules and policies involved, they may receive a grant-in-aid. Grants-in-aid are the instruments used by the President and Congress to circumvent the Tenth Amendment.

In 1913 total expenditures of all levels of government in the United States were a mere $2.8 billion. On the eve of the nation's involvement in World War II in 1941, the figure had risen only to $25 billion. Since 1950, as illustrated in Table 6-4, dramatic increases have occurred in revenues and expenditures at all levels of government. Between 1950 and 1985, for example, overall revenues and expenditures increased 21-fold.

Such figures indicate that the federal, or national, government is the big spender compared to state and local governments. However, it is difficult to estimate total government expenditures accurately because of the amount of intergovernmental transferring that occurs—from the federal government to the state governments and from the states to local governments. In 1985 it was estimated that state and local governments spent $782 billion, of which 14% came from federal grants-in-aid, 78% from their own revenue sources, and the rest from miscellaneous sources and charges. The states spent $269 billion directly plus $122 billion in intergovernmental transfers, mostly to local governments. If Defense Department expenditures and expenditures from the Social Security trust fund are removed from the direct federal expenditure estimate, it is clear that the delivery capacity, in terms of services, is at the state and local level.

The difficulty in estimating expenditures and revenue accurately is apparent when adding the federal, state, and local expenditures for 1985: they total $1.8 trillion, $233 billion more than the "total" in the table and $396 billion more than "total" revenues. This is in part the result of deficit budgeting by the federal government and partly because much of the money "spent" by one level of government is spent again by a lower level after being received as an intergovernmental transfer. The direct expenditures of the three levels in 1985 were $925 billion by the federal government (plus $107 billion in intergovernmental transfers), $269 billion by state governments (plus $122 billion that they transferred to lower levels of government), and $387 billion by local governments.

GRANTS-IN-AID

State and local governments, in the face of increased population, urbanization, demands for public services, and citizen expression, are hampered by an outmoded system of revenue resources. While the states have welcomed significant increases in federal grants-in-aid, they have been tied to the requirements of the federal government, which may not conform to state or local ideas about problems, needs, and priorities. State and local decision-making authority is limited when using federal grants. Beyond this is the difficulty of balanced and long-range planning and financing. Democratic governments find it difficult to plan or budget for more than one year at a time. An additional complaint is the considerable amount of red tape and paper work and the many conferences and reports required for each of the individual grants by each of the federal offices and agencies involved. An important step was finally taken by Congress in passage of the State and Local Financial Assistance Act of 1972. This enabled and required the federal government to share revenue with the states and local jurisdictions. Such shared funds replaced certain of the previously existing categorical grants-in-aid.

There are several different kinds of grants-in-aid. They differ in where authority resides to form policy with regard to the use of the money. *Revenue sharing* places maximum authority with the recipients. During the Nixon administration, state and local governments could use revenue-sharing funds for virtually any purpose that was not in violation of federal civil rights laws: books, nurses, streets, job training, or armored cars. *Block grants* retain some authority over use of the funds for

TABLE 6-4 Revenues and expenditures 1950-1980

Year	Revenues ($ billion)				Expenditures ($ billion)			
	All	Federal	State	Local	All	Federal	State	Local
1950	67	44	11	12	70	42	11	17
1960	153	100	26	27	151	90	22	39
1970	335	206	89	89	333	208	85	93
1980	932	564	277	258	959	617	258	261
1985	1,418	807	439	402	1,581	1,032	391	391

From Bureau of the Census: Statistical abstracts of the United States: 1988, ed 108, Table 431, US Government Printing Office, Dec 1987.

Congress and the administering agency of the federal government. Recipients can use the funds for a wide variety of activities within the broad category specified in the grant authorization: maternal and child health, preventive health services, or mental health, for example. Block grants require more reporting than does revenue sharing, and the array of approved activities may be specified in the law or rules, but the distribution of funds within the block is the responsibility of the state or local agency. *Categorical grants* are the most restricted. They are used for a specific purpose, such as screening for high blood pressure, measles immunization, or rat control. The methods to be used are specified, reporting requirements are usually detailed and extensive, and there is little if any latitude for local decision making. Grants-in-aid can also be awarded as *formula* or *project* grants. Formula grants are noncompetitive. They are allocated to the states in accordance with a formula, usually based on population, sometimes weighted by some other significant variable such as the percentage of people living below poverty level. Project grants are competitive. They are usually authorized as demonstration projects. Interested state or local organizations develop proposals, which are reviewed and evaluated by peers and experts in the area under consideration, and grants are awarded to those with the highest scores.

Grants-in-aid represent a transfer of public funds for the purpose of equalizing revenue among the several levels of government and among the states and their local areas. Some states and communities with high indices of poor health status, such as a high infant mortality rate, are unable or unwilling to allocate tax revenue to needed public health programs. In an effort to equalize access to what can be considered a basic level of public health services, Congress may authorize a grant-in-aid program.

A second reason for grants-in-aid is related to the efficiency of various tax systems. Local government units are more restricted in the types of revenue they can collect and are administratively in a disadvantageous position for levying and collecting taxes. For example, few would deny the right of local governments to share in the fiscal benefits of automobile excise taxes, since local areas must share in the building and maintenance of the roads over which automobiles travel. It would be confusing, however, should each locality attempt to apply and collect its own automobile excise tax. A revenue such as this is obviously collected more efficiently by a higher level of government.

A third purpose of grants-in-aid is to provide some measure of supervision or control over the activities of the lower units of government. Related to this, and arising as a result of it, is a fourth purpose of grants-in-aid: the enforcement of minimum standards on the recipient of the grant. Undoubtedly, few things have been as influential in promoting the employment of qualified local public health personnel, for example, as have been the conditions attached to grants by both state and federal health agencies.

Grants-in-aid were first applied in this country in New York State in 1795 for the improvement of schools in the poorer, particularly rural, areas of that state. Federal grants to states began as early as 1808, when Congress instituted an annual appropriation to assist the states in the development of their respective militias. No conditions were attached to these grants, and no federal supervision was exercised. Perhaps the next development of significance was the passage in 1862 of the Morrill Act, which entitled each state to a grant of public lands based on the total number of its members of Congress. The only condition was that not less than 90% of the gross proceeds was to be used for the establishment and maintenance of agricultural and mechanical colleges. Subsequent acts added to the original provisions an annual grant of cash to each state. In 1887 the Hatch Act was passed, which provided $15,000 per year to each state for the establishment of agricultural experiment stations. With this act was instituted the condition that an annual financial report be submitted, and 8 years later provision was made for a federal audit. This established a pattern that has never since been altered.

The rising tide of federal influence in state and local affairs is well illustrated by its involvement in welfare. Originally, the care of the poor in America was a local and often a private affair. The economic depression of the 1930s changed all that when, because of lack of funds, first private charity, then local governments, and in turn state governments found themselves incapable of meeting the tremendously increased demands. Only one other source of assistance remained—the national government—largely because of its power to borrow money and adopt an out-of-balance budget. As a result, numerous federal agencies were established that for the first time provided the basis for a broad system of federal welfare programs. These agencies concerned themselves with dependent children, the unemployed, the handicapped, and the aged.

The changes that have occurred in the relationship between the federal and state governments have also resulted in some change in the relationships between state and local governments and between local and federal governments. Theoretically the national government has no relations with cities. However, even antedating the Depression, closer contacts between national and municipal authorities had been developing. Federal agencies had developed standards in weights and measures, traffic and safety, zoning and building, highway construction, and milk sanitation and had carried out studies and surveys on local education, finances, crime, vital statistics, and public health. In addition, federal agencies were actively engaged in a cooperative sense in food and drug control, municipal water supplies, sewage disposal, and other fields. The economic depression of the 1930s and subsequently World War II accelerated the intimacies of these relationships. Although the federal agencies operated for the most part through the state governments as intermediaries, in some instances they dealt directly with cities.

As has been noted previously, big-city mayors, the U.S. Conference of Mayors, the Urban League, and other organizations brought city and nationally elected and administrative officials into increasingly close contact. When the national government built and staffed regional offices, they were located in the nation's large cities: New York, Boston, Atlanta, Kansas City, Chicago, Dallas, Denver, San Francisco, and Philadelphia. This brought the federal program managers, who often made grant decisions, into much more intimate contact with the urban officials who wanted the money and had the organizations needed to implement the programs. The power of the states was not usurped, but the state legislatures, long dominated by more rural interests, were simply bypassed as city and federal officials found that they had more in common. The state scarcely noticed or cared. In 1965 Congress established the new federal Department of Housing and Urban Development, and federal involvement in the nation's cities became still more pervasive. With a well-trodden path to Washington rather than to their state capitals, the cities were not prepared for the new federalism coupled with the severe budget cuts of the Reagan administration. From an administrative point of view, it makes sense for the federal government to deal directly and exclusively with the 50 states, especially with massive reductions in the personnel necessary to administer hundreds of grants. Similarly, it makes sense for the states to work with their administrative subdivisions, the counties. The new federalism of the 1980s promised not only major reductions in social programs at all levels, but major changes in the political relationships among the three levels of government.

The great increase in the numbers and types of grant-in-aid programs in health over the past four decades has created serious problems of manageability. The 89th Congress alone passed acts that created 21 new health programs, 17 new educational programs, 15 new economic development programs, 12 new programs for cities, 17 new resource development programs, and 4 new manpower programs. Until 1981 nearly 200 different federal aid programs existed, financed by over 500 separate appropriations, 21 federal departments, 150 Washington bureaus, and 400 regional offices. Funds for programs were channeled in different patterns under a variety of rules and regulations.

The Reagan administration forced a consolidation of categorical grants into four block grants in 1981: a general preventive health services block grant; an alcohol, drug abuse, and mental health block grant; a maternal and child health block grant; and a primary care block grant to encompass federal programs in support of community health centers. The process was remarkable. Under the 1974 Budget Act, Congress found itself forced to vote on a total figure for major areas such as health and then to reconcile the statutes that authorized programs and expenditures with the budget ceiling. In 5 short weeks in the fall of 1981, Congress rewrote most of the public health laws developed over the prior 45 years (The Omnibus Budget Reconciliation Act, P.L. 97-35) and reduced the authorizations substantially. When it came time to appropriate money, the programs were cut even further. The states, through the National Governor's Association, supported the block grant concept even though it was apparent that there would be much less money available for local programs. Few of them realized just how severe the cuts would be. The administration compared the 1982 spending levels and their 1983 proposals with 1981 expenditures. That, however, failed to account for inflation. The appropriation in terms of services was more sharply curtailed than the appropriation of dollars.

An added feature would come back to haunt the states in their quest for less federal supervision. While the Reagan administration truly wanted to return control to the states, budget cutting was an even higher priority. Program and planning concepts were jettisoned in congressional–White House negotiating sessions in favor of maintaining the targeted cuts. When the lobbyists for some of the categorical programs approached the budget committee staff members, they were asked to refrain from protesting the block grant move and the cuts since the cuts were sure to be made. In exchange they were often offered language that specified that "no less than the amount of money spent in the prior year shall be spent for disease X or program Y." When the hearings were held, the strongest advocacy groups were thus neutralized and only the weaker ones protested the new block grants with the smaller dollar amounts. When the states finally got the grants, they found the restrictions virtually intact and much less money with which to work. Not only that, but alternative sources had also dried up. In prior years for example, if the appropriation of funds to support community mental health centers was not up to the expectations of the center directors, the directors had learned to bill Medicaid more vigorously and bargain for a larger share of the state's Title XX money for social services. But this time all the appropriations were cut, and virtually all public health programs in the United States were faced with sharp reductions at the very time when the people who needed their services most were losing their jobs and other sources of support.

Block grants do offer the recipients the opportunity to become more creative and to tailor their programs to their problems and the expectations of their communities. But two essential features of a successful block grant program were ignored: restrictions on how the money is to be used have to be minimized, and the funds must be great enough so that all of the grant managers, thrown together in the same box, can at least start out with the assurance that their rent is paid and their doors can stay open.

Since then, the congressional budget process has become even more confusing. The funds available for public health services in the states have diminished in their purchasing power, and not many states have been able or willing to replace the lost federal funds. As will be discussed in Chapters 23 and 31, other federal changes have been adopted that may begin to offset these problems in the years ahead if the states are willing to use new federal laws and regulations creatively.

The relationships and roles of the federal, state, and local governments in the United States have changed considerably since the first local health departments and state agencies were formed. The changes have not been consistent: they have reflected not only changing technology and mores, but the different political philosophies of presidents, from Roosevelt and Truman through the Eisenhower era to the Kennedy-Johnson years, and then the succession of changes during the Nixon, Ford, Carter, and Reagan years. These changes have, of course, altered the structure of public health. They have also altered its functions and the roles of the state and local governments. These changing roles are the subject of Chapter 7.

REFERENCES

1. Snider C: American state and local government, New York, 1965, Appleton-Century-Crofts.
2. Institute of Medicine: The future of public health, Washington, DC, 1988, National Academy Press.
3. Brogan DW: The American character, New York, 1944, Alfred A Knopf, Inc.
4. Wright DS and Dometrius N: State administrators: their changing characteristics, State Government 50: Summer 1977.
5. US Bureau of the Census: Government units in 1987, Preliminary report No 1, 1987, Census of Governments.
6. Mullan F and Smith J: Characteristics of state and local health agencies, mimeographed paper, Baltimore, MD, 1988, Johns Hopkins University School of Hygiene and Public Health.

7. DeFriese GH and others: The program implications of administrative relationships between local health departments and state and local government, Am J Public Health 71:1109, Oct 1981.
8. Public Health Foundation: Public health agencies, 1987: expenditures and sources of funds, Washington, DC, 1987, The Foundation.
9. Clarke GJ: The role of the states in the delivery of health services, Am J Public Health 71(suppl):59, Jan 1981.
10. Public Health Foundation: Public health agencies, 1988: an inventory of programs and block grant expenditures, Washington, DC, 1988, The Foundation.
11. Gilbert B, Moos M-K, and Miller CA: State level decision making for public health—the status of boards of health, J Public Health Policy 3:51, March 1982.
12. National Conference of State Legislatures: Major health issues for the states: 1987, 1987, The Conference.
13. Public Health Foundation: Public health agencies, 1981: a report on their expenditures and activities, Washington, DC, 1983, The Foundation.

CHAPTER 7

The functions of public health in the United States

Prevention is not the sole property of the public health system, any more than education is the sole property of the public school system. Prevention and education are functions of multiple forces in the lives of people: family, friends, jobs, social policy, and advertising, as well as the public systems organized expressly for the purposes of preventing disease and injury and educating people. Again like the educational system, public health, which is charged with the mission of preventing disease and injury and the dependency caused by them, has a varied structure in the United States—even more so, perhaps, than the educational system.

To summarize points made in the last chapter, the states are the central force in organized public health in the U.S. system of government. The federal role evolved slowly, from preventing the importation of communicable diseases to a complex array of functions including research, health status assessment, education, technical assistance to the states, the prevention of occupational illnesses and injuries, payment systems for medical care for the elderly and the poor, protection of the environment, and the prevention of communicable diseases. The national government has virtually no direct delivery system for public health services. (The exceptions are the health services provided in federal prisons and for Native Americans by the Public Health Service; the Veterans Administration's medical care system; and the health care programs of the armed forces.) Most of the public health policies of the federal government are exercised through the use of grants-in-aid to the states and local communities. To the extent that there is an operating consensus on health policy, it is achieved by voluntary participation of the states and the use of federal grants.

The states use one of two structures for public health: an umbrella agency for health and social services or a "stand-alone" public health agency. They use a mixture of approaches for delivering public health services. Most have a number of local public health agencies, which are part of municipal or county government. In larger, more populous areas, the local health departments are the primary delivery vehicle for public health services. In less populous areas, the state agency is often a direct provider of services, usually using a district office staff group supplemented by technical and programmatic consultants from the central office.

The expenditures and programs of the state health agencies can be described with a reasonable degree of specificity and accuracy, primarily through use of the National Public Health Program Reporting System developed by the Association of State and Territorial Health Officials and managed by the Public Health Foundation in Washington. The state health agencies spend about $10 billion annually. The Public Health Foundation has estimated local health department expenditures at about $3 billion, certainly an underestimate. While the reporting system is reasonably accurate, it describes only the activities of the official state health agency. Most of the programs and expenditures of the state Medicaid agency,* the state mental health authority, and the growing number of state environmental protection agencies are not included in the system. These unincluded expen-

* Medicaid is a federal grant-in-aid program that provides matching funds to participating states to reimburse eligible health care providers for the services they provide to identifiable welfare recipients. All 50 states have developed Medicaid programs. In most states, these programs are administered by the state welfare agency, not the state health department. They do not provide services but are referred to as "vendor payment programs."

ditures dwarf the expendituresof the official public health agencies. Furthermore, as already stated, public health is much more than the work of the official state and local public health agencies: it includes extensive public sector programs as well as the millions of day-to-day decisions made privately by individuals and corporations.

The organizational structure of public health—its form—intimately reflects the structure of government in the United States.

THE GOVERNMENTAL PRESENCE IN HEALTH

In 1979 a group of public health leaders completed work on *Model Standards: A Guide for Community Preventive Health Services.*[1] The publication included the concept of "a governmental presence at the local level." "Government," according to the concept, "—whether at the local or the State level—is responsible for ensuring that standards are met in every community." The agency actually responsible for some aspect of public health might not be the official public health agency, but public health is responsible for ensuring that necessary, agreed-upon services are available, accessible, acceptable, and of good quality in every community. Community "implies an entity for which both the nature and scope of a public health problem, as well as the capacity to respond to that problem, can be defined." The community differs from problem to problem, covering multiple jurisdictions for hazardous waste management, for example, and a single county or school district for a health program for adolescents. The concept of a "presence" in public health is unusual in the organization of public affairs, and it is important.

Presence, as discussed in the introduction to Part Two of this book, has two meanings: (1) being present in a place and (2) the whole quality of that presence. A person or a piano or a voice can be present without having presence: it may not have the often ineffable qualities that command attention and respect. The concept of a governmental presence in health in every community embodies both meanings: it must be present and it should have presence. The former can be guaranteed; the latter cannot.

Most functional organizations can be typified by the work that they do. The educational system teaches, the highway department builds roads, the police department enforces the laws. They are also characterized by their discipline or training. The school system, for example, includes bus drivers, cooks, administrators, and computer programmers, but its dominant discipline is education—the teacher. All the other disciplines and skills are intended to support that one discipline. Highway departments hire lawyers, chemists, accountants, architects, and clerks, but at their core they have engineers. Law enforcement has police. Libraries have librarians. The dominant discipline of an organization, and the social and cultural mores of that discipline, characterize the organization. They provide the image that the public understands. An orchestra includes many different instruments, but the players are all musicians. They all know rhythm, tone, pitch, and scale. If they studied formally, they studied music and went to the same sorts of schools. They share many common interests, including their interest in the economics of their business. Public health is different.

There is no modal or dominant discipline in public health, nor have its workers attended the same schools. Public health includes physicians, nurses, sanitarians, engineers, lawyers, health educators, epidemiologists, laboratory technicians, chemists, sociologists, administrators, accountants, computer programmers, statisticians, physicists, meteorologists (yes! in air pollution control programs), and veterinarians. Only about 3% to 5% of the professional personnel in a health department attended a school of public health, and if they did, they usually studied in different departments. They do not share a common background or a common educational system. What they do have in common is a commitment to an outcome: the prevention of the dependency associated with disease and injury. And that is most unusual.

Usually, people who associate with one another share a common input (their skill or their culture), not a common output (like an immunization) or outcome (the prevention of something). Yet the activities and skills of public health cohere around an outcome, an outcome that is often intangible: something that did not happen. Those outcomes are attained by a wide variety of professional skills and disciplines: the law, chemistry, engineering, medicine, education, nursing, and many, many more. This fundamental feature of public health—that it obtains its cohering force, its glue, through its intended outcomes—makes it a unique endeavor. Not better, not more important than other endeavors, but unique.

The work of public health is not just interdisciplinary, it is interorganizational as well. Most agencies of government can accomplish their tasks with the skills and resources available to them. The highway department does not need to work with agriculture or education or public health to build roads. Education does not need to work with the state police or welfare to manage its mission. Public health, however, cannot accomplish its most important objectives without the cooperation of other agencies and organizations, both public and private. To cope with the AIDS epidemic, public health needs the collaboration of education, welfare, Medicaid, and mental health. To ensure that an adequate long-term care program is available to the growing numbers of elderly people, the governmental presence in health must be able to use the resources of welfare, the Medicaid agency, and mental health, as well as work with transportation organizations and local officials who are responsible for housing programs and the removal of access barriers. The medical care needs of the poor cannot be met by the public health agency alone: by its "presence" it must ensure that local physicians and hospitals will do their part, that the state welfare and Medicaid agencies will provide the money and services needed, and that the local community mental health center has the professional skills and commitment to provide the support needed. A toxic chemical spill cannot be dealt with by public health without the planned and coordinated involvement of law enforcement agencies, fire protection personnel, and often a state environmental response team, not to mention a federal network that facilitates rapid identification of the chemical. For public health to accomplish the tasks assigned to it, it must use its presence effectively to obtain both the internal collaboration of a wide variety of disciplines and the external involvement of many other agencies and organizations.

These two features of public health—its unique cohering force and its dependency on the resources and skills of other agencies—make its leadership and management an especially difficult task. While many communities and states have developed special coordinating groups and often appoint ad hoc task forces to deal with important and urgent problems, no state has effectively developed and implemented a system of management that facilitates transagency program planning. In most states, the public health agency has a difficult time obtaining support from the state Medicaid agency for family planning, prenatal care services, and assistance for AIDS patients. State environmental protection agencies have not been able to work effectively with environmental epidemiologists in their companion public health departments. Most states have approached the problems of obtaining medical care for the medically indigent* as a financing problem. Public health, which has experience in organizing health services delivery programs, is not usually involved in these discussions.

In Chapter 6, a list of major health issues developed by the National Conference of State Legislatures[2] was presented. It included

- Care of the medically indigent
- Malpractice
- Certificates of need for new health facilities and programs
- Long-term care and Alzheimer's disease
- Medicaid and other medical assistance programs
- Professional licensure
- Organ transplants and donations
- AIDS
- Health insurance
- State employee health plans
- Hospitals

These are not problems that can be attacked by a single state agency. They require negotiation, conflict resolution, policy analysis, and detailed planning. And the mechanisms to assure that these can be done on an ongoing basis are not available, either in government or in the private sector. The subject will arise again in Chapter 10. The unfortunate fact is that the future requires multiagency policy analysis, planning, and resource allocation, and the techniques to accomplish these have either not been invented or not been applied in the public sector, even on an experimental basis. This is one of

* The medically indigent are those who are not eligible for regular welfare payments (Aid to Families with Dependent Children, for example), which would automatically make them eligible for Medicaid support, but do not have enough money to pay for needed medical care. Their ineligibility is usually based on their "categorization" (an adult with no children, for example) or on their income or other assets.

the most important tasks for public health in the years ahead.

Its unique nature creates another problem for public health. Most public agencies are concerned about their "constituency"—their users and beneficiaries. They cultivate their support: farmers for the agriculture department, automobile clubs and truckers for the highway department, readers for the library. Public health's constituents are too diverse for such courting, and their fondness for the enterprise is variable, to say the least. Funeral directors know the public health department as the place they have to go to get a burial permit, and they judge the efficacy of the agency by the speed of that process and the availability of parking. Restaurant owners know it as the inspector. The poor know it as a place they have to go for health care (in some, but not all, communities). Parents know it as the place their daughters may be going for contraceptives. Hospital administrators may know it as the organization that tries to keep their rates down and prevent them from acquiring new equipment and space. Physicians may know it as the agency that badgers them to report communicable diseases and exhorts them to provide obstetrical services for yet more low-income, possibly high-risk, pregnant women. The skills needed to build a supportive constituency in such an environment are not just lacking in health departments; they have not been developed.

What is a health department?

In Chapter 6 it was stated that there are 3,233 local health departments in the United States, but no one really knows how many there are. It is a semantic problem. Universities count students in two ways: the number of people enrolled and the number of full-time equivalents, or FTEs. The FTE count is always lower than the enrollment count. Even a count of FTEs is not terribly useful unless you know the definition of a full-time student. For purposes of claiming federal support, which in some instances is based on an FTE count, schools define a full-time student as anyone taking 8 or more credit hours. When it comes to allocating resources to departments, however, the school may use 15 credit hours to define a full-time student. There may be 3,233 local health departments in the United States, but how many "FTEs" are there? What does it take to be a health department besides being present?

Many states require every county to have a health department. The departments are required to carry out specified state programs. Usually they are provided with some state money, which may be allocated on the simple basis of their presence or in proportion to population or in some relationship to the amount of local government expenditures. States often require that certain kinds of personnel be employed by the health department or appointed to positions in public health by the local elected officials or their board of health. A physician is commonly required, who may also serve as the health officer or chief executive officer of the department. In a county with 5,000 people, however, this is rarely possible. There may be only two or three physicians in the county, all of whom are fully occupied taking care of their patients. Moreover, if one were available, a county of 5,000 people could scarcely afford the salary, since it also has to have a sheriff and a sanitarian and a county clerk, as well as a few other employees. So the physician in such communities is part-time at best and often serves with no salary at all—perhaps the personal physician of a county judge or supervisor. There is usually a sanitarian, a nurse, and a clerk. The clerk is often the *de facto* administrator of the department. While this is a common situation, no one currently knows just how common it is. Is that a health department? It is present, but does it have presence? Can it ensure that standards for public health are met in the community? What does it take to have an FTE health department? The answer depends, in part, on what the standards are; on what is expected of a health department.

The Association of State and Territorial Health Officials[3] defines a local health department as

> an official (governmental) public health agency which is in whole or in part responsible to a substate governmental entity or entities. . . . A Local Health Department must meet these criteria:
> 1. It has a staff of one or more full-time professional public health employees.
> 2. It delivers public health services.
> 3. It serves a definable geographic area.
> 4. It has identifiable expenditures and/or budget in the political subdivision(s) which it serves.

This is a minimalist definition of a local health department. It is similar to describing an orchestra as a group of one or more musicians with the ability to play a tune.

A health department with presence has to have an infrastructure that, when overlaid with sufficient resources, can ensure the provision of basic public health services. The infrastructure of a local health department is directed by the health officer who is the governmental presence in health in that community—someone with the executive ability, responsibility, and authority to determine and implement health policy. The infrastructure includes the knowledge, skills, and support systems needed to:

1. Maintain an ongoing system for monitoring and analysis of community health status and services
2. Assure the use of appropriate and necessary public health knowledge and technology in all aspects of agency operations (including knowledge of the biological, physical, and chemical determinants of disease)
3. Inform and assist the community in appropriate actions necessary to promote health and prevent disease and injury
4. Assure efficient allocation and management of and appropriate accounting for the resources available to the agency
5. Incorporate the functions, knowledge, and expertise of the public health agency into an ongoing community health planning process

The infrastructure is not a tangible organizational unit. It is the core of the agency, its nerve system, its presence. It constitutes the ability of the agency to set objectives, to monitor progress, and to make decisions, based on feedback and knowledge—decisions that may serve to change the direction or the methods used by the agency to achieve its objectives.

By itself, the infrastructure is similar to a health department as described by David Sencer (see below), but it has little capacity to deliver required and needed services: immunizations, treatment and contact tracing for sexually transmitted diseases, prenatal care, food protection, and others. The additional resources needed to carry out the tasks assigned to the agency in its community, together with the infrastructure, constitute a functioning health department.

This definition appears to offer a better description of a health department, but it has not been used to count or classify local health departments.

The functions of public health

Periodically, the American Public Health Association (APHA) has issued official policy statements regarding the responsibilities and services of local health departments. In its most recent statement (1974)[4] the Association emphasized that the fundamental responsibilities are (1) to determine the health status and needs of the people in its jurisdiction, (2) to determine the extent to which these needs are being met by effective measures currently available, and (3) to take steps to see that the unmet needs are satisfied. It also emphasized the role of the local health department in social planning, especially in the areas of medical care, regional planning for health services, effective use of existing resources, and efficient delivery of traditional services. It noted that

> changes in demand for both health services and delivery techniques are requiring health agencies to modify their programs. . . . These changes will have a great impact on program organization and financing. . . . Thus it is likely that existing programs and existing ways of doing business within many health agencies will be put in new organizational, institutional and personnel settings.

It then forecast that

> how local agencies adjust to these changes and how aggressive they become in terms of moving ahead with comprehensive health services for their constituent populations within this context, will to a large degree determine the future of public support for health programs.

This was essentially the theme of the National Commission on Community Health Services[5,6] in the late 1960s, that in the years ahead each community would have to make maximum collaborative use of all of its health-related resources, regardless of formal organizational or other distinctions.

APHA's policy statement lists the following functional areas "to indicate the scope of the obligation of local government to see that these services are provided either by its own official health agencies, or by direct arrangement with other agencies, institutions, or providers":

I. Community Health Services
   A. Communicable disease control
   B. Chronic disease control and medical rehabilitation
   C. Family health, including prenatal, well child, crippled children, school health, and family planning
   D. Dental health
   E. Substance abuse
   F. Accident prevention
   G. Nutrition services and education
II. Environmental Health Services
   A. Food protection
   B. Hazardous substances and product safety
   C. Water supply sanitation
   D. Liquid waste control
   E. Water pollution control
   F. Swimming pool sanitation and safety
   G. Occupational health and safety
   H. Radiation control
   I. Air quality management
   J. Noise pollution control
   K. Vector control
   L. Solid waste management
   M. Institutional sanitation
   N. Recreational sanitation
   O. Housing conservation and rehabilitation
   P. Environmental injury prevention
III. Mental Health Services
   A. Primary prevention of mental disorders
   B. Consultation to community resources
   C. Diagnostic and treatment services
      1. Outpatient
      2. Emergency
      3. Short-term hospitalization
      4. Day care and night care services
      5. Aftercare services
      6. Diagnostic and evaluation services for the mentally retarded
IV. Personal Health Services
   A. Personal health services per se
   B. Health facilities operations
   C. Emergency medical services
   D. Home health services
   E. Employee health programs
   F. Medical care for inmates of prisons and institutions
V. Processes Common to all Services
   A. Health data acquisition and processing
   B. Agency program planning
   C. Interagency planning
   D. Comprehensive state and regional health planning participation
   E. Disaster planning
   F. Health education of the public
   G. Health advocacy
   H. Continuing education of health personnel
   I. Involvement of nonagency health personnel
   J. Research and development
   K. Community involvement
   L. Organization of the health agency
   M. Policy direction of the health agency
   N. Staffing
   O. Financing
   P. Relationships with state and federal health authorities

Multi-interest-group participation in developing the policy statement is evident in the list. The number of environmental health services far exceeds the number of mental health services, and the management functions are emphasized.* There are some services that a particular community might not choose to adopt, and other communities might add to the list. The list represents more than an ideal—it is a professional goal that has been approximated by a number of local health departments. In this statement, as in the later *Model Standards* statement about the governmental presence, it is not necessary that all the services be provided by the health agency itself, but it is the responsibility of the health department to ensure that the services are available to everyone in the community.

There are other descriptions of what public health should be doing. A less detailed but possibly more useful description emerged from the Sun Valley Conference held in 1983 at which the roles of state and local government in health were discussed.[7] The conferees proposed the following:

1. Health departments should provide the services needed to detect and prevent serious health problems through such programs as prenatal care, selected screening programs,

* The original policy statement was developed by what was at that time known as the Health Officers section of APHA. Other sections (including Medical Care and Health Planning) protested that the Health Officers should not be allowed to develop such an important policy statement on their own, and, over a 2-year period, representatives of several sections worked on the statement.

and experimentation with new approaches to the primary prevention of disease.

2. Given the impact of socioeconomic variables on health status, health departments should work with other agencies of state and local government to assure that these variables are addressed in a coordinated and effective manner.
3. Health departments should place a high priority on the assurance of adequate access to needed medical care services for those whose access is impeded.
4. Health departments should try to discontinue obsolete services and transfer others to more appropriate agencies of government. There will exist a residue of miscellaneous services, which may not be of high priority in the eyes of public health professionals but which the people of the community want. These services must be performed efficiently.
5. Health departments should reduce the exposure of their communities to hazards by preventing hazardous situations from occurring, by correcting those that do, and by educating and informing the public.
6. Health departments should be heavily engaged in the monitoring of health status in the community.
7. Health departments should protect the community by assessing the quality of health services and finding new ways to measure quality.
8. Health departments should act as catalysts to develop needed personal health services in the community.

These are similar to the functions described above as part of the infrastructure of a health department. They are functions that must be jointly developed and performed by state and local health departments.

Not everyone agrees with this description of the role of health departments, of course. Historically, the role of local health departments has been more narrowly prescribed. They were originally limited to sanitation and the control of communicable diseases. David Sencer,[8] a former director of the Centers for Disease Control, suggested a narrow role for urban health departments when he was Commissioner of Health for New York City in 1983. "Ideally," said Sencer, "an urban health department should offer its community skeleton service and surveillance." Sencer saw the health department as the critic of health status and health systems and as a catalyst for change through the power of its observations and its leadership and negotiating skills. Stripped of all save the most essential direct service responsibilities, the health department could move quickly through the underbrush of hazards, stimulating the development of needed services, forcing improvements in existing programs, assessing, monitoring, motivating, and punishing. If encumbered with a heavy service delivery obligation, the health department would become sluggish and a defender of the status quo. This is a very attractive role but not one that can survive the politics of community life. The community will insist upon certain health services. If the health department does not provide them, another agency of government will, or a new agency will be created. What is the role of the epidemiologist-critic then? How long will the body politic condone such a role? Agencies delivering lots of services attract the attention of the community and its elected leaders, and an agency that only criticizes and plans is destined for an early sunset. Both roles are needed. They are not easily combined in a single agency. Yet the work of government is rarely simple, neat, and fast.

Arden Miller,[9] in a speech at the 1984 annual meeting of the American Public Health Association, discussed some emerging themes, which he proposed be added to the agenda of the Sun Valley Conference. Miller felt that health departments should evaluate the work of new prospective payment plans for health services, such as health maintenance organizations. They should act as casefinders and as advocates and brokers for the poor. They should supplement the work of private providers in order to assure adequate care for multiproblem families. And, said Miller, they should continue to be the provider of last resort for those families and groups of people who cannot otherwise gain access to the medical care delivery system.

The *Model Standards* document referred to earlier contains a detailed list of preventive health services that the authors felt should be available in every community. While they may not be provided by the health department, their assurance is the responsibility of the governmental presence in health, provided that the service is, in some manner, incorporated into the public health policy framework of that community. The list is virtually identical to that of the American Public Health Association, adopted in 1974.[4]

In 1986 the Institute of Medicine*[10] launched an ambitious effort to chart the future of public health in the United States. The study was undertaken, according to the published report,

> to address a growing perception among the Institute of Medicine membership and others concerned with the health of the public that this nation has lost sight of its public health goals and has allowed the system of public health activities to fall into disarray.

As described in Chapter 6, the committee that carried out the study concluded that the states were and should be the central force in public health; that they bore "primary responsibility for public health." The core functions of public health, according to the committee, are assessment, policy development, and assurance, which were further described as follows:

> *Assessment:*
> Every public health agency, regularly and systematically, should ". . . collect, assemble and analyze, and make available information on the health of the community, including statistics on health status, community health needs, and epidemiologic and other studies of health problems. Not every agency is large enough to conduct these activities directly; intergovernmental and interagency cooperation is essential. Nevertheless each agency bears the responsibility for seeing that the assessment function is fulfilled. This basic function of public health cannot be delegated."
>
> *Policy development:*
> Every public health agency should, ". . . exercise its responsibility to serve the public interest in the development of comprehensive public health policies by promoting use of the scientific knowledge base in decision-making about public health and by leading in developing public health policy. Agencies must take a strategic approach, developed on the basis of a positive appreciation for the democratic political process."
>
> *Assurance:*
> Public health agencies should, ". . . assure their constituents that services necessary to achieve agreed upon goals are provided, either by encouraging actions by other entities (private or public sector), by requiring such action through regulation, or by providing services directly." Each public health agency should involve key policymakers and the general public in determining a set of high-priority personal and community-wide health services that governments will guarantee to every member of the community. This guarantee should include subsidization of direct provision of high-priority personal health services for those unable to afford them.

The committee developed new distinctions between assuring and guaranteeing. Many services should be assured; only a subset are so important that their availability to every member of the community should be guaranteed by government. The roles assigned to each level of government by the institute were as follows:

The states:

- Assessment of health needs in the state based on statewide data collection
- Assurance of an adequate statutory base for health activities in the state
- Establishment of statewide health objectives, delegating power to localities as appropriate and holding them accountable
- Assurance of appropriate organized statewide effort to develop and maintain essential personal, educational, and environmental health services; provision of access to necessary services; and solution of problems inimical to health
- Guarantee of a minimum set of essential health services
- Support of local service capacity, especially when disparities in local ability to raise revenue and/or administer programs require subsidies, technical assistance, or direct action by the state to achieve adequate service levels

The federal government:

- Support of knowledge development and dissemination through data gathering, research, and information exchange
- Establishment of nationwide health objectives and priorities, and stimulation of debate on interstate and national public health issues
- Provision of technical assistance to help states and localities determine their own objectives, and to carry out action on national and regional objectives

* The Institute of Medicine (IOM) was chartered in 1970 by the National Academy of Sciences, which was itself chartered by Congress in 1863. The IOM examines policy matters affecting the health of the public.

- Provision of funds to states to strengthen state capacity for services, especially to achieve an adequate minimum capacity, and to achieve national objectives
- Assurance of actions and services that are in the public interest of the entire nation such as control of AIDS and similar communicable diseases, interstate environmental actions, and food and drug inspection

Localities:

- Assessment, monitoring and surveillance of local health problems and needs and of resources for dealing with them
- Policy development and leadership that fosters local needs, and that advocates equitable distribution of public resources and complementary private activities commensurate with community needs
- Assurance that high quality services, including personal health services, needed for the protection of public health in the community are available and accessible to all persons; that the community receives proper consideration in the allocation of federal, state, and local resources for public health, and that the community is informed about how to obtain public health, including personal health services, or how to comply with public health requirements

The committee was correct in asserting that the states were the lead agencies in public health, certainly in the 1980s and for the foreseeable future. While not recommending the formation of umbrella agencies, the committee urged the development of new state health agencies that would bring together all of the clearly health-related aspects of state government: Medicaid, mental health, environmental health, and public health. Umbrella agencies had "gone too far in many states," according to the committee, including even income maintenance activities, which cast a pejorative welfare label over the functions of the health agency. Yet, as pointed out before, the Constitution speaks of the common "welfare," not public health. It is a noble term, turned into a derogatory epithet by those who do not or will not understand the problem or the programs. Moreover, public health is extensively involved in a major income transfer program, similar to the food stamp program—the Supplemental Nutrition Program for Women, Infants, and Children—a $1.6 billion effort.

While desirable for many reasons, it is unlikely that the states will combine, or recombine, mental health, environmental health, and Medicaid in a single state health department. They were split apart for what the states felt to be very good reasons. Moreover, the Medicaid program is as much a welfare program as are food stamps and Aid to Families with Dependent Children. Many public health professionals, and apparently some of the IOM study committee members, have complained about the lack of health programming by state Medicaid agencies on the one hand and, on the other, about the potential for burying public health functions in the much larger and contentious Medicaid program.

The report decries the instability of public health, pointing out that there is excessive turnover in state health directors and urging that they be appointed to fixed terms of office, overlapping those of their governors, in order to provide for greater continuity and consistency.

The problems identified are accurately portrayed. The proposed solutions are often naive. Congress, the President, state legislatures, and governors must have the means to debate and shape policy, in public health as in defense and education. They will continue to reorganize agencies and appoint administrators who will be their "presence," not someone else's. The future of public health depends not on its ability to insulate itself by statute from the political world around it, but on the development and use of new skills in transagency planning, constituency building, and negotiation.

State-local relationships

The relationships of state public health agencies to local departments of health present a variegated picture. The simple classification scheme described in Chapter 6 (centralized, decentralized, shared, and mixed) does not convey the tension that often exists and the patterns that are emerging. Some states make no provision for the operation of local health departments. Others require that every county have a public health department. It is clear that the responsibility for protecting the public's health is the state's. The state can meet its responsibilities directly, or it can support or even require the formation of local public health agencies. Local health departments represent two different notions at work: the belief that the most proximate form of government is the most effective and possibly the most efficient, and the pragmatic judgment that the state needs a decentralized delivery system to produce the services needed. The two reasons are sometimes confused when considering how or why the state should support the operations of local health departments.

In several states (New York and California, for example) local health departments are vigorously autonomous. A substantial amount of state money is allocated to support local departments, and both history and statutes operate to maintain well-staffed and independent local agencies. Attempts by the state to set policy are resisted. State associations of local health officers play a major role in developing health policies and programs. In other states, the local health departments, all except the largest, are heavily dependent on the state agency, not only for money but for policy formation and direction, as well as technical assistance. In these states, the local health departments exist less because of general support for local government than as the only practical means to deliver services. Lacking legislative support to build a large agency with district offices and an expanding work force, local agencies, even inefficient and ineffective ones, may be the only way to meet the state's responsibilities.

As will be shown below and in subsequent chapters, local governments do not always cherish their health departments. Beginning in the 1940s, federally mandated merit systems of employment largely did away with political patronage and removed the hiring role from elected officials. Federal grants-in-aid (see Chapter 6) provided a growing proportion of the money needed to run programs and included an increasingly wide array of requirements and restrictions for such programs. With policy formation and program management removed to higher levels of government, increasing requirements and expectations for services, diminished control over the financing of public health programs, and little or no opportunity to determine who would be employed, local elected officials began to see public health programs as someone else's responsibility. In many states, the county commissioners necessarily are more concerned with law enforcement, the county jail, and water and sewage systems than with public health—something that is controlled by the state and federal government anyway.

Then, too, the cost of public health services seems to keep going up at an uncontrollable rate. The growing number of people without adequate health insurance, the escalating problem of providing services to AIDS patients and preventing the spread of the disease, hazardous waste disposal, and the rising cost of providing prenatal care and delivery services to the growing number of women who cannot obtain private care all loom large in a county budget supported by property taxes. In some counties, the cost of a single hospitalization for a seriously ill or injured child exceeds the entire general fund budget of the county for the year. The phenomena that fuel the problems and drive the prices up seem beyond the reach of locally elected officials: they—the phenomena—are operating in the state capitol and in Washington. Many local officials are inclined to think that the programs should not only be supported by Washington and the state but should be run by them as well.

In an increasing number of states, this pattern is becoming more evident: rising expectations, increasing costs, tougher competition for local tax revenues, the growing complexity of public health problems, rapidly emerging technology, a need for interagency responses to solve problems, and a growing frustration at the local level at the inability to establish control over forces that are affecting the public's health. The result is increasing disenchantment with the ownership and operation of local health departments and increasing dependency on state agencies. Moreover, it is easier to complain about the inadequacies of the state health department than your own.

The states appear to be changing their organizational structures to reflect these trends. Where they exist, local public health agencies are being supported as necessary delivery systems for labor-intensive routine work such as childhood immunizations, restaurant inspections, and the operation of clinics. States are beginning to use their own staff to provide more complex services or are developing contractual relationships with a wide array of agencies to provide those services for which a private sector delivery system exists: obstetrical services, home health care, solid waste management, health care for the medically indigent, and AIDS treatment.

Many large and well-managed local health departments will continue to serve as major service providers in their communities, providing both state mandated services and locally developed programs. They will receive a substantial amount of state support for such roles as well as direct federal grants. But many of the smaller local health departments will no doubt relinquish their authority to state agencies in the years ahead, carrying out delegated tasks according to state protocols, often side by side with private, not-for-profit agencies and even some proprietary agencies. The result, of course, will be less local involvement in health policy formation and reduced local support for public health. That this need not be a step backward can be seen in Florida, where a state-run system has shown itself capable of producing an effective, well-staffed delivery system for public health with good local support.

THE SHIFTING LOCUS OF POLICY FORMATION

Grants-in-aid were described in Chapter 6 as a device used to circumvent the Tenth Amendment. The process has varied over time, as a succession of Presidents and Congresses and changing national expectations have altered the way health policy is formed in the United States (Fig. 7-1).

In the early stages of federalism, the national government had virtually no impact on local health

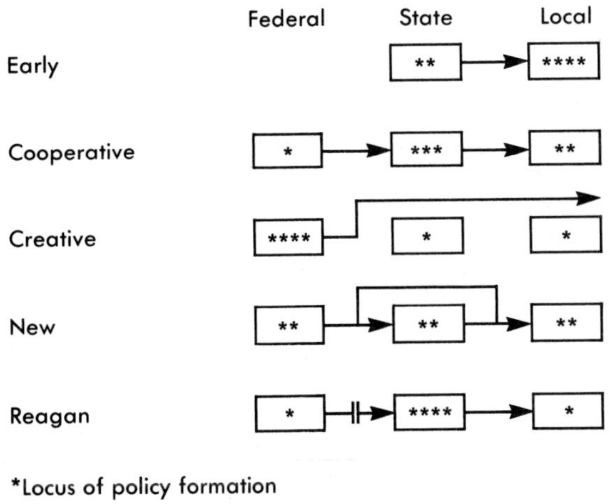

FIG. 7-1 The changing locus of health policy formation in the United States.

policy or programs. State governments had some influence, but most health policy was formed at the local level.

During the Depression of the 1930s, a new era of cooperative federalism developed: local governments lost or divested themselves of some of their previous authority, the national government acquired authority through the expanded use of grants-in-aid, and the states became the dominant partner in health policy.

During the 1960s, President Johnson used the emerging federal role much more creatively, shifting health policy-making to the federal government through a rapid expansion of grants-in-aid. Moreover, during the Johnson years, grant programs often bypassed state and local governments altogether. New citizen groups were formed to manage Economic Opportunity programs, Model City programs, and new health planning agencies. These organizations were outside the traditional pipelines of intergovernmental transfers and were frequently seen as rivals to elected officials and the official state and local health agencies.

President Nixon, in his New Federalism program, maintained interest in the use of private, not-for-profit organizations to deliver public health and social services, possibly as a prelude to an intended reduction in the governmental role. He devolved some of the recently acquired federal authority back onto state and local governments with the new revenue-sharing program described in Chapter 6. Thus the locus of health policy formation shifted once again, with power equally shared between the three levels of government.

Beginning in the late 1970s and accelerating with the advent of the Reagan years, federal power in health policy formation was sharply reduced. There was a marked reduction in federal grants for health and social services and a concomitant reduction in federal rules and policy guidelines. As noted earlier, local governments had neither the will nor the money to reacquire the authority they once had, leaving the states once again in the dominant role. Most of the creative action in health policy formation and program development is now taking place at the state level, as legislatures and governors wrestle with the complex problems of aging and long-term care, perinatal health, environmental hazards, indigent medical care, and AIDS.

Where should the locus of health policy formation be? Some argue that it should be as close to the community as possible. Of course the community varies depending on the problem: the community for air pollution is different from the community tied together by a water pollution problem, and both are different from the community requiring improved perinatal care. It is often asserted that local governments are more inventive than higher levels of government in solving problems and that local needs and priorities are frequently different from state or national ones. Others argue that health policy should be formed at the national level to be sure that needed services are delivered efficiently and, perhaps, equitably.

Rudolf Klein,[11] discussing the dilemma in a paper prepared for the Royal Commission on the National Health Service in England, reshaped the argument as follows:

> The Commission will have to decide whether the state of the art in health services planning is so well developed that it is sensible to endorse the kind of centralizing tendencies that have developed out of the desire to promote equity. If the Commission concludes—as it seems to me that they ought, on the basis of the available evidence—that the state of the art is still very primitive, that there are frequent fluctuations in fashions leading to the adoption of new policies on such issues as the best size for a hospital, then clearly they will also be led to endorse a policy of decentralization. If policy making is seen as a search process, of trial and error through experiment, then diversity becomes desirable in its own right—a value to be pursued, even if it means putting less weight on considerations of equity and uniformity. In turn this would suggest a more limited role for central government in assessing the outcome of local experiment and defining the outer limits of tolerance for diversity, rather than establishing uniform norms throughout the country.

The dilemma is visualized in Fig. 7-2. In a hypothetical nation with eight states, a centralized health policy (using categorical grants) might produce a higher "score" (on a scale from 1 to 10) than could be attained in a decentralized policy-forming structure (using block grants or revenue sharing). But note something else that occurs in the decentralized system: there are some states that perform better and others that perform more poorly than any of the states in the centralized system. There is greater diversity in the decentralized system, and at least two of the states have found a better way to deal with the problem than has the federal government in the more centralized system. To the dismay of some, however, two states in the decentralized system have done very little. Can that be tolerated? It would depend on the nature of the problem.

If the problem were measles control, an argument could be made for centralized policy-making: the nature of the disease is well understood, the methods of control are clear and effective, and there is broad national consensus about the objective. These conditions would be less forceful if the problem under consideration were teen-age pregnancy: the problem is poorly understood,

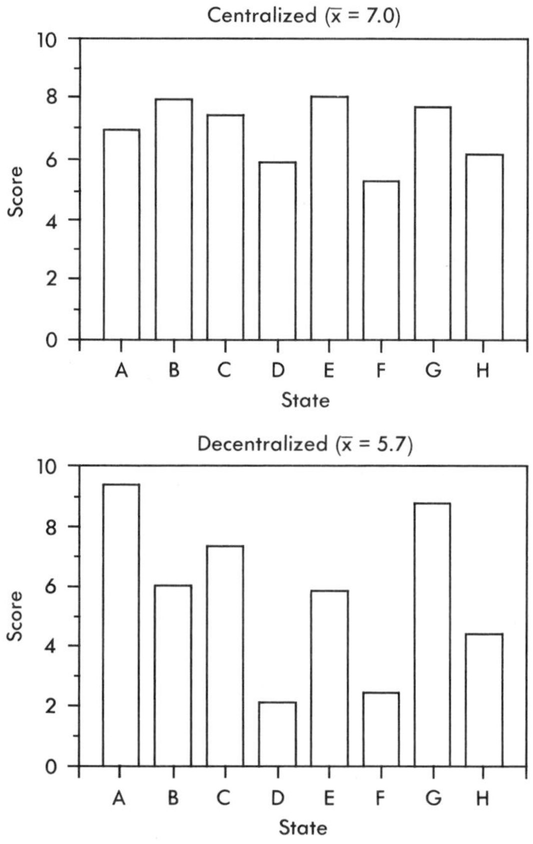

FIG. 7-2 Decentralized versus centralized health policy formation.

there is little consensus about an objective, and if there were such a consensus, there would be bitter arguments about the best methods to be used. In this instance, decentralization of policy formation would be more appropriate, and block grants or revenue sharing would be the more appropriate form of federal aid to state and local governments. Decentralized policy-making responsibility would stimulate "policy searching" and support the diversity needed when values and objectives themselves are so diverse.

The locus of health policy formation can shift between the levels of government. Unfortunately, it is often when the most creative policy searching should be encouraged that people insist most vehemently on centralized control. Public health professionals and elected officials, however, need to understand the difference and, as Klein has put it, employ national policy only to define "the outer limits of tolerance for diversity."

REFERENCES

1. American Public Health Association, Association of State and Territorial Health Officials, National Association of County Health Officials, United States Conference of Local Health Officials, and Centers for Disease Control of the U.S. Public Health Service: Model standards: a guide for community preventive health services, ed 2, Washington, DC, 1985, American Public Health Association.
2. National Conference of State Legislatures: Major health issues for the states: 1986, Denver, CO, 1986, The Conference.
3. Association of State and Territorial Health Officials: Comprehensive National Public Health Program Reporting System report: services, expenditures and programs of state and territorial health agencies, fiscal year 1979, Silver Springs, MD, 1980, The Association.
4. American Public Health Association: The role of official local health agencies, Am J Public Health 65:189, Feb 1975.
5. National Commission on Community Health Services: Health is a community affair, Cambridge, MA, 1969, Harvard University Press.
6. National Commission on Community Health Services: Health administration and organization in the decade ahead, Cambridge, MA, 1967, Harvard University Press.
7. Manning B and Vladeck BC: State and local governments and health—findings and propositions, Health Aff 2:134, Winter 1983.
8. Sencer DJ: Major urban health departments: the ideal and the real, Health Aff 2:88, Winter 1983.
9. Miller CA: An agenda for public health departments, J Public Health Policy 6:158, June 1985.
10. Institute of Medicine: The future of public health, Washington, DC, 1988, National Academy Press.
11. Klein R: Evidence to the Royal Commission on the National Health Service, J Health Polit Policy Law 3:11, Spring 1978.

CHAPTER 8

The statistics of public health

THE IMPORTANCE OF DATA

Health policy is formed, in part, on the basis of an evaluation of health problems. Diseases and injuries have to be defined, ascertained, and counted. The tabulation of that data forms the body of health statistics. Health statistics are not just the certificates of birth and death but all data that help describe life and those phenomena that affect it. An organized approach to the collection, analysis, and use of the information contained in health statistics is an essential activity of every public health agency. Epidemiology and biostatistics have been described as among the three fundamental and generic fields of knowledge in public health.[1] It is impossible to imagine a sound program of maternal and child health, communicable disease control, environmental health, or laboratory services in the absence of health statistics. Its influence, if properly used, permeates every part of the organization. At one point it determines what visits should be made by staff nurses or sanitarians; at another it assists in deciding matters of policy for the top administrator. The principal applications of statistics in public health include (1) population estimation and forecasting; (2) surveys of population characteristics, health needs, and problems; (3) analysis of health trends; (4) epidemiologic research; (5) program evaluation; (6) program planning, (7) budget preparation and justification; (8) operational and administrative decision making; and (9) health education.[2]

It is difficult if not impossible for a public health worker to be either successful or satisfied without an intelligent appreciation of health data. The material of statistics, properly organized, leads to a critically important end product—a plan for disease prevention and health promotion.

ORIGINS OF HEALTH STATISTICS

The compilation of health statistics is of ancient origin. Enumerations of people were carried out long before the birth of Christ, notably in China, Egypt, Persia, Greece, and Rome, primarily for purposes of taxation and to determine military manpower. Data relating to births, deaths, and marriages were recorded in elementary form in the old church registers of England. The oldest known copy of these so-called Bills of Mortality can be seen in the British Museum and is dated November 1532. These bills were compiled by parish priests and clerks for more than a century before John Graunt in 1662 published his book *Natural and Political Observations Mentioned in a Following Index and Made Upon the Bills of Mortality.** Graunt counted the deaths and casualties of the year 1632, totaling 9,532 buried (Table 8-1); he counted 9,584 who were newly christened. The reader is invited to translate the causes of death into current categories. Health statistics in the modern sense can be considered to have originated with the publication of this book.

The late eighteenth century saw the beginning of the modern national census. Priority is open to question. The outstanding claims are Canada, 1666; Sweden, 1749; and England and the United States, 1790. Regardless of the earliest claim, the U.S. Census had a significant influence on the spread of the idea throughout the rest of the world. The national census in the United States was the result of a political compromise that arose from conflict between the small and large states. The former demanded equal representation in the national legislature, but the latter considered that their larger populations justified more power. The compromise solution was to establish a bicameral legislature consisting of the Senate, in which states were equally represented, and the House of Representatives, with representation in proportion to population. This compromise solution made nec-

* Reprinted in 1939 by the Johns Hopkins University Press, Baltimore, MD.

essary some provision for the periodic inventory of the population. As a result, the following was included in the Constitution:

Representatives shall be apportioned among the several States according to their respective numbers, counting the whole number of persons in each State, excluding Indians not taxed. The actual enumeration shall be made within three years after the first meeting of the Congress of the United States, and within every subsequent term of ten years, in such manner as they shall by law direct.*

* Article I, section 2, paragraph 3, modified by the Fourteenth Amendment.

All that was required was a simple count of people. From this basic purpose there has developed a national census of great complexity and detail that provides data of value far beyond what was envisioned by the framers of the Constitution. Few parts of the nation's social, political, economic, and industrial systems could operate without it.

SOURCES OF PUBLIC HEALTH STATISTICS

For health problems to be understood, they must be defined and measured. Their measurement is determined by the frequency with which they occur and their seriousness. Seriousness, in turn, is a function of their severity, their urgency, their potential for involving others, and their cost, both to the individual and to society. How do these

TABLE 8-1 The diseases and casualties this year being 1632

Abortive and stillborn	445	Grief	11
Affrighted	1	Jaundies	43
Aged	628	Jawfaln	8
Ague	43	Impostume	74
Apoplex and meogrom	17	Kil'd by several accidents	46
Bit with a mad dog	1	King's Evil	38
Bleeding	3	Lethargie	2
Bloody flux, scowring and flux	348	Livergrown	87
Brused, issues, sores, and ulcers	28	Lunatique	5
Burnt and scalded	5	Made away themselves	15
Burst and rupture	9	Measles	80
Cancer and wolf	10	Murthered	7
Canker	1	Over-laid and starved at nurse	7
Childbed	171	Palsie	25
Chrisomes and infants	2268	Piles	1
Cold and cough	55	Plague	8
Colick, stone and strangury	56	Planet	13
Consumption	1797	Pleurisie and Spleen	36
Convulsion	241	Purples, and spotted Feaver	38
Cut of the stone	5	Quinsie	7
Dead in the street and starved	6	Rising of the Lights	98
Dropsie and swelling	267	Sciatica	1
Drowned	34	Scurvey and Itch	9
Executed and prest to death	18	Suddenly	62
Falling sickness	7	Surfet	86
Fever	1108	Swine Pox	6
Fistula	13	Teeth	470
Flocks and small Pox	531	Thrush and Sore mouth	40
French Pox	12	Tympany	13
Gangrene	5	Tissick	34
Gout	4	Vomiting	1
		Worms	27

Graunt, J: Natural and political observations mentioned in a following index and made upon the bills of mortality. Reprinted. Baltimore MD, 1939, Johns Hopkins University Press.

measurements determine whether a problem is of sufficient concern to warrant public health intervention? How many deaths due to heart disease would constitute a public health problem: 100,000? 800,000? How many from AIDS? How many cases of whooping cough would warrant intervention? How many fatalities due to motor vehicle crashes? There is no easy answer. A single case of smallpox would cause alarms to go off throughout the world, but 50,000 deaths owing to alcohol consumption scarcely sound a bell.

Rates or ratios are used to measure most health problems. They consist of numerators and denominators: a count of the events divided by the number of possible events. Rates make comparisons possible. If one community had 5 events and another 10, a comparison of events per 1,000 people in the two communities would indicate whether there was a difference between the two. Sometimes the numbers themselves are important. For purposes of evaluating trends or making comparisons, the *rate* of dependency among those over 75 years of age is necessary. However, to examine current policies and develop necessary programs, it is necessary to know the *numbers* of people who may need assistance.

The numerators and denominators used in public health are of three types: survival data (births, deaths, and a count of the population); health and socioeconomic status data; and data on health services resources and utilization.[3]

The denominators

The most important information on which activities in public health must be predicated is a count of the population to be served. On the surface it would appear that the decennial census, to which reference has been made, would supply whatever data are necessary. This was the case before paved highways, rapid transportation, and industrialization. Reasonably adequate intercensal populations could be estimated by means of simple projections. The situation changed drastically, however, as a result of World War II. In 1940 an extremely detailed census had been carried out. However, within little more than a year, the nation became engaged in an international conflict of great magnitude that required the enlistment and draft of several million citizens. In addition, new and old industries underwent spectacular expansion, necessitating the movement of additional millions of persons to serve them. Many communities within a short space of time found their populations doubled or trebled, whereas others were noticeably depleted. It soon became evident that neither the 1940 census data nor any estimates based on them could serve much useful purpose.

Many attempts were made to find suitable substitutes in the form of school attendance records, work records, or food ration card applications. The latter were probably the most useful during the World War II years. Social Security registration provided some additional measure of the population, with the handicaps, however, of not including children and certain groups of the employable and not giving an indication of population movement. It was hoped that the confused situation would be temporary; but soon statisticians, economists, and public health workers were convinced that the national mode of life had been so deeply affected as to require some new form of population determination and analysis. During the same period of time, a new business and social study technique, the sample survey or poll, began to serve a valuable purpose in health and other fields, especially during intercensal years and in obtaining answers to special questions. Intermittent population reports based on sample surveys are distributed by the Bureau of the Census.[4]

The numerators

Next in importance to the population base are data obtained from administrative registration and reporting procedures. Responsibility for this function in the United States rests with the respective states. The most significant of these activities relate to the vital events of birth, death, and morbidity. Again, so that these data may be of value in the planning of public health programs, there must be some assurance of their qualitative and quantitative dependability. This need led to the establishment of birth and death registration areas by the Bureau of the Census. The death registration area was organized in 1880 and included two states, the District of Columbia, and several cities. The birth registration area was not established until 1915 and originally included Connecticut, Maine, Massachusetts, Michigan, Minnesota, New Hampshire, New York, Pennsylvania, Rhode Island, Vermont, and the District of Columbia, accounting for 31% of the total population. By 1933 all states had become members of both the birth and the death registration areas. The program was included in the National Center for Health Statistics (P.L. 93-353) in 1974 along with other basic health data systems.

Part of the core research effort of the U.S. Department of Health and Human Services, the National Center for Health Statistics (NCHS) is the direct descendent of the National Office of Vital Statistics. The NCHS was incorporated into the Centers for Disease Control in 1987. It maintains 11 ongoing data systems, although budgetary constraints have caused the center staff to establish priorities for those systems and reduce the frequency of their operation. Those systems are[5]:

1. *Basic vital statistics.* Vital statistics come from records of births, deaths, fetal deaths, induced terminations of pregnancy, marriages, and divorces. These are prepared, collected, and archived by each state. The original documents, which are prepared by a wide variety of people in accordance with state laws (physicians, health care administrators, ministers, and civil officials) are verified by state or local registrars of vital statistics, coded, and transmitted periodically to the NCHS. The center publishes the *Monthly Vital Statistics Report: Provisional Data from the National Center for Health Statistics* and three annual volumes making up the *Vital Statistics of the United States,* with detailed information on births and deaths.
2. *Vital statistics follow-back surveys.* Follow-back surveys are periodic studies conducted by following back to their origin certain items contained in vital records. Follow-back surveys return to the state and often the household in which the event occurred and are used to obtain additional information about the events and the reporting system.
3. *National Survey of Family Growth.* The National Survey of Family Growth is a multipurpose survey of factors relating to fertility, family formation and dissolution, family planning practices, and related maternal and infant health topics. It is carried out on a probability sample of women aged 15-44. It is scheduled periodically and last "entered the field" in 1988. Data are published in Series 23 of the center's ongoing *Vital and Health Statistics* publications.
4. *National Health Interview Survey.* Initiated in 1957, the National Health Interview Survey is a continuous nationwide survey of the amount, distribution, and effects of illness and disability in the United States. The survey uses a multistage probability sample of the noninstitutionalized civilian population of the United States, surveying 40,000 households (approximately 110,000 people) each year. The response rate is about 95%, even though the interviews last about 45 minutes. There is a core set of questions, which is fairly constant each year, concerning health status, demographic characteristics, and socioeconomic status, and one or more sets of supplemental questions. For example, the survey has included additional questions about health status of the elderly and about health promotion activities practiced by household members. The results of the survey are published in Series 10 of *Vital and Health Statistics,* and computer tapes are available from the center.
5. *National Medical Care Utilization and Expenditure Survey.* This survey provides detailed national estimates of the use of and expenditures for medical services. First conducted in 1980, it has not been repeated, and there is no firm schedule for a second survey.
6. *National Ambulatory Medical Care Survey.* The purpose of the ambulatory care survey is to provide information about the location, setting, and frequency of ambulatory care encounters for different specialties and subgroups of the population. The survey uses the American Medical Association's master file as its sampling frame and randomly selects 3,000 physicians. Abstractors record data on about 50,000 visits. Conducted in 1985, it is scheduled to be repeated in 1989. Results are published in Series 13 of *Vital and Health Statistics.*
7. *National Health and Nutrition Examination Survey.* This survey (known as N-HANES) is used to collect direct physical, physiological, and biochemical data from a national sample. First carried out in the early 1970s, the study was repeated with modifications from 1976 to 1980. A special Hispanic NHANES was conducted from 1982 to 1984, and NHANES III will be in the field from 1988 through 1994. Results are published in Series 11 of *Vital and Health Statistics.*

8. *National Hospital Discharge Survey.* The hospital discharge survey, conducted annually, provides information about the characteristics of patients in civilian, short-stay hospitals; length of stay, diagnosis, surgical procedures performed, and patterns of patient use by size and ownership of hospital. The survey uses a sample of 550 hospitals out of a pool of 8,000. Abstractors record data on about 214,000 discharges. Consideration has been given to revising the study and combining it with the National Nursing Home Survey.
9. *National Nursing Home Survey.* The nursing home survey is a series of sample surveys of the residents and staffs of nursing homes to provide information about need, costs, level of care, and trends in the use of nursing homes. The last complete survey was conducted in 1985.
10. *National Master Facility Inventory.* The inventory attempts to identify and classify a broad array of facilities that provide 24-hour care, such as hospitals, nursing homes, and residential care facilities. In addition to serving as a statistical file of beds by type, it serves as a universe for sample surveys of special facilities. The inventory was last conducted in 1986 and included approximately 33,000 facilities.
11. *National health professions inventories and surveys.* These provide information about the distribution and training of people employed in the health labor force. They usually use state data systems developed as part of the states' health professions licensure programs.

Mental health statistics are developed separately by the National Institute of Mental Health. They differ from National Center for Health Statistics data in that they are derived primarily from an encounter-reporting network rather than a population-based survey. This is in part because of widespread disagreement about diagnosis in mental health, which makes population surveys difficult. The encounter-based system means that the mental health reporting system counts only those people who seek services and, for the most part, who do so in the public sector of community mental health centers and public mental health hospitals. During the 1980s, the Institute sponsored a series of research projects to develop population-based information about the prevalence of mental illness.[6] These efforts, coupled with an improved diagnostic manual,[7] have made possible more detailed analysis of mental health problems. (See Chapter 27.)

ACCURACY OF HEALTH DATA

All data systems suffer from both systemic and random inaccuracies. Random inaccuracies, if not too frequent, do not generate bias in the data – that is, they do not disturb the data in an integral way. Systemic inaccuracies, unless they are understood and corrected through compensatory adjustments, can inject bias into a data set that may lead to invalid inferences. For example, the census undercounts black people. Assuming that black births and deaths are more accurately counted, black birth and death rates, which use a denominator that is an underestimate of the true population, will tend to appear higher than they are.

The registration of births and deaths is virtually complete in the United States. Some deaths are missed because a few people simply disappear. Although this may result in a slight underreporting of certain causes of death, it represents a very small proportion of the total number of events. As many as 30,000 births (out of 3.8 million births annually) may go unrecorded initially, but most of these are subsequently registered when the individual enters into the civil systems of society such as school, Social Security registration, or employment. Other problems are related to the inadequate reporting of stillbirths and babies born out of wedlock and to the known underenumeration of certain groups, especially minorities, in the census.

The assurance of prompt and adequate reporting of both live births and stillbirths requires constant vigilance on the part of registrars and directors of vital statistics offices. Many different approaches have been used, and it would appear that no one approach alone is satisfactory. Education of the public, of attendants at birth, and of hospital personnel must be conducted constantly. In addition to this, many types of checks must be used, such as requiring a birth certificate for school attendance and counting the children attending well-baby or child health clinics. In many states, hospitals prepare a birth certificate at the time the prospective mother enters the hospital, complete except for the date of birth, sex, and name of the child. These can be readily added after birth at the time the physician signs the certificate. In addition to producing highly satisfactory results, this procedure has added value in that the certificates are usually typed and therefore more legible than they otherwise might be. Some states have made it possible for the hospital rather than the physician to report the birth. This helps produce more timely and accurate data, but may reduce the amount of information available about complications of the pregnancy or delivery.

Birth certificates

The birth certificate in use in the United States has been developed over many years. A national working group designed the latest form during the 1980s, and it was first used in 1989. It is important to bear in mind that the national government cannot require the reporting of births. The states can and do, and their cooperation with the National Center for Health Statistics is voluntary. Participation by the states is supported by various forms of grants-in-aid and by the ability of the national government to convene conferences and work groups to review and improve reporting procedures. The latest revisions (see Fig. 8-1) include special provisions to better understand Hispanic parentage, along with changes in the confidential portion of the certificate. The confidential portion must be completed by the certifier, usually the attending physician, but is never linked to the certificate when it is copied and made available for use, even to the person represented by the certificate. The information in the confidential section is used only for research purposes. The prior version of the certificate asked the certifier to list any complications of pregnancy. The new form uses a check-box format and lists specific important and common complications. It is the information on birth certificates that makes possible the detailed study of natality.

LF ______________

CF ______________

STATE OF MICHIGAN
DEPARTMENT OF PUBLIC HEALTH
CERTIFICATE OF LIVE BIRTH

29 121 – ______________ STATE FILE NUMBER

0151277

CHILD
1 CHILD – NAME (FIRST) (MIDDLE) (LAST)
2 SEX | 3a PLURALITY – SINGLE, TWIN, TRIPLET, ETC. (SPECIFY) | 3b IF NOT SINGLE – BORN 1ST, 2ND, 3RD, ETC. (SPECIFY) | 4a DATE OF BIRTH (Month, Day, Year) | 4b TIME OF BIRTH M

PLACE
5a HOSPITAL NAME – (IF NOT HOSPITAL GIVE STREET AND NUMBER) | 5b CITY, VILLAGE, OR TOWNSHIP OF BIRTH | 5c COUNTY OF BIRTH

CERTIFICATION
6a I CERTIFY THAT THE ABOVE NAMED CHILD WAS BORN ALIVE AT THE PLACE AND TIME AND ON THE DATE STATED ABOVE
SIGNATURE: ______________ DATE ______________
6b CERTIFIER'S NAME & TITLE (print or type)
6c NAME AND TITLE OF ATTENDANT IF OTHER THAN CERTIFIER | 6d MAILING ADDRESS OF ATTENDANT (STREET NO., CITY OR VILLAGE, STATE, ZIP)

7a REGISTRAR'S SIGNATURE | 7b DATE RECEIVED BY LOCAL REGISTRAR – (Month, Day, Year)

MOTHER
8a MOTHER'S NAME (FIRST, MIDDLE, LAST) | 8b SOCIAL SECURITY NUMBER | 8c STATE OF BIRTH – NAME COUNTRY IF NOT USA | 8d DATE OF BIRTH (Month, Day, Year)
8e MOTHER – SURNAME BEFORE FIRST MARRIED | 8f RESIDENCE (Check one box and specify) ☐ INSIDE CITY OR VILLAGE OF ☐ TWP OF | [redacted] | 8g COUNTY | 8h STATE

BY AUTHORITY ACT 368, P.A. 1978

FATHER
9a FATHER'S NAME (FIRST, MIDDLE, LAST) | 9b SOCIAL SECURITY NUMBER | 9c STATE OF BIRTH – NAME COUNTRY IF NOT USA | 9d DATE OF BIRTH (Month, Day, Year)

B213 (1/89)

MDPH

10a I CERTIFY THAT THE PERSONAL INFORMATION PROVIDED ON THIS CERTIFICATE IS CORRECT TO THE BEST OF MY KNOWLEDGE AND BELIEF
SIGNATURE ______________
(PARENT OR OTHER INFORMANT)
10b THE PARENT(S) REQUEST THAT INFORMATION ON THIS BIRTH BE RELEASED TO THE SOCIAL SECURITY ADMIN. FOR ISSUANCE OF A SOCIAL SECURITY NUMBER AND CARD. ☐ YES ☐ NO

FIG. 8-1 Standard birth certificate.

Continued.

The reporting of illegitimate births has been approached in three different ways by the various states. One is to make mandatory provision for the attendant at birth to file the birth certificate of an illegitimate child directly with the state office of vital statistics rather than to have it pass through the hands of the local registrar. Some believe that this weakens the local registration system and is therefore undesirable. Another approach is the provision that the certificate of an illegitimate child not differ from that of a legitimate child once the child

CONFIDENTIAL INFORMATION FOR PUBLIC HEALTH USE ONLY

	11. ANCESTRY – Mexican, Puerto Rican, Cuban, Central or South American, Chicano, other Hispanic, Afro-American, Arab, English, French, Finnish, etc. *(Specify below)*	12. RACE – American Indian, Black, White, etc. If Asian, give nationality i.e., Chinese, Filipino, Asian Indian, etc. *(Specify below)*	13. EDUCATION *(Specify only highest grade completed)* Elementary/Secondary (0-12) College (1-4 or 5 +)
MOTHER	11a.	12a.	13a.
FATHER	11b.	12b.	13b.

MEDICAL AND HEALTH INFORMATION

14. EXPECTED SOURCE OF PAYMENT FOR MEDICAL SERVICES (Private Insurance, Medicaid, etc.)

15. MOTHER'S MAILING ADDRESS (STREET NUMBER, CITY OR VILLAGE, STATE, ZIP)

16a. MEDICAL RECORD NUMBER OF MOTHER

16b. MEDICAL RECORD NUMBER OF CHILD

17. DATE LAST NORMAL MENSES BEGAN *(Month, Day, Year)*

18. MONTH OF PREGNANCY PRENATAL CARE BEGAN

19. TOTAL PRENATAL VISITS

20. LIVE BIRTHS *(Do not include this Child)*
20a. NOW LIVING — Number ____ None ☐
20b. NOW DEAD — Number ____ None ☐
20c. DATE OF LAST LIVE BIRTH *(Mo., Year)*

20d. OTHER TERMINATIONS *(Spontaneous and induced at any time after conception)* — Number ____ None ☐
20e. DATE OF LAST OTHER TERMINATION *(Mo., Year)*

21a. MOTHER TRANSFERRED PRIOR TO DELIVERY? If yes enter name of facility transferred from: ☐ YES ☐ NO

21b. INFANT TRANSFERRED? ☐ YES ☐ NO If yes enter name of facility transferred to:

22. ATTENDANT AT BIRTH — MD ☐ D.O. ☐ NURSE ☐ CERTIFIED NURSE MID. ☐ MIDWIFE ☐ OTHER ☐

23. INFANT ADMITTED TO NICU? ☐ YES ☐ NO

24. BIRTHWEIGHT *(Specify unit)*

25. ESTIMATED WEEKS GESTATION

26. APGAR SCORE — 1 MIN. 5 MIN.

27. PLACE OF BIRTH — Hospital ☐ Freestanding Birth Center ☐ Clinic/Doctor's Office ☐ Residence ☐ Other *(Specify)* ☐

28. MEDICAL RISK FACTORS FOR THIS PREGNANCY *(Check all that apply)*
Anemia (Hct. < 30/Hgb. < 10) 01 ☐
Cardiac disease 02 ☐
Acute or chronic lung disease 03 ☐
Diabetes 04 ☐
Genital herpes 05 ☐
Hydramnios/Oligohydramnios 06 ☐
Hemoglobinopathy 07 ☐
Hypertension, chronic 08 ☐
Hypertension, pregnancy-associated 09 ☐
Eclampsia 10 ☐
Incompetent cervix 11 ☐
Previous infant 4000 + grams 12 ☐
Previous preterm or small-for-gestational-age infant 13 ☐
Renal disease 14 ☐
Rh sensitization 15 ☐
Uterine bleeding 16 ☐
None 00 ☐
Other *(Specify)* ____ 17 ☐

29. OTHER RISK FACTORS FOR THIS PREGNANCY
Tobacco use during pregnancy .... Yes ☐ No ☐
Average number cigarettes per day ____
Alcohol use during pregnancy .... Yes ☐ No ☐
Average number of drinks per week ____
Weight gained during pregnancy ____ lbs.

30. OBSTETRIC PROCEDURES *(Check all that apply)*
Amniocentesis 01 ☐
Electronic fetal monitoring 02 ☐
Induction of labor 03 ☐
Stimulation of labor 04 ☐
Tocolysis 05 ☐
Ultrasound 06 ☐
None 00 ☐
Other *(Specify)* ____ 07 ☐

31. COMPLICATIONS OF LABOR AND/OR DELIVERY *(Check all that apply)*
Febrile (> 100° F. or 38° C.) 01 ☐
Meconium, moderate/heavy 02 ☐
Premature rupture of membrane (> 12 hours) 03 ☐
Abruptio placenta 04 ☐
Placenta previa 05 ☐
Other excessive bleeding 06 ☐
Seizures during labor 07 ☐
Precipitate labor (< 3 hours) 08 ☐
Prolonged labor (> 20 hours) 09 ☐
Dysfunctional labor 10 ☐
Breech/Malpresentation 11 ☐
Cephalopelvic disproportion 12 ☐
Cord prolapse 13 ☐
Anesthetic complications 14 ☐
Fetal distress 15 ☐
None 00 ☐
Other *(Specify)* ____ 16 ☐

32. METHOD OF DELIVERY *(Check all that apply)*
Vaginal 01 ☐
Vaginal birth after previous C-section 02 ☐
Primary C-section 03 ☐
Repeat C-section 04 ☐
Forceps 05 ☐
Vacuum 06 ☐

33. ABNORMAL CONDITIONS OF THE NEWBORN *(Check all that apply)*
Anemia (Hct < 39/Hbg < 13) 01 ☐
Birth injury 02 ☐
Fetal alcohol syndrome 03 ☐
Hyaline membrane disease/RDS 04 ☐
Meconium aspiration syndrome 05 ☐
Assisted ventilation < 30 min. 06 ☐
Assisted ventilation ≥ 30 min. 07 ☐
Seizures 08 ☐
None 00 ☐
Other *(Specify)* ____ 09 ☐

34. APPARENT CONGENITAL ANOMALIES OF NEWBORN *(Check all that apply)*
Anencephalus 01 ☐
Spina Bifida/Meningocele 02 ☐
Hydrocephalus 03 ☐
Microcephalus 04 ☐
Other central nervous system anomalies *(Specify)* ____ 05 ☐
Heart malformations 06 ☐
Other circulatory/respiratory anomalies *(Specify)* ____ 07 ☐
Rectal atresia/stenosis 08 ☐
Tracheo-esophageal fistula/Esophageal atresia 09 ☐
Omphalocele/Gastroschisis 10 ☐
Other gastrointestinal anomalies *(Specify)* ____ 11 ☐
Malformed genitalia 12 ☐
Renal agenesis 13 ☐
Other urogenital anomalies *(Specify)* ____ 14 ☐
Cleft lip/palate 15 ☐
Polydactyly/Syndactyly/Adactyly 16 ☐
Club foot 17 ☐
Diaphragmatic hernia 18 ☐
Other musculoskeletal/integumental anomalies *(Specify)* ____ 19 ☐
Down's syndrome 20 ☐
Other chromosomal anomalies *(Specify)* ____ 21 ☐
None 00 ☐
Other *(Specify)* ____ 22 ☐

FAILURE TO PROVIDE THE REQUIRED INFORMATION IS A MISDEMEANOR PUNISHABLE BY IMPRISONMENT OF NOT MORE THAN 1 YEAR OR A FINE OF NOT MORE THAN $1,000.00 OR BOTH

FIG. 8-1, cont'd. For legend see opposite page.

in question has been adopted or legitimized. An objection to this is the necessity of preparing new certificates. A third method is to delete the item of legitimacy entirely. This has been successfully promoted in a few states by welfare agencies and certain other groups. What will constitute "illegitimate" conception and birth in the 1990s is a moot point. Births out of wedlock still have certain characteristics that are of importance to health planners and sociologists, but the term *illegitimate* has little functional value when an increasing number of women and even couples prefer childbearing outside of marriage and so many marriages end in divorce. The term creates other problems when illegitimacy rates are calculated for different racial groups. Single parenting in a black family has not carried the same social stigma as it has in white families, and "illegitimate" black children are not as often the subjects of abuse as are white children. Whites have more often resorted to secrecy, forced marriages, abortions, relinquishments, and adoptions than have blacks, all of which feed into a syndrome of family breakdown. Publication of race-specific illegitimacy rates has thus served to perpetuate stereotypes that are the converse of reality. There are signs that these differences are changing as some white single women have begun to elect single parenthood. Many states have removed the item of legitimacy from the certificate proper and have placed it on the confidential portion.

Even though the basic demographic data on birth certificates are recorded reasonably accurately, information about years of education of the mother and congenital anomalies is often poorly recorded or, in the case of congenital anomalies, is dependent on the interest and training of the attending physician. Some may record every mole as a congenital anomaly, where others do not respond until an arm or a leg is missing.

There are a number of known sources of bias in the birth reporting process. The coding of weeks of gestation tends to peak at 40, since that is considered the norm. In the 1968 revisions, date of last normal menses was added to the birth certificate. This improved accuracy but resulted in an increased number of certificates without the requested information. There are digit preference problems as well: certifiers tend to select the numbers 15, 1, 10, 20, and 25 (in that order of preference) for the day of the month on which the last normal menses occurred.[8] There is a tendency for mothers to underreport prior pregnancies if they were illegitimate or if they were terminated by abortion.

One other phase of birth reporting that causes difficulty is delayed registration of births. Since routine court evaluation of the evidence is unwieldy, most states now have the evidence reviewed by the state registrar, with recourse to the courts in case of a rejection.

Death certificates

The value of death certificates is impaired not only by some inadequate reporting but also by the subjective nature of much of the data requested on the form (Fig. 8-2).

The standard certificate of death, similar to the standard certificate of birth, is the result of a collaborative process involving the National Center for Health Statistics, state and local registrars, and others. As shown in Fig. 8-2, the top portion of the certificate provides demographic information about the decedent, including a question about occupation. The new version, in use since the beginning of 1989, includes more detailed information about Hispanic parentage.

The cause of death section has always been troublesome. It asks for the immediate cause of death and then, sequentially, for the precursor steps leading up to death. It is intended that the underlying cause of the fatal process, the last listed in the section, will be coded as "the" cause of death. The difficulty in obtaining consistency is obvious. In recent years, the NCHS has begun to code multiple causes of death as an aid to researchers who may be interested in people who died *with* a particular problem although they may not have died *because* of it. The task force that proposed the 1989 revisions in the certificate recommended that the NCHS study the value of inverting the cause of death section, with the goal of making any new revisions in time for the next international revision in cause of death codes, in 1993. This would place the underlying cause of death at the head of the list, somewhat the way the principal diagnosis is listed on a medical record. Unfortunately, the center has not had the resources needed to conduct the research.

The new certificates include provision for two certifiers to the death. A body cannot be released to an undertaker for burial until a death certificate has been completed. The purpose is to reduce the

STATE OF MICHIGAN
DEPARTMENT OF PUBLIC HEALTH

CERTIFICATE OF DEATH

LF ______________

CF ______________

STATE FILE NUMBER

№ 0023734

TYPE/PRINT IN PERMANENT BLACK INK

NAME OF DECEDENT ______________
FOR USE BY PHYSICIAN OR INSTITUTION

DECEDENT

1. DECEDENT'S NAME *(First, Middle, Last)*
2. SEX
3. DATE OF DEATH *(Month, Day, Year)*
4a. AGE – Last Birthday *(Years)*
4b. UNDER 1 YEAR — MONTHS | DAYS
4c. UNDER 1 DAY — HOURS | MINUTES
5. DATE OF BIRTH *(Month, Day, Year)*
6. COUNTY OF DEATH
7a. LOCATION OF DEATH (Enter place officially pronounced dead in 7a, 7b, 7c.) HOSPITAL OR OTHER INSTITUTION – Name *(If not in either, give street and number)*
7b. IF HOSP OR INST Inpatient, Op./Emer. Room, DOA *(Specify)*
7c. CITY, VILLAGE, OR TOWNSHIP OF DEATH
8. SOCIAL SECURITY NUMBER
9a. USUAL OCCUPATION *(Give kind of work done during most of working life. Do not use retired)*
9b. KIND OF BUSINESS OR INDUSTRY
10a. CURRENT RESIDENCE – STATE
10b. COUNTY
10c. LOCALITY *(Check one box and specify)*
☐ INSIDE CITY OR VILLAGE OF
☐ TWP. OF
10d. STREET AND NUMBER
10e. ZIP CODE
11. BIRTHPLACE *(City and State or Foreign Country)*
12. MARITAL STATUS – Married, Never Married, Widowed, Divorced *(Specify)*
13. SURVIVING SPOUSE *(If wife, give name before first married)*
14. WAS DECEDENT EVER IN U.S. ARMED FORCES? *(Specify Yes or No)*
15. ANCESTRY – Mexican, Puerto Rican, Cuban, Central or South American, Chicano, other Hispanic, Afro-American, Arab, English, French, Finnish, etc. *(Specify below)*
16. RACE – American Indian, Black, White, etc. If Asian, give nationality i.e., Chinese, Filipino, Asian Indian, etc. *(Specify below)*
17. DECEDENT'S EDUCATION *(Specify only highest grade completed)* — Elementary/Secondary (0-12) | College (1-4 or 5+)

PARENTS

18. FATHER'S NAME *(First, Middle, Last)*
19. MOTHER'S NAME *(First, Middle, Surname before first married)*

INFORMANT

20a. INFORMANT'S NAME *(Type/Print)*
20b. MAILING ADDRESS *(Street and Number or Rural Route Number, City or Village, State, ZIP Code)*

DISPOSITION

21. METHOD OF DISPOSITION – Burial, Cremation, Removal, Donation, Other *(specify)*
22a. PLACE OF DISPOSITION *(Name of Cemetery, Crematory, or other place)*
22b. LOCATION – City or Village, State
23. SIGNATURE OF FUNERAL SERVICE LICENSEE ▶
24. LICENSE NUMBER *(of Licensee)*
25. NAME AND ADDRESS OF FACILITY

CAUSE OF DEATH

26. PART I. Enter the diseases, injuries, or complications that caused the death. Do **NOT** enter the mode of dying, such as cardiac or respiratory arrest, shock, or heart failure. List only one cause on each line.

Approximate Interval Between Onset and Death

IMMEDIATE CAUSE (Final disease or condition resulting in death) → a. ______________
DUE TO (OR AS A CONSEQUENCE OF)

Sequentially list conditions, **IF ANY**, leading to immediate cause. Enter UNDERLYING CAUSE (Disease or injury that initiated events resulting in death) LAST
b. ______________
DUE TO (OR AS A CONSEQUENCE OF)
c. ______________
DUE TO (OR AS A CONSEQUENCE OF)
d. ______________

PART II. Other significant conditions contributing to death but not resulting in the underlying cause given in Part I.

27a. WAS AN AUTOPSY PERFORMED? *(Yes or No)*
27b. WERE AUTOPSY FINDINGS AVAILABLE PRIOR TO COMPLETION OF CAUSE OF DEATH? *(Yes or No)*

CERTIFIER

28. ACTUAL PLACE OF DEATH (Home, Nursing Home, Hospital, Ambulance) *(Specify)*
29. WAS CASE REFERRED TO MEDICAL EXAMINER? *(Specify Yes or No)*

CERTIFYING PHYSICIAN
30a. To the best of my knowledge, death occurred at the time, date and place and due to the cause(s) stated.
(Signature and Title) ▶
30b. DATE SIGNED *(Mo., Day, Yr.)*
30c. TIME OF DEATH ______ M
30d. NAME OF ATTENDING PHYSICIAN IF OTHER THAN CERTIFIER *(Type or Print)*

MEDICAL EXAMINER
31a. *(Check one only)*
☐ The case reviewed and determined not to be a medical examiner's case.
☐ On the basis of examination and of investigation, in my opinion death occurred at the time, date and place and due to the cause(s) and manner stated.
(Signature and Title) ▶
31b. DATE SIGNED *(Mo., Day, Yr.)*
31c. CASE NUMBER
31d. PRONOUNCED DEAD *(Mo., Day, Yr.)* ON
31e. TIME OF DEATH ______ M

32a. NAME AND ADDRESS OF PERSON WHO COMPLETED CAUSE OF DEATH (ITEM 26) *(Type or Print)*
32b. LICENSE NUMBER

MEDICAL EXAMINER

33a. ACC. SUICIDE, HOM., NATURAL OR PENDING INVEST. *(Specify)*
33b. DATE OF INJURY *(Mo., Day, Yr.)*
33c. TIME OF INJURY ______ M
33d. DESCRIBE HOW INJURY OCCURRED
33e. INJURY AT WORK *(Specify Yes or No)*
33f. PLACE OF INJURY – At home, farm, street, factory, office building, etc. *(Specify)*
33g. LOCATION – Street or R.F.D. No. City, Village or Twp. State

34a. REGISTRAR'S SIGNATURE ▶
34b. DATE FILED *(Month, Day, Year)*

B-36
Rev. 1/89

FIG. 8-2 Standard death certificate.

possibility that a homicide will go undetected. However, this often results in difficult delays for the family while an attending physician is contacted, who may not have been present at the time of death, or autopsy results are made available. The new procedures will make possible the release of body upon proper certification by the physician who certified the death; the cause of death portion can be completed later and signed by the attending physician or medical examiner.

It is still not rare for the cause of a death to be misstated deliberately to circumvent potential social stigma. This occurs not only in relation to suicides and syphilis but also to some degree in tuberculosis, cancer, and some hereditary ailments, as well as with AIDS deaths. Incorrect diagnoses present a constant problem to the vital statistician. Numerous studies have been made regarding the degree of accuracy of the physician's statement of cause of death.[9] The figure varies considerably by time, place, and cause of death. For cancer reporting, it appears that death certificates are fairly accurate for cancer of the lung, breast, prostate, pancreas, bladder, and ovary and for leukemia, but cancer of the colon may be overreported in death certificates, whereas rectal cancer may be underreported.[10] The magnitude of this error is subject to steady reduction by virtue of improved medical education and the development and use of new laboratory and clinical diagnostic techniques. Even the most conscientious physician is faced with the difficult problem of deciding the primary cause of death as against contributing causes. This problem has been partially solved by the publication and wide adoption of the World Health Organization's International Classification of Diseases,[11] which presents primary and secondary causal preferences for all possible combinations of diseases. The tenth revision is expected in 1993.

Rates and ratios

Health statistics are usually presented as rates or ratios. The rates are constructed by dividing a count of the events being studied by the number of possible events and multiplying the result by a constant (K) to convert the fraction to a whole number.

Most of the rates used in public health and demography are either crude rates, standardized rates, or specific rates. Crude rates count all of the events and all of the people. The *crude death rate* is a count of all deaths occurring in the jurisdiction (city, county, state, nation) during the year, divided by the total number of people in the population at the midpoint of the reporting period. This figure is usually multiplied by 1,000 and, in the United States, produces a rate of approximately 8.7 deaths per 1,000 people.

Over time or between two different communities, the age distribution of a population may vary substantially. A community with few children and many elderly people would be expected to have many more deaths per thousand people than a younger community with many children. The *age-standardized death rate* compensates for this difference. If the age and sex of each decedent is known and the population figures are also known for each age and sex group, *sex- and age-specific death rates* can be calculated. For example, if there were 25,000 white men aged 40 to 44 in the population, and there were 119 deaths of white men aged 40 to 44 during the year, the sex- and age-specific death rate for that group would be $(119/25{,}000) \times 1{,}000$, or 4.76 per 1,000. If similar calculations are made for each age group of white men, each rate can be multiplied by the number of white men in the corresponding age group in a standard reference population. This yields the number of deaths that would have occurred in the standard reference group of white men if the age- and sex-specific rates of the study population prevailed in the standard population group. By dividing the theoretical number of deaths by the total population of white men in the standard reference population and multiplying by 1,000, the age-standardized death rate can be calculated. Similar calculations can be made in the study community for a different time or in another community, and if the age- and sex-specific death rates again are multiplied by the appropriate figures in the same standard reference population, another age-standardized death rate can be calculated, which can be compared to the first rate. The same sort of standardization process can be used to correct the rate for different sex or racial distributions, and multiple standardizations can be carried out on the same group. Age- or race- or sex-standardized rates have their uses, but they are summary indices of health status and should not be allowed to obscure the underlying differences that are found in the specific rates.

A *case fatality rate* is calculated by dividing the number of deaths that occur from a specific cause by the total number of cases of the disease, condition, or injury. The number may be multiplied by 100 to yield a percentage figure that is an indication of the lethality of the condition.

A *maternal mortality rate* is calculated by dividing the number of deaths because of pregnancy that occur during the reporting period (usually a year) by the number of live births during that same time and multiplying the answer by 100,000. The result is about 7.8 maternal deaths per 100,000 live births in the United States at the present time. The *crude birth rate* is calculated by dividing the total number of live births occurring during the reporting period (usually a year) by the total population at the midpoint in the reporting period. It is currently about 15.8. This is a very crude rate. More useful is the *general fertility rate,* which is calculated by dividing the total number of live births during the reporting period by the population of women aged 15 to 44 and multiplying the answer by 1,000. It is currently about 66 births per 1,000 women aged 15 to 44 in the United States, with an international variation of about 58 to 205. The *age-specific fertility rate* is calculated by dividing the total number of live births to women in a particular age group by the total number of women in that age group during the reporting period.

The *infant mortality rate* is calculated by dividing the total number of deaths occurring between birth and 1 year of age by the total number of live births occurring during the reporting period and multiplying the answer by 1,000. It is currently about 9.9 deaths per 1,000 live births in the United States, with an international range of about 8 to 200. The white-black rates are about 8 and 16 respectively. The *fetal death ratio* is more complex. It is usually calculated from some point in gestation that is assumed to represent the point of viability, but this is a controversial point in fetal development. Currently most states require reporting of fetal deaths past the twentieth week of gestation, although a few require reporting for any "product of conception." In the United States, the fetal death ratio is calculated by dividing the total number of fetal deaths by the total number of live births plus the number of fetal deaths and multiplying the answer by 1,000. The current United States ratio is about 8.2. The white ratio is 7.4 and the black ratio, 11.5. Because of the uncertainty attached to fetal age and the different reporting requirements, fetal death ratios are less commonly used than are other indices of conceptual failure. The *perinatal mortality rate* is surrounded by the same confusion. The more common version in the United States (referred to as perinatal I) is the total number of fetal deaths occurring after the 28th week of gestation plus the number of early neonatal deaths occurring before the end of the seventh day of life, divided by the total number of live births plus the number of fetal deaths with the answer multiplied by 1,000. The current United States perinatal I mortality rate is about 11.1 with a range of 10 for whites to about 17.5 for blacks.

The *neonatal mortality rate* has two components: an *early neonatal mortality rate* and a *late neonatal mortality rate.* The early neonatal mortality rate is calculated by dividing the number of deaths from birth through the seventh day of life by the total number of live births multiplied by 1,000, and the late neonatal mortality rate is calculated by dividing the number of deaths occurring from the 8th through the 27th day of life by the total number of live births multiplied by 1,000. The two rates (currently 5.6 and 0.8 respectively), when added, equal the neonatal mortality rate, currently 6.4. The *postneonatal mortality rate* is calculated by dividing the number of deaths occurring after the 28th day of life and before the end of the first year of life by the total number of live births minus the deaths occurring during the first 28 days. The result is multiplied by 1,000. The current rate is about 3.5. Adding the neonatal death rate and the postneonatal death rate results in the *infant mortality rate.* In a relatively stable health environment, partitioning the infant mortality rate into its two components, the neonatal mortality rate and the postneonatal mortality rate, can provide some indication as to the nature of a community's problems. If the neonatal mortality rate is comparable to the national average or better, but the postneonatal mortality rate is high, it suggests that the community is providing good hospital-based care from a technical standpoint but that environmental conditions in the community and its homes may not be good, or access to primary nursing and medical care for families may be inadequate. On the other hand, if the component causing a high infant mortality rate is the neonatal mortality rate, it suggests that prenatal and delivery services are inadequate.

Two final rates commonly used in public health are the *incidence rate* and the *prevalence rate.* The importance of incidence and prevalence was discussed in Chapter 5. The incidence rate is the number of new events occurring during a reporting period (such as cases of measles) divided by the population at risk of the event. The prevalence rate is the number of cases existing at a particular time divided by the population at risk of the event. In both rates, the constant has to be selected based on the frequency of the event. For very rare diseases or conditions such as autism or leukemia the constant may be 100,000, whereas it might be 1,000 or 100 for more common conditions such as sinusitis or backache. Prevalence is usually referred to as point prevalence, since it is calculated at a particular point in time. Incidence may be calculated for a week, a month, a year, or any period that is helpful in explaining the phenomenon. Prevalence equals the incidence of the disease multiplied by the duration of the disease, when incidence and duration are both expressed in the same units of time. If 15 new cases of a disease are diagnosed each month, and each attack lasts 2 weeks (0.5 months), the prevalence at any time during the month will be 7.5.

More complete discussions of rates and their development may be found in the most current edition of *Vital Statistics of the United States,* in most standard epidemiology textbooks, and in demography textbooks. Particular attention should be paid to techniques used for comparing rates between two different times or places, since the composition of the population groups studied may vary considerably. Kleinman[12] has discussed various indices for comparing age-adjusted mortality data between areas and has shown how each index, although essentially accurate, conveys a different perspective. Each of the indices has value, and the health administrator must have either a sufficient background in biostatistics or sufficient confidence in a staff biostatistician to avoid making incorrect inferences.

In addition to the mathematic problems involved in the analysis and understanding of vital statistics, there are a number of administrative and interpretive problems that can trap the unwary. Warshauer and Monk[13] found that New York City's reported suicide rate for blacks was almost identical to that determined by the medical examiner but that the suicide rate for whites was underestimated by 25% when the city's health department used the seventh revision of the *International Statistical Classification of Diseases, Injuries, and Causes of Death.* When the department switched to the eighth revision in 1969, suicides of blacks were underreported by 82% and suicides of whites by 66%! These marked changes occurred as a result of administrative procedures for closing out the reports at the end of the year, a change in classification practices, and differences in techniques used for suicide by blacks and whites. Such a marked change should cause the administrator of the suicide prevention program or the researcher to question the data, but lesser changes might well have been presented as real. A similar problem was found in Ohio when the recording of congenital anomalies was changed.[14] As a result of the change, the apparent rate increased from 8 or 9 per 1,000 live births in the period 1960 to 1967 to 18 per 1,000 in 1968.

Interpretive problems enter into the picture too. Morris, Udry, and Chase[15] studied the decline in infant mortality from 1965 to 1972 and concluded that 27% of the decline was caused by changes in the age at which women had their babies. The infant mortality rate varies with the age of the mother. The rate is generally expressed as the number of deaths under the age of 1 year divided by the total number of live births, without regard to the age of the mother. So long as birthing patterns remained the same, changes in the rate represented changes in mortality, but when the mother's age when a birth occurred began to shift in a systematic way, the composite risk of infant mortality also shifted, even though the rate for each individual age group might have remained the same. A similar problem may occur with changes in abortion practices in the United States. Following the 1973 Supreme Court decision making abortion legal on request, there was a marked increase in the number of legal abortions performed in some states, and many of these were provided to low-income women through Medicaid. It was anticipated that the changes would alter the distribution of high-risk pregnancies that go to term and have the effect of lowering the infant mortality rate. This appears to have happened, although the evidence is complex and may have some race-specific characteristics.[16] Legislative attempts to reduce access to abortions could have a negative effect on birth outcomes, reflected in higher neonatal and infant mortality rates and higher rates of developmental disabilities.

REPORTING PROCEDURES

Almost all states and territories place responsibility for vital records management in their state health department, and in the majority of instances the state health officer is designated by law as the state registrar of vital statistics. Actual collection is usually accomplished through local registrars, who receive reports directly from attending physicians, midwives, undertakers, and others. The routing of reports of births and deaths is subject to much variation. In some states certificates are either filed with the county health officers, who transmit them to the state health departments, or are routed by the local registrars through the county health departments. More commonly, local registrars send the certificates directly to their state health departments. Some states have developed direct reporting systems wherein the state registrar serves as the only registrar. Whatever routing procedure is followed, four basic principles should be adhered to:

1. Certificates should be completed promptly by medical or other attendants.
2. There should be a system of routine checking by registrars of all certificates for correctness and completeness.
3. Certificates should be forwarded to the state agency at intervals of not longer than 1 month.
4. Pertinent data on certificates should be made readily and promptly available to local health departments. If this is not provided for, much of the value of the reporting is lost.

Morbidity reporting, as distinct from morbidity surveys, presents an extremely difficult problem. There are two different reasons for morbidity reporting: (1) the analysis of trends and the study of the causes of disease and (2) the need to implement public health control measures when unusual events occur. It is not desirable to maintain a surveillance system for analytical purposes unless sufficient resources are available either to make the system fairly complete or to make its biases known.[17] This is true for cancer registries and studies of occupational diseases and accidents, as well as communicable disease reporting systems. Some states have developed especially good registries for one or more of these, and together with special surveys, their data can be studied by others. It would be expensive and unnecessary to replicate such registries in many states. It is possible to develop a good registry for one or a few diseases of special interest in a given area, but broad-scope morbidity reporting systems are too complex and expensive for most states. An underfunded registry is worse than useless—it is dangerous, in that practitioners may draw incorrect conclusions from incomplete data and practice accordingly.

Public health agencies do need a reliable method of assuring that certain diseases will be reported promptly so that control measures can be instituted. For example, special procedures for reporting cases of AIDS have been developed by the Centers for Disease Control in Atlanta. These include a detailed diagnostic definition of AIDS and special data collection and reporting files. States also have AIDS reporting procedures in effect, and several require laboratories to report positive test results. These are often used by health department personnel to contact those with positive tests and to attempt to notify partners and reduce the spread of the disease. (See Chapter 14.) Similar procedures have been in effect for syphilis for many years, and the reporting forms are used to trace contacts across state boundaries. The system has worked effectively, with no evidence that its confidential nature has been violated.

It is essential that such efforts to encourage prompt reporting by doctors, nurses, and health facility administrators continue. This is particularly true for cases of tuberculosis. With the advent of increasingly effective chemotherapy and the ability to rapidly restore the infectious patient to noninfectious status, some communities with otherwise progressive medical practices have become nonchalant about tuberculosis. As the disease becomes increasingly rare, it becomes increasingly important to stress that it is a dangerous disease and that new cases must be investigated promptly and thoroughly by trained public health workers.

In a speech to his colleagues in the American Medical Association in 1887, Rohe[18] said that "the watchwords . . . in dealing with communicable diseases [are] these three: notification, isolation and disinfection." The last two of Rohe's watchwords have changed somewhat, but reporting still remains important. It is often the first indication of a new and serious problem.

There are many reasons why physicians may not report communicable diseases to the health department: (1) it may be seen as a complicated nuisance, depending on the arrangements made to facilitate reporting; (2) it may be seen as an unimportant task; (3) the patient may attempt to interfere with or block reporting; (4) the physician may see reporting as an infringement of confidentiality; or (5) there may be no real incentive for the physician to report. In a study of venereal disease–reporting practices, each of these phenomena was specifically addressed, and it was found that the single problem of most importance was the administrative complexity of reporting. When that problem was alleviated by making arrangements for a call to an office worker at regular intervals, reporting increased sharply.[19] The same reasoning may not affect reporting for other diseases, because most physicians have some understanding of the health department's interest in case-contact investigation of venereal disease but may not be aware of the department's interest in many other diseases.

There is considerable variation among the states concerning the specific diseases included in the reporting requirement. All states require the reporting of conjunctivitis, diphtheria, measles, meningitis, poliomyelitis, scarlet fever, smallpox, syphilis, typhoid fever, tuberculosis, undulant fever, and whooping cough. Variation is noted with respect to morbidity reporting methods.

Only two requirements are uniform in all the states. First, every state requires that cases of notifiable disease be reported by the attending physician or, in the absence of a physician, by the householder, head of the family, or person in charge of the patient. Second, the reports are to be made to the local health authority. Many states use report cards. Several use the same card for all diseases. Many states have a special card for cases of venereal diseases. Format varies from no regular form to single- and multiple-case report cards, stamped cards, and cards requiring postage.

The usual practice is to route morbidity reports through the local health department to the state health department. Some states require only that copies of daily, weekly, or monthly summaries be sent to the state health department. A few states follow the unreasonable practice of requiring physicians to send reports to both local and state health departments.

Physicians and others who are required to report diseases and injuries are subject to disciplinary action for failure to do so. Such actions are rare, but they do occur. The California Board of Medical Quality Assurance took such action when a physician failed to report a case of hepatitis that was the precursor to a large outbreak.[20]

Most of the reporting mechanisms in use in the United States are mandatory at the state level but voluntary at the national level. There is no general nationwide disease or injury reporting system, although under certain circumstances the degree of cooperation is so high as to provide its equivalent. That is the current situation with AIDS. Communicable diseases are reported by the states to the Centers for Disease Control, which uses the data to compile the tables and special reports published in *Morbidity and Mortality Weekly Report.* Given the wide variability from practice to practice, community to community, and state to state, the data are understandably incomplete. It is thought that no more than 20% at best of the common communicable diseases is reported at the local level in the first place. Provided that nothing disturbs the reporting system, it is nonetheless useful for analyzing trends and for identifying outbreaks and epidemic seasons that are out of the ordinary.

There are several other reporting systems in addition to the data collection systems of the National Center for Health Statistics. These include the following:

- National Electronic Injury Surveillance System, which functions in several hospital emergency rooms and provides data that can be used to identify new consumer product hazards
- Survey of Occupational Injuries and Illnesses, which is carried out by the Bureau of Labor Statistics
- Drug Abuse Warning Network, operated by the National Institute of Drug Abuse, a network of hospital emergency rooms in 26 metropolitan areas, which can be used to identify new drug use patterns
- National Reporting System of the National Institute of Mental Health, mentioned earlier

There is not a well-organized, official reporting system or survey for sociodemographic data. The census is the primary source of such information, and the Department of Labor conducts extensive surveys of family status, working patterns, income, and mobility.

Practical considerations

Certain factors must be considered in regard to reporting systems. Fundamental is the need to prepare and educate those in the community from whom reports are to be obtained. The most important of these are physicians, hospitals, and schools. Two other sources worthy of mention are the dental profession and industry. Too often there is an inclination to require reports of too many diseases and in too much detail, whether or not any practical use is made of the information. Generally when this is done, physicians and other reporting agencies eventually question the practicality of the request and the use made of it. If they decide that the information is merely received and filed away, they soon become careless in their reporting. They can hardly be blamed if no one takes the trouble to explain the purpose of the items requested. An additional important factor is the amount of work involved in making the report. Busy practitioners are loath to spend much time in writing out details of cases for official agencies. The least that can be done is to standardize and simplify some of the forms and procedures insofar as possible.

Requirements and methods should be reduced to the barest essentials. An increasing number of official health agencies accept reports of cases of communicable diseases in the form of telephone calls or preaddressed postcards, requiring only the diagnosis and the name, age, and address of the person affected. From there on it is the responsibility of the public health personnel to obtain what further details appear necessary for the adequate public health management of the case.

The purpose of the reporting requirement has to be considered when designing the reporting procedure. Where a case report is needed to initiate disease control actions, it may be possible to identify certain types of medical practice or health practice environments in which many new cases will be diagnosed and to concentrate services in those areas. This may be true for sexually transmitted diseases, for example. Urologists, family practitioners, and internists are more likely to see cases than are surgeons and psychiatrists. However, data collected in an effort that targets high-risk groups or practices cannot be reported as demonstrating the incidence or changing patterns of the disease, since it is deliberately biased in an attempt to capture the greatest number of cases for control purposes. Clinics for sexually transmitted diseases are often established in inner-city areas where private medical care is not readily available. White patients are more likely to obtain treatment in a private office in the suburbs, where reporting is uncommon, whereas black patients are more likely to use the available public clinic, which assures a high reporting rate. If incidence rates are reported by race or by neighborhood, blacks will appear to have a higher rate of sexually transmitted diseases than whites, which may or may not be true. When it is important to measure such differences or to monitor trends, special efforts have to be made to assure adequate reporting. In some cases, special randomly selected panels of physicians may be called on for periodic reporting with greater effort on the part of the health department staff, which will assure more complete reporting.

In addition to reducing the amount of information requested, it is useful to review periodically the list of diseases that various people are supposed to report. Some disease reports are requested even though very little use has been made of the data, such as chickenpox reports. An important adjunct to the reporting process is an analysis of the data and the distribution of this analysis to those doing the reporting in such a manner that it has value for them. People who are required to report certain phenomena on a form on a regular basis maintain little regard for the accuracy of their reports if they never see any results. Analyses with written comments should be circulated regularly to the professional groups that do the reporting, in such a manner that the information can be of help to them in the diagnosis and treatment of similar cases.

The legal basis for reporting and the procedures used have been brought into the public arena for the first time in many years by the advent of the AIDS pandemic. The need for information, reporting requirements, and the right of government agencies to collect such information have been reexamined in recent years, not only because of concerns about confidentiality, but because of ethical concerns as well. (See Chapter 16.)

THE COOPERATIVE HEALTH STATISTICS SYSTEM

Since 1925 there have been many proposals for the establishment of a morbidity reporting area similar to the birth and death registration areas. The practicality and value of total community surveys have been established in Hagerstown (Md.), Tecumseh (Mich.), and Framingham (Mass.). Data from the National Health Interview Survey have been used by a growing number of public health analysts and legislators.

Langmuir,[21] in 1949, stated:

> The morbidity survey is a particularly useful epidemiological tool in that data on both the sick and the well are obtained concurrently. The problems arising from underreporting of cases, from arbitrary classifications of causes of death, and from unknown shifts of population between census years are largely eliminated. . . . Its unique advantage lies in the detailed information that can be collected about the population. Frequency rates, specific for a wide variety of social and environmental factors, can be determined. Such comparisons are not obtainable by matching routine morbidity reports and death certificates with census figures.

He further pointed out the interrelationships between the simple survey and the special study:

> The simple morbidity survey has one inherent limitation—only general data can be obtained. The questions asked by the interviewers must be simple and understandable to the informants. Few specific diseases can be adequately counted by this method. Special studies are necessary to collect such definitive epidemiological information.

Brotherston[22] has commented that the reorganization of the National Health Service in Great Britain made possible the integration of hospital data, general practice data, and public health data into one system. The organization of such a system was described in a U.S. publication in 1969[23] and finally authorized by P.L. 93-353 in 1974: the Health Services Research, Health Statistics, and Medical Libraries Act. The National Center for Health Statistics (previously known as the National Office of Vital Statistics) was directed to establish a Cooperative Health Statistics System "to assist state and local health agencies and federal agencies involved in matters relating to health, in the design and implementation of a cooperative system."[24] The regulations identified seven components of the Cooperative Health Statistics System: vital statistics, health manpower statistics, health facilities statistics, hospital care statistics, long-term care statistics, ambulatory care statistics, and health interview statistics. The first four of these were selected for priority implementation. The NCHS pulled together different units such as the birth and death registration unit, the National Health Survey unit, and the manpower unit, to develop new forms of contractual relationships with the states, including a multicomponent contract. In addition to technical assistance, substantially increased federal financial assistance was available through the contracts. In return, the NCHS got back machine-ready computer tapes from the contract states, which reduced the center's lag time considerably. By 1980, 39 states had developed centers for health statistics, and virtually all states had one or more of the seven components either in place or under development. The NCHS obligated approximately $15 million for Cooperative Health Statistics System contracts in fiscal year 1988. Of the 39 state-level centers for health statistics, 33 were managed by the state health agency in 1980. The others were run by either state financial offices or state development offices or as a special component of the governor's office. Almost all of the state agencies were engaged in multiple statistical collection and reporting activities, including health manpower, health facilities, hospital care, the development of health trend analyses, and population forecasts. The state health agencies reported total expenditures for health statistics programs of $76.8 million in 1986.[25]

Among the principal weaknesses of the Cooperative Health Statistics System are the lack of a fiscal data base that could be meshed with the service and population data bases to produce expenditure estimates and the lack of environmental and social data. The shortcoming in environmental data was corrected supposedly by P.L. 95-623 in 1978, which authorized studies to determine the effects of employment and environmental conditions on public health. Unfortunately, although NCHS programs have become stronger in conjunction with the state centers, fiscal support for the NCHS has remained static or dwindled in recent years, making it increasingly difficult to carry out its mission. Recent planning efforts within the NCHS have been devoted to developing longer cycles and refined sampling procedures to maintain the major statistical systems currently in operation with reduced budgets. Many states are looking for other markets for their data to obtain enough money to keep their programs operating. The Minnesota center utilized 15 different sources of funding in 1985: seven federal contracts (NCHS, CDC, the Bureau of Community Programs of DHHS, NIH, the Environmental Protection Administration, the Department of Agriculture, and the Department of Transportation), two private foundations, a state grant, a state line item appropriation, several other state agencies, and the private sector.[26] That may be effective so long as new purchasers of state data do not force the states to alter their collection procedures to better suit the needs of special interest groups. The Cooperative Health Statistics System has sharply upgraded the availability and quality of health statistics in many states, but it cannot provide complete national data until it has progressed to all of the states and until all of the components are in place. This will take continued leadership, a hallmark of the NCHS since its inception, as well as steady support from the President and Congress, which has been less reliable.

ADMINISTRATIVE USES OF VITAL STATISTICS

The collection and analysis of public health statistics are costly and difficult tasks. Certain records, such as certificates of birth, death, marriage, and divorce, are the result of ministerial acts and must be made out as a matter of governmental responsibility, regardless of any public health use for the information. Other data collection activities are more discretionary. They are of two types: (1) collected as a by-product of a service effort, such as managing a clinic, an immunization program, or a water pollution control program or (2) primarily information-generating programs designed to produce data about the population, its health, the use of health resources, or the environment. The only real justification for collecting data is the use to which the resulting information may be put. Birth and death certificates are important legal records. Their personal value arises in connection with proof of citizenship, the right to attend school, to vote, to marry, to enter the armed services, and to draw benefits of many types. Records of births and deaths are of particular significance in the establishment of inheritance rights and in the prevention of capital crime. Beyond this ministerial function, which is not specifically a health-related function, is the use of the information contained in the records for the evaluation of the health of the community, the state, and the nation.

Statistics are integers of information that constitute potential knowledge. Whether that potential becomes real depends on its management. In each case, it is essential to understand why the data are being collected and what the sources are. Data collected to answer specific questions about expenditures for the purchase of biologic supplies may not be particularly useful in determining the cost of immunizing children. Moreover, the people who collect or have access to that fiscal data may not have assembled it in a way that can be used readily by people in some other part of the organization who are interested in the costs and benefits of the overall program. At the same time, program managers may be collecting data that they believe will help them understand why and how people are using the program's services, but such data may not merge readily with budgetary or expenditure data kept elsewhere to produce a cost per unit of service.

Who collects the data, for what purpose, and who manages the available computer resources for storage, retrieval, and analysis of the data have a great deal to do with whether those data can be used for planning and management purposes as well as for the study of disease and disability patterns in the community. The fiscal officer of a public health agency has to have steady access to information about how much money has been spent on what and how much is left in each of the appropriated categories. This often results in competition for machine time, which can lead to the business office developing its own data system to maintain control of the budget. Since this tends to be the single most important control document in the agency, and usually the only agency "plan," the reporting and "inputting" of performance or activity data is often left to the individual program managers. This results in a lack of linkage between activity data and fiscal data and makes it difficult to measure the cost of an activity or function. Then when special information needs arise, to respond to either an external question or an internal research inquiry, neither information program is adequate and the requester has to develop or find yet another database. These conflicts are not just in the nature of the accountability each of the data users has to someone else, but often rest in the very style or orientation of the people looking for information. The researcher, the fiscal manager, and the program manager usually come from different parts of the organization and have little interest in the others' questions, at least at the time they are pursuing their own. This can lead to some very difficult organizational problems. A health statistics center is not usually placed under the supervision of the fiscal officer. It is important that the center manager and the fiscal manager learn to cooperate in the use of computers. However, such cooperation may not be practical, since the computers are usually under the control of one of the two managers whose programs will take precedence. It is now relatively inexpensive to acquire additional computer capability, and most programs have their own computer systems. This has made possible a significant increase in data management and evaluative capacity at an acceptable direct cost, but lack of coordinated planning often increases the indirect cost of information loss caused by idiosyncratic file development. It is essential that program managers collaborate with the central office and the fiscal staff in the design of their data collection procedures and file construction, so that cost and performance data can be linked without tedious and costly reconstruction in a third software program and file system.

It is not necessary to place the birth and death certificate registration process in the same management center with other statistical functions, although there are advantages to doing so in the use of microfilming equipment, computers, terminals, and printers. The management skills required to assure the continuity and accuracy of the certificate registration processes are those suited to a clearly defined line organization with fairly rigid practices and authority relationships. Management of the health statistics center requires a more flexible approach and the challenge of irreverent questions. If these two management styles clash, it is possible to keep the certificate registration process as a clerical center in the business management area of the agency so long as the information contained in the certificates can be filmed or stored on tape in such a way that the health statistics center staff can have continuous access to it.

In any case, management of the health statistics center, whatever functions it includes, should be placed in a fairly prominent staff position close to the agency director or the director of planning. If the center has responsibility for handling a considerable volume of management data, care should be taken that sufficient time and resources are sequestered for the evaluation and analysis functions; some should be left over for research inquiries. Administrators of smaller health agencies should not make the mistake of assuming that this advice is irrelevant to their needs. The director of such an agency may also function as the data center manager, but the requirements remain the same: keep the process close to the center of decision making; make sure that time is available for evaluation and that not all of it is used in balancing the budget; and keep a little left over for new inquiries.

The term *management information system* has become so common and popular in recent years that most health administrators with a few weeks of experience are comfortable with the term MIS. As this comfortable use of the term has increased, its value has decreased. Too many people have too many different ideas about what it means. Health administrators speak of a "mental health MIS," an "alcoholism MIS," and even a "health systems MIS." There is no doubt that too many different information systems are requested by various officials and legislative bodies and that too many irrelevant questions are being asked at the expense of the few questions that should be asked and answered. Elected and appointed officials and their staffs rail against the forms and reports that they have to complete. This paperwork is all there because someone asked a question and someone else either had to answer it or believed that they had to. Statistics center managers and other administrators have to learn to curb their appetite for data in the interest of asking more penetrating questions.

The question asked often has little relationship to what the questioner really wants to know. Recently a community mental health center director asked the director of the state statistics center for a printout of the names of all the patients who had been discharged from the state hospital into the center's catchment area over the previous 5 years. The community center director did not tell the state center director that his interest was not so much in the names as in calculating the percentage of patients discharged into the service area who were included in the mental health center's programs over the 3 months following hospital discharge. Because the state data manager did not know the specific purpose, he could not help the community mental health center manager, because the release of patient names was forbidden by agency policy on confidentiality. Had the two managers explored the question a little further, they would have found out what was really wanted and the state center manager could have produced the necessary information quite easily. Because information on discharged patients was regularly filed in the data system, as were patient data from the community center, the computer could have matched the two files.

The manager of the health statistics center should never accept an inquiry as it is stated but should use that as a starting point to find out exactly what the inquirer is trying to understand. Once that has been accomplished, it may be found that (1) the information really needed is already available, (2) a different question will be more useful, or (3) the question being asked is not as important as some of the other questions pending in the center's work load and cannot be answered in the immediate future. This last point is important and should be more commonly considered. Questions can be costly. To answer them requires time, and that represents an opportunity cost that has to be negotiated by the statistics center director, the agency director, and the inquirer. In cases where the latter two are one and the same, a particularly good working relationship is required if the agency's resources are to be used efficiently. Agency directors are just as prone as anyone else to ask whimsical or poorly formulated questions, and data center managers do not often feel that they have the ability to challenge such requests, which can lead to valuable time in the data center being used to answer relatively trivial questions.

For statistical data to be of real value in the health program, efforts far beyond the strict legal responsibilities imposed on public health agencies are required. When all the statistics available to a health department are correlated, they become of fourfold value in that they make possible (1) the definition of the problem, (2) the development of a logical program for its control, (3) the planning of records and procedures for the administration and analysis of the program as it progresses, and (4) the evaluation of the results of the program.

CONFIDENTIALITY

A number of technological developments, political events, and social trends have come together in recent years and heightened the concern for confidentiality. The use of very large computers and the increase in the number of skilled technicians who know how to operate them make the linkage of separate records possible and probable. Burnett and his associates[27] have reported on the ease with which they were able to link family planning records in Georgia with official vital statistics documents to determine fertility rates in subgroups of users of the family planning clinics. They found that black, young, and less educated users were more likely to have a baby after receiving services than were white, older, and better educated users. They regretted that they were not able to include all pregnancies but found that elective abortion records did not include sufficient patient identification data to make the matches possible. No doubt the information obtained from the study was useful (although neither surprising nor original), and it appears that they took pains to protect confidentiality, but the enthusiasm for such record linkage projects is disturbing. Similar concerns are raised by automating medical records in the Medicaid program in Alabama. Mesel and Writschafter[28] found that modern techniques allowed them to place information about 400,000 people—10% of the state's population—into a computer system for about 12½¢ per year per person, and they rhapsodized over the ease of doing the same thing for 20 million Medicaid recipients nationwide. Although they spoke of the need to assure confidentiality, they acknowledged that the techniques for doing that were yet to be developed and suggested that the patients be reminded of the advantage they obtained by having their records available to physicians all over the state.

The desire to assimilate such data is ancient and seemingly unquenchable. Lunde[29] has reported on the history and current status of unique identifying numbers that can be universally used to link records. Many countries have developed extensive systems that link birth, death, marriage, and divorce data with medical records, income tax returns, employment history, Social Security benefits, family linkages, etc. The Social Security number in the United States was established by executive order in 1943, and its use had become so pervasive by the 1970s that a Department of Health, Education and Welfare task force report recommended against any further expansion or the development of any other unique identifier system. But most states had already added a universal and unique identifier to birth certificates in 1968 for the express purpose of encouraging data system linkages.

The desire to learn more about health and the causes and treatments of disability leads many researchers into an omnivorous quest for data; and trading privacy for knowledge seems an easy bargain, especially when one is sure of one's own motives. The most conscientious researcher or administrator cannot forever protect information from an equally diligent intruder, however. The two conflicting values of privacy and freedom of information make the development of policy very complex.

A proposed "model state law for the collection, sharing, and confidentiality of health statistics"[30] makes the conflict apparent. In the model, no data can be divulged that will make it possible for the person described to be identified *unless:*

1. The individual described has consented. (In most cases it is not possible for the individual to know what is in the file and therefore what will be disclosed.)
2. The disclosure is to a governmental entity, and the recipient agency has a written agreement that it will protect the data.
3. The disclosure is for research purposes, and a written agreement to safeguard the data and allow them to go no further has been obtained.
4. The disclosure is to a governmental entity for the purpose of conducting an audit, evaluation, or investigation of the agency.

The report notes that all of the disclosure exceptions are at the discretion of the agency except for the last one, which is mandatory and means that a government auditor can gain access to the records of clients in an alcohol detoxification program in the course of conducting a fiscal audit. Under this proposed model, possibilities for a breach of confidentiality will grow in direct proportion to the size of the database.

The AIDS epidemic, as mentioned earlier, has brought many of the issues pertaining to confidentiality into the public arena with a new sense of urgency and interest. On the one hand, citizens are justifiably concerned about one of the most dangerous epidemics of modern times. The perceived need to know who is infected with the virus and may therefore infect others is not different in many respects from the need to know about other dangerous infectious diseases. Yet because of the nature of the disease and the high-risk groups associated with it, information about its victims can result (and has) in discriminatory actions that further harm the victims with no benefit for society.

State health directors have the principal burden of analyzing and forming policy regarding confidentiality for AIDS victims and testing programs for human immunodeficiency virus infection. State medical associations are also concerned, as are hospital associations, nursing groups, law enforcement officers, and the general public. The Association of State and Territorial Health Officials has developed a carefully worded policy on the subject.[31] While the report was prepared to deal with some of the unique features of AIDS, a slight rewording of its central conclusion has applicability to confidentiality more generally: confidentiality means that an individual will be protected from release of information that could link that individual's identity to facts about his or her disease, any behavioral risk factors that are thought to be involved, or the individual's application for related services. Disclosure of information without the documented and informed consent of the individual is permitted only when the disclosure is necessary for the individual's medical care or is required by law. That final condition (a disclosure required by law) is troublesome: the law is not always wise or just. So far, public health professionals have been extraordinarily effective at keeping bad AIDS laws off the books. The situation is complex and will continue to test a fragile sense of public health ethics and public health skills.

The problems involved in balancing privacy and the need to know about things will not yield to polemics or statutes unless there is a better understanding of the ethics of both. For example, most applicants for a job or for college sign a consent form entitling the organization to gain access to the applicant's medical records. But since the applicant has not, in most cases, seen those records, it is not an informed consent. The applicant has no idea what opinions may have been recorded. Until the physician, nurse, or counselor has been taught to write records so that the client can read and understand them and discuss them, this will not change.[32]

Some efforts to preserve confidentiality have been deleterious to the welfare of the person at risk. Mental health records are often so protected that it is technically illegal for a mental health worker in a community center to answer an inquiry from a psychiatrist in an emergency room as to whether anything is known about an overdosed patient. In most such cases the law is quickly violated in the interest of patient survival, but variations on the theme continue to occur with sufficient frequency to emphasize the point that the trade-off between privacy and the need to know cannot be settled by law or in electronics until the study of ethics has caught up with technology.

REFERENCES

1. Higher education for public health: a report of the Milbank Memorial Fund Commission, New York, 1976, Prodist.
2. Kraus AS: Efficient utilization of statistical activities in public health, Am J Public Health 53:1075, July 1963.
3. Murnaghan JH: Health indicators and information systems for the year 2000. In Breslow L, editor: Annual review of public health, vol 2, Palo Alto, CA, 1981, Annual Reviews, Inc.
4. Bureau of the Census: Current population reports (population estimates and projections), Series P-25, Washington, DC, issued intermittently, US Government Printing Office.
5. National Center for Health Statistics: Data systems of the National Center for Health Statistics, Series 1(16), DHHS Pub No (PHS) 82-1318, Hyattsville, MD, 1981, US Department of Health and Human Services.
6. Eaton WW and others: The epidemiological catchment area program of the National Institute of Mental Health, Public Health Rep 96:319, July-Aug 1981.
7. Task Force on Nomenclature and Statistics: Diagnostic and statistical manual of mental disorders, ed 3, Washington, DC, 1980, American Psychiatric Association.
8. Van Amburg G: Proposed new items on the 1988 standard vital records documents. In Proceedings of the 1985 public health conference on records and statistics, Hyattsville, MD, 1985, National Center for Health Statistics.
9. Kircher T, Nelson J, and Burdo H: The autopsy as a measure of accuracy of the death certificate, N Engl J Med 313:1263, Nov 14, 1985.
10. Percy C, Stanek E, and Glocekler L: Accuracy of cancer death certificates and its effect on cancer mortality statistics, Am J Public Health 71:242, Mar 1981.
11. World Health Organization: International classification of diseases, rev 9, Geneva, 1978, The Organization.
12. Kleinman JC: Age adjusted mortality indexes for small areas: applications to health planning, Am J Public Health 67:834, Sept 1977.
13. Warshauer ME and Monk M: Problems in suicide statistics for whites and blacks, Am J Public Health 68:383, April 1978.
14. Naylor A and others: Birth certificate revision and reporting of congenital malformations, Am J Public Health 64:786, Aug 1974.
15. Morris NM, Udry JC, and Chase CL: Shifting age-parity distribution of births and the decrease in infant mortality, Am J Public Health 65:359, April 1975.
16. Joyce T: The impact of induced abortions on black and white birth outcomes in the United States, Demography 24:229, May 1987.
17. Guidelines for evaluating surveillance systems, Morbid Mortal Week Rep 24(suppl):24, May 1988.
18. Rohe GH: Recent advances in preventive medicine, reprinted in J Am Med Assoc 258:328, July 17, 1987.
19. Rothenberg R, Bross DC, and Vernon TM: Reporting gonorrhea by private physicians: a behavioral study, Am J Public Health 70:893, Sept 1980.
20. Goodman RA and Berkelman RL: Physicians, vital statistics and disease reporting, J Am Med Assoc 258:379, July 17, 1987.
21. Langmuir AD: The contributions of the survey method to epidemiology, Am J Public Health 39:747, June 1949.
22. Brotherston JHF: Health planning and statistics: an overview from Scotland, Int J Health Serv 3:35, Winter 1973.
23. National Center for Health Statistics: A state center for health statistics: an aid in planning, Washington, DC, US Department of Health, Education and Welfare, Public Health Conference of Records and Statistics Document No. 626, Revised 1969.
24. The cooperative health statistics system: its mission and program; final report from the Task Force on Definitions to the Cooperative Health Statistics Advisory Committee, Aug 30, 1976, Washington, DC, US Department of Health, Education and Welfare Pub No (HRA) 77-1456, 1977.
25. Public Health Foundation: Public health agencies 1988: an inventory of programs and block grant expenditures, Washington, DC, 1988, The Foundation.
26. Gunderson PD: Implementing a state center for health statistics—selected funding implications. In Proceedings of the 1985 public health conference on records and statistics, Hyattsville, MD, 1985, National Center for Health Statistics.

27. Burnett CA and others: Use of automated record linkage to measure patient fertility after family planning service, Am J Public Health 70:246, March 1980.
28. Mesel E and Writschafter DD: Automation of a patient medical profile from insurance claims data: a possible first step in automating ambulatory medical records on a national scale, Milbank Q, Winter 1976.
29. Lunde AS: The birth number concept and record linkage, Am J Public Health 65:1165, Nov 1975.
30. Expert Panel for the Development of the Model State Health Statistics Act: Model Health Statistics Act: a model state law for the collection, sharing, and confidentiality of health statistics, Hyattsville, MD, 1978, US Department of Health, Education and Welfare.
31. Association of State and Territorial Health Officials: Guide to public health practice: AIDS confidentiality and anti-discrimination principles, Washington, DC, 1988, Public Health Foundation.
32. Payne M: Access to social services records—ethical and practical issues, J Royal Soc Health 108:41, April 1988.

CHAPTER 9

Law and public health

THE IMPORTANCE OF LAW

The law has two functions in public health: it must be used to guide the procedures of public health in a fair manner, and it should be used as a creative tool for the prevention of disease and the promotion of health. A conference in 1961 sponsored by the American Public Health Association and the U.S. Public Health Service concluded that public health workers were inadequately informed and trained in the legal aspects of public health and in the legal framework within which public health programs are designed and activated.[1] This is not surprising, since despite its impact on people, education about law for other than law students is one of the most neglected aspects of American education. The situation remains the same in this final decade of the twentieth century, not just because the study of law has not been fully incorporated into the study of public health, but because the law has changed and progressed at a pace not noticeably different from that of the other technologies of public health. According to Kenneth Wing[2]:

> Quite literally, new law—for better or for worse or for more of the same—is being created at an ever-increasing rate and, some would argue, in even more complicated forms. . . . The law as it relates to health care must be understood by anyone who deals with the critical issues that face our nation today. If for no other reason, the law effects a set of constraints on behavior. More importantly, the law is one determinant of health and of the health care delivery system; it is a means for causing change as well as preventing it.

Fortunately, one may point to the appearance during recent decades of not only an increasing number of specialists who have bridged the legal and public health fields but also a growing amount of literature concerning the relationships between law and public health. Especially useful have been the series of articles that have appeared in the *American Journal of Public Health* under the by-lines first of Forgotson and currently of Curran and Annas. The American Public Health Association now has a special primary interest group called the Health Law Forum.

It is impractical, indeed impossible, for health workers to attempt to function without at least a general familiarity with the legal system. To provide this is all that is attempted here. Beyond this, readers are urged to acquire a familiarity with the legislation, legislative structures, and legislative procedures of their respective communities, states, and nations, especially as they relate to health matters. There are several excellent books on public health law, including Wing (mentioned above) and Tom Christoffel's *Health and the Law.*[3]*

Wing thinks that an introductory education in law should include the following:

1. A thorough and realistic understanding of the law and the legal system, particularly the structure and function of the various legal decision-making processes
2. A familiarity with the substance of American law, including a basic understanding of important legal principles
3. The ability to sort out legal controversies and define relevant and critical legal issues in the application of these principles
4. The ability to understand how those issues are likely to be resolved
5. The ability to seek out, communicate with, and evaluate legal counsel

The legislative process involves interaction among the three basic branches of government, which are usually interlocked by a system of checks and balances. Thus in the United States, the *executive* may veto legislation or sign it into law, the *legislature* may introduce and enact a law and can override a veto by the executive, and the *judiciary*

* A new edition of Frank Grad's *Public Health Law Manual* should be published in 1990 by the American Public Health Association.

may discard a law if it considers it in violation of basic freedoms and rights. To these three may be added the operating or enforcement agencies that are held responsible for carrying out the intent of the legislation; these also may be a significant source of proposed legislative additions or changes. The classic separation of powers as it is traditionally described is not characterized by clean lines of demarcation. The executive branch of government exercises a considerable influence over the application of laws by the process of rule-making or administrative law (see below) and the use of executive orders, which set policy for the administration. The basic intentions of Congress can and have been altered by presidents. The judiciary also creates an enormous amount of law by its decisions in specific cases (see below under Stare decisis, or judicial precedence). And Congress has attached review requirements on executive branch action in an attempt to limit the discretion of the administering agencies. The legitimate and sanctioned sources of law-making by each of the three branches of government are sometimes seen as transgressions, and arguments ensue that may result in attempts to change procedures so as to alter the balance of power among the branches of government. These same tensions and changes occur at the state level as well.

Everything that is done in a health agency has a basis in law and is subject to legal sanctions of one type or another. As for official health agencies, in addition to their service functions, many activities involve the enforcement of law.

DEFINITION OF LAW[2,4,5]

Much has been written dealing exclusively with the nature and definition of law. It is interesting that, although the average citizen probably considers law an exact and strictly defined field, its mere definition presents the members of the legal profession with perhaps their most difficult problem. Law, at least in a democracy, depends in the last analysis on the collective wishes of the people; and the type and extent of their wishes vary through place and time. It should be realized that human behavior is subject to a never-ceasing process of evolution, as are the social factors determining or influencing it. It is worthwhile to consider briefly the changes and evolution that have occurred in legal attitudes and definitions as they relate to the United States. Blackstone,[6] the great English jurist, considered law as a "rule of civil conduct prescribed by the supreme power in a state, commanding what is right and forbidding what is wrong." It should be noted that he refrained from including the criteria involved in determining "right" or "wrong" at any particular time. As has been noted elsewhere, those who developed the government of the United States subscribed to the concept of natural law, essentially fixed and immutable. This concept led to and supported a laissez-faire type of government that interfered with the individual to a minimal extent. It carried over into the late nineteenth century. Thus, C.C. Langdell, the first Dean of Harvard University Law School, wrote in 1886 that "the law is a science" and that "all the available materials of the science are contained in printed books of judicial opinions."[7] As the twentieth century was approached, several prominent jurists, notably Oliver Wendell Holmes[8] and James B. Thayer,[9] insisted that legal doctrine should be regarded basically as the historical product of social conflict and political compromise.

Early in the twentieth century, a group of progressive legal theorists and practitioners including Louis Brandeis, Felix Frankfurter, Roscoe Pound, and James Landis urged consideration by the courts of nonlegal facts in relation to the interpretation and application of the law.[10] At the same time, Woodrow Wilson[11] still considered law as "that portion of established thought and habit which has gained distinct and formal recognition in the shape of uniform rule backed by the authority and power of government." During the 1920s and 1930s, a group referred to as "legal realists" appeared. They were strongly critical of classical and professionally self-centered lawyers. They advocated the application of various sociologic disciplines including anthropology, Freudian psychology, political science, and statistics to the interpretation of law in relation to behavior. In stronger words, they sought to deny "the autonomy of legal science" and to expose it as "a smoke screen disguising the realities of human motivation."[10] The Great Depression of the 1930s brought about a fundamental change in legal thought under the banner of the so-called legal process school. It considered the lawyer to have "a social role with definite social expectations" so that he should "coordinate his role with those of other role-players in the legal process." Further, it sought to demonstrate that "the courts were often not the institutions best equipped to make many judgments of social importance and that therefore judges should often defer to the policy resolutions made by legislatures, administrative agencies, other judicial systems, or by private parties themselves."[10]

The foregoing would appear to support the view of Wing that "the law" is the sum of all the sets of laws in a jurisdiction: its constitution, its statutes, its common law, its rules, and its body of judicial decisions. These will each be described below.

Finding the law

Laws are codified or arranged by subject matter into codes. In most states there is a health code or a health and welfare code. In too many states, the health code has not been kept up to date, and it is often difficult to find out what the current law is on a subject without access to a lawyer or a good legal reference librarian.

There are also codes of regulations, the rules adopted by administrative agencies of government to carry out the requirements of a statute. The *Federal Register*, which is published daily, contains all proposed and enacted rules in chronological sequence. The *Code of Federal Regulations* (CFR) codifies the rules by subject matter. There are 50 titles in the CFR, which are altered by new actions each day, as published in the *Federal Register*. A *"List of CFR Sections Affected"* is published monthly, and a cumulative list appears in the Readers Aid section of the daily *Federal Register*. Certain titles of the CFR are of special interest to public health:

Title 1—general provisions
Title 2—agriculture; Chapter 2 deals with the food and nutrition service
Title 21—food and drugs
Title 29—labor; Chapters 17 and 20 deal with occupational safety and health
Title 40—environmental protection
Title 42—public health
Title 45—public welfare

As in the codification of new statutes, the states tend to be dilatory with codifying their regulations.

New statutes are often referred to by title, such as The National Health Planning and Resources Development Act of 1974 or P.L. 93-641 (the 641st public law signed by the President during the 93rd session of Congress). In legal parlance, they are more often referred to by the section of the volume in the code: 8 U.S.C. ss 3456, for example, which means volume 8 of the U.S. Code, beginning at section 3456. In a state, the reference might be to the California Welfare and Institutions Code, Section 17000.

Regulations have similar citations: 42 C.F.R. "n" would refer to Title 42 of the Code of Federal Regulations, beginning at section n. A state citation might be 38 State n.

Judicial opinions are even more difficult to find. They are published in *Reporters* for the different court systems. For example, an important 1978 U.S. Supreme Court decision regarding inspections by the Occupational Safety and Health Administration *(Marshal v Barlow's Inc.)* is referred to as "436 U.S. 307," which means that the case appears on page 307 of the 436th volume of the *United States Reports.* It can become very difficult for a lay person to read such citations, let alone find them, but a little experience in a law school library with the help of a librarian can make the arcane appear simple.

CHARACTERISTICS OF LAW

A law implies an actual or potential command, and a command signifies nothing more nor less than a wish or desire. However, the commands and desires of law differ from ordinary personal commands and desires in that they (1) represent community desires or commands, (2) are applicable to all in the community, (3) are backed by the full power of the government, and (4) provide for all people the administration of justice under these laws. Wilson's definition might be considered appropriate, since it either states or implies all of the characteristics mentioned.

PURPOSE OF LAW

The primary purpose of law might be said to be the promotion of the general good by the regulation of human conduct to protect the individual from other individuals, groups, or the state, and vice versa. To effect such protection, it must be possible for the individual, the group, and the state to predict within reasonable limits the probable course of judgment in the event of an infringement of the law. Therefore another purpose of law is to assure, insofar as possible, uniformity of action to prevent errors of judgment or improper motives or actions on the part of judicial officers. It is often said that the wheels of justice turn slowly. The rate would be impossibly slow if the cumulative experience of earlier judges were not available to the people and to the courts. This also is a purpose of law.

The most fundamental means by which law endeavors to carry out its purposes is the definition of rights and duties existing between individuals or groups. Legal relationships form the essential subject matter of law, and rights and duties are the most important of legal relationships. A legal right is a power, privilege, or interest of an individual or group that is recognized and protected by law. Simultaneously the law imposes on all others the obligation to refrain from violation of the right. Thus the possession of a right by one person always implies a corresponding duty on the part of some other person or persons to respect that right. For example, A and B enter into a contract. The legal relationship may be expressed as either A has a right that B perform an act or B owes A a duty to perform an act.

Rights are of two kinds, primary and secondary. Primary rights are those that result merely from an individual's existence as a member of society. A citizen holds these primary rights against the entire community individually and collectively, and the community and each of its individuals owe each person a corresponding duty to refrain from violating them. Thus a citizen's person and property are held to be inviolate; that is a primary right, and all others owe a duty to respect it. Such rights exist not by virtue of any action taken or decision made but are the kind of rights that were termed "natural rights" by eighteenth century legal theorists. They are sometimes spoken of as "rights in rem" and "rights of ownership." Their violation is considered a civil wrong (a tort) or a crime, depending on their magnitude and on whatever statutory law declares them to be. Libel, slander, trespass, negligence, and the like are civil wrongs or torts. It is increasingly difficult, however, to determine just balances or limits for rights and duties and indeed to decide whether they result from rights or duties in rem or ownership. Examples of these dilemmas may be found in relation to tobacco smoking and to aspects of environmental pollution,[3] as well as to the privacy of personal health and medical records.[12]

Secondary rights are those superimposed on primary rights as a result of individual action and decision. They are not held against all other persons generally but only against a specified person or group. These rights arise as a result of contract. For example, A and B enter into a contractual agreement. Before the contract their legal relationship, consisting of rights and duties owed each other, was fixed and equal. Now, as a result of the contract, their legal relationships are different. A's previous primary rights are now increased by a secondary right that B carry out the action agreed on in the contract. This new right differs in kind from primary rights, first, because it is not simply caused by A's existence but results from a mutually agreed-upon contract, and second, because it is a right held against B alone and no others.

Remedial rights are sometimes referred to as a third form of rights. They come into existence on the violation of the legal primary and secondary rights just discussed. In other words, they are rights resulting from a personal injustice and are held against the individual committing the legal wrong. What they really amount to is a right of reparation, usually in the form of a money judgment. All that is meant by saying that a person has a remedial right is that if he or she appeals to the court, a favorable verdict will probably be rendered.

SYSTEMS OF LAW

Development

The concept of law has gone through many changes throughout the centuries of recorded history. With primitive man it apparently originated as a combination of gradually developing customs based on tradition and supposedly divine dictates. Perhaps the chief function of the patriarchs of a tribe was to define the practices evolved and followed by their predecessors, and these customs were gradually given the significance of established precedent and law. As to the meaning or reason for such laws, it was the theory of the Hindus and Chinese that laws were an essential necessity of human society, as a result of the innate depravity of humans. As evidenced by human nature, laws were necessary to prevent violence and injustice. Therefore it became a primary duty first of the tribal leaders and ultimately of their successor, the state, to formulate and enforce rules of human behavior and conduct.

The Greek theory of law was somewhat different and followed in general the basic philosophic pattern of their civilization. The Greeks argued that all necessary social laws really existed in nature and were merely waiting to be discovered, similar to the principles of physics. In fact, nature was thought of more or less as an expression of the total of all universal law. This concept that law exists perpetually, waiting to be discovered as natural truths, held sway for over 1,700 years, passing through Stoic philosophy, Roman law, the principles of the Christian Church, and on through the medieval civilizations and governments. It is significant that those who formulated the Declaration of Independence and the Constitution with its Bill of Rights had as their legal background the natural theory of law. It is noteworthy that the Declaration of Independence deals with natural rights, which are to be *secured*, rather than *granted* by government.

Since the establishment of the republic, the concept or theory of law in the United States has undergone considerable change, especially since the beginning of the twentieth century, so that legislation is now seen merely as a device for the regulation and control of human conduct to assure that the wishes of the greatest number, or of the dominant groups in the community, are carried out.

Statutory law

At the present time, almost the entire Western world is governed by a combination of two distinct systems of law: (1) statutory law, based essentially on Roman civil law, and (2) the common law of England. The earliest known recorded statutes were those of Hammurabi (2067-2025 BCE) for the Babylonian Empire. Roman law began its development very early in the Roman state. To these were added innumerable unwritten laws that ultimately, as a result of the Institutes of Justinian and others, were codified into a system of written law so perfect that even today it serves as the basic law of most European countries. Its geographic adoption was related, of course, to the paths of Roman conquest, which brought the Roman legal code into most parts of the continent. After the decline of the Roman Empire, the resulting daughter nations retained the Roman legal system, since they had little other pattern to follow. Subsequent states, such as the members of the American republic, provided legislatures to make whatever laws were necessary for government, and the resulting collections of legislative acts constituted the statutory law. For a time an attempt was made to adhere rather strictly to statutory law, but as societies became more complicated, especially as a result of urbanization and industrialization, innumerable additions had to be made in the form of specific interpretations, court decisions, and rules and regulations. The result is that at the present time, in the United States, written or statutory law constitutes only a small part (about 2%) of all existing laws.

Common law[8]

It was recognized at an early date that statutory law was in many cases too general to be directly applied to particular cases. As a result, courts were developed, the judges of which were expected to be guided in their specific decisions by the established customs of the community. England took particular strides in this direction. Essentially this recognition of the legal importance of custom represented a practical recognition of the right of a people to take part in making the rules and laws governing their conduct and relationships. This was a great step toward liberty. A custom, to be entitled to consideration in law, must meet certain conditions. First, it must have existed for a long time or, as Blackstone put it, "have been used so long that the memory of man runneth not to the contrary."[6] It must be followed continuously; that is, constantly observed and respected whenever an occasion for its observance or respect arises. Second, it must have a peaceful purpose and be reasonable and not inconsistent with the general spirit of the law. Third, it must be definite rather than vague and must be considered binding on all people. Fourth, it must be consistent with all other customs of society.

The American colonies, having been settled primarily by people of Anglo-Saxon origin, had as their original legal basis the written law existing in England at the time of their migration plus the vast volume of common law that had evolved in England up to that time. Superimposed on this was an ever-increasing amount of common law based on the social customs that evolved on the new continent. For example, the law governing the state of Indiana consists of the following:

FIRST. The Constitution of the United States and of this state.

SECOND. All statutes of the general assembly of the state in force, and not inconsistent with such constitutions.

THIRD. All statutes of the United States in force, and relating to subjects over which congress has power to legislate for the states, and not inconsistent with the Constitution of the United States.

6. FOURTH. The common law of England, and statutes of the British Parliament made in aid thereof prior to the 4th year of the reign of James I (except the second section of sixth chapter of 43rd Elizabeth, the eighth chapter of 13th Elizabeth, and the ninth chapter of 37th Henry VIII) and which are of a general nature, not local to that kingdom and not inconsistent with the first, second, and third specifications of this section.*

Added to this is all the common law evolved in Indiana since the inception of its statehood. Statements similar to this are to be found in the constitutions or statutes of each of the American states with the exception of Louisiana, for which the Napoleonic Code provides the legal base.

Stare decisis, or judicial precedence

With the gradual development and extension of use of the common law courts, another type of law developed. The administration of justice would have become impossibly slow were it necessary to judge every particular controversy by returning to the basic principles of the Constitution and the statute in question, as if the discussion had never before occurred. Therefore the doctrine of stare decisis (the decision stands) developed, whereby a rule of law, whether based on custom or on being recognized by the courts and thereby applied to the solution of a case, formed a precedent that should be followed in all similar cases thereafter unless subsequently deemed absurd or unjust or unless repealed by the legislature. Decisions made in higher courts are not only binding on lower courts within the same system but are usually held to be binding on peer-level courts in other systems. Supreme Court decisions are binding on all the lower level federal courts and are generally thought to be binding on state courts as well. The search for useful judicial precedence occupies a great deal of the time of law clerks and paralegals.

Equity or chancery

Up to the time of William the Conqueror (CE 1066) the administration of justice was limited to the application of existing laws. However, William the Conqueror assumed the doctrine that the sovereign was the ultimate source of all justice and that he himself was above the law. Hence the well-known saying "The king can do no wrong" developed. Therefore, he and the English rulers who followed him for a considerable period dispensed justice as they considered desirable or expeditious.

Thus if some wrong were committed for which the law offered no true remedy or if the plaintiff believed that the law had not provided complete justice, the king could be appealed to for assistance beyond the power of the courts. As common law courts came to depend more and more on precedents as guides in dispensing justice, they became more and more rigid. Accordingly the king was appealed to with increasing frequency, so much so that the king's chancellor, who was otherwise spoken of as the "keeper of the king's conscience," was made responsible. This was eventually followed by the establishment of separate courts of chancery or equity, the essential purpose of which was to render justice and restitution as completely as possible, going beyond the dictates of existing laws if necessary. As time went on, such courts became strictly limited to situations for which no adequate remedy or solution was offered by the regular law courts. Eventually, however, as chancellors and their courts rendered more and more decisions and judgments, they too, as a matter of course, became more or less bound by precedents, sometimes defeating the original purpose of their existence.

This system of equity as a supplement to the written and common law was also brought to America and established as a part of its legal structure. Separate chancery or equity courts still exist in a few states along the Eastern seaboard and in the Southeast. Otherwise, for practical purposes, the same court now sits as a court of law, dispensing strictly legal judgments, and again as a court of equity, administering relief in cases for which the law as it exists offers no remedy. Equity serves as the basis for the proper administration of justice in many cases of public health concern, reference to a few examples of which will be made.

Certain principles have been laid down to define the natural sphere of interest and applicability of equity. They may be summarized as follows:

Equity will not suffer a wrong without a remedy. This is fundamental, considering the reason for the development of equity.

* Section 1-101 (244) Burns Indiana Statutes Annotated 1933.

Equity delights to do justice and not by halves. Thus it is the intention of equity that all interested parties be present in court and that there be rendered a complete judgment adjusting all rights for the plaintiff and preventing future litigation. An example of this is presented by a case* questioning an amendment to a Wisconsin statute relating to the licensing of restaurants. A subsection had been added providing that no permit should be issued to operate or maintain any food-serving business where any other type of business was conducted unless the facilities dealing with the preparation and serving of food were separated from such other business by substantial partitions extending from the floor to the ceiling and with self-closing doors. The provisions of the subsection were applicable only to restaurants commencing business after the effective date of the subsection. In a mandamus proceeding in which it was sought to compel the state board of health to grant a permit to conduct a restaurant, the complainant contended that the added subsection was void under the federal and state constitutions in that it denied due process and equality before the law. The basis for licensing the business involved, said the court, was for the protection of the public health and safety. "If protection of the public health and safety requires partitions in case of a business subsequently to be commenced, then by the same token it requires them in case of existing businesses; and if one operating an existing restaurant is not required to maintain the partition, and one about to establish a restaurant is required to maintain one, then manifestly the latter is denied equal protection with the former." On this basis the supreme court sustained the contention of the complainant, declared the amending subsection void, but allowed the existing statute to remain in force and instructed the board of health to grant the requested permit, thereby adjusting all rights and preventing future litigation.

Equity acts in personam. A law court may render a judgment against a person's property rather than against the person. For example, the court may command a sheriff to seize and sell enough of the unsuccessful defendant's goods and turn over to the plaintiff sufficient proceeds to meet the money judgment of the court. Equity, on the other hand, commands an individual to perform or to refrain from performing whatever acts constitute the subject of the litigation. Such an action by a court of equity is known as an injunction. Failure to obey the command of the court places the defendant in contempt of court and thereby subject to personal punishment. Thus, if the sewage from the premises of one householder gives rise to an intolerable situation on the property of another, the ordinary court of law can merely render a judgment for money damages in favor of the offended property owner. This, however, does not solve the problem, since the problem still exists. In equity, however, not only may a judgment of cash restitution be rendered for damages already done but, in addition, the court may issue an injunction directing the person responsible to abate and prevent the nuisance from recurring in the future.

* Wisconsin Supreme Court: State ex rel. *F.W. Woolworth Co. v Wisconsin State Board of Health* et al, 298 NW 183 (1941).

Equity regards the intention rather than form. This constitutes a weapon against legal decision. Law concerns itself with a strict interpretation of a form of law transaction, or contract, but equity considers also the intent. This is illustrated by a case* involving the question of whether common-law marriages, which do not necessitate a license, were included under a state law requiring premarital examinations as a prerequisite for marriage licenses. The superior court said that the act was clearly a public health measure designed to assist in the eradication of syphilis, to prevent transmission by a diseased spouse, and to prevent the birth of children with syphilitic weaknesses or deformities and should be construed so as to effectuate its purpose if at all possible. "Certainly," said the court, "the legislature never intended that such an important hygienic statute could be circumvented by the simple device of the parties entering into a common-law marriage without first obtaining a license."

Equity regards that as done which ought to be done. If a contract is broken, the court of law may render a money judgment for damages, whereas equity orders or commands (mandamus) that the contract be specifically performed. This is illustrated by the previously cited case of *F.W. Woolworth Company v Wisconsin State Board of Health et al.*

Equity recognizes an intention to fulfill an obligation. If an individual promises or contracts to do a thing or if that individual has done anything that might be regarded as at least a partial fulfillment of a promise or contract, equity assumes that he or she intends to do it until the contrary is shown. This has sometimes served as a stumbling block to public health officials. For example, a person maintaining a public health nuisance may necessitate numerous fruitless visits and inspections on the part of public health workers. Finally, as a last resort, the wrongdoer may be brought to court. If the defendant can demonstrate to the satisfaction of the court that in some manner the suggestions or commands of the public health official have been followed, even though inadequately, the court may dismiss the case, saying in effect: "Why do you bring this person to court when he or she is taking steps to meet your requirements?"

* Superior Court of the State of Pennsylvania: *Fisher v Sweet and McClain et al,* 35A 2nd 756 (1944).

Equity follows the law. In accordance with this maxim, an equity court will observe existing laws and legal procedures insofar as possible, without hindering its own function in the administration of justice.

Where there is equal equity, the law must prevail. If both parties to the litigation are judged to have equal rights, the case will be sent back to the law courts, where the party with a right in law will have that right enforced.

The logic of this and the previous principle is obvious, considering the purpose for which equity was established. Equity is an adjunct to law, not a substitute for it.

One who comes into equity must do so with clean hands. If an individual claims a wrong, he or she must be free from a related wrong or the equity court will not listen. This was a factor in a well-known Chicago drainage canal case,* in which a court of equity refused a judgment against the city of Chicago for the city of St. Louis, partly on the basis that St. Louis itself contaminated its own public source of water.

One who seeks equity must do equity. This is similar to the previous principle. The plaintiff must not only have clean hands but must be and have been willing to do all that is right and fair as a part of a transaction or a judgment.

Equity aids the vigilant, not the indolent. This is known as the doctrine of laches and calls into effect the statute of limitations that fixes definite intervals within which legal action may be instituted after the cause for action has occurred or become complete. These time intervals are not the same for all actions and vary further among the states. If people wish to receive relief from an equity court, they must be prompt in applying to it. In other words, they must not "sleep on their rights."

Administrative law

In the statutory legislation of an earlier day dealing with comparatively simple social and economic structures, an attempt was usually made to include in the written statutes considerable detail with reference to the problem at hand. However, in more recent times, with the accelerating complexity of the social and economic systems and with ever increasing knowledge in all fields, it has become impossible to include within the statutes sufficient detail to cover adequately all of the situations that might arise in the practical application of the true intent of the law. Moreover, the application of many statutes now requires an increasing amount of technological expertise in measurement and identification—expertise that changes rapidly. At the same time, U.S. government structure has become more and more complicated and has had more and more demands placed on it in the form of public services and regulatory functions previously unanticipated. The relative recency of the modern public health program provides a good example of this. To meet the situation, a considerable and increasing number of administrative agencies have been established by government, on a statutory basis, for the purpose of putting into effect the intent of legislation.

The procedure of passing enabling legislation written in more or less general terms evolved. Such legislation includes clauses delegating administration and enforcement to a new or existing administrative agency, giving the agency the power and responsibility to formulate whatever rules, regulations, and standards are necessary for carrying out the purpose of the law. Such powers and responsibilities must be in conformity with all existing laws of the community, the state, and the nation. Thus, although the legislative branch of government is the only one that can actually formulate and enact a law, and although this power cannot itself be delegated, the legislature may delegate the power to make whatever rules and regulations are necessary to carry out the intent of the law. (The words *rule* and *regulation* appear to be interchangeable. Not knowing whether there might be a difference, people often use the phrase *rules and regulations.*) All such administrative rules and regulations, when properly formulated and when not in conflict with existing laws of the state and nation, have the force and effect of law, even though they arise from an administrative agency and not from the legislature itself. However, their interpretation by the courts tends to be somewhat more rigid than the interpretation of the legislative enactments themselves.

The regulations developed by an agency of government must meet several tests if they are to be useful. The agency must first be sure that it understands the intent of the law. Secondly, it must conduct careful research and fact-finding to document the methods by which it proposes to carry out the law. A regulation cannot exceed the authority contained in the statute. For example, a proposed new air pollution control regulation dealing with certain categories of pollutants cannot include organic chemicals if the statute authorizing the rule-making does not make that permissible. There must be an opportunity for the public, particularly

* *Missouri v Illinois,* 180 US 208, 2 S Ct 331, 45 L Ed 497 (1901).

those who may be affected by the regulation, to comment and to provide additional information on the subject. The public hearings provide an opportunity both to obtain expert testimony and to educate the public. Those who are affected by the regulation have a chance to develop better understanding of the problem, which is the first step in achieving compliance. Finally, the agency can use the hearing as an opportunity to determine just how far the community is willing to go.

One of the codes in most states is a code of administrative procedures, which specifies the steps that must be taken in promulgating a new regulation.

Ethics

Ethical standards may be considered another form of law. When they are codified in statutes, they are law. Ethical standards also operate outside of the formal legal system. They are principles of conduct that are generally accepted in the community or the group. They can be made binding on the members of the group by voluntary action. Their enforcement is also a voluntary action and depends on the sanctions available to the group and their willingness to use them.

COURTS

American government, as noted above, is based on the principle of the separation of powers. Accordingly, legislation can be formulated, considered, and ultimately enacted only by the legislative branch. After its enactment, the legislature supposedly has no further concern with a law except for the possibility of subsequent amendment or repeal. On passage, a law is referred to the executive branch of government for its administration and enforcement. Members of the legislature may take exception to the way the law is managed by the executive branch and may force the responsible officials to appear before a committee for questioning. The recourse of the legislature is to sue the agency or to rewrite the law. However, the constitutionality of the law and the manner of its enforcement are subject to review at any time on the initiative of the citizenry by the third, or judicial, branch of government. It is the duty of the courts to pass on the constitutionality of laws, to interpret them in the interest of justice and the public good, and to determine their validity whenever controversies related to them are brought before the court in the proper manner.

The judicial system, at both the federal and the state level, has two parts: trial courts and appellate courts. There may be several different types, and even levels, of courts within both of these systems. At the federal level, the trial courts are the 90 federal district courts. The appellate system has two levels: 10 federal circuit courts of appeal and the Supreme Court. The appellate courts only listen to legal arguments; they do not hear witnesses or acquire new evidence. The federal courts hear matters involving federal law and matters that involve two or more states. If a case includes possible violations of both state and federal law, the federal court can decide both issues.

States have similar systems. At the trial court level, there may be special courts for such things as probate, domestic matters, criminal law, or juveniles. Many of the original, or trial, courts are operated by municipalities or counties as part of the state system. States have jurisdiction over all legal disputes in the state, whether they involve state or federal laws, and cases can be brought before either a state or federal court by the litigants. A state court decision may end up in the U.S. Supreme Court if it involves federal constitutional issues. Where a case is argued can make a considerable difference. In a recent Detroit case, several environmental groups found themselves arguing about a new incinerator before an unsympathetic federal judge. They attempted to have the trial sent (remanded) back to a Wayne County court, but the judge denied their motion, saying their complaints were "artfully pled, in a purposeful attempt to deprive the federal court of jurisdiction. . . ."[15]

Trial courts have only one judge. Appellate courts have several judges. Judges are appointed in some jurisdictions and elected in others.

It is to be noted that a county court, although locally elected and locally responsible for the administration of its verdicts, is actually part of the state judicial system. On the lowest, or most local, level are the locally elected justices of the peace, who constitute the lowest rung on the state judicial ladder.

In addition, a state may set up certain special courts to deal with particular social problems such as juvenile delinquency, domestic relations, and industrial relations. On the municipal level of government, by virtue of a charter granted by the state government, an urban community may have the privilege of setting up certain courts of its own to administer justice in cases involving problems of concern limited to the municipality itself. Thus there are police courts with original jurisdiction in minor matters and municipal courts with original jurisdiction in more important cases; these municipal courts also serve as a place of appeal from the police court.

SOURCES OF PUBLIC HEALTH POWERS

Public health law may be defined as that body of statutes, regulations, and precedents that has for its purpose the protection and promotion of individual and community health. Although the term *public health* was not entirely unknown to contemporaries of the authors of the American Constitution, its present-day scope and significance were not conceived of. After all, there was no public health profession in existence, and science was not to enter the golden era of bacteriology for about 100 years. Three quarters of a century were to pass before the need to establish the first state health department was to be felt. Still 40 years more were to pass before the formation of the first county health department. The founders of the United States cannot be censured, therefore, for not considering public health functions specifically in their organization of the new government. They were so remarkably astute and farsighted, however, as to provide for future developments in many fields by the use of certain broad and general phrases that in subsequent periods were to make possible broad interpretations of the Constitution, thereby allowing the introduction and inclusion of certain public health activities in the functions of the federal government.

By far the most important of these broad phrases is found in the Preamble to the Constitution, which includes among the fundamental purposes of the government the intent to "promote the general welfare." This recurs in section 8 of Article I, which, dealing with the functions of Congress, gives it power "to lay and collect taxes . . . and provide for the common defense and general welfare. . . ." It was the generous interpretation of this phrase by the Supreme Court that made possible the activity of the Children's Bureau in maternal and child health, the development of Medicare and Medicaid, and the subsidization by means of federal grants-in-aid of state and local health programs by the Public Health Service. In fact, these and many other federal agencies owe their existence in large part to the intent that has been read into the "general welfare" phrase.

In addition, the varied and widespread activities of the federal government in fields relating to health have as their legal basis the manner in which numerous other clauses of the Constitution have been interpreted. Thus the direction to Congress "to regulate commerce with foreign nations, and among the several states, and with the Indian tribes" has been construed to include such matters as international and interstate quarantine, vital statistics, and direct responsibility for the health of Native Americans. The provision for the establishment of "post offices and post roads" has led to the right of the federal government to bar from the mails material deleterious to the public health. The power "to raise and support armies" and to "provide and maintain a navy" logically placed responsibility for the health of the armed forces (in recent years a not inconsiderable fraction of the population) in the hands of federal agencies. Complete and exclusive jurisdiction over the inhabitants of the seat of the national government (the District of Columbia) is also specified.

The reader may be reminded at this point that the United States, far from being one nation, is in a true sense a federation of 50 separate nations, called states, each with its own history, economic and social problems, and still somewhat jealously guarded intrastate interests. It will be recalled that the members of the Constitutional Convention carefully guarded the rights of their respective states, jointly turning over to the newly formed federal government only such powers and activities as they considered desirable and necessary for the common welfare and survival of all. Matters that they could adequately handle as individual states were retained by the states. Since the beginning it has been inferred that all matters not specifically mentioned in the Constitution and its subsequent amendments were questions to be dealt with primarily by the states. It is for this reason that the most complete and coordinated organization of public health activities is found on the state and local levels. Each state has developed its own characteristic body of legislation and judicial interpretation, as well as its own type of plan and organization for the implementation of its public health laws.[16] Indeed, each state may do as much or as little as it wishes, within the limits imposed by national interest.

Although there are 50 differing sets of public health laws and organizations, certain fundamental legal principles are involved in all. A brief discussion of some of these fundamentals is necessary for further understanding the sources of public health powers.

Eminent domain

The first of the basic powers of a state is that of eminent domain, sometimes referred to as the power of condemnation. This is the power, or right, of a sovereign state to summarily appropriate an individual's property or to limit the individual's use of it if the best interest of the community makes such action desirable. In so doing, however, the state must provide equitable compensation. In effect, the state has the right to demand the sale or limitation of use of private property. The distinction between the exercise of the power of eminent domain and actions on which legislatures may insist without compensation is not clear-cut and varies from time to time. The history of zoning measures to control the height of buildings is a good example of this. At first states attempted to control the height of buildings by purchasing from individuals their primary right to build on their own property above the height that was considered most desirable from the community standpoint. Since this action was upheld in the courts, it was resorted to by more and more people in more and more communities until it got to the point where, as Ascher[17] aptly stated, it resembled the economy of the mythical village of Ballycannon, where everyone made their living by taking in their next-door neighbor's washing. In other words, when resorted to on a wide scale, use of the power of eminent domain amounts to individuals (as taxpayers) purchasing the exercise of a right from themselves as private citizens. Inevitably, such a procedure becomes ineffective as a measure of control. Recognizing this, the public through its legislatures may finally say, "We shall forbid this particular action or use by the individual," and the courts more often than not will uphold the action.

In a certain sense, the procedure followed by some health departments in the past of paying an allotment to chronic carriers of typhoid bacilli to make sure of their refraining from engaging in food-handling occupations represented the purchase by the state of an individual's primary right. The states in most instances finally simply forbade such activity by these persons.

As pointed out by Ascher, it is interesting to note that those who attempted to bring about a form of building control that eliminated the necessity of compensation deliberately avoided a test case for about 10 years. Finally, when the Ambler Realty Company protested the restrictions of its use of land by the village of Euclid,* the U.S. Supreme Court upheld this arbitrary use of police power in a sweeping opinion that had as one of its basic contentions that over 900 cities were already subject to zoning and about one half of the urban dwellers of the nation lived under the benefits of zoning procedures. This is perhaps another way of saying that within a relatively short period of time the social concept of zoning had become part of the custom of American communities and that its requirement could be considered as having become part of the common law.

Laws of nuisances

Long before the United States and its government were conceived, medieval legal theorists had developed the concept that, although "a man's home is his castle," an individual's use of private property can be detrimental to others. The use of private property is unrestricted only so long as it does not injure another's person or property. If this occurs, a nuisance is considered to exist, and the individual whose person or property is injured can seek assistance from the courts. Innumerable examples of this exist in the field of public health, especially with regard to the physical environment. For example, individual property owners can dispose of the family's sewage in any manner they choose, provided that it cannot actually or potentially affect another. If the raw sewage is allowed to flow onto the land of another, a social injustice has obviously occurred, and the health and well-being of others have been placed in jeopardy. Legal relief against nuisances may be obtained in the courts by means of (1) a suit in law for damages resulting and (2) a suit in equity to forbid or abate the nuisance.

It is perhaps unfortunate that a large proportion of public health officials still consider use of the law

* *Village of Euclid v Ambler Realty Co,* 272 US 365 (1926).

of nuisances as one of their most important, if not their chief, legal recourse. The pursuit of this point of view eventually leads to many difficulties and dissatisfactions, since the law of nuisances is subject to increasing limitations.

In the first place, there are many things or uses of things that do not intrinsically constitute a nuisance but are merely in the wrong place. An example of this is provided by the case of *Benton et al v Pittard, Health Commissioner, et al.,** in which the plaintiff protested the establishment and operation by a health department of a venereal disease clinic in a residential district. The complaints were that the disease of the patients who would congregate in the neighborhood

> were not only communicable but were offensive, obnoxious and disgusting; that the clinic operation would be offensive to the petitioners and that their sensibility would be injured; and that their dwelling would be rendered less valuable as a home and place of residence.

The defending health officer and county commissioner filed an answer and a general demurrer, a form of pleading that although admitting all the facts, challenged their legal sufficiency to constitute a cause of action. The judge, after hearing both sides, denied the plaintiff's request for an injunction and sustained the demurrer. On appeal, however, the Georgia Supreme Court stated that the clinic's operation as a public institution would not alone prevent it from becoming a nuisance if located in a residential section and that the statutory provision requiring the care of venereally infected persons did not imply the right to perform such care in any location. "In other words, a nuisance may consist merely of the right thing in the wrong place regardless of other circumstances." On this basis the judgment of the original trial court was reversed. Similar cases have been heard regarding methadone treatment centers and AIDS treatment programs.

Another factor tending to limit the value of the law of nuisances is that a great many of the legal doctrines and decisions dealing with nuisances and their abatement were developed before the germ theory of disease became established scientific fact. During most of the law's development, no obvious factual or scientific data existed on which to base conclusions, and those appearing in court in such cases were merely pitting their opinions against the opinions of others. As a result, a mass of unsound and unscientific decisions has been built up, which because they are precedents continue to influence the public health problems of present-day communities. This also partly explains why many supposedly modern health departments are required to expend time, energy, and funds in activities that have little relationship to public health, such as garbage and refuse control.

Still another difficulty is that recourse to the law of nuisances does not overcome one of the rules of law. Decision by a law court that a nuisance exists may result in damages being paid to the plaintiff but does not necessarily effect a solution or abatement of the problem. There is, of course, the possibility of resorting to a court of equity with the hope of obtaining complete justice. However, here again it is found that a rule of equity may provide a way out for the defendant in that if he or she can demonstrate to the court's satisfaction an intention or, better yet, partial action to abate the nuisance, the case in all probability will be dismissed. The thought might arise that the situation could be improved by trying to bring about more up-to-date judicial interpretations and judgments regarding nuisances. Although theoretically possible, the task would be enormous. Furthermore, even if modern standards could be made the basis of definition, these standards and definitions might become outmoded with the passage of time.

Police power[18]

Another means of legal recourse for the public health official to consider is the police power that the sovereign state possesses. As a matter of fact, public health law owes its true origin and only real effectiveness to this inherent right of the state. Police power originated in the so-called law of overruling necessity, which claims that in times of stress such as a toxic spill or a contaminated drug, the private property of an individual may be summarily appropriated or even destroyed if the ultimate relief, protection, or safety of the group indicates such action is necessary. Through time this concept expanded to include even activities designed for the prevention of causes of social stress. The U.S. Supreme Court has on numerous occasions not only upheld the principle of the police power of the state but has also defined its scope in sweeping terms to include, as did Chief

* Georgia Supreme Court: *Benton et al v Pittard, Health Commissioner, et al,* 31 SE 2nd 6.

Justice Marshall, all types of public health laws and to acknowledge the power of the states to provide for the health of their citizens.* It should be noted, however, as Justice Brown stated, that "its [the legislature's] determination as to what is a proper exercise of its police powers is not final or conclusive but is subject to the supervision of the court."†

One of the best definitions of police power was given in the case of *Miami County v Dayton,*‡ in which the court defined it as "that inherent sovereignty which the government exercises whenever regulations are demanded by public policy for the benefit of the society at large in order to guard its morals, safety, health, order and the like in accordance with the needs of civilization."

Although the police power belongs to the sovereign state, the legislature of the state may for practical purposes delegate it to an administrative agency acting as its functional agent. Use of the police power is not a matter of choice when it has been delegated to a governmental agency. The agency has a definite and legal responsibility to use it but *is accountable for the manner in which it is used.* When the means for action are made available, the public officer responsible may be compelled to exercise the delegated police power if the public interest indicates such action. Failure to do so makes the public official guilty of malfeasance of office. However, although application of the police power may be indicated and demanded, the manner in which it is employed is usually left to the discretion of the administrative officer; that is, the public officer may select methods of enforcement, formulating rules, regulations, and standards as necessary unless the statutes specifically prescribe the method of procedure.

An important case§ in point was the decision of the U.S. Supreme Court in 1978 to uphold the decisions of a series of lower courts that the searches and inspections of business premises by inspectors of the Occupational Safety and Health Administration without warrants was a violation of the Fourth Amendment of the Bill of Rights. This is of significance to public health workers. As Curran[19] comments,

> Most lawyers familiar with the case law of the Supreme Court in the past two decades would have thought that the type of warrantless inspections in OSHA were of doubtful constitutionality. However, legislative draftsmen do not always follow such guidelines when the overall objectives of the inspection program are believed to be right and proper and where such inspections are thought "necessary" to the regulatory scheme of the legislation. There is also a practical assumption that most people will allow the inspections anyway, either because they wish to cooperate with the program in the best interests of safety and health, or because they think the inspector "must have" a legal right to enter. All sorts of federal and state laws have granted inspection authority to firefighters, health inspectors, mine-safety officials, and many others, all essentially on these grounds.

The position of a public health officer, as related to the summary abatement of a nuisance, was well stated by the Iowa Supreme Court in a case* involving such action by a health department in enforcing an ordinance dealing with the improper and indiscriminate dumping of garbage. In upholding the action of the board of health, the court stated that, although nothing in the statute granted to the officers immunity from the consequences of unfair or oppressive acts, "the particular form of procedure prescribed may vary from the customary procedure, but essential rights are not violated by granting to the board the right, in an emergency, to proceed in the abatement of a nuisance detrimental to public health, and it is safe to say that most cases calling for action on the part of boards of health are matters requiring immediate action." Of perhaps greater significance, the court went on to say that, even though the courts had not been uniform in their holdings, it believed the weight of authority, as well as reason and necessity, prescribed that in cases involving the public health, in which prompt and efficient action was necessary, the state and its officers should not be subjected to the inevitable delays incident to a complete hearing before action could be taken.

The careful distinction between the power of inspection and the right of privacy has become increasingly important as a result of a ruling of the California District Court of Appeals.† The court held that entry by a health inspector into a private residence for the purpose of a routine housing inspection at a reasonable time and on presentation of proper credentials was not a violation of the

* Perhaps the best known case is *Gibbons v Ogden,* 9 Wheat 1, 6 L Ed 23 (1824).

† *Lawton v Steele,* 152 US 133 (1893).

‡ *Miami County v Dayton,* 92 O S 215.

§ *Marshall v Barlow's Inc.*

* Iowa Supreme Court: *State v Strayer,* 299 NW 912 (1941).

† *Camara v San Francisco,* 277 ACA 136 (1965).

Fourth or Fourteenth Amendments of the Constitution. "The court reasoned that the ordinance in question was part of a general regulatory scheme which was civil in nature, limited in scope, and could not be exercised except under reasonable conditions." The court then defined the conditions in which privacy may be restrained. "In those areas of exercise of the police power where the chance of immediate tangible harm is present, such as in premises which might present fire or communicable disease hazards, the right of privacy most probably will be accorded only that constitutional protection that is given to property or economic rights. In intimate or personal activities not at all likely to cause immediate danger to life or limb, the right of privacy will approach the more protected constitutional position of freedom of expression."[20]

On appeal, however, the Supreme Court* held that administrative searches for housing violations are significant intrusions on the privacy and security of individuals—interests that are protected by the Fourth Amendment against arbitrary invasions by government officials and enforceable against the states under the Fourteenth Amendment. The court declared that such searches, when authorized and conducted without a warrant procedure, lack the traditional safeguards that the Fourth Amendment guarantees to the individual. This is true, the court added, whether the discovery of a violation on the initial inspection leads to a criminal conviction or results only in an administrative compliance order.

The court noted the following three significant reservations to its general holdings:

1. Nothing in the opinion is intended to foreclose prompt inspections, even without a warrant, that the law has traditionally upheld in emergency situations.
2. In the light of the Fourth Amendment's requirement that a warrant specify the property to be searched, "It seems likely that warrants should normally be sought only after entry is refused, unless there has been a citizen complaint or there is other satisfactory reason for securing immediate entry."
3. "The requirement of a warrant procedure does not suggest any change in what seems to be the prevailing local policy in most situations, of authorizing entry, but not entry by force, to inspect."[21]

* 87 S Ct 1727 p 1734 ff (1967).

The right of a legislature to delegate rule-making power to an administrative agency has been questioned many times, but only in one instance has such power been denied to a state or local board of health. This occurred in Wisconsin,* where it was held that the state board of health was simply an administrative agency and that no rule-making powers could constitutionally be delegated to it. On the other hand, the Ohio Supreme Court stated that "the legislature in the exercise of its constitutional authority may lawfully confer on boards of health the power to enact sanitary ordinances having the force of law within the district over which their jurisdiction extends. . . ."† The question was more or less settled by the U.S. Supreme Court, which held the following‡:

1. That a State may, consistent with the Federal Constitution, delegate to a municipality authority to determine under what conditions health shall become operative.
2. That the municipality may vest in its efficiency broad discretion in matters affecting the applicability and enforcement of a health law.
3. That in the exercise of the police power reasonable classification may be freely applied and that regulation is not violative of the equal protection clause merely because it is not all-embracing.

It is obvious and logical that a municipality or an administrative agency, in dealing with questions concerning the public health, for example, can act only when it has been given specific authority for such actions and that the ordinances adopted by the legislative body of the municipality must not only be limited to the subject matter of the power delegated but also must not conflict with or attempt to set aside any provision of the Constitution, of the state law, or of any other sanitary regulations of the state. The same conditions apply to regulations adopted by local boards of health. They can apply only where the subject matter has been placed by law under the jurisdiction of the local board of health.

Licensing

A related method of legal enforcement and control is found in the technique of licensing. The

* *State v Burdge*, 95, Wis 390, 70 NW 347 (1897).
† Exparte Co 106 OS 50.
‡ *Zucht v King*, 260 US 174, 43 S Ct (1922).

legality of the principle of licensing as a method of control and enforcement, as well as a source of revenue to meet the cost of the administration of a law, has been well established and accepted for a long while. However, intent and methods of licensing are constantly subject to questioning in the courts, as are all other methods of enforcement. Licenses may be granted or revoked under conditions imposed by public health authorities, provided that there is a statutory basis for the licensing and that there is no oppressive, discriminatory, or arbitrary action involved in its application.

For example, a city board of health voted that after a certain date no more milk distributor licenses would be granted to persons who were not residents of the city.* The plaintiff operated a well-qualified dairy 6 miles beyond the city limits and brought suit to compel the issuance of a license, charging that the regulation was discriminatory. The state law said, "Boards of health may grant licenses to sell milk to properly qualified persons." The court held that the word "may" in the state law should be construed as meaning "shall," so that a local board of health, existing by virtue of state law, had no alternative but to issue a license to any person who satisfied the sanitary requirements. More pertinent to the question at hand, it further held that the limitation on nonresidents was unreasonable and arbitrary and that if it had been included in a law instead of a regulation, it would have been ruled unconstitutional.

On several occasions, licensing has been used by health authorities to obtain indirect control of problems not obvious from the primary purpose of the licensing. Several communities, for instance, have required the licensing of individuals engaged in certain personal service occupations, such as masseurs and beauty parlor operators, in an attempt to stop advertising by prostitutes operating under the guise of these occupations. This particular use has been accepted, since the right of health departments to maintain sanitary control over individuals engaged in personal services to prevent the spread of communicable diseases has been well established. It is questionable practice, however. The use of indirection in a law to accomplish what otherwise could not be accomplished is a distortion of the law. It can be viewed as harassment, and it consumes the resources of the health department in an effort with little potential benefit to society. Such laws, in fact, are often attempts to legislate a moral code and use the police powers of the health department to enforce it.

* *Whitney v Watson,* 85 NH 238, 157 A 78 (1931).

When an ordinance requiring permits or licenses can be shown to have no public health basis, it will probably be considered an infringement of personal rights by the court and declared invalid. This is illustrated by the case* of a city board of health that passed a regulation providing that no person should engage in the business of undertaking unless duly licensed as an embalmer by the board of health. The Massachusetts Supreme Court held the regulation unconstitutional and invalid, saying,

> We can see no such connection between requiring all undertakers to be licensed embalmers and the promotion of the public health as to bring the making of this regulation by the board of registration in embalming or the refusal of a license by the board of health on account of the regulation within the exercise of the police power of the state.

A similar complaint could be made about the continued state licensure of many professions such as barbers, beauticians, physical therapists, and many others. Licensure, in general, has not been shown to benefit the public. It does, however, benefit the licensee.

NECESSITY OF BASIC PUBLIC HEALTH LAWS

In a DeLamar lecture given in 1920, Freeman,[22] who was at that time Commissioner of Health of Ohio, said:

> Every thoughtful sanitarian has in his mind the picture of that ideal system of health administration which would be founded on scientific principles, organized on the basis of administrative efficiency, and manned by a staff of trained workers filled with the spirit of public service. This ideal organization would have behind it a volume of law which, while fully recognizing the principles of individual liberty, would permit no man to offend against the health of his neighbor.

Freeman added with considerable justification,

> However thoughtfully a proposed measure may be prepared by its framers, it has by the time it is enacted into

* *Wyeth v Cambridge Board of Health,* 200 Mass 474, 86 NE 295 (1909).

law usually been so altered by ill-considered, hasty or prejudiced amendment as to have lost all semblance of its original form.

There are two things, it is said, that ought never to be observed in the making: sausage and law.

It is advantageous to consider some of the fields of public health activity in which fundamental legislation is desirable or necessary. The first of these is the registration or reporting of births and deaths. It is impossible to carry out a public health program in the absence of basic information concerning the circumstances surrounding birth and death. In most parts of the United States, it is the public health agency that is charged with the responsibility for assuring the collection of this information. To achieve this, it is necessary that each state have the appropriate legislation and administrative machinery to deal with mandatory reporting of these events by those in the best position to submit such reports, the attendants at births and deaths.

Related to this is the need for legislation requiring the reporting and control of cases of certain types of illnesses, especially communicable diseases. To accomplish this adequately requires careful and exact definition of certain terms such as *cases, communicable,* and *isolation* and the listing of the morbid conditions to be included. In accord with what has been said elsewhere, such defining and listing is best accomplished by inclusion in the rules and regulations drawn up by the administrative agency rather than in the body of the statute, which should limit its concern to broad principles, responsibilities, and penalties. The desirability of this is particularly evident in light of the spectacular changes that have occurred in recent years in the diagnosis, treatment, and social management of many of the communicable diseases. If details of reporting and control appear in the law, further scientific advances are certain to result in the necessity of either changing the law or allowing it to become hopelessly out of date. In recent years, Legionnaire's disease, Lyme disease, herpes, AIDS, and toxic shock syndrome have all required careful surveillance, and none were included in earlier versions of communicable disease reporting statutes.

In the field of environmental health, an enormous, confusing, and frequently contradictory mass of legislation and regulation exists. There are five major federal agencies involved in administering 20 laws that have to do with the control of the chemical vinyl chloride.[23] This is a somewhat extreme example of the confusion that can develop, but the problem of multiple agency involvement is growing. Undesirable as this situation is, all will agree that certain types of legal control are necessary. It is important for a community to exercise some control over those who produce and handle its food and milk supplies. This has been repeatedly upheld in the courts. With reference to milk, the Connecticut Supreme Court explained in an opinion*:

> The State may determine the standard of quality, prohibit the production, sale, or distribution of milk not within the standard, divide it into classes, and regulate the manner of their use, so long as these standards, classes, and regulatory provisions be neither unreasonable nor oppressive. The many recorded instances in which the courts have sustained this power of regulation bear witness to the liberality of their viewpoint where the public health and safety are concerned.

Judicial prejudice in favor of rules, regulations, and standards dealing with the sanitary quality of food and milk supplies has been extended far beyond the actual product itself. It has long been accepted as proper for the responsible health authority to formulate rules, regulations, and standards dealing with the sources of food and milk, the health and sanitation practices of all who come in contact with them, the sanitary facilities provided such persons, and the sanitary nature of all machinery, instruments, or utensils involved in their transfer from the source to the ultimate consumer.

In the field of general sanitation, including the sanitary problems involved in housing and industry as well as the supervision of water supplies, sewage disposal, and the like, basic legislation is necessary to place responsibility in the hands of the public health agency and to give it such powers as are needed to activate the intent of the law. Licensing of certain trades and occupations has been mentioned briefly. It is obvious that before such a procedure can be put into effect, the necessary legal justification must be brought into existence. In recent years, the AIDS epidemic has

* *Shelton v City of Shelton,* 111 Conn 433 (1930).

resulted in numerous problems of authority in the field of communicable disease control: isolation, testing, confidentiality provisions, and contact tracing. (See below under Future Themes and Chapter 16.)

Perhaps the most fundamental of all such legislation is that enabling the establishment and development of local public health programs. Obviously, a local area, being ultimately subject to the state, should be granted the legal right to establish official activity dealing with the public health. The rapid expansion of local health work in recent years, especially on the county level, has created increasing interest in the proper formulation of such enabling acts. In the first national conference on local health units, held in 1946, Mustard[24] summarized the essentials that should be included in enabling legislation for local health work. These essentials are listed here for their conciseness and inclusiveness and because they remain valid:

1. That this volume of law should provide assurance that there is a proper balance between local autonomy and state supervision.
2. That this volume of law should provide insurance that where a local unit of government is too small for effective public health administration, combinations of local jurisdictions may be made.
3. Insurance that health work locally will not be scattered among different elements of the local government.
4. Insurance that budgets for local health units be sufficient to meet at least a minimum in terms of funds, and to meet standards as to personnel.
5. No local jurisdiction will remain in want of health service, merely because of unfavorable financial position locally.
6. Supplementary to this insurance that even the poor areas will be included, there should be insurance that there will be adequate state aid.
7. Insurance that the whole state system of local health units will not be jeopardized by local option.

In the more recent report by the Institute of Medicine on *The Future of Public Health,*[25] the statutory requirements were described as follows:

> Clearly delineate the basic authority and responsibility entrusted to public health agencies, boards, and officials at the state and local levels and the relationships between them. Support a set of modern disease control measures that address contemporary health problems such as AIDS, cancer, and heart disease, and incorporate due process safeguards (notice, hearings, administrative review, right to counsel, standards of evidence).

Gostin[26] has said that public health laws in the United States "do not reflect modern conceptions of science and law." There is an absence of criteria and procedures in the current legal basis for public health interventions. "Most statutes and early court decisions presume the preeminence of public health interests over individual rights, utilizing neither cogent scientific examination of a measure's potential benefit nor legal assessment of unnecessary restrictions on individual rights." The public health situation is considerably different from that in the field of mental health. Old laws that allowed the capricious commitment of people with eccentric behavior patterns have given way to much tighter definitions and procedures. People suspected of being mentally ill now can generally have their civil liberties reduced only if it can be shown, in a formal hearing, that they are (1) gravely disabled because of a mental illness and (2) as a result, a source of danger to themselves or others. They are entitled to notice of a hearing, representation by a lawyer, cross-examination of witnesses, and other features of legal due process long held to be of fundamental importance in general law. These same provisions, however, have not been developed in public health law.

Much more is known about bacteria and viruses now than when the public health police powers of isolation and quarantine were first codified. The differences between airborne and waterborne infections are known, for example, and there is better understanding of modes of transmission and incubation periods. These technological developments have become evident as communities have wrestled with their fears about AIDS.

The original court decisions concerning the exercise of police power by public health supported any action by the state that wasn't arbitrary, oppressive, or unreasonable, without regard to whether any real benefits would accrue to society or whether the costs to individuals might exceed the benefits. As Gostin[26] observed, public health is one of the few areas in which personal liberty can be restricted without the commission of a criminal act. Gostin asserts that due process should be incorporated into the public health code along with the wisdom of accumulated technological evolution. Before steps can be taken to isolate those who are presumed to have dangerous communicable diseases, they should receive written notice of the circumstances and be entitled to representation by a lawyer, the presentation of evidence, cross-examination of witnesses, a "clear and convincing" standard of proof, and a verbatim transcript of the preceedings so as to be able to appeal any conclusions.

All of this takes time. What can be done to protect the public while these steps are being taken? The same questions have been asked and answered in the mental health community. People can be held for brief periods of time if competent professionals find that they are gravely disabled and therefore dangerous to themselves or others. This can continue for only two to three days before proceedings must take place, usually before a special mental health commissioner or judge.

As noted above, the AIDS epidemic has made these concerns a matter of public interest, and considerable progress has been made in recent years. It remains for that progress to be more thoroughly incorporated in public health codes and thinking.

WRITING AND PASSSAGE OF LAWS AND REGULATIONS

Curran[27] expressed concern about the inadequate attention given to the development of regulations by public health workers. He pinpointed three areas of weakness in most health departments: (1) the department's ongoing programs tend to operate ahead of the regulations; that is, the regulations have not yet caught up with what the department is actually doing; (2) the current regulations are too broadly worded to be used effectively; and (3) regulations are often based on model codes or the regulations of some other health department without sufficient regard for local conditions.

Many people complain about the terminology and complexity of laws and regulations and repeatedly call for simplification. Exactly what is meant by *promptly, insanitary, filth, reasonable access,* and *informed consent?* Attempts to simplify the terminology in laws and regulations have an unfortunate tendency to magnify and multiply administrative difficulties and overload the courts with unnecessary litigation. It might be well to consider briefly a few practical considerations with regard to the proper formulation of laws and regulations.

Because of the number and significance of federal legislative actions, it is important that health personnel be familiar with the complicated process involved. The procedure followed in the enactment of legislation is essentially the same on the national and state levels of government. Basically there are 15 steps involved, but they really boil down to the following: (1) after a first and second reading by title, the bill is referred to a committee (or subcommittee), which may or may not hold hearings; (2) the bill is placed on the calendar of the entire chamber for a third reading and debate; (3) if passed, it then goes through the same process in the other chamber, and if passed there, it goes to the chief of state for signature. If it is vetoed, a two-thirds majority overrides the veto.

More specifically, on the federal level, a bill is born when it is introduced in either house by its congressional sponsors. Bills are assigned numbers in order of their introduction. Occasionally, identical bills are introduced in the Senate and House of Representatives; more frequently, many different bills are filed on any major issue. In both houses the bill is assigned to the committee having appropriate jurisdiction. Often, the bill is then referred to a subcommittee for special detailed study. It is in this phase that hearings are often held, and the original bill is often changed during "markup" or drafting sessions.

When the subcommittee completes action on the bill, it is referred back to the full committee, which must approve all recommendations and amendments before the bill can be "reported out" to the full House or Senate. If the committee does not report out the bill, the legislation is "killed." It goes no further in the legislative process unless by special petition of the full membership. Legislation can also be "bottled up" by committee chairs who do not report the bill out of committee. Once reported out, a bill is placed on the legislative calendar in the Senate or on one of several calendars in the House of Representatives. In the House the bill then goes to the Rules Committee, where it is decided whether amendments will be permitted from the floor and the length of debate time is allocated. "Open rule" permits amendments from the floor; "closed rule" does not. The first House floor action is debate and vote on acceptance of the rule recommended by the Rules Committee, then on amendments, if an open rule is adopted. At this point the bill may be recommitted to committee for further study or voted on for final action. In the Senate there is no restriction on amendments, and debate time is unlimited unless there is a three-fifths cloture vote to cut it off.

When either chamber passes a bill, it must then be sent to the other chamber for acceptance, rejection, or alteration. If it is altered, the bill is sent to a conference committee, made up of members of the committees from both houses that worked on the legislation. Differences between the legislation passed by each chamber are ironed out in this committee. Occasionally they are unable to work out a compromise, and the measure dies.

If an acceptable agreement is reached, the revised bill is then sent to both chambers for final approval. If approved by both chambers, the new bill is sent to the White House for signing within 10 days. If the President does not act on the bill within 10 days, it automatically becomes law. However, if Congress adjourns before the 10-day limit expires, the President can "pocket veto" the bill by not signing it. Congress can override a presidential veto with a two-thirds majority vote. If Congress does not override a veto, the bill is dead and the process must begin again with the introduction of new legislation.

Essentially the same sequence of steps is involved in the introduction, consideration, and passage of legislation on the state level, with the governor fulfilling the role played by the President on the federal level.

On the state and local levels, it has been customary in the United States that responsibility for the public health be vested in a board of health, which is directed to employ as its agent a health officer and whatever other personnel are needed to carry out its policies. It is much better that rules, regulations, and standards be passed by someone other than the enforcement officer. The public believes that it is being treated more fairly if a disinterested party is involved. In turn health officers are relieved of the onus of enforcing their own regulations and the risk of repeated personal liability. This alone presents an important justification for the interposing of boards of health between the legislative body and the functioning agency. With these words of introduction, the following suggestions are made concerning the formulation of rules and regulations by public health agencies:

1. First is the necessity that they be promulgated by a board of health or other administrative agency in which this authority and responsibility are vested. Furthermore, the agency must have been properly created and legally existing in the eyes of the legislature. If any of its members have been improperly chosen, elected, or appointed, the entire board does not legally exist and all of its actions are considered invalid.
2. The actions of the board must arise by virtue of power and responsibility that has been delegated by either expression or implication by the state legislature.
3. The pronouncements of the board must relate and be limited to its legal jurisdiction and not infringe on the jurisdiction of another agency or another government entity.
4. The rules and regulations must not conflict with the Constitution and laws of the United States or the state.
5. The rules and regulations must be reasonable, consistent with the purpose of the enabling statute, and no more drastic than is necessary.
6. Generally, both the intention to develop a regulation and the proposed regulation itself should be published in newspapers of general circulation throughout the area affected by the proposal. The date and place of a public hearing should be announced and an opportunity given for all interested parties to comment on the proposal and to provide testimony about the proposed regulation.
7. All rules, regulations, and standards must be adopted by a legally constituted board of health legally convened in an official session. No individual member of a board has power to enact a regulation any more than an individual Senator or Representative has power to enact a statute. Final enactment can result only from a vote at a properly called meeting of the board, notice of which has been given to each of the members of the board, and at which a quorum is present. To attempt to act on a regulation by means of telephoning or visiting the office or home of each member individually does not constitute action by a legally convened meeting of the board, since it precludes debate.
8. Since a board of health regulation is in effect a law, it follows that the same care should be exercised in its formation as is exercised in drawing up a state or federal statute. The first consideration in this regard is proper form (including a title and enacting

clause), a series of consecutively numbered articles each related to one subject, a statement concerning the time when the regulation is to become effective, and a statement of penalties involved in instances of proved infraction.

9. The ordinance or regulation must be precise, consistent, definite, and certain in its expression and meaning. The present tense should be used. It should be written for the public and especially for those who will be affected by it. Complicated, high-sounding phrases should be avoided, punctuation used precisely, and parentheses almost never used. Foreign or technical terms should be avoided if possible. It has been said that there can be a lawsuit for each extraneous or ill-chosen word and for every ill-advised punctuation mark.
10. If the legislature prescribes the manner in which regulations and ordinances should be passed, such prescription must be exactly adhered to. If, for example, it is specified in the state law that a proposed ordinance be read and voted on favorably at three successive meetings of a legally constituted and convened board, this requirement cannot be fulfilled, as has been attempted, by having the clerk stand and read the ordinance and call for a vote three times during the same meeting.
11. The ordinance or regulation must be enacted in good faith and in the public interest alone and designed to enable the board of health to carry out its legal responsibilities. It should therefore be impartial and nondiscriminatory, applying to all members of the community.
12. The final step is proper and adequate publication of the rule or ordinance so that those who are to be affected by it have ample opportunity to be informed concerning it. This is usually carried out by means of publishing in the local newspapers.

Some states require that a proposed regulation be reviewed by the attorney general of the state, an elected official, before it can go into effect. Some state legislatures have also established a legislative review procedure, which requires the agency to submit the new regulation to a legislative committee for approval before it can go into effect. This is a questionable procedure, because it infringes on the authority of the executive branch and offers legislators a second chance to amend a bill by insisting on a particular interpretation, which might have been rejected in the original committee consideration of the statute.

In recent years, several issues have emerged, in part as a response to arguments that the regulatory practices of government have stifled competition and economic development. Some statutes require that the costs and benefits of the proposed rule be calculated and compared and that, if the costs are greater than the benefits, the rule should be changed or abandoned. A different theme concerns the burden of proof. Generally, when a court hears an appeal against the imposition of a regulation, it does not challenge the scientific and technical premises of the administering agency. There is a *judicial presumption* in favor of the findings, conclusions, and recommendations of the enforcing administrative official. For example, if the regulation specifies a certain permissible level for a chemical in the air in a workplace, that level is not questioned by the court *provided* that the administering agency has promulgated the regulation properly, in accordance with the administrative procedures code, and that the level has some basis in fact and is not arbitrary or capricious. This practice permits the court to avoid reexamining extensive scientific testimony. Some legislators, offended by what they perceive to be the officious acts of the executive branch, have attempted to change that practice so that the courts must conduct such a technical examination, a procedure many people feel the courts are not equipped to carry out.

A final caution might be given concerning the frequent practice of adopting or incorporating rules and regulations by reference. This procedure has the enticement of being convenient and easy, but it may give rise to legal difficulties in that only existing things can be legally incorporated by reference. Therefore each time the original regulation or law is changed, it is necessary to reincorporate by reference. Furthermore, it is legally impossible, although it is sometimes attempted, to adopt or incorporate a subject by reference on a blanket basis through time, because such action amounts to committing the public to regulations that are not yet in existence. It is comparable to asking the public to sign a blank check. This is not meant to condemn the technique of reference entirely, since its convenience amply justifies its use. However, it should be used with full knowledge of its limitations and potential disadvantages.

LIABILITY AND AGENCY

To accomplish a desired purpose such as the completion of a contract or the rendering of a public service, practicality usually makes it necessary that the one who is legally responsible for fulfilling the contract or for rendering the public service (the principal) obtain an agent or agents to carry out the details involved. This relationship between principal and agents gives rise to an additional series of legal complications, especially in terms of those things for which the principal is liable and those for which the agent is liable. In public health work the citizens of a community as represented by their legally designated board of health may be considered the principal, whereas the health officer acts as the agent of the people and is responsible to the board.

The fundamental rule governing the relationship of principal to agent is that the principal is liable for contractual agreements or other acts of an agent, provided that the agents have acted within the real or apparent scope of their authority. It should be noted from this that the principal is not liable or responsible for all contracts or all acts that might be carried out by the agent but only for those acts the agent has been given power by the principal to perform. The most important and difficult problem is to define or determine the meaning and extent of the agent's authority and power.

The powers of an agent have been divided into real and apparent. An agent's real power consists of the expressed or implied authority delegated by the principal. Expressed powers are given usually in the form of actual and explicit instructions. Thus a board of health may instruct a health officer to control the spread of a communicable disease through the community.

Added to this expressed authority, the agent also has certain implied powers to do whatever is reasonably necessary to carry out the instructions given. The health officer, therefore, on being instructed to control the spread of communicable disease, may correctly assume the implied power and authority to include whatever administrative procedures are reasonably indicated—for example, contact examination—to fulfill the responsibility given in relation to the expressed powers.

Over and above real authority, expressed or implied, the agent has certain so-called apparent powers. In the use of these, the agent exceeds actual power and would be considered liable in many instances were it not for the concept of apparent power. The use of apparent power is involved in major part in the solution of individual problems, each with its own peculiar circumstances, and the test of its correct use is the determination of whether or not a reasonably prudent person in similar circumstances would have been justified in acting as the agent did on behalf of the principal. This may be illustrated by the case of a health officer* who in the face of a smallpox outbreak hospitalized an individual erroneously considered to have smallpox, with the result that the patient became infected with smallpox while in the isolation hospital. Because the erroneous diagnosis was made in good faith by the attending private physician and similarly confirmed by the health department diagnostician after exercising due and customary care and judgment, neither the private physician nor the community through its authorized public health agents were held liable. "To hold otherwise," the court stated, "would not only invite indifference at the expense of society, but the fear of liability would well-nigh destroy the efforts of officials to protect the public health." There is no assurance that such a finding would prevail today, nor should it. The injured party would have recourse to compensation for the harm, although even that might not be available if the government agency were protected under the concept of sovereign immunity, an eroding concept in the United States. There is a difference between punishing the agent who might have inadvertently caused the harm and providing all necessary care and support for the harmed individual.

This emphasizes that an agent owes to the principal the exercise of a degree of care and skill that a reasonably qualified and prudent person (in terms of the community involved at the time) would be expected to exercise under similar circumstances. It should be noted that, except where a contract exists to the contrary, no guarantee is involved that a certain result will be effected. All that is required by the law is the exercise of that degree of skill, knowledge, and care usually displayed by similar members of the profession under similar circumstances.

In the absence of malice or corruption or a statutory provision imposing liability, health officers generally are not liable for errors or mistakes in judgment in the performance of acts within the scope of their authority where they are empowered

* Dillon's Municipal Corporations 771, as quoted by Tobey.[33]

to exercise judgment and discretion. Personal liability therefore depends on proof of bad faith, which "may be shown by evidence that official action was so arbitrary and unreasonable that it could not have been taken in good faith."*

It logically follows, however, that if reasonable and legal instructions have been given to an agent by the principal, it is the agent's duty to obey them unless he or she knows a better way to accomplish the purpose desired. In such an instance, should the agent willfully disobey the principal's instructions or laws and injury or any other undesirable result follow, the agent is liable for whatever damages have been sustained as a result of this disobedience.

With regard to liability of the principal if it is a government, it must first be reemphasized that the state traditionally has been considered sovereign and, as such, cannot be sued or held liable by its individual citizens except where it grants permission. Since county governments are essentially local administrative and political units of the sovereign state, the same rule tends to be applied to them. However, there is an increasing tendency on the part of states to allow counties to be sued and to hold them liable whenever there is question or doubt. Municipalities are somewhat different in that they are corporations carrying on various functions and services. Some of these functions—for example, the operation of a transportation system or a water works—are considered private, and the city may be sued concerning them. However, other functions and services—such as the maintenance of police and fire departments—are public functions, and concerning these the city cannot be readily sued. Public health activities fall into this category.

EXTENT OF USE OF LAW IN PUBLIC HEALTH

Seen in its proper relationship, legal enforcement represents only one of several ways by which an administrator acting as an agent of the community may bring about desirable results and effect conformity to the socially desired standards of the community. In effect, the administrator has three main tools or methods of approach—education, persuasion, and coercion—and the extent to which the administrator successfully blends and balances them is one of the best measures of true administrative ability. A health officer who is constantly in court, as either plaintiff or defendant, is suspect. Most public health laws can be applied through education and persuasion. Nonetheless, the law is available and should be used. Much of the progress of public health would not have occurred as rapidly as it has in the absence of law and its enforcement. For example, it is unrealistic to assume that coal mine operators and contractors will constantly act to protect the health of their workers in the absence of law and agency.

The early history of public health was characterized by enforcement of the law. In more recent years, education and persuasion have become more prominent as newer problems have emerged—problems requiring behavioral change by individuals as well as groups. Even to use the law effectively requires public education.

Addressing essentially the same point, Miller and coworkers[16] observe:

> A restraining influence on implementation of statutory authorizations is lack of money. And yet tremendous amounts of money are spent for health services. If that money is not spent in constructive ways then the responsibility may well rest with public health leadership that fails to provide enlightenment and programmatic vigor that can compete successfully in the nation's economic and political markets.

In most instances, social legislation is framed by persons who are somewhat more advanced in their social thinking than is the average citizen. Only relatively recently has it been recognized that legislation embodying social concepts that are too far ahead of the citizenry as a whole is almost inevitably doomed to failure. Many tragic examples of this nature may be found in the history of public health. One of the best known is the fate of the General Board of Health of England, established in 1848, which failed as a result of overenthusiasm for Edwin Chadwick's social thinking and planning, which were too far ahead of the people of England at the time. At least one local health officer in America was literally tarred and feathered because of his persistent attempts to institute complete pasteurization of milk when the strongly opinionated citizens of his area were not intellectually prepared for it.

As a result of the relatively recent realization that social progress of all types must be based on

* *Kirk v Aiken Board of Health,* 83 SC 372 (1909).

understanding and acceptance by the majority of those involved, leaders in the field of public health administration have turned increasingly toward emphasis on educational and persuasive action, minimizing the legal and enforcement approach.

The changing epidemiology of sexually transmitted diseases provides a good example of the need to attend to changes in health legislation. For a number of years, beginning in 1935, public health departments found mandated premarital tests for syphilis productive. Accordingly, states enacted the necessary legislation. Recent social and epidemiologic changes, however, have resulted in a less favorable cost-benefit ratio in comparison with other case-finding methods, which has prompted many states to repeal the earlier laws.[28,29] Still more recent interest in AIDS has brought about another reversal.[12]

A contrary situation is found in the widespread repeal of state laws that require the use of motorcycle helmets, despite the proven fact that the fatality rate per mile of travel for motorcyclists is seven times the corresponding rate for automobile occupants and increased 50% between 1975 and 1979.[30] Furthermore, it has been clearly shown that repeal of such protective laws is followed by a significant increase in motorcyclist fatalities. It is instructive that a long series of state legislatures has turned deaf ears to such incontrovertible facts in favor of the vigorous and skillful lobbying activities of a minority of motorcyclists.[31]

Obviously a balance is necessary. No single approach is suitable for all situations, and not infrequently firm action must be taken. Curran[32] has taken health professionals to task in words worth careful attention:

> Professionals in the health field have traditionally downgraded the use of legal sanctions. They have preferred to achieve their goals of better health for the American people through education. . . . Many professional public health people have forgotten that their basic responsibility is to protect and to improve the health of the masses of people and to use all effective public means to achieve it.

In noting the increasing legal activist role of health workers in company with the poor and with consumer groups, Curran suggests,

> In the future, we may look for greater participation in this field by "traditional" health professionals and their "traditional" professional organizations. Otherwise, this will be another in the growing number of health fields taken out of the hands of the old-line health groups.

COURT PROCEDURE

Since, despite all wishes to the contrary, every active health officer will sooner or later appear in court, it may be well to include a few words concerning court procedure. When court action appears to be necessary, all other efforts for the enforcement of a law or ordinance having failed, the first step is to bring charges against the offender. The party who initiates the action is called in law the plaintiff and in equity the complainant. The individual against whom action is brought is known as the defendant in both law and equity. In bringing charges against the defendant, one must first determine which court has jurisdiction. The same action may be interpreted as constituting any one of several criminal acts, depending on the intent, the circumstances, the existing laws, and the consequences. Thus to give dangerous contaminated material to an individual is considered an assault; to make it available to the public at large constitutes a criminal nuisance; and if sent through the mails, it is a breach of the postal regulations. The first two offenses are crimes under the common law or statutes of a state; the third offense is a crime under the acts of the Congress of the United States. Violations of public health laws or regulations are usually considered misdemeanors. In any case, an infraction of these laws constitutes a criminal act, so that the case is within the jurisdiction of a criminal court such as a police court.

The plaintiff then files with the court a complaint (sometimes referred to as a declaration, information, petition, bill, or statement of claim) that has been drawn up by the plaintiff, preferably with the aid of a municipal, county, or state attorney. This should consist of a detailed statement by, for example, the health officer of the facts and circumstances leading up to the controversy and including the terms of any regulation or ordinance violated. The plaintiff should expect to prove the facts and circumstances beyond reasonable doubt in court with the aid of credible witnesses. The magistrate of the court then issues a summons ordering the defendant to appear in court at a stated day and hour, and the summons is served in person to the defendant by an officer of the court. The purpose of the summons is to give written notice to the defendant that legal action has been instituted. Its personal service is essential, since a court is powerless to render a judgment against a defendant who has not been so notified. All individuals are entitled to their day in court and the opportunity to bring out whatever defense they may find possible. Defendants have a choice of six procedures:

1. They can ignore the proceedings and stand in default, inviting judgment against themselves.
2. They may confess to the accusation of the plaintiff and again invite a judgment against themselves.
3. They may enter a plea in abatement, questioning whether the court has power or jurisdiction to act against them and whether proper procedure has been followed.
4. They may file a demurrer, stating in effect that although they admit the truth of what the plaintiff states as a matter of law, the facts do not entitle the plaintiffs to recover.
5. They may file an answer or a plea consisting of a denial of the facts stated in the plaintiff's declaration.
6. Again, they may admit the facts brought out by the plaintiff but bring out still other facts in avoidance or in excuse of those alleged by the plaintiff. Pleading continues until one side denies the facts claimed by the other, thereby raising an issue calling for a decision, and the case is then ready to go to trial.

Most public health legal controversies do not take place before a jury, although either side is entitled to a trial by jury if it so wishes. The first step in such instances is the impaneling of a jury, consisting of calling prospective jurors from an approved list and questioning them individually concerning prejudices for or against either litigant. The function of the jury is to decide questions of fact, in contrast to the judge's function of deciding questions of law. When the court proceeding gets under way, counsel for each side may make an opening statement that explains briefly what the counsel expects to prove. After this, each side introduces its evidence.

All offenses consist of two factors, the criminal act and the criminal intent, and both must be proven beyond reasonable doubt to demonstrate the commission of a crime. A criminal act is an action or omission that the law forbids. To be considered criminal, the act must be defined by a law or regulation forbidding its commission. The rule of law is strictly interpreted in favor of the accused, so that the act is not considered criminal unless it corresponds exactly with the definition contained in the law. The criminal intent is the state of mind of the accused at the time when the criminal act was committed. It involves a conscious recognition of the unlawful nature of the act, followed by a determination to perform the act. The courts presume the existence of criminal intent on the basis of the actual commission of the act, and it is usually unnecessary to produce evidence of criminal intent unless the accused attempts to prove that at the time the criminal act was committed he or she was incapable of determining or understanding its nature and unlawfulness or that the act was involuntary. Such proof must be based on (1) youth, (2) insanity, (3) mistake of fact, (4) accident, (5) necessity, or (6) compulsion. If the defendant is able to prove lack of criminal intent to the satisfaction of the court, although the commission of a criminal act is recognized, the defendant will be declared innocent.

When all evidence has been brought forth, the judge instructs the jury concerning the law involved in the issues raised, and the jury then retires to decide on a verdict. When the jury renders its verdict but before the court pronounces judgment, the losing party may make a motion for a new trial. This may be granted if the court believes that an erroneous ruling has been made concerning the admission or rejection of evidence, if an erroneous instruction has been given to the jury, or if the verdict is obviously contrary to the weight of the evidence given. If the motion for a new trial is refused, the court tenders its judgment. If the losing party still believes that there was a substantial error in the conduct of the trial, he or she may take the case to a superior court of appeal, in which case the defendant is termed the *appellant* and the other side the *appellee*. The court of review or appeal is exactly what its name implies. It does not conduct a new trial. It simply considers the record of the proceeding that took place before the inferior trial court and the exceptions taken to rulings of the trial judge with regard to procedure, pleading, admission of evidence, instructions, etc. If the court of review or appeals decides that a substantial error prejudicial to the losing side was made by the lower trial court, the judgment of the lower court is reversed and the case is remanded for a new trial.

FUTURE THEMES

Public health law has not kept pace with changes in the law generally or in the technology of health. Some of these changes have been discussed, including changing attitudes towards criteria, judicial presumption, and the use of cost-benefit analyses in promulgating regulations. Gostin,[26] whose comments were quoted earlier, has made a series of proposals to modernize public health law:

1. There should be a uniform structure to the law. There should be no distinctions made between the law affecting communicable disease generally and sexually transmitted diseases specifically.
2. The exercise of compulsion should require that the necessity and the benefits of such compulsion be demonstrated. Blood testing of food service workers for AIDS has no useful role to play in the control or prevention of the disease.
3. Confidentiality provisions should be reviewed and updated, especially in the light of public concern about AIDS. There may be circumstances in which a breach of confidentiality is justified, such as in notification of an intimate contact if the infected person will not do so.
4. There should be a graded series of restrictions available to the agency so that the least restrictive alternative can be used first.

Dickens wrote, "The law is an ass." It is perhaps more like a mule. An ass is a natural creature with a life of its own. A mule is the invention of humans, an artificial and sterile animal. It takes human planning to breathe life into the law. It is a valuable tool, underutilized and poorly understood. The states should systematically undertake a thorough recodification of their health laws to bring them into conformity with scientific and legal developments of the past 40 years in preparation for the twenty-first century.

REFERENCES

1. Grad FP: Public health law manual, ed 3, Washington, DC, 1973, American Public Health Association.
2. Wing KR: The law and the public's health, Ann Arbor, MI, 1985, Health Administration Press.
3. Christoffel T: Health and the law, New York, 1982, The Free Press.
4. Gray JC: The nature and sources of law, New York, 1909, Columbia University Press.
5. Cardoza BN: The nature of the judicial process, New Haven, 1921, Yale University Press.
6. Blackstone W: In Lewis WD, editor: Commentaries, Philadelphia, 1897, Rees, Welsh & Co.
7. Sutherland AE: The law at Harvard, Cambridge, MA, 1967, Belknap Press.
8. Holmes OW: The common law, Boston, 1881, Little, Brown & Co.
9. Thayer JB: The origin and scope of the American doctrine of constitutional law, Harvard Law Review 7:129, Oct 1893.
10. Akerman BA: Law and the public mind: by Jerome Frank, Daedalus 103:119, Winter 1973.
11. Wilson W: The state: elements of historical and practical politics, Boston, 1918, DC Heath & Co.
12. Gostin L and Ziegler A: A review of AIDS related legislative and regulatory policy in the United States, Law Med and Health Care 15:5, Summer 1987.
13. Cardoza BN: The growth of law, New Haven, 1942, Yale University Press.
14. Seagle W: The quest for law, New York, 1941, Alfred A Knopf, Inc.
15. *Detroit Audobon Society et al v City of Detroit et al,* US District Court, Eastern District of Michigan, Southern Division, Case No 87-CV-71577-DT, 1987.
16. Miller CA and others: Statutory authorizations for the work of local health departments, Am J Public Health 67:940, Oct 1977.
17. Ascher CS: The regulation of housing, Am J Public Health 37:507, May 1947.
18. Freund E: The police power, Chicago, 1904, Calahan.
19. Curran WJ: Administrative warrants for health and safety inspections, Am J Public Health 68:1029, Oct 1978.
20. Forgotson EJ: 1965: the turning point in health law—1966 reflections, Am J Public Health 57:934, June 1967.
21. Edelman S: Search warrants and sanitation inspections—the new look in enforcement, Am J Public Health 58:930, May 1968.
22. Freeman AW: Public health administration in Ohio, DeLamar Lectures, Johns Hopkins University School of Hygiene and Public Health, Baltimore, 1921, The Williams & Wilkins Co.
23. Doniger DD: Federal regulation of vinyl chloride: a short course in the law and policy of toxic substance control. In Hogue LL, editor: Public health and the law: issues and trends, Rockville, MD, 1980, Aspen Systems Corp.
24. Mustard HS: Legal aspects of planning for local health units, Am J Public Health 37(suppl):20, Jan 1947.
25. Institute of Medicine: The Future of public health, Washington, DC, 1988, National Academy Press.
26. Gostin LO: The future of public health law, Am J Law Med 12(3-4):461, 1986.
27. Curran WJ: The preparation of state and local health regulations, Am J Public Health 49:314, March 1959.

28. Kingon RJ and Wiesner PJ: Premarital syphilis screening: weighing the benefits, Am J Public Health 71:160, Feb 1981.
29. Felman YM: Repeal of mandated premarital tests for syphilis: a survey of state health officers, Am J Public Health 71:155, Feb 1981.
30. Watson GS, Zador PL, and Wilks A: Helmet use, helmet use laws, and motorcyclist fatalities, Am J Public Health 71:297, Mar 1981.
31. Baker SP: On lobbies, liberty and the public good, Am J Public Health 71:573, June 1980.
32. Curran WJ: Making new health law: "sue the bastards," Am J Public Health 60:2016, Oct 1970.

PART THREE

The management of public health programs

The next four chapters describe how public health programs are organized. They are not a short text in management skills. Good public health management requires intelligence, a firm base in health and epidemiology, an understanding of fairness, and specific knowledge about financial management, organizational behavior, human resources, and community planning and organization. Those skills cannot be adequately presented in a few pages. Much of good management is intuitive, a lot of it is dependent upon good interpersonal skills, and experience is best acquired in a supportive work environment with good supervision.

Management of public health is made more complex because of the dominance of the business ethic in American enterprise. The public sector has never been popular in the United States. Private enterprise and the entrepreneurial spirit are prized. Most of the applied research in management as well as the teaching of management have been concerned with the private sector. Research grants and technical assistance requests have supported the faculty of business schools and helped to establish a rich and robust body of knowledge, but the insights gained and the skills acquired in the private sector are not readily translated into the public sector.

For years, business people have complained about inefficiency in the public sector and urged that a good dose of business principles be instilled into the public bureaucracy. Nevertheless, public programs are different from private enterprise: they have different purposes, different methods, and different constraints and incentives. These are rarely comprehended in the private sector. There are textbooks about financial management and accounting and marketing in the not-for-profit sector, but they are simple transformations of knowledge acquired in the private sector and do not begin with the basic concepts of public service. Generally they are oriented to the not-for-profit hospital and medical care enterprises, which are not the same as public health. There are some excellent academic programs in public administration, but they are very small compared to the business schools and have a relatively short history. The public sector needs much greater attention in the United States. The role of government in health will expand in the years ahead, using a blend of public and private resources and skills. Creative management of the health sector in the future will require the same intense effort that has been devoted to private business these past 200 years.

The ways public health programs are managed at the state and local level are described in Chapter 10. The complex interrelationships of state and local health departments indicate a highly varied approach to assuring that a governmental presence in health is available in every community in the United States. To translate that presence into effective programs requires a special planning effort—the community-based, comprehensive health planning program, which began in 1966 and nearly died in 1981. Its resuscitation and rehabilitation are necessary in the years ahead. That is not enough, however. Well-crafted policies and plans become useful only when they are translated into effective programs that reach their intended audiences. Marketing is now a commonly used term, but the marketing of public health programs requires research and experimentation, which by and large has not been done and the need for which is rarely understood. Some of the special features of the public health marketplace are described in Chapter 12.

Other countries have encountered most of the

public health problems faced by the United States. In some cases they did so before the problems were recognized in this country, and they have taken different approaches to dealing with them. Public health is organized differently in other countries. In some countries it hardly exists at all as a separate organizational entity; in others it has a higher priority than the therapeutic system. Understanding the commonalities and differences between the United States and other countries is an important step toward understanding public health in the United States.

CHAPTER 10

Managing public health

In earlier editions of this book, separate chapters were devoted to three aspects of management: organizing, personnel management, and financial control. Not too many years ago, most public health managers could do their jobs with no more orientation than that. Such is no longer the case. Fiscal stress, forced reductions in the size of the work force, the growing interdependence of the public and private sectors, the increasing complexity of the law, and explosive growth in technology have changed the requirements of management both qualitatively and quantitatively. Whether it is possible to teach people to be good managers is arguable, but it is clear that the management of public health programs now requires much more than can be learned from such a brief study of management as can be given here. This chapter makes no pretense of covering the complexities of managing in detail: its purpose is to introduce the subject and describe some of the idiosyncrasies of public health management that make it different from other managerial endeavors.

The study of management in the United States has been almost exclusively devoted to the private sector. There is a growing number of programs in public administration, but there are many more business schools, and they are larger, better funded, and more involved in research.

Public administration is quite different from private administration.* They share the purpose of efficiency in the use of resources, but they differ in many respects that will emerge in the discussion that follows. In recent years, there has been some evidence of a more purposeful and rigorous attempt to understand the special environment of public administration, but research is lacking. Competition and the goal of profit making in the private sector result in a substantial investment in managerial research. Faculty in business schools are better supported than their counterparts in public administration, both by their institutions and as consultants to business. The public sector is much less likely to pay for such assistance or to invest in the study of administration. Many faculty members in business schools have developed courses and textbooks that attempt to adapt their work in the private sector to the public arena, but these remain imbedded in the structure and traditions of the private sector and have questionable value for public health administrators. For many years, in fact for a century, the assertion has been made that what America needs is some good, old-fashioned business managers in the public arena. Although they have a lot to offer, they appear not to understand the differences between the sectors and often fail to further the purposes of government.

In the early 1970s the United States underwent a severe economic recession during which one of the authors was responsible for managing public health and welfare programs in a large urban community. As unemployment increased, it became evident that the agency would have to increase payments to unemployed families and provide more unreimbursed medical care. More eligibility workers would be required, even with streamlined processing. At the budget hearings, the executive director of the chamber of commerce complained that the agency director seemed to be the only person in the community who did not understand that times were hard; business was cutting back and laying off employees, but the agency was asking for *more* rather than less. He could not understand this seemingly paradoxical situation, but it should have been obvious: as the private sector protected its profit margins by reducing employment, it was

* The terms *management* and *administration* are used by different people to mean different things, and each author or speaker seems to have a different definition. No distinction is made in this book: the two terms are used interchangeably. They refer to the "organizational activities that involve goal formation and accomplishment, performance appraisal, and the development of an operating philosophy that ensures the organization's survival within the social system."[1]

shifting its potential losses to the public sector's revenue sources, property tax receipts. Local government was obligated to protect the families affected by the lay-offs. In an indirect manner, property taxes were being used to support the profit margins of the private sector. It should have been obvious, but it was not. The differences between the two sectors, public and private, often go unrecognized by managers in both sectors. It is important that these differences be understood.

Certain basic principles of management have been understood for a very long time. Without intending to intertwine religion and the state, it is worth reflecting on the advice of Moses' father-in-law:

> . . . the people stood about Moses from the morning unto the evening. And when Moses' father-in-law saw all that he did . . . he said: ". . . why sittest thou thyself alone, and all the people stand about thee from morning unto even?" And Moses said unto his father-in-law: ". . . when they have a matter, it cometh unto me; and I judge between a man and his neighbor . . ." And Moses' father-in-law said unto him: "The thing that thou doest is not good. Thou wilt surely wear away, both thou, and this people that is with thee; for the thing is too heavy for thee; thou art not able to perform it thyself alone. Hearken now unto my voice, I will give thee counsel: . . . thou shalt teach them the statutes and the laws, and thou shalt show them the way wherein they must walk, and the work that they must do. Moreover thou shalt provide out of all the people able men . . . men of truth, hating unjust gain; and place such over them, to be rulers of thousands, rulers of hundreds, rulers of fifties and rulers of tens. And let them judge the people at all seasons; and it shall be that every great matter they shall bring unto thee, but every small matter they shall judge themselves; so shall they make it easier for thee and bear the burden with thee. (Exodus 18:13-22)

THE ORGANIZATION OF WORK

The definition of an organization is the same as the definition of a system: a body of two or more people (or parts, in a system) engaged in the pursuit of common goals.[2] An organization can be as small as two or three people or as large and complex as the U.S. Department of Health and Human Services, but the basic principles remain the same: there has to be an understood goal or purpose; resources must be available to enable movement toward the goal; there must be a source of information to measure progress; and someone has to have both the authority to make decisions based on the information and the ability to change things.

The process is similar for any living organism. Mintzberg,[3] in one of the best books on organization, states, "The structure of an organization can be defined simply as the total of the ways in which it divides its labor into distinct tasks and then achieves coordination among them." Mintzberg's diagram (Fig. 10-1) has five parts: a strategic apex, a middle line, an operating core, and a technostructure and support staff, which sit on either side of the middle line. The strategic apex includes the top policymakers of an organization, as well as the chief executive. The operating core includes the people who produce the output of the organization, such as nurses, practicing physicians, engineers, and sanitarians. The middle line includes the managers who supervise the work of the major divisions of the organization, often with considerable latitude. Mintzberg makes an important distinction between the support staff, which may include clerical workers, data processing personnel, cafeteria staff, and maintenance personnel, and the technostructure, which consists of analysts and planners who seek ways to organize and standardize the work of the organization. The technostructure is growing in size and significance in public health organizations.

Mintzberg has also identified five coordinating mechanisms within the organization:

1. The process of mutual adjustment by and between people
2. The direct supervision of one or more people by a designated supervisor
3. The standardization of work processes, such as typing
4. The standardization of work outputs, such as the management of patients who have been discharged from a state mental hospital
5. The standardization of worker skills, such as the employment of licensed personnel.

The three standardizing mechanisms require and allow varying degrees of control by the analysts in the technostructure.

Max Weber is usually held accountable for the invention of the term *bureaucracy*.[4] His influence on the organization of governmental agencies has been strong, but in the last two decades, the inflexibility of the bureaucracy has increasingly yielded to the heterogeneous pressures of environment, purpose, and personality. Mintzberg[3] has described five forms of organization: the simple structure, the machine bureaucracy, the professional bureaucracy, divisionalization, and adhocracy.

Simple structures are usually small, centralized in control, and young. They are rarely found in government, since they are characteristically entrepreneurial. They lack the complex patterns of accountability to elected officials, boards, and legislative bodies that are a ubiquitous part of the governmental process.

Machine bureaucracies depend on standardization of process for coordination and are characteristic of large, old organizations with a fairly well understood product.

The *professional bureaucracy* is a common concept in health agencies. The professional is in essence a standardized worker who has acquired skills, indoctrination, and socialization from the tradition and practice of professional organizations and academic training centers external to the bureaucracy. Health organizations have a difficult time organizing and coordinating the work of professionals, who wish to work independently. The analysts in the technostructure try to standardize and coordinate the work of the organization. Analysts and professionals often engage in a struggle for control. A professional bureaucracy decentralizes control to the individual worker, but the need for managers and analysts to standardize work, either to establish control or to respond to real or perceived requirements for upward accountability, subjects the organization to constant conflict.

Divisionalized organizations, as they are defined by Mintzberg, are not common in the public sector. Although public health organizations are commonly compartmentalized into operating divisions, these are not autonomous organizations and cannot be dissolved or devolved by the agency director or the governing body without legislative approval.

Adhocracies have become the most popular concept in organizational theory in recent years. Adhocracies avoid standardization because of their need to diverge from established ways of doing things to solve new problems. Experts have a home base in units of similar experts and are extracted from the home unit and grouped in interdisciplinary teams to work on specific programs or projects. These are known as matrix organizations,

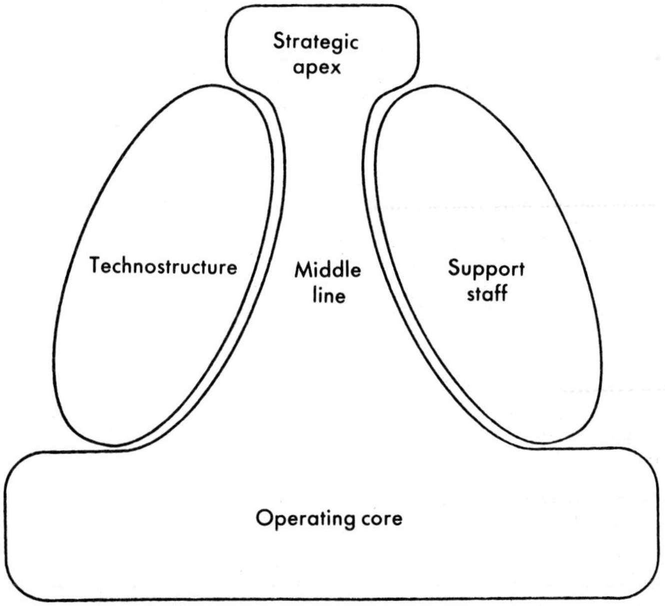

FIG. 10-1 Mintzberg's diagram of an organization. (From Mintzberg, H.: The structuring of organizations: a synthesis of research, 1979. Reprinted by permission of Prentice-Hall, Inc., Englewood Cliffs, New Jersey.)

since workers are members of two organizations at the same time, defying one of the classic principles of organizational theory. For example, the nurse may be a member of the nursing unit but be placed in a task group with specialists from nutrition, social work, data processing, and health education to develop a nutrition strategy for pregnant teenagers. The style of the adhocracy may appear more stimulating and less contentious than that of the professional bureaucracy, but matrix organizations purchase their creativity at high cost. They practically double the number of managers needed to get the work done, and they must not only tolerate diversity but protect it.

Most public health organizations have a variety of structural styles operating at any one time. The vital statistics office may function effectively as a simple structure. Its basic purpose is not the analysis of data, but the ministerial function of collecting it, cataloging it, safeguarding it, and providing people with necessary documents. The laboratory may work well as a machine bureaucracy with each technician following a carefully prescribed set of procedures. The pediatric clinic can function fairly efficiently as a professional bureaucracy and gets into real trouble only when managers attempt to erode the scope of professional judgment by task analysis and rigid job specifications. When it becomes necessary to look at the possibility of a genetic screening program for Tay-Sachs disease, staff from the vital statistics office, the laboratory, and the pediatrics clinic, as well as others, may be drawn together into an ad hoc task group to assess the size of the problem and consider intervention strategies.

Many variables enter into the design of an organization: its size, its age, its mission, its enabling legislation, the nature of its work, the training and indoctrination of its workers, the nature of the problem with which it is working, and very importantly, the external environment. Consistency of form and function is important. A centralized chain of command would be inconsistent with a professional bureaucracy, as would a matrix structure in a stable external environment with a consistent demand for an established service. Both would court disaster. The design and management of an organization have to evolve from a continuing attempt to define its purpose, its environment, and the nature of its human resources. Unlike a private sector enterprise, which can change its purpose, its structure, or even its resources, the public health agency must make many adaptive adjustments to achieve consistency in design. In fact, structural consistency is virtually impossible in most public agencies, given the diversity of expectations and requirements that make up their environments. Top managers need to be able to use a matrix form of management in their own environment, even though it may be an inappropriate structure for the operating core of the agency.

The chief executive officer of a large private company must satisfy several constituencies: the board of directors, the employees, and the customers. Public health directors have the same problem, with the addition of an entailed clientele (private physicians, hospital boards, and other groups, which often have in mind a specific role for the organization). These may exercise considerable control over the work of the agency, either through political influence or through service on a board that sets policy for the health agency. Most organizations, just like organisms, react to challenge or the threat of injury defensively. The instinct is to preserve and stabilize by the elaboration of policy. Over time, the organization becomes encumbered by policies and reflexes, just as a living organism develops a plethora of immune response mechanisms and defensive reflexes. An isolated incident or criticism is seen as a sign that something may be wrong not with the organization but with its clients or its governing body, and the reaction is systemic. In a long-term care institution, a patient became disturbed in the middle of the night and ripped the sinks from the wall of the bathroom. The staff and managers announced a new policy: "Bathrooms will be locked after 9 PM; patients who need to use the bathroom after this hour should go to the nursing station." The incident should have provoked thoughtful inquiry into how people react to long-term institutionalization and the anomie that often sets in, but policy formation is easier and places the blame on the patient, not the system. After years of reaction, most bureaucracies become so encumbered with an armor plating of policies that they cannot move. The final act in the drama is public attack, a new administrator, and reorganization, followed by repetition of the process of bureaucratization. Shonick and Price[5] have described reorganization as one of the public agency's responses to stress. It is often wasteful and enervating. The response is ancient. Petronius, according to Robert Lee, said in the first century, "I was to learn that later in life we tend to meet any new situation by reorganizing, and a wonderful method it can be for creating the illusion of progress while producing confusion, inefficiency, and demoralization."[6] It might be possible to examine the process more carefully and design institutional barriers to bureaucratization. Advisory boards and consumer-controlled governing boards have been used in this manner, but the results have not been completely satisfactory. More research is needed to make public institutions more accountable and responsive without making them less efficient.

Levels of organization

The legislative branch of government determines the areas in which a public agency must act and the boundaries limiting that action. The details of policy are usually delegated to a board or to a chief executive officer in the strategic apex who is charged with the development of necessary rules to carry out the broad purpose of the law. The actions of the legislature, the board, and the chief executive officer are, of course, subject to adjudication by the courts.

Boards. Most agencies of state and local government are directly responsible to the chief executive. Schools and health departments are common exceptions. Boards of health were created for one of two reasons: the employed workers lacked expertise and needed the direction of competent citizens, and public health programs were thought to be too important to be vulnerable to the vicissitudes of electoral politics and the board was inserted between directly elected officials and the health department to protect the latter from the former. Although the continued existence of such boards is rarely questioned, circumstances and concepts have changed. Most well-organized health agencies have little need for volunteer advisors in professional and technical matters, and when they do need such assistance it usually can be obtained from another agency of government. As to political interference with public health, the contrary criticism has been heard more often since the 1960s. Health departments and boards of health have been attacked for their alleged unresponsiveness to community wishes and needs, and elected officials have expressed frustration with the independence of such boards and officials, who do not have the same degree of direct accountability to the public.

As described in Chapter 6, the number of policy-making state boards of health decreased from 40 in the early 1970s to 27 in 1980.[7,8] Overall, state health agencies were placed more closely under the control of the governors.

The average size of the state boards of health found in the study by Gossert and Miller[7] was nine members. These are usually appointed by the board of supervisors, the mayor, or the governor for overlapping terms. In several states the appointment must be made from a list of nominees submitted to the governor by the state medical association, and in Alabama the board *is* the state medical association. No recent surveys of local boards of health have been reported, but their structure is generally the same as that of the state boards.

In 1988, the Institute of Medicine[9] called for the reestablishment of boards of health, which were called "Public Health Councils" to avoid confusing the present need with their previous purposes. Their role needs to be defined. In attempts to do this, board members have listed as many as 17 different functions, including provision of technical expertise, the watchdog function, provision of consumer feedback, education of the community, fund-raising, program and agency protection from real or imagined threats of elected leaders, a hearing panel for complaints, development and analysis of health-related legislation, promulgation of regulations, and a forum for public debate and deliberation. Members selected for one of these purposes may be ineffective for another, and it would be impossible for any one member to be useful for all of the suggested purposes. If the board members and those who appoint them are unclear about the purpose of a health board, confusion will ensue, resulting in either constant fighting or lethargy and inattention. The purpose of the board has to be thoughtfully defined, and the number of different purposes should be limited so that a small number of members can accomplish them with a reasonable degree of success.

Perhaps the most important role for boards of health, exclusive of their responsibility for developing necessary regulations, is to expand the deliberative capacity of government. Unlike the federal government, some state governments and most local governments have little if any capacity to conduct a full deliberation of public policy issues. They often have to rely on brief interactions with agency directors and interested citizens and then arrive at a decision or postpone it until some external event forces a decision. A board of health specifically organized and composed for this purpose could provide the community with an opportunity for expanded deliberation of public health issues; after analysis of the debate and distillation of the points raised, such a board could provide the elected officials with a better sense of the community's needs and expectations. In addition, the process could take much of the heat of debate out of the council chambers and into the community, where full and sometimes angry expression of opinions may do more good.

Most communities also have one or more community mental health center boards and they may have state-mandated boards for alcoholism programs, drug abuse programs, services for the developmentally disabled, and other groups. There may also be a health planning council. Membership requirements are usually different enough to preclude combining or merging boards, even if the various constituencies would tolerate such a move. Unless a local board of health can be thoughtfully designed and appointed, it may isolate the health agency director from other boards. State and federal laws that stand in the way of developing constructive linkages and networks of citizen boards should be amended, and health agency administrators and their boards should exert considerable effort to integrate and coordinate the work of the various boards.

Advisory committees. Advisory committees are formed for one or more of three reasons: (1) because the board of health or the health director needs technical advice in certain areas, (2) because not enough interested groups can be accommodated through appointment to the board of health, or (3) because the principal legislative or executive body of the jurisdiction does not want a board of health between itself and the health department but cannot afford to deny citizen input and oversight altogether. Often these committees are required by federal or state legislation. They may be advisory to the board, the chief executive officer, or a program manager.

Advisory committees are of two general types—constituent and technical. Members of constituent advisory committees may be chosen for their personal qualifications or because they represent social, professional, client, or other groups in the community. The chief advantage and use of constituent advisory committees is as a channel through which the community, on the one hand, and the health department, on the other, are kept aware of each other's thoughts, plans, and actions. Members of technical advisory committees assist the administrative officers of the public health agency in the formulation of plans and in the development and application of various techniques of value in the public health program.

Advisory committees have no direct power but can exert considerable influence, through either the quality of their advice or their political pressure, or both. When they are seen as an irrelevant nuisance by the health director and treated as such, they become useless at best and dangerous at worst. Kept from participation, an energetic advisory board will forcefully intrude on the operational domain. Although these groups have sometimes been created capriciously by federal or state law or regulation, they should always be taken seriously. Membership should be carefully chosen, not to assure homogeneity but to assure that responsible and thoughtful members become involved. Providing effective staff support and liaison to the advisory group are skills that cannot be assumed casually. They require thought and training.

Administration

In public health agencies the chief executive officer is responsible for carrying out the mission of the organization, usually expressed in statutory language, and has three functions: political leadership, management of the agency's resources, and ceremonial representation. The inherent politics of the role are often denigrated, yet any position that involves the development of a pattern of action emanating from an ideologic base in an often vaguely worded statute is a political position. The director has the opportunity to emphasize, to obscure, to create, and to resist—in short, to direct.

The importance of the ceremonial mission is often overlooked. Those who seek power as a goal may be disappointed with the perquisites of position, but those who acquire it by pursuing the goals of public health may be surprised at the status accorded the position. To most people in the jurisdiction served, the position is an important one and is treated with respect and trust. The presence of the health director at community functions may occasionally expose him or her to real anger and frustration, but even that is an indication of the expectations of the community.

The director's position differs in other ways from that of the staff of the agency. Although most workers are employed by the civil service system (see below), the director often is appointed, either by an elected executive or by a board, and may be fired just as easily. The director of a public health agency occupies a position whose functions are often specified in statute, whereas the staff works with job specifications developed by the civil service system. In the private sector, a chief executive officer can usually do anything that is not prohibited by law or forbidden by policies of the board. The public sector manager can do only those things permitted or required in the governing statute.

Whether continuing in office or starting out in a new position, the director should do three things: (1) read and know the law, because it describes what is supposed to be done and to some extent how it is to be done, (2) study the needs of the community, because they may not be the same as what the law allows and requires, and (3) evaluate the resources available, because they indicate what can actually be done.

Examining a community's needs has become so fashionable as to have its own jargon term: *needs assessment*. It involves identifying and studying important data sources. These include data from the census on housing, living conditions, and socioeconomic status; vital statistics data, which can reveal differences between the jurisdiction and the nation; welfare data, which can pinpoint the areas with a high concentration of frail elderly people, women with dependent children, and disabled individuals; and health services data, which were assembled in most communities by health planning bodies between 1966 and 1981. The review of such data by people trained in public health and epidemiology can do much to define the real needs of the community. The results should be compared with the statutory specifications of purpose, and the gaps will identify the major areas of work and planning in the years ahead. The assessment function is one of the three basic roles of public health at all levels of government.[9]

Finally, having identified what is allowed, required, and needed, the director has to measure the resources available both in the agency and elsewhere in the community. They will rarely be sufficient to meet either the needs or the requirements, and that realization forces the process of setting priorities – one of the most important tasks for any public health agency director. (Some of the techniques for doing this are described in Chapter 11.)

Since it has been impossible for economic reasons to employ a physician full time for such purposes in many local health departments, state laws allow part-time appointments or the appointment of a state health department physician as the local health officer of several counties. In the early 1970s, the Health Officer's section of the American Public Health Association changed its name to the Health Administration section. This reflected the growing number of nonphysician graduates of programs in health administration and the trend toward allowing nonphysician health officers to be appointed at both the state and the local level. By 1978, only 21 states required that local health officers be physicians, and nonphysicians filled about one third of all local positions.[10] Miller and associates[11] found that two thirds of local health directors were physicians in the 1970s, but only 23% had both a physician's degree and a master's degree in public health. In most large urban health departments, as well as in state agencies, the health officer is usually a physician.

Medical school is a poor place to learn how to be an effective administrator: the orientation is toward individual autonomy and decision making. The work of such professionals is standardized, and efficiency depends on the ability to classify problems and apply standard solutions; the urge to solve problems by diverging from accepted norms is necessary in administration but is not a characteristic of the clinical professions. When teamwork is involved, the physician is usually in a fairly autocratic position. These are not circumstances that characterize the job of public health administration. Some physicians have made the transition well, but that has been a function of their personal characteristics, not of their training as physicians.

Elected officials sometimes find it difficult to disagree with agency directors who have strong professional training. This is especially true when the director is a physician. It is easier to argue with the sheriff or the highway director. As the budgets of health departments have increased and public concern over a wide array of health problems has become more intense, elected officials have turned more frequently to nonphysicians as managers of public health agencies. It is easier to disagree with them; they usually have had special training in administration, and their salaries are certainly lower. Well-trained health administrators can be hired for $40,000 to $50,000, while a full-time physician director may cost from $80,000 to $90,000. In most areas of the country, nonphysicians are now serving as directors of public health agencies at the local level. Often there is a position for a medical director, who is to provide the professional medical expertise required, but the position has little line authority in the organization. Questions have been raised as to whether this is the best way to organize and manage public health resources. Roemer[12] has proposed that a new kind of doctor be trained—a doctor of public health—with a mixture of medical school and public health school training. His proposal was not well received initially, but a growing number of schools of public health have been examining it. The need is real: a short training program in public health or public administration with little or no training in human and social pathology is not sufficient to manage an enterprise as complex as public health.

Leadership is a popular but poorly understood concept. How does someone lead? Partly by position, which conveys authority, but the power to use that authority constructively comes from less objective assets. It is clear that an effective leader has to have a good grasp of the purpose and the methods of the organization being led. Beyond that, training in administration is a major asset. Both in the private and in the public sector, boards are looking for people who are comfortable with accounting terminology, are at ease with computers, understand (without being overly fascinated by) cost-effectiveness studies, and know enough about personnel administration to keep the agency and the elected leaders out of court. Most important, given the basic knowledge to use the agency's resources intelligently, is the leader's use of power. Power is the ability to get things done. The ability to get things done has much to do with productivity. Workers are more productive when they can exert more control over their environment, when they can, as individuals or as a group, bring enough of the tasks together to be able to carry out a whole task, not just an isolated piece of it. A supervisor or agency director becomes more powerful by giving than by accreting power, since productivity is increased. In short, a leader can only acquire the power needed to lead by learning how to give it to others. This is not simply the process of delegation, but the development of strong program leaders who can enter into contest with the agency director and each other for the expression of ideas and their implementation. It requires an individual who is

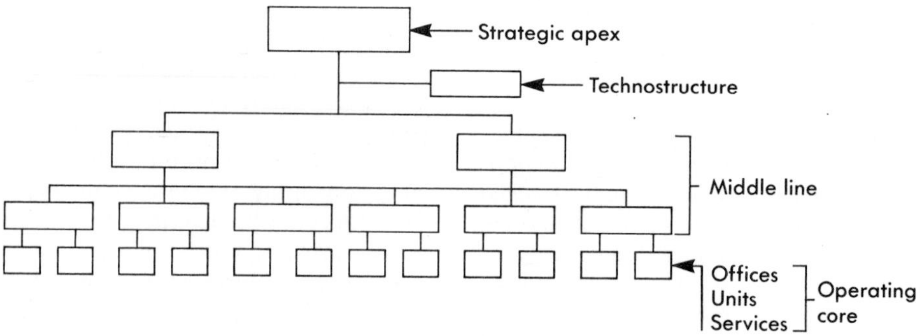

FIG. 10-2 The scalar process.

secure in knowing what is being done rather than in doing it all personally. It requires much hard work, but basically it depends on training, personality, and experience.

The scalar principle

The term *scalar principle* refers to the administrative arrangement of functional groups or units in steps, as in a scale (Fig. 10-2). Each of the steps, often referred to as divisions or sections, is usually determined on the basis of purpose, discipline, or function, such as water control, family planning, or nursing. The confusion of different terminologies is unfortunate; *department, division, bureau, service,* and *office* are often used interchangeably if not haphazardly in the structural plans of many organizations. Actually it matters relatively little how the terms are used as long as they are used in a consistent manner and are understood by those involved.

Some administrators believe that the charts make little difference and that the effectiveness of the organization depends on the personnel, not the design of the chart. Others go to the extreme of mechanizing their management, believing that complex charts will make things happen properly regardless of the individuals in the boxes. Neither approach is realistic. The organizational chart has two purposes: (1) it reveals the emphasis that the administrator places on different activities and programs, and (2) it outlines a facilitative approach to communications. The fact that the organizational chart conveys impressions about how the administrator-designer feels about certain activities or persons is often missed by administrators. Both the staff of the agency and groups within the community will interpret the chart with great care to see how they or their interests are valued. The perceptions they develop, whether or not they are accurate, will have a great deal to do with how they react to the administrator-designer.

Span of control

Span of control is a time-worn phrase in organizational theory. It has been common practice to organize spans of control in sixes since some early theorists believed that administrators could not deal effectively with more than six different personalities, programs, or divisions. No single rule can be applied, however. In some tasks, it may be better to develop a tall, narrow organization with a single leader, two or three boxes on the chart reporting to the strategic apex, and no more than a few program directors reporting to each of those managers. A flat organization is one in which the span of control is broad and shallow, with many program directors reporting directly to the chief executive. The latter is useful when it is desirable to reduce administrative control and forestall attempts to stultify the individuality of program leaders. The tall, narrow organization is more effective when there are many legalistic functions to be carried out, and tight supervision is necessary to assure precision in the output. The same purpose can be served by more rigid standardization of process.

The best plan is one that groups functions to enable responsiveness to the jurisdiction served rather than to the administrative controls placed on the agency. The contrary pattern has, unfortunately, prevailed in the United States. National agencies are established with their own mandates but with little understanding of how such activities are carried out on the local level. The state agencies that receive the national funds to carry out the program are encouraged to organize so that they can respond to national initiatives. This is often incongruent with the way the services must be delivered locally, yet the administrative requirements of the sponsoring national agency may override the service delivery requirements at the other end and dictate an administrative form that does not follow function. This has been especially evident in the development of environmental protection programs at the national level, where water pollution has been seen as a wastewater treatment problem, whereas in some states water pollution is clearly a matter of acid mine drainage that is not amenable to control through the construction of sewage treatment plants. Ideally each layer of government should be designed to conform to the needs of its receiving constituency rather than its sponsoring constituency. It should absorb the administrative problems of confusion rather than pass them along to the local level where the ultimate purpose is served.[13]

Organizational units may be formed around purpose, place, function, process, or discipline. Public health agencies have had a difficult time with organizational theory, because some programs are organized around their client group or their purpose, such as venereal disease control or maternal and child health programs, while others are organized to fit the place, such as a district office that attempts to provide comprehensive services. Other groupings are formed around a discipline such as nutrition, which has a specific purpose, while other discipline groupings such as nursing have at best a very broad purpose. This is not necessarily a significant problem until the jurisdiction becomes enamored of program planning processes and directs each operating unit to write a program plan following a specified format. This is easier to do in a functional unit such as tuberculosis control, where objectives can be stated numerically, than in nursing, where function ranges from prenatal care to hospice care for the terminally ill.

The technostructure

For a considerable period, all divisions of public agencies were more or less self-contained units performing all of the activities and functions necessary for their operation and maintenance. Beginning about 1900, with the expansion of public service and its increased specialization, various functions of a staff nature were separated from the operational units and brought together to form what are referred to as staff units, which are usually aligned structurally in close relationship with the chief executive officer of the organization. While some staff services belong in what Mintzberg[3] refers to as the support staff sector, others are in the technostructure: financial management services, planning, legal services, and research activities.

Staff units do more than study, plan, and advise. Their purpose is to facilitate the work of administration. They assist the line or functional units by working with them but without infringing on their authority or responsibility. Lines of authority should not pass through them. Instead, they are situated in an "off line" position as adjuncts to the office of the chief executive. Staff assistants carry implied authority in that they often serve as personal representatives of the chief executive. As such, their opinions are not viewed as their own but as reflections of what the chief executive wants done. To be effective, staff assistants have to have a full understanding of the policy and even the style of the chief executive so that these can be conveyed accurately and consistently. Moreover, program administrators have to be guaranteed access to the chief executive whenever they believe that the staff guidance offered is at variance with the facts or with program policy. The chief executive and staff assistants have to be very cautious about developing lines of communication that bypass the responsible administrator of a division or program. There may be times when this is necessary because of an emergency or the incompetence of the bypassed administrator, but such occasions are usually indicative of a management problem that needs attention.

The personnel who make up such staff units are not always under the control of the managers of the health agency at the state or local level. In the public sector, some are more likely to be placed in separate organizations formed to exercise budgetary control and assure financial accountability. While such staff units usually lack a statutory assignment for programmatic review, that function is often assumed, since the financial officer is appointed by the elected chief executive and the role may offer some additional opportunity to gain political control over the professional bureaucracy. When a vacant position is to be filled, the health agency director theoretically needs to requisition an eligible candidate from the civil service system. In practice, the request often has to be approved by the director of finance, who may question the wisdom of the program as well as the authority of the health director and the expenditure of funds, which if unspent might be available for some other purpose in the next fiscal period. The advent of the technostructure has presented new problems for government agencies whose program directors guard their statutory prerogatives and traditions from elected officials who seek to gain control of the bureaucracy. The best way to avoid the confrontation is for the director of the health agency to become a more effective manager and to gain better control of the bureaucracy so that the mayor or the governor will have less need to do so.

Organizational change

Organizations may have either a functional structure or a product-oriented structure. The product-oriented structure is more characteristic of private sector entities, especially profit-making ones, while functional structures are a characteristic result of the governmental process and of the civil service system of personnel management (see below). Functional structures are not well thought of in business schools or schools of public administration, and many health agency directors have attempted to reorganize public health functions into a product-oriented array of activities. As previously noted, many states have reorganized their health agencies in recent years, and the same thing has occurred at the local level. Some of the more complete reorganizations have occurred in Florida (1975), Minnesota (1976), West Virginia (1977), and Michigan (1978). All of the efforts have emphasized the reorganization or the development of local or community health services. Michigan's effort involved a recodification of all state laws affecting public health. The changes in Minnesota and Florida have been well documented.[14,15] Both efforts are described as decentralizations, but they are very different.

The Florida reorganization stemmed from the Health and Rehabilitation Services Act of 1975, which required the state agency to "establish measurable program objectives and performance criteria for each program it operates" and conduct studies of "relative cost and effectiveness."[14] The Minnesota law, by contrast, had as its purpose "to develop and maintain an integrated system of community health services under local administration with a system of state guidelines and standards."* The Florida effort emphasized the role of the technostructure at the state level, whereas the emphasis in Minnesota was on building community capacity under a variety of arrangements to be selected by the community, not the state. The impressive effort in Florida used almost every acronymic device popularized in the management literature of the 1960s and 1970s. Organizational development (OD) was used when professional resistance was detected, and a host of reports and computerized management information system documents have been generated. The base of the system rests on the Program Activity Report (PAR) to be filled out by each employee at the local level for each activity performed. The statewide system is impressive, and the work that was done to develop and implement it is worthy of study by those with a similar job to do.

The Minnesota change emphasized community development from the outset, and control by a technostructure was minimized. Considerable latitude was left to local communities, which could choose a single-purpose department and board or various consolidated or integrated models. The reports indicate that virtually the entire state was covered by the community-based system after 5 years and that local per capita support for the community health agencies increased substantially.

Reorganizations can be sponsored for a variety of reasons. The change in West Virginia was partly because of an effort by the governor to gain some control over the state health agency, which was run by a board and a director resistant to gubernatorial exhortations. Reorganizations can occur because of external dissatisfaction with the costs of management or the lack of attention to a favored program or constituency. They may be generated by community groups who do not feel the agency has been effective in meeting perceived health needs, in contrast to the agency's tradition of enforcing the health laws. They may be caused by a change in federal laws that makes it necessary for a state to change to conform to the structure of the national agency and receive its share of the money. They may come about because a new health agency director does not think that the agency is well positioned or designed for the role it is to assume.

Decentralization is a popular term in organizational formation or reformation efforts, but the term is poorly understood. It is not the relocation of service centers so that transit time is reduced and access is made easier. Decentralization involves the relocation of power and can occur with or without a geographic relocation of people. It is important to realize that an agency director can decentralize responsibility without granting the requisite power to meet that responsibility. If both responsibility and authority are decentralized to a community program or a division director, the recipient program director may hold that authority tightly, and the process of decentralization will stop there. Decentralization involves passing both authority and responsibility on to the lowest units in the organization that have the ability and resources necessary to make the decisions involved in carrying out the purpose of the unit. Decentralization of authority and responsibility in a human services agency is one of the most effective ways to

* Minnesota Statutes section 145.911.

move toward the agency's goals, but only when top management and unit supervisors have a reasonable degree of agreement about those goals and a willingness to absorb the additional work of diversity and dissent.

PERSONNEL MANAGEMENT

Personnel management involves the administration of an organization's human resources in a manner that assures the best output with the least costly input while protecting and enhancing the welfare of the workers. Merit systems of personnel management attempt to base employment and career development on merit. They are organized systems that attempt to assure due process in the selection and advancement of personnel. Civil service systems are merit systems that serve the public sector—civil (as differentiated from private or military) employment. Civil service systems had one goal and three subsidiary objectives when they began:

GOAL: to remove personnel management from partisan politics
Objective 1: to afford everyone an equal opportunity for employment
Objective 2: to apply behavioral science to personnel management
Objective 3: to offer employees an opportunity for career development

These original goals and objectives have undergone considerable modification.

Many people think that the American civil service system is too dominated by faith in scientism—a belief that human beings can be "engineered" into job descriptions. Others assert that it is dominated by the self-declared systems of ethics of professional, clerical, and technical groups and that these self-declared roles have robbed the public of the opportunity to be served by a creative work force. To the extent that this is true, it raises fundamental questions about flexibility, motivation, and productivity in all organized personnel systems. Critics decry the rigidities of job specifications, minimum qualifications, and the lack of effective rewards and punishments. Many public health program managers fervently wish that they could do away with the system entirely. Such wishes are unrealistic. Without a well-managed personnel system, most public health program managers would spend a large part of their time in court defending their personnel management practices. A personnel system designed to assure equity and due process is necessary given the democratic heritage of the American system of government. Personnel systems, like almost all systems, are compromises that attempt to satisfy often conflicting requirements but cannot maximize the satisfaction of any.

History

Beginning in the 1870s, voluntary groups were organized in several states to urge reform in public hiring practices. The first state civil service law was passed in New York in 1883 (introduced by Theodore Roosevelt and signed into law by Governor Grover Cleveland). Passage of the Pendleton Act, the first national personnel legislation, is generally attributed to the assassination of President Garfield a half-year earlier by a disgruntled job seeker. That dramatic event may have helped create public support for the act, but it is also apparent that the Republicans anticipated considerable gains in congressional seats by the Democrats in the 1884 elections and that they wanted to preserve the jobs of those they had helped place in office. A new civil service system would require that protected incumbents be removed only for cause, and it was Republican support that got the bill through Congress.

The civil service laws in the United States were modeled after those in England, but there were and are some significant differences. Competitive examinations are at the base of both systems, but the English examinations tend to be of the essay type, suited for college graduates with a liberal arts education. American examinations are more objective in nature, dealing with job-specific details and in some cases designed for graduates of a technical or vocational educational system. The British system admits new personnel only at the bottom of the career ladder and results in a closed service, with senior managers and policymakers coming up from the ranks. The American system is more democratic in its origins and in its practices. In its original form it was fervently Jacksonian in suggesting that participation in the government work force should be representative in nature and even characterized by turnover not dissimilar to that found in the patronage system. That has changed somewhat as job security has become a more important feature of public employment, and promotion from within the ranks has been urged by employee groups. Nonetheless, the dichotomy continues to exist: whether to support careerists in government or equal employment opportunity.

Civil service systems are usually insulated from partisan politics by placing them under the direction of an appointed commission. The commission members serve staggered terms and cannot be removed except for cause. The commission hires the personnel director and approves job classifications, adopts rules of procedure, reviews employee appeals, and either recommends salary schedules to the chief executive of the jurisdiction or in some cases establishes such schedules on its own authority. Appointment of commissioners is usually by the mayor or governor and is often subject to review by the legislative body.

There is a continuing state of tension between the civil service system and elected officials. Both Dresang[16] and Lee[17] indicate that personnel directors remain wary of political influence. Lee thinks that the protected role of civil service systems may isolate them too much from the political process. Others warn that continued vigilance is necessary. Shafritz, Hyde, and Rosenbloom[18] say that the only way to reconcile "discretion over peronnel decisions . . . with the goal of directing the action of political executives . . . lies in a further institutionalization of personnel processes." They urge employees to work together to make it more difficult for political appointees to bypass careerists in making policy level appointments.

Although civil service systems are usually described in the plural, there is virtually only one such system—the national one—with modifications by states and local governments. The U.S. Civil Service System has substantial authority over state and local systems, because Congress requires that a state merit system be in place as a prerequisite to the receipt of federal grants-in-aid for maternal and child health programs. The latter were authorized by the Social Security Act in 1935. The requirement has been continued in grant programs since then and has been extended to local health departments when they participate in a federal grant-in-aid program. Very few local health departments are not governed by civil service systems, although local health agencies in some states have resisted the use of merit systems and still rely on patronage.

Public health was the vehicle for carrying civil service systems into local government. The operation of such systems is expensive, involving job classification, task analysis, recruitment, and testing. Many local governments cannot afford such systems and use their state system for personnel management. Because of that, local public health workers are often thought of as employees of the state civil service system rather than as employees of local government. Their programs are often thought of as state-mandated and state-controlled programs, less amenable to local control. When local government believes that it has less control over some programs, it also believes that it is less responsible for them. Given state and federal control over hiring practices, state and federal financing for a substantial portion of local public health services, and state requirements for local government to carry out specific public health activities, usually without adequate state financing, local government's lack of enthusiasm for public health departments is understandable. This can be overcome by careful public health directors and a supportive state health agency, but tension between state and local governments over public health matters is a common problem.

Dissatisfaction with civil service systems is widespread. Managers and elected officials are dissatisfied with the system, because it restricts their freedom to hire the person they think may be best for the job as well as their ability to move people around or to fire those who they feel are not working effectively. Employees find the system rigid, restrictive in its rewards, and not sufficiently protective of their rights. Employee unions see civil service systems as agents of management and would prefer to transfer much of the responsibility for managing the public sector work force to the collective bargaining process. Personnel directors see the political process and employee unions as threats to the concept of merit. The tension cannot be totally relaxed: conflict between labor and management is a natural phenomenon to some extent. Enlightened and well-trained managers can alleviate the problems to a considerable degree. They need to understand both the rules of the system and the reasons for them, and they need to understand the needs of employees for fairness and a satisfying role to play.

The Federal Civil Service Reform Act of 1978 separated the national civil service system into three agencies: (1) the Office of Personnel Management, which is responsible for administering the civil service system (seen as the voice of management); (2) the Merit System Protection Board, which is to adjudicate disputes, study the workings of the system, and conduct reviews of the effectiveness of policies and procedures (seen as the neutral guardian of merit); and (3) the Federal Labor Relations Authority, which is responsible for designating work units for collective bargaining, supervising elections by employees for representation in collective bargaining, and resolving unfair labor practices (seen as the voice of labor). The act also established the Senior Executive Service, which was intended to loosen some of the restrictive characteristics of civil service on senior level managers as well as to offer them a wider opportunity for career development. The results have not lived up to expectations.[19]

Collective bargaining and civil service

Collective bargaining was the dominant public sector personnel issue of the 1970s. The concept of unionization was not only foreign but also objectionable to public health workers for many years. Patronage gave way to paternalism, not unionism, in the early days of civil service. In such a system, avuncular managers thrived on the reciprocal warmth of their employees, and the notion that unions might be necessary to protect the rights of employees was abhorrent. Beyond that, professional people (nurses and physicians especially) felt that unionization was antithetic to their code of ethics. As public health organizations grew beyond the original triad of physician, nurse, and sanitarian, it was inevitable that groups of workers with similar jobs and expectations would find it desirable to bargain collectively for their working conditions and their pay. Regardless of the law and its intentions, civil service systems were clearly the tools of management in their early days and very close to being politically controlled. Due process and employee rights were less often practiced than preached.

The central issue in public sector collective bargaining is the right to strike. The right to withhold one's labor is widely assumed, but it is often denied in the public sector on the premise that the services—police protection, fire protection, hospital care—are essential and monopoly services; that is, the consumer has nowhere else to go for essential service. Contrary to popular opinion, there generally are no statutes prohibiting collective bargaining by public employees; what is missing is a federal guarantee of the right to bargain collectively. Although the National Labor Relations Board has jurisdiction over the election of bargaining units in private industry, no such federal guarantees exist for public employees. From a legal standpoint, local and state elected officials are free to ignore representations by employees, but from a political standpoint it is very difficult to do so. To maintain the fiction that this is not really collective bargaining in the trade union sense of the term, local governments often call their agreements with employee groups "memoranda of understanding." Regardless of its title, once it exists and has been signed by both the government and the employee representatives, it serves as a contract and forms the basis for the resolution of grievances.

Elected officials who have to ratify whatever agreements are reached may delegate responsibility for the bargaining process to their appointed representatives (sometimes a special consultant) but reserve final approval to themselves. Union leaders prefer to bargain with the final decision makers rather than the appointed representatives, who can only make recommendations, and they often find a receptive ear, because elected officials thrive on bargaining and want employee group support. Circumvention of the appointed bargainers by individual elected officials can make a shambles of management's bargaining strategy.

Because of the complex procedures for publicly reviewing and approving budgets, public sector elected officials have to meet privately to define the parameters of their bargaining position in detail and in advance of the actual bargaining sessions, so their representatives can have a reasonable expectation that the agreements they reach with employee groups will be supported.

In collective bargaining, supervisors and supervisees are separated, the latter being covered by the collective bargaining statutes and the former being considered management. In the National Labor Relations Act, a supervisor is

> Any employee having the authority, in the interest of the employer, to hire, transfer, suspend, lay-off, recall, promote, discharge, assign, reward, or discipline other employees, or responsibility to direct them or to adjust their grievances, or effectively to recommend such action, if . . . the exercise of such authority is not of a merely

routine or clerical nature, but requires the use of independent judgement.

This definition raises difficulties in classifying physicians and nurses, as well as other professional and technical personnel. The act allows "professional employees" to bargain collectively and defines such employees.[20]

The public-private debate

It is commonly alleged that public sector employees are overpaid, unproductive, and only marginally ethical.[21] The facts do not support the allegations.

The public sector is predominantly a service industry and is therefore labor-intensive. Social work, epidemiologic surveys, and good prenatal care do not lend themselves to automation. By contrast, the private sector has one overriding objective: to maximize profits. That can be done by increasing prices and decreasing costs, so long as one remains competitive, or by increasing the amount of product sold. The public sector has neither that overriding motivation nor implicit or explicit public support to use the tactics of the private sector. While it behooves the private business person to minimize personnel costs, the public sector has other objectives. In addition to the frankly political motivation to produce jobs for constituents, government is often urged to use its work force as a social instrument in times of unemployment or to increase access to jobs by people who might not otherwise be employed. Whereas industry will automate to reduce costs and labor problems, government is reluctant to lay off workers, because employment is a valid social purpose and layoffs are not usually productive politically. Moreover, it is more difficult to automate service functions than to automate manufacturing.

Ethics are another point of debate. Newspapers are replete with stories about elected or appointed officials who misused an office or the authority that went with it, but it appears that private sector abuses are both more common and more acceptable to the public. A double standard exists. Governments often become inefficient in their quest to prevent the embezzlement of nickels and dimes. To paraphrase an old English rhyme:

> We punish the public man and woman
> Who steals the goose from off the common,
> Yet turn the private felon loose
> Who steals the common from the goose.

Even though elected officials are prone to attack sloth and lapses of ethics in those known as bureaucrats, legislative investigations have generally concluded that there is less pilfering, embezzling, and cheating by public employees than by business leaders, managers, and private sector employees.

The private sector always has the option of excusing theft or misconduct in exchange for a resignation or an apology or simply because of kinship or friendship. No such right exists in the public sector, because it is not the manager's money that is being lost or stolen but the public's money, for which the manager is legally accountable. The public sector manager never has the right to excuse dishonest behavior or to make a personal decision that mitigating circumstances excuse the situation but has instead an obligation to turn the matter over to the appropriate legal representative and leave the pleadings about mitigating circumstances to the witness stand in court.

One admonition is consistently valid: personnel management is the most underrated essential skill for public health administrators. Until fairly recently, most public health administrators were physicians, nurses, or sanitarians, whose basic training was far removed from the study of administration. Personnel management got short shrift by people who felt that their other skills equipped them to be effective managers of people. Given heavy reliance on the work of skilled people, it should be evident that the selection of capable people, their support and development, and sometimes their discharge are among the most important tasks that any public program manager has to perform. It is relatively easy to get along with an inadequate computer, typewriter, or building compared to the grief that can ensue from the wrong personnel choice. Most new managers are so anxious to learn the substance of their programs, the political milieu in which they must operate, and the nature of their constituents that they pay too little attention to the selection of new staff or the effective development of the existing workers. *Nothing* can be as costly as a personnel mistake. Failure to take the time to choose wisely in the first place or failure to admit a mistake and work as long and as patiently as it takes to help a miscast employee to move into a better role or out of the program altogether can result in more lost time, wasted money, and declining public and political support than virtually any other mistake. There are many good textbooks that explore public personnel systems in detail,[16-18] and anyone contemplating a career in public health administration, from a supervisory level to agency leadership, should study the subject thoroughly and decide at the outset to devote the time to personnel management that it deserves—it is an essential function.

The personnel process

The personnel system should be considered a human resource development program and not simply a clerical function involving paper processing. That is true partly because the work to be done by public health is demanding and important, but it is also true because the growth and development of a worker's capabilities are synonymous with good public health practice within the agency and essential to the development of an effective and respected agency.

Job classification. Job classification lies at the heart of the attempt to make personnel work scientific and equitable. The first step is task analysis, a detailed description of the work that is required of the person expected to do the job. For a sanitarian this might involve driving a car, collecting specimens from the cooling vat at a dairy, recording the temperature of the wash water, examining the cleanliness of the milk-collection tubing, discussing results with the dairy manager, completing a report, and so forth. If this work is sufficiently distinct from the work done by an inspector of restaurants, then two separate job classifications might be prepared: dairy inspector and restaurant inspector. Since some dairies are more automated and complex than others, or because the employing agency might want to distinguish between a novice and someone with a year or more of experience, dairy inspector levels I and II might be developed, where the dairy inspector II would be required to be able to disassemble an automatic milking machine or evaluate the reliability of a computerized control system for a cooling and storage facility. Finally, if several dairy inspectors I and II are needed, a separate classification of dairy inspector III might be established for supervisors.

For each classification there is a set of minimum qualifications that represents an effort by the personnel technicians, usually with the input of the health program managers, to estimate the kinds of prior training and experience required to carry out the tasks. In recent years, the U.S. Civil Service Commission has stressed the *minimum* part of *minimum qualifications.* The test is job relatedness: if the laboratory testing can be done by a high-school graduate, then a master's degree in microbiology cannot be required, since such a requirement would have the effect of denying an equal opportunity for employment to someone who has the skills to perform the necessary tasks. In part, this recent emphasis on minimum qualifications has had the salubrious effect of enabling people to enter the job market and develop careers through on-the-job training and experience rather than placing over-qualified people in what for them would be dull jobs. The change in emphasis reflects the development of social policy from the civil rights movement of the 1960s, which rightly saw employment as a crucial ingredient in social stability and growth, particularly for minorities and women. This is one of many instances in which the government's hiring apparatus has been used for some purpose in addition to its basic purpose of acquiring the human resources necessary to get a job done.

Recruitment. The purposes of the recruitment process are (1) to assure that all eligible people have an equal opportunity to apply for the job, (2) to be sure that only those who truly meet the minimum qualifications for the job take the time needed to apply, (3) to be sure that applicants know what they are applying for (functions, location, salary, nature of the agency), (4) to let prospective applicants know how and when the applications will be reviewed and an appointment made, and (5) to fill the position with a qualified individual. Sometimes recruitment is carried out only when a vacancy exists and it is the agency's intention to fill the vacancy. This is particularly true for job classifications in which there are few positions or perhaps only one, such as the director of a maternal and child health program. In other situations, advertising and recruiting are constant, because there are many positions in the classification and turnover is such that the personnel agency needs to have available a list of actively interested and eligible candidates.

One of the paternalistic abuses of the civil service concept in the past was the tendency of managers to tell a preferred candidate about an anticipated vacancy so that there might be only the one applicant. In recent years, rules requiring that notice of the vacancy be posted in a public place have been more consistently honored.

Jobs for which many people may be eligible can be advertised locally. Jobs for which the minimum qualifications reduce the pool of those who may be eligible require wider distribution often in national professional journals. The positions of director of epidemiology for a large state health agency or a new mental health center director require a wide area search, as might a position that requires running a piece of esoteric lab equipment. Most agencies now include in the advertisement that they are an equal employment opportunity employer to indicate that they operate under an approved minority hiring plan (see section on Equal Employment Opportunity). It is important to determine whether the civil service agency will do the recruitment as is often the case for jobs common to several user agencies, or whether the health agency is to conduct its own recruitment (for nurses or physicians, for example) for which it will pay the advertising costs.

Testing. Those applicants found to be eligible for an advertised position will be sent a letter announcing the date, time, place, and nature of the examination. Some examinations are objective in nature, using written, machine-graded, and standardized tests of ability and knowledge. Groups of applicants are examined at the same time using the same test. These are known as "assembled" examinations, because they are given once to all applicants in an assembly. Other examinations are open, or unassembled, and the test can be taken by individual applicants whenever they can demonstrate their eligibility for the classification. Some examinations include a performance test, such as typing or the use of tools, whereas other examinations may consist only of an oral interview, usually before a panel. This latter type of examination is particularly common for professional jobs. Some examinations consist of all three: a written test, a performance test, and an interview. Oral interview panels are usually briefed by the program manager about the kind of person the manager is looking for, which gives the examiners an opportunity to go beyond the confines of the written job specification to explore the nature of the work and the clientele.

When the examination process is completed, the eligible applicants are scored and ranked. In some jurisdictions, two lists will be developed, ranked by test score; one list ranks all applicants, and the other separately lists a minority group that has been identified by that jurisdiction as either underemployed or in need because of the nature of the task (usually the cultural or racial characteristics of the clientele).

The testing process has undergone considerable scrutiny in recent years, because it has been demonstrated that commonly used tests discriminate against members of minority groups and rate more highly those with academic backgrounds that take them well past the minimum qualifications for the job. Again the basic requirement is job relatedness, but there is the added complexity of constructing tests that are not culturally biased, or conversely, deliberately constructing a test that is so biased culturally as to enable those with cultural assets for the job to score higher than those who may have had a stronger academic background but who know little of the culture in which they will need to work. The problem is not different from that faced by educators in the classroom, and it is every bit as difficult and important. This is one of the reasons why small communities can rarely afford to run their own civil service system. Good tests are expensive to develop and rarely go unchallenged.

Selection. In most civil service systems, the agency is sent the names of the three top candidates after the tests have been scored. The appointing authority is free to select from among those three, so long as the choice is not based on illegal discrimination (race, sex, religion, national origin, handicapping condition, or age, assuming that all apply in that jurisdiction). This is known as the "rule of three." Some jurisdictions have a "rule of five" and some (Washington state, for example) have a "three plus three" rule, which provides the agency with the top three candidates among all applicants and a second list of the top three minority candidates. The appointing authority may choose from either list. In a few jurisdictions a "rule of one" operates, and either that candidate must be appointed or the appointing authority must show in writing why the individual would be inappropriate. The rule of one often operates when a closed competitive examination is used (that is, the list of eligibles is taken from those already employed within the civil service system of the jurisdiction who are seeking a promotion to the job). Open competitive examinations (open, that is, to both insiders and newcomers) usually offer the appointing authority a choice of the top candidates.

Appointment and probation. When the appointing authority and the selected candidate reach agreement about the appointment, a selection form is signed, usually placing the new employee in probationary status for 6 months. A common mistake is to negotiate salary with the prospective employee, something most appointing authorities are not in a position to do. Like most other features of civil service systems, there are rules governing placement within the steps of the appropriate pay grade. Appointing authorities often try to promise a little extra to get the person they want—a promise the civil service system may not be able to support. Some systems allow appointment above the entry level based on experience, and others do not. The appointing authority, often sharing some of the same work background as the prospective employee, may count a few years of experience that the personnel managers will not recognize. After all the paperwork has been completed, the new employee may find the first paycheck less than anticipated, leading to some very hard feelings. The relevant salary range should be described to the recruit but no figure agreed to before the appropriate personnel managers have reviewed the application and made a determination. In no case should the new employee be told to start work before the appointment has been officially completed.

If the new employee is an existing civil service employee who is making either a lateral transfer (a move to another position in the same classification previously held) or obtaining a promotion, the provisions for a probationary period may not apply, and the employee may have all the rights that an established worker has. If it is a new employee, the probationary period offers both the worker and the agency an opportunity to probe the correctness of the fit and to consider any changes that might need to be made, including discharge, before permanent status is obtained. A probationary employee can usually be discharged without cause so long as discrimination is not involved. Once the probationary period is over, the employee can be discharged only for cause, and termination becomes time-consuming and frustrating although neither impossible nor impractical as some have alleged.

During the early days of the probationary period, it is important that the supervisor and the new employee have a thorough discussion about what is expected on the job. This process is one of mutual negotiation and should be written down and signed so that the employee and the supervisor have something to review about halfway through the probationary period. They can then make any modifications either in the job or in the work plan that are both appropriate and permissible given the job description. It is this agreement of what is to be done that will be used to judge the abilities of the new worker, and this judgment should be scheduled to occur 2 or 3 weeks before the end of the probationary period. Most often, new employees slide into permanent status without this scheduled review, and it is this passive act that is later regretted by management when it finds itself encumbered with an incompetent worker but without sufficient cause for discharge. Not infrequently, representatives of management may start to discuss the inadequacies of a new employee only to learn that the probation period has elapsed and they have a permanent employee who cannot do the job.

Evaluation. The evaluation of work is difficult and is usually done poorly if at all. Most agencies use forms that attempt to evaluate the worker either on the basis of traits (such as attendance or manner), performance (amount of work done), or results. Sometimes all three are rated, using rating scales. Employees are usually graded as poor, below average, average, above average, or outstanding. There is usually space for written comments by the supervisor about outstanding accomplishments or deficits that need attention. There is also a space for the employee to respond and to sign the document. The signature usually means only that the employee has had an opportunity to read the form, not that he or she agrees with the evaluation.

Overall, evaluation procedures are poor, but they should be used nonetheless. They should serve as a basis for discussion between a supervisor and an employee as to what they expect of each other and how well they measure up. Evaluations should be considered when promotions and pay raises are at stake and certainly when disciplinary action is being considered. Too often it is easier for a supervisor to use "good" and an occasional "outstanding" to fill out the form rather than have what might be an unpleasant but useful discussion with an employee. Once rated as good or outstanding on some trait or behavior, any subsequent rating that lowers that grade may be contested by the employee. It is easier for the supervisor to raise the score to its traditional level than to attempt to justify the reduction. When a new supervisor enters the picture and finds the work not up to standards, he or she may be confronted with 5 years of good to outstanding ratings and a Civil Service Commission that will not sustain a discharge or a demotion.

Discipline. There is a constructive hierarchy to discipline that is both logical and often neglected. The basis for the hierarchy is fairness and a conviction that people would rather do a good job than a poor one. When a supervisor has reason to believe that an employee is either not performing up to the agreed expectations or has violated some rules of the organization, the first step is to discuss it with the employee. This obvious approach is frequently ignored, even by rational people. If the violation is dangerous for the employee or others, immediate action should be taken, up to and including suspension from work, until the situation can be remedied. For example, a child welfare worker caught drinking on the job in an emergency shelter and molesting one of the children should be removed without hesitation and the situation reported to the police and prosecuting attorney of the jurisdiction. Most problems are not as dramatic. The first discussion may clarify a misunderstanding on the part of the employee or the supervisor about what was being done or what was supposed to be done. If that successful outcome does not occur, then the employee needs to be verbally warned about the problem (tardiness, for example), and the next time it occurs the verbal warning should be recorded in a memorandum to the employee, and a signed and dated copy should be placed in the employee's file. The employee must be informed that the written reprimand is in the file and given an opportunity to place any explanations in the file that the employee thinks might mitigate the incident. If the employee believes that the written reprimand is erroneous, an appeal can be made to have it expunged from the file. A written reprimand should contain a statement of what is expected and precisely what will be the consequences if corrective action is not taken or if the violation is repeated. The nature of the threatened discipline should be in keeping with the rules of the personnel system. If in doubt, the supervisor should discuss the situation with the personnel manager before writing the reprimand.

In employment situations where collective bargaining agreements exist, the employee usually has the right to be accompanied by a representative or a witness of his or her own choosing in any such discussion with a supervisor. The supervisor should be sure that the employee knows of this right. Even without a collective bargaining agreement, it is good practice to allow the employee the help of an aide or an advocate, and it is equally advisable for the supervisor to have a witness to the exchange.

The next step in the process is usually a suspension from work without pay for a period of 1 to 30 days. Suspensions are appealable actions and may be immediately blocked until the matter can be reviewed by either the Civil Service Commission or some other panel. Alternatively, the suspension may go into effect with the possibility that a subsequent review will reinstate the employee with payment of back wages. In all such actions, the appointing authority must be sure that the employee is precisely informed of the rule that has been violated, the consequences of the violation, and the right to appeal, as well as the nature of the appeals process and any time limits involved. While suspensions are commonly a part of the disciplinary process, they are not especially sensible. Being removed from the work environment without pay for some number of days is not likely to lead to a correction of the problem and only serves to further isolate and alienate the worker, whose living standard may be seriously jeopardized.

The ultimate step in the disciplinary process is discharge. The same procedures to be followed in the written reprimand and in the suspension steps are applicable in a discharge action. Many people, especially in the national civil service system, complain that the procedures and the employee safeguards are such that an incompetent or even dishonest employee can never be discharged. The national civil service system does have some real problems with its procedures that make effective and fair personnel management difficult. At the state and local level, however, it is simply a matter of being fair, consistent, and persistent in the effort to secure good work.

Equal employment opportunity

Title VII of the Civil Rights Act of 1964, as amended by the Equal Employment Opportunity Act of 1972 (P.L. 92-261), makes it illegal to discriminate against anyone in employment because of race, color, religion, sex, or national origin unless one or more of those attributes can be reasonably shown to be related to the normal operation of the business. The Rehabilitation Act of 1973 (P.L. 93-112) extended coverage to the handicapped by declaring that "No otherwise qualified handicapped individual . . . shall . . . be excluded from participation in, be deprived of the benefits of or be subjected to discrimination under any program or activity receiving Federal financial assistance." That includes virtually all health and health-related organizations. The 1978 Federal Civil Service Reform Act also included a strong antidiscrimination clause, which, when coupled with executive orders, should have produced broad and complete protection for all minority groups and for women, but there has been much uncertainty and some unwillingness about the implementation of these acts.

Equal employment opportunity laws addressed the problem created by procedures that had the effect of discriminating against minority groups in hiring. It was clear that after a century or more of discrimination in education and employment, cessation of the practices would not redress the inequities. Affirmative action programs were developed to take positive steps to alter the imbalances created by past practices, and they sought, within the equal opportunity and due process dictates of the law, to compare the size of the employed minority work force group with the size of the potentially available minority work force and increase the penetration of minorities into all ranks of employment where an imbalance existed. Many procedures have been developed, such as targeted recruitment efforts, stratified lists of eligible candidates for jobs, and even quotas for employment. The situation has been made complex by a series of court cases. It appears to be illegal to establish quotas for any minority group, but it is permissible and desirable to establish goals for employment and to shape recruiting, testing, and selection procedures so as to attain those goals. Two maxims can be reliably stated: (1) regardless of any manager's personal convictions about affirmative action, it is essential to employ minorities if minorities are to be well served, and (2) failure to institute a vigorous affirmative action program may well result in a successful court suit against the agency for discrimination. The result of a successful court suit is often a court order that controls hiring practices in such a way that effective management and program performance are no longer possible until the employment imbalance is corrected. For example, if it is found that there are too few black nurses, the court may rule that only black nurses can be hired until they constitute 30% of the nurses in the agency. Since there are not many black nurses readily available for employment (a function, in part, of past discrimination in employment and education), it may be impossible to fill vacancies for 3 or more years, thus bringing the work of the nursing department to a standstill. The only way to avoid such situations is to develop a strong affirmative action policy and to pursue it vigorously and persistently.

Motivation

In recent years, public agencies have paid a good deal of attention to motivation. Management by objectives became popular in the private sector in 1954 and became commonly used in the public sector in the 1970s. Simply put, it involves a group discussion of objectives so that they become internalized throughout the work force rather than known only to top management. By whatever title, it is sound practice. Organizational development is another type of group process, similar to group sensitivity training. It is meant to help people adjust to a changing environment. Change has been a marked feature of public sector employment in recent years, and organizational development efforts have been helpful so long as they have not become such a preoccupation that the way workers and management feel about each other becomes more important than what gets done.

A variety of efforts have been made to modify the conditions of work so as to improve morale and increase motivation and productivity. In addition to such obvious things as improving the physical environment, work-time alterations have been helpful. Many organizations now use "flexible time," which allows workers to start anytime between 7 and 9 in the morning and finish anytime between 3 and 5 in the afternoon, so long as they work the standard number of hours for that agency. Other experiments have involved 4-day work weeks with 10 hours of work each day. This offers those who want them 3-day weekends on a regular basis. All of these changes and experiments have their benefits, and they all have their advocates and their critics. The principle to keep in mind is to get the job done efficiently. Within that requirement, and allowing for any laws or rules that may control working hours or conditions, whatever a worker wants to do to get the work done should be seriously considered and allowed if it can be done in that setting. Supervisors and managers should be encouraged to avoid preconceptions about what works and to try to meet the needs of their employees, if that can be done while accomplishing the work without an increase in cost. In some typing pools, all workers are required to work the same 8-hour days, 5 days a week, even though that means that some will accomplish much more than others. There is no reason, save reluctance to struggle with change, that typists could not be employed to turn out some predetermined volume of work with some set error rate and allowed to do the work on their own schedule. If that is too much of a change for managers and personnel people to accept, then let those who wish to do so work their 40 hours whenever they want to so long as they get the work done when it is needed. There are no reasons other than tradition and laziness for failing to experiment with working arrangements that give the worker more control over the work. This is simply an extension of the concept of "job enlargement," a theory that is widely accepted if not widely practiced. Rather than each employee being given a small part of a big task to do, each worker is given as much of the total job as possible, so that each may have the satisfaction of producing something recognizable. Civil service job descriptions make job enlargement difficult, because they are seen as a restrictive list of tasks to be performed by anyone holding a particular job classification title, but this merely points the way to the arduous task of reform, not resigned acceptance. Public health agencies need managers who not only feel strongly about their employees' welfare, but who take public health seriously enough to apply it within the agency to the well-being of the work force.

FINANCIAL MANAGEMENT

The administration of public health programs involves the use of public funds on behalf of the public's health. The management of those funds is a grant of a public trust. There has been a long history of distrust of government agencies in the United States—of both their efficiency and their management skills. Efficiency is the ratio of outputs to inputs, and the value of the outputs of public health agencies (better health, less dependency, the prevention of disease) cannot be reduced easily to a dollar amount to satisfy economists or accountants (although the effort to do so by Cooper and Rice[22] is an important contribution to the literature). In a strictly fiscal sense, the value of certain human services may be negative for society as a whole, and it is not the purpose of public health to do only those things that have a positive cash value. Effectiveness is the extent to which the actual output of an organization corresponds with its goals and objectives, but public agencies often have conflicting and ambivalent goals and objectives by virtue of the statutes that authorize them. (The Comprehensive Health Planning Act of 1966 [see Chapter 11] was designed to reform health care but was prohibited from interfering with private practice traditions.)

In the private sector, the dominant goal is the bottom line: the excess of revenues over costs. It is a goal that can be measured in a universally understood manner—money. In the public sector, the bottom line is the public's welfare. Revenues and costs are supposed to be equal (with some exceptions to be noted later), and the net gain in assets is supposed to be an improvement in the public's health, something that does not enter the balance sheet when the accountant is through with the audit. Anthony and Herzlinger[23] indicate that not-for-profit organizations differ from profit-making organizations in nine characteristics:

1. The profit measure is absent.
2. They tend to be service organizations rather than product oriented.
3. They tend to have legislative constraints on their goals and strategies.

4. They are less dependent on their clients for their revenue.
5. They tend to be dominated by professionals.
6. They have a different governance structure, often elected.
7. They are often led by people not specifically trained for administrative leadership.
8. They (especially government agencies) are heavily influenced by the political process.
9. There has been a tradition of inadequate management controls in the public sector.

These characteristics are neither absolute nor as typical now as they once may have been. The list has been developed by two eminent scholars of business administration, which for 500 years has derived its traditions from the private sector. This illustrates again one of the problems of public administration and management—the short span of study and research and its dominance by techniques developed to suit a different world, the world of profits.

The study of public administration in the United States against a backdrop of private sector traditions leaves unnoticed the basic purpose of government, which is to assure the public welfare and to protect the rights of its citizens with adherence to the concepts of due process. A social and political structure established for such purposes is not easily adapted to the production of services or products, and due process is an expensive concept to preserve. For example, from a business standpoint, it would be far more efficient simply to close an unclean restaurant or to sterilize an offending welfare recipient.

The past two decades have witnessed a steady increase in stronger management practices in the public sector. Much more remains to be done, however, to acquaint the public and the private sector with the differences and the challenges.

Budgeting is a fairly recent concept that began with the New York Bureau of Municipal Research in 1906. Budgeting became a common practice in the public sector before its development as a private sector planning device. In the 1950s budgeting began to be seen as a planning tool, and planning was increasingly adopted as a management tool. Subsequent to the enormous investments of the Great Society era of Lyndon Johnson, the concern for better resource allocation and program evaluation gave rise to the concepts of cost-effectiveness evaluation and cost-benefit analysis,[24] zero-base budgeting,[25] and social accounting.[26] (These terms are defined later in this chapter. Social accounting is the attempt to apply accounting techniques to the analysis of social costs and benefits.) Most of these techniques have had their fervent advocates, and all have fallen from their pedestals into a more realistic acceptance of their value. Concern for the effective use of tax dollars and the persistence of mixed motives in the support for most human service programs will continue to cause people to search for the "magic rule" that will enable them to measure the true worth of public programs. Public sector administrators need to remain conversant with the latest trends in financial management and skeptical about their universal applicability.

Fiscal policy

The fiscal policy of governmental jurisdiction sets the structure for the financial management practices of the agencies involved. The policies governing revenue administration and treasury management are often set by statute, but most of the day-to-day procedures and policies are placed in the hands of the executive branch of government. Unlike the private sector, however, a state or local treasurer is frequently elected independently of the governor or the city or county officials in an effort to separate the power to spend from the responsibility for maintaining a strong revenue base. Governments, like private sector businesses, invest their tax revenues in a variety of forms designed to conserve the funds, increase their value through interest earned, and assure that enough cash is available to meet current obligations. Some jurisdictions permit the continued obligation of expenditures based on anticipated tax receipts, whereas others require that the full amount of money required for a period of time be in the bank before any obligation (for salaries, supplies, or equipment) is incurred.

Even though a health agency administrator may have an approved appropriation for a program, the finance officer of the jurisdiction may require that all proposals to obligate any of the funds be approved by the finance director before the request can be acted on by the personnel system or the controller or the treasurer. The finance director is not the same as the treasurer. The latter is an elected official whose task is to safeguard the public treasury. Finance directors do not exist in all units of government, but where they do exist, they serve as staff to the chief executive officer to manage the budget. As has been demonstrated in recent years by the role of director of the federal Office of Management and Budget, the position can wield substantial power. As is true in personnel management, the external restraints imposed on operating agencies by appointed finance directors can lead to acrimonious conflicts.

The best way to avoid unreasonable external restraints (the "second-guessing" of the responsible administrator's decisions) is to maintain an effective and rigorous set of reliable controls internally so that the agency has a reputation for effective financial management. Occasionally there is a policy conflict when the finance director believes the purpose of the finance office is to save money by underspending the approved budget. The program director rightly holds that the funds were appropriated to be used to buy or produce services. The argument may be phrased in terms of the effective use of the appropriated funds, but the real goal of the finance director may be to reduce expenditures, allowing the unused funds to accumulate and thereby reducing the need for tax revenues in the next fiscal year.

Every jurisdiction has its own traditions. It is important to understand the reasons behind the traditions and the purposes to which they may be put by those in a position to control the flow of expenditures. One of the more important fiscal policy struggles in recent years has taken place at the national level as Congress sought to curtail President Nixon's ability to stop spending funds appropriated by Congress. The President attempted to impound funds for programs he did not approve of in his effort to restrain government outlays during the year. The Anti-Impoundment and Congressional Budget Act of 1974 (P.L. 94-344) attempted to restrict the President's power but subsequently had some unexpected consequences. The act requires that the President send a recision proposal to Congress and that, unless that recision proposal is specifically approved by both houses within 45 days, the President must make the expenditure. A presidential deferral, on the other hand, goes into effect unless one or both houses of Congress disapproves of the deferral.

Of less prominence when the act was passed was the new budget-making process that required Congress to build its own annual budget rather than just react to a presidential budget. The act established a new budget committee in both the House and the Senate. The two committees develop a preliminary budget resolution in the spring that sets general spending and revenue goals. Then, after work by numerous committees on programs, taxes, and other revenue measures, a second resolution is adopted that establishes specific budget targets for major activities. The second resolution is binding on Congress and requires a reconciliation of revenue and expenditure laws to the targets specified in that resolution. This can result in specific assignments to committees to redraft numerous laws. The new budget act displaced the previously powerful heads of the appropriations committees and the House Ways and Means and Senate Finance committees but was not used until the summer and fall of 1981 when Congress became obsessed with the budget-cutting pressures of President Reagan. The result was the Omnibus Budget Reconciliation Act of 1981 (P.L. 97-35), which in 5 short weeks rewrote most of the important health legislation developed over the previous 48 years. It is difficult to predict just how the Budget Act will be used or amended in the future, but its recent impact has been a dramatic example of the effect of fiscal policy on health programs.

Fiscal operations

The fiscal operations of government agencies vary somewhat in terminology from local to state to national government, but the essential concepts are the same. Most local governments must follow an accounting structure defined by the state. The major practices are accounting; budgeting; execution of the expenditure plan, including purchasing and personnel practices; and auditing.

Accounting. In private sector traditions there are two forms of accounting: managerial accounting and financial accounting. Financial accounting has to do with presentation of an organization's economic status to the outside world. It has given rise to the certified public accountant, who expresses a professional opinion about the authenticity of the report. Managerial accounting is designed to provide timely information to management to improve effectiveness and efficiency. It is concerned with internal management information flow. Public sector management practices were established originally to provide a public accounting of the funds appropriated—similar to financial accounting in the private sector.

Accounting is a systematic means for recording the history of an organization in quantitative terms. It is a very elderly profession with its roots in the 1400s, and there are numerous textbooks on the subject,[27,28] including do-it-yourself manuals, short courses for professionals, and special accounting texts for hospitals and other enterprises. There are few texts specifically devoted to accounting in not-for-profit organizations and governmental agencies. Among those available and useful are Hay's *Governmental Accounting* text[29]; the Comptroller General's *Accounting Principles and Standards for Federal Agencies*[30]; *Auditing, Accounting, and Financial Reporting*[31] and *Governmental Accounting and Financial Reporting Principles,*[32] published by the Municipal Finance Officers Association; and the Anthony and Herzlinger text on the management of nonprofit organizations.[23] The reader may be confused by the phrase *not-for-profit* rather than the more commonly used phrase *nonprofit.* While the latter phrase has had a long history, many organizations with profit as their purpose are nonprofit organizations for a time. The term *not-for-profit* is of recent vintage but is more accurate, since it deals with purpose rather than happenstance.

The double-entry concept was to accounting what the wheel was to locomotion. The accounting sheet has a left side that records assets and a right side that records liabilities. The two totals are at all times equal. The bottom line, in a profit-oriented enterprise, is what the accountant calls *net income,* or income in excess of expenses. The liability side of the balance sheet usually shows an increase in the owner's equity to balance the increase in assets. Double-entry accounting is less useful in the public sector, since revenue is usually appropriated, is known fully in advance, and is not dependent on sales or the production of services.

The amount of funds available by appropriation at the start of the fiscal year is distributed into a series of special funds, usually one for each major program, such as maternal and child health or a hospital, and further segregated into accounts for salaries, operating expenses (consumable supplies, phone service, heating and cooling), equipment, and "other." Expenditures and other financial transactions are entered sequentially in a journal, then subsequently "posted" to the correct account classification ledger. The ledger is the record of the account, and each major fund usually has several accounts. The list of the fund accounts is known as the chart of accounts.

The multiplicity of funds is a unique characteristic of public sector accounting. Private businesses may have numerous accounts, but they are for management purposes, and they may be changed during the course of the accounting period if circumstances require assets or liabilities to be moved about. In the public sector, accounts are legislative controls on executive branch spending. Transfers between funds can rarely be made without going back through the legislative process, although transfers of funds between subcategories of an account (between office supplies and utility bills within a single fund, for example) can be made either within the agency or with the approval of a central budget or finance director.

The private sector has long used an accrual basis for counting its expenditures and its revenue, whereas the public sector has more often worked with cash accounting. In accrual systems, an expense is recognized when a cost is consumed, not when the money is obligated or disbursed, and revenue is recognized when a service is performed or a product is delivered to a customer. Cash may not be transferred until a later date and may be noted in the accounting balance sheet as an account receivable or liable until it is received. In the public sector, the distinction is less important except in programs that involve billing the client or a third party for services or products provided. The difference can be confusing. If an agency shifts from a cash system to an accrual system during an accounting period, it can dramatically alter the appearance of the accounts by reducing the cash available to cover the costs obligated but not yet incurred or "expensed."

The involvement of government agencies in rendering services for a fee and in a host of national and state grant-in-aid programs has complicated government accounting enormously. The big revenue and expense accounts involved in hospital administration involve concepts and account structures not previously used by government. Grant programs, whether special project grants or more general block grants, usually require separate fund accounts, and the granting agency may have a different fiscal year from that of the recipient government. The health officer of Springfield-Greene County in Missouri, for example, has different fiscal years for city, county, state, and federal accounting purposes. Fees received for work done under city ordinances are accounted for separately from those received in state or county programs. A strong accounting arm is necessary in most public health agencies, whether it is part of the agency or part of a central structure in smaller jurisdictions.

Budgeting. A budget is a plan that describes how much is to be spent in each of several accounts. It may include a statement about outputs (activities) and the number of personnel that may be employed, but the essential and binding ingredients are the dollars appropriated.

Budgeting used to be a periodic exercise, beginning at some point in the fiscal year and continuing through the process of legislative review and adoption and final executive development of an approved plan of expenditures based on the legislative budget. In recent years, budgeting has become a nonstop process, with the development of a budget for one year overlapping the development of the next one, the management of the one for the year before, and the debate over recisions, deferrals, and impoundments.

Budgets are developed from the top down, from the bottom up, and from the middle out. Program managers count needs not met and the resources available to meet them. As these estimates of additional resources needed are aggregated, they begin to form the budget request, first from the program, then from the agency, and finally from the governor, the president, or the mayor. At the same time, legislative budget committees, the President, governors, mayors, and county leaders are examining their revenue expectations and their tax policies in the light of program requirements and new initiatives they may wish to undertake. At some point, these two different approaches meet and a gap is recognized: the gap between what people want to do and the money available to do it. In most jurisdictions, the revenue estimate, including any revenues to be gained or lost through tax changes, is used to set the budgeting process formally in motion. Each agency director is given instructions as to the assumptions to be used to form the agency's requested budget. One of the most productive approaches is to ask the agency to develop three budgets: (1) a budget that accepts a percent change in the cost of particular ingredients such as salaries, supplies, and utilities and is built on the assumption that only 90% (or some other figure) of last year's appropriation will be made available for the next year (a reduced-level budget); (2) a budget that accepts all current programs, sets certain assumptions about cost increases, and aggregates what it would take, given those assumptions, to do the same things in the next fiscal year (a current-level budget); and (3) a budget that is built on the same assumptions about cost increases for the inputs but asks managers to describe what it would take to carry out fully what they believe needs to be done (an expansion, or optimal, budget).

The reduced-level budget forces the agency to ask, "What would we recommend if X% less money were available next year for this program?" Would it be altered in concept, reduced in size, or eliminated altogether in favor of maintaining or even expanding some other more essential program? It is a depressing but necessary process that requires each program manager to think through the efficiency and the effectiveness of the program and debate its essentiality with other program managers whose needs are competitive within the same fund.

The expansion, or optimal, budget offers a rare opportunity to see what managers feel would be needed to meet current statutory authorizations or requirements fully. It is not an occasion for irresponsible proposals but a chance to describe realistically what is needed, for example, to meet current fire and safety code requirements, to provide adequate patient care in the mental hospital, or to provide good prenatal care to all rather than just a fraction of the low-income, high-risk pregnant women in the community. As such, the optimal budget provides a rare glimpse at a community's real needs and the resources needed to meet them, even though the proposals have to be seen as reflecting a particular approach to public health interventions by their authors.

Budgets are usually developed in a series of hearings, first at the program level, then at ascending responsibility centers in the organization, until the agency director decides on a final presentation. Those hearings, especially in the early stages of budget formation, should focus on needs, problems, programs, and activities as well as productivity, costs, and efficiency. Only after some of the proposals have been discussed in terms of their importance and acceptability should the staff begin the detailed process of developing complete budget displays.

At some point, the chief executive decides on what will be put forward as a proposed budget for legislative consideration, whether that be by a county commission, a city council, the state legislature, or the Congress. Until recently, most legislative bodies then began a process of hearings and reviews as they attempted to wrestle with revenue expectations, taxes, and their own program preferences. In recent years, more and more legislative bodies have acquired the staff necessary to build their own budgets, sometimes only using the chief executive's budget proposals as executive branch input to an essentially legislative process.

In some cases, the health director may work for a board of health and speak in opposition to the governor's proposed budget. In those jurisdictions in which the health agency director is appointed by the chief executive, the ground rules need to be worked out before the legislative hearings start. The chief executive may have cut the agency's proposed budget, and the agency representatives may be called on to support those cuts rather than their own proposals. In the best of worlds, the differences can be agreed to, and the agency director is free to discuss those differences so long as the discussion does not involve heavy-handed opposition to the chief executive's proposals. It can prove very difficult to support some recommendations without distorting facts and opinions. A proposal to close a public hospital cannot be championed as an effort to maintain public sector employment, expand the provision of health services, and reduce public waste when the facts and the convictions of the hospital administrators do not confirm such claims. It can be supported as a difficult, unpleasant, but necessary step, if the chief executive and the agency director can reach agreement on what is actually entailed and what the consequences will be.

The final budget, once agreed to and passed by both houses of the legislature, goes to the chief executive officer (in states, in the national government, and in some cities), where a variety of outcomes can occur depending on the budget law of the jurisdiction: the budget can be signed as submitted, vetoed in its entirety, or any specific item in the budget may be reduced or eliminated, usually subject to an override by the legislature. The rules differ from place to place.

Executing the expenditure plan. Once the budget is approved, the chief executive officer has to initiate the second phase of the budget process, which involves the development of expenditure plans for each separate fund in accord with the final figures in the approved budget. While it varies from jurisdiction to jurisdiction, the general format for the budget display is a series of columns:

1. The first column lists actual expenditures, line by line, for the immediately preceding completed fiscal year.
2. The second column shows the approved budget for the current fiscal year.
3. A third column may be used to list any changes made in the approved budget subsequent to its adoption.
4. A fourth column usually shows all expenditures in each category as of a certain date in the fiscal year.
5. A fifth column lists the agency's request.
6. The sixth column indicates the differences (plus or minus) for each category from the current year to the proposed budget.
7. The seventh column lists the chief executive officer's recommendations, line by line.
8. An eighth column may be left to record the details of the final approved budget.

Reference is often made to "program budgets" and "line-item" budgets. A program budget is one that describes the cost of a program and is made up of "X" activities (immunizations, clinic visits, or restaurant inspections) multiplied by the cost per activity. A line-item budget is built by aggregating the costs of the objects of expenditure (salaries, books, pencils, cars, or drugs). Most budget acts require that the final action be taken on a line-item budget, although whether the categories should be many and specific or few and broad is often a matter of legislative and executive discretion. Program managers need to have valid line-item budgets and accounts set up, since they enable better cost finding and control. Program budgets are useful for public display and discussion.

The expenditure plan for a budget often allocates money to discrete parts of the year—a quarter or even a month. It is important to develop an expenditure plan that reflects actual payouts, since they will not always occur uniformly over the year. Certain supplies are bought in large amounts once or twice a year; insurance premiums are due once, not monthly; and utility bills change depending on the season of the year. Budget variances need to be detected as soon as possible and corrected swiftly. Most accounting systems are designed to start at a zero point at the beginning of each fiscal year, so the information available in the first 3 months, even with an "on-line" rapid management information system, may be limited. It is better to have an accounting system that can display both the expenditures for the current fiscal year and the expenditures for the immediately preceding 12 months, even though that crosses over into the preceding fiscal year, so that variances from the expenditure plan are easier to detect. This is not possible with new programs.

As noted above, some budget officers operate on the assumption that their job is to save money. Unless the chief executive officer or some other compelling influence intervenes with contrary guidelines, the monies appropriated are there for a purpose, and it is the agency director's job to spend them—to spend them efficiently and effectively, but to spend them—for the purpose for which they were made available.

There are several external restraints on an agency that may curtail expenditures. The personnel system may or may not approve salary changes that were planned in the budget or the acquisition of personnel needed to fill vacancies or newly created job slots. The budget director or director of finance may retard the rate of expenditure by reviewing each request for supplies, equipment, personnel, or contract approval. The purchasing officer has to obtain requests in an approved fashion (usually specifying what the equipment or supply item is to do, rather than the brand name or the vendor), then advertise for a specified period of time, review bids, and award a purchase order. Negotiations along the way between program managers and purchasing agents, as well as the budget director, may delay the process. The result is a retarded rate of expenditure that may be deliberate on the part of any of the people mentioned, whether they have that explicit assignment or not. Such interagency tensions, which sometimes are created within the health agency between program staff and financial management staff, may get out of control, and the power to influence the agency's programs may slip away to an external agency. The agency director and program managers have to walk a narrow line between insisting on an unreasonable degree of autonomy on the one hand and making a collaborative effort to carry out some overall budget planning for the total jurisdiction.

Auditing. An audit is an evaluation, usually conducted by an external agency, of the management controls used by the health agency. There are several kinds of audits: (1) a financial audit, which reviews record keeping for financial transactions, (2) a compliance audit, which ascertains whether the expenditure policies of the jurisdiction were correctly observed (through the use of competitive bids, for example), (3) an operations audit, which reviews the activities of the agency, and (4) a program audit, which considers the effects of a specified program.[33]

Auditors usually sample the transactions in an account and look at the nature of the controls used to account for cash receipts and the use of resources. "Sunset" laws are one form of agency evaluation in which the legislature periodically requires an agency to rejustify its continued existence. They have become common in recent years, but very few programs have been eliminated as a result. The first sunset law was introduced in Colorado in 1976. Straussman[33] says the Colorado legislature eliminated three boards and commissions in 1977 at an annual savings of $6,810. The review by the legislature cost $212,000.

Other evaluations are carried out as part of a cost-benefit analysis or cost-effectiveness evaluation. A cost-benefit analysis enables comparison of the costs and benefits, usually in monetary terms, of different programs with different objectives. Cost-effectiveness analysis compares the efficiency of different methods of attaining the same objective.[34] Such studies are arduous and rarely determine a program's future, but they are important efforts as public health professionals attempt to come to grips with the value of their efforts in real terms. The Office of Technology Assessment of the Congress has stated that "CEA/CBA [cost-effectiveness analysis/cost-benefit analysis] cannot serve as the sole or primary determinant of a health care decision. Decision making could be improved, however, by the process of identifying and considering all the relevant costs and benefits of a decision."[22] Health care costs in the United States increased as a percentage of the gross national product from 6.1% in 1965 to more than 11% in 1989. Public, or tax, funds increased as a proportion of the total from 26% to 41%. Health care expenditures, largely for medical care, intrude on all other areas of social investment and reduce the ability of government and private industry to support expansion in employment, improved housing, educational systems, and other environmental conditions that have a greater impact on the public's health than medical care. Careful analysis of the cost-effectiveness and benefits of medical care and public health programs is needed, especially given the proclivity of the medical care system to acquire and use new, unproven, and expensive technology.

SUMMARY

There are many good textbooks covering management, public administration, personnel management, and financial management. Many of them have been referred to in the preceding pages.* Most of the material is specific to medical care delivery systems, such as hospitals or outpatient programs, or deals with public administration generally. There is virtually no well-researched material dealing with the administration of public health programs in the United States. This is a deficit that should be corrected.

The Institute of Medicine has described public health as being in a state of disarray and cites the need for improved management as one of the principal areas of concern.[9] The problems are serious, complex, and profound. Public health, as it has been described in earlier chapters, necessarily involves the formation of policies that affect numerous other public and private sector agencies and the collaborative use of resources controlled by other agencies. The management tools to do this have neither been developed nor studied extensively. Matrix management techniques have not been applied to such situations, nor is the problem widely understood, either by public health practitioners or organizational theorists.

Productivity, motivation, and equal employment opportunity are the major challenges facing public personnel management in the years ahead. Combining an effective merit system with collective bargaining techniques while helping build satisfying careers for health professionals is a very difficult problem.

Finally, public health agencies, like other agencies of government, must wrestle with the complex and often threatening processes of cost-benefit and cost-effectiveness analysis. The efficient allocation of resources, not only within the public arena, but between the public and private health sectors, requires the development of new techniques to evaluate health promotion and disease prevention programs.

* Others are by Longest,[35] Hodgetts and Cascio,[36] Levey and Loomba,[2] and Kovner and Neuhauser.[37] Shortell and Kaluzny[38] have written a text that approaches health services administration from the viewpoint of organizational theory and behavioral science. Waldo[39] describes public administration generally from the viewpoint of a political scientist. Gordon[40] has written a second edition of his textbook dealing with public administration in the United States.

REFERENCES

1. Duncan WJ: Essentials of management, ed 2, Hinsdale, IL, 1978, Dryden Press.
2. Levey S and Loomba NP: Health care administration: a managerial perspective, ed 2, Philadelphia, 1984, JB Lippincott Co.
3. Mintzberg H: The structuring of organizations: a synthesis of research, Englewood Cliffs, NJ, 1979, Prentice-Hall, Inc.
4. Gerth H and Mills CW: Max Weber: essays in sociology, New York, 1946, Oxford University Press.
5. Schonick W and Price W: Reorganizations of health agencies by local government in American urban centers: what do they portend for public health? Milbank Q 55:233, Spring 1977.
6. Lee RD: Public personnel systems, Rockville, MD, 1987, Aspen Publishers.
7. Gossert DJ and Miller CA: State boards of health: their members and commitments, Am J Public Health 66:486, June 1973.
8. Gilbert B, Moos M-K, and Miller CA: State level decision making for public health—the status of boards of health, J Public Health Policy 3:51, Mar 1982.
9. Institute of Medicine: The future of public health, Washington, DC, 1988, National Academy Press.
10. Cameron C and Kobylarz A: Nonphysician directors of local health departments: results of a national survey, Public Health Rep 95:386, July-Aug 1980.
11. Miller CA and others: A survey of local public health departments and their directors, Am J Public Health 67:931, Oct 1977.
12. Roemer MI: The need for professional doctors of public health, Public Health Rep 101:21, Jan-Feb 1986.
13. Pickett GE: Upside down the organization, Am J Public Health 65:82, Jan 1975.

14. Bigler WJ, Mittan JB, and Wisthuff R: Florida's new local health unit management system, Tallahassee, FL, 1981, Department of Health and Rehabilitation Services.
15. Hossler JL: Community health services: Minnesota's experiment with decentralized health services, Minneapolis, MN, 1981, Minnesota Department of Health.
16. Dresang DL: Public personnel management and public policy, Boston, 1984, Little, Brown & Co.
17. Lee RD: Public personnel systems, Rockville, MD, 1987, Aspen Publishers, Inc.
18. Shafritz JM, Hyde AC, and Rosenbloom DH: Personnel management in government: politics and process, New York, 1981, Marcel Dekker, Inc.
19. Lamourette WJ: SES: from civil service showpiece to incipient failure in two years, Nat J 13:1296, July 18, 1981.
20. Munchus G: Collective bargaining: when is a supervisor a manager? Health Serv Man 13:1, Oct 1980.
21. McKinney JN and Johnston M: Fraud, waste and abuse in government, Philadelphia, 1986, ISHI Publications.
22. Cooper BS and Rice DP: The economic cost of illness revisited, Soc Secur Bull 39:21, 1976.
23. Anthony RN and Herzlinger RE: Management control in nonprofit organizations, Homewood, IL, 1980, Richard D Irwin, Inc.
24. The implications of cost effectiveness analysis of medical technology, Pub No OTA-H-125, Washington, DC, 1980, Congress of the United States, Office of Technology Assessment.
25. Cheek LM: Zero-base budgeting comes of age, New York, 1977, AMACOM.
26. Melton JW and Watason DJA, editors: Interdisciplinary dimensions of accounting for social goals and social organizations: a conference of the department of accountancy, Columbus, OH, 1977, Grid Inc.
27. Gordon MJ and Shillinglaw G: Accounting, a management approach, ed 4, Homewood, IL, 1969, Richard D Irwin, Inc.
28. Granof MH: Financial accounting: principles and issues, ed 2, Englewood Cliffs, NJ, 1980, Prentice-Hall, Inc.
29. Hay LN: Government accounting, ed 6, Homewood, IL, 1980, Richard D Irwin, Inc.
30. Comptroller General of the United States: Accounting principles and standards for federal agencies, Washington, DC, 1972, General Accounting Office.
31. National Council on Governmental Accounting: Auditing, accounting and financial reporting, Chicago, 1968, Municipal Finance Officers Association.
32. National Council on Governmental Accounting: Statement 1: governmental accounting and financial reporting principles, Chicago, 1979, Municipal Finance Officers Association.
33. Straussman JD: Public administration, New York, 1985, Holt, Rinehart & Winston.
34. Warner KE and Luce BR: Cost-benefit and cost-effectiveness analysis in health care: principles, practice and potential, Ann Arbor, MI, 1982, Health Administration Press.
35. Longest BB: Management practices for the health professional, Reston, VA, 1984, Reston Publishing Co.
36. Hodgetts RM and Cascio DM: Modern health care management, New York, 1983, Academic Press, Inc.
37. Kovner AR and Neuhauser D, editors: Health services management: readings and commentary, Ann Arbor, MI, 1983, Health Administration Press.
38. Shortell SM and Kaluzny AD: Health care management: a text in organization theory and behavior, New York, 1983, John Wiley & Sons, Inc.
39. Waldo D: The administrative state: a study of the political theory of American public administration, ed 2, New York, 1984, Holmes & Meier Publishers.
40. Gordon GJ: Public administration in America, ed 2, New York, 1982, St Martin's Press.

CHAPTER 11

Planning

EVOLUTION OF PLANNING

The words *health planning* can evoke feelings among public health professionals that the newcomer could not, at first, comprehend: anger, nostalgia, frustration, and even bemusement. At some level, everybody plans: to cook a meal, travel, or build a house of cards. Organizations plan: they develop budgets, consider marketing strategies, and implement new programs. Yet health planning meant something else to tens of thousands of people from 1966 to 1987. It was a revolutionary attempt to involve the citizens of every community in the United States in helping to determine the composition, location, and even ownership of the numerous activities that make up the health sector. It was in many ways a naive and misguided effort, but it provided an opportunity for many people to learn about their health system and play an important role in designing it. It was both exciting and confusing. The excitement stemmed from the opportunity to transfer policy-making from the providers of health care to its consumers. At the core of the confusion was a reluctance to accept the political nature of planning and an attempt to use planning as a regulatory approach to cost containment. Many planners insist that planning is an objective way to make decisions and that politics and planning are antithetic to one another. That belief is delusional. Even at the microlevel, where, for example, two hospitals are considering a shared laundry service, the final choice is political, since one hospital usually gives up something to get something. At the state level, the linkage of planning and politics becomes more apparent and more important. Planning is the process of determining how to achieve an objective once the objective has been defined. The effect of planning is to clarify the differences between alternatives, and in most important decisions, clarification narrows the superficial differences and exposes underlying value differences as the principal issues. Whenever two or more people have to make a choice involving values, the process of decision making is political. The reluctance of planners to understand and accept that allows the mythology rather than the reality of planning to dominate discussions about the subject and reduces the usefulness of planning in public health.

It is widely believed that planning and collecting more and better information make decision making easier. The opposite is probably true. Simple problems are simple because the issues are clear and there is little value conflict. Elaborate planning is rarely needed. Important problems are hard to solve because issues are not clear and because value judgments are involved. In such cases, more and better information only serves to strip away the rationalizations of those with different values, finally exposing the basic conflicts and making the choice very difficult. For example, is prison meant to be punitive or rehabilitative? Most societies do both badly because they cannot decide. Although elected officials may ask for better data so that they can make a decision, they are probably better off not making a clear choice, because it could not be accepted for long. Is a welfare worker supposed to get public assistance for those who need it or reduce the size of the dole? The answer is to help those in need and to keep those who would cheat from doing so, but that answer masks a deep-seated and shifting belief as to just who are the "truly needy." More and better information will not make the choice any easier, but it does help to keep people from deluding themselves.

Planning as a formal process was not common in public health until the work of the American Public Health Association's Committee on Administrative Practice and Evaluation in the 1920s. As funds for public health programs increased, as the perimeters of the field were extended by legislation, as public demands and expectations increased, and as government and management in general became more sophisticated, health agencies became more visible and more accountable. Planning became more important. In the mid-1960s concern for efficiency in government coupled with apprehension over the rising cost of medical care and the persistent evidence that many people still did not get the care they needed prompted President Johnson and the 89th Congress to begin a series of initiatives with far-reaching effects. The President required his cabinet officers to incorporate sophisticated planning techniques into their budget-making procedures. An Office of Health Planning was established in the Department of Health, Education and Welfare, but it remained in an "off-line" position (out of the mainstream of decision making) and had little impact on budget and program strategies.

Planning has several meanings. Most agencies engage in managerial planning: the organized acquisition and deployment of resources to achieve desired objectives with the minimum consumption of scarce resources. Many agencies engage in strategic planning: the analysis of threats, opportunities, strengths, and weaknesses in an effort to improve the competitive position of the organization. The latter is not discussed in this chapter, since it is arguable whether it is appropriate to a public agency (not that it is not practiced vigorously, regardless of whether it is appropriate). It is a practice common in the medical care delivery arena, especially since the 1970s. An introduction to its application in the medical care sector can be found in *Strategic Management in the Health Sector.*[1] An interesting attempt to use corporate planning models in the broader health sector is described in *Strategic Planning in the Health Sector,*[2] based on research in one of the health authorities of the British National Health Service. Managerial planning will be discussed later in this chapter, but first, let us review the fascinating story of the Comprehensive Health Planning movement in the United States.

The Comprehensive Health Planning Act

Congress attempted to develop health planning systems throughout the country by passing the Comprehensive Health Planning and Public Health Services Amendments in 1966 (P.L. 89-749). The law attempted to locate responsibility for health planning in the states and in subareas within the states. The local or "area-wide" organizations were known as "B" agencies, and the state agencies that were to assimilate the area-wide plans into a single statewide plan were known as "A" agencies. The designations came from the pertinent sections of the law, 314(b) and 314(a), respectively.

The comprehensive health planning legislation did not include authority over the federally funded (Hill-Burton) hospital construction program or the new Regional Medical Programs, which were to extend medical training and services from the major medical centers to the communities of each state. The "B" agencies had to rely heavily on local support for their budgets and had no real authority over federal grants to community agencies. The law contained an unfortunate restriction in its statement of purpose, which was "to support the marshalling of all health resources . . . to assure comprehensive services of high quality for each person, but without interference with existing patterns of private professional practice of medicine, dentistry and related healing arts." This paradox was repeated in other health legislation in the 1960s and reflected a major problem of Congress in the latter part of the twentieth century.

In earlier days national legislation had been more local in scope, and compromises occurred between a dam in one jurisdiction and a post office in another. Neither may have been needed, but when completed, the dam held water and the post office delivered mail. With the increasing involvement of the federal government in the broad issues of health and welfare, which had been traditionally reserved to the states, compromises began to occur within the context of bills themselves in an effort to get enough votes for passage. Thus we got an increasing number of creations that combined a dam and a post office, the result of which could hold neither water nor deliver mail. Health statutes that might have been landmarks in the history of public health were internally compromised with conflicting values and the inevitable problem of interpretation by administering agencies, interest groups, and the courts.

All of the states formed comprehensive health planning "A" and "B" agencies, but if their purpose was to rationalize the distribution of health resources and to contain cost increases, they failed. If their purpose was to involve citizens in making decisions about health affairs, an arena heretofore reserved for the providers, and to broaden community awareness of the workings of the health system, they partially succeeded. They were required to have a majority of consumers and to reflect the broad ethnic, racial, and socioeconomic groupings in the communities. Congressional expectations and those of the interested public health groups were not realistic and were not met, however. The comprehensive health planning agencies did involve a lot of people in thinking about health services in an orderly way and subjected many provider plans to public scrutiny and debate. However, the provider groups were better organized, had more knowledge about the systems, and easily dominated the debates.

Official local health agencies generally were not heavily involved in this experiment. The law favored the use of new, private, not-for-profit planning organizations rather than existing agencies of government. This reflected the skepticism of social reformers regarding whether traditional political and bureaucratic organizations had the will or the freedom to alter major systems. Many local health officers felt that they were already charged with responsibility for health planning in their communities and doubted that the new organizations would become important, nor did they relish having their professional plans challenged by every citizen in the community. They remained aloof from the new process. The public health community thought in terms of the traditional boundaries of its official agencies, although the public tends to think of public health in much broader terms that include mental health, medical care, many social service functions, and consumer protection activities. These larger concerns were not included in the managerial planning of most public health agencies. A few public health directors became comprehensive health planning leaders in their communities, but more commonly, they were only one of 30 or more voting members of the organization.

Congress moved to strengthen the process with the National Health Planning and Resources Development Act of 1974 (P.L. 93-641). The new law required the governors to designate health service areas to include between 250,000 and 3 million people. Once the area designations were approved by the Secretary of the Department of Health, Education and Welfare, groups within the areas could apply for designation as the Health Systems Agency (HSA) for the area. The law required a consumer majority and went further in specifying limits on provider representation. Two other provisions were remarkable: (1) although the areas were designated by the governor, the HSAs made their application to the Secretary of Health, Education and Welfare and became accountable to the Secretary rather than to the governor or to the community served, and (2) although it was possible for a council of governments or a general-purpose government to apply for status as an HSA, the law made that difficult, with the result that most of the planning agencies were private, not-for-profit organizations accountable to the Secretary of Health, Education and Welfare in Washington.

The priorities of Congress were specified in section 1502 of the act: improved access to primary care for medically underserved groups and communities, consolidation and better use of hospitals, the development of medical group practices and health maintenance organizations, improved quality, better management and cost controls, and health promotion and disease prevention. Each HSA was to develop a health systems plan and an annual implementation plan. The Statewide Health Coordinating Council, which was partly made up of representatives from the HSAs, was to meld the health systems plans into one state health plan. The staff work was to be done by the State Health Planning and Development Agency (SHPDA). In 13 states the health service area was the entire state, which meant that the statewide HSA, Statewide Health Coordinating Council, and the SHPDA were all writing health plans for the same area.

The new agencies had more authority than the predecessor comprehensive health planning agencies. The Hill-Burton hospital construction program and the Regional Medical Programs were abolished, and some of their functions were assigned to the HSAs. As the new agencies grew in experience, they were to get increasing grants of authority from the Secretary of Health, Education and Welfare, finally including approval authority over most applications for the use of federal health funds. The exceptions were those used to purchase medical care (such as Medicaid and Medicare), federal subsidies to educational institutions for the training of health workers, and research grants from the National Institutes of Health. The latter two exclusions reflected the power of the medical schools, which could scarcely condone community control over such enterprises. The law also established a National Council on Health Planning and Development, which was to advise the Secretary and adopt national standards for health services.

One of the more complex and revolutionary subjects encompassed in the health planning legislation was the certificate of need—or CON. During the early years of the formation of hospital planning councils and the Hill-Burton program, need, at least operationally, meant the need of the hospital—its physicians, its administrator, and its board. So long as they could substantiate their need for equipment or additional beds, the need was accepted as real. By 1966 and in the spirit of that time, need meant what the community needed. Since it was really the community that paid for the program or the construction through health insurance, foregone property taxes, or direct, tax-supported subsidies, the added investment required some assessment of whether the community really needed it. The 1974 health planning legislation required each state to pass a certificate of need law to qualify for designation of the State Health Planning and Development Agency and the rest of the health planning apparatus. A proposal to build or initiate a program or acquire equipment that would cost more than $100,000 had to be reviewed by the HSA. The tests were whether or not the new effort was congruent with the needs described in the health systems plan, whether the project was feasible and affordable, and whether it was the least costly of all the alternative ways of meeting that need. The recommendation of the HSA went to the SHPDA, which had a specified period of time to either approve or disapprove the proposal and, if it disagreed with the HSA, to state its reasons. Lacking approval, the program could not be implemented, or if it was implemented, it would not be eligible for reimbursement by any of the federal medical care payment schemes such as Medicare and Medicaid. In some states, denial of a certificate of need meant that the facility could not be licensed.

The National Health Planning and Resources Development Act represented a conviction by some in Congress that the concept of community health planning was sound but needed more authority over community programs and better financial support. It incorporated fiscal information into the planning data base for the first time. Earlier health planning efforts had ignored fiscal realities, assuming that if the plan was all right, the money would be available. The 1974 law included a requirement to review from time to time the appropriateness of existing facilities and to make plans for their discontinuation or other changes that might be desirable. Amendments to the law in 1979 were extensive but largely procedural.

Ultimately 203 HSAs were designated by the Secretary, although three subsequently lost their designations for failure to meet the requirements of the law (Los Angeles County, Clark County, Nevada, and Topeka, Kans.). Puerto Rico was placed in a special category.[3] One hundred and eighty of the agencies were private, not-for-profit organizations, and 23 were a function of regional planning bodies or a local general-purpose government agency. There were 13 statewide HSAs and 16 interstate agencies, which required complex efforts on the part of two states. The National Council on Health Planning and Development found that 50,000 volunteer participants were contributing 1½ million hours of time to the effort: 9,000 on HSA governing bodies, 2,000 on Statewide Health Coordinating Councils, 16,000 on subarea advisory councils, and the rest on committees and task forces.[4] The National Council and the American Health Planning Association (an association largely representing HSA directors) claimed impressive reductions in capital expenditures and other improvements as a result of the health planning effort. Others have claimed that it has been an expensive failure. Once again the truth lies somewhere between expectations and reality.

Problems with comprehensive health planning

To plan effectively there must be some understood and broadly accepted sense of purpose—a direction. Some believed that the purpose of the health planning process was cost containment, others thought it was improved access, especially for the "have-nots" of society, and some thought the sole purpose was to turn over health planning to consumers at the community level. There were some who believed that key congressional aides were acting on an agenda set in the 1930s to centralize planning and resource allocation and that the health planning laws were an elaborate attempt to create failures leading to centralization, first at the state level, then at the national level. A former Surgeon General, Dr. Julius Richmond, stated that we did indeed have a national health policy: to extend and improve health services to all Americans, to conduct an elaborate program of research, and to promote health and prevent disease.[5] This policy or purpose, if it does exist, meets the test of general acceptability but tends to reflect interest groups more than any real consensus. The National Council on Health Planning did not promulgate national standards until March 1978,[6] and they were so highly specific in some areas, such as computerized axial tomography, and so general in others, such as the supply of hospital beds (4 per 1,000 people), as to require a series of special conditions and qualifications and to provoke inquiry as to the comprehensive nature of the few standards developed. Many believed that if the purpose of the law was to develop a pattern of community health planning, national numerical standards encumbered with a series of qualifications would be an inappropriate way to fulfill that purpose. Still others thought that there should be even more rigid standards at the national level.

The certificate of need process became the most important task of the HSAs and the SHPDAs. Yet it was a very complex and flawed concept. It amounted to a form of licensure, or franchising, but standards were lacking. It meant that volunteers who often had very little concept of such matters would review complicated financing and service delivery plans that were worth millions of dollars to boards, physicians, construction companies, and equipment manufacturers. Denials of any significant nature often ended up in court, and the proceedings were tortuous at best. Well-monied corporations with multimillion-dollar investments at stake were pitted against small, understaffed, and underpaid state health planning agencies. The concept also had some aspects of an anticompetitive nature, since the practice involved review of a proposal against the suppositions of an approved plan. If a second proposal to do the same thing was received a few days later, it followed the same mandatory process with a specified number of days in review. If the first proposal in the pipeline of review was approved, the second proposal, even though it might have been a better one, would be disqualified, since by the time its due date arrived, the need had been filled by the first proposal. Some agencies attempted to solve this problem by batching competing proposals. The whole process became entangled in antitrust laws, since it sometimes involved extending franchises to existing providers at the expense of would-be competitors. An important experiment in regulation was implemented nationwide before sufficient experience had been accumulated to give it a reasonable chance to work, and state health planning agencies became hopelessly entangled in the review and approval process without an adequate base of guidelines, precedent, and practice.

Many states found themselves faced with the task of completing a host of separate plan documents for the Department of Health, Education and Welfare (a title V plan, an alcohol plan, a mental health plan, a 314[d] plan, a plan for the developmentally disabled, an aging plan, a title XX social services plan, a title IV-B plan for child welfare services, to name just a few) with little support for their efforts to bring the planning processes together at the state agency level. The national program planning requirements were all separate and different, and there was virtually no interest on the part of program managers at the national level in having their plans merged with those of any other program. As a result, a new initiative, the Planning Reform Demonstration Project, placed in the office of the Assistant Secretary for Intergovernmental Affairs in 1978, funded efforts in 10 states to attempt to develop a consolidated plan. The effort was commendable, but the Assistant Secretary and the 10 regional directors had an uphill battle with the central program managers, since the consolidators had little authority over the separators.

Citizen participation, although impressive when looked at from one angle, was weak when seen from another. The National Council on Health Planning saw the benefits of involving 50,000 people in health planning, but this participation in community decision making concerning what was then a $200 billion plus industry represented 0.03% of the adult population of the country. In Los Angeles, 9,058 people (0.2% of the population) voted for the 150 seats available in the health planning system, and those who remained involved were those with the greatest need to stay involved—scarcely a representative group.[7] The National Council concluded that the consumers on the HSAs suffered from a relative lack of knowledge and that they lacked an organizational base that could have made them more effective vis-a-vis the providers. The Council report[4] urged dedicated staff support for the consumers and less paperwork and jargon, recommendations that were not at all likely to end either the flow of paper and jargon or the influence of staffs with their own biases. The Council did find a surprisingly good distribution of consumer members, in contrast with the predecessor comprehensive health planning "B" agencies (Table 11-1). Although scarcely reflecting the composition of the groups targeted in the purpose of the act, the makeup of the governing bodies is fairly reflective of the voting public.

The General Accounting Office conducted two major reviews of the health planning process and found it to be inadequate to the purposes stated in the enabling legislation. In particular, the General Accounting Office concluded that the objectives adopted by HSAs lacked the essential ingredient of measurability (discussed later), that there were far too many objectives (100 or more in some cases) to allow any hope of implementation, that objectives were frequently unrealistic and did not take into account either available resources or the feasibility of acquiring the ones needed, and that they lacked a realistic set of implementing recommendations.[8] The report recommended that the Department of Health and Human Services (the successor agency to the Department of Health, Education and Welfare) play a stronger role in HSA and state plan development (contrary to those who felt the purpose was to encourage diversity in problem solving at the local level), that single HSA states be allowed to combine the Health Systems Plan and the State Health Plan into one document, and that the HSAs be required to pursue implementation of a more realistic set of objectives.

TABLE 11-1 Consumer representation on HSA governing councils

Category	Number	Percent
Sex		
Male	2,041	43
Female	2,664	57
Age		
18-34	797	17
35-64	3,179	68
65+	729	15
Income		
Less than $10,000	692	15
$10,000-24,999	2,121	45
$25,000 or more	1,599	34
Race		
Black	695	15
White	3,743	80
Other	267	5

From the National Council on Health Planning and Development: Report on consumer participation in the health planning program, Feb 6, 1981, US Department of Health and Human Services.

The National Academy of Science's Institute of Medicine also studied the health planning program and found that it had substantial potential.[9] The Institute encouraged the diversity and decentralization other critics had decried. It found that the process had been an important experiment in forming relationships between government and the private sector and between consumers and providers. The Institute identified three functions for the planning program: to provide an open and participatory structure, to contribute to a redirection of the health system, and to contribute to cost containment. These are a more modest set of expectations, and they were within the grasp of most HSAs, although some may claim that the cost of attaining such a modest set of objectives was too high.

If diversity of problem solving is seen as an important objective, the Institute of Medicine's study seems to reflect fairly on the experience. The problems have stemmed from lack of understanding and acceptance of these functions and from the belief by most HSA governing bodies that they were apolitical planning groups rather than voting bodies of citizens, all of whom had an interest in what was going on and whose personal interests were often in conflict with the interests of some other people or groups in the community. Some national strategists expected entirely too much, and some HSA staff and board members shared those unrealistically high expectations. The accountability of the HSAs to the Secretary of Health, Education and Welfare (now Health and Human Services) rather than to the community served, the flawed effort to wrestle with national standards, and the intense legal battles over project reviews and certificate of need reviews embroiled the HSAs in a government experiment too far-reaching to be achieved in so short a time.

The roles of the state and local planning bodies were often in conflict. At the local level, citizens may want more and better health resources, and they are physically and emotionally close to their providers. The state, however, has the principal financial burden of paying for such services and may be more interested in cost containment. As much as 50% of the cost of the state's Medicaid program is state money. Most of the mental health budget comes from state tax sources, and one half to two thirds of the public health budget is state money. Yet it is not clear that the local HSAs were more liberal and the states more tight-fisted in their reviews of new proposals.

Local public health directors were more concerned about and involved in the HSA than they were in the predecessor "B" agency, but they often still stood aside, missing its importance and assuming that they had the health planning responsibility in their community anyway. They tended to ignore the new planning bodies when they developed proposals for new services or changes in old ones and were subsequently puzzled and even angered when the councils sought to interfere in those plans. That mistake became more serious in 1974 when the new and stronger law was under consideration. During the debates about accountability and the role of local general-purpose government agencies in forming HSAs, congressional leaders indicated their dissatisfaction with the participation of local government in health planning. While the legislative liaison worker (lobbyist) for the National Association of County Health Officers was able to force a floor colloquy that opened the door slightly for local government, the law clearly favored the better organized comprehensive health planning agencies, which had everything to gain and nothing to lose by dedicating themselves to the shaping of the new legislation. If they could not gain designation as the successor agencies, they would suffer bureaucratic death.

The reduction of health planning

Local health officers and their state-level counterparts may have been realistic about the immediate impact of community planning on public health programming. Gorham,[10] who had had much to do with the development of sophisticated planning procedures in the U.S. Department of Health, Education and Welfare, said that "anyone in government knows that most decisions on spending emerge from a political process and are most heavily influenced by value judgments and the pressures brought to bear by a wide range of interested parties." He knew that government leaders, both elected and appointed, had program preferences often unrelated to costs, benefits, or efficiency. They may be related to an influential constituent or to a personal experience with alcoholism, cancer, or heart disease. Nonetheless, the community health planning experiment offered a new chance to develop a larger constituency of public involvement in health.

Given more time the process might have matured and achieved some of the effectiveness experienced in counterpart agencies in England. However, President Reagan was intent on eliminating the process, partly in response to intense pressure from vested interest groups such as the American Medical Association and the American Hospital Association and partly because of his own commitment to a society regulated by a "free market." In his 1982 budget he proposed no funds for the HSAs. Congress provided $64 million dollars by means of a continuing resolution (in contrast to the inadequate $127 million that had been available in the prior year) and allowed any governor to certify by October 1, 1981, that the state agency could perform the work of the HSAs, with the result that the Secretary would remove designation from the HSAs in that state. Five governors did just that (Ohio, Alabama, Nebraska, Louisiana, and Missouri), and the HSAs lost their designations and their federal funds. The remaining agencies did not have sufficient funds to continue and made plans to cut back, shut down, solicit private donations from the community (an unlikely prospect for a quasi-regulatory agency), or form private consulting agencies in an already cluttered competitive market. State agencies showed no signs of support for the community planning bodies. In 1982 the President returned to his elimination agenda and proposed $2 million to close the remaining HSAs. Congress kept the HSAs alive until January 1987, when a new law, repealing the planning act, went into effect. At that time, there were 142 barely viable HSAs. One year later, there were only 42. A search of the computer data bases for articles dealing with comprehensive health planning found 16 in 1979 to 1980, 6 in 1981 to 1982, 1 in 1983 to 1984, 1 in 1985 to 1986 (and that dealing with Nicaragua), and none in 1987 to 1988.

The states have begun to reexamine their experience with comprehensive health planning. Most of the states still maintain an expenditure review program of some sort. They have been streamlined, and the amount of money that can be invested in new construction, renovations, or new programs without requiring a certificate of need review has been increased substantially (up to $2 million in Colorado) but the programs remain in place. They offer the states some control over the development of hospitals and nursing homes. In addition, there are signs that the states are beginning to reevaluate the planning aspect of the experiment, separating it from the certificate of need process. As the medical care problems of the uninsured and underinsured become more pressing, as long-term care costs continue to rise, as racial and other socioeconomic differences in infant mortality rates remain intractably powerful, and as the mounting burdens of the AIDS epidemic become more apparent, comprehensive health planning becomes more essential: planning that cuts across the public and private sectors, as well as across the boundaries separating state and local public agencies. Without federal rules, a number of states are beginning to mount new and possibly more effective health planning programs at their own expense. They are not inclined to support local or regional planning agencies, since they are sometimes contentious opponents, and, after all, it is the state's money, but the comprehensive health planning movement is not dead. It may be better described as undergoing rehabilitation.

Those who believe that the whole strategy was part of a long-term effort to demonstrate that neither community nor state health planning could work and that only centralized control over health resource allocation efforts, based in Washington, could lead to achievement of a national agenda of equity may look with satisfaction on the events of the last few years. Those who believe that the ability to carry out such planning is still so primitive that only a policy of diversity and scanning for useful approaches to complex problems makes sense must now try to resurrect the idea of local health planning. It may be that the nation's most conservative president since the 1920s will have fostered the development of a more creative experiment at the community and state level than would otherwise have been possible.

MANAGERIAL PLANNING

The comprehensive health planning ferment during the last two decades has obscured attention to planning as an administrative process. The framers of P.L. 89-749 and P.L. 93-641 had community and nonprovider control over the allocation of health service resources as much on their minds as planning. The intense community struggle for control of the new health planning agencies tended to distract attention from the day-to-day realities of health planning, both in legislative bodies and in operating agencies.

Structure

Just where does planning fit in the operating agency? The answers illustrate some of the previous discussion about the political nature of the planning process. Levin[11] thought that the comprehensive health planning process failed because it was grafted onto administration when it should have subsumed it. However, that would intertwine decision making (a political process) with planning. If the planners or planning bodies subsume decision making, the planners become the new administrators and the purpose of planning turns out to be the substitution of a new leadership for the old one. Others think of planning as a scientific process separated from the more subjective realm of day-to-day management—an "off-line" location. Levey and Loomba[12] see planning as an "on-line" process, with the planners very much involved in programming and implementation. In practice, planning is a process, not a product, and it is a process that should permeate all management and political systems. Planning is to administration as epidemiology is to disease prevention. Some agencies may establish a staff unit organizationally close to the director's office with analysis and planning as its function. This fits into what Mintzberg has called the technostructure[13] (see Chapter 10).

The breadth of the planning process will influence its organizational placement. Some have argued for a broad scope that would include the environment in an ecologic approach to health planning. The broader the boundaries of the planning effort, the more likely it will be to come into conflict with other spheres of interest such as education and welfare. If health planners realize that employment has a major impact on community, as well as family health and take a broad approach to their mission, they might try to incorporate vocational training and employment opportunity programs into the health plan, leading to wasteful battles with other agencies of government. The scope of planning should fit the agreed-upon mission of the agency. When it exceeds those boundaries, the planners and the agency director need to begin discussions with the planners and directors of other community agencies.

Health planning does impinge on other spheres of interest and should be seen as one facet of social and economic planning. Many states developed large hospitals for the mentally ill and for tuberculosis patients in the nineteenth century and the first half of the twentieth century. These were usually located in isolated rural communities. With modern treatment techniques, the number of people confined to such institutions has declined dramatically, especially since the 1950s. It is essential that those responsible for the management of such institutions consider alternatives for the future, including the possibility of converting them to more generalized use or closing them. The last alternative is often the most practical one because of the location and age of the facilities, but it is a difficult choice, because the surrounding area is often dependent on such institutions for its economic stability. The mental health of a community is jeopardized by undercutting its economic stability, and health agency administrators should become involved in studies of the economic development of the area as part of the closure alternative. It can be argued that it is better to continue less-than-optimal care for the patients in the institution if moving them to a better system would imperil employment opportunities for a large sector of the community. Such considerations raise the question of boundaries: how global does a health plan have to be to be comprehensive? Although health planners have to consider such issues as employment and economic development, they need to work with, rather than try to usurp the work of, those who have responsibility for and skill in such efforts.

Some large state agencies and the national Department of Health and Human Services maintain separate planning units, which are often involved in the study of technology or policy. In most state and local health agencies, planning is carried out at the program level and as part of the budget process.

Terminology in planning

A variety of terms have been invented and applied to the analytic processes of planning[14-15]: program planning, program analysis, decision trees, program cost accounting, cost-benefit analysis, cost-effectiveness analysis, planning-programming-budgeting systems (PPBS), operations research, systems analysis, program evaluation and review technique, and automatic scheduling with time integrated resource allocation. Many of these names and methods are more or less synonymous, some represent parts of others, and many overlap. The more encompassing programs are planning-programming-budgeting systems, operations research, systems analysis, and program evaluation and review techniques. These techniques are concerned with the complete spectrum from fact-finding to problem definition, goal setting, programming, controls, and evaluation, with proper feedins and feedbacks of information, resources, and results to subsidiary or final outputs or solutions.

Planning-programming-budgeting-systems is a procedure intended to make possible the better allocation of resources among alternate ways of attaining a desired objective.

According to Hatry and Cotton,[16]

> Its essence is the development and presentation of information as to the full implications, the costs and benefits of the major alternative courses of action relevant to major resources allocation decisions. . . . Such problems as budget implementation, manpower selection, the assessment of the work efficiency of operating units and cost control of current operations are generally considered to be outside the purview of PPBS. Cost accounting and non-fiscal performance reporting systems are very important in providing basic data required for PPBS analyses (as well as for fiscal accounting and management control purposes). However, such systems are usually considered complementary to PPBS rather than directly part of it. . . . The main contribution of PPBS lies in the planning process, i.e., the process of making program policy decisions that lead to a specific budget and specific multi-year plans.

Operations research originated from the efforts of scientists of many disciplines to solve military operations problems during World War II.[17] It is a term applied to "research into some or all aspects of conducting or operating a system, a business, or a service, while treating the system as a living organism in its proper environment. . . ." Operations research usually involves the development of a model, manipulation of the known variables, and forecasting of the results of the system under different conditions.

Systems analysis focuses on the first phases of PPBS or operations research. The process involves defining the problem, projecting determinants of the problem, generating alternative approaches to solving the problem, evaluating the cost effectiveness of the alternatives, and interpreting the quantitative and qualitative results.

Program evaluation and review technique (PERT) is adapted from the work-flow studies used in industrial management. It provides a detailed graphic representation of the components of a program during the planning of its implementation. It involves a breakdown of the project into subprojects with their objectives and the development of a network of activities necessary to move from one event to another. Time estimates are developed for each activity and then for the whole process, including the critical path, which is the longest path in terms of time from the beginning to the end. The network is a diagram of the events necessary to reach the project's objective, and it is under constant analysis to identify problem areas and to indicate whether predicted progress is being made.[18]

The iterative process

Planning is an iterative process with the results constantly feeding back into the cycle. The steps can be described in various ways, but the following are generally used in some form or another: (1) statement of a goal, (2) listing of problems in attaining that goal, (3) definition of objectives, and (4) exploration of various methods for moving toward the objectives. Then (5) someone has to choose which method will be used and (6) the program has to be implemented and (7) evaluated. All along the way, the results feed back into the cycle and force a reappraisal of the goal, the problems, the objectives, the methods, and the priorities. Information about social and health status indicators, the law, the availability and cost of resources, political and social constraints and sanctions, and the effectiveness of different intervention techniques is essential to the process.

Goals. Goals are broad statements incorporating social values and policy into a statement of a desirable future status. Goals need not be immediately attainable nor involve numerical targets; but it is important that they reflect a social consensus and not contain an inherent conflict with the aspirations of the community. *Assuring all persons an opportunity to develop their capabilities so that they can live as independently as possible* is a useful statement of a goal. To reduce dependency by guaranteeing every person an adequate income may be acceptable as a statement of personal principle, but it fails as a goal because it specifies the method to be used (a guaranteed annual income), one that is not generally accepted in the United States.

Problem definition. What are the obstacles that stand in the way of goal attainment? *Many children have a hearing problem that interferes with the development of language skills, psychologic growth and development, and learning skills.* This problem can result from a number of causes, and its prevalence is measurable. This statement has all of the ingredients of a useful and explicit statement of a problem: clarity, measurement, and an understanding of causality.

Objective. A statement of an objective must include (1) a realistic target, (2) a measurable target, and (3) the advantage of clarity. It should not make reference to a preferred method of reaching the objective, and it should not include a mixture of objectives that would necessarily involve the development of several different strategies. *The reduction of the prevalence of hypertension through better public education aimed at obesity* would be a poor statement of an objective. It specifies reduction without indicating from what to what; it selects public education as the method of choice when there are many other strategies that could be used for the reduction of hypertension; and it confuses obesity with hypertension without defining either.

To curtail the number of acute care hospital beds from a ratio of 4.3 per 1,000 persons to 3.8 by 1994 would be a useful statement of an objective. Presumably a goal of reducing the cost of health care has been accepted, and one of the problems has been found to be an oversupply of hospital beds (although the nature of these relationships is by no means clear). The objective is to reduce that supply by a measurable amount over a defined period. An objective that does not allow measurement should be avoided if possible.

Objective statements should be aimed at results, or outputs, not inputs, or activities, although this is not always possible. For example, most communities cannot reduce the incidence of polio, since the incidence is usually zero. Since the relationship of immunization to the prevention of polio is well known and adequately measured, *the maintenance of a 98% level of immunization among schoolchildren* would be an acceptable objective. Stating objectives and measuring results in prevention programs are difficult. If an input, or an activity, is to be measured, its efficacy in attaining the real purpose of the program must be known. The relationship of restaurant inspections to the prevention of outbreaks of food-borne disease is a good example. The objective may be to reduce the frequency of outbreaks, but measurement is difficult. A "proxy" target of some number of restaurants inspected each year with correction of 75% of the deficiencies within 30 days could be used, but the staff should review what they know about the relationship of such enforcement activities to the possible spread of disease before adopting the indices.

Methods. Most program managers when asked to reach an objective will describe the existing method, but it is important that alternatives be explored and their costs compared. If an acceptable objective is to reduce the number of decayed, missing, and filled teeth in school-aged children from 2.9 to 2.5 over a 10-year period, all available technology should be explored to develop an array of methods. This might include the expansion of water system fluoridation, the use of topical fluorides, a program of preschool dental health education coupled with training and incremental dental care, and possible use in the future of immunizing agents or other chemicals. The cost, the effectiveness, and the acceptability of each technique and the availability of necessary resources must be considered in the review.

Implementation and evaluation. Before the program is implemented, the evaluation methodology has to be developed. As noted above, evaluation is linked to the definition of the problem, the objectives, and the design of the intervention method. Once started, the program should return information that enables progress and performance to be reviewed. The feedback continues throughout program operation, although it may be modified, just as any other part of the program may be modified, based on the feedback.

It is important to distinguish between activity reporting, performance reporting, and the reporting of results. It is also important to determine what is to be accomplished by the evaluation. Evaluation is similar to research. A hypothesis is postulated, the program (experiment) is run, and the results either confirm or deny the hypothesis. If the purpose of the evaluation is to study different treatment or intervention techniques to see which is best, it can be structured as a research project, in which case the production of information is one of the end results of the project. Costs are usually high, and the research method is probably inappropriate to most ongoing programs, however. Evaluation as a management tool should be incorporated into the work of the program staff and not treated as a research project. In this case the data do not constitute an end product but are fed back into the iterative cycle as part of the program itself, helping the staff to correct the program. An evaluation should not become more rigorous than the program requires. A service program should not be implemented unless the staff is reasonably convinced that, properly run, it will accomplish the intended results.

Activity reporting is the most common form of feedback and is of little value for evaluation purposes. It counts the number of lab tests run, the number of home visits made, or the number of restaurants inspected. Performance reporting is more difficult but more useful. Performance enumerates results: deficiencies corrected, children immunized, full birth weight babies delivered. Performance is more directly related to objectives and serves as a better measurement of progress, but performance can be difficult to measure. A reasonable objective for an alcoholism program would be to reduce the number of disability days caused by alcoholism, but keeping track of alcoholics is notoriously difficult. Follow-up without a very costly effort may be as low as 20% to 30%. Even if the effectiveness of the intervention program were as high as 70%, the overall "success rate" would be $0.20 \times 0.70 = 0.14$. With nothing known about the other 80%, no assumptions about their success or failure can be made.

Evaluation of a health education program is especially difficult. A campaign to increase the use of lap-and-shoulder restraints in cars could be measured by asking for police reports on the use of such devices by people stopped by the police for some reason, but such a sample would be heavily biased toward nonuse. The automobile accident fatality rate could be used, but it is so dependent on miles driven and speeding laws and their enforcement that no valid inferences can be drawn from such a measurement. When reliance on indirect measures such as these is necessary, it is helpful to select several different ones. If they form a consistent pattern, they have higher overall validity.

Cost has become a crucial variable in program evaluation. Cost-effectiveness analysis compares the ratio of cost to effectiveness for several different methods of achieving the same objective. *Effectiveness* is a relative term in cost-effectiveness analysis and may mean the attack rate for a disease, the fatality rate for those who get the disease, or the rate of secondary spread. Cost-benefit analyses attempt to quantify the benefits as well as the costs in monetary terms so that different types of programs and outcomes can be compared. The terms have become very popular and the procedures are arduous. The Office of Technology Assessment of the U.S. Congress has concluded that "CEA/CBA cannot serve as the sole or primary determinant of a health care decision. Decision making could be improved, however, by the process of identifying and considering all the relevant costs and benefits of a decision."[19]

One of the problems in evaluation is the difficulty of measuring something that can be accepted as an index of health or lack of health. Sackett and his colleagues[20] have developed and tested a survey approach that combines the ingredients of comprehensiveness, a positive orientation, general applicability, sensitivity, simplicity, and precision that the authors required, but it basically measures health as the complement of ill health. Cochrane[21] has suggested a terse if irreverent measurement of ill health. He suggests that we define ill health for any condition as that point at which treatment does more good than harm.

Evaluation remains difficult and important. It is not impossible. It does require a thoughtful approach to objective setting and the use of evaluation criteria that are congruent with the scope of the program and the knowledge that exists about the program.

Legislative leaders will continue to ask that public efforts be evaluated and will continue to launch new programs without evaluation. The priorities listed by Congress for the National Health Planning and Resources Development Act of 1974 fail the test of good objective writing, and evaluation was not built into the law. That may illustrate the difference between politics, or decision making, and planning.

Priorities

The choice of a method is intimately related to the process of establishing priorities. Program managers have to choose or recommend a method to accomplish an objective. This has to be done within the political framework for reviewing community priorities. Sometimes the elected community, state, or national leaders will have established priorities, as was true with the passage of the National Health Planning and Resources Development Act of 1974. More often it is a program or agency administrator who takes the analysis of problems and priorities to a decision-making body, such as a county commission or a governor and legislature, with a recommendation. There are a number of ways to analyze priorities: the simplex method, the nominal group process, criteria weighting, decision alternative rational evaluation, and the priority rating process.[15]

The priority rating process has some of the advantages of several of the other techniques and serves as an effective learning process for the participants. As is true of the other procedures, it yields relative results that are useful for comparing different and competing programs or alternative methods for achieving the same objective. It cannot be applied to a single program as a method of evaluation. The members of the group have to work together throughout the process rather than separately, since definitions of the component parts of the process tend to be unique to each working group. Consistency across the scope of programs reviewed is necessary to get a useful relative ranking.

The first step is for the participants to list every activity or program under consideration. The list may easily number into the hundreds. The group then proceeds to analyze each program using a dynamic formula consisting of four components:

Component A: size of problem
Component B: seriousness of problem
Component C: effectiveness of intervention
Component D: propriety, economics, acceptability, resources, and legality (PEARL)

The basic priority rating formula is:

$$\text{Basic priority rating (BPR)} = \frac{(A + B)C}{3} \times D$$

The range of scores for each of the four components is:

A: 0 to 10
B: 0 to 20
C: 0 to 10
D: 0 or 1

The maximum obtainable product of the components (A, B, and C) is 300. By an arbitrary division of the maximum product by 3, the maximum score becomes 100. Every rating will then be in the range of 0 to 100. Component D, or PEARL, becomes 0 or 1, as shown later.

As in the case of many evaluative procedures, a large subjective element enters into this exercise. The choice and definition of the components in the formula and the relative weights assigned to them are based on group consensus. Some control may be achieved by the use of a precise definition of terms, the delineating of exact rating procedures, and the use of statistical data to guide ratings when feasible.

Component A: size of problem. For purposes of assigning priorities, the size of the problem may be scored by the use of rates or the percentage of the total population at risk for the problem under consideration. Many problems will be defined for very small population groups, making an incidence or prevalence rate per 100,000 people at risk a useful approach, as in the following scale:

Incidence or prevalence per 100,000 population	Score
50,000 or more	10
5,000 to 49,999	8
500 to 4,999	6
50 to 499	4
5 to 49	2
0.5 to 4.9	0

The use of incidence or prevalence depends on whether the program is designed to prevent the occurrence or to reduce the prevalence of the problem through secondary or even tertiary prevention techniques (see Chapter 5).

Component B: seriousness of problem. The seriousness of a problem is defined in terms of four factors: urgency, severity, economic loss, and involvement of other people. "Seriousness" is assigned a range of 0 to 20 in the formula, and each of the four factors is assigned a range of 0 to 10. It is possible to attain a score of 40, which exceeds the range, but it is rare that the combination of the factors accumulates to that extent. The most urgent or severe problems are usually individual problems that do not involve significant community disruption. The terms are all subjective, and several iterations of the process will be necessary before the group can begin to agree on their rating. *Urgency* can be used to define the emergent nature of the problem, such as emergency response to a car wreck, or the sense of community urgency if an unknown chemical is spilled by a tank truck. *Severity* may encompass estimates of the case fatality rate or the seriousness of the disability if the problem is rarely fatal. *Economic loss* is related to severity and may reflect both community costs or losses and family costs. The involvement of other people is related to the other factors as well and is most frequently an issue in rapidly contagious diseases such as measles in an unimmunized population. If the total score exceeds 20, it is arbitrarily truncated to that level.

Component C: effectiveness of intervention. Effectiveness is often difficult to measure. The efficacy of most vaccines has been measured fairly carefully, but other interventions, such as the hospitalization of psychiatric patients or the use of supplemental nutrition for high-risk, low-income pregnant women, are less well evaluated. Most groups can make reasonably useful estimates, especially if the members have programs in competition, since they will contest unrealistic claims of effectiveness by each other. If the program reaches only 20% of those with the problem and is only 70% effective, then the effectiveness is $0.20 \times 0.70 = .14$, or 14%, and the rating would be quite low. Effectiveness is a multiplier in the basic priority rating formula, so its impact is powerful.

Component D: propriety, economics, acceptability, resources, and legality (PEARL). PEARL consists of a group of factors not directly related to the actual need or the effectiveness of the proposed intervention, but which determine whether a particular program can be carried out at all.

Propriety and acceptability are virtually synonymous. If economic resources are not available, if other resources such as physicians or nurses cannot be obtained, or if the program depends on an activity not permitted in law, then it cannot be implemented without changing the condition. Each of these qualifying factors is given a score of 0 or 1 and, since together they represent a product rather than a sum, if any one of them is rated a 0, it not only gives PEARL a 0 but makes the overall priority rating 0.

CONCLUSIONS

Health planning has several dimensions: the necessary managerial planning that has to be carried out to achieve efficiency; the possible use of strategic planning to compete for public attention in an era fraught with complex resource allocation problems; and the need for comprehensive health planning. The first two are not dissimilar from activities that take place in the private sector and in other public agencies. The latter, comprehensive health planning, is unique. It has gone through several phases in the United States: planning for resource development from 1945 to 1965; planning for broader access from 1966 to 1975 or 1976; planning for cost containment from 1978 to the early 1980s, and use of the marketplace to shape the allocation of resources since then.

The evidence suggests that progress has been irregular and that the present problems are severe. Resources indeed expanded during the first part of this century—the work force expanded, facilities were constructed, and research increased. The general consensus is that access to health care by those most in need of it increased following the Great Society programs of the 1960s. However, attempts to curtail the rapid increase in the percentage of gross national product consumed by the health sector during the 1970s did little to improve the economics, the quality, or the acceptability of the system. More recent reliance on the market to allocate resources has clearly failed: costs have gone up even more sharply, the health sector has become increasingly entrepreneurial, and both the number of people and the proportion of the population with inadequate access to decent health care have increased.

The burden of these problems has shifted to the states, which have demonstrated a variable willingness to solve them. To do so will require new experiments in cross-organizational planning. It is not the first time that public health has had to find new ways to solve both old and new problems.

REFERENCES

1. Simyar F and Lloyd-Jones J, editors: Strategic management in the health sector, Englewood Cliffs, NJ, 1988, Prentice-Hall, Inc.
2. Rathwell T: Strategic planning in the health sector, London, 1987, Croom Helm.
3. Bureau of Health Planning: Toward a better health care system, annual report, fiscal 1979, Washington, DC, US Department of Health and Human Services Pub No (HRA)80-14006, April 1980.
4. National Council on Health Planning and Development: Report on consumer participation in the health planning program, Feb 6, 1981, Washington, DC, US Department of Health and Human Services.
5. Richmond JB: Do we have a national health policy? the first annual Lester Breslow Distinguished Lectureship, Los Angeles, Oct 6, 1980, University of California at Los Angeles School of Public Health Alumni Association.
6. National Council on Health Planning: The national guidelines for health planning: standards regarding the appropriate supply, distribution, and organization of health resources, Washington, DC, US Department of Health, Education and Welfare, Pub No (HRA)79-645, March 28, 1978.
7. Cooper TL: The hidden price tag: participation costs and health planning, Am J Public Health 69:368, April 1979.
8. General Accounting office: Health systems plans: a poor framework for promoting health care improvements, Washington, DC, US General Accounting Office, Pub No (HRD)81-93, June 22, 1981.
9. Committee on Health Planning of the Institute of Medicine: Health planning in the United States: selected policy issues, vol 1, Washington, 1981, National Academy Press.
10. Gorham W: PPBS: its scope and limits, The Public Interest 8:4, Summer 1967.
11. Levin AL: Health planning and the US federal government, Int J Health Serv 2:367, Aug 1972.
12. Levey S and Loomba NP: Health care administration: a managerial perspective, Philadelphia, 1984, JB Lippincott Co.
13. Mintzberg H: The structuring of organizations, Englewood Cliffs, NJ, 1979, Prentice-Hall, Inc.
14. Blum H: Planning for health, ed 2, New York, 1981, Human Sciences Press.
15. Spiegel AD and Hyman HH: Basic health planning methods, Germantown, MD, 1978, Aspen Systems Corp.
16. Hatry HP and Cotton JF: Program planning for state, county and city, Washington, DC, 1967, George Washington University Press.

17. Flagle CD: Operational research in the health services, Ann NY Acad Sci 107:748, May 22, 1963.
18. Merten W: PERT and planning for health programs, Public Health Rep 81:449, May 1966.
19. The implication of cost effectiveness analysis of medical technology, Pub No OTA-H-125, Washington, DC, Congress of the United States, Office of Technology Assessment.
20. Sackett DL and others: The development and application of indices of health: general methods and a summary of results, Am J Public Health 67:423, May 1977.
21. Cochrane AL: The history of the measurement of ill health, Int J Epidemiol 1:89, 1972.

CHAPTER 12

Marketing public health

DEFINITIONS AND PURPOSES

The role of the market in health care has received increased attention in recent years, partly as a result of the conservative shift that began in the late 1970s and the emphasis on "natural markets," or competition, as a way to correct some of the problems of medical care. Yet it is a concept that is not routinely accepted in most public agencies. A market is the arena in which voluntary exchange transactions take place. Marketing is the planned attempt to influence the characteristics of voluntary exchange transactions—exchanges of cost and benefits by buyers and sellers or providers and consumers. Marketing is considerably different from selling in that selling concentrates on the needs of the producer (to sell more products or to inject more vaccine), whereas marketing, which may have the same ultimate objective, concentrates necessarily on the needs of the buyer or the public. The sales force of an organization is one part of the marketing effort, which includes consideration of the product, its price or cost to the public or the consumer, its distribution and accessibility, and the information available to and used by the public, or the four "Ps" of McCarthy[1]: product, price, place, and promotion.

Public health is difficult to market, as will be shown below. Most marketers develop their skills in the private sector, initially marketing products, then services. In recent years, the medical care industry has employed marketing to improve its utilization, and hospitals and medical practice groups have turned to marketing to improve their competitive position. The public sector, however, has been slow to use marketing. Public health has been particularly reluctant and, according to Manoff,[2] ineffective: the design of public health's message has been mediocre, and its use of media has been ineffective. Manoff makes the interesting point that public health has in recent years changed from social reform tactics to individual behavior modification to prevent disease and injury. This shifts the burden and cost of improving health from government to the individual. It also makes exchange transactions more complex and difficult to modify.

Social marketing, the use of marketing techniques to introduce or bring about social change, was first described in 1971 by Kotler and Zaltman.[3] That concept, as will be shown later, raises a number of important issues about the political structure of the United States and about the ethics of behavior-change strategies. Since the marketing of public health usually involves an effort to create social change, all such efforts are social marketing activities, and marketing will be used in that sense throughout this discussion.

Marketing is a relatively new business management practice, although some aspects of marketing have been carried out by public and private firms for centuries. When Benjamin Waterhouse persuaded Thomas Jefferson to be vaccinated, he was using one aspect of marketing, promotion, to gain wider acceptance of the product. Since marketing has traditionally been used to increase product sales, it has seemed irrelevant to the work of public health, which usually deals neither in profits nor in products. As it is applied in the business sector, the seeming irrelevance of marketing to public health is at least partly real, but adaptations of marketing concepts to the service environment and to not-for-profit enterprises have enhanced its attraction for public sector workers. There are several publications dealing with the subject,[1,2,4-7] although most efforts to date focus on hospital service marketing, which is sometimes antithetic to the interests of public health. The American College of Health Care Marketing publishes proceedings of its annual meetings in the *Health Care Marketing Quarterly*, several issues of which are of interest to public health: *Marketing for Mental Health Services* (1:1, 1983), *Marketing Long Term and Senior Care Services* (1:4, 1983), *Marketing Human and Social Service Agencies* (2:4, 1984), *Health Marketing and*

Consumer Behavior (2:1, 1985), and *Professional Practice in Health Care Marketing* (3:2/3, 1985).

Most business marketing experts find it difficult to translate concepts from their customary environment to the unique world of the public agency with its legislatively derived mandates. Nonetheless, it would be a mistake for public agency personnel to ignore the subject and strategies of marketing. They can be very useful in enhancing the general credibility of the agency; in maintaining protection against once common communicable diseases; in improving environmental controls; and in reducing deaths caused by heart disease, stroke, and cancer. There are real ethical and political problems involved in the use of a public agency's resources to attempt to influence public opinion and behavior, but the fact remains that it is being done all the time, often by enterprises that seek to increase their market at the expense of the public's health, and there is no reason for public health workers to remain in self-righteous darkness about the strategies and purposes of marketing.

GENERAL CONSIDERATIONS AND CONSTRAINTS

Public sector marketing has a number of unique features. Consumers of services or products usually exercise some control over their market transactions through loyalty, exit, and voice.[8] Loyalty is a form of voting for the conditions that prevail in the market by staying with the "brand" or the policies of the business when other options are available. Exit is the ability to leave the market if one is dissatisfied with the conditions of the transactions. Voice is the ability to challenge the conditions of the market if one is dissatisfied with them, perhaps through a simple complaint or by organizing a citizen's group to protest the market's policies. These classic democratic ways of influencing the market are not readily available to the consumer of public agency services. Loyalty cannot be demonstrated when there is no other agency from which to obtain a copy of a birth certificate or a burial permit. Exit is not practical for a restaurant owner who does not like the sanitary regulations or for many low-income people who cannot find a private physician who will accept Medicaid patients. Voice is usually the sole means of redress.

Public health has a number of marketing problems. It has not one but multiple constituencies, a problem of special significance in public health that is not well recognized either by public health practitioners or by those from other fields who have offered to help. The public sector, including not-for-profit health organizations, operates in an environment where the way it acquires resources (taxation or charitable donations) is separated from the way it allocates them. Increasing exchange transactions will not necessarily increase benefits to the organization. Public health has multiple objectives, too: "selling" immunizations, cleaning up the water supply, safeguarding the food supply, managing birth and death records, protecting workers, preventing pregnancy in children, and protecting those who do become pregnant. These problems make the simple application of private sector marketing techniques a questionable activity at best.

The service exchange

The concept of marketing developed to influence exchange transactions involving products. The health industry, public and private, is a service industry. Services are intangible, and there is no transfer of ownership involved. Services cannot be transported or stored and recalled for later use. If the prenatal clinic has a surplus of supply (time for additional appointments) on Wednesday afternoon, it cannot be used when there is a surplus of demand on Thursday. Moreover, the buyer and seller (provider and consumer) are not exchanging the same thing. When one buys a toaster, the seller hands the buyer a toaster and the buyer gives the seller money. In a venereal disease clinic, the consumer may obtain relief of symptoms and protection, whereas the clinic manager is engaged in exercising professional skills to control the spread of disease. In one sense, the consumer is only one of many consumers of the services provided. The cost to the consumer may be some discomfort, embarrassment, and time rather than money.

The not-for-profit environment

Not-for-profit organizations have not engaged in selling or marketing in the past, and their boards, even though they often consist of business people, are not accustomed to marketing what they believe to be a needed and valued service in their community. Not-for-profit organization managers are often professionals from the field of service, such as scouting or nursing, and marketing has never been part of their training or experience. Yet when attendance remains low in an immunization clinic, and it is known that less than 80% of the children in elementary school have been protected against measles, the staff are likely to start talking in marketing terms: "Who are these folks?" "What do they know about measles?" "Are they afraid of shots?" "Is the price (waiting time, travel distance, etc.) too high?" Such problems should be recognized as marketing problems from the outset, and programs should be designed to contend with the problems inherent in the market.

Competition

The market is crowded with health messages from both profit-making and not-for-profit organizations. Many of the messages are confusing and conflicting, offering cautionary advice about things to do and not to do. Marketing is a consumer-oriented practice, but it is product based. To accomplish the goals of marketing, people have to be made aware of the product and then moved from awareness to action—the decision to obtain either the product or the service, or, as often happens in health promotion/disease prevention, the decision to stop doing something. Advertising often involves describing the marginal advantages of one toothpaste over another, but health promotion often involves promoting doing something versus not doing something or vice versa. It is not a matter of brand preference so much as contrast preference in an environment that may make the alternative behavior (a fast car, a good martini, or a cool cigarette) seem an effective competitor. For example, car dealers are rarely faced with having to extol the virtues of driving versus walking.

Penetration

Penetration is a measure of the amount of the effective market captured by one provider or product. For example, 97% immunization of elementary school children is an effective degree of penetration: it will prevent epidemics of measles. In product or service marketing, 20% of the market may be a very good degree of penetration. Moving from 20% to 25% may require a costly marketing effort and may not return enough revenue to make the effort worthwhile. Unfortunately, in most public health efforts, it is the last percentage point rather than the first one that is most valuable. That is, the women who most readily accept the offer of a Pap smear to detect cancer of the cervix are least likely to have the disease. It is costly to get the interest and the action of 50% to 60% of women between the ages of 18 and 54, but that proportion, which would represent an extraordinary accomplishment in the marketing of a product, would represent failure of marketing Pap smears, since the people at highest risk are in the last 5%. As a general rule, the most important people to reach in a health promotion/disease prevention effort are the hardest people to reach. There has been a marked decrease in the percentage of men smoking in the United States in the last 20 years, but the lung cancer death rate decreased only slightly. This is because those most likely to quit smoking are the lightest smokers, who have less excess risk than heavy smokers. In a statistical sense, the last recruit is known as the "last x," and the "last x" is always more difficult yet more important to get than the "penultimate x." In the private sector, the benefits of reaching the last consumer can be compared to the costs of doing so. The result may be to ignore him or her. But in public health campaigns, failure to reach the last consumer may cause the entire program to fail.

Segmentation

Many health promotion/disease prevention efforts have focused indiscriminately on the entire population of a community rather than recognizing that there are many different facets of the public in even the smallest of towns. Identifying the different interest groups is known as market segmentation. The segments may have geographic, demographic, socioeconomic, or behavioral characteristics that make them distinct. Each segment will respond to different marketing strategies. Families of alcoholics, alcoholics, judges, police officers, and employers will each have different perceptions of the nature of the alcoholism problem and what should be done about it. Family members will not respond to the same message that will interest a judge.

Many public health marketing efforts wastefully target or "segment" the entire community rather than concentrate resources on that segment with the greatest risk. A feature story about screening for cancer of the cervix in the Sunday supplement of the local newspaper may please health educators, but it is likely to miss altogether the segment of the community most likely to be at high risk and devoid of needed information and access to services. A more effective marketing plan can lead to increased participation by the target group.[9]

Most product or service enterprises have a relatively homogeneous product line, and it is not difficult to reach different segments with different but effective messages. But public health agencies have sponsoring clients (such as legislators and their "back-home" constituents), consumer clients (such as teenagers), and competitive members of the community (such as physicians in private practice), each of which may see the public health clinic as serving a different purpose. It is very difficult for a public health agency to appeal to all three at the same time with consistent yet effective messages. It would be unrealistic to expect the public to have equal regard for Delta Airlines, Delta Toasters, and Delta Home Health Services: what do they have in common? Yet the public health clinic may need to provide services to parents bringing schoolchildren in for required immunizations, teenaged family planning clients who may know some of the parents in the clinic, other teenagers with sexually transmitted diseases, young women seeking public prenatal care because they cannot obtain access to private medical care, and mothers with infants seeking postdelivery checkups and well-child assessments. They all require the services of trained nursing, medical, and laboratory personnel, but their interests and commonality end there, as do the reasons for public support of those different programs. The problems become more complex when one considers developers seeking variances to sewerage requirements, funeral directors who need a burial permit to arrange a ceremony for a bereaved family, restaurant owners who have to send their kitchen workers to a class on food handling, and the Association of Parents of Autistic Children, who are demanding that the health officer require mainstream schooling plus special psychiatric care for their children. Market segmentation in a public health agency presents problems of diversity unknown to even the largest proprietary organizations. The agency has to think of those different market segments, formulate responses to their needs, and design promotional messages to bring about desired social change, yet never appear inconsistent to any of the different clienteles or alienate one group by serving another.

In recent years, many public health workers have focused on "constituency building" as a tactic to improve public health's position in the competitive resource allocation process at the state and local level. They have watched sister agencies—highways, education, agriculture, economic development, and natural resources—develop strong and effective constituent groups, which have helped to increase the agency budgets and obtain passage of favorable legislation. But these agencies, as complex as their work is, have relatively simple constituency-building problems. Highways has to satisfy paving contractors, the trucking organizations, and occasionally the state automobile association. Education has to satisfy the teachers, parents, and taxpayers. Agriculture has to satisfy the farmers, economic development the chamber of commerce, and natural resources the hunters and campers. Public health has numerous constituent groups, as noted above, and each expects and demands different things—often things that are in conflict with the expectations of some other group. Simple constituency-building tactics developed for other agencies are of little use in this environment. The marketing research needed by public health has not been done, since no other agency or organization needs it and public health is poorly equipped to do such research. Until well-designed and -evaluated experiments can be carried out, public health will find it difficult to develop an effective constituent base.

Prevention is a difficult notion around which to develop strong adherence. As a general notion, it has widespread but diffuse support. People are specific in their prevention activities, which may focus on breast cancer, AIDS, or hypertension, radon, lead, smoking, child abuse, incinerators, or land fills. It is possible to develop qualitatively determined market segments for health promotion activities,[10] but enthusiasm for one cause does not readily translate into support for another. Each prevention target attracts its own constituent group, and the groups are often quite dissimilar and even antagonistic to one another. The formation of a communitywide prevention council might seem like a nifty idea for a local health department, but it is difficult to maintain strong and balanced support for a broad, multifaceted prevention program.

The governmental image

Even though many people have had one or more pleasing experiences with a government agency or know a public sector employee whom they respect and trust, most people do not have a high opinion of the creativity, productivity, and adaptability of government workers or programs. That perception does not appear to be justified, but a full discussion of the governmental image exceeds the confines of this book. Since such perceptions are relative, it may be that Americans have an unwarranted notion that private enterprise is efficient and creative, and the public sector image suffers in contrast. Frequent revelations of white-collar crime seem to have little impact on this imbalance of perceptions. Mistrust of government was part of the origin of the United States, as was private enterprise without governmental interference. Mistrust has the advantage of keeping public programs under public scrutiny, but it also makes public sector tasks more difficult.

When a private enterprise has a negative image, it may resort to special tactics to change the environment, including a heavy dose of advertising, a name change, a product change, and a change in management. In the public sector, many of those tactics are not available to counteract what seems to be a pervasive attitude. It is again unfortunate that the public sector's resources cannot easily be used to stimulate the sort of research that has been carried out in business schools to support the private sector. Yet many public health agencies have been able to develop and maintain a good public image. It is not an impossible task. Although multiple constituencies, purposes, and "products" make it difficult, respect can be earned and maintained by ability, behavior, and appearance, as noted later.

Decentralization

Many marketing strategies are dependent on macromarketing, which occurs at the national level and is sometimes individualized by local dealers, as in automobile advertising. Private, not-for-profit, national health agencies can engage in macromarketing by developing advertising and legislative programs to modify smoking behavior or nutrition, but public agencies are often mistrusted if they engage in the same efforts. The tobacco lobby or the milk producers may pressure key legislators to obstruct federal agency advertising campaigns. In their private capacity, citizens may object to the use of public funds to market a concept that they may not espouse, such as family planning. To avoid the perception that some anonymous "they" are trying to manipulate lives, public sector marketing efforts need to be decentralized, so that local boards of health or legislative bodies can respond to such concerns. Lacking that intimacy, people who are mildly in favor of the particular effort or neutral on the matter may be aroused to opposition simply because the effort comes from afar under the auspices of a remote government agency. At the local level, if the opposition group is successful in blocking family planning services for teen-agers, for example, it will only affect that community rather than the entire country.

Marketing is much more than advertising, however. It requires a careful plan with consistent actions, as will be discussed below. There must be a "step-down" element to the plan. When a national food company advertises a new convenience food on prime-time television, it is important that consumers see the display when they walk into the grocery store the next day. This enhances "memorability, penetration and action consequences."[4] Public health marketing needs to use well-developed, decentralized programs, even though this may be relatively inefficient compared to private sector marketing programs.

Honest marketing

No organization, private or public, can long endure if its service or product programs are dishonest—if the sponsors claim more than they can deliver. The effort to deinstitutionalize the mentally ill was marketed partly on the basis that it would save money, but the savings have not materialized, because good community care of the mentally ill is not cheap. Legislators who were involved in the change process remain skeptical of the community mental health movement, because they were promised more than could be delivered. The Secretary of the Department of Health, Education and Welfare in 1976 promised that 95% of the American population should and could be immunized against swine flu, despite the fact that most practicing public health workers knew it was not possible. The failure of that program was a serious though temporary setback to the credibility of public health.

Given the other problems faced by government agencies, which have been discussed, public health workers need to be particularly careful not to promise results that cannot be reasonably anticipated. Many programs have been established on the basis that they would cost virtually nothing to implement and might even make money, only to confront some of the same legislators a few years later with substantial budgetary requirements and a vociferous constituency. The legislators may provide the money, but they may not forget the false claims made when another program is proposed by the same claimant.

THE POLITICS OF PUBLIC SECTOR MARKETING

Many of the special conditions that affect public sector marketing have been previously described, but the ubiquitous influence of the political decision-making process warrants special emphasis.

The generally negative image of government programs extends to legislators, elected executive officers, agency directors, and their employees, as a class if not always as individuals. Legislative and executive branch sponsors of public health programs may surprise public health workers who thought they had an ally by asking very skeptical questions. Elected officials have many constituencies whose interests may clash on particular issues. Although the program manager and staff may think that they are running a model alcohol detoxification program, members of Al-Anon may be telling normally supportive county supervisors or state legislators that the manager doesn't know enough about alcoholism to be trusted with the program. Politicians have to listen to such information, partly because they do not wish to lose votes unnecessarily and partly because they have learned that such allegations are not always incorrect. Occasionally, a knowledgeable manager may not be paying enough attention to what is going on and may have ignored the same complaint or be inaccessible to the complainants.

Beyond organizational or personal competition, there exists a deep-seated ambivalence about many important social issues. Helping sexually active teenagers avoid pregnancy and protecting the concept of the family as a value-forming unit are examples of issues about which many people have internal conflicts. The criminal justice system and public welfare are even better examples: is the purpose of the criminal justice system to punish or to rehabilitate? Is the purpose of the welfare system to seek out those who need help or to prevent people from becoming dependent? The answers vary not only between groups but within individuals, depending on the time the problem is considered and on whether a particular case or class of cases is under consideration. Given the ambivalence, most elected officials would prefer not to take a clear position, especially if what is needed can be done without vote-losing position taking. An elected official who supports residential care for mentally retarded adults may be quick to investigate charges of mismanagement in the program when homeowners on the same block complain. Often those complaints come to the elected official because the program manager or the agency director has failed to pay attention to the need for constant program marketing, both in the council chambers and in the neighborhood.

If a complaint is dismissed too often, it is easy to miss the signal that several people have begun to complain. Programs that are known to present such problems require constant marketing. Opponents of a program may correctly assume that the staff and managers will not listen to their complaints. Not hearing any complaints, the program director may forget marketing until it is too late. In the mid-1980s the residents of one community insisted on the establishment of programs to combat drug abuse, including detoxification and residential treatment. Many people think that any health problem can be solved by calling it a medical problem and assigning it to medical personnel. But drug abuse is a serious problem not always treatable and sometimes resulting in death. Most residential treatment programs for cocaine users will experience violence from time to time. The manager of the program was concerned that the first such incident could result in allegations of mismanagement and even closure of a needed service. He took great pains to bring such problems to the attention of the community through contacts with newspeople and in public meetings, including the annual budget sessions in the county court house. When a fatal stabbing did occur, the reaction was temperate and understanding. Marketing is a constant effort and requires the same sort of careful attention given to other aspects of programs.

Even though it is true that marketing is a constant process, it is also true that the public may resent what appears to be an effort to sell services that cost tax dollars. The same community or legislature that approves money for prenatal care for high-risk, low-income women may disapprove of an organized effort to find all of the eligible clients. As previously mentioned, it is often the hardest-to-reach clients that are most important to reach, yet those same individuals may appear to be the least deserving clients in the eyes of the community. The family that is most splintered and least capable of providing effective support for its members may be thought to be so abnormal as not to merit the use of the public services available to less atypical citizens. Public programs are not established to support deviancy but because they are perceived as a way of controlling it. The interests and capabilities of the workers may lead them toward more constructive alternatives, but angry taxpayers may have a more conservative version of the purpose of the program. Although a dishonest representation of the methods and purposes of the program will not be tolerated, discretion in advertising program goals is often necessary.

The public arena is a competitive place. Success comes not from higher profits but from greater use, public support, and the attainment of objectives, which are often intangible. What might be an effective marketing effort in the private sector might be, or seem to be, an unwarranted effort at personal aggrandizement by a program director, either because of relative laxity on the part of other agency directors and elected officials or because of overzealousness on the part of the director. Other agency directors will not respond favorably when a peer is seen each evening on the local news, has frequent press conferences, and issues all of the news about all of the programs in that agency. Nor will most mayors or governors tolerate a health director who gets more press coverage than they do, even if they are at fault. It may be necessary to mute an otherwise effective marketing program if it appears overzealous by community standards.

Even with discretion, the marketing of a person rather than a program is never justified. It is often desirable and appropriate to feature an individual employee, including the agency director, to inform the public about a program or a problem, but repeated media exposure of the same person will generate adverse reactions. The public knows that no health director can be an expert on sewerage system design, skin rashes in schoolchildren, acid rain, the high cost of medical insurance, and alcoholism. Different messages are better conveyed by different spokespersons, provided they are knowledgeable and effective in a public setting. If not, it is better to obtain the help of people from the voluntary or private sector who may have those attributes. Attaching a problem or a program to a symbol that can gain public recognition is important, however.[11] Using the same spokesperson for major and continuing problems can affix a level of credibility and expertise to that individual that can help the public understand the issue and support the necessary intervention.

PUBLIC RELATIONS

Public relations is the summation of many individual relations that go on in a complex agency and a crucial component of marketing. It is one part of a much broader effort to influence the public's health. In the private sector, public relations, good or bad, may be the result of a designated sales force, but in most public agencies there are few or no dedicated salespersons. This is not unique to the public sector. Commercial airlines generally have very effective marketing programs, including an emphasis on good public relations. No one is totally dedicated to sales, yet everyone does a bit of it, from the agent who handles computerized reservations on the phone (who is usually contacted through the automatic switching of what appears to be a local telephone number to a remote site), to the staff behind the desk at check in (often confronted with impatient customers who have confusing problems and heavy bags), to the flight attendants who may have to serve drinks and meals to 100 or more passengers on a 45-minute trip. When a ticket or a child is lost, a customer can become a loyal fan when any one of those people solves the problem. Most of them are trained to do just that and do not simply refer the person with the problem to someone else located someplace else.

Good public relations are similar to good manners. They are developed from the appearance, behavior, and ability of the agency, collectively and individually.

Appearance

Dress codes are out of style and usually out of place, but effective communications are not. Appearance is an essential part of the ability to communicate effectively with people. An appearance that might be very effective in talking with teenagers about AIDS could very well offend their parents at a civic meeting. It is fortunately difficult to discipline someone for eccentric dress in these litigious days, but it is quite appropriate to intervene when a worker's appearance is such as to offend or in some other way jeopardize his or her ability to communicate with someone who needs help. In most cases peer pressure will serve to normalize appearance. In cases where that does not work, provided the problem is real and not just a manifestation of intolerance on the part of one or two other workers, counseling and even reassignment may be in order.

Some agencies still use uniforms, particularly for nursing personnel. This necessitates some sort of dress code, but it should be interpreted liberally enough to allow individual personalization. Some people believe that a uniform adds an air of professionalism and identity to the interaction, whereas others think it indiscrete to have a uniformed worker knocking on the door of a family whom the neighbors believe to be in trouble. It is often tempting to discontinue the practice, but if it has been in existence for a long time, it may not be worth the effort, especially if some of the community's leading citizens were initial sponsors of the agency.

Appearance is not just a personal matter. It extends to the appearance of the agency itself. For many years, and still today in many communities, the health agency has been reconciled to the basement of the courthouse, often in quarters that a sanitarian might condemn for human use were it not a governmental program. The problem is complex. The national government and several of the larger state governments have made enlightened, at times even profligate, decisions about buildings and office space. Many states, however, and most local governments do not handle real estate transactions in the same matter-of-fact manner as they do other expenditures. The acquisition and construction of office space, as well as its location and interior and exterior design, are often highly politicized processes. Building design and construction are areas in which patronage still operates and it is important to recognize the competition that exists for such contracts. The temptation to purchase cheap property that is of no use to anyone else is great, but marketing concepts of service distribution are too important to abandon just to avoid competition for a more useful or attractive site. Although the investment is relatively trivial as part of the continuing cost of most public health programs, an unwise decision about location or design can exact a heavy toll. Concern and hesitancy may be the residue of an era when real estate manipulation was a more common source of corruption in local government. It is not only difficult for government at the local level to make sensible decisions about the location and design of buildings but it is also difficult for elected officials to furnish and equip such buildings in the manner they would choose for their businesses. Whatever the causes, too many public agencies have to cope with a work environment that is improperly located and poorly designed. It need not be so. There are many examples of local health departments and clinics that were designed and equipped with both function and cost in mind. Even in these days of high property taxes and interest rates, capital investments for government are probably the least expensive decisions made.

Behavior

Although the first impression of an agency may be visual, its lasting impression has more to do with behavior. The essential ingredient is attitude: the clients of the agency are the reason for its existence. They are neither supplicants nor beneficiaries, but owners. To characterize the difference between good and bad public relations, it is only necessary to compare the customary interaction in an office of the Postal Service (a private corporation, incidentally) to a similar encounter with a good commercial airline. The difference is not innate, but acquired.

Most of the people who contact a health department would rather be doing something else: children come for shots, undertakers come for burial permits, some people come because they have been ordered to, some because they are not healthy, and others because they cannot afford to go elsewhere. There is no justification for making the contact more unpleasant. This begins with the ability to get to the facility, including bus service or parking convenience. Most government agencies reserve proximate parking for employees, often stratified by their rank or tenure, and those with assigned places are usually annoyed by interlopers. The most convenient parking should be reserved for clients, not employees. Parking is one of the most persistent problems in public agencies, primarily because it is treated as an employee perquisite rather than as part of the marketing program.

Every agency needs a first-encounter process, either an information desk or someone near the entrance, who can help guide visitors to the appropriate location and deter idle visitors. A common mistake is to place the most inexperienced person at the information desk, whereas common sense dictates that the most skillful and experienced people should perform that function. Civil service systems unfortunately uphold the former alternative, with pay rates to match. Handling a diversity of inquiries, some curious, some troubled, and a few angry, is difficult work, however, and requires equanimity and a positive attitude toward the rights and needs of the people making the inquiries. Many difficult problems, including psychiatric emergencies, can be solved quickly and simply if the first encounter is with someone who has the experience and knowledge needed to bring the necessary resources into the transaction immediately. Fumbling at this point often makes the problem much more difficult and costly to solve.

Another common mistake is to transfer inquirors from point to point, either on the phone or in person, leaving them with the burden of unraveling the bureaucracy. The reader should recall the airline representative, who has been taught to take each problem through to a full resolution before ending the transaction. Phone callers should be transferred to the correct extension after making sure that there is someone there to handle the inquiry. Visitors should be carefully routed to the correct location, either in person or with well-placed signs. When they get to the correct extension or location, they warrant prompt and courteous attention. Neither the client nor the agency is helped by staff who appear to be involved in last night's party or tomorrow's ball game.

The referral and problem-solving processes highlight the need for continuing orientation of employees and staff development. Many private agencies have effective staff development programs and may be able to help establish similar programs in the public sector if the personnel system does not have the capability to do so. Complaint handling is particularly difficult. The recipient may think the complaint completely unjustified, but careful listening is important. It does little to enhance the agency's reputation to interrupt the complainant before the story has been told and begin to argue about the problem. Many warning signals about program problems are missed by defensive and premature arguments. Nor is it appropriate to become so empathetic as to leave the complainant with the impression that he or she has indeed been treated unfairly and that this is characteristic of the process or the person complained of: the defendant deserves an equally fair hearing before judgment. Skillful and attentive complaint handling may solve the problem at the first encounter or at least make the final resolution of the problem much simpler, whereas inept listening may make the problem worse.

Ability

Appearance and behavior help, but the reputation of the agency must rest on the ability of the staff. As previously noted, the public generally does not associate ability with its agencies, despite evidence to the contrary. Public sector agencies have a number of special problems associated with their mission and their environment, and they have not always been able to pay competitive wages for well-qualified people. Beginning with the development of major new human service programs in the 1930s, the public sector attracted outstanding planners, managers, theoreticians, and support staff, partly because private sector jobs were scarce and partly because of a sense of reformism in government programs. Those workers stayed in government service through World War II and began to retire in the 1960s, but they left a legacy of propriety and performance that has shaped the work of their successors.

During the 1960s and 1970s government jobs were opened up to people with the necessary minimal (as differentiated from maximal) qualification, as part of an overdue social concern about equal employment opportunity and affirmative action. As noted in Chapter 10, the practice of choosing the most highly qualified person from the eligible applicants gave way to choosing from a list of people who met the minimal established requirements for the job. Although civil service systems have been in a state of upheaval ever since, there is no indication that the quality of government work has diminished. In fact, there is substantial evidence that those entering the management, professional, and technical ranks are better trained than ever before.

Program managers and agency directors should continue to insist on quality work and adequate training for public sector employment. Job classification descriptions warrant careful scrutiny to be sure that the skills necessary for increasingly complex work will be available. Competency needs to be rewarded by commendation, through regular personnel evaluations and through attention to the reputation of the staff as it is portrayed to the community through the news media. Inadequate work requires the same attention, through training, reassignment, demotion, or discharge when all else fails. The best safeguard of ability is diligence in recruitment and hiring and insistence on employee development as the principal objective of the personnel office.

Private lives

Public employees, particularly those in visible and executive positions, do not have completely private lives away from work: their behavior is always associated with their public position. As with public school teachers, double standards may be applied, with the community less tolerant of behavior by its officials than it would be of other neighbors in the private sector. Staff who participate in wild parties on the weekend can expect to be challenged, even though others in the community may engage in the same activities. There is little point in complaining about such double standards: they are a fact of life and one of the conditions of public employment. Tolerance for atypical lifestyles follows a bell-shaped curve, with those who share the atypicality in one tail, those opposed in the other, and most people, who are indifferent, in the middle. Those opposed, whether in the "left" or the "right" tail, are often vociferous in their objections to atypicality. The tendency of the people in the middle is to be more tolerant of the objections of the right than of the left, which results in not-so-subtle pressures to adopt a more conservative life-style.

In addition to this general caveat, public sector employees have other private lives in the social organizations of the community. Even people who are not inclined to join organizations need to make some sacrifices for their programs. If the Rotary Club is the leading service group in town, the director ought to consider joining. The chief medical officer of the public health agency needs to belong to the local and state medical associations even if he or she does not join the American Medical Association, since the physicians of the community will consider not joining an affront. No employee should be urged to join an organization if he or she cannot afford it or is opposed to the organization's purpose or process, but program managers and executive officers especially should be supported in their participation in community organizations as part of the agency's overall marketing effort: that is why many of the other members of those organizations are there. Prudence is required to avoid joining the wrong group as it is in making the wrong friends, especially for newcomers. It is especially important to avoid joining an organization that continues to practice racial, ethnic, or religious segregation, since that would compromise the very purpose of public health.

Residency is a sensitive issue, especially in major cities of the United States where "white flight" has resulted in a black inner city surrounded by white suburbs. Some states allow such jurisdictions to restrict employment to city residents, and the courts have been inconsistent in reviewing such restrictions. There are many reasons that justifiably enter into the selection of a family residence, but professional, technical, and senior management personnel can expect to continue to feel uneasy if they live outside the community that employs them. Research in recent years has reinforced what should not have been forgotten: the cop on the beat, the neighborhood school teacher, the local family practitioner, the visiting nurse, and the sanitarian can be far more effective when they are part of the community in which they work.

One final note about private lives: it is difficult for a public official to separate private gifts from public ones. Needless to say, employees should never accept gratuities, gifts, or favors of any value from clients or people whose lives or businesses are regulated in part by the health department. Some gifts may appear to be private expressions of gratitude, but employees should be taught to say, "No, thank you" politely and to point out that while no offense is felt and surely not intended, agency policy forbids the acceptance of gifts. Some gifts are more overt in their intentions, such as persistent attempts by a state milk producers association to entertain a health officer. It sometimes takes great ingenuity to avoid a gift.

Training

Much of what has been said is in the domain of common sense and good manners, but it is easy to overlook the development of bad public relations. As simple as it may sound, there is a great deal to be gained not only from regular orientation sessions for new employees, but from in-service training programs in telephone answering, correspondence management, complaint handling, and reception techniques. It may be possible to use some particularly competent employees for some of the training programs, and other agencies, including private industry, are often willing to help. While it is difficult to arrange, it is useful to obtain the participation of the managers of the agency in similar training exercises—they too can forget.

THE MARKETING PROCESS

The marketing process depends on the ability of the organization to manage the four "Ps" of McCarthy[1]: product, price, place, and promotion. Without alliteration this translates to the ability to develop an acceptable service, the ability to offer it at a cost (in time, money, or effort) that will encourage those in need to make the necessary voluntary exchange, the ability to make the service accessible to those who need it (thereby reducing the cost), and the ability to inform or even teach the community and particularly the high-risk segments the value of the service. The development and implementation of a marketing plan are very similar to the planning that takes place for a program and should be a part of that process.

The marketing plan begins with the effort to establish realistic marketing goals. The problem could be a simmering epidemic or the fact that Americans have high death rates during their adult years. (Those who make it to age 65 are very durable, but a surprisingly large percentage of those who survive childhood never make it to retirement.) The goal may be to eliminate indigenous measles or to reduce the death rate between the ages of 17 and 64 by 15%.

Analysis of the goal may reveal a number of constraints, problems, and opportunities. For example, the number of cases of measles may have increased because immunization levels in schoolchildren have declined below 85% (ascertained through a survey of school records, which is a form of market research). The problems are information (not enough of the parents, teachers, or even pediatricians are aware of the severity of measles or the efficacy of the vaccine) and "cost" (it is difficult to get to the county health department offices during the one afternoon each week that immunizations are available, and a private office visit is too expensive compared to the benefits the parent expects to obtain). Even though many people are not impressed by the seriousness of measles, that is not as important as access to a convenient source for the service, given the propensity of people to comply with school entrance requirements. Therefore, more effort should be expended on distribution than on technical information. In the case of death rates in the 17- to 64-year age group, the difference between the U.S. experience and that of comparison countries in Western Europe is almost entirely because of violence and injuries, principally automobile crashes: speed and power are part of the advertising message for cars; drunk driving is far more common than most people realize; automobile safety is still poor; and very few people use seat belts. All of the known contributing factors need to be analyzed to determine their severity and frequency.

Once the factors have been identified and classified in terms of their overall importance, the various methods that might be used to modify their impact on the problem can be explored, and those most likely to have the biggest impact for the least investment per person can be selected. Simple changes may be attractive because of their simplicity, but if they are known to have little effect on the problem, resources should not be wasted on them. For example, a billboard campaign against drinking and driving may appear attractive, particularly if donated, but may accomplish very little and may even distract effort.

The techniques of change involve persuasion, legal controls, the use of technology, and economic strategies.[4] Most complex problems cannot be solved using only one technique. In the case of seat belts, persuasion through advertising has had very little impact. Legal intervention to require the installation of seat belts on passenger cars has resulted in use by only about 15% of drivers and still fewer passengers. The use of technology and law to require warning buzzers or the installation of passive restraints such as airbags has been postponed or blocked by American car manufacturers on the basis that foreign car makers would have a relative price advantage if new technology were required. Economic tactics have not been used yet but might involve a sizable copayment for insurance claims in accidents in which the participants were not wearing seat belts. Surveys (market research) have indicated that a majority of citizens would not object to laws that required the wearing of seat belts. It is likely that a careful combination of several techniques together with well-designed information campaigns could result in a substantial increase in seat belt use and a reduction in motor vehicle death rates. An example of a multifaceted approach was reported by McLoughlin and her associates.[12] They found that burns in childhood were a serious problem but that educative messages alone were ineffective. She advocated product modification and environmental redesign in a more comprehensive effort to deal with a serious problem.

As in program planning, the next step in marketing planning is implementation. Efforts to achieve water fluoridation are excellent examples of implementation and indicate the kinds of communities in which the effort may be successful[13] and the reason for failure that may have some educational benefits for the agency.[14] In New Mexico, officials were concerned by what appeared to be overuse and misuse of rabies vaccine, which created certain risks for the victims and cost problems for the state health department. A thorough problem analysis verified the existence of the problem and the factors that maintained it, including ignorance by practicing physicians, lack of effective and prompt consultation, difficulty in obtaining rapid laboratory reports, and inadequate product information about the human cell vaccine. The marketing program was designed to cope with all of the problems, and included an effective public relations effort with the state and county medical societies. Misuse of the vaccine declined dramatically.[15]

The feedback loop is just as important as in any other planning process. Manufacturers need timely information about their marketing objectives. Pretesting can provide valuable information before a program is begun, but with well-thought-out objectives and an information plan that is built into the implementation and management of the marketing program, the validity of the plan can be monitored and the effort modified quickly even after it has started. Expensive surveys are not always necessary: client response forms can provide useful information about the service, as can skilled community workers. An effort to reach deep into a Mexican-American ghetto that had been the source of several outbreaks of tuberculosis among school children was jeopardized by a raid by the Immigration and Naturalization Service. Community residents felt they had been betrayed by the public health nurses whom they had assisted in their efforts to trace contacts. The bicultural, bilingual community workers identified the problem promptly, and a few meetings in the homes of community leaders quickly reestablished the integrity of the public health nurses.

The ability to change a plan based on feedback is an important attribute and presents some difficult problems for government agencies. Occasionally, a government objective expressed in a statute may be considerably out of date yet the agency may either mechanically continue performing the duty or be forced to do so by a community that does not understand the changing nature of prevention. A few health departments still require routine venereal disease tests for restaurant employees, and their communities are often surprised when told that it is a waste of time. An agency ought to routinely evaluate its services or products to be sure that they are still needed. Many laboratory services were introduced in an effort to market improvements in disease prevention such as rapid streptococcal testing. With the advent of easily managed office techniques and the proliferation of private laboratories, the agency may find that its resources can be better used in other efforts.

Government objectives are not always immutable: at times they are remarkably ephemeral. In the 1960s many states passed laws authorizing and directing the health department to engage in expensive multiphasic testing programs, including the use of mobile vans. They fell into disfavor shortly thereafter, partly because those who had evaluated the programs found that they were of little use in preventing morbidity or reducing mortality, but many departments were still operating the units in the late 1970s. One mayor or governor may make a major issue out of alcoholism or child abuse only to be followed by a successor who is far more concerned about roads and industrial development. Yesterday's problem of lead in the drinking water may be replaced by tomorrow's concern about radon in housing or next week's headlines about another strange virus.

The environment can change quickly, leaving the agency with last year's organization and still older technology. Sometimes the change in the political environment occurs without regard to the importance or the continuation of the problem, and the agency needs to persist in its efforts, often with a different marketing strategy. If the need is not there or has been met, the program can be changed or discontinued, but if it persists, the marketing program has to be changed to fit the altered circumstances.

Products, services, and programs are conceived and born, grow to maturity, become old, and often die. Marketing plans must change as the product life cycle changes. One hospital marketer has developed a thoughtful plan for managing the delivery of medical care to the medically indigent.[16] She felt it was important, because (1) the hospital wanted to maintain its not-for-profit status; (2) it needed public sector support from time to time to obtain a certificate of need for new construction programs; (3) it needed to keep the support and interest of local employers; (4) the public expects hospitals to help solve the problem; *and* (5) the medically indigent may be covered by some form of insurance in the future and thus become a new and profitable market segment.

As noted at the outset, ethical concerns are close to the surface of any public health marketing effort. Just how far can and should government go in trying to modify human behavior? The arguments over motorcycle helmets and seat belts have centered around individual responsibility, as have the arguments by legislators from tobacco-producing states. They argue that people have the facts and have the right to make up their own minds about their own lives. Dan Beauchamp[17] argues to the contrary that the justice of the marketplace is not appropriate for most prevention efforts, that the goal of public health is to prevent hazards, not just to change behavior. Not wearing a seat belt is a fairly safe practice for most individuals, since the probability of an accident for that individual is very small. Nonetheless some people will be hurt, and some of that damage will result in a public tax burden of considerable magnitude. Is that a sufficient justification for intervention? Probably not in the American culture. Yet, since each individual action of nonuse may be rational in view of the probability of an accident, even though many people will be hurt or killed, and since each such loss diminishes the community in some way, the majority of the people who will not be hurt have an ethical obligation to reduce the probability that anyone will be hurt. This obligation can be fulfilled by developing and implementing a multifaceted marketing program to urge or even to require the use of seat belts and safety devices.

THE MEDIA

Good relationships with the press (newspapers, television, and radio) are an essential part of any marketing effort. Just as in other personal relationships, attitude is the key to good or bad media relationships. Many people regard the press with suspicion if not with outright hostility. Occasionally it is warranted. Some publishers and editors are every bit as capable of using the resources available to them to force their biases on the public as are some public health officials. More often than not, however, poor relationships are caused by a lack of understanding of the purposes and the problems of the news media. Most reporters are bright, well meaning, and literate. They have deadlines and an obligation to explore all sides of an issue, not just one side. They respond to candor, honesty, and courtesy with the same delight that others do.

Health agency directors and program managers may find certain reporters who are more favorable to their cause than others, but it is important to assure that all interested members of the press have equal access to public officials and to the information needed to write their stories. A new director should take the time to go to the offices of the community's papers and radio and television stations to meet the managers or editors and get to know something about their deadlines and any special interests they may have. Such contacts should be renewed periodically. The weekly newspapers that serve suburban and rural areas are an important part of that marketing effort, since they are a major source of local news for many people. In some communities foreign language newspapers have an important role to play and may be instrumental in reaching certain high-risk groups with public health programs.

It is quite appropriate for the health agency director to suggest an editorial conference to deal with major issues in the community. The agency or program director may meet with the editor and key reporters to describe the entire issue as the health department understands it and then respond to questions. Some questions may appear to be skeptical yet require a thoughtful response, since skepticism is an essential technique in developing valid opinions about any major issue.

Most health departments have a policy, sometimes written and sometimes much less formal, about who is expected to talk to the press. It is important to avoid the impression that employees have been instructed not to talk to the press, yet it is equally important to demonstrate to the staff of any health agency that they must be sure of the facts and avoid speculating about rumors or gossip when talking to the press. Usually people who are not qualified to discuss an issue will refer the reporter to someone who is. Occasionally an employee will attempt to use the press to discredit a program or an individual. This sort of behavior should not be condoned but may be very difficult to correct. Reporters have old friends or "sources," and it is difficult to locate them and intervene in the relationship without appearing to be repressive. There is no easy answer to the vindictive employee who may attempt to use the press in this manner except for an open and honest portrayal of the facts to other members of the press, including the editors and managers.

The health agency director's schedule is usually crowded, but the press have special needs for prompt access if that is at all possible. They have an important public information function to fulfill, and it is enmeshed in deadlines. It is always appropriate to ask if the matter can be postponed, but if it cannot be, every effort should be made to find someone who can respond to the inquiry. Some stories may involve patients or other clients. Health officials have to be particularly careful about confidentiality: when in doubt, the health agency director should refuse to disclose the identity of any private citizen who may be involved in a public health problem until the matter can be discussed with the attorney for the agency.

Many people make the mistake of worrying about each error made by a reporter and sometimes insist on corrections of unimportant details. An official who may have been lauded one day may find a critical editorial the next about another matter. A thin skin is a liability in the public sector. News information should be reviewed in its totality and over time. Errors that are important should be corrected politely, but if the article or broadcast is generally accurate and does a reasonable job of informing the public, minor inaccuracies, personal criticisms, and matters of interpretation should be ignored.

Local radio and television stations often have feature stories that involve half-hour interviews or panel discussions. They can be important opportunities, but it is well to remember that such offerings are not aired during prime time. The audience is usually small and does not contain the high-risk target group of the agency. A panel discussion about alcoholism will not capture the attention of active alcoholics, but it may attract family members, and the session should be seen as a marketing effort targeted to a special segment of the public.

SUMMARY

Marketing techniques are not readily transferable from the private sector, where they were developed, to the public sector. The political nature of public health programs and the need to reach the most difficult segment of the public present some special problems. However, the basic concepts are still valid. Health care marketing is a comprehensive program involving the product or service, its cost, its distribution, and the education of the public to influence voluntary exchange transactions that will result in the prevention of disease and the promotion of health.

A successful marketing program in the public sector requires skillful planning, careful attention to community attitudes and sensitivities, a thoughtful exploration of ethical issues, prudent balance between a campaign that is too zealous and one that is ineffective, constant feedback and concern, and consistency both in purpose and image in a complex, multifaceted organization with a diverse product line.

REFERENCES

1. McCarthy EJ: Basic marketing: a managerial approach, ed 6, Homewood, IL, 1978, Richard D Irwin, Inc.
2. Manoff RK: Social marketing: new imperative for public health, Westport, CT, 1985, Praeger Publishers Division of Greenwood Press, Inc.
3. Kotler P and Zaltman G: Social marketing: an approach to planned social change, J Marketing 35:3, July 1971.
4. Kotler P: Marketing for non-profit organizations, ed 2, Englewood Cliffs NJ, 1982, Prentice-Hall, Inc.
5. Cooper PD, Jones KM, and Wong JK: An annotated and extended bibliography of health care marketing, Chicago, 1984, American Marketing Association.
6. Frederiksen LW, Solomon LJ, and Brehony KA: Marketing health behavior: principles, techniques and applications, New York, 1984, Plenum Press, Inc.
7. Kotler P and Clarke RN: Marketing for health care organizations, Englewood Cliffs, NJ, 1987, Prentice-Hall, Inc.
8. Hirschman AO: Exit, voice and loyalty: further reflections and a survey of recent contributions, Milbank Q 58:430, Summer 1980.
9. Alexander K and McCullough J: Application of marketing principles to improve participation in public health programs, J Community Health 6:216, Spring 1981.
10. Miaoulis G: Benefit segmentation for health promotion. Proceedings of Advances in Health Care Research, Association for Consumer Research, Snowbird UT, April 1982.
11. Selame E: The coming collision of health care marketing. In Cooper PD, editor: Responding to the challenge: health care marketing comes of age, Chicago, 1986, American Marketing Association.
12. McLoughlin E and others: Project burn prevention: outcome and implications, Am J Public Health 72:241, March 1982.
13. Smith RA: Community structural characteristics and the adoption of fluoridation, Am J Public Health 71:24, January 1981.
14. Dolinsky HB and others: A health systems agency and a fluoridation campaign, J Health Policy 2:158, June 1981.
15. Mann JM, Burkhart MJ, and Rollag OJ: Antirabies treatments in New Mexico, Am J Public Health 70:728, February 1980.
16. Kinney CF: Marketing principles applied to indigent care: an innovative and effective perspective. In Effective leadership in action: health care's focus on accountability, Chicago, 1987, American Marketing Association.
17. Beauchamp D: Public health as social justice, Inquiry 13:3, March 1976.

CHAPTER 13

Public health in other countries

The organization and management of public health in the United States have been described in several of the preceding chapters. The U.S. "model" is not necessarily the best way to get things done. Other countries, facing some of the same problems, have devised different approaches to fulfilling the obligations of the governmental presence in health, and other countries—many other countries—have some very different problems. Before discussing specific public health program areas in the United States, it will be useful to pause briefly to consider some of the common and uncommon features of public health in other countries.

This will be a short chapter. There is considerable, justifiable criticism of public health and medical care professionals in the United States because of their insularity. Canada, a country with which the United States has an extensive and uniquely friendly relationship, does things differently. Many think the Canadian organization of medical care services is superior to that in the United States. Given the similarities in geography, economy, and political structure (both use federal forms of government) it is odd that students of public health in the United States know so little about Canada. This chapter will not, unfortunately, correct that problem. Its purpose is only to indicate the existence of both commonalities and differences in public health throughout the world and to describe some of the emerging concepts of organization, management, and health sector financing that are developing on the world scene.

Much of the work done in comparative analyses of health care systems concentrates on the organization and financing of medical care services. Medical care system comparisons are complex and will not be dealt with specifically in this chapter. For those who are interested, there are many books dealing with the health care systems of individual countries. Three books that deal with comparative health care systems are Raffel's *Comparative Health Systems*,[1] Roemer's *National Strategies for Health Care Organization*,[2] and his earlier work, *Health Care Systems in World Perspective*.[3] Comparative analyses of what is referred to as public health in the United States are not to be found.

TRENDS AND ISSUES

In 1978 the International Conference on Primary Health Care, meeting in Alma-Ata, USSR, declared:

> Governments have a responsibility for the health of their people which can be fulfilled only by the provision of adequate health and social measures. A main social target of governments, international organizations and the whole world community in the coming decades should be the attainment by all peoples of the world by the year 2000 of a level of health that will permit them to lead a socially and economically productive life.[4]

Health for all by the year 2000 became the official policy of the World Health Organization (WHO). The Alma-Ata conference determined that primary health care was "the key to attaining this target as part of development in the spirit of social justice." (See Chapter 4 for a discussion of primary care as the term is used in WHO parlance.) With that ambitious goal in mind, a number of global trends and issues warrant attention.

The epidemiologic revolution

In 1982 Milton Terris[5] described the second epidemiologic revolution. The first was the conquest of communicable diseases. The second, according to Dr. Terris, is the conquest of chronic diseases. The eras can be subdivided. The long era of communicable diseases had many turning points: improved nutrition, the industrial revolution and urban crowding, the rise of modern sanitation, the biologic revolution of the midnineteenth century, and the advent of the antibiotic era in the midtwentieth century.

The decline in the prevalence of communicable diseases unmasked the underlying pathology of the chronic diseases: cardiovascular diseases, cancer, neurologic and metabolic disorders. At first it was felt that such diseases could be prevented by the application of screening techniques and early intervention. In more recent years, life-style issues have received increasing attention, and still more recently, the modern environment has been reexamined as an important factor in the production of disability and dependency. Less attention has been paid to the social environment, unfortunately, with governments and health professionals shifting the burden of prevention from their organizations to individuals. Then, much to the surprise of many who had thought the era of infectious diseases was past history, at least for those who lived in industrialized nations, Legionnaires disease, Lyme disease, toxic shock syndrome, AIDS, and Reye's syndrome were discovered, new and complex diseases that are the result of interactions between microorganisms and behavioral and environmental phenomena largely created by societal forces.

As stated earlier, the United States and other industrialized nations have had the advantage of dealing with these eras sequentially and with considerable success. The developing nations of the world, however, are faced with a concurrence of epidemics. They are still mired in a wormy world[6] (see Chapter 4). Massive immunization efforts and water sanitation programs are beginning to reduce infant and child mortality rates slowly, but the population burden of parasitic diseases absorbs an enormous proportion of the total caloric production of many countries and the energy of their people. At the same time, cigarette manufacturers have seized on the third-world market as their last major opportunity, and increased urbanization of rural dwellers with inadequate housing, nutrition, and job opportunities is producing a heavy burden of chronic illness. Environmental pollution in cities more concerned about economic development than public health adds to the problem. The combination of environmental, biologic, behavioral, and organizational factors generates more problems: suicide, homicide, infanticide, starvation, cancer, cardiovascular disease, chronic respiratory disease, diabetes, cirrhosis, blindness, and a rising toll of injuries. Nations with the least resources are facing this coalescence of epidemics and hardly know where to begin to intervene. The industrialized and developed nations are finding that they too are facing concurrent eras with new twists.

The maldistribution of resources

In all countries, the geographic distribution of resources presents persistent problems. Hospital beds, technology, and the bulk of the work force are concentrated in a few urban areas. Those who have not yet migrated into those areas are faced with severe and worsening health problems. Table 13-1 shows the location of hospital beds and health centers in Peru in 1980. Nearly 32% of the population is in Lima, but 37% of the hospitals with 53% of the beds are located there. The small, primary care health centers are located predominantly outside of the Lima area.

Similar accounts are not available for health professionals, but they tend to concentrate in areas

TABLE 13-1 The distribution of hospital beds and health centers in Peru, 1980

	Total	Lima	% Lima
Population (millions)	19	6	31.6
Hospitals	329	120	36.5
Hospital beds	33,704	17,810	52.8
Ministry of health	17,559	8,480	48.3
Social Security system	5,408	2,679	49.5
Military system	3,308	2,746	83.0
Private	6,400	3,796	59.3
Health centers	593	160	27.0
Ministry of health	425	122	28.7
Social Security system	81	17	21.0

From Ministry of Health Planning Documents.

with hospital facilities, producing a severe maldistribution of resources. Several countries have attempted to correct the imbalance, using either command or structural rules. Command rules dictate where a physician can or cannot practice. Structural rules attempt to alter incentives. In Great Britain, general practitioners are free to practice in London if they wish, but under the structural rules of the National Health Service, they can enroll only private patients, and there are very few for new GPs. A good list of patients, and therefore a good income (since income equals the current capitation rate multiplied by those who enlist with the practitioner), can be had in rural and otherwise undersupplied areas. In either case, most practitioners spend the better part of their professional lives attempting to return to the urban environment.

In Cuba, where command regulation is used, all medical school graduates must spend two years in social service, and the assignments are generally in rural areas of the country.[7] China has a similar policy.[1] While many medical school graduates appear to appreciate their rural assignments in Cuba, it is reported that most look forward to returning to Havana as soon as their tour of duty is up.

Similar patterns have been observed in Peru and in other countries. Assignments to rural outposts go to the newest recruits, where they are often mentored by older, poorly trained practitioners. Success and promotion involve a return movement to the urban centers and the hospital environment. Command regulations tend to be more effective than structural regulations, but there is some evidence that the practice patterns that emerge are wasteful. New young professionals are left to run the poorly equipped and crowded health posts, while their senior colleagues skim off those in the community who can afford to pay a private fee, often practicing out of their own homes. All too often, the new recruits reduce the time and quality of their work in the public clinics in favor of private practice.

Rising costs

The United States spends more of its total wealth on medical care than any other country and has struggled to bring rising costs under control since 1966, but it is not alone: all countries are faced with rising medical care costs, rising prices, a seemingly insatiable demand, and increasing competition for scarce resources. The World Health Organization reports that countries with low- and middle-income economies have reduced the proportion of their national budget allocated to the health sector. This diminution, coupled with inflation and rapid population growth, may lead to a rapid deterioration in health status. Many think this has already occurred. In the more developed economies, allocations to the health sector have been increasing, with rising costs and prices which increase apprehension about the ability of such economies to continue to expand.[8]

The problem does not occur simply in laissez-faire or market-oriented economies. Some socialist countries have made a policy choice to support an expensive health sector, and some capitalist nations, while concerned about the cost problem, have kept the proportion of their gross national product that is consumed by the health care system more modest than is the case of the United States. The problems are a function partly of conscious policy choices and partly of per capita wealth and the evolution of professional power.

Financing the health sector

Countries vary in the way they mix different sources of revenue to pay for health services. Information is not available that would allow an accurate international comparison to be made. Roemer has described a health sector financing model that reflects his own heuristic notions of a mix of sources.[2] It has an implicit validity based on work in several countries and is presented as a reasonable approximation of reality in Table 13-2. Roemer has used a total of $20 billion in his scheme and suggests that about 21% of the total comes from family resources, 3% from charity, 15% from voluntary insurance, 2% from industry (from a few industrial health plans for employees), 27% from social insurance (Social Security), 32% from general tax revenues, and 2% from foreign aid. The distribution would vary from country to country. His scheme indicates that 80% of the total is spent on medical care and about 4% for public health, a higher amount than is allocated to public health in the United States.

Voluntary insurance is highly variable, but personal or out-of-pocket expenditures pay for a substantial amount of medical care in all countries. Private practice exists even in China and Cuba, and unofficial or black market private practices flourish even in socialist countries, often with a heavy reliance on folk healers.

In the United States most of the money spent on the health sector comes from family resources and private insurance, but even here collectivization of financing has expanded rapidly since 1928, when the first hospital insurance programs were launched. More recently, there has been an increase in the socialization of financing mechanisms, with rapid growth in the Medicare and Medicaid programs. Moreover, most employees in the United States are covered by some form of "voluntary" or private health insurance and these expenditures are tantamount to government expenditures. Businesses are increasingly obliged to provide such benefits for their employees, and the payments are tax-deductible business expenses. Moreover, virtually all public sector employees, a substantial proportion of the total work force, are covered by health insurance plans, and the premium costs of those plans are paid for with tax dollars. (While this picture is generally accurate, an increasing number of people in the United States have no health insurance at all, a topic that is discussed in more detail in Chapter 31.)

Collectivization and socializaton of the financing sources for the health sector are global themes. Although variable, they are present in all countries, since governments have recognized the necessity to assure access to needed health services for all citizens and the increasingly difficult problem that presents due to rising costs. Health services and medical care have real value. As medical care prices have risen faster than real wages, a growing proportion of people are unable to pay for needed services. When society determines that certain services, such as education and health care, are essential but too costly to leave to private market forces, use of the services is gradually reclassified from a privilege to a right. Having done this, however, governments must then cope with the rising costs. In some countries, such as the United States, the attempt has been made to solve the access problem by providing some of the poor with increased buying power under the assumption that market forces will respond to demand and solve the problem. In other countries, command rules have been used to organize and allocate resources. In all countries the dilemma has become increasingly difficult and, for the poorest countries, cruel. The World Health Organization has adopted a managerial posture in the face of this growing problem, urging that improved management be used to make better use of shrinking resources. The Director General has stated the belief that "structural adjustments" and the passage of authority to local officials will increase efficiency.[8] While that may be a weak response to a strong problem, it is the only politically acceptable position available to WHO.

TABLE 13-2 Financing the health sector (in millions of dollars)

	Purpose						
Source	**Medical care**	**Public health**	**Resource production**	**Research**	**Regulation and planning**	**Total**	**Percent**
Personal	$ 4,100					$ 4,100	20.5
Charity	$ 100		$ 300	$100		$ 500	2.5
Private insurance	$ 3,000					$ 3,000	15
Industry	$ 100	$100		$100		$ 300	1.5
Social insurance	$ 5,200	$100			$100	$ 5,400	27
Tax revenue	$ 4,000	$600	$ 700	$700	$400	$ 6,400	32
Foreign aid	$ 100		$ 200			$ 300	1.5
TOTALS	$16,600	$800	$1,200	$900	$500	$20,000	
PERCENT	83	4	6	4.5	2.5		

Reprinted from Roemer MI: National strategies for health care organization: a world overview, Ann Arbor, MI, 1985, Health Administration Press, with permission of the publisher.

Resource production

Surprisingly, most countries have increased their production of trained health workers, so much so that an oversupply problem is now of concern in many nations, since the volume of services delivered seems to depend as much on the supply of service providers as it does on the health needs of a community. Following the Cuban revolution in 1959, over half of the physicians fled the country, presumably because they anticipated a change to a government controlled and salaried versus fee-for-service system. To reduce the exodus, the new government established higher salary schedules than might otherwise have been acceptable and offered special privileges to those who remained. Medical schools were expanded. By 1971, 30% of university students were studying medicine, and the total number of physicians in practice soon exceeded the number in prerevolutionary Cuba.[7]

While many countries have a severe shortage (see Chapter 4), geographic distribution is now the main problem, along with specialization (see below).

Other resources are more difficult to obtain. In many countries the production of pharmaceutical supplies and medical equipment is especially difficult. Patents and complex technology make it difficult for many third world nations to obtain an adequate supply of basic medications. Import-export policies that are intended to increase domestic production and produce a favorable trade balance, coupled with inflation, make it difficult for ministries of health and other parts of the health sector to obtain desired and needed materials. At the national level, government policymakers are faced with the dilemma of allocating resources to economic development or such programs as health and education. Economic development often wins.

Foreign aid has been a major contributor to resource development, both of a skilled work force and of pharmaceutical supplies and equipment, but such aid has not been an unmixed blessing. The health professionals are often trained in Western, high-technology medicine and imbued with income expectations more relevant to the United States than their own countries. The Rockefeller Foundation made major investments in the development of medical training programs in many countries, but the training was provided by Western physicians, using Western models of care and organization, including specialization of the work force and its reliance on technology that is rarely available outside of a few medical centers.

An imbalance in health care resource production is a characteristic of many countries, but the oversupply of physicians and the limited availability of essential supplies, including vaccines, is a major problem for the third world especially.

The role of professionals

Traditionally, physicians have determined the supply and nature of health care services. As private practice developed and medical knowledge expanded, a growing proportion of medical practitioners specialized in narrower areas of interest. The areas in which specialization occurs are related to the income potential in those specialties. Lacking forceful social planning and policy formation, the production of specialized physicians is determined largely by market forces, which bear little relationship to the health care needs of the community.

Specialization is a ubiquitous and pervasive problem. Teachers specialize. Lawyers specialize. Accountants specialize. Builders specialize. Public health workers specialize. As the universe of what is known about the law or accounting or building or medicine expands, the only way to maintain control, and therefore power, is to more tightly constrain the sample of that universe that will be studied and practiced. Moreover, society rewards specialization more than generalization.

Referring to Cuba again, new graduates who may accept their rural social service assignment with enthusiasm appear equally enthusiastic about returning to Havana and specialty training.[7] In England, GPs often earn more than specialists, who are for the most part salaried employees of the National Health Service, but when a specialist position opens in one of the hospitals, eligible practitioners from throughout the country apply for the post and consider a rejection as professional failure. In some countries, it is not uncommon to see the brass plate on physicians' office doors "Dr. ———, RCP (Failed)," indicating that they took the examination for the Royal College of Physicians but failed: simply being qualified to take the specialty exam is considered by some to be a mark of distinction.

The decline of humanism

It may seem unkind to observe that medical care has lost some of its humanistic flavor, but it is an inevitable consequence of the other worldwide trends described. As the knowledge base expands and technology becomes richer and more complex, specialization is inevitable. And a characteristic of specialists is that they obtain their gratification from their peers, not their clients.

A general practitioner in a small town is well known to most of the local citizens. If two or three people meet in the hardware store or at a social gathering, they can compare notes about their physician: the recent car purchase, the treatment of a mutual friend, drinking habits, or domestic affairs. As consumers, they are evaluating their physician. Orthopedic surgeons, however, subspecialize. Some deal with legs, others with backs, and some with arms and hands. There is little chance that a grocery shopper who has had a hand operation will run into another shopper who has seen the same physician. Recognition for skillful surgery comes not from satisfied (or dissatisfied) patients but from fellow specialists at the annual meeting of those who also prefer hands to legs or backs. There the latest techniques can be demonstrated and results discussed.

In other words, surgeons, just like lawyers or dentists or teachers of junior-high-school math, obtain their support and recognition from their peers, not their clients, who may be seen just as a hand or a root canal or a dyslexia problem. In most such encounters, the patient does not even pay the bill. Surely it is an expression of logic, not just a prejudice, to assert that humanism will be eroded in such a system.

Regionalization

The health sector (a term that is defined and discussed below) is increasingly regionalized. A regional system is one in which there is a sophisticated, fully equipped medical complex at the hub or center (a tertiary care center or the central office of the health department), a surrounding cluster of affiliated hospitals or health centers located in smaller towns (the secondary medical care component of the system), and around each secondary center a cluster of clinics or health "posts" that provide first-level, or primary, care.

In a regionalized system of care, most health problems are solved at the primary entry point. Those requiring more sophisticated technology and training are referred to the secondary system, and a few—very few—are referred on to the tertiary care level. The concept has been widely discussed in the United States as a way to organize a perinatal care system. In the United States, it is a revolutionary way of providing medical care, however. First of all, it depends on centralized planning of a complete system of care: hospitals, physicians, social workers, nutritionists, nursing personnel, transportation, communications, medical records, and billing procedures. This sort of system integration and coordination is not only rare in the United States, it has been officially condemned by organized medicine for years as an attempt to destroy the autonomy of the physician.

A regionalized system of care, no matter how logical it appears, requires a substantial change in the way medical care is practiced in the United States. The concept is much more common and much better accepted in countries that have a tradition of government involvement in the health sector. Practitioners at the primary care level (physicians or, in many countries, a more basic level of practitioner) must be able to communicate with the higher level care centers and to refer patients to them without either (1) risking the loss of their patient and thus some income, if they are practicing in a fee-for-service system, and (2) over-referring problems to the secondary level as a way to reduce the amount of work required of them, if they are working for a salary. Physicians at the secondary and tertiary levels must, in turn, return the problem or the patient to the primary care center together with the necessary information to continue to manage the situation. This is unlikely in a traditional practice setting in the United States.

Most countries of the world now have some form of regionalized public health and medical care system.[1] In China the rural system is based on counties *(hsien),* which are further broken down into communes and brigades. "Barefoot doctors" (known as *feldsher* in Russia, and somewhat similar to general nurse practitioners and physician assistants in the United States) are assigned by a formula to production teams and they staff the health stations. Complex problems are referred upward to the commune clinics, which are staffed with physicians. In urban areas, the components are referred to as lane health stations, street health stations, district hospitals, and municipal or specialized hospitals. The official and operative health policy of China is to place prevention ahead of therapeutic care and to concentrate on the rural areas. Belgium, a hereditary, representative, and constitutional monarchy, provides for a health officer in each of nine provinces who directs the public health activities of the community and provides staff support to the provincial medical council, which oversees the provision of medical care. The national and provincial authorities do not provide many direct services, leaving those to the municipalities. Denmark stratifies health services more formally into primary, secondary, and tertiary care systems, with the county councils responsible for hospitals and curative care and the municipalities left to deal with nursing, the aged and disabled, and most public health functions.

Regionalized health systems can be centralized or decentralized in their control. The use of regions or districts only indicates where a function is carried out—responsibility. Centralization and decentralization are concerned with the location of power. Most regionalized systems are centralized for planning purposes and control, but there are ways of decentralizing some of the authority needed to carry out policy. For example, a regional hospital council may be given a general budget for hospital services, leaving it with the problem of allocation within the region. It may have to close one hospital in order to improve or expand another. While regionalization of health systems has been a worldwide trend, decentralization of power varies widely and is less common.[9]

The Alma-Ata declaration included the notion that the community would exercise a substantial amount of control over its health system. The notion is based on the belief that the professions that provide services are neither well motivated nor equipped to allocate resources equitably—that is, in proportion to the needs of communities. However, due to the devastating increase in costs, most national governments have tightened their control over regionalized systems. Interestingly, it is the medical care components of such systems that are held most tightly under central control. Public health responsibilities are often left to the local officials, as is true in the United States. It seems likely that this difference is due to the higher cost of the therapeutic system (80% of total health sector investments—see Table 13-2), but it is becoming increasingly apparent that public health programs involving immunizations, developing a safe water supply, and the behavioral and environmental aspects of chronic diseases will be of growing importance in all countries. In some nations of Africa, the AIDS epidemic is the most serious economic threat to the government, as well as the most serious health threat, and lacking an effective therapeutic tool, public health measures are of growing importance.

It seems likely that the balance of power in regionalized systems will fluctuate in the years ahead with a growing tendency to concentrate planning, policy formation, and economic control centrally. Finding the best balance of power to strengthen the acceptability and effectiveness of programs at the local level is an important task. It has as much to do with understanding the nature of the political context in which regionalization occurs as with the professional and technical training of the managers.

Government regulation

The use of command and structural rules to shape the workings of the health sector has been discussed above. Roemer[2] feels that the tendency of governments to use rules has increased. This has been the result of growing pressure by workers in capitalist countries, the inherent commitment of socialist countries, and rising costs in both. Rules govern the training and practice of health workers, the construction of hospitals, the use of pharmaceuticals and equipment, and the utilization of service systems by people. It seems likely that the reliance of the United States on structural rules to regulate the system will give way to more command rules as the stakes grow higher and the failure of the marketplace-restructuring rules becomes more evident.

Population "control" and family planning

A complete discusson of family planning is beyond the scope of this book. The literature has grown exponentially in the past 20 years. All countries are involved in population policies whether they are explicitly labeled as such or not. In some countries, rules are used to prescribe family size directly. In others, structural rules are used to implement government policies, such as increased family allowances in Quebec. Many countries with a severe imbalance of calory production and need have avoided adopting explicit population policies, since the cultural norms of the citizens support high population densities, but apprehension prevails nonetheless. The future of population policy is unclear. Some countries have begun to see population as another form of national competition, while others cannot hope to produce enough food to raise population norms to a subsistence level.

The two critical factors appear to be the general literacy level and the social status of women. Where those two factors improve, fertility rates decline and longevity increases. Where such changes do not occur, little progress can be made and technological interventions often produce unintended consequences or are rejected by the people. The Department of International Economic and Social Affairs of the United Nations has emphasized the importance of maternal education as a determinant of health status in general.[1]

Aging

Health policy in the United States is deeply concerned with the effect of the rapid aging of the population on the health care system and vice versa. The problem is not unique to the United States. Virtually all countries are experiencing rapid growth in their older age cohorts. While infant and childhood mortality rates remain unacceptably high in many places, more people are being born and more are surviving to old age. It is not clear that this is as grave a problem as some contend, at least in developed nations (see Chapter 26), but in less developed countries, the added burden of a large and growing dependent elderly population is severe. While living longer, the elderly in many countries carry with them the scars of their youth, increasing their dependency in urban and rural areas where health and social service resources are meager at best.

THE HEALTH SECTOR

The notion of a "health sector" is not well understood in the United States. Like a sector of an orange, it is a piece of the whole, in this case the activities, both public and private, that constitute a community's health efforts. Its most common manifestation in the United States is the annual attempt to aggregate all of the health expenditures into a single account: the national health account. The total figure is widely quoted in newspapers.* Similar figures are developed in most other countries, but variability in the construction of such estimates makes international comparisons difficult.[11]

In many countries, the health sector is composed of a ministry of health, a social security system, often a military medical care system, and a private medical care system. Related but separate sectors are education, agriculture, and commerce. Education is often responsible for professional schools; agriculture may be the lead agency concerned with human nutrition and rural water supplies; and commerce is usually concerned with the production of nonhuman health resources. Only the ministry of health has a broad public health interest, the other components of the health sector being largely concerned with medical care. The sector is often described and spoken of, but coordination and collaboration among its component parts are infrequent.

Ministries of health are usually responsible for health status assessment, health sector planning, the control and prevention of diseases and injuries, many aspects of both rural and urban sanitation, health education of the public, and, except in the United States, medical care of the poor. The social security systems in most other countries are separate entities, often with considerable autonomy. Unlike the Social Security system in the United States, which was developed to provide pensions for retired workers, social security elsewhere developed to provide social insurance, including health insurance, to employed workers and, to some extent, the members of their families. Initiated by Bismarck in Germany in 1883, such systems used employee-employer-based mandatory contributions to a trust fund to pay for medical care, which was usually purchased in the private sector. (See Chapter 31 for a tabular presentation of the development of such systems.) Fairly early in their history, some social security systems decided to build their own hospitals and hire professional staff to produce services directly for their beneficiaries, a pattern that has been followed throughout much of Latin America. Such systems resist collaborative

* The detailed report can usually be found in Health Care Financing Review, the Journal of the Health Care Financing Administration of the U.S. Department of Health and Human Services.

planning with ministries of health. They usually represent a limited number of industrialized workers in urban areas. Their revenues enable them to develop better equipped hospitals and to offer higher pay to health professionals than can be afforded by the ministries of health, which are reliant on general tax revenues. Attempts to open social security systems to the clients of ministries of health, the poor, have been met with much the same resistance that greeted Medicare and Medicaid in the United States in 1966. The beneficiaries of the social security system are apprehensive that the level of their benefits will be diluted by the incursion of large numbers of the poor. They also feel that their system is an earned system in contrast to the ministry of health, which is thought of as a welfare system.

The military system often has still greater status. It is more exclusive, has better equipment than the social security system, and treats its health professionals as officers. Table 13-1 showed the distribution of hospital beds in Peru owned by each component of the health sector. Table 13-3 provides a rough indication of the distribution of the health professions.

It is puzzling that figures were not available for physicians, but it is clear that the 3,400 employed by the ministry of health (out of a total of 13,000 in the public sector) were an inadequate proportion, given estimates of the percentage of the population that is indigent. The social security systems in South America are generally estimated to represent about 17% of the population (the percentage in Peru is somewhat less than that). The military serves an even smaller percentage. The imbalances are obvious. Added to the numerical imbalance is the imbalance in productivity. While no reliable figures exist, physicians and dentists in the less well-paid components of the health sector are often induced to "moonlight" whenever they can, which decreases their effectiveness for the system in which they are primarily employed.

The private sector is extensive in most countries. Perhaps nowhere is it as well paid as in the United States, but private practice exists even in countries where it is illegal. It is impossible to assess the size of the private sector. Much of it is practiced on a cash-only basis to escape income taxes or to avoid detection where it is illegal. Moreover, in addition to the licensed practitioners, extensive networks of folk healers exist in most countries. Without belaboring the point, much of what has been said about the health sector in other countries can be applied, with some modifications, to the situation in the United States. The reader is encouraged to look for parallels.

In many countries, the minister of health has either the constitutional or the statutory responsibility to plan for the health sector. Unless there is vigorous political support, however, the minister cannot provide leadership: neither the social security system, which has strong labor backing, nor the military will agree to it. This, too, suggests that there are commonalities in the health sectors of nations.

At a different level, ministers of health (and this includes analogous positions at the national and state level in the United States) need to engage in intersectoral planning and collaboration. Difficult and important as it may be to achieve coordination within the health sector, however, such success would not be sufficient to solve the problems of world health, and this maxim too warrants careful

TABLE 13-3 Sectoral distribution of selected categories of health professionals in Peru, 1979-1980

		Public sector			
	Total	Ministry of Health	Social Security	Military	Other
Physicians	13,000	3,400			
Dentists	3,500	379	187	380	84
Midwives	2,100	675	298	76	121
Nurses	9,500	2,556	2,335	2,040	412
Psychologists	5,400	24	20	21	1

From Ministry of Health planning documents.

consideration in the United States. The World Health Organization has paid considerable attention to intersectoral planning.[9] To solve or ameliorate many of the most significant health problems of the world will require the concerted attention of the health, education, agriculture, industrial, and environmental sectors. Examples of effective intersectoral collaboration can be found between the health and education sectors in Sri Lanka. Norway has developed effective intersectoral collaboration in human nutrition involving the health and agriculture sectors.[12] Malaria control requires the attention of agencies dealing with water supply and irrigation, the health sector, and agriculture. Urban air pollution requires the concerted attention of the health and commercial development sectors.

In the United States it is clear that the prevention of AIDS requires effective collaboration between the education, welfare, and health sectors, including the mental health agencies, which are often a separate component within the health sector. Social and health services for the elderly similarly require intersectoral planning and collaboration. Many states have developed ad hoc approaches to deal with specific problems, but mechanisms and structures to facilitate and even force intersectoral approaches to solving important health problems have not been developed or studied. There is general political support for such efforts but little commitment to their development or implementation. They are absolutely essential for public health in the future. As Gunatilleko[9] points out, an explicit commitment to intersectoral planning and collaboration is necessary before mechanisms can be developed to make such linkages work. Joint training and information-sharing projects would help. New approaches to resource allocation and public sector financial management are also needed.

PRIMARY CARE

Primary care means something quite different in most of the world than it does in the United States. (See Chapter 4.) In the United States it refers to first-contact physicians such as family or general practitioners, pediatricians, general medicine specialists, and obstetricians and gynecologists (although the latter specialty is increasingly subspecialized and may no longer be included in the category). In the rest of the world, primary care denotes a combination of public health and first-contact health care services, sometimes provided by nonphysicians, such as the bare-foot doctors of China or the *feldsher* of Russia. As defined by the World Health Organization,[13] primary care "is essential health care based on practical, scientifically sound and socially acceptable methods and technology made universally accessible to individuals and families in the community," and it includes, at least,

> education concerning prevailing health problems and the methods of preventing and controlling them; promotion of food supply and proper nutrition; an adequate supply of safe water and basic sanitation; maternal and child health care, including family planning; immunization against the major infectious diseases; prevention and control of locally endemic diseases; appropriate treatment of common diseases and injuries; and provision of essential drugs. . . .

The concept has little currency in the United States and is not likely to obtain any organized support in the future, given the medical care system's advanced state of development and the separate nature of the public health system.

Nor is primary health care necessarily an established concept in the developing world, where it is used to provide essential health services mainly to dispersed rural populations and integrates preventive and therapeutic health services. The concept has been challenged on several grounds: effectiveness, cost, resource availability, and even cultural norms.

As mentioned in Chapter 4, Walsh and Warren,[14] concerned that the aspirations of the Alma-Ata conference were unattainable using the methods advocated, described various approaches to the improvement of health status in developing countries. They used the Alma-Ata definition of comprehensive primary care and stated that lack of resources made its provision to everyone in the near future unlikely. They defined basic primary health care in more limited terms: the use of health care professionals in clinics to treat illness. This they found inappropriate, ineffective, and unaffordable. Another strategy, multiple disease control, would focus on nationally selected priority issues with a series of unrelated programs, vertically organized and designed to control specific diseases. Such programs might concentrate on selected vector-borne diseases, basic water and sanitation programs, and nutrition supplementation. The programs might come together in the ministry of health at the national level but would have little or no interaction at the local level. That is, they would not be decentralized, and they would not involve treatment of basic illnesses. Walsh and Warren's favored strategy is selective primary health care, a strategy that involves the careful definition of problems, based on mortality and morbidity. They recommended focus on programs of measles and diphtheria-pertussis-tetanus immunization for children over 6 months of age, tetanus toxoid for all women of childbearing age, encouragement of long-term breast-feeding, the provision of chloroquine (an antimalarial) for episodes of fever in children under 3 years of age in areas where malaria is prevalent, and oral rehydration packets for the treatment of diarrheal diseases. It should again be noted that Walsh and Warren worked for the Rockefeller Foundation at the time, and a number of authors attacked their recommendations as being short-sighted and reflecting a traditional policy.

Others have attempted to show that comprehensive primary care is both feasible and practical. Bossert and Parker[15] feel that the political and administrative context in which primary care is nurtured are as important as the technical and professional strategies and processes and that crucial variables are policies affecting resource allocation, the decentralization of authority and control, and the interface of the health service system with people in the community setting. However, no one has yet found a way to solve the significant resource problems involved in implementing the World Health Organization's approach to primary care, and, as noted above, there is some evidence that the resource problem has become worse in recent years.

SUMMARY

This short and incomplete discussion of public health in other nations should serve at least to indicate the ubiquitous nature of some problems and the unique character of others in the United States. The need for sectorwide planning in all countries is apparent. In the United States this is made difficult by the disarticulated structure of the health sector, with separate public health, mental health, medical care, and environmental health agencies. The Institute of Medicine has recommended that a health sector be constituted in the United States as a first step in the rehabilitation of public health.[16] Beyond that, experience with intersectoral planning and collaboration is lacking, as are political support for it and research on it. Whether or not an effective health sector can be constituted, however, multiagency collaboration is essential.

In all countries, the rising cost of medical care is a severe problem, producing conflict with basic subsistence programs and economic development in poor countries and diminishing opportunities for other important investments in the industrialized nations. In neither the poor nor the wealthy nations is there a feeling that the price of medical care is worth the benefits obtained. As a result, government has increased its role in organizing, financing, and managing health services. Financing has become increasingly collectivized and socialized, with little evidence that this increases efficiency, although it may produce a more equitable distribution of resources.

Public health programs suffer in this zero-sum-game competition. With public sector spending constrained, the demands of the medical care sector force a constriction in other social service programs. As national governments concentrate on tightening both command and structural rules designed to deal with equity and cost problems, they tend to leave public health programs to more local levels of government. This may produce beneficial diversity and experimentation. Nevertheless, such problems as maternal, infant, and child care, AIDS, and long-term care are of increasing importance in all countries. Only in rigidly controlled socialized countries such as China is public health considered to be the most important activity in the health sector.

Finally, whether considering the development of decentralized care in the United States or Bangladesh or primary care in Italy or Sri Lanka, it is apparent that the inherently political nature of public health demands as much attention as its professional and technical base.

REFERENCES

1. Raffel MW: Comparative health systems: descriptive analyses of fourteen national health systems, University Park, PA, 1984, Pennsylvania State University Press.
2. Roemer MI: National strategies for health care organization: a world overview, Ann Arbor MI, 1985, Health Administration Press.

3. Roemer MI: Health care systems in world perspective, Ann Arbor, MI, 1976. Health Administration Press.
4. Primary health care. Report of the international conference on primary health care, Alma-Ata, USSR, September 6-12, 1978, Geneva, 1978, World Health Organization.
5. Terris MI: The complex task of the second epidemiologic revolution: the Joseph W. Mountin Lecture, J Public Health Policy 4:8, March 1983.
6. Stoll NR: This wormy world, J Parasitol 33:1, Feb 1947.
7. Werner D: Health care in Cuba: a model service or a means of social control—or both? In Morley D, Rohde J, and Williams G: Practising [sic] health for all, Oxford, 1983, Oxford University Press.
8. World Health Organization: The work of WHO, 1986-1987. Biennial report of the Director General to the World Health Assembly and to the United Nations, Geneva, 1988.
9. Gunatilleko G, editor: Intersectoral linkages and health development, Geneva, 1984, World Health Organization.
10. Department of International Economic and Social Affairs: Mortality and health policy: proceedings of the expert group on mortality and health policy, Rome, May 30 to June 3 1983, New York, 1984, United Nations.
11. Poullier J-P: Levels and trends in the public-private mix of the industrialized countries' health systems. In Culyer A and Jönsson B: Public and private health services: complementarities and conflicts, Oxford, 1986, Basil Blackwell, Ltd.
12. Winikoff B: Nutrition and food policy: the approaches of Norway and the United States, Am J Public Health 67:552, June 1977.
13. World Health Organization and United Nations Children's Fund: Primary health care. Report of the international conference on primary health care, Alma-Ata, USSR, September 6-12, 1978.
14. Walsh JA and Warren KS: Selective primary health care: an interim strategy for disease control in developing countries, N Engl J Med 301:967, Nov 1, 1979.
15. Bossert TJ and Parker DA: The political and administrative context of primary health care in the third world, Soc Sci Med 18(8)693, 1984.
16. Institute of Medicine: The future of public health, Washington, DC, 1988, National Academy Press.

PART FOUR

The prevention of disease, disability, and dependency

The prevention of death, disability, and the dependency that would otherwise be caused by disease and injury is the primary purpose of public health. Virtually all other activities are secondary to that mission. Hundreds of years ago, this mission was fulfilled by sanitation. People did not know about germs, vaccines, and antibiotics, but they did understand that filth and squalor were often associated with an increased risk of disease, and operating under that premise, much was accomplished. Leprosy victims were separated from the rest of society; people tried not to live near swamp water (where mosquitos prospered); and those who had died of plague were often burned. More to the point, housing reforms were instituted and municipal water, sewerage, and garbage collection systems established.

By the second half of the nineteenth century, however, bacteria and viruses had been discovered and the principles of immunization established. Enormous progress was made during the next 80 years. As death due to infectious diseases diminished, the residual, underlying impacts of injury and chronic disease were more apparent, and attention shifted to environmental and behavioral aspects of disease prevention. Some, in fact, said goodbye and good riddance to the era of communicable diseases and looked to a different set of challenges in the future. Human experience with plagues has not ceased, however, only changed and become more complex. Acquired immunodeficiency syndrome (AIDS) startled and shocked theworld in 1981. Here was an exquisitely complex alteration of a living microorganism let loose on the world because of behavioral attributes that were, in turn, intimately linked to societal and environmental factors. The concern was laden with value judgments but otherwise not especially different from the concern addressed to such problems as lung cancer, heart disease, and injuries, both intentional and unintentional.

In recent years, government, industry, and the health professions have pointed to behavior as the dominant health problem of the end of this century and most of the next, but it is not that simple. Social and environmental forces have a powerful effect on modern as well as ancient diseases, and some ancient diseases are quite capable of taking on new twists in the modern ecology of humans.

The next four chapters treat the prevention of disease in four segments: communicable diseases generally, the special case of AIDS, noncommunicable diseases, and finally, the concept and role of health education and promotion. The separation is somewhat artificial. Much of the preceding chapters and succeeding chapters also deals with the prevention of disease and injury.

While prevention is the purpose of public health, it is not the domain of public health alone. Prevention is accomplished by the educational system, by families, by social welfare and mental health agencies, by law enforcement, by politicians, engineers, ministers, and ethicists. It is the dominant concern of public health, however, and it can take a number of guises, as was shown in Chapter 5: primary, secondary, and tertiary prevention, for example. Sometimes, as in the case of the disabilities associated with aging, prevention is accomplished through postponement. Sometimes it is accomplished by self-action and sometimes through communal action; sometimes through persuasion and sometimes by compulsion. Deciding what can and should be done by society to prevent the dependency associated with disease and injury is a complex ethical, technical, economic, and political question.

CHAPTER 14

The control of infectious diseases

Public health has two responsibilities: preventing the consequences of disease and injury and providing health care for those "not otherwise provided for." The prevention of disease and injury involves exercise of the police power functions of the state (the state in the classic Greek sense of the word, that is—the embodiment of the authority of people gathered together under one government). Medical care of the poor requires that attention be paid to the common welfare. It is a less well understood function of public health and is discussed in Chapters 23 and 31. This chapter is about prevention—a police power function.

The activities involved in preventing the consequences of disease and injury (or the four Ds: death, disability, dependency, and, if you enjoy alliterative devices, dolor, or sorrow and grief) are sometimes classified into three categories: prevention, protection, and promotion.[1] Prevention, in this scheme, includes individual, clinical, or personal health services such as immunizations, screening for high blood pressure and follow-up services, or the use of Pap smears to detect the precursors to cancer of the cervix. Protection means the activities of organizations, both public and private, to reduce exposure to hazards such as polluted water, contaminated food, traffic accidents, mosquitos, or the use of electric saws without safety devices. Promotion means personal actions that people can take to prevent the four Ds of disease and injury, such as not smoking, following a good diet, and taking appropriate exercise. Health promotion will be discussed in Chapter 17. The prevention of noninfectious diseases is discussed separately in Chapter 15.

To control means to constrain or regulate. In one instance (smallpox), control has been accomplished through the total eradication of the agent of disease. In other situations, however, control may necessarily have a much more modest objective, such as reducing the annual estimated incidence of hepatitis B to 20 cases per 100,000 people by 1994, down from a 1978 estimate of 45 cases per 100,000.[2]

It is somewhat artificial to separate infectious diseases from noninfectious diseases, since the basic principles are for the most part the same, but there are differences. Note that the subject is infectious diseases, not communicable diseases. The difference may be narrow, but noninfectious diseases are sometimes communicable from one person to another or to the community. Adolescent suicides have been known to occur in brief clusters; crowd hysteria or violence is not unknown; and children of abusing parents are sometimes abusing parents themselves. Infectious diseases, in this chapter, are those caused by living microorganisms. (That definition may soon be of little use. Certain molecular configurations that are thought of as viruses may become living creatures, capable of reproduction, only when they can capture the genetic machinery of a host cell. Perhaps other less animate collections of chemicals will be found in the future that can produce diseases in the same manner.)

In Chapter 5 the theoretical structure of the concept of prevention was discussed. This chapter deals with the application of that theory and with the role of health departments—the governmental presence in health—in organizing public resources to control infectious diseases. The rationale for the involvement of government in control activities is discussed first, followed by the process that should be used to create a control program. The chapter concludes with a discussion of current state activities in the control of infectious diseases. Because of its special characteristics and its significance for public health generally, the acquired immunodeficiency syndrome (AIDS) will be discussed separately in Chapter 16.

There are several good textbooks and handbooks concerning the control of communicable diseases. The American Public Health Association's *Control of Communicable Diseases in Man*[3] is an internationally recognized and authoritative handbook, first published in 1917 and updated periodically. The *Handbook of Prevention,* edited by Edelstein and Michelson,[4] is a behaviorally oriented text that covers numerous infectious and noninfectious diseases. Rosenau's original textbook on public health and preventive medicine has been updated by John Last[5] and a large number of contributors. It is a clinically oriented encyclopedia of prevention, with chapters covering infectious diseases, chronic diseases, behavioral disorders, and general epidemiologic concepts. A shorter "how-to" manual has been written by Murray Grant.[6] Handbooks have been written for various professional groups, such as nurses[7] and physicians.[8] Most such books are written for clinicians, and most take a categorical approach—that is, they treat individual diseases serially. There is little written about the organization of disease control programs by public health agencies. The associations of State and Territorial Epidemiologists and of State and Territorial Chronic Disease Program Directors meet regularly and provide their members with excellent opportunities to discuss programs, but little or none of the information is reproduced in a form that would be available to people outside of those associations.

CONTROLLING DISEASES—THE GOVERNMENTAL PRESENCE

The rationale for the involvement of the state in the control of diseases has been discussed in earlier chapters (see especially Chapter 5). The decision to intervene may be based on concern for the utility of the state, equity, beneficence (as was true in the early church hospitals), or on what Dan Beauchamp[9] has called "communitarian values." All of these motivations may be present in infectious disease control programs (the mixture is more complicated when considering noninfectious diseases). The basic rationale of such programs lies in the police power function of the state, however: the authority to reduce the personal liberty of an individual when necessary to protect the common good. While such control activities may necessitate creating a medical care services program for affected individuals, the service programs have less to do with the humane treatment of people than with the protection of the rest of the community.

That harsh differentiation is tempered sometimes by concerns for beneficence. Victims of leprosy in ancient times were cast out of society and made to wear a bell so that people could hear them coming. Cruel and ignorant though that may have been, it did serve to isolate a potential source of contagion and prevent the spread of a dread disease. There are still people suffering from leprosy in the United States (238 cases were reported in 1987[10]). So long as they cooperate in the continuing surveillance program, their identity is protected to avoid the discrimination that they would otherwise be subjected to. The similarity of leprosy to AIDS is obvious.

Although the state can reduce the civil liberties of an individual in order to protect society, the concept of the "least restrictive" intervention has gained currency in recent years. Originating in the mental health field (see Chapter 27), this legal principle arose to protect people from unnecessary incarceration in state mental hospitals. In lay terms, the state can reduce an individual's civil liberties no more than is demonstrably necessary to prevent harm to the public, based on objective evidence of the nature of the disease and the behavior of the affected individual. It would be unlawful under such a legal principle to deny employment to a food handler with syphilis or to require a blood test for a sexually transmitted disease as a condition of receiving a food-handler's permit, since such diseases cannot be transmitted to others in the normal course of work as a waiter or cook. The "least restrictive" principle is less well established in the arena of infectious diseases than it is in mental health, but it would be prudent for public health personnel to act as if it were. While it is not clear that all states initially will act to protect the rights of AIDS victims, the trend is clearly in that direction and may serve to stimulate a redevelopment of statutes covering the control of infectious diseases generally (see Chapter 9).

The police power of the state does not simply empower the state: it obliges it. That is, when circumstances warrant, the state *must* exercise its police power to protect the public. The state has a number of tools available for the control of communicable diseases:

- *Reporting.* Physicians and other health professionals must report specified diseases to a designated authority, usually the local or state health department.

- *Laboratory reporting.* In many states, licensed laboratories must report positive tests for certain diseases to the health department, even though a diagnosis may not have been established.
- *Surveillance.* Despite its connotation of spies, surveillance is the systematic measurement of health status and risk factors.[11]
- *Monitoring.* Often thought of as synonymous with surveillance, monitoring involves the ongoing assessment of a condition after intervention has been initiated.[11]
- *Laboratory analysis.* Public health agencies have been authorized to establish laboratories for the study and detection of infectious diseases since 1893 when Dr. William Park was appointed to the position of Bacteriological Diagnostician and Inspector of Diphtheria in New York City.[12]
- *Contact investigation.* Once a case of a particular disease has been diagnosed, personnel from the health department are authorized to interview the victim to establish a list of possible contacts. This practice has been called into question recently because of AIDS, as will be discussed in Chapter 16.
- *Treatment.* Public health agencies are required to provide treatment services for specified infectious diseases. In many cities, special hospitals were built for this purpose, such as Herman Kiefer Hospital in Detroit, and separate buildings established for different diseases, such as smallpox, diphtheria, and leprosy. Local health departments are also required to provide services for people infected with sexually transmitted diseases or tuberculosis. These requirements were not established under the welfare provisions of state and local government, but rather to provide the tools necessary to prevent the spread of dangerous communicable diseases. Since it is not possible to immunize people against syphilis, it is necessary to find the contacts to an active case quickly, examine them to see if they too are infected, and if they are, to treat them effectively and promptly to prevent further transmission. It is important to understand, however, that the state usually cannot *require* treatment. It can take steps to prevent the further spread of the disease, but if the victim refuses treatment, the state can only force the issue if it can prove in court that the victim is (1) gravely disabled and (2) a danger to self or others as a result of the disability. (This is a generalization, of course. The specific statutes and cases in a given state should be carefully examined to understand the authority and obligations of public health in that state.)
- *Isolation.* Often confused with quarantine (see below), isolation means the separation of infected people from noninfected people during the period of communicability. This is an ancient concept, which is still occasionally useful. In most cases, infected individuals will readily accept treatment and avoid infecting others, but not always. Isolation may have to be used when treatment is rejected, as noted in the paragraph above. This legal authority is also under review because of the AIDS epidemic, and the provisions may be rewritten so as to better assure that the least restrictive options available will be used.
- *Quarantine.* People who have been exposed to a dangerous infectious disease can be quarantined for the length of the incubation period for that disease. This does not necessarily, or usually, involve the incarceration of the individual or a restriction in freedom to move about. More often, it involves close personal supervision in cooperation with the health authority to detect the possible development of the disease as early as possible and prevent further spread.
- *Immunization.* All states have requirements for the immunization of children against certain infectious diseases. The most common are measles, rubella (German measles), diphtheria, pertussis (whooping cough), tetanus, and polio. The health department is usually authorized to provide immunizations. The controlling agency is usually the school system, which is required to prevent the entry of any child who has not been properly immunized.

This authority can become complex. In some states, the statute is written in such a way that it prevents only the original entry into the school system. Children transferring into the school system at higher grades, or those who may have been missed on school entry for some reason, cannot be required to be immunized later on. Such laws should be rewritten. In the meantime, it may be possible for the health department to issue emergency rules during an outbreak, under the general police power statutes, effectively closing the school to all children who have not been immunized until the outbreak is brought under control.

- *Investigation.* In addition to the specific authorities described above, most health departments are required to investigate unusual occurrences of disease or injury. This includes the authority to review medical records, to perform laboratory investigations, to examine patients, and to interview both patients and others who may have been exposed to the disease or injury.

In earlier chapters it has been shown that poor people are more likely to be afflicted with most diseases and are more likely to be harmed by injuries than are nonpoor people. The impact of poverty, socioeconomic status, and discrimination on health status will be explored again and again in this book. Their impact is so pervasive, so ubiquitous, and so powerful that many students of public health wonder why they are asked to concern themselves with specific disease control programs. Would it not be more appropriate and more useful to concentrate on those powerful underlying causes—the circumstances that support and nourish the more immediate causes of disease?

Public health has been described as a social science and as a revolutionary movement. It uses the tools that society will support at a particular moment in history to protect and promote the health of that society. In the United States at this time, society is more willing to support public health interventions that are technological and medical in nature than it is to support redistributive social welfare programs. Public health workers, of course, have their own political commitments and social values. They are free to act on those beliefs and values just as other citizens are. But their job involves using the resources that society makes available to achieve the objectives society has selected, even if the permitted tools are not as effective as less acceptable ones. If a different personal choice is needed, other careers can be considered, including running for office.

In the meantime, public health, like other governmental presences such as education and welfare, must use the tools it has to promote and protect, to push and nudge, to lead and support the communities of which it is a part.

ORGANIZING A DISEASE CONTROL PROGRAM

Organizing a program to control an infectious disease is similar to other organizational activities that have been described in earlier chapters, such as planning and marketing. It is an iterative process, which begins with the definition of the problem, the development of objectives, and consideration of methods and concludes with implementation and evaluation, with feedback into the planning process at every step of the way. All of the steps should be linked conceptually and organizationally, so that information needed to make choices about the problem, objectives, methods, implementation, and evaluation is available to the decision makers.

Problem definition

An accurate definition of the problem is one of the most undervalued steps in the process. Legionnaires disease[3,13] was a good example of this: Was it due to a chemical in the ambient air, a bacterium or a yeast? Where did it come from in the hotel? Was it a new organism or an old familiar one that had become dangerous because of an altered environment? Once identified, it was necessary to figure out what the bacteria ate, at what temperature they could reproduce, what changes in the environment could alter their characteristics, and what antibiotics might be useful in the treatment of those affected. Investigation showed it to be an old organism, which had caused outbreaks many years ago, but whose manifestation in Philadelphia in 1976 was somewhat different, startling, and alarming. It was quickly brought under control once the problem was defined.

Problem identification involves a sequence of steps:

1. Identification of the signal case. This requires an accurate description, including laboratory investigation, which may enable the investigator or others to identify a known problem
2. Diagnosis
3. Formation of a disease model, or a detailed analysis of the pathologic changes that occur
4. Epidemiologic investigation to determine the circumstances of its spread in a population group
5. Microbiologic investigation to pin down the precise characteristics of the organism

Control activities may precede the full investigation described above, which could take years. John Snow unraveled the epidemiology of cholera in London before the microbe had been seen and took steps to prevent its further spread.[14] Steps were taken to control outbreaks of polio before the virus had been isolated or characterized, and preventive interventions were suggested for Lyme disease and toxic shock syndrome before the evidence chains had been completed.[3] While effective, such early interventions are not as powerful as those developed after the problem has been completely identified.

Objectives

The objectives of a control program must fit the known facts and should be directed to the problem as it has been defined. Objectives should be stated in measurable terms, indicating what is to be accomplished and when. The example noted above for hepatitis is a clear example of a well-defined objective (provided the methodology is available to support the objective, which it is.) A general statement to the effect that the disease in question will be prevented is useless, since it offers no reference points for measurement purposes, making it impossible to tell whether you are getting closer to or further away from the result you are seeking. The objectives described in *Promoting Health/Preventing Disease*[2] are precise. For example:

- By 1990, reported measles incidence should be reduced to less than 500 cases per year—all imported or within two generations of importation.
- By 1990, 95% of licensed patient care facilities should be applying the recommended practices for controlling nosocomial infections (infections initiated *in* a hospital).

While precise, the second of these objective statements had no reliable data base at the time it was proposed, making progress difficult to measure. Objectives, like the other steps in the process of planning and organizing a control program, are subject to change based on feedback from the other steps. For example, a change in the definition of a case of measles might increase or lower the number of cases reported, necessitating a revision in the stated objective.

The value of carefully thought-out objectives is made apparent by the worldwide program to eradicate smallpox.[15] There were 10 to 15 million cases in 1967. The final case was reported on October 26, 1977.[16] At the beginning of the eradication program, objectives were established that called for 75% of all outbreaks to be discovered within 2 weeks of the onset of the first case, for containment activities to begin within 48 hours of ascertainment, and for no new cases to occur more than 17 days after the containment activity had begun. These objectives were instrumental in guiding the work of the personnel involved and in evaluating progress. Their level of specificity was based on a thorough knowledge of the natural history of the disease (such as its period of communicability and its incubation period), careful evaluation of control methods, and specific research called for by the needs of the program.

Methods

The methods that can be used to control or prevent the spread of infectious diseases focus on the host, the agent, or the environment—sometimes on all three.

Primary prevention efforts (see Chapter 5) can increase the resistance of the potential host (the human victim in this discussion) by specifically altering immune status or by more general steps to improve resistance, such as better nutrition.[17] (Note that this reference is over 20 years old! There is no more recent book on the important subject of public health nutrition in the United States. That is a significant gap.)

Primary prevention efforts aimed at the agent of infectious disease are rare. The only useful example to date is smallpox, but Henderson[15] points out that the smallpox eradication program has stimulated considerable discussion about similar health problems. For example, national objectives call for the *elimination* of measles using the same three strategies: achieving and maintaining high immunization levels, strong surveillance, and aggressive outbreak control. (Elimination is not yet a well-defined concept. It usually means the elimination of domestic cases of the disease, while acknowledging that occasional importations from other countries will still occur.)

Many primary prevention programs have focused on the environment in which an infectious disease occurs. Water protection and sewage treatment programs are examples of environmental activities designed not to eradicate the organism itself but to protect humans from contact with agents of disease. Other activities, such as malaria control programs, interfere with the mosquito vectors that carry the microorganisms by eliminating stagnant pools of water, by the use of insecticides, or by simple screening of dwelling places. Environmental interventions are often the most efficient and effective means of primary prevention for infectious diseases that can live in other hosts.

The secondary prevention of infectious diseases accepts at least the initial case but attempts to prevent further cases from developing. (Screening is a special and important example of a secondary preventive intervention and will be discussed in the following chapter.) The smallpox eradication program eventually operated on the agent of disease, but in addition to a worldwide immunization effort (primary prevention directed to the host), it concentrated on rapid outbreak control (secondary prevention). Secondary prevention is aided by effective reporting and surveillance systems (see above). Good laboratory backup and other diagnostic services are necessary. The New York City program established in 1893 was a prototype for such work.[12] Park and his colleagues developed a physician reporting system and a set of detailed procedures for sending specimens to his laboratory. Note that the program resulted in an apparent *increase* in cases of diphtheria. Most changes in a reporting system will cause a change in the reported incidence of the disease: new and more rigid case definitions will lower the number of case reports accepted (as happened for measles reporting in 1978 and for tuberculosis in 1975), whereas publicity regarding an outbreak may result in more cases being reported.

More recently, investigation of gastroenteritis in Pittsfield, Mass., revealed the agent to be *Giardia lamblia,* a protozoan. Careful analysis showed that the reported attack rate was 14.3 per 1,000 people using one of three water reservoirs and 7 per 1,000 for those using one of the other two. A phone survey that asked people about symptoms indicated that as many as 3,800 cases might have occurred, compared to the 70 cases that were reported.[18]

Careful secondary prevention efforts may turn up carriers of a disease—people who have no symptoms but who are infected with the agent and can spread it to others. This fairly recently discovered phenomenon was described by Park, who found

> that children, and to a lesser extent adults, who are brought in direct contact with true cases of diphtheria very often receive the diphtheria bacilli into their throats, and that these bacilli may persist and develop in these throats for days and weeks. In some cases . . . true diphtheria followed the appearance of the bacilli in the respiratory passages, while in others no disease developed, though they might be a source of diphtheria in others.[12]

The most famous carrier was Typhoid Mary, who will enter this discussion again when describing the use of isolation as a control method.[19]

Tuberculosis control provides the most complex example of secondary intervention depending on the use of registries, surveillance, reporting, diagnosis, treatment, case follow-up, immunization, and even isolation.[20] There are approximately 36,000 new *infections* each year in the United States, but only 1,800 of these progress to clinical disease during that same year. In addition, 22,000 new *cases* arise from people who were previously infected, known as "reactors," since they would react to a tuberculin skin test if it were administered, showing that they were harboring often dormant bacteria.

In recent years, as the incidence of active tuberculosis has declined, many large cities and counties have found it increasingly costly to maintain categorical control programs with trained clinicians, organized clinics, nurse specialists, and laboratory technicians. Management of tuberculosis has been transferred to private physicians, with the health department providing drugs, follow-up, outbreak investigation services, and monitoring. Although this can result in excellent treatment of patients with tuberculosis at less cost to the health department, it makes the data needed to monitor the dynamics of tuberculosis more difficult to obtain. Clinicians are less likely to obtain routine cultures (which are tedious to collect and slow to develop), which means that drug-resistant organisms are not as well identified, and the rapidity of conversion from a sputum-positive case (infectious to others) to a sputum-negative case (noninfectious) is not measured.

The familiar techniques of control are important in the ongoing battle against tuberculosis. It is essential that new cases be promptly reported to the health department. Case contacts should be examined and skin tested. If the skin tests become positive, detailed diagnostic studies should be undertaken and the converters should be treated with isoniazid (INH). Although there is some risk of liver damage due to INH, the risk and the cost of active disease is greater.[21] The signal case requires careful follow-up to be sure that treatment is complete and that there is no danger of infection to others. Less onerous than it once was, short-term isolation is often indicated while a treatment plan is established for the new case. The treatment plans themselves are not complex but require specialists with considerable experience in the treatment of tuberculosis. Special isolation procedures are used to reduce environmental contamination in the hospital room. Skilled and experienced laboratory work is needed to detect the development of antibiotic resistance. Occasionally, it is still necessary to seek a court order to force the isolation of a new case, but the vast majority of individuals infected are cooperative. Since the disease is more common among those in the worst socioeconomic circumstances, however, it may require considerable skill and tact, as well as genuine interest in the welfare of the client, to achieve treatment objectives. In New York, the health department has reestablished a form of tuberculosis hospital, a phenomenon that has all but disappeared in the United States, by converting one of its shelters for the homeless into a special shelter for those with tuberculosis.[22] Maintaining a supportive and caring environment for tuberculosis patients is more effective than the earlier approaches, which resembled prisons.

The occasional difficulty encountered is typified by the case of Typhoid Mary.[19] Mary Mallon was a cook who worked for and infected several households in and around Oyster Bay, N.Y., in 1906. The carrier state was not understood at that time, nor were there techniques for eradicating the bacilli from carriers. She refused to cooperate and was arrested on March 19, 1907. She had considerable public support as an innocent victim of typhoid who unknowingly infected others. She was released by a new health commissioner, because she promised to refrain from working as a cook. But she went back to work anyway: in a hospital! When 25 cases occurred in 1915, Mary was again detained. Her public support evaporated, and she was held in isolation indefinitely. While such extreme situations occasionally occur, permanent imprisonment would be a most unlikely technique to secure effective isolation.

Tertiary prevention, which accepts the existence of a disease or injury and attempts to halt or retard the progress of dependency (see Chapter 5), is probably not applicable to this discussion. In the case of infectious diseases, this is not different from the provision of direct medical care services.

Consideration of the methods to be used in preventing infectious diseases is based on available technology and a careful definition of the problem and of the objectives of the program. Consideration of the methods available should lead to a careful reevaluation of the objective statement to be sure it is still accurate and useful. The basic methods are those that attempt to specifically or generally increase the resistance of the host, eradicate or eliminate the agent, or modify the environment in such a way as to reduce the probability that people will come into contact with the hazard.

Implementation and evaluation

The implementation of an infectious disease control program is dependent on PEARL (propriety, economics, acceptability, resources, and legislation—see Chapter 11) and a careful examination of the potential benefits and costs of the program. A simple statement of the dominant criterion is "the most for the least": what steps will provide the best control for the least cost? The answer to this question will again cause a careful reexamination of the objectives and methods discussed in previous steps.

Some theoretical interventions fail the test of propriety (compulsory gynecological screening of all college women for sexually transmitted diseases, for example); some are too expensive; some are unacceptable to the public (similar to the propriety question); others may be economically feasible, but necessary resources may not be available at the time (such as laboratory facilities for determining measles susceptibility of school children during an outbreak); others may not be supported by present statutes (such as requiring immunization of older school children who were admitted to school during some prior year).

A method that promises a high benefit-to-cost return but flunks the PEARL test should not be rejected automatically. It may not be possible to implement such a method at the moment, but further evaluation of the problem may show where changes can be made that might make the method practical.

An otherwise acceptable method may suffer from financial constraints: the rising cost of vaccines, for example, or a lack of sufficient funds to hire the necessary personnel to carry out case interviews and contact investigations. These problems may necessitate selection of a less efficient intervention and therefore restatement of the objectives of the program. For example, many public health workers would like to be able to conduct the same sort of case interviews and contact tracing procedures for people with gonorrhea that they use for the less frequent cases of syphilis, but given the incidence of gonorrhea, this is not possible in most jurisdictions. Nor would it be particularly effective owing to differences in the natural history of the disease—another important factor in considering methods. Syphilis has a relatively slow incubation period of 2 to 3 weeks. This provides enough time for contact tracing to occur before the contact can have developed active syphilis and infect someone else. In gonorrhea, the incubation period is only 2 to 7 days. Most contacts cannot be found before they have had an opportunity to infect another. Different measures need to be considered.

Evaluation of a preventive intervention is essential. Without regular checks, it is impossible to know whether the program is working or whether some change in the implementation, the methods, or the objectives needs to be considered. Evaluation depends on the case definition, its acceptance by those who may diagnose or suspect the existence of the target disease, carefully designed reporting procedures, the availability of good laboratory services, and the ability to analyze the data collected. Tuberculosis, as described above, is a good example of the complexity and importance of evaluation.

Assuming that the program works—that is, enables progress to be made toward reaching the objective—it is necessary to reevaluate the entire program regularly. In Chapter 5 the power of prevalence and incidence in shaping prevention efforts was demonstrated. As the incidence of the disease, or its prevalent pool of sources of infection, decreases, the dynamics of the process can change quickly. When tuberculosis was common (high prevalence and incidence), isolation and other physical interventions were useful, even though the bacteriology of the disease was not well understood. Communitywide X-ray screening programs were useful in detecting people who were likely to have the disease. While false positives and negatives occurred, a large number of cases was detected. As incidence and prevalence declined, false negatives and false positives began to increase in proportion to the number of active cases found. The selected method shifted from mass X-ray screening to the more precise skin test. However, as incidence and prevalence declined still further, the skin test became less useful, and it became important to "increase" prevalence in the selected groups by better defining high-risk criteria. Skin testing is no longer routinely performed on the general population, but it is valuable for people whose health status has been compromised by adverse socioeconomic circumstances or life-style. Evaluation is not only necessary for the annual report and to support the budget request: it is essential to continued success.

INFECTIOUS DISEASE PREVENTION PROGRAMS OF STATE AND LOCAL HEALTH DEPARTMENTS

Control and prevention of infectious diseases were the original reasons for establishing local health departments. There is little organized information about those activities at the present time, however. Interest has shifted to noninfectious diseases and health promotion activities in the mistaken belief that infectious diseases are no longer a problem. Disease-specific information is still collected by the Centers for Disease Control (CDC), but information about program activities has been limited since the onset of the block grant programs in 1981. (A feature of the block grants was reduced reporting requirements, which also means less knowledge of what is happening.) In addition to the important weekly publication *Morbidity and Mortality Weekly Report,* the CDC publishes the annual *Summary of Notifiable Diseases* and a *Surveillance Summaries* report. The latter publication includes information about all current surveillance systems, which are operated as a cooperative endeavor with the 54 state and territorial health agencies. Originally established to monitor infectious diseases, the surveillance program has been expanded to cover human reproduction, injury control, environmental health, chronic diseases, risk reduction efforts, and occupational safety and health. A summary of reported cases of notifiable diseases for 1987 is shown in Table 14-1.

State health agencies voluntarily report their annual program expenditures to the Public Health Foundation, a not-for-profit organization created by the Association of State and Territorial Health Officials. The activities involved in the control of infectious diseases are not routinely grouped together under one heading. The Communicable Disease Control category includes such activities as immunizations, epidemiologic investigations, tuberculosis control, programs to control the spread of sexually transmitted diseases (including AIDS), and several other activities. In addition, most state health departments have substantial programs in the environmental health field that are designed to prevent infectious diseases: food and milk sanitation, drinking water protection, and vector control programs, for example. Laboratory expenditures are rarely broken down into separate categories, such as clinical and chemical laboratory work and microbiological investigations. The states spend approximately $932 million annually on these infectious disease control programs, or about 12% of their total budgets.[23] This estimate probably includes some activities in the environmental field and in the laboratory programs that are not specifically aimed at infectious diseases, but it misses much larger expenditures that are made by other state agencies (agriculture and environmental protection agencies, for instance) and leaves out the extensive activities of local health departments. The Foundation's reports necessarily identify the activities of an organization rather than the total state effort in any area. In Iowa, for example, the state health department laboratory is a part of the state university and is not identified in the Foundation's reports.

The activities of the state health agencies are extensive and involve a substantial proportion of the citizens of each state. Indirect involvement through such activities as food inspection and water supply protection involves virtually the entire population of the country. In 1984, tuberculosis control programs in 42 of 46 state health agencies screened 2.4 million people, and about 31,000 patients received treatment services; 46 state health agencies screened 13.1 million people for sexually transmitted diseases, and 45 of the agencies treated 2.7 million people, including 825,000 in California alone (New York did not report its activities); the agencies administered 6.2 million doses of immunizing agents and supplied another

TABLE 14-1 Notifiable diseases: summary of reported cases, 1987, United States

AIDS	21,070
Amebiasis	3,123
Anthrax	1
Aseptic meningitis	11,487
Botulism	82
Brucellosis	129
Cholera	6
Diphtheria	3
Encephalitis	1,539
Gonorrhea	760,905
Hepatitis A	25,280
Hepatitis B	25,916
Hepatitis, non-A, non-B	2,999
Hepatitis, unspecified	3,102
Legionellosis	1,038
Leprosy	238
Leptospirosis	43
Malaria	944
Measles	3,655
Meningococcal infections	2,930
Mumps	12,848
Pertussis	2,823
Plague	12
Poliomyelitis	—
Psittacosis	98
Rabies, human	1
Rheumatic fever	141
Rubella (German measles)	306
Rubella (congenital syndrome)	5
Salmonellosis	50,916
Shigellosis	23,860
Syphilis	35,147
Tetanus	48
Toxic shock syndrome	372
Trichinosis	40
Tuberculosis	22,517
Tularemia	214
Typhoid fever	400
Typhus fever	653
Varicella (chicken pox)	213,196

From Summary of Notifiable Diseases, Morbidity and Mortality Weekly Report 36(54), Sept 1988.

18.7 million doses to local health departments and to some private physicians and other agencies.[24] These service counts are woefully inadequate: they do not include similar programs of the major city and county health departments or of the 2,000 or more smaller health departments that are active in infectious disease control.

Although there is considerable variability among the states, all have a focal point for the control of infectious diseases and general epidemiology. The immunization programs, tuberculosis control programs, and programs to control sexually transmitted diseases are sometimes managed as separate activities.

Local health departments are more limited in their scope of activities. In the larger city and county units, qualified epidemiologists are usually in charge of infectious disease control programs. In some cities, however, the activities have deteriorated in recent years to unacceptable levels. A series of reports in the Chicago newspapers in 1988 raised serious concerns about the ability of that city to maintain even rudimentary infectious disease control programs or to investigate outbreaks. The widespread and erroneous notion that infectious diseases have been conquered has lulled some public health professionals into complacency, and they have turned their attention to more popular problems such as health promotion, control of chronic diseases, medical care activities, and hazardous waste control. The AIDS epidemic has reawakened the public's apprehension about communicable diseases in general; concerns are concentrated on the AIDS problem, and resources have been allocated based on the urgency of that situation, further diminishing the efforts to control other infectious diseases.

Table 14-1 reveals the extent to which we are still vulnerable to infectious diseases. Several diseases on the list were unknown or unrecognized just a few years ago: AIDS, toxic shock syndrome, legionellosis, and certain varieties of hepatitis. Lyme disease is not included in the list at this time, nor are several other important infectious diseases. Note that some diseases of ancient importance still occur in the United States: malaria, cholera, plague, rabies, anthrax, botulism, and leprosy.

As the incidence of infectious diseases has declined, so has public interest and the knowledge and concern of the governmental presence in health. Many new health officers and program directors at the state and local level have little or no training or experience in human biology, epidemiology, pathology, and microbiology. In many such health departments, physicians are employed simply to oversee medical services and also have little or no training in epidemiology. The ability of microorganisms to infect, harm, and kill people has not been diminished sufficiently to warrant such casual treatment of the public's health.

REFERENCES

1. Healthy people: the Surgeon General's report on health promotion and disease prevention, 1979, Pub No 79-55071, Washington, DC, 1979, US Department of Health, Education and Welfare.
2. Public Health Service: Promoting health/preventing disease: objectives for the nation, Washington, DC, 1980, US Department of Health and Human Services.
3. Benenson AS, editor: Control of communicable diseases in man, ed 14, Washington, DC, 1985, American Public Health Association.
4. Edelstein BA and Michelson L, editors: Handbook of prevention, New York, 1986, Plenum Press.
5. Last JM, editor: Public health and preventive medicine, ed 12, Norwalk CT, 1986, Appleton-Century-Crofts.
6. Grant M: Handbook of community health, Philadelphia, 1987, Lea & Febiger.
7. Edelman C and Mandle CL, editors: Health promotion throughout the lifespan, St Louis, 1986, The CV Mosby Co.
8. Holbrook JH, editor: Disease prevention and health promotion: a handbook for physicians, New York, 1986, Praeger Publishers.
9. Beauchamp D: Community: the neglected tradition of public health, Hastings Cent Rep 15:28, Dec 1985.
10. Summary of notifiable diseases, United States, 1987, Morbid Mortal Week Rep 36(54), Sept 1988.
11. Eylenbosch WJ and Noah NP, editors: Surveillance in health and disease, New York, 1988, Oxford University Press.
12. Biggs JM, Park WJ, and Beebe AL: Report on bacteriological investigations and diagnosis of diphtheria from May 4, 1893 to May 4, 1894. In The Carrier State, New York, 1977, Arno Press (originally published in 1895).
13. Fraser DW and others: Legionnaires' disease: description of an epidemic of pneumonia, N Engl J Med 297:1189, Dec 1, 1977.
14. Snow J: On the mode of transmission of cholera, ed 2. New York, 1936, The Commonwealth Fund (originally published in 1855).

15. Henderson DA: Principles and lessons learned from the smallpox eradication programme, Bull WHO 65:435, 1987.
16. World Health Organization: Smallpox surveillance, Weekly Epidem Record 54:1, Jan 5, 1979.
17. Scrimshaw NS, Taylor CE and Gordon JE: Interactions of nutrition and infection, Geneva, 1968, World Health Organization.
18. Kent GP and others: Epidemic giardiasis caused by a contaminated public water supply, Am J Public Health 78:139, Feb 1988.
19. Soper GA: Typhoid Mary, Military Surgeon 45:1, July 1919.
20. Snider DE, editor: Supplement on future research in tuberculosis: prospects and priorities for elimination, Am Rev Resp Dis 134:401, Aug 1986.
21. Rose DN and others: Tuberculosis prevention: cost-effectiveness analysis of isoniazid chemoprophylaxis, Am J Prev Med 4:102, Mar/Apr 1988.
22. New York Times, national edition, p 14, Oct 24, 1988.
23. Public health agencies, 1988: an inventory of programs and block grant expenditures, Washington, DC, 1988, Public Health Foundation.
24. 1990 objectives for the nation: profile of state health agency progress, Washington, DC, 1987, Public Health Foundation.

CHAPTER 15

Prevention of noninfectious diseases

The relative brevity of this chapter does not mean that the subject is unimportant. On the contrary, some have claimed this to be the era of chronic diseases.[1] From the early 1950s until the advent of the AIDS epidemic in 1981, the control of noninfectious diseases was the dominant concern of public health, the public at large, and health policymakers. (The dominant prevention concern, that is: still greater attention was focused on access to medical care and the rising cost of securing that access.) The basic concepts of prevention have been described in Chapter 5, and the application of those concepts, as described in Chapter 14, is germane to the control of noninfectious diseases as well.

Why a separate chapter on noninfectious diseases? Epidemiologists have spent years demonstrating the relevance of the methods used to control infectious diseases to this newer field:

Host, agent environment

Primary, secondary, and tertiary prevention

There are important differences, however. When the state acts to control an infectious disease, it has the authority to reduce the freedom of individuals to protect the common good. Infectious diseases are communicable. The victims are a source of danger to others. Regardless of what may have caused them to become infected, others may be innocently affected. The state can intervene dramatically in the affairs of an individual to prevent that from happening. Indeed the state has no discretion in such matters: it must act.

Noninfectious diseases are different. The freedom of individuals to harm themselves is, by and large, a protected right so long as they harm no others. How can the state take action to prevent or control noninfectious diseases such as lung cancer, diabetes, congenital anomalies, or injuries? It does so by developing a harm-to-others rationale.

The classic modern case is the motorcycle helmet. Riding motorcycles may be pleasurable, but it is more dangerous than riding in a car. The injury rate per passenger-mile driven on a motorcycle is considerably higher than the rate for automobile drivers or passengers. Many of the victims have severe head injuries. Those who survive are often permanently disabled and dependent. People who are permanently dependent in the United States usually rely on public funds for their support: Medicaid, Social Security, and the Supplemental Security Income program. By their risk-taking, harm-to-self actions, they do economic harm to others. Therefore, those others have a right to use the police power of the state to protect themselves. Thus did the argument develop, and many states passed laws requiring motorcyclists to wear approved helmets. The case is interesting for two reasons: (1) many states subsequently revoked the laws and (2) motorcyclists as a class are a minority group with a bad public image. The public is much more reluctant to pass such restrictive legislation when the affected class of people is larger and more like most middle-class Americans.

Prohibition was an earlier and more important example of the evolution of a control rationale. Drunkenness was first a sin, then a crime, and more recently, a disease. It is a moral offense in some religions. Over a period of years, this moral offense became elevated to the status of criminal behavior. The rhetoric escalated: wives and little children were harmed; employers were harmed; public safety was threatened by the drunk. An action that could not be prohibited to protect the drinker could be prohibited, and was, to protect the public. (Actually, drinking was not prohibited—the 18th Amendment, which was adopted in 1919, prohibited the manufacture, sale, and transportation of alcoholic beverages.) The storm receded; the constitutional amendment was repealed (1933) and, along with it, many other laws, which prohibited a variety of other "sinful" actions such as smoking. (The sale of cigarettes had been prohibited in 12 states by the time Prohibition was repealed.)

This was not the first time American society had transformed self-harm into public harm and taken steps to control the damage, nor would it be the last. In the 1970s public attention began to focus on the use and abuse of other substances. Interest waned toward the end of the decade but began to escalate again in the mid-1980s with the discovery of the "crack" form of cocaine. Rhetoric became more and more strident. Reports of the public harm attributed to the use of illicit drugs became increasingly global until it appeared as if society had no other problems—that all the ills of modern life, all the things that frightened people could be attributed to the drug problem. Political leaders, following what they perceived to be the public's demands, called for an all-out war on drugs, including use of the military to seal the country's borders. Drug dealers were labeled murderers, and the death penalty was resuscitated to stem the tide of moral decay.

Riding along with the action were a number of other prohibitory efforts. The damage wrought by alcohol received increasing attention, and public attitudes toward drunkenness hardened. By 1985 42 states had passed laws restricting the use of tobacco in a variety of locations, and more than 320 restrictive state and local ordinances were passed in the next 3 years. The smoking restrictions were based on evidence that "passive smoking"—the cigarette smoke inhaled by nonsmokers—was dangerous. At last the antitobacco forces had the ammunition needed to move toward prohibition, an action that had been precluded by earlier evidence showing only the tragic consequences to smokers themselves. Note the difference between smoking and motorcycle helmets: smoking is more normative than motorcycle riding, and as a class, smokers were not initially thought of as a disreputable element in society. While their actions clearly caused economic harm to others, restricting their freedom to harm themselves was not considered possible until it could be shown that the harm done to others was also severe, that little children and other innocent people could be hurt. As a class, cigarette smokers then began to appear less desirable, their "rights" were less valued, and prohibition became more acceptable. There have been other times when the moral force of society has boiled over into prohibitory laws to protect not the miscreant, but the public from harm. David Musto[2] has written an excellent history of the cycles of prohibition in the United States.

There are other justifications for intervention: beneficence, for example, or doing something because it is good to do it, because it benefits someone. The distinction between beneficence and paternalism is narrow at times, and paternalism can erode personal autonomy just as surely as other forms of coercion. Dan Beauchamp[3] has spoken of communitarian values. We might all choose not to wear seat belts while driving. Most of us would not be involved in an accident, but some of us would, and some of us would be killed. Since we know that the community would lose as a result, the community has the right to take action to protect itself.

It is not easy to distinguish between infectious and noninfectious diseases as epidemiologic or pathologic phenomena. Infectious diseases are caused by living microorganisms, and the specific organism is an essential ingredient in the development of the disease: people do not get strep throat without the streptococcal organism. That is because we have defined that disease in that manner. Similar sore throats can occur for other reasons. The presence of the microorganism is not always sufficient to cause the disease. Diseases are a function of the strength of the causative agent and the resistance of the humans.

Noninfectious diseases have some of the same characteristics. Although not caused by a microorganism (some exceptions will be noted in a moment), the various ingredients in the development of such diseases are not always individually sufficient to cause the disease. Many smokers do not get lung cancer, and most drivers who do not use seat belts do not die in traffic accidents. In fact, it is possible for nonsmokers to die from lung cancer, since there are other ways to inhale a sufficient quantity of carcinogenic chemicals (although none so efficient as smoking).

Some so-called chronic noninfectious diseases begin with an acute infectious disease. Rheumatic heart disease, for example, is a complication of certain streptococcal infections. It is a disabling, chronic illness, which cannot be communicated to anyone else. Syphilis freqently caused a chronic brain disease that was not communicable. A number of important progressive and chronic diseases are thought to be caused by "slow" viruses.

Noninfectious diseases are sometimes called chronic diseases, but that is not very helpful. Does the word *chronic* mean that it lasts a long time once you have it (paraplegia after an automobile injury) or that it takes a long time to develop (such as most cancers)? The largest current textbook dealing with disease prevention does not make a simple distinction between infectious and noninfectious diseases but is divided into sections dealing with communicable diseases, environmental health, behavioral factors affecting health, and noncommunicable and chronic disabling conditions, which are not defined.[4] The book is largely clinical in its development and application.

Classification schemes are meant to be useful and should be used only so long as they serve that purpose. They rarely have any intrinsic validity. This book is about the organization of public health programs. Calling a disease infectious or noninfectious does not alter its character or its epidemiology one whit. The distinction is made here partly out of convenience and, more importantly, to reflect the different rationales used to support control efforts. Noninfectious diseases can be divided into several subcategories. Injury control will be discussed separately in Chapter 21. The remaining diseases can be divided into those that are "caused" by something pathologic (the tobacco-related diseases, for example, or rheumatoid arthritis or juvenile diabetes) and those that appear to be the result of declining victim resistance or accelerated aging (such as osteoarthritis, cataracts, or adult onset diabetes). The distinction is of little use biologically but may result in different social attitudes toward intervention.

This chapter covers control programs, not health promotion generally. Several important aspects of disease control are discussed in subsequent chapters and will not be considered here: AIDS (Chapter 16), health promotion (Chapter 17), environmental health (Chapters 18 and 19), occupational health and safety (Chapter 20), injury control (Chapter 21), maternal and child health (Chapter 23), school health and adolescence (Chapter 25), aging (Chapter 26), mental health (Chapter 27), substance use and abuse (Chapter 28), and violence (Chapter 29). (That this includes so many chapters of the book is not surprising since this is a book about public health.)

THE PROBLEM

The decline in the power of infectious diseases has been discussed in earlier chapters. Changing mortality patterns for children aged 1 to 4 are shown in Table 15-1. The 10 leading causes of death had a combined mortality rate of 359.4 in 1925, and 78% of those deaths were from infectious diseases. By 1984, the mortality rate for the 10 leading causes of death in children aged 1 to 4 had declined to 37.1, and only 4% of those deaths were from infectious diseases. Only accidents in 1984 would have made the list in 1925, the other 9 causes having lower mortality rates than any of the diseases on the list in 1925. Surprisingly, motor vehicle accidents, which are a function of passenger miles driven, declined from 1925 to 1984, despite the substantial increase in number of passenger miles driven.

Similar changes have occurred in adult mortality rates (Table 15-2). As with rates for children, the

TABLE 15-1 Mortality rates in the 1 to 4 age group, United States, 1925 and 1986

Cause of death, 1925	Rate per 100,000	Cause of death, 1986	Rate per 100,000
Diarrhea and enteritis	109.8	Accidents	13.4
Accidents	57.7	Motor vehicle accidents	7.0
Pneumonia	44.7	Congenital anomalies	6.1
Diphtheria	43.0	Malignant neoplasms	4.0
Tuberculosis	28.9	Influenza and pneumonia	1.4
Whooping cough	28.6	Homicide	2.7
Measles	14.4	Heart disease	2.5
Scarlet fever	11.7	Diarrhea and enteritis	0.1
Motor vehicle accidents	11.7	Nephritis	0.2
Heart disease	8.9	Tuberculosis	0.0

From Bureau of the Census: Mortality statistics, 1927, part 1, Washington, DC, 1927, US Government Printing Office; National Center for Health Statistics: Vital statistics of the United States, 1986, vol II—Mortality, part A, Washington, DC, 1988, US Government Printing Office.

changes have been dramatic. Total mortality rates have been cut in half since 1940. Deaths from infectious diseases such as tuberculosis, syphilis, and rheumatic heart disease have almost disappeared. Deaths from diabetes, cirrhosis, and motor vehicle accidents have declined. Deaths from cancer, heart disease, and homicide have increased. The often-labeled "epidemic" of cancer is really an epidemic of lung cancer due to cigarette smoking. In the absence of that phenomenon, the cancer mortality rate, in the age groups shown, has declined. A substantial proportion of the increase in the mortality rate due to heart disease has also been related to cigarette smoking. Note that here too, as with children, the motor vehicle accident mortality

TABLE 15-2 Death rates for selected causes, by age group, 1940 and 1985

	Age			
Cause of death	**25-34**	**35-44**	**45-54**	**55-64**
Tuberculosis				
1940	52.9	56.1	62.4	72.0
1985	0.2	0.4	0.8	1.3
Syphilis				
1940	7.1	17.8	29.6	39.0
1985	0	0	0	0.1
Cancer				
1940	17.3	61.1	168.8	369.6
1985	13.1	45.7	169.1	450.5
Lung cancer				
1940	0.8	3.5	13.0	25.7
1985	0.8	8.1	52.8	158.4
Breast cancer				
1940	1.9	9.8	23.3	37.2
1985	3.0	17.5	46.7	83.6
Rheumatic heart disease				
1940	9.9	16.2	25.3	40.5
1985	0.4	0.8	2.3	5.3
Coronary artery disease				
1940	5.0	29.8	102.2	247.2
1985	4.9	37.8	170.1	501.7
Diabetes				
1940	2.8	6.7	25.0	87.2
1985	1.3	3.7	8.8	26.1
Cirrhosis				
1940	1.8	7.2	16.5	87.2
1985	3.0	9.8	22.0	33.8
Motor vehicle accidents				
1940	24.8	22.2	29.1	41.2
1985	22.8	17.1	15.2	15.5
Homicide				
1940	12.0	9.8	6.7	4.7
1985	14.7	11.3	8.1	5.7
TOTALS				
1940	305.9	520.1	1059.9	2226.2
1985	123.4	207.2	516.3	1282.7

From US Bureau of the Census: Vital statistics of the United States, 1940, volume 2, Washington, DC, 1943, US Government Printing Office; National Center for Health Statistics: Vital statistics of the United States, vol 2, part A, Hyattsville, MD, 1988, US Government Printing Office.

rate has dropped considerably, even though the number of passenger miles driven has increased markedly during the past 45 years.

Two observations about these two tables are important: (1) classification of some of the diseases has changed considerably during the 45-year period, as has diagnostic accuracy on the death certificate, and (2) grouping or subdividing categories can alter the picture considerably. The heart disease classification is particularly troublesome, since the grouping of diseases that make up this category has changed several times. When considering younger age groups, the combination of all other accidents with motor vehicle accidents would change the relative position of accidents vis-a-vis other causes of death. Categorical disease interest groups do just that. The heart association, the lung association, the cancer society, and the safety council can group various causes of death in different fashions to make a particular cause of death number one in certain age groups. Nonetheless, the changes are astounding.

The combination of a declining infant mortality rate and sharp drops in mortality for young children means that many more people are living into and through their adult years. The number of people becoming 65 (the threshold of what was once called old age) has increased markedly in the past few decades. More recently, beginning in the mid-1960s, adult mortality rates have declined rapidly, principally as a result of a decline in deaths due to heart disease. This has been true at all ages for adults, including those over 65. Therefore, concurrent with an increase in the *incidence* of aging, the average duration of life for those over 65 has increased. Prevalence, or the number of people with a given characteristic, is a product of the incidence of the characteristic and its duration (see Chapter 5). When both incidence and duration increase (the number of people reaching 65 and the average duration of life after that), the prevalence of those over age 65 increases very rapidly indeed. If 400,000 people become 65 years old each year and they can expect to live, on the average, 10 years, there will be 10 × 400,000 or 4,000,000 people over the age of 65. If the number of 65-year-olds increases to 800,000 and their life expectancy increases to 20 years, there will be 20 × 800,000 or 16,000,000 people over the age of 65! Since chronic diseases and other causes of activity limitation increase with age (even though people are healthier now than they have ever been before), the prevalence of dependency due to chronic diseases has increased.

That is the nature of the problem: as death rates have declined, the relative importance of the noninfectious diseases has increased, and because of the aging of the population, it is widely feared that the prevalence of dependency due to such conditions will present a serious economic burden to society. (However, see Chapter 26 for some interesting counter-arguments.)

Prevention, control, and postponement

Faced with such a problem, public health has been challenged to find less costly ways to deal with dependency, by developing new methods or by restricting utilization of available services. The true contribution of public health, however, lies in the prevention of dependency, not its management. Milton Terris[1] has drawn special attention to the problems of heart disease, cancer, cerebrovascular disease, injuries, chronic obstructive pulmonary disease, and chronic liver disease. The list does not include a number of important and serious causes of dependency, such as Alzheimer's disease or arthritis, but it does include problems that can be prevented, controlled, or postponed. The differences are profound.

Prevention has been defined and described in Chapters 5 and 14. Control refers to a reduction in the incidence and prevalence of a disease by organized community actions. Postponement is significantly different. Measles can be prevented. Lung cancer can be prevented. Collectively, efforts to prevent them constitute a control program. Loss of organ reserve capacity over time cannot be prevented, but its progression to the point at which dependency occurs can be postponed in many instances. Assuming that most important organs will eventually wear out, it may be possible to slow the process and thus postpone to a later point in life both the awareness and the reality of the limitation. Lung disease due to cigarette smoking is dose-dependent: the greater the number of pack-years of exposure, the greater the damage and the earlier in life the loss of effective lung tissue will be noticed. Reduction in exposure (fewer years, fewer packs, or both) slows the rate of progression and postpones the onset of symptoms. If the onset of the problem is postponed long enough, the reformed smoker may die of old age before the lung damage materializes, and postponement becomes the same as prevention. But the difference is important. It may not be possible to prevent altogether, in the usual sense of that word, the onset of cataracts, diabetes, chronic obstructive pulmonary disease, periodontitis, or a host of other noninfectious diseases, but it may be possible to retard their rate of development, to postpone the onset of disability, and therefore prevent or shorten the period of dependency. Some noninfectious diseases can be prevented, as noted above. Postponement can accomplish the same goal.

Some indicators of noninfectious disease[5]

In 1986, 38.8% of those over the age of 65 in the United States had some limitation of activity due to chronic conditions, and slightly more than one quarter of those were unable to carry on their major activity as a result. Nearly one third of males over the age of 20 were current cigarette smokers (1985), and 28.4% of women had the same problem. From 1976 to 1980, 20.1% of all people aged 25 to 74 had elevated blood pressure. The rate increases with age, reaching 34.5% of the population aged 65 to 74. It is more common in black people: 27.7% versus 19.2% for whites.

Serum cholesterol levels were found to be increased in 21.9% of all people from 1976 to 1980. The rates have been declining in recent years, down from 26.9% in 1960. Slightly more than 28% of all people were overweight, a problem that seems to be increasing slightly.

ROLE OF THE GOVERNMENT

Government clearly has the responsibility and the authority to intervene when a disease threatens people. That is why the colonial cities in the United States originally developed boards of health. It was a protective or defensive reaction. Originally few services were provided. The signal case was separated from society until the victim died or became well. With the development of the biological sciences, a more enlightened approach became possible although not always practiced. The freedom of the victims to move about through society could be restricted, and they could be treated as well. This was not only more humane but could shorten the period during which the government had to assume responsibility for the victim. As noninfectious diseases assumed greater importance, the state was faced with a problem: if no one was harmed but the victim, why should the state intervene? And yet the state was eager to intervene. It is almost impossible for a group of citizens to observe a large number of people being harmed by their own behavior, or by events over which they have no control, and do nothing about it. When personal behavior is thought to be the major cause of the problem, they will try education and persuasion first, then various mechanisms such as the use of taxes to raise the price of the product, and finally, restriction on the availability of the product or its use.[6] As noted above, the movement toward more forceful and coercive interventions is congruent with escalating assertions that the problem is harmful to others and not just the victim.

Prevention can take other forms as well. The distinction was made in the last chapter between prevention, protection, and promotion. Prevention includes individual, clinical, or personal health services such as immunizations, screening for high blood pressure and follow-up services, or the use of Pap smears to detect the precursors to cancer of the cervix. Protection means the activities of organizations, both public and private, to reduce exposure to hazards such as polluted water, high-fat content milk in the public schools, contaminated food, traffic accidents, or the use of electric saws without safety devices. Promotion means personal actions that people can take to prevent the four "Ds" of disease and injury (death, disability, dependency, and dolor), such as not smoking, following a good diet, and exercising appropriately.

The primary prevention of noninfectious diseases is often a function of health promotion and education (see Chapter 17). Secondary prevention usually involves screening programs to detect the changes leading to the disease at an early stage so as to make treatment possible before dependency occurs. Screening programs have not lived up to people's hopes and expectations, however. On the face of it, they offer a great deal, but the problems presented by false positives and false negatives are serious (see Chapter 5), and although well-managed screening programs can lead to detection of disease at an early stage, it does not always follow that the health status of the screened population is improved. Additionally, the cost of the benefits gained can be exorbitant. Perhaps not for a nation that can send a rocket to Mars and make war on poverty, but most nations will have to make painful choices.

David Eddy[7] accepts the conclusion from large cancer screening studies that X-ray mammography to find a small, nonpalpable breast lump can increase the 5-year survival rate from 60% to 95%. However, part of that increase is the result of detecting the disease earlier, thus giving only the appearance of longer survival. Moreover, Eddy says, "the expected impact of a single mammogram on a woman who has a negative physical examination is to increase her longevity by about two days—an effect approximately equivalent to avoiding one ride in a small plane." In the group aged 40 to 49, the risk of breast cancer in the next 10 years is 128/10,000 and the risk of dying is 82/10,000. Adding an annual mammogram to a physical examination reduces that risk to 60/10,000, a 26% reduction. If just one quarter of the women in this age group were screened annually, there would be 373 fewer deaths due to breast cancer in the year 2000. The net cost, in 1984 dollars, would be $408 million, or approximately $1.1 million per life saved.

Screening raises other difficult questions. Using one set of criteria, 7.3% of males and 5.8% of females who were screened for high blood cholesterol were referred for further examination and treatment. Using another set of criteria, the referral rates increased to 49.2% and 40.2% respectively.[8] People who voluntarily participate in most screening programs are not necessarily those who are at highest risk. Friedman[9] has shown that "regular" participants in such programs are at lower risk than are "reluctant" participants, a generalization that is important but not always true.

Chronic diseases, by definition, may take a long time to evolve into something that can be detected. Infrequent screening will save very few lives, because the condition can develop and progress too far between examinations. As the frequency of screening increases (or the interscreening interval decreases), more lives can be saved. The increase in the value of the screening device levels off as frequency and cost increase still more. Once-a-day screening would be the most effective at detecting the greatest number of people with the disease, but the cost would be prohibitive, and many, many people who do not have the disease would be referred for more expensive and possibly dangerous diagnostic evaluations. Each condition has its own unique set of conditions. There are other problems too. Overall, screening in adults has been of limited value, with some slight gains in longevity for white males.[10]

In spite of the questions raised by screening activities, it is a popular practice with both the public and health professionals. Between 1973 and 1982, the percentage of people who had been tested for glaucoma increased from 53.7% to 80.7%; for breast cancer, from 76.3% to 90.2%; and for cancer of the cervix, from 75.2% to 89.2%.[11]

Protection activities are another form of government intervention and have had a long record of success. Supplemental iodine in salt has decreased the prevalence of thyroid disease in some areas of the country, and fluoridation of public water supplies has had a major impact on the incidence of dental caries. A 1979-1980 survey of children aged 5 to 17 showed a 33% reduction in the number of decayed, missing, or filled surfaces. Nearly 37% of the children had no caries at all.[12]

Pollution control programs have reduced air and water pollution burdens substantially during the past 20 years in the United States, but there is little evidence to demonstrate a positive effect on the health status of those exposed. Nonetheless, environmental control programs, both in the workplace (see Chapter 20) and in the general outdoor environment, are effective means of protection against hazards. The success with indoor air pollution in private dwelling places is another problem altogether. Once again, the healthy reluctance of government to intervene in private matters leaves certain serious problems uncorrected.

The governmental presence, then, can pursue a variety of methods to reduce dependency due to noninfectious diseases. Through control programs it can both prevent and postpone the onset of dependency. It can do so through primary prevention (principally health promotion and environmental regulation) and secondary prevention (screening for the most part, coupled with follow-up).

CONTROL PROGRAMS

Prevention and protection activities aimed at noninfectious diseases are ubiquitous at all levels of government. In the U.S. Department of Health and Human Services, the Office of Disease Prevention and Health Promotion is responsible for coordinating prevention activities and for disseminating research and demonstration project information. This office was responsible for the original development of national objectives for the prevention of disease and health promotion.[13] A second major effort, describing objectives for the year 2000, will be available in 1990. The office also publishes an inventory of federal activities in disease prevention and health promotion.[14]

The federal government both supports and engages in prevention research at the National Institutes of Health (NIH) and at the Centers for Disease Control. Demonstration projects are supported in a number of state and local health departments and under the auspices of schools of public health. The National Cancer Institute was slow to become involved in control, as opposed to research, activities at the outset, even though prevention was part of its original mandate.[15] Responsibility for cancer control was transferred out of the Institute in 1957 into the Bureau of State Services (a bureau long since gone) with $2.5 million for formula grants to the state health departments and $60,000 for its own operations. The program focused on Pap smears initially. Similar programs were developed in the bureau for heart disease, neurological and sensory diseases, diabetes, and other NIH priority areas. The National Cancer Act was amended in 1971 and responsibility for control activities was reestablished in the Institute. Many interest groups, including practicing physicians, business, and the biomedical research establishment, have been opposed to efforts in chronic disease control by the federal government in general and by the NIH specifically. Part of the opposition is ideological, part competitive. Advocates have been less numerous and forceful.

State and local health departments devote a considerable part of their resources to prevention and protection activities designed to reduce dependency due to noninfectious diseases. Table 15-3 indicates the size of such efforts in a few categorical areas.

In 1981, various U.S. Public Health Service categorical grants-in-aid were consolidated into a preventive health services block grant. The total amount of money available was reduced, but the states were given increased flexibility to plan for the most appropriate use of that money. The experiences of the states have been varied. In Massachusetts, 39% of the grant was allocated to the development of emergency medical services; 12% to hypertension detection and control; 15% to health education and risk reduction activities; 9% to fluoridation; and the remainder to a variety of other activities. Many of these programs had been established under the previous mechanism of categorical grants, and their continuation reflected the presence of constituent groups with a strong interest in maintaining them. The state added $200,000 annually to the block grant and established a State Center for Health Promotion and Environmental Disease Prevention with $1.3 million in state funds. A resource allocation model was developed, which considered a variety of criteria,

TABLE 15-3 Selected State Health Agency (SHA) programs and activities to control noninfectious diseases, 1984

High blood pressure	46 SHAs screened 6.1 million people in 197 personal health service programs. 42 SHAs reported screening 2.6 million people in high blood pressure programs; 4.2% were diagnosed as hypertensive; 44% of those were treated. 15% of those screened by 33 SHAs were black.
Genetic screening	47 SHAs screened 2.6 million infants for genetic diseases.
Infant health	44 SHAs provided health assessment services for infants.
Lead poisoning	35 SHAs carried out treatment activities; 99% of those found were treated.
Occupational safety and health	See Chapter 20.
Perinatal services	See Chapter 22.
Injury control	See Chapter 21.
Dental health	67% of the 157 million people served by water systems in 45 states received fluoridated water.
Nutrition	46 SHAs provided nutrition assistance to 4.6 million people.

From 1990 objectives for the nation: profile of state health agency progress, Washington, DC, 1987, Public Health Foundation.

as resources were slowly shifted from the targets previously selected by federal requirements to more closely reflect the needs of Massachusetts. Criteria included the size of the problem, identification of modifiable causes, the efficacy of intervention, the estimated benefit-to-cost ratio, and the availability of useful objectives and an evaluation process.[16]

Publication of *Promoting Health/Preventing Disease: Objectives for the Nation*[13] by the Surgeon General in 1980 touched off a continuing wave of activity in the states. The publication included 226 objectives, most of which dealt with risk factors for noninfectious diseases. *Model Standards*,[17] published in 1985, included more than 400 standards to be considered in the development of community prevention programs. Many states wrote their own objectives documents, using state data to obtain a better estimate of the problems their citizens faced and to build a sense of investment in the effort. State leaders described a number of requirements for an effective program: leadership first of all; then good strategic management, able to examine the opportunities outside the health department, in the private sector and in community programs, set measurable targets or objectives, and develop the evaluative mechanisms to review progress and readjust the programs; effective communications between the health department and elected officials; attention to consensus building; accountability mechanisms; good programming; and the development of collaborative working relationships with other public and private agencies.[18] The importance of a "hard-nosed" assessment of health status was stressed. State program directors found that the political process by which health policy is formed was an important aspect of their ability to gain support for prevention and control programs.

State health agencies participate in an annual conference on the control of noninfectious diseases at which information is shared concerning surveillance, applied research and technology transfer, program organization and implementation, evaluation, marketing, communication and training.[19]

Interest in the prevention and control of noninfectious diseases is high at this time for several reasons: beneficence, communitarian values, and economics. The public and its elected representatives are cautious about intervening, however, because of conflicting information and because of a traditional reluctance to become too intimately involved in private affairs. The caution is justified. A common plaint, after reading the day's health news, is that you can't do anything anymore—everything is dangerous. The public is bombarded by conflicting information about disease prevention, and the loci in which action occurs are too numerous to count. Yet there are a few fairly simple objectives of major importance, some with cross-cutting impact on a number of important causes of death, disability, dependency, and dolor,[20] which have been known since the famous Alameda County study began in 1965.[21] They include the major problems of smoking and the use of drugs and other dangerous substances, exercise, nutrition, and stress management. They also include a variety of measures to assure that every child has a chance to live independently (a topic that will be more fully discussed in subsequent chapters). They do not justify the popular notion that government has no role to play and that people are individually responsible for their own health. It is certainly useful to consider what people can do to improve their health status, but it is not sufficient. The physical and social environment that is supported by collective actions and government policies can and does have a significant impact on individual health and on the health status of the community. The argument has been phrased nicely by Tesh[22]: "a public health policy that consists mainly of exhorting individuals to change their behavior appears at best to be shortsighted. At worst it seems less a policy directed at attaining health for the public than one bent on protecting the institutions . . . threatening that health."

REFERENCES

1. Terris M: Redefining the public health agenda, J Public Health Policy 8:151, Summer 1987.
2. Musto DF: The American disease: origins of narcotic control, New York, 1987, Oxford University Press.
3. Beauchamp D: Community: the neglected tradition of public health, Hastings Cent Rep 15:28, Dec 1985.
4. Last JM, editor: Maxcy-Rosenau's public health and preventive medicine, ed 12, Norwalk, CT, 1986, Appleton-Century-Crofts.
5. National Center for Health Statistics: Health United States, 1987, Hyattsville, MD, 1988, US Department of Health and Human Services.
6. Warner KE and others: Licit and illicit drug policies: a typology, unpublished manuscript, 1988.

7. Eddy D: Screening for cancer: theory, analysis and design, Englewood Cliffs, NJ, 1980, Prentice-Hall.
8. Råstam L and others: Population screening and referral for hypercholesterolemia, Am J Prev Med 4:249, Sep-Oct 1988.
9. Friedman GD: Multisite screening. In Schottenfeld D and Fraumeni JF, editors: Cancer epidemiology and prevention, Philadelphia, 1982, WB Saunders Co.
10. Collen MF, editor: Multiphasic health testing services, New York, 1977, John Wiley & Sons.
11. Dawson DA, Hendershot GE, and Bloom B: Trends in routine screening examinations, Am J Public Health 77:1004, Aug 1987.
12. National Caries Program, National Institute of Dental Research: The prevalence of dental caries in United States children, 1979-1980, NIH Pub No 82-2245, Dec 1981, US Department of Health and Human Services.
13. Public Health Service: Promoting health/preventing disease: objectives for the nation, Washington, DC, 1980, US Department of Health and Human Services.
14. Office of Disease Prevention and Health Promotion: Prevention 86/87: federal programs and progress, Washington, DC, 1987, US Department of Health and Human Services.
15. Breslow L and Breslow DM: Historical perspectives. In Schottenfeld D and Fraumeni JF, editors: Cancer epidemiology and prevention, Philadelphia, 1982, WB Saunders Co.
16. Havas S and Blik C: The preventive health and health services block grant: the Massachusetts experience, Public Health Rep 102:284, May-Jun 1987.
17. American Public Health Association, Association of State and Territorial Health Officials, National Association of County Health Officials, US Conference of Local Health Officers, and Centers for Disease Control: Model standards: a guide for community preventive health services, ed 2, Washington, DC, 1985, American Public Health Association.
18. Intergovernmental Health Policy Project: A review of state activities related to the Public Health Service's health promotion and disease prevention objectives for the nation, Office of Disease Prevention and Health Promotion Monograph Series, Washington, DC, 1986, US Department of Health and Human Services.
19. Mason JO, Koplan JP, and Layde PM: The prevention and control of chronic disease: reducing unnecessary deaths and disability—a conference report, Public Health Rep 102:17, Jan-Feb 1987.
20. Public Health Service: Healthy people: the Surgeon General's report on health promotion and disease prevention, Washington, DC, 1979, US Department of Health, Education and Welfare.
21. Berkman LF and Breslow L: Health and ways of living: the Alameda County study, New York, 1983, Oxford University Press.
22. Tesh SN: Hidden arguments: political ideology and disease prevention policy, New Brunswick, NJ, 1988, Rutgers University Press.

CHAPTER 16

AIDS: the public health challenge

The history and the future of public health can be told through the saga of AIDS. This chapter will not tell that story. By the time it is read, the chapter will be obsolete, but the disease and the lessons it has taught—is teaching—will not be. The literature on AIDS has mushroomed. A search through those journals indexed on Medline, the computerized bibliographic reference system of the National Library of Medicine, shows an increase from 25 articles in 1982 to 4,000 in 1988 (Table 16-1). Very little of that literature will be included in this chapter, because most of it will have been replaced by new information by the time this is read.

The prevention and control of both infectious and noninfectious diseases has been discussed specifically in the last two chapters and generally in most of the other chapters of this book. Why a special chapter on AIDS? Because virtually every important system involved in public health has been challenged by the epidemic. It has called into question our basic concepts of disease prevention and control and challenged the legal system, health care financing, long-term care, laboratories, community care concepts, professional ethics, epidemiology, and behavioral change theorists and practitioners. It has profoundly affected the social values that shape the work of public health. How public health manages the AIDS epidemic will determine the future role of public health in our society. The effort to do so is the subject of this chapter.

THE DISEASE

The first cases of AIDS were recognized in 1981, and the virus was identified soon after. Some blood specimens collected from homosexual men in San Francisco for a study of another viral disease (hepatitis B) were reanalyzed and revealed the presence of antibodies to the human immunodeficiency virus (HIV) as early as 1978. A peculiar virus, it has some special features that make it very worrisome. It attacks the immune mechanisms of the body by infiltrating key defense cells, taking over the genetic machinery of those cells, and forcing a replication of itself. The clones then attack more of the defensive cells of the body.

The first phases of infection are similar to infectious mononucleosis, with fatigue, an elevated temperature, and characteristic white cell changes. During this period, humans develop protein antibodies to the virus, which are the telltale markers used to test for its presence in screening programs and in individual clinical tests. An asymptomatic period follows while the infection slowly progresses, resulting in the later signs of fatigue, nighttime sweating, and chronic diarrhea. The final phase is AIDS itself, a syndrome characterized by repeated severe infections. An intermediate picture of somewhat milder symptoms, known as the AIDS-related complex, or ARC, is not important as a discrete manifestation of AIDS.

It is known as the AIDS epidemic, but AIDS is only the final manifestation of the disease. Infection by the human immunodeficiency virus (HIV) is the disease. While there may be spontaneous remissions, it appears likely that all of those infected with the virus will progress through the various stages and die of the disease. That may take as long as 13 years, but most people who have clinical symptoms will die within 5 to 8 years.

The epidemiology of AIDS*

The virus is both fragile and lethal. It can survive only under very special circumstances. It needs certain types of mammalian cells to reproduce itself. It cannot be transmitted by sneezing or in food or through casual, day-to-day contact. The

* Much of the following information can be found in Confronting AIDS: Update 1988, published by the Institute of Medicine, Washington, DC, 1988, National Academy Press. More recent reviews will be available by now.

virus can be passed from person to person only when certain kinds of cells, containing the virus particles, are transmitted. This can and does occur by blood or semen "injection" and by organ or body tissue transplantation. The virus can be found in breast milk and other secretions.

The most common routes of transmission are by the use of contaminated needles and syringes, sexual intercourse, from an infected mother to her unborn child through the placenta, and by blood transfusions and organ transplantations. The last two modes, transfusions and transplantations, can be prevented almost completely by careful screening of blood and organ donors. Intravenous drug users, known as IVDUs, transfer the virus among themselves by sharing unclean injection equipment such as syringes and needles. The "efficiency" of this form of transmission is not known, since the variables are not readily standardized and measurable, but it is clearly a very high-risk practice. Transmission from mother to fetus occurs in about 30% to 50% of cases in which the mother is infected. The efficiency of transmission by blood transfusion has been estimated to be as high as 66% to 100%. Transmission by accident, as when a laboratory worker is accidentally stuck by a needle, has occurred, but it is very unlikely. In thousands of needle-stick accidents that have occurred when the patient was infected with HIV, the infection rate has been less than 1%.[1]

The efficiency of transmission by sexual intercourse is not precisely known. Transmission is most efficient via anal intercourse. The receptive partner is at greater risk than the insertive partner. Transmission is less likely to occur in vaginal intercourse. It appears to be easier for a male to transmit the virus to a female during vaginal intercourse than for a female to transmit it to her male partner.

The likelihood of transmission in any of the above situations depends on the dose, or amount, of virus transmitted and on numerous biological factors, such as the presence of skin abrasions.

The disease was first described in homosexual men and was thought by many to be a disease unique to that group, but such proved not to be the case. The figures in Table 16-2 illustrate the changing nature of the epidemic as of 1989.

Half the tale of the AIDS epidemic in the United States can be told through the table: the rapid increase in cases and the lethality of the infection. Virtually all of the people diagnosed with the disease in the first year of the epidemic are now dead. More than half of the new cases occurring in 1987 were dead by June 1989. Current estimates (1988) indicate that there are 945,000 to 1,400,000 people infected with HIV in the United States. By the end of 1991, there will be 270,000 people with AIDS and 179,000 deaths. It is anticipated that all of those infected with the virus will die prematurely because of that infection.

That is half the tale of AIDS. The other half concerns who is infected. The disease, as noted above, is concentrated in groups of homosexual and bisexual men, intravenous drug users (IVDUs), female sex partners of male IVDUs, and infants of infected mothers. Like other major health problems, the disease is concentrated in minority groups, especially blacks and Hispanics. Table 16-3 shows the categories of cases by probable means of transmission and racial or ethnic group. Keep in mind that these are reported cases of AIDS, a reportable disease in all states, not cases of HIV infection. Infection with the virus is not yet a reportable disease. Most of the cases of AIDS have occurred in homosexual or bisexual males. However, the proportion has been declining as that population group has been increasingly penetrated by the virus and as its members have changed their sexual behavior (see below). In the last few years, the increase has been greatest in IVDUs and infants.

Most of the cases have occurred in whites, but the attack rates are much higher among blacks and Hispanics. As of June 1989, there were 87,100 cases in males and 8,461 cases in women.

TABLE 16-1 Articles mentioning acquired immunodeficiency syndrome, indexed in Medline, 1981-1988

Year	Articles
1981	0
1982	25
1983	655
1984	1,139
1985	1,677
1986	2,552
1987	3,594
1988	4,000

Whereas 67% of the males presumably have been infected through homosexual activity and 17% by IVDU, 52% of the cases in women have been associated with IVDU and 30% with heterosexual activity.

Most of the cases have occurred in New York, California, Florida, northern New Jersey, and Texas, but all 50 states have been affected. Most of the new cases are now occurring and will continue to occur outside of the initial areas of geographic concentration. As of this date, AIDS is the leading cause of death in New York City for males aged 25 to 44 and for females aged 25 to 34. AIDS is the eighth leading cause of years of life lost before the age of 65. Of every 66 babies born in New York City in 1987 and 1988, 1 had antibodies to the HIV, but not all of them were infected: some simply had antibodies from their mothers, passed through the placenta, without the virus itself.

The HIV epidemic, as it has been measured through the incidence of AIDS, has several characteristics that make it unlike other plagues in history[1]:

1. The victims are permanently infectious throughout their lives, even when they appear well.
2. The primary victims of the epidemic are young adults (although infant AIDS is increasing rapidly).
3. The disease does not affect a random sample of the population but is heavily biased toward already stigmatized groups in society, confounding the discussion of interventions.
4. As noted above, the epidemic is a series of discrete epidemics, each with its own characteristics: IVDUs and their sex partners in New York City, homosexual and bisexual men in San Francisco.

There is one other peculiarity of AIDS with profound importance. Most of the diseases that are the result of human behavior are noninfectious, and the probability of developing the disease increases with cumulative exposure: addictions, lung cancer, obesity, and so forth. AIDS is the result of probabilistic exposure. A behavioral pattern that has a low probability of resulting in infection in an area with a low prevalence of HIV infection has a high probability of disaster in another community where the prevalence of infection is high. Youngsters, who are particularly prone to risk-taking behavior, may be lucky in their home town but

TABLE 16-2 Cases of AIDS and case-fatality rates by half year of diagnosis, United States

Year	Period	No. of cases	No. of fatalities	Case-fatality rate (%)
1981	Jan-Jun	94	87	93
	Jul-Dec	199	183	92
1982	Jan-Jun	393	352	90
	Jul-Dec	667	598	90
1983	Jan-Jun	1,279	1,165	91
	Jul-Dec	1,640	1,483	90
1984	Jan-Jun	2,540	2,182	86
	Jul-Dec	3,343	2,900	87
1985	Jan-Jun	4,762	4,063	85
	Jul-Dec	6,150	5,117	83
1986	Jan-Jun	7,963	6,310	79
	Jul-Dec	9,555	6,947	73
1987	Jan-Jun	11,946	7,814	65
	Jul-Dec	13,108	6,787	52
1988	Jan-Jun	13,927	5,528	40
	Jul-Nov 14	13,146	3,807	29
TOTALS		90,795	55,388	61

Centers For Disease Control: HIV/AIDS surveillance, June 1989, p. 12.

become another tragic statistic elsewhere. It is the probabilistic nature of the risk that is so difficult for people to comprehend. Those who may be infected are rarely noticeable and often unaware of the infection. A single episode of risky behavior can introduce the virus into an otherwise innocent population group.

Other features of the epidemic are special and will be discussed below, as programs to prevent the spread of the disease and to treat its victims are described.

THE PREVENTION AND CONTROL OF HIV INFECTION

At this time, HIV infection cannot be cured. There are drugs that can be used to control some of the extreme conditions caused by HIV infection, but there is no cure. There is also no vaccine to prevent the disease. Its prevention is dependent on the ability and willingness of people to change their behavior and on the willingness of society to provide the resources needed to facilitate the necessary changes. The stigmatization of the dominant groups affected by the epidemic makes prevention and control very difficult. Victim blaming is a common phenomenon. The inappropriateness of such attitudes and beliefs will not be discussed here. Suffice it to say that there are many innocent victims and that intravenous drug use and sexual behavior are not always voluntary in the simplest sense of that word.

Primary prevention of HIV infection requires that attention be paid to those who have not yet begun to engage in high-risk behavior. Techniques must be developed to dissuade them from engaging in practices that can result in infection or to persuade them to develop safer practices. Since the complete avoidance of sexual activity is an unlikely prospect, as is the cessation of IVDU activity, safer practices are an essential part of any educational program. However, this presents public health with a classic dilemma: does teaching someone to use condoms or to clean injection equipment constitute support for behavioral patterns that society wants to condemn? Can a school health education program that avoids describing the use of condoms be effective given the heightened sexuality of adolescent children? If the use of condoms is described, and the descriptions need to be detailed and graphic to be

TABLE 16-3 Reported AIDS cases by transmission category and racial or ethnic group, November 14, 1988

Transmission category	White not Hispanic	Black not Hispanic	Hispanic	Asian/Pacific Islander	American Indian/ Alaskan Native	Totals
Adults/Adolescents						
Homosexual/bisexual male	42,327	9,367	6,064	432	58	58,389
IVDU	3,909	9,731	5,764	20	19	19,497
Homosexual male and IVDU	4,062	1,743	986	8	16	6,824
Coagulation disorder	761	58	71	12	6	912
Heterosexual cases	845	2,753	673	19	7	4,305
Transfusion cases	1,742	360	206	45	3	2,361
Undetermined	1,239	1,264	701	35	5	3,273
Subtotals	54,915	25,276	14,465	571	114	95,561
Children						
Coagulation disorder	67	11	13	3		94
Parents with/at risk of AIDS	192	785	306	3	3	1,293
Transfusion	102	44	40	3		189
Undetermined	12	32	12			56
Subtotals	373	872	371	9	3	1,632
TOTALS	55,288	26,148	14,836	580	117	97,193

Centers For Disease Control: HIV/AIDS surveillance, June 1989, p. 9.

useful, does that constitute tacit acceptance of activities that a substantial proportion of the parents and teachers wish to proscribe altogether?

A second target group for primary prevention activities consists of those who are already involved in high-risk behaviors and convincing them either to abstain or to adopt safer practices. The same problem arises in this instance, albeit with less of a sense of urgency, since those involved are already stigmatized to some extent and society cares less about them. A third group consists of those who are infected. Preventive intervention involves convincing them not to expose others.

Secondary prevention is not an especially useful activity unless it is seen as one aspect of approaching the last of the three groups mentioned above. It involves early case-finding in an effort to curtail further spread.

Tertiary prevention is not a practical concept in HIV infection, although a great deal can be done to control some of the consequences of the disease and to ease the suffering that accompanies such a dreadful end to so short a life.

Attempts to modify behavior have been studied in several cohorts of gay men in San Francisco with encouraging results. (On the other hand, half of the estimated total population of gay men in that city were thought to be infected by 1988, leaving little room for optimism.) There were profound changes as the groups became more fully aware of the nature of the epidemic and the risk factors involved. Monogamous relationships increased in their binding power; fewer people were engaging in anal intercourse outside of their monogamous relationships, and more men were using condoms.[2] Studies of the effectiveness of such efforts in IVDU groups have been less well developed and even more difficult. Some changes in behavior have been observed, with a higher proportion of young males making some effort to sterilize their injection equipment, but these changes may be less noticeable in the primary groups at risk, young black and Hispanic males. Again, the highest risk groups are the most difficult to reach and to evaluate. There is little evidence of abstinence, however. This makes more important the need to clarify the goals of a behavioral change program.

Recidivism has also been examined. There is some evidence that males who can be encouraged to alter their behavior return to their previous high-risk patterns over time. The number of unknowns in this important effort is daunting. What are the determinants of behavioral risk reduction? What can be effective in the groups at highest risk? What can be done to maintain behavioral changes over a lifetime? Little is yet known, but the studies are under way. As in other aspects of this epidemic, the answers promise to shed light on numerous other important aspects of public health. Little has been done to try to understand the factors underlying IVDU behavior, and even less is known about the minority groups most affected. AIDS is now driving the necessary research, which may have beneficial impacts far beyond this singularly important problem.

Screening for those infected with the virus has received a great deal of attention, and bills have been introduced in all states to require screening activities in certain groups. However, at the end of 1988 the only useful screening activity appeared to be that directed at safeguarding the supply of blood, blood products, and tissues used in transplant surgery. Once again, the apparent attractiveness of screening is found to be disappointing on closer examination. Fortunately, public health leaders in the states have been successful in preventing the passage of such legislation. There are at least two important reasons why population screening is not useful. General population screening has the problems associated with low prevalence and the serious consequences of both false negatives and false positives. While the current tests are very good, false negatives and positives still occur. The latter can lead to profound psychological consequences, whereas the former may lead to the unwitting exposure of others. A few states have required HIV screening as a condition for receiving a marriage license. Since sexual activity so often precedes marriage and since the disease is so uncommon in heterosexual couples applying for a marriage license, this accomplishes little, however. Universal premarital screening might find 1,200 people with a positive blood test for HIV infection, or about 0.1% of all of the people thought to be infected. It would also label 380 people falsely positive and miss 120 infected people.[3] One factor that can increase the value of screening is the ability to treat those infected to render them noninfectious, but this cannot be done with AIDS.

The other problem thought to militate against compulsory screening is the possibility that those who are especially at risk might avoid the screening procedures to avoid the real or imagined consequences of being detected. Those who have considered the issue have insisted that careful attention must be given to confidentiality provisions before any mandatory screening program can be implemented, and the same requirements must be applied to voluntary screening programs as well. Those who are to be screened need to know what is being done and why; pre- and postscreening counseling services must be available; and rigorous provisions to assure confidentiality must be in place.

Reporting of positive test results has been required in a few states. This too has been opposed by many public health leaders who see reporting as a precursor to compulsory testing and are concerned about the lack of safeguards to protect the confidentiality of those test results. It should be noted, however, that the public health record in this respect has been outstanding. A well-enunciated set of conditions has been in effect in programs to control other sexually transmitted diseases for many years, with very few breaches of the confidentiality provisions.

Another aspect of programs to control infectious diseases has been the necessity to warn others who may be at risk. This has become especially complex in the case of HIV infection. If someone who is found to be infected indicates to those health professionals who know of the condition that he or she will not cease taking part in activities that can infect others, what is the duty of those who know? Increasingly, health professionals, ethicists and lawyers are of the opinion that the duty to warn is paramount, provided every reasonable effort has been made to obtain voluntary notification.

The problems become even more difficult, however. As noted in Chapter 5, isolation of infected people has been used in the past and may still have some utility. What steps should be taken to prevent an infected individual from knowingly infecting others? The AIDS epidemic seems likely to result in the recodification of statutes concerning the control of communicable diseases. Courts have been willing to enforce restriction of the civil liberties of those who are infected when their behavior constitutes a threat to others. The principles embodied in mental health laws prescribing that the least restrictive approaches be utilized are entering into the public health field at last. Both male and female prostitutes infected with HIV have had their freedom restricted under court order.

Treatment services for those infected with HIV are likely to remain under public auspices. Historically, the treatment of dangerous and unpopular diseases, especially when they afflict society's underclasses, has been a government responsibility. AIDS patients occasionally require complex medical intervention, but most of their needs can be met in a caring community setting. Specialized inpatient and outpatient services are needed to deal with some of the complex problems encountered. Long-term care beds, community-based board and care facilities, and hospice care are all needed for AIDS patients and will be difficult to establish. New Jersey has moved aggressively to establish such facilities, but the need for them is rapidly outstripping the planned supply in most major metropolitan areas. The special needs of children with AIDS have become a difficult problem in some cities. Many otherwise effective caregivers are afraid of infected children, even though the risk of infection is slight. Many communities resist the location of board and care facilities for such patients. The children are often without any useful parental support, making their care and the financing of that care even more difficult. In those few cases in which a mother is present, she is usually infected herself and may be unable to provide the support needed. There is nothing about the care of the victims of HIV that is beyond the knowledge of health and social service professionals, but the availability of the necessary resources is becoming a crucial problem.

A final, important question: what are the obligations of health professionals when faced with a disease that clearly can be a threat to them? It is generally agreed that, as a class, physicians have an obligation to treat those who are ill, even if doing so places the physician at some risk, but the courts have not been willing to require them to treat those they wish not to treat except in an emergency situation. The American Medical Association has adopted the policy that a physician "may not ethically refuse to treat a patient whose condition is within the physician's current realm of competence" merely because that patient is infected with HIV.[4] Nursing has adopted a similar policy.[5] The problem does not end with policies, however. Although the risk is slight for physicians and nurses as a group, especially if they take the sort of precautions they should take to guard against infectious diseases generally, the risk is nonetheless real. Moreover, in some inner-city emergency rooms the percentage of patients infected with HIV may be very high. Health professionals have insisted that they be warned if a patient is infected. How can confidentiality be protected in such an environment? A system will have to be developed to indicate situations in which such risks exist, such as the general warning that has been used in the past to indicate particular kinds of isolation techniques to guard against other blood-borne infections.

The list of issues goes on. As noted at the beginning of this chapter, virtually every system encountered when dealing with AIDS and HIV infection requires examination and change.

STATE AND LOCAL PROGRAMS

Although many people are dissatisfied with the response of society and its governments to the HIV epidemic, responses have been impressive. The federally supported biomedical research establishment has done an extraordinary amount of work. It has been observed that medical progress accelerates during wartime; that has been the case with AIDS. The rapidity with which the virus was identified and dissected was extraordinary. During conservative administrations not known for supporting social service programs, the amount of money appropriated for research and service has been significant. The Surgeon General of the Public Health Service at the time, Dr. C. Everett Koop, was a courageous spokesman for aggressive and compassionate intervention. Under his auspices, a frank and useful pamphlet was written about AIDS and distributed to every household in the United States in 1988. The Centers for Disease Control has been effective and expert in its definition of the problem, its data collection activities, and its information dissemination work. As is usually the case in this federalist form of government, the delivery of services and creativity in organizing them have been the responsibility of state and local governments and numerous private, not-for-profit organizations.

As noted above, AIDS legislation has been introduced in every state. The legislative activities fall into three categories: laws to find and identify those who are infected, laws to protect the privacy of those who are infected, and laws concerning the provision of treatment services for those who are ill. The latter, so far, have been in the minority. AIDS itself is a reportable disease in all 50 states and the District of Columbia. HIV infection was reportable in only 10 states as of mid-1988. Those states with the most cases generally have been less active in passing legislation to detect new cases than have those states with relatively few cases.[6] State public health agencies have been effective in preventing bad legislation except in a few states, such as Illinois and Louisiana, which have passed mandatory premarital screening laws.

Voluntary screening programs have expanded rapidly. With the initiation of blood screening by the Red Cross and other organizations, there was considerable fear that people at high risk might volunteer to donate blood to obtain screening, thereby endangering the blood supply. Alternative screening sites were established quickly to meet this demand. Such programs have evolved into HIV clinics, which should provide testing services, counseling, and community and professional education. Dr. Vernon, the state health director in Colorado, has insisted on reporting, partner notification, and contact tracing, as has been the practice for other sexually transmitted diseases. His position has been unpopular in some quarters, but the information provided by the programs in Colorado has been very useful. It does not indicate that confidentiality has been a problem, nor is there any evidence to indicate that those at high risk have avoided voluntary screening because of the reporting and notification requirements.[7]

Often with state guidance and financial support, many local communities, especially those with a high incidence of AIDS cases, have developed state and local level interagency councils, involving both government and private organizations: public health, mental health, social services, education, hospitals, physician groups, the clergy, and many others. These groups can be effective in facilitating an enlightened and helpful community response and increased allocation of needed resources for the treatment and care of the victims of the epidemic. This has not been true in all cases, of course, and some communities remain woefully behind in preparing for the problems they will have in the next several years.

In most states, special task forces or other interagency groups have been formed to prevent and control the spread of HIV infection. This too has been a useful and important experience for the public health establishment. As in other important public health areas, effective work requires the collaboration of numerous agencies, particularly the state health, mental health, education, and welfare authorities.

Funding has been a problem, in spite of the rapid growth in federal support and increased allocations by many state legislative bodies. There has been some tendency to reallocate existing funds away from other public health activities, an activity that can be counterproductive. HIV activities need to take place in clinics for the treatment of sexually transmitted diseases, family planning clinics, maternal and child health programs, tuberculosis control clinics (the suppression of the normal immune mechanisms is leading to a resurgence of tuberculosis in some communities), physicians' offices, hospital clinics, emergency rooms, and community clinics. Diverting funds from these programs will reduce important activities to prevent the spread of the disease.

State Medicaid programs have become the most important source of payment for treatment services. The programs need to be expanded, and more states need to develop Medicaid-supported programs to provide community-based social and health services for AIDS patients as a more humane and less costly alternative to hospitalization. Many health insurance programs have attempted to reduce their losses by refusing coverage to those who indicate that they engage in some of the high-risk activities associated with HIV infection. Some of these programs have also refused to accept AIDS patients for coverage. State legislative bodies have attempted to block such exclusionary actions, but it will be necessary to face the financing problem directly rather than simply attempt to require insurance companies to meet the needs.

The cost of AIDS is high and growing. Lifetime medical costs for an AIDS patient in 1987 were estimated at $65,000 to $80,000. The indirect costs (lost wages and other noncare costs) amounted to seven times that amount.[8] The direct medical care cost of AIDS by 1991 will be $4.5 billion.[9] That will represent less than 1% of the total medical care budget. In some areas of the country it will be a major problem. In 1986 AIDS patients occupied 3% of all medical and surgical hospital beds in New York City. This will increase to 8% to 12% by 1991.

The federal budget for AIDS in 1988 was $1.3 billion, with $400 million for prevention and treatment services. State expenditures of their own funds (not including grants from the federal government) had increased to $156 million by 1988. Of the total, 21% was for education, 17% for research (mostly in California), 4% for surveillance, 12% for testing and counseling services, 16% for patient care, 19% for support services (such as laboratory testing), 6% for administrative support, and 5% for other activities.[10] State expenditures per AIDS case averaged $3,323; expenditures per capita averaged only 65 cents! Such efforts are clearly too small to meet the challenge.

SUMMARY

For most of the people working in public health, the AIDS epidemic is the most extraordinary phenomenon they will ever experience. It will affect every aspect of the systems they use: biologic, sociologic, administrative, financial, epidemiologic, and legislative. It will tax our systems economically, intellectually, and ethically. It will destroy the lives of untold numbers of people in this country and throughout the world. This short chapter can only highlight some of the major issues of the epidemic as of 1988. It is unlikely that they will have been solved by 1991, just as it is unlikely that the epidemic will have been fully controlled. If it is possible to survive AIDS, however, public health may have revamped and revitalized its purposes and its methods to better meet the challenges of the twenty-first century.

REFERENCES

1. Institute of Medicine: Confronting AIDS: update 1988, Washington, DC, 1988, National Academy Press.
2. Becker MH and Joseph JG: AIDS and behavioral change to reduce risk: a review, Am J Public Health 78:394, April 1988.
3. Brandt AM: AIDS in historical perspective: four lessons from the history of sexually transmitted diseases, Am J Public Health 78:367, April 1988.

4. Report of the Council on Ethical and Judicial Affairs: Ethical issues involved in the growing AIDS crisis, Chicago, IL, 1987, American Medical Association.
5. Committee on Ethics: Statement regarding risk versus responsibility in providing nursing care, Kansas City, KS, 1986, American Nurses' Association.
6. Colby DC and Baker DG: State policy responses to the AIDS epidemic, Publius: the Journal of Federalism 18:113, Summer 1988.
7. Judson FN and Vernon TM: The impact of AIDS on state and local health departments: issues and a few answers, Am J Public Health 78:387, April 1988.
8. Scitovsky AA and Rice DP: Estimates of the direct and indirect costs of acquired immunodeficiency syndrome in the United States, 1985, 1986, and 1991, Public Health Rep 102:5, January-February 1987.
9. Hellinger FJ: Forecasting the personal medical care costs of AIDS from 1988 through 1991, Public Health Rep 103:309, May-June 1988.
10. Rowe MJ and Ryan CC: Comparing state-only expenditures for AIDS, Am J Public Health 78:424, April 1988.

CHAPTER 17

Health education and health promotion

THE GROWTH OF HEALTH EDUCATION

That remarkable universal man of American history, Thomas Jefferson, once observed, "Health is no more than learning." In considering the important subject of health education and health promotion, the following statement written over a century ago is pertinent:

> The time has gone by when people can be dragooned into cleanliness, or be made virtuous by police regulations, and hence it is that the most thoughtful among practical reformers of the present day base their hopes of sanitary progress on the education of the masses as the real groundwork of national health. The people must be taught that good conduct, personal cleanliness, and the avoidance of all excesses, are the first principles of health, hand-in-hand in the rearing and guidance of youth. . . . They must be interested systematically in the general results of sanitary progress, and become more intimately acquainted with the social and material causes by which it is impeded.[1]

This quotation from the first report of the Maryland State Board of Health, dated 1875, emphasized that the public's health is dependent on the public's convictions about health.

Health education in some form has always been an important activity of public health personnel. It was not until the second quarter of this century, however, that it became formally recognized as a specialty and as a major function in public health. The transition has been gradual. In the earlier eras of public health that focused on the sanitation of the environment and the control of communicable disease, public health activity was interpreted to consist of doing things *to* and *for* people, with great reliance on legislative and police power. With the newer interpretation of public health as the summation of personal health, there developed an appreciation of the need to do things *with* people and to get people to accept an increasing responsibility for their own health.

Health education in the United States may be considered to have begun with the establishment in 1914 of the first Bureau of Health Education in the New York City Health Department. Soon after, the New York State Health Department and the Detroit Department of Health also formed designated organizational units. The field received its specialty name, health education, at a conference called in 1919 by the Child Health Organization of America, which also offered the first fellowship in health education the following year. It is interesting to note that this organization was formed by a pediatrician, L. Emmett Holt, and a nurse, Sally Lucas Jean, both of whom were convinced that emphasis on child health promotion through education and nutrition would accomplish much more than dogged, never-ending diagnosis and treatment of existing ills.[2] By 1922 there were sufficient numbers of people working in the field to merit the establishment of a separate specialty section in the American Public Health Association. Meanwhile, health education was recognized academically with the development of a specialized graduate curriculum by Clair E. Turner at the Massachusetts Institute of Technology.

During the ensuing period, enthusiastic hopes were held for what health education might accomplish through targeted attacks on specific health problems such as infant mortality, diphtheria, and tuberculosis. Health education of that period has been described by Hochbaum[3] as

> guided principally by the notions that its main goals were the prevention of certain categorical diseases, . . . the achievement of these goals depended on efforts to get people to carry out certain actions, . . . their failure to carry these out were due primarily if not totally to

> ignorance, and . . . therefore the mission of health education was first and foremost to remove such ignorance. Once done, it was assumed, the desired actions would be taken as a matter of course.

But, of course, the results did not meet these expectations; regression set in, and at the time the United States became involved in World War II, a mere 13 state and local health departments reported employment of health educators—44 persons in all. Wartime needs spurred renewed action, and special curricula were established in several of the accredited schools of public health. Several leaders in the field had been emphasizing the importance of community organization and the use of groups from the community itself in the health education and action process. This then became the principal method and function in health education.

The rapidity of response to the need and the acceptance of the approach influenced by the wartime effort were indicated by the fact that by 1947 over 300 persons, all of whom had completed graduate courses in recognized schools of public health, were employed as health educators in official and voluntary health agencies. Concurrently, an important change took place in the attitude of health officers and other more traditional health workers, from one of skepticism and suspicion to one of welcome and professional acceptance.

This trend has continued, and although firm information is lacking, it has been estimated that about 25,000 individuals are currently employed in some aspect of health education in the United States.[4] Using a different methodology, Frank Moore estimated that there were 16,850 health educators in the work force in 1983.[5] Moore further projected the size of the work force in 1990 to be 25,000, increasing to 37,000 by the year 2000.

There is considerable confusion as to what or who is a health educator. Traditionally, there have been two different groups: school health educators, trained as teachers and working largely in the classroom setting, and community health educators. Altogether there are 140 undergraduate programs in health education, 91 master's level programs, and 36 that offer a doctoral degree. The programs in schools of public health concentrate on community health education and the new field of patient education. There are 6 accredited programs in community health education, which are located in other schools or colleges. Some of the other master's level and baccalaureate programs are involved in community health education, but most are dedicated to teacher training. These programs and degrees are offered by schools and colleges of education, health science, physical education and recreation, and other components of institutions of higher learning.

Confusion is evidenced in accreditation and professional organization. The Council on Education for Public Health (CEPH) accredits the 6 graduate programs in health education in other than schools of public health. The National Commission for Accreditation of Teacher Education (NCATE) accredits programs in colleges of education. This leaves an accreditation gap beyond the programs covered by CEPH and NCATE. With reference to professional organizations, health educators have a wide choice for affiliation: the Association for the Advancement of Health Education of the American Alliance for Health, Physical Education, Recreation, and Dance; the American School Health Association; two sections of the American Public Health Association (Public Health Education and School Health Education and Services); and the Society for Public Health Education. On the state level there are the Conference of State and Territorial Directors of Health Education and the State Directors of Health, Physical Education, and Recreation. In 1972 the Coalition of National Health Education Organizations was formed with the hope of finding some common ground. However, neither it nor any other organization can speak for the entire profession.[6] It should also be mentioned that on the global level there exists the quasiofficial International Union for Health Education of the Public, which other organizations may join and help support.

SCHOOL AND HEALTH DEPARTMENT RELATIONS

The school represents a most important learning situation for a large and significant group of the population. What is learned as a child tends to have a deep and lasting influence on one's happiness, opinions, and behavior throughout life. A child is reached and influenced primarily through three channels: parents, teachers, and peers. Since the teacher is the one most likely to provide a positive role model in some environments, the importance of teacher training in health is obvious.

Today's schools contain all of tomorrow's "public" and affect most of today's. However, in most communities the next generation will be little better equipped to separate the basic facts concerning health and disease from the vast amount of misinformation that troubles the present generation. Not only is school health education a logical adjunct of a comprehensive community health program, but it should have high priority.

It is unfortunate that a certain amount of misunderstanding and self-defeating competition sometimes develops between public health agencies and departments of education because of their mutual interest in the transmission of health knowledge to children. No valid cause for conflict exists. In some areas both the health department and the school department reach for the school health education program with attitudes of equal proprietorship. The fact is that each has an important role to play.

The personnel of health departments must always remember that teaching is a professional specialty in itself and that it is the classroom teacher who does the teaching of the children. On the other hand, school personnel should bear in mind that the school health program and its educational component are merely parts of the total community health program. This does not imply that the official health department has a right to usurp the activities of the schools in this field any more than this overall responsibility and concern entitles the health department to take over the private practice of medicine or the management of food industries.

The need is obvious. What is wanted is coordination, in friendly, professional, and cooperative terms, of the contributions and abilities of those interested in health education, whether employed in a health agency, a school system, or elsewhere. The important fact to consider at this point is that the job that needs to be done is great, that neither group alone can accomplish it, and that much remains to be achieved. The conclusion is clear—greater resources, much better joint planning, and truly coordinated action are needed.

THE FOCUS OF HEALTH EDUCATION

The definition of health education has changed through time. One of the earliest was that of Wood,[7] who described it as the "sum of experiences which favorably influence habits, attitudes, and knowledge relating to . . . health." As time passed, the philosophy, objectives, and methods of health education underwent significant change. This has been summarized by Rosen[8] as follows:

> It has been recognized that it is not enough simply to present information; what counts is whether and how this knowledge is applied. Furthermore, it has been realized that the community is an organized structure, and that in health education, as in other health work, a coordinated program is needed which will touch each segment of the community in accordance with its nature and its needs. Finally, it is accepted in principle that when the members of a community have a chance to learn about their health problems and how they might deal with them, they will do so, but this was obscured during the early decades of the century by an excessive emphasis on tools and techniques.

More recently, another dimension has been added to the health education movement. Increasingly its members recognized that it was not enough to present fears or facts, and it was not enough to organize communities and groups for action. Something beyond this was needed—an understanding of how individuals, groups, and cultures viewed and interpreted conditions and events and, on the basis of this, how they might be motivated to apply, adapt, or even alter their views and interpretations for their own welfare. As a result, current emphasis is on the role of the health educator as an agent of social change through the application of behavioral science.

All recent definitions emphasize the importance of methods to effect behavioral change. The most appropriate current definition of health education was developed during the Role Delineation Project in 1981: health education is "the process of assisting individuals, acting separately or collectively, to make informed decisions about matters affecting their personal health and that of others."[9] An even simpler definition was suggested by Larry Green[10] and his colleagues, who wrote that "health education is any combination of learning experiences designed to facilitate voluntary adaptations of behavior conducive to health."

The term *health promotion* has entered the lexicon of public health in recent years with subtle but important distinctions from prevention, protection, and perhaps, health education (see Chapter 5).

Some would define health promotion, to paraphrase Green, as any combination of phenomena intended to facilitate changes in behavior conducive to health. Using this definition, health promotion would encompass health education. It would also include such actions as legislation influencing the consumption of alcoholic beverages, requirements for fitness training in schools, labeling of cigarette packages, and increasing the tax on smokeless tobacco. Some health educators do not find the distinction all that useful and prefer to think of health promotion as something that health educators do.

The definition of health education has changed over the years, as techniques have improved and as public expectations have increased. These changes are reflected in the various revisions of the statement on educational qualifications of health educators first enunciated in the 1920s. As summarized by Bowman[11]:

> behavioral emphasis has supplanted for the most part community organization and dissemination of health emphases in health education. But it is interesting to note the continued attention given (1) to community organization as a method for effecting change . . . and (2) to the communication of health knowledge and instructional technology.

FUNCTIONS IN HEALTH EDUCATION

In 1937 the American Public Health Association began an attempt to describe the diverse functions and activities of health educators. Many studies, adaptations, and revisions have followed. In 1960 responsibility for stating the qualifications and functions of health educators was passed to the Society for Public Health Education. In its 1967 statement, it attempted for the first time to differentiate the functions of community health educators with different degree levels of preparation—baccalaureate and master's. The resulting document[12] also contained a section on the areas of knowledge, concepts, and skills that community health educators on the two levels should have. More recently, various health education groups sponsored the exhaustive Role Delineation Project mentioned above and a still more recent effort to establish a credentialing system for health educators, supervised by a National Commission for Certifying Health Educators.[12] The first phase of the Role Delineation Project was the Conference on Commonalities in the Preparation and Practice of Health Educators, which took place in 1978 at Bethesda, Md. The second phase, from 1980 to 1982, culminated in a conference in Birmingham, Ala., at which an attempt was made to verify the identifiable roles. The roles were summarized by Henderson in 1981.[13] The responsibilities and necessary competencies of health educators, as developed under the auspices of the National Center for Health Education, are listed in Table 17-1.

THE SETTINGS OF HEALTH EDUCATION

Needs for health education are ubiquitous. Every stage of life, every type of person or social group, and all occupations and professions are appropriate targets of programs for the prevention of illness and disability, the control of disease, and the promotion of wellness. Since the need is omnipresent, health education must be provided in a wide variety of settings that ideally blanket a community or society: homes, schools, community agencies, voluntary and private organizations, government agencies, hospitals, professional schools, group practices, planning agencies, communications media, unions, business, and industry.

Preschool and school-aged children and their parents are especially important. This points to the importance of a carefully planned, comprehensive, sequential program of health education for all students from kindergarten through secondary school, aimed at the development of healthy life-styles and an understanding of the larger community aspects of health protection and promotion. Since parents provide role models in the establishment of good health practices, they should be assisted in fulfilling their role. Beyond this, college students, families, people in the occupationally productive years, and senior citizens also have special health education requirements.[14]

Germane to the selection of targets or settings for health education is the basis on which they are selected. In the instances just mentioned, special attention is justified, because the individuals are actually or potentially at risk. Too often, however, as Galanter[15] has pointed out, health education and many other public health programs "focus attention exclusively on the victims of problems rather than on the problems themselves." As examples, she mentions workers exposed to carcinogens told

Text continued on p. 300.

TABLE 17-1 Responsibilities and competencies for entry-level health educators

Responsibility I—assessing individual and community needs for health education

Competency A: Obtain health-related data about social and cultural environments, growth and development factors, needs, and interests.

Subcompetencies:

1. Select valid sources of information about health needs and interests.
2. Utilize computerized sources of health-related information.
3. Employ or develop appropriate data-gathering instruments.
4. Apply survey techniques to acquire health data.

Competency B: Distinguish between behaviors that foster, and those that hinder, well-being.

Subcompetencies:

1. Investigate physical, social, emotional, and intellectual factors influencing health behaviors.
2. Identify behaviors that tend to promote or compromise health.
3. Recognize the role of learning and affective experience in shaping patterns of health behavior.

Competency C: Infer needs for health education on the basis of obtained data.

Subcompetencies:

1. Analyze needs assessment data.
2. Determine priority areas of need for health education.

Responsibility II—planning effective health education programs

Competency A: Recruit community organizations, resource people, and potential participants for support and assistance in program planning.

Subcompetencies:

1. Communicate need for the program to those who will be involved.
2. Obtain commitments from personnel and decision makers who will be involved in the program.
3. Seek ideas and opinions of those who will affect, or be affected by, the program.
4. Incorporate feasible ideas and recommendations into the planning process.

Competency B: Develop a logical scope and sequence plan for a health education program.

Subcompetencies:

1. Determine the range of health information requisite to a given program of instruction.
2. Organize the subject areas comprising the scope of a program in logical sequence.

Competency C: Formulate appropriate and measurable program objectives.

Subcompetencies:

1. Infer educational objectives facilitative of achievement of specified competencies.
2. Develop a framework of broadly stated, operational objectives relevant to a proposed health education program.

Competency D: Design educational programs consistent with specified program objectives.

Subcompetencies:

1. Match proposed learning activities with those implicit in the stated objectives.
2. Formulate a wide variety of alternative educational methods.
3. Select strategies best suited to implementation of educational objectives in a given setting.
4. Plan a sequence of learning opportunities building upon, and reinforcing mastery of, preceding objectives.

Continued.

TABLE 17-1 Responsibilities and competencies for entry-level health educators—cont'd

Responsibility III—implementing health education programs

Competency A: Exhibit competence in carrying out planned educational programs.

Subcompetencies:

1. Employ a wide range of educational methods and techniques.
2. Apply individual or group process methods as appropriate to given learning situations.
3. Utilize instructional equipment and other instructional media effectively.
4. Select methods that best facilitate practice of program objectives.

Competency B: Infer enabling objectives as needed to implement instructional programs in specified settings.

Subcompetencies:

1. Pretest learners to ascertain present abilities and knowledge relative to proposed program objectives.
2. Develop subordinate measurable objectives as needed for instruction.

Competency C: Select methods and media best suited to implement program plans for specific learners.

Subcompetencies:

1. Analyze learner characteristics, legal aspects, feasibility, and other considerations influencing choices among methods.
2. Evaluate the efficacy of alternative methods and techniques capable of facilitating program objectives.
3. Determine the availability of information, personnel, time, and equipment needed to implement the program for a given audience.

Competency D: Monitor educational programs, adjusting objectives and activities as necessary.

Subcompetencies:

1. Compare actual program activities with the stated objectives.
2. Assess the relevance of existing program objectives to current needs.
3. Revise program activities and objectives as necessitated by changes in learner needs.
4. Appraise applicability of resources and materials relative to given educational objectives.

Responsibility IV—evaluating effectiveness of health education programs

Competency A: Develop plans to assess achievement of program objectives.

Subcompetencies:

1. Determine standards of performance to be applied as criteria of effectiveness.
2. Establish a realistic scope of evaluation efforts.
3. Develop an inventory of existing valid and reliable tests and survey instruments.
4. Select appropriate methods for evaluating program effectiveness.

Competency B: Carry out evaluation plans.

Subcompetencies:

1. Facilitate administration of the tests and activities specified in the plan.
2. Utilize data-collecting methods appropriate to the objectives.
3. Analyze resulting evaluation data.

Competency C: Interpret results of program evaluation.

Subcompetencies:

1. Apply criteria of effectiveness to obtained results of a program.
2. Translate evaluation results into terms easily understood by others.
3. Report effectiveness of educational programs in achieving proposed objectives.

TABLE 17-1 Responsibilities and competencies for entry-level health educators—cont'd

Competency D: Infer implications from findings for future program planning.

Subcompetencies:
1. Explore possible explanations for important evaluation findings.
2. Recommend strategies for implementing results of evaluation.

Responsibility V—coordinating provision of health education services

Competency A: Develop a plan for coordinating health education services.

Subcompetencies:
1. Determine the extent of available health education services.
2. Match health education services to proposed program activities.
3. Identify gaps and overlaps in the provision of collaborative health services.

Competency B: Facilitate cooperation between and among levels of program personnel.

Subcompetencies:
1. Promote cooperation and feedback among personnel related to the program.
2. Apply various methods of conflict reduction as needed.
3. Analyze the role of health educator as liaison between program staff and outside groups and organizations.

Competency C: Formulate practical modes of collaboration among health agencies and organizations.

Subcompetencies:
1. Stimulate development of cooperation among personnel responsible for community health education program.
2. Suggest approaches for integrating health education within existing health programs.
3. Develop plans for promoting collaborative efforts among health agencies and organizations with mutual interests.

Competency D: Organize in-service training programs for teachers, volunteers, and other interested personnel.

Subcompetencies:
1. Plan an operational, competency-oriented training program.
2. Utilize instructional resources that meet a variety of in-service training needs.
3. Demonstrate a wide range of strategies for conducting in-service training programs.

Responsibility VI—acting as a resource person in health education

Competency A: Utilize computerized health information retrieval systems effectively.

Subcompetencies:
1. Match an information need with the appropriate retrieval system.
2. Access principal on-line and other data base health information resources.

Competency B: Establish effective consultative relationships with those requesting assistance in solving health-related problems.

Subcompetencies:
1. Analyze parameters of effective consultative relationships.
2. Describe special skills and abilities needed by health educators for consultation activities.
3. Formulate a plan for providing consultation to other health professionals.
4. Explain the process of marketing health education consultative services.

Continued.

TABLE 17-1 Responsibilities and competencies for entry-level health educators—cont'd

Competency C: Interpret and respond to requests for health information.

Subcompetencies:

1. Analyze general processes for identifying the information needed to satisfy a request.
2. Employ a wide range of approaches in referring requesters to valid sources of health information.

Competency D: Select effective educational resource materials for dissemination.

Subcompetencies:

1. Assemble educational material of value to the health of individuals and community groups.
2. Evaluate the worth and applicability of resource materials for given audiences.
3. Apply various processes in the acquisition of resource materials.
4. Compare different methods for distributing educational materials.

Responsibility VII—communicating health and health education needs, concerns, and resources

Competency A: Interpret concepts, purposes, and theories of health education.

Subcompetencies:

1. Evaluate the state of the art of health education.
2. Analyze the foundations of the discipline of health education.
3. Describe major responsibilities of the health educator in the practice of health education.

Competency B: Predict the impact of societal value systems on health education programs.

Subcompetencies:

1. Investigate social forces causing opposing viewpoints regarding health education needs and concerns.
2. Employ a wide range of strategies for dealing with controversial health issues.

Competency C: Select a variety of communication methods and techniques in providing health information.

Subcompetencies:

1. Utilize a wide range of techniques for communicating health and health education information.
2. Demonstrate proficiency in communicating health information and health education needs.

Competency D: Foster communication between health care providers and consumers.

Subcompetencies:

1. Interpret the significance and implications of health care providers' messages to consumers.
2. Act as liaison between consumer groups and individuals and health care provider organizations.

Reprinted from A framework for the development of competency-based curricula for entry level health educators, by the National Task Force for the Preparation and Practice of Health Educators, Inc., with permission of the National Commission for Health Education Credentialing, Inc., copyright 1985.

not to smoke so as to reduce the risk, and mothers taught to stop children from eating the lead-based paint in shabby houses. "Of course," she notes,

> individual behavior influences health—and of course individuals can control some of their behavior. But many other behaviors and the problems with which they interlace are simply beyond the realm of individual action or can be far more effectively tackled by societal or institutional action.

As an example, Spiegel and Lindaman[16] focused attention on a significant but underrated cause of injury and death—falls of small children from high windows. In New York City such falls accounted for 12% of all accidental deaths in children under 15 years of age, an incidence about equal to the annual number of aspirin poisonings nationwide, which merited federal legislation. Although parental and neighborhood health education efforts were obvi ously important, more effective would be a housing code requiring window barriers—a statutory change subsequently implemented.

As has been pointed out, the tendency to blame the victims of social policy for their poor health was revivified in the 1970s. Major medical care provider groups were concerned about the rising portion of the nation's gross national product that was being consumed by medical care without apparent proportionate results in health status. Government joined in this shift of responsibility to the victims in an attempt to decrease demands for government funding of public health programs and to avoid expanding existing, consumer-oriented, health protection regulatory systems. People are not just individually responsible for their bad habits, however. Recent successful efforts to expand the number of places in which tobacco smoking is not permitted make manifest the social responsibility for change. Victim blaming is not new. It has occurred in earlier times in this society and in others. As will be described in Chapter 20, common law held until recently that people accepted wages in exchange for their work and the risks they took, so if they lost an eye or a limb in the workplace, it was their own fault. The pendulum began to swing in the opposite direction just a few decades ago and has recently shifted back a little as state laws have established procedures for apportioning guilt between the business, the injured worker, and even co-workers. Regulatory controls became unpopular during the 1980s, but it is likely that attempts to protect people against hazards will be revitalized during future years.

With reference to the organizational setting of health education activities, especially in official health agencies, although each functional unit should be engaged in health education to some degree, there are certain overall aspects of the field that must be treated in a more central manner. Questions arise, therefore, concerning whether the work should be completely centralized in one health education unit or dispersed and whether such a unit should be line or staff. Every possible variation is seen in state and local health departments. Centralized health education units are organized sometimes as a separate line unit and sometimes as a staff agency close to the health officer. On the other hand, activities for health education are often decentralized and dispersed throughout the organization. Beyond these are numerous expedient arrangements, with health education placed in a division of vital statistics, of maternal and child health, or of communicable disease control. This has little to recommend it, since it usually results in provincialization of the service.

Certain general conclusions may be drawn. It is impossible to centralize health education activities completely. Even if this could be accomplished, the rest of the health agency would lose much of its effectiveness. Therefore the functional units, augmented and supported by a central unit of health education staffed by specialists, should be encouraged to engage freely in these activities. In most circumstances, the central health education unit had best be a staff unit that is closely associated with the administrator, with whom overall community planning and programming may be effected.

One other aspect of the setting of health education merits emphasis—the relative importance of activities at different levels of government. With health education, as with other health programs, one is apt to overemphasize the state and especially the federal role. Ogden,[17] speaking from the position of director of the federal Bureau of Health Education, has cautioned against this:

> In a field like health education—with activities widely diffused within government and still more widely dispersed across the national scene—this foreshortened perspective can leave the false impression that government in general, and the Federal Government in particular, is "where the action is."
>
> The truth, of course, is quite the reverse. Health education of individuals and families happens, or does not happen, where people live, in their homes, workplaces, or communities. That is where people learn and practice, or do not learn and do not practice, means for keeping well, raising the quality of their lives, and how to use the services available to them. Government may, and often does, propose. Sometimes its proposals are sweetened by the offer of various forms of support. But local institutions and individual persons dispose. What they do determines whether or not health education fulfills its great potential for improving our national health status.

This comment, while an appropriate and useful description of reality, has some overtones of the victim blaming that began to receive fresh currency in the 1970s.

PLANNING HEALTH EDUCATION PROGRAMS

Green and his colleagues[10] have described the planning process in health education: it is not dissimilar to the descriptions of planning in this book (see Chapter 11). You begin with a goal, define the problems that prevent the goal from being realized, develop specific objectives, consider the available methods, adopt and implement those that are useable, and evaluate progress toward the goal.

The term *health education,* or what might be regarded as the selling of sound health understanding and behavior,* usually gives consideration to at least four phases or types of activities: analysis, sensitization, publicity, and education. They are in no sense mutually exclusive but tend to be sequential, overlap generously, and be dependent on each other. The first, *analysis,* is, of course, fundamental. It involves a study of the problems of an area or a group, the factors that generated the problems and tend to maintain them, and the characteristics of individuals or groups that may hinder the application of knowledge to the solution of the problems.

Green describes the PRECEDE framework, an acronym that stands for Predisposing, Reinforcing, and Enabling Causes in Educational Diagnosis and Evaluation.[10] Health education is concerned specifically with possible changes in behavior that can help attain its established objectives. Predisposing factors are attitudes, beliefs, and perceptions that affect how people see a particular problem or behavior. Reinforcing factors are those phenomena that support one structure or an alternative one, such as the menu for a school lunch. Enabling factors facilitate adoption of a belief, attitude, or perception. They may be barriers to needed change, or they may be assets to the change program. The predisposing, reinforcing, and enabling factors affecting any adverse behavioral pattern need to be fully understood if an intervention is to be effective.

The next phase is *sensitization.* Here the intent or expected result is not an addition to health knowledge per se or an evident change in the health habits of a person or a community; rather, it is a process by which people are made aware of the existence of certain things: a health agency, a behavior, a disease, a service. Sensitizing techniques such as slogans, spot announcements on radio or television, and billboards are not expected to give the public more information about a subject or to make them do something they otherwise might not do. Examples are found in commercial advertising, where a manufacturer merely attempts to make potential customers aware of the existence of a product in competition with those of other manufacturers. The manufacturer may accomplish this by bombarding the public's eyes and ears with simple reminders of the product. In doing this, the manufacturer and advertising agent do not expect the public to rush to the nearest store to purchase the product. What is hoped for is that when people are in a situation where they must make a decision—"Shall I buy or not" or "Shall I buy this brand or that?"—they will choose the product whose name is now familiar as a result of the sensitizing process. Therefore when a health agency, using any of the audiovisual methods, asks "Is your baby protected against measles?" or states "Polio kills children," it is merely sensitizing the listeners or readers so that they will be receptive to subsequent, more detailed information.

One thing is certain—people cannot be sensitized by the term *health education.* It is not well understood by professionals, much less by the general public. The concept must be made meaningful by relating it to readily recognized problems and services that are already known to be practical and useful to the individual or the community.

The third phase of health education is *publicity.* This is closely related to the foregoing and, like it, is of considerable importance in the public relations program of the organization. In one sense, publicity might be considered an elaboration of sensitizing procedures, presenting more details about the items that were mentioned in simple concise statements or exhortations. Examples of activities that might be included in this category are press releases that relate to the programs of the health agency, announcements of clinics available for various purposes, and descriptive statements about the seriousness of certain conditions in the community.

The fourth phase of health education is *education* in the more usual sense. Usually this is accomplished by personal contact between the one who imparts the information and those who receive it. It must be realized that education in health or in

* The reader is referred to a charming essay, "The Pebble in the Bell," which deals with the application of advertising to health.[18]

anything else is never something given by one person to another. The mere act of presenting information and knowledge accomplishes nothing. A gorilla, for example, might be exposed to the expostulations of the world's greatest philosophers, but it is doubtful that it would learn anything because of its inability to comprehend the sounds it heard. For many humans, the word *inability* might be changed to *unwillingness.* In other words, learning takes place only through the matched efforts of teacher and learner. To impart information to increase the knowledge of others or to change concepts, personal discussions carried out in terms and circumstances familiar to the listener and related to the individual's personality and circumstances are required. This approach accounts for the success of certain companies that sell cosmetics and household products. It also explains why home visits by public health nurses are so often fruitful.

In previous editions of this book a fifth phase of health education was described—*motivation.* According to Green,[10] however, the word *motivation* refers to internal forces that are not malleable through external stimuli such as educational messages: hunger, defense, altruism, and so forth. Yet the concept is still useful in health education so long as it is limited to efforts which stop short of initiating compulsive behavior as a result of external, planned, educational efforts.

Among those who die each year from preventable diseases are many who have been exposed to considerable publicity relating to those diseases and have even acquired considerable knowledge about them. Very few of the parents of children who needlessly acquire and even die from preventable conditions are completely ignorant of protective measures or opposed to them. They simply do not act on the information or knowledge. In other words, the acquisition of knowledge in itself is not an accomplishment; it is the extent to which that knowledge is translated into action that makes the difference.

It is recognized that for people to be motivated to use health knowledge, it must be presented to them in a manner comprehensible and acceptable to them. Their basic emotional needs and wants; their cultural attitudes, beliefs, and prejudices; their fears, ambitions, jealousies, determinations, pride, and malice; or any combination of these must all be taken into consideration. Rosenstock, Derryberry, and Carriger,[19] in a historically important paper, summarized the problem well: "It is known that human behavior is determined more by one's belief about reality than by reality itself, and that people vary markedly in their interpretations of reality." As a consequence, it has been pointed out that effective health education can be achieved only by linking what is taught to the endogenous motivation of the individual or group addressed. Rosenstock, Strecher, and Becker[20] have recently modified the Health Belief Model to include certain aspects of social learning theory. Self-efficacy, or belief in one's ability to implement a desired change, has been added as an independent variable to the traditional model. The model states that before people can accept and act upon a health education message, whether in a clinical setting or in a community campaign, they must believe that (1) they are susceptible to the problem (such as a motor vehicle accident), (2) the consequences can be severe, (3) there are real benefits to be gained through adopting some change in behavior, and (4) the barriers to that change can be manipulated.

The advertising industry long ago found that one cannot reach everyone with the same message, so it selects specific audiences and talks in their terms to their interests. If public health workers have a message for a certain group, they should write and promote the message for that group. If it is a low socioeconomic group with a low level of education, they should couch the message in terms different from those for a middle-class suburban population.

In an interesting study of commercial advertising as a health education technique, inquiry was made with regard to the use of patent medicines. Of those interviewed, 60% said they used products of this nature before calling a physician. Although the majority recognized that the claims for the products often were not substantiated, the investigation indicated that the patent medicines resorted to most frequently were those for which the advertising played on emotions (especially fear), vanity, and desire for personal gain and that promised or implied unequivocal cure and relief. Somewhat related to this, health educators and others in the health field should not be too ready to condemn the various "nonprofessionals" who provide question-and-answer columns in newspapers, in magazines, and on radio and television. Neither should the public be criticized for contacting them. The mere fact that such "nonprofessionals" are contacted by the public gives reason for professional introspection. Their advice and counsel is often very good and, more importantly, believed. They not only provide the kind of answers people want, but they are excellent communicators. At the University of Michigan in Ann Arbor, students can join a computer conference known as Meet:Ourselves. A wide variety of students from the health professions, the arts, social work, engineering, law, and the natural sciences participate. Any participant can enter an item, and others who have access to computers (which includes most of the 35,000 students at the university) can participate. It is a literate and instructive source of helpful information. Similar services could be made available in most communities.

PROBLEMS IN HEALTH EDUCATION

It is paradoxical that despite extensive advances in literacy and education, as well as vastly improved methods of communication, there still exists a great gap between existing medical and health protective knowledge and the public's acceptance and use of it. Professional journals are replete with surveys of school children, college students, and the adult public that present discouraging and embarrassing evidence of failure in this field. Many parents still do not obtain immunization for their children, and many drivers still invite injury and death by drinking and driving and by not using seat belts. The use of cigarettes and useless or harmful patent medicines is still widespread. One of the handicaps of public health work, of course, is the usual absence of pain and urgency (except when an epidemic occurs). Indeed, this is becoming even more true as the public health profession progresses from attacks on communicable diseases to the effort to control chronic illnesses. There is little difficulty in motivating to prompt action an individual with a high fever from meningitis or a severe abdominal pain from acute appendicitis. To bring about a change in dietary or behavioral habits or to secure health maintenance examinations against possible future difficulty is something else. Results are less dramatic or rapid; cause and effect are less readily apparent.

Several reasons have been put forward to explain the inadequacies of health education at the present time. A practical starting point is Swinehart's[21] observation that "information presented through the channels commonly used by public health and voluntary associations is fairly easy for most potential audiences to avoid, since these audiences are not 'captive.' Even if they are exposed to communication, there is no guarantee that this will lead to learning and action." So in the field of health education, public health workers start with two handicaps.

In more detail, a committee of the New York Academy of Medicine presented the following points to consider.[22]

1. It is easier to sell symptomatic relief of illness or the promise of a cure than it is to sell health and prevention of disease.
2. Education is a catchall—a ready solution and means of disposition but one that is all too seldom put into action. Whenever there is a problem in a community, someone is sure to say, "The answer is education." And usually, that is where the problem rests.
3. Health education does not have high prestige. In the schools it is treated as a subordinate subject or as an additional chore to be passed out to a teacher whose main interest is not too remotely related. It is frequently made the responsibility of an athletic coach or physical training teacher.
4. In general, the people charged with health education programs lack special training and are not qualified.
5. Departments of education and health do not work together in programming, planning curricula, and raising standards of teaching health in the schools.
6. There is a lack of overall organization in the field of health education with a unified program and a single-minded objective. An effective and dynamic program of health education must include: intercommunication of ideas, selection of priorities, formulation of programs, and assignment of responsibility. As matters stand now, there is a great deal of shifting of responsibility from school to home to church to community organization.

Beyond this, it appears that health education has been regarded too much as a private preserve by the professionals in public health, medicine, and education. Actually, they have often tended to be stuffy, overly didactic, and lacking in understanding of what really concerns the average and less educated members of the population. This was forcefully brought out by an executive of a successful public relations and advertising firm in an address to a public health conference, which he titled "Public Health Is No Private Preserve (or Things I Never Knew 'till Now, No Thanks to You)." This unusually well-educated man stated:

> I was asked by your chairman to talk about selling public health. I, like most people, know very little about public health. I have no ready answers for your problems. I'm not even sure I understand the problems themselves. But I do know this: You are not communicating—you are not getting through to people. . . . I am amazed at the amount of effort, time, and money needed to safeguard my health and that of my family . . . yet the average citizen has no awareness of your efforts and actually impedes your work through ignorance.[23]

Concern was given a national focus in 1971, when the President's Committee on Health Education concluded that health education in America was "a neglected, underfinanced, unhealthily fragmented activity" and that "school health programs for 60 million American children are in disarray, and are scheduled for rainy days when children have nothing else to do."[24] The committee director, Victor Weingarten, president of the Institute of Public Affairs, pointed out that of the $75 billion spent on health in the United States during 1971, about 92% was spent after illness occurred and only 0.5% was spent on health education. And most of that, he complained, went into "packaged information" that was irrelevant and ineffective. The situation is unchanged now (1989) when the nation is spending more than half a trillion dollars each year on its health care.

The President's Committee on Health Education produced three significant results: (1) establishment of an extragovernmental health education consortium, the National Center for Health Education; (2) creation of a Bureau of Health Education within the Centers for Disease Control to serve as the operating focus for health education activities in the Department of Health, Education and Welfare (now known as the Department of Health and Human Services), and (3) establishment of a focal point in the Secretary's office for health education. The latter, the Office of Health Information, Health Promotion, Physical Fitness and Sports Medicine, was created by Congress in 1976. It is now known as the Office of Disease Prevention and Health Promotion. Accompanying these moves was significant congressional interest, evidenced by several bills to provide increased funding for training and project support. The unit at the Centers for Disease Control has been reorganized (1988) and is now known as the Center for Chronic Disease Prevention and Health Promotion. It is interesting to note that health education has been subsumed under health promotion and linked to chronic diseases at a time when the Centers for Disease Control is involved in a major struggle to control AIDS and HIV infection.

The evident inadequacy and ineffectivenss of health education up to the present obviously calls for continued evaluation and experimentation. Skillfully developed and properly used, health education can become a powerful force for social improvement and change. Its ultimate goal, of course, should be to encourage and assist the public in taking individual and group initiative to protect and improve its own health.

HEALTH HAZARD APPRAISAL: A HEALTH EDUCATION TOOL

Four health education approaches to the reduction or elimination of risks to health have been described as (1) educational, (2) preventive, (3) radical, and (4) self-empowerment.[25] The educational approach involves the exploration and clarification of beliefs and values in the hope that the individual will choose freely to avoid a health risk such as smoking. However, many find this difficult because of social pressures or parental examples. The preventive approach requires the persuasion or motivation of individuals on the basis that prevention is better than cure—that certain actions are involved in the development of undesirable or fatal disease. The radical approach directs itself to the social, economic, and political roots of health problems; for example, poverty or tax advantages to producers and disseminators of disease-causing materials such as tobacco, environmental pollutants, and the like. The self-empowerment approach attempts to avoid the passivity of the educational, the coercion of the preventive, and the posturing or subversive action of the radical approaches by creating a genuinely free and informed choice. It includes promoting attitudes for deferring present and immediate gratification (such as smoking) in favor of future benefits, challenging beliefs that life and health are controlled by others, and promoting self-esteem, which helps in responding to health education and resisting pressures for unhealthy practices. The four approaches are by no means mutually exclusive and often overlap in practice.

The intent of self-empowerment programs is really to bring about a personal commitment to a change in life-style. By now the advantages of a healthful life-style are well documented. One old example[26] that relates to the members of the Reorganized Church of Jesus Christ of Latter-Day Saints (Mormons) in Missouri will suffice. This group strictly avoids the use of tobacco, alcohol, and hot drinks such as tea and coffee. It emphasizes the importance of a well-balanced diet. A mortality study compared the 1972-to-1978 mortality of this group with that of three other groups. Missouri Mormons experienced age-adjusted death rates 22.6% lower than rates for Missouri non-Mormon whites; 19.6% lower than non-Mormon residents of Independence, Mo.; and 14.4% lower than residents of Utah, 72% of whom were Mormons. The Missouri Mormons experienced lower death rates than the other two Missouri groups for each of seven selected causes, especially for lung cancer, pneumonia and influenza, and violent deaths.

Risks to health are often multiple and interrelated. This is illustrated in Fig. 17-1 with reference to cumulative life-style risks in relation to motor vehicle accidents.[27] An example is furnished by persons convicted of improper driving.[28] They were found to have a higher risk of death from diseases caused by smoking or alcohol, and they drove more miles and used seat belts less often than a control group. In general they had a more hazardous life-style and a diminished life expectancy.

During recent years a methodology has been developed and increasingly refined that emphasizes prevention by placing responsibility clearly on the individual. The basic tool used is referred to as health hazard appraisal or health risk assessment, and the overall approach is known as prospective medicine. The concept originated in 1958 with Dr. Lewis C. Robbins while he was chief of the cancer control program of the U.S. Public Health Service. Searching for some approach to primary prevention in place of secondary prevention or terminal

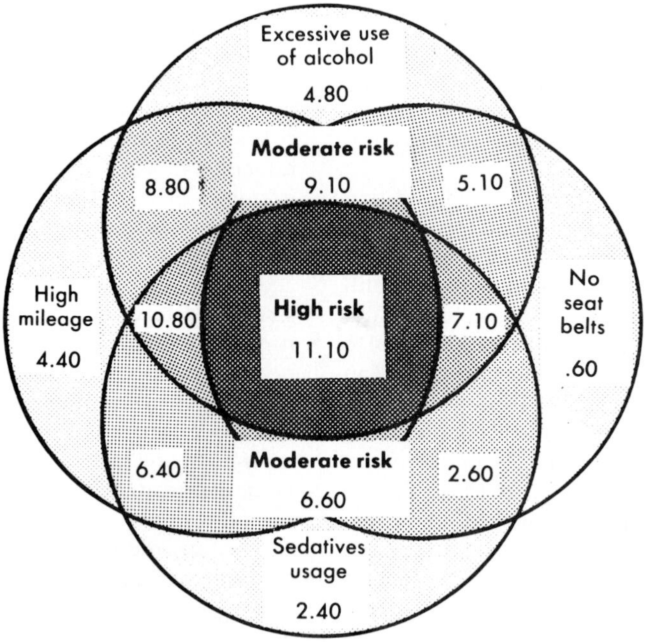

FIG. 17-1 Cumulative effect of risks of motor vehicle accidents. (Figures represent degree of risk for each behavioral factor.) (From Shires DB, editor: Bodycheck, Division of Family Medicine, Dalhousie University, Halifax, Nova Scotia.)

care, he ignored the common doctrine that "you cannot apply group data to the individual."[29] Following an encouraging trial at the medical centers of Temple University and George Washington University, the method was adopted by the Graduate Medical Center of Methodist Hospital, Indianapolis, in its continued education curriculum. Dr. Robbins, who had joined Dr. Jack Hall at that institution, addressed the question of how to extend an individual's life expectancy. The important innovation was to approach the question prospectively, on the basis of statistical or actuarial probabilities, rather than by postmortem retrospection.[30]

Briefly, the concept is based on the fact that whereas a given individual theoretically may be subject to a vast array of health risks that may lead to a large number of possible illnesses or injuries (i.e., potential causes of death), actually at any given point in life for a particular type of individual, a few conditions—perhaps 10 or fewer—constitute most of the risk for the succeeding 10 years. This is a time span for which the usual person can comprehend and plan. For each type of person, categorized by age, sex, race, and perhaps occupation and location, the probability or risk of death from each of the predominant conditions during the next 10 years is provided by tables that are known as the Geller-Gesner Tables.[31] Similar tables have been produced for 1-year age intervals.[32] Gesner[33] has outlined the steps involved in a health hazard appraisal (see Fig. 17-2 for an example).

1. For each of the 10 to 12 leading causes of death for people of the individual's age, sex, and race, indicate the average risk of death during the next 10 years. These figures are obtained from the Geller-Gesner Tables.
2. For each cause of death listed indicate the precursors or prognostic characteristics brought to light by the individual's medical history, life-style, and, depending on the extensiveness of the program, physical examination and laboratory and clinical tests. (Fig. 17-3 presents examples for several causes of death.) Decreases as well as increases in the group average risk are listed to refine the individual's risk for better or worse.
3. For each precursor listed indicate the positive or negative risk factor. A risk factor is a quantitative weight or multiplier that indicates the extent to which a precursor influences the risk of death. Risk factors are computed from mortality ratios and prevalence data and periodically reviewed and updated by groups of specialists knowledgeable with reference to particular diseases and causes of death.[34]
4. Compute the composite risk factor if there is more than one precursor for a given cause of death. Composite risk factors are determined by a formula similar to the credit-debit system used by the life insurance industry to determine total risk to the individual.
5. Obtain the present personal risk of the individual with reference to a particular potential cause of death by multiplying the average risk for the individual's population group by the individual's composite risk. The sum of all the disease-specific personal risks provides the total risk to the individual.
6. Apply intervention recommendations (e.g., stop smoking, use seat belts, exercise) and calculate the decreased risk possible, assuming compliance with recommendations. The difference between this potential risk figure and the existing risk represents the achievable survival advantage.

Use of the health hazard appraisal approach has been increasing rapidly during recent years. The purposes have included health education, behavior modification, health maintenance and disease prevention, and professional education. University populations, public and private health clinics, government and industrial groups, insurance companies, and many other groups and organizations have been adapting it to their special needs. An important landmark was its adoption in 1973 as a significant component of the national health program of Canada.[35,36] A significant step has been the application of computer science to the methodology. The program and manuals are now available for use on personal computers from the Centers for Disease Control in Atlanta.

As with all innovations, health hazard appraisal has its critics. This is by no means undesirable, since it encourages further research and refinement. Furthermore, as Fielding[37] editorializes:

> Although health risk appraisal has many inherent problems compounded by some instances of misuse, concern with these problems should not lead us to overlook the number of actual and potential benefits

Text continued on p. 313.

HEALTH HAZARD APPRAISAL CHART

Quality control: Evaluate performance of a predetermined goal.

(Goal: "Get this patient safely through the next ten years.")

W M AGE 40-44	AVERAGE TO INDIVIDUAL RISK					
POPULATION AVERAGE 10 YEAR DEATHS PER 100,000		INDIVIDUAL PROGNOSIS RISK APPRAISAL				
Disease/Injury	Average Risk	Prognostic Characteristics	Risk Factor		Composite Risk Factor	Present Risk
From Manual	*From Manual*	*Listed in Manual Physician Select*	*From Manual* ×	+	*See Instructions*	*(2) x (5)*
(1)	(2)	(3)	(4)		(5)	(6)
1. ARTERIOSCLEROTIC	1,877	Blood pressure 108/70	.4		2.1	3941.7
HEART DISEASE		Cholesterol 214 mgs.%	.9			
		Diabetic No	1.0			
		Exercise Sedentary		2.5		
		Family history neg. over 60	.9			
		Smoking 3 pipes/day	1.0			
		Weight 69" 211# 39%ov.		1.3		
2. ACCIDENTS:	285	Alcohol Mod. & Occ.	1.0		3.0	855
MOTOR VEHICLE		Drugs & med. none	1.0			
		Mileage 32,000		3.2		
		Seat belt use 100%	.8			
3. SUICIDE	264	Depression no	1.0		1.0	264
		Family history neg.	1.0			
4. CIRRHOSIS OF LIVER	222	Alcohol Mod. & Occ.	1.0		1.0	222
5. VASCULAR	222	Blood pressure 108/70	.4		.4	88.8
LESIONS		Cholesterol 214 mgs.%	.9			
AFFECTING CNS		Diabetic No	1.0			
		Smoking 3 pipes/day	1.0			
6. CANCER OF LUNGS	202	Smoking 3 pipes/day	.3		.3	60.6
7. CHRONIC	167	Murmur No	1.0		.1	16.7
RHEUMATIC		Rheumatic fever No	1.0			
HEART DISEASE		Signs or symptoms None	.1			

FIG. 17-2 Example of a health hazard appraisal. (From Gesner NB: The credit-debit system of health hazard appraisal, Proceedings of the Thirteenth Annual Meeting of the Society of Prospective Medicine, Indianapolis, 1977, Methodist Hospital of Indiana.)

AVERAGE TO INDIVIDUAL RISK

POPULATION AVERAGE 10 YEAR DEATHS PER 100,000		INDIVIDUAL PROGNOSIS RISK APPRAISAL				
Disease/Injury	Average Risk	Prognostic Characteristics	Risk Factor		Composite Risk Factor	Present Risk
From Manual	*From Manual*	*Listed in Manual Physician Select*	*From Manual* x	+	*See Instructions*	*(2) x (5)*
(1)	(2)	(3)	(4)		(5)	(6)
8. PNEUMONIA	111	Alcohol Mod. & Occ.	1.0		1.0	111
		Bacterial pneumonia No	1.0			
		Emphysema No	1.0			
		Smoking habits 3 pipes	1.0			
9. CANCER OF	111	Polyp No	1.0		1.0	111
INTESTINES &		Rectal bleeding No	1.0			
RECTUM		Ulcerative colitis No	1.0			
		Proctosigmoidoscopy No	x1.0			
10. LYMPHOSARCOMA &	76				1.0	76
HODGKINS DISEASE						
11. CANCER OF	56	Hypochlorhydria No	1.0		1.0	56
STOMACH &						
ESOPHAGUS						
12. HYPERTENSIVE	56	Blood pressure 108/70	.4		.7	39.2
HEART DISEASE		Weight 39% ovwt.		1.3		
13. TUBERCULOSIS	56	Current X-ray '67 neg.	1.0		1.0	56
		Econ. & soc. status Mid.	1.0			
		T B activity No	1.0			
Other Causes	1,855				1.0	1,855
Total	5,560					7,753

*Reappraise on assumption that physician's prescription is complied with. Columns (7) through (10) same as columns (3) through (6) except where the physician's prescription changed prognostic characteristics.

**Divide figures in column (11) by total of column (6).

Health appraisal age 44½

FIG. 17-2, cont'd. For legend see opposite page.

Continued.

Name John Doe Patient No. ______ Birthdate ______

Street ______ Race, Sex, Age WM 41

City ______ State ______ Zip ______ Date June 25 1971

RISK REDUCTION FOR INDIVIDUAL

PROGNOSIS AFTER INTERVENTION RISK REAPPRAISAL *					SURVIVAL ADVANTAGE	
Prognostic Characteristics	Risk Factor		Composite Risk Factor	New Risk	Amount Reduction	Per Cent Reduction
After Physician's Prescription	*From Manual* x	+	*See Instructions*	*(2) x (9)*	*(6) - (10)*	**
(7)	(8)		(9)	(10)	(11)	(12)
	.4		.2	375.4	3566.3	46%
	.9					
	1.0					
Prescribed exercise	1.0					
	.9					
Stop Smoking	.7					
Reduce to desirable weight 150-154#	1.0					
None before driving	.5		2.6	741	114	2%
	1.0					
		3.2				
	.8					
	1.0		1.0	264	0	0
	1.0					
Stop before symptoms	.2		.2	44.4	177.6	2%
	.4		.4	88.8	0	0
	.9					
	1.0					
Stop Smoking	1.0					
Stop Smoking	.2		.2	40.4	20.2	.3%
	1.0		.1	16.7	0	0
	1.0					
	.1					

FIG. 17-2, cont'd. For legend see p. 308.

RISK REDUCTION FOR INDIVIDUAL						
PROGNOSIS AFTER INTERVENTION RISK REAPPRAISAL *					SURVIVAL ADVANTAGE	
Prognostic Characteristics	Risk Factor		Composite Risk Factor	New Risk	Amount Reduction	Per Cent Reduction
After Physician's Prescription	From Manual x	From Manual +	See Instructions	(2) x (9)	(6) - (10)	**
(7)	(8)		(9)	(10)	(11)	(12)
ppropriate reduction	1.0		1.0	111	0	0
	1.0					
	1.0					
top Smoking	1.0					
	1.0		.3	33.3	77.7	1%
	1.0					
	1.0					
nnual Proctosigmoidoscopy	x0.3					
			1.0	76	0	0
	1.0		1.0	56	0	0
	.4		.4	22.4	16.8	.2%
educe to desirable weight	1.0					
nnual Chest X-ray	.2		.2	11.2	44.8	1%
	1.0					
	1.0					
			1.0	1,855	0	0
				3,736	4017	52%

Compliance age 37

Appraiser ______ (SIGNATURE)

Physician ______

FIG. 17-2, cont'd. For legend see p. 308.

Risk factors	Major disorder
Depression Family history of suicide	Suicide
High annual mileage Seat belt nonusage Increased alcohol habits Drugs and medications (Influencing driving)	Motor vehicle accidents
Increased alcohol habits History of bacterial pneumonia Presence of emphysema/bronchitis Increased smoking habits	Pneumonia
Presence of crime record Weapons carried	Homicide
Increased alcohol habits	Cirrhosis of the liver
Increased smoking habits	Cancer of the lung
Increased smoking habits Blood cholesterol raised Blood pressure elevated Presence of diabetes Family history of diabetes	Cerebrovascular and peripheral arterial disease
Increased smoking habits Blood cholesterol raised Blood pressure elevated Diabetes Family history of diabetes Weight Lack of exercise Family history of ischemic heart disease	Arteriosclerotic heart disease

Risk factors	Major disorder
Rectal polyp Rectal bleeding Ulcerative colitis Protosigmoidoscopy not done	Cancer of the intestine and the rectum
Pap smear not done Early age of intercourse Poor economic and social status Jewish ethnic origin	Cancer of the cervix
Signs/symptoms or history treatment of rheumatic heart disease	Chronic rheumatic heart disease
Abnormal vaginal bleeding	Cancer of the body of the uterus
Family history of breast cancer or breast disease Late age of pregnancy or nulliparity Early age of menarche Late age of menopause Fibocystic breast disease Radiation exposure Upper socioeconomic class Above average height/weight	Cancer of the breast

FIG. 17-3 Precursors of selected causes of death.

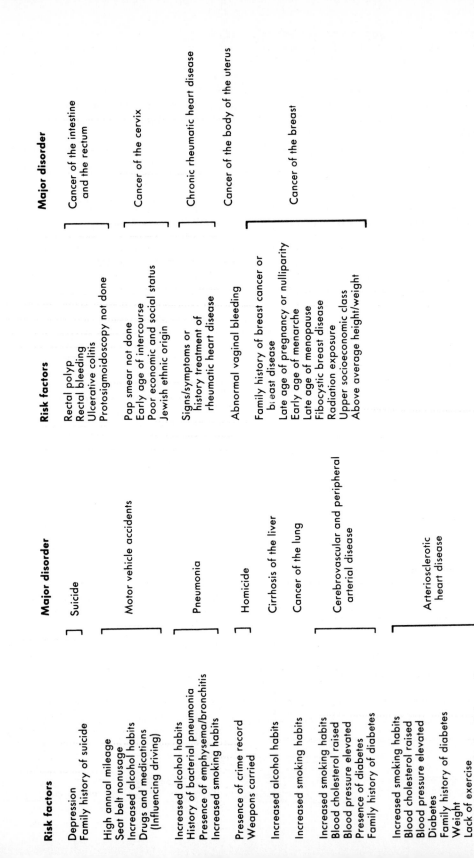

which it can confer and the variety of other uses to which it can be put.

Certainly for the purposes of health education and behavior modification, the health hazard appraisal appears to provide an important tool with prospects of success in an area where so many other approaches have failed.

REFERENCES

1. Report of the Maryland State Board of Health, 1875. (Courtesy Clemens W Gaines, Executive Office, 1965.)
2. Rosen G: A history of public health, New York, 1958, MD Publications.
3. Hochbaum G: At the threshold of a new era. Quoted in Ogden H: Health education: a federal overview, Public Health Rep 91:199, May-June 1976.
4. McClendon BJ: Available data and information on public health personnel: the second report to Congress. In Proceedings: a forum on the public health workforce, HRA contract No 238-81-0004, Sept 1982, US Department of Health and Human Services.
5. Moore FI: Analysis of the public health workforce: final report, HRSA contract No 85-266(P)ES0, Aug 1985, US Department of Health and Human Services.
6. Henderson AC and others: The future of the health education profession, Public Health Rep 96:555, Nov-Dec 1981.
7. Wood TD: In Fourth yearbook of the Department of Superintendent of the National Education Association, Washington, DC, 1926, National Education Association.
8. Rosen G: Evolving trends in health education, Can J Public Health 52:504, Dec 1961.
9. Henderson AC and McIntosh DV: Role refinement and verification for entry level health educators: final report, San Francisco, 1981, National Center of Health Education.
10. Green LW and others: Health education planning: a diagnostic approach, Palo Alto, CA, 1980, Mayfield Publishing Co.
11. Bowman R: Changes in the activities, functions, and roles of public health educators, Health Educ Monogr 4:226, Fall 1976.
12. Henderson AC: Developing a credentialing system for health educators. In Simonds SK and others: Advances in health education and promotion, vol 2, Greenwich, CT, 1987, JAI Press.
13. Henderson AC, McIntosh DV, and Schaller WE: Progress report of the role delineation project, J Sch Health 51:373, 1981.
14. Toward a policy on health education and public health: position paper of the American Public Health Association, Am J Public Health 68:203, Feb 1978.
15. Galanter R: To the victims belong the flaws, Am J Public Health 67:1025, Nov 1977.
16. Spiegel C and Lindaman F: Children can't fly: a program to prevent childhood morbidity and mortality from window falls, Am J Public Health 67:1143, Dec 1977.
17. Ogden H: Health education: a federal overview, Public Health Rep 91:199, May-June 1976.
18. Marti-Ibanez F: The pebble in the bell, MD 15:13, July 1971.
19. Rosenstock IM, Derryberry M, and Carriger BK: Why people fail to seek poliomyelitis vaccination, Public Health Rep 74:98, Feb 1959.
20. Rosenstock IM, Strecher VJ, and Becker MH: Social learning theory and the health belief model, Health Educ Q 15:175, Summer 1988.
21. Swinehart JW: Voluntary exposure to health communications, Am J Public Health 58:1265, July 1968.
22. Health education: its present status: report by the Committee on Public Health, New York Academy of Medicine, Bull NY Acad Med 41:1172, Nov 1965.
23. Anderson RE: Public health is no private preserve (or things I never knew 'till now, no thanks to you), Mich Health, May-June 1965.
24. Report of the President's Committee on Health Education, Washington, DC, 1973, US Department of Health, Education and Welfare.
25. Tones BK: Health education: prevention or subversion? R Soc Health J 101(3):114, 1981.
26. McEvoy L and Land G: Life-style and death patterns of the Missouri RLDS church members, Am J Public Health 71:1350, Dec 1981.
27. Shires DB, editor: Bodycheck, Division of Family Medicine, Dalhousie University, Halifax, Nova Scotia.
28. Wilcock AR and others: Evaluation of relative health-risk levels of a group of impaired drivers through health hazard appraisal, Can J Public Health 72:264, July-Aug 1981.
29. Robbins LC and Petrakis NL: Coverting ratios to risks—a foundation for prospective medicine, Proceedings of the Twelfth Annual Meeting of the Society of Prospective Medicine, Bethesda, Md, 1977, Health and Education Resources.
30. Hall JH and Zwemer JD: Prospective medicine, Indianapolis, 1979, Methodist Hospital Press.
31. Probability tables of dying in the next 10 years, Indianapolis, 1974, Methodist Hospital Press.
32. Althafer C: 1975, 1976, 1977: averaged probability of dying within the next 10 years of the 12 leading causes from 34 specific causes of death by age, race, and sex (1-year age groups), mimeographed paper, Atlanta, Bureau of Health Education, Centers for Disease Control.
33. Gesner NB: The credit-debit system of health hazard appraisal, Proceedings of the Thirteenth Annual Meeting of the Society of Prospective Medicine, Indianapolis, 1977, Methodist Hospital of Indiana.

34. Gesner NB: Derivation of risk factors from comparative data, Proceedings of the Seventh Annual Meeting of the Society of Prospective Medicine, Indianapolis, 1971, Methodist Hospital of Indiana.
35. Lalonde M: A new perspective in the health of Canadians: a working document, Ottawa, 1974, National Health and Welfare Ministry.
36. Lalonde M: Beyond a new perspective, Am J Public Health 67:357, April 1977.
37. Fielding JF: Appraising the health of health risk appraisal (editorial), Am J Public Health 72:337, April 1982.

PART FIVE

Environmental health

"What is this thing called health?" once asked the journalist-commentator H.L. Mencken. "Simply a state in which the individual happens transiently to be perfectly adapted to his [or her] environment." But what is meant by environment?

Until recently, most people considered their environment limited to some of the visible, tangible, inanimate aspects of their surroundings. For a century or more, public health workers' interpretation of environmental health did not go much beyond solving problems of insanitation in the water and food supply and in housing. But a revolution has occurred, complete with speeches, marches, legal actions, civil disobedience, and even occasional violence born of frustration. The Green Parties of Europe have begun to attain a measure of political power in open elections. In the United States, environmental concerns have begun to play a prominent role in presidential races as well as in state elections and in Congress. We have come to learn and understand the word and the concept of *ecology*. The traditional egocentric concept that the planet and everything on it is ours to exploit and despoil without danger of repercussion has disappeared. The greenhouse effect, disposal of toxic wastes, management of nuclear energy, acid rain, reducing the size of the waste stream, and even the sanctity of the supply of clean water are all issues that have raised the consciousness of people in all the nations of the world. Nature has begun to strike back.

The widening gap between technological developments and the ability of our institutions to adapt is at the root of the multiplication of environmental problems that confront us—in our homes, at work, on the street, at play, and even in outer space. Increasingly it is becoming apparent that there is no escape, only trade-offs. Moreover, all of these environmental and institutional problems in turn are intertwined with and form a part of the social and economic problems of this final decade of the century. The situation is well put by C.P. Snow in his book *The Two Cultures and the Scientific Revolution*: "as history routinely and regularly records, because the engineering community and the political community could not get sufficiently on each other's wavelengths, one advanced civilization after another, sooner or later, collapsed."

So now, our only recourse is to join the rest of the planet, to live on it with greater wisdom than before, and to anticipate and guard against those environmental forces, natural and man-made, that may imperil our health, well-being, and continued existence.

The chapters in this part consider several aspects of the environment: pollution and its control, occupational health and safety, the prevention and control of injuries, and public health nutrition.

CHAPTER 18

Environmental health policy*

Few areas of public health policy are as riddled with ironies as environmental health. The environment is a public health problem of long standing yet one that constantly produces new wrinkles and challenges. It is a public health problem about which there is near unanimity among citizens that government must intervene, yet there is no consensus on the most appropriate methods of intervention. It is a public health problem that cannot be confined by local and state government boundaries yet one about which the national government remains quite deferential to subnational and private sector strategies. It is an area ripe for preventive strategies yet one where reactive, crisis-management approaches have prevailed. Finally, it is an area in which health departments and public health officials have played an effective and dominant role in earlier decades but have seen their responsibilities eroded in more recent times in favor of officials from agencies with broad responsibilities for environmental and natural resource protection.

At the same time, few areas of public health policy pose a comparable set of opportunities for public health officials—and other individuals with a commitment to environmental health—to demonstrate a capacity to take action that will contribute to the public good. Whether examining the unfinished agenda of the 1960s and 1970s, which addressed water and air pollution with rigorous new legislation, or the diverse agenda of the late 1980s, which includes toxic substances, hazardous waste, radon, nuclear waste, and ozone layer depletion, one finds questions in environmental health that defy simple remedies. These questions are biological, chemical, political, economic, and legal. With the possible exception of AIDS and medical care for the underserved, environmental health looks as if it will be the dominant public health issue on the national political agenda for at least the balance of this century. It may prove a litmus test of the capacity of the public health community to forge viable policy strategies and work cooperatively with other governmental agencies, the private sector, and the general public at this stage in our nation's political and economic development.

This chapter will pose a series of challenges for public health officials in environmental health by examining the track record of recent governmental interventions, reviewing the institutional and legislative infrastructures created to address environmental health, and outlining the tasks that lie ahead. It will begin with an exploration of the nature of environmental health problems, reviewing progress and failure in past decades. In addition, it will describe new and growing problems for which new policy remedies will be required. Second, the chapter will consider the institutional and political response to environmental health problems over the past few decades. It will devote considerable attention to the ways in which authority for environmental health policy has been divided intergovernmentally (national, state, region, local) and interorganizationally (public health, environmental superagency, natural resources, agriculture among others). It will also consider the common dividing lines between "media," such as land, air, water, and biosphere, despite the fact that transfer, transport, and transformation of pollutants across these formal boundaries is commonplace. This discussion will underscore the many lines of fragmentation in environmental health policy and management and explore both the strengths and weaknesses of such a pluralistic strategy. Throughout these sections, considerable attention will be devoted to

* This chapter was contributed by Professor Barry Rabe, Department of Public Health Policy and Administration, School of Public Health, University of Michigan, Ann Arbor, Michigan.

the role that public health officials and agencies have played and might play in environmental health.

THE PROBLEMS OF ENVIRONMENTAL HEALTH

Humanmade and natural environmental health threats come in many forms and pose many potential health problems. Foremost among these threats in recent decades has been cancer, although exposure to various environmental contaminants may also result in genetic damage, birth defects, neurological effects, liver damage, infections, and injuries. In response, governments at all levels have developed a variety of methods, including animal bioassays, human epidemiologic studies, and tests for mutagenicity, to measure and predict human risk. They have also devised a myriad of regulatory programs to attempt to control and minimize these risks.

Assessments of the effectiveness of these strategies must be couched in terms of extreme caution. There is neither a foolproof method for measuring the risk posed by a particular contaminant in a particular setting nor a certain regulatory method for minimizing risk and assuring protection of public health. Nonetheless, the experiences of recent decades do make possible some general assessments of environmental quality and the scope and severity of relatively new environmental health problems. In turn they facilitate tentative assessments of the types of governmental regulatory interventions that may or may not be effective.

Areas of progress

Perhaps the two most encouraging twentieth century developments in environmental health involve the tremendous advancements in sanitation achieved early in the 1900s and the substantial strides in reducing conventional pollutants in the air and water during the 1970s and 1980s. Public health officials and agencies were in the forefront of efforts to combat the enormous environmental health problems posed by unsafe sanitation systems. These problems proved particularly severe in industrialized urban areas that underwent rapid population growth in the late 1800s and early 1900s. Safe systems of sanitation and waste disposal lagged several decades behind this growth, and the public health community played a central role in securing its implementation.[1]

Many of the public health or epidemiological accomplishments in the United States and certain other countries can be attributed to the sanitary measures that have been instituted. Included among these have been the spectacular reductions in typhoid fever, cholera, dysenteries, and summer diarrheas; the control of many of the milk-borne and food-borne infections; the control of malaria; and the elimination of yellow fever. It was not until the beginning of the present century that the chains of events involved in the transmission and perpetuation of these diseases became unraveled. Prompt steps were taken to break links in these chains.

At first, activities in the field of sanitation were concerned primarily with the abatement of noxious nuisances. Gradually the provision and supervision of sanitary water supplies and sewage disposal facilities were added as the first well-defined and scientific measures. Meanwhile, the Rockefeller Sanitary Commission, established in 1909 to combat hookworm disease, led to programs by state health departments with emphasis on the eradication of hookworm and other enteric infections in the rural population. These activities laid the foundation for the eventual establishment and spread of many full-time county health departments in the United States, particularly in the Southeast.

In this regard, the noteworthy surveys, demonstrations, and epidemiologic investigations of the Public Health Service also had enormous impact. Throughout this formative era of the modern sanitation and public health program, much emphasis was placed on the construction and use of sanitary privies in rural areas and small towns as a practical means of preventing the spread of enteric disease. This emphasis on sanitation remains a major health department concern to this day through such functions as monitoring of septic tanks and drinking water wells, restaurant inspection, housing hygiene, and animal vector control.

A comprehensive attack on major industrial air and water pollutants was delayed until the early 1970s but has registered a number of notable achievements. There were forerunners of the 1970s Clean Air Act and 1972 Water Pollution Control Act (now known as the Clean Water Act), but these were quite modest in scope.[2] For example, the national government became involved in water pollution control as early as 1899 with enactment of the Rivers and Harbors Act. Similarly, many localities have attempted to monitor and regulate air and water pollution throughout the twentieth century. Several states frequently used the interstate compact process to advance environmental regulation, and a federal-state compact was initiated in 1963 to establish environmental planning for the Delaware River Basin.[3,4] Nonetheless, these were of minimal consequence in combating the growing threats to the environment—and environmental health—posed by our enormous consumption of natural resources and production of wastes.

The nation's decision in the 1970s to combat these pollution problems with greater rigor and resource commitment led to serious assaults on several of the most obvious problems, many of which possessed a compelling environmental health component. The Clean Air Act established national ambient air quality standards (NAAQS), set an array of emissions standards for motor vehicles and industrial facilities, and required states to design and implement plans for air quality. The Water Pollution Control Act imposed strict controls on industrial, municipal, and other sources of water pollution, established a program for wastewater discharge, and expanded grants available for wastewater facility construction. Other major pieces of legislation added new rigor and specificity to environmental regulation.[5]

If not as sweeping a series of successes as had been attained in prior generations through new sanitation efforts, these legislative efforts have had a significant impact. If not measurable in lives saved, they have made at least some contribution to human health through improved environmental quality. Success has been particularly dramatic in reduction of the release of particulates, sulfur dioxide, and automobile-related and other conventional pollutants to the air and reduction of suspended solids, bacteria, and oxygen-consuming materials discharged to surface waters. As the 1987 State of the Environment report by the Conservation Foundation[6] summarized, "The United States is less polluted, at least with conventional pollutants, than it was in 1970. Considering that . . . the nation's gross national product has grown approximately 50% during the same period, this is not a trivial achievement."

In air quality, progress has been made in a number of areas with considerable environmental health ramifications. For example, between 1975 and 1984, there was an average decline in emissions of 33% for total suspended particulates (TSP), 16% for all sulfur oxides, 14% for carbon monoxide, and 10% for nitrogen dioxide, according to data from the U.S. Environmental Protection Agency (EPA).[6] Many other important indicators of air quality suggest similar progress, with potentially significant benefits for public health.

In the area of surface water quality, which involves lakes and rivers as opposed to subsurface groundwater, conventional pollutants from industrial and municipal sources have received considerable regulatory attention, and some noteworthy successes have been registered. According to the National Ambient Stream Quality Accounting Network (NASQAN) of the U.S. Geological Survey (USGS), water quality trends have been particularly encouraging for lead, dissolved oxygen, and fecal coliforms and streptococci (two common bacterial contaminants that are indicators of sewage pollution).[7]

These achievements were costly; both public and private sectors made major increases in pollution control spending after 1970. The nation invested $557 billion for this purpose from 1972 to 1984, reaching a high of 2% of the gross national product in the late 1970s before dropping off slightly in the 1980s.[8] There is little evidence to suggest that this commitment of resources has had an adverse impact on economic growth.[9]

Future challenges

Despite some heartening developments in improving environmental quality, potential threats to environmental health loom even greater today than they did on Earth Day in 1970. Incremental progress in water quality has been offset by growing concentrations of arsenic and cadmium, and minimal progress has been registered for metals such as chromium, iron, manganese, selenium, mercury, and zinc despite massive investments in water pollution control.[6]

Of even greater import is the growing recognition that past environmental regulatory efforts have largely ignored a series of problems that may require massive new interventions by the public and private sectors in future decades. Many of these relate to the safe disposal of solid wastes that are by-products of manufacturing, households, and even environmental treatment processes. The United States generates approximately 50,000 pounds of waste per person per year and by restricting traditional disposal methods (incineration or direct dumping into lakes, rivers, and oceans) has created a waste disposal problem of almost unfathomable magnitude. Approximately 250 to 260 million metric tons of what is commonly known as hazardous waste are generated each year, and every plausible method of safe disposal has serious drawbacks.[10,11] Land-based fills and surface impoundments allow wastes to seep into groundwater or vaporize into the air; deep-well injection leads to serious groundwater contamination threats; incineration poses obvious air pollution threats that could further harm water and land.[12] The federal EPA, working through the Superfund program for cleanup of abandoned toxic waste sites, has already uncovered more than 25,000 abandoned dump sites that cause or have the potential to cause contamination. The agency also estimates the existence of more than 50,000 municipal landfills, nearly 75,000 mining waste sites, more than 75,000 industrial landfills, and more than 175,000 leaking underground storage tanks.[13] Many of these may pose serious environmental health threats, although assessments of the severity of the hazards remain largely conjectural. These estimates do not touch upon the problem of safe disposal of waste from plants that provide nuclear power or materials for nuclear weapons.

The 1970s assault on environmental degradation also tended to overlook hazardous substances such as chemicals. By focusing so heavily on conventional pollutants, which were in many instances the most visible threats, national, state, and local governments devoted far less attention to toxic substances control. It is increasingly realized, however, that these substances are ubiquitous in air, water, land, and biosphere and that they may pose more serious public health problems than conventional pollutants. According to the inventory conducted under the 1976 Toxic Substances Control Act, more than 63,000 chemical substances have been used commercially since 1975. In addition, new substances are introduced into commercial use far more rapidly than any national, state, or local program can evaluate their safety. Among synthetic organic chemicals alone, nearly 225 billion pounds were produced in 1985, an increase of nearly 45% since 1975.[6] The Registry of Toxic Substances of the National Institute of Occupational Safety and Health (NIOSH) has registered nearly 60,000 substances "that are known to have toxic effects at some level of exposure." These effects include irritation, mutation, reproductive effects, carcinogenesis, and death. However, it should be noted that many substances may not be particularly hazardous, and little is known about the health effects of a great many of them.[6] Scientific understanding is particularly uncertain of the effects of the myriad possible combinations and permutations of these substances.

These sobering numbers are not intended to imply that a public health crisis owing to hazardous wastes and toxic substances is upon us. In fact, environmental scientists, industry leaders, and public health officials have little idea of how many Americans are at risk from exposure to these materials and how serious the health consequences might be. Rather, these figures are introduced to underscore the scope of potential human health effects and the nature of the challenge facing public and private sector leaders, including public health officials, who will have to make basic policy decisions concerning them in the face of uncertainty. Unlike the triumphs over substandard sanitation early in this century, there will be no comparable scientific and political quick fix for the latest difficulties in environmental health.

THE INSTITUTIONAL AND POLITICAL ROLE OF ENVIRONMENTAL HEALTH

Political systems respond to the public demands of the moment. In environmental health, this has resulted in a pattern of policy shifts dictated by problems or crises that have been seen as particularly serious at different points in time.[14] In the decade following World War II, concerns over natural resource abuse grew, and expanded government commitment to conservation soon followed, particularly through increased responsibilities for the U.S. Department of the Interior. In the late 1960s and early 1970s, concerns over visible environmental degradation in air and water led to formation of a national environmental agency and enactment of major new legislation related to air and water quality. In the late 1970s and through the

1980s, concerns have mounted over hazardous wastes, toxic substances, and a series of even more far-reaching concerns, including ozone layer depletion and the "greenhouse effect." Mounting evidence indicates that a combination of natural and humanmade gases, including chlorofluorocarbons, methane, carbon dioxide, and nitrous oxide, are depleting the earth's protective layer of stratospheric ozone. Not only does this increase the amount of dangerous ultraviolet radiation reaching life on earth, but these chemicals also act to trap radiative heat close to the earth's surface. It is feared that this could substantially elevate atmospheric temperatures and have potentially severe consequences. True to form, the U.S. political system has begun to respond with a series of new or expanded research and regulatory efforts.[15]

This series of perceived environmental problems and policy responses has increased the public sector's regulatory power and added to the resources for addressing environmental degradation that could have an adverse effect on human health. In particular, growing authority has been amassed at national and state levels, as the once dominant role of local governments (and their health departments) has been increasingly overshadowed by national and state legislation and agencies. To be sure, the traditional local role has remained substantial, particularly in the implementation of various environmental health programs, but it has become increasingly dependent on national and state sources of funding and policy direction.[16] Coordinating the efforts of these respective levels of government has proven a major stumbling block to effective environmental regulation.

Creation of a new agency

The early 1970s were a critical turning point in expanding the government's role in environmental regulation and shifting authority from local town halls to state capitols and Washington, D.C. At the national level, funding for environmental programs had been modest, and regulatory authority was scattered throughout the federal bureaucracy. Responsibility for water pollution control, for example, was divided among the Department of Health, Education and Welfare, the Department of the Interior, and the Department of Defense. The Public Health Service maintained a role in certain aspects of environmental regulation but was hardly a dominant figure, since responsibility was delegated to so many other departments and agencies and the overall national role was so modest.

The outcry over environmental contamination in the late 1960s fueled a social movement that placed enormous political pressure on Congress, President Nixon, and state legislatures. As a result, there was substantial expansion of water and air pollution control programs, and Congress passed the National Environmental Policy Act (NEPA) in 1970. NEPA ushered in an era of "environmental impact statements" that were to take into account all anticipated environmental ramifications from proposed development projects supported by national government funding. It also created the Council on Environmental Quality (CEQ) to assist in coordinating all of the federal government's environmental efforts.[17,18] Twenty-eight states subsequently responded with state environmental policy acts (or little NEPAs) of their own, several of which were far more detailed and rigorous than NEPA.

This new and expanded legislative commitment coincided with an executive branch decision to consolidate a wide range of environmental regulatory functions into a single agency. The Environmental Protection Agency emerged in 1970, with responsibility for all environmental media (air, water, and land) and most of the major pollution control programs. However, the agency was not the all-encompassing environmental superagency or vehicle of integration across media boundaries that many supporters of reorganization had recommended. Political resistance from individual program constituencies was too formidable to challenge, and the Nixon administration (especially EPA administrator William Ruckelshaus) was eager to demonstrate its environmental commitment in some manner more dramatic than agency reorganization. As a result, the departments of Interior, Health and Human Services, Agriculture, and Defense (and later Energy) retained considerable control over environmental regulatory functions that touched their immediate jurisdictions, and many previous lines of divisions were perpetuated within the EPA.[19,20] Other agencies, such as the Nuclear Regulatory Commission, Consumer Products Safety Commission, Food and Drug Administration, and Occupational Safety and Health Administration, have also maintained some direct role in environmental regulation.[21]

As was the case with NEPA, many states quickly followed this national action by consolidating environmental regulatory responsibilities into new agencies. The health department soon ceased to be the dominant environmental regulatory agency in the majority of states, replaced after 1970 by a series of little EPAs modeled on the national agency or similarly structured environmental superagencies with broad jurisdiction. As of 1986, less than 20% of the American people resided in the 12 states in which public health departments were the dominant environmental agency: Arizona, Colorado, Hawaii, Kansas, Maryland, Montana, New Mexico, North Dakota, Oklahoma, South Carolina, Tennessee, and Vermont.[22] Much like the national EPA, the new state agencies achieved some degree of environmental program consolidation within a single agency but continued to share authority with a variety of other organizations. In Minnesota, for example, nearly 50 separate agencies, boards, and commissions addressed some aspect of state environmental regulation.[23] As a result, state agencies with responsibility for commerce, agriculture, natural resources, mining, economic development, and energy have continued to play a role in environmental regulation, often at cross-purposes with environmental regulatory agencies.

The federal EPA, much like its state-level counterparts, failed to resolve varying agency rivalries or coordinate different regulatory approaches. It has become an amalgamation of programs and divisions rather than a carefully integrated agency. The agency was built partly along program lines that adhered to divisions in environmental media (air vs. water vs. land) and partly along functional lines, such as standards, enforcement, and research, that transcended individual programs or media. This resulted in a divided agency in which programmatic concerns increasingly came to dominate cross-cutting functional ones. Moreover, the agency was restrained in any effort to integrate regulatory efforts by highly exacting legislation and extensive congressional oversight, both of which reflected a fragmented congressional committee and subcommittee system, which tended to further subdivide national environmental policy.

Air vs. water

The fragmentation was particularly evident in the two areas where tremendous expansion of national regulatory authority occurred in the 1970s: air and water pollution. The division of these two media has been evident at both the national and state levels throughout the twentieth century. Not only have they been studied separately and approached through differing legislation, but water pollution has consistently been addressed before air pollution at the national level. Water pollution reached the national political agenda in 1924, 29 years before air pollution arrived at a comparable point.[24] Even discounting the 1899 Rivers and Harbors Act, the 1924 Oil Pollution Act, and the 1944 Public Health Service Act, all of which involved the federal government in very modest efforts to control water pollution, the first federal water pollution legislation was enacted in 1948, 7 years before comparably extensive legislation in air pollution. Similarly, federal enforcement powers were authorized in water pollution in 1956 and in air pollution in 1963.[23] Regulations under that legislation were then issued much more rapidly for water than for air. It is not surprising, therefore, that dramatically different national programs have evolved to address these two media. They are similar only in their extreme individual complexity. As political scientist Alfred Marcus[25] has noted:

> In spite of the fact that air and water were in the same agency and for a time were in the same office, the two programs remained distinct and separate entities with different operating procedures and differing laws governing them. Their focus was not on the pollutant and its movement through the ecological chain. No efforts were made to determine where best to interdict the unhealthy, foul substances that needed elimination.

The air and water pollution programs of the federal government continue to differ in many important respects. For example, the Clean Air Act established health-based national ambient air quality goals, while the Clean Water Act set technology-based effluent guidelines. Moreover, the water program emphasizes the regulatory "carrot" of public works funding, whereas the air program emphasizes the regulatory "stick" of stringent requirements and few funding rewards. Even the political strategies adopted by the officials who operate the programs differ considerably. Whereas the air program attracts extensive public attention and controversy and its officials tend to confront opposition directly, the water program maintains a more modest political profile and responds to opposition in a less confrontational manner.

Toxic substances and hazardous waste

Various changes in the air and water programs and the enactment of a new wave of federal environmental programs in the 1970s and early 1980s did not bridge this fundamental, program-based gap. On the contrary, the emergence of legislation that did not address a single medium exclusively served in some respects to fragment the system further. For example, 25 separate federal laws address some aspect of toxic substances control and hazardous waste management; 8 separate laws give EPA authority in toxic substances control. These programs are housed in several different national agencies, including EPA, the Food and Drug Administration, the Department of Transportation, and the Consumer Products Safety Commission.[26,27]

If not necessarily divided along medium lines, the management system that has resulted from this mélange of programs has proven similarly complicated and cumbersome. Each incident or issue related to toxic substances control and hazardous waste management has required a different combination of program agencies. For example, national control of all exposures from the manufacture, use, and disposal of vinyl chloride would require the participation of five national agencies through 15 national laws.[28] As political scientist Rae Zimmerman found in examining the tapestry of programs designed to manage toxic substances and hazardous wastes, "Standards are often set without regard to the relationship among various environmental media and the way that contaminants migrate among them."[29]

This proliferation of national legislation represents a continuation of the incremental, fragmented process of environmental policy formation that began with the earlier air and water programs, but the process has accelerated. This is manifest in legislation that includes the 1976 Toxic Substances Control Act (TSCA) and its 1982 amendments; the 1976 Resource Conservation and Recovery Act (RCRA) and its 1984 Hazardous and Solid Waste Amendments; and the 1980 Comprehensive Environmental Response, Compensation, and Liability Act (CERCLA, or Superfund) and the 1986 Superfund Amendments and Reauthorization Act (SARA). Each of these programs takes a separate cut at the problem: TSCA addresses premanufacture registration of toxic substances and authorizes EPA to ban certain substances; RCRA sets hazardous and solid waste disposal standards in close conjunction with states; CERCLA/SARA sets standards, determines responsibility, and implements cleanup of abandoned hazardous waste disposal sites. As Joel Hirschhorn of the U.S. Office of Technology Assessment has noted, "These programs are not integrated in any sense. They are very fragmented and are not implemented in any sort of integrated fashion."[30]

In summary, environmental regulation at the national level is fragmented along media lines and in other ways because of the variety of forces within the executive branch that have some role in policy. The consequences can be particularly severe along media lines, as mounting evidence indicates that many regulatory strategies may merely push environmental contaminants to the least regulated medium of the moment, such as leaching into groundwater that results from government-sanctioned land-based waste disposal.[12] This fragmentation has also resulted in uncertain coordination between regulation designed to protect human health and that intended to attain conservation goals.

Congress vs. itself

Fragmentation in national environmental policy is not confined to the executive branch. The political institution responsible for creation of legislation, the Congress, is fragmented itself, and it has impeded more integrative approaches. As early as 1970, committees dealing with environmental matters in both houses of Congress were divided along highly specialized, single-medium lines. No sooner did William Ruckelshaus become the first EPA administrator than he realized that he would have to deal with at least 16 congressional subcommittees that had some jurisdiction over the agency's pollution control activities.[20] Not only did these various bodies hold dramatically differing environmental responsibilities, but many were headed by members of the House and Senate who had already become wedded to a particular regulatory program or approach. Congressional leaders tend to build their environmental reputations through creation or expansion of specialized programs, with no responsibility for the ultimate fit between multiple programs. For example, Edmund Muskie (D-Maine) became a dominant figure in Senate battles over air pollution policy, just as John Blatnik (D-Minn.) became known as a champion of water pollution control in the House.[2] Proposals to enact new environmental legislation or to amend existing legislation were parceled out among specialized committees, with little coordination or interaction. The problems have continued in the 1980s, exemplified by the two-year process required to reauthorize and amend the Superfund program. Five full House committees and even more subcommittees assumed some role in some aspect of the reauthorization and encountered enormous difficulty in reaching common ground. As a result, the program was temporarily brought to a halt during 1986 after its funding ran out and was only reinstituted after a badly cobbled piece of legislation was approved, which is full of internal contradictions and promises to fit poorly with other programs.[31]

State agency vs. state agency

Agency and legislative fragmentation in environmental regulation may be most evident at the national level, but it is not confined there. Although states have assumed increasingly prominent roles in environmental regulation in recent years, they have not, on the whole, been any more successful in integrating regulation along functional and across media lines than the national government. The emergence of dozens of broad new environmental agencies has been only minimally effective in bringing various constituencies together in coordinated fashion.[32]

Fragmentation has been particularly evident in the implementation process, where states are often responsible for overseeing the approval of permits for various projects that will have some environmental impact. Each permitting program, often medium-based and guided by national policy, has its own internal logic and independent system of operation. As a result, very real trade-offs between media and regulatory strategies are not systematically taken into account.

Some states have responded to this problem with efforts to mesh the environmental programs under their jurisdiction. Permit coordination efforts have proven particularly popular, and more than 30 states had implemented such programs in some form by the early 1980s. Permits are a basic tool of environmental management in all states, as proposed development projects cannot begin until authorized agencies deem them in compliance with relevant regulatory requirements and provide a formal permit. Certain projects may require acquisition of dozens of such permits, ranging from those governing air and water pollution control to those for wetland and wildlife protection. State permit reforms have included developing master permit information forms, one-stop permitting processes, joint application procedures, mediation services, or permit expediters to break logjams, publishing permit directories, opening permit information centers, and holding preapplication conferences. All of these have the common aim of streamlining the permit process, and they have attained some success in bringing together diverse regulatory constituencies, including, on occasion, public health officials. However, their overall impact has been far greater in smoothing the process for permit applicants than in integrating a management system that considers all environmental ramifications in a coordinated fashion.[32]

No two states have devised identical regulatory systems, despite national government pressures and incentives for a certain degree of uniformity. For example, the emergence of toxic substances control and hazardous waste management as a major public concern and challenge for state government has led to very different responses. In states such as Michigan, jurisdiction is divided between multiple agencies, including the Toxic Substances Control Commission, the Department of Public Health, and the Department of Natural Resources, with minimal policy integration or innovation occurring.[33] By contrast, Illinois has launched a far-reaching Integrated Toxic Substances Control Strategy, in which the state EPA has systematically organized various state programs and agencies to coordinate their efforts and devise an integrated set of policies to address the problem.[34]

State innovators vs. state laggards

No two states are equally committed to environmental health or equally capable of effectively formulating and implementing regulatory programs. Certain states have consistently emerged as leaders in devising innovative strategies for environmental health: California has been a pioneer in air pollution control and hazardous waste disposal; Minnesota has played a similar role in water pollution control; Illinois and New York have repeatedly proven leaders in cross-media integration of pollution control programs; North Carolina has championed preventive strategies of industrial waste reduction; New Jersey has taken dramatic steps in toxic substances control. These leadership roles can be attributed to the potential severity of environmental health problems in these states (such as air pollution in northern California and toxic substances in New Jersey) and to the political cultures of the states. States have often devised environmental policies that have served as models for other states or the nation. By contrast, some states have continually been laggards in environmental health, taking new steps only when prodded by Washington.

Many evaluations of state environmental regulatory innovativeness and effectiveness have been attempted. Perhaps the most thorough was completed by Christopher Duerksen[35] of the Conservation Foundation in 1983. Duerksen ranked state environmental controls according to 23 indicators of environmental commitment, including levels of spending for environmental quality control, existence of a hazardous waste program, existence of a state process for environmental impact statements, and the voting record of the state's congressional delegation. His findings paralleled those of a great many other studies in ranking the industrialized states of the Northeast, Upper Midwest, and Pacific Northwest near the top in terms of commitment and the states of the Southeast and Southwest toward the bottom. Minnesota, California, New Jersey, Massachusetts, and Oregon held the top five positions; New Mexico, Idaho, Missouri, and Alabama were at the bottom (Table 18-1).

State-by-state variation is also evident in comparing the capacity and willingness of individual states to fund environmental regulatory programs. The states fund these efforts through a variety of mechanisms, including general tax revenues, bonds, user fees, and federal grants-in-aid. Many of them continue to face serious limitations on the amounts of funding they can be expected to generate for environment-related activities.[36] A comparison shows only a modest correlation between various measures of state expenditures (Table 18-2) and state ranking in environmental regulatory commitment (Table 18-1).

State government vs. national government

The realities of American federalism necessitate some basic working agreement between national and state governments if environmental regulatory programs are to be implemented effectively. This has not always been easy to attain, in part because individual state governments view their regulatory responsibilities in such profoundly different ways and in part because national funding has often not been as great as states would like and the extensive demands of national legislation would recommend.[26,33,37]

Three distinct types of strategies have emerged that characterize national-state relations in various environmental regulatory programs. At one extreme, the national role in certain programs has been extremely deferential to state government's differences and preferences. Under this form of "cooperative federalism," as defined by political scientist David Welborn,[38] the national government attempts to stimulate state action but does so with generous funding incentives, offers of state control over the program, and minimal national pressures for state-by-state conformity. Programs such as the solid waste portion of the Resource Conservation and Recovery Act and the Coastal Zone Management Act reflect this style of federalism, delegating considerable authority to individual states.

At the other extreme, the national government has at times taken a much more domineering role in relation to the states, assessing a particular environmental problem as national in character and warranting a uniform national remedy that leaves little if any role to the states. In fact, such legislation often attempts to preclude any direct state involvement in program implementation and relies on national agencies to secure enforcement. This style of "national federalism" includes programs such as the auto emissions portion of the Clean Air Act and the Toxic Substances Control Act. More recently, it includes CERCLA (Superfund) and its 1986 reauthorization as SARA. In the case of SARA, the national government bypasses state (and, for the most part, local) government in setting standards, assessing liability, and implementing cleanup strategies at abandoned hazardous waste facilities.[38] States may choose to develop their own Superfund-type programs with state funding but must operate independently of the national program and nationally designated cleanup sites and are unlikely to receive much if any of the $9.5 billion that the national government will spend on this program over the next 5 years.[39]

A far greater number of national environmental regulatory programs operate somewhere in between these two extremes, with a more balanced distribution of authority between national and state levels. Under this more common "conjoint" arrangement, national environmental legislation is intended to force state action and to provide regulatory control in the absence of state participation. However, authority is delegated to cooperating states, and they receive considerable latitude in implementation. Enforcement is shared between national and state officials, considerable national funding is provided to states to ease costs of implementation, and states devise implementation plans that must be approved nationally. This approach has been used in the Clean Water Act, most portions of the Clean Air Act, the hazardous waste portion of RCRA, the Federal Insecticide, Fungicide, and Rodenticide Act (FIFRA), the Safe Drinking Water Act, the Noise Control Act, the Surface Mining Control and Reclamation Act, and others.[38]

This effort to balance national and state authority under national legislation does not necessarily result in intergovernmental harmony and careful integration of efforts from both levels, however. In fact, both the conjoint and cooperative approaches

TABLE 18-1 Ranking of states' environmental commitment

State	Rank	Score (0-63)	State	Rank	Score (0-63)
Minnesota	1	47	Arkansas	26	27
California	2	46	Colorado	27	26
New Jersey	3	45	Rhode Island	27	26
Massachusetts	4	44	Georgia	29	25
Oregon	5	42	North Carolina	29	25
Washington	6	39	South Carolina	29	25
Maryland	7	37	Arizona	32	24
Montana	7	37	Alaska	33	23
New York	7	37	Kansas	33	23
Wisconsin	7	37	Tennessee	33	23
Indiana	11	36	Utah	33	23
Hawaii	12	34	West Virginia	33	23
Kentucky	12	34	Wyoming	33	23
Connecticut	14	32	Nebraska	39	22
Maine	14	32	Nevada	39	22
Vermont	14	32	North Dakota	39	22
Florida	17	31	Texas	39	22
Michigan	18	30	Louisiana	43	21
Ohio	18	30	New Hampshire	43	21
South Dakota	18	30	Oklahoma	45	19
Delaware	21	29	New Mexico	46	18
Iowa	21	29	Idaho	47	17
Illinois	23	28	Mississippi	48	15
Pennsylvania	23	28	Missouri	49	14
Virginia	23	28	Alabama	50	10

From Duerksen CJ: Environmental regulation of industrial plant siting, Washington, DC, 1983, Conservation Foundation.

TABLE 18-2 Ranking of states' environmental expenditures, fiscal year 1986

Rank	Ranked by total environmental expenditures: State	$	Ranked by per capita expenditures: State	$
1	California	1,199,938,000	Alaska	326.00
2	Pennsylvania	332,549,763	Wyoming	135.33
3	Wisconsin	260,289,169	South Dakota	75.90
4	New York	227,274,090	Montana	69.55
5	New Jersey	200,750,000	Wisconsin	55.31
6	Illinois	181,897,000	Idaho	51.97
7	Michigan	173,007,900	California	50.70
8	Florida	171,267,941	Oregon	49.01
9	Washington	160,334,318	Delaware	47.74
10	Alaska	130,973,900	Vermont	42.94
11	Oregon	129,052,806	Washington	38.80
12	Missouri	123,279,074	New Hampshire	32.41
13	Massachusetts	122,313,035	North Dakota	31.08
14	Texas	100,921,072	Pennsylvania	28.03
15	Ohio	92,169,500	New Jersey	27.25
16	Kentucky	88,448,194	Rhode Island	26.16
17	Virginia	87,316,466	Missouri	25.07
18	Maryland	85,748,214	Utah	24.60
19	North Carolina	77,193,938	New Mexico	24.59
20	Minnesota	73,482,950	Mississippi	24.38
21	Louisiana	73,079,329	Kentucky	24.16
22	Tennessee	70,911,499	West Virginia	23.68
23	Georgia	68,986,592	Maine	22.31
24	Colorado	64,319,886	Colorado	22.26
25	Wyoming	63,604,967	Nevada	21.77
26	Mississippi	61,453,623	Massachusetts	21.32
27	Alabama	60,252,564	Maryland	20.33
28	Montana	54,739,315	Hawaii	19.21
29	South Dakota	52,450,000	Michigan	18.68
30	South Carolina	50,018,484	Minnesota	18.03
31	Idaho	49,063,734	Florida	17.57
32	Iowa	47,090,046	Louisiana	17.38
33	Indiana	46,551,743	Virginia	16.33
34	West Virginia	46,183,752	Iowa	16.16
35	Oklahoma	43,892,933	South Carolina	16.02
36	Arizona	41,287,553	Illinois	15.92
37	Connecticut	38,666,000	Alabama	15.47
38	Utah	35,947,156	Tennessee	15.45
39	New Mexico	32,046,123	Arizona	15.19
40	Kansas	30,445,137	North Carolina	14.62
41	Arkansas	30,372,330	Oklahoma	14.51
42	New Hampshire	29,850,570	Nebraska	13.32
43	Delaware	28,359,508	Arkansas	13.29
44	Maine	25,096,481	New York	12.94
45	Rhode Island	24,767,942	Kansas	12.88
46	Vermont	21,944,786	Georgia	12.63
47	Nebraska	20,918,705	Connecticut	12.44
48	North Dakota	20,293,798	Ohio	8.54
49	Hawaii	18,540,533	Indiana	8.48
50	Nevada	17,413,195	Texas	7.09

From Brown RS and Garner LE: Resource guide to state environmental management, Lexington, KY, 1988, Council of State Governments.

tend to fragment environmental regulation further by giving each level of government a significant and potentially competing role. The extreme intergovernmental conflicts over the Clean Air Act and hazardous waste portion of RCRA, for example, illustrate that these approaches to environmental federalism only add further tension to the regulatory system. By contrast, more nationalized programs such as Superfund, which attempt to bypass this problem by reducing or eliminating the state government's role, pose their own set of implementation pitfalls and intergovernmental conflicts, since the national government must ultimately work cooperatively with local level agencies and citizen groups. This is no small task given the degree of public alarm triggered by abandoned hazardous waste sites.

The subdued role of public health agencies

State health departments and their local counterparts were dominant institutional forces in environmental health as recently as the mid-1960s but saw their influence decline following the creation of new national and state institutions with broad responsibilities for environmental regulation. Nonetheless, their role remains central in those 12 states that continue to rely on the health department model for environmental regulation, through state departments of health, public health, or health and human resources. In addition, the continuing responsibility of state and local health departments in areas central to environmental health, particularly their data gathering and analysis capabilities, give them an enduring—if subdued—role in all 50 states.[16]

Health departments have tended to respond to their new institutional competitors at the state and national levels with lamentation over their relegation to the sidelines rather than bold initiatives to define their natural role in the increasingly crowded field of environmental regulatory institutions. A major challenge for public health officials and health departments with an interest in environmental health will be clarifying that role in future decades. What role might state and local health departments play in cleaning up abandoned dumps laden with toxic substances and hazardous wastes? What role might they play in shifting our regulatory strategies from reaction to the crisis of the moment to a more preventive mode, one that emphasizes waste reduction and recycling rather than merely waste treatment and management? What role might they play in forming more integrative regulatory strategies that cut across divisions between media, institutions, and levels of government? These are among the questions explored in the following chapter.

REGULATORY ALTERNATIVES FOR ENVIRONMENTAL HEALTH

Many of the leading institutions in environmental regulation, unlike those in other spheres of public health, remain in fairly early stages of development. Even the well-established U.S. Environmental Protection Agency is in very early stages of maturation compared with national-level counterparts such as the Food and Drug Administration, the Social Security Administration, and the Federal Trade Commission.[39] Similarly, many of the most important pieces of national environmental legislation are of very recent vintage, particularly in the areas of toxic substances control and hazardous waste management. The overlapping institutional and legislative infrastructure at the state level is in comparably early stages of development.

As a result, many of the leading agencies and programs remain highly experimental in character and uncertain entities in terms of any demonstrated capacity to protect public health or the environment. In fact, the past two decades are perhaps better thought of as an exploration of alternative regulatory methods, or tools, than as a definitive determination of what does and does not work in environmental regulatory policy. Not surprisingly, many of the prevailing approaches have been received with growing concern over their cost-effectiveness and with considerable skepticism about their capacity to achieve much in terms of public health or environmental protection. This has triggered a search for institutional arrangements and regulatory alternatives that may prove more successful. The following chapter will introduce some of the prevailing approaches and the most promising alternatives, paying particular attention to the potential contributions that health departments and public health officials might make.

REFERENCES

1. Tarr JA: Industrial wastes and public health: some historical notes, part I, 1876-1932, Am J Public Health 75:1059, Sept 1985.

2. Davies JC: The politics of pollution, Indianapolis, IN, 1975, Pegasus.
3. Derthick M: Between state and nation, Washington, DC, 1975, Brookings Institution.
4. Bowman A and Kearney R: Resurgence of the states, Englewood Cliffs, NJ, 1985, Prentice-Hall.
5. US Advisory Commission on Intergovernmental Relations: The federal role in the federal system: the dynamics of growth, Washington, DC, 1981, The Commission.
6. Conservation Foundation: State of the environment: a view toward the nineties, Washington, DC, 1987, The Foundation.
7. Smith RA, Alexander RB, and Wolman MG: Analysis and interpretation of water quality trends in major US rivers, 1974-81, Washington, DC, 1986, US Geological Survey.
8. Farber KD and Rutledge GL: Pollution abatement and control expenditures, Survey of Current Business 66:94, July, 1986.
9. Clark EH: Reaganomics and the environment: an evaluation. In Vig NJ and Kraft ME, editors: Environmental policy in the 1980s: Reagan's new agenda, Washington, DC, 1984, Congressional Quarterly.
10. US Office of Technology Assessment: Technologies and management strategies for hazardous waste control, Washington, DC, 1983, US Government Printing Office.
11. Congressional Budget Office: Hazardous waste management: recent changes and policy alternatives, Washington, DC, 1985, US Government Printing Office.
12. National Research Council: Multimedia approaches to pollution control, Washington, DC, 1987, National Academy Press.
13. US Comptroller General: Cleaning up hazardous wastes: an overview of Superfund reauthorization issues, Washington, DC, 1985, US General Accounting Office.
14. Price DE: Policymaking in congressional committees: the impact of "environmental" factors, Tucson, 1979, University of Arizona Press.
15. Hays SP: Beauty, health, and permanence: environmental politics in the United States, 1955-1985, Cambridge, 1987, Cambridge University Press.
16. Rabe BG: The eclipse of health departments and local governments in American environmental regulation, J Public Health Policy 9:376, Fall 1988.
17. Liroff RA: A national policy for the environment: NEPA and its aftermath, Bloomington, 1976, Indiana University Press.
18. Caldwell LK: Science and the National Environmental Policy Act: redirecting policy through procedural reform, Tuscaloosa, AL, 1982, University of Alabama Press.
19. Marcus A: Environmental Protection Agency. In Wilson JQ, editor: The politics of regulation, New York, 1980, Basic Books.
20. Marcus A: Promise and performance: choosing and implementing an environmental policy, Westport, CT, 1980, Greenwood.
21. Zimmerman R: Policy, legal, and administrative considerations for the control of the outdoor environment. In Greenberg MR, editor: Public health and the environment: the United States experience, New York, 1987, Guilford.
22. Brown RS and Garner LE: Resource guide to state environmental management, Lexington, KY, 1988, Council of State Governments.
23. Congressional Research Service: Federal-state relations in transition: implications for environmental policy, Washington, DC, 1982, The Service.
24. Davies JC: Setting the national agenda, Unpublished manuscript, 1975.
25. Marcus A: The limitations of comprehensive environmental management: an analytic history of EPA, Unpublished manuscript, 1976.
26. Lester JP: The process of hazardous waste regulation: severity, complexity, and uncertainty. In Lester JP and Bowman A, editors: The politics of hazardous waste management, Durham, NC, 1983, Duke University Press.
27. Schmandt J: Managing comprehensive rule making: EPA's plan for integrated environmental management, Public Administration Review 45:309, 1985.
28. Doniger DD: Federal regulation of vinyl chloride: a short course in the law and policy of toxic substance control, Ecology Law Quarterly 7:500, 1978.
29. Zimmerman R: The management of risk: toxic and hazardous substances control, Washington, DC, 1982, National Science Foundation.
30. Hirschhorn JS: Presentation to the Integrated National Hazardous Materials Research Workshop, Argonne National Laboratory, Argonne, IL, Aug 7, 1985.
31. Rabe BG: Legislative incapacity: legislative policymaking and the case of Superfund, Unpublished manuscript, 1989.
32. Rabe BG: Fragmentation and integration in state environmental management, Washington, DC, 1986, Conservation Foundation.
33. National Governors Association: Controlling toxic pollution: a profile of state activities, Washington, DC, 1988, The Association.
34. Illinois Environmental Protection Agency: Chemical safety: an agenda for continued progress in the control of toxic pollutants, Springfield, IL, 1984, The Agency.

35. Duerksen CJ: Environmental regulation of industrial plant siting, Washington, DC, 1983, Conservation Foundation.
36. Aronson JR and Hilley JL: Financing state and local governments, Washington, DC, 1986, Brookings Institution.
37. Meier KJ: Regulation: politics, bureaucracy, and economics, New York, 1985, St Martin's Press.
38. Welborn DW: Conjoint federalism and environmental regulation, Publius: the journal of federalism 9:27, Winter 1988.
39. Atkeson TB and others: An annotated legislative history of the Superfund amendments and reauthorization act of 1986 (SARA), Environmental Law Reporter Dec 1986.

CHAPTER 19

Environmental control*

The arsenal of regulatory and managerial tools available for the protection of environmental health is formidable. It includes stringent regulatory controls with highly specific and demanding standards, many of which are backed by penalties for noncompliance. At the other extreme, it includes more analytical and participatory measures intended to help public officials and the general citizenry make prudent policy decisions.

No single regulatory approach is foolproof, and, in fact, nearly two decades after the first Earth Day, the search for the proper mixture of regulatory approaches continues amid high uncertainty. How do we reduce environmental risk to scientifically, politically, economically, and socially "safe" levels? How do we reconcile the need for uniform compliance with national and international environmental objectives and the need for communities to devise locally tailored procedures to protect human health? Should health departments and public health constituencies seek to regain their earlier preeminence in environmental health, or should they seek a partnership with the varied public agencies that currently play some role in this area?

This chapter attempts to address such questions by examining a number of diverse approaches that have been undertaken in the name of protecting environmental health. It will suggest that no single strategy has proven perfect, in terms either of overall capacity to safeguard human health or of likely cost-effectiveness. Instead, a confluence of such approaches is likely to prove necessary, given the diverse set of environmental health threats that exist and the array of existing legal and organizational mechanisms currently available to address them.

* This chapter was contributed by Professor Barry G. Rabe, Department of Public Health Policy and Administration, School of Public Health, University of Michigan, Ann Arbor, Michigan.

STRICT STANDARDS AND TECHNOLOGY FORCING: THE CASE OF CLEAN AIR

The national government's role in air pollution regulation is a classic example of the transformation from a regulatory system of high deference to local government and industry (in the 1950s and 1960s) to one of stringent national air quality goals and requirements (in more recent decades). What was once a modest national presence, largely confined to research, limited funding assistance to states, and mediation of multistate conflicts, has become a model of "command-and-control" regulatory style, which concentrates considerable authority in central government hands. What was once indifference to the types of pollution control technologies adopted and the rapidity with which they were put into use has become an ambitious scheme for prodding technological innovation and accelerating its widespread utilization.

The Clean Air amendments of 1970 reflected a congressional commitment to transform the very nature of national regulatory policy in this area. They demonstrated a sizable distrust of state and local governments, as well as the private sector. Rather than provide regulatory carrots of funding and other positive incentives, this legislation established national primary and secondary air quality standards, set national emissions standards for stationary sources that required use of the "best available control technology," and created statutory deadlines for vehicular emission reductions. States retained a direct role in the regulatory process but were required to submit "state implementation plans" to the national government, which were to assure attainment of national air quality standards. Subsequent Clean Air amendments, including modest revisions in 1971, 1973, 1974, and 1976 and a major expansion in 1977, added further layers of specificity and, in many instances, regulatory rigor.

This was a federal regulatory undertaking of unprecedented ambition and scope.[1,2] If fully implemented, it was expected to make radical improvements in air quality and to provide a permanent basis for promoting new pollution control technologies and responding to the emergence of new air quality threats. It was also thought likely to serve as a model for regulation in other environmental media, such as land and water, whereby the national government would attempt to bring all states and regions into uniform adherence to its standards.

The track record of such a regulatory approach is decidedly mixed. As noted in the previous chapter, emissions of a number of dangerous air pollutants have dropped since 1970, and this can be at least partly attributed to the national clean air legislation. Many new pollution control technologies have in fact been developed, such as the catalytic converter devices now standardized in American automobiles. In addition, many industries with long-standing records of environmental abuse have been forced to introduce new pollution control devices, leading to significant air quality gains in some of the most polluted urban areas of the nation. Finally, these gains have been achieved at relatively modest direct cost to the public sector, including the national government. Direct governmental expenditures on air quality have been quite modest in comparison to those in other major regulatory areas, placing most of the burden on the private sector and, ultimately, on consumers of various goods.

Despite its bold preamble and lofty environmental goals, however, national clear air legislation has demonstrated a number of shortcomings.[3] Many standards have neither been met nor, in some instances, approached, and implementation has proven extremely difficult. State and local governments have resisted strict interpretation of the federal legislation and lacked the resources necessary to monitor and enforce it fully; they have been caught in the middle repeatedly between divergent demands from the national government and locally based industry. The clean air program has also tended to operate with minimal consideration for the overall environmental health ramifications of its regulatory provisions and has, at times, only pushed pollutant problems into another medium (land or water) with less stringent regulation. For example, many air pollution control technologies result in residues or sludges, which must be disposed of on land and are often quite hazardous in this form.

The command-and-control approach adopted through the national clean air legislation has radically undercut the traditionally dominant role of public health authorities in this area. State and local governments, including their health departments, played a central role before 1960, although many of their efforts were extremely modest and highly deferential to the preferences of local industry.[4] However, it is possible to envision these agencies playing a more significant role under a command-and-control approach, given their natural abilities of data collection and analysis and awareness of unique local circumstances. In particular, local agencies might assume expanded responsibility for monitoring the compliance of individual industries and businesses with state or national emission standards, a fundamental activity that has not been successfully managed by federal or state environmental agencies.

STRICT STANDARDS AND SUBSTANTIAL FUNDING INCENTIVES: THE CASE OF CLEAN WATER

The national government's regulatory approach to water pollution followed an evolutionary path comparable to that of air, with dramatic intensification and expansion of regulatory requirements in the 1972 Federal Water Pollution Control Act Amendments. The 1972 legislation was modeled in part on the 1970 air legislation and called for far-reaching controls on industrial, municipal, and other sources of water pollution. As the U.S. Advisory Commission on Intergovernmental Relations[5] noted, "Embracing more than 89 pages of fine print, the statute has been called 'one of the most complicated pieces of legislation ever to emerge from Congress.' "

The clean water legislation differed in one important respect from clean air legislation, however: it called for substantial direct expenditures by the national government (and other levels of government) to address some of the most severe water pollution problems facing the nation. Rather than a pure command-and-control strategy, which would deposit the vast majority of compliance costs on the private sector, the clean water approach emulated a public works strategy whereby government would open its coffers generously to advance clean water goals.

Much of the expanded governmental investment on behalf of clean water was concentrated in waste water treatment plants, as the federal government offered grants for up to 75% of total construction costs to participating communities. This federal share jumped to 85% for innovative projects in 1977 before beginning to be scaled back during the 1980s. Overall spending on water quality control soared at all levels of government during the 1970s, exceeding $16 billion by 1980. By contrast, federal, state, and local spending was only $769 million for air quality control and $3.8 billion for land-focused quality control during the same year.[6]

The availability of such major amounts of public funding has eased intergovernmental and public-private tensions, although as in the case of strict clean air legislation, progress has been far slower than envisioned in the legislation of the early 1970s. Moreover, there has been growing concern over the appropriateness of concentrating scarce governmental dollars for environmental matters so overwhelmingly in the area of water pollution and relying so heavily on massive construction projects to reduce pollution. The big-construction, high-technology focus of these governmental efforts has tended to obscure other sources of water pollution, including uncontrolled pesticide runoffs from farmland and less visible but perhaps more health threatening toxic wastes from small businesses, industries, and localities.

Much as in the case of clean air, the public health community has been relegated to the sidelines in much of this regulatory activity, despite its historic role in sanitation and water pollution control. This is attributable to political and institutional changes in recent decades and to growing funding commitments to personal health services, as opposed to environmental health, on the part of state and local health agencies. Barring access to major new funding sources, the public health community is unlikely to rival other agencies in paying for capital-intensive environmental health activities.

ENVIRONMENTAL ASSESSMENT: THE CASE OF ENVIRONMENTAL IMPACT STATEMENTS

Not all of the national environmental initiatives of recent vintage have involved stringent command-and-control regulatory approaches. The National Environmental Policy Act of 1969 represented a markedly different approach, one that emphasized interdisciplinary planning in trying to minimize future environmental degradation. It relied on analytical skills and interagency cooperation rather than on strict standards and technology-forcing and was ultimately replicated by 28 states that enacted their own state environmental policy acts (or little NEPAs, as they are commonly known).

NEPA and the development of "environmental impact statements" stemmed from the burgeoning interest in ecology that fueled the environmental movement of the late 1960s and early 1970s. It called upon all agencies of the national government to consider the environmental ramifications of their actions and to incorporate this consideration formally into their policy-making processes. Impact statements were to provide a "detailed" environmental assessment for "proposals for legislation and other major Federal actions significantly affecting the quality of the human environment." These statements were to assess (1) the environmental impact of the proposed action; (2) any adverse environmental effects that could not be avoided should the proposal be implemented; (3) alternatives to the proposed action; (4) the relationship between local short-term environmental uses and the maintenance and enhancement of long-term productivity; and (5) any irreversible commitments of resources that would be involved in the proposed action should it be implemented.[7]

This was a tall order for government agencies, ranging from the Army Corps of Engineers to the Department of Health and Human Services, that had never before been asked to make such assessments. While philosophically appealing, given its vast scope, NEPA has suffered from many of the shortcomings that have made command-and-control regulatory approaches so attractive. It calls for thorough planning but lacks any precise measures of what is and is not environmentally appropriate activity, and it gives enormous leeway to individual agencies to weigh other pressing considerations against environmental ones. Moreover, NEPA is confined to activities sponsored by the federal government, excluding environmentally threatening activity that occurs through state and local government actions and in the private sector. It is widely viewed as having made some modest contributions to general environmental awareness but few tangible contributions to promoting environmental health.

Counterpart state programs vary greatly from one another. Those in New York, Oregon, and Washington have proven particularly innovative in linking the environmental impact statement process to additional incentives and standards that appear to have proven more effective. For example, New York's State Environmental Quality Review Act represents an effort to integrate broad environmental assessment into virtually every aspect of the state's environmental policy-making and has been used aggressively by the state's Department of Environmental Quality.[8,9]

Public health officials and agencies have frequently participated in the federal and state environmental impact statement process, but their involvement has rarely been formalized and has often been fairly superficial. Greater public health sophistication in assessing the health risks of proposed development projects could facilitate a more forceful participatory role, as could greater political savvy by public health officials in convincing other key environmental officials of the legitimacy of their expanded involvement.

NATIONAL GOVERNMENT AS DIRECT CLEANUP AGENT: THE CASE OF SUPERFUND

The sheer volume of abandoned hazardous waste sites and the perceived potential threat to human health necessitated a federal regulatory response that transcended both the command-and-control and environmental assessment styles that had prevailed earlier. As noted in Chapter 18, the seemingly ubiquitous nature of these sites caught the nation by surprise, and exact measures of their prevalence and potential health consequences remain elusive. Nonetheless, they constitute a new type of challenge for policymakers and represent the failure of the regulatory system in the decades before the 1970s to address these waste disposal problems in a serious fashion. As a result, enormous public and private resources will have to be invested to clean up toxic messes that in many instances have been simmering for decades.

The national response to this problem has included enactment of the 1980 Comprehensive Environmental Response, Compensation, and Liability Act (CERCLA, or Superfund) and the 1986 Superfund Amendments and Reauthorization Act (SARA). Superfund is a multibillion-dollar program that enables the federal government to assess the severity of the abandoned site problem, rank the most serious environmental health hazards, and conduct far-reaching cleanups. It also sets detailed standards that guide the assessment and cleanup processes and has already been supplemented by a number of state government efforts that provide additional funding.

This legislation not only involves government in the environmental cleanup process in a more direct, expansive way than ever before, but it also gives federal officials sweeping powers to attempt to determine liability for creating such environmental hazards. Government officials may either attempt to force responsible parties to clean up their own messes or initiate cleanup efforts and then sue responsible parties to recover the costs.

Despite its relatively new arrival, Superfund has already experienced a turbulent period of implementation. During the early stages of the Reagan administration, leading environmental officials were accused of defining their authority under Superfund in minimalist terms and giving generous settlements (called "sweetheart deals") to industries responsible for abandoned sites. Enormous political controversy ensued, and Superfund became a political volleyball bounced between an executive branch committed to limited enforcement and a Congress committed to rigorous enforcement. This political conflict compounded a complicated process of assessment and intervention and allowed the program to accomplish very little in terms of successful site cleanups. This clouded record leaves Superfund's capacity as an effective regulatory tool largely uncertain.[10,11]

Congress approved a 5-year, $9.5 billion extension in 1986 through SARA that gave EPA vast new resources to attack these cleanups. However, no reliable technology exists for safely cleaning up many types of hazardous waste sites, and government officials have found it extremely difficult to assess liability and press cases that will hold up in court. Superfund has also received harsh criticism for consuming such a large share of scarce federal environmental funds given the wealth of other forms of expenditures that might afford greater environmental health benefit.[12]

Superfund offers opportunities for public health officials to assume a significant role in its implementation. The program provides broad opportunities for public participation in assessing the hazards posed by Superfund sites and exploring the various remedial tools that might be used in the cleanup process. It also calls for a massive data-gathering effort concerning locally generated hazardous wastes and toxic substances. Public health officials and agencies would appear uniquely equipped to contribute to these processes, and many have begun to expand their involvement. This involvement may only expand in the future, however, since the federal EPA has received scathing criticism in 1989 for relying heavily on contractual cleanup arrangements with private firms rather than state and local agencies or its own staff.[13]

ECONOMIC INCENTIVES: BUBBLES, NETTING, OFFSETS, AND BANKING

Economists have long been among the harshest critics of the prevailing set of environmental regulatory approaches. Many tend to view command-and-control schemes and direct cleanup intervention as highly inefficient and as deterrents to innovation. They also tend to perceive other mechanisms, such as environmental assessment, as lacking the incentives necessary to secure broad commitment to improving environmental quality. Instead, they have devised proposals that would apply marketlike incentives to the regulatory process. These incentive-based proposals would set specific pollution reduction timetables and monetary penalties for noncompliance but would give individual industries and other regulated sources great latitude in deciding how to meet them.[14-17]

Congress and the federal EPA became increasingly interested in these alternatives in the late 1970s, as political resistance to tough command-and-control provisions mounted and proved more expensive for the private sector than had been anticipated. The EPA completed a number of modest experiments designed to test these market-based strategies, particularly in the area of air quality regulation. These experiments go by an array of intriguing names, including "bubbles," "netting," "offsets," "banking," and "emissions trading," all of which significantly reshape incentives and opportunities for compliance with the Clean Air Act standards. Under the bubble approach, for example, an imaginary bubble covers multiple emissions points in an individual plant. The owners of the plant may choose which points are cheapest to clean up (and what methods are cheapest to achieve the cleanup) as long as overall reductions meet federal and state standards. This differs from the more rigid command-and-control approach, which offers no latitude for concentrating on those sources that offer the biggest cleanup payoff.

What begins as elegant theory is often difficult to translate into policy, and economic incentives have been no exception. Implementation has been fraught with difficulties, in part because of the enormous monitoring efforts that are required to determine compliance and (if necessary) set penalties. As a result, government oversight must be far more expansive than under command-and-control, where often the litmus test of compliance is simply use of a federally imposed technology rather than careful measurement of emissions. These approaches have also received scathing criticism from environmental lobby groups that view them as a way to undermine regulatory rigor and appease industry.[18] Nonetheless, careful analyses of these early experiments suggest that they hold considerable promise and could develop into a useful mechanism to promote greater regulatory efficiency and flexibility.[19] Thus far, public health officials and agencies have had minimal direct involvement in developing or implementing these strategies, but they could play a central role in the monitoring process that is so pivotal to their effectiveness.

PREVENTION: WASTE REDUCTION AND REUSE

Regulatory strategies designed to reduce the amount of waste generated each year and promote its reuse or recycling would seem a natural component of a prevention-oriented environmental policy. It would also seem to be a natural mission for public health officials and health departments, enabling them to apply their considerable expertise in prevention to the environment. However, preventive approaches have consistently been overshadowed at all levels of government by regulatory efforts designed to respond to existing problems and manage disposal of existing wastes rather than promote their reuse or reduce their generation.

The American track record in this area is particularly disappointing when compared with that of other Western democracies. The United States is estimated to generate approximately three times as much hazardous waste per person as West Germany, for example, in large part because of its comparatively modest commitment to waste reduction and reuse. The West Germans, much like their Western European neighbors, have eschewed the land-based disposal techniques long favored by the United States in favor of a variety of innovative strategies that are only beginning to be seriously considered in this country.[20] According to the U.S. Office of Technology Assessment, less than 1% of all environment-related expenditures of federal, state, and local governments are concentrated on waste reduction, which the agency defines as a wide range of "in-house practices [by business, industry, and government] that will reduce, avoid, or eliminate the generation of hazardous wastes or pollutants."[21] Other estimates suggest a comparably limited—but gradually expanding—government commitment to waste reduction and reuse.[22]

Local governments have perhaps been most active in this area, and many individual communities play an active role in recycling consumer wastes such as paper, glass, and metals, but their efforts have rarely extended into chemicals and hazardous wastes. In the past decade, however, many state governments have launched a variety of initiatives to promote waste reduction and reuse. In North Carolina, for example, a state government program provides small grants and technical assistance to private firms that have innovative waste reduction ideas. In Illinois, a state environmental agency has developed a waste exchange network, whereby state officials provide information throughout the state on waste materials that may be reusable. In a number of other states, legislation has been enacted that either provides incentives for or mandates waste reduction or reuse, including some particularly far-reaching efforts that were recently approved in New Jersey. Finally, New York has directly integrated waste reduction with its waste management process, requiring all generators of hazardous waste to complete a Waste Reduction Impact Statement (WRIS) before they are allowed to dispose of wastes. These statements call for comprehensive assessment of waste reduction alternatives and a schedule for implementing waste reduction plans.

Waste reduction and reuse require very different sets of regulatory and information gathering efforts. The main leadership in these areas thus far has come from the private sector through industrial redesign and resource substitution and from the comprehensive environmental agencies of larger industrial states.[23] By contrast, public health agencies and officials have not been viewed as significant contributors to policy innovation in this area, despite their natural conversance with prevention and presumed familiarity with local conditions. If waste reduction and reuse are ever to emerge as a central component in U.S. environmental regulatory policy, the public health community may need to play a central role in helping the American people and their industries become more aware of these options and finding ways to tailor them to varying local conditions.

NONADVERSARIAL METHODS OF DISPUTE RESOLUTION

Just as the environmental regulatory system has largely failed to devise strategies to prevent or reduce waste generation, it has also suffered from a highly adversarial process of policy formation and dispute resolution. Such a process is understandable given the high saliency of environmental issues to the general public and the opposing positions often taken on regulatory matters by industrial and environmental lobbying groups. And it features some healthy attributes, including a wide-open system of dispute resolution that provides enormous participatory opportunities for parties dissatisfied with the direction of policy.

This contentious process also has many unsavory qualities, however, including the tendency to stall decision making through protracted litigation. The penchant for using the courts to challenge virtually every major action of a national or state environmental agency leads to huge expenditures on dispute resolution and gives the judiciary far more authority in environmental policy than is the case in any other Western nation. Many critics have suggested that such a style of policy-making is highly inefficient and does not necessarily result in policy decisions that are technically feasible or politically acceptable.[24-26]

These growing doubts surrounding the capacity of our highly adversarial system to forge coherent, effective environmental policy have triggered a search for dispute resolution alternatives in recent years. Nonlitigative methods of dispute resolution are not new, but only in recent years have they been utilized with any frequency in American environmental policy. In theory, these various methods are linked by their emphasis on bringing contending parties together to explore possible settlements. This may involve mediation of a specific environmental controversy, such as the authorization of water quality permits at a single manufacturing plant. Broader issues may also be addressed in a "policy dialogue," in which a neutral convener will help a large number of interested parties chart long-term strategies for environmental policy.[27]

As recently as a decade ago, these environmental dispute resolution (EDR) approaches were clearly confined to the fringes of American environmental policy. Few EDR cases had been undertaken, much less resolved, and very little had been written on the subject. However, EDR has gained a foothold in American environmental policy since the mid-1970s and gives every indication of being used in more environmental conflicts in future decades. One of the major forms of EDR has been mediation; between 1977 and mid-1984, the number of environmental disputes that have been mediated increased from 9 to 161. These disputes have involved a wide array of environmental issues, and 78% of them have reached some form of agreement.[28] Far-reaching policy dialogues have attained some degree of consensus in complex areas such as groundwater protection and the use of coal for electrical power. Federal regulatory agencies, including EPA, the Occupational Safety and Health Administration, and the Federal Aviation Agency, have begun experimenting with "regulatory negotiation," a form of negotiated rulemaking that seeks to develop a policy consensus among contending parties for the purpose of avoiding legal challenges to agency-proposed rules.[29]

EDR is also beginning to be used on more than an ad hoc basis. Six states have institutionalized some form of mediation in the siting of hazardous waste facilities before parties may pursue arbitration or litigation, and many others have provided for some form of negotiation in the siting process. Virtually every state has attempted to introduce some version of EDR into its environmental policy-making. Once seen as highly untested and experimental, EDR has now reached center stage as an option for avoiding litigation and adversarialism. Advocates such as National Wildlife Federation President Jay Hair predict that by the year 2000 more than half of all environmental disputes will be handled through EDR procedures. The selection of a long-standing champion of nonadversarial dispute resolution, Conservation Foundation President William Reilly, to head the EPA in the Bush administration promises to promote even greater use of EDR approaches. It behooves the public health community to decide what use, if any, it will make of them.

Nevertheless, EDR remains a regulatory alternative rather than a proven vehicle for more efficient and effective environmental policy. It may suffer from shortcomings, including exclusion of certain interested parties and settlements that emphasize political acceptability rather than optimal protection of environmental health. Moreover, EDR has been used more extensively to date on environmental conflicts with a predominantly natural resource or conservationist cast than with those concerning central questions related to environmental health. These latter issues may prove more politically divisive and more methodologically difficult to resolve.[27]

If EDR is to be used more expansively in cases that confront environmental health matters, public health officials and agencies may need to play a central role in providing health-related data needed for negotiation and in assembling coalitions. Under the Massachusetts Hazardous Waste Facility Siting Act, for example, negotiations are mandated between the site developer and the community where a site is proposed. The act establishes a 21-member Safety Council to assist participants in the siting process, review all site proposals, offer technical assistance to participating communities, and reject proposals deemed unacceptable. At least two of these council seats must be reserved for public health officials, one from the state level and the other from the local level. To date, all six efforts to approve a site have collapsed because of strong opposition from local citizens. Nonetheless, this process does formally provide for public health participation in mandatory negotiation over siting and could serve as a model in establishing formal linkages between public health and other relevant agencies.

The Massachusetts case is somewhat unusual in that public health officials and agencies have clearly not been in the vanguard of this reform movement to date. Local health departments would appear to be particularly well equipped to contribute to any expanded use of EDR that involves health issues, however, given their familiarity with local institutions and problems, which probably exceeds that of state or national regulatory agencies.

PROGRAM AND AGENCY COORDINATION

The potpourri of government agencies and legislative committees with some involvement in environmental policy has led to repeated problems in coordinating regulatory efforts and periodic attempts to organize these numerous activities better. At its best, this fragmented system may result in unnecessary duplication of effort. At its worst, it can lead to the types of cross-media problems discussed in Chapter 18, where pollutants are merely transferred or transported into less-regulated media rather than addressed in any definitive sense.

As a result, the national government and its state-level counterparts have continued to tinker with the overall fit of individual regulatory agencies and programs. Many states have sought better coordination of the processes by which various permits are authorized, responding in large part to criticisms in the late 1970s from permit applicants of uncoordinated, inefficient processes that were alleged to deter economic development within the state. Common state reforms have included joint application conferences, permit information centers, and imposition of strict deadlines for permit issuance or denial. Virtually every state has attempted at least one of these reforms and some, such as Illinois, New York, and Oregon, have tried almost all of them.[30] Public health officials and agencies have been active in a great many of these reforms, particularly in those states where a state health department is the dominant environmental regulatory agency.

The growing problems posed by toxic substances and hazardous wastes have also generated state-level interest in promoting cross-agency and cross-program coordination. A 1988 National Governors' Association study of state efforts to control toxic pollution indicated a highly fragmented regulatory system in most states and a wide array of reorganization and coordination activities.[31] In Ohio, for example, this coordination problem has led to new cooperative initiatives between the state's EPA and Department of Health. In particular, officials from the Department of Health and the state EPA Division of Air Pollution and Division of Solid and Hazardous Waste Management have begun to coordinate their previously separate efforts to control toxic air pollutants. In Wisconsin, the Environmental Standards Division of the state Department of Natural Resources has appointed a toxics coordinator who is responsible for linking various functions into a coordinated regulatory system, including Division of Health efforts in the area of risk assessment. The need for coordinated toxic control efforts has also led to far-reaching reorganization in Illinois, where it is centered around the development of an Integrated Toxics Control Strategy, designed to promote policy innovation and to coordinate toxics-related efforts of the many branches of the state EPA, and other involved state agencies such as Public Health, Agriculture, and Energy and Natural Resources. These types of reorganization efforts indicate that it is possible to devise creative linkages between fragmented agencies.

RISK ASSESSMENT

A growing issue in numerous state coordination efforts, particularly those linked to toxic substances and hazardous waste, has been determining the best manner for introducing new methodological tools into the environmental regulatory process. Foremost among these tools is risk assessment, which at least in theory can quantitatively assess environmental health risk. If successful, such tools could facilitate a systematic consideration of the severity of various threats and the viability of alternative regulatory remedies.

One of the greatest political tests facing any expanded use of risk assessment is that it may threaten existing environmental agencies and officials who prefer to adhere to current practices. Control over risk assessment development and application has already become a major battleground among federal agencies and in numerous states, with all relevant environmental agencies eager to exercise some influence over the way the process is devised and implemented. Not surprisingly no two federal agencies or states have defined risk assessment in the same way or established identical institutional mechanisms for putting it to use. In Virginia, for example, a consultative Bureau of Toxic Substances Information has been created within the state Health Department and is expected to guide the use of risk assessment by various state agencies.[31] In Michigan, by contrast, risk assessment has been caught in a political tug-of-war between the state Department of Public Health and the state Department of Natural Resources, both of which make considerable use of the technique but do not coordinate their regulatory efforts.

Much as in the case of economic incentives, risk assessment comprises a promising but as yet untested set of methods for guiding regulatory priority setting and decision making. Its proponents credit it with great potential to analyze risk systematically and ultimately facilitate effective management of those risks and communication of their relative dangers to the public. Skeptics caution that it remains in a highly preliminary stage of development and must also surmount a series of political and institutional hurdles before being adopted as a central environmental regulatory tool. As one leading analyst of risk assessment has cautioned, "In the face of scientific uncertainty and inadequate data, some interested parties magically invoke the term risk assessment in an effort to bring authority and confidence to an uncertain process."[32-35]

If risk assessment is to mature and be widely deployed in future decades, public health officials and agencies could play a central role, given the part that such core public health methodologies as epidemiology and biostatistics must play in developing such sophisticated assessment capabilities. In fact, hazard identification and exposure assessment, central components of any formal risk assessment process, have long been central activities for the public health community.

MULTINATIONAL COORDINATION

Environmental problems do not respect local, state, or national boundaries and will increasingly call for multinational approaches if substantial environmental health improvements are to occur. Just as uncontrolled air pollution emissions from Mexico threaten the health of American citizens, minimally controlled emissions from Midwestern U.S. industries may exacerbate Canadian acid deposition with its resultant natural resource and public health problems. Even more broadly, widespread destruction of Third World rain forests may be a leading contributor to the "greenhouse effect," which may leave no continent, developed or otherwise, unscathed.

Nonetheless, multinational and international coordination on behalf of environmental health has proven elusive. Nations may be even less successful in this area than in negotiating common approaches to monetary policy, trade policy, and defense commitments.[36-37] To date, few nations have proven willing to yield their sovereignty over internal environmental policy in favor of some broader cooperative approach. The role of the United Nations in this regard has been almost exclusively rhetorical, like that of other broad institutions such as the World Health Organization and the Organization of American States. Even international institutions with considerable capacity to link economic development assistance to environmental health, such as the World Bank and International Monetary Fund, have only recently begun to examine any potential involvement of this type.

Gradual progress may be emerging, however, between neighboring nations of Western Europe and North America. The growing cohesion of individual European nations under the auspices of the European Economic Community (EEC) has led to major efforts to coordinate environmental regulatory programs and work cooperatively to protect environmental health. For example, the EEC has been instrumental in the development of international protocols for chlorofluorocarbon regulation. The impetus of the 1992 deadline for integration of economic regulatory policy has also accelerated multinational interest in reducing the capacity of any individual nation to export its environmental problems to neighboring nations. In North America, the Great Lakes Basin has served as a source for growing environmental cooperation between the Canadian and U.S. governments. The International Joint Commission has been increasingly active in attempting to reduce water pollution in the lakes and has been bolstered by a series of multinational regulatory and research initiatives, including a number of promising efforts launched by American states and Canadian provinces that border the Great Lakes. Most of these North American initiatives have moved gradually, in the face of enduring political disincentives to extensive collaboration, indicating that some progress may be possible in expanding the scope of regulatory efforts beyond national boundaries.[38]

SUMMARY

The odyssey of American efforts to protect environmental health has featured numerous changes of course in recent decades. Once a fairly modest presence on the national political agenda, environmental policy has become a dominant domestic concern. Once the province of public health officials and agencies, it is now influenced by a myriad of laws, agencies, and interest groups. Once an area in which direct government expenditures were quite modest, it is likely to consume ever-increasing portions of scarce public sector resources in future decades.

Following the expansion of national and state environmental regulatory efforts in the late 1960s and early 1970s, growing doubts emerged concerning their effectiveness. The initial plunge into far-reaching regulatory activity with a range of regulatory tools was followed by a period in which deregulation received considerable support and alternative regulatory tools were considered that were purported to be more efficient. During the mid- and late-1980s, however, any prospects for far-reaching deregulation have been rejected, in large part because of overwhelming public support (as evident in public opinion surveys) for rigorous environmental regulatory efforts.[39] As a result, all levels of American government are eager to demonstrate their capacity to provide effective environmental regulation. As we have seen, they have an array of potential regulatory tools with which to address environmental health and natural resource threats, ranging from stringent command-and-control approaches to consensus-building techniques of mediation. None has proven inherently superior to others, and a major challenge for environmental policymakers remains to sort out the conditions under which certain tools prove more effective.

All of these regulatory tools are available in some form to public health officials and agencies, as well as to the galaxy of other organizations that play some role in environmental health. Following the historic days of triumph over basic sanitation problems earlier in this century, the public health role in environmental health has increasingly shrunk to such areas as restaurant inspection, septic tank inspection, and animal vector control.[40] These functions are important and must be carried out with competence and diligence, but they have increasingly been overshadowed by potentially more severe environmental health problems, such as toxic substances, hazardous and nuclear wastes, and air and water pollution. Still further threats, such as the greenhouse effect and radon, loom on the horizon. The general response of public health officials and agencies to these developments has been to lament their reduced standing in environmental health rather than to redefine their proper role. This is unfortunate given their natural strengths in data collection and analysis, their expertise in prevention-oriented strategies, and their unique familiarity with local conditions. If the public health community is to play a more central role in environmental health for the balance of this century and into the next one, it will have to assess its regulatory capabilities and shortcomings carefully and more forcefully articulate its potential mission in the political arena. Without such concerted efforts, its once dominant role in environmental health policy will continue to wither away.

REFERENCES

1. Jones CO: Clean air: the policies and politics of pollution control, Pittsburgh, 1975, University of Pittsburgh Press.
2. Jones CO: Speculative augmentation in federal air pollution policy-making, Journal of Politics 36:438, May 1974.
3. Lave LB and Omenn GS: Clearing the air: reforming the Clean Air Act, Washington, DC, 1981, Brookings Institution.
4. Crenson M: The un-politics of air pollution, Baltimore, 1971, Johns Hopkins University Press.
5. US Advisory Commission on Intergovernmental Relations: Regulatory federalism, Washington, DC, 1985, The Commission.
6. US Bureau of the Census: Environmental quality control, government finances: fiscal year 1979-1980, Washington, DC, 1980, US Government Printing Office.
7. Liroff RA: A national policy for the environment: NEPA and its aftermath, Bloomington, IN, 1976, Indiana University Press.
8. Rabe BG: Fragmentation and integration in state environmental management, Washington, DC, 1986, Conservation Foundation.

9. Muldoon PR: Cross-border litigation: environmental rights in the Great Lakes ecosystems, Toronto, 1986, Carswell.
10. US Office of Technology Assessment: Superfund strategy, Washington, DC, 1985, The Office.
11. US Office of Technology Assessment: Are we cleaning up?—10 Superfund case studies, Washington, DC, 1988, The Office.
12. Atkeson TB and others: An annotated legislative history of the Superfund Amendments and Reauthorization Act of 1986 (SARA), Environmental Law Reporter, 1986.
13. US Office of Technology Assessment: Assessing contractor use in Superfund, Washington, DC, 1989, The Office.
14. Tietenberg TH: Emissions trading: an exercise in reforming pollution policy, Washington, DC, 1988, Resources for the Future.
15. Russell CS: Controlled trading of pollution permits, Environmental Science and Technology 15:24, Jan 1981.
16. Schelling TC, editor: Incentives for environmental protection, Cambridge, MA, 1983, MIT Press.
17. Anderson FR and others: Environmental improvement through economic incentives, Baltimore, 1977, Johns Hopkins University Press.
18. Doniger D: The bubble on the cusp, The Environmental Forum 4:32, July 1985.
19. Liroff RA: Reforming air pollution regulation: the toil and trouble of EPA's bubble, Washington, DC, 1986, Conservation Foundation.
20. Piasecki B: Beyond dumping: new strategies for controlling toxic contamination, Westport, CT, 1984, Quorum.
21. Oldenburg KU and Hirschhorn JS: Waste reduction: a new strategy to avoid pollution, Environment 29:16, March 1987.
22. Gordon RG: Legal incentives for reduction, reuse, and recycling: a new approach to hazardous waste management, Yale Law Journal 95:810, 1986.
23. Royston MG: Pollution prevention pays, Oxford, 1979, Pergamon.
24. Melnick RS: Regulation and the court: the case of the Clean Air Act, Washington, DC, 1983, The Brookings Institute.
25. Schuck PH: Agent orange on trial, New Haven, CT, 1987, Yale University Press.
26. Lieberman J: The litigious society, New York, 1981, Basic Books.
27. Rabe BG: The politics of environmental dispute resolution, Policy Studies Journal 16:585, Spring 1988.
28. Bingham G: Resolving environmental disputes: a decade of experience, Washington, DC, 1986, Conservation Foundation.
29. Gusman S and Harter PJ: Mediating solutions to environmental risks, Annual Review of Public Health 7:306, 1986.
30. Rabe BG: Fragmentation and integration in state environmental management, Washington, DC, 1986, Conservation Foundation.
31. National Governors' Association: Controlling toxic pollution: a profile of state activities, Washington, DC, 1988, The Association.
32. Davies JC: Risk assessment and risk control, Washington, DC, 1984, Conservation Foundation.
33. Lave LB: Quantitative risk assessment in regulation, Washington, DC, 1982, The Brookings Institute.
34. Hadden SB: Risk analysis, institutions, and public policy, Port Washington, NY, 1983, Associated Faculty Press.
35. National Academy of Science: Risk and decision making, Washington, DC, 1982, National Academy Press.
36. Gilpin R: The political economy of international relations, Princeton, NJ, 1987, Princeton University Press.
37. Keohane R: After hegemony: cooperation and discord in the world political economy, Princeton, NJ, 1984, Princeton University Press.
38. Caldwell LK, editor: Perspectives on ecosystem management for the Great Lakes, Albany, NY, 1988, State University of New York Press.
39. Mitchell RC: Public opinion and environmental politics in the 1970s and 1980s. In Vig NJ and Kraft ME, editors: Environmental policy in the 1980s: Reagan's new agenda, Washington, DC, 1984, Congressional Quarterly.
40. Walker B: The future of public health: an analysis of the NAS report and its implications for public health, Journal of Environmental Health 51:133, Jan/Feb 1989.

CHAPTER 20

Occupational health

HEALTH AND THE WORKPLACE

A joint committee of the International Labor Office and the World Health Organization has defined the objectives of occupational health as follows:

> the promotion and maintenance of the highest degree of physical, mental and social well-being of workers in all occupations; the prevention among workers of departures from health caused by their working conditions; the protection of workers in their employment from risks resulting from factors adverse to health; the placing and maintenance of the worker in an occupational environment adapted to his physiological and psychological condition.[1]

Occupational health and safety has technical, legal, political, and economic aspects, but the World Health Organization definition is absolutist in tone: it indicates that worker health takes precedence over all other factors, including the economic conditions of the worker, the family, and the community. That may not always be the case.

There are two ways of looking at work: (1) as a basic need of humans, something that can and should be ennobling but is often boring at best and brutal at worst or (2) as the best way to support a consumer economy by providing both the goods to be purchased and the wages with which to purchase them.[2] This is not a chapter based on any other ideology than that of public health, however. Why people work and the value they attach to their work will not be discussed.

Occupational health and safety have been separate issues historically, legally, and technically. Safety preceded health as a social, economic, and legal concern because the cause and cost of an injury could be immediately recognized. Compensation laws were written to deal with such issues, not with the illness that might occur 20 or 30 years after exposure to a toxic chemical. An effort has been made in law and in educational programs to combine the two aspects of worker health, but safety issues remain more in the province of the industrial hygienist, whereas occupational diseases are treated as medical problems. In this chapter the term *occupational health* will be used to refer to both occupational diseases and injuries.

The subject is of major importance to the public's health even though official health agencies are not always involved at the state or local level. A substantial proportion of the population spends about one third of its time either at work or in transit between home and work. Although the transit process and the home environment are the source of many hazards, the workplace has special significance: some of the hazards are unique and complex (such as radiation and chemicals that may affect a fetus); the problems have a direct economic impact on workers, their families, the workplace owners, and the entire community; and the voluntary exchange transaction that takes place between worker and manager (work for wages) is such that a contest can develop over fault. According to the National Safety Council, there were 8.9 million disabling injuries in the United States in 1986: 1.8 million caused by motor vehicle accidents, 1.8 million work-related, 3.1 million in the home, and the remainder elsewhere.[3] In addition to the injuries, however, the work environment is full of products and procedures that can cause disease and illness both in the unborn and in workers after retirement. The magnitude of these problems is only beginning to become apparent. The working hypothesis of public health is that all of these injuries and illnesses can be prevented. Society will determine whether it is worth the price.

CONFLICTS OF FACT, PERCEPTION, AND VALUE

That an employer is responsible for the health of workers is a relatively recent concept in the Western world. Both workers and workplace owners have long assumed (1) that work is necessary,

(2) that all work entails some risk, and (3) that people accept work knowing about the hazards and assuming them as part of the price they must pay, in addition to their work, for the wages they receive. Indeed, hazardous jobs are often recompensed at a higher level than less hazardous jobs requiring similar skills.

An individual worker may find it difficult to comprehend the importance of a potentially serious illness or injury when the probability of experiencing it is slight. If management points out the low probability of the problem and the high cost of preventing it (with the implied or explicit warning that prevention costs might result in a plant shutdown), the risks may be assumed without further challenge. However, society will pay for those inevitable events, both directly and indirectly.

The direct costs of occupational disease and injury appear as higher product prices caused by absenteeism and worker's compensation payments. The indirect costs appear as welfare costs, unemployment costs, aid to families with dependent children, medical and rehabilitation costs, and a variety of other costs related to subsequent dependency. The total for work-related injuries alone amounted to $34.8 billion in 1986.[3] The cost of occupational diseases is at least as great, but the amount is unknown.

Owners have accepted some of the cost of injury through safety programs and worker's compensation plans. The adage "safety pays" is true up to a point. An industry with high injury rates will have to pay more money into the worker's compensation fund, and these costs have to be added to product price or subtracted from profits. The costs appear fairly quickly after the accident occurs, and the fault is usually easy to determine. Moreover, the compensation laws of most states have set aside the right of an employee to sue an employer for damages if compensation payments are accepted, thus limiting the cost to management. Disease problems, however, tend to occur much later, often 20 or 30 years after exposure to the hazard. The worker may be killed in an automobile accident before the cancer develops or may be working in another industry in another part of the country. It is far more difficult to establish the cause of the disease, since some people with the same exposure will not develop the disease and others without such exposure may develop an identical problem. Owners are inclined to avoid the costs of preventing such illnesses, since they are not likely to accrue the benefits of their prevention efforts. The costs of preventing accidents may yield benefits through lower worker's compensation payment rates and less lost work time, but preventing illness 20 or 30 years later benefits the Social Security system, state welfare programs, and families, not the business. Job injury victims average about 60% of their lost income through all sources of payment, while victims of occupational disease obtain only 40%, most of which comes from Social Security and welfare payments rather than from the compensation fund.[4] The courts have begun to hold businesses accountable for such problems, and to avoid the high cost of civil suits, some industries have favored inclusion of compensation for illness in the state-run compensation programs. Compensation after the fact may be less costly to the industry than prevention, since the payments will occur much later at a discounted rate. Without the intervention of law, the costs of failing to prevent occupational disease can be externalized to other segments of society. Occupational health legislation seeks to internalize those costs to the business so that the product or the service will carry the full social costs of production.

A simple illustration of the problem and one approach to solving it is shown in Table 20-1. (Note: don't try to add the columns. If you are not familiar with the calculation of net present values, ask a banker or a business major.) In this case, the financial manager of the company advises the chairman of the board that if they ignore a hazardous situation, they can expect to begin paying compensation costs of $25,000 about 20 years from now and that the amount will increase by about $2,500 each year. To prevent the problem from occurring, they will have to spend $100,000 now on some special equipment. In addition, they will need to maintain that equipment at a cost of $5,000 each year. Using an annual discount rate of 4% (the rate at which the value of the money spent can be expected to increase each year), a net present value calculation shows that it will cost the company only $157,000 if they ignore the problem, but preventing it will cost them $184,919. The company might choose ignorance over prevention. Just such calculations are made everyday. To increase the probability that a better choice will be made (better from the standpoint of the entire community, that is), an annual $2,000 dollar fine turns out to be very effective, tipping the net present value calculation so that it becomes slightly less costly to prevent the disease from occurring. It is the job of public health to make the net cost of prevention less than the cost of compensation. Fines are one way to do that.

Conflicts occur because of different self-interests, a lack of knowledge, and different perceptions of what is fair. The worker is concerned about income; the manufacturer about price. The manufacturer will not add to labor costs unless some monetary benefit can be realized or unless forced to by law. Voluntary absorption of an additional labor cost to prevent a disease without any immediate benefit will make a single manufacturer less competitive. Legislation affecting all manufacturers can restore that balance but may make the industry less competitive with foreign manufacturers.

Some problems appear to occur more commonly in certain industries but cannot yet be linked to a specific hazard. Brain cancer has been found to be more common in certain petrochemical plants, but no cause has been identified. It is difficult to hold an owner accountable for a problem that cannot be defined. Sometimes knowledge is adequate, but different values or ideas of what is fair result in a conflict about responsibility. For example, asbestos workers are at high risk of certain lung diseases. Asbestos workers who smoke are at greater risk. Should asbestos workers who smoke be compensated at the same rate as nonsmoking workers, or are they guilty of contributory negligence?

In addition to the economic importance of the work environment to the community, it has both direct and indirect spillover effects on the health of the community. In most instances, the work environment cannot be walled off: its effluents intermingle with the air, the water, the sewage, and the land-use problems of the surrounding community. The disposal of toxic wastes presents special problems—the same chemicals handled by workers in the plant can affect the community years later. Industrial accidents may cause a sudden spill of hazardous material into the community's water supply or air. Heavy trucks rumbling through residential streets present special hazards for young children. Workers do not leave the hazards in the workplace; asbestos fibers and toxic chemicals are carried into the house in clothing and have been shown to cause the same diseases at home that they do in the workplace.

There are indirect consequences as well: marginal companies that have avoided their responsibility for worker health in the short run eventually pay the price, which may involve shutdown and unemployment. Local health departments, which do not often have the explicit authority or the resources to combat such problems and may accept them just as the rest of the community does, can nevertheless play an important role in surveillance, fact-finding, planning, and correction.

TABLE 20-1 Net present value (NPV) calculation of ignoring or preventing an occupational disease hazard

	Annual cost and net present value		
Year	**Compensate**	**Prevent**	**Fine***
1	0	$100,000	$ 2,000
2	0	$ 5,000	$ 2,000
3	0	$ 5,000	$ 2,000
4	0	$ 5,000	$ 2,000
5	0	$ 5,000	$ 2,000
6	0	$ 5,000	$ 2,000
7	0	$ 5,000	$ 2,000
8	0	$ 5,000	$ 2,000
9	0	$ 5,000	$ 2,000
10	0	$ 5,000	$ 2,000
11	0	$ 5,000	$ 2,000
12	0	$ 5,000	$ 2,000
13	0	$ 5,000	$ 2,000
14	0	$ 5,000	$ 2,000
15	0	$ 5,000	$ 2,000
16	0	$ 5,000	$ 2,000
17	0	$ 5,000	$ 2,000
18	0	$ 5,000	$ 2,000
19	0	$ 5,000	$ 2,000
20	$ 25,000	$ 5,000	$ 27,000
21	$ 27,500	$ 5,000	$ 29,500
22	$ 30,000	$ 5,000	$ 32,000
23	$ 32,500	$ 5,000	$ 34,500
24	$ 35,000	$ 5,000	$ 37,000
25	$ 37,500	$ 5,000	$ 39,500
26	$ 40,000	$ 5,000	$ 42,000
27	$ 42,500	$ 5,000	$ 44,500
28	$ 45,000	$ 5,000	$ 47,000
29	$ 47,500	$ 5,000	$ 49,500
30	$ 50,000	$ 5,000	$ 52,000
NPV	$157,939	$184,919	$193,906

* Fine of $2,000 per year plus the compensation costs.

Business associations constantly strive to reduce the scope of government intervention, and many business and political leaders believe that the forces of marketplace competition will serve to correct any health problems that may exist in the workplace, but even a cursory review of history since the industrial revolution shows otherwise. In the absence of regulatory controls, mine owners would not take steps to reduce the buildup of coal dust, nor would the asbestos industry adopt an adequate safety standard. This may seem a harsh indictment of human nature, but it is a reasonable reflection of history, both remote and recent. More is at stake than profit: it is difficult for owners (and workers too) to accept the fact that a product to which they have devoted their working lives can be unduly hazardous. The conflict that exists between wages and profits is such that government intervention is essential: the market does not internalize the costs of disability and dependency in its pricing of products and services. The cost of prevention does not always yield recognizable or sufficient benefits to the owners to prompt corrective or preventive action, and both direct and indirect spillover effects require that the community intervene with the force of law to establish an adequate program.

BACKGROUND

Ramazzini is usually considered the father of occupational health, based on the publication of *De morbis artificium diatriba* in 1700. Modern occupational health is an outcome of the industrial revolution in nineteenth-century England. As a result of the rapid development of deplorable working conditions in general and the exploitation of women and children in particular, numerous laws were passed for the protection of workers. During the first half of this century, America profited by the experience of England, even to the extent of some states adopting some of the earlier English legislation. The Massachusetts Department of Factory Inspection was established in 1867, but further expansion of the role of the state was slow because of the three common-law notions that still affect occupational health programs: (1) that workers contribute through their own negligence to their problems, (2) that fellow workers share in the responsibility by creating or failing to correct unsafe conditions, and (3) that accepting a job means assuming the risks that go with it.

In 1908 Congress passed the Federal Employers' Liability Act, which made railroads and other interstate carriers liable for industrial injuries sustained by their employees. At that time the Wainwright Commission in New York showed that only one out of every eight injured men was awarded any compensation and that he actually received only about a third of what was awarded. The other two thirds went for insurance adjusters, legal advice, and commissions. Various states had previously enacted workmen's compensation laws, but these early laws were declared unconstitutional by the courts. The year 1911 marked the beginning of useful compensation laws; no less than 10 states passed legislation in that year alone. By 1920, 40 states had worker's compensation laws, but interest waned after that until the 1960s, when a broadened concern for environmental protection raised new questions about disease, as well as injury and accidents. By then the principle had been established that owners were responsible for the cost of medical care and the subsequent disability caused by accidents.

Worker's compensation statutes provided benefits to workers, but they represented a substantial victory for management. Juries had begun to award large settlements to injured workers. The new laws enticed workers to settle quickly for a dependable form of compensation and give up the right to sue for larger awards. Since the laws covered all businesses, they did not significantly alter competitive forces. The costs were passed along to consumers and so did not reduce profits, and owners could predict those costs rather than be subject to unpredictable court settlements.

The whole subject of worker's compensation has become more complex and controversial in the United States in recent years. Some compensation laws have been amended to remove waiver of the right to sue, and some court decisions have maintained that the owners are still susceptible to suit if they willfully expose workers to a hazardous situation. By 1985 approximately 84 million workers were covered by worker's compensation plans, and benefits paid totaled $22.5 billion, almost 7½ times the amount paid out in 1970. As courts ruled that more and more disabilities were work related, business leaders and some economists began to attack the plans as too liberal. To some extent the plans have become part of the general welfare system and thus are exposed to the same public ambivalence and, at times, hostility.

The National Association of Insurance Commissioners[5] appointed a special task force on worker's compensation to consider the unique problems of occupational diseases, which concluded in 1985 that equity should prevail: diseased workers should receive necessary medical care and income benefits. They also felt that the costs of the system should be allocated among various employers in an appropriate way and not arbitrarily assigned to the last known employer, that the costs had to be affordable, and that employers and insurers had to be able to predict them. The task force did not suggest a role for compensation programs or insurance commissioners in the prevention of occupational diseases. However, if the benefits are to be based on the medical and income maintenance needs of the workers, and if at the same time the program is to be affordable and predictable, prevention, including surveillance and intervention, would seem to be a necessary capability.

Compensation has also become entangled in special interest group legislation and collective bargaining, which places certain problems in separate categories, such as black lung (coal workers' pneumoconiosis) or exposure to agent orange during the Vietnam War. Administration of the programs has become very costly because of the extensive and expensive legal maneuvering that occurs. Certain categories of workers are treated as special risk categories and compensated differently than others, often obtaining compensation for total and permanent disability when they are perfectly capable of working in another occupation. These problems have caused many experts and legislators to urge a more uniform, national approach to compensation, but it seems unlikely that any basic reform in the nation's social insurance system can occur in the immediate future that would both correct some of the abuse and bring about greater equity.

The period from 1910 to 1920 witnessed the establishment of occupational health as a medical specialty. The Department of Labor was established as a separate cabinet entity, and the Bureau of Mines of the Department of the Interior and the Office of Industrial Hygiene and Sanitation (later the Division of Occupational Health) of the Public Health Service came into existence. An Industrial Hygiene Section was established in the American Public Health Association (now called the Section on Occupational Health and Safety), and the National Safety Council was organized. The New England Association of Industrial Nurses was formed in 1916, and the American Association was formed in 1942 when 300 nurses from 16 states met.[6] Now called the American Association of Occupational Health Nurses, it has continued to play a vital role in the provision of occupational health services.

The American Association of Industrial Physicians and Surgeons was formed in 1915, and minimum standards for medical service in industry were adopted that same year by the Committee on Industrial Medicine and Traumatic Surgery of the American College of Surgeons. In 1937, the American Medical Association created the Council on Industrial Health to coordinate all medical efforts in the industrial health field. The *Journal of Industrial Hygiene* and the first specialized teaching of the subject appeared in schools of public health at about the same time. The Association of Industrial Physicians and Surgeons became first the Industrial Medicine Association and then the American Occupational Medicine Association (AOMA). In 1988, AOMA merged with the American Academy of Occupational Medicine to form the American College of Occupational Medicine.

Before passage of the Social Security Act in 1935, little progress had been made by state health agencies in occupational health. Up to that time only five states had engaged in any activities designed for the benefit of industrial workers. Programs were instituted in 1913 in New York and Ohio. The Social Security Act made funds available for the expansion of state and local programs with the result that, by 1950, all of the states, Alaska, Hawaii, Puerto Rico, and the District of Columbia were engaged in some type of activity to improve the health and safety of workers.

Since 1960 occupational diseases have drawn increasing attention, partly as a result of continued research in toxicology and the rapid increase in production and use of complex chemical products. Reproductive research has heightened awareness of the special problems of women in the workplace. The subject was surrounded by more mythology than fact until recent years. Even though women are on the average smaller and physically less powerful than men and have some unique considerations related to reproduction, there is little evidence that they have different risks because of occupational exposures. Many special risks have been alleged, such as greater susceptibility to lead poisoning, organic solvents, and carcinogens. The allegations have resulted in exclusion of women from certain work areas rather than an effort to alter the work environment, even though research has not substantiated important differences.[7] Generally those substances that may harm a fetus should be considered hazardous for men as well, and the objective should be to protect all workers from the hazards. In certain plants women who could become pregnant have been excluded from high-risk areas, which has resulted in legal challenges to a management policy that essentially requires sterilization as a condition of employment. Problems can occur after giving birth as well because of contaminated clothing or toxic substances that may be discharged in breast milk.[8]

The epidemiology of occupational disease is an extremely complicated subject.[9] There is usually a long latent period, during which time the worker may be exposed to a variety of agents in different plants and in different locations. Some exposures may have occurred because of a momentary accident that resulted in the unique combination of two or more products not intended by the manufacturer and never counted in the inventory of substances produced or used in the plant. There are rarely any adequate data about exposure levels, and lacking reliable, quantitative data about dosage, it is difficult to develop a dose-response hypothesis. Studies designed to demonstrate that there is no hazard from a particular product have to be very large and very sensitive, minimizing the random errors that are less important in studies of a positive relationship. Lacking that and quantitative data about exposure, such studies are only nonpositive, not negative.

The scientific study of occupational disease presents special problems to the lawyers, courts, politicians, and public health workers whose job it is to prevent the problems in the first place or to provide equitable compensation for those injured or made ill. The standards of evidence in science are higher than those in civil law, with no necessity to conclude the debates. The courts and other public officials have to make decisions based on what is known at the time. Furthermore, they have the special problem of deciding whether to prohibit something until it can be proved safe or to allow something until it can be proved hazardous: an ethical question not subject to laboratory proof.

NATURE AND SCOPE OF THE PROBLEM

The hazards to the work force may be looked at in terms of injuries, illnesses and deaths from injuries, and occupational diseases caused by or occurring in the workplace. Valid national statistics on the nature and causes of occupational diseases and industrial accidents have not been available in the past. Detailed statistics have been compiled by several states, but these have not been usefully comparable because of different definitions and different reporting requirements. In recent years, as the programs of the Occupational Safety and Health Administration of the U.S. Department of Labor have become more extensive, reporting has improved. Even so, it is widely acknowledged that occupationally related deaths exceed the reported incidence by a factor of 5 and that job injuries are 10 times more frequent than official reports indicate.[10] The error factor for occupationally related diseases is unknown but probably exceeds 100.

For occupational injuries and deaths caused by work injuries, some data are available from the Bureau of Labor Statistics, the National Safety Council, the National Health Survey, and individual states. It should be pointed out, however, that not all of the states require reporting by employers. Because of increased emphasis placed on occupational safety since the Korean War, the number of deaths caused by injuries on the job decreased from 14,200 in 1955 to 10,700 in 1986 despite a 77% increase in the number of workers (from 62.2 million to 110 million). This means a reduction in the death rate from 8.6 per 100,000 workers in 1955 to 4.4 per 100,000 workers in 1986.[3]

In 1985, 11.4 million people reported that they had been injured on the job, but injury rates appear to be declining. Disabling injuries have declined to 1.8 million in 1986 from 2.2 million per year in 1965 despite the increased size of the work force at risk.

Even though the accuracy of injury reporting is improving, the reported occupational illness incidence rate will vary as understanding of the relationship between the hazards of the work environment and illness improves. As the incidence of some occupational illnesses is reduced through education and prevention techniques, other linkages will be established through epidemiologic research, which should increase the reported incidence of occupational illness.

There are several reasons for poor data on occupational diseases. Nonrecognition and nonreporting of diseases are probably paramount. In addition, there are long development times before some occupational diseases become apparent. For example, silicosis does not occur usually until after about 15 years of exposure. Other dust diseases, such as byssinosis and asbestosis, also have prolonged developmental periods. In addition, there is a lag time between the onset of the disease process in the body and clinical evidence of disease. This holds true even though exposure may have long since ceased. Cases of mesothelioma, one type of lung cancer, have become manifest as long as 25 years after the last known exposure to asbestos. Barry Levy, in 1983, wrote that 20 million work-related injuries occurred each year and 390,000 new work-related diseases.[11]

Despite their inexactness, some examples of the incidence of various occupational diseases may be illustrative. It has been estimated that 12.8% of active coal miners and 21.2% of those retired, disabled, or unemployed have radiographic evidence of pneumoconiosis[12]; 123,000 may be disabled. Of the 3½ million American workers exposed to asbestos on the job, significant numbers develop asbestosis, which often leads to mesothelioma, as previously mentioned. Studies of asbestos insulation workers indicate that half of the people who have worked in the trade for 20 years have X-ray evidence of asbestosis, and 1 in every 10 of their deaths is caused by mesothelioma, in contrast with 1 in 10,000 in the general public.[13] As many as 11 million American workers have been heavily exposed to asbestos, and the possibility of suffering from a severe epidemic of disease related to that exposure hangs over their heads like Damocles' sword. Byssinosis, a lung disease caused by cotton mill dust, was long said not to occur in America. It is now known to be common. Talc, diatomite, sugarcane fiber, and dust from moldy silage all produce various forms of respiratory system diseases among workers. Of the 6,000 people who are or have been uranium miners, an estimated 600 to 1,100 will die of lung cancer within the next 20 years because of radiation exposure on the job. Large numbers of workers are exposed to heavy metals, each of which exacts its toll—lead, mercury, arsenic, and beryllium, to name only a few (see Harrington[14] and Clayton and Clayton[15] for details). Hundreds of thousands of workers each year suffer skin diseases from contact with materials used in their work. Dermatoses are the most common of all occupational diseases. An estimated 7 million industrial workers are exposed to noise levels that cause impaired hearing.

Another important aspect of occupational health and safety is the additive effect of mental stresses the worker brings from home to the workplace and vice versa. These may be domestic or neighborhood problems, concerns about economics or illness in the family, the use of drugs or alcohol, or other forms of delinquency. Such stresses cannot help but affect the worker's safety on the job, and it is reasonable to expect them to exacerbate work-generated stresses. In the same way, stresses in the work environment can affect an employee's health and safety off the job. Such terms as *ulcerogenic jobs, climbing the wall, the daily grind,* and *the rat race* are based on much more than apparent humor. Workers subjected to the stresses of noise, vibration, solvents, speed-ups, or overbearing supervisors can become occupational casualties just as much as if they inhaled dust or were exposed to toxic chemicals. Occupational health and safety programs are not complete without consideration of these psychologic factors. Many authors have spoken and written of the problems of alienation and powerlessness as they affect workers in America.[16,17]

Toxicology has become one the major "growth industries" in public health. Over 12,000 products known to be toxic are currently in use, and combinations of two or more of them run into the millions. New products are being introduced to the economy and the environment at a rate far greater than the growth in epidemiologic or toxicologic understanding of their nature. Given the long latent period for the development of many occupational diseases in humans, it is necessary to use biologic systems in the laboratory that mature much faster and have a higher rate of cellular mitosis and meiosis, such as cultures of *Salmonella* or some types of fish. Although these systems are efficient and useful indicators of the teratogenic, mutagenic, and carcinogenic potential of chemicals, mammalian testing is a necessary second step, but it is very expensive and time-consuming. It is necessary to determine several different levels: the maximum allowable concentration (MAC), a threshold limit value (TLV), a time-weighted average (TWA), short-term exposure limits (STEL), and emergency exposure limits (EEL).[18] Standards often use several different levels to specify a tolerable continuous background level along with the maximum exposure level for short periods. Even when such levels can be established with reasonable certainty, prudence, as well as the law, requires a margin of safety, so that permissible levels are often set at one-tenth the level found to be acceptable in the experimental situation. Some European countries specify pollutant limits in terms of their impact on the average person, but the practice in the United States has been to set levels so that even those with idiosyncratic responses are protected.

Three of the greatest items of loss to business and industry are labor turnover, absenteeism, and liability compensation for occupational illness and injury. (The National Safety Council estimated the cost of work injuries at $34.8 billion in 1986.[3]) Among the tangible profits of good community and occupational health programs are remedies against these three sources of loss.

Manufacturing industries have gained the most through safety programs, with a reduction in their occupational death rate of about 60% during the past 45 years. The work-related death rate for manufacturing occupations in 1986 was 6 per 100,000 workers, in contrast with 52 per 100,000 in agriculture, 33 in construction, and 27 in transportation and public utilities.[3]

Other benefits to business and industry are a diminution in employee grievances, improved employee relations, and consequently improved public relations. Health problems and responsibilities are always present in the plant or in the office, whether or not industry and business recognize them and whether or not they wish to do anything about them. If they do accept these responsibilities, they not only perform an important public service but may also turn that recognition and action to their own financial advantage. On the other hand, if they refuse to recognize their health problems and responsibilities, it becomes incumbent on official agencies acting in the public interest to step in and do something about the situation.

Sometimes the worker is his or her own worst enemy. All too frequently workers can be found circumventing safety devices because they are considered a nuisance or because they take extra time. However, management has the more serious problem. Ever since the industrial revolution, the health of the work force has not been the primary concern of the business owner; rather, the concern has been how much productivity can be obtained per unit of investment. Many of the costs of occupationally related diseases and injuries are still so indirect that they have less bearing on the everyday decisions of plant managers and owners than more direct and visible costs. It is rare for management to install a safety device or injury prevention program unless the cost can be offset either by a reduction in the direct costs of illness and injury or by increased productivity. The only exception to this rule is when government intervenes to protect the health of the worker, and then it is often argued that the cost of the change required by government regulation will be either inflationary or may make the plant or the industry so noncompetitive as to jeopardize its survival. When faced with such a possibility and denied access to the information necessary to verify such an assertion, workers often side with the managers and against their own health. There are instances where the real choice has been jobs or illness, but all too often the facts are obfuscated by propaganda and industrial secrecy.

Although business associations have argued that declining productivity in the United States has been caused by regulatory controls affecting occupational health and environmental pollution, studies by mixed groups of labor, management, and occupational health experts have concluded that, although they are inflationary, the negative impact of such efforts on the economy has been slight. There have been some plant closures because of environmental and worker protection programs, but they have been marginal plants at best, and the programs may be seen as a part of the competitive process that drives inefficient organizations out of the marketplace.

In some instances the nature of the work may be such that jobs and health are incompatible. When this occurs in a small community, the solution requires far more than the expertise of public health workers. The health of the entire community may be involved, and a thoughtful program of retraining, public assistance, economic development, and sometimes even relocation is required. As a result, the community may prefer to accept the risk they think they know "than fly to others they know not of."

OCCUPATIONAL HEALTH AND SAFETY PROGRAMS

It is appropriate to preface a discussion of the objectives and content of occupational health and safety programs with a pertinent comment made some years ago by the director of industrial hygiene of one of the world's largest corporations.[19] It is fairly representative of the basic approach and attitude of the private sector. "Business," this person pointed out, "is conducted on a practical, or profit and loss, basis and when losses equal or exceed profits, you do not stay in business long. Industrial hygiene programs that are not basically sound are not likely to survive the test of time." While not always true, this candid assessment of the problem points up the necessity for statutory intervention. As has been described in earlier chapters, the interventions may be "command" rules or "structural" ones. Command rules require that certain hazards be removed or controlled, and civil and criminal penalties may be applied if they are not. Structural rules attempt to manipulate market forces to encourage business and labor to take the steps needed to prevent disease and injury.

Even though public health emphasis has been placed on education and the voluntary progress that can be made by an enlightened public and enlightened industry, many of the issues that have been raised have been settled only through confrontation. There is growing emphasis on educating workers to become more involved in protecting their own health through plant surveillance, worker education programs, and the process of collective bargaining. From the public health standpoint, the purposes of an occupational health program are the same as those of all other health programs: to promote the optimal growth and development of people and their capacities, to prevent illness and disability, and to reduce the dependency that may result from disease or injury, physical or mental. The inclusion of mental and social factors merits particular note. There are indications that up to 30% of absenteeism is caused by emotional disturbances resulting from interpersonal problems in the plant, in the home, and in the community.

Many factors influence the nature and extent of an occupational health program. Among these are the type of industry or business; the nature of its product and of the ingredients and equipment used in its manufacture; the disposition of the product; the size and location of the establishment; the complex attitudes and relationships among top management, labor unions, and the community with its medical profession, public health agency, and government; and the organizational status of the unit responsible for the activities. For these reasons, it is obvious that a standard pattern does not exist. Each program must be tailored to fit the needs and circumstances of the particular situation.

Serafini[20] has shown how to apply the nursing process of assessment, diagnosis, planning, implementation, and evaluation to the design of an industrial health program in an orderly fashion. Webb[21] has adapted guidelines developed by the Council on Occupational Health of the American Medical Association, the Occupational Health Institute, and the work of Felton to describe a basic program of services. He categorizes the services into two groups: those of economic benefit to the company (which he calls "short range") and those of benefit to the health of the worker ("long range"):

Short range
Preplacement evaluations
Preplacement laboratory procedures
Personal protective devices as indicated by work environment
Periodic occupational health evaluations
Job transfer evaluations
Job termination health evaluations
Treatment for occupational illness or injury
Emergency treatment for nonoccupational illness or injury
Regular inspection of premises for potential hazards

Long range
Regular health evaluations
Health counseling
Special surveys for case finding
Retiree health program
Alcohol control program
Rehabilitation program

Liaison with personal family physicians
Liaison with community health insurance programs
Advice to management about health insurance programs

It is easy to debate the categorization of the different elements, but the listing taken as a whole seems reasonably complete. The concept of counseling should be expanded to include generalized health education programs with special emphasis on the hazards of each individual workplace.

In developing occupational health programs for different work settings, it is useful to consider the job classification system proposed by Gamble, Spirtas, and Easter.[22] They found that the proliferation of chemicals and other environmental conditions together with the mobility of workers made it virtually impossible to categorize workers by their exposure to any particular element—chemical, physical, or biologic. They therefore developed occupational titles for workers in a rubber plant that were based not on exposure to any one element but on process, function, and product. With knowledge of when what worker did what task, it is often possible to use manufacturing or industrial information to reconstruct the work environment to develop and test hypotheses epidemiologically.

For many years, occupational health workers and labor unions have urged manufacturers to provide their workers with information about the nature of the chemicals and other materials to which they are exposed. Business has opposed the workers' "right to know," claiming that it would require giving up trade secrets and that the workers could not understand such complex information. The issue has been debated in state legislative bodies and in Congress for many years. A Hazard Communication Standard was enacted in 1983 for chemical plants and has since been expanded to cover other workers. A recent revision requires all employers handling any hazardous substance to inform their employees about the materials. In addition, Congress, in its amendments to the Superfund legislation in 1986, has required the Environmental Protection Administration to develop both worker and community right-to-know programs. Every state and thousands of individual communities must establish committees to review the information provided by industry and to plan for community responses to emergency situations. As many as 1.5 million factories may be subject to the new law. The factory reports should include:

- The chemical and common name of the substance or its ingredients
- The characteristics of the substance
- The physical hazards, such as fire, associated with substance
- The health hazards associated with the substance
- Precautions for safe handling

States and local agencies have also become active in right-to-know legislation. By April 1988, 44 states had adopted such legislation on their own, and some had gone much further than the federal legislation. In fact the maze of rules had begun to make enforcement and compliance very difficult.[23] It is likely that some steps will be taken to preempt state legislation with uniform federal rules, but there is opposition to the federal government's assuming a quick hegemony in the field. As states pass tougher laws, the ultimate strength and power of a federal bill will be increased.

In many parts of the country, committees or health and safety teams have been formed to monitor the plant environment and make recommendations for improvements. Some teams or committees are combined labor and management groups with a carefully specified scope of action and authority. Other are composed of labor but have management support. Team members function during work hours and receive training from management. They function best when their activities carefully avoid issues that are a part of the regular contract or grievance process. Other more elaborate efforts have involved a consortium of unions, management, and a university, such as the agreement between the United Rubber Workers, B.F. Goodrich, and the Harvard School of Public Health.[24] Formed in 1971, the contract resulted in the formation of an Occupational Safety and Health Committee with three representatives from labor and three from management, which decides what issues require investigation and warrant research support. The Research Study Group consists of Harvard faculty. Results of the research efforts go to labor and management at the same time.

Several businesses have expanded their efforts into health promotion generally and provide help for those who want to lose weight, stop smoking, or exercise. Although this has been partly a public relations effort to improve morale, there have been some reports that employee health promotion efforts are developing a more professional public health approach, with impressive results in decreasing absenteeism and increasing productivity.[25,26] A less biased and more rigorous review of the literature, however, has raised questions about the efficacy of such programs. The reports, mostly sponsored by industry advocates and entrepreneurs who sell such services to businesses, have a dearth of sound, empirical research. Such programs may have real value, but much of the popular literature on the subject deserves a reserved and even skeptical response.[27]

Because of the numbers of employees involved, many of the larger business and industrial concerns find it practical to operate most or all of their employee health and safety programs themselves. Some industries have conducted genetic screening programs to detect employees or job applicants who might have a particular sensitivity to certain hazardous situations. Such efforts have been vigorously criticized by labor and civil rights groups as an unwarranted intrusion into the private affairs of the individual. Although a company may have the right to protect itself by excluding people from tasks that might harm them, genetic screening is not sufficiently well developed to support such exclusionary action in many cases, and resources might better be used in protecting all workers from such hazardous substances.

One of the greatest problems relates to small plants and businesses, which are in the majority and which taken together employ the major proportion (60%) of workers. Individually they are usually too small to afford or justify the employment of even a single full-time nurse, much less a physician. Unfortunately they have been largely left out of the picture except for essentially token services rendered by state and occasionally local health departments. To overcome the problem, there has been a trend toward the joint employment by groups of small industrial plants of full-time health personnel who devote the necessary number of hours a week to each plant in the group. This plan has proven of value in several locations. For supervision of the environmental hazards of small plants, various types of portable or mobile equipment have also been used to advantage. Private businesses now sell a variety of occupational health services, including screening, preemployment physical examinations, and counseling.

ROLE OF GOVERNMENT

Reference has been made to the relatively slow growth of occupational health programs in government agencies, beginning with the initiation of activities in 1913 in New York and Ohio. Activity and interest accelerated with the passage of the Social Security Act in 1935 and again during the period of World War II. In 1940 the majority of state health agencies were involved in occupational health activities. By 1980, however, only 11 state health agencies reported lead agency responsibility in occupational safety and health. As is the case with environmental health, in many instances occupational safety and health at both the federal and state level has been separated from public health and placed in other agencies, such as a labor department, or in an independent agency.

The director of the National Institute of Occupational Safety and Health (NIOSH), Dr. Millar, asked his division directors, in 1981, to rank what they believed were the most important occupational health problems. At a meeting of the National Advisory Committee on Occupational Safety and Health on March 31, 1982, he provided the Institute's list[28]:

1. Occupational lung disease
2. Musculoskeletal injuries
3. Occupational cancer
4. Traumatic deaths
5. Cardiovascular diseases
6. Reproductive problems
7. Neurotoxic illnesses
8. Noise-induced hearing loss
9. Dermatologic problems
10. Psychologic disorders

These problems areas have been discussed at greater length in publications of the Centers for Disease Control[29,30] (the parent organization of NIOSH) and in a more recent publication by the Association of Schools of Public Health.[31]

The list is a useful starting place for any organization at the state, local, or national level that is attempting to develop an occupational health program. In general, the function of government agencies on the state and local levels in occupational safety and health includes surveys and field investigations of environmental conditions in industry; collection and analysis of data relating to occupational illness and injuries; surveillance of atmospheric pollution and radiation in industrial plants; development of techniques for the detection of occupational disease; methods of prevention and control; and consultation with labor and management. Health departments concentrate on the supervision of environmental conditions conducive to employment-related illness. They suggest measures for control, promote in-plant sanitation and medical services, provide advisory engineering and nursing services, and conduct health education activities.

The Division of Epidemiology and Disease Control in the New Jersey state health department has a particularly strong program in occupational health. The division includes four functions that are not customarily a part of such units: (1) response to environmental emergencies; (2) response to nonemergency environmental contamination problems, including clusters of disease that may be related to environmental exposure; (3) epidemiologic investigations based on the accumulation of data, such as that contained in the state's cancer registry; and (4) epidemiologic study of occupational diseases.[32] Utah has developed a sophisticated computerized system for monitoring data potentially related to occupational exposures, including death certificate data (which include occupation), fetal deaths, and industrial injury and disease reports.[33]

Departments of labor and mines are primarily concerned with safety measures and the regulation of working conditions. The industrial or occupational health units of these agencies, in addition to their specific functions, coordinate their activities and services with those of units concerned with sanitation, health education, and preventable and chronic disease, thereby attempting to bring to industry a well-rounded health program. In addition, they usually maintain cooperative working relations with labor, management, and various pertinent professional societies.

To varying degrees, state agencies are charged with the enforcement of laws relating to the field of occupational health. Whereas state health departments are frequently responsible for general occupational health and safety functions, labor departments are more often charged with enforcement.

The problem of occupational health and safety is large, complex, and destined to become even more complicated and to require the services of still more types of specialists. The availability of trained workers in the United States is thought to be a particularly serious problem. One of the principal recommendations of a national task force on prevention called for increased support of training programs for epidemiologists, engineers, chemists, and regulatory personnel.[34]

The Occupational Safety and Health Administration has not had the work force necessary to carry out its mission, and the National Institute of Occupational Safety and Health has not been able to proceed with the enormous task of analyzing occupational hazards and developing appropriate and realistic standards. The problem is more political than technical; it became apparent in 1977 and 1978 that Congress was unwilling to support an aggressive occupational safety and health program while it was deluged with the problems of inflation, assertions that government regulation was a cause of inflation, and demonstrations that the taxpayers wanted less rather than more government, although the demand for services continued unabated.

In spite of that general reaction and the marked conservative swing in recent elections, public opinion polls show that such programs still have the support of a substantial majority in the United States, and Congress has not adopted legislation that would substantially reduce the programs. President Reagan issued an executive order in February 1981 requiring agencies to carry out cost-benefit analyses on all proposed regulations, but the courts have ruled that such studies are not required under existing legislation. Even though the Reagan administration reduced the size of the occupational health and safety work force and attempted to delay the issuance of regulations, the scientific base of concern is such that initially skeptical appointees have found themselves supporting regulatory efforts they had vowed to terminate before taking office. Although the President initially reduced or deleted funding for training programs, the 14 Occupational Safety and Health Educational Resource Centers established at universities to train industrial hygienists, occupational medicine and nursing specialists, and other needed categories of workers have been maintained by Congress. Most occupational health and safety workers would agree that the Reagan administration sharply reduced the level of research, standard development, and enforcement of occupational health and safety rules. Complaint investigations declined. The promulgation of new standards was waylaid by the Office of Management and Budget. The use of criminal penalties was negligible. Several authors have described the problems and proposed new initiatives for the 1990s.[35]

The Coal Mine Health and Safety Act of 1969 (P.L. 91-173) placed significantly increased responsibilities on the Secretary of Health, Education and Welfare and the Secretary of the Interior. For the first time in this country, a federal law recognized a specific disease, coal workers' pneumoconiosis or "black lung," required radiographic examination of all exposed workers, and provided federal funds to compensate its victims and the survivors of deceased miners. In 1987, 412,000 beneficiaries were receiving more than $1.5 billion in payments.[36] Because the review procedures in the original bill enabled reluctant medical panels and eligibility workers to delay and deny benefits (the program is financed by a royalty on coal), Congress amended the law in 1978, requiring time limits for case review, allowing local radiologists to determine the degree of impairment, and extending benefits to other miners who were not directly involved at the coal face.

To date, no other categoric federal programs have been organized to deal specifically with other occupationally disabled workers, such as asbestos workers or those affected with byssinosis. The reasons for this are political, not medical or epidemiologic. The causes and pathogenesis of the diseases differ, but the concept is fundamentally the same: exposure to toxic or hazardous substances on the job leads directly to severe and permanent disability, and such exposure could be reduced by control techniques. Therefore those who were and are in a position to implement control programs are held liable for the consequences (although the cost is ultimately passed along to consumers). The special attention given to pneumoconiosis is probably related to the interest in Appalachia generated by President Kennedy and to the effectiveness of the United Mine Workers and their occupational health program. This is in effect a special worker's compensation program to deal with one disease in one industry. It is likely that other disabled occupational groups will follow the same route and that eventually the pressures will result in reform of the worker's compensation laws at the federal level.

The Occupational Safety and Health Act (P.L. 91-596) of 1970 created a regulatory body (the Occupational Safety and Health Administration, OSHA) in the Department of Labor and regrouped the research activities of the Public Health Service into the National Institute for Occupational Safety and Health (NIOSH). The roles and relationships were confusing at first, with NIOSH serving as the research arm of the federal program and OSHA serving as the regulatory agency. The separation of functions was rationalized as logical and effective, but it was a compromise resulting from political battling for jurisdiction. The two agencies developed increasingly effective relationships during the last half of the 1970s, as the work of OSHA was oriented more toward health and NIOSH functioned more capably as a technical advisory group. Among the responsibilities of NIOSH are research on occupational safety and health problems, hazard evaluation, toxicity determinations, work force development and training, industrywide studies of chronic or low-level exposures to hazardous substances, and research on psychologic, motivational, and behavioral factors as they relate to occupational safety and health. Field stations and research centers have been established in Cincinnati, Salt Lake City, and Morgantown, W. Va.

States can enter into an agreement with OSHA to administer a compliance program. The original agreements were funded on a fifty-fifty basis. By July 1982, only 21 states had approved programs. Many state occupational health authorities did not like the complaint-investigation orientation and the inspection requirements of OSHA, and the funding agreements were not particularly attractive. This severely impeded implementation of the program, since OSHA could not acquire the resources needed to carry out the inspection programs directly. In states without a federally approved program, OSHA is directly responsible for inspection and enforcement. The federal agency is prohibited from providing consultation services to businesses without triggering the enforcement provisions of the act, but states may provide such services. Federal reimbursement was increased to pay for 90% of the development of a state program and 50% of the maintenance costs, but no additional state plans have been submitted and approved since 1978, and some that had been approved or submitted have since been withdrawn. Since 1981 the administration has attempted to provide funds to the states in the form of block grants with a decreased regulatory overlay from the federal agency, and that may encourage more states to become active. Both industry and labor have been opposed to state assumption of the program: industry because it prefers not to have to deal with 50 different programs and labor because it believes that business interests are more influential at the state level and that most state agencies lack the resources to carry out such complex programs of research, standards development, and enforcement. Even though the Occupational Safety and Health Act was a progressive national step, leadership historically has come from the states, with programs in Michigan, California, Minnesota, Oregon, and Washington providing especially good examples. State programs are amenable to change with changing governors and legislative leadership, perhaps more so than a national program, but that same malleability means that they can move more quickly and experiment with more creative approaches to problems. When hazards are universally understood and control technology is well developed and accepted, federal management of a program may assure better uniformity and equity across geographic lines, but when those conditions do not exist, as is the case for much of the occupational health field, state programs can produce more information in a shorter period of time. Some occupational health and safety workers see a strong federal role emerging out of state program efforts. They suggest that state programs should concentrate on surveillance and education and implementing innovative state programs and standards. Such efforts may force the federal OSHA program to become more progressive. The state programs can serve as OSHA "'watchdogs'—continuing to point out the agency's failures. In this strategy, preemption is our goal, not a defeat. . . ."[37]

In 1978 the Senate moved to exempt small businesses having 10 or fewer employees from OSHA regulations unless their injury and illness rate exceeded 7% per year (which could mean 0.7 workers). The injury-illness rate requirement would have applied to each individual business, a formidable task. The bill would have excluded the majority of American workers. It was not passed.

The Supreme Court ruled in May 1978 that OSHA inspectors would have to obtain warrants to enter a workplace if the owners refused entry. This was an extension of earlier Supreme Court rulings restricting the right of entry of health inspectors. In July 1980 the Court, in a confusing opinion, overturned an OSHA standard for benzene, a chemical known to cause leukemia. OSHA had attempted to lower the standard from 10 parts per million to 1 part per million. The industry had sought to block the regulation on the basis that (1) it was not based on scientific evidence and (2) it would be too costly to implement. The Court's ruling caused the agency to slow down the promulgation of other standards to do a more thorough risk assessment and to consider the need for cost-benefit analysis, but OSHA did not argue its case very effectively: the evidence it needed was already at hand.[38] In July 1981 the Court upheld the proposed cotton dust standard against a similar challenge and stated that OSHA was not required to carry out a cost-benefit analysis on its regulations.

It has been difficult for NIOSH to develop reasonable standards for toxic and hazardous substances. The research work has been tedious and costly; thousands of new compounds enter the work environment each year, and NIOSH has not had the resources required to conduct the necessary studies. In 1977 new regulations were proposed that would allow a generic classification system for carcinogens to be used so that they could be grouped. This change would help speed up the definition and promulgation of standards, but it has been vigorously opposed.

One of the more promising developments has been the agreement to support union educational efforts. Particularly strong programs have been under way in some unions, and OSHA has supported those efforts with grant money.

In 1980, 20 objectives for the nation in occupational health and safety were adopted.[39] They are listed in Table 20-2. For several of the objectives, no good source of data exists to monitor progress, but data are available to track 16 of the 20 objectives. Deaths owing to injuries and the incidence of work-related disabling injuries have decreased (Figs. 20-1 and 20-2). A panel of experts has concluded that progress has been made in several other areas as well.[40] NIOSH has proposed strategies for preventing the leading work-related diseases and injuries (listed above), and detailed descriptions of some of this work have been published.[31] The basic principles are the same in virtually all situations: (1) remove the hazard (a process or a substance) from the workplace, (2) protect the worker from the hazardous process or substance, and (3) provide the full range of services and benefits needed by workers who are harmed. Most of the attention has been focused on protecting the worker: the use of masks and respirators, protective garments, ventilation fans, various

TABLE 20-2 1990 Objectives for the Nation in Occupational Safety and Health*

Objective 1: By 1990, workplace accident deaths for firms or employers with 11 or more employees should be reduced to less than 3,750 per year.
Objective 2: By 1990, the rate of work-related disabling injuries should be reduced to 8.3 cases per 100 full-time workers.
Objective 3: By 1990, lost workdays due to injuries should be reduced to 55 per 100 workers annually.
Objective 4: By 1990, the incidence of compensable occupational dermatitis should be reduced to about 60,000 cases.
Objective 5: By 1990, among workers newly exposed after 1985, there should be virtually no new cases of four preventable occupational diseases—asbestosis, byssinosis, silicosis, and coal worker's pneumoconiosis.*
Objective 6: By 1990, the prevalence of occupational noise-induced hearing loss should be reduced to 415,000 cases.*
Objective 7: By 1990, occupational heavy metal poisoning (lead, arsenic, zinc) should be virtually eliminated.*
Objective 8: By 1985, 50% of all firms with more than 500 employees should have an approved plan of hazard control for all new processes, new equipment and new installations.
Objective 9: By 1990, all firms with more than 500 employees should have an approved plan of hazard control for all new processes, new equipment and new installations.
Objective 10: By 1990, at least 25% of workers should be able, prior to employment, to state the nature of their occupational health and safety risks and their potential consequences, as well as be informed of changes in these risks while employed.*
Objective 11: By 1985, workers should be routinely informed of lifestyle behaviors and health factors that interact with factors in the work environment to increase risks of occupational illness and injuries.
Objective 12: By 1985, all workers should receive routine notification in a timely manner of all health examinations or personal exposure measurements taken on work environments directly related to them.
Objective 13: By 1990, all managers of industrial firms should be fully informed about the importance of and methods for controlling human exposure to the important toxic agents in their work environments.
Objective 14: By 1990, at least 70% of primary health care providers should routinely elicit occupational health exposures as part of patient history, and should know how to interpret the information to patients in an understandable manner.
Objective 15: By 1990, at least 70% of all graduate engineers should be skilled in the design of plants and processes that incorporate occupational safety and health control technologies.
Objective 16: By 1990, generic standards and other forms of technology transfer should be established, where possible, for standardized employer attention to such major common problems as: chronic lung hazards, neurological hazards, carcinogenic hazards, mutagenic hazards, teratogenic hazards and medical monitoring requirements.
Objective 17: By 1990, the number of health hazard evaluations being performed annually should increase tenfold; the number of industrywide studies being performed annually should increase threefold.
Objective 18: By 1985, an ongoing occupational health hazard/illness/injury coding system, survey and surveillance capability should be developed, including identification of workplace hazards and related health effects, including cancer, coronary heart disease and reproductive effects. This system should include adequate measurements of the severity of work-related disabling injuries.
Objective 19: By 1985, at least one question about lifetime work history and known exposures to hazardous substances should be added to all appropriate existing health data reporting systems, e.g., cancer registries, hospital discharge abstracts and death certificates.
Objective 20: By 1985, a program should be developed to: (1) follow up individual findings from health hazard and health evaluations, reports from unions and management and other existing surveillance sources of clinical and epidemiological data; and (2) use the findings to determine the etiology, natural history and mechanisms of suspected occupational disease and injury.

*Denotes objectives for which no accurate measure of progress is now available.
From Public Health Service: Promoting health/preventing disease: objectives for the nation, 1990, Washington, DC, 1980, US Department of Health and Human Services.

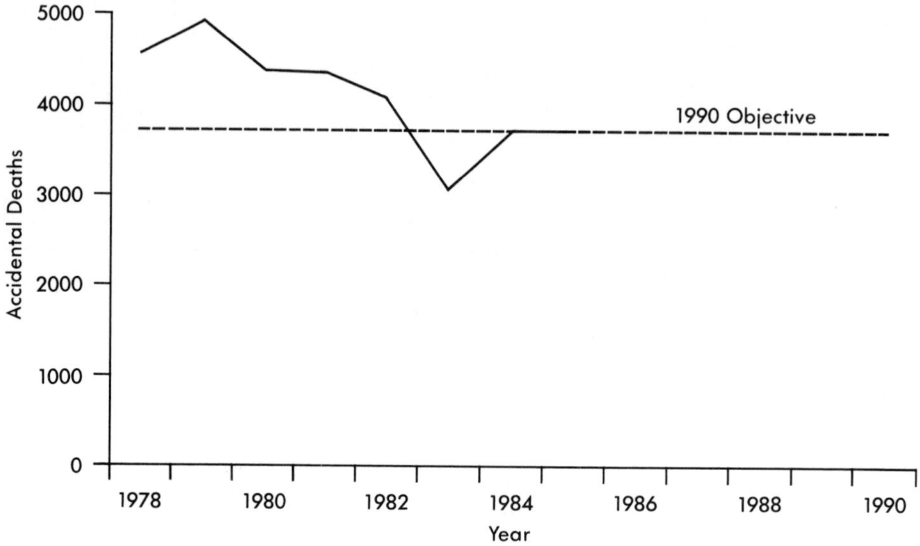

FIG. 20-1 Accidental deaths in the workplace in firms with 11 or more employees, by year—United States, 1978-1985. (Source: Bureau of Labor Statistics. From Morbidity and Mortality Weekly Report, 36(37):621, September 25, 1987.)

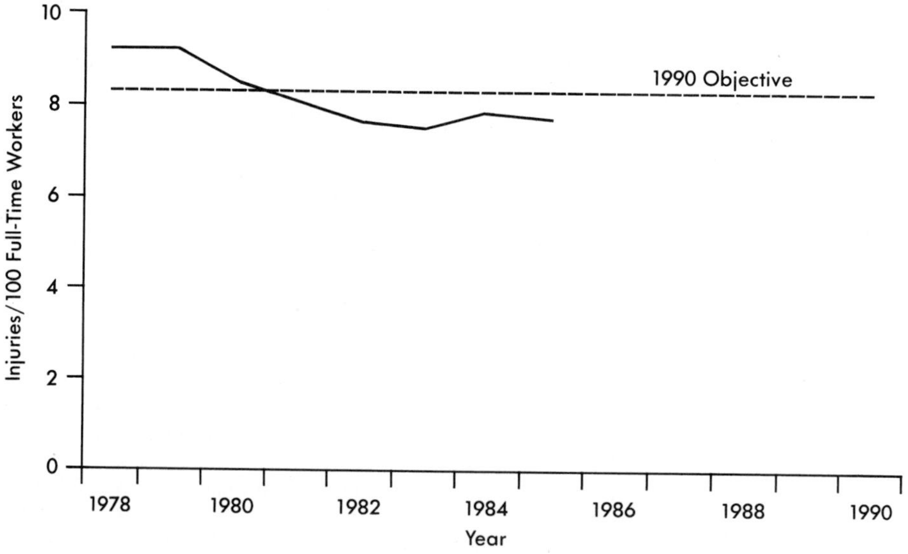

FIG. 20-2 Incidence rate of work-related disabling injuries, by year—United States, 1978-1985. (From Morbidity and Mortality Weekly Report, 36(37):621, September 25, 1987.)

guards on dangerous machinery, and so forth. But such devices are inherently faulty: they fail, they are improperly used or maintained, and they provide incomplete protection. Primary emphasis should be placed on removing hazardous products and processes from the workplace, either by using substitute materials or processes or by redesigning procedures so that they no longer require human exposure.

THE FUTURE

The conservative tilt in 1980 has not eroded basic support for these programs, and it seems likely that progressive legislation will continue to be adopted in the United States during the 1990s.

Although evidence suggests that occupational disease will prove to be at least as important as occupational injuries and far more complex both scientifically and ethically, lead agency responsibility for government programs will remain outside health departments for the most part. However, several aspects of the effort are very much a part of public health. Epidemiologic investigation will play an increasingly important role in elucidating cause-effect relationships in spite of the complexity of the interactions. The field of toxicology is growing rapidly and will continue to do so as industry, labor, and government agencies seek to learn more about the chemicals developed and used in modern society.

Technology will play a stronger role in control efforts. Finding the problems is only part of the process. Monitoring is increasingly important, and passive dosimeters are being developed for a wide variety of environmental conditions. These are badges or other devices worn by an employee and periodically tested in a laboratory. They will make it possible to carry out low-cost monitoring programs even in small businesses.

The biggest area of development over the next two decades will be risk assessment: the careful and painstaking attempt to differentiate between the hazards posed by a concentration of 10 parts per million and 1 part per million. The process will continue into the parts per billion range in an effort to determine what level of exposure, if any, is safe for most people. The issue was raised in the Supreme Court decision regarding the benzene standard. It is present again in considering ethylene oxide, ethylene dibromide, and formaldehyde, all suspected carcinogens but presently uncontrolled pending the ability to demonstrate at what level, if any, they cease to be hazardous.

Labeling and right-to-know laws will continue to occupy the attention of labor and management and their lawyers for the next few years. They bring different interests into direct conflict: personal privacy, industrial secrecy, and the right to know what risks a worker is facing. To some degree, the conflict illustrates that the old common-law concept of the assumption of risk is still viable: if a worker is adequately informed about the hazards and still accepts the risk, the owners are not responsible. That concept appears moribund in a society that recognizes its responsibility to protect itself and its individual members from the grave consequences of an improbable event.

REFERENCES

1. Occupational health, WHO Tech Rep Ser No 66, Geneva, 1963, World Health Organization.
2. Sperounis FP and Miller LM: The context of work in America. In Levy BS and Wegman DH, editors: Occupation health: recognizing and preventing work-related disease, Boston, 1983, Little, Brown & Co.
3. Statistics department: Accident facts, ed 1987, Chicago, 1987, National Safety Council.
4. Des Jardins RS, Bigoness WJ, and Harris RL: Labor-management aspects of occupational risk, Ann Rev Public Health 3:201, 1982.
5. National Association of Insurance Commissioners: Occupational disease issues: report of the NAIC Occupation Disease Advisory Committee, New York, 1985, The Association.
6. Bodnar EM and Pinkham J: Occupational nursing, Occup Health Saf 57:20, April 1988.
7. Messite J and Bond MB: Occupational health considerations for women at work. In Zenz C, editor: Developments in occupational medicine, Chicago, 1980, Year Book Medical Publishers, Inc.
8. Messite J and Bond MB: Reproductive toxicology and occupation exposure. In Zenz C, editor: Developments in occupational medicine, Chicago, 1980, Year Book Medical Publishers, Inc.
9. Hernberg S: Epidemiology in occupational health. In Zenz C, editor: Developments in occupational medicine, Chicago, 1980, Year Book Medical Publishers, Inc.
10. Gordon JB, Ackman A, and Brooks M: Industrial safety statistics: a re-examination—a critical report prepared

for the U.S. Department of Labor, New York, 1971, Praeger Publishers, Inc.
11. Levy BS: Occupational health in the United States: its relevance to the health professional. In Levy BS and Wegman DH, editors: Occupation health: recognizing and preventing work-related disease, Boston, 1983, Little, Brown & Co.
12. American Public Health Association: Chart book: health and work in America, US Department of Health, Education and Welfare, Washington, DC, 1975, US Government Printing Office.
13. Selikoff IJ, Churg J, and Hammond EC: Relation between exposure to asbestos and mesothelioma, N Engl J Med 272:560, March 18, 1965.
14. Harrington JM: Occupational health, Chicago, 1987, Year Book Medical Publishers.
15. Clayton GD and Clayton FE: Patty's industrial hygiene and toxicology, vol IIa(1981), IIb(1981), and IIc(1982), New York, John Wiley & Sons, Inc.
16. Navarro V: The underdevelopment of health in working America: causes, consequences and possible solutions, Am J Public Health 66:538, June 1976.
17. Work in America; report of a special task force to the secretary of HEW, Cambridge, MA, 1973, The MIT Press.
18. Lauwerys RR: Occupational toxicology. In Doull J, Klaassen CD, and Amdur MO, editors: Casarett and Doull's toxicology: the basic science of poisons, ed 2, New York, 1980, Macmillan Publishing Co, Inc.
19. Patty FA: The industrial hygiene program in industry, Am J Public Health 41:971, Aug 1951.
20. Serafini P: Nursing assessment in industry, Am J Public Health 66:755, Aug 1976.
21. Webb SB: Objective criteria for evaluating occupational health programs, Am J Public Health 65:31, Jan 1975.
22. Gamble JF, Spirtas R, and Easter P: Applications of a job classification system in occupational epidemiology, Am J Public Health 66:768, Aug 1976.
23. O'Neill BM, Stone JM, and Rosenbaum BT: Right-to-know laws: a guide to maintaining compliance, Occup Health Saf 57:28, June 1988.
24. Spotlight: The rubber workers study: a model of industry-labor-university cooperation, Boston, 1980, Harvard School of Public Health.
25. Azarow J and Cardy W: Health on the job: change the worker or change the workplace. Paper presented at the annual meeting of the American Public Health Association, Los Angeles, Nov 1981.
26. McGill AM, editor: Proceedings of the national conference on health promotion programs in occupations settings, Jan 17 to 19, 1979, US Department of Health and Human Services, Office of the Assistant Secretary for Health.
27. Warner KE and others: Economic implications of workplace health promotion programs: review of the literature, J Occup Med 30(2):106, Feb 1988.
28. Bureau of National Affairs: Occupational Safety and Health Reporter 11:957, April 15, 1982.
29. Leading work-related diseases and injuries—United States, Morbid Mortal Week Rep 32:24, January 21, 1983.
30. Leading work-related diseases and injuries—United States, Morbid Mortal Week Rep 32:189, April 15, 1983.
31. Association of Schools of Public Health: Proposed national strategies for the prevention of leading work-related diseases and injuries, part 1, Washington, DC, 1986, The Association.
32. Koplin AN, Altman R, and Finley JE: The epidemiologic basis of environmental and occupational health policy: the New Jersey experience, J Public Health Policy 3:39, March 1982.
33. Brockert JE, Levy MI, and Kan SH: Utah occupational health surveillance system. Paper presented at the annual meeting of the American Public Health Association, Los Angeles, November 1981.
34. Peters JM: Occupational safety and health. In Preventive medicine, USA: task force reports sponsored by the Fogarty International Center and the American College of Preventive Medicine, New York, 1976, Prodist.
35. Symposium: A new OSHA: the tasks of the first 100 days, J Public Health Policy, 9:319, Autumn 1988.
36. US Bureau of the Census: Statistical abstracts of the United States, 1988, Table 585, Washington, DC, 1988, US Department of Commerce.
37. Tarlau ES: OSHA preemption strategies, Occupational Health and Safety Section Newsletter, American Public Health Association, March 1988.
38. Linet MS and Bailey PE: Benzene, leukemia, and the Supreme Court, J Public Health Policy 2:116, June 1981.
39. Public Health Service: Promoting health/preventing disease: objectives for the nation, 1990, Washington, DC, 1980, US Department of Health and Human Services.
40. Progress toward achieving the 1990 objectives in occupational safety and health, Morbid Mortal Week Rep 36:620, September 25, 1987.

CHAPTER 21

Public health and injury control

Injuries and infectious diseases have been the most important public health problems since the beginning of human life. Injuries result in the death of about 150,000 people each year in the United States. In terms of years of life lost, injuries are considerably more costly than either heart disease or cancer. (Remember that years of life lost takes into consideration how early in life the problem occurs. Since cancer and heart disease tend to occur late in life, they claim relatively few years of life, even though they kill a lot of people. Injuries are very common in childhood and often rob society of several decades of life.) In terms of cost—both the direct costs of care and the indirect costs to individuals, families, and societies of a diminished life—injuries are among the most expensive of all social problems.

Social problems? Are not injuries due to carelessness and risk-taking behavior? Are they not the consequence of individual actions? In part they are; but they have significant environmental and social components, as well as collective consequences. This is not a chapter about accidents but about unintentional injuries. The word *accident* implies that the injury is the result of purely random events beyond our control (a bolt of lightning) and frequently related to injudicious behavior such as driving under the influence of alcohol (DUI-A). On the contrary: injuries are as predictable as mumps, AIDS, and strokes. They do not occur randomly but in high-risk groups and situations. And they are preventable—as preventable in theory as mumps, AIDS, and strokes. The challenge for public health is to translate that theory into practice. This chapter will describe the history of injury control in the United States, the epidemiology of injuries, and current programs to prevent or control injury. It will not discuss occupational safety, which is described in Chapter 20. Nor will it discuss intentional injuries, such as murder and other forms of interpersonal violence, which are discussed in Chapter 29.

An injury is an impairment of body structure or function as the result of a sudden exchange of energy. The energy may come in a variety of forms, such as heat or cold, electricity or a bullet. The energy is transferred to the host by a vector (a cold lake, an automobile, or a broken power line) in an environment that does not offer sufficient protection. The transfer causes a distortion in form or function, which may cause a disability, which in turn may lead to a state of dependency. The energy transfer may be from the host to the agent or vector or vice versa: that is, the energy in a car crash may compress the chest and disturb pulmonary or cardiac function; submersion in cold water transfers thermal energy away from the host to the water. In some respects, injuries and diseases are nearly indistinguishable. A sudden transfer of energy may break a bone; repeated transfers of small amounts of energy may produce lower back pain or arthritis.

THE HISTORY OF INJURY CONTROL

An abbreviated history of injury control can be found in a recent editorial by Julian Waller.[1] A more complete story is told in *Injury Prevention.*[2] Waller attributes the beginning of public concern for injury control to a German public health pioneer, Johann Frank. In the United States, public health departments became interested in injury control in connection with their programs for maternal and child health early in the twentieth century. Children, especially poor children, were brought to the early child health "stations" with the obvious sequelae of burns and falls—the results of environmental problems, poor product design, and lack of education. The problems were treated by public health nurses, who made home visits in both tenements and private homes. Since these were childhood "accidents," the victims were usually considered blameless, but not the parents. The problems were attributed to their ignorance or apathy. "Accidents" that affected adults were similarly attributed and therefore regarded as personal, not public health, problems.

In the 1950s and 1960s there was a focal point for accident prevention in the U.S. Public Health Service, but it was short-lived. As has so often been true in American public health, the field was dominated by concerned groups with a well-developed thesis, and contrary notions were either not heard or treated as heretical and therefore as the trivial notions of the ill-informed. Injuries were thought of as accidents, which were the result of individual behavior; the intervention of choice was education of the people. This of course satisfied governments and industry, since it exonerated them from any responsibility, the former from action and the latter from reengineering their products. The National Safety Council became, for those interested in accidents, the sole source of information and leadership, just as the Tuberculosis Association and the National Council on Alcoholism dominated their fields.

The efforts of public health were broad and oriented to the entire population. There were few attempts to identify high-risk groups. This too has been a recurrent problem in American public health. When the incidence of disease or injury is high and diffusely distributed across the population, as was the case with tuberculosis many years ago, population-based actions can be useful if the intervention itself is effective. The incidence of injury is indeed high, but it is not randomly distributed across all groups, as was the case with infectious diseases in the nineteenth century. The intervention, education of the individual, has been shown to be dismally ineffective unless a number of other social policies can be implemented strategically as part of the total effort. Early public health programs largely disappeared because of lack of interest and lack of efficacy. In the third edition of this textbook, John Hanlon wrote:

> If there is ever a tendency for any people at a particular time or in a particular place to consider disease fatalistically, such attitude is even more apt to be applied to accidents. In fact, the average person in even the most advanced societies tends to define the word *accident* as something due to chance, over which the individual has very little, if any control. This negative attitude explains to a considerable degree why so little concerted attention has been given to the problem until quite recent years.[3]

The basis for destroying the dogma of accidents was unfolding, however. During World War I, it was noted that some of the pilots who fell from their planes survived. Hugh DeHaven[4] found that survival depended on the rate of deceleration and the distribution of the energy transfer over the surface of the body. If deceleration was abrupt (as in falling onto pavement) or if the point of impact was confined to a small area of the body (as when landing on a picket fence), severe injury or death was a likely outcome. If the deceleration was more gradual (landing on the side of a haystack) and the impact was distributed over the surface of the body, survival was possible. This seemingly simple finding was startling at the time. It suggested that the environment could be altered (with protective gear, for instance) in such a way as to reduce the probability of injury. The biomechanics of injury prevention was born of such simple parentage: the notion that if you cannot always prevent a crash, you can nevertheless alter the environment to reduce the probability of impairment, disability, or death.

An infectious disease expert, John Gordon,[5] noted the similarity between the epidemiology of infectious diseases and injuries. The familiar triad of host, agent, and vector (see Chapter 14) became useful in injury control, with the vector enlarged to the environment in which the host and the agent interacted. Shortly afterward, James Gibson[6] simplified the emerging construction of an epidemiology of injury by recognizing that the real agent of injury was an energy transfer. He published a simplified typology of energy transfers: electrical, thermal, radiant, mechanical, and chemical.

Considered the leading theorist of injury control today, William Haddon used the work of De Haven, Gibson, Gordon, and others to develop the concept of injury control as it is now known. Haddon was an engineer who became a physician and then an epidemiologist. Working with several prominent researchers, such as Sue Baker and Julian Waller, Haddon had a profound influence on the field of injury control in the United States and elsewhere. Haddon divided the injury episode into three phases: the preincident phase, the incident itself, and the postincident phase. Crossing this with the host-agent-environment construction from infectious disease epidemiology, he produced a three-by-three matrix of injury control, which has been used by epidemiologists, engineers, and ethicists to expand the theory and practice of injury control. The matrix is shown in Table 21-1 with a brief analysis of one common injury problem.

A fourth column should be added, dividing the environment into the physical environment and the socioeconomic environment. In that last column would go such factors as public comprehension of injuries, willingness to intervene, the economic status of the elderly person, and the availability of a multidisciplinary response to the incident once it has occurred.

The value of the matrix is that it makes it possible to consider the relative merits of different forms of intervention. It is similar to the more generic matrix shown in Chapter 5, which places the field theory (biology, behavior, environment, and organization) along the horizontal axis and primary, secondary, and tertiary prevention along the vertical axis. Of course such depictions have little or no absolute meaning, but they do compel an orderly consideration of the possible interventions and their relative merits.

Haddon made a number of significant contributions to the field before his untimely death in 1985. The most significant for purposes of this chapter is his typology of interventions. His reformulation of the primary-secondary-tertiary prevention construction has been reformulated again by Dan Beauchamp[7] and finally by the author to yield the following:

1. Primary prevention prevents the incident from occurring and can be accomplished by controlling the hazard (eradicating it or reducing the frequency or pervasiveness of its occurrence).
2. Secondary prevention prevents the impairment from progressing to a disability and can be accomplished by minimizing the energy transfer through modification of the environment, the agent, or the host.
3. Tertiary prevention minimizes the dependency that might otherwise ensue by organizing and applying the treatment and rehabilitation resources of the community.

Within this framework, Haddon and Baker put forth 10 intervention strategies[8]:

1. Prevent the occurrence or aggregation of potentially injurious hazards. Examples: Teflon-coated bullets, plastic "toy" handguns, carbon monoxide in heating gas.
2. Reduce the amount or frequency of hazards. Examples: lower highway speeds, reduce the flammability of children's clothes, lower the height of children's beds.
3. Prevent the inappropriate release of hazardous agents into the environment. Examples: modify human capabilities through driver training, protect wall receptacles with voltage interrupt circuits, place antislip surfaces on the floors of bathtubs.
4. Modify the release of hazardous agents. Examples: seatbelts and air bags in cars, safety devices on water heaters.
5. Separate hosts and agents by time or space. Examples: use pesticides during the early morning hours when winds are minimal, keep electrical lines away from water lines in household construction.
6. Separate hosts and agents by barriers. Examples: helmets for bicycle riders, fences

TABLE 21-1 An injury control matrix: falls and the elderly

	Host (human)	Agent	Environment
Before the incident	Vision Medications Fitness	Loose carpet Uneven flooring Uneven sidewalks	Home Street
During the incident	Osteoporosis Fitness Skill training	Surface characteristics	Temperature Surrounding hazards Time of day Visibility of site
After the incident	Fitness Age Mental ability Psychological health	Surface	Medical insurance Emergency response Medical care Rehabilitation

around backyard pools, guards on electric saws.

7. Modify products. Examples: padding and cowling on snowmobiles, designing guns so that it is apparent if they are loaded and making the release of a safety control more complex, changing the structure of gasoline tanks on automobiles, redesigning the placement of brake and accelerator pedals in cars.
8. Increase resistance to injury. Examples: physical fitness training for sports, use of sun screens, exercise to reduce bone fragility in the elderly.
9. Prevent the progression of impairment to disability. Examples: prompt care for trauma victims, training in first aid for all high-school students.
10. Prevent the progression of disability to dependency. Example: rehabilitation.

Coincident with Haddon's death, the Institute of Medicine, one of the arms of the National Academy of Science created to provide policy advice to the nation, published its landmark report on injury control, urging the establishment of a focal point for injury research and control in the Centers for Disease Control (CDC) of the U.S. Public Health Service.[9] The report proposed a five-part research program: epidemiology and data acquisition, injury prevention, the biomechanics of injury, injury treatment, and rehabilitation. Congress reacted swiftly, with both a new appropriation for a series of injury research centers in the United States and creation of the Division of Injury Epidemiology and Control at the CDC. Nearly 400 research proposals were received in response to an advertisement for proposals, and 31 of them were funded, covering all five of the areas of concern. In a subsequent review of progress, a new committee,[10] composed of some of the same people, urged still greater financial support, and Congress once again complied promptly, even in an era of budgetary retrenchment. The committee expressed preference for an Institute for Injury Control, reflecting the power and prestige that go with that appellation, at the National Institutes of Health, but proposed that the division be made a center at the CDC in the interim.

The subject received other important emphasis. In 1979, the Surgeon General included injury control in a report that has proven to be pivotal for the prevention movement in the United States: *Healthy People: The Surgeon General's Report on Health Promotion and Disease Prevention.*[11] The report described 15 major areas (see Chapter 5), ranging from family planning and the control of high blood pressure to stress control and smoking cessation. In the section on injury control (referred to as *accidental injury control,* a term later changed to *unintentional injuries*), the report described the magnitude of the problem and discussed

Motor vehicle accidents
Firearms
Falls
Burns
Poisoning
Drug reactions
Product-related accidents
Recreational accidents

In the fall of 1980, the following specific objectives for injury control were published[12]:

By 1990, the motor vehicle fatality rate should be reduced to no greater than 18 per 100,000 population. (In 1978, the rate was 24.)

By 1990, the motor vehicle fatality rate for children under 15 should be reduced to no greater than 5.5 per 100,000 children. (In 1978, the rate was 9.2.)

By 1990, the home accident fatality rate for children under 15 should be no greater than 5.0 per 100,000. (In 1978, the rate was 6.1.)

By 1990, the mortality rate from falls should be reduced to no more than 2 per 100,000. (In 1978, the rate was 6.3.)

By 1990, the mortality rate for drowning should be reduced to no more than 3.0 per 100,000 persons. (In 1978, the rate was 3.2.)

By 1990, the number of tap water scald injuries requiring hospital care should be reduced to no more than 2,000 per year. (In 1978, there were 4,000.)

By 1990, residential fire deaths should be reduced to no more than 4,500 per year. (In 1978, there were 5,400.)

By 1990, the number of accidental fatalities from firearms should be held to no more than 1,700. (In 1978, there were 1,800.)

By 1990, the proportion of automobiles containing automatic restraint protection should be greater than 75%. (In 1978, the proportion was 1%.)

By 1990, all birthing centers, physicians, and hospitals should ensure that at least 50% of newborns return home in a certified child passenger carrier. (No baseline data were available for this recommendation.)

By 1990, at least 110 million functional smoke alarm systems should be installed in residential units. (In 1979, there were approximately 30 million systems.)

By 1990, the proportion of parents of children under age 10 who can identify appropriate measures to address the three major risks of serious injury to children (motor vehicle accidents, burns, and poisoning) should be greater than 30%. (No baseline data were available for this recommendation.)

By 1990, virtually all primary health care providers should advise patients about the importance of safety belts and should include instruction about use of child restraints to prevent injuries from motor vehicle accidents as part of their routine interaction with parents. (In 1979, the proportion of pediatricians who reported that they advised parents on car safety measures was approximately 20%.)

By 1990, at least 75% of communities with a population of over 10,000 should have the capability of ambulance response and transport within 20 minutes of a call. (In 1979, approximately 20% had this capability.)

By 1990, virtually all injured persons in need should have access to regional trauma centers, burn centers, and spinal injury centers. (In 1979, about 25% of the population lived in areas served by regional trauma centers.)

By 1990, at least 90% of the populaton should be living in areas with access to regional or metropolitan area poison control centers that provide information on the clinical management of toxic substance exposures in the home or work environment. (In 1979, about 30% of the population lived in such areas.)

By 1990, at least 75% of the states will have developed a detailed plan for the uniform reporting of injuries.

Note that the term *accident* was used regularly as short a time ago as 1980. The terms *unintentional injury* and *intentional injury* (as a result of interpersonal violence) are preferred to avoid the connotations of the word *accident.* Instead of motor vehicle accidents, experts in the field refer to motor vehicle crashes. Note also that baseline data for several of the objectives were either lacking or inadequate. As stated in Chapter 11, objectives should be measurable, both in time and amount. The objectives for the nation did not include an estimate of either the costs of attaining the objectives or of the benefits to be realized. Reading the list and considering other proposals for reducing the frequency or severity of injuries provokes surprise: much can and should be done to prevent these seemingly unpreventable problems, but the benefits and costs of doing so have not been compared adequately.

The objectives for the nation were followed by model standards for preventive health services,[13] which used the term *injury control* and established a mechanism for community-based public health agencies to establish program objectives in light of the national objectives. Objectives for the year 2000 will be available by the time this book is published. They will take advantage of an evaluation of progress made to date. In a special report published in 1986, progress was discussed and projections to the year 1990 were made.[14] It was assumed at that time that several of the objectives would be met. Motor vehicle fatalities had declined, for example. However the rate may increase once more as a result of increased speed limits on interstate and similar highways. (This points out the fragility of assumptions about injury control, given the multifactorial environment described by Haddon. In part, the decline in motor vehicle fatality rates occurred because of concern for gasoline consumption in 1974 and had little to do with public health concerns at all. Similarly, Congress reversed itself and allowed speed limits to be increased by the states despite objections by public health professionals and others who were concerned about the consequences.) The objective for the home injury fatality rate was attained by 1983, largely as a result of an improved economy and technological changes such as the use of smoke detectors. The installation of passive restraint systems in cars (air bags or the equivalent) will not, of course, be met. Although Congress passed legislation many years ago empowering the Department of Transportation to require such systems, domestic automobile manufacturers have continued to lobby successfully against such regulations. Several other recommendations, such as the installation of residential smoke alarms, require special tracking mechanisms, and for a few of the objectives, no suitable data are available.

THE EPIDEMIOLOGY OF INJURIES

Injuries are described by some as the most important preventable public health problem. The data most often used to describe the problem are mortality data. There are about 150,000 deaths due to injuries in the United States each year. The ability to count and describe nonfatal injuries is less well developed but is improving. A classification system for injuries is included in the International Classification of Diseases,[15] whose tenth revision will be in use in the 1990s. The system uses N and E codes: N codes describe the injury that occurred; E codes describe the event. In vital statistics systems, E codes determine categorization of the cause of death. In hospital records, N codes are used more often, since they relate to a medical diagnosis (e.g., a fracture or a ruptured spleen). Some hospitals also supply the E code with their hospital discharge information, and it has been recommended that this be uniformly required for all hospital discharge and record-keeping systems.

The E codes include the following categories:

Railway accidents (E800-E807)
Motor vehicle traffic accidents (E810-E819)
Motor vehicle nontraffic accidents (E820-E825) (this category includes such things as off-road vehicular injuries and injuries incurred while boarding a vehicle)
Other road vehicle accidents such as those involving bicycles and animal-drawn vehicles (E826-E829)
Water transport accidents (E830-E838)
Air and space transport accidents (E840-E845)
Vehicle accidents not elsewhere classifiable (E846-E849)
Accidental (unintentional) poisoning by drugs, medicinal and biological substances (E850-E858)
Accidental poisoning by other solid and liquid substances, gases, and vapors (E860-E869)
Misadventures to patients during surgical and medical care (E870-E876)
Surgical and medical procedures as the cause of abnormal reaction of patient or later complication, without mention of misadventure at the time of procedure (E878-E879)
Accidental falls (E880-E888)
Accidents caused by fire and flames (E890-E899)
Accidents due to natural and environmental factors such as heat, cold, snakebites, or lightning (E900-E909)
Accidents caused by submersion, suffocation, and foreign bodies (E910-E915)
Other accidents such as "hit by a falling object," exposure to radiation, or overexertion (E916-E928)
Late effects of accidental injury (E929)
Drugs or medicinal and biological substances causing adverse effects in therapeutic use (E930-E949)
Suicide and self-inflicted injury (E950-E959)
Homicide and injury purposely inflicted by other persons (E960-E969)
Legal intervention, such as execution or homicide by a police officer, during the commission of a crime (E970-E978)
Injury undetermined whether accidentally or purposely inflicted (E980-E989)
Injury resulting from operations of war (E990-E999)

The range of numbers in each category indicates the wide variety of specific injuries that can be captured in the system, such as the category of poisoning (E860-E869), which includes accidental (unintentional) poisoning by alcohol (E860), cleaning agents (E861), petroleum products (E862), fertilizers (E863), or poisonous plants (E865).

Some categories are much more important than others as public health problems, as shown in Table 21-2.

The table reveals the marked age differences that are related to exposure and risk taking, as well as health status. For example, death due to falls increases with age. Motor vehicle deaths are concentrated in the age groups most likely to be exposed; deaths due to fires affect children under the age of 5, as does drowning. Note that drowning also affects teenagers and adults aged 20 to 64. In most of these cases, alcohol is involved. The figures do not reveal the startling sex differences, especially in deaths due to motor vehicle crashes, which predominantly affect males by a ratio of nearly 2.5 to 1. The ratio for those aged 20 to 24 is 3.6 to 1.

Other data, developed by Susan Baker,[16] show the disparity in risks by income and urban-rural location: the injury death rate for the poor is much higher than it is for the middle class and wealthy, and the rural injury-related death rate is higher than the urban rate. Baker also concludes that there are more than 3.6 million hospital admissions because of injuries each year and more than 7 million physician contacts.

There are obvious high-risk groups: motor vehicle drivers and passengers, for example, especially teenagers and people who have been drinking alcoholic beverages; low-income people, especially their children; people with backyard swimming pools; gun owners; people who drink alcohol generally; smokers. Many of these categories can be combined with unfortunate multiplier effects.

The cost of injuries is significant. The National Safety Council estimated the cost at $118 billion in 1986, with most of that due to motor vehicle crashes.[17] Of the total, $32 billion represented lost wages, $20.5 billion medical expenses, $21.2 billion insurance, $6.7 billion fire loss, $21.2 billion motor-vehicle property damage, and $16.4 billion indirect work loss. This does not take into consideration the still higher toll due to permanent and residual disability.

THE ROLE OF PUBLIC HEALTH

Injury control is both a new field of endeavor for public health agencies and a peculiarly appropriate one, given their multidisciplinary nature. Based on the matrix presented in Chapter 5 (and recast above), interventions can occur in any of nine different areas, using a wide variety of skills and disciplines. For example, the law can establish building codes, engineers can design better water supply and electrical systems, educators can teach parents and children about electrical shock, and health professionals can work with the victims to minimize disability and dependency.

Given the eclectic nature of the interventions possible, and of the problems that can arise, what constitutes an injury program?

Many state health departments have developed extensive injury control programs. New York State (the agency for which William Haddon once worked) has been especially noteworthy. The focus varies, but most programs concentrate on childhood safety measures, with special emphasis on automobile restraint systems: all 50 states have laws requiring some sort of infant and child restraint system in passenger cars. Programs at the local health department level are even more idiosyncratic. In New York, a requirement for injury prevention activities was built into the standards for local health departments.

The essential functions of public health are the same in injury control as they are in other areas: assessment (including surveillance), policy development, and assurance.[18] The assessment function requires that injuries be identified and classified and that some procedure be established to ascertain their incidence. Death certificates are one important source of information. Hospital discharge

TABLE 21-2 Deaths due to injuries, selected causes, by age group, 1986

Cause of death	Totals	Age group				
		<5	5-9	10-19	20-64	65+
All	151,032	4,607	2,133	15,671	95,253	33,073
Motor vehicle accidents	47,865	1,188	1,069	8,278	30,873	6,410
Water transport accidents	1,102	12	20	119	851	100
Air and space transport accidents	1,148	11	13	44	1,023	43
Accidental poisoning	5,740	93	24	249	4,605	763
Falls	1,444	117	22	183	2,803	8,313
Fire and flames	4,835	768	290	296	2,087	1,383
Drowning	4,777	742	311	890	2,349	443

From National Center for Health Statistics: United States Vital Statistics, vol II, part A, Mortality, Washington, DC, 1988, US Department of Health and Human Services.

records, especially if both N and E codes are included (see above), are another important source of information. Some states have developed injury reporting systems. Other important sources of data can be found in each state highway department's planning documents, which include information about highway safety, and police records, which contain highway crash information and data about other injuries that result in police calls. With patience and skill, public health workers should be able to establish effective interagency data systems, which can collect such information, analyze it, and make it widely available to multiple state and local agencies.

Direct services are not commonly provided, although many local health departments have established loaner systems to help low-income families obtain and use infant and child automobile restraint systems. Some agencies have attempted to provide in-home services to assist elderly and infirm people in minimizing hazards in the home, such as loose rugs, poorly engineered controls for gas heaters and cooking elements, and stairs. Agency advisors may suggest grab-bars in the bathroom, relocating frequently used items and appliances to more accessible shelves and cupboards, and eliminating safety hazards for children. Such services are valuable but costly, and few public health agencies can afford to maintain them.

Advocacy is an extremely important function of public health in injury control. The assessment function can help identify important opportunities for intervention, but their effective application often requires legislation. In the earlier era of concern for "accident prevention," public health and the National Safety Council concentrated on education. However, years of experience and research have convinced most safety experts of the virtual futility of attempting to control injuries through public education. It has been stressed repeatedly that regulation of behavior (such as mandatory seat belt usage) works better than education and that the automatic protection that can be accomplished through regulation and product liability law suits is even more effective. Examples are numerous: deaths from carbon monoxide poisoning decreased when the carbon monoxide content of natural gas used in home heating was decreased; deaths from injuries with machines that are regulated by law have decreased, but deaths related to the use of machinery that is not regulated by law have increased; lead poisoning decreased following mandatory controls on the use of lead in paints and gasoline; aspirin poisoning decreased following the use of "child-proof" containers for medicines. It is widely recognized that the installation of air bags in cars would significantly reduce the death rate due to automobile crashes.

Automatic protection is almost always difficult to obtain. The public at large has been reluctant to see its personal freedom eroded by laws that require certain behavior, such as the use of motorcycle helmets, but is less concerned about laws that require automatic protection devices to be installed, even when this raises the price of a product. Manufacturers almost invariably oppose such legislation, however, since they fear that a higher price will reduce demand for the product or place them at a competitive disadvantage with foreign manufacturers who may be able to design and install mandated automatic safety devices more quickly and less expensively. Yet it is clear that such devices are the most effective way to reduce the incidence of injuries and the disability and dependency that can result. Product liability suits have been effective at accomplishing what advocacy sometimes cannot do.[19] Successful suits against automobile manufacturers, toy makers, and food processors have made the cost of hazard removal or protection part of the price of doing business instead of leaving its consequences for society to cope with later. Such action can prompt businesses to abate serious hazards much more quickly than a regulatory effort and may also cause them to be more alert to the potential for such circumstances in the future.

Education has one important function, even though its efficacy in reducing the incidence of injuries directly has not been rewarding: it can produce an informed constituency. This constituency may not change its own behavior to minimize hazards but will support legislative and regulatory changes to assure a safer environment. Seat belt laws required extensive persuasion and education. Other interventions will require a similar effort.

Public health has a difficult mission to carry out: it is accountable to the elected leadership of its community, whether the county, the state, or the nation. It can be difficult to lobby for initially unpopular statutory changes when the lobbied body has to approve the agency budget. Yet that has been the history of public health in the United States: advocacy for change to alter the environment, the host, and the agents of disease and injury. It will remain the task and the value of public health in the future.

REFERENCES

1. Waller J: Injury control in perspective, Am J Public Health 79:272, March 1989 (editorial).
2. National Committee for Injury Prevention and Control: Injury prevention: meeting the challenge, Am J Prev Med 5 (suppl): May-June 1989.
3. Hanlon JJ: Principles of public health administration, ed 3, St Louis, 1960, The CV Mosby Co.
4. DeHaven H: Mechanical analysis of survival in falls from heights of fifty to one hundred and fifty feet, War Med 2:586, July 1942.
5. Gordon JE: The epidemiology of accidents, Am J Public Health 39:504, April 1949.
6. Gibson JJ: The contribution of experimental psychology to the formulation of the problem of safety: a brief for basic research. In Behavioral approaches to accident research, New York, 1961, Association for the Aid of Crippled Children.
7. Beauchamp DE: Public health as social justice, Inquiry 13:3, March 1976.
8. Haddon W and Baker SP: Injury control. In Clark DW and MacMahon B, editors: Preventive and community medicine, Boston, 1981, Little, Brown & Co.
9. Committee on Trauma Research, Commission on Life Sciences of the National Research Council and the Institute of Medicine: Injury in America: a continuing public health problem, Washington, DC, 1985, National Academy Press.
10. Committee to Review the Status and Progress of the Injury Control Program at the Centers for Disease Control: Injury control: a review of the status and progress of the injury control programs at the Centers for Disease Control, Washington, DC, 1988, National Academy Press.
11. The Surgeon General: Healthy people: the Surgeon General's report on health promotion and disease prevention, Washington, DC, 1979, US Department of Health, Education and Welfare.
12. The Public Health Service: Promoting health/preventing disease: objectives for the nation, Washington, DC, 1980, US Department of Health and Human Services.
13. American Public Health Association, Association of State and Territorial Health Officials, National Association of County Health Officials, United States Conference of Local Health Officers, and the Centers for Disease Control: Model standards, a guide for community preventive health services, ed 2, Washington, DC, 1985, American Public Health Association.
14. Office of Disease Prevention and Health Promotion: The 1990 health objectives for the nation, a midcourse review, Washington, DC, 1986, US Department of Health and Human Services.
15. United States Public Health Service: The international classification of diseases, ed 9, clinical modification, DHHS Pub No (PHS)80-1260, vol 1, ed 2, Washington, DC, 1980, US Department of Health and Human Services.
16. Baker SP: Injuries: the neglected epidemic, J Trauma 27:343, April 1987.
17. Accident facts, ed 1987, Chicago, IL, 1987, National Safety Council.
18. Institute of Medicine: The future of public health, Washington, DC, 1988, National Academy Press.
19. Teret SP and Jacobs M: Prevention and torts: the role of litigation in injury control, Law, Medicine and Health Care 17:17, Spring 1989.

CHAPTER 22

Public health nutrition

FOOD AND THE HEALTH OF NATIONS

In a dissertation written in 1851, *Food and the Development of Man,*[1] Ule stated:

> Of all the influences which determine the life of the individual, and on which his weal and woe depend, undoubtedly the nature of his food is one of the weightiest. Every one has for himself experienced how not only the strength of his muscles, but also the course of his thought and his whole mental tone, is affected by the nature of his food. . . . The foods we use must contain the indispensable elements of nutrition in due proportion; our food must be mixed, varied, and alternating. And what is here said with regard to individuals, holds good also for nations.

The concern for national health and the political aspects of food and nutrition have been apparent for millennia. Much of human history and development can be understood in terms of the ability of people to obtain food. The evolution of modern society depended on its ability to reduce the amount of work that was needed to produce that food. Caesar, Napoleon, Hitler, and the military tacticians in the Vietnam War knew the power of food as a weapon, particularly the ability to destroy the opponent's supply. McKeown[2] has made the case that the rise of modern population groups was dependent on the development of an adequate food supply; that human nutrition preceded other forms of social development and control as a public health measure.

The stupendous efforts of the allied nations during World War II to produce not only more food but also food of a better quality in the face of many difficulties is well known. Less well realized, however, is the effect on the general health of the countries involved. Not only did millions of young men and women of the allied nations who were in uniform get better meals than they otherwise would have obtained, but civilians also benefited enormously, both in terms of education and in the substitution of nutritionally more desirable foods for some that were scarce and less beneficial.

The situation in Great Britain was summarized by Magee,[3] Consultant in Nutrition to the British Ministry of Health:

> The war-time food policy was the first large-scale application of the science of nutrition to the population of the United Kingdom. . . . A diet more than ever before in conformity with physiological requirements became available to everyone, irrespective of income.
>
> The other environmental factors which might influence the public health had, on the whole, deteriorated under the stress of war. The public health, far from deteriorating, was maintained and even in many respects improved. The rates of infantile [and] neonatal mortality and the still-birth rate reached the lowest levels ever. The incidence of anemia declined, the growth-rate and the condition of the teeth of school children were improved, and the general state of nutrition of the population as a whole was up to or above prewar standards. We are therefore entitled to conclude that the new knowledge of nutrition can be applied to communities with the expectation that concrete benefit to their state of well-being will result.

The situation in the United States was much the same, although the immediate devastation of war was not as apparent as in Great Britain. So striking were the gains in nutrition since the years of the Great Depression that an ominous finding emerged from the Korean War: autopsies of young men showed very early evidence of coronary atherosclerosis. Americans had apparently become too well fed in some respects.

NUTRITION IN THE WORLD COMMUNITY

A measure of the importance of food to people is the proportion of their productive resources that is devoted to providing it. The proportion of the labor force involved in farming has continued to drop in the United States, from 8% in 1960 to less than 2.5% in 1989. In less developed countries, the majority of the labor force is needed to produce food, leaving little energy for anything else. The differences in capacity to produce food depend on many factors, such as wealth, social constitution, the nature of the soil, the national economy, industrialization, scientific development, and transportation. Of great importance are habits, customs, and education. The international importance of these differences has becoming increasingly apparent as population growth, the ability to move farm surpluses, and the speed with which modern telecommunications systems can portray the grim reality of starvation all make evident the importance of food as an instrument of peace or war.

Jelliffe[4] has defined malnutrition as a pathologic state caused by a relative or absolute deficiency or excess of one or more essential nutriments, the clinical results being detectable by physical examination or biochemical, anthropometric, or physiologic tests. Four types of malnutrition are distinguishable:

1. *Undernutrition,* which results from consumption of an inadequate quantity of food over an extended period of time. Marasmus and inanition are synonymous with severe undernutrition. Starvation implies the almost total elimination of food.
2. *Specific deficiency,* which results from the relative or absolute lack of a specific nutrient. With the exception of ascorbic acid and vitamin D deficiency in infants, specific deficiency conditions are uncommon in human malnutrition in the United States.
3. *Overnutrition,* which results from the ingestion of excess food over an extended period of time.
4. *Imbalance,* which results from a disproportion among essential nutrients, with or without the absolute deficiency of a particular nutrient required in a theoretically balanced diet.

It is difficult to determine the number of people in the world who are malnourished. The Third World Health Survey[5] by the Food and Agriculture Organization concluded in 1963 that in the less developed countries at least 20% of the population was undernourished (insufficient calories) and about 60% had diets of inadequate nutritional quality. Overall it estimated that up to one half of the world's population (1 to 1.5 billion people) suffered from undernutrition or malnutrition or both. More recently, newspapers and the broadcast media have been filled with descriptions of widespread hunger and starvation due to drought and armed conflict in Ethiopia, the Sudan, and Bangladesh.

The most vulnerable group is young children. The World Health Organization estimates that about 100 million children under 5 years of age in developing countries are moderately or severely malnourished. Their malnourished state, complicated by disease, often leads to premature death. Measles, whooping cough, or chickenpox often become fatal. Studies by the Pan American Health Organization show that in the Americas malnutrition is directly or indirectly responsible for the deaths of children under 5 years of age in 53% of the cases, and the situation in Asia is even more severe. In addition to increased susceptibility to illness and death, malnutrition has long been recognized to have a significant and long-lasting adverse effect on intellectual development and social behavior.[6,7]

Protein deficiency is one of the most severe forms of malnourishment in terms of its consequences. Since animal protein is the most expensive food, the extent of its availability and consumption is essentially a function of the economy of a family or nation. Whereas the proportion of protein from animal products in the North American diet reaches the exceptionally high figure of 40% and in the British diet nearly 30%, the figure for Latin America is only 17%, for Africa 11%, for the Near East 9%, and for the Far East 5%.[8] As the source of the protein varies, so does the amount needed. Scrimshaw[9] has estimated that Caucasians and the Japanese need to obtain only 9% to 10% of their calories from protein, whereas those who rely on predominantly vegetable sources of protein need to get 11% to 12% of their calories from protein; and in underdeveloped nations where much of the nutrition comes from roots and tubers, 13% to 14% of the calories needed should come from protein. Thus those countries with the poorest food supply have the compounding problem of needing a higher proportion of protein in their diet. Millions of children throughout the world are estimated to be stunted by protein deficiency. This condition is known in South America as *culebrilla;* in Africa, it is called *kwashiorkor.* It is characterized by retarded growth and development, apathy, gastrointestinal irritability, a reddish golden appearance of the skin and hair, edema resulting in a swollen abdomen, and fatty infiltration of the liver. Untreated, the mortality of this condition is high.

Food is the energy of people and, like the energy problem, it poses the same questions of production, acquisition, and distribution. In recent years it has become apparent that the United States can and will use its food-producing capabilities as a major instrument of foreign policy, whether dealing with the Soviet Union or bargaining for oil.

In view of the great advances in the science of nutrition, it is paradoxical that so much malnutrition still exists. In addition to ignorance, prejudice and poverty, agricultural practices, economic policies, social values, and political factors play their part in the total picture of malnutrition.

In 1966 the President of the United States appointed a panel of technical experts to study world food problems. After a year of study these experts expressed the view that hunger and malnutrition were not primary diseases of the last half of the twentieth century. Rather, along with the so-called population explosion, "they are symptoms of a deeper malady—lagging economic development of the countries of Latin America, Asia and Africa in which nearly two-thirds of the people of the earth now live."[10] The panel's deliberations led to four basic conclusions:

1. The scale, severity, and duration of the world food problem are so great that a massive, long-range, innovative effort unprecedented in human history will be required to master it.
2. The solution of the problem that will exist after about 1985 demands that programs of population control be initiated now (i.e., in the 1960s). For the immediate future the food supply is critical.
3. Food supply is directly related to agricultural development, and in turn agricultural development and overall economic development are critically interdependent in the hungry countries.
4. A strategy for attacking the world food problems will of necessity encompass the entire foreign economic assistance effort of the United States in concert with other developed countries, voluntary institutions, and international organizations.

It is difficult to tell whether the circumstances have worsened in succeeding years or whether all the efforts have resulted in no real change, but the target of having programs in place by 1985 certainly has not been attained.

THE DETERMINANTS OF DIET

Many practical problems remain to be solved by education, by agricultural and industrial production, by better food sanitation procedures, and by proper food storage. One of the most difficult problems is changing eating habits. Merrill[11] grouped the factors that shape diet under four headings: geographic factors, biotic factors, economic factors, and cultural factors. "Men eat," according to him, "not only what the soil and the climate allow them to eat, not only what the saleability and desirability of the products they grow allow them to purchase from their neighbors, but essentially they eat what they saw their parents and grandparents eat before them."

In addition to culturally derived preferences, food faddism has become a marked feature in American dietary habits in recent years. No other topic has had so much written about it with such a bewildering mixture of common sense and nonsense. Various forms of vegetarianism, interest in organically grown foods, and countless surefire formulas for weight loss have confused many. There are repeated articles in newspapers linking certain food products to disease, most often cancer, usually produced in laboratory animals with excessive doses of the suspect ingredient.

On the one hand, this ubiquitous interest in food and nutrition can auger well for the future nutritional status of Americans. However, the frenzied confusion that exists currently, in addition to endangering some, may cause many to treat the entire subject with increased skepticism. It is clear that there are a variety of ways to obtain a nutritious diet and that not all of them involve the kinds of balanced approaches commonly taught a few years ago. A diet of fruit and vegetables, whole-grain cereals, nuts, legumes, and seeds can be adequate but it takes thoughtful effort to obtain that adequacy, and it is difficult for most people to sort through all of the "how-to" guides to find thoughtfulness. It seems likely that many people who are trying to attain a healthier diet lack the basic education necessary to design one, since most Americans know very little about nutrition. It is common for people to avoid bread when dieting and eat a piece of meat, even though the meat, ounce for ounce, has more calories and more fat than the bread. The concern about food additives has provoked many persons to reject any food product that lists an ingredient with a complicated chemical name on its label, without knowing whether the questionable ingredient is beneficial, neutral, or harmful. Since there are so few recognized and acceptable authorities on the subject of nutrition, anyone can claim to be one and add to the confusion.

It is a rare person who can honestly deny having some food biases or idiosyncrasies. Some foods are shunned for fear that they might be fattening or poor chemical mixers or for other real or imagined physiologic reasons. Some foods are identified with low social or economic status (such as cabbage); others are identified with affluence (such as lobster). Certain foods are symbols of hospitality, such as wines and ice cream.

Because of some and in spite of other factors that influence dietary habits and customs, some remarkable changes have taken place in the types and amounts of foods consumed by the American public during this century. Except for World War I and the middle of the Depression in the 1930s, there was a general increase in per capita consumption of dairy products, citrus fruits, vegetables, and animal protein from 1900 until the 1960s. Per capita caloric intake has slowly increased. The consumption of meat began to decline slightly in 1976. Dairy product consumption has declined sharply since 1960, while the consumption of fish has increased slightly.[12] Unfortunately, fat as a proportion of total calories consumed increased from 32% in 1910 to 42% in 1976; the consumption of complex carbohydrates has given way to consumption of simpler, less valuable forms; and beef consumption was much higher in 1976 than in prior decades. (Most of the figures about food consumption come from studies of food sales carried out by the U.S. Department of Agriculture. They overestimate the amount actually eaten, since they cannot account for wastage and the feeding of pets. They are the only long-term data available, but they are not a precise indicator of dietary habits.)

Several factors have led to these changes: new technology and the development of prepared food products; an increase in per capita income; government programs (described later); the increased entry of women into the labor force and the consequent change in family eating habits; the end of the baby boom and the rise of new consumption patterns; and a general interest in good health.[13] The Food and Nutrition Board[14] of the National Academy of Science has concluded that economic factors play a major role in changing dietary habits. The relative consumption of beef, pork, and poultry seems directly related to price changes.

The overall pattern, triggered partly by cost shifts, particularly for beef and other meats, has been toward an improvement in the diet of most Americans, although fat intake remains too high, and obesity is the most prevalent nutritional problem.

The increased use of dairy products between 1900 and 1960 resulted in considerable increases in calcium and riboflavin. The bread and flour enrichment program also contributed to the riboflavin increase, as it did to the increase in thiamin, niacin, and iron. Increased use of leafy green and yellow vegetables added a considerable amount of vitamin A. A similar change in the amount of ascorbic acid resulted from increased consumption of tomatoes and citrus fruits.

In 1980 the Food and Nutrition Board of the National Research Council issued its ninth revised edition of *Recommended Dietary Allowances*.[15] Because of decreasing physical activity and a corresponding tendency to overweight on the part of many Americans, the recommended daily calorie allowance for adults has been lowered in recent years. Other changes from the previous recommendations include a decrease in protein, vitamin E, ascorbic acid, and vitamin B_{12} for both sexes and a decrease in riboflavin and thiamin for women. Zinc has been added to the list. The definition of a recommended dietary allowance (RDA) is difficult. The Food and Nutrition Board writes:

> Recommended dietary allowances (RDA) are the levels of intake of essential nutrients considered, in the judgement of the Committee on Dietary Allowances of the Food and Nutrition Board, on the basis of available scientific knowledge, to be adequate to meet the known nutritional needs of practically all healthy persons.

The recommendations are for healthy population groups, not for individuals, and the Board states that most nutrients need not be consumed equally each day but can be averaged over a 5- to 8-day period. Hegsted[16] suggests that recommended ingestion of nutrients should be higher than the RDA.

PUBLIC HEALTH NUTRITION IN THE UNITED STATES

During the years since World War I, much fundamental research has been conducted and nutrition has become well established as a medical and public health specialty, but the profession is still in its infancy.

Changes in social organization in the United States have had far-reaching effects on national food habits. The process of "Americanization," involving the intermarriage of many nationalities, results in considerable interchange of dietary customs, ideas, and habits. Increased travel enables individuals to experience many new types of foods and methods of food preparation.

The increase in eating away from home has been the single most striking change in American dietary habits during the past 25 years. The implications for both nutritional harm and benefit are enormous. On the one hand, it should be possible to apply engineering technology to food processing so that more and more Americans will receive a well-balanced, sanitary, and palatable diet. So far, however, such efforts have not been a feature of the industry. The massive processing and distribution systems now in use offer the potential for greater control over the safety of food, but they also mean that a breakdown in controls can lead to the rapid spread of contaminated products to hundreds of thousands of people. Some nutritionists think that as little as one third of the food eaten in the United States is being prepared at home. Although modern snack foods and fast-food restaurants are often decried as examples of poor nutrition, they appear to make only slight differences in nutrient intake.[14] It seems unlikely that the phenomena responsible for this change will be reversed, and this creates the need for a major shift in the attempt to develop and implement an effective national food policy.

Until recently, educational efforts have focused on home economics courses in schools and the efforts of the Agricultural Extension Service to teach rural housewives how to prepare nutritious meals economically. With fewer farm families and a smaller proportion of calories consumed from raw foodstuffs prepared in the home, educational efforts have to change. It is now as important to teach men about nutrition as it is women, since they are as likely to buy processed or convenience foods. Labeling of prepared foods has become an important issue. The food industry has opposed government requirements for complete nutritional labeling. Some have claimed that the average person could not understand such complex information if it were available. In addition to underestimating the interest and intelligence of the average consumer, that assertion underscores the lack of good nutrition education in schools.

The ability of a family to obtain adequate nutrition has been described by Schorr[17]:

> The portion of income that a family uses for food may be regarded as a rough indicator of its prosperity. That is, as total income goes up, a smaller and smaller percentage is devoted to food. The poorest families spend a third or more of their income on food; other families generally spend a smaller proportion. The point at which total income is less than three times the cost of the basic nutritional requirements of a family (of specific size and ages) may be viewed as the brink of poverty. . . . It is by this standard that almost one fourth of the children in the United States are counted as poor. The rapid increase in food prices during the 1970s has exacerbated the problem.

Food is a commodity and can be had only for a price. Those who are economically disadvantaged cannot afford expensive food habits. Furthermore, they cannot afford the auxiliary factors that influence dietary development, such as education and travel. As a result, large numbers of low-income people in the United States suffer from malnutrition, often in the face of food surpluses.

In 1961 Congress enacted a 3-year pilot program to improve the nutritional status of low-income families by the provision of food stamps. The families who participated showed better diets than similar families who had not participated. "Findings showed food stamp families made significant increases in the value of food purchased with more than 80 percent of this increase accounted for by animal products—meat, poultry, fish, milk and eggs—and by fresh fruits and vegetables."[18]

In 1968 the Citizen's Board of Inquiry into Hunger and Malnutrition in the United States published its famous report, *Hunger, U.S.A.*[19] This was a passionate indictment of the circumstances that allowed poverty and malnutrition to exist so flagrantly in so wealthy a nation. The Citizen's Board was almost as concerned about the lack of knowledge of the problem. The report had a profound and continuing effect on federal programs. It also typified the sharp dichotomy between the ideologies of welfare and public health. The Citizen's Board found that the poor know how to use their food dollars but have too few of them. Its primary recommendation was for expansion of the food stamp program, making it available on the basis of need rather than a means test. It urged that the program be required in all states (this was done in 1974; in 1986, $10.6 billion in food stamps and food certificates were distributed to more than 19 million low-income people) and that those in need get the stamps free rather than have to pay varying amounts for them, as is currently the case. Public health workers, though grateful for the food stamp program, feel that it should be used in a more instructive fashion, with more controls placed on the nature of the products that can be purchased with the stamps. In short, public health workers would often prefer to limit the freedom of the recipient for the purpose of obtaining better nutrition, whereas welfare workers have preferred to provide cash (or the equivalent of cash) and leave the recipient free to choose. The food stamp program, like most other nationally supported public nutrition programs, is run by the U.S. Department of Agriculture's Food and Nutrition Service, not by the Department of Health and Human Services. It mixes the objectives of production supports for the industry, income expansion, and public health to the detriment of consistently comprehensible policy formation and good management. It does, however, increase total family income.

The school lunch program began as a response to the needs of children, especially in urban areas. It was the largest of the child nutrition programs and served about 23.7 million children in more than 88,000 schools in 1986. The program was expanded in 1975 to serve children in other types of institutions. Although the school lunch program has generally been considered a joint enterprise of federal, state, and local authorities, it is of critical importance that the principal, teachers, parents, and school lunch managers be interested in and understand the program. On the federal level, information regarding the establishment and management of the program and the use of surplus foods has been available through the U.S. Department of Agriculture. On the state level, inquiry can be made through the state health department and the state department of education. On the local level, health departments and school authorities can provide information necessary to the establishment and management of a school lunch program. However, the mere serving of food is not enough; the art of incorporating nutrition education into the entire curriculum so that the feeding experience is really a learning laboratory is essential if the aim of developing good food habits in children is to be achieved. Todhunter[20] has described some goals that must be attained if the school lunch is to contribute to the lifetime nutritional well-being of the child:

1. Educators and school administrators must understand the importance of nutrition for school children and recognize the value of the school lunch in nutrition education.
2. The school lunch must be a part of the total school program. Teachers need to have training which will provide sufficient background in nutrition to be able to give children adequate guidance in food selection and the development of desirable food habits.
3. The school lunch program must be managed by trained lunch managers, assisted by employees who have been given adequate training for their specific jobs.
4. The school lunch must be eaten by "trained" children—that is, children who are learning about foods in relation to nutrition and health as a laboratory for educational experiences.
5. The school lunch program must run on a nonprofit basis, financed in the same way that other school services are financed. The sale of nonessential foods and beverages at lunch times or at any other period of the school day should not be permitted.
6. There must be further research and study of the nutritional needs of children, of ways of developing new food habits, and of how to teach nutrition to boys and girls so that they will put into practice what they are taught.
7. Nutritionists, dieticians, public health workers, and health educators must be alert to the significance of the school lunch as a contribution to the nutritional well-being of the child and must direct their efforts to the fulfillment of such a program as has been described.

Nutrition education can and should be an integral part of the total school curriculum and be carefully planned as such. It should be developed to fit the student's level, beginning with kindergarten and progressing through secondary school and college. P.L.95-166 authorized the use of federal funds for nutrition education in the schools. Coates, Jeffrey, and Slinkard[21] have shown that a comprehensive program can have an important effect on the knowledge and eating habits of elementary school children, which may influence the rest of the family. Glanz and Morris[22] have found that this can work in a college dormitory too.

RELATION OF NUTRITION TO SELECTED HEALTH PROBLEMS

Pregnancy

The most vigorous public nutrition activities center around the health of mothers and children. The first recognition of nutrition as a public concern came at the White House Conference on Child Health in 1930. The evidence relating nutritional habits to maternal and infant health has been confusing. It is widely believed that good maternal nutrition has a beneficial impact on the outcome of pregnancy, but the few good studies carried out still have flaws in them that leave the answers in doubt. Except for situations involving extreme deprivation or the ingestion of toxic substances, the adverse effects of inadequate nutrition are subtle and difficult to establish in population-based studies. The most authoritative reviews of the supplemental nutrition program for women, infants, and children (WIC) have shown that the program has had the following effects:

- The intake of key nutrients is increased.
- There is improved maternal weight gain.
- The babies' head circumference is increased.
- There is lower fetal mortality (appreciable but not significant).
- Birth rate is increased about 30 to 60 grams.
- There are some indicators of better intellectual development.
- The strongest beneficial effects occur in those who are at highest risk due to poverty or as members of single parent families.
- There is some slight indication of an increase in food expenditures in the family unit.[23]

As noted elsewhere, these are all desirable outcomes. (See "Infancy" below for a more complete discussion of the WIC program.) In women with a stronger educational background, higher socioeconomic status, and no known nutritional deficiency, however, it seems unlikely that added nutritional efforts will have any additive beneficial impact on the outcome of pregnancy.

Many questions remain inadequately answered. For example, does maternal malnutrition play a role in the development of congenital anomalies? Can a woman poorly nourished all of her life compensate for long-term malnutrition by consuming adequate food during the pregnancy? What are the added risks for the woman who is malnourished when she conceives? Despite the fact that research groups have not yet been able to unravel many of the unknowns in this important aspect of preventive medicine, there exists adequate knowledge of the relation of nutrition to the health of both the mother and the baby to justify use of all resources at hand to encourage the best state of nutrition possible in all pregnant women. Futhermore, good nutrition throughout the entire prior life span, as well as during the period of pregnancy, is essential if optimal nutrition is desired in the offspring. Nutritional status, good or bad, cannot be turned on and off like a faucet. Adequate nutrition during pregnancy must be based on adequate nutrition before pregnancy.

How should the pregnant woman's diet be managed? Although supplemental food programs are necessary for low-income families, circumstances place the responsibility fundamentally on the woman and the attendant to whom she goes for care. Her diet should be neither ignored nor considered merely in terms of a table of standards. Each woman is an individual and should be treated as such, and the physician who fails to study the pregnant patient's dietary problems as carefully as her blood pressure is clearly negligent. Public health nurses and nutritionists can help by interpreting the nutritional needs of pregnancy and lactation to women individually or in mothers' classes.

There is much misinformation about proper nutrition during pregnancy and during the period of lactation. The average pregnant woman in the United States obtains enough vitamins from her ordinary diet. On the other hand, there is no evidence that extra vitamins are harmful, with the exception of vitamins A and D. Additional iron and folic acid are needed both during and after pregnancy, whether or not the infant is breast-fed. Ordinarily, supplementary calcium is unnecessary, and it is not known whether prenatal fluoride will reduce the future incidence of dental caries in the child. The pregnant woman requires additional calories, and restriction of caloric intake as well as the routine use of diuretics can be dangerous. The average woman should gain 22 to 27 pounds during the course of her pregnancy.[24]

Infancy

The infant has certain nutritional requirements and dietary problems peculiar to early age. Many factors are involved, including the infant's lack of teeth, limited digestive powers, spectacular rate of growth, and need to acquire a taste for foods of a variety of flavors and textures. The mother also has nutritional needs peculiar to her recovery from the physiologic strain of pregnancy and to the production of adequate breast milk for the feeding of her infant. The advantages of breast-feeding are substantial.[25] The practice declined for several decades in the United States, partly as a matter of fashion and partly because many women associated breast-feeding with a less desirable social environment. That has changed since 1960 as public health workers, nutritionists, and physicians became more aware of the benefits of breast-feeding and as attitudes changed once more. Even so, only about 35% of mothers breast-fed their infants in 1975, and most stopped after 3 months.[26] Breast-feeding became a matter of social advocacy in the 1970s as the American Public Health Association and other groups put pressure on manufacturers of processed infant food to modify their advertising to emphasize the importance of breast-feeding. One of the unfortunate changes that occurred was the more aggressive marketing of the products to developing countries, where they have compounded an already serious pattern of malnutrition.

In 1964 federal funds were made available to local and state groups for comprehensive maternity and infant care projects. By 1981, such projects provided needed services, including nutrition services, to approximately 450,000 mothers and 300,000 infants.[26] The WIC program (Public Law 92-433) began with 88,000 children and a total cost of about $10.4 million in 1974. By 1987, the program was serving 3.4 million children and mothers for a total cost of $1.7 billion.

WIC is a grant-in-aid program to the states from the U.S. Department of Agriculture. It is administered in a variety of patterns, usually calling upon local health departments and other community agencies for enrollment, education, and distribution. Pregnant women, postpartum women up to 6 months (12 months if they are breast-feeding their babies), and children up to the age of 5 are eligible if they meet two criteria: (1) have an income that is a maximum of 185% of the federal poverty level, although states can go as low 100% of the federal poverty level and decrease the number of beneficiaries substantially, and (2) be "nutritionally at risk." *Nutritionally at risk* is defined as

1. Having a detrimental or abnormal nutritional condition that is detectable by biochemical or anthropometric measurements, or
2. Having some other nutritionally related medical conditions or a dietary deficiency that can endanger their health, or
3. Having some other condition that may predispose them to an inadequate nutrition pattern, or
4. Having some other nutritionally related medical condition such as alcoholism or drug addiction.

It is apparent that the U.S. Department of Agriculture and the state operating agencies have considerable leeway to include or exclude large numbers of people as they write regulations and policies.

The WIC program has a series of priority categories, and states must begin with category I and add additional categories if they wish to do so. The categories are:

I. Pregnant or breast-feeding women and infants at nutritional risk [as defined in the program policies] as determined by hematological (usually anemia) or anthropometric criteria or because they have a nutritionally related medical condition
II. Infants up to the age of 6 months if their mothers were eligible WIC participants during their pregnancy
III. Children aged 1 to 4 who are nutritionally at risk as determined by hematological or anthropometric criteria or have some other nutritionally related medical condition
IV. Pregnant women, breast-feeding women, and infants who are at risk because of an inadequate dietary pattern
V. Children aged 1 to 4 who are at risk because of an inadequate dietary pattern
VI. Postpartum women who are not breast-feeding but who are at nutritional risk, as defined earlier

This program differs from other public nutrition programs in that it is distinctively public health in its ideology. Food is treated as a prescription item following a professional evaluation of the pregnant or lactating woman or infant. The rules refer specifically to a "competent professional authority," which in practice means a physician, a nutritionist, or a nurse. If determined to be at nutritional risk because of inadequate nutrition and income, the woman or infant is provided specified amounts of certain foods: iron-fortified infant formula, iron-fortified cereal, fruits or vegetables high in vitamin C, fortified milk, cheese, and eggs. Unlike many other federal programs, nutrition education is an integral part of the WIC program since the 1975 amendments. The amount of time and effort devoted to education is small, however, and its value has not been evaluated. In 1984, only 3.3% of total funds were to be spent on educational programs. At least two educational sessions during each 6-month period of eligibility are required, but they can be conducted by aides or clerical personnel.

The regulations for WIC programs require that the service agencies coordinate their programs with other health service providers and that the recipients have access to needed health care. About 3% of participants receive their food directly from the local agency; 8% receive their food by home delivery (usually a dairy); and the remainder receive vouchers from the local program, which can be used in participating grocery stores in exchange for specified food products.[23]

School nutrition

The school health program is perhaps the activity to which nutrition is next most closely allied. The relationship is threefold: (1) the attempt to assure adequate nutrition, (2) the imparting of good nutrition information, and (3) growing out of integration of the first two, the development of desirable nutrition habits.

Nutrition education should be a basic part of school studies for all socioeconomic groups, from kindergarten through the primary, secondary, and college levels. Major obstacles to the inclusion of more nutrition education in school curricula appear to be lack of understanding of educational concepts on the part of nutrition specialists and lack of workable information about nutrition on the part of teachers. In the past, teachers' colleges have not provided their students with an adequate background in health, and nutrition has been particularly neglected. Consequently, graduate in-service nutrition education is now being provided in many states. The training is offered by one or several agencies or institutions that employ personnel who are experienced in both the field of education and the field of nutrition. Included are county, city, and state health departments; colleges and universities, particularly those engaged in training home economics teachers; the American National Red Cross; and government agencies such as the Agricultural Extension Service.

Programs in nutrition education are now receiving increased attention, and both commercial and academic groups, as well as official agencies, have developed and made available helpful guides based on graded levels. The use of tools appropriate to the age and interest of each grade level is an absolute necessity in this field, as in all health fields. In the primary grades, the emphasis is best placed on food itself; that is, how it grows, how it tastes, and so on. In the upper elementary grades, simplified technical information should be presented, such as the need for particular foods to promote growth. In secondary schools, a more scientific approach will hold the student's interest, if earlier nutrition education has provided the information necessary for this more mature approach.

As has been mentioned, nutrition education that can accompany a well-managed school lunch or breakfast program holds great potentialities—potentialities that unfortunately are often ignored. Schools that feed but do not teach fall short of one of the aims of providing breakfast or lunch at school. Through the school feeding programs, children have an opportunity to become acquainted with foods not familiar to them and simultaneously to learn good patterns of eating by practicing them throughout their school years.

The school lunch program began in 1946 and remained fairly small until President Nixon pledged his support for the expansion of the program during the White House Conference on Food, Nutrition, and Health in 1969. By 1986, 23.7 million children were participants in the school lunch program, which had a total cost of about $2.7 billion. The similar school breakfast program spent another $406 million. The program is unique in that its income requirements are high enough to permit almost all children to participate, making the federally guided program a major vehicle for improved nutrition. Only about half of the participants were categorized as "poor." Since the program subsidizes meals, it enables more families to use the school food service program, which in turn makes it possible for a school to maintain the program. During the budget-cutting frenzy of 1981 and 1982, most related programs were reduced, but the more pervasive use of the school lunch program meant that budget cuts were opposed by middle-class families as well as the poor. This caused the President to focus budget cuts more exclusively on the low-income programs, giving credence to the assertion that he discriminated against the poor.

Although school nutrition programs are aimed at the problems of child development (intellectual, physical, social, and emotional), evaluation of the efforts to date have not produced significant evidence of improvement. Pollitt, Gersovitz, and Gargiulo[27] reviewed six studies of the short-term effects of the school breakfast program and found some suggestion of an improvement in very general terms but they found all of the studies to be poor in design. These authors reviewed seven studies of the longer-term effects of school feeding programs and found only two that showed a beneficial effect. Again, the studies were poorly designed. Podell and associates[28] found that high-school students reported a favorable change in knowledge and behavior after completing schoolwork on the relationship of diet to cardiovascular disease but reported that blood cholesterol value increases 1 year later were the same in the study group as in the control group. The experimental program described by Coates, Jeffrey, and Slinkard[21] suggests that a well-coordinated effort to integrate teaching programs with lunch activities and a general "ecologic" approach to good nutrition can have a significant impact. The evidence is neither overwhelming nor irrefutable, however. The flaws in each study design were such as to blunt the sharpness of any differences found between "treated" and "untreated" children. Given that most of the evidence is either positive or neutral, and that none of it suggests that good nutrition is bad for children, the programs warrant vigorous support and continuation.

Handicapped children

Children with special health problems, such as physical, mental, or economic handicaps, also need the services of a nutritionist. Mentally handicapped children are increasing in number and require special help in meeting their dietary needs. Nutritional factors are directly involved in retardation in conditions caused by inborn errors of metabolism, such as phenylketonuria and galactosemia. Severe brain damage will occur if these conditions are not detected early and medical and specific dietary treatment provided. Other cause-and-effect relationships linking nutritional problems to developmental disabilities will undoubtedly be found as research continues. There is a possibility that many of the children and adults presumably hopelessly disabled and housed permanently in public or private institutions may be there as a result of nutritional disorders, whether genetically or environmentally caused.

Welfare departments and juvenile courts, migrant worker programs, and child care facilities all can use consultant services of nutritionists or dietitians.

The aging population

Inadequate nutrition is one of the greatest concerns in aging and aged populations. In many respects the former group is of more importance, because there are many more people growing old than there are those already infirm by virtue of age, and far more can be accomplished for those who are still aging than for those already advanced in years. Furthermore, the circumstances of middle life determine in large part whether the subsequent advanced years will be healthy or infirm. Arteriosclerosis, hypertension, arthritis, diabetes mellitus, degenerative conditions of the kidneys and liver, cancer, and various other disorders are increasingly becoming dominant challenges to the health professions. These are all conditions of as yet somewhat uncertain cause. However, it is known that life-style has much to do with the development of all of them, and considerable research indicates a direct or indirect relationship with nutrition.

Certain facts about the older population should be borne in mind. In general, they tend to use fewer calories because of reduced physical activity. The period of tissue and organ development is largely past, and certain changes in food habits have been enforced by virtue of impaired dental function, elimination difficulties, various physiologic changes, boredom, or economic limitations.

The most common nutritional problem in the United States is obesity. Obesity is defined as an excess of body fat frequently resulting in a significant impairment of health.[29] Obesity is difficult to define in quantitative terms. The prevalence of overweight (deviating by 20% or more from desirable weight) increases with age in women but not in men. Overall, about 14% of American men and 20% of women are overweight.[30] The problem is more common among the poor and among black women. The causes are complex and not fully understood, but they boil down to an excess of calorie consumption in comparison to the number of calories burned up by physical activity.

Obesity is usually measured by the use of tables showing what is thought to be the desired weight for a particular height for males and females. The body mass index (BMI) is a more complex but more accurate figure. It is derived by dividing body weight in kilograms by the square of the person's height expressed in meters. Obesity begins for males with a BMI greater than 27.7 and for females at 27.2. There are 39.37 inches in a meter and 2.2046 pounds in a kilogram. Therefore, if you know your weight and height in pounds and inches, you can calculate your BMI by dividing your weight by 2.2046 and dividing that quotient by the square of the quotient of your height in inches divided by 39.37:

$$\text{BMI} = \frac{\text{Weight in pounds}/2.2046}{(\text{Height in inches}/39.37)^2}$$

Body fat can also be calculated by measuring skin-fold thicknesses at certain locations on the body or by measuring "lean body mass," usually by submerging the body in warm water, exhausting as much of the air in the lungs as possible, and measuring weight under those unnatural circumstances. The simple height-weight charts have the advantage of being visual and easily understood.

The impact of obesity on mortality is direct, as shown in Table 22-1. When relative weight drops well below the norm, the mortality ratio (the actual or observed death rate of the group divided by the expected death rate for people of that age and sex) increases slightly. As it rises, however, the mortality ratio goes up sharply, with those who are 55% to 65% over their best weight suffering a mortality rate 2.27 times greater than those who are not obese.

TABLE 22-1 Mortality ratios for men aged 15 to 39 compared to relative weight

Relative weight (percent)	Mortality ratio (percent)
65-75	105
75-95	93
95-105	95
Average	100
105-115	110
115-125	127
125-135	134
135-145	141
145-155	211
155-165	227

From 1979 data.[29]

Upper socioeconomic groups have made headway, caused largely by unplanned and unorganized social forces that focus on general well-being or sometimes vanity. Public health workers need to identify those forces and play on their impact, seeking ways to bring the same forces or others to bear on lower socioeconomic groups as well.

In contrast with obesity in the middle and advanced years is the problem of underweight and excessive leanness caused by caloric restriction. The reasons may be impaired dental function, allergic difficulties, economics, disinterest in eating because of living alone, or emotional reasons such as anorexia nervosa. Significant underweight may lower resistance to tuberculosis and various other infections, and it may also cause serious disability from ocular, vasomotor, endocrine, and skeletal changes. In addition, there is the risk of mild to full-blown avitaminoses. These in turn may aggravate further the underlying causes by bringing about additional oral or psychic conditions.

Interest of Congress in the nutritional aspects of aging is reflected in the Medicare amendments to the Social Security Act. Written into the Conditions of Participation for Extended Care Facilities are requirements for dietary supervision and adequacy of meals. The Home Health Care section has given the professional worker an obvious responsibility for the acute and chronic nutritional status of the aged. Another important step has been the inclusion in the Older American's Act of a program to provide one hot meal each day to the elderly poor. It became operational during 1972 and during its first year served 212,000 people daily. By fiscal year 1986 approximately 625,000 meals were being served each day at a cost of $137 million per year. In addition to the obvious nutritional advantage offered many low-income elderly people, the programs provide a substantial opportunity for social interaction, which has an important role to play in the health of the elderly. This is a population particularly vulnerable to the hazards of malnutrition, since decreased mobility, income, ability to prepare meals, boredom, isolation, and dental problems may combine to produce serious nutritional deprivation.

ORGANIZATION AND FUNCTIONS OF STATE NUTRITION PROGRAMS

The first states to employ nutritionists were Massachusetts and New York in 1917. The Sheppard-Towner Act in 1921 supported the establishment of state maternal and child health programs, and nutrition services spread. The Social Security Act of 1935 expanded federal support and established guidelines for professional nutrition personnel. By 1980, 51 of the 57 reporting state and territorial health agencies claimed that they had nutrition programs serving 3.37 million clients.[31]

Most of the current activity in state and local health departments is attributable and limited to WIC programs. WIC is virtually 100% federally funded, and health departments, faced with intense competition for resources, have moved most of their nutrition work into WIC to capitalize on the federal funding and because WIC addresses one of the most important target areas for public health nutrition. Mildred Kaufman and others[32] surveyed the states in 1985 and found that three fourths of the professional public health nutrition work force was working in maternal and child health activities, and most of them were supported by either the WIC program or the maternal and child health (MCH) block grant (Table 22-2). (See Chapters 6 and 23 for more information about the block grant.)

"Public health nutritionists utilize a community diagnostic approach in assessing needs of the general public and in applying the scientific knowledge of nutrition to planning, implementing, and evaluating public health services."[33] Although licensure requirements are not yet in vogue (the profession seeks licensure at least in part to become eligible for fee-for-service reimbursement), most job descriptions require a master's degree. The role and status of nutritionists and dietitians were controversial for years but the two groups now appear to work cooperatively in pursuing common goals. There are no practically useful distinctions between a public health nutritionist and a community dietitian at this time. In some states nutrition has been organized as a separate division or as a staff agency responsible to the health department director. In others it has been placed in divisions of medical services, public health nursing, or local health services. Most commonly it has been allocated to the bureau or division of maternal and child health.

The major roles of a state-level nutrition program are to carry out nutritional surveillance; to develop standards for public nutrition programs, including Head Start, public schools, and similar activities; to provide consultation to local health agencies and other state agencies; and to carry out applied research in community nutrition. The ideal qualifications of the director of nutrition would include a medical education with special clinical experience in nutritional diseases, a basic background in biochemistry, and training and experience in public health. Such professionals are rare. The most important qualifications are the nutrition and public health backgrounds, which will enable the director of nutrition to give the necessary guidance and to integrate the program into the other activities of the health department.

The special 10-state nutrition survey carried out by the Public Health Service in 1968-1970[34] has been continued as part of the Cooperative Health Statistics System known as the Health and Nutrition Examination Survey (HANES).[35,36] The third round, known as N-HANES III, is under way at this time (1988-1994). The data available, plus the data that can be obtained through WIC programs, through Maternal and Infant Care and other maternal and child health programs, and from the state agencies on aging should provide most state

TABLE 22-2 Funding for state and local health department public health nutrition positions, 1985

Source	Percent
WIC	62
MCH block grant	11
State funds	8
Local funds	7
Other	3
Not identified	5
Prevention block grant	2
Home health	1
Family planning	1

health departments with the ability to assess the special problems and needs of their states and the subgroups and areas within the state. Various techniques for incorporating nutritional assessment into health programs are described by George Christakis,[37] and continuing information about nutrition is available in a special bulletin, *Nutrition Surveillance,* published by the Centers for Disease Control.[38]

Given the work that has been done in nutrition surveillance and its importance, it is reasonable to expect that the states would have well-developed plans for nutrition services. Such is not the case. Although nutrition has had a powerful impact on health historically, it is not given urgent attention in countries as affluent as the United States. Obesity is the major problem, followed by an imbalance of appropriate nutrients, such as too much fat and not enough complex carbohydrates. Many people are hungry for a diet that is both physiologically and psychologically satisfying,[39] but there is little evidence of gross malnutrition in the United States except for obesity. There is considerable dispute about the value and feasibility of obtaining significant changes in the human diet quickly. Moreover, the preoccupation of state and local health departments with the WIC program has dulled their appetite for useful and comprehensive information about nutritional status. Kaufman and others[32] found that the states were collecting and analyzing data for only 5 of the 15 nutrition objectives for the nation in 1985. Only 43 states were aggregating the available data concerning iron deficiency anemia in pregnancy; 35 were doing so for child growth abnormalities; 13 for overweight adults; 4 for cholesterol levels; 14 for breast-feeding; and 9 had studied data regarding adult nutrition knowledge.

LOCAL NUTRITION PROGRAMS

At the local level, the principal roles of nutritionists are assessment of dietary practices in the community and in subgroups of the community; nutrition education and counseling for selected groups such as pregnant women, mothers, and infants; the provision of referral services to needed food service programs; and the provision or securing of special equipment and food supplements. In an effort to further define the role of nutritionists in local health agencies, the California Conference of Local Health Department Nutritionists (a group related to the California Conference of Local Health Officers) developed *Guidelines for Nutrition Services in Local Health Jurisdictions.*[40] The standards cover nutrition in chronic disease control, children and youth programs, dental health services, environmental health programs (food and restaurant inspections), family planning, maternal and child health programs, communicable disease control, nursing, disaster relief, detention facilities, and laboratory services. Members of the Conference, with the support of the state nutrition staff, have formulated the following goal:

> Local health jurisdictions will provide and/or assure community nutrition programming and articulated nutrition care services sufficient to meet the needs of the jurisdiction and administered by a designated and qualified person.

The standards provide a comprehensive look at opportunities and also provide some insights into the ways professional groups define problems and solutions in terms of their own training and aspirations.

Planning community nutrition services is essential given the numerous needs and the scant resources in the official agency. Problem and program priorities must be established; otherwise nutritionists may find themselves spending all their time giving talks and providing one-on-one consultation, with little impact on the community as a whole or any of its subgroups. There are many data sources available. Although nutrition surveillance can be highly sophisticated and expensive, Christakis[37] lists some of the kinds of data that may be available in one form or another in most communities to help a well-trained nutritionist formulate priorities: demographic information from the census, public utility companies, and regional planning bodies; information about socioeconomic status developed by human service organizations; health statistics gathered by Health Systems Agencies and their predecessors between 1966 and 1981; information about cultural patterns from interested community organizations and local colleges; housing conditions from the housing agency; information about food supplies and costs from personal surveys; information about school nutrition programs from the office of the superintendent of schools; welfare data from the welfare agency; and information about transportation (particularly to and from low-income neighborhoods) and occupational patterns from regional planning and transit bodies.

There are many resources available to the nutritionist in most communities. It is a common mistake to look only at the one or two positions available in the local health department itself. Many local hospitals now encourage their dietary staff to become actively involved in community nutrition education and service efforts. Day-care programs often have consultant nutritionists, as do Head Start Programs, local schools, and economic opportunity programs. The Extension Service in each state, supported by the federal and state Departments of Agriculture, has had a long-standing interest in nutrition. Local colleges and universities often have faculty and staff who are involved in nutrition. Federally funded migrant health centers and community health centers frequently have nutrition services available, and some churches and alcohol guidance centers have developed nutrition programs. (See Owen and Frankle[41] for more complete information about the organization and management of community nutrition programs.)

Much of the function of the health department is that of a coordinator and catalyst for existing community resources. It is particularly important that programs that involve the actual distribution of food, or vouchers or certificates for food, be coupled with personal and group educational efforts. At one time the distribution of food was thought of as a function of a welfare program, and health departments were limited in their thinking and in their roles to education and consultation. As noted before, health departments are increasingly involved in the direct management of feeding programs and food distribution activities, and the linkage of supply to education must be established. Every effort should be made to work with other community agencies that have similar responsibilities, especially the public welfare office and those professionals who determine food stamp eligibility. Consultative service should be offered by well-qualified nutritionists to the various persons and agencies mentioned, the end in view being to demonstrate how nutrition education can be injected into daily routine without adding appreciably to the daily burden.

These phases of the work should be under the immediate supervision of a well-trained and experienced nutritionist with a knowledge of the area and its government and voluntary agencies. In the case of a state program, the state should be divided into regions. It is suggested that at first activities be restricted to counties or communities with full-time public health services, since their existence will facilitate public acquaintance and acceptance of the work of the nutritionist. The length of time to be spent in each local area, the frequency of visits, and the particular type of activity and approach should be worked out on the basis of cumulative experience in the locality by the regional nutritionist. At all times the nutritionist should keep in mind that efforts to render direct service to the public will reach only a few and that the real contribution is to promote the use of local talent and facilities for improving community nutrition.

With the rapid expansion of the services of public health nutritionists, there is a critical need to evaluate the services they render and determine what services could be delegated to other personnel. The 6 or 7 years of training required is barely enough to provide all the many skills and experiences needed to face the complex nutritional problems in urban and rural society in an age of advancing technology. The University of California has developed a 5-year program that produces graduates with a master's degree, an American Dietetics Association–approved internship, and some experience in public health. Various countries have developed other approaches suitable to their situations. Japan, for example, meets its personnel needs by graduating 2-year nutrition technologists. Just as the hospital dietitian has promoted the use of food service supervisors, so must the public health nutritionist look for ways of extending services through lesser-trained workers. Underdeveloped nations have selected village workers, trained them for 1 year, and returned them to their homes to teach health and nutrition to their peers. Might not this principle be used to teach people in the ghetto areas of American cities, to saturate the neighborhoods with adequate nutrition information on food buying and budgeting, and to provide enough sound nutrition information so that people would not become vulnerable to fallacious practices and beliefs?

LEGISLATION AND THE NEED FOR FOOD AND NUTRITION POLICY

It is possible for a community, a state, or a nation to attack nutritional problems at their source; that is, the place of production or distribution of a product. Perhaps the earliest example of this was the addition of iodine in the form of sodium or potassium iodide to public water supplies, chocolate, and, more practically, to table salt.

On January 18, 1943, a government order known as War Food Order No. 1 went into effect in the United States. This order required that all white bread be enriched to meet the requirements of the order in thiamin, niacin, riboflavin, and iron. It remained in effect until October 18, 1946. Since then, a number of states have passed legislation for the continuance of a policy of enrichment of all white flour and bread within their borders.

In 1976 the West Virginia State Board of Education took the audacious step of banning the sale of all "junk foods" in vending machines in school buildings. Although various commercial groups have tried to weaken that ban, it has remained in effect and is a clear example of the articulation of policy with practice. Many organizations have supported compulsory labeling to reveal nutrition information, but as noted earlier this has been successfully opposed by the industry so far, although some manufacturers have developed their own programs. During the Reagan administration, the emphasis on deregulating rather than regulating further postponed useful labeling practices.

Understanding food labeling is difficult, because many nutrients interact with each other in complex ways, but it is no more complex than many other aspects of modern life that we are called on to handle. It may be possible to produce meat, dairy, and egg products with lower and more unsaturated fat content through altered animal breeding and feeding practices. To do so, however, may take legislation, both to finance the necessary research and perhaps to require that the changes be made, and it may be extremely difficult to effect such legislation in the United States.

In the past 10 years, there has been a diminution of federal support for nutrition programs. Except for WIC, which has the political advantages of its focus on babies and children and its authoritarian and prescriptive posture, and programs for the elderly, a powerful political constituency, nutrition programs were providing fewer meals toward the end of the Reagan years than they were at the beginning (Table 22-3).

The 1990 objectives for the nation specified 17 nutrition objectives.[42] (Kaufman reported on 15—see above.) They are listed in Table 22-4. The Office of Disease Prevention and Health Promotion determined in 1986 that none had been achieved, 6 were "on-track" and could probably be achieved, 5 were unlikely to be achieved, and that there were no useful data for 6 of the objectives.

In addition to the 1990 objectives for the nation, model standards[43] have been adopted for local public health programs, which include a single goal: the nutritional status of all community residents will be optimal. This will help assure that health will be maximized and that morbidity and mortality due to nutrition-related problems will be minimized. For the one outcome, there are seven process objectives: (1) the incidence of specified nutritionally related disorders will be reduced to some new level; (2) the community will have an ongoing assessment system in place; (3) needed nutrition services will be available; (4) appropriate dietary practices will be promoted for infants and children, based on the needs ascertained by the assessment system; (5) a nutrition education program will be provided for children, parents, school personnel, and others, again based on the findings of the assessment system; (6) preventive and

TABLE 22-3 Federal expenditures (in millions) and participants (in millions), USDA-supported nutrition programs, 1970, 1980, and 1986

Program	1970	1980	1986
Food stamps			
Participants	4.3	21.1	19.4
Federal expenditures	$550	$8,761	$10,605
School lunch			
Participants	22.4	26.6	23.7
Federal expenditures	$300	$2,279	$2,714
School breakfast			
Participants	0.5	3.6	3.5
Federal expenditures	$11	$288	$406
WIC			
Participants	NA	2	3.5
Federal expenditures	NA	$603	$1,304
Elderly			
Meals served	NA	166	228
Federal expenditures	NA	$75	$137

From US Bureau of the Census: Statistical Abstracts of the United States, 1988, Washington, DC, 1988, US Government Printing Office.

TABLE 22-4 1990 nutrition objectives for the nation

Objective	Status
By 1990, the proportion of pregnant women with iron deficiency anemia (as estimated by hemoglobin concentrations early in pregnancy) should be reduced to 3.5%.	Data not available in sufficient detail. In 1983, low hemoglobin values were reported in as many as 17.3% of pregnancies in a limited sample of low-income pregnant women.
By 1990, growth retardation of infants and children caused by inadequate diets should have been eliminated in the United States as a public health problem.	Modest progress made. Unlikely that objective will be attained. Growth retardation remains at levels ranging from 10.9% to 23.6% in a selective group of low-income children.
By 1990, the prevalence of significant overweight (120% of "desired" weight) among the U.S. adult population should be decreased to 10% of men and 17% of women, without nutritional impairment.	Little reduction in overweight between 1971 and 1980. Unlikely that the objective will be attained. Good current data not available.
By 1990, 50% of the overweight population should have adopted weight loss regimens, combining an appropriate balance of diet and physical activity.	No baseline data are available. Considerable interest and awareness but little progress.
By 1990, the mean serum cholesterol level in the adult population 18 to 74 years of age should be at or below 200 milligrams per deciliter.	Level has dropped to about 211 milligrams for men and 215 for women, but it is not certain that the objective can be attained.
By 1990, the mean serum cholesterol level in children aged 1 to 14 should be at or below 150 milligrams per deciliter.	Data insufficient.
By 1990, the average daily sodium ingestion (as measured by excretion) for adults should be reduced to at least the 3 to 6 gram range.	Some evidence is encouraging, but good data are not available.
By 1990, the proportion of women who breast-feed their babies should be increased to 75% at hospital discharge and 21% 6 months later.	There has been a rapid increase in breast-feeding. This objective may be attained.
By 1990, the proportion of the population that is able to correctly associate the principal dietary factors known or strongly suspected to be related to disease should exceed 75% for each of the following diseases: heart disease, high blood pressure, dental caries, and cancer.	Likely that the objective can be attained.
By 1990, 70% of adults should be able to identify the major foods that are low in fat content, low in sodium content, high in calories, high in sugars, and good sources of fiber.	Progress has been made, but data are insufficient to indicate whether the objective can be attained.
By 1990, 90% of adults should understand that to lose weight people must either consume fewer calories or increase physical activity or both.	Likely that this objective will be met.
By 1990, the labels of all packaged foods should contain useful calorie and nutrient information to enable consumers to select diets that promote and protect good health. Similar information should be displayed where nonpackaged foods are obtained or purchased.	There is improvement, but it is unlikely that this objective will be attained.
By 1990, sodium levels in processed food should be reduced by 20% from present levels.	Baseline and current data not available.
By 1990, the proportion of employee and school cafeteria managers who are aware of and actively promoting U.S. Department of Agriculture and Department of Health and Human Services guidelines should be greater than 50%.	Data not available.
By 1990, all states should include nutrition education as part of required comprehensive school health education at the elementary and secondary levels.	By 1985, 12 states had attained this objective.
By 1990, virtually all routine health contacts with health professionals should include some element of nutrition education and nutrition counseling.	Data not available.
Before 1990, a comprehensive national nutrition status monitoring system should have the capability of detecting nutritional problems in special population groups and for obtaining baseline data for decisions on national nutrition policies.	The legislation was introduced and passed by Congress, but it was vetoed by President Reagan in 1988.

remedial nutrition assistance will be provided to pregnant women, breast-feeding women, and women of childbearing age; and (7) the adult and elderly populations will receive indicated preventive and remedial nutrition assistance, based on the findings of the assessment system.

The objectives for the nation and the model standards can be debated. Experts in nutrition, economists, public health officials, and elected policymakers may argue about the relative merits or the costs and benefits of particular measures. Taken as a whole, they are certainly not an unreasonable set of objectives, however. It is also clear that the policies and the resources needed to attain the objectives are not now available.

Winikoff[44] has written a thoughtful comparison of attempts to develop a policy on food and nutrition in Norway and in the United States. The Norwegian government produced a white paper that combined goals (which were very similar to those developed by the U.S. Senate Select Committee on Nutrition and Human Needs[45]) with a national policy on attainment. Implementation of the policies would involve interference with agricultural practices, manufacturing, processing, distribution, and even the purchase and use of foods. The goals and policies were developed by the Ministry of Agriculture and had the support of the government. By contrast, goals for the United States were developed by a Senate committee and never ratified by Congress or adopted by the President. The Senate Select Committee's goals are excellent. They call for reducing our fat intake from 42% of our total calories to 30%, for increasing carbohydrate intake from the present level of 46% of total calories to 58% with the complex carbohydrates increasing to 40% of the total and sugar declining to 15%, and for a concomitant reduction in cholesterol and salt intake. The balance of calories, 12%, should continue to come from protein. These goals were supported by the American Public Health Association but not by Congress, the President, nor, at the time, the U.S. Department of Health, Education and Welfare, or the U.S. Department of Agriculture.

The American Heart Association modified its dietary guidelines in 1986. It called for a cholesterol intake of no more than 100 milligrams per 1,000 calories, not to exceed 300 milligrams per day. (A single egg yoke contains 250 to 275 milligrams of cholesterol.) It also called for a limitation on sodium, principally by salt restriction, a limitation on alcohol to 1.5 ounces per day, protein to represent 15% of daily calories, saturated fat less than 10%, and carbohydrates, especially complex carbohydrates, to represent 50% to 55% of total calories.

There is a deep-seated fear of the use of law to try to influence consumption practices in the United States. Actually, it may be more of a notion that is turned into a fear by the unflagging efforts of the food industry, in much the same way that other special interest groups have been able to turn certain notions into catch phrases to effectively prevent the nation from considering an enlightened and progressive policy. The fact that special interest groups have been able to use legislation to influence purchasing and consumption habits goes unnoticed. Medicare and Medicaid restrictions on who can participate in the programs and how, federal subsidies for tobacco growers, and special interest group legislation dealing with virtually every edible product make it obvious that the power of law is often used to influence behavior and restrict freedom on a broad scale. The use of these same procedures to create and implement a healthful policy for food and nutrition must apparently await another time and other leaders.

REFERENCES

1. Ule O: Food and the development of man (translated from the German by J Fitzgerald, from Die Natur, 1851), Pop Sci Month 5:591, 1874.
2. McKeown T: The modern rise of population, New York, 1987, Academic Press.
3. Magee HE: Application of nutrition to public health, some lessons from the war, Br Med J 1:475, March 1946.
4. Jelliffe DB: The assessment of the nutritional status of the community, WHO Monogr Ser No 53, Geneva, 1966, World Health Organization.
5. Third World Food Survey, FFHC Basic Study No 11, Rome, 1963, Food and Agriculture Organization.
6. Scrimshaw NS and Gordon JE, editors: Malnutrition, learning and behavior, Cambridge, MA, 1968, Massachusetts Institute of Technology.
7. Birch HG: Malnutrition, learning and intelligence, Am J Public Health 62:773, June 1972.
8. Wolstenholm G and O'Connor M, editors: Health of mankind, Boston, 1967, Little, Brown & Co.
9. Scrimshaw NS: Through a glass darkly: discerning the practical implications of human dietary protein–energy relationships, Nutr Rev 35:321, Dec 1977.

10. President's Science Advisory Commission: The World food problem: report of panel on the world food supply, Washington, DC, 1967, US Government Printing Office.
11. Merrill MH: Meeting the challenges of the coming decades—the role of medicine in nutrition. Talk given at the Western Hemisphere Nutrition Conference, Chicago, Nov 1965.
12. US Bureau of the Census: Statistical abstracts of the United States, 1981, Tables 208, 209, Washington, DC, 1981, US Department of Commerce.
13. Brewster L and Jacobs MF: Our changing food habits. In Wright HS and Sims LS, editors: Community nutrition: people, policies, and programs, Belmont, CA, 1981, Wadsworth Health Sciences Division.
14. Food and Nutrition Board: What is America eating? proceedings of a symposium, Washington, DC, 1986, National Academy Press.
15. Committee on Dietary Allowances, Food and Nutrition Board: Recommended dietary allowances, ed 9 (revised), Washington, DC, 1980, National Academy of Sciences.
16. Hegsted DM: On dietary standards, Nutr Rev 36:33, Feb 1978.
17. Schorr AL: Poor kids, New York, 1966, Basic Books, Inc.
18. Currents in public health, vol 5, No 2, Ross Laboratories, Feb 1965.
19. Hunger U.S.A.: a report of the Citizen's Board of Inquiry into Hunger and Malnutrition in the United States, Washington, DC, 1968, New Community Press.
20. Todhunter EN: Child feeding problems and the school lunch program, J Am Diet Assoc 24:422, May 1948.
21. Coates TJ, Jeffrey RW, and Slinkard LA: Heart, healthy eating, and exercise: introducing and maintaining changes in health and behavior, Am J Public Health 71:15, Jan 1981.
22. Glanz K and Morris NM: Cafeteria nutrition education for university students: an evaluation study. Paper presented to the annual meeting of the School Health Section, American Public Health Association, Los Angeles, Nov 1981.
23. Rush D and others: The national WIC evaluation: evaluation of the special supplemental food program for women, infants and children, Am J Clin Nutr 48(suppl 2), Aug 1988.
24. Committee on Maternal Nutrition, Food and Nutrition Board, National Research Council: Maternal nutrition and the course of pregnancy, Washington, DC, 1970, National Academy of Sciences.
25. Nutrition Committee of the Canadian Pediatric Society and the Committee on Nutrition of the American Academy of Pediatrics: Breast feeding: a commentary in celebration of the International Year of the Child, 1979, Pedes 62:591, Oct 1978.
26. Select Panel for the Promotion of Child Health: Better health for our children: a national strategy, Pub No (PHS) 79-55071, vol 1, Washington, DC, 1981, US Department of Health and Human Services.
27. Pollitt E, Gersovitz M, and Gargiulo M: Educational benefits of the United States school feeding program: a critical review of the literature, Am J Public Health 68:477, May 1978.
28. Podell RN and others: Evaluation of the effectiveness of a high school course in cardiovascular nutrition, Am J Public Health 68:573, June 1978.
29. National Institute for Arthritis, Digestive Diseases and Kidney: Health implications of obesity: consensus development conference statement, Bethesda, MD, Feb 11-13, 1985, National Institutes of Health.
30. Bray GA, editor: Obesity in America, US Department of Health, Education and Welfare Pub No (NIH) 79-359, Bethesda, MD, Nov 1979.
31. National Public Health Program Reporting System: Public health agencies, 1980, Washington, DC, Aug 1981, Association of State and Territorial Health Officials.
32. Kaufman M and others: Progress toward meeting the 1990 nutrition objectives for the nation: nutrition services and data collection for state/territorial health agencies, Am J Public Health 77:299, March 1987.
33. Bureau of Health Professions: Public health personnel in the United States, 1980, US Department of Health and Human Services Pub No (HRA)82-6, Jan 1982.
34. Highlights: ten-state nutrition survey, 1968-1969, US Department of Health, Education and Welfare Pub No (HSM)72-8134, Washington, DC, 1972.
35. US Public Health Service: Forward plan for health, 1978-1982, Washington, DC, 1976.
36. National Center for Health Statistics: Caloric and selected nutrient values for persons 1-74 years of age: first health and nutrition examination survey, United States, 1971-1974, US Department of Health, Education and Welfare Pub No (PHS)79-1657, Hyattsville, MD, June 1979.
37. Christakis G: Community assessment of nutritional status. In Wright HS and Sims LS, editors: Community nutrition: people, policies and programs, Belmont, CA, 1981, Wadsworth Health Sciences Division.
38. Centers for Disease Control: Nutrition surveillance, US Department of Health and Human Services (periodical).
39. Physicians Task Force on Hunger in America: Hunger counties 1986: the distribution of America's high risk counties, Boston, 1986, Harvard School of Public Health.

40. California Conference of Local Health Department Nutritionists: Guidelines for nutrition services in local health jurisdictions, June 1980, Sacramento, CA, Sept 1981, Health and Welfare Agency.
41. Owen AY and Frankle RT: Nutrition in the community: the art of delivering services, St Louis, 1986, Times Mirror/Mosby College Publishing.
42. Office of Disease Prevention and Health Promotion: The 1990 health objectives for the nation: a midcourse review, Washington, DC, 1986, US Department of Health and Human Services.
43. American Public Health Association, Association of State and Territorial Health Officials, National Association of County Health Officials, United States Conference of Local Health Officials, and Centers for Disease Control of the US Public Health Service: Model standards: a guide for community preventive health services, Washington, DC, 1985, American Public Health Association.
44. Winikoff B: Nutrition and food policy: the approaches of Norway and the United States, Am J Public Health 67:552, June 1977.
45. Report of the US Senate Select Committee on Nutrition and Human Needs: Dietary goals for the United States, Pub No 052-070-03913-2, Washington, DC, 1977, US Government Printing Office.

PART SIX

Health and human development

In building a public health program, as with so many other things, the best place to start is at the beginning. Life is a continuous spiral with a myriad of interlocking biologic, environmental, and circumstantial factors blending to determine genesis. That event in turn brings to bear a new panoply of factors over which the life that has been brought about has absolutely no control—the characteristics of the bearing mother, her socioeconomic circumstances in the broadest connotations, her habits, mental condition, and state of nutrition. Then, when the cord is cut, the still helpless and dependent baby has need for physical and mental care and comfort through a long period of maturation, learning, and development. Childhood can and should be a time of joy and happiness, but biologically it is also a time of preparation for adulthood. It is a period of incredible versatility and vulnerability.

Living begins at birth. So, in a sense, does aging. From childhood to adolescence, from young adult to senior citizen, humans change and evolve, shucking off old problems for new ones and reaping the harvest or the bitter fruits of past practices, the environment, and the pool of genes. The middle and last thirds of life are important to those who live them and to public health workers. These phases and transitions are considered in the following chapters on maternal, child, preschool, school-aged, adolescent, and maturing health problems and opportunities.

CHAPTER 23

Maternal and child health

A CRITICAL PERIOD

The field of public health is concerned with the well-being of all people, regardless of age, sex, race, or other characteristics. Traditionally, however, there have been two groups to whom special attention has been given: pregnant women and young children, particularly infants. There are sound reasons for this. Special attention to a pregnant woman brings double health benefits: first, to her as an adult member of society and second, to the child born of her pregnancy. Other reasons are that pregnancy is a period of particular physical stress during which the woman may face unusual risk. Undesirable influences during the prenatal period may jeopardize the health of both the mother and the expected infant. Short of fatalities, these effects may result in health and economic disadvantages for the woman and child and even for the rest of the family if the mother's health is permanently impaired.

Remarkable progress has been made in many parts of the world in protecting the lives of expectant mothers and their infants. In the United States during the last 50 years, maternal mortality declined about 99% and infant mortality about 89%. This may be attributed to many factors, of which public health progress is only one. Hospital and medical standards have improved, as have nutrition and the general standard of living. Many new preventive and therapeutic agents and techniques have been introduced. Almost every aspect of public health has had an effect on the health and welfare of expectant mothers, infants, and young children. In undeveloped areas, the institution of an effective program of environmental sanitation involving the purification of water, the sanitation of milk and food, and the promotion of satisfactory facilities for the disposal of human wastes will show its first effects in a reduction in infant morbidity and mortality. Vital statistics are involved in the maternal and child health program in various ways, especially by pinpointing specific problem areas. The public health laboratory is an essential tool, particularly in prenatal management where tests must be performed to detect blood incompatibilities between mother and child, inborn metabolic disorders of the fetus, diabetes, infection with the human immunodeficiency virus (HIV), and other problems that increase the risk of pregnancy. Throughout the antenatal, natal, and postnatal period there must be a strong thread of health education. The expectant mother must be constantly protected against communicable diseases, particularly those of a viral, streptococcal, and influenzal nature; the use of many hazardous substances, including alcohol and tobacco, must be restricted; and early attempts must be made to protect the newborn child against gonorrheal ophthalmia, whooping cough, diphtheria, measles, and other communicable diseases, as well as genetic disorders. It is obvious therefore that the maternal and child health program cannot be considered by itself.

BACKGROUND OF MATERNAL AND CHILD HEALTH PROGRAMS

The development of maternal and child health programs has been discussed in Chapters 2 and 6. Some additional background will be presented here.*

The opening of the first milk station in 1893 in New York City to combat the tremendous incidence of summer diarrhea in infants and children of the underprivileged by providing them with safe milk during the summer heat was a significant event. Observance of the benefits that resulted from this meager start led to the establishment of numerous infant welfare societies designed to bring medical and nursing knowledge and care to

* For a short history, see Schmidt W: The development of health services for mothers and children in the United States, Am J Public Health 63:419, May 1973.

those in need. In 1908 the New York City Association for Improving the Condition of the Poor, in conjunction with the New York Outdoor Clinic, began to provide prenatal care for expectant mothers in the lower income groups. Simultaneously a Bureau of Child Hygiene was established in the New York City Health Department. These two moves were subsequently duplicated by many other communities throughout the nation. In 1909 a conference on the prevention of infant mortality was held by the American Academy of Medicine. This was followed the same year by the first White House Conference on Children and Youth, called by President Theodore Roosevelt. Its purpose was to discuss what might be done at the federal level to stimulate and help finance state and local health and social welfare programs for children. It resulted in several legislative proposals, one of which was signed into law in 1912 by President Taft to establish the Children's Bureau. Its initial charge was limited—essentially to conduct studies and report—but on this modest base astute leadership was able over the years to develop a broad program of far-reaching significance.

Another development of significance at about the same time was the formation of the American Association for the Study and Prevention of Infant Mortality. This group was composed of pediatricians, infant welfare nurses (who in a sense were the precursors of the present-day public health nurses), social workers, public health officials, and other interested persons. The organization was the beginning of what in 1923 became the American Child Health Association, which provided effective leadership until the time of its disbandment in 1935. The growing interest in child health and welfare commanded national attention that resulted in passage of the Sheppard-Towner Act. This provided the beginning of a federal grant-in-aid program to encourage and enable states to develop programs in maternal and infant care. The act functioned only from 1922 to 1929, but its goals and principles were subsequently influential in the broad national consideration of maternal and child health problems in the Social Security Act, which was approved in August 1935. The struggle to renew and continue the Sheppard-Towner Act pitted conservative against liberal forces in Congress. The American Medical Association was opposed to the legislation, and a group of pediatricians split off from the AMA to form the American Academy of Pediatrics, a group that has continued to make substantial contributions to the improvement of child welfare programs.

In 1963, recognizing that about 3% of babies born were mentally retarded and that much of this problem was attributable to inadequate maternal and infant care, Congress passed the Maternal and Child Health and Mental Retardation Planning Amendments. This made possible the start of a 5-year, $265 million program to improve maternal and child health services, especially for high-risk prospective mothers who face or are likely to face conditions hazardous to themselves or to their infants during pregnancy. Particular emphasis was placed on those who otherwise would not receive care because of low income or for other reasons beyond their control. The act also provided grants to states to plan comprehensive programs to combat mental retardation.

For health, 1965 was a banner year. The nation, through its Congress and the President, entered into an unprecedented assault on its health problems.[1] More progressive health legislation was passed during that year than at any time previously. The single most significant public health measure passed was the Social Security Amendments Act of 1965 (P.L. 89-97), which modified Title V of the act (the Maternal and Child Health and Crippled Children's Services) and added Title XVIII (Medicare) and Title XIX (Medicaid) to provide payment for health services to the elderly and the poor respectively. (See Chapter 31.) The Medicaid program has become the largest government program (more than $9.9 billion by 1986) for the provision of health services to mothers and children. It was not a service delivery program initially but a federally supported, state-managed vendor payment system that paid for medical services provided to children in families meeting the low-income requirements of the program in that state. If one child is eligible, the mother and other children become eligible as well. The Medicaid act was amended later to require early and periodic screening, diagnosis, and treatment (EPSDT) for all low-income children. This latter program was never successfully implemented because of confusion about objectives and methods and the responsibilities of different government agencies,[2] but it signaled the interest of Congress in addressing the health needs of virtually all children in the United States.

In a series of amendments during the 1980s, the Medicaid program was separated from its historic welfare ties. Congress allowed states to provide Medicaid coverage for women and children in families that had income as much as double the federal poverty level. Previously, only families who qualified for Aid to Families with Dependent Children (AFDC) because of their indigency were eligible for Medicaid. The change officially recognized the concept of *medical* indigency: a situation that occurs when someone is presumed to have enough money to pay for the expected routine costs of food, shelter, and clothing but does not have enough money to pay for the unexpected costs of medical care. In addition, Congress allowed states to develop experimental programs to support the delivery of a broader array of social services and counseling. By 1988, the Medicaid program had been altered in such a way that the states could begin considering providing perinatal health care services to all of their citizens. Congressional concern for child health had, even during the Reagan administration, resulted in a fundamental shift in health care policy.

Another event of considerable significance to maternal and child health was passage of the Economic Opportunity Act of 1964 (P.L. 88-452). Through the provision relating to the Head Start program, medical and dental examinations and in some cases treatment and nutritional services were provided to economically disadvantaged preschool children.

P.L. 93-53 amended Title V of the Social Security Act in 1973 by essentially transferring responsibility for the development of maternal and child health programs to the states. The competitive project grants were to be discontinued, and the money was to be allocated to the states as part of a formula grant program with each state receiving a share of the appropriated funds. Each state was supposed to develop a "program of projects" and a Maternal and Child Health Services Plan. The program had to include maternity and infant care, family planning services, infant intensive care, health services for children and youth, and dental care. By fiscal year 1986, state health agencies reported spending $2.5 billion on maternal and child health programs and more on other related services that were not organizationally a part of their maternal and child health programs, such as dental health, immunization programs, and others.[3] In 1980, the total expenditure by those same agencies for maternal and child health programs was $1.234 billion. Note that the source of this information, the Public Health Foundation, includes only expenditures for public health made by state public health agencies (and to a lesser extent, local health departments). It does not include the far larger sums spent by the state Medicaid programs, nor does it include the expenditures for child health of most state mental health agencies, state social service programs, and the state education authority.

Of the total amount reported for maternal and child health services in 1986 (the $2.5 billion), $1.96 billion came from federal sources:

- $286 million from the Maternal and Child Health block grant
- $87 million from family planning appropriations (Title X of the Public Health Service Act)
- $1.53 billion from the U.S. Department of Agriculture for the Supplemental Nutrition Program for Women, Infants and Children
- $52 million from other federal sources

The picture that emerges from the information presented in Table 23-1 is that the WIC program and state support for maternal and child health have been increasing at an annual rate of 13%, whereas federal block grants and family planning support have increased at rates of just 3% and 4% respectively, considerably less than the rising need and inflation combined. The WIC program (see Chapter 22) does not provide a significant amount of services. It is primarily a form of income transfer in that it increases the supply of food for the family.

There are no current figures on total public sector expenditures for maternal and child health. Budetti, Butler, and McManus,[4] in 1978, estimated the per capita expenditure for child health to be $82. Compare this to $218 for those aged 19 to 64 and $1,280 for those aged 65 or more. The available evidence indicates that, whatever the actual amounts are, the gap has widened, as both medical care costs and long-term care expenditures for the elderly have increased rapidly.

If the WIC program (which is virtually 100% federally funded) is excluded from the calculations, state and local expenditures were about 56% of the total, an increase from 50% in 1980. Although the amounts seem large in absolute terms, many experts contend that they are relatively small compared to need.

Title V of the Social Security Act was meant to stimulate state programs for maternal and child health, and the substantial level of effort by the states suggests that this objective was attained. About 46% of the $5.5 billion spent for personal health service programs by the states and local health agencies in 1986 was for maternal and child health programs. State appropriations for maternal and child health services increased very slowly until the federal grant programs were reduced, beginning in 1981. Federal support was so strong, and matching requirements were so slight, that paper increases in state support were obtained by identifying existing state services and including them in the state maternal and child health plan. When the block grants resulted in a decrease in federal funds, the states began to increase appropriations for necessary services.

The Medicaid program was more successful than the Maternal and Child Health program in stimulating an increase in state funding for health services, but this was for payments to physicians, hospitals, and other private health service providers. Those groups were the primary lobbyists for increases in state appropriations. The intended recipients of both Maternal and Child Health (Title V) and Medicaid (Title XIX) services were either left out of the discussions at the state level or ineffective as lobbyists. Individual groups, such as the Parents of Autistic Children or the Parents of Children with Cerebral Palsy, were effective in obtaining state support for specific programs, but the concept of child health was too general to elicit vigorous and successful support until the problems became more severe. Public health workers concentrate on Title V programs in their planning, programming, budgeting, and legislative activities, since the state health agency is the single state authority for all Maternal and Child Health programs and almost all Crippled Children's Services Programs. Nevertheless, expenditures by state health agencies for maternal and child health (excluding the large WIC program) are only one-tenth those made by the state Medicaid programs for families with dependent children. If other state expenditures for maternal and child health could be measured (mental health, social services, education programs, and so forth), the relative size of the public health effort would be even less.

The significance of the role that can be played by state health agencies should not be underestimated, however. Medicaid funds were originally appropriated for a system of vendor payments and could not be used to alter or develop needed programs. Other funding sources have similar restrictions, which make innovation difficult. The state health agencies generally have much more freedom to use available funds in a creative manner and can often influence the expenditure and programmatic policies of other state and local agencies, as well as the private sector.

In 1978, Congress authorized the establishment of a Select Panel for the Promotion of Child Health. There was considerable concern about the repeated assertions that the United States still experienced an unnecessarily high infant mortality rate in spite of its investments in research and services, and Congress, as well as experts in maternal and child health, believed that the federal and state agencies responsible for providing or developing services were poorly coordinated and linked. In addition, maternal and child health leaders in the federal government and in the states were dissatisfied with the reduction in status of the remains of the Children's Bureau, which had dropped from bu-

TABLE 23-1 State expenditures for maternal and child health programs, 1981 and 1986, by source of funds

Source of increase	1981	1986	Annual rate (percent)
Federal	$1,170	$1,959	11
WIC	845	1,535	13
MCH block grant	240	286	4
Family planning	75	87	3
State	249	462	13
Other	73	102	7
TOTALS	$1,492	$2,523	11

From Association of State and Territorial Health Officials: Public health agencies, 1981: a report on their expenditures and activities, Washington, DC, 1983, The Association; Public Health Foundation: Public health agencies, 1988: an inventory of programs and block grant expenditures, Washington, DC, 1988, The Foundation.

reau status just below a Secretary to office status in the Bureau of Community Health Services, which reported to the Health Services Administration, which reported in turn to the Office of the Assistant Secretary for Health.

The Select Panel, chaired by Lisbeth Bamberger Schorr, concluded its 2-year effort in December 1980 with a four-volume report to the Secretary[5] that, together with *Maternal and Child Health Practices,*[6] serves as the principal text for students of the subject. The report of the Select Panel verified the concerns of its sponsors and called for stronger, more centralized federal leadership.

The Select Panel found that the organizational, administrative, fiscal, and training aspects of the current system of health care had not kept pace with changing needs, technology, and epidemiologic research. They proposed that more attention be given to the prevention of disease and injury through environmental programs, concentration on the relationships between behavior and health, and improved nutrition. The panel members reached a consensus that three broad classes of services were so essential that unfettered access to them should be guaranteed to all citizens:

- Prenatal, delivery, and postnatal care
- Comprehensive health care for children from birth through age 5
- Family planning services

Predictably, the Select Panel urged that the Children's Bureau be reconstituted as a new Maternal and Child Health Administration within the Public Health Service and that its reporting channel to the Secretary of the Department of Health and Human Services be shortened from four to three or even two steps. The Select Panel decided not to recommend that Medicaid, EPSDT, or the WIC program be transferred to the new Maternal and Child Health Administration but did recommend that the states be urged to consolidate their functions under the control of a single state agency. This disparity probably resulted from the proximity of the Select Panel to the federal agency program managers, who played a significant role in organizing the work of the panel, and its relative isolation from the organizational relationships of the state agencies.

THE PROBLEMS

Many of the problems that plagued maternal and child health 50 years ago have been stripped away by improvements in the standard of living generally and in health care particularly, leaving a central core of problems that are more difficult to correct. They are related more to education and the distribution of resources than to medical care or specific public health practices.

A substantial proportion of the nation's children move through puberty to adolescence without either the intellectual and emotional ability or the environmental support needed to achieve and maintain an effective family structure. Approximately 1 million teenagers become pregnant each year. Many have abortions. For pregnant teenage girls, there are nearly as many abortions as there are live births. Even though abortion is legal, many pregnant adolescents find it difficult to obtain needed medical care, since Congress has prohibited the use of federal funds for such purposes. Many of the girls do not know about or use effective contraceptive techniques, and most of them do not have ready access to a source of continuing health care.

Alcohol, tobacco, and drug abuse have a pronounced impact on the outcome of pregnancy, reducing the birth weight and increasing the infant mortality rate.[7] Substance abuse is more common in adolescent pregnancies than in those of older women, and it seems likely that adolescent girls are less willing or able to change those practices during pregnancy. Statistically, teenagers are a high-risk group, but studies have shown that the risk is not inherent in the biologic age of the mother (except for those under the age of 14) but rather in her education, behavior, and socioeconomic status.[8]

Other toxic influences in the preconceptual and prepartum periods reside in the environment.[9,10] Many workplaces expose both men and women to chemical and physical hazards that can have an impact on the development of sperm and ova: dry-cleaning establishments, electronics industries, laboratories, chemical plants, and paint manufacturers, to mention a few. The harm is often done in the first few weeks of pregnancy, before the woman knows she is pregnant. Men also are affected and may have damaged sperm or a lower sperm count as a result of toxic exposures. Some plants have attempted to exclude women from areas where such exposures may occur rather than alter the environment. Unless evidence exists to the contrary, it is prudent to assume that if a chemical or other hazard can harm a developing fetus, it can harm spermatozoa as well.

The hazards faced during a pregnancy have changed substantially in the last 50 years. Although the risk of environmental harm has increased, most other factors have improved, including the general state of nutrition and the standard of living. Problems exist in the organization and availability of services. Maternal mortality was 67.3 deaths per 10,000 live births in 1930 but declined to less than 1 by 1986. There is still a pronounced racial difference, the rate for white women being 0.49 per 10,000 live births, whereas the rate for nonwhite women is 1.9. These differences in the rates of maternal deaths by race are also reflected in variations among the states, with higher rates occurring in the south. There is no reason to believe that true racial or geographic differences naturally exist.

Before World War II, most black mothers delivered at home, and nearly half did not have adequate medical care (Table 23-2). Falk, Rorem, and Ring,[11] writing for the Committee on the Costs of Medical Care in 1929, said that 30% or more of the births in the southern states were attended by midwives who were "often ignorant, untrained, dirty and superstitious." The Committee went on to point out that with proper supervision and backup, even the midwives of 50 years ago could provide a valuable service, and the situation has changed dramatically since then. Overall in the nation, by 1986, not only did almost all white births (98.9%) occur in hospitals, but the proportion of black births in hospitals rose from 31.5% in 1943 to 99.4% in 1979, and medically attended black births rose from 55.9% to 96%. Recently there has been a slight trend toward home deliveries and deliveries in nonhospital-based birthing centers, partly as a choice based on life-style and partly because of the high cost of delivery in general hospitals. The American College of Obstetricians and Gynecologists has opposed such practices, and official vital statistics reports indicate a higher incidence of complications in out-of-hospital deliveries, including a higher neonatal death rate (deaths occurring in the first 28 days of life), but the figures include accidental and poorly planned out-of-hospital births along with planned and attended births. With careful risk assessment (see "Approach to the Problem" below) and a well-trained attendant, the available evidence suggests that the outcomes for home deliveries may be as good as they are in a hospital environment. Oregon, which has a higher rate of out-of-hospital births than most states, has published standards for home births.[12]

The striking reductions in maternal mortality that have occurred, particularly during the last 30 years, are because of improved medical care in preventing and treating infection and better management of shock with intravenous fluids and blood. For many years, small babies were considered to be better than large ones, since they were presumed to have a less difficult transit through the birth canal, and physicians sought to keep maternal weight gain below 15 pounds. Nutritionists knew that the restrictive diet practices were causing, not preventing, problems, and as physicians have become more cognizant of the information, weight gains of 25 pounds or more have become the norm, with much better results.

Whether pregnancy should be treated as a natural process or as a medical problem has become an increasingly important argument. As shown in Table 23-2, efforts to improve the environment in which delivery occurs and the qualifications of the attendants at birth have succeeded dramatically, and the statistics indicate that there has been a parallel improvement in the outcomes. However, in recent years many have advocated the return of the

TABLE 23-2 Births by race, location, and type of attendant, United States, 1943 and 1986

		Location		Attendant	
Race	Year	Hospital (%)	Elsewhere (%)	Physician (%)	Other (%)
White	1943	77.2	22.8	97.8	2.2
	1986	98.9	1.1	96.5	3.5
Nonwhite	1943	31.5	68.5	55.9	44.1
	1986	99.4	0.6	96.0	4.0

birthing process to a more natural, homelike environment with family involvement. Repeated studies have shown that a very high proportion of births involve the use of anesthesia, forceps to extract the baby, and induction of labor. In 1986, 24.1% of births were by cesarean section, and a disproportionate number of births occurred on weekdays, as opposed to weekends and holidays.[13]

Electronic monitoring of the fetus is becoming an increasingly common practice, and many believe that this results in still more interventions. Increasingly, births are being managed as elective medical procedures in a high-technology environment that is very costly and, some believe, unnecessarily risky for most of the families involved.

Advocates of "demedicalizing" maternity point out that 70% of all pregnancies are perfectly normal, with no known risk factors that might serve to complicate the process. As long as medical backup is promptly accessible, most of these births could occur in a less intense environment with less risk, fewer interventions, and considerably less cost.

Abortion

Most maternal deaths from abortion in earlier years were caused by illegal abortions induced either by unqualified individuals or by women themselves, usually under extremely unsatisfactory and unsanitary conditions. This resulted in its recognition as an important social and public health problem. During the 1960s and early 1970s, an increasing number of nations liberalized their laws with regard to medically induced abortion.[14] Several states in the United States revised their laws to allow induced abortion under medically acceptable circumstances. The Public Health Service established an Abortion Surveillance Program in 1968 in cooperation with state and local health departments, which were encouraged and assisted to develop abortion reporting systems. The purpose was to be able to observe and study changes in fertility as well as maternal morbidity and mortality.

Meanwhile, many professional and other organizations passed strong resolutions endorsing the trend. This long-overdue movement culminated in a landmark decision by the United States Supreme Court in January 1973.* The court did not remove restrictions entirely. For the first 3 months of pregnancy, it said, the decision rests with the woman and her physician—a "right of privacy" with which the state cannot interfere. For the next 6 months, states may "regulate the abortion procedures in ways reasonably related to maternal health," such as licensing and regulating the persons and facilities involved. For the last 10 weeks of pregnancy, when the fetus "has the capability of meaningful life outside the mother's womb, states may prohibit abortion except as it may be indicated to preserve the life or health of the mother." The Supreme Court stressed that the ruling did not give a woman the right to abortion on demand, nor could a physician (or presumably a hospital) be required to perform an abortion.

Reports from various countries indicate that the risk from induced abortion under proper circumstances, and especially during the first trimester of pregnancy, is extremely low. There were only 51 deaths caused by abortions in the United States in 1986, and several of these were spontaneous rather than planned abortions. The reported ratio of induced abortions in 1983 was 348.7 per 1,000 live births. The ratio for whites is lower than for blacks (302 versus 497) and higher for unmarried women (1,308 versus 90).[15]

In recent years, some groups have succeeded in reinstituting barriers to abortion, particularly for low-income women, by obtaining congressional interdictions of the use of any federal funds for abortion purposes. This includes counseling by professional staff in a clinic that is only partially funded by federal money. The tactics of committed single-interest groups are frequently effective, even though the majority of Americans favor broader access to needed abortion services. It is not clear what the effect of restricting access will be on maternal and child health. The impact of expanded access to abortion services on maternal and child health has been beneficial.[16]

Infant mortality

As would be expected, the factors involved in the problem of infant mortality and the improvements that have been made closely parallel those described for the mothers of the infants. Although there is cause for satisfaction in the reduction in infant mortality, much remains to be accomplished. The nation still suffers a loss of about 39,000 infants each year. In 1986 this resulted in an infant

* *Roe v Wade* 41 USLW 4213, 1973; *Dow v Bolton* 41 USLW 4233, 1973.

mortality of 10.4 per 1,000 live births. Between 1915 and 1949, infant mortality dropped dramatically from 100 to 28 per 1,000 live births. Then the rate of decrease slowed noticeably. With a revamped and bolstered federal grant-in-aid program in the mid-1960s, the pace of progress accelerated again, and between 1965 and 1981, the infant mortality rate declined 50%. In 1981, federal government support began to dwindle: the administration consolidated the maternal and child health grants into a single block grant and reduced the amount of money available; the Medicaid program was cut; rapid increases in medical care prices caused more and more companies to reduce employee health benefits; and the growing number of people working in marginal jobs without any health insurance benefits further increased the number of people with access problems. To the dismay of many (but not to the surprise of public health workers), the decline in the infant mortality rate virtually stopped, and in some cities the rate increased (Table 23-3).

In almost all regions of the country, the rate for black infants is double the rate for white infants. Although both the white and the black infant mortality rates have been declining, the disparity has not diminished appreciably. Again, as in the case of adult women, there is no convincing evidence that the nonwhite infant is intrinsically less viable than infants born to white mothers.

The infant mortality rate can be partitioned into a neonatal mortality rate (the first 28 days of life) and a postneonatal rate, from the twenty-eighth day to the end of the first year. In 1986 the national rates were 7.0 and 3.4 per 1,000 live births respectively. A higher neonatal death rate suggests inadequate access to delivery services; a higher postneonatal death rate indicates the existence of environmental problems in the home and a lack of access to child care services.

TABLE 23-3 United States infant mortality rates, 1980-1986, for whites and blacks

Year	White	Black	Total
1980	11.0	21.4	12.6
1981	10.5	20.0	11.9
1982	10.1	19.6	11.5
1983	9.7	19.2	11.2
1984	9.4	18.4	10.8
1985	9.3	18.2	10.6
1986	8.9	18.0	10.4

From Annual editions of vital statistics of the United States, vol II, mortality, part A, Washington, DC, US Government Printing Office.

In one sense, infant deaths are most commonly caused by congenital anomalies, respiratory distress, the sudden infant death syndrome, and premature delivery. Underlying all other causes, however, is low birth weight, and underlying low birth weight is poverty. The dividing line is 2,500 grams, although there is some evidence that low birth weight in black infants may begin at 2,250 grams. The infant mortality rates within each weight-specific group in the United States are better than those of most other countries, and the rates have improved within each weight group over the past two decades, but the frequency of low birth weight has not changed. It still occurs in 12.4% of black births and 5.4% of white births.[17] It is more common in women with fewer years of education. It is also more common in women who obtain prenatal care late or not at all during the pregnancy, and it is more common in unmarried than in married women. These factors (race, education, prenatal care, and marital status) overshadow all other variables in their relationship to low birth weight and therefore to higher infant mortality and morbidity rates. Race is consistently the most powerful determinant, but it appears to be mediated through the problems of generally lower socioeconomic status and fewer years of education.

The principal effort of public health workers in the United States has been to initiate prenatal care as soon as possible for all women. That effort is reflected in the policies of interested associations and governmental agencies that seek to either provide or pay for prenatal care, particularly for high-risk mothers.[18] Until recently, few people have inquired into the reasons for the relationship, since pregnancy has been considered a medical problem, and it is assumed that medical problems respond favorably to a medical intervention. Yet the dominant cause of low birth weight is the socioeconomic status of the mother. There is no basis for assuming that race causes low birth weight and higher infant mortality rates: racism is the problem, not race.

Low birth weight is divided into two categories: very low birth weight (less than 1,500 grams) and moderately low birth weight (between 1,500 and 2,500 grams). Black women are 3 times more likely than white women to have babies with very low birth weights and 2.3 times more likely to have babies with moderately low birth weights. From 1973 to 1983, the incidence of babies with moderately low birth weight decreased more rapidly for whites than for blacks. The incidence of babies with very low birth weight decreased for whites but *increased* for blacks.[19] Of white women, 76% began prenatal care in the first trimester (the first 3 months) of their pregnancy; only 62% of black women did so.[13] Data from state health departments have indicated that women who rely on public sector services begin prenatal care later than women who can afford and use private care.

The situation has grown worse in recent years. Half a million women who have no insurance coverage and who are not eligible for Medicaid give birth. Many Medicaid beneficiaries find it difficult to obtain maternity care. Neither hospitals nor physicians like Medicaid patients: they carry with them the stigma of poverty, and the system does not pay providers well. In spite of congressional action to broaden Medicaid eligibility, many states have not provided coverage to needy women. Overall, the states had established an average eligibility threshold at less than 56% of the federal poverty level.[20] In Alabama, the income ceiling was $1,416 for a family of three. This began to change in 1988, but the fees paid to providers were so low that expanded coverage did little to increase access.

Can prenatal care, which is largely medical care, overcome the burdens of poverty, racism, and other environmental and behavioral risk factors? Would it be more appropriate to concentrate on education, employment, and income transfer programs? The answer is pragmatic: the public will accept some measure of medical assistance more readily than it will support more fundamental changes in society. Improvements in education and housing and more equitable employment patterns are an essential part of the public health movement in its broadest application, but progress is relatively easier, albeit more expensive, in the more traditional and acceptable realm of medical care. And it can work. Brown[21] urges a comprehensive program including risk factor identification and counseling, unimpeded access to prenatal care, strengthened prenatal services to include social services and nutrition, a public education program, and more research. An experimental Medicaid access project in California resulted in 87% of the women beginning prenatal care in their first trimester, and the incidence of low birth weight dropped to 4.7% compared to 7% in a comparison group.[22] Two large projects funded by the Robert Wood Johnson Foundation produced similar conclusions.[23,24] The crucial ingredients were the organizational efforts to link necessary resources and assure smooth access to needed services.

As noted before, the infant mortality rates in the United States within each weight-specific group are very good compared to other countries. This has occurred largely because of improved care at the time of delivery. Maternity care services have been provided in a traditional fashion in the United States, with each practitioner providing individualized service using a community hospital. When a very low birth weight baby is delivered, he or she may be transported to a major medical center with a neonatal intensive care unit, in which the probability of survival is increased greatly, but at considerable cost.

Survival of the first few days or weeks of life does not mean that the health and life of the infant are no longer subject to risk. Until only a few years ago, infectious diseases were common. Now they are of secondary importance, with the exceptions of pneumonia and influenza and gastroenteritis. Even these have been greatly reduced in recent years—the first by better nutrition and antibiotics and the second by improved sanitation, nursery techniques, and chemotherapy. Nevertheless, the large proportion of infant deaths attributable to a variety of respiratory ailments is notable.

Once again, severe racial disparities exist. Table 23-4 shows the leading causes of infant mortality for whites and blacks. The differences are striking. (Note that in this table, the death rate uses a denominator of 100,000 live births. The infant mortality rate for all causes, as noted earlier, is 10.4 per *1,000* live births. The larger denominator is used in Table 23-4 to make the rates more comprehensible. A death rate for pneumonia and influenza of .142 per 1,000 live births is difficult to understand.) More recently, acquired immunodeficiency syndrome (AIDS), a result of infection with the human immunodeficiency virus (HIV), has become a major problem in pregnancy with as many as 2% of all newborns infected in some areas of the country.

The infant requires a spectrum of precautions and services to get through the hazardous first year: adequate and sanitary feeding, protection against infections and accidents, supervision, preferably by a family pediatrician, home follow-up if necessary by a public health nurse, prompt correction of any defects that may exist, early diagnosis and treatment of any illnesses that may occur, and the provision of a satisfactory emotional environment. Failure to meet these needs invites more serious difficulties later in life.

The preschool child

There are in the United States approximately 18.5 million children under the age of 5, customarily referred to as the preschool period. After that first birthday, the child enters a phase of development that is most favorable from the standpoint of the risks of mortality. Currently the risk of death between the first and the fifth birthday is 0.52 per 1,000. It is now rising owing to HIV infection (see Chapter 16).

This was not always the case. At the beginning of the century the death rate of this age group was about 20 per 1,000. The preschool period benefited most from many of the greatest triumphs of preventive medicine and public health. The dramatic decreases in deaths, illnesses, and disabilities in this group may be credited chiefly to the prevention of the acute communicable diseases of childhood. This is emphasized by a comparison of the leading causes of death in this age group in 1925 and 1986 (Table 23-5).

TABLE 23-4 Infant mortality rates (per 100,000 live births) for leading causes of death, United States, 1986, white and black infants

Cause of death	White	Black
Pneumonia and influenza	14.2	35.9
Congenital anomalies	219.5	232.1
Short gestation period or low birth weight	60.3	225.4
Respiratory distress syndrome	158.8	336.3
Sudden infant death syndrome	123	233.6
Accidents	20.3	43.1
Intrauterine hypoxia and birth asphyxia	22.2	47.6
Maternal complications	31.9	61

From National Center for Health Statistics: Advance report on final mortality statistics, 1986, Monthly Vital Statistics Report 37(suppl):33, Sept 30, 1988.

In the earlier year (1925), diarrhea and enteritis accounted for 109.8 deaths per 100,000 children aged 1 to 4; 60 years later, the rate had dropped to less than 1 per 100,000, primarily because of improved environmental conditions. The overall decline in mortality is striking for almost all causes. It is somewhat surprising to note that the death rate from motor vehicle crashes was less in 1986 than in 1925. Such figures can serve to illustrate a particular point, such as the change in the nature of the phenomena that may place the preschool child in jeopardy, but the observer has to beware of the kinds of groupings that can occur to make a particular item the number one cause. If the category of "accidents (other than motor vehicle)" were subdivided into its various components, the category of "motor vehicle accidents" would rank number one. In addition to ranking, the actual rates merit attention. Although it is shocking to find homicide on the list of the leading causes of death in any age group, the rate (2.7 per 100,000) would not have made the list at all in 1925, when such diseases as diphtheria had death rates in excess of 40 per 100,000.

Of greater significance than the forces of mortality in the preschool years is the fact that although deaths are infrequent, morbidity is high. Thus the National Health Survey indicates an annual frequency rate of acute conditions during the first 6 years of life of 376.2 per 100 children. Similarly, restricted activity days and bed disability days are high during this period of life. Fortunately, not only is the recovery rate for preschool children high but the duration of their illnesses is brief.

The preschool years represent a period of significant nutritional and emotional change for the child, with increased effective contacts for the acquisition of communicable diseases and involvement in injuries. From the point of view of public health, therefore, this stage of life is one to which more attention must be given, not so much for the prevention of death as for the prevention of physical and mental illnesses and trauma that may handicap the future lives of those concerned. Since the individual in this age span is undergoing extremely rapid growth and development, what may often appear at the moment to be inconsequential influences of a nutritional, emotional, dental, or physical nature may have an ultimate cumulative effect far out of proportion to their initial appearance. The need, therefore, is for programs designed to minimize the daily impact of influences of this nature, programs for nutritional improvement, injury prevention, and continuous health and dental supervision, including techniques for the prevention of dental caries, such as topical application of sodium fluoride. Mental illness is one of the greatest causes of disability in the adult population at the present time. It is during the preschool period that the seeds of much of this are sown. There is an important need, therefore, for the application of sound mental health principles and for the more widespread establishment and use of mental health and child guidance services.

APPROACH TO THE PROBLEMS

Since so many factors can affect the well-being of mothers and children, programs related to them must be multifaceted and involve the coordinated efforts of many disciplines, organizations, and agencies. For children, of course, well-informed and concerned parents necessarily must provide the keystone for the arch of proper child care and development. There are many important and sometimes critical roles for the health department.

To meet adequately the many problems in maternal, infant, and child health, the official health agency of a community should carry out a well-conceived and coordinated series of activities, each of which looks forward to the subsequent periods of life. Personal and community services and education are involved.

Arden Miller,[25] speaking before the National Health Forum in 1974, gave a specific prescription in five parts: (1) a national health service for mothers and children to include prenatal care, obstetric and midwifery services, homemaking assistance and mothercraft, postnatal care, family planning services, well-child and developmental checkups, routine immunizations and anticipatory guidance, preschool screening, and school health services, including a mandate to treat and correct the defects found and provide care for illnesses of those not able to use private medical care effectively; (2) a public feeding program; (3) national housing reform; (4) community-based family support centers, including day care; and (5) performance standards for state and local health departments and private providers. Miller said that we could afford to do it and that we could not afford not to.

In Cambridge, Massachusetts, the city operated a separate hospital and health department until 1968, when they were combined in an effort to bring about better coordination of public health programs. The Chairman of the Department of Pediatrics in the hospital (Dr. Philip Porter) became the director of the combined maternal and child health program and moved to consolidate the administration of the programs and decentralize the delivery system into selected schools in areas that had the greatest child health problems. With the expanded use of nurse practitioners, a comprehensive pro-

TABLE 23-5 Mortality in the 1 to 4 age group, United States, 1925 and 1986

Cause of death, 1925	Rate per 100,000 population	Cause of death, 1986	Rate per 100,000 population
Diarrhea and enteritis	109.8	Accidents (other than motor vehicle)	13.4
Accidents (other than motor vehicle)	57.7	Motor vehicle accidents	7.0
Pneumonia	44.7	Congenital anomalies	6.1
Diphtheria	43.0	Malignant neoplasms	4.0
Tuberculosis	28.9	Homicide	2.7
Whooping cough	28.6	Heart disease	2.5
Measles	14.4	Influenza and pneumonia	1.4
Scarlet fever	11.7	Meningitis	1.0
Motor vehicle accidents	11.5	Perinatal causes	0.9
Heart disease	8.9	Septicemia	0.6

Modified from Monthly vital statistics reports, National Center for Health Statistics.

gram was developed with the resources that were available.[27] If all of the money currently spent on a disarticulated and uncoordinated system of care for children could be aggregated and managed in a more thoughtful and appropriate manner, substantial improvements in health status could be attained at a much lower total cost to society.

The state health agency is responsible for the overall effort. The federal Office of Maternal and Child Health described 14 functional elements in a state-based maternal and child health program[27]:

1. Leadership
2. The assessment of problems, needs, and resources
3. Planning
4. Resource development and allocation
5. Standard setting for providers
6. Quality assurance reviews
7. An information system and data analysis
8. Education for the public and providers
9. Technical assistance for local health departments and community organizations
10. Coordination of multiple programs
11. Evaluation
12. Administration
13. Direct services where needed
14. Research

The health department cannot function alone. In fact, no other part of the health department program requires the cooperation of so many people and agencies in the community. Except in economically disadvantaged areas, much of the direct medical and dental service to mothers, infants, and children will be rendered by private physicians and dentists. Similarly, the health department can never substitute for the health teaching of children in the home and in the classroom under the guidance of intelligent parents and professionally trained teachers. No other phase of the public health program requires so many cooperative contacts with non-official health agencies and with the many social agencies that usually exist in the community.

Community health centers, frequently initiated with federal project grant support, and health department clinics provide a substantial proportion of the maternal and child health services in the United States, especially in areas that are otherwise disadvantaged or are medically underserved. No one knows the exact proportion, but as much as 20% of all such health services may now be provided by the public sector in organized settings. Beyond this, the active cooperation and assistance of many lay persons and community groups must be obtained. In addition to using lay advice and support by means of advisory committees, maternal health councils, or similar techniques, many health departments have found it possible to improve and expand their service programs considerably by using volunteer workers, both in clinics and in the field.

One further general point deals with the necessity to conduct continuous research and surveys to keep the total health program in balance with maternal and child health needs. In areas with good reporting, morbidity and mortality data provide the most obvious source of guidance. The Bureau of the Census and the National Center for Health Statistics are especially good sources of data. In addition, state and community agencies can provide regionally and locally pertinent information.

Generally speaking, the statistical needs for maternal and child health programs can be divided into two categories: vital statistical data and supplemental statistical information that is usually necessary for the proper interpretation of the vital statistics. The following vital statistics relating to maternity and infancy are usually available for any state, county, or large city and are part of the basic information needed in planning any health service for mothers and infants:

1. Live births and fetal deaths (number and rate)
   a. Urban, rural
   b. Resident, nonresident
   c. In hospitals, in homes
   d. Attended by physician, not attended by physician
   e. Race, marital status, and age of mother
2. Maternal deaths (number and rate)
   a. Urban, rural
   b. Resident, nonresident
   c. In hospitals, in homes
   d. Attended by physician, not attended by physician
   e. Causes of death
3. Neonatal deaths (infant deaths under 1 month of age) (number and rate)
   a. Urban, rural
   b. Resident, nonresident
   c. In hospitals, in homes
   d. Attended by physician, not attended by physician
   e. Race and age of mother

f. Causes of death
g. Age at time of death

This list must be supplemented by information relating to available medical, nursing, and hospital resources; the occupations of women in the child-bearing ages; and educational, cultural, and many other socioeconomic factors. In addition, data must be sought with regard to the quality of health care available and the complications of pregnancy and infancy that occur in the geographic area under consideration. There should also be conducted and available to the health agency periodic analyses of hospital and medical records. This is best done by an acceptable and unbiased peer review procedure.

MATERNAL HEALTH PROGRAM

The natal process divides into several discrete physiologic phases, each of which presents certain problems and needs.

Preconceptional period

An adequate maternal health program should begin long before the child is conceived and even before the expectant mother reaches physiologic maturity. The preconceptional aspects of the program involve a threefold approach of education, health service, and developmental counseling. Much education that may have a direct and significant influence on future parenthood can be accomplished with the high-school and even grade-school girl and boy. Scientifically correct and socially acceptable facts may be presented to school-children in relation to many phases of social hygiene, including the anatomy and physiology of reproduction, the problem of sexually transmitted diseases, the importance of qualified supervision during pregnancy and infancy, and the responsibilities of parenthood. One of the most important problems in junior and senior high schools is pregnancy and sexual behavior that is unaccompanied by adequate knowledge of reproduction, birth control, AIDS, and contraception or a thoughtful approach to psychologic development, self-esteem, and the ethics of responsibility. (See Chapter 25.) The tendency has been to focus on educational programs for teenage girls, but many school boards have found themselves faced with stiff parental opposition when the school attempts to teach what the parents have not or cannot. Moreover, it is probably better to conduct such teaching in a coeducational environment, since that is a more natural setting. It is important to encourage both boys and girls to understand their responsibility for their sexual behavior, especially when it results in the birth of a child. Faced with parental opposition, some programs have explored techniques for identifying the high-risk girl, so that she can be singled out for individual counseling. Health department staffs can work collaboratively with school staffs in settings outside the school, which may ameliorate parental opposition.

Many states have begun to provide genetic counseling services and, by referral, the technique of amniocentesis for high-risk pregnant women (those with a prior history of a congenital anomaly, those with a genetic trait that may jeopardize the outcome, or women over the age of 35, who are more likely to have a baby with Down's syndrome).

Family planning is an essential part of public health programs. In fact, most contraceptive supplies are now distributed through the many public programs. Virtually all state and local health departments provide family planning services, including counseling and contraceptive devices. In most states, such services are made available to teenagers without parental consent. Infertility services are also provided. Millions of women receive such services through public health agencies, and an increasing number of men seeking sterilization find help here too. The techniques of vasectomy and tubal ligation are now quite simple, safe, and relatively inexpensive; and a growing number of men are seeking sterilization as a simpler and safer approach to family planning than the continued use of contraceptive devices by the woman or sterilization of the woman. It is especially important to deal with the consent process in an informed and thoughful way, and many agencies require a waiting period of a few days to allow the client to think about what is, practically speaking, an irreversible decision. Involuntary sterilizations are now uncommon, but there are some indications for their performance. Careful guidelines need to be developed in any state that still makes provisions for such procedures, and public health personnel should be involved along with those whose expertise is in law or ethics.

By 1982, 54% of all women were using some form of contraception: 18% had been surgically sterilized, and 37% were using a variety of temporary devices such as the oral contraceptives (15.5%), condoms (6.7%), diaphragms (4.5%), and intrauterine devices (3.9%). Slightly more than 40% of married women between the ages of 15 and 44 were sterile, and another 40% used various forms of contraception.[28]

The family planning movement has been significant in many ways in the United States. It was started by Margaret Sanger, who saw it as a political and social action movement to improve the status of women; but the movement quickly became "medicalized," and the term that was applied to it—*family planning*—implied that the purpose was to raise a family, albeit a planned one.

Family planning programs should include a variety of contraceptive methods; good record keeping, including pertinent medical, social, and reproductive historical information; initial and annual examinations, including breast examinations, abdominal and pelvic examinations, Pap smears, and screening for hypertension; and effective referral for any medical problems detected.

Although services are now widely available, they are still not being used effectively by teenagers. Most girls who use family planning clinic services have had sexual intercourse before they are 16 years old. Many teenagers are contraceptive "failures" who become pregnant either accidentally or deliberately to attain some sense of accomplishment and control in their lives. Services need to be easily accessible for teenagers, and the staff requires special training to cope in a supportive manner with the special problems and demands of these young people. Recent efforts by the federal government to require that clinic personnel inform the parents before providing services, if implemented either by federal requirement or local initiative, may drive many young girls away from one of the few places where they are able to get sound advice. (See Chapter 25.)

Programs and services such as those described may be implemented in several ways: through supplementary service in maternal health clinics, through specifically established planned parenthood clinics, and through referral to private physicians. Public health nurses and other trained family planning workers and counselors can provide effective and acceptable services, although a physician is still a desirable participant, at least to conduct the initial physical and annual follow-up examinations and to initiate prescriptions for oral contraceptives. In practice, all of these functions can be performed by trained nurse practitioners and auxiliary personnel if medical backup is available on referral, but most states have not modified their medical and nursing practice laws to permit such activities.

Women's health groups have formed health centers where much of the indignity of the gynecologic examination has been ameliorated. In addition, some of the groups have published outstanding self-help texts that have contributed significantly to teaching women how to take better care of themselves. *The New Our Bodies, Ourselves*[29] is a notable example. It is significant that similar activities and publications have not been developed by and for men. The exploited feelings of women, when faced with the masculine medical care system, have led them to develop a strong consumer-oriented focus that promises to be effective in improving self-help and a sense of self-responsibility for both sexes.

One other problem that should concern public health workers is that of rape. Many communities have established rape counseling centers and hot lines. A great deal of attention has been focused on the problems of women who have been raped: the probability that police investigation will involve male officers, the trauma of the emergency room examination—also usually performed by a male physician—the suspicion that a rape victim may have enticed the attack, and, more recently, the difficulty in distinguishing between the overtly violent act of rape as it has been customarily described and the more covert forms of psychologic rape that involve a subtle but no less serious form of violence to the woman's self-esteem. Health department staff, particularly public health nurses who have had special training or who have special empathy, can and should be involved in helping the victims.

Antepartum and intrapartum period

The antepartum period of pregnancy is most important. The objective is to involve the pregnant woman in an organized system of care as early as possible. In the United States this usually means medical care, although it should include the involvement of a nurse-midwife, access to nutrition counseling, the availability of childbirth and parenting classes for both parents, and an organized approach to special needs such as support and counseling for unmarried women, abortion services if they are not prohibited by law, care for women engaged in industry during pregnancy, and such technical problems as the management of Rh incompatibility.

It is necessary to set up some administrative procedure to locate pregnant women as early in their pregnancies as possible, especially those who may be at high risk because of age, income, education, physical problems, or a combination of factors. The need for and manner of doing this varies from one community to another. The health department has at its disposal several sources of information. Knowledge of pregnancies may come to the health department staff through their personal observations during their daily rounds, by statements or suggestions from neighbors of expectant mothers, from previous patients, and from school personnel. A highly desirable goal is for private physicians, as well as those in community programs, to notify the health department of each new obstetric case. Part of the problem is already solved in that the patient in question is under medical supervision. However, even here the health department may render service through public health nursing supervision and education and follow-up of women who miss appointments.

A Committee on Perinatal Health was formed by the American Academy of Family Physicians, the American Academy of Pediatrics, the American College of Obstetricians and Gynecologists, and the National Foundation–March of Dimes to develop standards for prenatal and delivery services. The Committee recommended a regionalized system of perinatal care and stratified centers into three levels: level I centers are designed to take care of the uncomplicated delivery (even here, however, the backup services and laboratory requirements are extensive); level II centers have a more complete range of maternal and neonatal care services and should be able to handle most of the complicated cases; level III centers are designed to have the full spectrum of services, including neonatologists and other highly skilled personnel. These centers are designed to serve an area with 8,000 to 12,000 deliveries per year, and the Committee established a model budget of $2.637 million. (The Committee's report[30] has an excellent bibliography, principally dealing with high-risk situations.)

The regionalization of perinatal care has received a great deal of attention from the American College of Obstetricians and Gynecologists and the Robert Wood Johnson Foundation,[23,24] which has invested heavily in the development and evaluation of such systems. Regionalization of care seems perfectly rational to people outside of the health care system, but within the system in the United States, it is a radical notion. Traditionally, each physician has been the caregiver for his or her own clients. In the last several decades, referrals to specialists have become more common, and many specialists serve as primary care providers, especially in small towns. These referral patterns are usually informal and work at the professional level. A regionalized system of perinatal care is an organized system, however, with referral protocols and a managed information system. Pregnant women are assessed for the presence of risk factors, which if present require their referral to a technologically higher level of care. It is unlikely that such formations will occur voluntarily without considerable developmental work by major medical centers and public health departments. Interestingly, the recent corporatization of medical care may facilitate the development of regionalized perinatal care systems. Since the emerging systems of medical care are managed systems, which try to increase efficiency and reduce exposure to liability, rational referral systems are attractive, especially if they do not result in the overutilization of expensive resources.

Some members of the American College of Obstetricians and Gynecologists believed that the report of the Committee on Perinatal Health did not sufficiently deal with rural areas, and they developed a separate report,[31] which is fascinating because of its model's reliance on nonmedical personnel. In fact, the organization of this model is similar to that of some health care delivery models in underdeveloped countries. The organizational chart starts with the family units at the top rather than at the bottom and recommends the services of a health advocate for each family—a skilled person such as a successful mother—who will serve as a guide for the family. Then comes the primary perinatal health care provider, who does not need to be a physician but may be a public health nurse or, preferably, a nurse-midwife. Below this in the organizational structure come the level I, II, and III centers as described by the original committee. (This second report also contains an excellent bibliography.)

One of the more important developments in recent years in the United States has been a changing attitude toward the use of professionally trained nurse-midwives. The American College of Nurse-Midwives had 1,684 members in 1984. Nearly two thirds of the nurse-midwives were practicing nurse-midwifery.[32] Several states have modified nursing practice laws in recent years. By 1987, 10 states explictly permitted nurse-midwives to practice, 10 states prohibited such practice, and in 21 states, the legal status of midwives was unclear.[33] Resistance by physicians to the independent practice of nurse-midwifery, coupled with growing problems in obtaining adequate liability insurance, has limited the role of nurse-midwives in the United States.

The problem of access to obstetrical care grew rapidly during the 1980s: physicians elected to withdraw from the time-consuming practice, and rising expectations of perfection coupled with rapidly growing jury awards when it was not attained made liability insurance increasingly difficult to find and afford. In many states, people who were thought to have several risk factors for an adverse outcome found it increasingly difficult to find any source of care, especially in rural areas. Once again, it is the poor who are most seriously imperiled: they have scant economic resources, Medicaid pays for prenatal and delivery services at rates far below those expected by practitioners, and practitioners *think* that low-income women are inherently high risk, even though there is no evidence that liability payments are more frequent or more sizeable when treating poor and minority women. The problem has become severe, with a growing number of reports of patient dumping, inadequate treatment, unplanned out-of-hospital births, and early neonatal deaths. The problem will not be solved until state legislatures are able to solve the liability problems and obstetricians decide either to provide the needed services or to assist in the appropriate licensure of people who will.

It is difficult to know how many deliveries are actually performed by someone other than a physician. The figures in Table 23-2 indicate that between 3.5% and 4% of births are attended by someone other than a physician, but many more deliveries were undoubtedly performed by nursing personnel, both untrained and trained. Physicians often "miss" the delivery by arriving too late at the hospital, but still sign the birth certificate, which results in the official tabulation of births by attendant. In recent years, as hospitals and medical staffs have accepted nurse-midwives in the delivery room, they have been less apprehensive about allowing the nurse to sign the official documents. Still less is known about the number of births that are assisted by nursing personnel with no medical supervision at all. In many states, such practices are thought to be illegal, and the people offering such services are necessarily nervous about their visibility. Should a death occur, some county medical societies and prosecuting attorneys might well force prosecution on a charge of manslaughter.

The Maternity Center Association of New York City established the first school of midwifery in 1932 and the first formally organized out-of-hospital delivery program, the Childbearing Center, in 1974. After several years of effort they were successful in obtaining formal recognition from the city and the state and were recognized as an acceptable provider by Blue Cross shortly thereafter—the first such contract in the nation. By 1989 there were more than 150 such centers operating in most of the states. The Association was instrumental in establishing the Cooperative Birth Center Network to provide information and technical assistance to interested groups. Model standards for alternative birthing centers were published by the Network in their newsletter in 1982.[34]

An important part of the standards are the criteria used for risk assessment. Each applicant for an out-of-hospital delivery program needs to be carefully screened for behavioral, environmental, physical, mental, or genetic factors that might increase the probability of an unsuccessful outcome. Individuals with certain risk factors warrant a referral for further evaluation by a specialist before being accepted into the program. In practice, competent nurse-midwives are very thorough in their assessments and insist on client compliance with nutritional and substance-abuse guidelines. A review by Bennetts and Lubic[35] includes a study of 1,938 pregnancies in 11 birthing centers, which indicated the safety and reliability of the practice. It has not been possible to develop a controlled, randomized trial, since most physicians would not cooperate in a randomized experiment and most women who choose a birthing center would not accept referral to a hospital unless it was medically necessary.

Hospitals have been quick to adopt the birthing center concept in an effort to satisfy consumer demand. It provides a lower-cost labor and delivery area and a more homelike environment for the family. Many hospitals authorize attendance by nurse-midwives in the birthing center. They are able to move quickly to a more traditional medical environment if that becomes necessary. The hospital-based birthing center is a partial response to the overall problem of high-cost and high-technology obstetric care, but its most important feature may be the evidence that a hospital can respond to consumer pressure and meet community needs, especially when competition is available in the community.

Most states now have one or more requirements related to the screening of the newborn infant for metabolic diseases such as phenylketonuria (PKU) or thyroid problems that if undetected and untreated can lead to cretinism. At least 20 such screening tests can now be performed, but the availability of the technology is not a sufficient reason for doing it. There should be a reasonable probability that affected subjects will benefit from treatment, that affected subjects and their families will be apprised of hazardous situations that should be avoided, or that affected families can be counseled about the risk of recurrence.

Postpartum period

As in the antepartum program, the first essential in the postpartum program is casefinding. The location of women who have recently delivered can be accomplished with relative ease where an efficient birth registration program is in effect. In addition to this, in some localities hospitals promptly notify the health department of all deliveries. In many instances the health department is notified when the patient is about to return home. Many women and children are now being discharged within 24 hours and routinely within 2 days. In birthing centers the mother is often discharged in 4 to 6 hours if there is no bleeding and within 12 hours in most cases. Notification through the routine birth registration route no longer suffices: some women may be home for a week in a hostile and risk-laden environment before the health department even knows of the birth. It is far better to arrange for someone in the delivery area to notify the health department on the day of birth. Early discharge is advantageous to the family economically, and it facilitates a more rapid reformation of the family, but it reduces the time for contemplation, rest, learning, and the management of special problems such as congenital anomalies and out-of-wedlock births. The immediate postpartum period is often a very effective time to learn about family planning techniques and services, especially for those women who were unaware of such programs.

It is generally not possible to provide services to every mother and child on their return home, nor is it necessary to do so; but depending on resources, procedures should be established to make contact with those mothers who may be facing an unusual problem or who are at high risk, such as the adolescent, the socioeconomically disadvantaged, the woman over 35 with her first baby, or the mother whose child has a congenital anomaly (often reported on the birth certificate or by the hospital). Contact should also be made in situations of multiple births and families that have had previous problems.

The value of meeting the mother and infant at the doorstep of the home has been demonstrated by several health agencies, and the secret of its accomplishment is one of interagency cooperation and administrative timing. The problem of contacting women and infants after delivery has been greatly complicated during recent years by frequent changes of address and by the fact that many women come into cities for hospital delivery as a convenience but return to small communities or rural areas after discharge from the hospital. Since the early 1970s, the frequency of such home visiting has declined. With the advent of the Medicaid program and the subsequent sharp rise in medical care prices, local elected officials have sharply curtailed appropriations for health services that are not reimbursed by some third party or that do not have an immediate effect on a demonstrably dangerous situation. In many local health departments, routine postnatal visits have been discontinued altogether.

The health department's postpartum program has two purposes: to provide public health nursing service and education to the mother as indicated in each case and to accomplish a smooth and automatic carryover to the infant health program. The nurse should instruct the mother in proper postpartum care, in infant care, in the advantages and hygiene of breast-feeding, and in the preparation of infant formulas if they are necessary. The nurse should make certain that the birth of the infant has been registered and that the mother and infant are both under medical supervision. The nurse should also maintain a watchful eye for the development of postpartum complications in the mother and of illness in the infant and make referrals to appropriate agencies wherever medical, economic, or social problems are found to exist. Finally, the nurse should lay the groundwork for pediatric supervision of the infant, including all indicated protective treatments, from either private physicians or health and well-baby conferences and clinics.

Newborn and infant feeding have attracted particular attention in recent years. Several decades ago, it became fashionable for women to use bottles and later prepackaged formulas to feed their babies. It was thought to be uncivilized to nurse a baby. In recent years mothers and nutritionists have rediscovered the benefits of breast milk: it enhances bonding, provides the baby with a substantial dose of antibodies against infections, maintains natural uterine contractility and recovery, and avoids the problems of allergy to cow's milk. Breast-feeding should be encouraged in every birth unless there are real physical or psychologic problems.

THE INFANT AND PRESCHOOL PROGRAM

With regard to the neonatal program, early case-finding is again a prerequisite and may be accomplished by means of (1) a routine check of birth certificates; (2) notification by the attendant at birth (accoucheur), the hospital, or the family itself; or (3) the records of prenatal clinic attendance. Neonatal cases should be classified into priority groups, with premature infants at the top of the list, followed by those known to have been born with physical defects and those who have become ill or injured during or after birth. Many health departments maintain several portable infant care beds, which may be loaned to parents of premature babies, and have worked out arrangements with other agencies such as fire or police departments for resuscitation services and for emergency transfer to hospitals. Intensive infant care programs have been developed in most states, including provisions for the transfer of fragile, high-risk, or damaged infants to intensive neonatal care centers with trained neonatologists (a subspecialty of pediatrics) and other trained personnel and technicians and special instruments to aid in the care and treatment of these very fragile babies. Specially equipped ambulances with controlled environment systems and trained staff and similarly equipped helicopters are becoming more available and are especially useful in rural areas.

Of course, it is better to try to identify the high-risk situation before birth and transport the pregnant women to a level II or III center for the delivery. Intensive infant care services are expensive. It should be stressed that public health departments ought to concentrate on preventing the need for such heroics and that no community should be encouraged to make such investments in hospitals and personnel before it has adequately developed family planning, prenatal care, nutrition services, and public health education programs for prospective mothers, genetic counseling services, and detection and screening services to find the high-risk cases before or during pregnancy.

The health department has a role to play in helping every child develop to the fullest potential. This involves the availability of guidance, counseling, screening, referral, and treatment services and special programs to deal with child abuse, mental health, dental education, immunizations, AIDS, and nutrition. The majority of children have access to a private physician, either a family practitioner or a pediatrician. Even here, the health department has a role to play in providing screening services and in helping parents understand what is necessary for the healthy development of their children. In many cases, public agencies or private, not-for-profit organizations are the main source of care for young children and their families, and the health department should be closely involved in such activities, either as a provider of services or as a co-provider and referral agency.

Well-child clinics have been commonly used by health departments as a means of providing guidance and counseling for parents. The paradox of discontinuing services when the child is sick and referring the family elsewhere has led many health departments to expand their services, so that the well-child clinics have become child care centers, providing comprehensive child health care and educational services. This transition should be encouraged where need can be demonstrated. There are many areas where private practice has adequately covered virtually the whole population; but in areas where that is not the case, health department programs can be made more comprehensive, often in collaboration with local practitioners.

The American Academy of Pediatrics[36,37] has published a fairly extensive guide to the standards that should be maintained in an effective program. The latest edition makes a point of avoiding a rigid prescription for how many visits should be made to a physician at any particular age, stating that such schedules need to be individualized. Nonetheless, it suggests that the child be seen at least five times during the first year and about three times during the second year of life. It suggests about three visits during the preschool years (at the ages of 2, 3, and 5 or 6), and then at least four visits during the school years, between ages 6 and 18. Not all of the visits need to be to a physician.

Immunization programs have been increased in recent years, partly as a result of the interest expressed by Secretary Califano of the Department of Health, Education and Welfare after his experience with the swine flu program in 1976 and 1977. The percentage of children who were fully immunized against polio, diphtheria, tetanus, pertussis, and measles declined to the point that scattered outbreaks of measles began to occur in 1977 and 1978. As the result of an aggressive program by the Centers for Disease Control and state health agencies, the number of doses of vaccine administered increased sharply, boosting coverage to over 90% in most areas of the country. It is still difficult to maintain such protection levels, and a threat of diminished federal support in the 1980s made it apparent that the effort can never be neglected.

Here too, the mounting cost of liability insurance eroded support for essential preventive health services in the 1980s. Vaccine prices increased rapidly, and fewer manufacturers were willing to participate at all. It is unclear where fault really lies. Are the products or procedures really dangerous? (The best evaluations of the dominant childhood immunization practices say no.) Are vaccine manufacturers trying to reap excessive profits? Are insurance companies trying to recoup the losses they incurred through aggressive investment practices in the early 1980s? Is the legal profession capitalizing on excessive awards? Is the American public overly sympathetic to people who are injured as a result of medical interventions? Some states have begun to experiment with different forms of state-administered compensation awards, which are intended to be both equitable and affordable. The answers are critical to the future development of essential public health services.

Almost every state attempts to develop its own recommended schedule for immunizing children, and a great deal of confusion exists among both practitioners and parents. It would be sensible to follow the schedules recommended by the American Academy of Pediatrics in its *Report of the Committee on Infectious Diseases*[38] (known as "the Red Book"), which is published periodically.

The influence of poverty on health has been particularly well described by Kessner and Calk[39] and by Kosa, Antonosky, and Zola.[40] Health departments have traditionally concentrated a large part of their resources on the children of low-income families, but much more needs to be done. Special nutrition services such as the WIC program (for women, infants, and children) have been of great value. (See Chapter 22.) Even in Great Britain, with a National Health Service, it has been found that the poor do not use health services as effectively as the nonpoor or as much as they need to, and special efforts have had to be incorporated into the programs to be sure that services reach those who need them most. As mentioned earlier and as pointed out by Miller,[25] environment, education, housing, and the employment prospects for parents have a powerful impact on health, even when access to health services is technically available.

Special programs for the provision of services to handicapped children are a feature of many health departments, although responsibility is often placed with welfare and educational agencies. Most state health agencies provide Crippled Children's Services, but most services made available to children with developmental disabilities are the responsibility of educational institutions. Federal legislation (P.L. 94-142) requires that educational services for all children be provided in as normative and nonrestrictive an environment as possible and that all other services, including the detection, diagnosis, and correction of defects necessary to make education possible, must be provided. More recent legislation (P.L. 99-457, 1988) requires all states to assure that handicapped children have access to necessary services by the 1990-1991 school year. Health departments at the state and local level should be involved with departments of education in planning and providing these services, although recent changes in block-grant legislation have removed many of the specific requirements.

The special problems of child abuse also require the attention of health departments, usually in collaboration with other agencies, particularly social service agencies. Many states have made the suspicion of child abuse a reportable event, and every effort is made to provide a supportive, therapeutically oriented program for the child and the parents. The best approach to child abuse is a team approach involving public health nursing, mental health workers, social workers, pediatricians, and a lawyer. A great deal can be done to help these troubled families with such an approach, although an out-of-home placement for the child is sometimes the only solution possible.

THE FUTURE

Whether such a program of projects can become a national and comprehensive set of services, linked together in some coherent way to provide sensible and holistic services for women and children, remains to be seen. The United States has made great progress since the Children's Bureau was established; but whether a truly comprehensive program containing the five elements recommended by Miller[25] can be established is doubtful. The EPSDT program, as discussed earlier, was part of an effort to do just this, but a lack of ability or determination by Congress and the Department of Health, Education and Welfare to declare explicitly what was intended impeded the development of the program. The managers of the program wrote encouraging words about its possibilities, but others have written about the failures. Foltz[41] particularly describes the legislative and administrative problems that befuddle attempts to create clear policy. The rising incidence of AIDS in pregnant women certainly complicates the picture. This is a continuing problem throughout public health but particularly so in maternal and child health, where broad, general visions are often defeated by the particularistic notions of groups with special interests and by a political process that responds to people who can vote now rather than the needs of those who will shape the future.

Nonetheless, the 1990s may see the final development of a national program to assure that all mothers and children have access to necessary services. The traditional resistance of the medical profession to government programs has diminished in recent years. The new corporate forms of practice are sensitive to profits, and obstetrics and pediatrics are among the least profitable aspects of health care. Congress and state legislative bodies are not likely to solve the problem by increasing the fees they are willing to pay the private sector, yet they are increasingly aware of the damage that is being done and the price that we must ultimately pay if we jeopardize the health and welfare of those who will soon dominate our social structure. Rising concern and diminishing obstacles, even at a time when "scarcity of resources" (or our willingness to pay for them) has become the slogan of the land, may lead us to a future of healthier children.

REFERENCES

1. Forgotson EH: 1965: the turning point in health law—1966 reflections, Am J Public Health 57:934, June 1967.
2. Foltz A-M: Uncertainties of federal child health policies: impact in two states, US Department of Health and Human Services Pub No (PHS)78-3190, Washington, DC, April 1978.
3. Public Health Foundation: Public health agencies, 1988: an inventory of programs and block grant expenditures, Washington, DC, 1988, The Foundation.
4. Budetti PP, Butler J, and McManus P: Federal health program reforms: implications for child health care, Milbank Q 60(1):155, Winter 1982.
5. The Select Panel for the Promotion of Child Health: Better health for our children: a national strategy, vols. 1 through 4, US Department of Health and Human Services Pub No (PHS)79-55071, Washington, DC, 1981.
6. Wallace HM, Ryan GM, and Oglesby A, editors: Maternal and child health practices, ed 3, Oakland, CA, 1988, Third Party Publishing Co.
7. Mills JL and others: Maternal alcohol consumption and birth weight, J Am Med Assoc 252:1875, Oct 12, 1984.
8. Geronimus AT: On teenage childbearing and neonatal mortality in the United States, Population and Development Review 13:245, June 1987.
9. Messite J and Bond MB: Reproductive toxicology and occupational exposure. In Zenz C, editor: Developments in occupational medicine, Chicago, 1980, Year Book Medical Publishers.
10. US Congress, Office of Technology Assessment: Reproductive hazards in the workplace, OTA-BA-266,

Washington, DC, 1985, US Government Printing Office.
11. Falk IS, Rorem CR, and Ring MD: The cost of medical care, Chicago, 1922, University of Chicago Press.
12. Maternal and Child Health Program: A task force report on guidelines for out-of-hospital births, Portland, OR, 1988, Oregon Department of Human Resources.
13. National Center for Health Statistics: Advanced report of final natality statistics, 1986, Monthly Vital Statistics Report 37(suppl), July 17, 1988.
14. Cook RJ and Dickens BM: A decade of international change in abortion law: 1967-1977, Am J Public Health 68:637, July 1978.
15. Ellerbrock TV and others: Abortion surveillance, 1982-1983, Morbid Mortal Week Rep 36:11SS, Feb 1987.
16. Legge JS: Abortion policy: an evaluation of the consequences for maternal and infant health, Albany, NY, 1985, State University of New York Press.
17. US Bureau of the Census: Statistical abstract of the United States, 1988, Table 86, Washington, DC, 1988, US Government Printing Office.
18. Institute of Medicine: Preventing low birthweight, Washington, DC, 1985, National Academy Press.
19. Kleinman JC and Kessel SS: Racial differences in low birth weight, New Engl J Med 317:749, Sept 17, 1987.
20. Gold RM, Kenney AM, and Singh S: Paying for maternity care in the United States, Fam Plann Perspect 19:190, Sep-Oct 1987.
21. Brown SS: Can low birth weight be prevented? Fam Plann Perspect 17:112, May-June 1985.
22. Lennie JA, Klun JR, and Hausner T: Low birth weight reduced by the obstetrical access project, Health Care Fin Rev 8:83, Spring 1987.
23. Robert Wood Johnson Foundation: The perinatal program: what has been learned, Special Report No 3, 1985.
24. Robert Wood Johnson Foundation: The rural infant care program, Special Report No 2, 1986.
25. Miller CA: Health care of children and youth in America, Am J Public Health 65:353, April 1975.
26. Porter PJ: Realistic outcomes of school health service programs, Health Educ Q 8:81, Spring 1981.
27. Office of Maternal and Child Health: An organized system of child health care in every state: need, potential, mission, a staff paper of the Office of Maternal and Child Health, US Department of Health and Human Services, June 1980.
28. Bachrach CA and Mosher WD: Use of contraception in the United States, 1982, National Center for Health Statistics Advance Data 102, December 4, 1984.
29. Boston Women's Health Book Collective: The new our bodies, ourselves: a book by and for women, New York, 1984, Simon & Schuster.
30. Committee on Perinatal Health: Toward improving the outcome of pregnancy, White Plains, NY, 1977, National Foundation–March of Dimes.
31. Health care for mothers and infants in rural and isolated areas, Chicago, 1978, American College of Obstetricians and Gynecologists.
32. Adams C: Nurse-midwifery in the United States, 1982, Washington, DC, 1984, American College of Nurse-Midwives.
33. Butter IH and Kay BJ: State laws and the practice of lay midwifery, Am J Public Health 78:1161, Sept 1988.
34. Cooperative Birth Center Network: Information for establishing standards or regulations for free-standing birth centers, Perkiomenville, PA, CBCN News 1(2-3), Feb-May 1982.
35. Bennetts AB and Lubic RW: The free-standing birth center, Lancet 1:378, Feb 13, 1982.
36. Committee on Standards of Child Health Care: Standards of child health care, ed 3, Evanston, IL, 1977, American Academy of Pediatrics.
37. Committee on School Health: School health: a guide for health professionals, ed 4, Elk Grove, IL, 1987, American Academy of Pediatrics.
38. Committee on Infectious Diseases: Report of the Committee on Infectious Diseases, 20th ed, Evanston, IL, American Academy of Pediatrics.
39. Kessner DM and Calk CE: Contrasts in health status, vol 2, A strategy for evaluating health services, Washington, DC, 1973, National Academy of Science.
40. Kosa J, Antonosky A, and Zola IK: Poverty and health, Cambridge, MA, 1969, Harvard University Press.
41. Foltz A-M: The development of ambiguous federal policy: early and periodic screening, diagnosis and treatment (EPSDT), Milbank Q 53:35, Winter 1975.

CHAPTER 24

Children and public health

THE SCHOOL CHILD

When children leave home for school, their small world begins to change inexorably. They become involved in a more diverse array of personal interactions, a wider geographic range, and an increasing number of conflicts, with many varied learning experiences. There are about 30,200,000 children aged 5 to 13 in the United States at this time (1988). They will spend a large proportion of their formative years in the school environment.

By 1986, one-parent families accounted for 26% of all households with children.[1] In 1987, 32.5 million Americans lived below the poverty level. That represents 13.5% of the total population. Yet 20.6% of all children under the age of 18 were living in poverty: 15.4% of white children, 39.6% of Hispanic children, and 45.6% of black children![2] Approximately 20 million children under the age of 18 receive welfare benefits: food stamps, school lunches, Medicaid, subsidized housing, WIC food supplements, and cash grant assistance.[3]

The ethnic and racial mixture of children in the United States has changed dramatically in recent years, with a decline in immigration from European nations and a great increase in immigration from Latin and South America and the Far East. The new immigrants bring with them different traditions, religions, dietary practices, and languages. They also bring different patterns of illness and vitality and different health care traditions and expectations. The diversity of the childhood population holds the promise of continued invigoration of American society if it can be nourished and protected. The task of public health in the next decade is of extraordinary importance, challenge, and potential gratification.

Health status

Children are incredibly resilient, and they are very vulnerable. When the environment is salubrious, poverty is absent, and services well organized, most children survive childhood. Too often, that is not the case.

The mortality rate for children has improved by nearly 10-fold since the onset of the twentieth century, dropping from about 4 per 1,000 to less than 0.5 at the present time. The reduction is largely a result of the decline in deaths due to communicable diseases (Table 24-1). The decline in deaths due to tuberculosis is especially noteworthy: one of the most common causes of death in all age groups in 1900 (6,100 deaths), only 2 children in the age range 5 to 14 died of tuberculosis in 1985. Deaths due to heart disease and unintentional injuries (accidents) have also decreased, the former because of a decline in infections by certain strains of the streptococcal bacteria, which can lead to heart and kidney disease, and to better treatment of infections with antibiotics. The decline in deaths due to unintentional injuries is surprising. It is largely attributable to environmental changes, including improved building codes and housing. Deaths due to motor vehicle injuries were, of course, virtually unheard of in 1900. They were very common in the 1920s but have decreased since then in spite of the enormous increase in exposure to the risk.

The changes in the pattern of mortality for children are striking. Cancer deaths are mostly from leukemia and very unusual forms of cancer, which appear to be the result of congenital anomalies. Deaths from cardiovascular diseases are also largely a result of congenital anomalies of the heart. Thus, with the exception of leukemia, most deaths are now due to violence, including unintentional injuries, or congenital anomalies. Infectious diseases are no longer on the short list of causes.

Mortality is unevenly distributed among children. There are both sex and racial differences, the latter no doubt because of sharp differences in the socioeconomic status of black and white children. Table 24-2 shows the differences in mortality from all causes of death for male and female, white and black children. The rates for white boys are nearly twice those for white girls, but less than the rates for black boys. The sex differences are largely a result of unintentional injuries; the racial differences, of socioeconomic status. Note that the death rate for black girls declines between age group 5 to 9 and age group 10 to 14. There are a variety of minor differences, but the major cause is a sharp drop in deaths due to both motor vehicle and all other unintentional injuries from the younger to the older age group. A similar decline is not apparent for boys and for white girls.

As was true for preschool children, mortality data provide a poor measure of the health status of school-age children. Although the nature of mortality in children is surprising and the differences based on socioeconomic status ominous, they are, all things considered, a remarkably durable group of people. Almost all of them survive childhood once they get past the infant and preschool years. They have a high rate of acute illness, however, and underlying their vitality and durability can often be found the signs of developmental disabilities, missed in the earlier years and destined to affect the remainder of their lives if not corrected. The frequency of illness and injury is indicated in Tables 24-3 and 24-4.

Respiratory illnesses (the majority of which are common colds) are the most frequent cause of restricted activity days for schoolchildren, followed by injuries and other infectious diseases. Such common ailments are usually dismissed as trivial and necessary aspects of childhood. It is true that little can be done at present to prevent such problems: there is neither cure nor preventive intervention for the common cold. Injuries are to some extent an inevitable consequence of exploration and growth, but they are too common. A large proportion are preventable through parent and child education, better environmental design in households and schools, and better consumer protection programs. Nor are they trivial problems. As can be seen in Table 24-4, there are an enormous number of restricted activity days associated with such problems, and in most cases, a restricted activity day for a child means a restricted activity day for an adult. Since a large proportion of the mothers are in the work force, this means time off, decreased productivity, lost wages and employee benefits, and often the use of medical insurance. The cost is great, with numerous trips to doctors' offices and hospital emergency rooms. Many of the trips and the services provided are unnecessary: more focused and thoughtful education programs could enable parents to care for many of the problems brought to physicians and other professional health care providers.

Mental illness in children is an especially difficult problem.[4,5] Most childhood emotional and behavioral problems appear at first to be just variations of normal behavioral patterns. Although friends and family members often suggest the possibility of a behavioral disorder, it is rare for the problem to be brought to the attention of a qualified professional. Parents, while troubled, are reluctant to suspect mental illness, and the patterns of emotional disorder in young children are not as well formed as they are later, often resulting in vague, nonspecific labels. As children enter the school system,

TABLE 24-1 Leading causes of death (rates per 100,000) for children 5 to 14 years of age, United States, 1900 and 1985

1900		1985	
Cause of death	**Rate**	**Cause of death**	**Rate**
Diphtheria	69.7	Motor vehicle accidents	6.8
Accidents, not motor vehicle	38.3	All other accidents	5.7
Pneumonia and influenza	38.2	Cancer	3.5
Tuberculosis	36.2	Congenital anomalies	1.4
Diseases of the heart	23.2	Major cardiovascular disease	1.3
		Homicide	1.2

Data for 1985 from National Center for Health Statistics: Vital statistics of the United States, 1985, vol 2, part A, Mortality, Washington, DC, 1987, US Government Printing Office.

vever, it is easier to make comparisons, and the dren are more likely to express their deviations n the norm, given the larger environment and more diverse interactions. Repeated efforts to measure the nature and incidence of behavioral problems in children have resulted in an estimate of what is referred to as "clinical maladjustment" in up to 11% of children.[6] These are children who in a group setting have a difficult time adapting to the presence and needs of others in the group. There are no accurate estimates of the prevalence of psychotic conditions in children. They are rarely encountered in a form that is recognized as such. Research efforts are aimed at detecting the precursors of adult and adolescent mental illness in young children.

Behavioral problems are a major source of concern to both parents and school teachers, because they impede the education and development of the individual child and affect classmates as well. In recent years, parents, teachers, psychologists, and sociologists have turned their attention to the impact of television on the growth and development of children. It has been a vigorously contested debate, but the consensus is growing that violence on television does increase the incidence of abnormal behavior in children. In a recent book, Hefzallah[7] writes:

> Research has indicated a modest correlation between television violence and aggressive behavior of children. Viewed in the light of millions of children who watch television for long hours every day, especially those who use it to escape their personal, familial, school and friendship problems, there is tremendous cause for being concerned.

The exposure is enormous: preschoolers will have spent 6,000 hours watching television by the time they enter first grade; by high-school graduation, students have usually watched 15,000 hours of television, compared to 11,000 hours spent on formal education. Children watch approximately 20,000 food product commercials, most of them devoted to snack foods, soft drinks, and breakfast cereals.[8] In an elaborate study of three communities, researchers found that aggressive behavior of children increased significantly after the introduction of television to the community. The effects occurred in both boys and girls, for both physical and mental aggression. The increase occurred in children who initially had low aggression scores as well as in the small subsample of highly aggressive children.[9]

TABLE 24-2 Death rates per 100,000, all causes, age groups 5 to 9 and 10 to 14, United States, 1985

	Males		Females	
Age	White	Black	White	Black
5-9	26.0	39.6	19.2	31.3
10-14	33.8	43.0	19.7	25.0

From National Center for Health Statistics: Vital statistics of the United States, 1985, vol 2, part A, Mortality, Washington, DC, 1987, US Government Printing Office.

TABLE 24-3 Acute conditions per 100 persons per year, by age and type of condition, United States, 1987

Condition	<5	5-17	18-24
All types	358.9	230.1	186.6
Infections and parasitic diseases	57.0	44.8	22.5
Respiratory conditions	160.2	111.4	88.2
Injuries	25.9	33.5	33.3

From National Center for Health Statistics: Current estimates from the National Health Interview Survey, United States, 1987, Vital and Health Statistics, Series 10, No 166, Sept 1988.

TABLE 24-4 Number of restricted activity days associated with acute conditions per 100 persons per year, by age and type of condition, United States, 1987

Condition	<5	5-17	18-24
All types	936.3	654.7	689.9
Infections and parasitic diseases	165.2	151.6	64.8
Respiratory conditions	459.6	304.8	236.6
Injuries	38.2	105.7	184.6

From National Center for Health Statistics: Current estimates from the National Health Interview Survey, United States, 1987, Vital and Health Statistics, Series 10, No 166, Sept 1988.

The physical, mental, and social problems of childhood are not just of concern for the moment; they are worrisome as possible precursors to developmental problems that may alter or retard the development of the child into an effective adult. As noted earlier, children are resilient; they are experimenters and risk takers, and they are very heterogeneous, with patterns of behavior that are not yet reliably formed. How can parents and teachers determine what is a normal variation and what warrants intervention? Given the variability and the inadequacy of so many adults, it is encouraging that children do so well.

Developmental disabilities

State and local governments have long had special programs for the mentally retarded. Beginning in 1963, other conditions were recognized as presenting similar problems (cerebral palsy, epilepsy, and autism), and programs began to refer to developmental disabilities rather than mental retardation. A series of federal laws has extended civil rights protection to those with such handicaps, and more recent federal legislation (P.L. 94-142 and P.L. 99-457) requires special education programs for them.

Perhaps the most important and significant concept in child and school health for those with developmental disabilities is the by-now familiar concept of "the least restrictive alternative." Children with handicapping conditions are to be brought into the mainstream of community life as much as possible, including the classroom and the athletic fields.[10] A large number of children have one or more handicapping conditions. Most of them are educable, and for the majority, educational services can be provided in conjunction with the special care necessary.

In the past, many localities followed a policy of complete segregation of children with developmental disabilities, if not in special institutions, then in separate classes for the blind, the hard of hearing, the mentally retarded, or the emotionally disturbed. Although such segregation can provide specialized care, it has the undesirable effect of making the child feel still more isolated and different. This is hardly conducive to good mental health or personal development. Most authorities consider that the best policy is to encourage the handicapped child to intermingle with other children in the same classrooms and to provide special classes or rest periods when needed. This has a beneficial effect for the handicapped child as well as for the other children, who can learn to accept handicapping conditions in a more normative fashion.

Mainstreaming has been criticized as impractical, time-consuming, expensive, and disruptive. In many instances specially trained teachers are needed. With careful curriculum and administrative planning, however, and by using specialized personnel partly as consultants and in-service trainers for the general teaching staff, much can be accomplished. Federal and state laws now require that all handicapped children receive a complete education in the least restrictive environment and that all necessary support services be included in the plan for each child. Local health departments should be intimately involved in organizing these services.

THE SCHOOL AND THE COMMUNITY

After the fifth year of life, children spend a large proportion of their time in school. During these years, the essential influences on physical, mental, and social well-being are produced by the home, the school, and the larger community. The school is particularly important for several reasons. It can have an influence on health in the future through its practices and its education programs. It is a large, formal gathering place. Disease (both infectious and noninfectious) as well as good health practices can be transmitted in such an environment. Finally, the school is one of only two environments in our society in which the state can influence its human resources directly. (The other is the military.) In the United States, as in most other industrialized democratic societies, the state has very little influence on the development of children in the home. For good or ill, parents—all kinds of parents—are the dominant influence on children from birth to age 5. The state also has little authority to influence the behavior of adults. In the community at large, the influence of the state is vague and minimal. In the school, however, it is direct and powerful. What to do with that authority has been a continuing source of debate and concern.

In eighteenth- and nineteenth-century Europe, the state had an immediate interest in the welfare of its children: they were its most important resources. At one time, children were thought of as an infinitely replenishable source of labor; they were just small people and were expected to work along with older, larger people. The death rates were appalling (see Chapter 2). With the advent of the philosophy of mercantilism, the state's enlightened self-interest led to labor reforms and sanitary improvements, which rapidly changed the patterns of mortality and led to the development of present-day population patterns in industrialized nations. How far can the state's self-interest take it? Does the state have the authority and the responsibility for shaping the mental, physical, and social well-being of its children? Does that include moral values? How far can the state go to prevent the problems associated with alcohol and tobacco use? Clearly the state has an interest in preventing AIDS. Does that involve teaching children about the disease and the behavioral activities that can result in infection, or should the state insist on a single set of values and label homosexual intercourse a sin, or perhaps a crime? There are both pragmatic and ideological answers to such questions. The public health pragmatists are leery of the concept of *sin,* knowing that such labels drive potentially dangerous practices into the closet, where the outbreak can continue, rather than out of existence. The same questions can be asked about the use of intravenous drugs by older children: should the state teach them to avoid drugs at all costs, or must the state acknowledge that the use of illicit substances has plagued all societies and teach people how to protect themselves against the most dangerous consequences?

Similar arguments are waged over school health service programs. The school system can maintain that its role is education, not health. Its interest in the health status of children extends only to those problems that may interfere with the learning process: hearing and vision screening, for example. Or the community may recognize that a large proportion of its children live in poverty, with little access to good health care and supervision, and seize the opportunity provided by the school system to offer comprehensive services.

The school program is an important part of the triad (home, school, and community) and should be integrated with other community programs and with the home, to the extent possible. Its success depends in large measure on the common understanding of parents, community, and school officials about (1) the scope of its sphere of action, (2) its role in the total community health picture, and (3) the need for consistent cooperation in its implementation. At its best, the school health program should be a concerted attempt to put into practice for the school-aged child the thought embraced in the Children's Charter: "Every child has the right to be well-born and to attain the best possible quality of health of which it is capable."[11] All community health personnel need to pool their efforts to realize this obviously desirable goal. This has been emphasized by the American Public Health Association[12] in a position paper on Education for Health in the School Community Setting: "Thus it seems that the school should be regarded as a social unit providing a focal point to which health planning of all other community settings should relate."

THE SCHOOL HEALTH PROGRAM

William Alcott, in "Essay on the Construction of School Houses" (1832), suggested the attendance of a physician at school.[13] In the United States, it is the states and not the national government that set school policy, and the states have decentralized that responsibility to local school districts. School boards are elected, and most school districts have their own taxing authority, relying substantially on property taxes. (This is gradually changing as courts have ruled that children can be treated very unequally depending on the wealth of a community. State taxes are being used as an increasingly large part of the school financing system to achieve greater equity.) Given the local autonomy that has existed, school health programs vary greatly from community to community.

There have been three phases in the development of school health programs in the United States:

1. An initial concern about basic protection, involving the control of communicable diseases and school sanitation, which expanded into a more comprehensive service program in some jurisdictions
2. The development of a national effort to deal with the problems of handicapped children,

beginning with the Crippled Children's Services Program in 1935 and expanding into new federal legislation to assure an adequate education for all handicapped children in 1975 and 1988

A recent effort to bring a broader emphasis on health education and services into the school system, often in collaboration with health departments, community hospitals, and other provider organizations, both public and private

In the 1930s and 1940s, school health services were widely available in many school districts, with several school health nurses providing routine nursing care. Dental and general medical examinations were frequently provided, and schools often had a dispensary for injuries and minor illnesses. Such programs declined in scope and resources beginning in the 1960s, as school boards experienced greater competition for educational resources and more children appeared to have access either to private care or to one of the new community health center programs. After the Select Panel's 1981 report on the health of the nation's children,[8] and with the help of several private foundations, school-based health programs enjoyed a renaissance, the durability of which is not yet apparent.

There are many good descriptions of school health programs.[14-17] The American Academy of Pediatrics until recently recommended that a physician serve as the director of the school health program, but in its 1987 guide[17] it focused on the tasks to be performed and the skills and relationships needed.

A complete school health program includes a systematic concern for the environment of the school, health services to promote and protect the health of the children, and a comprehensive approach to health education. With this triad in mind, the basic components of a school health program

TABLE 24-5 Components of a school health program

School environment	Health services	Health education
Maintenance of a safe, sanitary plant	Health appraisal	Planned, direct health teaching
Buildings	Health exam	Indirect health education
Grounds	Screening exams	In food service
Playfields	Special exams	In athletics
Gymnasium	Referrals	Role models
Health service unit	Care of exceptional children	Integrated health education
Seating, lighting, ventilation, heating, sanitation, drinking fountains	Prevention and control of disease	Health units in other subject courses
Safety and injury prevention	Immunizations	In-service health education
General safety	Surveillance	Parent education
Protective equipment	Reporting	Preparation of health curriculum guides
Fire drills	Planned emergency care	Resources
Civilian defense and disaster drills	Illness	Teaching aids
Safety patrols	Injury	Print media
Traffic safety	Health counseling	Film media
Transportation	Health of school personnel	Community facilities
Recreation program	Cooperation with community agencies	Museums
Food service	Official	Libraries
Custodial care	Voluntary	Health centers
The school day	Civic	Cooperation with community health education efforts
Length	Parent	Official agencies
Class size	Program coordination	Voluntary agencies
Daily routine		

Modified from Hanlon JJ and McHose E: Design for health: the teacher, the school, and the community, ed 2, Philadelphia, 1971, Lea & Febiger.

and the activities involved in each of them are presented in Table 24-5. Of necessity, there is a certain amount of overlapping and interrelationship among them. This is desirable, since each part of the program should be designed and used as much as possible to augment other parts. Thus certain aspects of the school enviroment or health appraisal activities should provide valuable first-hand instructional material.

The school environment

The term *environment* should be interpreted in its broadest context when considering the school health program. It refers not only to the immediate, physical nature of the school building—its sanitation and safety—but also to its surroundings and its interplay with child growth and development. The environmental health aspects of the school health program should take into consideration every potential physical, mental, and social hazard with which the child may come in contact. When the state requires that its citizens spend time in a public arena, it is the state's responsibility to assure that the environment is a salubrious one. This obligation increases in direct proportion to the vulnerability of those involved.

A discussion of the details of each of the many factors involved in the school environment is beyond the scope of this book. Most states have detailed specifications regarding the physical plant of a school, and architects must adhere to those requirements when planning new buildings and grounds. The decision to build a new school and the decision of where to locate it are not matters over which a public health agency has a great deal of control. School boards are fairly autonomous, and they have the usual difficulties that all forms of local government have when attempting to site a new building project: the most appropriate land is often the most expensive, the least expensive land is often the least appropriate. In addition, however, the school board has the horrendous problem of satisfying the many interests of both the parents whose children will be using the school and nonparents who may wish to obtain special advantages from the school or to be spared having anything to do with it. All too often, an attempt is made to satisfy landowners, taxpayers, and the users of several community schools by building a new, consolidated school on neutral ground, which usually means too far away from everyone, necessitating long walks for a few and bus rides for many others. The health department probably will not be consulted about the choice, but it should be prepared to intervene nonetheless to assure, at a minimum, that the location is safe and sanitary, with a good water supply, adequate sewerage, and not unduly close to waste disposal facilities or significant sources of noise or other forms of pollution. There should be adequate and safe recreational space and a reasonable guarantee that adjacent land will not be used for purposes inimical to the best interests of the children in the years ahead.

One possibility that is rarely considered is use of the school facilities by other community groups. The school's educational functions are served only for about 8 hours a day, 9 months out of the year. There are other important groups in the community that can benefit from many of the same facilities and services: a food service system, audiovisual aids, recreational space, and a library. The elderly are one example. In many communities, the Area Agency on Aging pursues its interests independently of the school board. Yet both groups propose to use public funds to build and manage public buildings to serve the needs of partially dependent and vulnerable groups of citizens, one young and one old. Senior citizens could derive substantial benefits from the shared use of school facilities. Young children can be helped significantly by interested and experienced older citizens, who can play an informal foster grandparent role. This is especially important for children with developmental disabilities and for the growing number of children who lack a healthy home environment with an intact family.

The health department may have a role to play in the construction process, including review and approval of sanitary facilities and the food service system. In some rural areas, where fluoridated municipal water is not available, it may be possible to install an on-site water fluoridation system. Although state school authority requirements (and often direct supervision of the building project) should assure that acceptable standards regarding ventilation, lighting, heating, and acoustics are met, it would be prudent for qualified staff of the health department to become involved in the review process. In urban areas, the water and sewer systems to be used may be presumed to be adequate but often are not, and the health department should carefully review the plans for connections and the plumbing systems themselves to avoid cross-connections and other improper and unsafe conditions. In rural and developing suburban areas, water and sewer systems can be considerably more troublesome and require especially persistent supervision by the health department.

Many school systems employ their own environmental health specialists, and in some jurisdictions, the school board may feel that it is not subject to the supervision of the local health department. Contention can result that may be related more to hegemony than to the health of the children. Such problems require careful and thoughtful consideration and negotiation if the best interests of the children are to be protected. Many schools have extensive food service systems, for example, and a school system nutritionist may avoid any input from the local health department in regard to the meals, the physical facilities, and the personnel. Supervision by the school system may be quite adequate, but it should not be assumed to be so: the health department should examine the food service systems carefully and attempt to develop good working relationships with the school personnel.

The school may also contain extensive and complex recreational facilities, including swimming pools and shower rooms. Standards for construction and maintenance should be carefully reviewed with the school authorities, and the health department should continue to monitor the use of the facilities. This is particularly important in light of the trend to expand the use of expensive school facilities to the community at large. The school should also have space set aside and designed for its health services program, including provisions for first aid and employee services. (This is discussed further below, under "School health services.")

The most ideally located and constructed school can rapidly deteriorate and become a sanitary menace unless provision is made for its proper maintenance. The school and its facilities should have a well-developed inspection program, with individual schedules for those aspects of the system that have the greatest potential for danger, such as water, food, and ventilation. A complete, annual inspection should be carried out by the health department with school system personnel participating. This includes private schools and academies. It is often best done in the summer months when schedules make a thorough inspection more practical and time remains for necessary repairs before the start of the fall session. Written reports and recommendations for improvements should be submitted to the school principal and superintendent. In some districts, state school board environmental health personnel may be involved in such inspections. Follow-up inspections should be made to be sure that essential improvements are made correctly.

School health services

The principal argument about school health services (as one part of the school health program) was mentioned earlier: should the services be those minimal activities designed to facilitate learning, or should a more comprehensive array of health services be provided in the school and even by the school system. There is some general sense that children are a valuable resource, that they are vulnerable, and that the community has both the authority and the responsibility to care for them. The community will tolerate a broad range of abuse before it will intervene in the home setting, but once the child is in school, there is a less ambivalent attitude toward intervention. Dress codes are by no means passé; behavior is modified to fit the school's needs and expectations; children are required to be immunized against certain communicable diseases (imagine the response if the state tried to require adults to be immunized against influenza!); and hearing and vision testing are common. It is generally assumed that most schoolchildren have a family physician, but except in affluent areas, this is increasingly incorrect. Accepting the earlier statement that the state is obliged to protect those over whom it assumes even temporary custody, can or should the state, as it is represented by the school board, take steps to provide basic health services? Can the community try to correct the problems brought into the school and send a healthy child on into the secondary school system and the adult world?

The question is not a simple one. There might be some conviction, although often not the resources, to provide physical health services, but some of the more serious problems brought into elementary school by children are the result of mental and social deprivation or abuse. These are not only more difficult to correct, but community and parental support for such efforts is weak and ambivalent. To treat an infection or repair an injury is one thing; for a bureaucrat to meddle unasked in the psyche of a family's child is quite another thing, perhaps justifiably so. Psychological testing and counseling in the school system have not been uniformly useful, and schools are not loathe to label variations and eccentricities as clinical aberrations warranting reformation and treatment. Mental illness in children, as noted before, is a difficult phenomenon to detect and diagnose accurately. Moreover, schools may take a fairly conservative approach to behavior modification to avoid the risk of parental wrath. This is prime time: significant events may have occurred already that, at least in theory, could be offset by skillful intervention in elementary school, and other events will occur during these years that may have a profound effect on personality development. Epidemiologic and clinical research is badly needed. It is equally true that sociological research and ethical inquiry are needed to make interventions both appropriate and useful.

At one time, it was the custom to attempt to examine every schoolchild every year. Eventually it was realized that the practice was inefficient and ineffective.[18] So many children had to be examined that they usually received only cursory attention; so much work was involved in getting the job done that management of the process became an end in itself, leaving no time for the essential counseling, referral, and follow-up. Moreover, epidemiologic concepts of incidence and prevalence, sensitivity and specificity, and the other problems of screening, which have been described in previous chapters, were not well understood by those involved. A more reasonable and enlightened approach to the examination of school children is now followed in progressive communities with adequate resources. This involves general physical examinations three or four times during the school years, usually in the office of a family physician or pediatrician. Those without such access are often seen in health department clinics or in community health centers. Special examinations, such as screening for hearing and vision defects, and a simple examination of the spine for scoliosis (the incorrect curvature of the spine) are carried out on different schedules, based on the nature of the particular problems. It is especially important that protocols for such examinations be carefully developed, with consultation from experts and routine quality checks to be sure that the tests are being performed accurately. Screening tests, even simple ones, can produce a large number of erroneous results if great care is not exercised.

Some school districts still employ local physicians for such purposes, usually on a part-time basis. It is rare now for schools to have regular, salaried physicians. At one time, it was common for schools to hire the most recent arrivals in the community under the assumption that they did not have a busy practice yet and that they might be willing to devote time to community programs. These practices are breaking down now as an increasing number of new physicians begin practice in a group, as a salaried member, and devote all of their time to the development of the group's interests. Sometimes the older physicians in the community may be willing to spend some of their time in such work.

As a growing number of children enter the school system without adequate access to pediatric care and the business of medicine becomes more highly organized, school health service programs will require more planning and involvement by the health department. Schools are under intense pressure to use their scarce resources for their primary mission of education. Health departments are under similar pressures to carry out expanded programs with restricted resources, but the health of school children is thought to be a health department, not a school board, problem. Where the family can afford to pay for private care, they should be urged to do so, and programs of record keeping should be developed to assure that the school is aware of any problems. Where such care is not possible, public resources will have to be used.

In many communities private care is the norm. In others it may be the exception, and public agencies must develop both the essential services and the coordinating, referral, and follow-up mechanisms needed to assure consistency and continuity of care. Follow-up is often difficult because of working parents or ignorance of health and medical care. Well-designed programs have been developed in many communities.

An important technique that is of value as an adjunct to surveillance and examination by health professionals is the screening of pupils by their classroom teachers. The health department can assist in the development of such programs and in in-service training for teachers to acquaint them with the signs and symptoms of common problems. Without attempting to make diagnosticians out of them or to overburden them, the accuracy of teachers at first level screening can be enhanced considerably. Pupils with indications of problems can be referred to health professionals within the school system for further evaluation. Comparative tests have demonstrated the sensitivity of teachers to health problems without reference to a specific cause.

Some screening tests have been sufficiently validated to warrant their use in the school setting by trained health professionals or technicians. Vision and hearing testing are especially important. A substantial number of children enter school with hearing or vision defects, which if uncorrected will impede learning. Screening programs require careful attention to detail and quality control to be sure that they are appropriately conducted. Equally diligent efforts are necessary to assure that the referral and follow-up procedures are carried out. It is astonishing to realize the extent to which some programs have emphasized testing without quality controls and without a well-developed referral program: without such features, the screening is of little or no use. It is widely assumed that screening is useful. When such programs are carefully examined, however, the cost-to-benefit ratio is often found to be considerably greater than 1.0. Such programs require periodic reevaluation, since the results are dependent on the prevalence of the condition screened for and the technology of the screening process.

Another important aspect of the school health services program is the control and prevention of communicable diseases. The most important objective is to be sure that all children entering the school system have been properly immunized against measles, mumps, whooping cough, rubella, polio, diphtheria, and tetanus. Of course, this should be done much earlier in life, beginning before the first birthday and being completed before the second year of life. Statutes should be in place that require the school system to verify that children have been immunized before they can enter school, even though this sometimes results in parents delaying immunizations unitl the fifth year. The protocol used to verify immunization status will vary from state to state. The health department should work with the school board to assure that an adequate protocol is in effect and that it is followed, with periodic audits to be sure. A high degree of protection can be obtained by education of parents and school officials without resorting to legal threats. For purposes of protecting the children in the school (and in the case of rubella, the adult female teachers and other school employees), it is not necessary that every last child be completely immunized. There are people who object strongly to such practices for religious reasons. Although the law requires that they submit to the wisdom of the state, outbreaks can be prevented if 95% of the children are immunized. If there are a few families in the community with strong objections (e.g., Christian Scientists), it should be possible to attain those levels without rigorously insisting on 100% compliance.

The periodic audit of immunization requirements is necessary if outbreaks are to be prevented. Inevitably, a few children will enter the school system without adequate immunization. There are always a few children in whom the immunization was not effective even though it was done properly. Sooner or later, the small probability that a group of such unimmunized people will come together materializes, and an outbreak can occur with serious consequences. Most new cases of measles in the United States, other than those imported from other countries, occur in just this way. When programs are not reviewed periodically, the immunization status of the group will slowly decline until less than 85% of the children are protected and an outbreak occurs. Such outbreaks are far more costly to contain than they are to prevent. Note that laws often indicate that all children must be immunized upon *school entry,* which has been interpreted to mean kindergarten or first grade. Older children transferring into the school district are usually not subjected to inquiry about their immunization status. The laws should be changed to require immunization in order to attend school. While a public health law, mandatory immunization statutes are enforced by the school system. The impact of such laws is obtained through the parallel law requiring children to attend school. Since they cannot do so without being immunized, the parents are in violation of the attendance law until they have the child immunized. If an outbreak occurs and the situation gets out of control, the health department may be able to exercise its emergency powers to prevent people from coming into the school environment unless they have been protected.

One question that inevitably arises is when to close a school because of an outbreak of infectious disease. Generally, the public expects the school to be closed when an outbreak occurs, but this is often neither necessary nor desirable. Closure is treated as a holiday by many children and their families, resulting in even more intense intermixture of unimmunized adults and children and an extension of the outbreak. In communities with a well-organized and efficient public health program and a good school health service program, it is usually better to keep the school open where the children can be kept under surveillance. When an outbreak occurs, two questions should be asked: (1) are nurses and medical staff adequate and teaching staff alert enough that the inspection, observation, and supervision of students will keep sick children out of school? (2) if the school is closed, will students be kept at home and away from other children, so that closing the school will not increase the opportunities for contact? When the first question can be answered affirmatively or the second one negatively, schools should be kept open. This is most often the case in large schools and in urban communities. Schools should be closed when the first question is answered negatively or the second affirmatively. In smaller communities with scattered homes, where chances for personal contact are limited, this is frequently the case. There are no simple rules for making a decision when both questions are answered either no or yes.

It is easy to lose control in such situations, and the health department can find itself in the middle of a squabble that may have its roots in other sources of parent-teacher-administration contention. Some parents cannot accept the fact that scabies may have been acquired at home and insist that the school be closed as the source of what is perceived by them to be a disease born in filth. Such accusations can fall on eager ears if there are other sources of friction, such as bus routes, hiring practices, or school lunch programs. On one occasion, mothers were irate about what appeared to be a criticism of their housekeeping practices and insisted that the school be closed. The health department was dragged into the fracas and concurred. Only later did the health department director realize that (1) most of the fathers were on strike at the local auto parts plant and (2) fishing season had started. The families took a 5-day vacation. Perhaps it did everyone some good, but it didn't solve the health problem.

Health education

Schools are primarily places where children go to learn. Good health is an essential ingredient to both learning and life. It follows, therefore, that children should learn about health in school. They should learn a lot about it. "Health" is a required part of most school curriculums, but only recently has it received the attention it deserves. Too often, whatever passed for health instruction was the responsiblity of the gym teacher or a general classroom educator who was not especially qualified for the subject and often had little interest in it. The relationship of the teaching, observable practices, the general environment, and role models was not appreciated. On a par with these inadequate practices is the use of didactically unsuited staff of the local health department, who are asked to come into the classroom and give a "health talk" to the students. Most public health professionals enjoy and accept such invitations without realizing that they are an entertaining diversion for the students and a welcome substitute for the teacher, and little more.

Teaching is a profession and a skill. Everyone is not suited by temperament, training, and experience for the challenge. Certain skills, aptitudes, and training are necessary to accomplish what is needed. As much as possible, the teaching of health, like the teaching of math and language, should be left to trained professionals who are acquainted with the students. The health department can be of greatest assistance to the teacher by offering advice and providing consultation and in-service education, teaching materials, and other assistance in planning the health education program. This can best be done by a trained health educator on the health department staff, who may meet with teachers collectively and individually to discuss goals and problems. Visual aids are becoming available from ever-enlarging sources, and the health department, as one of its community activities, should help make them available to the school.

Green and Iverson[19] and McAlister[20] have emphasized the need for rationality and consistency in the school health education effort as a part of the total school health program. The ecology of the school has as much impact on shaping health behavior as the more didactic classroom work. The purpose of health education is to impart knowledge, with the expectation that the knowledge will shape attitudes that will in turn affect behavior. There has been a great deal of skepticism about the efficacy of school health education efforts. Many programs have been so poor as to justify the skepticism, but there is much new evidence that a well-designed school health education effort can improve nutrition, reduce risk-taking behavior such as drinking and smoking, and prevent pregnancy.

Green and Iverson emphasize the need to develop consistency in the approach to the three basic factors in a school health education program:

1. *Predisposing factors,* or knowledge about biology and health
2. *Enabling factors,* such as the skills needed to floss teeth or to say no to peer pressure
3. *Reinforcing factors,* which include the attitude and environment of the teachers and administrators in such places as the school cafeteria, lounge areas, and playgrounds

Good results have been achieved when schoolchildren have been taught how to resist peer pressure. Consistency and rationality are the crucial ingredients: an effective classroom program can be eroded by a poor diet or smoking in the teacher's lounge area.

The effectiveness of school health education programs with well-designed curriculums and trained teachers has been demonstrated by the School Health Education Evaluation Study (SHEE).[21] Between 1982 and 1984, 30,000 children in the fourth through seventh grades were followed in 1,071 classrooms in 20 states. Some children were involved in carefully designed programs; others remained in their normal classrooms. Health knowledge increased in the experimental classrooms, followed by the acquisition of healthier attitudes and better skills and practices. There was evidence that the programs slowed the onset of smoking till later grades. Specific knowledge could be increased relatively easily; general knowledge about human health required greater concentration and more classroom hours. The overall effects were "dose-dependent"; that is, the more time and effort spent, the greater the effect. Interestingly, it was noted that a learning module was most effective when the teacher believed the material and thought it to be important. The evaluators suggested that if all of the students in the United States had been exposed to one of the four experimental curriculums used in the project, there would have been 146,000 fewer smoking students in the seventh grade.

Many local health departments and school authorities have developed programs of field trips and special health study projects designed to demonstrate to schoolchildren community activities that have an influence on the health and well-being of themselves, their families, and the community. When properly planned and carried out, these study programs can have a considerable educational impact. A few health departments have progressed further, to the point of allowing high-school students to take turns working at simple jobs in the health department offices or in clinics, as volunteers or at a nominal salary. This is a doubly worthwhile venture as a form of vocational guidance. To be of value, however, a judicious choice of jobs and constant supervision are necessary.

In recent years, many states have undertaken extensive curriculum development projects as the pressure of health problems on economics and community productivity has become a more serious topic of concern and discussion. Since the early 1980s, of course, the problem of AIDS has increased state and community interest in school health education. The Centers for Disease Control of the U.S. Public Health Service has published guidelines for AIDS education in the schools, and a number of new kindergarten-through-high-school (K-12) curriculum plans have been developed.[22]

Governance

Bearing in mind that there are three components to the school health program (the environment, health services, and health education), there are three organizational models for implementing the program: the board of education can operate the entire program, the health department can operate the school health program, or they can manage the program collaboratively. If the past history of the community is favorable, joint governance is preferred. If not, then it is probably better for the board of education to govern the program, even though it will need a good working relationship with the health department to assure an acceptable level of environmental protection and sanitation. It makes little sense for a health department to attempt to take over a program that has been a traditional concern of the school board for many years, even though the health department may be better qualified in some respects. Upsetting tradition can harm a program more than the assumed benefits can help. The board of education is legally responsible for the health and safety of the children in school, and if collaboration is not possible, it must assume that responsibility directly. In most states the health department has statutory responsibility for many aspects of the school environment and must carry out that responsibility by working with the school officials.

In a combined program, the school staff should have the lead role in developing and implementing the health education program with the support of the public health department and its staff when needed. Health professionals should serve in a consulting capacity and only become involved in direct teaching when they are particularly effective or when school personnel cannot handle the assignment. The environmental program must be carried out by school personnel, but health department staff must set the standards and should conduct periodic inspections and provide technical assistance in overcoming problems. Environmental health workers should be involved in the planning of any new school. The health service program, which is designed to protect and promote the health of the children, is more appropriately placed under the general supervision of health department personnel, who must plan and carry out their work in close collaboration with the school faculty and staff.

In some large cities, the board of education may have a well-developed school health program, including health services, and there is no need to make fundamental changes in the organizational responsibility of such programs. In smaller and rural communities, it is more likely that the school system will have to depend on the health department for the school health program. "Ownership" of the school health program has been a theoretical as well as a political argument in many communities, to the detriment of the program and the health of the children. More recently the argument has centered around who can afford it. As school costs have increased and citizens have resisted increases in school taxes, school boards have often reduced their support for school health service programs, leaving them by default to the local health department, which often has not had the resources to absorb the added work load. Taxpayer support for school systems in general and school health programs in particular has become a significant problem, especially as the population ages and the fertility rate declines. In many communities the organized voters are older, white citizens with few or no school-aged children, while those with the greatest interest in the schools are younger, less well organized, poor, and largely minority. Support for school taxes has decreased.

Every school and school system should have a health council or committee with representation from all groups concerned with school health. At the top level in the community, where general cooperative relationships and policies are developed most effectively, membership should include such persons as the superintendent of schools, the local health officer, the president of the parent-teacher organization, representatives from the medical and dental societies, and other individuals who are in key positions in regard to the health and well-being of schoolchildren. Special efforts should be made to include articulate parents who resist an extension of the school's role in health services and education. If not, they can be surprisingly effective at blocking plans for improvements. The relationship of the central school health council to each of the individual school health councils or committees is best determined by experience in each community. In general it has been recommended that the central council guide and give leadership but leave each individual school health council with substantial authority and latitude.

THE FUTURE

There are many good texts on the subject of child health and development,[8,23] but the essential problems are perhaps best expressed by Arden Miller, who has proposed a comprehensive national program of organized health services for mothers and children,[24] and George Silver,[25] who makes the same recommendation. Concern for the health of children, according to Silver, is in third place after concern for the role of the family (even though the family is regrettably the source of the problem in many instances) and concern for protecting the entrepreneurial role of the private doctor. Much of what is needed cannot be provided, because many people feel that values and behavior are the province of the family, not social institutions, and many services are lacking because of a traditional reliance on private practice. The public organization of school and community health services for children is a tattered fabric woven to protect those concerns while still serving the needs of the child. Although many efforts have been very creative and resulted in well-balanced programs, the effort to construct such programs without addressing the core problem is tedious, expensive, and inadequate. Reliance on the traditional concepts of private, fee-for-service medical practice supported by sickness insurance cannot produce the sort of social health organization needed. Given the social indicators of poverty, family disruption, illiteracy, substance use, behavioral disorders, and child abuse in society at present, the development of such programs cannot move forward fast enough. But it is moving. As noted in the conclusion of the previous chapter, social forces are aligned now that could result in new national initiatives to support rather than harm the growth and development of this nation's children.

REFERENCES

1. US Bureau of the Census: Household and family characteristics: March 1986, Current Population Reports, Series P-20, No 419, Nov 1987.
2. US Bureau of the Census: Money income and poverty status in the United States: 1987, Advance data from the March 1988 Current Population Survey, Current Population Reports, Series P-60, No 161, Aug 1988.
3. US Bureau of the Census: Economic characteristics of households in the United States: fourth quarter, 1984, Current Population Reports, Series P-70, No 6, Jan 1986.
4. Strayhorn JM: The competent child: an approach to psychotherapy and preventive mental health, New York, 1988, Guilford Press.
5. Blom GE, Cheney BD, and Snoddy JE: Stress in childhood: an intervention model for teachers and other professionals, New York, 1986, Teachers College, Columbia University.
6. Dohrenwend BP and others: Mental illness in the United States: epidemiological estimates, New York, 1980, Praeger Publishers.
7. Hefzallah IM: Critical viewing of television: a book for parents and teachers, Lanham, MD, 1987, University Press of America, Inc.
8. The Select Panel for the Promotion of Child Health: Better health for our children: a national strategy, vol 1, Washington, DC, 1981, US Government Printing Office.
9. Williams TM, editor: The impact of television: a natural experiment in three communities, Orlando, FL, 1986, Academic Press.
10. Braddock D: Federal policy toward mental retardation and developmental disabilities, Baltimore, MD, 1987, Paul H Brooks Publishing Co.
11. The White House Conference, New York, 1931, The Century Company.
12. American Public Health Association: Education for health in the school community setting: position paper of the American Public Health Association, Am J Public Health 65:201, Feb 1975.
13. Schaller WE: The school health program, ed 5, Philadelphia, 1981, Saunders College.
14. Sandoval J. editor: Crisis counseling, intervention and prevention in the schools, Hillsdale, NJ, 1988, L. Erlbaum.
15. Cornacchia HJ, Olsen LK, and Nickerson CJ: Health in elementary schools, ed 7, St Louis, 1988, Times Mirror/Mosby College Publishing.
16. Creswell WH, Newman IM, and Anderson CL: School health practice, ed 8, St Louis, 1985, Times Mirror/Mosby College Publishing.
17. Committee of School Health: School health: a guide for health professionals, Elk Grove, IN, 1987, American Academy of Pediatrics.
18. Yankauer A and others: A study of periodic school medical examinations, parts I, II, III, and IV, Am J Public Health 45:71, Jan 1955; 46:1553, Dec 1956; 47:1421, Nov 1957; and 51:1532, Oct 1961.
19. Green LW and Iverson DC: School health education, Ann Rev Public Health 3:321, 1982.
20. McAlister AL: Social and environmental influences on health behavior, Health Educ Q 8:25, Spring 1981.
21. Effectiveness of school health education, Morbid Mortal Week Rep 35:594, September 26, 1986.
22. Guidelines for effective school health education to prevent the spread of AIDS, Morbid Mortal Week Rep 37(suppl 2), January 29, 1988.
23. Wallace HM, Gold EM, and Oglesby A, editors: Maternal and child health practices, ed 2, New York, 1982, John Wiley & Sons.
24. Miller CA: Health care of children and youth in America, Am J Public Health 65:353, April 1975.
25. Silver GA: Redefining school health services: comprehensive child health care as the framework, J Sch Health 51:157, March 1981.

CHAPTER 25

Adolescence and public health

> Adolescence is a new birth, for the higher and more completely human traits are now born. The qualities of body and soul that now emerge are far newer. . . . Development is less gradual and more saltatory, suggestive of some ancient period of storm and stress when old moorings were broken and a higher level attained. The annual rate of growth in height, weight, and strength is increased and often doubled, and even more. Important functions previously non-existent arise. . . . Some linger long in the childish stage and advance late or slowly, while others rush on with a sudden outburst of impulsion to early maturity. . . . Nature arms youth for conflict with all the resources at her command—speed, power of shoulder, biceps, back, leg, jaw—strengthens and enlarges skull, thorax, hips, makes man aggressive and prepares woman's frame for maternity. . . . every step of the upward way is strewn with wreckage of body, mind, and morals. . . . Modern life is hard, and in many respects increasingly so, on youth. . . . Sex asserts its mastery in field after field and works its havoc in the form of secret vice, debauch, disease and enfeebled heredity . . . and sends many thousand youth a year to quacks, because neither parents, teachers, preachers or physicians know how to deal with its problems.[1]

Thus did G. Stanley Hall, a professor of psychology at Clark University, describe adolescence in 1905. The phenomenon had only recently been discovered.[2]

Whether adolescence exists in nature and was truly discovered by adults or simply invented to describe changing social circumstances has been debated for years. Surely something significant is going on that is special to those years, and just as surely, Americans have heightened the attention paid to the phenomenon far beyond the value attributed to it in other countries. Birth is clearly demarcated, and death too. In between, however, the dividing lines are vague and difficult to define. As will be discussed in the next chapter, the concept of aging is especially elusive.

Adolescence has been defined as "the process whereby an individual makes the gradual transition from childhood to adulthood."[3] Its beginning is marked by the biochemical and physiologic changes of puberty; its endings are less precise, varying between the middle teenage years and the mid-20s. For reasons not altogether clear but thought to be related to improved health status generally and nutrition specifically, the onset of puberty has become gradually earlier. As children prolong their training into college and graduate school before entering the world of employment and family formation, the end of adolescence has become gradually later. Thus the duration of adolescence has been increasing. If you remember the relationship of prevalence to duration and incidence described in Chapter 5, it becomes apparent that there are more adolescents now then there used to be, even though there are slightly fewer people in the age range 13 to 19 than there were in the early 1970s, simply because the duration of adolescence is greater. Adolescents, like families, are more mobile than ever before, and they have more economic power, at least in the United States and other industrialized countries, than at any other time in history. They are an important market segment for manufacturers of radios, compact discs, clothes, cars, sports equipment, and, unfortunately, tobacco, alcohol, and other licit and illicit substances. They staff and use fast food outlets, patronize hair stylists, attend massive concerts, view and even produce movies and videocassettes, fill the beaches and swimming pools, and throng the shopping malls. They have a lot of babies and a lot of abortions. Adolescence is a biological phenomenon, but it is also and equally powerfully an economic, social, and demographic phenomenon.

There were about 25 million teenagers (ages 13 to 19) in the United States in 1989. They were born in the years 1970 to 1976. Although birth rates had been going down for several years, they began to increase in 1976, and that increase continued through 1986. That means that there will be more adolescents in 1994—about 2% to 4% more. If the duration of adolescence continues to increase, there will be still more.

HEALTH STATUS

By and large, adolescents are an incredibly healthy bunch of people. There is great national angst about the health problems of adolescents, and many groups talk about the leading cause of death or disability for 13-year-olds or 18-year-olds. The overwhelming majority of them, however, will survive not only to adulthood, but to a very old age. The problem, of course, is that so few diseases affect adolescents seriously that the few things that do cause death are particularly tragic: motor vehicle crashes, suicide, and homicide, especially. The picture emerges in Table 25-1, which shows the leading causes of death for male and female, black and white adolescents, aged 15 to 19.

Most of the deaths are the result of violence: homicide, suicide, motor vehicle crashes, and other injuries. That is true for 82% of the deaths of white males aged 15 to 19, 76% of black males, 70% of white females, and 51% of black females. The second most striking feature is the sex discrepancy: males are 2.4 to 2.8 times more likely to die during these years than are females, and most of that difference is due to violence. Note also the differences in death rates due to motor vehicle crashes. They are a function of passenger miles driven, and white males and females are much more likely to have access to a car than are black males and females. That white females are more likely to die a violent death than black females is almost solely attributable to their access to cars and to the fact that black females have higher death rates from disease.

These are the facts and figures that are partly responsible for the national concern over the health of adolescents. Yet while the causes of death are shocking, another fact is apparent, as noted above: teenagers are very unlikely to die from any cause at all: 99.9% of males and an even larger percentage of females aged 15 to 19 survive these years. Death is much more likely to occur in the first year of life (only 99% of newborns survive their first year) or during childhood.

There is more to life than an absence of death, however. Acute and chronic dependency patterns related to physical, mental, and social disease have

TABLE 25-1 Ten leading causes of death and death rates per 100,000 for white and black males and females, aged 15 to 19, United States, 1986

	Cause of death (rate per 100,000)			
Rank	**White males**	**Black males**	**White females**	**Black females**
1	Motor vehicle crashes (51.9)	Homicide (46.4)	Motor vehicle crashes (22.8)	Homicide (10.3)
2	Suicide (17.3)	Motor vehicle crashes (21.9)	Suicide (4.1)	Motor vehicle crashes (7.5)
3	Other injuries (16.9)	Other injuries (18.5)	Cancer (3.7)	Other injuries (3.2)
4	Homicide (7.3)	Suicide (8.2)	Other injuries (3.4)	Cancer (3.0)
5	Cancer (5.8)	Heart disease (5.8)	Homicide (2.7)	Heart disease (3.0)
6	Heart disease (2.3)	Cancer (5.2)	Heart disease (1.4)	Suicide (1.5)
7	Congenital anomalies (1.4)	Congenital anomalies (2.0)	Congenital anomalies (1.0)	Congenital anomalies (1.2)
8	Influenza and pneumonia (0.6)	Asthma (1.4)	Influenza and pneumonia (0.3)	Complications of pregnancy (1.2)
9	Cerebrovascular diseases (0.6)	Cerebrovascular diseases (1.0)	Cerebrovascular diseases (0.3)	Asthma (1.1)
10	Asthma (0.2)	Chronic lung disease (1.2)	Septicemia (0.3)	Influenza and pneumonia (0.9)
	All causes (113.7)	All causes (124.7)	All causes (47.0)	All causes (44.3)

From National Center for Health Statistics: Vital statistics of the United States, 1985, part II, Mortality, Part A, Washington, DC, 1987, US Government Printing Office.

a significant influence on adolescence and subsequent adulthood. Table 25-2 shows the number of acute conditions per 100 people each year for children, adolescents, and young adults. (The figures published by the National Center for Health Statistics do not include a separate category for children aged 13 to 19. The data tapes are public documents and are available from the Center, making it possible to calculate tables for any age group. They are complex, however, and require advanced statistical and computer skills.) The age group 5 to 17 is intermediate in its experience with acute illness, as well as in age, between preschoolers and young adults, with an average of 2.3 acute conditions each year. Table 25-3 indicates that these conditions result in a large number of restricted activity days each year: 6.5 per person per year, with the common cold, injuries, and various infectious diseases accounting for most of the lost days.

Throughout the time of adolescence, the individual is preparing for living by learning. This receptive, impressionable period should be the most fruitful for the dissemination of health knowledge, the development of healthy life-styles, and the establishment of understanding and support of community health measures. Often it is not.

During this period, the stresses of rapid growth become evident. Growth is manifest in both physical and mental changes, including the sexual maturation of the individual. Braceland[4] has suggested that as the adolescent tries to find a place in the scheme of things, there is a growing need for intimate peer exchange, friendship, acceptance, and social relationships with the opposite sex. All of these are important in the development not only of the adolescent but also of the subsequent adult. If there is nonacceptance of the adolescent's role as an individual and as a male or female, a defiant loneliness is apt to develop, with feelings of rejection and resentment or even hatred of oneself or of one or both parents, which may transfer to all members of a particular sex or social group or to society as a whole with disastrous consequences.

Out of this turmoil, a panoply of special medical and social problems may develop. Some are related to genetic factors and some to physiologic changes, whereas others develop from the search for identity and purpose with concomitant rebellion against a real or apparent restraining society. Not infrequently the causes are interrelated and mutually reinforcing, such as defiance of parents, drinking or drugs, pregnancy and sexually transmitted diseases, leading back to greater intergenerational discord. But the turmoil of adolescence can be, and often is, overstated. A teenage child dead of suicide evokes the guilt of all adults: how could we have created or portrayed a world so lacking in value that this young child did not wish to inhabit it? Yet most adolescents do not kill themselves, nor are they particularly disturbed. Repeated studies have shown them to be insightful, realistic, and at peace with their families.[5]

HEALTH NEEDS OF ADOLESCENTS

Many experts point out that society has not provided health services designed to meet the needs of adolescents, but the problem may not be lack of interest so much as the habit of thinking that a health problem requires a medical solution. In the

TABLE 25-2 Acute conditions per 100 persons per year, by age and type of condition, United States, 1987

Condition	<5	5-17	18-24
All types	358.9	230.1	186.6
Infections and parasitic diseases	57.0	44.8	22.5
Respiratory conditions	160.2	111.4	88.2
Injuries	25.9	33.5	33.3

From National Center for Health Statistics: Current estimates from the National Health Interview Survey, United States, 1987, Vital Health Stat, Series 10, No 166, Sept 1988.

TABLE 25-3 Number of restricted activity days associated with acute conditions per 100 persons per year, by age and type of condition, United States, 1987

Condition	<5	5-17	18-24
All types	936.3	654.7	689.9
Infections and parasitic diseases	165.2	151.6	64.8
Respiratory conditions	459.6	304.8	236.6
Injuries	38.2	105.7	184.6

From National Center for Health Statistics: Current estimates from the National Health Interview Survey, United States, 1987, Vital Health Stat, Series 10, No 166, Sept 1988.

Surgeon General's report *Healthy People*, the low priority given to adolescents is in part attributed to such factors as their low mortality rate generally, the difficult problems of consent and confidentiality, and the lack of a recognized medical specialty group.[8] Having described their problems in traditional medical terms, the lack of a traditional medical response is seen as a problem, and the health needs of adolescents are defined as unmet needs. Given that description of the problem, one response would be to support training in adolescent medicine and develop better health insurance programs. Such solutions might have some value, but they would miss the mark: the health problems of teenagers have more to do with their social and mental development, their knowledge and behavior, their attitudes and their values than with viruses and oncogenes. While they suffer a lot of injuries and minor colds, the resources most needed are counselors, teachers, and better-educated parents. Unfortunately, health insurance schemes do not include such vendors in their payment systems, making the work less lucrative. Since the school systems are under pressure to provide a strong, traditional education with vocational overtones, there is little support for the sort of health services needed by adolescents.

Adolescent health problems fall into certain categories in relation to their origin, severity, and behaviorism, of which parents, physicians, health agencies, schools, and society should be aware. One such category is the extensive group of congenital conditions, some genetic and some acquired in the uterus. This category includes diabetes, anatomic conditions such as cardiac and alimentary canal malformations, and physiologic conditions such as phenylketonuria (PKU) and certain anemias. It also includes certain psychiatric and neurologic conditions such as Huntington's chorea and schizophrenia. Finally, it includes certain infections that may be acquired congenitally. Most of these are manifest in early childhood, such as AIDS, which results in death before adolescence, but there are also a number of chronic conditions in adolescence that are a result of congenital infections. Congenital anomalies are common enough to take their place on the list of the ten leading causes of death in adolescents (see Table 25-1). They also cause developmental retardation and learning difficulties, which may necessitate special educational, social, and health services.

Substance use

This peculiar phrase is much argued over. More common terms are smoking, alcohol, and drug abuse. Taken collectively, the various chemical products, licit and illicit, that are used by people to alter their moods, their sensations, and their physical responses are often referred to by the colorless term *substances*. Then the question arises, is it abuse or use about which we are concerned. Is the mere use of tobacco, alcohol, and other drugs abusive? Abusive of what or whom: of society's expectations and policies, of the mind and body of the user, or of the welfare of friends and family? These are complex arguments for adults, for whom the consumption of alcohol and tobacco is a legal practice. For adolescents, the argument is a little simpler: given the laws of the land, their consumption is illegal, and any use can be considered a problem. More than half of high-school seniors have tried an illicit drug.

In the ongoing survey conducted by the University of Michigan's Institute for Social Research, illicit drug use increased from 1975 to 1982 and then slowly decreased, from a high of 66% of all seniors to 57% in 1987.[7] According to the authors of the study, "these clearly remain the highest rates of illicit drug use of any country in the industrialized world." Some of the decline was the result of decrease in the use of cocaine. No decline in alcohol use was measured. Almost all high-school seniors have had some experience with alcohol, and two thirds are current users. About 5% are daily drinkers, and nearly 40% reported at least one occasion of heavy drinking in the prior 2 weeks.

Cigarette use, which will kill more people than any of the other substances used by adolescents, did not decline after 1984. Almost 20% of high-school seniors were daily smokers in 1987, and most of them began smoking when they were 13. It is important to note that the survey included currently enrolled high-school seniors. It did not include drop-outs, who are more likely to use the various licit and illicit substances, and thus the real prevalence of use and abuse is underestimated.

The patterns of 1987 will be different by 1994. Certain patterns seem fairly durable: the disappointingly slow decline in the use of tobacco products and the persistent experimentation with alcohol. Other drugs are more variable. Cocaine had been used in the past 30 days by 1.9% of high-school seniors in 1975, increased to 6.7% by 1985, and then declined to 4.3% in 1987. The 1987 profile is in Table 25-4.

For most of the drugs listed, the current use (30-day prevalence) is considerably less than the experimental use (lifetime prevalence). Such is not the case for alcohol, however, which remains the most frequently used drug by high-school students and perhaps second only to tobacco in its danger.

The use of drugs spills over into the injury category of problems, especially motor vehicle crashes. Half of all fatally injured drivers aged 16 to 19 had been drinking. They tend to have slightly lower blood alcohol concentrations than do older drivers who are fatally injured, but their relative risk for a crash is greater, and it increases more rapidly with rising blood alcohol levels.[8] The assumption is that older drinking drivers compensate for their drinking better by driving more cautiously. The younger, less experienced drinking driver may not have learned such adaptive behavior or may feel less endangered.

Suicide and depression

Adolescent suicide is a prominent concern of parents, teachers, and public health professionals. As a cause of death it is underreported for two reasons: (1) some suicide deaths are not detected, or the suicidal nature of the act is suppressed by the family and a well-meaning but misguided physician; (2) many so-called accidental deaths surely occurred because of a suicidal act. Completed suicides are more common for white males than for black males or for females (see Table 25-1). Females more often attempt suicide but less often complete the act. Suicide is related to depression. The risk factors for both phenomena are similar and on a continuum.[9] Depression is sometimes considered a normal, episodic characteristic of adolescence, but a distinction should be made between depressive *feelings* as an affective (emotional) phenomenon and a depressive *disorder* as a psychopathological condition.[10] Such disturbances are *not* normal. A troubled adolescent should not be taken lightly.

Adolescent boys and girls have different suicide patterns. Girls, as noted above, are more frequent "attemptors." Their worries more often involve interpersonal relationships and family stress. Boys, who are more often successful, tend to be more active, aggressive, and impulsive, and their depression and suicidal acts often involve a confrontation with some authority and subsequent perceived humiliation.[9] Suicide may result from a particular incident, but it more usually reflects a pattern of vulnerability: unsuccessful adaptations, lack of effective peer relationships, and a sense of repeated failure with no hope for a better future. Warning signs are usually evident and may include expressions of worthlessness, giving away valued possessions, and mention of suicide. Even though most such behavioral patterns do not end in suicide, they are indicators of a potentially serious problem and should be treated accordingly.

Adolescent suicide is not a new phenomenon. Teenagers regularly think about their death and often have death wishes. Such thoughts are rare before the age of 10, as is suicide. The suicide rate was high in the United States in 1910 (about 11 per 100,000), then dropped to just under 4 in 1987. It has increased since then.[11] Why is not clear. Perhaps a greater contemporary sense of the limitation of global resources, the apparent degradation of the earth's environment, and the threat of nuclear and

TABLE 25-4 Lifetime and 30-day prevalence of use of selected drugs by high-school seniors, 1987*

Drug	Lifetime prevalence	30-day prevalence
Marijuana/hashish	50.2	21.0
Hallucinogens	10.3	2.5
Cocaine	15.2	4.3
Heroin	1.2	0.2
Other opiates	9.2	1.8
Stimulants	21.6	5.2
Sedatives	8.7	1.7
Tranquilizers	10.9	2.0
Alcohol	92.2	66.4
Cigarettes	67.2	29.4

From Johnston LD, O'Malley PM, and Bachman JG: Illicit drug use, smoking and drinking by America's high school students, college students and young adults, 1975-1987, Washington, DC, in press, National Institute on Drug Abuse.

*Only drug use that was not under a doctor's supervision is included.

chemical warfare, phenomena of which adolescents are painfully aware, contribute to the problem. Although still a relatively rare phenomenon, it has considerable shock value, sometimes occurring in a quick cluster involving friends.

Sexuality

The emerging sexuality of the adolescent presents both opportunities and problems. Girls mature earlier than boys. Both develop sex roles based on the models and examples established by their parents, their relationships with their peers, and such influences as magazines, television, and most importantly, their sexual experiences. The percentage of teenage girls who had experienced sexual intercourse increased during the 1970s, so that 55% of those who had never been married in 1976 had had intercourse by the age of 19. By now the rate has increased to 70%; for boys, 80%. Most sexually active adolescents wait at least 9 months after first intercourse before seeking contraceptive advice. According to the Planned Parenthood Federation of America, 35% of teenagers who come to a family planning clinic do so because they suspect they are pregnant.[12] Despite the high numbers, most teenagers are relatively monogamous, maintaining a continuing relationship with their partner and not experimenting outside of that relationship while it is still active.

About 11% of teenage girls between the ages of 15 and 19 become pregnant each year—1.1 million pregnancies—10% of white teens and 19% of nonwhites. The rate for black females has been decreasing in recent years. Almost half (449,000) of all teen pregnancies end in abortion, 40% white, 34% nonwhite. Over half a million pregnant teens keep their babies. This is more common for black than for white females.

Teenage pregnancy is a volatile topic. Roundly condemned as a serious national problem, it is only recently that pregnancy during the teen years has become a disutilitarian phenomenon. At the turn of the century it was not only normal in the confines of marriage, but expected and thought to be economically productive and appropriate. With the industrialization and urbanization of the economy, however, the adolescent years have been seen as a time of preparation for adulthood through education, and pregnancy is seen as disruptive to say the least. Whether it is dangerous is debatable, however. It is generally agreed that teenage mothers are more likely to have babies with low birth weights than are women in their 20s. They are also less likely to receive adequate prenatal care and more likely to die as a result of their pregnancy. These problems seem to be related to the risk factors for becoming pregnant, however, not to age. Pregnancy does not "select" a random assortment of teenage girls, but a biased sample: girls who have other risk factors related to their socioeconomic status and behavioral characteristics. They are more likely to be poor, smokers, drug users, and poorly nourished. Teenage girls, biologically, are fine mothers, but those who become pregnant have multiple risk factors, and the pregnancy can often compound them, disrupting their education. Even given that scenario, Geronimus[13] has postulated that black teens may make better mothers than their older sisters, who by their 20s have accumulated still more environmental and psychosocial damage, leading to even worse outcomes. The younger girls have family support and can often complete school and enter the labor force before their child enters school.

Most teenage girls do not use birth control regularly: one third never use it, one third use it inconsistently. Many use unreliable forms of contraception such as withdrawal or vaginal spermicides. Their level of knowledge about fertility and contraception is woefully inadequate. Boys are even less likely to understand what is going on, and they are rarely incorporated into community and school programs that focus on fertility and contraception.

Risk taking

Most of the adolescent health problems about which both adults and adolescents worry involve some element of risky behavior. Adolescents, boys especially, are risk takers. They experiment and challenge. They are as close to being immortal as they will ever be. Their physical, mental, and social development equips them to take risks younger children could not contemplate and older people would not attempt. The use of drugs, alcohol, and tobacco; daredevil driving; sexual experimentation; and the proclivity to climb high mountains, swim wide seas, and leap deep chasms all reflect the incredible energy of adolescence and the changes taking place. Risk taking is dangerous, assuredly. It leads to tragic consequences of death and disability.

It also leads to growth and development, however. A life without risk is death. Occasionally a child is born without an immune system. He or she is housed in a sterile cocoon in a high-tech hospital and never climbs a tree or rides a bike or kisses a friend. It is possible to keep such children alive for years, awaiting the development of their immune system. In the meantime, if they were exposed to the environment of the outside world, they would die. A life of perfect safety, with no risk, may be possible, but it is hardly desirable. It leads to such fragility that a normal life is impossible. Where to draw the line? We would prefer that adolescents not kill themselves or each other; we would prefer that they not smoke or drink or inject drugs; we would prefer that adolescent boys not impregnate adolescent girls. Yet they must experiment, and if they do, some will go too far, some will be disabled, and some will die. Help, support, education, and understanding are needed, not a perfectly safe and sanitized world.

ADOLESCENT HEALTH SERVICES

Until quite recently, health services programs specifically designed for adolescents were rare in the United States. Younger children, as an especially vulnerable and precious population group, have been protected in a variety of ways since the late 1800s, and school health services programs have been common in elementary schools (see Chapter 24). Teenagers, as befits their low mortality rates and seeming durability, have been largely ignored, however. In recent years, the problems described above have become more apparent, partly because they have increased in their incidence and partly because, as other problems have been overcome, the problems of adolescence have stood out more clearly against the background of salubrity.

In 1981, the Robert Wood Johnson Foundation, a major philanthropic organization with an interest in public health, announced a new program of projects to see what could be done about teenage pregnancy, drug (ab)use, suicide, homicide, alcoholism, depression, sexually transmitted diseases, and injuries.[14] They invited teaching hospitals throughout the United States to join with community organizations to develop special programs of needed services for high-risk adolescents. Altogether, 20 projects were funded, which involved nearly 15,000 health professionals; 17 project clinics were established in city or county health departments, 12 in community health centers, 10 in hospitals, and 8 in schools.

Since that time, adolescent health programs have been started in most states. By 1985, 12 states reported that they had adolescent mental health and school health education programs and provided services for adolescent pregnancy, and 14 states had general adolescent health promotion programs.[15]

Service programs are diverse in both structure and methods, but certain common features are apparent. First, federal support can be very useful. Grants-in-aid can provide both the stimulus and the funds necessary to start adolescent health programs in the states and their communities. Federal leadership was singularly important in getting the states to raise the legal drinking age to 21. Title X funds are available for family planning services, and the block grants for maternal and child health and general preventive health services can be used to support such programs.

State leadership is even more important. Although it is at the community level that services are actually provided, those who are interested and willing often find state level policies that make collaborative efforts at the local level very difficult. Two kinds of actions are needed at the state level: obstacle removal and policy formation. Adolescent health services require the effective collaboration of public and private providers in the public health, education, welfare, mental health, and medical care arenas. Education system policies that may preclude the development of a school-based health center or the provision of sex education or that make access to needed services by adolescents difficult need to be counteracted by the state level policymakers, including the legislature if necessary.

It may be necessary to pass special legislation establishing the right of adolescents to consent to certain forms of health services and, at the same time, protect their right to privacy and confidentiality.[16] Until recently, children were mere chattels and could not give their consent.[3] New statutes are not usually necessary, but consultation across agencies and with the state attorney general can help to clear up the confusion and provide the impetus needed for state agencies to provide facilitative policies for local program directors. It may also be possible to obtain more reimbursement from the state Medicaid agency, and the state education authority may help work out the complex issues pertaining to sex education and family planning in the school environment.

Most effective programs of health services for adolescents begin with an attempt by the responsible state agencies to arrive at a common definition of problems and objectives and to identify areas in which new policies and programs are needed. These interorganizational efforts should not be limited to the official state agencies, however. Representatives of parent organizations, health professional groups, ministerial organizations, and elected officials should be involved. It would be unwise to exclude those who are opposed to sex education in the schools, since they will be encountered again at the local level, and their values and viewpoints have to be considered.

At the local level, it is essential that the same groups be involved in reviewing the problems and in establishing community-based objectives. In some communities it may be acceptable to locate a clinic within the school itself. In other areas, it may be necessary to locate the program in the health department or in a community hospital or other facility. In some states, concerned citizens have obtained new legislation prohibiting the distribution of birth control information or devices in schools and in school-based health clinics. That may be an unfortunate policy, but it must be honored where it exists and alternative procedures established for referral of students to a health department or other clinic.

Procedures for obtaining consent and restrictions on the scope of consent that can be given by an adolescent must be developed at the community level. Parents should be given the option of allowing their children to give consent or requiring that the parents be involved. Generally speaking, confidentiality provisions should be rigorous, formal, and widely discussed in order to achieve consensus.

Funding can be very difficult. Ideally, new state legislation should be introduced to establish a grant-in-aid program. Local government resources may be available, either through the health department or the school board. Community agencies, including Planned Parenthood and federally funded community health centers and mental health and substance abuse centers, should be involved, along with community hospitals and organizations of health professionals. Out-of-pocket payments by adolescents are possible, as are some insurance payments.

Such programs can be very effective. The Robert Wood Johnson program for high-risk teenagers demonstrated the work that can be done to protect adolescents from their own risk-taking behavior, to provide crisis intervention services, to prevent and treat sexually transmitted diseases, and to cope with substance use problems. Programs to help adolescents with their awakening sexuality have been successful in increasing knowledge, altering attitudes, influencing behavior, and decreasing the fertility rate.[17]

SUMMARY

Adolescents are special people: they are nearly immortal (but only for a few short years), they are generally well adjusted, they undergo a gradual transformation from children to adults, they take all kinds of risks and generally escape unscathed, and they can depress, excite, and agitate adults beyond reason.

They do have special health problems and needs, which are not well served either in traditional child health programs or in the private practice of medical care. Since much of their time is spent out of the home and in the school, it is reasonable to develop special service programs to serve their needs in the school environment. To do so requires the collaboration of a wide array of interests and groups, because the very nature of adolescence is such that people have strong convictions about its meaning, its role, and its outcomes. States and communities have made considerable, innovative progress in recent years in meeting some of the health needs of their adolescent population. Much remains to be learned and accomplished.

REFERENCES

1. Hall GS: Adolescence: its psychology and its relations to physiology, anthropology, sociology, sex, crime, religion and education, New York, 1905, D Appleton & Co.
2. Troen SK: The discovery of the adolescent by American educational reformers, 1900-1920: an economic perspective. In Graff HJ, editor: Growing up in America, Detroit, 1987, Wayne State University Press.
3. Paxman JM and Zuckerman RJ: Laws and policies affecting adolescent health, Geneva, 1987, World Health Organization.

4. Braceland F: The devious paths of loneliness, MD 22:11, Jan 1978.
5. Adleson J: Inventing adolescence: the political psychology of everyday schooling, New Brunswick, NJ, 1986, Transaction Books.
6. Brown SS: The health needs of adolescents. In Healthy people: the Surgeon General's report on health promotion and disease prevention, background papers, US Department of Health, Education and Welfare Pub No (PHS)79-55071A, Washington, DC, 1979.
7. Johnston LD, O'Malley PM, and Bachman JG: Illicit drug use, smoking and drinking by America's high school students, college students and young adults, 1975-1987, Washington, DC, in press, National Institute on Drug Abuse.
8. Simpson HM: Young drivers' alcohol and drug impairment: magnitude, characteristics and significance of the problem. In Benjamin T: Young drivers impaired by alcohol and other drugs, New York, 1987, Royal Society of Medicine Services.
9. Hirschfeld RMA and Blumenthal SJ: Personality, life events, and other psychosocial factors in adolescent suicide and depression. In Klerman GL: Suicide and depression among adolescents and young adults, Washington, DC, 1986, American Psychiatric Press.
10. Rutter M, Izard CE, and Read PB: Depression in young people: developmental and clinical perspectives, New York, 1986, Guilford Press.
11. Diekstra RFW and Hawton K, editors: Suicide in adolescence, Dordrecht (Netherlands), 1987, Martinus Nijhoff Publishers.
12. Planned Parenthood Federation of America: Fact sheet, New York, Dec 1986.
13. Geronimus AT: On teenage childbearing and neonatal mortality in the United States, Pop and Development Review 13:245, 1987.
14. Robert Wood Johnson Foundation: The high-risk young people's program: a progress report, Information Exchange, Fall 1985, The Foundation.
15. Exemplary and innovative health department programs for service delivery to adolescents: a report prepared for the Intergovernmental Health Policy Project Conference on Intergovernmental Options for Improving Preventive Health and Mental Health Services for Adolescents, Dallas, Nov 14-15, Washington DC, 1986, Public Health Foundation.
16. Morrisey JM, Hofmann AD, and Thrope JC: Consent and confidentiality in the health care of children and adolescents, New York, 1986, The Free Press.
17. Zabin LS and Hirsch MB: Evaluation of pregnancy prevention programs in the school context, Lexington, MA, 1988, DC Heath & Co.

CHAPTER 26

Aging and public health

Sometime after adolescence starts, aging begins. It isn't clear just when that is, or what it is. The cells in most of the organs continue to divide, and the body continues to grow and take shape, as do the mind and the personality. But in some profound and subtle ways not yet understood, people start to age. The organs and their cells begin to lose some of their original capacity for adaptation. Because of the incredible reserves available, these changes are scarcely noticed. The growth changes of the earlier years create such momentum that development continues like a rocket on an upward, sloping trajectory, but inside, the resources, as in a rocket, are beginning to be depleted. When aging becomes noticeable varies greatly from person to person. Kareem Abdul-Jabar made some outstanding basketball plays in his 40s. Others show signs of aging in their late 20s.

Throughout this chapter, which focuses much more on those over 65 than on those between adolescence and retirement, comparisons will be made between age groups. People in the age group 70 to 74 are more dependent than those aged 65 to 69, for example. Human variability must be kept in mind, however. There can be greater differences in vitality between individuals in a single age group than between groups of individuals in adjacent age groups. Or as biostatisticians would put it, intragroup variability is greater than intergroup variability. When a comment is made about the dependency of those aged 85+ compared to those aged 70 to 74, you will no doubt know of some exceptions to the statement. Sometimes people are discouraged from thinking in terms of exceptions: Don't concentrate on the few smokers who live long and well or the few unfortunate individuals who used a seat belt and were strapped into a burning car. Think instead of the probabilities associated with health practices and, like a gambler, play the odds. In the case of aging, however, the exceptions are important. The tendency of health reseachers is to focus on pathology and to study the epidemiology of disease. The question of why some elderly people are so vital and others so dependent should also be considered. The epidemiology of vitality should attract a substantial research effort.

Social policies recognize the aging process in a variety of ways. Children can drive cars, buy alcoholic beverages, smoke cigarettes, join the army, and vote (not all of the perquisites of age are dangerous) at certain ages. Still more advanced ages must be attained before they can be elected to the Senate or to the Presidency. The selection of these demarcation points is often contentious, both politically and scientifically. The oldest demarcation point is the most difficult one to define: when are people "old"?

Title VII of the Older Americans Act considers people eligible for nutrition programs at age 60. The Department of Housing and Urban Development makes housing supports available to people who are 62. The Medicare program begins paying hospital bills when people reach age 65. Universities urge retirement at 70. Biologically, people begin to show some signs of diminished functional capacity by the time they reach 30. From that time on, the prevalence of chronic diseases, the use of medical services, and the degree to which people are dependent on others to carry out what might be considered normal daily activities increases. Is aging a disease or a normal process? Gerontologists have given up trying to define aging and have urged others to abandon the effort. It consumes too much work with no real benefit.

Aging is a process that cannot be reversed. To the extent that its consequences make people excessively dependent on others, much can be done to prevent the dependency or to reduce it. To the extent that dependency is irreversible, its impact on personal security can be mitigated by a spectrum of community supports. The purposes of those community support systems are to maintain maximum possible functional independence, to help restore functions that have been lost, to provide humane care for people who are permanently dependent, and to support the final release from dependency by death with dignity.[1] Those purposes are a rephrasing of the basic concept of prevention (primary, secondary, and tertiary) to suit the target group.

THE DEMOGRAPHY OF AGING

In 1900 there were 2.5 million people aged 65 and over in the United States, representing 4.1% of the total population. By 1985 there were 28.5 million people aged 65 and over, representing 12% of the population. Within those summary figures, a number of important shifts have been taking place and will continue to emerge over the next 50 years.

It is difficult to project population estimates with confidence at this time, because several surprising changes have been occurring in the last 20 years that have altered mortality expectations dramatically—especially the rapid decline in deaths from cardiovascular disease. This decline has affected the over-65-year age group as well as younger adults.

Table 26-1 may be the most important table in public health. In 1900, white male babies (age 0) had a 48-year life expectancy, people who were 40 years old could expect to live for another 28 years, and those age 65, another 12 years. By 1960, life expectancy at birth had increased 20 years, to age 68 for white males. It was common knowledge that most of that increase was attributable to declines in infant and childhood mortality rates: 40-year-old adults had gained only 3 years (from 28 to 31) during that same time. Between then and 1986, however, when life expectancy at birth had increased another 4 years, all of the gain came from declining mortality rates in the adult years (from 31 to 35 years). This is the largest increase for adults in such a short period of time in recorded history. It is the sort of increase that could be attained if all causes of cancer were suddenly eliminated.

If these changes continue to occur over the next 20 years, their impact on the age distribution of the nation's population will have important consequences. The Census Bureau has developed high, low, and midrange estimates. Looking at the midrange figures, the over-65 age group will increase from 28.5 million to 55 million by 2040, and the over-75 group (the group that begins to use health and social services in significant amounts) will increase from 11.5 million to 28 million. At that rate of increase, the over-65 group will represent 15.2% of the population.

Surprisingly, those figures, which used to be considered very stable estimates, could be off by a factor of 2 or more. Studies carried out by the National Institute of Aging and the University of Southern California have considered what might happen if adult mortality rates continue to decline at such a rapid rate. They forecast that the over-65 group could increase to 87 million by 2040, nearly 25% of the population. The 85-year-old group, using these estimates, could increase to 24 million by then.[2]

Two things have occurred that serve to increase the number of elderly people rapidly. The declines in infant and childhood mortality that have been discussed in previous chapters have left many more people alive who can now reach the age of 65. To put it in epidemiologic terms, the *incidence* of aging (defined as passing the 65 mark) has increased. The *prevalence* of aged people will change in direct proportion to the *incidence* if the *duration* of being aged does not change. But the *duration*, or the average length of life, has increased dramatically, as illustrated in Table 26-1. *Prevalence* equals *incidence* times *duration* (see Chapter 5). If both the incidence and the duration

TABLE 26-1 Average years of life remaining at specific ages and in different decades, United States, white males

Age	1900	1940	1950	1960	1970	1980	1986
0	48	63	66	68	68	71	72
40	28	30	31	31	32	34	35
65	12	12	13	13	13	14	15

of aging increase 2-fold, the prevalence of aging—the number of people over the age of 65—will increase 4-fold. This is exactly what has been happening, to the surprise of demographers, who used to assume that adult mortality rates would not change in the industrialized nations. The declines in adult mortality rates are continuing, which means that duration will continue to expand, and the rates are falling for the oldest old just as they are for the younger old. The age group 65 to 74 has been increasing in size at a rate of 1.6% each year, the age group 75 to 84 has been increasing at a rate of 2.3%, and the over-85 group at 3.8% each year. At those rates, it would take nearly 45 years for the 65 to 74 age group to double in size, but it would take just 18.5 years for the over-85 group to do so.

What does this portend? A society heavily weighed down with frail elderly people, or one that is being rejuvenated by its vital elderly and its multiethnic young at the same time? Many worry about the ratio of dependent people to workers. The age-dependency ratio is derived by dividing the number of people aged 65 and over by the number of people aged 18 to 64. It is a figure sometimes used to illustrate the extent to which working people will have to support nonworking adults, although it ignores the contributions of many people over 65 and the dependency of many younger people. In 1920 the ratio was 0.08. By 1980 it had increased to 0.19. By 2020 it will increase to somewhere between 0.23 and 0.29.[3]

The biggest increases will be in the over-85 group. This is the group most likely to need assistance with activities of daily living such as toileting, dressing, eating, and bathing. By that time there will be two older women for each older man. Women have higher rates of dependency and activity limitation than men. There are sharp differences in mortality between adult men and women and between whites and nonwhites (Table 26-2). Note first the rapid increase in mortality rates from age 65 to 74 to age 75 to 84. In the over-85 group, the rates increase much faster, and nearly half of all deaths reported are from heart disease. Secondly, note the differences between whites and blacks, both in the death rate for all causes combined and in the rank ordering of the leading causes of death. In both age groups, blacks have higher mortality rates than whites.* Thirdly, note the sex differences. At both ages and for most causes of death, women have a lower mortality rate than men. The sex differences are greater than the socioeconomic differences.

Disability and dependency

Having consumed a fair amount of space describing the mortality rates for people over age 65, it must be pointed out that they are not especially important. In younger age groups, the causes of death provide some insight into the major health problems and are therefore of help in designing preventive interventions. In the older age groups, specific diseases and causes of death are less important than function. The health needs of the elderly are best described in terms of dependency, not diseases or causes of death. Nearly 40% of people over the age of 65 report some degree of activity limitation. For most, however, this is not a serious problem. Only 10.6% of the elderly are unable to carry on with their major activity. This increases with age to about 20%, or one out of five, for people over the age of 85. Among the more common problems are arthritis, vision impairment, hearing loss, and other musculoskeletal problems that limit mobility and cause pain (Table 26-3).

The elderly have more health problems and use more health services than do young adults. They are not more likely to have acute problems or injuries, but they are more likely to have troublesome and lingering consequences and are more likely to have chronic problems that result in more doctor's office visits and days of hospital care.

* It is important to note that current vital statistics publications include separate figures for total deaths, white deaths, all other racial and ethnic groups, and black deaths. In virtually all instances, the death rates for "all others" are intermediate between the rates for whites and blacks, but the "all other" category includes a wide variety of ethnic groups. In this brief summary of differential mortality rates, the important differences between the white groups in the United States and the many other racial and ethnic groups cannot be considered in detail. The most striking differences are between whites and blacks, and these are described to illustrate the health status differences, which are based largely on socioeconomic status and are, in this case, exacerbated by racism, not race itself. There is no reason to believe that race as a biological variable has a significant impact on health status or mortality, but racism can and does.

TABLE 26-2 Leading causes of death and rates per 100,000 (in parentheses), white and black males and females, United States, 1986

	Age 65-74		Age 75-84		Age 65-74		Age 75-84	
Rank	**Black males**	**White males**	**Black males**	**White males**	**Black females**	**White females**	**Black females**	**White females**
1	Diseases of the heart (1,673)	Diseases of the heart (1,441)	Diseases of the heart (3,407)	Diseases of the heart (3,405)	Diseases of the heart (1,108)	Diseases of the heart (694)	Diseases of the heart (2,624)	Diseases of the heart (2,180)
2	Cancer (1,455)	Cancer (1,063)	Cancer (2,249)	Cancer (1,827)	Cancer (718)	Cancer (659)	Cancer (1,018)	Cancer (956)
3	Cerebrovascular diseases (338)	Chronic lung disease (217)	Cerebrovascular diseases (810)	Cerebrovascular diseases (617)	Cerebrovascular diseases (269)	Cerebrovascular diseases (136)	Cerebrovascular diseases (711)	Cerebrovascular diseases (531)
4	Chronic lung disease (178)	Cerebrovascular diseases (171)	Pneumonia and influenza (351)	Chronic lung disease (523)	Diabetes (135)	Chronic lung disease (107)	Diabetes (236)	Pneumonia and influenza (185)
5	Pneumonia and influenza (125)	Pneumonia and influenza (78)	Chronic lung disease (317)	Pneumonia and influenza (343)	Kidney disease (57)	Diabetes (56)	Pneumonia and influenza (179)	Chronic lung disease (181)
6	Diabetes (101)	Diabetes (54)	Kidney disease (196)	Diabetes (114)	Pneumonia and influenza (53)	Pneumonia and influenza (39)	Kidney disease (135)	Diabetes (117)
7	Kidney disease (75)	Liver disease (53)	Diabetes (178)	Kidney disease (100)	Chronic lung disease (53)	Liver disease (26)	Septicemia (113)	Atherosclerosis (68)
8	Accidents (73)	Suicide (38)	Septicemia (150)	Accidents (98)	Accidents (34)	Accidents (20)	Accidents (75)	Accidents (63)
9	Liver disease (48)	Kidney disease (30)	Accidents (144)	Atherosclerosis (88)	Liver disease (24)	Kidney disease (18)	Atherosclerosis (74)	Kidney disease (57)
10	Homicide (30)	Septicemia (25)	Atherosclerosis (95)	Suicide (59)	Atherosclerosis (20)	Septicemia (17)	Chronic lung disease (71)	Liver disease (24.6)
All causes	4,790	3,635	9,291	8,342	2,892	2,032	6,149	5,109

From National Center for Health Statistics: Vital statistics of the United States, Vol II, Mortality, Part A, Washington, DC, 1988, US Government Printing Office.

Chronic conditions become more common with age, and they cause an increasing amount of dependency. According to the latest figures from the National Health Interview Survey, those over 65 have 33.1 restricted activity days per year compared to 12.4 days for people under the age of 65. Keep in mind that there are many more people in the younger age group: altogether those under 65 are responsible for almost 2.6 billion days of restricted activity per year compared to 895 million for those over 65. (That is not an error: those are really billions and millions of days respectively. Disability is costly!)

The increasing prevalence of chronic conditions as people age causes them to use more and more medical care. Those 65 and older, representing about 11% of the population, make 15% of all doctor's office visits. Of more importance, they use about 34% of all short-stay hospital days and 89% of all nursing home beds. All told, they use 29% of all the money spent on medical care.[4] Assuming that some of the changes just described continue to occur, the rapid increase in the older age groups, coupled with their heavy use of medical services, means that those 65 and over might use 50% or more of all the medical care available in the United States by the year 2040. That could cause some serious problems. Would the national government find it necessary to again stimulate an increase in the training of health personnel and the construction of hospital and nursing home beds, and would younger age groups manifest increasing dissatisfaction with the rising costs and increasing scarcity of medical care for themselves and their children?

Total spending for long-term care in 1986 was about $50 billion. Nursing homes accounted for 80% of that. Of the nursing home payments, 52% came from public sources, and 90% of that amount came from Medicaid. If the projections for the size and dependency of the elderly population materialize, federal spending for long-term care will increase to $42 billion by the year 2000. Such cost increases could occur as a result of three phenomena: increasing size of the elderly population (which could increase spending by 50%), price increases (which could double the impact of demography), and increases in the services provided (which could double the amount again).[5]

Will this scenario unfold as predicted? Fries and Crapo[6] have proposed an alternative that has provoked considerable controversy. They look not at the "doom and gloom" statistics but at the incredible vitality of the elderly. The life tables presently used reflect the mortality experiences of people who are 65 or 75 or 85 now. The available data regarding dependency likewise come from the experiences of people who were born during the first two decades of this century. To predict the future on the experience of such a past is folly: it will be different—maybe better, maybe worse, but different surely. Those who become 65 in the year

TABLE 26-3 Rank order of selected conditions with highest prevalence, age 65 to 74 and 75+, United States, 1983-1985

Rank	Age 65 to 74	Age 75+
1	Arthritis	Arthritis
2	High blood pressure	High blood pressure
3	Heart disease	Deafness and other hearing impairments
4	Deafness and other hearing impairments	Heart disease
5	Deformities and orthopedic impairments	Cataracts
6	Chronic sinusitis	Deformities and orthopedic impairments
7	Diabetes	Chronic sinusitis
8	Cataracts	Blindness and other visual impairments

From Collins JG: Prevalence of selected chronic conditions, US 1983-1985, Advance Data, No 155, May 24, 1988.

2000 will have been born in 1935, and those who are 65 in 2010 will date from 1945. They will have eaten different foods than their predecessors, smoked less, lived in a cleaner world, worked at less hazardous occupations, and known more about health promotion and disease prevention. They will be less likely to have had serious childhood diseases or to have suffered the consequences of multiple, poorly attended pregnancies. There are dangers in the current environment: hazardous wastes, the episodic use of dangerous drugs, and the ingestion of synthetic compounds, but on the whole the elderly of the next generation should be healthier than ever before in history and less likely to be dependent.

Fries and Crapo forecast a continued compression of morbidity into smaller and smaller proportions of the life span. Many of the problems that may lead to functional limitations are occurring with less force than in earlier years. People have altered their behavior substantially: 30-year-olds today are much less likely to be smokers than were 30-year-olds in the 1940s and 1950s (at least those in middle or higher socioeconomic brackets—the poor have not yet benefited from the movement toward a smokeless society). The onset of impairment may occur later in life and the beginnings of disability and dependency still later than that. If they occur late enough, they may not occur during life. If the onset of dependency is postponed 5 years as the result of a nonsmoking environment, for example, and life expectancy increases 3 years during the same period, the dependency associated with smoking-related impairments will affect people for a lesser proportion of their lives: 2 years less. The period of morbidity or dependency will then be compressed into fewer years, toward the tail end of the life span, thus lessening its impact. A greater proportion of people might then live to the age of 85 (plus or minus a couple of standard deviations, a statistical phenomenon that always affects biological systems) in good health and die suddenly when the vital organs finally wear out. Expenditures for long-term care would decrease, and the costs of a terminal and lingering illness would become negligible.

Which scenario will unfold in the years ahead: the frail elderly scenario with millions of fragile, dependent women living alone or in nursing homes consuming large amounts of medical and social services, or the vitality scenario? The debate is important from both a metaphysical standpoint and a public policy perspective. (For a useful discussion of the various points of view, see *Health Care for the Elderly: Regional Responses to National Policy Issues.*[7]) A reasonable appraisal suggests that both scenarios will apply to some degree. For the next 20 to 40 years, the rapid increase in the size of the elderly population will produce serious pressures on health and social service delivery systems and on federal, state, and local budgets. Public health must play a lead role in managing those problems, by reducing the amount of dependency through preventive interventions and by helping to organize effective services. It also seems reasonable to believe that future generations of the elderly will be healthier than their predecessors and require less help. Again, public health has an important role to play. In the absence of the vitality scenario, some unfortunate policies will be considered, leading in part to cut-backs in services, intergenerational conflict, and the inhumane treatment of the elderly. The only ethical and reasonable response to that is to reduce the development of dependency by preventive interventions and thus reduce the need for services.

Even that may not be enough, however. The medical enterprise is full of promises and prospects for immortality or at least freedom from disability. More and more techniques will be developed and applied to alleviate the accumulation of disabilities and impairments associated with aging. The elderly, no matter how vital they are, will need and want cataract operations, joint replacements, organ repairs and replacements, and other expensive technological marvels. Without considering how society can apply limits to the demand for relative immortality, the negative scenario of aging will undoubtedly materialize to some degree during the first half of the twenty-first century.

Social problems

There are other dimensions to the aging phenomenon. Family size is decreasing, and the divorce rate is increasing. Although more of the elderly have a living child now than two or three decades ago, the ability or the willingness of that child to care for an aged parent is decreasing. Houses are becoming physically smaller as building costs rise. Family separations are more likely to result in an aged individual living alone, lost to the children as a functioning member of the family unit. When an elderly parent does live with what remains of the family, there is likely to be greater stress because of space and money problems. The value of a family's earned income has begun to decline in recent years, and more women are finding it necessary to work outside the home, both to augment income and to find personal satisfaction. Women have been the traditional caregivers for elderly parents, and their removal from the home during the time when elderly parents need increasing amounts of assistance with activities of daily living suggests either that the elderly will be less welcome in the home or will be a source of increased stress within the family. Caregivers are still predominantly women, but more than a quarter of them are now aged 65 to 74 themselves, and 10% are over the age of 75. Many of those younger than 65 have competing child care demands and often have to quit work or have serious conflicts due to their caregiver roles.[8] The abuse of fragile elderly family members is not uncommon, and some think it is becoming more common.[9] On the other hand, an older parent in the home may make it possible for both parents to work and provide valuable support for a child.

Repeated studies of mortality patterns show that elderly people living together are more likely to survive and retain their independence than those living alone. As previously noted, death rates for elderly men are substantially higher than for elderly women. Widowhood has a sex-specific effect, increasing the mortality rate of surviving men but having little or no apparent effect on the mortality rate for surviving women.[10] The death of a spouse is frequently followed by increased dependency in the survivor and the need for family support. Such needs, having been unexpressed for several decades, often fall suddenly on a family poorly equipped by inclination, income, or space to respond well.

Many other difficulties emerge for the elderly: housing, transportation, housekeeping, and the need for social interaction. The elderly are much less likely to live in their own homes than are the young. In 1984, 17 million people over the age of 70 were living in community settings: 6 million of them lived alone and 11 million with others. Of that 11 million, 7 million were living with spouses and 4 million with someone else. Those who were living alone in 1984 were more likely to be in a nursing home in 1986 than those who were living with someone else.[11]

A variety of living arrangements are possible for the elderly, not all of them satisfactory. About 4.3% of those over the age of 65 are in nursing homes (about 1.5 million people), but many more are in boarding homes or personal care homes, most of which are not licensed or regulated in any way.[12] Personal care homes are usually homes in which the owner or manager provides some limited forms of assistance with activities of daily living but no direct health services. Boarding homes provide no services at all other than some housekeeping and meals. Although some are very well managed, and many are operated on the basis of friendship rather than for proprietary purposes (particularly in rural areas), those in urban areas that cater to the needs of the frail elderly, who are often people who have been "deinstitutionalized" from public mental health or developmental disability facilities, are frequently a source of abuse and mistreatment.

Aloneness is increasing, particularly for women, and its impact on dependency, disability, injury, and death is powerful. The mortality rate is much higher for the elderly who live alone than for those who live with a friend or in a family setting. Depression is one of the more important phenomena affecting the elderly living alone.[13,14] It is frequently confused with dementia, which is the familiar syndrome of failing memory, disconnected thought patterns, and eccentric behavior so often used to characterize the elderly. Dementia is reversible in up to 20% of cases and is not as common as its diagnosis would suggest, but the label is used casually in the United States, where geriatrics is still a relatively rare form of medical practice. Depression is more common and more treatable. Unfortunately, although the elderly are often given psychoactive drugs, they are rarely afforded an adequate psychologic assessment by someone trained in geriatrics.

Suicide, largely as a result of depression, is an all too common problem among the elderly, especially white males. The elderly attempt suicide less often than the young, but they more often succeed. They are more likely than the young to have a death wish, and their suicide often appears to be the result of a well-thought-out appraisal of their circumstances and prospects.[15]

The health of the elderly

The problem of maintaining the health of the elderly is real and growing. Medical care costs are high and rising rapidly. The formal institutions, mainly nursing homes, that have been developed to solve the problem have not only failed to solve it but have exacerbated it by increasing family separations, costs, and, sometimes, patient abuse. Yet it is not all a bleak picture.

To repeat what has already been said, the elderly are truly healthier than ever before and getting more so. Recent trends in the incidence of cardiovascular diseases suggest that more and more people may emulate Dorian Grey, remaining robust and functional to a ripe old age and then dying suddenly without the interventions of a formal medical or social service structure. Disability is more common in the elderly than in the young but still is uncommon. When asked by an interviewer, 67% of the elderly respond that they are in good or excellent health.

Branch and Jette[16] are following a group of elderly participants in the original Framingham heart disease study and find that most do not have any unmet needs arising from a social disability. Of this group, 74% have no unmet housekeeping problems, 79% have no unmet transportation problems, 68% have no unmet needs because of a lack of social interaction, 84% are able to get their meals prepared, and 91% have solved any grocery shopping problems they may have had. When they do have problems stemming from unmet needs, these are most likely to involve housekeeping (3%) or transportation (7%). The Framingham population is mostly white and reasonably well off, but the authors have examined other studies and found results not grossly dissimilar.

In summary, most of the elderly are healthy; their needs are met either by themselves, their friends, or their families; and they live in private homes, not nursing homes. The development of community-based service systems, described later, should increase wellness even more, and preventive efforts can decrease dependency. Nonetheless, the small proportion of the elderly that is dependent and disabled is a small proportion of a very large and rapidly growing group, which means that the small proportion of partially dependent people includes many people—millions of people—whose needs are often great, and the costs of meeting those needs are high and growing higher. Considering all of the disabled and dependent people in society, regardless of the cause of their disability or dependency, and the fragmented, complex, and costly nature of the formal service structures we have erected to deal with the problems, dependency generally, and aging particularly, are the biggest challenges to be faced by public health in the decades ahead.

THE LONG-TERM CARE SYSTEM

A system is an organization of two or more people or parts engaged in the pursuit of a common goal. In that sense, there is no long-term care system: the parts are rarely organized and the people, or parts, have different goals. In a somewhat looser sense of the word, however, the parts define a system that (1) is largely proprietary, (2) is institutionally based, (3) is built on welfare concepts rather than entitlements, (4) is fueled by a fee-for-service approach, (5) treats aging as a health problem rather than a social problem, (6) is not generally attractive to most well-trained professional health workers, and (7) is "closed-ended"—that is, one rarely leaves the system alive.[17] That may be an optimistic portrait. The U.S. Senate Special Committee on Aging[18] wrote:

> the elderly and their offspring suffer severe emotional damage because of the dread and despair associated with nursing home care in the United States today . . . the actions of Congress and of the States, as expressed through the Medicare and Medicaid programs, have, in many ways, intensified old problems and have created new ones. . . .

For an even more graphic portrayal of the problem, the reader may wish to read *Tender Loving Greed,* which describes an industry driven by profit motives and fueled by a government or series of governments that has taken on the problem and made it worse.[19]

Institutionalization

No matter what government tries to do, the institutional response gets worse. Faced with pressure to provide more nursing home beds for the disabled elderly, Congress included coverage for such care in both Medicaid and Medicare. The response was rapid. The available beds were filled quickly, and more were built as entrepreneurs found the new program would assure quick profits, principally through manipulations of real estate and taxes rather than through services. In 1960 there were 388,000 people aged 65 and over living in nursing homes, or about 2.3% of that age group. By 1970 the number had more than doubled to 796,000. By 1986 it had increased to 1.5 million.

As more and more elderly people went into the new beds, Congress attempted to protect them and the budget by establishing standards for admission and for the care services that had to be provided. Although the industry objected, it did add the services, often in an inadequate fashion, and simply increased its charges. The costs continued to increase, and the regulatory pressures became worse. Regulations defined door widths, floor coverings, hours of nursing care per patient, safety requirements, and record-keeping procedures, but none of this has been shown to be related to the quality of the care provided.[20]

Nearly 52% of the costs of the nursing home industry are paid for by public funds, with Medicaid absorbing 90% of that public share and Medicare paying about 5%. Medicare services and conditions are defined nationally, and use has been controlled by very tight admission and length of stay criteria. The Medicaid program is administered by the states, which pay one quarter to one half of the cost of the program. The pressure of families with no place to put the elderly and of builders who were quick to show legislators how to provide the care and pay only 25 to 50 cents on the dollar resulted in support at the state level for extensive Medicaid coverage and an expansion of the bed supply.

Historically, counties provided sheltered housing for the dependent elderly in what were often known as county poor farms. County commissioners were anxious to support the building plans of the investors, especially since that meant shifting the costs from the county's weak tax base to the state and federally funded Medicaid program. The cost involved in this shift of the elderly from homes, poor farms, and other boarding home environments into nursing homes has increased substantially, but the cost has shifted away from the community, which had customarily paid the bill. Many communities rehabilitated their "old folks' home" to meet Medicaid standards. Although the cost of rehabilitation was substantial, much of the increased operating cost could then be received as revenue from the state Medicaid program. Whether the elderly got better care is unknown, but it certainly cost more.

For private paying patients, the process often wipes out the family estate, transferring what used to be an inheritance within the family to the nursing home industry. Once the personal holdings of the elderly have been sufficiently depleted to make them indigent, they become eligible for the Medicaid program, and the cost is shifted to the public purse. Many elderly people shift title to their homes and other assets to their children, making the elderly parents eligible for tax-supported nursing home care. The black and rural elderly are less likely to "benefit" from these changes than are the white and urban elderly. This does not appear to be a direct result of discrimination but rather a locational phenomenon: investors put nursing homes where they can get patients, preferably those who can pay their own bills, because they pay higher rates than the Medicaid program. That means that the nursing homes are built in more urban and affluent environments.

Nursing homes are not the only institutions used to house the frail or dependent elderly. Some nursing homes are called skilled nursing facilities (SNFs, called "sniffs" by the bureaucrats). They generally require the highest level of nursing care. Intermediate care facilities (ICFs) were invented to provide care at a lower cost by decreasing the amount and type of care needed, but intermediate care facilities are still health related. Generally the Medicare program will only pay for skilled nursing facility services, since Medicare has a decidedly medical orientation. In many states the Medicaid program will pay for care in both skilled nursing facilities and intermediate care facilities.

Personal care homes move away from the medical aspects of aging and provide basic social supports. This may include routine body care, such as grooming, help with the toilet, and washing. Personal care homes cannot participate in either the Medicaid or the Medicare programs. They are often supported by Title XX funds (Title XX of the Social Security Act, which provides for social services designed to keep people out of institutions) or by payment from a cash grant received by the resident, who may qualify for old age assistance or aid to the totally disabled.

Boarding homes may provide meal service and some housekeeping, but no personal care. There are no government programs specifically designed to help with the cost of boarding home care.

In recent years "congregate" care and "group homes" have become increasingly popular. These are usually organized for a specific group, such as the developmentally disabled, alcoholics, or occasionally the aged. In a sense these are cooperative housing arrangements, often supported by community groups with a genuine social welfare motivation. Arrangements are usually made with community-based service organizations for home health services, meal services, transportation assistance, and occupational and physical therapy, which are easier to arrange and pay for on a group basis.

As previously discussed, most nursing homes are privately owned, although government funds are used in several ways to pay for them. In many states it is possible for a private organization to float a bond issue through a local government as an effort to develop the industrial or commercial base of the community. These bonds produce tax-free income for the bond owners and thus represent a government subsidy for construction. As also noted, most of the operating costs are paid with public funds. There is no good count of personal care homes or the beds available in them or of congregate housing arrangements, since these are often not licensed. Lacking a statutory reimbursement program such as Medicare or Medicaid, they are less directly involved in government processes; hence they are not as well counted. Some official counts by the national government put the number of personal care home and similar beds at about 12,000, but workers in licensure programs are aware of numerous private arrangements that have been made to provide some housing and support for a dependent unrelated person. It seems likely that the total number of such arrangements equals or exceeds the number of formally counted and regulated beds.

The cost of institutional care varies widely, depending on the location and the level of care available. Since most of the bills are paid by Medicaid, rates are generally set to reflect what can be negotiated with the state program, which means that they are different in each state. They may range from as little as $50 per day to $135 per day or more, depending on private pay status and ability to pay. At an average price of $75 per day, nursing home care can cost about $2,300 each month. The national cost is about $40 billion per year.

Nursing homes often solve problems of behavior or nonconformity by routinely using tranquilizers in large doses. The sexes are often segregated, and late-night visits are discouraged because they appear to be disorderly or disturbing, at least to the staff. These shortcomings make nursing homes and similar facilities the kinds of institutions that dehumanize people. Any unusual behavior is treated by the formation of additional rules or policies rather than accepted as part of the heterogeneity of the community within the nursing home. Policies accumulate over time until virtually all aspects of human conduct are regulated by the institution rather than by the individual. The results are apparent to any visitor of most nursing homes. However, there are exceptions. It cannot be proved that the exceptions are homes that are run by nonprofit organizations or by religious groups, but it seems that way to any collector of personal impressions and anecdotes. Unfortunately, efforts to measure the quality of care have been very unsatisfactory. Whenever objective criteria are applied to such assessments, either for research or regulatory purposes, the difficulty in defining *quality* becomes apparent. Social workers, nurses, physicians, administrators, and family members all have different impressions of quality care, and the client is usually least able to express his or her preference, which should be the most important one.

America has created a dilemma for itself. A decision was made in 1965 to support the development of private sector services through Medicare and Medicaid payments to providers of health services. Although it did not appear to be possible politically at that time, an alternative was available, at least theoretically: the organization of public sector service systems. As private nursing homes developed under the influence of public policy and more and more dependent elderly people were admitted to them, society worried about two problems: the quality of the care provided and its cost.

In an attempt to assure that the quality was adequate, state licensure agencies were encouraged to increase their regulatory controls, and Congress passed laws requiring a higher level of service for Medicare and Medicaid beneficiaries. At the same time, however, the cost increases were worrisome, and efforts were made to reduce the utilization of nursing homes and to constrain increases in the rate of payment. These two policies were obviously in conflict. You cannot clamp down on the money you will pay for a service and expect the service to improve in quality. Since the nursing home industry is a private industry that has to pay its bankers, its vendors, and its employees, as well as make a profit, it searches for ways to cut costs. The industry has been severely criticized, but that seems inappropriate: it is behaving the way any profit-making enterprise is expected to behave.[21] The social policy of using commercial vendors to produce what might be considered public services or goods for a vulnerable and dependent population should be reexamined. An alternative is still possible, at least theoretically. Public systems of care are common in other countries and provide high-quality care.[22]

Deinstitutionalization

"Deinstitutionalizing" people has become very popular in the United States during the last three decades. Major national efforts have been launched to deinstitutionalize the mentally ill, the developmentally disabled, and now the elderly. The motivations are not always related to the benefits to the individual from living outside an institution: many government officials think that it will save money.

The original efforts to deinstitutionalize tuberculosis patients were based on improvements in drug therapy and the demonstrated ability to do a better job with outpatients than with inpatients. Tuberculosis hospitals were designed to keep infectious people away from healthy people and were managed somewhat like prisons. It became important for the patients, who often felt well, to outwit the medical and nursing staff who were trying to control their lives, sometimes by taking unauthorized leave or by not taking medications. In addition to creating social problems, the disease was not controlled. A different kind of medical and nursing team found it easier and more effective to form a partnership with the patients and treat them in the community once the initial assessment had been completed and treatment had begun. To convince legislators, who often had a vested interest in the large tuberculosis hospitals, which employed many people, the health staff calculated how much cheaper it would be to treat someone as an outpatient. Of course, as the census in the hospital declined, the cost per day for the remaining patients increased, but overall the program change did save money as well as improve care.

The same approach was tried in mental health. Pinel did it in France in the 1790s. It began in the United States in the 1950s as a result of President Kennedy's interest in the development of community service programs. Having learned from the tuberculosis battle, experts touted the low cost of outpatient or community-based care in contrast with institutional care, and several studies seemed to substantiate this. Two problems existed in such comparisons, however: most studies were unable to assess the change in the functional level of the person being deinstitutionalized, and none of the studies was able to capture all of the public costs incurred on behalf of the deinstitutionalized individual.

As will be discussed later, these same problems jeopardize cost-benefit studies of community-based care for the elderly. Often the communities into which most dependent people are deinstitutionalized are not integrated communities, with all necessary health and social service supports well coordinated in an efficient manner. Even though nursing home environments are often shabby, sometimes brutal, and usually demeaning, they are at least open and available for public inspectors, and they do fix responsibility for the safety of the resident on the institution. This is not the case in the more fractured living arrangements often available in community settings.

Since nursing homes have created such a bad impression, and since collectively they cost so much, national, state, and community officials and leaders have tried to develop alternatives. Several studies have indicated that many of the people in nursing homes would not need to be there if other kinds of services were available in the community. Estimates of unnecessary use of nursing homes vary a great deal, depending on the bias of the investigator, but an overuse of about 30% is commonly described. At the same time, other investigators have found at least as many if not more people living in the community, often in very poor environments, who do need nursing home care. Similar to other types of health care, the total may be about right, but decisions about use or nonuse are not made by what an investigator could call rational means in about 30% of the cases. The problem is one of misuse rather than overuse.

Case management

To study the needs of a community, standardized assessment forms are used, such as the Older Americans' Resources and Services (OARS) information system, developed by Duke University. OARS is used to develop a baseline of well-being, cataloging social and economic resources, mental and physical health status, and capacity for self-care. OARS has been successfully used in before-and-after comparisons to test the efficacy of specific interventions.[23] The Capacity for Self Care Index is derived by ascertaining if the subject can (1) go out-of-doors, (2) walk up and down stairs, (3) get about the house, (4) wash and bathe, (5) dress and put on shoes, and (6) cut toenails. (If the last item seems foolish, imagine an elderly person with arthritis trying to do it.) Scores range from 0 to 7, with 7 indicating the greatest level of incapacity.[24] There are other survey techniques, such as Activities of Daily Living,[25] but all are aimed at testing physical capability, social strength, and mental status in an effort to understand something about the three areas most likely to be related to dependency: disability, aloneness, and income. These are the three areas that require community services such as home nursing and therapy, homemaker services, appliances such as canes and wheel chairs, companionship and social interaction systems, and income support, either through Social Security or through supplemental cash grants, known as Supplemental Security Income.

Most of the efforts to develop more rational service delivery arrangements involve case management. Simply put, this involves fixing responsibility on one individual to secure needed services for a client. The case manager is usually a member of an organization skilled in assembling the services needed for the particular client group. The principal advantage of case management is that it starts from an assessment of the client's needs and attempts to weave a cloth of services that will fit the client without suffocating and without leaving any vulnerable spots bare. Theoretically, this avoids trying to reshape the client to fit the needs and services of the institution.

Case managers (1) accept referrals, (2) assess the client's needs, often with other specialists, (3) recommend services, (4) connect the client with the needed service, and (5) periodically reexamine the client to be sure that their needs are being met. Case managers use mental health services, nursing homes, optometrists, physicians, hearing aid dealers, home health agencies, homemakers and chore workers, day care centers, hospitals, and meal services such as Meals on Wheels or senior citizen food programs supported by local agencies for the aging. Their goal is assumed to be to keep the client out of an institution, but sometimes an institution may be the most appropriate setting for a client.

Although most experts agree on the need for case management, there is dispute as to whether the agencies should be brokers or service providers. The tendency is to follow the broker model, with the creation of a new agency for case management that arranges or brokers services on behalf of the client, using existing agencies. There are several advantages to this approach: it involves little disruption in the existing pattern of doing things, it allows the case manager the freedom to arrange the most suitable services rather than try to shape the client's needs to the agencies' array of services, and it should leave the case manager in a better position to serve as an advocate for better care and needed services in the community.[26] The Health Care Financing Administration (part of the U.S. Department of Health and Human Services) seems to favor the brokering type of case management agency in its research and demonstration programs, but this may be because it is reluctant to establish any more large provider organizations, given its difficulties in trying to make sense out of the nursing home industry.

Others have advocated a more consolidated or centralized approach, with the case management agency actually providing most of the services needed, either directly or through contractual arrangements. This has the advantage of assuring the availability of the recommended service and fixing responsibility for the nature of the care package developed for the client. However, it has the theoretical disadvantage of allowing the agency to continue to use the service slots it has rather than develop new and possibly more needed services.

The social health maintenance organization (SHMO) is the ultimate in centralized case management organizations, depending on a prepaid capitation fee to provide all necessary services for enrolled clients. SHMOs were organized on the same principles as health maintenance organizations (see Chapter 31) and were intended to bring social services and supports into an otherwise medicalized approach to long-term care. It was thought that they might reduce costs *and* improve the quality and appropriateness of care. The latter may well be possible, but the former objective has not been attained.[27] This is a recurrent finding in studies of long-term care.

Hospitals, home care agencies, or personal care agencies could manage a consolidated social health maintenance organization, but the development of a new agency that builds its service package through coalitions and contracts would appear to be more desirable to avoid the service biases of the existing agencies. However case management agencies are developed, they must always depend on the assessment of the case manager, which raises questions about the training and orientation of the workers. Nurses are likely to see problems and service needs differently than social workers. If, as most people believe, the problems of aging are more social problems than health problems, it would seem logical to use social workers as case managers, but some have argued that nurses do a better job. The professional discipline is likely to be less important than the experience and training of the worker. Both disciplines are clearly needed.

Partial day-care services and home services are often described as useful alternatives to institutional care. Partial day-care services provide either daytime or nighttime shelter and a social environment. Day care can provide for needed social interaction, nutrition support, and nursing and physical therapy services in a convenient location. This may be particularly effective for a family that can provide evening support but needs to be at work during the day. Home services may consist of housekeeping assistance, skilled nursing care, physical therapy, speech therapy, or the assistance of a nutritionist. Home health agencies are principally nursing agencies, but to be accredited by Medicare for reimbursement purposes, at least one other skilled service must be available. This requirement plus time-consuming and costly travel requirements have made home care difficult to establish in rural areas. Homemakers and chore services are often paid for by social service agencies with Title XX funds. They provide help with shopping, cleaning, cooking, and other housekeeping needs.

This array of service possibilities would seem to offer many opportunities for better and more appropriate care at a lower cost than is possible through nursing homes, but the evidence, although enthusiastic, does not support the claim. A major study was launched by the Health Care Financing Administration in 1980-1981 to explore the possible benefits of "channeling"—the use of case management to assess a patient's needs, develop a social and health services plan, and then "channel" the client into the correct array of services. The project especially supported community care services.* The program costs were not offset by lower costs for nursing home care. The clients were benefited through the receipt of more services, a decrease in the number of unmet needs, and an increase in confidence and satisfaction, but total costs increased.[28] These findings are similar to those of some 27 other studies. Some early studies enthusiastically reported substantial savings, but they left out several public costs, such as subsidized housing, meals, and Supplemental Security Income payments. Community support services seem not to replace institutional services, but to supplement or complement them. If it were possible to identify just those people who would in the absence of community support services be admitted to a nursing home, and concentrate on their needs, cost benefits might be obtained, but that has not been reliably done. Good community care is expensive, and bad community care is less desirable than good nursing home care.

Present research is aimed at refining the mix of available services and better identifying those individuals who are most likely to benefit from a well-managed, community-based system and who would otherwise incur significant costs.

PUBLIC HEALTH AND AGING

Aging, whatever it is, is not really a health problem. It is a physiologic and metaphysical inevitability that increases the probability of health problems, which may have important social consequences. The responsibility of government for the welfare of the aged has varied over time and is changing now. The federal government is respon-

* The Channeling Demonstration Project is discussed thoroughly in a special issue of Health Services Research, 23(1), April 1988.

sible for Social Security and for Supplemental Security Income payments (a form of welfare for certain categories of poor people including the aged), as well as for the Medicare program. Medicare pays for medical services, not health and social services. (See Chapter 31.) The states manage the federally supported Medicaid program, the food stamp program, and the Title XX programs for social services. In addition, state and local governments provide mental health and public health services. The private sector provides an extensive array of services, ranging from special housing programs to home visitors and community day care. In an attempt to help coordinate such services, the national Administration on Aging supports state programs, which in turn support community-based Area Agencies on Aging (AAA). The state level agencies, often governed by an appointed Commission on Aging, have a variety of forms, some operating as free-standing agencies and some as units of larger social or health services agencies. The local AAAs both provide direct services and attempt to act as a coordinating and advocacy body at the local level. Public health should be an active participant in such organizations, as should other state and local agencies. Where such coordination occurs, services are improved.[29]

Aging itself cannot be prevented, but some of the health problems associated with it can be. Heart disease is the biggest disease problem of aging. The known risk factors are high blood cholesterol levels, hypertension, smoking, and lack of exercise. Although most of these risk factors fade with age, since age itself appears to become the predominant risk factor, hypertension remains a valid indicator of vulnerability, and it can be controlled. Primary prevention is not yet possible, but early detection and effective management can do much to reduce the consequences of hypertension: renal disease, cerebrovascular disease, and heart failure. It was once thought that blood pressure rose naturally with age, but it is now apparent that high blood pressure is as significant in the aged as it is in the young and that it can be controlled. The death rate from cardiovascular disease has decreased by over 20% in the last two decades, and this decrease has occurred in the age group over 65 just as it has in the younger age groups.[30] There are many other risk factors associated with the dependency and disability of aging: inappropriate retirement, aloneness, lack of social activity, heredity, sex differences, race, education, and socioeconomic status. The last three are connected to some extent. The well-established relationship of poverty and lack of education with poor health is very evident in the aged. Some of the risk factors cannot be changed, but their effects can be modified.

Many of the health problems common in the aged, such as arthritis, cancer, vision problems, and hearing problems, can only be dealt with through secondary and tertiary prevention techniques once the process has begun, which highlights the need for stronger prevention efforts in the young. There are many approaches to health maintenance, such as the *Canadian Periodic Health Examination Report,*[31] *Prospective Medicine and Health Hazard Appraisal* by Robbins,[32] *Preventive Medical Services in National Health Insurance* by Breslow,[33] and *Proposed Preventive Benefits to be Covered on a First Dollar Basis under National Health Insurance* developed by the American Public Health Association.[34] All of these proposals focus on periodic health and social needs assessments, tailored to the known risks and disability patterns evinced by sex- and age-specific groups as ascertained through epidemiologic analysis (see Chapter 5). In older age groups, they recommend health assessment every 1 or 2 years and pay particular attention to cancer, heart disease, vision, hearing, housing, nutrition, and socialization. A number of experts believe that the health of the elderly can be improved through health promotion and disease prevention activities.[35] Injuries can be reduced (especially falls), immunizing agents are practical, smoking cessation is beneficial in aging as in youth, programs to help problem drinkers and drug users, and better nutrition and stress management programs can help.

Many public health agencies have established chronic disease screening programs for such problems as diabetes, glaucoma, and cancer. Most screening programs, either single purpose or multiphasic, have not been effective either in preventing disease or in saving money. The reasons are described in Chapter 5. Generally speaking, they tend to attract those at lowest risk and too often are unable to assure continuity of care for those identified as having a problem. Screening that is not done by an agency with a continuing responsibility for the well-being of the client fails to protect either the client or the public purse. Screening for glaucoma has been especially popular, but there is little evidence that such activities or the medical and surgical interventions to which they lead improve the functionality of the beneficiary. The old-fashioned notion of the periodic health checkup has little to commend it either. As noted earlier, the health problems of old age are not a matter of specific diseases but of the loss of function. Functional assessments would be more useful than disease-based checkups.[36] For example, there are several risk factors for loss of ability to cope with Activities of Daily Living: being over 85, having been discharged recently from a hospital, being recently bereaved, and taking multiple medications.

Some public health agencies operate service programs that provide direct treatment and maintenance services for adults, such as general outpatient clinics or special-purpose programs for the maintenance of blood pressure control. Health departments also operate home health agencies, although it is administratively difficult to separate public health nursing, which is not generally reimbursable by Medicare or other third-party insurance programs, from home health nursing with its special certification requirements. The latter programs are usually operated by independent agencies, voluntary or proprietary, but they need close working relationships with public health nursing (see Chapter 30).

Public health agencies also have an important role to play in monitoring the long-term care system. In addition to such traditional functions as inspection and licensure of food-serving establishments (this includes the kitchens in nursing homes and in senior citizen centers), laboratory performance testing, and supervision of in-home health programs, most state health departments and many local health departments have a role in the licensing and certification of nursing homes. State programs to license nursing homes date from the 1950s and the Social Security amendments, which required such regulation if a state wished to participate in the old-age assistance program. Licensure is a state function that can deny an organization the privilege of operating a nursing home if it cannot meet reasonable state standards for services, equipment, safety, and patient care. Certification is a national program that determines whether or not a nursing home can participate in the Medicare program. It is a responsibility of the Health Care Financing Administration but is administered with federal support through state agencies, which carry out the work under contract. The standards for licensing and certification are often different and sometimes result in two different units, sometimes within the same state agency, conducting two separate inspection programs. They should be combined.

In some states, licensing has been delegated to selected local health departments if they have the capability to carry out the program. The nursing home licensure programs have been controversial from their beginning. They are not generally thought to have been particularly effective in improving care or preventing abuse and have been criticized for their failure to serve as effective advocates for better services for the elderly. The programs are fraught with difficulty, since it is hard to bring about corrective action except through tedious and time-consuming negotiation and court orders. The final weapon is closure and removal of the patients, but this is rarely an effective option, since there is usually no place else for the patients to go. A few states have experimented with legislation that empowers the state health agency to assume direct operating control of nursing homes whose deficiencies cannot otherwise be corrected. These actions have resulted in corrections, but they leave the state with the problem of continued management or some other acceptable disposition of the facility.

THE FUTURE

The aging phenomenon is fascinating and important; along with AIDS and health care for the poor generally, it looms as the most significant health problem of the twenty-first century. Not only is there a rapid increase in the number of people over the age of 85, but America will soon have a sizable population of centenarians.

The elderly have more impairments than the young, they use more medical care, and they require more extensive social supports. The Federal Council on Aging developed 13 themes that should serve well as a guide through the future[37]:

1. Long-term care should be defined in terms of the person, not the program.
2. Long-term care should be based on an assessment of the disability, not a medical diagnosis.
3. Physical and mental health concepts must be integrated.
4. Long-term care is not just a problem for the elderly.
5. Disability is a social problem, not a medical problem.
6. Agencies should try to use natural supports and not supplant them in favor of professional workers.

7. Programs should strive to maintain volunteerism.
8. Some of the fundamental actions have to be carried out at the community level: (a) the administration of a simplified eligibility process, (b) client assessment, and (c) case management.
9. Program management should be locally based.
10. The fiscal resources available in all related federal programs (Titles XVI, XVIII, XIX, and XX of the Social Security Act and Title III of the Older Americans Act) should be used creatively and together, rather than separately by state agencies in support of local programs.
11. Quality control may be elusive, but has to be pursued.
12. The responsibilities of the three different levels of government have to be sorted out.
13. Who is supposed to pay and how is a question that requires an answer.

A number of other important issues must be considered. During the 1980s, federal support for social service programs declined.[38] Federal policy on aging has altered in favor of state, community, private, and self-managed services. Responsibility for dependent population groups generally has been decentralized or passed by the federal government to the states and hence to local communities, with decreased federal financial support and a move toward increased beneficiary cost-sharing.[39]

The first-generation Area Agencies on Aging were large, loosely managed organizations that provided services for the well elderly. With the reductions in federal support, the agencies became more stable, better differentiated, smaller, and more capable of delivering specific services. They now focus on the ill and the impaired.[40]

During the 1960s and 1970s, growth occurred in the public and not-for-profit sector. The new organizations were protected from competition and price wars. Now those same agencies are being forced to behave more like their profit-making kin, with increased attention paid to cost centers and revenue centers and such nouveau terms (at least for public health and social service workers) as "market share." Service expansion occurs where reimbursement is possible; service contraction occurs where it is not. Reductions in federal support for social services were greater than the cuts in health services, and community agencies recast their programs as health or medical care activities to better position themselves for reimbursement in the more lucrative health sector of the economy. Service development is guided more by revenue projections than by community needs. Such developments place public goods, such as services to protect the elderly, into the marketplace, where supposedly voluntary exchange transactions can take place between buyers and sellers, but this may have little to do with the functionality of the elderly.

One other important problem has arisen. Medicaid, when it was developed in 1965, was conceived as a program to provide access to needed medical care for the young and dependent population groups, primarily poor women and their children. With the rapid development of the nursing home industry, a growing proportion of the Medicaid budget has been siphoned off to pay for long-term care for the elderly and the disabled. With effective organization, the elderly have emerged as the most powerful lobby in the nation. The American Association for Retired People is the largest membership organization in the United States. At the other end of the age spectrum, we see a less well-organized sector of society, women and ethnic minority groups, which traditionally have lacked power in our society. Will the relatively powerful elderly absorb more and more of the benefits of an affluent society at the expense of the young, the poor, and the disenfranchised? As Binney and Estes[41] have put it, resurgent ideologies of individualism, family, and filial responsibility, coupled with the renaissance of the notion of the market, have created a zero-sum environment: that is, if one group gets more, another has to get less. It is policy, not a law of nature that has created this attitude, which is leading to heightened intergenerational conflict. The conflict distracts attention from the role of the state and focuses attention on purported rival groups. Policymakers have long feared the rise of conflict between the old and the young, but policymakers have encouraged it. It need not occur. Both can be served in a society willing to do so.

REFERENCES

1. Callahan D: Setting limits: medical goals in an aging society, New York, 1987, Simon & Schuster.
2. Guralnik JM, Yanagishita M, and Schneider EL: Projecting the older population of the United States: lessons from the past and prospects for the future, Milbank Q 66:283, 1988.
3. Siegel JS: Recent and prospective demographic trends for the elderly population and some implications for

health care. In Haynes SG and Feinleib M, editors: Epidemiology of aging, NIH Pub No 80-969, July 1980, US Department of Health and Human Services.
4. Kovar MG: Morbidity and health care utilization. In Haynes SG and Feinleib M, editors: Epidemiology of aging, NIH Pub No 80-969, July 1980, US Department of Health and Human Services.
5. Gordon NM: Statement before the Health Task Force, Committee on the Budget, US House of Representatives, Oct 1, 1987.
6. Fries JF and Crapo LM: Vitality in aging: implications of the rectangular curve, San Francisco, 1981, WH Freeman.
7. Andreoli KG, Musser LA, and Reiser SJ: Health care for the elderly: regional responses to national policy issues, New York, 1985, The Haworth Press.
8. Stone R, Cafferata GJ, and Sangl J: Caregivers of the frail elderly: a national profile, Gerontologist 27:616, Oct 1987.
9. Kosberg JI: Preventing elder abuse: identification of high risk factors prior to placement decisions, Gerontologist 28:43, Feb 1988.
10. Helsing KJ, Szklo M, and Comstock GW: Factors associated with mortality after widowhood, Am J Public Health 71:802, Aug 1981.
11. Kovar MG: Aging in the eighties, people living alone—two years later, AdvanceData, No 149, April 4, 1988.
12. Sirrocco A: Nursing and related care homes as reported from the 1986 Inventory of Long-term Care Places, AdvanceData, No 147, Jan 22, 1988.
13. Ruegg RG, Zisook S, and Swerdlow NR: Depression in the aged: an overview, Psychiatric Clinics of North America 11:83, March 1988.
14. Ben-Arie B, Schwartz L, and Dickman BJ: Depression in the elderly living in the community: its presentation and features, Br J Psychiatry 150:169, Feb 1987.
15. Achté K: Suicidal tendencies in the elderly, Suicide Life Threat Behav 18:55, Spring 1988.
16. Branch LG and Jette AM: The Framingham disability study: I. Social disability among the aging, Am J Public Health 71:1202, Nov 1981.
17. Kane RL and Kane RA: Directions for reallocating health resources: some next steps. In Morris R, editor: Allocating health resources for the aged and disabled, Lexington, MA, 1981, DC Heath & Co.
18. US Senate Special Committee on Aging: Nursing home care in the United States: failure in public policy, Washington, DC, 1974, US Government Printing Office.
19. Mendelson MA: Tender loving greed, New York, 1974, Alfred A Knopf, Inc.
20. Beatrice DF: Licensing and certification in nursing homes: assuring quality care? In Altman SH and Sapolsky HM, editors: Federal health programs: problems and prospects, Lexington, MA, 1981, DC Heath & Co.
21. Hazelbacker RE: The dilemma of long-term care: an industry view. In Kapp MB, Pies HE, and Doudera AE, editors: Legal and ethical aspects of health care for the elderly, Ann Arbor, MI, 1985, Health Administration Press.
22. Raffel NK and Raffel MW: Elderly care: similarities and solutions in Denmark and the United States, Public Health Rep 102:494, Sep-Oct 1987.
23. Fillenbaum GG and Smyer MA: The development, validity, and reliability of the OARS multidimensional functional assessment questionnaire, J Gerontol 36:428, 1981.
24. Shanas E: Self-assessment of physical function: white and black elderly in the United States. In Haynes SG and Feinleib M, editors: Epidemiology of aging, NIH Pub No 80-969, July 1980, US Department of Health and Human Services.
25. Katz S: The index of ADL: a standardized measure of biological and psychosocial function, J Am Med Assoc 185:919, Sep 21, 1963.
26. Kodner DL and Feldman ES: The service coordination/delivery dichotomy: a critical issue to address in reforming the long-term care system. Paper presented at the annual meeting of the American Public Health Association, Los Angeles, Nov 1981.
27. Leutz WN and others: Changing health care for an aging society: planning for the social health maintenance organization, Lexington, MA, 1985, DC Heath & Co.
28. Kemper P: The evaluation of the National Long-term Care Demonstration: 10. Overview of the findings, Health Serv Res 23:161, April 1988.
29. Lebowitz BD, Light E, and Bailey F: Mental health center services for the elderly: the impact of coordination with area agencies on aging, Gerontologist 27:699, Dec 1987.
30. Kannel WB: Cardiovascular risk factors in the aged: the Framingham study. In Haynes SG and Feinleib M, editors: Epidemiology of aging, NIH Pub No 80-969, July 1980, US Department of Health and Human Services.
31. Periodic health examinations: report of a task force to the Conference of Deputy Ministers of Health, Hull, Quebec, 1980, Canadian Government Printing Center.
32. Robbins LC, editor: Prospective medicine and health hazard appraisal, Indianapolis, IN, 1974, Methodist Hospital Press.
33. Breslow L: Preventive medical services in National Health Insurance. Paper prepared for the Office of Management and Budget on behalf of the Association of Schools of Public Health and the Association of Teachers of Preventive Medicine, 1973. In Preventive medicine USA: task force reports sponsored by the John E Fogarty International Center for Advanced

Study in the Health Sciences, National Institutes of Health, and the American College of Preventive Medicine, New York, 1976, Prodist.

34. American Public Health Association: Proposed preventive benefits to be covered on a first dollar basis under national health insurance. In Preventive medicine USA: task force reports sponsored by the John E Fogarty International Center for Advanced Study in the Health Sciences, National Institutes of Health, and the American College of Preventive Medicine, New York, 1976, Prodist.
35. Williams TF: Health promotion and the elderly: why do it and where does it lead? In Andreoli KG, Musser LA, and Reiser SJ: Health care for the elderly: regional responses to national policy issues, New York, 1985, The Haworth Press.
36. Buckley EG and Williamson J: What sort of "health checks" for older people? Br Med J 296:1144, April 23, 1988.
37. Fahey C: Some political, economic, and social considerations. In Morris R, editor: Allocating health resources for the aged and disabled, Lexington, MA, 1981, DC Heath & Co.
38. Oriol WE: Federal public policy on aging since 1960: an annotated bibliography, Westport, CT, 1987, Greenwood Press, Inc.
39. Wood JB and Estes CL: Medicalization of community services for the elderly, H Social Work 13:35, Winter 1988.
40. Alter CF: The changing structure of elderly service delivery systems, Gerontologist 28:91, Feb 1988.
41. Binney EA and Estes CL: The retreat of the state and its transfer of responsibility: the intergenerational war, Int J Health Serv 18(1):83, 1988.

PART SEVEN

Public health and behavior disorders

Despite Juvenal's well-known and widely quoted aphorism, *Mens sana in corpore sano,* far too many people, including a substantial proportion of health workers, tend to think of health and illness only in relation to the soma—the physical self. This is three times an error: first in that it ignores the complex of mental and behavioral disorders that afflict a large proportion of people; second in that it ignores the various mental and behavioral conditions that have their genesis in physical illnesses; and third in that it ignores the fact that few, if any, physical illnesses or injuries are without their behavioral dimensions, consequences, or manifestations. Many behavioral problems are treated inappropriately and inefficiently as if they were physical problems, and many prevention interventions are based on the same erroneous beliefs.

Behavioral problems do not always fit into what has been described as "the disease model." That is, in many instances it is not possible to detect clear-cut antecedents or causal phenomena that inevitably lead to a particular, labeled disease. Much mental disease, although classified by psychiatrists, is not the result of a reliable, reproducible pattern of development. Alcohol abuse, homicide, reckless driving, and depression are complex problems that arise out of social and environmental situations more often than out of willfulness or biologic phenomena.

This may suggest that such problems are not manageable and that public health should eschew involvement if there is so little chance for success. But the lack of a convenient biologic explanation of the problems does not make them less understandable or manageable. They have patterns of incidence and prevalence that enable us to determine risk factors. Any time any condition of disease can be ascertained to have identifiable risk factors, it can be prevented, at least in part.

More importantly, public health in the United States must begin to realize that even when it cannot prevent what it perceives to be the problem (alcoholism, for example, or hostility), it can often reduce the prevalence of the dependency that will ensue if nothing is done.

The chapters that follow present a complex picture of behavioral, social, and environmental risk factors and prospects for prevention. The appropriate interventions are often difficult. They involve more than fluoridating the water or immunizing children or providing prenatal care to pregnant women: they often involve altering deeply held social attitudes and beliefs. Perhaps that is what makes the area of behavioral disease so difficult for public health. It should, realistically, entice public health into more intensive exploration and experimentation, for these are the problems that truly bedevil society.

CHAPTER 27

Mental health

Nearly forty years ago, quoted in an article called "Mental Health: a Local Public Health Challenge," someone said, "If it's not mental health, it's not public health."[1] Apparently he was attempting to describe the saliency of the one to the other. Yet public health and mental health are organizationally estranged in most of the United States now as they were then. At both the state and local levels, separate agencies are responsible, different sources of funding and different organizational models are used, different personnel are employed, and different laws are invoked, even though the problems and their solutions are very similar. Many people who use medical services have mental health problems and vice versa. They are often treated relatively ineffectively in the wrong clinic or office. Public health could make a significant difference. This chapter will explore why it does not and what should be done.

MENTAL DISORDERS

It has always been difficult to know just how many people were mentally ill at any one time. There are two essential tasks to the measurement of anything: its definition or description and its ascertainment. Everyone knows (or used to) what a "case of measles" looks like. Since most of them were treated by a physician or at least witnessed by a school nurse, they were ascertained and reported to the local public health department. The same is true for deaths due to homicide or cases of colon cancer. Although they are not necessarily reported to the local health department, their definition is reasonably precise, and most of the cases are recognized as such and reported on a death certificate if not somewhere else. The definition of mental illness has been more difficult. Until recently, there were no clear-cut laboratory tests that could be used to detect and classify most mental illnesses, and practitioners disagreed about the subjective descriptions of a "case of schizophrenia" or psychosis versus neurosis. Beyond that, however, people with a mental disorder were reported only when they entered a public treatment system. Lacking any laws that required mental illness to be reported (since it is noncontagious and the number of cases seemed not to be especially important), private psychiatrists and psychologists had no place to report their cases even if they had been inclined to do so. Annual figures are available for the number of patients housed in state and county mental health hospitals or asylums (lots of them), but that was the limit of our understanding of the epidemiology of mental illness until recently.

In 1952 the American Psychiatric Association published the first *Diagnostic and Statistical Manual of Mental Disorders (DSM).* After years of heated debate, the third major version, DSM-III, was published in 1986. The Association described DSM-III as "only one still frame in the ongoing process of attempting to better understand mental disorders" and quickly proved its point by publishing the first revision of DSM-III in 1987.[2] The Association defines a mental disorder as a "clinically significant behavioral or psychological syndrome or pattern that occurs in a person and is associated with present distress . . . or disability . . . or with a significantly increased risk of suffering death, pain, disability or an important loss of freedom."[2] This is very similar to the definitions of health and of public health that were given in Chapter 1. Disease or injury may lead to an impairment (at the organ level), which in turn may cause disability (at the person level), which may lead to a state of dependency. Health is the absence of a disability caused by disease or injury. Mental health is the absence of a disability caused by a behavioral or psychological syndrome or pattern.

DSM-III lists 17 categories of mental disorder:

Disorders usually first evident in infancy, childhood, or adolescence
Dissociative disorders
Sexual disorders
Organic mental syndromes and disorders

Psychoactive substance use disorders
Schizophrenia
Delusional disorders
Psychotic disorders not elsewhere classified
Mood disorders
Anxiety disorders
Somatoform disorders
Sleep disorders
Factitious disorders
Impulse control disorders not elsewhere classified
Adjustment disorders
Psychological factors affecting physical condition
Personality disorders
Conditions not attributable to a mental disorder that are a focus of attention or treatment

The DSM manual has been a major advance in the epidemiology of mental disorders. Coupled with a Diagnostic Interview Survey, which can be administered by trained lay interviewers, it is now possible to obtain reasonably consistent and reliable definitions of mental disorders and estimates of their occurrence in different population groups.

The ascertainment problem has also been overcome, since the National Institute of Mental Health sponsored the Epidemiologic Catchment Area (ECA) program, the goals of which are to provide more dependable estimates of the incidence and prevalence of mental disorders, to search for clues to their causes, and to aid in planning mental health care services and programs. Its methods are 5-fold: emphasis on specific diagnosis, integration of community surveys with institutional surveys, collection of prevalence and incidence data, systematic linkage of service use data with other epidemiologic variables, and multisite comparative-collaborative efforts.[3] Using community surveys and the diagnostic procedures mentioned above, the ECA program has begun to yield valuable data about the size of the mental health problem in the United States.

The combined syndrome of alcohol, drug abuse, and mental disorders (ADM) affects about 18.7% of the adult population of the United States.* Only one in five of the affected people uses mental health services, however. Nearly 12% of the childhood population is affected with mental disability. In the adults affected, the problems are distributed as follows:

Substance abuse	24.4%
Anxiety disorders	29.4%
Schizophrenia	4.9%
Antisocial personality	4.9%
Severe cognitive disorders	4.9%
Affective disorders	15.0%
Major depression	16.4%

The relative importance of the different disorders varies within age groups and between the sexes, as shown in Table 27-1.* Note that alcohol is the leading problem for males in all four age groups. (See Chapter 28 for a discussion of substance abuse.) It is ranked as one of the four leading problems for females only in the youngest age group.

The disorders listed have different values as public health problems. Schizophrenia, which affects only 4.9% of those with mental disorders, is a major problem in terms of the services required and the cost of providing those services. Depression, which affects 16.4%, is a major cause of academic and work-related problems. The incidence rate of depression has been reported to be about 9 per 1,000 people per year, with a duration of 10 years. It is much more common in women than in men.[5] It also tends to affect relatively young people, with the highest prevalence in the age group 25 to 34.

Peculiarly, there are no recent estimates of the impact of the various mental disorders on the service systems, particularly the state psychiatric institutions. There are data about the total number of people in institutions, but not about the reasons for their being there. The total cost of mental disorders is thought to be about $72.7 billion annually: $33.4 billion in direct costs for health care services, $37.1 billion in indirect costs, such as lost work and the need for income support, and $2.2 billion in related costs, such as the court system, traffic accidents, and other ingredients of the overall problem.

The National Institute of Mental Health collects data on service utilization and expenditures by type of organization. Their data indicate an increase in expenditures from $3.3 billion in 1969 to

* Unless otherwise specified, the numbers used to describe the prevalence of mental disorders come from the *Economic Fact Book for Psychiatry.*[4]

* Space does not permit a definition of each of the disorders listed. The reader is urged to pursue the matter in a copy of DSM-III, which should be available in most public and university libraries.

$14.4 billion in 1983.[6] This amounts to $62.12 per man, woman, and child in the United States. Inflation accounts for part of that increase, of course. In terms of constant dollars (set at the 1969 medical care component of the consumer price index), the increase has been 39%, or a rate of 2.4% per year. These are expenditures in recognized mental health organizations and do not include the large amount of money spent each day in the offices of psychiatrists, psychologists, other physicians, and social workers. The largest portion of these "organizational" expenditures (38% of the total) is spent in state and county mental hospitals; 12% is spent in private psychiatric hospitals; 15% in general hospitals; 9% in Veterans Administration hospitals; and the rest in a variety of residential treatment facilities, community mental health centers, and other ambulatory care programs.

So prevalent are mental disorders that it is difficult to think of any aspect of public health that is not affected by mental health issues. It is clear that somatic and psychic health are so closely interrelated that they operate as a virtual entity, and the integration of mental health care with general medicine has been a long-standing but unrealized objective. The problems are increasing, not just because of the incidence in the population, but also because of the social and environmental stress associated with modern life: biomedical stress, psychologic stress, psychosocial stress, economic stress, political stress, and demographic stress.[7] The incidence of mental illness depends on many factors. Type of condition in relation to age is especially important. Most mental illnesses have their origins in early childhood but do not become manifest until the developmental or productive years of life. About one half of first hospitalization episodes occur between the ages of 35 and 64. Yet geriatric first admissions are increasing, as is the size of the older population. The frequency of disability due to a mental disorder increases with age. The elderly may not be hospitalized in a recognizable mental health facility, however. They may be placed in a nursing

TABLE 27-1 Rank orders of the four most common mental disorders for males and females, by age

	Males	Females
Age 18-24		
1	Alcohol abuse or dependence	Phobia
2	Drug abuse or dependence	Drug abuse or dependence
3	Phobia	Major depressive episode without grief
4	Antisocial personality	Alcohol abuse or dependence
Age 25-44		
1	Alcohol abuse or dependence	Phobia
2	Phobia	Major depressive episode without grief
3	Drug abuse or dependence	Dysthymia
4	Antisocial personality	Obsessive compulsive disorder
Age 45-64		
1	Alcohol abuse or dependence	Phobia
2	Phobia	Dysthymia
3	Dysthymia	Major depressive episode without grief
4	Major depressive disorder without grief	Obsessive compulsive disorder
Age 65+		
1	Severe cognitive impairment	Phobia
2	Phobia	Severe cognitive impairment
3	Alcohol abuse or dependence	Dysthymia
4	Dysthymia	Major depressive episode without grief

From Office of Economic Affairs of the American Psychiatric Association: Economic fact book for psychiatry, ed 2, Washington, DC, 1987, American Psychiatric Press.

home, as will be discussed below under "Deinstitutionalization."

Interestingly, there is little useful information about the incidence or prevalence of mental disorder by race or ethnic group. About 80% of all people admitted to inpatient psychiatric services are described as white, 18% as African American, and the rest as American Indian, Alaskan Native, and Asian or Pacific Islander. About 5% of those admitted are of Hispanic origin. More specific information about the distribution of mental disorders by type and race is lacking. This may be a result of the relatively primitive state of psychological diagnosis and the difficulty the mostly white professionals have in defining and identifying mental disorders in people unlike themselves. The distribution by race varies in different institutions, however. Of approximately 1 million admissions of white people to inpatient psychiatric services, 25% were in state and county mental hospitals, 12% in private psychiatric hospitals, 12% in the Veterans Hospital system, and 52% in general hospitals. Only 41% of African Americans are hospitalized in general hospitals and another 7% in private psychiatric hospitals. Nearly 40% (compared to 25% for whites) are hospitalized in state or county mental hospitals.[6] The primary diagnosis varies by race too. African Americans are more likely to be admitted with a primary diagnosis of schizophrenia than are whites and less likely to be admitted for alcohol-related disorders. Information about people who are admitted to noninstitutional mental health services is less reliable.

THE EVOLUTION OF THE MENTAL HEALTH SYSTEM

Mental disorders have been handled differently at different times. They have undergone several phases in the process of their medicalization, from sin to crime to disease. Like problems of substance abuse in certain cultures and at certain times, mental illness has been thought to be a sign of divine retribution, a condition requiring incarceration in a jail, and more recently, a disease requiring treatment and care.

Until the end of the eighteenth century, the mentally ill of Western Europe and the new United States were usually housed in institutions that provided no care whatsoever. They were often put on display, in fenced-off courtyards, for the entertainment of the town. Phillipe Pinel, in France, removed the chains and the degradation from the mentally ill in the 1790s, in the face of strenuous opposition and ridicule from both other citizens and his fellow physicians.

About 50 years later, in the United States, Dorothea Dix convinced the legislature of Massachusetts that it should assume direct responsibility for the mentally ill. There were only 18 mental hospitals in the United States at that time. Most of the mentally ill were housed in local jails or pesthouses or were boarded out to householders for a fee. Dix's reforms led to the creation of large state asylums in virtually all the states, usually in rural and peaceful areas, and the era of "moral treatment" began. The patients were to be cared for and nourished until they became well again. This marked the first of several differences between the mental health and public health movements. The latter was strictly a local responsibility at that time. It was unusual for a state to declare itself solely responsible for the care of a dependent population.

The asylums continued to grow into large complexes for the rest of the century. They became the chief source of employment and commerce in their counties, where most of the families had at least one member employed at the institution. Moreover, they built buildings, bought food, and often managed large agricultural enterprises. Since state legislatures were dominated by rural politics, the representatives from such districts became the patrons of the asylums and thwarted any effort to change the state's role in the treatment of the mentally ill. Yet there was no treatment—only a form of guardianship, often not known for its humanity. In 1908, Clifford Beer wrote *A Mind that Found Itself*,[8] the story of his hospitalization in such an asylum, his survival, and his return to health. He was instrumental in establishing the National Committee for Mental Hygiene in 1909. Rapid growth occurred during the next two decades with the formation of state associations in 19 states. It was an unusual movement then as well as now in being a decentralized organization, with primary power at the state, not the national, level.

Beer coincided with the advent of Sigmund Freud in the United States. The superintendents of the asylums were usually physicians, but they were administrators, not mental health specialists. There was little evidence to lead people to believe that the mentally ill could be treated successfully, so there was no inclination to pay anyone to do so. Lacking payment, the private practice of psychiatry had not developed. Freud changed all that. He popularized the notion that physicians trained in neurology could treat patients, and a new specialty was born.

Herein lies yet another of the significant differences between public health and mental health. As will be discussed in Chapter 31, by the time the public became convinced that physicians and surgeons had something to offer, could in fact make them well again, the profession was already well established as an economic and political entity. Although government began to play a role, it was a minimal role for many years, and it was widely assumed, as it is now, that medical care is best provided by the private sector. Not so in mental health. Because of the need to house the mentally ill, the state had established a dominant role long before the development of private practice in the field. To this day, the public sector in mental health is a large and important part of the overall treatment system.

With the advent of modern psychiatry and the influence of Beer, the United States entered what Goldman and Morrissey[9] have called the second cycle of mental health reform (the first being Dorothea Dix's moral treatment reform): mental hygiene and the psychopathic hospital. This second cycle was staffed by trained specialists, including physicians, psychologists, psychiatric social workers, and others. It placed special emphasis on the prevention of chronic mental illness. Even with these developments, insurance for mental illness was slow in coming, which impeded the flow of third party (insurance company) payments and the development of a robust private sector.

Neither public health nor public welfare was involved in these developments. The largest role played by public health was in the sanitation of the asylums. There were, as yet, no hypotheses about the causes of mental illness, no epidemiologic base from which to work, no known preventive techniques, and moreover, a general distaste for the problem. Public health workers are dependent on estimates of incidence and prevalence, knowledge of risk factors, and notions about preventive interventions. So mental health remained under separate, state level auspices, sometimes in the same agency responsible for the prisons.

World War II changed the nature of mental health care. As was true with medical care in general, psychiatry enjoyed creative growth during wartime. University-trained practitioners played a lead role in treating the casualties of war, and their successes were noted. After the war, they lobbied Congress to support more effective, modern treatment programs. Many veterans had been treated by psychiatrists and psychologists during the war, and they frequently benefited from the encounter. In 1946, Congress passed the National Mental Health Act, which authorized funds for the construction of a hospital and research facilities (the National Institute of Mental Health) and $10 million in grants-in-aid for the states. The impetus was toward community-based treatment programs, and the states slowly began to change their role as the custodians of the mentally ill. Mental hygiene clinics and child guidance programs were developed in many communities, and local public health programs often played a lead role in organizing the services.

The third cycle of reform was triggered by two phenomena: the swing toward community treatment rather than institutional care and the discovery of psychopharmacology. Chlorpromazine was first available in the United States in 1954, and it was received with the same enthusiasm that had earlier been accorded to penicillin: it was thought to be the magic bullet of psychiatry. It promised to cure all and return even the most regressed schizophrenics on the back wards of the state asylums to a productive life. The new drugs were indeed responsible for some remarkable progress, but they were not magic. They became widely used for trivial problems, and some were sold as over-the-counter products, such as Miltown (meprobamate). Even now, more money is spent on mood-altering drugs—legally—than is spent on all of the community mental health centers in the United States.[10] Much of the prescribing and use constitutes a form of legalized drug abuse.

In the asylums, the new drugs were heavily used not only to treat the mentally ill, but to control them without physical restraints. It seemed cheaper to push pills than to hire custodians. That such "treatment" could not eliminate mental illness soon became apparent. In time, serious side effects were observed (tardive dyskinesia, for example), which raised questions about the safety of drug treatment. In many quarters, the use of drugs to treat and control the mentally ill was condemned as a new, sanitized form of chemical incarceration, and some refused to use them at all, enthusiasm turning to rejection all too quickly.[10] The truth, of course, lies in the middle: used thoughtfully, by well-trained professionals, psychopharmacology is an important and increasingly effective ingredient in the treatment of many mental disorders. Used casually, it is dangerous.[11]

The drugs made it possible to release some of the mentally ill to community settings, sometimes in their own families and sometimes in special board and care facilities. Many attribute the modern rise of homelessness to the deinstitutionalization process and the use of psychopharmacology. In fact, deinstitutionalization began before the advent of the new drugs. In some of the better psychiatric hospitals in England and the United States, drug therapy resulted in longer rather than shorter hospitalization, since it was now possible to institute more definitive treatment. In most institutions for the mentally ill, such competence was not present, however, and the new drugs did indeed help open the doors to what was thought to be less expensive as well as more humane treatment of the mentally ill. Institutional care peaked at a daily census of about 560,000 in 1955. It had declined to 535,000 by 1960, and then the movement accelerated.

President Kennedy, partly because of his personal familiarity with mental retardation, urged Congress to pass the National Mental Retardation Facilities and Mental Health Center Construction Act of 1963. The new law established the concept of the community mental health center (CMHC). A CMHC defines the locus of administrative responsibility for organizing and managing the network of services needed to carry out the mission of the agency. They do not necessarily provide direct services: they plan, develop, implement, and coordinate. They may manage some of the needed services or, rarely, none at all. They often use an array of contractual relationships with other provider organizations, including local public health departments, general hospitals, area agencies on aging, private clinics, and even state hospitals. (CMHCs are somewhat analogous to the concept of a governmental presence in health; see Chapter 7.)

The advocates of the new cycle of reform hoped to prevent chronicity by becoming more aggressively involved in both prevention and acute care. It was thought that rapid and effective intervention in an acute episode of mental illness could bring about a quick resolution of the problem and avoidance of chronic mental illness. The asylums had become the problem in the eyes of many: they were thought to create chronic mental illness by their ineffective and inhumane treatment of the mentally ill. The movement was thoroughly anti-institutional. It not only fought the asylums, it fought all hospitals, and it fought the state mental health bureaucracy as well. Following a pathway created by the Kennedy administration and expanded by President Johnson, federal funds bypassed state government and even local government, stimulating new, not-for-profit, citizen organizations to form community mental health centers. It was hoped that 2,000 such centers would serve catchment areas that included all the people of the country. At the movement's peak, there were only 700 of them, however. Each center was required to provide the five basic services thought to be necessary:

- Inpatient care
- Outpatient care
- Emergency care
- Day care
- Consultation to other agencies

The list was later expanded to 12 services.

The CMHC movement was counterinstitution, counterculture, and counterprofessional to a large extent. In its revolutionary zeal, it eschewed traditional, licensed professionals and concentrated on social reform. Its leaders and staff were trained in community organization and social work, and they saw empowerment of the poor as the best preventive intervention. Their boards were often made up of the parents of chronically mentally ill patients who were living in the community, but the staff was more interested in acute care and prevention of social ills. Yet the chronically mentally ill kept coming: the state hospitals, partly because of their own therapeutic successes, partly because of court orders that forced them to release those they were not treating actively, and partly because of the conviction of state financial managers that this was the way to save money, were by now sending a flood of patients back into communities that were poorly prepared to serve them.

With the inauguration of President Reagan, federal support for the CMHCs and federal guidance regarding the effective treatment of the former state hospital patients declined. The fourth era of "reform" began. State and local governments became increasingly concerned about the chronically mentally ill in their communities and insisted that the mental health centers devote more of their resources to the problem and less to the stresses and strains of seemingly normal people. With a reduction in federal dollars, the centers searched for new sources of revenue. They discontinued services that were not reimbursable in a fee-for-service medical climate in favor of more traditional medical activities.[12]

Was it, is it, deinstitutionalization or abandonment? It remains to be seen. The federal government withdrew, and the state had turned the problem back to the community, but the latter had neither the resources nor in many cases the will to cope with the problem. Out of this dilemma, discussed further below, has emerged a new cycle of reform—the fourth one—with both promise and threat. Disappointed with the promises of the 1960s and faced with the pressures of the 1980s, some mental health professionals and other human service workers appear to be taking the position that not all of the mentally ill can be cured, nor can all mental illness be prevented. This is, for Americans, a heretical notion. The belief that all problems can be solved has been a powerful force in the United States since World War II. The realization that this may not be so is a novel one. It is also an important step in the care of the mentally ill. It means that the community must provide the social supports necessary to protect at least some of the mentally ill on a permanent basis, with no expectation that they will recover and become productive, tax-paying citizens. This is a very European notion, but a new concept in the United States. It suggests some maturation, but it raises the specter of biased triage: Who will decide? At what threshold will we decide that care is a more appropriate objective than cure? Will that threshold change based on appropriations of money or advances in scientific knowledge? Will some treatable, curable people be relegated to the back wards of the community support system? The development and maintenance of such systems are important steps forward, not only for the mentally ill, but they raise complex ethical questions and require more difficult management decisions than were needed when it was assumed that all people could be cured.

DEINSTITUTIONALIZATION

The word *deinstitutionalization* has been used several times in this book. It was applied to the change in treatment for tuberculosis, to the management of the long-term care system, and now to mental illness. Simply put, deinstitutionalization means decreasing the role an institution plays in managing or solving a problem. By institution, people usually mean a building and its style of management. More generically, however, an institution can refer to any system—a social structure, a religion, a school system, or a hospital. Moving people with mental disorders from a physical institution to a community institution merely changes the form of institution in which they must live. Community-based institutions, such as the Girl Scouts or a particular church, have their own mores and can be every bit as constraining and demanding of conformity as hospitals and jails.

The courts, many years ago, adopted the principle of the "least restrictive alternative" as the method that should be chosen whenever society moves to restrict the freedom of an individual. If the purpose is to prevent contagion, for example, restriction in excess of what is needed for that limited purpose should not be considered. Restricting the freedom of someone with a mental disorder can usually be condoned only when the individual is "gravely disabled" and can be shown to be dangerous, either to himself or herself or to others, *as a result of that disability.* The restriction imposed should be that which is least restricting of all the feasible alternatives and which, at the same time, can prevent the harm that is feared. People who stand on the street corner and chant may be distracting and even offensive, but if they are not (1) dangerous (2) because of a grave disability, their freedom cannot be restricted any more than anyone else's.

To make such decisions and distinctions, society must determine the threshold at which a problem is deemed dangerous. Outright self-starvation might be considered dangerous to one's self, and society might intervene. A poor diet might not be considered so dangerous. By the passage of a law or through court action, that threshold can be altered. If it is decided that only people with a blood sugar content greater than 180 milligrams per deciliter of blood are to be called diabetic, then a screening program will label very few people diabetic. Those who are labeled diabetic will very likely turn out to have diabetes, but many people with the disease will be missed. If the threshold is lowered to 120 milligrams, many more people will be labeled. Few diabetics will be missed, but many of those who have a positive test result will not have diabetes.

Societal decisions about mental illness, either in the legislature or in the courts, have the same effect. If the threshold is set high enough (gravely disabled and a danger to self or others, for example), only the seriously disabled will be so labeled and have their freedom restricted. Many people with mental disorders will live in the community unrestricted, and that may annoy some people and even scare a few. If that level is lowered (just disabled, for instance, and a potential danger to self or others), then many more people will be restricted in their freedom; fewer seriously disabled people will be left on the streets or elsewhere in the community, but many people will have their freedom restricted unnecessarily.

The deinstitutionalization movement in the United States was started because many mental health professionals felt that the institutions, the state asylums, were not helpful and, in fact, were part of the problem. The movement was accelerated by court decisions that changed the threshold at which people could be restricted. The final push came from those who thought that deinstitutionalization could save money, tax dollars specifically. The rise of homelessness in the 1980s is often attributed to the deinstitutionalization of the mentally ill. Because of that, and because of occasional newspaper headlines that scream EX-MENTAL PATIENT KILLS 3, people have attempted to change the threshold once again.

There is little doubt that many of the homeless are people who would have been in state or county asylums many years ago, but most of the homeless are not: they are people without enough money. They are often entire families, and they often work at regular jobs, but they cannot afford a home. What really happened to the mentally ill? Where did they go? It is known that the number of occupants of state and county mental health hospitals has declined sharply during the last two decades. What is less well understood is where those people went. Part of the answer is shown in Table 27-2.

The decline in the daily census is apparent, but it is also clear that there was a change in institutionalization, with patients moving into the private sector and into residential care facilities. This reduced state and county tax costs but did not reduce the total cost of hospitalization. One important aspect of the deinstitutionalization movement is not readily apparent. Many of the patients who once were in state and county asylums were transferred to nursing homes, where Medicaid reimbursement could offset state and county tax costs. The exact number of such transfers is not known, but it appears to be in excess of 300,000.[13] This would more than offset the reduction in institutional care shown in the table, but of course the total population has increased since 1969. The overall impression is that the proportion of people in mental health institutions has decreased slightly over the past 25 years, and there has been a substantial relocation from one kind of institution

TABLE 27-2 Average daily inpatient and residential treatment census by type of mental health organization, United States, 1969, 1979, and 1983

Type of organization	1969	1979	1983
State and county mental hospitals	367,629	138,600	116,236
Private psychiatric hospitals	11,608	13,901	16,467
General hospital psychiatric services	17,808	21,110	34,328
VA medical centers	47,140	28,693	20,342
Community mental health centers	5,270	—	—
Residential treatment centers for children	12,406	18,054	15,826
All other organizations	970	1,140	20,970
TOTALS	468,831	233,384	224,169

From Manderscheid RW and Barrett SA, editors: Mental health, United States, 1987, Rockville, MD, 1987, US Department of Health and Human Services.

to several others. Whether their care has improved as a result is not known, but the cost of that care has surely increased.

At the same time, the number of *admissions* to inpatient institutions has increased: from 1,282,698 in 1969 to 1,633,307 in 1983. The number of admissions to state and county asylums decreased slightly, from 486,661 to 339,127, but admissions to other types of institutions, especially general hospitals, increased dramatically, from 478,000 to 786,180. Since the number of beds available for psychiatric admissions has declined, the increase in admissions has to have been accompanied by shorter durations of stay. In addition, the number of outpatient admissions has skyrocketed: from 1,146,612 in 1969 to 2,665,943 in 1983. The increase in admissions and the fact that many patients are readmitted repeatedly have led to the criticism that the deinstitutionalization movement has increased recidivism with no resultant benefits to society. *Recidivism* is a word that entered the health arena from the corrections arena, where repeated admissions are indeed an indication of failure, but this may not be so in mental health. People who used to live their entire lives in a mental hospital could not be readmitted: the recidivism rate was zero. As they reenter society, some remain at relatively high risk of mental disability. Similar to someone with diabetes, their treatment may be delicate at times, and under stress they may suffer a relapse. The goal of treatment should be to reduce dependency. Someone who lives in the community and functions there, but who is admitted to the hospital two or three times a year for 24 hours to 3 days at a time, is less dependent and more functional than someone who spends a lifetime in an asylum. Having asserted that not all recidivism is bad, however, it must be acknowledged that many readmissions indicate inadequate case management in the community and a lack of community supports.

There are indications that some people, policymakers among them, would like to reinstitutionalize mental health. They are fearful of the homeless, whom they perceive to be mentally ill, and they are fearful of violence, which they incorrectly attribute to people who are mentally ill. (Former mental hospital patients are less likely to commit a violent act than are others in the community who have never been so institutionalized.) To some extent, this may be a desirable move. A number of people who have been placed in community settings are unable to function there and have been abandoned, lonely and afraid. They could be better protected and live a happier life in a well-designed and well-staffed institution. The major problem with deinstitutionalization of the mentally ill has been the lack of social supports in the community.[14] Mental health and public health professionals have often attempted to "sell" the notion of deinstitutionalization by claiming that it would be cheaper. It is cheaper only if it is not done well, and there is some question about whether that might not turn out to be more expensive for society in the long run.

Deinstitutionalization has been jeopardized by an inadequate definition of goals, fragmentation of responsibility at the community level, lack of a systematic approach to financing, lack of commitment to the agencies that serve the poor, and lack of effective community organization and advocacy.[15] A new effort to develop more effective community support systems was launched in 1977 after several community mental health centers had developed models. A community support system recognizes that services alone are not enough.[16] The concept includes the following components:

1. Locating clients and outreach to them
2. Assistance in meeting basic human needs such as food, shelter, and clothing
3. Mental health care
4. 24-hour crisis assistance
5. Psychosocial and vocational services
6. Rehabilitative and supportive housing
7. Assistance, consultation, and education
8. Natural support systems (families, friends, and other groups)
9. Grievance procedures and protection of client rights
10. Case management

Many states have begun to take steps to improve community support. It is difficult to do so in an era of tight budgets. The money to support such systems could come from the state hospitals themselves, but some money in advance would be required to strengthen community capacity before the patients could be relocated to the community. Gradually, expenditures for inpatient care will decrease, but careful planning and some advanced funding are necessary. As recently as 1983, 65% of state mental health funds were spent for inpatient care. In Wisconsin, new legislation together with new funds has established a better integrated community and state hospital system, gradually moving responsibility for inpatient services into the community mental health center. Other states have increased support for housing and social services.

Richard Lamb and John Talbott[17] have summarized the present situation by describing homelessness among the mentally ill as symptomatic of a larger problem, which will not be solved until "a comprehensive and integrated system of care . . . is established," including a range of supervised housing; comprehensive and accessible mental health services, rehabilitation programs, and general medical care; crisis services; and a dependable source of income.

MENTAL HEALTH PROGRAMS

At the national level, the focal point for research and service is the Alcohol, Drug Abuse and Mental Health Administration (ADAMHA), which includes the National Institute of Drug Abuse (NIDA), the National Institute of Mental Health (NIMH), the National Institute on Alcoholism and Alcohol Abuse (NIAAA), and St. Elizabeth's Hospital, the mental health institution in Washington, DC. The NIMH sponsors research on the treatment, diagnosis, and epidemiology of mental illness and supports the principal grant program that helps fund the community mental health centers.

In most of the states, there is a separate mental health agency, which may or may not be responsible for substance abuse programs. Even when the state mental health authority is part of a larger umbrella organization that includes public health, there is little coordination between the two. Local public health agencies are a part of general-purpose government and use state or local civil service systems. The local mental health agency is usually governed by a private, not-for-profit board of directors and uses a different personnel system. The state agency is responsible for managing the state psychiatric hospitals, where they still exist (as many as 32 in New York and as few as 1 in many states), and for managing the state mental health plan and the legislative appropriation for community-based mental health programs. Most of the local programs are coordinated if not directly managed by the community mental health center for that catchment area.* For the foreseeable future, they will have to place increased emphasis on management, interagency collaboration, and the construction of community coalitions. Tightening dollar supplies and increased regulatory controls along with continuing client demands will make success difficult to attain.[18] Their linkage to public health agencies is more important than ever but possibly more difficult to assure, given the propensities of both organizations to worry about their own problems and their own funding bases. In addition to the complex problems presented by the chronically mentally ill who are living in the community, the problem of AIDS presents new challenges to both agencies. Patients with AIDS need the services of a community support system if they are to function as independently as possible. A first step would be to develop specific, written agreements regarding the services to be provided to certain key groups in need of help from all three agencies. While that can be done at the local level, state level leadership can facilitate and encourage such sensible and necessary agreements.

PREVENTION

The treatment and management of mental disability and the dependency that ensues are difficult and not especially rewarding tasks. Much of the problem concerns the partial habilitation and rehabilitation of seriously disabled people with limited prospects for an outright cure. The prevention of mental illness has been a goal and a dream for years. Several advances over the past two decades suggest that that dream may be at least partially realized.

There are a number of known risk factors for several of the most important mental disorders, which can guide the work of public health and mental health professionals toward more effective interventions. Depression is more likely to occur in women, in those with a family history of depression, following bereavement, in those with a medical illness and an adverse drug reaction,

* A bibliography on the mental health programs has been prepared by the National Institute of Mental Health: Feldman S, editor: Mental health administration: an annotated bibliography, Rockville, MD, 1983, US Department of Health and Human Services.

during stressful life events, and following separation and loss. It is more common in nonwhites and in those living in isolated and segregated circumstances, and it is more common in older people. There are several other risk factors that appear to be of importance in the development of schizophrenia: a family history of the disease, social incompetence, family conflict, school maladjustment, low intelligence, certain biochemical abnormalities, and problems in childhood emotional development.[19]

It is important not to overstate the promise. Beverly Long, Chairwoman of the National Mental Health Association's Commission on the Prevention of Mental-Emotional Disabilities,[20] has written:

> an investment in a prevention strategy would simultaneously reduce the frequency of mental-emotional disabilities, decrease health care costs as well as welfare, delinquency and other social costs, enhance family stability, increase productivity throughout all sectors of business and, therefore, prove in this era of increasingly tight budgets to be a very prudent expenditure.

The statement has a familiar and worrisome ring to it: prevention can do all things for all people, and with just a little bit of money. Such claims rarely come to fruition. Wellness—physical, mental, and social—is neither cheap nor easy.

Yet there are many cross-cutting issues, commonalities to social, mental, and physical wellness, that are fairly easy to understand: the need to support the biologic integrity of individuals, the need to enhance their psychosocial development, the need to provide adequate and appropriate social supports, and the need to aid the development of helpful social attitudes. Such commitments could produce astonishing benefits in many aspects of daily social life. They are not, however, easy to accomplish.

REFERENCES

1. Jensen HE: Mental health: a local public health responsibility, Ment Hyg 37:530, Oct 1953.
2. Diagnostic and Statistical Manual of Mental Disorders, ed 3, Revised, Washington, DC, 1987, American Psychiatric Association.
3. Eaton WW et al.: The epidemiological catchment area program of the National Institute of Mental Health, Public Health Rep 96:319, July-Aug 1981.
4. Office of Economic Affairs of the American Psychiatric Association: Economic fact book for psychiatry, ed 2, 1987, American Psychiatric Press.
5. Murphy JM and others: Incidence of depression and anxiety: the Stirling County study, Am J Public Health 78:534, May 1988.
6. Manderscheid RW and Barrett SA, editors: Mental health, United States, 1987, Rockville, MD, 1987, US Department of Health and Human Services.
7. Duhl LJ and Cummings NA, editors: The future of mental health services: coping with crisis, New York, 1987, Springer Publishing Co.
8. Beer CW: A mind that found itself, New York, 1948, Doubleday & Co, Inc.
9. Goldman HJ and Morrissey JP: The alchemy of mental health policy: homelessness and the fourth cycle of reform, Am J Public Health 75:727, July 1985.
10. Brown P: The transfer of care: psychiatric deinstitutionalization and its aftermath, Boston, 1985, Routledge & Kegan Paul.
11. Barchas JD and Bunney WE, editors: Perspectives in psychopharmacology, New York, 1988, Liss.
12. Jerrell JM and Larsen JK: How community mental health centers deal with cutbacks and competition, Hosp Community Psychiatry 36:1169, Nov 1985.
13. Kiesler CA and Sibulkin AE: Mental hospitalization: myths and facts about a national crisis, Newbury Park, CA, 1987, Sage Publications, Inc.
14. Rose SM and Black BL: Advocacy and empowerment: mental health care in the community, Boston, 1985, Routledge & Kegan Paul.
15. Turner JC and TenHoor WJ: The National Institute of Mental Health community support program: pilot approach to a needed social reform, Schizophr Bull 4(4), 1978.
16. Stroul BA: Models of community support services: approaches to helping persons with long-term mental illness, Boston, 1986, Sargent College of Allied Health Professions.
17. Lamb HR and Talbott JA: The homeless mentally ill: the perspective of the American Psychiatric Association, J Am Med Assoc 256:498, July 25, 1986.
18. Newman FL and Sorensen JE: Integrated clinical and fiscal management in mental health: a guidebook, Norwood, NJ, 1985, Ablex Publishing Corp.
19. Watt NF: Prevention of major mental illness: risk factors in schizophrenia and depressive disorders. In Resource papers to the report of the National Mental Health Association Commission on the prevention of mental-emotional disabilities, Alexandria, VA, 1986, The Association.
20. Commission on the Prevention of Mental-Emotional Disabilities: The prevention of mental-emotional disabilities, Alexandria, VA, 1986, National Mental Health Association.

CHAPTER 28

Drug-related problems and public health

In addition to diseases and injuries there are other "slings and arrows of outrageous fortune" that threaten the health of individuals and of society, insults that are thought of as self-inflicted but for which society must shoulder some of the blame. Humans and other animals can become addicted to chemicals, which may then dominate their lives in ways they had not foreseen, leading to both dire personal consequences and considerable societal disruption. These are behavioral disorders that involve the compulsive consumption of such drugs as alcohol, marijuana, and tobacco. Many of the objects of use and then abuse have beneficial aspects when used judiciously and generally affect only a small proportion of the population directly. They affect a larger proportion indirectly, and have the power to arouse still larger segments of society to vehemence, action, and hyperbole. They have done just that, repeatedly.

Most prominent of the drugs of abuse is alcohol. It is the most frequently used drug in our society. It is also the one most commonly used by adolescents, the one most frequently implicated in highway fatalities and murders, and the one most often involved in interpersonal violence. This chapter will focus first on alcohol, then on the other commonly abused drugs, and finally on tobacco, the drug that causes more deaths each year than all of the others combined.

Alcohol has played a fascinating role in the history of humans. Its production appears to have been one of the earliest discoveries, perhaps not long after fire and the wheel. Undoubtedly, it was recognized early that among those who consumed it were some who developed a seemingly uncontrollable urge to continue to do so, regardless of the destructive impact it had on their health and safety. The drunkard is recognized in the Old Testament:

> Who has woe? Who has sorrow? Who has strife? Who has complaining? Who has wounds without cause? Who has redness of eyes? Those who tarry long over wine, those who go to try mixed wine. (Proverbs 23:29-30)

The drunkard was typified as well by Shakespeare and in ancient Babylonian writings, all of which note the behavioral disorder with scorn and little pity. Society has looked on drunkenness with variable attitudes throughout history, assigning it a different ranking as a problem from time to time, based partly on policies and circumstances, partly on changing perceptions and mores. The use of drugs has called forth a similar variation in social attitudes over time. (The changing patterns of use, abuse, and disapproval are described best in David Musto's book, *The American Disease.*[1] Some interesting aspects of the cyclic nature of alcohol policies are described by Stanton Peele[2] and by Tabakoff, Sutker, and Randall.[3]) As early as 1606 in England, the Act to Repress the Odious and Loathsome Sin of Drunkenness was passed. It remained in effect until 1872. Alcohol was heavily integrated into the daily life of the colonists and played an important role in the economic structure of the new nation, including its slave trade. Taverns were common, as they were in England, but drunkenness does not appear to have been especially troublesome in colonial society.

By the 1830s, the beginnings of prohibition were evident as the incidence and prevalence of alcohol-related problems appeared to increase. Per capita consumption was high—higher then than now—and the social problems, variously thought of as sins or crimes, seemed to grow in importance. As the momentum for prohibition grew, consumption waned, but the fervor to rid society of the demon rum did not. Interestingly, opiate use became more common. Laudanum and paregoric, common opium-containing remedies used for headaches and menstrual pains, were widely available in nineteenth-century America. They were largely middle-class balms used by women. With industrialization, their use shifted to the new ghettos and minority population groups. Long a practice in other countries and soon one in America, the exploitation of labor by the use of mind-numbing drugs is still a practice in the Andean mining regions, where coca leaves are commonly chewed. Prohibition was aimed at alcohol, however, not these other drugs.

By the turn of the century, the rhetoric of the prohibitionists had become infectious. Alcohol use was transformed from a sin to a crime and then both at the same time. It was described as the smoking pistol of civilization, and purveyors of booze were condemned in terms later applied to child pornographers. Politicians were afraid to avoid the bandwagon, so unpopular was even the tacit acceptance of alcohol in society. Prohibition became the law of the land in 1920 by means of a constitutional amendment, and the fervor spilled over into the use of tobacco and other drugs. Several states had outlawed smoking altogether by the beginning of the twentieth century.

A lot of things happened during prohibition: Al Capone, the flapper era, bathtub gin, and recovery from World War I, for instance. It is also true that the number of deaths due to cirrhosis of the liver declined sharply. Figures on traffic fatalities are not available, but it is likely that other health status indicators showed improvement during the 13 years of prohibition. It was repealed in 1933, and the cycle began again.

Tolerance for various forms of drug abuse, including tobacco, relaxed. Alcohol use increased, and by the 1960s, even more fearsome, illicit drugs were popular: marijuana, LSD, and prescription drugs that had some of the same effects. Cocaine was widely touted as a marvelous drug that created a very pleasant effect and had absolutely no dangerous side effects! Interestingly, tobacco was becoming less popular at this time. It had less of a mood-altering effect on people (and the altering of moods was not so disdained as it had been and later came to be again), and its lethal effects were increasingly well known to the general public.

By the late 1970s the public had become alarmed by the damages suffered as a result of alcohol, drugs, and tobacco, and prohibitionism was waxing once more. Hundreds of communities began to pass ordinances limiting smoking. (By 1989, nearly 400 such local ordinances had been adopted.[4]) The drinking age was raised in several states in an effort to reduce the number of adolescent deaths due to highway crashes. Soon the movement gained such momentum that Congress included such provisions in laws governing the use of federal highway construction funds by the states, and 21 became the norm for purchasing alcohol, even though it was widely understood that 13- and 14-year-olds were experimenting with the drug in their homes and at parties. President Carter's top drug advisor, Dr. Peter Bourne, resigned when it became known that he had written an illegal prescription for drugs for a staff aide. (It was also alleged that he had used cocaine at a Washington party.)

Cocaine, previously looked on benevolently, became the drug of choice among the affluent, but then trickled down to the poor, and as "crack" (an almost pure form of cocaine that can be smoked and produces its effects swiftly) quickly became the scourge of the 1980s. Drug users were reviled as the source of most of society's ills, and before long, some of the most prominent officials in the Reagan administration had labeled those who sold drugs as "murderers" and a move was on to legally execute those who might meddle in drugs. Nightly newspapers were full of stories about "crack houses," and local evening news broadcasts showed sheriffs and police officers breaking into a house to arrest the users and sellers, usually minorities and often young. The army was called out to police the borders, invading squads of drug enforcement officers were sent to producing countries in South America, surveillance planes and balloons were launched to guard the borders, and there was talk of erecting something similar to the Great Wall of China to protect our southern exposure against the invading hordes.

The organizations MADD and SADD (Mothers Against Drunk Driving and Students Against Drunk Driving) were increasingly effective in forcing stiffer penalties for people who were caught driving "under the influence," and in some instances, drunk drivers who killed other people were convicted of murder. The use of "designated drivers" at parties became increasingly common, and the alcoholic beverage industry and public health groups became increasingly combative with one another. Surgeon General Koop convened a conference in 1988 to discuss alcohol policies and the industry tried to block it, first calling for a postponement, then a boycott, and finally, legal steps to prevent the workshop from focusing on the problems.

Alcohol and drug abuse are involved in a wide variety of important public health and other kinds of problems: from high mortality rates, to fetal loss, spouse abuse, injuries, violence, lost work time, and simple annoyance. Their economic impact is devastating, at both the family and community level. One of the difficulties public health will continue to encounter as it attempts to ameliorate the problems related to the abuse of drugs is the inconstancy of policy and public opinion. The peculiarly American trait of ambivalence toward drugs that can affect moods and emotions hinders reasoned understanding of the epidemiology of the problems and their potential resolution. This chapter cannot overcome that problem, because no one understands it, but an attempt will be made to describe it.

Some definitions

People involved in the subject are apt to speak in terms of "substance use." The three major problem areas are alcohol, licit and illicit drugs (such as heroin, cocaine, and tranquilizers), and tobacco. Technically, these could all be called drugs: substances other than food intended to affect the structure or function of the body. However, to speak of "drug abuse" offends smokers and social drinkers, who recognize drug abusers as someone quite different from themselves. Hence the use of the word *substance,* although a substance can be almost anything: a substance user could be someone who applies face powder or takes vitamin C.

Then there is the argument over *use* versus *abuse.* The argument takes two forms, one having to do with guilt and innocence and the other with pharmacologic principles. Describing people as drug abusers implies that their own volitional behavior (at least originally) is at fault: if they had not chosen to use the product, addiction and other problems would not have ensued. According to this argument, there is nothing inherently wrong with cocaine, for example; the problem is the abusive misbehavior of some people. Others argue that society should absorb a greater degree of blame, that children cannot be blamed for their risk-taking experiments with tobacco, drugs, and alcohol. Since these substances are so widely advertised and available, their users are doing only what they are urged to do, enticed to do, seduced to do. They are not abusing anything; they are being abused by society. The pharmacologic argument concerns thresholds. *Abuse* implies that there is some way to use the questionable substances that will not be harmful and that only when use exceeds that level will harm result. This argument is particularly attractive to the liquor industry and to the large number of people who consider themselves to be responsible users of a product that is only harmful in excess. However, no one has been able to demonstrate a threshold below which tobacco is not harmful, and since heroin and "crack" are illicit, any use may be termed abuse.

These are nice arguments and not without their substantive importance, but they leave us with weak phrases such as *substance use,* which conveys nothing of the process. With apologies to the sensitivities that have led to this discussion, the term *drug abuse* will be used here to include any inappropriate use of chemicals that causes harm to the individual. (*Inappropriate* because some prescribed drugs hurt people but are necessary to mitigate a more serious source of harm, such as cancer or AIDS.) It begs the question of whether any use of alcohol can be harmless, because it is assumed that alcohol will always be used and that, more often than not, no lasting harm will ensue.

Addiction

Addiction is another term that confuses discussions of drug abuse. Conventionally, an addiction is defined as a compulsion to act that is beyond self-control.[2] It includes elements of tolerance, withdrawal, and craving, words that conjure up images of evil and degradation. *Tolerance* is the phenomenon of increasing resistance to the effects of the drug, which necessitates that higher and higher doses be used in order to get the desired effect. *Withdrawal* refers to the unpleasant physical symptoms experienced by someone who is addicted to a drug but unable to obtain it. There is a biochemical reality to the pain of withdrawal, at least for some drugs. *Craving* refers to the strong, well-nigh insurmountable desire to have the drug.

These are strong words in our society. Peele[2] points out that addiction is not just a biochemical process. He describes it as an "individual's adjustment, albeit a self-defeating one, to his or her environment." That may be a bit soft for many people's taste, but it is clear that addiction has social and cultural aspects as well as biochemical ones. Addicts can often cope with whatever biochemical urges they may have during withdrawal but succumb to their feelings when they find themselves in the same ecological context that supported their addiction originally. At one time, authoritative people made a distinction between *addiction,* with the characteristics mentioned above, and *habituation,* which meant something similar but without the withdrawal and tolerance phenomena. Such distinctions are of less use now. *Addiction* will be used to describe the general phenomenon in this chapter, with apologies to those who are compulsive about certain things that they would not like to think of as addictions. (Future research will probably shed more light on the phenomenon of addiction, and the term can then be used more precisely.)

Addiction is not without its problems as a label. There is evidence of its rising popularity.[5] There are some very popular self-confessed addicts: Betty Ford, Elizabeth Taylor, Kitty Dukakis, and numerous personalities whose troubles became brief sagas in the 1980s. A wide variety of groups has been formed to assist people with the tribulations of addiction: Alcoholics Anonymous, Gamblers Anonymous, Overeaters Anonymous, Narcotics Anonymous, Love and Sex Addicts Anonymous, and many more. A new magazine, *Lifeline America,* has been published for addicts of various sorts, and there is a growing number of treatment specialists, addictionologists. Since some notable figures have confessed to addictions, it is apparently acceptable to acknowledge compulsive behaviors so long as they can be described as addictions. They have now been labeled officially as diseases. There is a certain fundamentalist Christian revival tone to the movement: salvation can be attained through testimony, public contrition is a necessary part of testimony, and one must acknowledge submission to a higher power—first the drug (a lower power) and then God. (Recently, a new group has formed, which attempts to accomplish the same goals without relying on a belief of God—the American Atheists Addiction Recovery Group.)

This sanitation of personal failure through relabeling is not uncommon in the United States. Indeed, the movement to label alcoholism a disease, rather than a sin or a crime, had many of the same virtues: it pleased the alcoholics; it supported the contentions of the industry that its product was harmless and even beneficial except for a small group of people with a disease who should not, of course, drink at all; and it solved the problem for the rest of us, since diseases are to be treated by physicians, and that's that. Voila! We've found the cure for alcoholism: we'll call it a disease and doctors will cure it. The same process is now occurring with the broader concept of addiction, although there is, as yet, no acknowledged professional group with the skill and power to treat and cure the problem.

Disease

Is addiction a disease? Is alcoholism a disease? It was widely thought that the labeling of alcoholism as a disease was a progressive and enlightened step forward. Public inebriation was treated as a crime—a misdemeanor, but a crime nonetheless. Alcoholism was often treated sternly when it could not be confined quietly to the home and family. Drunks were tossed into the local jail until they sobered up, then hauled before the judge and fined. When the courts and the medical professional decided to call alcoholism a disease, the judges were quite happy. Rather than sentencing people to overcrowded jails, they could now send them to hospitals and treatment facilities. Yet these were not widely available, and those that existed were not notoriously efficacious.

By now, most people think of alcoholism as a disease, but does that appellation help or hinder effective intervention? If it is a disease, it is not a unitary disease. Peele[2] points out that alcoholics do, in fact, control their drinking. Many of them recover on their own, and many return to social drinking. If it is a disease, it is many different kinds of diseases, not one. Others question whether it is a disease at all. A disease is a distinctive disorder of the body caused by an explicit phenomenon. Alcoholism, like other forms of drug abuse, surely leads to diseases, but it does not fit well what has been called the "disease model." Laboratory studies have shown that an alcoholic's drinking does not conform to the loss-of-control notion—they do know what they are doing and how much of it they can do. Moreover there are many examples of people who have successfully moderated their drinking behavior to attain a specific objective. Longitudinal studies on the natural history of alcoholism have shown that many alcoholics recover spontaneously, and there are numerous cross-cultural studies that reveal the significant role played by cultural variables. The most characteristic volitional disorder, drinking, is simply not explained by the disease concept. Rather than become entangled in a morass of unknowns, drug abuse will be treated here as a distinct entity, a collection of problems, which causes diseases.

INTERVENTION

Interventions to reduce the incidence and prevalence of drug-related problems are difficult to characterize. As will be discussed later, public health must decide whether its purpose is to prevent the abuse, drinking, or the problems that stem from the abuse, such as motor vehicle fatalities and fires. Beyond that, however, is the problem of social sanction: is it the user or the resultant problems that are to be the object of scorn? How far can we go in shaping behavior? It is acceptable to pass laws governing the age at which children can first buy forbidden products such as tobacco or alcohol, but can we pass laws prohibiting adults from using them? This is the same argument that was presented in Chapter 15 about the prevention of noncommunicable diseases. Beyond even this problem lies the problem of blame: should our attention be focused on the supply of the product or the demand for it? This argument clouded the government's attack on drug abuse during the Reagan administration. While many advocated use of the military to interdict the supply of illicit drugs, others asserted that the supply could never be blocked so long as there was a demand. The focus of attention for the demand-siders is on education, treatment, and punishment and social ostracism of the users and abusers of both illicit and licit drugs. Prudence dictates that both the supply-siders and the demand-siders have valid arguments. Public health is involved on both sides: through the regulation of legal drugs and their authorized prescribers, through education and advocacy, and through treatment and rehabilitation.

On the question of where to intervene, popular notions of the evolution of drug abuse reveal the lack of scientific thinking that often guides public policies. Most people who use cocaine experimented with marijuana at an earlier point in their life. And most people who have used marijuana have used alcohol and cigarettes. Hence the famous, compelling, and erroneous "stepping stone" theory of drug abuse: the one drug leads to the other. Cigarettes and alcohol lead to marijuana, which leads to crack and heroin. Parents who find their child has smoked a cigarette have every reason to fear an imminently craving dope fiend! However, most children who experiment with one drug do not progress up the chain of addiction. In the dominant culture in the United States, beer and wine are the first drugs of abuse. Later, children may experiment with liquor and cigarettes. Some, still later, experiment with marijuana. And later yet, a few experiment with other illicit drugs, such as cocaine and heroin. The characteristic patterns at different ages and stages may differ within social and cultural groups, but there is no inevitable progression from one to the other. The sequence is probably related to availability and social factors rather than any pharmacologic phenomena. Not all children who experiment at stage I move to stage II. The key to intervention involves identifying the factors that differentiate between the different subgroups. Trying to prevent all people from experimenting with drugs will prove difficult, and most of the people who do experiment will not produce a plethora of drug-related problems. At the present time, however, attention is focused on broad attempts to reduce the incidence of drug abuse through primary prevention and to reduce its prevalence through secondary and tertiary prevention.

ALCOHOL

The effects of alcohol

The response to alcohol follows a typical dose-response curve: the more ingested, the greater the response. People vary, however, in how they respond. Some may be able to ingest considerably more than others with no apparent effect and never become alcoholics. Alcohol is rapidly absorbed into the blood stream and is detectable within 5 minutes of ingestion. The average adult can metabolize about 10 milliliters of alcohol per hour. Ingestion at a more rapid rate results in a buildup in the bloodstream and in the tissues. Blood concentrations in excess of 0.10% (100 milligrams per deciliter) are known to result in impaired judgment and coordination. At 0.20%, intoxication is apparent to the casual observer. Blood concentrations in excess of 0.50% can result in death.

All parts of the body are affected, especially the central nervous system tissue. Contrary to popular belief, alcohol acts as a depressant, not a stimulant. It inhibits or depresses higher level control over behavior. The heart rate increases and the blood vessels dilate, resulting in a loss of heat and a decrease in body temperature. Vision and balance are impaired relatively early. In more advanced stages of intoxication, the part of the brain that regulates breathing and heart function is depressed. Chronic effects are even more severe. At small levels of consumption, little effect on longevity can be detected, but heavy drinkers live shorter lives than nondrinkers. The functional capacity of several organs is decreased with prolonged heavy drinking, the liver most importantly. Many of the long-term ill effects of heavy alcohol consumption are the result of altered nutrition. Alcoholics often eat poorly, with relatively large amounts of simple carbohydrates and fats. In addition, certain vitamin deficiencies occur as a result of heavy drinking. In advanced stages, severe central nervous system disorders become apparent.

Drinking behavior

How do alcoholics differ from (1) people who drink but who are not alcoholics and (2) nondrinkers? There are many reasons for drinking: to fulfill ritual obligations, to be polite, to have a good time, to make friends, to experiment, to get warm or cool, to avoid reality, or to quench one's thirst. None of these is the purpose of the alcoholic, however. Alcoholics drink, more or less, because they have to. Many of them hate the taste and the effect of liquor, and they often hate themselves for drinking, but drink they will. Psychiatrists have suggested that if alcoholics did not drink, they might seek some other outlet for a maladapted personality, but this is speculation without evidence. It is probably true, however, that some people are predisposed to alcoholism. The predisposition appears to have some genetic qualities. The usual way such factors are found is by studying twins, those raised in their natal family and those raised in adoptive settings. The genetic effect is slight overall, but it is probably more pronounced in certain people. Environmental conditions no doubt can contribute to the predisposition. Some people with no apparent predispositions become alcoholics because of their jobs and their family circumstances. Some jobs include a general ambience of drinking, both at lunchtime and for dinner.

The epidemiology of alcohol abuse

The epidemiology of drinking is not as well understood as it should be. The situation is compounded by inconsistent definitions of what constitutes heavy drinking and by a lack of commonality in various data bases. As noted below, one study defines heavy drinking as anything in excess of 0.99 ounces of absolute alcohol per day. Other studies have defined problem drinking as having had more than a certain number of drinks on one occasion during the past 30 days. Still others define heavy drinking in terms of the number of drinks consumed in a week. Agencies involved and interested in alcohol-related problems do not maintain information about their clients in ways that would allow comparisons. In one study, the only demographic variables routinely collected by all of the agencies were age and gender: other interesting variables, such as race, marital status, education, occupation, employment status, and religion, were not elicited and made part of the record by all of the organizations.[6] Finally, most of the data on consumption actually comes from state tax figures, which identify sales, not the drinker.

Drinking is a widely prevalent form of behavior in the United States and in many other countries. Most people drink. Drinking is (at least statistically) normal behavior; both abstinence and heavy drinking are atypical. Whether an individual drinks at all is primarily related to sociological and cultural variables, but whether he or she becomes a problem drinker depends more on psychologic variables. Moreover, drinking behavior is not constant: people become abstainers with no external interventions, and there is a general tendency for older people to reduce their drinking and to abstain altogether.[7] Even so, the pattern becomes confusing, since the proportion of elderly drinkers who drink heavily tends to increase with age.[8]

The average citizen of the United States over the age of 14 drinks 2.65 gallons of pure alcohol each year. This is the amount of alcohol contained in 50 gallons of beer, 20 gallons of wine, 4 gallons of distilled spirits, or some combination of the three.[9] (*Distilled spirits* is a term usually applied to distilled alcoholic liquor and includes whiskies, brandies, and other beverages.) When abstainers are excluded from the denominator, consumption of pure alcohol is about 4 gallons per year. About 21% of the entire population drinks moderately (defined as 0.22 to 0.99 ounces of pure alcohol per day) and 8% drink heavily (an ounce or more per day). The rates for men are higher than for women. Both rates appear to have decreased slightly over the past 10 years.

The amounts consumed vary enormously by state. As shown in Table 28-1, the average ranged from 5.34 gallons in the District of Columbia to 1.53 gallons in Utah. Some peculiarities in the table are explained by a knowledge of the communities involved. For example, residents of New Hampshire might be assumed to consume 4.91 gallons per year while their Massachusetts neighbors to the south drink just 3.04 gallons per year. However, these figures represent sales, not consumption. People who live along the road between Boston and New Hampshire will tell you that the traffic is fierce on Friday nights as Massachusetts residents drive to New Hampshire to take advantage of the lower state liquor taxes. These figures do not include the liquor involved in home production and illegal sales. In the 4 years between 1980 and 1984, sales decreased in 40 of the states and the District of Columbia.

These figures can be misleading. They use total sales for the numerator and total population of people over the age of 13 for the denominator. They do not reflect the distribution of drinkers into

TABLE 28-1 Apparent per capita consumption of alcohol by U.S. state, population aged 14 and older, 1984

Rank	State	Gallons	Rank	State	Gallons
1	District of Columbia	5.34	26	Louisiana	2.63
2	Nevada	4.19	27	Oregon	2.63
3	New Hampshire	4.91	28	Michigan	2.60
4	Alaska	3.86	29	Maine	2.57
5	California	3.19	30	North Dakota	2.55
6	Wisconsin	3.19	31	Virginia	2.55
7	Delaware	3.17	32	South Carolina	2.50
8	Florida	3.12	33	Georgia	2.48
9	Vermont	3.12	34	Idaho	2.43
10	Colorado	3.09	35	Nebraska	2.41
11	Arizona	3.08	36	South Dakota	2.33
12	Massachusetts	3.04	37	Missouri	2.27
13	Hawaii	2.97	38	Ohio	2.26
14	Montana	2.95	39	Pennsylvania	2.25
15	Rhode Island	2.92	40	Indiana	2.19
16	Wyoming	2.86	41	North Carolina	2.13
17	Maryland	2.84	42	Iowa	2.09
18	New Jersey	2.83	43	Mississippi	2.06
19	Texas	2.80	44	Kansas	1.95
20	Connecticut	2.80	45	Tennessee	1.95
21	Illinois	2.77	46	Oklahoma	1.91
22	New Mexico	2.75	47	Alabama	1.90
23	Washington	2.71	48	Kentucky	1.85
24	Minnesota	2.68	49	Arkansas	1.78
25	New York	2.67	50	West Virginia	1.68
			51	Utah	1.53

From National Institute on Alcohol Abuse and Alcoholism: Sixth special report to the US Congress on alcohol and health from the Secretary of Health and Human Services, Rockville, MD, 1987, US Department of Health and Human Services.

heavy, moderate, and light categories, nor do they indicate the number of nondrinkers in the states. In Table 28-2, it can be seen that the highest per capita consumption does not necessarily correspond with the percentage of people in the population who drink. Even these figures are highly derived, however, and there is little correlation between such geographic estimates and the prevalence of alcohol-related problems such as highway fatalities and spouse abuse.

The incidence and prevalence of drinking by children are of special concern, both because of the immediate damage that may result and because of the widely feared but unproven potential for progression to other stages of drug abuse.[10] Table 28-3 is a copy of a table from an earlier chapter (Chapter 25).

Note that for all the concern expressed about the use of illicit drugs such as crack and marijuana, alcohol is clearly the drug of choice and abuse by students. Slightly more than half as many students show signs of having experimented with marijuana, but only a third as many appear to be regular or recent users.

The cost of alcohol abuse

Anything so widely used and abused as alcohol is bound to have substantial social costs. In 1980, the cost was estimated to be nearly $90 billion. Straightforward projections, assuming no major changes in the prevalence of problems related to the use of alcohol, indicate a current cost of approximately $200 billion. Most of the cost (nearly 90%) is in what Harwood and others[12] call "core costs": the direct and indirect costs of treatment and the loss of lives and productivity. The remainder is accounted for by the costs of motor vehicle crashes, crime, social welfare programs, and incarceration. There is always a danger in such estimates, however, because the same problems may be claimed by the advocates of many different social problems. For example, the cost of fires may be claimed by those interested in warning people about the costs of alcoholism, the costs of tobacco use, or the costs of failure to install fire safety devices in the home. Similarly, the costs of the associated crime may be claimed by people interested in preventing rape and spouse abuse as well as by those concerned about drug abuse. Nonetheless, the economic costs of alcohol abuse cut across all sectors of modern life and extract a considerable toll.

The focus of concern

Given the amount of disability and death and the high economic costs associated with alcoholism, what is the appropriate concern of public health: alcohol*ism,* alcohol *use,* or the problems that stem from the abuse of alcohol? The problems are seemingly without end: the fetal alcohol syndrome (Chapter 23), injuries (Chapter 21), spouse and child abuse (Chapter 29), homicide (Chapter 29), liver cirrhosis, lost work time, early death, and severe dependency. The traditional public sector concern has been with obvious inebriation: the nuisance and the danger manifest in or latent in the drunk, the skid row bum. More recently, attention has turned to the social problems created by alcohol abuse, especially deaths due to motor vehicle crashes and interpersonal violence. The former set of problems was somewhat easier to manage. They required custodial care and support, which often

TABLE 28-2 Apparent alcohol consumption by geographic region for the total U.S. population over age 21 and for the U.S. drinking population over age 21 (excluding abstainers), 1983

Geographic region	Percentage of adult population over age 21 who drink	Apparent per capita consumption based on total population over age 21 (gallons)	Adjusted apparent per capita consumption based on drinking population over age 21 (gallons)
Northwest	78.1	3.22	5.79
Midwest	72.2	3.00	5.86
South	51.6	2.91	8.01
West	66.0	3.42	7.34
TOTALS	67.0	3.14	6.75

From National Institute on Alcohol Abuse and Alcoholism: Sixth special report to the US Congress on alcohol and health from the Secretary of Health and Human Services, Rockville, MD, 1987, US Department of Health and Human Services.

was provided in state and local mental health facilities or in jails. While many set out to cure and rehabilitate chronic alcoholics, more often the objective was to protect them from their problems by providing room and board and a relatively secure environment. The latter problems, injuries and violence, require a different form of intervention, since most of the problems are caused not by the few advanced alcoholics found on the streets, but by the large number of problem drinkers and social drinkers, who are rarely labeled as public health problems. The reasons for this are simple statistical ones. Given the high prevalence of drinking in the United States and most other non-Moslem countries, and the distribution of drinking by amounts, there are large numbers of social drinkers and relatively few alcoholics. Assume that the ratio is on the order of 10 to 1. If the risk ratio for an automobile crash for an alcoholic versus a nonalcoholic drinker is 3 to 1, most of the crashes will involve either someone who has not been drinking or a drinker who is not an alcoholic. A program intended to prevent alcoholics from driving, therefore, will have a relatively minor effect on the incidence of crashes. Only when the prevalence of drinking is broadly depressed will there be fewer crashes. The same is true for acts of violence. Most of the people who abuse their spouses or murder their friends while drunk would not be classified as alcoholics.

TABLE 28-3 Lifetime and 30-day prevalence of use of selected drugs by high-school seniors, 1987

Drug*	Lifetime prevalence	30-day prevalence
Marijuana/hashish	50.2	21.0
Hallucinogens	10.3	2.5
Cocaine	15.2	4.3
Heroin	1.2	0.2
Other opiates	9.2	1.8
Stimulants	21.6	5.2
Sedatives	8.7	1.7
Tranquilizers	10.9	2.0
Alcohol	92.2	66.4
Cigarettes	67.2	29.4

Johnston LD, O'Malley PM and Bachman JG: Illicit drug use, smoking and drinking by America's high school students, college students and young adults, 1975-1987, Washington, DC, in press, National Institute on Drug Abuse.
*Only drug use that was not under a doctor's supervision is included.

They may be drunk or they may simply be impaired at the time of the event, but a program that focused on alcoholics would miss them entirely.

Alcoholism is not only difficult to define, it is difficult to treat. Treating alcoholics might be a benevolent thing to do, and result in some reduction in the incidence of alcohol-related problems, but the benefits of such efforts, given their probability of success, might be considerably less than their costs. Indeed there has been a general sense of pessimism about the prospects of successfully "treating" alcoholics, but the pessimism is not justified. There is considerable evidence that well-designed programs are effective.[13] A key ingredient in successful treatment is matching the program to the needs of the alcoholic. There is evidence that brief consultations can be helpful for those not yet addicted, more helpful in fact than more intensive interventions, but the latter are needed for those who are addicted.[14]

Focusing on the alcohol-related problems may provide even more useful results. Society, and its public health agencies, can take the position that drinking is widely acceptable and widely practiced, but the problems caused by it are not. Driving while drunk can be made a heinous offense. Programs to teach bartenders and waitpersons to detect and manage excessive drinking can be effective. The designated driver rule is a social policy that can be formed and implemented in any community that takes its problems and its welfare seriously and is willing to devote time and attention to both. In short, public health may find it more useful to focus on the problems that can result from alcohol abuse than on the abuse itself. As in the definitions of health and public health in Chapter 1, the goal is to prevent the dependency associated with disease and injury (or drug abuse). The best method *may* be primary or secondary prevention. However, focusing on the socially decried problems can attain a higher level of public support than focusing on drinking itself, which is widely condoned.

Interventions

The traditional forms of intervention have involved restricting the supply of the drug (alcohol), educating the user, and treating the casualties. Supply restrictions have taken many forms, from the extreme of prohibition to the limitation of sales to people over a certain age, now 21 in the United States. Other supply-side measures include the use of excise taxes to drive the price up and the limitation of sales to certain places, hours of the day, or days of the week. Suffice it to say that such restrictions as they have been applied in the United States have not been effective.

Educational programs have been widely used, but until recently have proven no more effective than other sorts of efforts. In fact there has been a general conviction among some experts that teaching children about drugs only encourages them to experiment. In the last several years, however, some conceptual research coupled with large-scale experiments has shown that the situation is not as hopeless as it was thought to be. Educational programs that focus on the demon rum or the perils of becoming a drug fiend have no value, but programs intended to increase knowledge about health in general and specifically to bolster positive peer leadership and value-setting within the school environment have shown encouraging results.[15,16] The social influence approach has six ingredients:

1. An emphasis on outcomes of the behavior that are thought by the target audience to be most important and objectionable
2. A Socratic instructional style whereby beliefs and opinions are elicited from the target audience and consensus is reached through discussion
3. Active skills training in social resistance and other such attributes
4. Engagement of same-age or older peer leaders to help implement the program
5. Disabusing the student population group of the belief that the drug-abusing behavior is really normative for their group
6. Elicitation of voluntary, public commitments to try to avoid the behavior

A community program for the prevention of alcohol abuse involves a number of components:

- Information and referral services for alcoholics, family members, and employers
- Counseling and treatment services
- Acute detoxification services, both medical and nonmedical
- Medical care
- Psychological services
- Outpatient treatment services
- Inpatient treatment services
- Halfway houses and shelter care
- Counseling services for children and spouses
- Pastoral counseling services for alcoholics, children, and spouses
- Vocational rehabilitation
- Employee assistance programs
- Consultation for professionals
- Educational programs in both the community and school settings
- Surveillance and epidemiologic studies of alcoholism, drinking behavior generally, and the incidence and prevalence of alcohol-related problems

A health department can and should play an active role in organizing such an array of services. In some communities, the health department may be the center for such programs. In others, a separate organization for drug abuse may exist, often as part of the mental health center for the region. The health department should be a participating agency in such circumstances. Often it will be necessary for the health department to serve as the governmental presence in drug abuse (see Chapter 7). In addition to its role as an advocate, coordinator, and coalition builder, the health department may be a direct provider of services, including outpatient treatment services, along with its more expected functions of surveillance, data analysis, and information provision. In any case, it is clear that an effective community-based program requires the collaboration of numerous agencies.

The use of law to prevent alcohol-related problems

In earlier chapters, the creative use of the legislative process has been explored as one of the important tools of public health. This is an especially important consideration in drug abuse. Several recent developments offer a number of enticing possibilities for effective alcohol policy. As noted earlier, there are "supply-side" and "demand-side" approaches to the control of drug abuse. In a variety of ways, government policy on both sides of the equation has served to increase rather than decrease the consumption of alcohol. This paradoxical situation is attributable, in part, to the notion of alcoholism as a disease, which holds that the user, not the product, is the problem. Alcohol is portrayed as a normal and ubiquitous part of everyday life, a beneficial and, on the whole, civilized part of normal human intercourse. People spending an evening in front of the television set will probably see alcohol used as the beverage of choice at least 20 times when in fact it is chosen by most people *after* water, fruit juice, carbonated drinks, coffee, and tea. People with problems are portrayed as unusual and suffering from a disease. It follows that government should not be worried about consumption of alcohol in general, just about those few people who have the disease.

Reality is quite different. As noted above, most of the adverse consequences of alcohol use are the result of drinking by people who are *not* alcoholics. It is true that alcohol is involved in about half of all highway fatalities, and is commonly involved in other acts of violence, but the majority of those cases involve social drinking by people who would not be considered alcoholics. In the work environment it is not even clear that alcoholics have a higher accident rate than their fellow workers.[17] (This may be because they are careful to avoid situations in which an accident can occur. They may also be protected by their fellow employees.) Programs that concentrate on alcoholics as people with a disease might keep the beverage industry happy but will have little impact on the burden of alcohol-related problems.

Interestingly, it has long been assumed that the market for alcohol, drugs, and tobacco is inelastic. Elasticity refers to the responsiveness of demand for a product to its price. In an elastic situation, an increase in price causes demand for the product to decline. As the price of alcohol and tobacco change, however, the demand does not seem to alter, a situation described by economists as being relatively inelastic. Therefore, it is said, increasing the price of the product will not decrease its consumption but only hurt poor users by requiring them to spend more of their resources on their habits. Elasticity varies depending on the range of prices, however. At a very low price, demand is quite inelastic. As prices rise, elasticity increases. If the price of alcohol is set high enough, consumption declines. The industry cannot be expected to make such a change, but government can, by increasing the excise tax on alcohol. That has not been done, and the net effect has been to lower the real price of alcohol to the customer, thus increasing demand. This is because excise taxes represent a very large proportion of the retail price of alcoholic beverages. If a product's price is made up of $6 in taxes and $4 for the product itself, a 20% increase in the price of the raw product to $4.80 will increase the total price to $10.80, an increase of just 8%. Because of this, the real price of alcoholic beverages, corrected for inflation, decreased 28% between 1967 and 1987. The effect on distilled spirits was even greater: a 50% reduction in price.[18] If taxes on alcoholic beverages were increased substantially and then "indexed" to inflation (that is, rose and fell with the value of a dollar), their effect on demand could be powerful indeed.

The beverage industry, needless to say, is opposed to such a policy. Some will argue, as industry representatives have, that such a policy would hurt the poor by increasing the price of an innocuous and pleasing beverage, and it would have little beneficial effect, since the addicts—those we are most worried about—will not be affected at all: they will continue to find their booze and harm themselves and others. Such does not appear to be the case, however. A sensible excise tax would be based on the actual alcohol content of the beverage, which would deter product-switching in the face of price increases. Alcoholics in such an environment appear to be as price-sensitive as nonalcoholics. And while the poor who wished to have a drink might find their favorite beverage too expensive, it can be said that, having exploited their consumption patterns for a long time, government would now be moving to protect them. This might be attacked as a paternalistic gesture, but it is clear that the industry segments its potential audience and targets its ad campaigns to different racial and economic groups quite effectively. An attempt by government policymakers to protect them from such exploitations would not be without merit.

The evidence indicates that a forced increase in prices of this sort would depress consumption in all categories of drinkers and thus reduce the incidence of alcohol-related problems.[14,19-22] There are other steps the government could take to reduce access to alcoholic beverages. The cost of alcohol is not just a matter of price, but also of time cost. Even though the distribution of alcoholic beverages is regulated in all states, there has been a general increase in the number and variety of retail stores that can sell alcoholic beverages and an increase in the hours they are open and the days of the week on which such products can be sold. All of these actions are a matter of conscious governnment policies to increase tourism and convention business, to stimulate restaurant development, and to make life more comfortable for its citizens, as well as to increase state tax revenues and the profits from sales in state-run stores. They also have the effect of driving down the cost of obtaining alcoholic beverages and so increasing demand. This surely has an effect on the incidence of alcohol-related problems.

There are other uses of the law that could reduce the burden of dependency attributable to alcohol consumption. Government policies treat expenditures for alcoholic beverages as tax-deductible if they are part of business entertainment or travel.[21] This could be changed. Several states have adopted "dram shop" laws, which make bartenders and servers liable if they serve alcoholic beverages to anyone who is subsequently involved in injuring someone else or in being injured. Several of these laws were passed in order to *limit* the liability of the servers, but in some states they have had the effect of driving insurance rates upward with the promise that they will be reduced if the servers undergo an educational program intended to increase their effectiveness in dealing with people who drink too much.

There are a number of policy options available to government to affect the incidence of alcohol-related problems, some more acceptable and effective than others. There are, in addition, a variety of elements that should be part of a community-based program intended to accomplish the same ends. This raises one final problem for the United States. Given the peculiar, cyclical history of temperance and intemperance in this country, it is not surprising that tolerance for diversity has been uncommon. The general conviction in the United States in recent years has been that alcoholism is a disease and abstinence the only treatment. The 12-step program of Alcoholics Anonymous has been considered the model for the treatment of alcoholics. Programs that have considered social and moderate drinking an acceptable and possible goal have been ridiculed. Such is the zeal of recovered alcoholics that their pathways to success are treated as religious journeys, and heresy is not condoned. Research into alternative approaches to alcoholism has been stifled in the United States. In Great Britain, 93% of treatment centers use controlled-drinking programs among other approaches, but the idea has been virtually extinguished in the United States.[2] Programs such as Alcoholics Anonymous have been extremely important, but a community needs a more variegated network of services if it is to meet genuine community objectives.

LICIT AND ILLICIT DRUGS

Despite the complexity of the subject, this section will be relatively short. Much of the discussion in the section on alcohol pertains to other drugs: (1) the breadth and antiquity of the abuse, (2) the changing patterns and products, (3) the problems of selecting either the demand for or the supply of the products as a target for intervention, and (4) the ambivalence about use and abuse on the one hand and use and the problems generated by that use on the other.[23] Table 28-4 provides a review of the various categories of drugs in question.

Addicts can be classified into the following four groups:

1. Emotionally well-adjusted individuals who take addicting drugs on medical advice for treatment of pain, sleeplessness, diet, or other purposes. After protracted use they find they are addicted. Much of this is due to careless prescribing and inadequate record-keeping.
2. Neurotic individuals who use drugs to help themselves cope with their problems.
3. Individuals, often characterized by what is referred to as a psychopathic personality, who take drugs in a deliberate search for illicit thrills.
4. Otherwise normal individuals, often adolescents, who experiment with drugs in a peer-induced setting.

Most of the users or experimenters in category 4 present few problems, but they are a source of considerable concern to communities. It is difficult to forecast just who is likely to experiment and move on to more dangerous drug abuse patterns. Adolescents who are socially dependent and badly need peer support are probably of more concern than those with a fairly robust ego.

Those adolescents who use drugs regularly appear to be less aggressive than their nonusing peers and to use more passive techniques in their personal relationships, which tend to be weak and superficial. As is so often the case, children from deprived backgrounds are more vulnerable for a variety of reasons, including the relatively low value they attach to any long-term future and the exploitation of their neighborhoods by those who are aware of their vulnerability. Among the factors commonly observed in drug-dependent individuals are underachievement, loneliness, mistrust and fear of closeness, identity problems, social conflicts, and self-destructive tendencies.

Opiates

It is difficult to determine the real extent of addiction to opium and its derivitives in the United States. Estimates have ranged upward into several hundred thousand, with the largest number thought to be concentrated in the East Coast megalopolis running from Washington to Boston. Opium, the base for much of the illegal narcotics trade, is grown in many parts of the world, principally the Far East, where it is an important part of the economy. In recent years, there has been a major shift to South America, especially as cocaine and its derivative "crack" have become more popular. It is interesting to note that last year's balm often becomes this year's menace. Heroin was so named because it was thought to be a heroic drug with the potential to drive out opium abuse. Cocaine was thought to be a marvelous addition to the social pharmacopeia until the 1980s.

Most of the narcotic drugs cause a general stimulation, euphoria, and contentment, with release from pain or concerns that arise from worries, conflicts, and neuroses. Although they are perceived as stimulants, like alcohol, they are depressants, which can lead to death if too much is used. Most of them are injected in a cultural milieu that supports needle sharing as part of the socialization process. This carries with it the rapidly rising threat of AIDS along with the less well-known menaces of hepatitis and other blood-borne diseases.[24] Intravenous drug use has now become the most common form of transmission for the AIDS virus (see Chapter 16), which tends to concentrate both sorts of problems (drug abuse and diseases) in low-income and minority population groups. Although narcotics use and intravenous drug–related problems are concentrated in major metropolitan and racially segregated areas, they are not unknown in more affluent and suburban areas, but such users are more likely to have access to sterile equipment such as disposable syringes.

Successful programs to treat narcotic addiction are rare. Beginning in the 1960s a number of experimental closed communities were formed that treated abstinence as a way of life. These were experimental in the sense that there was no evidence that they would work. They were by no means experimental in their design, and in fact very little evidence about their efficacy is available. Earlier, federally supported programs at the narcotics treatment centers in Lexington, Ky. and Fort Worth, Tex. were notoriously unsuccessful.

More recently, the drug methadone has been used with considerable success. It is itself a narcotic, but it can be taken orally and is characterized by a much longer and more even mood swing. In controlled programs, addicts have been able to remain free of street drugs and live an active, productive life with a daily dose of the substitute drug. The programs have been severely criticized by some who feel that replacing one narcotic with another is unacceptable, but years of work show that the programs are successful and accomplish what both society and the addict want: a socially acceptable life free of the multiple risks associated with illicit drug use. Many have urged that the programs be expanded to provide safe treatment for people at high risk of both drug addiction and AIDS, but the number of treatment slots available at the end of 1988 remained at just 148,000, not nearly enough to respond to the need and the demand.[24] Another unpopular proposal, but one with some compelling plausibility, has been the distribution of sterile, disposable syringes to addicts. This too results in an outcry from some who are disturbed about the seeming acceptance of a way of life they feel must be prohibited, but early evidence from other countries suggests that such efforts may be helpful.

The principal approach to narcotics addiction in the United States has been the attempt to interdict the supply, a seemingly hopeless effort so long as demand remains high. No society, including prisons and devoutly religious communities, has been able to close all of its borders to the flow of illicit drugs when a demand existed. The profits to be made by the suppliers are such that they will risk arrest, imprisonment, and death. It is clear, however, that social attitudes and information can alter acceptance of drugs. In white, affluent environments, publicity about the dangers of cocaine use has resulted in diminished use. As so often happens, however, a drug that began in such communities is transferred to the ghetto environment where it becomes a more tenacious problem. Support for research and programs in the ghetto communities is less forthcoming. It is difficult for established agencies, including health departments, to alter drug abuse patterns in such areas,

TABLE 28-4 Characteristics of narcotics and drugs

	Slang names	Description
Alcohol (sedative)	Booze, liquor, cocktail, nightcap, moonshine, white lightning, mountain dew, firewater	Liquid, made through natural process by the fermentation of sugars and starches
Amphetamines, or uppers (stimulant)	Bennies, dexies, hearts, speed, pep pills, wake-ups, uppers, copilots, meth	Capsules or pills in a variety of shapes and colors; bitter taste, odorless
Barbiturates, or downers (depressant)	Peanuts, barbs, goof balls, red devils, yellow jackets, rainbows, blue devils, spacers, downers	Capsules or pills in a variety of shapes and colors; bitter taste, odorless
Cocaine (anesthetic)	Snow, dust, flake, stardust, girl, Corine, Cecil, C, coke, crack	White, flaky powder; bitter, odorless; numbs lips and tongue
Codeine (mild depressant)	C, poppys, school boy	Liquid, ingredient in cough medicine
Hallucinogens (includes LSD, STP, DMT, psilocybin, PCP, etc.)	Acid, cubes, sugar, pearly gates, heavenly blue, royal blue, DOM, serenity, tranquility, peace, angel dust	White crystalline powder or a tasteless, odorless, colorless liquid that can be placed on any type of tablet, capsule, or transporting agent
Heroin (analgesic-depressant; narcotic made from morphine)	Horse, H, smack, white stuff, joy powder, junk, dope, goods, hard stuff, heavy stuff	White (or possibly brown) powder, packed in paper bundles or balloons; bitter taste, vinegarlike odor
Marijuana (*Cannabis sativa;* hallucinogen, stimulant)	Pot, grass, weed, hashish, joint, stick, reefer, roach, Mary Jane, rope, ashes, jive, hay, loco, sweet Lucy, gaga, griefo, bhang	Greenish-brown plant material, coarsely ground, powdered leaf; weedy, burned-rope odor
Mescaline (hallucinogenic drug from peyote cactus)	Peyote, mescal, mesc, buttons	Powder made from cactus plant top; bitter, odorless
Morphine (analgesic narcotic)	Junk, morpho, morphie, Miss Emma, white stuff, hard stuff, dope, goods, stuff, Big M	Bitter white powder or tablets
Solvents (includes glue, paint thinner, gasoline, etc.; volatile chemicals)	Sniffing	Any volatile substance whose fumes are capable of producing an intoxicating effect, such as glue, paint thinner, gasoline, lighter fluid, air fresheners

Effects	How used	Medical use
Slurred speech, incoordination, confusion, tremors, drowsiness, agitation, nausea, respiratory depression; continued use can damage the liver and enlarge and weaken the heart	Orally	For mild sedation and appetite stimulation
Excitability, rapid and unclear speech, restlessness, tremors, insomnia, sweating, dry mouth, bad breath, itchy nose, dilated pupils; continued use results in increased pulse and blood pressure, hallucinations, psychoses	Usually orally or by injection (speed)	For weight reduction, mild depression, narcolepsy
Similar to alcohol intoxication: drowsiness, confusion, incoordination, tremors; continued use results in depressed pulse and blood pressure, possible convulsions	Orally or by injection	For sedation and sleep, analgesic for minor pain; sometimes used as anesthetic for minor surgery
Excitability, talkativeness, headache, nausea; continued use results in increased blood pressure and pulse rate, possible hallucinations and violent or dangerous behavior	Usually sniffed or injected	Has been used (very rarely now) for local anesthesia in oral-nasal surgery
Drowsiness, pinpoint pupils, stupor, sometimes nausea develops; continued use develops a tolerance to drug	Orally	To relieve pain, coughing
Trance, anxiety, confusion, tremors, euphoria, depression, dilated pupils, increased pulse rate and blood pressure; continued use may result in psychoses, possible chromosomal breakdown, and organic brain damage	Orally, dissolved on sugar cubes, tablets, stamps, etc., and swallowed or licked; can be injected for faster high; DMT is often smoked in pipe or cigarette	None, LSD has been used for psychiatric experimentation
Relaxation, drowsiness, confusion, euphoria, slurred speech, flushing of skin or face, nausea, constricted pupils, respiratory depression; continued use results in scars or abscesses at injection points	Dissolved in water and injected, called skin popping or mainlining; sometimes sniffed	None in the United States
Euphoria, dizziness, excitability, hallucinations, increased appetite, dryness of mouth, increased pulse and blood pressure, nausea	Usually made into cigarettes (joints) and smoked; sometimes sniffed or swallowed (baked in cookies)	Occasionally used with cancer chemotherapy and in glaucoma
Resembles LSD effects: distortion of senses, anxiety, confusion, tremors, euphoria, depression, dilated pupils, increased pulse rate, psychoses, and possible hallucinations	Orally, powder form in capsule	None
Lethargy, drowsiness, confusion, euphoria, slurred speech, flushing of skin, nausea, constricted pupils, respiratory depression; continued use results in scars or abscesses at injection points	Dissolved in water and injected or sometimes used orally	For relief of pain
Similar to alcohol intoxication: slurred speech, blurred vision, incoordination; ringing in ears, nausea, and vomiting; continued use results in psychoses, hallucinations, liver and blood damage, respiratory depression	Inhaled; fumes from the glue tubes are inhaled by the user after the glue has been squirted into a sack or paper bag	None

but there is no reason to believe it is an impossible task. It requires a form of market segmentation to make the effort fit the needs of the target group. The AIDS epidemic has resulted in increased interest in and support for such efforts, possibly because, as an infectious disease, it can escape from the ghetto into affluent sectors of society.

Prevention remains the key to reducing the dependency caused by narcotics addiction. Not enough is known about the reasons for experimentation or the progression of a few from experimentation to addiction. Some of the same factors that influence the outcome of programs designed for the prevention of alcohol abuse may work with narcotics as well. It is clear that much of the work must be done in the school system. It is also obvious that the social deprivation of the ghetto itself produces much of the addiction that so worries society and damages its citizens. It is less clear that those problems will be directly attacked by effective social policies.

Depressants

The depressants include sedatives and hypnotics. Commonly used as sleeping pills, they are widely abused as both licit drugs prescribed by physicians and other practitioners and as illicit drugs, especially by adolescents who may raid their parents' medicine cabinets or buy them as street drugs. They are powerfully addicting and can produce life-threatening withdrawal symptoms. Frequently taken in combination with other drugs, sometimes indiscriminately, they can create complex symptoms and pharmacologic responses.

Stimulants

The stimulants act on the central nervous system, producing a heightened awareness of other stimuli, excitation, and sometimes an increase in blood pressure and the rate of respiration. The most common stimulants, after caffeine, are the amphetamines, which have been used as appetite suppressants and, paradoxically, to reduce excitability in children with certain specific neurologic disorders. They are now heavily restricted and have virtually no legitimate use in medical care, although they are still widely available. Stimulants have also been used by people who want to avoid the inattention of drowsiness, sometimes by truck drivers and often by students who need to study for long hours. Their side effects are unpleasant, however, and users involved in the management of heavy equipment, including trains, planes, and automobiles, may engage in dangerous risk-taking, leading to catastrophic accidents.

Ataractics

Tranquilizers, as they are popularly known, are classed as ataractics. They are mood-calming drugs, the opposite of the stimulants. They were introduced in the 1950s and had a profound effect on the treatment of both chronic and acute mental disorders (see Chapter 27). They constitute the second most abused drug group after alcohol. Tons of tranquilizers are sold and used each year in the United States by people who obtained them from a physician and depend on them to cope with normal stress. They too are powerfully addicting and are now recognized as dangerous drugs.

Hallucinogens

The hallucinogenic drugs are often called psychedelic drugs. LSD was the most famous hallucinogen, a semisynthetic derivative of ergonovine. It has been manufactured by amateur chemists and widely used to create a psychedelic world of sound, colors, and shapes. Hallucinogens such as mescaline have been used by some Native American tribes for centuries. Such drugs, especially in their more powerful forms such as LSD, produce a "trip," usually with a gentle onset and a high that can last for several hours, followed sometimes by a very rough landing. They can also produce unanticipated psychotic responses in some people, with violent outcomes, and are suspected to cause chromosomal damage and fetal harm. Their use has at times taken on a mystical aura and they have been used in quasireligious rites, thus producing the argument that the state ought not interfere, but their potential for harm to some users and to the larger community is real.

Marijuana

Marijuana is a relatively mild hallucinogenic drug of considerable popularity. A plant extract, it has been used in one form or another (marijuana, bhang, ganja, charras, maconha, kif, or hashish) for at least 5,000 years. It was introduced into Western medicine in 1839 as a treatment for rheumatism, tetanus, and seizures. It was considered a satisfactory remedy for headaches and a treatment for opiate addiction. Marijuana is fabled as the drug of choice for jazz musicians. As people became more and more fearful of its use by undesirable types, the federal government moved to restrict its importation and use. In the 1960s, however, apparently spurred by its use by a number of well-known entertainers, a sharp increase in marijuana consumption occurred, arrests increased, and some communities moved to decriminalize its use.

Marijuana is usually smoked (although it can be eaten too) and acts on the central nervous system. Its effects range from exhilaration to depression, with a distortion of the sense of time and distance. It impairs motor coordination and can lead to unsafe management of heavy machinery such as automobiles. The dangers of marijuana are hotly debated and there are organizations devoted to removing sanctions against the drug. It has been used to reduce the pressure of glaucoma, an eye disease characterized by an often painful increase in the fluid pressure inside the eye. It has also been used to decrease the nausea that sometimes accompanies certain types of chemotherapy for cancer. As noted in Table 28-3, about half of all high school seniors have experimented with marijuana at least once, and one fifth have used it frequently.

Other drugs

The variety of drugs that have been used by people to alter their moods and feelings is virtually endless. Some have no effect, some are highly toxic, and some are powerfully addictive. People engage in "solvent sniffing," for example: lining a paper bag with airplane glue or lighter fluid or gasoline or nutmeg (!), sticking their head in the bag, and breathing. Some of these practices are just silly, but others are highly dangerous. Some solvents inhaled in such a manner can produce severe kidney damage. The variety of these experiments is ever changing, and the first notice is sometimes the user's arrival in a hospital emergency room. The persistence with which such experiments have been pursued over several millennia is testimony to a powerful human urge to experience different feelings, some allegedly sublime and others horrifying. It is unlikely that the practice will stop, but it is hoped that its damage can be mitigated by responsive, thoughtful, and caring educational, health, and law enforcement systems.

PUBLIC HEALTH AND DRUG ABUSE

Having spent some time in a brief review of drug abuse patterns in the United States, it must be admitted that public health can do very little about the problem. The use and abuse of drugs is, as has been noted, a ubiquitous and persistent characteristic of human beings. There are two concerns about drug abuse: the harm it does to the user/abuser, and the social problems it may create. Self-harm is of two sorts: the sudden harm that can occur to an experimenter as a result of either an idiosyncratic response or the use of contaminated drugs or mixed drugs, and the long-term damage that can occur to chronic users and their children.

The short-term problem is best dealt with by a surveillance system and by an effective educational network. Formal surveillance systems such as DAWN (the Drug Abuse Warning Network) can provide fairly quick information about new patterns of drug abuse in a community or the possible importation of a contaminated product. DAWN receives daily reports from selected hospital emergency rooms about the types of drug reactions seen during the day. The information is compiled each day at the national level and is rapidly available to those involved in treating drug problems. Informal surveillance systems, which depend on discussions with high-school students, including high-school drop-outs, can be useful too. School health personnel together with health department nurses and law enforcement workers can be very helpful in keeping track of the patterns of experimentation in a community. This information can be analyzed and incorporated into both formal and informal educational efforts. Teenagers are responsive to reliable information about the types of problems that can be created by street drugs and new fads, and their use can be truncated quickly by an effective communications network. The acute reactions to drug experimentation are best handled by a well-trained emergency response system and a rapid communication system, which can connect the responders to experts on current patterns of drug abuse in that community. Often a university hospital has such personnel, as do poison control centers.

The longer-term problems are more difficult to manage. Drug addicts are notoriously difficult to treat, especially during the early stages of addiction. In later years, if they survive that long, drug addicts are often grateful for any help they can get to break the addiction, since it is accompanied by repeated harm, insults, danger, and degradation. Medical treatment has little to offer, and classical psychotherapy seems not much better. Methadone programs are useful for treating narcotics addicts, as noted above. More recent efforts to develop residential counseling programs have shown promise, but they are expensive and not readily available to low-income neighborhoods. More research is needed to increase the probability of success. The prevention of drug abuse is also a difficult task.[25] The social influences approach mentioned earlier has been studied most extensively in smoking prevention programs, but there is good reason to believe that the same concepts can work to prevent other forms of drug abuse as well.

TOBACCO

Tobacco use is responsible for more deaths than all of the other drugs combined. (That could change, however, if the AIDS epidemic spreads from intravenous drug-using groups into the nonusing community by means of heterosexual and homosexual intercourse.) In 1985, more than 390,000 people died in the United States as a result of their smoking habits, present or past.[4] In the foreward to the report on the twenty-fifth anniversary of the Surgeon General's first report on smoking and health,[4] the situation is summarized clearly:

> Twenty-five years have elapsed since publication of the landmark report of the Surgeon General's Advisory Committee on Smoking and Health. By any measure, these 25 years have witnessed dramatic changes in attitudes toward and use of tobacco in the United States. The health consequences of tobacco use will be with us for many years to come, but those consequences have been greatly reduced by the social revolution that has occurred during this period with regard to smoking.

The report concluded that:

1. The prevalence of smoking among adults decreased from 40% in 1965 to 29% in 1987. Nearly half of all living adults who ever smoked have quit.
2. Between 1964 and 1985, approximately three quarters of a million smoking-related deaths were avoided or postponed as a result of decisions to quit smoking or not to start. Each of these avoided or postponed deaths represented an average gain in life expectancy of two decades.
3. The prevalence of smoking remains higher among blacks, blue-collar workers, and less educated persons than in the overall population. The decline in smoking has been substantially slower among women than among men.
4. Smoking begins primarily during childhood and adolescence. The age of initiation has fallen over time, particularly among females. Smoking among high-school seniors leveled off from 1980 through 1987 after previous years of decline.
5. Smoking is responsible for more than one of every six deaths in the United States. Smoking remains the single most important preventable cause of death in our society.

The most common form of tobacco use is in cigarettes. Pipe and cigar smoking are less of a problem because (1) they are less common, and (2) they appear to have less potential for serious damage. In recent years, so-called "smokeless tobacco" in the form of chewing tobacco and snuff has become a matter of considerable concern. As teenagers have eschewed cigarettes they have turned to these products in the mistaken belief that they are harmless. However, they can cause cancer of the mouth and serious disfigurement as well as death.

Smoking has multiple effects on the human body. The respiratory tract is acutely affected by the inhalation of tobacco smoke, producing constriction of the main airways and irritation that increases the rate of mucous production. Smoking also depresses the defense mechanisms of the pulmonary system, making the smoker (and nearby nonsmokers) more vulnerable to other air pollutants, including asbestos and other carcinogens. The nicotine in tobacco smoke is rapidly absorbed into the bloodstream, where it causes changes in the cardiovascular system. Nicotine is an addictive drug, and in recent years the Surgeon General and others have concluded that tobacco smoking is yet another addiction, perhaps the most compelling and dangerous of all.

The long-term effects of smoking are well known by now. The risk of lung cancer is increased 10-fold in smokers, and the risk of cardiovascular disease, chronic bronchitis, emphysema, and other cancers is increased as well. In addition, the babies of smokers are smaller at birth than those of nonsmokers, and the children of smokers suffer respiratory effects from the smoking of their parents.

The age of initiation of smoking shifted downward in the United States for many years, but the prevalence of regular smoking, at least among boys, has been decreasing until recently. Cessation rates have continued to increase as people have become more aware of the dangers, and numerous programs have been established to help people stop smoking.

Public health departments have been quite active in the prevention of smoking-related damage. Both at the state and local level, health departments developed educational and treatment programs, beginning in 1964, with increasing signs of their effectiveness. More recently, attention has turned to legislative intervention. Many states and local communities have adopted laws that restrict smoking to increasingly fewer places. Such efforts are intended to protect nonsmokers from the annoyance and the potential harm of "passive smoking"; that is, the inhalation of other people's smoke. First were restrictions on smoking in public buildings. Later these were extended to such places as restaurants and entertainment centers. Still more recently laws have empowered private businesses to assure their employees of a smoke-free workplace. Nearly 400 such laws had been passed by 1988, to the consternation of the tobacco industry, which has waged expensive and often unsuccessful battles in city halls and county chambers to defeat such efforts.[4] The industry began a new campaign in 1989 to protect the rights of smokers, claiming "Enough is enough," but it scarcely seems that way given the 390,000 smoking-related deaths that occurred that year. Educational programs in the schools have become increasingly effective as well, with special research emphasis on peer values. Different programs have been adopted to assist older smokers in stopping, and other efforts have been aimed at pregnant women, especially in public prenatal care programs.

Although the picture has brightened generally, some dark spots remain. As noted above, smoking cessation has not been as successful in minority population groups. This repeats a persistent trend noted repeatedly in this book—that health problems have become increasingly a matter of socioeconomic status exacerbated by racism. As upper socioeconomic groups move to protect themselves, the problems become sequestered in less advantaged neighborhoods, where they are often then neglected. The tobacco industry effectively segments its marketing to concentrate on vulnerable population groups, and it appears to have been successful. Public health programs to prevent initiation of smoking and to encourage cessation must concentrate on those same segments with the same intelligence and research that the tobacco industry has applied. The other phenomenon of concern is the exportation of tobacco products to third-world nations. Perhaps the same considerations that support smoking in America's underclasses make it profitable for the tobacco industry to sell its products in other countries, where people can least afford such malignant luxuries. Government policies have supported such efforts, just as they have supported tobacco production in the United States.

The present scene of death and disability is truly shocking, but there is reason for optimism. Unless the public health efforts are derailed, either by the tobacco industry or by a shift in government philosophy away from its obligation to protect the health of its citizens, the Surgeon General's goal of a smoke-free society by the turn of the century is possible.

REFERENCES

1. Musto D: The American disease: origins of narcotic control, New York, 1987, Oxford University Press.
2. Peele S: The meaning of addiction: compulsive experience and its interpretation, Lexington, MA, 1985, DC Heath & Co.
3. Tabakoff B, Sutker PB, and Randall CL, editors: Medical and social aspects of alcohol abuse, New York, 1983, Plenum Press.
4. US Public Health Service: Reducing the health consequences of smoking: 25 years of progress, a report of the Surgeon General, 1989, Washington, DC, 1989, US Department of Health and Human Services.
5. "Are you addicted to addiction?" The Utne Reader, No. 30:51, Nov-Dec 1988.
6. Westermeyer J: Problems with surveillance methods for alcoholism: differences in coding systems among federal, state and private agencies, Am J Public Health 78:130, Feb 1988.
7. Cisin IJ and Cahalan D: Some correlates of American drinking practices. In Mello NK and Mendelsohn JH,

editors: Recent advances in studies of alcoholism, DHEW Pub No (HSM) 71-9045, Rockville, MD, 1971, National Institute of Mental Health.
8. Atkinson RM: Alcohol and drug abuse in old age, Washington, DC, 1984, American Psychiatric Press, Inc.
9. National Institute on Alcohol Abuse and Alcoholism: Sixth special report to the US Congress on alcohol and health from the Secretary of Health and Human Services, Rockville, MD, 1987, US Department of Health and Human Services.
10. Blane JT and Chafetz ME, editors: Youth, alcohol and social policy, New York, 1979, Plenum Press.
11. Johnston LD, O'Malley PM, and Bachman JG: Illicit drug use, smoking and drinking by America's high school students, college students and young adults, 1975-1987, Washington, DC, in press, National Institute on Drug Abuse.
12. Harwood and others: Economic costs to society of alcohol and drug abuse and mental illness, 1980, Pub No RTI/2734/00-01FR/, Research Triangle Park, NC, 1984, Research Triangle Institute.
13. Greenstreet RL: Cost-effective alternatives in alcoholism treatment, Springfield, IL, 1988, Charles C Thomas.
14. Ashley MJ and Rankin JG: A public health approach to the prevention of alcohol-related health problems, Ann Rev Public Health 9:233, 1988.
15. Green LW and Iverson DC: School health education, Ann Rev Public Health 3:321, 1982.
16. Effectiveness of school health education, Morbid Mortal Week Rep 35(38), Sept 26, 1986.
17. Smith GS: Alcohol and residential, recreational, and occupational injuries, Ann Rev Public Health 9:99, 1988.
18. Cook PJ: Testimony prepared for the United States Senate Committe on Governmental Affairs, Sept 27, 1988.
19. Holder HD and Wallack L: Contemporary perspectives for preventing alcohol related problems: an empirically-derived model, J Public Health Policy 7:324, Autumn 1986.
20. Mosher JF: Federal tax law and public health policy: the case of alcohol-related tax expenditures, J Public Health Policy 3:260, Sept 1982.
21. Mosher JF: Tax-deductible alcohol: an issue of public health policy and prevention strategy, J Health Polit Policy and Law, 7:855, Winter 1983.
22. Rush BR, Gliksman L, and Brook R: Alcohol availability, alcohol consumption and alcohol-related damage: I. The distribution of consumption model, J Stud Alcohol 47:1, Jan 1986.
23. O'Brien R and Cohen S, editors: The encyclopedia of drug abuse, New York, 1984, Facts on File Publications.
24. Schuster CR: Intravenous drug use and AIDS prevention, Public Health Rep 103:261, May-June 1988.
25. Bell CS and Battjes R: Prevention research: determining drug abuse among children and adolescents, National Institute on Drug Abuse Research Monograph 63, Rockville, MD, 1985, US Department of Health and Human Services.

CHAPTER 29

Violence and public health

The chapters in this section have attempted to consider aberrant behaviorisms that are often referred to as "antisocial" or as "escapes from reality." All have a psychologic base. The most evident are mental ill health, alcoholism, and substance abuse. To these should be added the various types of outwardly directed violent aggression.[1] A few words about the term *aggression* are indicated. Inherently, it is not necessarily bad or undesirable. Literally it merely means "to move actively"—and many actions are constructive. In fact, to be progressive, to achieve, one must have some degree of aggressiveness. Certain groups in society—racial, sexual, occupational—even obtain training in being aggressive. If this represents a self-assertive determination to improve and secure one's rightful status and opportunity, it is the proper thing to do. If, on the other hand, the concept of aggression is misdefined and misapplied by the inclusion of vengeful hostility or rage, the ultimate result can only be harmful to all concerned. Indeed, such action typically generates a reaction that makes things worse. It is important, therefore, to distinguish between appropriately aggressive self-determination on the one hand and hostility on the other.

Each of the types of hostile action considered here has at one time or another been the subject of legal and criminal justice measures. Historically the legal profession has identified each of them with "the guilty mind." Even now there is much debate between those who advocate the legal or criminal justice approach to all such problems and those in the health and social service professions who regard those involved as frustrated or disturbed personalities who are either calling for help or attempting to escape from some personally unwanted and intolerable situation. Fortunately some rapprochement has been occurring. Matthews,[2] a lawyer and director of the project on mental illness and the criminal law of the American Bar Association, described its rationale in 1967:

> If one observes both the persons who crowd our criminal courts . . . and the population of our mental hospitals, one is struck not by the differences between the two but by the similarities. Our preoccupation with trying to separate the "mentally ill" from the "criminals" may have led us to overlook a more central reality: both mental illness and criminality are tributaries of some deeper and more mysterious channel. Certainly there are differences between "criminals" and the "mentally ill" but it seems possible that the problems of mental illness and crime frequently lend themselves to similar if not identical methods of handling. This possibility is reinforced when one reflects to what extent entry into . . . and continued presence in the criminal process may be a result of what we call the "random factor"; that is, decisions based not so much on reason and scientific differentiation as on chance circumstances, social class, available mental health resources, divisions of political authority, and education and training levels of the officials whose responsibility it is to make decisions. There is a need for individualization at every step of the criminal process in order to neutralize the random factor as much as possible. If the wide range of alternatives available for handling persons thought to be mentally ill, especially alternatives in the individual's home community, should be made available to persons involved with the criminal law, then the accident of labels, whether civil or criminal, would be reduced. A wide spectrum of diagnostic and treatment facilities should be made available to the administrators of the criminal law to assist them in the related tasks of preventing crime and dealing effectively with persons legally convicted of criminal acts. If mental health resources are available both in mental hospitals and correctional facilities, much of the sting of criminal convictions will have been removed.

Matthews concludes that an imaginative change in present competency procedures by prosecutors, judges, attorneys, and even defendants would lead to new dispositional alternatives to the criminal-process. Many of these are or should be available at progressive mental health centers. He notes, however, the unfortunate reality that there is a limited supply of mental health resources and inefficient use of those that exist.

This emphasizes the possibility that neither criminal justice nor public and mental health can stand or function alone. Each to a significant degree must depend on and work with the other. It is significant that the major causes of death for young males in the United States are all violent: for white males, motor vehicle crashes, suicide, and homicide; and for black males, homicide, motor vehicle crashes, and other injuries (Table 29-1).

One can fantasize about ways to prevent some of this tragic violent loss: the elimination of human judgment in driving by a complex computerized highway system, the tranquilization of all young men so they will not kill themselves or each other, the fencing of all lakes and rivers. Obviously, none of these are practical, much less acceptable, although it should be mentioned that the second, in the form of leucotomy (brain surgery in certain cases) or chemotherapy, has been attempted to some degree in several countries.[3] Also, some very exciting research is under way to accomplish the first of these seemingly fantastic proposals. The general reaction to such Orwellian approaches is negative, however, in part because of the macabre path down which they might lead civilization. The only practical approach is to attempt a better understanding of the underlying causes of hostility and violence and to seek effective ways to motivate the public to avoid or neutralize the causes.

HOSTILITY

Source of hostility

Underlying most if not all violence, whether directed toward oneself or others, is a deep-seated sense of hostility, which the affected individual may or may not recognize. Hostility is a unique and much misused term. In an attempt to describe it

TABLE 29-1 Death rates due to violence, by age and sex, for white and black adults, United States, 1986

	Suicide				Homicide			
	Male		Female		Male		Female	
Age	White	Black	White	Black	White	Black	White	Black
15-24	23.6	11.5	4.7	2.3	12.5	79.2	4.3	16.2
25-34	26.4	21.3	6.2	3.8	14.6	106.0	4.4	21.9
35-44	23.9	17.5	8.3	2.8	11.6	79.4	3.5	14.8
45-54	26.3	12.8	9.6	3.2	8.6	56.3	2.8	8.5
55-64	28.7	9.9	9.0	4.2	6.0	35.4	1.9	6.8
65-74	37.6	16.1	7.7	2.8	4.3	30.0	2.2	8.7
75-84	58.9	16.0	8.0	2.6	4.6	27.9	3.1	8.6
85+	66.3	17.9	5.0	—	4.4	25.4	3.3	13.1

	Motor vehicle crashes				Other injuries			
	Male		Female		Male		Female	
Age	White	Black	White	Black	White	Black	White	Black
15-24	62.6	35.3	21.5	9.1	20.1	21.6	3.8	4.2
25-34	37.5	41.7	10.8	10.3	24.2	36.6	4.5	8.8
35-44	23.7	35.1	8.4	8.7	21.4	47.9	5.0	9.4
45-54	20.8	31.4	8.5	8.7	22.9	48.4	6.0	10.5
55-64	19.9	31.9	9.6	10.9	27.5	56.6	9.4	19.5
65-74	22.4	27.2	14.4	9.7	41.4	72.8	20.1	33.6
75-84	42.9	53.1	20.5	10.0	97.9	143.9	62.8	74.7
85+	51.6	62.7	14.7	11.0	306.5	258.2	199.9	169.7

From National Center for Health Statistics: Vital statistics of the United States, 1986, vol II, Part A, Washington, DC, 1988, US Department of Health and Human Services.

precisely, Saul[4] defined it as "a motivating force—an impulse, urge, tendency, intent, motivation or reaction—toward injury or destruction of some kind or degree, toward an object which can be animate (including oneself) or inanimate, usually accompanied in humans by the feeling or emotion of anger." To elucidate, Saul emphasizes that hostility is not merely aggression, anger, or hatred, although any or all of these may be components or manifestations of overt hostility. Hostility may be manifest in many ways and for many purposes, varying in intensity from a simple unnoticed glance, a fixed stare, or facial tenseness, to active vindictiveness in the form of malicious gossip, the smashing of objects, brutality toward animals or other humans, and in the extreme, murder or suicide. Mere anger should not be confused with hostility, since typically anger is transient and often is expressed toward a loved one. A storm of sudden anger quickly passes, usually leaving in its wake some degree of remorse. With hostility there is no place for remorse. It is the inherent Cain—or as some have said, the essential evil in humanity.

Some may find this an objectionable or unpleasant thought, but it must be realized that everyone, to varying degrees because of complex circumstances, is pulled by two opposing forces—strong social and self-satisfying motivations and strong asocial or antisocial motivations that may be equally or even more satisfying. An understanding of these opposing forces or motivations and the social application of that understanding offers the only ultimate hope of headway against the individual and collective brutality and violence that constantly threaten us and our societies. It is significant that toward the end of his life, Sigmund Freud[5] wrote:

> I can no longer understand how we could have overlooked the universality of non-erotic aggression and destruction and could have omitted to give it due significance in our interpretations of life . . . those who love fairy tales do not like it when people speak of the innate tendencies of mankind toward aggression, destruction and cruelty. . . . The tendency toward aggression is an innate, independent, instinctual disposition in man and . . . it constitutes the most powerful obstacle to culture.

In his classic studies of behavior and conditioning, Cannon[6] observed that an animal confronted with a threat, irritation, or frustration is physiologically stimulated and prepared for either of two maximum responses—to fight or to flee. In our own special development in competitive biologic circumstances, this was necessary for survival, but in supposedly cooperative and civilized contemporary societies this automatic physiologic response, if misunderstood and uncontrolled in relation to existing stresses and problems, is likely to flood the mind with unwise and unwarranted feelings of fear and hostility and result in destructive reactions against others or oneself. This is unfortunately common, as a reading of history or any current newspaper gives ample testimony.

An additional tendency or characteristic seems almost unique to our species—purposeful aggressive attacks on and destruction of our own kind. Thus Allee[7] noted:

> One species of animal may destroy another, and individuals may kill other individuals, but group struggles to the death between members of the same species, such as occur in human warfare, can hardly be found among nonhuman animals.

To this, one may add the observation that only a human could have written "Thanatopsis." Only a human could have conceived and composed a *Götterdämmerung.* And only a human could have attempted it.

Hostility—a disease

Because of such considerations, Saul[4] regards hostility as the central problem in human affairs and urges recognition of its many forms. He provides health workers with the challenge in these terms:

> Hostility is a disease to be cured and prevented like cancer, tuberculosis or smallpox, . . . its cure will result in healthier, better living—not only for society in general but for each individual in particular. . . . Hostility cannot be passed off as something we inherit and hence can do nothing about. The fact is that hostility is a disease of the personality, transmittable from person to person and group to group, and, basically, by contact from parents to children, from generation to generation. . . . Indeed if the major motivating forces in each of us could develop normally, healthily, without interference or coercion from the outside, friendly social cooperation would be the result. Only when this development is disturbed during the earliest formative years of infancy and childhood, by active mismanagement or by gross neglect (whether unconscious and well meaning or conscious and willful)

does the fight-flight reaction, with its resulting hostility, flower into full strength.

To this Saul adds the pertinent health-related observation that through all the various forms of physiologic and psychologic reaction—withdrawal, depression, manic episodes, hysteria, phobias, compulsions, perversions, addictions, paranoias, schizophrenia, and the rest, as well as the psychosomatic conditions in which emotions play a role, such as ulcers, hypertension, stroke, thyroid disease, and some allergies and arthritis—"however prominent the element of flight, invariably the power of the fight reaction with its rage, hate and hostility is also unmistakable." He concludes:

> The elucidation of hostility in its causes, effects, transformations, connections, and the means of reducing and preventing it, could well be the great contribution of this generation of students of the human mind and human motivations.

Extent and form of hostility

The choice between flight or fight has special implications for modern survival. There now exist awesome weapons with which to fight. Furthermore, they are not limited to physical form. Saul[4] has pointed out that aggression may now range from direct, overt action to indirect, hidden, subtle, and even masked forms disguised as justice, righteousness, and love: "It can be acted out within or outside the law by single persons on their own, by unorganized crowds or mobs, or by highly organized gangs or armies. It finds easy expression in crime, delinquency and warfare, the prevalence of which serves as an index of how widespread the problem is."

Obviously the true dimensions of the problem elude determination because of a variety of factors including failure to report, erroneous recording, population shifts, and variable criminal justice definitions and systems. However, some indications do exist. In the United States, for example, about 1.5 million violent crimes are reported each year, and the rates have been increasing. In addition to nearly 20,000 murders, there are over 1 million nonfatal violent crimes against persons, including about 90,000 reported forcible rapes, 834,000 instances of aggravated assault, and more than 500,000 robberies.[8] But this is not all. There are estimated to occur annually more than 1,700,000 cases of physical child abuse and probably as many cases of spouse abuse.[9]

In the world arena, one can point to the more than 130 wars of varying intensities since the end of World War II, with a minimum of 30 million people killed and several times that number injured. A large proportion if not most of these were civilian noncombatants. In addition, it is interesting to note our attitude toward the physical environment, which we "conquer," "subdue," "exploit," and "tame" in the name of productivity and development.

Before exploring these phenomena and their prevention, it should be pointed out that this chapter deals only with interpersonal violence. The larger problems of social and corporate violence are beyond its scope. Such violence has been mentioned in numerous places in earlier chapters: in relation to occupational health, maternal and child health, drug abuse, and AIDS, to mention a few. Crimes of social and corporate violence occur daily throughout the world, both from negligence and from willful violation of human rights. They result in loss of life, loss of property, the destruction of minds and bodies, and the degradation of the air we breathe and the water we drink. They occur in coal mines and cotton mills, in steel foundries and battery plants, in film processing labs and in migrant labor camps. They occur in automobiles, in schools, at home, and at work. News reports usually refer to such crimes as accidents or mistakes, but many of them are homicides, both intentional and unintentional.[10] In the mid-1980s, Illinois chose to prosecute the owers of one workplace for murder because of their knowing exposure of their employees to lethal chemicals. It was the first such case and aroused considerable controversy. The reader is urged to scan the computerized listings of library holdings for books dealing with social and corporate violence.

CRIMINAL HOMICIDE

Every 38 seconds in the United States someone is stabbed, clubbed, or shot. A significant number of them die. During 1986 felonious murders and nonnegligent manslaughter accounted for over 19,257 deaths, or 1 every 25 minutes. Homicide decreased through the early 1950s, but about 1958 it began to increase again. By 1980 it had increased from 4.5 to 10.7 deaths per thousand, a rate of 4% per year.[10] The rate began to decline slowly after 1980 and in 1986 was 9.0 per 100,000.[11] There is some feeling that the rates began to rise again after that as a result of youth gang violence in some cities and the "crack" epidemic. These, of course, are only the incidents known to the police and do not take into consideration the unknown numbers of individuals whose deaths are classified erroneously as "accidents." The statistical chance of an American being murdered in any one year is about 1.7 in 20,000. The risk varies considerably, however, among different components of the population (see Table 29-1).

Differences among racial and ethnic groups outweigh differences by sex, with homicide rates for the nonwhite population 6 to 7 times greater than for the white population. When data are limited to men, the differences are even greater. Age adjustment further emphasizes the disparity, especially for black males, whose rates are raised about an additional fourth. Homicide is committed most frequently by persons between the ages of 25 and 44 years, for whom the rate is twice the national average. At these ages racial differences are most pronounced, with the black rate 7.3 times higher than that found in the white population.

The male to female homicide rate is a ratio of about 3 to 1. With reference to residence, rates are higher in urban areas, especially center city circumstances, as compared with rural areas. Some changes are taking place in all of these dimensions, however. The homicide rate for white males decreased from 10.9 per 100,000 in 1980 to 8.6 in 1988, while the rate for nonwhites decreased from 57.8 to 45.1.* Rates declined more for males than for females: the ratios of male to female rates have declined from 3.4 and 4.8 for whites and nonwhites respectively in 1980 to 2.8 and 4.3 in 1986.

There are a number of problems involved in interpreting such information. The figures are from vital statistics reports, and not all murders are properly reported in such form. Then too, the rates vary considerably with age, as noted above. The overall rates by sex and race obscure changes and differences in the age distributions of the groups. A population with a greater proportion of its members in the age range from 15 to 24 will have a higher overall rate than a group with more older people or more newborns. As noted, age adjustment tends to reduce the differences between blacks and whites. Additionally, rates are a result of dividing numerators by their larger denominators, the population at risk. For blacks, the numerators are more accurately defined than the denominators, since the census undercounts young black males. This has the effect of increasing the apparent black homicide rate. Finally, since the racial differences are so widely known, they may cause the police to report black male homicides as murders more often than may be the case for white males or females. Nonetheless, the evidence for an increase in recent years is convincing.

It is important to distinguish murders from other homicides. The term *homicide* includes not only "murder and nonnegligent manslaughter" but also "justifiable homicide" (such as the killing of a felon by a policeman in the line of duty and some other types of killing in self-defense). It also includes legal executions. Practically speaking, homicide includes any violent death that is neither a suicide nor an unintentional injury, although as pointed out previously, some of each of these are actually conscious or subconscious homicides. *Murder*, or *criminal homicide*, is a more restricted term. It involves a deliberate act, whether premeditated or not, to kill someone.

Homicides may be considered to fall into three categories. The best known and the type on which the criminal justice system and the public in general have centered their attention is planned killing that is consciously acceptable to the perpetrator at the time. Contrary to popular belief, this type of killing, criminal homicide, represents only a small fraction of the total homicides in American society. By far the most common type of homicide is a form of resolution of conflict between acquaintances. According to FBI reports,[8] murders usually involve either a family member (15.7%), an acquaintance (30.8%), or a friend or neighbor (10.7%). Murders involving strangers, the sort of dark act that inspires fear in some people, occur in only 13% of all cases. (Another 29.8% are classified as "unknown" at the time the crime report is filed by local investigating officials. If subsequent investigation determines a more specific category, it does not result in a change in the statistical reports.) In other words, more than half of all murders (57.2%) involve people who know one another, and they occur in homes or in peer groups. They are usually the result of an intense emotional response to conflict, a response that was not planned and that

* Note use of the category *nonwhite* instead of *black*. They are different, and readers should be wary of substituting one for the other.

usually entails remorse after the act. Those involved, often both the victim and the assailant, lack the ability to resolve the conflict less violently (a response that is, in part at least, learned), and they have access to the means of murder, most often a gun. The third type of homicide consists of presumably justifiable acts taken by a law enforcement officer or an individual in self-defense.

With these facts in mind it must be recognized that in a great many instances there are two active parties to a murder, the killer and the victim, and the latter by no means necessarily plays a passive role. Many murders are the result of antagonisms that have gone on for years, with the victim teasing, taunting, blaming, goading, or suppressing the eventual murderer until a breaking point is reached.

The foregoing facts prompted Judge George Edwards of the National Commission for Reform of Federal Criminal Laws, in an address before the American Psychiatric Association in 1971, to deflate what he referred to as the "four myths about murder." They are that the average citizen is justified in living with a top priority fear of being murdered, that most murders are premeditated killings for money, that the most likely murderer is a stranger, and that you can protect yourself from murder by keeping a pistol handy. None of these myths, he emphasized, is true. As a consequence, murder is the least suppressible of crimes. Greater police visibility and more sophisticated police techniques have little effect on homicide because it occurs most often in the privacy of the home, with an existing prior relationship between victim and killer. This means that murder is almost always an act of blind rage or illogical violent passion that cannot be anticipated. It has also been pointed out by Pasternack,[12] a psychiatrist and a specialist in violent behavior, that perhaps as many as 40% of murders of passion are actually victim precipitated, wherein one person taunts another beyond endurance or where a philandering husband parades his mistress in front of his wife, daring her to do anything about it. This type of situation, says Pasternack, is far from rare, and when it happens, the killer as well as the killed is the victim.

Prevention of homicide

The question arises, "Can anything be done to reduce this significant loss of life?" For one thing, those in the health professions must recognize, as many still do not, that an individual killed with a weapon is just as dead and just as tragic as one who has succumbed to tuberculosis or cancer and that most if not all criminal homicides involve some degree of mental ill health. Secondly, there are patterns to homicide, as noted above. It is not randomly distributed in society. It concentrates on the young and especially on young black males. A cause of death that has risk factors is a cause of death that can be prevented. This is not the place for a detailed discussion of the psychiatric measures, individual or collective, that are needed. There are two aspects of prevention, however, that deserve mention.

The first is social conditioning. Banay[13] pointed out nearly four decades ago that the American public is conditioned to murder, that it is no exaggeration to consider that "the society we live in almost reaches out to encourage murder." Violence is the most common topic in children's so-called comic books, the focal point of mystery and adventure stories that are sold by the millions each year, and the stock-in-trade of television, radio, and motion picture "thrillers." Typically it receives the top headlines in American news media. More than one murderer has stated as a motive a wish for a day in the public eye.

The gun is probably the most common toy sold and encourages the most popular form of play, especially among boys, which takes the form of mock killing. In 1976, the American Public Health Association passed a strong resolution calling for legislation to prohibit the manufacture, assembly, sale, transfer, or possession of handguns or handgun ammunition for private use. In 1987, the Association noted that "handguns, while constituting only one-fourth of all firearms in the United States, account for three-fourths of firearm homicides" and pointed out that the manufacture and sale of realistic plastic handguns were both immediately dangerous (in airplane hijackings, for instance) and a continued sanctification of such weapons in American society.[14]

Public opinion polls have consistently shown that the majority of Americans think that handguns and other weapons should be more tightly controlled. In early 1989, two episodes of violence involving the use of "assault" guns, weapons that clearly have no use in hunting, provoked several cities to move toward such controls. Offsetting this is the unfortunate fact that the National Rifle Association, which consistently and staunchly opposes any limitation or even registration of not merely rifles but even handguns not used in hunting, is one of the strongest and financially best-supported political lobbies in Washington.

The argument over the sale and possession of handguns is a fascinating bit of Americana. The United States has more guns in private ownership than any other nation in the world, and it has one of the world's highest murder rates. It has long been claimed by the National Rifle Association that guns are needed for hunting and for self-protection, but the issuance of new hunting licenses has been declining steadily in recent years as less land is available for hunting. There are fewer hunters now than ever before. And there is no evidence to support the self-defense argument. Quite the contrary, as noted above, most murders occur when two people who know each other cannot resolve their conflict in a less violent manner and a gun is available. To carry the idiocy one step further, ammunition sellers have begun to make available coated bullets that can penetrate the protective vests worn by some police officers. Efforts to ban their sale have been opposed by the National Rifle Association. Surely such bullets are not intended for innocent sporting endeavors or to kill a deer wearing a Mylar flak vest!

Washburn,[15] in his discussion of aggressive behavior and human evolution, observed that

> all the evidence would indicate that evolution has built into man a propensity for learning to be aggressive. Our early ancestors' way of life was not easy . . . the group was defended by the young adult male who hunted and formed the army. The order of killing was very high . . . in many primitive tribes about 25 percent of the males were killed off in combat. This of course does not mean that humans must continue to be aggressive, but it does suggest the importance of institutional controls over aggression.

Although violence is prevalent, it is not necessarily natural to the human condition. Preconditions of violent behavior must be sought in social rather than in genetic or instinctual characteristics. This appears to be borne out by the current epidemic of homicides among black males. The rates have changed dramatically, even during a few short years, and they vary in different geographic areas of the country. The homicide rate for black males aged 15 to 24 decreased 33.5% in the 13 years between 1970 and 1982, while the rate for white males increased from 9.9 per 100,000 to 13.1.[16] Recognizing the three dominant and increasing causes of death among young blacks—homicide, unintentional injuries, and suicide—as violent reactions to social stress, the National Medical Association, a black organization, has called the situation a public health problem requiring national action.

Recently much attention has been focused on the influence of television on aggressive behavior in the United States. As pointed out by the Surgeon General's Advisory Committee on Television and Social Behavior,[17] 96% of American homes have one or more television sets, and the average home set is turned on for more than 6 hours per day. Most of the studies inquired into by the Committee indicated positive relationships between exposure to television violence and aggressive tendencies, although most were of low magnitude. However, the observation raised other questions: (1) Does violence-viewing lead to aggression? (2) Does aggression lead to violence-viewing? (3) Are both violence-viewing and aggression products of a third set of conditions? The studies tended to support the first and third of these propositions. The subject of violence and television is discussed in Chapter 24. A good bibliography on the subject is available.[18]

Gerbner[19] has emphasized that "there is now sufficient evidence to conclude that television alone (as well as in combination with other social and cultural factors) makes a significant difference in the way viewers deal with reality." Gerbner's group, which has been monitoring and scoring television programs since 1967, found that after 10 years of hearings, investigations, and presidential commissions, 8 out of every 10 network programs (9 out of every 10 cartoons) still contained violence, with a rate of 5 violent episodes per program and 10 per children's cartoon: "About 65% of all leading characters (85% in children's programs) are still involved in some violence . . . and about 10% in killing." During the past few years, although killing in "family hour" programs declined from 28% to 1%, it increased after the family hour period from 9% to 23%. Also, violence in weekend daytime children's cartoons increased from 65% to 85%. Of great significance is Gerbner's observation that "for every incident in which a male is violent, there are 1.19 male victims, but for every incident in which a female is violent there are 1.32 female victims. Similarly children; lower-class, foreign, and nonwhite characters of both sexes; and older women are more likely to fall victim than to be perpetrators of violence. Old, poor, black women are cast for violent parts only to be killed." One must consider this in relation to child abuse, spouse beating, and the frequent mugging and robbing of aged women. Gerbner concludes that "potential incitement to mayhem among a minority of viewers is bad enough but the cultivation of fear and rigidity among many is scarcely less damaging in its long range effects."

There is a second important area for preventive action in relation to homicide. Experts in the field almost unanimously agree that the most urgent need is effective gun control. Repeated studies have indicated that curtailing the availability of and access to guns would be likely to reduce killings among spouses and young males.[20] The slogan "Guns don't kill people, people kill people," has been refuted over and over again, but many Americans cling stubbornly to the notion. In one study, comparing Seattle and Vancouver, two cities with markedly different approaches to gun control, the incidence of assault was about the same, but the incidence of assaults involving guns was seven times higher in Seattle than in Vancouver, and the probability of death due to homicide was 1.6 times greater. Almost all of that increased risk was explained by a 4.8-fold higher risk of being murdered with a handgun.[21]

Other steps that can be taken to reduce the incidence of murder are as follows[20]:

1. Decrease the cultural acceptance of violence. Efforts to reduce the prevalence of violence on television would help. The death penalty, whatever else its advocates may say about it, validates murder in society by making clear to millions of children that the state can murder people under certain circumstances. If violence generally, and murder specifically, is to be reduced, it is essential that a reverence for life be supported by the state.
2. Reduce racial discrimination in all aspects of life.
3. Reduce gender inequality and support more flexible male models.
4. Reduce the consumption of alcohol and other drugs (see Chapter 28).
5. Develop educational programs to teach conflict resolution skills in schools and elsewhere.
6. Increase education for family life.
7. Support families with community-based support services.
8. Address and remedy problems in the recognition of violence so that it can be seen and counted by the community.
9. Develop interdisciplinary teams within the human services system to deal with murderous acts.
10. Improve treatment for victims of violence in hospital emergency rooms and by the police.
11. Decrease financial barriers to caring for victims of violence.
12. Improve communication and cooperation among health care providers, police departments, and schools.
13. Provide statutory and policy directions to compel the police to treat physical assaults among acquaintances as criminal behavior.

Some of these recommendations would be more difficult to implement than others, but their availability as options and the rationale underlying them make evident the fact that murder and other forms of assaultive behavior need not be accepted as human traits beyond the scope of public health and prevention.

CHILD ABUSE

A type of violence of special concern to the fields of public health, medicine, and social service is the "battered child syndrome." The term was applied in 1962 by Kempe[22] in the first comprehensive survey of child abuse. Throughout most of history, children have been misused and abused, regarded as inherently evil or at least as the fruits of evil, and treated as replaceable chattel.[9,23,24,25] The historian deMause,[26] on examining 200 statements of advice on child rearing, found that "virtually every child rearing tract from antiquity to the eighteenth century recommended the beating of children." The tradition was widely accepted. John Calvin preached that breaking the will of the infant at the earliest possible age was a parent's duty to God. Similarly the wife of John Wesley, writing about child rearing, states "when turned a year old (and some before) they were taught to fear the rod, and to cry softly."[27] Pleck[25] also notes, however, that the Puritans drafted a criminal code against wife beating and "unnatural severity" to children, the latter clause verifying that the precepts of John Wesley were followed.

The inception of the industrial revolution accentuated the overt aspects of child abuse. In England, wagonloads of unsuspecting children were gathered from the countryside and delivered to impatient factory and mine managers. Sir William Petty, the "father" of vital and health statistics, advocated free maternity hospitals for unmarried women, whose resulting children, he said, would become wards of the state and their labor available for 25 years.[27] In the United States, the evils of child industrial labor were multiplied by the textile needs of the Union and Confederate armies, which also diminished the supply of adult labor. During the twentieth century, societies for the protection of children, in company with other socially minded groups, succeeded in eliminating many of the evils of the industrial employment of children in the United States, Great Britain, and some other countries.

Child abuse is defined as "the physical or mental injury, sexual abuse, negligent treatment, or maltreatment of a child under the age of 18 by a person who is responsible for the child's welfare under circumstances which indicate that the child's health or welfare is harmed or threatened thereby."*

The problem of "the battered child" within the home remains a much less evident and more elusive aspect of child abuse—one that has attracted increasing attention during recent decades as a significant cause of disability and death in children. Usually the battered child is a rejected child, not infrequently the only one of several children in a family who is subjected to abuse, and often the most recently born. Various reasons for rejection have been noted. Prematurity or small birth size seem to be significant, as are very frequent pregnancies close together.[28] Poor marital adjustment or resentment of a marriage forced by pregnancy or by other persons also plays a role. Post-partum depression, with confusion of the identities of mother and child, resulting in outwardly directed hostility arising from feelings of guilt or self-deprecation, may be an important and sometimes fatal factor. Other causes may be mental illness in one or both parents, social and economic frustrations, unusually young and immature parents who may treat an infant like a doll or toy and mistreat it during a tantrum to "teach the other parent a lesson," jealousy in one parent over the attention given the child by the other parent, jealousy on the part of older children in relation to the new child in the family, or sexual aberrations on the part of one or both parents, older children, other relatives, or family acquaintances. Not infrequently, the child abuser believes that children exist primarily to satisfy parental needs, that the needs of children are unimportant, and that those children who do not fulfill parental needs deserve punishment.

One characteristic of child abusers stands out. Practically all who have studied the problem have noted that it has an intergenerational characteristic, almost as if it were a communicable behavioral aberration. "It would appear," says Kempe,[22] "that one of the most important factors . . . is 'to do unto others as you have been done by.' " Among the many pertinent studies is one in the United States in which three generations of child abuse were documented.[29] Another in England describes a family with five generations of known child abuse.[30] Wolfgang[31] stated the case poignantly:

> Perhaps the most malignant outcome of child abuse, however, is the seed of violence so often sown in the heart and mind of the young victim. Centuries ago, the sage Ben Sirach observed: "The branch sprung from violence has no tender twig." His observation has now been confirmed repeatedly by investigators who find an unusually high rate of violent behavior, including juvenile delinquency and crime, among children abused earlier by adult parents and guardians.
>
> The number of such untender twigs in American society is proliferating at an alarming rate. While violence in general has been steadily increasing in our society, recent years have witnessed an especially remarkable spurt in the incidence of violent behavior among the young. Violent crimes committed by children of all ages have been increasing between three and four times faster than they have in the general population.

Abuse of children may run the gamut from overprotection in the form of isolation to general neglect, with poor hygiene and malnutrition, constant nagging and scolding, sexual abuse, and severe and often irrational punishment, sometimes leading to death. It is these latter instances that have been given the name "battered child syndrome."

* From P.L 93-237, 1974, which created the National Center on Child Abuse and Neglect.

Reliable statistics are understandably difficult to obtain. Gelles and Straus,[9] in a continuing study of domestic violence, interviewed samples of the U.S. population in 1975 and again in 1985. In the earlier study, they found that 3.6% of parents reported an abusive act of violence to a child during the year. This would suggest an annual incidence of about 1.4 million cases involving children aged 3 to 17. A recent estimate by the National Center on Child Abuse and Neglect suggests about 1.7 million cases. However, when Gelles and Straus repeated their survey in 1985, they found that the incidence of child abuse had *declined* from 36 per 1,000 to 19 per 1,000. Their report stirred up considerable debate and controversy, since many people felt that the incidence was increasing. There were certain methodological problems with the 1985 survey, but they cannot account for the decline actually measured. Indeed, while public sensitivity to the problem and newspaper reports of cases have resulted in the impression of an increase, there are reasons for believing that the incidence has declined. Child abuse is related to early onset of child-rearing and to frequent unwanted pregnancies. Nowadays, marriages and parenting are being postponed till later years, family size has been diminishing, and the number of unintended pregnancies that result in births has declined.

The highest fatality rate is in the very young, commonly those under 3 years of age, who are too young to explain their bruises, fractures, and swellings. Among older children, many are too frightened or convinced of some accused or imagined guilt to discuss what actually occurred. It is estimated that 5% of battered children are killed outright and another 30% eventually suffer permanent injury. Furthermore, of those who are not killed outright, it is estimated that one of every two dies after being returned to the parents. This is extremely important, especially for emergency care personnel to bear in mind. If physically abused children do survive, their intellectual and psychologic functions appear to be impaired.

Herein lies one of the debates that has confused child care workers in recent years. During the early years of the movement in the United States (in the 1960s and early 1970s), many advocated strong family support services in an attempt to provide a healthy environment for abused children. Seeing the abusing adults as disturbed and "sick," therapists advocated that the children be kept in the family environment and that health and social workers attempt to treat the problem. It was felt that disruption of the family was potentially more damaging than the risk of harm to the child, a risk that could be reduced by close surveillance, supervision, and treatment.[25] This argument has since faded, in child abuse as in spouse abuse. The most effective interventions occur when the abusing adult, whether a spouse, boyfriend, or parent, is arrested on criminal charges and treated accordingly.[9,24,32]

It is estimated that very few cases of battered or abused children are brought to the attention of appropriate authorities. Since most incidents occur in the home, all but the most serious tend to go unnoticed even by neighbors. Physicians represent a critical point of first suspicion and action. However, even here reporting tends to be limited and varies by type of practice or specialty. The physician's concern may be so much with clinical signs that little thought is given to their source. If there are suspicions, they are difficult to prove, and the parent's word is accepted about accidents, clumsiness, or other children. Furthermore, most people, including physicians, find it difficult to believe that any parents would injure their own children.

In addition, some may fear becoming involved in time-comsuming legal processes. These reactions overlook the possibility that although few abusive parents are actually psychotic, most are immature, impulsive, and suspicious; and although frightened by the medical and legal professions, they recognize that something is wrong and want help themselves.

In 1963 the Children's Bureau and the American Humane Association developed a model law[33] to provide for mandatory reporting of suspicious cases of child abuse by physicians while protecting them against criminal or civil liability. Reporting would lead to investigation, and if suspicions were confirmed, appropriate steps would be taken to protect the child and rehabilitate the family if possible. The Committee on the Infant and Preschool Child of the American Academy of Pediatrics made the following recommendations.[34]

1. Physicians should be required to report suspected cases of child abuse immediately to the agency legally charged with the responsibility of investigating child abuse—preferably the county or state department of welfare or health or their local representatives, or to the nearest law enforcement agency.

2. The agency should have ample personnel and resources to take action immediately upon receipt of the report.
3. Reported cases should be investigated promptly and appropriate service provided for the child and family.
4. The child should be protected by the agency either by continued hospitalization, supervision in home, or removal from home through family or juvenile court action when indicated.
5. The agency should keep a central register of all such cases. Provision should be made for the removal of case records from the register when it is found that abuse did not, in fact, occur.
6. The reporting physician or hospital should be granted immunity from suit.

All 50 states enacted laws based on either the proposed model law or the American Academy of Pediatrics recommendations. These laws and increased professional publicity concerning the problem have led to a significant increase in reports.

These various efforts crystallized in the passage of national legislation on January 31, 1974—the Child Abuse Prevention and Treatment Act (P.L. 93-247). It established a National Center for Child Abuse and Neglect in the Department of Health, Education and Welfare to (1) compile, analyze, and publish an annual summary of research on child abuse and neglect; (2) act as a clearinghouse for information; (3) publish training materials for personnel in fields dealing with child abuse programs; (4) provide technical assistance (by grant or contract) to public and nonprofit organizations; and (5) conduct research in the area of child abuse. The center is also authorized to make grants and contracts for state and local demonstration programs designed to identify, prevent, and treat child abuse and neglect.

It is obvious that none of the professions or organizations—health, legal, social service, education, or any other—can solve this tragic problem alone. It presents a classic example of the necessity for interdisciplinary teamwork. Among the services that should be available in every community are[28]:

- Medical and psychiatric diagnostic and therapeutic services
- Social work diagnosis and treatment
- Nursing services
- Child care services and homemakers
- Parenting services: parent aids, Parents Anonymous (a self-help group for abusive parents)
- Substitute care services such as foster homes and group care resources
- Legal initiatives to make possible necessary custody and criminal processes

Parents need quick access to emergency counseling and intervention services, and women and children need "safe houses" where they can seek emergency protection and support. Special services are needed to cope with sexual abuse of children, including greater awareness of the problem and efforts to empower children to say no to sexual overtures from adults. Professionals who work with children should be carefully screened. Most pedophiles do not have criminal records (that's part of the problem, they are often driven away from one community into another without being prosecuted), which makes screening difficult. References can be checked, however.

SPOUSE ABUSE

A social and public health problem similar to child abuse is the aggressive behavior of some adults toward their marital partners. As with child abuse, the adequate solution of such occurrences often requires joint action by the social work, legal, and health professions.

In the 1975 survey of Gelles and Straus[9] mentioned above, 3.8% of wives reported being struck by their husbands during the course of their marriage. The average for wives reporting battering was three episodes a year. In 1975, 2% of the wives reported having had guns or knives used against them, and a survey in 1985 found the incidence to have increased to 3%. Again the methodology can be criticized, but the evidence, although verifying that abusive relationships are shockingly common, does not indicate a rapid increase in recent years. Husbands are battered too, but this has been less of a problem, since they are usually the stronger member of the dyad and presumably capable of both inflicting more harm and protecting themselves from it. This is not, of course, always the case. Many battered women have murdered their husbands (and been acquitted by juries).

Other reports indicate that between 20% and 25% of all adult women in the United States (12 to 15 million women) have been physically abused at least once by a male with whom they had an intimate relationship.[35] Some data indicate that such abuse may be the most frequent cause of injury in women. It is rarely an isolated event: it is often tied to the use of alcohol or other drugs and may include episodes of rape, child abuse, and suicide.

Some women are still raised to be subservient to men, and some for various reasons believe they deserve to be abused. Similarly, some men are raised to believe that "a man's home is his castle" and that no one has the right to question anything he may do inside it. This ignores the legal fact that physical violence against another person is a crime regardless of any relationship that may exist. However, in practice, only 2% of men who are known to physically abuse their female living partners are ever prosecuted. It is also significant that more police personnel are killed as a result of answering domestic violence calls than from any other aspect of their duty. About one out of every five police deaths occurs under such circumstances.

Spouse beating may occur in all races and socioeconomic classes. It has been noted, however, that the phenomenon occurs somewhat more frequently in families with socioeconomic difficulties, hence greater worries and frustrations. Education appears to play an interesting role. Thus while Parker and Schumacher[36] found no significant differences in the education of battered as opposed to nonbattered women, the husbands of battered women had less education than those of nonbattered women. They also found that if a wife's mother had been a victim, the wife herself had a significant probability of being battered by her husband. Also, the more a beaten wife had been struck as a child, the more likely she was to remain with an abusive husband—in fact, the more likely she was to marry a violence-prone man. Parker and Schumacher concluded that "women who did not observe violence in their family of origin found wife battering inconsistent with their role and were able to cope with and avoid further violence."

Wife beating is scarcely new. The Puritans perceived it as a problem at Massachusetts Bay, as noted above. An early spokesperson for the safety and dignity of women, Frances Power Cobbe, experienced ridicule as well as some success in early nineteenth-century England.[37] Regretfully, little has been done up to now to ameliorate this serious physical and mental health problem. Many police personnel regard such episodes as an annoyance of relatively little importance. Hospital emergency room personnel tend to treat the injuries but not the essential problems. Neither they nor the police, much less neighbors, want to be caught in the middle of a domestic struggle, especially if they may end up being blamed or injured. The spouse, if a woman, when released usually has no place of refuge and can only return to the person who abused her. This, of course, reinforces the undesirable behavior and encourages repetition.

Some community agencies, including a few health departments, have been instrumental in the establishment of temporary refuges for battered women. Usually similar to halfway houses, such refuges should be developed in all communities of significant size and should have related to them the necessary health care, social services, counseling, and legal assistance that this serious problem warrants. In addition, much more effective interdisciplinary professional education and planning for health personnel is obviously indicated.

The services and interventions needed to treat abused women and to prevent spouse abuse are similar to those noted above for child abuse. Of special note is the recommendation to treat violence against a person as a crime rather than a civil or domestic matter. Many states have passed laws requiring the police to act accordingly, with markedly beneficial effects for both the battered spouse and the children. It may be possible in the long run to "treat" abusive people to reduce the incidence of violence, but protection of the abused must occur immediately. In addition to the fact that such protection may prevent death or permanent disability, either mental or physical, it is clear that those at highest risk for abuse are those who have already been abused.

CONCLUSION

In *Promoting Health/Preventing Disease,*[38] a number of public health experts in the United States wrote:

> Violent behavior—in its many forms—exacts a huge toll on America's physical and mental health. Suicide and homicide lead to thousands of premature deaths annually. Assault, including rape and child and spouse abuse cause much injury and emotional suffering. Numerous factors underlie these violent forms of behavior. Health programs alone cannot deal with these factors. Many major aspects of American social structure are involved—the family, the community, the system of stratification, the educational system and the economic structure. Much remains unknown regarding means of reducing mortality associated with violent behavior. Even in the absence of such information important steps can be taken.

Fourteen objectives were put forth for the nation and its public health organizations:

1. By 1990, the death rate from homicide among black males aged 15 to 24 should be reduced to below 60 per 100,000.
   Outcome: The Public Health Service in 1986 concluded that this objective might be met,[39] but that appears most unlikely. The rate in 1986 was 79.2, an increase from 1983.
2. By 1990, injuries and deaths to children inflicted by abusing parents should be reduced by at least 25%.
   Outcome: It is unlikely that this objective will have been met by 1990.[39]
3. By 1990, the rate of suicide among people 15 to 24 should be below 11 per 100,000.
   Outcome: It now appears unlikely this objective can be attained.
4. By 1990, the number of handguns in private ownership should have declined by 25%.
   Outcome: There is no accurate source of data to evaluate progress toward this objective, but the evidence at hand suggests that progress has been in the wrong direction.
5. By 1990, the proportion of the population over the age of 15 that can identify an appropriate community agency to assist in coping with a stressful situation should be greater than 50%.
   Outcome: Indirect data indicate that this objective may have been attained.[39]
6. By 1990, the proportion of young people age 15 to 24 that can identify an accessible suicide prevention "hotline" should be greater than 60%.
   Outcome: Data are not available to evaluate progress.
7. By 1990, the proportion of the primary care physicians who can take a careful history related to personal stress and psychological coping skills should be greater than 60%.
   Outcome: No adequate data.
8. By 1990, to reduce the gap in mental health services, the number of persons reached by mutual support or self-help groups should double from the 1978 baseline figures.
   Outcome: Objective probably has been met.[39]
9. By 1990, stress identification and control should become integral components of the continuum of health services offered by organized health programs.
   Outcome: No adequate data.
10. By 1990, of the 500 largest U.S. firms, the proportion offering work-based stress reduction programs should be greater than 30%.
    Outcome: Met.[39]
11. By 1985, surveys should show what percentage of the U.S. population perceives stress as adversely affecting health and what proportion is trying to use appropriate stress control techniques.
    Outcome: Met.[39]
12. By 1985, a methodology should have been developed to rate the environmental stress loads of major categories of occupations.
    Outcome: May have been met.[39]
13. By 1990, the existing knowledge base about stress effects and stress management should be greatly improved through scientific inquiry.
    Outcome: Not quantifiable, but probably met.[39]
14. By 1990, the reliability of data on the incidence and prevalence of child abuse and other forms of family violence should be greatly increased.
    Outcome: Met.[39]

This is a pretty sorry record given the incidence of death and disability due to violence in American society. There is a heavy emphasis on stress management, an individual approach to violence, and very little on the social determinants of violence. A few of the objectives have been met, several have no data with which one can assess progress, and the rest are unmet. Moreover, they do not go to the heart of the problem: the persistent ratification of violence as an acceptable outcome of anger and hostility. It is ratified on television and in movies, in schools and at work, in our laws and in our policies. Progress against the gun lobby has been embarrassingly meager; violence in the media is more prevalent than ever; the death penalty has been reinstated in several states; funds and services for coping with domestic violence were sharply reduced during the Reagan administration; the emasculation of the federal civil rights program from 1981 to 1989 encouraged rather than discouraged racism and sexism in society; and state and local public health agencies have aspired to too little. This is abysmal for an enlightened and affluent, if violent, society, one that has been characterized by its caring and its altruism.

Much can be done by public health in concert with other agencies. Starting at the local level, it is possible to build support for gun control and for the prosecution of violent behavior within the domestic environment and on the streets. Safe houses for victims and other measures to assure the victims of violence that they have rights can be developed in any community that cares to do so. Children can be taught to cope with interpersonal conflict in healthier ways. First and most importantly, people must slowly teach themselves that the ethic of violence is unacceptable and that its endemic nature can be reduced.

REFERENCES

1. Hovey JE: Violence: is it a public health problem? Am J Public Health 71:319, Mar 1981.
2. Matthews AR: Mental illness and the criminal law: is community mental health an answer? Am J Public Health 57:1571, Sept 1967.
3. Crime and medicine, MD 9:120, Nov 1965.
4. Saul LJ: The hostile mind, New York, 1956, Random House, Inc.
5. Freud S: Civilization and its discontents (1931). In Strachey J and others: The complete psychological works of Sigmund Freud, London, 1955, Hogarth Press, Ltd.
6. Cannon WB: Bodily changes in pain, hunger, fear, and rage, New York, 1929, Appleton-Century-Crofts.
7. Allee WC: Cooperation among animals, New York, 1951, Henry Schuman, Inc., Publishers.
8. Federal Bureau of Investigation: Uniform crime report, US Department of Justice, 1987.
9. Gelles RJ and Straus MA: Intimate violence, New York, 1988, Simon & Schuster.
10. Holinger PC: Violent deaths in the United States: an epidemiologic study of suicide, homicide and accidents, New York, 1987, The Guilford Press.
11. National Center for Health Statistics: Vital statistics of the United States, 1986, vol II, Part A, Washington, DC, 1988, US Department of Health and Human Services.
12. Pizer V: Murder and the tyranny of fear, Washington Star, May 7, 1972.
13. Banay RS: Study in murder, Ann Am Acad Pol Soc Sci 284:26, Nov 1952.
14. American Public Health Association: Plastic handguns, a policy resolution of the American Public Health Association, Am J Public Health 78:198, Feb 1988.
15. Washburn SL: Aggressive behavior and human evolution. In Coelho GV and Rubinstein EA, editors: Social change and human behavior, DHEW Pub No (HSM) 72-9122, Rockville, MD, 1972, National Institute of Mental Health.
16. Centers for Disease Control: Morbid Mortal Week Rep 34(41), Oct 18, 1985.
17. National Institute of Mental Health: The impact of televised violence: report of the Surgeon General's Advisory Committee on Television and Social Behavior, DHEW Pub No (HSM) 72-9090, Rockville, MD, 1972.
18. Signorielli N and Gerbner G: Violence and terror in the mass media: an annotated bibliography, New York, 1988, Greenwood Pass.
19. Gerbner G: Television violence: measuring the climate of fear, Am Med News, Dec 13, 1976, p 1.
20. Rosenberg ML and Mercy JA: Homicide and assaultive violence. In Violence as a public health problem, background papers prepared for the Surgeon General's workshop on violence and public health, Leesburg, VA, Oct 27-29, 1985.
21. Sloan JH and others: Handgun regulations, crime, assaults, and homicide: a tale of two cities, New Engl J Med 319:1256, Nov 10, 1988.
22. Kempe CH and others: The battered child syndrome, JAMA 181:17, July 7, 1962.
23. Radbill SX: A history of child abuse and infanticide. In Helfer R and Kempe C, editors: The battered child, Chicago, 1973, University of Chicago Press.
24. Hutchings N: The violent family: victimization of women, children and elders, New York, 1988, Human Science Press.
25. Pleck EH: Domestic tyranny: the making of social policy against family violence from colonial times to the present, New York, 1987, Oxford University Press.
26. deMause L, editor: The history of childhood, New York, 1974, Psychohistory Press.
27. George MD: London life in the eighteenth century, New York, 1925, Alfred A Knopf, Inc.
28. Newberger EH: Child abuse. In Violence as a public health problem, background papers prepared for the Surgeon General's workshop on violence and public health, Leesburg, VA, Oct 27-29, 1985.
29. Silver L, Dublin C, and Lourie R: Does violence breed violence? Am J Psychiatry 126:404, Sept 1969.
30. Oliver JE and others: Five generations of ill-treated children in one family pedigree, Br J Psychiatry 119:473, Nov 1971.
31. Wolfgang ME: Child and youth violence. Quoted in Segal J: Child abuse: a review of research. In Corfman E, editor: Families today, vol 2, DHEW Pub No (ADM) 79-815, 1979.
32. Sonkin DJ: Domestic violence on trial: psychological and legal dimensions of family violence, New York, 1987, Springer Publishing Co.
33. Children's Bureau, US Department of Health, Education and Welfare: The abused child—principles and

suggested language for legislation on reporting of the physically abused child, Washington, DC, 1963, US Government Printing Office.
34. Maltreatment of children: recommendations of Committee on the Infant and Preschool Child of the American Academy of Pediatrics, Pediatrics 37:377, Feb 1966.
35. Stark E and Flitcraft AH: Spouse abuse. In Violence as a public health problem, background papers prepared for the Surgeon General's workshop on violence and public health, Leesburg, VA, Oct 27-29, 1985.
36. Parker B and Schumacher D: The battered wife syndrome and violence in the nuclear family, Am J Public Health 67:760, Aug 1977.
37. Bauer C and Ritt L: The work of Frances Power Cobbe: a Victorian indictment of wife beating. In Russell GW, editor: Violence in intimate relationships, New York, 1988, PMA Publishing Group.
38. US Public Health Service: Promoting health/preventing disease: objectives for the nation, Washington, DC, 1980, US Department of Health and Human Services.
39. Office of Disease Prevention and Health Promotion: The 1990 health objectives for the nation: a midcourse review, Washington, DC, 1986, US Department of Health and Human Services.

PART EIGHT

Public health and health care services

Historically, one of the most significant events in the development of public health in the United States was its separation from medical care. Although much of the early history of public health involved the provision of personal health care services, the activities were usually a part of the police power functions of government to prevent the spread of dangerous communicable diseases. Governments at the state, county, and city level have been involved in medical care, but until recently that involvement has been through separate agencies concerned with corrections, welfare, or mental health. Public hospitals more often than not were operated under some other authority than that of the local health department.

Health officers have customarily been physicians selected for their jobs by boards of health, which were dominated by physicians. Many state and local health officers have long maintained that public health has no business providing medical care. The argument over the role of medical care in public health and vice versa has been deeply entwined in the history of the American Public Health Association, whose Medical Care section rose to prominence because the Health Officers' section had maintained, predictably, that medical care was not a public health service. However, in the 1970s, the Health Officers' section renamed itself the Health Administration section and began to broaden its sphere of interest. Although it remains difficult in many states to obtain the consensus of the official health officers that personal health care services are a proper concern of health departments, many of the nation's most effective departments have extensive personal health care delivery systems, and several either operate public hospitals or participate in their operation.

Several generations of public health workers and physicians have been practicing both public health and medical care either without realizing it or without openly acknowledging it. Even though many clinics have been ostensibly limited to tuberculosis, venereal disease, prenatal care, or well-child care, there has been more continuity and breadth in those services than is apparent at a cursory glance. The trend toward more personal health care delivery is continuing, not because health officers are trying to expand their domain but because the needs are there and the public expects its public agencies to do something about unmet needs for essential services. The public policy theme for two decades has been to move those without access to dependable health care into the mainstream of private practice. Although this was partially accomplished, it is apparent that a vigorous public system of health care exists, is growing, and must continue to meet the needs of a large number of people who cannot obtain access to private services.

Part Eight will describe the principal components of that system: nursing and organized systems of medical care.

CHAPTER 30

Community health nursing

HISTORICAL DEVELOPMENT

Among all of the various professional persons engaged in public health work, one group, nurses, merits particular mention. Environmental workers, sanitarians, and engineers outnumber nurses in public health, but unlike nursing, their work is clearly devoted to program areas that have been previously described: environmental health and occupational health activities. Nursing is both a profession, like medicine or dentistry, and, at the same time, a system and philosophy of caring for, treating, and preventing disease and disability.

Nurses have closer personal contact with greater numbers of the public than does the rest of the professional staff of the health department. To many citizens, the nurse represents the health department: she or he is the person who reduces the work of the organization to its lowest common denominator—direct service to the individual. Many health departments owe their start to communities becoming convinced of the value of the services rendered by one or two visiting nurses. One old but still pertinent review[1] of the subject has stated it in this way:

> It is precisely in the field of the application of knowledge that the public health nurse has found her great opportunity and her greatest usefulness. In the nationwide compaigns for the early detection of cancer and mental disorders, for the elimination of venereal disease, for the training of new mothers and the teaching of the principles of hygiene to young and old; in short, in all measures for the prevention of disease and the raising of health standards, no agency is more valuable than the public health nurse.

Since that time, nurses have taken a leadership role in planning, program development, policy formation, and administration, in both community and institutional settings. Nursing as a public health profession and practice is no longer limited to a clinical encounter: its concept of health is applied to families, groups, and entire communities.

There is some confusion about terms. As will be discussed later, there are several different routes to becoming a nurse: diploma programs, associate degree programs, baccalaureate degree programs (as well as master's and doctoral degree programs), and vocational or practical nursing programs. Most public health agencies believe that preparation at the baccalaureate level (commonly known as a BSN, or baccalaureate in nursing science) is necessary to function as a public health nurse. Many other nurses work *in* public health without such training, however. Once prepared, nurses may work in a clinical setting (such as a hospital, a physician's office, or an outpatient clinic) or in community or public health nursing. Community health nursing is the more widely used term at this time and is intended to include public health nurses working in official state and local health departments and nurses working in community-based agencies, including home health care organizations.

The community health nursing movement owes its inception to William Rathbone of Liverpool, who in 1859 was impressed by the care and comfort given by a nurse to his fatally ill wife. A philanthropist, he promoted the establishment of a visiting nurse service for the sick poor of his city. Despite the enormous existing demand for therapeutic nursing of the sick, the first nurse, Mary Robinson, was directed not only to give direct care to her patients but to instruct them and their families in the care of the sick, the maintenance of clean homes, and other matters that contribute to healthful living. As stated in the previously mentioned review[1]:

> This went far beyond mere nursing, and the work of the visiting nurse was thus bound up with and made part of a general health movement—the nurse herself becoming

perforce a social worker as well as a nurse. And the highly constructive educational work all this involved put new life and vitality into the age-old charity of visiting the sick poor, gave it enormously increased importance, and brought about its later amazing development.

So that qualified nurses would be available for the work, Rathbone enlisted the assistance of Florence Nightingale and established a training school in affiliation with the Royal Infirmary of Liverpool. Interestingly, Miss Nightingale from the beginning referred to the graduates who engaged in home visiting as "health nurses."

Early in 1873 Bellvue Hospital in New York City opened the first school of nursing in the United States. It was patterned after Miss Nightingale's principles. One of its first graduates, Frances Root, went out to work with poor patients in their homes and thus pioneered community nursing in the United States.[2] In 1877 the first visiting nurses were employed by a voluntary agency, the Women's Branch of the New York City Mission. The idea soon spread to other communities. Meanwhile official health organizations were being established, and they soon recognized the unique contribution that nurses could make to their programs. At first, resort was made to the visiting nurses of the voluntary agencies. Thus the nurses of the New York City Mission carried out the orders of the school medical inspectors, visited the pupils' homes, instructed the mothers in general health and infant care, and took sick children to the dispensary.[3]

In the United States, the nurse was to become the "teacher of positive health," not just the caregiver for the sick. Nurses were to serve as "the relay station, to carry the power from the control stations of science, the hospital, and the university to the individual homes of the community," a role for which they were "preimminently fitted" according to C.-E.A. Winslow, because they were women and had the patience and tact necessary to bring hygiene into the tenement.[4]

The first visiting nursing associations per se were established in Buffalo in 1885 and in Boston and Philadelphia in 1886. Originally, those of Buffalo and Philadelphia were named District Nursing Societies and that of Boston was referred to as the Boston Instructive District Nursing Association. Eventually all their names were changed to visiting nurse associations. They depended on lay contributions for their support, and small service charges where indicated. At the beginning not only were they administratively under the direction of lay boards, but the actual work of the nurses themselves was supervised by laypersons. Within a short time, however, the Philadelphia organization led the way by providing for a supervising nurse. These three early voluntary nursing organizations are still active.

As the visiting nurses' work loads increased, their responsibilities expanded rapidly. With immigration, the cities were filled with people at high risk for tuberculosis and other health problems. The cost of providing such care could not be met by the voluntary associations. They saw themselves as demonstration agencies, taking on new tasks, developing the methods, then transferring their work to government agencies.

The first city to employ public health nurses was Los Angeles in 1898. The initial purpose was to provide visiting nursing care to the sick poor rather than to engage in educational or health promotional acitivites. The first official community health nurse, although paid with tax funds and responsible to the health officer, was assigned to the Los Angeles Settlement Association. As more nurses were added, however, a bureau of municipal nursing was established in the health department in 1913.

The new public health nursing programs were directed by health officers who were physicians. The physicians had been well schooled in the notion that health departments were not to provide personal health services, and the public health nurses were accordingly used as teachers, counselors, coordinators of care, and disease investigators, leaving nursing care to the private, not-for-profit agencies. The latter were dependent on physician referrals and on physician support for their financing and continued existence and thus restricted their services to what were thought of as nursing tasks and to carrying out physician orders. The Town and Country Nursing Service of the American Red Cross, in 1914, noted that nursing was to be carried on under the direction of a physician. (They also advertised that qualified nurses could expect to earn $70 to $85 per month, although those with longer preparation and unusual skills could expect to earn as much as $1,000 to $1,200 per year.[5])

In earlier days of public health work, it was easier to focus public attention on special problems and to obtain public and private funds for their solution than it was to gain support for a broad, general program. As a result, most community health nursing programs were originally organized on a specialized basis; nurses were employed specifically as tuberculosis nurses, school nurses, maternal and child health nurses, communicable disease nurses, and, later, industrial nurses. This trend was given further strength by the activities of the National Tuberculosis Association, by the passage of the Sheppard-Towner Act, and by the growing interest of school officials in the health of the schoolchild. On the other hand, demonstration of the value of county public health units, sponsored by the Public Health Service and the Rockefeller Foundation, and of the Town and Country Nursing Service, sponsored in many parts of the nation by the American National Red Cross, indicated distinct advantages to the generalization of visiting nursing activities.

The argument over specialization has continued to the present. At first, it was argued by many that a specially trained nurse could be more effective, especially in such settings as the tuberculosis clinic. Others argued that people and families, not a specific disease, were the focus of community health nursing, and that the specialist might deal effectively with specific organs and pathology but poorly with the person. Initial training usually took place in the hospital setting. Those nurses who wished to work in the community setting had to acquire additional training. Over the past two decades two trends have emerged in community health nursing: more rigorous training for the generalist, usually at the baccalaureate level but increasingly at the master's level, and, at the same time, a growth in nurse practitioner training programs, including those with a specialty emphasis such as nurse midwifery, pediatric nursing, geriatrics, family planning, and industrial nursing. Some of the turmoil surrounding these developments is discussed later.

Bullough[6] has described three phases in the evolution of nursing in the United States. The period from 1900 to 1938 involved legalization of the process of registration. This did not limit what people could do but limited use of the title *registered nurse* to those who had been approved by a board. Beginning in 1938 the practice of nursing began to be limited to those who could demonstrate special knowledge, skill, and training to their state licensing boards. This necessitated a definition of nursing so that the laws could be specific about what those who were not nurses could not do. In most states, nursing practice acts avoided such terms as *diagnosis* and *treatment,* which were considered medical acts, and either required or implied that nurses carried out the orders of a physician. The third phase began in 1971 with an Idaho statute that broadened the practice of nursing to include the diagnosis and treatment of problems under certain circumstances. Since then most states have rewritten their nursing practice acts to provide for similar extensions. The New York law, for example, states that

> the practice of the profession of nursing as a registered professional nurse is defined as diagnosing and treating human responses to actual or potential health problems through such services as case finding, health teaching, health counseling, and provision of care supportive to or restorative of life and well being.*

Efforts to define nursing in a manner acceptable to the practitioners proved to be difficult, and the American Nurses' Association[7] took until 1955 to provide the following definition:

> the performance, for compensation, of any acts in the observation, care and counsel of the ill, injured or infirm or in the maintenance of health or prevention of illness of others, or in the supervision and teaching of other personnel or the administration of medications and treatments as prescribed by a licensed physician or a licensed dentist; requiring substantial specialized judgment and skill and based on knowledge and application of principles of biological, physical and social science. The foregoing shall not be deemed to include any acts of diagnosis or prescription of therapeutic or corrective measures.

By the time the Association had adopted this definition, it was out of date. Although they often called the process "assessment" and "planning," nurses had of necessity been engaged in diagnostic and therapeutic practices for some time. Until fairly recently such practices had occurred as part of an elaborate physician-nurse game ritual that involved the nurse calling the physician's attention to a particular problem or set of symptoms and asking

* New York State Education Law, Section 6902, Article 139.

if it was all right to start a particular treatment. The many games developed over the years are still engaged in frequently, but the evolution of extended roles for nursing and the independent practice of nursing[8,9] indicate that the compulsion to do so is less common. Soares[10] has defined a nursing diagnosis as one that is amenable to nursing intervention—an answer that raises a question. (Simply put, a physician might make a diagnosis of diabetic coma and prescribe insulin, whereas a nurse might diagnose a subconscious state that requires assistance with eating, eliminating, moving, and possibly breathing.)

It is perhaps even more difficult to define public health nursing. If we know what nursing practice is, can it be said that a nurse managing a maternal and child health clinic is practicing nursing, maternal and child health, management, or something else? In 1980, the Public Health Nursing section of the American Public Health Association developed a new definition of public health nursing:

> Public health nursing synthesizes the body of knowledge from the public health sciences and professional nursing theory for the purpose of improving the health of the entire community.[11]

It is not clear that this suffices as a definition, however, since the body of knowledge from the public health sciences and professional nursing theory, included by reference, is not well understood itself. The definition has also been attacked on the grounds that public health focuses on the prevention of disease whereas nursing focuses on wellness, and therefore a synthesis of the two cannot be achieved.[12] The arguments and the confusion are part of the problem of nursing as a profession, a set of problems that will be described more completely later.

In the United States, nursing has emerged with two distinct roles: (1) as a dependent participant in the provision of services to sick people (dependent on the authority of the physician, who has the more powerful license), and (2) as an independent health professional involved in fostering human wellness at the personal, family, group, and community level. They are two different forms of practice, and it is not clear that educational programs make the differences distinct or that an identifiable body of nursing theory or concepts is taught for both purposes. In the emerging hospital of the twenty-first century, nurses are high-level professionals and technicians providing intensive care to critically ill patients. The majority of nurses are employed in such settings. There is little similarity between that practice and the work carried out by the community health nurse working with adolescents or high-risk mothers as a health assessor, planner, evaluator, or counselor. For that matter, there is little similarity between the physician practicing emergency medicine and the physician guiding an epidemiologic investigation, but it is not claimed that the latter are practicing medicine. Nursing, however, asserts that community health nursing is a nursing practice with a distinct body of knowledge and a unifying concept. It is not clear just what those are, nor is it clear that they are necessary to the effective functioning of nurses in public health roles.

There have been numerous other attempts to define nursing, but they have been complicated by the fact that the practice of medicine was licensed before the practice of nursing; physicians staked out the whole field of health care, making it necessary for all other professional groups to work around the medical practice acts, either nibbling off small bits (as have dentists, optometrists, and podiatrists) or working in a dependent relationship to a physician.

It is difficult to define a practice by exclusion. Nursing is concerned with human wellness and engages in assessment, planning, and implementation but does not use the tools of medical practice such as diagnosis or treatment, which involves prescribing certain drugs or performing surgery. That definition by exclusion is neither accurate nor helpful. Nursing assessments *are* diagnoses, and nurses who counsel and advise people with health problems are engaged in every bit as risky an endeavor as physicians who prescribe an antibiotic or operate on a hernia. Helping a young single mother understand parenting can have the same useful consequences and result in the same catastrophes as can the practice of medicine. Even more confusing is the fact that a nurse cannot legally prescribe tetracycline for an elderly male cigarette smoker who is coughing up yellow phlegm in February (surely a low-risk and useful intervention) but can counsel an AIDS patient regarding sexual behavior.

It is risky for a non-nurse to attempt a definition of nursing, but perhaps it can be said that nursing is a health profession concerned with wellness and health enhancement and characterized by a caring rather than curing approach to the prevention of dependency.

THE SUPPLY OF NURSES

Supply versus need

In 1970 the National League for Nursing[13] estimated that there were 850,000 nurses in the United States but that only 530,000 of them were in active practice. By 1988, there were approximately 2.1 million licensed nurses, most of whom were working at least part time. That represents a doubling in the ratio of nurses to population in 18 years. During the 1960s it was believed that there was a growing shortage of nurses, and federal support for nursing education increased rapidly. The Nurse Training Act of 1975 limited that support and required the Department of Health, Education and Welfare to develop work force projections that were more reliable. Both the Department and the Congressional Budget Office estimated that there would be between 1.467 million and 1.541 million nurses by 1990, and the congressional report concluded that supply and demand would be in balance through that period with no new initiatives.[14,15] The Institute of Medicine rendered a similar verdict shortly afterward. By 1988, however, the American Hospital Association warned of a serious shortage of professional nurses, claiming that nearly three quarters of its member hospitals had unfilled but budgeted positions. A Commission on Nursing appointed by the Secretary of Health and Human Services reported that the shortage was beginning to affect patient care.

The situation was puzzling but understandable. The supply, as noted, had increased dramatically, and a large proportion of all licensed nurses was in the labor force. Hospital bed days had declined, and more than 40,000 hospital beds had been taken out of service in recent years. Yet the shortage seemed real to some observers.[16,17] Aiken and Mullinix[16] and others have observed that nursing salaries have lagged far behind those of other service professions, including teachers, another traditional female profession in the United States. Many nurses who are in the labor force are working part time. With wages lagging, hospitals use nurses for tasks that would be better performed by clerical workers, managers, and technicians. The shortage is a function of demand and supply. Even with a reduced number of hospital patients, if more budgeted positions are created by hospital administrators, demand can appear to exceed supply. Peculiarly, however, it has not driven up wages.

To make matters worse, the American Medical Association and the American Nurses' Association (ANA) launched a new battle over the role of nursing in 1988, with the former calling for a new Registered Care Technologist (RCT) to replace nurses in the hospital environment. Presumably cheaper to train and hire, the RCTs would return to the basic business of providing patient care and carrying out physician orders and stop concerning themselves with their professional role and their autonomy. The ANA fired back with a rallying cry to all nursing factions to join together in opposition to the AMA initiative.[18]

To many people, the reported shortage and the AMA-ANA conflict were symptomatic of the overproduction of professional health workers in the United States during the preceding two decades and the persistent problem of trying to define nursing carefully so as not to abrade the traditional relationships of nursing to medicine. That careful effort may well have been terminated by the physician attack on nursing. Indeed nursing has begun to trumpet the political decline of organized medicine and a new opportunity to increase the political power of nursing. In an editorial titled "Hyperbole,"[19] two spokespersons noted that "thanks to the American Medical Association, the nursing community is moving to unite as never before. . . . We don't know how this is going to play in the community. We do know, however, that nursing will capitalize on medicine's increasing vulnerability in the marketplace." Startling words from the profession. The editorial emphasized the advantages of nursing: more time with patients, home care, and a closer alliance with its consumer group. It is in the light of this emerging and possibly epochal dispute that the nursing shortage must be considered. There may well be a major shift in the professional alignments involved in acute patient care, with nursing moving more independently and forcefully into long-term care and the provision of community health services.

Whether "demand" will equal "need" is not known. The concept of work force needs is just as complex as the concept of the need for hospital or nursing home beds, and for many of the same reasons. The health industry has an astonishing degree of elasticity in that it can and usually will use resources as they become available without any apparent relation to an objective assessment of need or the usual law of supply and demand. Moreover, the need or demand for the services of one particular professional group will vary with the supply and role of other professional groups. Physicians, various kinds of physician assistants, and nurses cannot be defined usefully as independent of each other, which is exactly what most needs-assessment methodologies attempt to do. The dynamics of the interrelationships and what they portend for health workforce planners and health economists have not been explored in sufficient detail to provide a realistic base for calculating need.

There are several estimates of the number of nurses who are employed in community health programs. In an overview of a 1980 survey, the Bureau of Health Professions[20] estimated that 65,449 registered nurses were working full time in community health settings and 16,745 were working part time. By 1989, it was estimated that the total had increased to 115,000. Nearly half (50,000) were thought to be trained in public health nursing, with the remainder (65,000) made up of nurses working in a public health setting.[22]

In a different project, the Bureau developed estimates of the number of community health nurses who were working in different types of agencies in 1979.[21] Bureau personnel believe that the former set of figures provides a better count of the total numbers but that the latter study provides a more accurate picture of the distribution of the nurses by sponsoring agency. Applying that distribution to the total of 115,000 produces the estimates shown in Table 30-1. Considering only those practicing in state and local public health agencies, community health centers, and home health care agencies, there may be 72,400 practicing community health nurses.

Until the 1920s, the majority of community health nurses were employed by voluntary agencies. Since that time, the distribution has changed considerably, with a large increase in the number of nurses employed by local health departments and boards of education. Slightly more than 92% of all community health nurses are working in local agencies. Slightly more than half of those working for home health agencies are employed by not-for-profit organizations, and the remainder are working for proprietary home health organizations. As noted earlier, it is difficult if not impossible to indicate whether these numbers are sufficient for the work that needs to be done. Even with that warning, it is tempting to refer to a very old suggestion that there ought to be one community health nurse for every 2,500 people, which results in a "need" for 96,000 nurses! It is also tempting to note that the entire "deficit" could be overcome by moving 2% of hospital nurses from that setting to community nursing.

Education and training

Most nurses currently working in community health programs are graduates of diploma programs usually sponsored by a hospital and not affiliated with a college or university. As mentioned earlier, community health nursing directors generally believe that it requires at least baccalaureate-level training to qualify as a community health nurse, and many would require additional formal academic or planned in-service training. Only about a third of the staff nurses working in community health nursing have received 1 year or more of academic training. At the supervisory level and above, a majority have had 1 or more years of such training.

TABLE 30-1 Distribution of registered nurses employed in community health work, by full-time–equivalent positions and type of agency, United States, 1986

Type of agency	Number of full-time–equivalent positions
National	2,100
University	2,215
State agency	4,650
Local health agency	40,800
Community health centers	2,300
Home health agencies	24,650
Boards of education	34,390
Other	2,300

Some significant steps have been taken during recent years to extend the effectiveness of community health nursing staffs by the training and use of a variety of auxiliary personnel. Several thousand practical or vocational nurses are employed in public health agencies, and nursing aides have been employed with increasing frequency. In view of rising health care costs generally and the increasingly sophisticated skill training that occurs in aide and vocational nurse programs, it is anticipated that many more such individuals will be employed in nursing programs in the future. This influx will result in continued role changes for registered nurses. In addition, much of the burden of epidemiologic casefinding and follow-up is being taken off the shoulders of the public health nurse by disease control investigators.

In 1978, the American Nurses' Association decided that the baccalaureate degree should be the entry level degree for professional nursing.[23] By 1986, only 32.9% of all graduates were from such programs, however, a slight decrease since 1980 (Table 30-2). Note that graduates of associate degree programs have increased significantly. It may well be that young people contemplating a career choice are aware of the lag in salaries for nursing and the unpopular working conditions and are simply unwilling to invest in a four-year college education for such a future.

It is difficult to predict the effect of the growth of various "nurse practitioner'" programs on the credentials of community health nursing in the future. Nurse practitioners were relatively new in 1970, but by 1985 there were more than 30,000 nurse practitioners in the United States. A growing proportion had master's or doctoral degrees. (Most of the master's degrees were in nursing or public health, but many of the doctoral degrees were in education.) This trend toward higher levels of academic preparation is expected to continue, with concomitant changes in the roles that nurses expect to play in the health care system.

TABLE 30-2 Graduates of nurse training programs, 1970, 1980, and 1986

	1970	1980	1986
Diploma programs	22,551	14,495	11,496
Associate degree programs	11,483	36,034	42,150
Baccalaureate programs	9,069	24,994	26,365
TOTALS	43,103	75,523	80,011

From Igelhart JK: N Engl J Med 317:646, Sep 3, 1987.

Whereas some nurse practitioners are generalists or specialize in primary care, many are graduates of specialty training programs. The differences between nurse practitioners and community nurses are often debated, and at least one program titles itself *Clinical Nurse Practitioner Training in Community Health Nursing.* In general, nurse practitioners provide more depth in the management of selected cases, whereas community health nurses provide greater breadth and engage in individual, family, and community educational efforts more frequently.

Some of the changes in training and titles make evident much of the turmoil going on in nursing, a profession under considerable pressure. Community nurses are caught between physicians, who oppose their attempt to function as an independent professional group; other professional workers, such as social workers and rehabilitation workers, who feel that their turf is being invaded by the nurse; other nursing groups, such as nurse practitioners and clinical nursing specialists, who have fostered specialization of their practice just as physicians did before them and with the same zealous notion that generalists are not well qualified; and client and community forces, who want better access to a more caring health worker at less cost. A few short years ago it appeared that these conflicts would continue to evolve in the direction of a stronger role for nursing in primary care, but as Aiken[24] has pointed out, circumstances have changed rapidly: there is a decline in the rate at which resources are being added to health care, there are enough providers to meet present and future needs (although they are not always where they are needed), those who cannot obtain necessary health care require additional monetary resources, not more providers, and nursing so far appears not to displace or reduce costs but to add to them (whether that produces an increased benefit has not been determined). Given that impression, it is unlikely that nursing can progress rapidly in the development of primary nursing care unless there are major structural reforms in the health care system generally.

NURSING AGENCIES

In the evolution of community health programs, the contribution of nurses has been increasingly recognized on all levels.

National level

In the past, on the federal level, several programs of the Public Health Service conducted activities in public health nursing. They operated by providing grants-in-aid and consultation service to the states and through them to local health departments and by participating in the development of standards and qualifications. For a period of years the Office of Indian Affairs provided direct nursing service by means of public health field nurses stationed on reservations. In 1953 this activity was transferred to the Public Health Service and has been significantly expanded. Among other activities it promotes nursing as a career among young native Americans. The Division of Nursing is now in the Bureau of Health Professions of the Health Resources and Services Administration of the Department of Health and Human Services. Three private organizations that are active on the national level are the National League for Nursing, the American Nurses' Association, and the new Council of State Boards of Nursing.

State level

By 1937, all of the states employed community health nurses in their state health organizations. By 1985, the states reported that they employed approximately 18,000 nurses.[25]

The manner of their placement in the organization varies. The majority of state health departments have had separate bureaus or divisions of public health nursing. Recently the trend has been to place nursing personnel in the operating programs, such as maternal and child health, preventive medicine, or local health administration. By 1986, only 19 states and the District of Columbia reported that they had an identifiable nursing unit, and an additional 7 states indicated that they operated a home health nursing unit or program (Table 30-3). Note once again the extreme heterogeneity among state health agencies. In several instances (Arkansas, Georgia, and Indiana), the nursing program provides consultation and technical assistance to local health departments. In some cases, as in the District of Columbia, Alaska, and Maryland, the nursing program is a direct service program. Note also the large investment made by some states in home health service programs (Mississippi, South Carolina, and Virginia), while other states with an identifiable home health agency are providing guidance or quality assurance services to local service delivery organizations. In most states with no identifiable nursing unit at the state

TABLE 30-3 State health agency public health nursing programs and home health service units, 1986

State	Budget
Nursing programs	
Alabama	$ 599,817
Alaska	8,413,798
Arkansas	38,788
Connecticut	882,935
Delaware	189,810
DC	8,547,238
Georgia	224,410
Hawaii	3,896,966
Indiana	350,699
Iowa	9,786,885
Kansas	448,038
Maine	2,025,232
Maryland	10,850,335
Minnesota	491,361
Nebraska	658,762
Nevada	802,477
North Dakota	260,456
Ohio	505,529
Oklahoma	268,304
West Virginia	642,236
SUBTOTAL	$ 49,884,076
Home health programs	
Louisiana	164,657
Mississippi	9,975,568
New Mexico	279,292
North Carolina	2,194,183
South Carolina	30,720,607
Vermont	14,210
Virginia	12,453,161
SUBTOTAL	$ 55,801,678
TOTAL	$105,685,754

From Public Health Foundation: Public health agencies: 1988, an inventory of programs and block grant expenditures, Washington, DC, 1988, The Foundation.

level, nursing personnel play leadership roles in operational programs such as maternal and child health, disease prevention and health promotion, adolescent health, and tuberculosis control.

The organizational placement of nursing in a state health department has involved a considerable amount of conflict. Most state health agencies are not the principal providers of public health services at the local level. If public health nursing is conceived of as a program of services, then the state may have only a technical assistance unit for nursing, providing consultation, continuing education, and quality assurance. In recent years, even these functions have been eliminated, and no such focal point exists at the state level.

The functions and responsibilities of nurses in state health departments depend on the legislative basis of the department. In the majority of instances they act as advisors to local health departments, boards of education, voluntary health agencies, and other state agencies. In a few state health departments that have been given broader responsibilities and powers, nurses may actually supervise and administer certain direct services, local as well as state, and may have regulatory responsibilities related to nursing practice, nurseries, day care, nursing homes, and hospitals. Other important activities of state health department nurses include demonstrations of particular services or of total community health nursing programs, development of home health services programs and agencies, and the conducting of in-service training courses.

All state health departments are active in the promotion of community health nursing services for prenatal and postnatal care, infants, and preschool children. To do so, they function through the direct assignment of state nurses to local areas, the loan of state nurses to specially selected local communities, or subsidy of local nursing programs.

Local level

Generally speaking, community health nurses today may be placed into two general categories—those employed by official health agencies primarily to carry out preventive and promotive health functions and those engaged by voluntary or commercial agencies primarily to render home nursing care to the sick. In addition, a large number of nurses have been employed by boards of education as school health nurses, and in recent years a number of community health nurses have been employed by neighborhood health centers and community mental health centers. It has been difficult to make a durable distinction between community health nurses and visiting nurses. Generally, it has been held that those who provide preventive and promotive services are practicing community nursing, whereas those who provide nursing care to the sick are providing visiting nursing services. The functional differences have become increasingly obscure. The visiting nurse often engages in health promotive activities while in the home, and the community nurse may help with a dressing change, either because it needs to be done or because some member of the family needs to learn how to do it. Increasingly, both activities are being provided by the same nurse; the only useful distinction that can be made is that visiting nursing services are often reimbursable, whereas community nursing services usually are not.

Nursing, as an organizational unit in a local public health department, is not usually a program; rather, it is a service. Nursing staff members are involved in many health department programs. The historical role of community nursing in public health agencies and the natural desire of a group of workers sharing a common background, training, and commitment to form a unit have long left both state and local agencies in an awkward organizational position. Many public health administrators have believed that the nursing staff of the agency should be distributed into the major program areas, but community nursing leaders have feared that such dispersal would lead to inattention to the integrity of the nurse's role, a loss of skills, and a gradual decline of the impact of the nurse on public health planning. The advent of more professional administrators in decision-making positions within official health agencies seems to have encouraged a gradual movement toward dispersal of the nursing staff. There are three ways to avoid the loss of nursing concepts in public health program development: (1) maintain a bimodal organizational structure in which nurses can belong to a nursing organization within the agency while also serving as members of a program team; (2) place trained community health nursing administrators into key program management positions within the agency; or (3) reestablish an identifiable community health nursing program by explicitly changing the role of the nurse in favor of a more independent practice—independent, that is, from the control of the physician.

The employment and supervision of school nurses have always been sources of friction. Many school officials feel that the personnel working in the school system should be a part of that system, whereas public health administrators claim that teachers cannot adequately supervise nursing personnel and that nurses working for school officials will be relegated to first-aid tasks rather than playing a role in health promotive activities and counseling. Community health nurses working for boards of education have generally been paid better and/or have worked less than their counterparts in public health agencies, and this has often added to the friction. The determining factor will probably be fiscal. Boards of education have their own tax base and until recently were able to obtain the personnel they wanted. Since public health administrators had a more difficult time getting support for community health nursing services, the school board could and did hire its own nurses. The property taxpayer has become increasingly concerned about the rising cost of the educational system, however, and school boards have elected to decrease nursing and counseling services to retain their teaching personnel. The result has been a gradual decline in the amount of community health nursing service available in the school setting—a valuable environment for assessment and diagnosis and for planning, implementation, and evaluation of group and individual health programs.

Another source of nursing service that has played an important role in some parts of the country is the large private occupational medical and health program, many of which employ not only industrial or occupational health nurses but also nurses whose function it is to attend sick employees and sometimes members of their families in their homes. With the broadening scope of occupational health and safety and the interest of labor unions in health services, such programs often include health protection and promotion activities provided by industrial clinic and home visiting nurses. A guide to nursing assessment in the industrial setting has been developed by Serafini.[26]

Several national organizations of nurses have played prominent roles in the development of nursing practice in public health, in addition to the nursing service of the American Red Cross. That organization, founded in 1912 in Ohio, was a direct service delivery organization, which operated at the local level. The National Organization for Public Health Nursing did not render direct service to the public but played a dominant role in the advancement of the field. It was organized in 1912 as the national professional society for those engaged or interested in public health work and became recognized as the voice of the profession. No other single agency contributed so much to the improvement of educational and service standards and to public acceptance of and respect for the work of the community health nurse. By 1952, however, concern developed about the growing number of nursing agencies and the need for coordination. As a result, in that year the National Organization for Public Health Nursing joined the National League of Nursing Education and the Association of Collegiate Schools of Nursing to form the National League for Nursing. At the same time, the bylaws of the American Nurses' Association were changed to provide for cooperation with the new National League for Nursing. Meanwhile the National Association of Colored Graduate Nurses also went out of existence, and its functions were integrated into the other organizations.

FUNCTIONS AND RESPONSIBILITIES

The statement of functions and responsibilities of community health nurses, first prepared in 1931 by the Subcommittee on Functions of the National Organization for Public Health Nursing, has undergone several revisions. The original listing of functions included assessment (collecting and analyzing information about the individual or the community), planning (for intervention), implementation, and evaluation of the intervention. More recently, the task of diagnosis has been added. The Association of State and Territorial Directors of Nursing[27] (an affiliate of the Association of State and Territorial Health Officials) describes the essential competencies of public health nursing for individual, family, and community services as follows:

Assessment
Planning
Implementation
- Performing nursing tasks
- Teaching
- Imparting knowledge and skills
- Counseling
- Consulting with others as needed
- Referring to others as needed
- Recording
- Evaluation

Public health nurses also need to be able to
Function independently without close supervision
Make independent nursing judgments
Manage a mixed caseload of individuals, groups, and communities while calculating priorities for service delivery
Modify procedures as needed to fit the needs of the client
Function as a health advocate for clients
Understand and participate in the political process

With regard to the last of those competencies, Marla Salmon White[28] has stated that public health nursing is necessarily political in nature and that nursing must constantly assess the value of its interventions. A distinguishing characteristic of nursing according to White is its focus on the public good, which can lead the nurse to make decisions about services that run contrary to the best interests of the individual. Since the carte blanche delivery of services to one client carries with it opportunity costs for other clients (individuals, families, and groups), choices have to be made to optimize the use of available resources.

The term *consumer* is often used by nursing rather than *patient* or *client.* That is not done in the spirit of the consumer movement of the 1960s but in the more sophisticated sense that a consumer-provider contract is being developed by two equal partners. A plan will be developed in the context of this partnership. That is, the nurse will discuss possibilities with the consumer, but the consumer will ultimately be the one to select the goals and objectives on which the two partners will work together. Periodically progress will be reviewed, the plan will be evaluated, and new goals and objectives may be agreed on. This contract-negotiating process is a unique concept in American health care and is of fundamental importance to the clinician and the administrator, whether dealing with an individual consumer or an entire community.

Ruth Freeman,[29] one of the most articulate and thoughtful nursing leaders and authors, writes that "the traditional function of community health nursing is to help others help themselves."[29] It is not a solo practice but a care system. Accepting Freeman's description, there may be no such thing as a community health nurse, but rather a variety of nursing practices that go together to make up a community nursing program.

The term *independent practice* may be used to describe a professional nursing practice that is not dependent on the direction or orders of a physician or to describe a private nursing practice that is not part of a private or public agency. In this discussion, the adjective *independent* will be used to characterize professional nursing as a distinct form of practice in contrast to a physician-dependent practice. The term *private practice* is better suited to distinguish individually provided patient care services from nursing that takes place under the auspices of a nursing agency.

ADMINISTRATIVE RELATIONSHIPS

An important administrative consideration influencing the value and efficiency of community health nursing programs is the nature of the relationships that exist among the various nursing and social agencies in the community, the public, and the members of other health professions. The need for community health nursing services is so great that it is important for agencies engaged in this work to cooperate and coordinate their respective programs as much as possible for maximum efficiency.

Relationships within the health department

The professional relationships of nurses in community health agencies take place in two areas: (1) within the agency itself and (2) in contacts with other agencies and individuals in the community. Within a health department, the relationship between the community health nursing staff and the administrator of the agency or department is of paramount importance. All too often satisfactory relationships between the nursing staff and the administrator are falsely assumed to exist. It is not unknown for health officials merely to support the nursing program quantitatively and to neglect to participate in the planning and organization for the effective delivery of nursing services.

Some health officials follow the path of least effort by allowing the nursing unit to proceed almost as if it were an independent agency. Inevitably this policy leads to difficulty both within and outside the department. The agency administrator is ultimately responsible for all phases of the health program of the department and, to a considerable extent, of the community as a whole. With respect to the nursing aspects of the program, the health director, who may be a nurse, should carefully select a well-qualified director of nursing services, provide adequate administrative support, and see that general policies and interagency relationships are developed by the nursing services director rather than perhaps haphazardly and inadequately by staff nurses and the workers of other agencies. The health agency director needs to maintain constant interest in the nursing program and endeavor to learn enough about it to assist the nurses in their efforts to fit into the total community health picture. If nursing is a service unit rather than a program, the nursing services director may be relegated to a role that exists outside of the policy-making group within the health agency. The agency director may discuss problems and policies frequently with directors of maternal and child health programs and environmental health directors, but the nursing services director may be excluded from such discussions. The conceptual framework and the value system of community health nursing should permeate virtually all discussions about programs and policies. If the nursing services director cannot maintain that sort of involvement in a productive manner, then the agency administrator either has the wrong person in that job or has not allowed the nursing services director sufficient intellectual exercise within the agency to maintain a forceful role. Many local health agency directors in the United States are physicians, and the traditional physician-nurse relationship can seriously weaken the potential effectiveness of the nursing services director. Only a fraction of the physician directors of local health agencies have had training in public health or public health administration, whereas the nursing services director may have had training and experience in community health programs that exceed that of the department director.

The community health nurse and the staff working in environmental health may on the surface seem unrelated. However, they are part of the same organization and should maintain a helpful and cordial relationship. In the course of daily field visits, the alert community health nurse is certain to become aware of many insanitary situations. Often they have a direct or indirect bearing on the nurse's professional interests and activities. A policy of prompt and effective intraagency referral should be developed to handle such situations. The same applies conversely to the engineer and sanitarian. The problem becomes more difficult in communities that have separated environmental health from the rest of public health.

Consolidation of nursing services

There is little if any justification for more than two community nursing groups in any given community: (1) the community health nurses working as employees of the official health department and (2) the staff of a visiting nursing association. The trend has been to explore ways of effectively merging these two groups. Regardless of the number involved, coordination is necessary to best serve the needs and interests of the public. There is no one answer as to how this may be accomplished; each community must work out the solution best suited to its particular needs and background. The number and variety of possible arrangements in a given community may be somewhat as follows.

If there are several voluntary or nonofficial agencies that render nursing services in the community, they may (1) remain completely independent of each other; (2) retain their individual identities but coordinate their programs by means of a central nursing advisory committee in which each agency participates; or (3) combine their programs to form a single community health nursing agency. (Once common, the delivery of nursing services by voluntary health associations such as those for tuberculosis or cancer is now rare, except for the visiting nursing association.) The voluntary agencies singly or united may limit their activities to bedside care, leaving most or all educational, promotional, and legal control measures to the nurses of the official health department. On the other hand, the health department may delegate some or all of its community health nursing responsibilities to the voluntary nursing agency. In the few communities where this procedure is followed, it is usually attributable to two influences: the existence of a long-established, well-supported, and accepted visiting nursing association, and a weak official health department.

The completely satisfactory consolidation of community nursing services is as yet relatively rare, usually strongly resisted, and in some situations premature. One of the most successful solutions has been developed in Seattle, Wash. The official and voluntary nursing agencies agreed on a cooperative, completely generalized community health nursing program that includes all preventive, promotive, educational, and bedside services but retains the board of directors of the voluntary nursing agency as an advisory committee. The committee controls its own contribution to the total cost of the program by means of an annual contract with the official health department. When carefully prepared and put into effect, this plan has worked well and has brought about increased efficiency and economy, and both groups of nurses have found more professional job appeal and stimulation from it.

The divergence and conflict between visiting nursing and public health nursing are of more than passing interest.[4] The consignment of sick care to the voluntary agencies while disease prevention and health promotion activities were transferred to the official public health agencies has had a great deal to do with the relatively limited role of public health agencies in providing primary care to the indigent and the medically indigent. In recent years, with restricted budgets, health departments have looked for additional sources of revenue under every rock, behind every tree, and in hitherto forbidden areas. In some states (see Table 30-3), home health care has become a dominant enterprise. The same has occurred in local health departments when there has not been an interdiction of such activities either by the private sector or by political considerations that require public health to stay out of health care. In that this has provided a substantial source of new revenue, it has been helpful, but it has also led newer public health managers, as well as county, city, and state fiscal managers and elected officials, to ignore the traditions of public health and authorize pursuit of reimbursable activities as a high-priority objective of the agency. Such work carries with it the sort of productivity measures characteristic of private enterprise, such as the number of reimbursable visits per day and the cost-to-revenue ratio for such visits. Evaluations such as these are not relevant to the interactions that often occur between a nurse and a high-risk, multiproblem client, be it a person, a family, or a group.[30] New and more relevant productivity measures are needed, and public health agencies must be cautious in the pursuit of reimbursement, since the promise of revenue can distort priorities away from the community's best interests and toward those of the third-party payor systems.

Physician relationships

The nurse in community health work has traditionally served under the direct or indirect orders of the physician. As noted earlier, licensure of a professional group is a process that involves declaring particular activities to be illegal and then specifying a procedure whereby certain individuals can be authorized to carry out those activities. The boards that issue licenses are traditionally composed of members of the profession licensed. Physicians were successful in getting licensure programs established before other health professionals in the United States could do so, and their definition of medical practice was global. The license to practice medicine and surgery is still the most unrestricted grant of authority any government can give to a citizen. The effort to license nurses, which began in 1938, of necessity had to be more restrictive in its definition of nursing practice and made that practice a dependent practice of medicine; that is, whatever a nurse could do depended on what a physician ordered done for the patient. This relationship has dominated and retarded the development of nursing for decades.

The relationship of nurses in community health agencies with locally practicing physicians was carefully circumscribed and designed in such a way as to reduce the effectiveness of the nurse, although it has also offered considerable protection. Traditionally, the health officer, who usually worked for a board of health dominated by physicians, could not allow expansion of the nurse's role with impunity. A primary function of the community health nurse was to interpret medical advice when asked to do so by the physician of the patient. The nurse was expected to assist people in obtaining medical care when they needed it or wanted it and then to assist them in carrying out the physician's orders. In doing this, the nurse was explicitly forbidden from recommending a particular physician, from advising patients to change physicians if the care they were getting was obviously unsatisfactory, or from offering advice about their treatment or other actions they might consider unless that advice could be considered carrying out the physician's orders. To be sure that this was done properly, it was common to appoint a medical advisory committee to discuss, clear, and implement policy. The members were usually appointed by the local medical society. Such committees were of obvious help to the health officer and the nursing service director when a local physician felt affronted by nursing advice given to a patient that seemed to be at variance with what the physician had prescribed. The medical committee would often intervene to suggest to the physician that he or she might have erred.

In most cases the nurse did not enter the home without first discussing the matter with the private physician and obtaining permission and direction. The nurse was expected to report observations and findings about the patient's progress to the physician, but if the nurse thought that the diagnosis or management of the patient was incorrect, it became a very difficult matter to deal with, usually involving consultation with the supervisor and often with the physician health director, who might try to find some tactful way to remedy the situation without offending the private physician. It is clear that the feelings and well-being of the physician took precedence over the best interests of the patient. It is also clear that the entire charade was, and to some extent still is, based on the political vulnerability of the health department to the concerns of organized medicine. The ethics of professional practice preclude one professional criticizing the work of another professional in front of a client. There is some virtue as well as some self-interest in this ethic, but its observance requires that special consideration be extended to the rights of the consumer or client. Some of the issues involved in this complex series of relationships are discussed at the conclusion of this chapter, but reality dictates that health agencies and their community nursing staff continue to pay attention to the difficult problem of serving the community while maintaining the support of the principal provider organizations.

In many instances, the nurse is serving as an assistant to the physician in carrying out the latter's prescriptions. In such cases a traditional supervisory relationship exists, and good professional practice will dictate the manner in which that relationship works for the benefit of the client. Sometimes the community health nurse will be asked for a reference to a physician. Standard practice in the past has been to advise the client to call the medical society for a list; or, if approved by the medical society and the agency director, the nurse may provide the patient with a list of physicians in the area whose field of practice is pertinent to the needs of the patient. In reality, such attempts to be nonpartisan often do not work. The nurse may have good reason to doubt the competency of some of the physicians on the list and may also know that a particular physician will not take any new patients or any new patients who depend on certain insurance or welfare programs for payment of their medical bills. Experienced nurses often find ways to signal the client in such a way as to get a particular message conveyed. It is important that personal biases, which may not be useful, do not enter into such transactions. It is often helpful for the nurses practicing in a given area to compare notes and update their unofficial list so that it reflects judgments about competency and social attitudes rather than personal preferences. Occasionally community health nurses have been criticized for referring low-income patients to the county or city hospital instead of to private practitioners; and faced with such criticism, agency and nursing service directors have sometimes prohibited those referrals. Such a policy would be a mistake. It is very hard for some people who do not have a personal physician relationship to establish one, especially when they are low-income and minority group members. The local public hospital or health department clinic is frequently the best place to refer such individuals, since the staff is usually adept at dealing with such problems, and has social support services available that are often needed by their clients.

In some areas a community nursing council exists to assist in studying, planning, improving, and coordinating all the nursing activities in the community. Its membership is usually fairly large, including representatives from all official and non-official agencies that provide nursing services; from organized professional groups such as medicine, dentistry, nursing, and social work; and from the public at large.

More recently the trend has been to develop a council of social agencies. The council plays a most important role in the development of joint analyses, planning, and implementation by all of the many social agencies that exist in the typical community. It usually functions by means of several standing and ad hoc committees with representatives of various interested and pertinent agencies. The health committee, which is almost universally one of the standing committees, may serve effectively in the absence of a community nursing council.

NURSING AND OTHER COMMUNITY SERVICES

The association of the official public health nursing program with the other social agencies in the community emphasizes the fact that in a certain sense the nurse in a community health agency is part of a social service system. The approach to individual and family problems differs depending on the provider's training. Social workers, nurses, and nutritionists may all describe the same problem differently and plan a different approach. Nevertheless, because of the complex nature of all social problems, of which illness and its prevention is one, mutual understanding and cooperation between the groups are of great importance. The more they know about each other's special training and abilities, the better will be their individual and joint performance. The nurse should be familiar with each of the social agencies in the community and know what each does and where its interests and contributions cut across, supplement, or complement those of the nursing program. Both the nurse and the social worker should have available for ready reference a directory or file indicating the interests, resources, location, and leadership of each social service agency.

Usually the social welfare programs consist of child welfare services, family services, medical social services, psychiatric social work, public assistance, and in- and out-of-home care services. Occasionally, most or all of these are found in a single agency. However, the usual pattern is for several official and nonofficial agencies to be involved. One of the important practical reasons for familiarity with the social agencies of a community is for purposes of referral. A client with AIDS, for example, may appear to be primarily the concern of the health department. However, problems of hospitalization and its costs, counseling, mental health care, housing, child care, and family support, to mention a few, will usually arise. The nurse cannot solve all of these singlehandedly and should refer certain aspects of the total problem, which has been crystallized by the onset of AIDS, to other appropriate community resources.

At one time many communities tried to establish a social service exchange system, which was essentially a registry of clients of various official and voluntary health and social service agencies. Their purpose was to enable workers to be sure that they were not duplicating the efforts of some other agency and to find out what other problems might exist in the family and who was doing what about them. Without computers, the maintenance of the registry was too difficult for most communities, and their popularity declined. The need still exists, and computer programs for such services are increasingly available and useful. Considerable attention has to be paid to the problems of confidentiality. Mental health workers, alcoholism and drug abuse counselors, and AIDS counselors are understandably and properly concerned about the problem. If all potential users are involved in the design of the system and thoughtful attention is given to the concept of "need to know" and what is clearly in the client's best interest, such sophisticated clearinghouses are possible.

ADMINISTRATIVE AIDS IN COMMUNITY HEALTH NURSING

As in other professional areas, community health nursing has found it practical to apply certain well-proven administrative aids.

Supervision

Unquestionably the most valuable administrative aid is the supervision provided at each level within a community health nursing agency. Supervision is necessary for the properly balanced development of the nursing service in public health programs and for the maintenance of its standards. Total responsibility for such supervision rests on the nurse administrator and, depending on the size of the agency, assistants and one or more supervisors. At the staff level, supervision ensures the quality and quantity of the service through both administrative and educational processes. With a ratio of 1 supervisor to every 6 to 8 staff nurses, it should be possible for the supervisor to offer sufficient guidance and counsel to the field or staff nurses to maintain the standard of the service offered and to encourage them individually to develop their ability to serve the patient and the family. The nursing supervisor is also a liaison person who serves as a two-way link between the staff nurses and the administrative officers of the agency. The supervisor interprets policies and methods of application and may also transmit the impressions of the staff, together with suggestions for additions or changes in policies, to the administration centers of the agency. In this way it is possible for the field staff to play an important role in the formation or modification of policies and programs.

Standard procedures

In any situation where several persons perform similar work toward a common purpose, it is desirable that they each follow the same procedures with regard to certain aspects of their work. To avoid misunderstanding and confusion, it is helpful, even in the smaller agencies, to have available a manual that sets forth clearly the policies of the agency and the procedures that are used. This should include statements of the exact responsibilities and authority of the personnel, standing orders used by the agency, and descriptions of techniques that are considered safe, effective, and ethically acceptable. Although each agency will find it necessary to develop its own manual, attention is directed to the *Manual of Public Health Nursing,* which has been prepared and is periodically revised by the National League for Nursing (formerly the National Organization for Public Health Nursing). Many state health departments have also prepared excellent nursing manuals for use by local health departments. There also should be a record manual in which the purpose and proper use of each record used by the community health nursing staff is explained and illustrated. It must be remembered that, valuable as these administrative manuals are, they quickly become useless unless continually kept up to date.

Nursing records have been transformed in recent years as a result of the problem-oriented approach first developed by Weed.[31] Its application to nursing practice has been well described by Woolley[32] and in *Problem Oriented Systems of Patient Care,* published by the National League for Nursing.[33]

Clerical staff

Although much of the recording, particularly that relating to details of field visits, must of necessity be done by the nurses themselves, there is much clerical work that is more efficiently carried on by an office clerical staff. Despite this, it is by no means uncommon to find the professional nurses of many organizations devoting a large proportion of their work time to details of record-keeping and analysis in the office. This is particularly unfortunate in the face of a shortage in community nursing personnel. The false reasoning appears to be prevalent that, as long as nurses must be employed in the community health nursing program, they might as well do all or most of the clerical work involved. It should always be realized that the records are also a necessary part of the program and that proper personnel for their handling is wholly justified. Use of the relatively expensive time of a professionally trained nurse for office work, which can more efficiently and effectively be turned over to less highly trained employees at lower salary scales, is simply poor administration.[34]

THE FUTURE OF COMMUNITY NURSING

It should be evident from the preceding sections of this chapter that nursing is in a continuing state of flux and evolution. Chaska[35] collected and edited an outstanding collection of papers on nursing titled *The Nursing Profession: Views Through the Mist.* The papers deal with the topics of professionalization, education, research, nursing theory, practice, relationships, and the future of nursing. Chaska describes three role possibilities: (1) primary care as a lower level practitioner (that is, lower than the physician), (2) a combination of medical activities with nursing assessment and teaching, or (3) a concentration on nursing's primary role. She asks if nursing should compromise or develop its own unique role and makes a strong case for the latter.

The problems and prospects seen through the mists by Chaska more than a decade ago have changed in some respects, but in others they are the same. Since the early days of Lillian Wald in the Henry Street Settlement, community health nursing has evolved but never quite fully emerged.[36] What is nursing to become? In the acute care setting, its future is questionable. The American Medical Association has attacked professional nursing in the hospital. With the oversupply of physicians and other health care professionals (in spite of the continued access problems), economic competition will increase, and the stronger professional group—stronger in terms of the power of its license and its purse—may prevail, reconciling nursing to the assistant's role. In community health nursing, however, the distinctive features of nursing are more evident and possibly more valuable. The many good textbooks on community health nursing provide different perspectives on the future of the practice.[37-41] Nurses have begun to create new program concepts in the community and to implement them, through both official public health agencies and new, not-for-profit ventures to meet real needs.[42]

Several roles for which nursing is well suited suggest themselves. For one, the nation needs health professionals who concentrate on health, not disease, and who seek to enhance health status.[43] Then, too, as the various systems of care become increasingly fragmented, weavers are needed to bring together the strands to form a safety net through which people will not fall. Stanhope and Lancaster[38] write: "Nursing's challenge is to become the central unifying figure in the health care system." Certainly at the community level, and for those without the resources to weave for themselves, this too is an appropriate and possible role. Finally, nursing could take on the challenge of developing a true primary care system—a system of care in which the client retains a primary role in making decisions.

The practice of medicine is a high-technology form of practice. Most problems that cause people to seek help are low-technology problems. When a low-technology problem is managed in a high-technology system, money is wasted and harm may ensue, because high-technology diagnostic and treatment procedures are also relatively high-risk procedures. Moreover, the selection, recruitment, education, and training of physicians orient them toward the management of organ-specific pathology, whereas most health problems have multisystem (physical, emotional, and social) involvements and causes. Nursing practice is more oriented to multisystem assessment and planning techniques and relies more on interpersonal skills than on high technology. It is likely that some nurses, physician extenders, physicians' assistants, aides, and other technicians will become the new working group that will serve to carry out the physician's prescriptions in the high-technology system of medical care, whereas professional nurses, and those with public health training particularly, may develop an entirely new low-technology system of holistic primary care. Such a system is badly needed, and no other professional group is as well equipped to develop it.

Public health agencies should assist the emergence of community health nursing in one or more of these roles, since they are the roles of the health departments themselves in the years ahead.

REFERENCES

1. Department of Philanthropic Information, Central Hanover Bank and Trust Co: The public health nurse, New York, 1938, reprinted by the National Organization for Public Health Nursing.
2. Birth of nursing at Bellevue, MD 17:68, April 1973.
3. Waters Y: Visiting nursing in the United States, New York, 1909, Charities Publication Committee.
4. Buhler-Wilkerson K: Public health nursing: in sickness or in health? Am J Public Health 75:1155, Oct 1985.
5. American Red Cross: Town and country nursing service, general outline, revised 1914, Washington, DC.
6. Bullough B: The law and the expanding nurse role, Am J Public Health 66:249, March 1976.
7. ANA Board approves a definition of practice, Am J Nurs 55:1454, 1955.
8. Jacox AK and Norris CM, editors: Organizing for independent nursing practice, New York, 1977, Appleton-Century-Crofts.
9. LaBar C and McKibbin RC: New organizational modes and financial arrangements for nursing services, Kansas City, MO, 1986, American Nurses' Association.
10. Soares CA: Nursing and medical diagnosis: a comparison of variant and essential features. In Chaska NL, editor: The nursing profession: views through the mist, New York, 1978, McGraw-Hill Book Co.
11. American Nurses' Association: A guide to community-based nursing services, Kansas City, MO, 1985, The Association.
12. Hanchett ES and Clarke PN: Nursing theory and public health science: is synthesis possible? Public Health Nurs 5:2, March 1988.
13. National League for Nursing: The need for nurses, New York, 1971, The League.

14. First report to the Congress, Feb 1, 1977: Nurse training act of 1975, US Department of Health, Education and Welfare, PHS Pub No (HRA) 78-38, Washington, DC, 1978.
15. Congressional Budget Office: Nursing education and training: alternative federal approaches; budget tissue paper for fiscal year 1979, Washington, DC, 1978, US Government Printing Office.
16. Aiken LH and Mullinix CF: The nurse shortage: myth or reality? N Engl J Med 317:641, Sep 3, 1987.
17. Iglehart JK: Problems facing the nursing profession, N Engl J Med 317:646, Sep 3, 1987.
18. ANA house opposes AMA caregiver proposal, The American Nurse, Jul-Aug 1988.
19. Shamansky SL and Graham KY: Hyperbole, Public Health Nurs 5:127, Sep 1988.
20. Bureau of Health Professions: The registered nurse population: an overview, Bureau Rep No 82-5, Hyattsville, MD, 1982, US Department of Health and Human Services.
21. Bureau of Health Professions: Public health personnel in the United States, 1980, US Department of Health and Human Services Pub No (HRA) 82-6, Hyattsville, MD, 1982.
22. McClendon BJ: Personal communication, Feb 1989.
23. The American Nurse 10:7, July 15, 1978.
24. Aiken LH: The practice setting: an overview of health policy issues. In Aiken LH, editor: Health policy and nursing practice, New York, 1981, McGraw-Hill Book Co.
25. Madden S and McClendon BJ: State health agency staff, 1979-1985, Washington, DC, 1988, Bureau of Health Professions.
26. Serafini P: Nursing assessment in industry, Am J Public Health 66:755, Aug 1976.
27. Association of State and Territorial Directors of Nursing: Statement of competencies: public health/community health nursing. In A guide for community based nursing services, Kansas City, MO, 1985, American Nurses' Association.
28. White MS: Construct for public health nursing, Nurs Outlook 30:527, Nov-Dec 1982.
29. Freeman RB and Heinrich J: Community health nursing practice, Philadelphia, 1981, WB Saunders Co.
30. Mattner KM: Public health nursing and productivity measurements: are home visit numbers the right focus? Nurs Management 19:99, Mar 1988.
31. Weed L: Medical records that guide and teach, N Engl J Med 278:593, Mar 14, 1968.
32. Woolley FR: Problem oriented nursing, New York, 1974, Springer Publishing Co.
33. Department of Home Health Agencies and Community Health Services: Problem oriented systems of patient care. Papers presented at the 1973-1974 workshop series, National League for Nursing, New York, 1974, The League.
34. Hernandez SR and others: Enhancing nursing productivity: a social psychologic perspective, Public Health Nurs 5:52, March 1988.
35. Chaska NL, editor: The nursing profession: views through the mist, 1978, McGraw-Hill Book Co.
36. Frachel RR: A new profession: the evolution of public health nursing, Public Health Nurs 5:86, June 1988.
37. Turner JG and Chavigny KH: Community health nursing: an epidemiological perspective through the nursing process, Philadelphia, 1988, JB Lippincott Co.
38. Stanhope M and Lancaster J: Community health nursing: process and practice for promoting health, ed 2, St Louis, 1988, Times Mirror/Mosby College Publishing.
39. Spradley BW: Community health nursing: concepts and practice, ed 2, Boston, 1985, Little Brown & Co.
40. Jarvis LL: Community health nursing: keeping the public healthy, ed 2, Philadelphia, 1985, FA Davis Co.
41. Fromer MJ: Community health care and the nursing process, St Louis, 1983, The CV Mosby Co.
42. Community-based nursing services: innovative models, Kansas City, MO, 1986, American Nurses' Association.
43. Novack JC: The social mandate and historical basis for nursing's role in health promotion, J Prof Nurs 4:80, Mar-Apr 1988.

CHAPTER 31

Public health and medical care

Food, shelter, and medical care are essential to life. (Some might add risk and faith to the list.) It was not always so. Before the twentieth century, one's chances of benefiting from an encounter with a physician were less than fifty-fifty. The extraordinary scientific advances of the mid-nineteenth century coupled with an improved educational system for health care professionals generally brought enormous benefits to those who were able to use the system of medical care. As a basic need, access to medical care is now considered a right rather than a privilege in most countries, but it is a much more difficult right to assure than, for example, access to food or shelter. The need for food and shelter is predictable and consistent. Their cost can be anticipated, and plans for their provision are possible. This is not true just for groups, but for individuals, within a fairly narrow range of variability. Such is not the case for medical care.

Routine preventive health services can be predicted: immunizations, well child care, hearing and vision screening, and the few other evaluations that are of use. The need for medical care is unpredictable. A presumably healthy person may develop cancer or have a baby with a congenital malformation or catch a cold. Since all risks cannot be avoided, a healthy child may become paralyzed in a bicycle accident, and even with the best of precautions, a few people will suffer from therapeutic misadventures while in the hospital and require medical care for the remainder of their lives. You may argue that although this is true, the need for medical care by a large group of people is predictable, and to some extent you would be correct. However, fashions and technology change: in recent years, dentists have altered the technology of what can be done, cataract surgery has become almost commonplace for elderly people, and even heart transplants are considered by some to be a normal procedure. Redefining (always upward) the art of the possible has characterized the history of medical care in the twentieth century and shows no sign of diminishing either in rate of change or in cost.

It is easy to suggest that a social guarantee of health services be limited to some defined set of services or that people who harm themselves not be entitled to communal support for the consequences of their intemperate behavior, but such policies are excessively difficult to administer in a civilization that prizes fairness. If we were to deny treatment for lung cancer to those who used tobacco, would that mean all treatment? Even hospice care for the terminal illness? By the same principle, we should deny care to those who eat or drink too much. How much is too much? Would the decision be based only on the number of calories or would it also reflect the quality of those calories? (How do we value oat bran today and fish oil tomorrow?) How should we determine which risks we approve of and which we frown on? Are sports to be encouraged or discouraged? Should people who don't notice that a restaurant has a substandard sanitary rating pay for the cost of their food poisoning, or some percentage of it based on the score?

Let us decide that transplants are not covered by communal funds. If you have lived to the age of 72 and eaten unwisely, why should the social purse be tapped for the cost of a replacement heart? How about 63 years and a somewhat healthier diet? How about 45 years and a history of eating fiber and grains and fish? How about a 7-year-old with congenital heart disease? The transaction costs of managing such a complex decision-making process would be exorbitant.

The problems are complex and defy easy answers, yet answers are badly needed. In the United States, the health sector of the economy now consumes more than 11% of the gross national product. In 1990 that will amount to about $650 billion. That is more, proportionally, in absolute cost per person, than in any other country of the world. Moreover, while other nations have managed to stabilize the cost of their health sectors, in the United States it is still increasing. Table 31-1 shows that increases in the cost of medical care have outstripped those in other segments of the economy on a regular basis for the past 20 years. Only during the 6 years from 1975 to 1981 did the service sector inflate more rapidly than the medical care sector, and the latter outpaced the service sector by a wide margin during 1982 and 1983. These figures beg the question "So what? Is that too much, not enough, or just about the right amount?" For two reasons, it appears to be too much: (1) Americans are no healthier than others who spend much less on their medical care, and (2) the opportunity cost of the medical care expenditure in the United States is significant.

It is difficult to compare health status across national boundaries, given the complexities of the differences in living standards, environment, education, and social policies. Yet many other nations have greater longevity and a lower infant mortality rate than the United States. Comparisons between health status indices of very poor countries and affluent countries reveal wide disparities, but it would be foolish to suggest that these differences are the result of the general availability of high-quality medical care services in the latter. Comparisons between the affluent countries of the world show little difference that can be accounted for by either the number of medical care services produced and used or the total investment in the health sector.

Beyond a certain point, or margin, there is little evidence that increasing expenditure has a positive influence on health status or that any improvement that might be observed is worth the extra cost. In fact, increasing expenditure may even make things worse. Some of the dissatisfaction with medical care in the United States may be related to the extension of services beyond the margin of utility. Medical care is clearly of value when fixing a broken leg or treating pneumonia, but its value is less apparent (and its adverse consequences less acceptable) when more trivial and self-limiting conditions are treated.[1]

The opportunity cost problem is also worrisome to both economists and public health professionals. Spending such large amounts of money on one element of the total economy, an element that has declining value at the margin, deprives society of the opportunity to spend that money on other elements of the economy: education, social services, housing, job training, or for that matter, defense or recreation. Some of the opportunities that are foregone because of the high investment in medical care—education especially—would have at least as much influence on health status, as has been discussed repeatedly in this book.

At the same time, many Americans—about 35 million of them*—have no health insurance at all.[2] That number has grown in recent years, and many other people have seen their employment-based health insurance coverage diminish in value as employers have cut back on their labor costs by reducing their payments for health insurance.[3] Those most likely to have the best health insurance are those who need it least, while those who need it most have the least coverage. Millions of other people are dependent on publicly supported medical care programs such as Medicare and Medicaid, while still others are dependent on the residual charity of state and local governments.

* This is an inexact figure. The National Center for Health Statistics estimated the total uninsured population at 23.4 million in 1986. The Robert Wood Johnson Foundation has a different set of calculations. Whichever figure you use, the number is very large.

TABLE 31-1 Annual percentage of change in selected components of the consumer price index for all urban consumers, 1970-1986

	1970-1975	1975-1980	1981	1982	1983	1984	1985	1986
All items except medical care	6.7	8.8	10.3	5.9	2.9	4.1	3.4	1.5
All services except medical care	6.3	10.1	13.4	8.7	2.9	5.2	5.0	4.6
Medical care	6.9	9.5	10.8	11.6	8.7	6.2	6.2	7.5

From Health Care Financing Administration: Health Care Financing Rev 8:1, Summer 1987.

Finally, the U.S. health care system is inherently inflationary. While alternative forms of practice have flourished in recent years, fee-for-service is still the dominant form of payment for physician services, and insurance and tax laws discount that payment to the consumer in such a way that the normal restraints on purchases do not affect most consumers of medical care.

These features mandate a public role in the organization and delivery of medical care services because of the following:

- Medical care has become an essential good.
- Many people are unable to obtain it without public support.
- Its price has become excessively high and is presently uncontrollable.

Although the public has been intimately involved in attempts to manage the medical care marketplace in the United States for more than 20 years, official public health agencies have played a very small role. The reasons for that and the prospects for the future are the substance of this chapter.

MEDICAL CARE IN THE UNITED STATES

The U.S. medical care system has several features in common with such systems elsewhere, and several features that are unique. Among the features it has in common with others is that it is

- Very costly
- In high demand
- Avaricious about improved technology
- Nonhumanistic
- Judged by its peers, not its consumers

Its cost has been attested to. Every country has been and is concerned about the cost of its medical care system. The demand for medical care seems insatiable, at least within a wide margin. Utilization of the health care system increases as resources, both facilities and personnel, increase. Specialization has affected health care just as it has affected all walks of life. Teachers now teach math or languages or history; lawyers do corporate law, criminal law, or tax law; builders do homes or apartments or office buildings, and doctors do arms or legs or heads. Specialization is more highly prized than generalization. In most instances specialists earn more money than generalists. Specialization is made necessary in part by the enormous increase in the growth of knowledge. The only way to maintain intellectual control over a chosen field is to increasingly narrow the scope of that field and dig deeper into it. When that happens, however, a practitioner inevitably becomes less of a humanist. Since the area of concern may be only the eye or a gallbladder or a foot, concern for the whole human is necessarily less—that is someone else's responsibility.

Accompanying this change in focus is the growing tendency for professionals to be judged by their peers, rather than their consumers. When most physicians were engaged in general practice and people lived in small towns, they compared notes about their family doctor. However, after surgery on their left hand, the probability that they will run into an acquaintance who consulted with the same hand surgeon in the major medical center many miles away is very small. Rather than face the daily judgment of their clients, specialists such as hand surgeons now seek the approval of their peers at annual meetings of their professional society at a huge conference center half way round the world.

These features are common to almost all countries of the world. There are several unique aspects to medical care in the United States as follows:

- It is vigorously private.
- It is highly entrepreneurial.
- It has an unusual payment system.
- It is mostly paid for by insurance.
- The components of the system are linked together in unusual ways.

These characteristics are a result of the history of the system. That history will be considered in four parts: the rise of the modern hospital, the evolution of medical practice, the special role of medical insurance in the United States, and the development of a public role.

The rise of the modern hospital

In the Western world, hospitals began as institutions of the Catholic Church, places where the sick and dying were attended by nuns and priests. There were no secular voluntary or private hospitals until the nineteenth century. In the Western hemisphere, the first hospitals were in Mexico City and in Montreal, both Catholic cities. In England, poor houses were the antecedents to hospitals. The Guardians of London (the custodians of the poor) found "out-relief" to be too expensive as the industrial revolution increasingly concentrated the poor in the cities. Rather than continue to hand out a dole to the poor, they decided to offer them food and shelter in large poor houses ("in-relief") in which costs could be controlled. Of course when you gathered the poor of London together in one place, you also gathered together many sick and infirm people. To reduce the probability that they would infect others, they were concentrated within special areas of the poor houses, known logically enough as infirmaries. Bellevue Hospital in New York City began as a poor house, and Philadelphia General Hospital, now closed, began as a public almshouse for non-Quakers. Some care was provided, but no cures. There were no medical schools, nor was there any confidence that medical care could make much of a difference.

Then, in the middle of the nineteenth century, the Golden Age of science emerged. In just a few short years, European physicians acquired a new understanding of human physiology, pathology, treatment, and prevention. Warren and Bigelow[4] discovered anesthesia in 1846, making it easier for surgeons to operate on living people. In 1849, before bacteria were understood, John Snow[5] deduced the etiology of cholera by studying the incidence of the disease in households along different water lines. In 1867, Lister[6] discovered antisepsis, making it possible for surgeons to prevent the infections that had previously killed their patients. In 1870, Louis Pasteur discovered viruses and the principle of immunizations.[7] During the same decade, Rudolf Virchow, a German social scientist, developed the science of pathology and concepts of social medicine.[8] And in 1882, Robert Koch[9] described the basic principles of proof required to determine the cause of a disease. The rapidity of discovery was breathtaking. So extraordinary were the findings of the middle of that century that Sir William Osler[10] wrote:

> For countless generations the prophets and kings of humanity have desired to see the things which men have seen . . . in the course of this wonderful 19th century. To the call of the watchers on the towers of progress there has been the one sad answer—the people sit in darkness and in the shadow of death. Politically, socially and morally the race has improved, but for the unit, the individual, there was little hope. Cold philosophy shed a glimmer of light on his path, religion in its various guises illumined his sad heart, but neither availed to lift the curse of suffering from the sin-begotton son of Adam. In the fullness of time, long expected, long delayed, at last science emptied upon him from the horn of Amalthea blessings which cannot be enumerated, blessings which have made the century forever memorable, and which have followed each other with a rapidity so bewildering that we know not what next to expect.

With this new knowledge, public health moved out of the darkness and into the grime of industrial metropolitan life. What was possible had changed. The politics of the time had begun to alter conceptions of the value of life, and there was a growing democratization of national governance with a nascent sense that equity would serve all people better than an aristocracy would. It was the scientific discoveries of the Golden Age that made these changes possible, however. Now the infirmaries of the poor houses could be used as hospitals, and the major medical schools found them much more useful for teaching purposes than the apprentice system, which was dependent on private practitioners and private patients. The poor houses of London became its great teaching hospitals. The same changes occurred in the United States.

The evolution of medical practice

Until the end of the nineteenth century, American physicians were largely itinerant, poorly educated tradesmen and housewives. There were no medical schools. Most physicians were trained as apprentices, and few of their masters had studied at the great medical schools of Europe. Cults were common, and there were many botanic practitioners. In New Jersey, as late as 1818, most of the practitioners were women who worked part-time as healers. The Thomsonians emerged in 1822 espousing only one cause of disease: cold, for which heat was the logical remedy. Licensing systems were initiated in some states in an effort to impose order on the business (and protect a few physicians), but the laws were soon rescinded since they were based on personal benefit, not competency.

Typical of the American physician was Dr. Hiram Buhrman,[11] who practiced in small towns in Maryland and Pennsylvania in the 1870s. His regular fee was 25 cents for an office call. This included medicines unless expensive drugs were necessary. A house visit within the township was 50 cents without medicine, 75 cents with. The physician compounded his own prescriptions. In case of death there was a $3 fee for which he did most of the work of the present-day mortician. All obstetric cases, regardless of the length of labor, were $5, as were abortions, but miscarriages were billed at $1.50. Dr. Buhrman also functioned as a dentist. A tooth extraction cost 25 cents, except when several in a row were removed at the same time, in which case the fee per tooth was reduced. In this unspecialized small-town practice conducted with few instruments and drugs for a limited number of diseases, the hospital did not enter into the picture at all.

Proprietary medical schools flourished in the latter part of the nineteenth century, mostly with no adequate laboratory space, no hospital or clinic facilities, an incompetent faculty, and no external reviewing mechanisms such as licensure or accreditation. At the beginning of the twentieth century, there were 450 medical schools in the United States and little or no control over any of them. In 1904, the American Medical Association recommended that a high-school education be a prerequisite to admission to medical school.

There were some nascent signs of excellence, however. William Osler and John Halsted at Johns Hopkins University in Baltimore were familiar with the form of education in European medical schools: basic sciences taught by full-time professors during the first two years, followed by an introduction to clinical medicine, also taught by full-time faculty. At the end of the formal academic training period, postgraduate training began in a hospital under the tutelage of senior clinicians who had specialized training in medicine or surgery. Because of the concern of physicians such as Osler, Halsted, and others, the Carnegie Foundation commissioned the famous Flexner report of 1910.[12]

Abraham Flexner was an educator, not a physician. He visited most of the medical schools in the United States in the course of his work and wrote a devastating report, detailing the incompetence of most of the proprietary medical schools: their resources, their laboratories, their faculty, and their clinical teaching arrangements. He made detailed recommendations for change—closures, consolidations, and improvements. His work and that of Osler and Halsted led to the emphasis on full-time academic training and the specialization of medical training and practice.

Hospitals moved to a central position in medical education. Many small private hospitals were built in small towns throughout the country to accommodate the work of the newly trained physicians. They were owned by individual surgeons and often included a home, an office, and a dozen or so beds either in an open ward arrangement or in multiple-occupancy rooms. In the large cities, hospitals were for the most part either "voluntary" (private but not-for-profit institutions organized by philanthropists and community leaders) or university hospitals. These institutions grew slowly until after World War II but played an increasingly dominant role in the practice arrangements of their areas. Later, after voluntary accreditation programs for hospitals became influential, the "mom-and-pop" hospitals of America's small towns began to close. Large private hospitals were uncommon, since it was difficult for investors to aggregate sufficient capital to build such institutions until later.

During the years from Flexner to the present, the number of medical schools decreased from 450 to 120. Had it not been for a major federal investment in the creation of new medical schools in the 1960s, there would have been fewer.

Given its checkered past and present, it is not surprising that most Americans thought little about organized medical practice during the nineteenth century. There had been numerous physician organizations, but most of them split apart over issues relating to the theory or practice of medicine. In quality, the American medical practice lagged far behind European countries, where medical care had already been recognized as a valuable service, something governments should be concerned about. In the United States, since it was of so little consequence, neither the federal nor state governments were interested in assuring all people access to medical care in the same way that they had access to education. When medical care was needed, to mend a broken limb or prevent the spread of smallpox, it was cheap enough to obtain: village, township, and city officials could arrange for what was needed as a minor matter of local government. In this environment no one noticed or cared that the physicians were now establishing a monolithic professional organization with county, state, and national components or that they had developed licensure laws largely administered by their nominees. It was strictly a private affair, of little consequence to most people.

With the advent of modern medical education, beginning in 1910, the leadership of the American Medical Association (AMA) was assumed by academic physicians who were more interested in the social aspects of medical care than its business features. A progressive organization, its journal (*The Journal of the American Medical Association*) became increasingly important and known around the world. In 1916, its Social Insurance Committee recommended the establishment of compulsory, state-run, health insurance programs, and in 1917, the AMA House of Delegates adopted principles for a government health insurance program.[13]

After World War I, however, Americans became more fearful of collectivism. The Russian revolution and the rise of communism and socialism in Europe frightened the free-enterprisers in the United States. Physicians by then had more status and income to protect. In a leadership revolt, power shifted from the academics, who had little economic interest in medical care, to the private practitioners. California voters defeated a referendum for a statewide health insurance program in 1919, and in 1920, under its new leadership, the AMA reversed its earlier positions. In 1932, it stated[14]:

> The alinement [sic] is clear—on the one side, the forces representing the great foundations, public health officialdom, social theory—even socialism—inciting to revolution; on the other side, the organized medical profession of this country urging an orderly evolution guided by controlled experimentation which will observe the principles that have been found through the centuries to be necessary to the sound practice of medicine.

We have seen just how long that tradition really was. It was a position from which the AMA fought many battles over the next five decades.

The special role of medical insurance

Both hospitals and medical practice developed differently in the United States than they did in Europe: there was much greater reliance on private ownership of the institutions of medicine in the United States and little interest in government involvement in the practice of medical care. Social insurance developed in a uniquely American way too. The term *social insurance* connotes insuring people against the cost of unexpected social problems (death, disability, injury, or disease, for example) rather than insuring property.

Social insurance programs developed early in Europe as programs of the guilds—groups of artisans such as hatters or glovemakers or saddlers. They collected small amounts of money from their members each month to be used for burial expenses when a member died, sparing the widow and children the ignominy of a pauper's grave. Sickness insurance (euphemistically referred to as health insurance in the United States) soon followed. The guild members (the men, that is) would contract with a physician to provide the medical care services their members usually needed. These were house calls, some medicines, and in-home obstetrical services. Hospital care was not included, since it was rarely used. In present-day terminology, this would be considered primary care insurance. The programs were designed and managed by the consumers of care, not the providers.

With the rise of socialism and the increasing power of trade unions in the mid-1880s, pressure grew for the state to develop more universal sickness insurance programs. To fend off a political attack by the socialists in Germany, Otto von Bismarck introduced new legislation creating a social security program in 1883. Social security was quite different then from what was later developed in the United States: it protected working-age men by providing sickness insurance. The Social Security Act in the United States, which was passed in 1935, long after most of the rest of the world had adopted such measures (Table 31-2), was limited to income protection for elderly retired workers. The Social Security systems of other countries often developed their own medical care delivery systems, complete with hospitals, clinics, and employed physicians.

Social insurance programs developed much more slowly in the United States, beginning with "mother's insurance" in the 1800s. After World War I, the general revulsion from anything that sounded remotely like collectivism helped the AMA defeat proposals for sickness insurance programs. In 1929, however, the hospitals in Houston, Tex., became worried about their ability to collect payments from an increasingly unemployed work force, and Baylor Hospital sold a Blue Cross Plan to the local school board to provide hospital insurance for teachers at a cost of $6 per year. The plan provided for a semiprivate room, a 21-day limit, and it paid the bill directly to the hospital rather than indemnify the teacher for payment of the hospital bill. These were important features, especially the last, which was opposed by organized medicine, since if extended to their practices it threatened to interpose a third party between the physician and his patient (physicians were, by and large, male then). In 1939, a group of surgeons in California went through the same process: worry about collecting fees led to adoption of a physician-owned, not-for-profit, sickness insurance program, known as Blue Shield.

The Blue Cross/Blue Shield phenomenon set the stage for six decades of change and crisis in American medical care. Both plans differed strikingly from their earlier European counterparts in that they were provider initiated. It was the consumers, operating first through guilds and then through labor unions, who initiated sickness insurance in Europe: they decided what they wanted to buy and entered into negotiations with potential providers. In the United States, first the hospitals and then the surgeons decided what they wanted to sell or provide and then negotiated with employers to sell their plans. Rather than primary care, the new American plans covered hospital care and surgery.

TABLE 31-2 Dates of enactment of selected social security programs

Year	Country
1883	Germany
1888	Austria
1891	Hungary
1910	Norway
1911	Great Britain*
1920	Poland
1922	Russia
1922	Yugoslavia
1922	Japan
1922	Greece
1924	Chile
1925	Italy
1928	France
1933	Denmark
1935	United States
1936	Peru
1938	New Zealand
1941	Costa Rica
1943	Mexico
1945	Brazil
1948	Great Britain†

* Social security program first adopted.
† National Health Service first adopted.

These features of sickness insurance have dominated the history of medical care organization in the United States since 1930. To this day, primary care and preventive health services are less well insured than surgery and hospital services (this includes the large government Medicare and Medicaid programs—see below). Secondly, the insurance transactions generally took place between the providers and employers, insulating the insured employees from both the details of the plans and the financial transactions. Since the plans were later treated as a benefit of employment, their costs were treated as a business expense by the employer and they were excluded from the taxable income base of the employee. These features had a subsequent inflationary impact on health care in the United States, since neither consumers nor providers of medical care were involved in price competition.

As America moved slowly into the Great Depression and toward World War II, its medical care system was unique: most people did not value medical care highly; partly as a result of that, there was little history of philanthropy or government sponsored care (why use private or public money for something of little value?); medical practice and hospital services were considered to be private enterprises of no interest to the government, federal, state or local; and most medical care, when it was needed and available, was cheap—it could be paid for "out-of-pocket" by most people. The profession, represented by the American Medical Association, and the hospitals, represented by the American Hospital Association, had risen to sovereign power in medical care, both politically and economically, *before* either the science or the social policy of medical care had emerged into the modern era. In Europe and elsewhere in the world, the value of medical care was evident and appreciated before the professions had seized absolute control of its instruments, and government was a major participant. Not so in the United States.

The development of a public role

During the depression years of the 1930s, the new health insurance programs spread slowly throughout such industries as were still in business.

As the economy recovered in the latter part of the 1930s, and such programs might have been expected to increase more rapidly, the United States began its entry into World War II. Labor strikes were limited because of the war effort, and employee benefit packages did not expand rapidly. Shortly after the war, several important changes began to occur.

Hospitals, which had begun their transition from a proprietary practice environment in 1910, had languished during the Depression from lack of money and during the war for much the same reason. To repair the dwindling stock of hospital beds and make modern medicine more widely available, the Hill-Burton Act was passed in 1946. It established a federal-state partnership that provided nearly $16 billion in grant money for more than 11,500 projects during its 25 years. It brought science and standards into the business of hospital design and construction, including such concepts as the separation of medical beds from surgical beds and maternity from pediatrics and the newborn nursery, to reduce the probability of infection. (Of course this also reduced the probability of breastfeeding and family participation in the birthing process.) There were a number of other important features to the Hill-Burton program:

- The states organized their own hospital planning bodies, which were dominated by hospital interests. The standard of need was not that of the community but that of the hospital and its affiliated physicians.
- The law limited aid to states with no more than 4.5 hospital beds per 1,000 people, since that appeared to be the norm in well-developed communities. This ceiling soon became a target for every community and became part of the planning process. In later years, this became a surplus, and health planning sought ways to reduce the number of hospital beds available.
- Because of the matching requirements for the grants, most of the money went to middle-class areas rather than to low-income areas, where voluntary hospitals were few and far between.
- Primary care facilities, such as clinics and public health departments, were not included. This was later changed, but by then, most of the money that was to come had already been allocated to long-range construction programs.
- Provisions were added to the bill that required grant recipients to provide some measure of free care to low-income people, but these provisions were little known and not enforced for more than 20 years. By the time they became an issue in the 1970s, the length of time during which the provisions for free care were to apply had largely expired.
- The law specifically recognized the existence of separate facilities for blacks and whites in the South.

The Hill-Burton program stimulated enormous growth in the hospital sector, most of it in the community hospital segment.

The federal government also invested heavily in biomedical research after World War II. The National Cancer Institute had been established just prior to the war, and institutes for heart disease, diabetes, neurological and sensory diseases, mental health, and dental health soon followed. These investments increased the pace of technological discovery, innovation, and diffusion, shortening the time it took for breakthroughs in the laboratory to enter mainstream medical practice. This further accelerated the rising importance and cost of hospitals.

Yet the most important phenomenon was the veterans—more than 15 million of them. They came from every village, farm, and city; they were black, white, Native American, Hispanic, Polish, Japanese, and Serbo-Croatian. They ran the political gamut from laissez-faire capitalists to card-carrying Communists. They had several things in common, however, among which was having been provided with comprehensive medical and dental care at no out-of-pocket cost while in the service.

These young men and women came from families in which medical care had been an infrequent experience. Many of them had been born at home, attended by a midwife. Immunizations were rare, and routine dental care almost unheard of. Their parents had grown up in an era when the quality of medical care was generally abysmal, had limited access to such services, and hardly missed them. They had no interest in sickness insurance and certainly did not expect that they or their children should be guaranteed access to medical care by their government. Their children, however, were different. At the formative and impressionable age of 18 to 25, they came from the farm and city to the Army and Navy. (The Air Corps at that time was part of the Army.) They were examined from stem to stern. If they were well enough, they were drafted and immunized. From that day until they reentered civilian life, they were not only given the medical and dental care they needed, they were commanded to use it. Their caries were filled, their colds treated, their wounds sewn up, their psyches dealt with by psychiatrists. And the care they received was good. The physicians and dentists and nurses who provided the care were young, recent graduates, the beneficiaries of some of the best medical education available.

The recipients of that care valued it, and when they returned to civilian life they assumed that such care was necessary for themselves and their families. Unlike their parents, they expected it to be available to them. And as beneficiaries of the GI bill, they received it, along with support for a college education. As they reentered the labor force, they expected their employers to provide health insurance, and the revitalized unions saw that they got it. As they entered the peak years of their working lives, in the 1950s and 60s, they became the industrial leaders, the labor union officials, and the elected policymakers who designed the social systems for the last half of the century, and those designs included the notion that everyone needed access to good medical care.

TABLE 31-3 Aggregate and per capita expenditures for personal health care by source of funds, selected years, 1929-1987

			Third Parties			Government		
Year	**Totals**	**Direct patient payment**	**All third parties**	**Private health insurance**	**Other private funds**	**Totals**	**Federal**	**State and local**
			Aggregate amount (in billions of dollars)					
1929	3.2	2.8	0.4	*	0.1	0.3	0.1	0.2
1935	2.7	2.2	0.5	*	0.1	0.4	0.1	0.3
1940	3.5	2.9	0.7	*	0.1	0.6	0.1	0.4
1950	10.9	7.1	3.8	0.9	0.3	2.4	1.1	1.3
1955	15.7	9.1	6.6	2.5	0.4	3.6	1.6	2.0
1960	23.7	13.0	10.7	5.0	0.5	5.2	2.2	3.0
1965	35.9	18.5	17.3	8.7	0.8	7.9	3.6	4.3
1970	65.4	26.5	38.9	15.3	1.1	22.4	14.5	7.9
1975	117.1	38.1	79.0	31.2	1.6	46.3	31.4	14.9
1980	219.1	62.5	156.7	67.3	2.6	86.7	62.5	24.3
1987	438.9	127.9	311.0	136.0	5.5	169.6	128.8	40.8
			Per capita amount ($)					
1929	26	23	3	*	1	2	1	2
1935	21	17	4	*	1	3	1	2
1940	26	21	5	*	1	4	1	3
1950	70	46	24	6	2	16	7	8
1955	93	54	39	15	3	21	10	12
1960	129	71	58	27	3	28	12	16
1965	177	91	85	43	4	39	18	21
1970	305	124	182	72	5	105	68	37
1975	522	170	352	139	7	206	140	66
1980	934	268	666	287	11	367	266	102
1987	1,744	508	1,236	540	22	674	512	162

* Included with direct payments; separate data not available.
From Gibson RM and Waldo DR: Health care financing review, Health Care Financing Administration, Pub No 03123, Washington, DC, Sept 1981, US Government Printing Office; Health Care Financing Administration: National health expenditures, 1986-2000, Health Care Financing Rev 8:1, Summer 1987.

As costs rose, insurance coverage expanded. And the costs did rise (Table 31-3), from a per capita cost of $26 in 1929 to $177 in 1965. The national cost increased from $3.2 billion to nearly $36 billion during those years and then kept right on rising, to an estimate of over $573 billion by 1990. And the percentage of the bill that was paid for out-of-pocket and by private insurance decreased from 88.4% to 51.6% (by 1990 it is expected to be about 28%).

The population was growing older too. The number of people over the age of 65 and out of the labor force was increasing rapidly. The declines in infant and childhood mortality discussed in earlier chapters meant that more and more people survived to the age of retirement. With the expansion of the Social Security program, workers began to retire at the age of 65, but when they did, they lost their employment-based health insurance, and they faced a world in which the cost of medical care was now beyond the reach of a personal pocketbook or checking account. During their years in the labor force, while costs had been escalating rapidly, they were protected from both the impact and the knowledge of the increase by expanding health insurance benefits. In retirement, however, just when the burdens of disability began to increase, their ability to pay for the services needed was at its lowest. They could no longer afford the medical care they often needed.

THE GOVERNMENT'S ROLE

Medical care became a public issue in the United States when it became valuable and costly. This finally became evident after World War II, when it was understood by many that good medical care could make the difference between life and premature death. Many people could not obtain it, however, because it was a private service, available only to those who could afford to pay for it. This was not, of course, strictly true. Many local governments operated county or city hospitals, there was considerable charity care available in the large cities, and most physicians did not expect to collect their fees from every patient. In many towns and cities, a third or more of the care provided was offered with no real expectation of payment. However, as the technology of medical care improved, professional training became more arduous, and hospitals grew more expensive; with enormous capital costs and large payrolls, it became less realistic to expect that the needs of the poor could continue to be met in such an informal manner. The costs, which could not be dispensed with by the wave of a wand or a charitable impulse, had to be met. This was often done by shifting them inconspicuously to those who could pay. The insurance companies and private payors began to absorb an increasing amount of the cost of the care for those who had neither insurance nor sufficient wealth to pay for the care they needed.

Previous chapters of this book have repeatedly demonstrated that poverty per se is a major cause of disease and injury. It affects health at birth, during childhood, adolescence, and adulthood, and it affects occupational health, maternal health, old age, and death. Tables 31-4 and 31-5 show the difference undramatically: low-income people have more acute conditions per year and more restricted activity days per year than higher income people. (The greater number of acute conditions for higher income children under the age of 18 may be related to the greater likelihood of reporting such conditions by higher income mothers, the usual respondents in the household survey.)

TABLE 31-4 Acute conditions per 100 people per year, by age and family income, United States, 1987

	Family income level			
	<$10,000	$10,000-$19,999	$20,000-$34,999	$35,000+
All ages	198.2	171.3	177.6	173.9
<18	266.3	253.1	268.2	293.4
18-44	214.9	179.6	169.7	148.2
45+	126.8	97.5	94.6	97.2

From National Center for Health Statistics: Current estimates from the National Health Interview Survey, United States, 1987, Hyattsville, MD, 1988, US Department of Health and Human Services.

With greater burdens of disability, disease, and death, the poor have greater need for health care and medical services, but the rapidly rising cost of medical care makes it increasingly difficult for those who need it the most to obtain it at all. As family income has increased, the cost of medical care has increased even more rapidly. In 1970, the per capita cost of personal medical care services in the United States was $305, or 7.5% of personal income. By 1986, this had increased to $1,620, or 11.1% of disposable income (Table 31-6). Note that the table is based on total personal income, not just disposable income, and on total cost of personal medical care. Much of that care is covered by insurance, the cost of which is borne by the employer, not the employee. It is included in the calculations, however, since it is paid for by the individual in many instances and could be made available as income if it were not spent on medical insurance. To more accurately reflect the changes that have occurred, the cost of employer-provided medical insurance should be included in the denominator as well as in the numerator. This would reduce the apparent increase in the proportion of personal income that is spent for medical care.

The rising proportion of income consumed by necessary medical care is more of a problem for low-income people. Until 1981, the federal government published figures detailing how an average family spent its money. The population was divided into thirds (upper, middle, and lower income groups), and a model budget for a family of four was calculated based on current prices and expenditure patterns. Table 31-7 reveals the terrible impact on low-income families of the uncontrollable rise in the price of medical care.

TABLE 31-5 Number of restricted activity days per person per year due to acute and chronic conditions, by income, United States, 1987

Income	Restricted activity days
<$10,000	24.2
$10,000-$19,999	16.9
$20,000-$34,999	12.3
$35,000+	9.9

From National Center for Health Statistics: Current estimates from the National Health Interview Survey, United States, 1987, Hyattsville, MD, 1988, US Department of Health and Human Services.

All of the consumable items except medical care show the pattern of discretionary choices by higher income people. They spend more on their food, housing, automobiles, and personal items than lower income people do. Only the cost of medical care seems virtually fixed. While upper income people may choose to pay for a little more costly care or more of it, the differences are insignificant. Given the fact that lower income people have more health problems than upper income people do, their expenditures should be even greater. As it is, by 1981 lower income people were forced to spend 11% of their disposable income on medical care, while upper income people had to use only 6% of theirs, leaving more for other aspects of their lives, including savings and the education of their children.

As the cost of medical care continues to increase faster than personal income, the burden on the

TABLE 31-6 Per capita personal income and expenditures for personal health care services, 1970, 1980, and 1986

	Per capita personal income	Per capita personal health care	Proportion for health care (%)
1970	4,056	305	7.5
1980	9,916	934	9.4
1986	14,628	1,620	11.1

From US Bureau of the Census and Health Care Financing Administration: National health expenditure 1986-2000, Health Care Financing Rev 8:1, Summer 1987.

TABLE 31-7 Family budget for "consumables" in 1981

Item	Lower	Middle	Upper
Food	$4,545	$5,843	$7,366
Housing	2,817	5,546	8,423
Transportation	1,311	2,372	3,075
Personal items	1,316	1,841	2,666
Medical care	**1,436**	**1,443**	**1,505**
Other	644	1,196	1,972
TOTALS	$12,069	$18,241	$25,007

From Bureau of the Census.

poor will become even greater. They must either reduce expenditures in other categories or go without the medical care they need. Since the other categories are demonstrably at the lowest level possible, medical care must be foregone unless government intervenes. The problem is not new, but it was exacerbated in the 1980s by a variety of changes in income, employment practices, and the increasing entrepreneurialization of medical care.

MEDICARE AND MEDICAID

Government can intervene in three ways: it can attempt to modify the system by regulating it; it can provide health services directly to those in need; or it can act as a consumer, buying needed services from the private sector for those who are unable to enter the medical care market on their own. In the United States, all three mechanisms have been tried, both separately and concurrently, with mixed but on the whole unsatisfactory results.

Following the Flexner report and the change in the social position of the AMA during the first two decades of the twentieth century, the evolution of health policy in the United States took place largely in private. The American Association for Labor Legislation succeeded in establishing workers' compensation laws in most of the states and turned its attention to sickness insurance, where it enjoyed some early success. After World War I, however, as noted earlier, the country turned against such radical notions. In 1927, the Committee on the Costs of Medical Care was established with financing from six foundations. It included 42 people representing medicine, public health, hospitals, economics, and the general public. Its many studies and reports between 1928 and 1932 were summarized by Isidore Falk[15]:

1. Comprehensive medical service should be provided largely by organized groups of practitioners, organized preferably around hospitals, encouraging high standards and preserving personal relations.
2. All basic public health services should be extended to the entire population, requiring increased financial support, full-time trained health officers and staffs, with security of tenure.
3. Medical costs should be placed on a group payment basis through insurance, taxation, or both; individual fee-for-service should be available for those who prefer it; and cash benefits for wage loss [due to illness or injury] should be kept separate.
4. State and local agencies should be formed to study, evaluate, and coordinate services, with special attention to urban-rural coordination.
5. Professional education should be improved for physicians, health officers, dentists, pharmacists, registered nurses, nursing aids, midwives, and hospital and clinical administrators.

Organized medicine took strong exception to recommendations 1 and 3 but accepted the others. It is generally felt that these recommendations are as valid today as they were 60 years ago but that nothing has been done about them. However, Milton Roemer[16] has written an excellent review of Dr. Falk's contributions and points out that considerable progress has been made on at least four of the five recommendations. (While the nation began to experiment with recommendation 4 in 1966 and again in 1974, the comprehensive health planning movement was killed by the Reagan administration; see Chapter 11.)

The Social Security Act, which was passed on August 14, 1935, was meant to be an incremental program that would expand to form a comprehensive safety net, providing both income protection and insurance against the costs of medical care, forestalling the need to develop a welfare program. The impetus for such a change weakened in the latter part of the decade, and the AMA warned Roosevelt that it would oppose him vigorously if he moved in that direction. The war postponed further action. Public health was notably silent during these discussions. The architects of Social Security came from a background in labor law and welfare, not medical care or public health. The U.S. Public Health Service saw no need to become involved, and state and local health directors, mostly physicians, were of the opinion that medical care was an improper concern for public health.

The changes that occurred after World War II have been described above. They occurred in an environment rich with legislative experience but one in which conservative opposition to an expanded role for government was at its height.

Even before the war, Senator Robert Wagner and others had been active in the pursuit of public support for medical care, earning the wrath of the AMA, which held emergency meetings, raised money for an enormous political campaign, and cried out that the Wagner-Murray-Dingell bill was "the most virulent scheme ever to be conjured out of the mind of man." The bill proposed comprehensive medical, hospital, dental, and nursing home care for almost the entire population, to be paid for out of a special fund based on equal contributions from employers and employees. The bill was defeated as were a variety of successor attempts to develop even a modest role for the federal government. With the rise of the McCarthy era, few legislators were willing to espouse anything that sounded as radical as social insurance.

Nevertheless, as noted above, the federal government sponsored the Hill-Burton program, expanded its role in biomedical research, and launched major new initiatives to increase the number and quality of health professionals in the United States. Ultimately, almost 60% of the cost of medical education was paid for by the federal government, until finally it was concluded that there were too many practitioners and too many hospital beds and both programs were first reduced, then eliminated altogether. These public policies implicitly and explicitly recognized the private practice of medicine and supported its growth and its sovereignty.

Again, public health remained more or less aloof. Some changes were occurring, however. The Medical Care section of the American Public Health Association began to make heretical assertions that the public sector generally, and public health particularly, had an obligation to provide medical services, especially where they would not otherwise be available. Some local health departments, under local leadership and within the framework of their communities' traditions, began to do just that. It was scarcely a movement and did not influence the general theory about the proper role of public health, but a growing number of people, generally poor people with limited access, began to obtain needed medical services through the programs of their local health departments. Although legislative bodies at the state level, organized medicine, and the official public health establishment did not feel this was appropriate, most citizens assumed that their health department was supposed to provide medical care when it was needed to those who could not pay for it on their own. In some communities, health departments could and did. In others, citizens were surprised to find that the local health department did not do such things and began to turn elsewhere for leadership or provide it themselves.

As the country approached the 1960s, the inequities of the system were increasingly apparent, especially as they affected the elderly. The enormous public sector investments in the private practice of medical care had produced a system of enviable quality but one that was excessively expensive and not equally available to all. Moreover, the investments had been almost exclusively in therapeutic care, not in the prevention of disease and injury.

1960 to the present: the public role and the rise of medical entrepreneurialism

The past 30 years have been a period of mixed messages and frustration. The nation abandoned its war on poverty, won its race for the moon, failed in the war in Vietnam, and survived a major presidential challenge to its Constitution. Most of all, it was a period of shortages. At times Americans ran out of gas, toilet paper, wheat, beef, oil, optimism, tolerance, and prosperity. It was a time of intractable budget problems and a growing realization that not all of the nation's problems could be solved: we would have to choose. Most of the people of other nations had already come to that realization or never thought otherwise.

In 1960, afraid of more radical legislation, Congress passed and President Eisenhower signed the Kerr-Mills bill, which made grants to states that wished to establish a welfare-based health insurance system for the elderly poor. It was a weak bill, which would have helped very few of the elderly. The AMA did not oppose it, preferring this small intrusion to some of the more formidable bills that had been introduced. It soon became evident that the new law would accomplish very little, and the next President, Kennedy, let it be known that stronger, more effective legislation would be high on his list of things to do. The AMA filled its war chest with dollars once again, but the new legislation received unprecedented support from such groups as the National Council of Churches, the YWCA, the American Nurses' Association, the American Hospital Association, and the American Public Health Association. Several groups of physicians disassociated themselves from the AMA position to support better programs for the elderly. A gigantic rally was held in Madison Square Garden, and the testimony of elderly people who had been forced into penury by illness was witnessed on the television sets of every home.

After the assassination of President Kennedy, President Johnson made a strong plea to Congress to pass the new legislation promptly. Senator Clinton Anderson (Democrat, New Mexico) introduced Senate Bill Number One and Representative Cecil King (Democrat, California) the identical House Bill Number One on opening day. Several other bills were introduced. The AMA attempted to torpedo the process by pointing out that the bills would do little to solve the problems: they would help only the aged, not the poor generally, and they would not pay for outpatient care. To the surprise of everyone, Congressman Wilbur Mills (Democrat, Arkansas), Chairman of the House Ways and Means Committee, accepted the AMA's critique and resolved the problem by creating what he called his "three layer cake." (The Ways and Means Committee controlled the bill, because it proposed to use a tax on payrolls to finance the care, and new taxes were the responsibility of that committee.) Working with Wilbur Cohen, the Secretary of Health, Education and Welfare, Mills and his staff incorporated (1) hospital insurance for the elderly from the King-Anderson bill with (2) an outpatient insurance program, to form the new Medicare program and (3) a state-managed Medicaid program for the poor. Medicare became Title XVIII of the Social Security Act and Medicaid Title XIX. They were and are quite different.

Medicare is a mandatory insurance program for people over the age of 65, managed by the Health Care Financing Administration of the U.S. Department of Health and Human Services. Medicaid is a welfare program managed by the states. Medicare is an entitlement program: that is, people are entitled to its benefits by virtue of becoming 65 years old. People are not entitled to Medicaid, a welfare program that is "means-tested." People who are poor apply to the state or local Medicaid agency (usually the public welfare program) and must prove that they are eligible by meeting two tests: categorical and income. The categories are the blind, the totally and permanently disabled, certain families with dependent children, and those elderly who are too poor to pay the out-of-pocket obligations of the Medicare program. In addition to being in one of the four categories, applicants must also show that their total assets, both money and property, are scant enough to make them poor.

The Medicaid threshold level is set by each state, usually at some fraction of the federally established poverty level, in some states as low as 20% of that level. Eligibility for Medicaid is usually determined when someone is sick or injured and needs medical care, and eligibility lasts only so long as both categorical and income standards are met. There are 50 different Medicaid programs, with different standards and different services. Each participating state is required to provide the basic services of inpatient and outpatient care, but many other services are optional. States can, if they wish, broaden their Medicaid programs to include the medically needy (also known as the medically indigent) in addition to those who are categorically eligible.

Medical indigency means that the individual does not fit one of the categories, or may have more money than is allowed, but is judged too poor to be able to pay for needed medical care. In a literal sense, this category is now quite large. A serious illness or injury is beyond the means of millions of Americans who have no or inadequate insurance. In 1987, during one of the most conservative administrations in decades, Congress broadened the Medicaid program to allow the states to include pregnant women and their children who had assets considerably in excess of the standard for welfare generally: up to 185% of poverty, or $20,726 for a family of four. These were fundamental changes in the tradition of publicly supported medical care in the United States: they recognized that people who were not eligible for welfare could still be medically needy. This severed the provision of public medical care from its traditional link to welfare.

Both Medicare and Medicaid are vendor payment programs: the administering agency pays a set fee to eligible providers (physicians and hospitals, for example) for the services they provide to eligible beneficiaries. In the Medicaid program, providers usually cannot charge the patient an additional fee. In recent years, in an attempt to curb the growth in Medicaid spending, Congress has allowed states to use co-payments as a method of deterring what some perceive to be frivolous usage of medical care. Co-payments are one form of what has been referred to as out-of-pocket payments, also called cost-sharing, and require the consumer to pay either a fixed amount for each service (a dollar for a prescription, for example) or a percentage of the cost. The other form of cost-sharing is the deductible, which requires the beneficiary to pay all of the costs of medical care up to some amount ($100 or $200 per person, for example) after which the insurance program comes into effect and pays all or some proportion of costs above that amount. Both co-payments and deductibles are used by private insurance companies to reduce their costs, but deductibles are not allowed in the Medicaid program. It would not make sense: raising the income threshold for eligibility would accomplish the same thing.

The Medicare program has two parts: Part A, or Hospital Insurance, and Part B or Supplemental Medical Insurance. They are virtually identical to the original Blue Cross and Blue Shield programs. Part A pays hospital bills, and Part B pays doctor bills and other related costs. All people are automatically enrolled in the Medicare Part A program when they reach age 65. Part B is voluntary: those who reach 65 are invited to pay a monthly premium, which entitles them to coverage. Both deductibles and co-payments are used in the Medicare program. (There are a few other special groups that have been made eligible for the Medicare program: people with chronic progressive kidney disease and younger people who are disabled and entitled to Social Security payments. These groups will not be discussed further in this chapter.) The co-payment provisions are complicated and costly to Medicare beneficiaries.* States can use Medicaid funds to pay the Part B premium costs, deductibles, and co-insurance for low-income elderly people. These are called "cross-overs."

The Medicare program is paid for in three ways. Part A, hospital insurance, is financed by a payroll tax on employment, which goes into a hospital trust fund. Part B is paid for by premiums and federal general fund taxes. Nearly three quarters of the Part B program is now paid for with federal tax funds. The Medicaid program is financed almost entirely by taxes. The federal share varies from state to state, reflecting differences in per capita income in the states, ranging from a high of 83% to a low of 50%. Several states require local governments to contribute to the state's Medicaid program. The states' share is now quite large and has become a major budget problem in all states.

As noted above, the Medicare program uses co-payment requirements in the same way that private insurance companies use them: to deter utilization and to decrease the cost to the program. Physicians can be paid by "assignment" or they can charge the patient directly. If they accept assignment, they cannot bill the patient but agree to accept the current Medicare fee for their area of the country as payment in full. If they refuse assignment, they can charge the patient whatever they choose. The patient must then pay the bill personally and seek indemnification from Medicare. Since Medicare fees are less than the fees charged by some physicians, many will not accept assignment. Congress has encouraged physicians to accept assignment, and some states have begun to require that they do so. The Medicaid program does not recognize nonassignment: providers are paid directly by the program, reflecting a lack of trust in welfare recipients to manage their own affairs. The key provisions of the two programs are summarized in Table 31-8.

The Medicare and Medicaid programs caused some important changes in the medical care system in the United States. They clearly accomplished what they set out to accomplish: access to needed medical care was improved for many poor and elderly people. They also poured an enormous amount of money into a system that had no built-in controls to curb its growth, which resulted in rapid and destructive inflation in the price of medical care. Finally, the two programs made the provision of medical care a very attractive business investment, converting it from a practice based in professionalism to one driven by market forces and the exuberance of entrepreneurialism.

Access

Many poor people still have limited access to medical care. Their access is impeded by their lack of buying power in the medical care marketplace, by geography (in rural areas and the inner city, good medical care is hard to find), and by discrim-

* For current information on benefit periods, co-payments, and deductibles, call the local Social Security Administration. As of 1988, the deductible, which is supposed to be equivalent to the current cost of a single day's stay in a hospital, was $525. For each benefit period, the first 60 days of hospital care were covered by the program with no additional cost to the beneficiary; the next 30 days were covered with a co-insurance requirement equal to one fourth of the deductible ($131.25 per day). In addition, each beneficiary has a lifetime reserve of another 60 days, with co-payments equal to half the deductible. The Part B premium was $24.80 per month. There is a $75 deductible for outpatient care, and the program paid 80% of the what were considered to be "reasonable charges." In 1989 the program began to change, as a new catastrophic illness provision was implemented that was intended to "cap" the amount of money Medicare beneficiaries would have to pay in a given year.

inatory practices, which reflect class distinctions between the poor, who are most in need of medical care, and the providers of care, who are generally not poor. The elderly have serious problems too. As the per capita cost of medical care increased from $177 in 1965, when Medicare became law, to $1,744 in 1987, the co-payment requirements for the elderly rose accordingly, resulting in greater out-of-pocket costs for medical care than before the law was passed. Of course, the dollars spent in 1987 were inflated relative to their value in 1965, but out-of-pocket costs could easily exceed $5,000 for an elderly couple with serious health problems.

The disparity in the amount of medical care used by different economic groups had all but disappeared by the 1980s. Roemer[16] showed this nicely in his article about Isidore Falk (Table 31-9). The changes are striking and have been discussed in detail by Yelin, Kramer, and Epstein.[17] Yet this is not the end of the question. Poor people have more health problems and need more medical care than more affluent people do. Is the amount shown enough, too much, or too little? Perhaps more importantly, is it the same sort of medical care made available to higher income people?

The physician contacts of the poor are more likely to occur in hospital emergency rooms and clinics than in private physician offices. That, in and of itself, is not necessarily indicative of lower quality, but given recent cutbacks in the funding for such programs, continuity of care and the appropriate use of referrals and auxiliary services are less likely to occur in such environments. Moreover, although access appears to have equalized numerically, the number of poor children in welfare families with access to a physician decreased during the 10 years from 1973 to 1983, and the children in welfare families are less likely to get well child care or to see the same physician for each visit. They do not get their immunizations at the same place they get the rest of their care, indicating a lack of continuity and consistency in their care.[18] Moreover, although the number of physician visits for different income groups appears to be the same, poor children with health problems actually make fewer visits than nonpoor children with health problems.[19] There is some evidence that implicit rationing takes place when resources are limited and that the decisions made about who will receive care are based in part on attitudes toward the social value of the potential clients, including their ability to pay commercial rather than Medicaid rates.[20] None of these signs of discrimination based on factors other than need and health status should be especially surprising—they reflect the decisions made by human beings—but they do indicate that the Medicaid and Medicare programs cannot solve the problems of inequity, they can only alleviate them.

Inflation

The disturbing increases in the price of medical care were exacerbated by the Medicare and Medicaid programs, which poured billions of dollars into a system that has a seemingly infinite capacity to absorb them. In order to placate hospitals and physicians and encourage their cooperation, the

TABLE 31-8 Key provisions of the Medicare and Medicaid programs in 1988

Feature	Medicare	Medicaid
Law	Title 18 of the Social Security Act	Title 19 of the Social Security Act
Beneficiaries	The elderly	The poor
Concept	Insurance	Welfare
Management	Federal government through regional intermediaries	States (usually the state welfare agency)
Finance	Part A—the Medicare trust fund	Federal and state taxes
	Part B—premiums and taxes	
Eligibility	Age 65 and over	A means test
Features	Co-payments	No deductibles
	Deductibles	Some co-payments
	Assignment or nonassignment	Assignment only
	Basically medical	Some social services
Expenditures (1986)	$76 billion	$41 billion
Beneficiaries (1986)	32 million	22.3 million

new programs offered to pay the hospitals whatever it cost them to provide the care needed, with a little extra to help them replace and improve their facilities. Physicians were promised their "usual and customary" fees. However, physician fees were higher than they needed to be because most physicians did not collect from many of their patients and therefore set their usual and customary fees for patients who could pay higher than they might otherwise have done. The inflated fees enabled them to achieve their income targets by depending solely on those who could pay them. Medicare and Medicaid virtually wiped out the bad debts of physicians and did so at the higher fees, thus making medical practice, for the first time, a truly lucrative profession.

Hospitals had no restraints on the acquisition of new technology, staff, or facilities, since the bills would be paid at "cost-plus." With these features in place, the annual bill for personal health services increased rapidly: 6.9% per year from 1970 to 1975, 9.5% per year from 1975 to 1980, and over 10% in 1981 and 1982.[21] These increases were a result of changing demographics (more elderly people, who use a lot of medical care), increasing intensity of the medical care inputs for a given episode of illness or injury, inflation generally, and inflationary price increases unique to medical care. All of these factors have played a role, and expanded government spending has added fuel to the inflationary fires.

GOVERNMENT AS A PRODUCER

Medicare and Medicaid made government a major purchaser of medical care services. The conclusion reached by Congress in 1965, and ratified in subsequent decisions, was that medical care in the United States was just fine. It was of high quality and generally available. The problem was, as Congress and others saw it, that some people lacked the means to participate in the market. That might be all right when it came to shoes or television sets or vacation tours, but medical care was deemed necessary, and a lack of market power was harmful to the health of the poor.

The solution was to increase the buying power of the poor and the elderly. Armed with a Medicare card or Medicaid eligibility, they would enter the market, and their expressed (and now financed) demand for medical care would cause the market to respond. Services would be redistributed to match the demand. In part, this happened. Organizations and individuals made a lot of changes to acquire this new market segment. However, market forces are not the only ones that impede access, as has been indicated.

Moreover, insurance (and that is what Medicaid and Medicare are—insurance) cannot solve all of the access problems. All insurance policies have exceptions, and most have co-payment requirements. Not everyone is eligible for Medicaid or Medicare, and many cannot buy private health insurance. At least 23% of the population of the United States (more than 55 million people) are not covered by private health insurance.[22] A simple maxim: some people are uninsured all of the time, and all people are uninsured some of the time. When they are poor, they must turn to the public sector for the services they need.

Historically, local government had the responsibility for the poor who were not "otherwise provided for."* In many towns, a public hospital was erected to meet the needs of the poor, and those hospitals were forbidden to care for the nonpoor. Many public hospitals later became large and important teaching hospitals in the United States, with a long history of service: Philadelphia General, Boston Lying-In, Bellevue in New York,

TABLE 31-9 Medical care and family income, United States, 1928-1931 and 1981

	Income Level	
	Lowest	**Highest**
Physician contacts per person per year		
1928-1931	1.9	4.7
1981	5.6	4.4
Hospital cases per 1,000 people per year		
1928-1931	59.4	98.0
1981	165.1	104.6

From Roemer MI: Am J Public Health 48:979, Aug 1988.

* The language is from the Elizabethan Poor Law of 1601, which declared that the most local government was responsible for the aid and support of those not otherwise provided for. The language was captured in the constitutions of most of the new states of the United States and has been operable in law if not in fact since the founding of the country.

Detroit Receiving Hospital, the Cook County Hospital (Chicago), Denver General, San Francisco General, Los Angeles, and many, many more. With the advent of Medicaid, many people presumed that the public hospitals would be needed no more, and there were moves to close them. However, as Medicaid revenue became available, the public hospitals discovered three phenomena: (1) they too could get paid for the work they did, (2) their costs increased just as rapidly as those in the private sector, since they had to hire their personnel and buy their equipment and supplies in the same markets, and (3) the poor had not been entirely absorbed into mainstream medical care.

In most cities, the public hospital was *not* a part of the local health department. Recall that public hospitals emerged from a welfare history—they began as poor houses for relief. Public health was a police power agency of government, concerned with sanitation and the prevention of communicable diseases. Local public hospitals were usually either free-standing entities or part of the local welfare system. Recall too that Medicare and Medicaid were written by people with a background in Social Security and welfare. Their tendency was to think of transfer payments (transferring money to eligible poor people) and empowering the poor to make their own purchasing decisions. In fact, in the early days of the Medicaid and Medicare programs, public hospitals were considered ineligible to participate in the programs, and local health departments were not expected to bill Medicaid for services provided to eligible beneficiaries.

Despite the generally accepted policy that health departments were not supposed to provide personal medical care services, many did. Health departments in several cities established extensive outpatient treatment programs over the years, and all health departments deliver a large number of personal health care services as part of their other obligations, such as maternal and child health, family planning, chronic disease control, and clinics for sexually transmitted diseases and for tuberculosis. Miller and Moos[23] reviewed the programs of several health departments in the 1970s and concluded that approximately 20 million people received part or all of their care through such systems. (The picture by 1987 had deteriorated significantly, with a decline in federal support and considerable disarray at the state level as responsibility for the medically indigent became a hotly contested issue.[24] Yet even more people had become dependent on their local health department for access to needed medical care.)

Beginning in the 1960s, the federal government began supplying grant funds to new local organizations to develop comprehensive primary care centers. Initially among the Office of Economic Opportunity (OEO) programs, they were later transferred to the Department of Health, Education and Welfare (later renamed the Department of Health and Human Services). The new grant programs helped establish rural and urban health centers in areas that had little or no usable access. As part of President Johnson's Great Society program, the grants went to new, nontraditional, community-based organizations. In most cities and counties they had no official contact with the formal agencies of government and were seen by some elected officials as rival sources of political power. Public health departments generally were not involved, although there were some notable exceptions, as in Denver, Colo., where creative leadership built an extensive network of comprehensive primary care centers linked to Denver General Hospital.

President Nixon returned to the traditional embrace of private practice and reduced the grants, insisting that the new centers needed to learn how to capture payments for the services they delivered, just like other practice systems. As grant income declined, many of the health centers turned to the private sector for advice, consultation, and even management services. The consultants quickly demonstrated to the community boards that they were underutilizing such profitable services as laboratories and X-rays and overutilizing such services as nutrition and social work counseling, which were nonrevenue-producing activities. Many of the centers made the changes indicated, which served their financial interests well but their communities less well.

In more recent years, many of the neighborhood or community health centers have come into closer alignment with more traditional agencies of government, and better support mechanisms have developed. At the state level, associations of primary care centers have been formed, and negotiations with the state Medicaid agencies have resulted in the formation of newer, more flexible, reimbursement models. At the national level, an organization has been formed to work for stronger federal grant support for the centers. A National Health Service Corps was formed in the 1970s, which "drafted" commissioned officers into the United States Public Health Service and assigned them to selected primary care centers: physicians, nurses, social workers, psychologists, and dentists, who worked in subsidized positions providing clinical services. It was a unique experiment, which resulted in a national corps of health professionals providing essential health care services in communities where access was impeded or nonexistent. It was more than nationally sponsored health insurance: it was a national health service in miniature form. Needless to say, as the 1980s unfolded such heretical experiments were all but eliminated. Yet the experience that was obtained was invaluable, and the experiment could be mobilized again rather quickly if the political environment were supportive. The original concept of the comprehensive primary care center has been resurrected in recent years as Community Oriented Primary Care; it contains many of the original features of the OEO programs.

Public provider programs and systems have long been derided in the United States as inferior or second-rate delivery systems. Although there were some excellent public sector medical care programs before the advent of Medicare or Medicaid, many public hospitals and clinics were indeed wretched: shabby, rundown, with rude personnel, and of poor quality. As late as 1968 and 1969, macabre scenes were witnessed on Saturday nights, when seriously mentally ill patients were left in the corridors of public hospitals shackled to makeshift beds awaiting attention. Clinics were grey and dirty, with bare bulbs hanging from the ceilings. Patients were herded into the waiting room en masse, without appointments, and summoned to an examining room over a loudspeaker. Nursing care was often callous and indifferent.

These aspects of public medical care were only partly the result of inadequate budgets: they were equally the result of public attitudes in the United States toward the poor in general, and welfare in particular. Medicare and Medicaid were designed to overcome both problems—access and attitudes. They were intended to "mainstream" the poor; that is, to incorporate them into private medical care as it was enjoyed by others.

Yet public provider systems are not necessarily second-rate, even though they may be for a second class. They have not been the beneficiaries of the large investments characteristic of private sector systems, but they have a record in recent years of providing good care under very difficult circumstances. In a review of the accreditation reports for New York City hospitals, it was found that the public institutions had more recommendations regarding safety procedures that needed attention, but they had fewer recommendations regarding direct medical care services than did voluntary and private hospitals.[25] Costs and charges have been reported to be higher in private hospitals than in not-for-profit facilities,[26] and private sector management contracts intended to improve the efficiency and reduce the costs of public hospitals have accomplished neither.[27] Reviews of the quality of medical and dental care in public programs have found them to be outstanding. At the same time, poor people who gain access to the private sector via Medicaid eligibility have often been badly treated by poorly trained practitioners.

Local government is by now led by people who have no historical sense of the role of local government in providing medical care to the poor. They see the budgets for their public hospitals (those few that still exist) as reflecting losses: "We lost $13 million on the hospital last year." Their predecessors understood those necessary payments to be an investment. To the newer political leader and health department administrator, costs in excess of revenue seem to imply bad management. State legislative bodies view the problem as an insurance failure and, in state after state, are seeking ways to pay for the cost of the care provided to the uninsured.[28] Massachusetts and Washington have launched major new initiatives to insure the poor, and other states will no doubt do the same.[29]

Yet the insurance schemes simply transfer money from the public generally to the provider systems without altering the latter or improving their coordination or changing the configuration of the services provided to better meet the needs of the poor. Mullan[30] has expressed it nicely: "The principal problem underlying the service dilemma is that we have neither a system of universal entitlement that wraps the care of the poor in with the care of the rest of the population, nor an explicit, comprehensive strategy for care for the poor outside of the dominant private system." Attempts to buy the poor into the private system by increasing the payment schedules simply drive prices up for everyone, without solving the access problems of the poor.

One state, Florida, has tried a slightly different approach, using a hospital tax to create an indigent care fund and providing grants to local public health departments to serve as the primary care providers in their area.[31] In general, however, access problems for the poor became more severe during the 1980s, with little evidence that creative new solutions were being considered. Medical care, unlike education and welfare, is still considered to be a private matter, with government acting to manipulate the market for those who cannot otherwise gain access. The experience has been devastatingly expensive and, on the whole, quite unsatisfactory.

THE REGULATION OF MEDICAL CARE

Both state and federal governments are involved in attempts to regulate the quality, the distribution, and the cost of medical care. The Medicaid and Medicare programs represent one approach to regulation: structural regulation to alter the distribution of services. Since the unregulated market forces of the medical care system deprived many people of needed access, the federal government decided to manipulate those market forces by increasing the purchasing power of certain categories of needy people. In order to implement the programs, government also used command regulations, which affect the costs of the services purchased and their quality. There are many other approaches to the regulation of medical care.

Quality

Government can try to assure that medical care is of high quality by determining who can and cannot provide services, by reviewing their performance, and by setting standards for institutions.

Access to the practice of a trade or a profession is usually mediated by the issuance of a license. The basis for a license lies in a finding that the practice in question is potentially dangerous if not carried out by someone who is qualified. The state outlaws the practice by statute and then allows certain people to do what is otherwise forbidden based on a demonstration of their competence. Physicians must be licensed to practice in every state, and the same is true of nurses and dentists, but there are more than 100 other health care professionals and technicians who are licensed by one state or another, ranging from medical social workers and psychologists through nursing home administrators and people who remove unsightly hair.

Certification is a voluntary form of competence recognition. People who practice a particular specialty may form a private association, which can set standards for educational preparation and practice and offer to certify those who can meet those standards. Most medical specialty practice is certified, not licensed. People who are not certified by a private organization cannot be prohibited from the practice, provided they have a state license to practice, but they cannot call themselves by certain titles. (In practice, hospital boards may refuse to grant the privileges of practice to those who are not certified members of a recognized medical specialty group, such as heart surgeons, thus effectively denying them the right to practice that medical specialty in that community.)

A third form of personal regulation is registration, which is offered by the government, usually a state, as evidence that the registered individual has met certain standards. Registration simply places the individual on the registry; it does not restrict others from engaging in the registered practice provided they can get a job or find clients. They may not, however, call themselves a "registered sanitarian" or whatever. Some health departments add economic force to the registration process by including registration as one of the minimum qualifications in a job description.

All three forms of personal regulation have been established by professional groups, not by the public—there has never been a popular outcry to license health professionals—and the results of these practices are mixed. At times they can be said to have raised the standards of practice, but generally they can be better understood as economic regulators, keeping access to the market restricted. Most licensing, certifying, and registering boards are governed by those who form them—the practitioners. Since there is real economic value attached to being licensed, courts have treated a license as property rather than as a privilege to be granted by the state, and it has proven difficult for a licensing board to revoke such a license or to exercise other sanctions against those who appear to affront the standards of practice. Much of this difficulty stems from the traditional and highly informal practices of the past. Legislative reform can improve licensing mechanisms and turn them into true consumer protection programs, as has happened in California. Generally speaking, however, once licensed, there has been no automatic review or attempt to reevaluate the continued competence of the licentiate. Disciplinary actions tend to be infrequent and mostly for drug abuse.

The states have not been happy with either the processes or the results of licensure programs. For many years it seemed a harmless way to grant political favors to a well-meaning group. Since all they wanted was their own licensure board, which would be entirely supported by the fees paid for the license, what harm could it do? Plenty, as it turned out. Access to the practice could be restricted, at times whimsically, and in the past because of racial discrimination. Orthodoxy could be compelled by accepting only certain schools of thought as appropriate to establish eligibility for licensure. In some states a restricted license was granted to graduates of certain foreign medical schools, and the holders of such licenses were treated as the indentured servants of physicians with an unrestricted license. Others were confined to state psychiatric hospitals from which they could not expect to extract themselves since they were not given sufficient time to study for the regular licensure examination. Perhaps the epitome of misuse of the state's power to license professions is the ancient practice of licensing barbers and beauticians. At one time they were practitioners of medicine, but in recent years little real hazard has been involved in haircutting and styling. Yet the licensure programs continue, asking arcane questions and usually paying more attention to the competence of the examinees as stylists than to their potential as health hazards.

Licensure has helped third-party payor organizations such as Blue Shield and Medicaid. Were it not for licensure, such programs would have to find some way of determining which providers could be paid for services rendered to an insured beneficiary. People might receive medical advice from a brother-in-law and send a bill to the insurance company, or consult a social worker about a behavioral disorder. By accepting only the bills of specified, licensed professionals in certain categories, insurance companies limit their exposure to claims.

Governments have also attempted to regulate professional performance. There are four mechanisms for performance evaluation:

1. Utilization review, which is concerned with the appropriate use of available facilities and services
2. Medical audit of the quality of care received by patients, usually accomplished by a review of the medical record
3. Claims review to evaluate the apparent appropriateness of services before approving that a bill be paid
4. Professional standards review organizations

The latter are made up of professionals in the field of practice, with occasional public interest representation. Required by Congress for a period of time to protect public investments in Medicare and Medicaid, these organizations were generally expensive and ineffective. Most of the current efforts, although evincing a concern for quality, have been designed to save money, by disallowing certain services or practices or denying payment for unnecessary services. To some extent they have been successful in this cost-saving endeavor, but they are not inexpensive, and they have not had a clearly demonstrable effect on quality.

Attempts to regulate the quality of health care institutions have taken the form of accreditation, certification, and licensure. Accreditation is a voluntary program by a private organization. The dominant entity in the United States is the Joint Commission on Accreditation of Health Care Organizations, which was formed by the American College of Surgeons in conjunction with other medical specialty groups and the American Hospital Association. In recent years, the Joint Commission has expanded its purview to include community mental health centers and other more complex provider organizations. The Commission's work involves on-site review of institutions, procedures, and facilities in comparison to standards established by the Commission. Loss of accreditation is not only an embarrassment but financially disastrous: Medicare, Medicaid, and some private insurance organizations automatically accept accreditation as "deemed status": that is, any hospital that is accredited is deemed to meet the standards of the program for payment. It is difficult to become an eligible provider without accreditation.

Certification is similar to the practice described above for individuals and carries somewhat the same import. Nursing homes, for instance, must be licensed by the state to do business. Beyond that, they can apply (in this case to a state agency) to become certified as eligible providers of Medicare or Medicaid services. To be certified, the nursing home must first be licensed. Lack or loss of certification would not prevent the home from operating but would prevent it from receiving funds from Medicaid, which is the most important payor of nursing home bills.

Public health is intimately involved in licensure and certification programs. At the state level, most institutional licensure programs are managed by the health agency. In some states, the health agency also manages the personal licensure programs. In those states where the welfare agency manages the Medicaid program (which is the case in most states), that agency often contracts with the health agency to carry out certification inspections on nursing homes and other facilities. In addition, the facilities licensure agency may have a separate contract with the federal Medicare agency to certify nursing homes for participation in that program. These two certification programs and the state licensure programs should, of course, be closely coordinated and managed. In many states, licensure standards are more rigorous than the federal certification standards, making such coordination both difficult and expensive.

The distributional role

As noted earlier, government can attempt to regulate the distribution of medical care resources through its role as a consumer of services. In addition, it can attempt to use command regulations to affect distribution. For example, states and local governments can affect the distribution of health care services by their choice of location for health departments, primary care centers, community mental health centers, and public hospitals and clinics. They can also attempt to influence distribution by what have been referred to as "certificates of need" (see Chapter 11). Providers who wished to make major new investments in programs or facilities after 1966 had to make their case to one of the health planning bodies. By 1974 they had to demonstrate (1) that the community needed the service, (2) that they knew how to manage the program and had the resources to do so, and (3) that the proposal was the best of the available choices for that service. At times the review panels used their authority to force locational and service changes.

Distribution can also be influenced more indirectly through other structural regulations, such as differential reimbursement rates for rural or inner city hospitals. States could, if they chose to do so, increase Medicaid payments for primary care physicians and decrease them for medical and surgical specialties. The concept has been discussed for years but has been attempted only hesitantly to date.

Finally, the federal government has attempted to affect distribution by means of the National Health Service Corps. Physicians, nurses, and other health care providers could enter the Corps, be assigned to an underserved area, and have their salary subsidized or guaranteed by the federal government. Some states have considered developing similar programs. At times, political and public health leaders have considered requiring a certain number of years of service in underserved areas as a condition of receiving tax subsidies for professional education, but no major programs have been implemented.

Cost regulation

Government programs to control the cost of medical care have been no more successful than other attempts to modify the effect of market forces on the large and well-endowed medical care system in the United States. The open-ended provisions of the Medicare and Medicaid programs have long since ceased, but to little avail. Providers have found ways to "unbundle" and separately bill what were once general office services, and to include additional procedures that have the effect of keeping total payments high. In one general hospital (part of a health department managed by the author), physicians were paid using a Relative Value Schedule, which assigned one unit to the simplest procedure and multiples of that to more complicated procedures. The contract called for physicians to receive $6 per unit of service. Because of budget problems, the $6 rate was frozen for a 3-year period. During that time, the number of patients seen in the hospital's clinics did not increase, but the average number of units of service billed by the physicians per patient visit increased from 4 to 5.2, which effectively increased physician income 19% over the period! If Medicaid reimbursement rates lag too far behind private fees, physicians decline to see Medicaid patients. If the fees are raised, the result is often a similar across-the-board increase in fees charged to non-Medicaid patients and a restitution of the gap between private and Medicaid patients in the ensuing 6 months.

In 1983 Congress finally adopted a prospective payment system for Medicare services provided by hospitals. A prospective payment system categorizes medical conditions ahead of time and offers to pay a set amount for, say, a gallbladder operation or a heart attack, regardless of how much time and how many services the hospital may use in treating the condition. Efficient hospitals can profit from such a scheme, while less efficient institutions will presumably have to become more efficient or close. Called diagnosis related groups, or DRGs, the system uses 467 categories and was phased in over a 4-year period. It did not affect physician payments initially, but many people have proposed that it be expanded to be an all-inclusive rate, to be administered or apportioned by either the hospital or the physician. The scenario is a strange one for Americans. Imagine a physician with authorization to spend $5,400 on treating a patient's gallbladder disease calling each community hospital looking for the best deal, both for the patient and the physician.

The major intervention by government to control the cost of medical care has been the fervent attempt to introduce competition into the system. President Nixon asked the 93rd Congress for the new Health Maintenance Organization (HMO) Act, which was intended to force competition between provider organizations for the medical business of employers. An HMO sells a package for a fixed amount for the year and is supposed to provide all necessary services, usually with no additional charges. This is supposed to provide an incentive for the organization to keep its costs down and to keep its clients healthy. Considerable competition has ensued, but it has not resulted in widespread cost-cutting, nor has it reduced the rate of inflation in medical care to that of the rest of the economy. In general, well-organized HMOs are thought to be an improvement in the organization and management of medical care, however.

The results of the various cost-regulating schemes to date have been disappointing, for both individuals and government. Medical and related prices have continued to increase much faster than income or tax receipts, thus eroding the ability of individuals, families, and governments to make other investments. Access to care for low-income people has decreased,[32] the number of people who are medically indigent has grown rapidly,[2,22] and employer-sponsored health insurance plans have decreased their coverage and insisted on greater out-of-pocket payments by the beneficiaries.[3] No matter what regulatory steps have been proposed and implemented, prices keep going up and access and dissatisfaction increase. The measures taken can best be described as tinkering with a market-based private system that cannot achieve the twin goals of equity and affordability. The last 30 years of rule-making have been a substitute for recognizing that the original choice was wrong: if the public is to be protected, there will have to be public provider systems, to serve as the ultimate safety net if for no other purpose. The job of public health, which is better attuned to organizing a provider system than it is to managing a vendor payment system, is to see to it that the second system is not a second-rate system.

EMERGENCY SERVICES

One of the most visible components of medical care is emergency care. In most states and local communities, the governmental presence in health has an obligation to assure the existence and effective functioning of an emergency response system. This has become increasingly difficult in recent years as prices have gone up, liability insurance has become more of a problem, and increasing numbers of emergency patients have had little or no insurance coverage.

The technology of emergency medical care has advanced enormously over the past 30 years, and its effectiveness has increased concomitantly. With that rising technology, however, has come the realization that not all hospitals can provide adequate emergency services. In many rural and inner city areas, access to emergency medical care has diminished, just as the quality of care that is technically available has improved. Part of the problem is organization and coordination, another part is training, and the third is payment. Public health is involved in the first two.

A system of emergency medical services is an organized procedure for receiving and acting on requests for assistance when there is a likelihood of trauma requiring rapid medical attention or an illness that poses conditions threatening to life or requiring immediate resuscitation to sustain life. It usually includes a communication system to receive requests, a defined procedure for acting on those requests, including centralized control of the dispatching of ambulances, and the availability of an appropriately staffed transport system with the capacity for immediate on-site treatment and in-transit life support. There must also be 24-hour, 7-day emergency care centers equipped to receive patients from within a defined area and staffed with appropriately trained people. Usually such centers are part of a large, tertiary care hospital.

Criteria and standards have been developed for all the components of an emergency medical care system.[33] These include the following:

An adequate statutory base

- Assignment of responsibility and specification of qualifications
- Establishment of systems to supervise and coordinate local systems
- Authorization of necessary communication systems

Ambulances

- Specifications
- Equipment
- Training of personnel

Personnel

- Qualifications and training
- Relationships (emergency medical technicians and physician roles, for example)

Hospital facilities

- Planning
- Categorization into levels of care
- Training and qualifications
- Role as supervisors of medical care in the system
- Role as an ambulance operator

Communications

- Authorization of a 911 system
- Provision for centralized control and dispatching of ambulances
- Establishment of environmentally secure communication systems

Local health departments should take the lead in planning for regional service systems, often in conjunction with law enforcement, fire safety, and state agency personnel. Often such systems are governed by local government but rely on private businesses to provide the services by means of a franchise.

THE FUTURE

Attitudes toward medical care in the United States are ambivalent. On the one hand, it is thought to be the best care available; on the other hand, it is not available to all. On the one hand, government expenditures for medical care, while large, are less per capita than they are in many other countries; on the other hand, the opportunity cost of medical care in the United States is higher than anywhere else in the world. On the one hand, many people do not get enough care; on the other hand, too much medical care is frivolously dispensed to deal with trivial and self-limiting illnesses and injuries, creating its own sort of problems. On the one hand, public health agencies have had little to do with the development of the medical care system in the United States; on the other hand, they should have and must.

Public health agencies are major providers of medical care, both categorical (maternal and child health, immunizations, treatment of sexually transmitted diseases, family planning, and treatment of high blood pressure, as examples) and general primary care. They are also involved intimately at the state and national levels in attempts to regulate the cost, quality, and distribution of medical care. Public health's involvement is mainly as a provider or as a regulator, not as a consumer or purchaser of care. That is contrary to the chosen modes of overcoming problems of medical care over the past 30 years, yet given the government's lack of success in market manipulating, it seems timely for public health to become more involved.

For many years, public health professionals have debated whether they should do so. It has been said, often and by many, that public health should stick to its prevention mission; that the provision of medical care to the poor is such a gargantuan and expensive task that the other more important purposes of public health would be submerged under the burden of hospitals and bills and ever-rising costs. It has been claimed, with considerable pungency, that when government found it necessary to cut its budgets, the less visible preventive efforts of public health would give way before the more dramatic but less valuable heroics of emergency rooms and transplants. Warren and Sydenstricker[34] said it many years ago: with the costs of medical care rising into the "millions of dollars annually" [sic], it was unlikely that legislative bodies would continue to support public health and other disease prevention activities. Others have said it more recently.[35,36] Yet public health cannot stand aloof from the problems of medical care for three reasons:

1. The public does not expect it to. If public health persists in telling the community that, despite its name, it does not provide health services to those who need them and have nowhere else to go, the public will invent some other agency to do so and abandon its health department.
2. Congress and state legislative bodies will not find it acceptable to fund the preventive programs of public health when they are inundated with the expense of public medical care and get no help from public health in solving that problem.
3. Public health has a population-based approach to identifying health problems and solving them, which is not characteristic of the private sector (or of social welfare programs) and which is absolutely essential to the development and implementation of effective and efficient public medical care programs. Market forces result in a distribution of services that has little relationship to the public's good or its needs.

Epidemiology drives public health's analysis of problems and its solutions: what are the important problems, and what are the most expeditious ways of solving them? The private medical care system identifies problems by their price tag, and its only solution is to use medical care, which is almost always expensive and sometimes the wrong solution for the real problem. Public health's emphasis on results rather than methods is needed if "Health for All," the World Health Organization's goal for the year 2000, is to be attained in the United States by the year 2100.

REFERENCES

1. Wolfe B and Gabay M: Health status and medical expenditures: more evidence of a link, Soc Sci Med 25:883, 1987.
2. Enthoven A and Kronick R: A consumer-choice health plan for the 1990's: universal health insurance in a system designed to promote quality and economy, New Engl J Med 320:29, Jan 5, 1989.
3. Employees are paying more for health benefits, National Center for Health Services Research, Research Activities, No 111, Nov 1988.
4. Bigelow HJ: Boston Med and Surg J 35:309, 1846.
5. Snow J: On the pathology and mode of communication of cholera, The London Medical Gazette 9:730, 1849.
6. Lister J: On the antiseptic principle in the practice of surgery, Lancet 2:353, 1967.
7. Koprowski H and Plotkin SA, editors: World's debt to Pasteur: proceedings of a centennial symposium commemorating the first rabies vaccination, held at the Children's Hospital of Philadelphia, Jan 17-18, 1985, New York, 1985, AR Liss.
8. Rather LJ, editor: Collected essays on public health and epidemiology by Rudolf Virchow, Canton, MA, 1985, Science History Publications.
9. Koch R: Berliner Klinische Wochenschrifte 19:221, 1882.
10. Osler W: Quoted in Ravenal MP, editor: Foreword to A half century of public health, New York, 1921, American Public Health Association.
11. Behneman HMF: Leaves from a doctor's notebook of seventy years ago, Milit Surgeon 86:547, June 1940.
12. Flexner A: Medical education in the United States and Canada, New York, 1910, Carnegie Foundation.
13. Corning PA: The evolution of medicare, Res Rep No 29, Washington, DC, 1969, US Department of Health, Education and Welfare.
14. Editorial, J Am Med Assoc 99:1952, Dec 3, 1932.
15. Falk IS: The committee on the costs of medical care—25 years of progress, Am J Public Health 48:979, Aug 1958.
16. Roemer MI: IS Falk, the Committee on the Cost of Medical Care and the drive for national health insurance, Am J Public Health 75:841, Aug 1985.
17. Yelin EH, Kramer JS, and Epstein WV: Is health care use equivalent across social groups? a diagnosis based on study, Am J Public Health 73:563, May 1983.
18. Levey LA, McDowell NM, and Levey S: Health care of poverty and nonpoverty children in Iowa, Am J Public Health 76:1000, Aug 1986.
19. Newacheck PW and Starfield B: Morbidity and use of ambulatory care services among poor and non-poor children, Am J Public Health 78:927, Aug 1988.
20. Kilner JF: Selecting patients when resources are limited: a study of United States medical directors of kidney dialysis and transplantation facilities, Am J Public Health 78:144, Feb 1988.
21. Health Care Financing Administration: National health expenditures, 1986-2000, Health Care Financing Rev 8:1, Summer 1987.
22. Ries P: Health care coverage by age, sex, race, and family income: United States, 1986, NCHS Advance Data, No 139, Sept 19, 1987.

23. Miller CA and Moos M-K: Local health departments: fifteen case studies, Chapel Hill, NC, 1981, American Public Health Association.
24. Brooks EF and Miller CA: Recent changes in selected local health departments: implications for their capacity to guarantee basic medical services, Am J Prev Med 3:134, May-June 1987.
25. Hyman HH: Are public hospitals in New York City inferior to voluntary, non-profit hospitals? a study of JCAH hospital surveys, Am J Public Health 76:18, Jan 1986.
26. Pattison RV and Katz HM: Investor owned and not-for-profit hospitals, N Engl J Med 309:47, Aug 1983.
27. Shonick W and Roemer R: Private management of public hospitals: the California experience, J Public Health Policy 3:182, June 1982.
28. Uninsured, indigent care initiatives gain momentum, State Health Notes, Number 81, April 1988, The Intergovernmental Health Policy Project.
29. Washington enacts landmark health law, State Health Notes, Number 74, June 1987, Intergovernmental Health Policy Project.
30. Mullan F: Poor people, poor policy, Health Aff 6:113, Spring 1987.
31. Florida's health care access act: radical steps in a conservative state, Intergovernmental Health Policy Project Focus on . . . , Number 10, July 1986, Washington, DC.
32. David K: Changes in Medicaid and eligibility—more poor people, The Blue Sheet, July 20, 1983.
33. US Department of Health, Education and Welfare: Recommended standards for development of emergency medical services systems, DEHS Pub No 4, Rockville, MD, 1971.
34. Warren BS and Sydenstricker E: Health insurance, the medical profession and public health, Public Health Rep 34:775, April 18, 1919.
35. Hanlon JJ: Is there a future for health departments? Health Services Report 88:898, 1973.
36. Sencer DJ: Major urban health departments: the ideal and the real, Health Aff 2:88, Winter 1983.

PART NINE

The future of public health

The future is shaped by the present. Unfortunately we are not prescient enough to know which of all the seemingly important and trivial events of the present will influence the future. Trends can be examined, but they lend themselves to the forecasting of several scenarios, not just one, and it is impossible to know which unanticipated event or new and forceful personality will emerge to reshape the trend and alter the timing, if not the outcome. In the 1960s it was widely believed that some form of national health insurance was "just around the corner." The design of the Medicare and Medicaid programs can be understood only if the student (and present policymaker) understands that the designers felt they were following an incremental path and that the next steps would follow swiftly. They did not. President Johnson became enmeshed in the Vietnam War, national priorities were shifting rapidly, the reality of resource limitations began to unfold, and a new, more conservative President replaced the man who had been elected to the office in a landslide. The 1960s passed into the 1970s and a strikingly different national agenda. Another example: As recently as the 1970s, some writers spoke of the end of the era of communicable diseases and the need to focus on chronic diseases. Then an obscure virus in Africa, now known as HIV or human immunodeficiency virus, underwent a genetic mutation and within a few years had dramatically altered the research and service priorities of public health in the United States.

Forecasting a future for public health is like betting on a horse race. In a field of seven horses, one may have an 18% chance of winning, another a 17% chance, a third a 15% chance, and the remaining five each have 1 chance in 10 of crossing the finish line first. If you could know that, and if you were a cool, calculating, unemotional bettor, you would place your money on the horse with the 18% probability. But a good biostatistician, although perhaps not a good bookie, would tell you that (1) you had made the correct choice, but (2) there is an 82% probability that you will lose!

Many speeches, chapters, and papers have had the title "The Future of Public Health." In 1988 the Institute of Medicine[1] published a book with that name. The scenario that emerges depends on the focus of the observers. Some have talked about the future of health departments.[2-4] The Institute of Medicine report emphasized that this was not its focus: it dealt with public health as a public enterprise of considerable value rather than as an organizational entity. It would also be appropriate to focus on the future of the public's health—how dependent or independent will we be in the twenty-first century? How long can be expect to live? How well? All three questions have been addressed in the chapters of this book. This final part will not attempt to summarize that work, but to draw from it and to contemplate what may happen in the next 10 years.

THE PURPOSE OF PUBLIC HEALTH—PREVENTION

The purpose of public health is to prevent the dependency that would otherwise result from disease or injury (see Chapter 1). Many other organizations, public and private, play a role in attaining that goal: the educational system, highway departments, voluntary health associations, and private health care practitioners. For most organizations and people, the prevention of dependency is a secondary purpose, however. For public health, it is central. Public health agencies are responsible for occasional programs that do not have the prevention of something as their purpose (such as the collection and maintenance, as distinct from the analysis of, birth and death certificates), but virtually all of the resources, laws, and practices of public health are the result of a deliberate social decision to allocate and organize certain resources to prevent disease, death, disability, and dependency. Prevention is not the exclusive domain of public health, nor can public health be successful in its primary mission without the resources of other segments of the public and private sector. It is like education in being an important public good and public enterprise: the public education system has the primary mission, but other agencies play a crucial role, and the educational system cannot accomplish the complete task by itself. Like education also, public health is a complex task, and its complexity has a great deal to do with its future.

Historically, most great enterprises have been identified with a dominant method, discipline, or input. Teaching depends on teachers, war on soldiers, the church on ministers, and the highway department on engineers. Others play a role, of course: cooks and bus drivers in the schools, scientists and politicians in war, the laity in the church, and accountants in the highway department. Nevertheless, the driving force, the skill or discipline that dominates the process, is clear and well understood. This is true of organizations too: associations of physicians or nurses or farmers or lawyers derive their cohesion and therefore their power from the commonality of their basic discipline, their shared experiences, the common values of the profession. Much of the professional training process is devoted to the socialization of new professionals to the norms of the group, and an elaborate code of conduct is often an important part of the process.

Not so with public health. At the core of public health stands epidemiology, that unique way of looking at problems in their social context, but beyond the core unfolds an almost endless variety of disciplines, skills, and interests. In Chapter 1, the purpose of prevention was divided into its primary, secondary, and tertiary modes (see also Chapter 5). Although the dependency that may result from disease or injury is the target, its prevention may best be accomplished by eliminating the hazard altogether or by protecting the individual or the community from contact with the hazard. This may be done by altering environmental forces, modifying individual or group behavior, immunizing susceptible people, or organizing the resources of the community to respond to the hazard when it occurs. For any given problem, the essential skills needed may be legal, medical, psychological, political, social, biochemical, or administrative. The purpose of public health is defined by its intended outcome, not the discipline of its practitioners. This is unique. When physicians encounter a health problem, they treat it as a medical problem, not a social or environmental or educational problem. When lawyers encounter a health problem, they see it as a legal problem, not a behavioral disorder or environmental problem. Engineers respond to engineering problems, teachers to educational problems. When public health is confronted with a health problem, it first tries to understand the cause of the problem and its natural history, then to apply the intervention that is most effective and acceptable. Public health is not dependent on any one methodology, and therefore it is not dependent on any one discipline.

If a health problem does not yield to a biological solution or a medical practice, it is a health problem nonetheless. Public health lacks the comfortable cohesion that stems from a common discipline, but it has the advantage of an incredible array of skills. Public health is not inclined to approach a health problem with a single, monolithic method but with an eclectic array of skills and a pragmatism tempered by its basic ethic of social justice. Alone among major public enterprises, public health obtains its cohesion from its focus on outcomes, not its inputs, and thus is able to seek the optimal solution rather than draw from a narrow, disciplinary base.

Consider some examples. A highway department is centered around its engineering background and the automobile. Transportation problems are seen as engineering tasks, when social planning for the development of housing and business zones might have a greater influence on some of the problems. Crime problems are seen as matters for law enforcement, not welfare or education. Public health, however, examined the problem of dental caries and determined that an engineering solution would work; it examined the problem of developmental disabilities and found that requiring the immunization of children against German measles would be useful; it examined the problem of syphilis and determined that a medical intervention would work; it examined the problem of automobile crash deaths and determined that a legal solution and product design would be more effective than driver education; it examined the problem of AIDS and found that education was the only feasible intervention in the initial phases of the epidemic.

Having decided what will work best, public health may find that it does not have the resources needed to implement the intervention, but the fact that an in-house skill or resource is not the best approach does not end public health's involvement with the problem. A health problem that will not yield to medicine or surgery is still a health problem. AIDS cannot be dealt with without the involvement of the state Medicaid agency (to pay for drugs and medical treatment), the mental health authority (AIDS patients are faced with severe psychological problems), and the educational system (because children as well as adults must learn the facts about AIDS). The infant mortality problem cannot be solved without an equally diverse reliance on most of the same agencies. Hazardous waste problems require the effective collaboration of public health, environmental protection agencies, and law enforcement. Some agency representing the public's interest must organize those resources.

The governmental presence in health

There was a time when public health could draw upon its own resources to solve the problems assigned to it by society. Before the middle of the nineteenth century, the problems yielded to the practice of sanitation. From the mid-1800s to the 1960s they yielded to epidemiology and the control of communicable diseases. The resources needed by public health were available to it: laboratories, epidemiologists, health educators, sanitarians and engineers, vaccines, public health nurses, and rule-making authority.

The public health problems of this time will not yield to such simple solutions. Lung cancer has replaced diphtheria as a leading cause of death, and preventing lung cancer requires the work of the educational system, the agricultural system, finance and taxation policies, lawyers, psychologists, surgeons, and chemists. Long-term care problems are now of as much concern as problems of child health, and they require architects, bankers, social workers, nurses, physicians, nutritionists, lawyers, real estate brokers, psychologists, geriatricians, and demographers among others. Public health's role is to serve as the governmental presence, as described in Chapter 7. It has to have the ability to coordinate the resources and skills of a wide array of systems in both the public and private sectors if it is to fulfill its purpose. This is different from the roles played by other essential agencies of government: law enforcement, highways, libraries, schools, and welfare. They have a central responsibility requiring the work of a single basic discipline or methodology, and they have the resources they need to carry out their tasks, although often not in sufficient amount. Public health, because of its purpose and because of the problems and resources assigned to it, cannot act alone.

The Institute of Medicine[1] has defined the tasks of public health as assessment, policy development, and assurance. The first involves the systematic collection and analysis of the information needed to assess the public's health and the hazards that threaten it. Some of the necessary information is readily available to public health—birth and death statistics, for example—but other essential data systems often are not: traffic arrests, hospital discharge information, chemicals used in manufacturing and in consumer products, information from worker's compensation systems, welfare data, household income data, health status information, mental health data, and data about the number and training of various health professionals. The acquisition of such "data-sets" and their integration require skills not yet developed, collaborative agreements among multiple agencies, and the tedious job of developing common approaches to data collection, coding, and filing.

Policy development requires the use of the assessment function, a strong base of scientific knowledge, and the ability to orchestrate the often conflicting demands of different constituencies through the public policy-forming process. AIDS and human nutrition are just two examples of problems requiring the formation of a comprehensive set of policies involving numerous public agencies with different purposes and often with different values.

The assurance function of public health often does not entail the direct provision of needed services, but rather their identification and development, their coordination and oversight of their accessibility and quality. As the governmental presence in health, public health has the responsibility for assuring that its communities are adequately served by an emergency health services system, by adequate hospitals with prenatal care, with fluoridated water, that it is adequately immunized, that there are effective information and referral systems for people with substance abuse problems, and that the unintended spill of a hazardous chemical can be promptly neutralized. With few exceptions, these tasks require the work of other organizations, some of which may be poorly developed and some of which may be reluctant to carry out a public health mission.

So public health is unique. It has the mandate and perhaps the ability to reach beyond its own organizational boundaries to solve problems, and it has the unique necessity to examine problems not from the point of view of a single discipline but in terms of the intended goal of society. These special attributes of public health should be seen as advantages, especially in this era when resources are scarce and must be shared, but they are also handicaps. It is more difficult for the public to form a consistent image of its public health agency than of its school or its library or mental health center.

The constituency problem

The image of public health is blurred further by the diversity of its assignments. Public health workers in recent years have fretted about their constituency. They see the parents of the mentally ill as forming a constituency for the support of community mental health centers, farmers as a natural constituency for a state department of agriculture, the trucking industry and automobile associations (not to mention paving contractors) as a reasonably homogenous constituency for highway departments, but public health departments are once again unique. Since the prevention purpose is advantageously treated as an outcome-oriented rather than a method- or discipline-oriented enterprise, it has no single or even dominant constituency.

On the one hand it regulates social intercourse by such tasks as inspecting restaurants and granting or denying them a permit to remain in business; on the other hand, it provides care to people who are sick and need help. On the one hand, it treats people who have a sexually transmitted disease; on the other hand, it can exercise certain police power supervision over their behavior. Public health agencies provide infant restraints to low-income car drivers, measure the blood pressure of the elderly, oversee the school lunch program, enforce standards for septic tank installation in a new housing development, issue burial permits to morticians and birth certificates to people taking a summer vacation abroad, provide nutrition counseling to pregnant women, supervise hearing and vision screening programs in the school, draft new legislation governing the notification of the sexual partners of AIDS patients, provide dental care to some, and confiscate suspect foods in a supermarket. Most of these tasks are demonstrably related to the basic mission of public health, but they do not facilitate the ready identification of a supportive constituency group. The pregnant woman with a 2-year-old in tow does not feel a close bond with the young males she suspects may be in the clinic because of a gonorrhea infection, and the elderly couple in for a blood pressure check may be made more alarmed than empathic by the pregnant teenager or the effeminate male they suspect has AIDS. One family may be pleased with the help available to test their well water; another family may be enraged by the determination that the new lot they bought cannot have a septic tank installed on it.

A health department has not one constituency, but hundreds, and not all of them are thrilled with the encounter. Each single constituency may represent a very small segment of the community, and several of the constituencies may be in actual or potential conflict with one another. Those who are concerned about sexual abstinence among the young may take a dim view of the family planning or prenatal care clinics. Those who support the involvement of the health department in the child abuse program may be vehemently opposed to its referral of young women to abortion services. Those who are champions of the health department's role in forcing the cleanup of a chemical lagoon may be angry about its denial of a permit for their new and novel method of sewage disposal. When a health department expresses concern about its constituency, it must be asked "Which one?" And it has to determine whether it is a negative or a positive constituency.

This is not a trivial matter. When the health department appears before the state legislature's budget committee, each member of that committee may have not one but several images of the health department, some of them in conflict with others. The concept of prevention is too abstract to serve as the glue for an effective image of constituency.

People tend to become interested in the prevention of something specific but not in prevention generally. They become members and eager volunteers for the heart association or the cancer society or the parents of adult schizophrenics group but not of a prevention association. It lacks focus and relevance. Those who want the health department to do more for autistic children are baffled as to why it would spend more money on a restaurant inspection program. And those who have invested in a new housing development want their plans reviewed; they are not interested in the educational program for overweight adolescents (unless one of them is the parent of a fat child).

Legislators reflect the ambivalence of the citizenry. The health department does not have the easy handle with which one can grab hold of the state hospital or the state police or the agriculture department. Legislators currently are concerned about AIDS, long-term care, medical care of the uninsured, malpractice insurance and its effect on the cost of medical care, and landfill problems. As noted above, the health department—and these problems are properly seen as health problems by legislators—does not have all the answers. Parts of the puzzle have been assigned to other agencies of state government. It seems to the elected official that the health director is supposed to know about such things, but the agencies involved are often unable to form a coherent, consistent, and sensible policy. Not only that, but the health department may oppose what seems to the legislator to be a perfectly straightforward approach to the problem. For example, in many states, concerned legislators insisted on mandatory AIDS testing for a wide variety of classes of people: prisoners, marriage license applicants, people in substance abuse programs. The health departments were convinced that anything other than voluntary testing with a provision for anonymity would drive some high-risk people "underground," where they (1) might not be helped and (2) might continue to serve as a source of infection. Legislators have not generally studied epidemiology. Careful explication of the problems of false positive and false negative tests can lead to conclusions that are counterintuitive for people who assume that screening programs are always a good idea. Some were enraged by what they saw as an ineffective response by the state health departments.

The prevention of dependency does not hang together in a tidy bureaucratic structure. The public health agency uses disparate methods and different rationales to arrive at a common good, but the concept of a governmental presence in health, no matter how badly needed, is not an easy one to comprehend, identify, or support. Elected officials have often turned to more identifiable agencies and organizations. Mental health is separate; environmental health programs have been increasingly separated from public health; public medical care is assigned to the welfare agencies of government; and more recently, some states have considered grouping all children's services in a single agency of government.

The result was recognized by the Institute of Medicine's Committee for the Study of the Future of Public Health as "disarray,"[1] but the committee did not understand the underlying reason for the disarray. Their prescription for the problem was to reaggregate the functions in the public health agency. It is unlikely that legislative bodies will do this, nor would it overcome the underlying problems of public health. Public health is both pleiomorphic and abstract. Its problems will not yield to the traditional solutions of reorganization and constituency building because of its unique features. The special problem of public health requires special attention and understanding. It is tempting to speculate that organizing the task of public health is more consonant with the needs of the future than is the traditional way of organizing and managing public solutions to important problems.

THE ORGANIZATION OF PUBLIC HEALTH

Public health is not in disarray: government is. The Weberian approach to organizing a bureaucracy does not facilitate the solution of problems inherently requiring transorganizational approaches. Court systems are frustrated by the organization of children's services. When judges have a complex child custody and juvenile delinquency problem to deal with, they need an organized response from welfare, education, mental health, the probation department, and a separate juvenile care facility. The apparent solution is to regroup all relevant services in a new agency. That would disrupt other important service systems, however, taking child mental health systems out of family-oriented mental health systems and separating child welfare from the mother's welfare. As foci shift and different problems attract public attention and concern, new arrangements of services are constantly proposed, creating instability and confusion, producing at least short-term inefficiency, and laying the groundwork for other problems in the future, which may prompt yet other attempts to reorganize a solution to the problem.

Another example: a large city has proposed construction of a huge incinerator capable of handling nearly a million tons of garbage a year. Review of the proposal has been assigned to the state air pollution control agency, where an attempt to assess the risk imposed by the incinerator has produced a number unacceptably large given present standards. The review, however, has not considered the risk of continuing with the current landfill system: that is not part of the process; the Environmental Protection Administration at the federal level and its counterpart agencies in the states were organized to conduct single media reviews. That problem cannot be solved by a simple reorganization of the agencies. It requires new concepts, new skills in coordination and information processing, better science, and the ability to resolve conflicts swiftly and effectively. Developing a single organization with all of the necessary resources to cope with a problem is simpler, but it simply will not work any longer: the problems are too complex and there are not enough resources to go around.

An alternative solution is to establish a "blue-ribbon" commission to solve the problem. At both the federal and state level, this has become an increasingly popular approach to unpleasant problems: the federal deficit, health care of the uninsured, children's services, and AIDS. Blue-ribbon commissions are temporary, however, and they are a costly approach to problem solving. Given that transorganizational solutions to most complex problems are necessary, the commission approach could result in a hideously entangled bureaucracy, with lines of authority and communication lying about the landscape like fire hoses at a five-alarm high-rise conflagration. The purpose of the commissions, transorganizational problem solving, must become an institutionalized part of state and local government operations, not an exception.

Earlier in this book, matrix organizations were described briefly (see Chapter 10). Resources are grouped along one axis of the organizational chart (nurses, engineers, social workers, etc.) and the issues or problems along the other (AIDS, long-term care, hazardous waste disposal, for example). The problem managers have a budget and can negotiate with the resource managers for the people and other resources needed to solve their problems. The method has been applied in certain limited settings with some degree of success. It is expensive, because it can increase the amount of time spent in negotiation, and it can reduce the loyalty to a process that serves a simpler organization well, but these same drawbacks arise in other, more traditional approaches to problem solving. An attempt needs to be made to develop the concept of a matrix structure as a way of organizing the work of the public sector and coordinating it with private sector resources. It is a complex task and one that would require considerable political courage and stamina by a governor and several other elected officials, but one of the advantages of the federal system of government in the United States is that 50 different experiments can be going on at any one time.

THE DEMISE OF PUBLIC HEALTH

Public health confuses and often frustrates elected officials. Its focus on its purpose rather than its methods is atypical; its eclectic array of interventions delights some but often antagonizes others; its variegated constituency problem robs it of a consistent image and an effective presence in legislative corridors; and its thoughtful, often counterintuitive approach to problems is seen as stubborn arrogance by some.

The disarray of public health has been described both in this book and in the Institute of Medicine review.[1] In most states, substantial parts of the environmental health system, originally constructed by public health, have been moved to new agencies of government: departments of natural resources or environmental protection administrations. Public medical care programs are generally the responsibility of state welfare agencies. Mental health has its own agency, as does substance abuse in most states. Several states have contemplated the formation of a new children's services agency. What's left for public health to do?

The prevention of disease.

It is true that many of the functions of public health could be assigned to other agencies of government, but there are problems in such a dispersal of functions. Environmental protection agencies have little background in public health and disease prevention. They often seek engineering solutions to complex social problems. Welfare agencies have only a limited understanding of the efficacy of medical care interventions and respond to health problems by paying for traditional health services rather than investigating the cause of the problem and searching for more efficient and durable solutions. However, imperfect organizational responses to public problems are not unheard of, nor are they always unacceptable.

It is more difficult to contemplate a different approach to the assessment function of public health and its focus on the prevention of dangerous diseases, communicable or not. It is difficult to imagine that diphtheria, polio, smallpox, and measles could have been dealt with effectively without the work of public health. Although much of the national effort to deal with AIDS involves the organization and financing of treatment services, the identification of the problem initially depended on the public health assessment function, and the effort to prevent AIDS is basically a public health function—testing, counseling, educating, changing.

It is less apparent that the organization of public health is essential to progress in combating noninfectious diseases. Although public health investigators were responsible for elucidating many important nutritional problems, public health does not play an indispensable role in correcting them at this time in the United States. The distribution of food stamps and the special foods that are part of the WIC program (see Chapter 22) could be accomplished by social welfare agencies. Although epidemiologists have played a leading role in identifying the risk factors for heart disease, reductions in mortality rates have come about because of medical and surgical interventions and because of an enormous number of individual decisions about diet, exercise, and smoking. Although public health agencies at the state and local level have been aggressively involved in efforts to bring about such changes, there is no convincing evidence that progress would not have been made without those efforts. Much of the progress stemmed from advertising, television shows, fashion designers, and the general affluence of the United States.

It is painful for public health to evaluate itself so harshly, but the standards of a randomized, controlled trial have to be applied to any intervention. The fact that an effort was made to prevent something and progress was observed does not justify the conclusion that the intervention caused the improvement. What might have happened if public health had not attempted to intervene in the prevention of chronic diseases? Would the prevalence of the diseases be more, less, or the same as it is now? If less, how much less and at what cost? These are not questions for which answers can be obtained easily. They are asked here to inspire contemplation, not solution.

The organization of public health services in the United States is unique to this country. In most other nations, public involvement in medical care developed earlier, and that role was intertwined with the functions separately assigned to public health in the United States. Public health agencies in other countries are known for their work in the organization and delivery of health care services to the population generally or to special groups within the population. Their work in disease prevention is secondary. Many of the police power functions of public health in the United States are assigned to other agencies of government elsewhere, and the public health role in environmental health is often minimal or concentrated at the national level. Yet it would be difficult to prove that other countries are any less healthy than the United States as a result of their different approach to the public's health.

THE RESURRECTION OF PUBLIC HEALTH

The unique nature of public health has value beyond its impact on the prevalence of dependency. The role of public health in the control of communicable diseases is clear and remains of value. Communicable diseases will continue to affect human health, and their nature is changing in complex and challenging ways. AIDS is only one example, albeit a particularly deadly one, of the complexity of communicable diseases in this modern era. The role of public health in the prevention of chronic diseases and patterns of dependency that are the result of environmental, behavioral, and biological interactions is less clear. However, its ability to identify the problems, to analyze them, to determine their natural history, and to focus attention on the need for policy debate and formation is essential to the public's health.

It is especially important that health policy analysis and formation be continued in each state rather than left to the national level of government. Centralized policy formation, especially when value concerns are important to the solution of the problem, reduces the probability that the best solutions will be found. As described in Chapter 7, national health policy should be applied only to define the outer limits of our tolerance for diversity.

Public health must also become involved in the organization and management of medical care services. The problems of access, cost, quality, and mix of services have not been solved by reliance on the private sector and market forces. If anything, they have been exacerbated. The public and its elected representatives are demanding that progress be made in solving these seemingly intractable problems. Other countries have done so. The attempt to solve them as if they were simply financial problems has not provided solutions that satisfy the criteria of public health. Simply finding ways to pay for insurance for low-income people will not adequately address problems of access or quality or the appropriate mix of services. Some people will remain uninsured for all services, and all people will remain uninsured for some services. When they are poor or otherwise dependent, they must be able to rely on government to secure the access they need. Public health must help design organizational approaches to the problems.

There are other essential tasks for public health in the future. In recent years governments and professional organizations have become enamored of the notion that the residual health problems left to the twenty-first century are personal, not public matters. They are attributed to decisions made by individuals about smoking, drinking, eating, work, and play. Public health is based in concepts of social justice, however, and knows that the proper attribution of such problems involves social decisions and an environment that is the result of both implicit and explicit policies with regard to the distribution of costs and benefits. Tax policies with regard to alcoholic beverages, engineering decisions made by automobile manufacturers, and the agricultural subsidy programs of the federal government have a great deal to do with the distribution of costs and benefits in society and therefore with the dependency associated with disease and injury. The behavioral decisions that may result in dependency are not isolated phenomena but have their communitarian components.[5]

Public health has the knowledge and the ability to work for more comprehensive policies. As the governmental presence in health, it should work to assure that predisposing, reinforcing, and enabling forces are properly aligned to increase the probability that healthy choices will be made[6] (see Chapter 17).

The Institute of Medicine[1] was correct in stating that the essential functions of public health are assessment, policy formation, and assurance. They are functions that cannot be served in the absence of a public health presence. The task of public health is to assure that they are served in the future. This requires that public health support the flexibility and the changes necessary for governments to work in new and nontraditional ways; that it be able to work in a transorganizational environment in which values must be identified with the same care and attention addressed to the identification of problems; that it build coalitions through negotiation rather than organizations by acquisition of resources.

Public health is in the familiar position of having to be in the forefront of change to achieve its mission. This was true in 1790, in 1850, in 1914, 1965, 1974, and 1981, and it will be true in the future. Public health was the first agency of government that had to challenge the policies of government to achieve its mission. Its advocacy has often brought it into conflict with some of its constituencies and with elected officials. Its programs have often placed demands on the resources and policies of other agencies of government. The successful work of public health often alienates some elements of the society it serves. It would be easy to be less effective, and it may be restful to contemplate the dissolution of the effort in favor of more orthodox approaches to the complex health problems of the future, but then progress would be less sure and less just. Public health is unique, and although there is little comfort in that realization, there is considerable value.

REFERENCES

1. Institute of Medicine: The future of public health, Washington, DC, 1988, National Academy Press.
2. Pickett GE: The future of health departments: the governmental presence, Ann Rev Public Health 1:297, 1980.
3. Sencer DJ: Major urban health departments: the ideal and the real, Health Aff 2:88, Winter 1983.
4. Hanlon JJ: Is there a future for local health departments? Health Services Reports 88:898, 1973.
5. Beauchamp DE: Community: the neglected tradition of public health, Hastings Cent Rep 15:28, Dec 1985.
6. Green LW and others: Health education planning: a diagnostic approach, Palo Alto, CA, 1980, Mayfield Publishing Co.

Index

Page numbers followed by "t" indicate tables; "f" indicates figure.

M